OUTLINE CONTENTS

DETAILED CONTENTS

PART I

PREFACE

Many important changes have occurred in the European Union since this book was first published in 1988. Membership of the Union, originally called the European Economic Community, has risen to twenty-five and is likely to increase still further. The goal of the internal market, set down in the 1986 Single European Act, has been largely achieved. 1992 saw the signing at Maastricht of the Treaty on European Union, committing members to new goals, not least to economic and monetary union, and increasing governmental cooperation in the fields of foreign and security policy and justice and home affairs: the concept of citizenship of the Union was born. The first stage of economic and monetary union came into effect in 1992; the final stage for participating Member States occurred on 1 January 1999. The Treaty of Amsterdam, signed in 1997, added significantly to the EC Treaty, renumbering most of its articles, and together with the Treaty of Nice effected radical changes to the institutional structures and decision-making processes of the Union, paving the way for a larger, more flexible Union. The most recent treaty, the Treaty establishing a Constitution for Europe has, as had some of the previous treaties also, proved controversial. The Constitution on the one hand is significant as it completely replaces the existing treaty structure and makes express a number of key principles of constitutional law. On the other hand, in terms of new developments, the Constitution changes little. As we will see, the future of the Constitution is uncertain, as France and the Netherlands voted 'no' on their respective referenda. It seems that for some, it is the very terminology of constitutionalism that is key, rather than the actual substance of the treaty. Nonetheless, despite disagreement both within and between Member States over the nature and pace of future developments, there are no doubts as to the need for the Union's continued existence.

The purpose of this ninth edition is not to chart the political developments in the Union and its relationship with Member States and would-be Member States, except in outline. Instead, it aims to continue the approach adopted in previous editions of providing an accurate and succinct account of the present state of European law. There is still a need for a single textbook of manageable size, concise but not simplistic, covering the major areas of EU law – constitutional, institutional and administrative as well as substantive – to cater for the growing body of students (and not only lawyers) from around the world who wish to study EU law, and for practitioners who realise that they can no longer afford to ignore it. The advent of the internal market and the continuing expansion of the Union has simply reinforced that need.

A book of this type cannot of necessity provide an in-depth account of the EU institutions (although this section has been expanded over previous editions), nor can it cover all areas of substantive law. Much EU law, for example in the field of company or commercial or environmental law, or the law relating to employment or consumer protection, is increasingly, and more appropriately, incorporated into the general textbooks on these subjects. Some topics, such as agriculture or monetary union are too large or too specialised for inclusion. Others, such as transport, are still in the process of development. The book continues to concentrate on the more highly developed areas of EU law, what one might describe as fundamental

Community law, the law relating to the free movement of goods, persons and services, competition law and sex discrimination, and on the remedies available for breaches of Community law.

There are a number of changes to this edition. The book has been re-ordered so that the jurisdiction of the European courts is dealt with before the substantive areas of law, thus according with the order in which many universities teach European law. More fundamentally, the name of the book has changed to the simple *EU Law*, a decision taken partly in anticipation of the structural changes which would be introduced by the Constitution, but also because the subject is now generally known as 'European Union Law'. All chapters have been revised in the light of the possible impact of the Constitution, should it come into force. This affects the chapters on the Union's development (Chapter 1), that on the institutions (Chapter 2) and on law-making (Chapter 3) the most. This edition also includes a chapter on the free movement of capital. The chapter on services and establishment has been divided into two separate chapters and, as part of this process, more detail on the position of companies has been included. The chapters on workers and citizenship have been substantially amended in the light of recent case law and the new Citizenship Directive. One significant change, in the final stages of the legislative process at the time of finalising this edition, is a new consolidating directive in the field of sex discrimination. This came too late to be fully incorporated into the text, although the substance of Chapter 25 on 'Discrimination' is up to date.

As before, the book aims to provide sufficient insight into the principles of EU law, including its current difficulties, and the processes of the European institutions, to enable the reader to pursue studies, resolve problems, and enforce rights in areas of law whether or not covered by the book, as and when the need arises. The principal sources of EU law and a selection of textbooks are listed at the end of the book. Each chapter provides a list of further reading.

As with the eighth edition, Jo Steiner, who wrote the original Textbook in 1988, and was joined in 1996 by Lorna Woods for the fifth and subsequent editions, has had no involvement with this edition. She continues to enjoy a well-earned retirement. Given the range of the Textbook and continuing development of the law in this area, it is beyond the capabilities of one person to update the entire text. Lorna Woods has again been joined in the preparation of this edition by Christian Twigg-Flesner.

Our thanks go to all of those who helped in the preparation of this book: to colleagues in respective institutions for their helpful comments and suggestions (with particular thanks to Anne Bonnie and Costas Kombos at Hull), and to our families and friends for their unflinching support, and for providing a welcome distraction from the demands of academic research.

Lorna Woods
Christian Twigg-Flesner
March 2006

ABBREVIATIONS

Bull. EC	*Bulletin of the European Communities*
CAP	Common Agricultural Policy
CCT	Common Customs Tariff
CDE	*Cahiers de Droit Enropéen*
CET	Common External Tariff
CFI	Court of First Instance
CFSP	common foreign and security policy
CMLR	*Common Market Law Reports*
CML Rev	*Common Market Law Review*
COREPER	Committee of Permanent Representatives
D/G	Directorate-General
EAGGE	European Agriculture Guidance and Guarantee Fund
EC	European Community/Communities, Treaty Establishing the European Community
ECB	European Central Bank
EC Bull	*Bulletin of the European Communities*
ECHR	European Convention for the Protection of Human Rights and Fundamental Freedoms 1950
ECJ	European Court of Justice
ECLR	*European Competition Law Review*
ECR	*European Court Reports* (official reports of the judgments of the European Court, English version)
ECSC	European Coal and Steel Community
ECtHR	European Court of Human Rights
EEA	European Economic Area
EEC	European Economic Community
EFTA	European Free Trade Association
EIPR	*European Intellectual Property Review*
EL Rev	*European Law Review*
EMU	Economic and Monetary Union
EPL	*European Public Law*
ESCB	European System of Central Banks
EUCFR	European Charter of Fundamental Rights
Euratom	European Atomic Energy Community
FSP	foreign and security policy
FYR	Former Yugoslav Republic
GATT	General Agreement on Tariffs and Trade
GG	Grundgesetz (Basic Law for the Federal Republic of Germany)
Harv Int'l LJ	*Harvard International Law Journal*
ICLQ	*International and Comparative Law Quarterly*
ICTY	International Criminal Tribunal for the former Yugoslavia
IGC	Intergovernmental Conference
JHA	justice and home affairs
JO	*Journal Officiel* (French version of OJ)
LIEI	*Legal Issues of European Integration*
LQR	*Law Quarterly Review*
MCA	Monetary Compensatory Amount
MEQR	measure having equivalent effect to quantitative restrictions
MLR	*Modern Law Review*
OJ	*Official Journal* (of the European Communities)
OMC	Open Method of Co-ordination
PL	*Public Law*

qmv	qualified majority voting
RPM	relevant product market
SEA	Single European Act
SGP	Stability and Growth Pact
SME	small and medium-sized enterprises
SSNIP	small but significant and non-transitory increase in prices
TCN	third country national
TEU	Treaty on European Union
ToA	Treaty of Amsterdam
UNICE	Union des industries de la communauté européenne (federation of European employers' groups)
WashLRev	*Washington Law Review*
WTO	World Trade Organization
YEL	*Yearbook of European Law*

Unless otherwise stated, cases cited were decided by the ECJ and Articles cited are Articles of the EC Treaty.

TABLE OF CASES

Belgian Courts

French Courts

German Courts

Italian Courts

United Kingdom Courts

European Court of Human Rights

TABLE OF CASES

Court of Justice of the European Communities–Alphabetical List

Cases have been arranged in alphabetical order. See page xvii for chronological list of Court of Justice of the European Communities cases.

TABLE OF COMMISSION DECISIONS

TABLE OF UK STATUTES

*Page references in **bold** indicate that the text is reproduced in full*

TABLE OF EUROPEAN COMMUNITY TREATIES

*Page references in **bold** indicate that the text is reproduced in full*

TABLE OF EU SECONDARY LEGISLATION

TABLE OF EQUIVALENCES

On the EU Constitution

Note that Articles are in the order given in the Constitution.
* New Articles introduced by the Treaty Establishing a Constitution for Europe.

Maastricht Treaty – TEU/TEC	Nice Treaty – TEU/TEC	The EU Constitution
		Part I
		Title I
Art. A, O TEU	Art. 1, 49 TEU	Art. I–1
Art. F(1) TEU	Art. 6(1) TEU	Art. I–2
Art. B TEU, 2 TEC	Art. 2 TEU, 2 TEC	Art. I–3
Art. 7a, 6 TEC	Art. 14(2), 12 TEC	Art. I–4
Art. F(1), K.5 TEU, 5 TEC	Art. 6(3), 33 TEU, 10 TEC	Art. I–5
		Art. I–6*
Art. 210 TEC	Art. 281 TEC	Art. I–7(*)
		Art. I–8*
		Title II
Art. F(2) TEU	Art. 6(2) TEU	Art. I–9(*)
Art. 8, 8a, 8b, 8c, 8d TEC	Art. 17–21 TEC	Art. I–10
		Title III
Art. 3b TEC, B TEU	Art. 5 TEC, 2 (last sentence) TEU	Art. I–11
		Art. I–12*
		Art. I–13*
		Art. I–14*
Art. 3a TEC	Art. 4(1) TEC	Art. I–15
Art. 103 TEC	Art. 99(1), 3(1) (i) TEC	
Art. 109n TEC	Art. 125 TEC	
Art. 109q TEC	Art. 128 TEC	
Art. 118c TEC	Art. 140 TEC	
Art. J.7, J.1 TEU	Art. 17, 11(2) TEU	Art. I–16
		Art. I–17*
Art. 235 TEC	Art. 308 TEC	Art. I–18

Maastricht Treaty – TEU/TEC	Nice Treaty – TEU/TEC	The EU Constitution
		Title IV
Art. C TEU, 4(1) TEC, E TEU	Art. 3(1) TEU, 7(1) TEC, 5 TEU	Art. I–19
Art. 137 TEC	Art. 189 TEC	Art. I–20
Art. 138 TEC	Art. 190 TEC	
Art. 138b TEC	Art. 192 TEC	
Art. 140 TEC	Art. 197 TEC	
Art. D TEU	Art. 4 TEU	Art. I–21
		Art. I–22*
Art. 145 TEC	Art. 202 TEC	Art. I–23
Art. 146 TEC	Art. 203 TEC	
Art. 148 TEC	Art. 205(1) TEC	
Art. 146 TEC	Art. 203 TEC	Art. I–24
	Art. 207(1) TEC	
Art. 148 TEC	Art. 205(2) TEC	Art. I–25
Art. 144 TEC	Art. 201 TEC	Art. I–26
Art. 155 TEC	Art. 211 TEC	
Art. 157 TEC	Art. 213(2) TEC	
Art. 158(1) TEC	Art. 214(1) TEC	
Art. 205 TEC	Art. 274 TEC	
Art. 158 TEC	Art. 214(2) TEC	Art. I–27
Art. 161 TEC	Art. 217 TEC	
		Art. I–28*
Art. 164–8 TEC	Art. 220–4 TEC	Art. I–29(*)
Art. 4a, 105, 105a, 106, 107, 156 TEC	Art. 8, 107, 105(1), 105(4), 106, 108, 212 TEC	Art. I–30
Art. 4, 188a, 188b, 188c TEC	Art. 7, 246–8 TEC	Art. I–31
Art. 4(1), 193, 194, 198a TEC	Art. 7(2), 257, 258, 263 TEC	Art. I–32
		Title V
Art. 198 TEC, J.3, K.6 TEU	Art. 249 TEC, 13, 34 TEU	Art. I–33
		Art. I–34*
		Art. I–35*
		Art. I–36*
Art. 5 TEC	Art. 10 TEC	Art. I–37

Maastricht Treaty – TEU/TEC	Nice Treaty – TEU/TEC	The EU Constitution
Art. 145 TEC	Art. 202 TEC	
Art. 190 TEC	Art. 253 TEC	Art. I–38
Art. 191	Art. 254 TEC	Art. I–39
Art. J.3, J.6, J.11, J.13 TEU	Art. 13, 16, 21, 23 TEU	Art. I–40(*)
Art. J. 7, J.11 TEU	Art. 17, 21 TEU	Art. I–41
Art. K.1 TEU, 73i TEC	Art. 29 TEU, 61 TEC	Art. I–42
		Art. I–43*
Art. J.17, K.15 TEU	Art. 27, 43 TEU	Art. I–44
Art. 5a TEC	Art. 11 TEC	
		Title VI
		Art. I–45*
Art. A TEU	Art. 1(1) TEC	Art. I–46
Art. F TEU	Art. 6(1) TEU	
Art. 138a TEC	Art. 191 TEC	
		Art. I–47*
Art. 118a TEC	Art. 138 TEC	Art. I–48
Art. 155, 156 TEC	Art. 211, 212 TEC	
Art. 138e TEC	Art. 195 TEC	Art. I–49
Art. A TEC	Art. 1 TEU	Art. I–50
Art. 191a TEC	Art. 255 TEC	
Art. 213b TEC	Art. 286 TEC	Art. I–51
		Art. I–52*
		Title VII
Art. 199, 201a, 202, 209a TEC	Art. 268, 270, 271, 280 TEC	Art. I–53
Art. 210 TEC	Art. 269 TEC	Art. I–54
		Art. I–55*
		Art. I–56*
		Title VIII
		Art. I–57*
		Title IX
Art. O TEU	Art. 49 TEU	Art. I–58
Art. F.1 TEU, 236 TEC	Art. 7 TEU, 309 TEC	Art. I–59
		Art. I–60*

Maastricht Treaty – TEU/TEC	Nice Treaty – TEU/TEC	The EU Constitution
		Part II
		Title I
		Art. II–61*
		Art. II–62*
		Art. II–63*
		Art. II–64*
		Art. II–65*
		Title II
		Art. II–66*
		Art. II–67*
		Art. II–68*
		Art. II–69*
		Art. II–70*
		Art. II–71*
		Art. II–72*
		Art. II–73*
		Art. II–74*
		Art. II–75*
		Art. II–76*
		Art. II–77*
		Art. II–78*
		Art. II–79*
		Title III
		Art. II–80*
		Art. II–81*
		Art. II–82*
		Art. II–83*
		Art. II–84*
		Art. II–86*
		Title IV
		Art. II–87*
		Art. II–88*
		Art. II–89*

Maastricht Treaty – TEU/TEC	Nice Treaty – TEU/TEC	The EU Constitution
		Art. II–90*
		Art. II–91*
		Art. II–92*
		Art. II–93*
		Art. II–94*
		Art. II–95*
		Art. II–96*
		Art. II–97*
		Art. II–98*
		Title V
		Art. II–99*
		Art. II–100*
		Art. II–101*
		Art. II–102*
		Art. II–103*
		Art. II–104*
		Art. II–105*
		Art. II–106*
		Title VI
		Art. II–107*
		Art. II–108*
		Art. II–109*
		Art. II–110*
		Title VII
		Art. II–111*
		Art. II–112*
		Art. II–113*
		Art. II–114*
		Part III
		Title I
Art. C TEU	Art. 3 TEU	Art. III–115
Art. 3 TEC	Art. 3(2) TEC	Art. III–116
		Art. III–117*

Maastricht Treaty – TEU/TEC	Nice Treaty – TEU/TEC	The EU Constitution
		Art. III–118*
Art. 12 TEC	Art. 6 TEC	Art. III–119
Art. 129a TEC	Art. 153(2) TEC	Art. III–120
Protocol on protection and welfare of animals	Protocol on protection and welfare of animals	Art. III–121
Art. 7d TEC	Art. 16 TEC	Art. III–122
		Title II
Art. 6 TEC	Art. 12 TEC	Art. III–123
Art. 6a TEC	Art. 13 TEC	Art. III–124
Art. 8a TEC	Art. 18(2–3) TEC	Art. III–125
Art. 8b TEC	Art. 19 TEC	Art. III–126
Art. 8c TEC	Art. 20 TEC	Art. III–127
Art. 8d TEC	Art. 21 TEC	Art. III–128
Art. 8e TEC	Art. 22 TEC	Art. III–129
		Title III
Art. 7a, 7c TEC	Art. 14, 15 TEC	Art. III–130
Art. 224 TEC	Art. 297 TEC	Art. III–131
Art. 225 TEC	Art. 298 TEC	Art. III–132
Art. 48 TEC	Art. 39 TEC	Art. III–133
Art. 49 TEC	Art. 40 TEC	Art. III–134
Art. 50 TEC	Art. 41 TEC	Art. III–135
Art. 51 TEC	Art. 42 TEC	Art. III–136
Art. 52 TEC	Art. 43 TEC	Art. III–137
Art. 54 TEC	Art. 44 TEC	Art. III–138
Art. 55 TEC	Art. 45 TEC	Art. III–139
Art. 56 TEC	Art. 46 TEC	Art. III–140
Art. 57 TEC	Art. 47 TEC	Art. III–141
Art. 58 TEC	Art. 48 TEC	Art. III–142
Art. 221 TEC	Art. 294 TEC	Art. III–143
Art. 59 TEC	Art. 94 TEC	Art. III–144
Art. 60 TEC	Art. 50 TEC	Art. III–145
Art. 61 TEC	Art. 51 TEC	Art. III–146
Art. 63 TEC	Art. 52 TEC	Art. III–147

Maastricht Treaty – TEU/TEC	Nice Treaty – TEU/TEC	The EU Constitution
Art. 64 TEC	Art. 53 TEC	Art. III–148
Art. 65 TEC	Art. 54 TEC	Art. III–149
Art. 66 TEC	Art. 55 TEC	Art. III–150
Art. 9 TEC	Art. 23 TEC	Art. III–151
Art. 10 TEC	Art. 24 TEC	
Art. 12 TEC	Art. 25 TEC	
Art. 28 TEC	Art. 26 TEC	
Art. 29 TEC	Art. 27 TEC	
Art. 116 TEC	Art. 135 TEC	Art. III–152
Art. 30, 34 TEC	Art. 28, 29 TEC	Art. III–153
Art. 36 TEC	Art. 30 TEC	Art. III–154
Art. 37 TEC	Art. 31 TEC	Art. III–155
Art. 73b TEC	Art. 56 TEC	Art. III–156
Art. 73c TEC	Art. 57 TEC	Art. III–157
Art. 73d TEC	Art. 58 TEC	Art. III–158
Art. 73f TEC	Art. 59 TEC	Art. III–159
Art. 73g TEC	Art. 60 TEC	Art. III–160(*)
Art. 85 TEC	Art. 81 TEC	Art. III–161
Art. 86 TEC	Art. 82 TEC	Art. III–162
Art. 87 TEC	Art. 83 TEC	Art. III–163
Art. 88 TEC	Art. 84 TEC	Art. III–164
Art. 89 TEC	Art. 85 TEC	Art. III–165
Art. 90 TEC	Art. 86 TEC	Art. III–166
Art. 92 TEC	Art. 87 TEC	Art. III–167
Art. 93 TEC	Art. 88 TEC	Art. III–168
Art. 94 TEC	Art. 89 TEC	Art. III–169
Art. 95, 96, 98 TEC	Art. 90–2 TEC	Art. III–170
Art. 99 TEC	Art. 93 TEC	Art. III–171
Art. 100a TEC	Art. 95 TEC	Art. III–172
Art. 100 TEC	Art. 94 TEC	Art. III–173
Art. 101 TEC	Art. 96 TEC	Art. III–174
Art. 102 TEC	Art. 97 TEC	Art. III–175
		Art. III–176(*)

Maastricht Treaty – TEU/TEC	Nice Treaty – TEU/TEC	The EU Constitution
Art. 3a TEC	Art. 4 TEC	Art. III–177
Art. 102a TEC	Art. 98 TEC	Art. III–178
Art. 103 TEC	Art. 99 TEC	Art. III–179
Art. 103a TEC	Art. 100 TEC	Art. III–180
Art. 104 TEC	Art. 101 TEC	Art. III–181
Art. 104a TEC	Art. 102 TEC	Art. III–182
Art. 104b TEC	Art. 103 TEC	Art. III–183
Art. 104c TEC	Art. 104 TEC	Art. III–184
Art. 105 TEC	Art. 105 TEC	Art. III–185
Art. 105a TEC	Art. 106 TEC	Art. III–186
Art. 106 TEC	Art. 107 TEC	Art. III–187
Art. 107 TEC	Art. 108 TEC	Art. III–188
Art. 108 TEC	Art. 109 TEC	Art. III–189
Art. 108a TEC	Art. 110 TEC	Art. III–190
Art. 109(1) TEC	Art. 123(4) TEC	Art. III–191
Art. 109c(2–4) TEC	Art. 114(2–4) TEC	Art. III–192
Art. 109d TEC	Art. 115 TEC	Art. III–193
		Art. III–194*
		Art. III–195*
		Art. III–196*
Art. 109k(1), (3–5) TEC	Art. 122(1), (3–5) TEC	Art. III–197
Art. 109j(1), 109k(2), 109l(5) TEC	Art. 121(1–2), 122(2), 123(5) TEC	Art. III–198
Art. 109f(2), 109l(3) TEC	Art. 117(2), 123(3) TEC	Art. III–199
Art. 109m(1) TEC	Art. 124(1) TEC	Art. III–200
Art. 109h TEC	Art. 119 TEC	Art. III–201
Art. 109i TEC	Art. 120 TEC	Art. III–202
Art. 109n TEC	Art. 125 TEC	Art. III–203
Art. 109o TEC	Art. 126 TEC	Art. III–204
Art. 109p TEC	Art. 127 TEC	Art. III–205
Art. 109q TEC	Art. 128 TEC	Art. III–206
Art. 109r TEC	Art. 129 TEC	Art. III–207
Art. 109s TEC	Art. 130 TEC	Art. III–208

Maastricht Treaty – TEU/TEC	Nice Treaty – TEU/TEC	The EU Constitution
Art. 117 TEC	Art. 136 TEC	Art. III–209
Art. 118 TEC	Art. 137 TEC	Art. III–210
Art. 118a TEC	Art. 138 TEC	Art. III–211
Art. 118b TEC	Art. 139 TEC	Art. III–212
Art. 118c TEC	Art. 140 TEC	Art. III–213
Art. 119 TEC	Art. 141 TEC	Art. III–214
Art. 119a TEC	Art. 142 TEC	Art. III–215
Art. 120 TEC	Art. 143 TEC	Art. III–216
Art. 121 TEC	Art. 144 TEC	Art. III–217
Art. 122 TEC	Art. 145 TEC	Art. III–218
Art. A23–5 TEC	Art. 146–8 TEC	Art. III–219
Art. 130a TEC	Art. 158 TEC	Art. III–220
Art. 130b TEC	Art. 159 TEC	Art. III–221
Art. 130c TEC	Art. 160 TEC	Art. III–222
Art. 130d TEC	Art. 161 TEC	Art. III–223
Art. 130e TEC	Art. 162 TEC	Art. III–224
Art. 38 TEC	Art. 32(1, 2.sentence) TEC	Art. III–225
Art. K.4 TEC	Art. 32 TEC	Art. III–226
Art. K.5 TEC	Art. 33 TEC	Art. III–227
Art. K.6 TEC	Art. 34 TEC	Art. III–228
Art. K.7 TEC	Art. 35 TEC	Art. III–229
Art. K.8 TEC	Art. 36 TEC	Art. II–230
Art. K.9 TEC	Art. 37 TEC	Art. III–231
Art. K.10 TEC	Art. 38 TEC	Art. III–232
Art. 130r TEC	Art. 174 TEC	Art. III–233
Art. 130s, 130t TEC	Art. 175, 176 TEC	Art. III–234
Art. 129a TEC	Art. 153(1, 3–5) TEC	Art. III–235
Art. 74, 75 TEC	Art. 70, 71 TEC	Art. III–236
Art. 76 TEC	Art. 72 TEC	Art. III–237
Art. 77 TEC	Art. 73 TEC	Art. III–238
Art. 78 TEC	Art. 74 TEC	Art. III–239
Art. 79 TEC	Art. 75 TEC	Art. III–240
Art. 80 TEC	Art. 76 TEC	Art. III–241

Maastricht Treaty – TEU/TEC	Nice Treaty – TEU/TEC	The EU Constitution
Art. 81 TEC	Art. 77 TEC	Art. III–242
Art. 82 TEC	Art. 78 TEC	Art. III–243
Art. 83 TEC	Art. 79 TEC	Art. III–244
Art. 84 TEC	Art. 80 TEC	Art. III–245
Art. 129b TEC	Art. 154 TEC	Art. III–246
Art. 129c, 129d TEC	Art. 155, 156 TEC	Art. III–247
Art. 103f TEC	Art. 163 TEC	Art. III–248
Art. 130g TEC	Art. 164 TEC	Art. III–249
Art. 130h TEC	Art. 165 TEC	Art. III–250
Art. 130i TEC	Art. 166 TEC	Art. III–251
Art. 130j, 130k, 130l, 130m, 130o 2. TEC	Art. 167–70, 172 (2.sentence) TEC	Art. III–252
Art. 130n, 130o TEC	Art. 171, 172 (2. sentence) TEC	Art. III–253
		Art. III–254*
Art. 173 TEC	Art. 173 TEC	Art. III–255
		Art. III–256(*)
Art. K.1 TEU, 73i TEC	Art. 29 TEU, 61 TEC	Art. III–257
		Art. III–258*
		Art. III–259*
		Art. III–260*
Art. K.8 TEU	Art. 36 TEU	Art. III–261
Art. K.5 TEU, 73l(1) TEC	Art. 33 TEU, 64(1) TEC	Art. III–262
Art. 73n TEC	Art. 66 TEC	Art. III–263
		Art. III–264*
Art. 73j TEC	Art. 62 TEC	Art. III–265
Art. 73k(1–2), 73l TEC	Art. 63 (points 1–2), 64(2) TEC	Art. III–266
Art. 73k(3–4) TEC	Art. 63 (points 3–4) TEC	Art. III–267
		Art. III–268*
Art. 73m TEC	Art. 65 TEC	Art. III–269
Art. K.3 TEU	Art. 31(1)(a–d) TEU	Art. III–270
Art. K.3 TEU	Art. 31(1)(e) TEU	Art. III–271(*)
		Art. III–272*
Art. K.3 TEU	Art. 31(2) TEU	Art. III–273

Maastricht Treaty – TEU/TEC	Nice Treaty – TEU/TEC	The EU Constitution
		Art. III–274*
Art. K.2 TEU	Art. 30(1) TEU	Art. III–275
Art. K.2 TEU	Art. 30(2) TEU	Art. III–276
Art. K.4 TEU	Art. 32 TEU	Art. III–277
Art. 129 TEC	Art. 152 TEC	Art. III–278
Art. 130 TEC	Art. 157 TEC	Art. III–279
Art. 128 TEC	Art. 151 TEC	Art. III–280
		Art. III–281*
Art. 126 TEC	Art. 149 TEC	Art. III–282
Art. 127 TEC	Art. 150 TEC	Art. III–283
		Art. III–284*
		Art. III–285*
		Title IV
Art. 131, 136a TEC	Art. 182, 188 TEC	Art. III–286
Art. 132 TEC	Art. 183 TEC	Art. III–287
Art. 133 TEC	Art. 184 TEC	Art. III–288
Art. 134 TEC	Art. 185 TEC	Art. III–289
Art. 135 TEC	Art. 186 TEC	Art. III–290
Art. 136 TEC	Art. 187 TEC	Art. III–291
		Title V
Art. C, J(1) TEU	Art. 3(2.sentence), 11 TEU	Art. III–292
Art. J.3(1) TEU	Art. 13(2) TEU	Art. III–293
Art. J.1, J.2 TEU	Art. 11, 12 TEU	Art. III–294
Art. J.3 TEU	Art. 13 TEU	Art. III–295
Art. J.8, J.16 TEU	Art. 18(1–2), 26 TEU	Art. III–296
Art. J.4 TEU	Art. 14 TEU	Art. III–297
Art. J.5 TEU	Art. 15 TEU	Art. III–298
Art. J.12 TEU	Art. 22 TEU	Art. III–299
Art. J.13 TEU	Art. 23 TEU	Art. III–300
		Art. III–301*
Art. J.8 TEU	Art. 18(5) TEU	Art. III–302
Art. J.14 TEU	Art. 24 TEU	Art. III–303
Art. J.11 TEU	Art. 21 TEU	Art. III–304

Maastricht Treaty – TEU/TEC	Nice Treaty – TEU/TEC	The EU Constitution
Art. J.9 TEU	Art. 19 TEU	Art. III–305
Art. J.20 TEU	Art. 20 TEU	Art. III–306
Art. J.15 TEU	Art. 25 TEU	Art. III–307
Art. M TEU	Art. 47 TEU	Art. III–308
Art. J.7 TEU	Art. 17(2) TEU	Art. III–309
		Art. III–310*
		Art. III–311*
		Art. III–312*
Art. J.18 TEU	Art. 28(2, 5) TEU	Art. III–313
Art. 110 TEC	Art. 131 TEC	Art. III–314
Art. 113 TEC	Art. 133 TEC	Art. III–315
Art. 130u TEC	Art. 177 TEC	Art. III–316
Art. 130w, 130y TEC	Art. 179, 181 TEC	Art. III–317
Art. 130x, 130y TEC	Art. 180, 181 TEC	Art. III–318
Art. 130y TEC	Art. 181a TEC	Art. III–319
		Art. III–320*
		Art. III–321*
Art. 228a TEC	Art. 301 TEC	Art. III–322
Art. J.14 TEU	Art. 24 TEU	Art. III–323
Art. 228 TEC	Art. 300(7) TEC	
Art. 238 TEC	Art. 310 TEC	Art. III–324
Art. 238 TEC, J.14 TEU	Art. 300 TEC, 24 TEU	Art. III–325(*)
Art. 109 (1–3, 5) TEC	Art. 111(1–3, 5) TEC	Art. III–326
Art. 229–31 TEC	Art. 302–4 TEC	Art. III–327
		Art. III–328*
		Art. III–329*
		Title VI
Art. 253 TEC	Art. 190(4–5) TEC	Art. III–330
Art. 138a TEC	Art. 191 (point 2) TEC	Art. III–331
Art. 138b TEC	Art. 192 TEC	Art. III–332
Art. 138c TEC	Art. 193 TEC	Art. III–333
Art. 138d TEC	Art. 194 TEC	Art. III–334
Art. 138e TEC	Art. 195 TEC	Art. III–335

Maastricht Treaty – TEU/TEC	Nice Treaty – TEU/TEC	The EU Constitution
Art. 139 TEC	Art. 196 TEC	Art. III–336
Art. 140, 143 TEC	Art. 197, 200 TEC	Art. III–337
Art. 141 TEC	Art. 198 TEC	Art. III–338
Art. 142 TEC	Art. 199 TEC	Art. III–339
Art. 144 TEC	Art. 201 TEC	Art. III–340
		Art. III–341*
Art. 147 TEC	Art. 204 TEC	Art. III–342
Art. 148, 150 TEC	Art. 205(1, 3), 206 TEC	Art. III–343
Art. 151 TEC	Art. 207 TEC	Art. III–344
Art. 152 TEC	Art. 208 TEC	Art. III–345
Art. 153 TEC	Art. 209 TEC	Art. III–346
Art. 157(2) TEC	Art. 213(2) TEC	Art. III–347
Art. 159 TEC	Art. 215 TEC	Art. III–348
Art. 160 TEC	Art. 216 TEC	Art. III–349
Art. 161 TEC	Art. 217 TEC	Art. III–350
Art. 163 TEC	Art. 219 TEC	Art. III–351
Art. 156, 162(2) TEC	Art. 218(2), 212 TEC	Art. III–352
Art. 165 TEC	Art. 221 TEC	Art. III–353
Art. 222 TEC	Art. 222 TEC	Art. III–354
Art. 167 TEC	Art. 223 TEC	Art. III–355
Art. 168 TEC	Art. 224 TEC	Art. III–356
		Art. III–357*
Art. 168a TEC	Art. 225 TEC	Art. III–358
Art. 164 TEC	Art. 220 (2.sentence), 225a TEC	Art. III–359
Art. 169 TEC	Art. 226 TEC	Art. III–360
Art. 170 TEC	Art. 227 TEC	Art. III–361
Art. 171 TEC	Art. 228 TEC	Art. III–362
Art. 172 TEC	Art. 229 TEC	Art. III–363
	Art. 229a TEC	Art. III–364
Art. 173 TEC	Art. 230 TEC	Art. III–365
Art. 174 TEC	Art. 231 TEC	Art. III–366
Art. 175 TEC	Art. 232 TEC	Art. III–367
Art. 176 TEC	Art. 233 TEC	Art. III–368

Maastricht Treaty – TEU/TEC	Nice Treaty – TEU/TEC	The EU Constitution
Art. 177 TEC	Art. 234 TEC	Art. III–369
Art. 178 TEC	Art. 235 TEC	Art. III–370
Art. L TEU	Art. 46e TEU	Art. III–371
Art. 179 TEC	Art. 236 TEC	Art. III–372
Art. 180 TEC	Art. 237 TEC	Art. III–373
Art. 181 TEC	Art. 238 TEC	Art. III–374
Art. 182, 183, 219 TEC	Art. 239, 240, 292 TEC	Art. III–375
Art. L, M TEU	Art. 46 TEU	Art. III–376
Art. K.7 TEU	Art. 35(5) TEU	Art. III–377
Art. 184 TEC	Art. 241 TEC	Art. III–378
Art. 185, 186 TEC	Art. 242, 243 TEC	Art. III–379
Art. 244 TEC	Art. 244 TEC	Art. III–380
Art. 245 TEC	Art. 245 TEC	Art. III–381
Art. 109a TEC	Art. 112 TEC	Art. III–382
Art. 109b TEC	Art. 113 TEC	Art. III–283
Art. 188c TEC	Art. 248 TEC	Art. III–384
Art. 188b(2–7) TEC	Art. 247(2–7) TEC	Art. III–385
Art. 198a TEC	Art. 263 TEC	Art. III–386
Art. 198b TEC	Art. 264 TEC	Art. III–387
Art. 198c TEC	Art. 265 TEC	Art. III–388
Art. 194 TEC	Art. 258(1–2) TEC	Art. III–389
Art. 195 TEC	Art. 259 TEC	Art. III–390
Art. 196 TEC	Art. 260 TEC	Art. III–391
Art. 198 TEC	Art. 262 TEC	Art. III–392
Art. 198d TEC	Art. 266 TEC	Art. III–393
Art. 198e TEC	Art. 267 TEC	Art. III–394
Art. 189a TEC	Art. 250 TEC	Art. III–395
Art. 189b TEC	Art. 251 TEC	Art. III–396
Art. 162(1) TEC	Art. 218(1) TEC	Art. III–397(*)
		Art. III–398*
Art. 191a TEC	Art. 255 TEC	Art. III–399
Art. 154, 188b(8), 194 TEC	Art. 210, 247(8), 258 (4.sentence), TEC	Art. III–400

Maastricht Treaty – TEU/TEC	Nice Treaty – TEU/TEC	The EU Constitution
Art. 192 TEC	Art. 256 TEC	Art. III–401
		Art. III–402*
Art. 203 TEC	Art. 272(1) TEC	Art. III–403
Art. 203 TEC	Art. 272 TEC	Art. III–404
Art. 204 TEC	Art. 273 TEC	Art. III–405
Art. 202 TEC	Art. 271 TEC	Art. III–406
Art. 205 TEC	Art. 274 TEC	Art. III–407
Art. 205a TEC	Art. 275 TEC	Art. III–408
Art. 206 TEC	Art. 276 TEC	Art. III–409
Art. 207 TEC	Art. 277 TEC	Art. III–410
Art. 208 TEC	Art. 278 TEC	Art. III–411
Art. 209 TEC	Art. 279 TEC	Art. III–412
		Art. III–413*
		Art. III–414*
Art. 209a TEC	Art. 280 TEC	Art. III–415
Art. K.15, J.1 TEU	Art. 43b, c, e, f TEU, 11(3) TEC	Art. III–416
Art. K.15, K.16 TEU	Art. 43h, 44(2. last sentence) TEU	Art. III–417
Art. K.15 TEU	Art. 43b TEU	Art. III–418(*)
**5a TEC	Art. 40a, 27c TEU, 11(1–2) TEC	Art. III–419
	Art. 40b, 27e TEU, 11a TEC	Art. III–420
	Art. 44a TEU	Art. III–421
		Art. III–422*
Art. K.17 TEU	Art. 45 TEU	Art. III–423
		Title VII
Art. 227 TEC	Art. 299(2), (2.sentence, 3) TEC	Art. III–424
Art. 222 TEC	Art. 296 TEC	Art. III–425
Art. 211 TEC	Art. 282 TEC	Art. III–426
Art. 212 TEC	Art. 283 TEC	Art. III–427
Art. 213 TEC	Art. 284 TEC	Art. III–428
Art. 213a TEC	Art. 285 TEC	Art. III–429
Art. 214 TEC	Art. 287 TEC	Art. III–430
Art. 215 TEC	Art. 288 TEC	Art. III–431

Maastricht Treaty – TEU/TEC	Nice Treaty – TEU/TEC	The EU Constitution
Art. 216 TEC	Art. 289 TEC	Art. III–432
Art. 217 TEC	Art. 290 TEC	Art. III–433
Art. 218 TEC	Art. 291 TEC	Art. III–434
Art. 234 TEC	Art. 307 TEC	Art. III–435
Art. 223 TEC	Art. 296 TEC	Art. III–436
		Part IV
		Art. IV–437*
		Art. IV–438*
		Art. IV–439*
Art. 227 TEC	Art. 299(1, 3–6) TEC	Art. IV–440
Art. 233 TEC	Art. 306 TEC	Art. IV–441
Art. 239 TEC	Art. 311 TEC	Art. IV–442
Art. 39 TEC	Art. 48 TEU	Art. IV–443
		Art. IV–444*
		Art. IV–445*
Art. Q TEU, 240 TEC	Art. 51 TEU, 312 TEC	Art. IV–446
Art. R TEU, 247 TEC	Art. 52 TEU, 313 TEC	Art. IV–447
Art. S TEU, 248 TEC	Art. 53 TEU, 314 TEC	Art. IV–448

PART I

1

From EEC to EU: a brief history of the development of the Union

1.1 Introduction

The purpose of this chapter is to provide a brief overview of the development of the European Economic Community into the European Union. The development of the organisation will be traced chronologically and certain underlying themes and tensions will be identified. It is these perennial issues, or the way the Community institutions and the Member States choose to deal with them, that will shape the future of the EU.

1.2 Development prior to the Single European Act

The European Economic Community (EEC) came into existence following the signing of the Treaty of Rome in 1957 by the six original Member States, France, Germany, Italy, Belgium, The Netherlands and Luxembourg. A second Rome Treaty signed by the same six States created Euratom (the European Atomic Energy Community) on the same day. These treaties, but particularly the EEC Treaty, represented the culmination of a movement towards international cooperation which had been growing throughout the twentieth century, and which was given particular impetus in Europe following the devastation inflicted by the Second World War.

The institutional model for the EEC had already been provided by the European Coal and Steel Community (ECSC) set up in 1951 with the Treaty of Paris by the same six States. However, the scope of the EEC was altogether wider. The ECSC was concerned only with creating a single market in coal and steel; the EEC was designed to create an economic community. Although its aims were primarily economic, to create a single 'common' market in Europe, they were not exclusively so. The founder members of the EEC were fired by ideals as well as economic practicalities. As stated in the preamble to the EEC Treaty, its signatories were 'Determined to lay the foundations of an ever closer union among the peoples of Europe', 'Resolved by thus pooling their resources to preserve and strengthen peace and liberty'.

These words were not pious platitudes; they represented the spirit and purpose underlying the Treaty, and, in interpreting the Treaty and legislation enacted thereunder, the Court of Justice (ECJ), the original court of the EU, has never lost sight of these aims.

Although the institutional framework of the EEC, as of Euratom, was modelled on that of the ECSC, the three communities at the outset held only two institutions in common, the Assembly (subsequently renamed the Parliament) and the ECJ. It was not until the Merger Treaty 1965 that the other two main institutions merged. The High Authority, the executive body of the ECSC, merged with the EEC and Euratom Commission to form what is now the Commission, and the Council of Ministers of the ECSC with that of the EEC and Euratom to become a single Council. Henceforth the three communities continued to function as separate entities, but with shared institutions.

1.3 Enlargement

The United Kingdom, together with Denmark and the Republic of Ireland, finally joined the Communities in 1973 with the Treaty of Accession under a Conservative government led by Edward Heath. Incorporation of the Treaties into UK law was achieved by the European Communities Act 1972. (Norway joined at the same time but subsequently withdrew following a referendum which came out against membership.)

There were many reasons for the UK remaining outside the Community for so long. The UK was reluctant to loosen its existing ties with the Commonwealth, which membership of the EEC would clearly entail; it wished to retain its (perceived) 'special relationship' with the USA; and, as an island nation which had not been subject to enemy occupation during the First and Second World Wars, it no doubt lacked the sense of urgency which inspired the original Member States. Suspicious that membership of the EEC would involve an unacceptable loss of sovereignty, the UK preferred the looser ties of the European Free Trade Association (EFTA), which the UK entered on its creation in 1959. When the UK did seek to join the EEC, persuaded by its clear economic success, its entry was blocked for some years, largely due to the efforts of the French President, General de Gaulle. Even after accession in 1973 public opinion in the UK was divided; it was only following a referendum in favour of membership conducted in 1975 under the government of the Labour Party that the UK's membership was fully and finally confirmed.

In 1979 Greece, and in 1986 Spain and Portugal, signed acts of accession to join the Communities, bringing the then total membership to 12. Membership of what was by then the Union increased again with the accession of Austria, Finland and Sweden on 1 January 1995. Norway held a referendum which again resulted in a vote against membership. Expansion continued, with the largest number of countries joining the EU in one go, ten, acceding in 2004. The new Member States, sometimes referred to as the EU10, are, in alphabetical order, Cyprus, the Czech Republic, Estonia, Hungary, Latvia, Lithuania, Malta, Poland, Slovakia and Slovenia, resulting in an EU of 25. Further expansion is planned.

The process of joining the EU involves several stages. A country must first of all apply, then be recognised as a candidate country at which point formal negotiations are opened between the candidate country and the EU. The negotiations have the aim of concluding an accession treaty. After the signing of the accession treaty, there is usually a period before the treaty comes into force. Before a country can accede to the EU, it must satisfy the terms of Article 49 TEU, Article 6 TEU and three additional criteria, the Copenhagen Criteria. Article 49 requires that a state be European, Article 6 requires respect for democracy, the rule of law and respect for human rights. The Copenhagen Criteria are: the political criterion (respect for democracy and human rights); the economic criterion (the need for viable market economies and the capacity to cope with competitive pressure and market forces within the EU); and the ability to adopt the Community *acquis*. During the accession period, the Commission reviews progress of the country and publish its views.

Bulgaria, Croatia (application submitted 21 February 2003), Romania, Turkey (application submitted 14 April 1987) and the Former Yugoslav Republic of Macedonia (FYR Macedonia, application submitted 22 March 2004) have all applied to join the Union. Additionally, the EU has established European partnerships with Albania, Bosnia-Herzegovina, and Serbia and Montenegro including Kosovo (as defined by the United Nations Security Council Resolution 1244 of 10 June 1999), as all have been recognised as potential candidate countries. Croatia and the former Yugoslav Republic of Macedonia likewise entered into European partnerships, the purpose of which is to assist countries in preparing for membership of the EU. Both Romania and Bulgaria signed accession treaties on 25 April 2005 with the intention of joining the Union in January 2007 (acceding countries). The position as regards the remaining countries has to varying degrees been contentious.

The Commission Communication (COM (2004) 656 final) stated that in the Commission's opinion Turkey satisfied the Copenhagen Criteria. The Commission additionally suggested using a three-tier strategy for the negotiations to ensure that the reform process in Turkey continues, with particular regard to the zero tolerance policy towards torture and ill-treatment. The first tier deals with the political criterion and seeks to support the reform process. The EU will monitor the political reforms on an annual basis, and the Commission may suspend negotiations if there is a serious and persistent breach of the principles of liberty, democracy, respect for human rights and fundamental freedoms or the rule of law on which the Union is founded. If such a recommendation is made, the Council may, by a qualified majority, decide to suspend negotiations. This wording mirrors that in the TEU regarding Member States' obligations to comply with human rights obligations. The second tier introduces an intergovernmental conference (IGC) within which the negotiation process will be held. The Commission notes that amongst other factors, the EU will have to consider its financial position before negotiations with Turkey can be concluded. The third tier concerns cultural dialogue and dealing with differences in society and specifically the rights of minorities. The Commission aims to facilitate dialogue involving civil society. Finally, the Commission in its Communication emphasised that Turkey's accession could not take place before 2014. In November 2005, the Council agreed to start negotiations, the process actually starting in spring 2006.

Croatia has been officially recognised as a candidate country and in November 2004 the Commission recommended opening negotiations. The December 2004 European Council envisaged commencing negations the following March, provided Croatia fully cooperated with the International Criminal Tribunal for the former Yugoslavia (ICTY). On the day before negotiations were due to start, the European Council found that Croatia had not so cooperated and the Council of Ministers decided to postpone the commencement of accession negotiations with

Croatia indefinitely. In November 2005, the European Council agreed to start the negotiation process, which seems to be starting contemporaneously with the negotiations with Turkey. Although FYR Macedonia has submitted its application for membership, at the time of writing it had not obtained the official status of candidate country.

1.4 The Single European Act

An important development in 1986 was the signing of the Single European Act (SEA) by the then 12 Member States. A White Paper issued by the Commission in 1985 had revealed that despite the Community's long existence, many barriers still existed to the achievement of the single internal market. The result was a new treaty, the SEA. The principal purpose of the SEA was to eliminate the remaining barriers to the single internal market within the deadline of 31 December 1992, to be achieved by a massive programme of harmonisation (see Chapter 15). In addition, the SEA extended the sphere of Community competence and introduced a number of procedural changes designed to accelerate the Community decision-making process (see Chapter 3). The SEA undoubtedly injected a new dynamism into Community affairs. By February 1992, 218 of the 282 proposals forming the complete programme for the completion of the internal market had been adopted. Although the 1992 programme reached its termination date, it is important to remember that the provisions the SEA introduced remain and are still used as a basis for legislation (see Chapter 15), as barriers to the internal market remain even now (see, e.g, the proposed Services Directive, discussed in Chapter 22). Note also that legislation may be enacted but is, to a large extent, dependent on Member States for implementation, and that this may be where the real difficulty lies (see Chapters 5 and 10).

1.5 Treaty on European Union

The late 1980s saw a growing movement within the Community towards closer European union. In December 1989, two intergovernmental conferences were convened pursuant to cooperation procedures introduced by the SEA to consider the questions of (a) economic and monetary union and (b) political union. The conferences, which lasted for a year, resulted in the signing, at Maastricht, on 7 February 1992, of the Treaty on European Union (TEU).

The TEU comprised two distinct parts. One part (Article G, renumbered Article 8 following the ratification of the 1997 Amsterdam Treaty ('ToA') which, in pursuit of greater coherence, renumbered most of the articles of both the EC Treaty and the TEU), consisting of 86 paragraphs, introduced substantial amendments to the EEC Treaty, and renamed it the European Community (EC) Treaty, reflecting its wider purposes.

The second part of the TEU (Articles 1–7 and 9–53 (Articles A–F and H–S respectively as originally provided in the TEU)), representing the political pillar of the

Treaty, stood as a separate treaty establishing the European Union (Article 1 (ex A)). It set out a number of general principles (Articles 1–7 (ex A–F)) and provided specifically for cooperation, with a view to adopting joint action, in the field of foreign and security policy (FSP), and eventually defence (Articles 11–28 (ex J)) and for cooperation and the framing of common policies in justice and home affairs (JHA) (Articles 29–45 (ex K)). These two areas of cooperation came to be referred to as the second and third pillars, respectively, of the European Union. The remaining pillar is the EC, together with Euratom and, prior to its expiry in 2002, ECSC. The communities comprising this pillar, referred to as the first pillar of the Union, are together called the European Communities.

The TEU was due to come into effect on 1 January 1993, following ratification as required by all Member States. As a result of difficulties, political and legal, causing delay in ratification in some Member States (notably the UK, Denmark and Germany), the Treaty did not enter into force until 1 November 1993. From that date the EEC Treaty became the EC Treaty, and will henceforth be referred to as such in this book, except where the term EEC is needed for reasons of historical accuracy. The term European Union (EU), introduced in Article 1 (ex A) of the TEU to describe the union of Member States as comprised under the European Community treaties and the TEU, is not strictly applicable to matters of law relating to the EC Treaty, although it is widely used in that context. The law emanating from JHA and CFSP may be referred to as EU law. For the most part, these areas fall outside the scope of this book. Therefore, although there are occasions when it might properly be used, for example to describe 'the EU' or 'EU countries' or 'EU citizens', the term EC will continue to be used throughout this book to avoid confusion.

1.5.1 Monetary union

Like the SEA, the TEU extended the scope of Community competence and strengthened its institutional machinery; in particular, the powers of the European Parliament (see Chapter 2). Perhaps one of the most politically sensitive issues was the introduction of provisions designed to lead to full economic and monetary union by 1999. The fact that of the then Member States both Britain and Denmark negotiated provisions allowing them to opt out of this process indicates the importance of this issue. Even Germany, one of the driving forces behind monetary union, experienced difficulties: the validity of Germany's entry into the single currency was challenged, albeit unsuccessfully, before the German Constitutional Court.

The road to monetary union fell into three stages (Articles 98–124 (ex 102a–109m) EC). Stage one consisted of the completion of the internal market and the removal of controls on the movement of capital. This stage has been completed. Stage two began on 1 January 1994. It aimed to ensure the convergence of the economies of the Member States, measured by criteria set out in the EC Treaty. These are commonly referred to as the 'convergence criteria'. Only countries which satisfy the convergence criteria will be able to join the single currency. The Member States joining economic and monetary union in the first wave were identified in a Commission recommendation based on its Convergence Report of 25 March 1998 on the state of the Member States' economies. Eleven States were identified as having satisfied the convergence criteria: Belgium, Germany, Spain, France, Ireland,

Italy, Luxembourg, The Netherlands, Austria, Portugal and Finland (the UK, Denmark and Sweden having, for the time being, opted out of monetary union). This recommendation was confirmed by the European Council meeting in May 1998. Subsequently, Greece became the twelfth Member State to join the Eurozone, on 1 January 2002. None of the new Member States has as yet joined the Eurozone, although, if they meet the criteria, they are entitled to do so. Cyprus, Estonia, Latvia, Lithuania, Malta and Slovenia have joined the Exchange Rate Mechanism as a preliminary step and Slovenia is planning to join the Eurozone on 1 January 2007. The final stage in monetary union was the irrevocable locking of the exchange rates of the Member States' currencies and the introduction of a common currency, the euro. The date set for the introduction of the single currency was 1 January 1999, although euro coins and notes were not issued in all the participating States until 2002. Following the introduction of the single currency, a new exchange rate mechanism was introduced between the euro and the currencies of those Member States which have not yet joined the single currency. In addition to this, the Treaty contains provisions detailing the institutions necessary to run the single currency (Articles 112–115 (ex 109a–109d) EC). These are the European Central Bank and a committee to determine economic policy, the Council of Economic and Finance Ministers (ECOFIN). Member States, including those which have not adopted the Euro, are supposed to run their economies in line with the Stability and Growth Pact (SGP), though difficulties in practice led to its revision in 2005 so as to allow greater flexibility in national responses to difficult economic times.

1.5.2 Union citizenship

The TEU also introduced the notion of citizenship of the Union (Article 17 (ex 8)). On the face of it, citizenship seems a relatively straightforward notion. It entitles EC nationals to certain rights such as freedom of movement throughout the Community (see Chapters 14 and 24) and the right to vote and to stand in municipal elections or elections to the European Parliament in any Member State in which they are resident. The precise extent of the rights to be granted to citizens, however, is not clear. Will citizenship incorporate rights contained elsewhere in the EC Treaty hitherto granted to EC workers, the self-employed and their families (see Chapters 20–24)? Does it include rights and duties found in the TEU provisions relating to the other pillars (e.g., Article 6(2) TEU)? There has been much debate about the significance of European citizenship. Some see it as the beginning of the development of a common European identity or as a means to ameliorate the democratic deficit (see Chapter 3) within the Union. Others have criticised it for being no more than a label for the rights of free movement already incorporated in the EC Treaty. The Treaty does allow the Member States to increase the rights attaching to the notion of citizenship, but more than ten years on it is still too early to tell how citizenship will fully develop. Recent secondary legislation is based in part on Article 18, though the legislation in question is, in part, a codification of existing secondary legislation and ECJ jurisprudence in the context of free movement of people (see further Chapters 14, 20 and 24).

1.5.3 The other two pillars of the Union

Articles 11–28 (FSP) and 29–42 (JHA) of the TEU constitute the second and third pillars, respectively, of the European Union. Although they can be seen as extending the powers transferred to the European level, they can also be seen as maintaining the autonomy of the nation State. Decision-making within these pillars was, under the TEU, predominantly in the hands of the Council representing the Member States, and, although these two pillars share the institutions of the EC, the other Community institutions were limited in the role they played in both policy-making and enforcement. In addition, all decisions were required to be made unanimously and consequently progress towards effective policies within these areas would inevitably be slow. The TEU contained provisions whereby some of the policies in JHA could be transferred to the EC (former Article K.9 TEU). A comparison between the decision-making processes within these two pillars and those of the EC (Chapter 3) would suggest that such a transfer must surely increase the speed of common policy-making in those areas. This was recognised and, following the ratification of the Treaty of Amsterdam, several policy areas originally dealt with under JHA (e.g., immigration and asylum of third-country (non-EU) nationals) are now dealt with under the EC Treaty (see further Chapter 24). The decision-making procedures under JHA have also been amended following Amsterdam, specifying in limited circumstances the use of qualified majority voting (qmv).

1.6 Impact of the Treaty of Amsterdam

Former Article N(2) TEU provided that an intergovernmental conference should be held in 1996 to examine the provisions which the TEU required to be reviewed. Other issues could also be included on the agenda (Article N(1) TEU). The purpose of the review was to revise the policies and institutional structure of the Union to ensure its effectiveness (Article 2 TEU). This was an issue gaining ever more relevance with the increase of Union competence under the TEU and the further expansion of Union membership. As the IGC discussions progressed, it became clear that the issues to be decided coalesced round three broad, interlinked themes: democracy, transparency and efficiency (discussed further in Chapters 2 and 3). The review process continued into June 1997, when a draft treaty was agreed at Amsterdam. This treaty, the Treaty of Amsterdam (ToA), was signed on 2 October 1997 and came into force on 1 May 1999. Since the ToA renumbered all treaty articles, the new numbers of the treaty articles will henceforth be used throughout this book, with the former numbers bracketed alongside them where necessary to clarify the meaning (e.g., Article 30 (ex Article 36) EC), save where reasons of historical accuracy (such as articles cited in the context of cases) dictate that the original article number be shown.

1.6.1 Strengthening the EC pillar

The ToA, when compared with the ambitious TEU, may seem to achieve little; indeed, when one considers the stresses to which the EU will increasingly find its decision-making subject once membership is enlarged, the ToA could be criticised for failing to deal adequately with the difficult institutional questions involved. Nonetheless, the ToA can still be seen as constituting a cautious but significant expansion of the Community's scope. The first (EC) pillar was strengthened by streamlining its decision-making powers and by the allocation of new competence (see Chapter 3). Certain provisions, e.g., those relating to the admission of third-country nationals, have been moved from the third pillar (JHA) to the EC pillar. In addition, the Schengen Agreement which dealt with controls at internal borders (an agreement outside the EC/EU framework between a number of the EU Member States) and its associated decisions have, in effect, been incorporated into the EC Treaty. All of these have been combined to form a new Title in Part Three of the EC Treaty, Title IV. These are discussed further in Chapter 24. Some completely new provisions have also been introduced into the EC Treaty, such as those relating to unemployment. The Protocol on Social Policy, originally annexed to the EC Treaty by the TEU, has now been incorporated into the main body of the EC Treaty, replacing the existing social policy provisions.

1.6.2 Equality and fundamental rights

These changes reflect a shift of emphasis away from the mainly economic conception of the EC to a more political idea, founded on fundamental rights and principles. In particular, the provision prohibiting discrimination on grounds of nationality (Article 12 EC) has been developed by the insertion of a new clause (new Article 13 EC) authorising the Council to 'take appropriate action to combat discrimination based on sex, racial or ethnic origin, religion or belief, disability, age or sexual orientation'. Although not phrased in the absolute terms of Article 12 EC, it reinforces the idea of non-discrimination as a fundamental principle which the ECJ has invoked and used to significant effect in its case law. Further, the promotion of the equality of men and women is now identified in Article 2 EC as a task of the Community.

This concern with fundamental principles is also evidenced by amended Article 7 TEU. This provides that any Member State found to have committed a persistent and serious breach of the fundamental principles listed in Article 6 TEU may be suspended from voting in the Council of Ministers, although it will remain subject to obligations arising out of the Union membership, such as compliance with EC legislation. The principles listed in Article 6 TEU are: liberty, democracy, respect for human rights and fundamental freedoms, and the rule of law. Respect for the rule of law, in particular, is evidenced by the expansion of the ECJ's jurisdiction in relation to the new Part Three Title IV of the EC Treaty and to the JHA provisions remaining in the TEU. In both these cases, however, the jurisdiction of the ECJ is subject to serious limitations (discussed further in Chapters 7 and 9). Nevertheless, the ToA has extended the scope of Union competence under the EC Treaty and effected significant changes in the TEU (see Chapter 3).

1.6.3 Closer cooperation

The last main change introduced by the ToA was the introduction of provisions allowing for 'closer cooperation' by Member States. This is often referred to as an example of the principle of 'flexibility', described as the leitmotif of the ToA. It allows differing conceptions of the European ideal and different degrees of commitment to coexist within the Union framework. As such, it is a variant of the concepts variously described as 'multi-speed Europe', 'Europe of variable geometry' and 'Europe of concentric circles' prior to the 1996 IGC. The ToA allows Member States which wish to cooperate more closely in specific areas within the general scope of the treaties, but which are not yet subject to Community legislation, to do so. Although the Union had, in effect, accepted this approach in specific policy areas, for example, the UK and Danish opt-out of monetary union under the TEU and the UK opt-out of the Protocol on Social Policy in the TEU, this is the first time that a *general* provision (Article 11 EC and, in respect of JHA, Article 40, subject in both cases to Articles 43 and 44 TEU) allowing for such separate development within the Union framework, has been incorporated.

Cooperation is limited to the matters within the scope of the treaties and cannot in any way conflict with Community law (see Article 11 EC as inserted by ToA). Article 11 limits the circumstances in which closer cooperation may operate; in particular, a majority of the Member States must be involved, the action must be in the furtherance of the Union's objectives and closer cooperation must not affect the rights and obligations of Member States not involved. The provisions in relation to closer cooperation within the JHA provisions of the TEU are couched in similar terms (Article 43 TEU). Note that these provisions have been amended by Nice (see below at 1.7.1) and possibly by the Constitution (see below at 1.8).

This provision for closer cooperation may bring some advantages, notably by preventing the frustration of the integrationist aims of the majority of Member States by the minority, thus relieving the tensions between the Member States which disagree about the depth of European integration and allowing compromise within the Union. It also carries disadvantages. In particular, the boundary between matters falling only within the sphere of EC law proper and areas permitting closer cooperation may be unclear. Furthermore, is it possible in the context of the internal market for some Member States to become involved in closer cooperation without affecting the position of other Member States? In which case, should the other Member States be involved in the discussions leading to the adoption of closer cooperation measures even though they will not be bound by them? This problem has already surfaced in the context of the UK's role in the introduction of monetary union. On the other hand, if the ECJ interprets the provisions set out in new Article 11 EC strictly so as to preserve and even stretch the boundaries of Community law, then the opportunities for such cooperation will be severely curtailed. In any event, the very fact that the Community contemplates an approach where some Member States go ahead regardless of the wishes of others will undermine the ideas of community and solidarity which are fundamental to the creation of both the internal market and an ever closer union. Unless benefits and burdens are equally shared, there is a danger that the achievements of the past 49 years could be undone. It seems, however, that 'flexibility' is now an unavoidable part of ensuring agreement within the Union and allowing it to develop.

1.7 **Treaty of Nice**

It has been suggested that the ToA failed to deal with one of the main issues identified by the 1996 IGC – that of preparing the EU for enlargement. On that basis, the swift progression from treaty negotiation (in respect of the ToA) to treaty negotiation (regarding the Treaty of Nice) is not that surprising. Just two months after the ToA was signed, the European Council at the Cologne Summit in 1999 called for an IGC with a mandate to address certain unresolved issues: size and composition of the Commission; the weighting of votes in Council; and the extension of qualified majority voting. At the same time, wider discussions were taking place about the legitimacy of the Union and the scope of its powers. There was consequently a debate as to whether the issues to be dealt with by the Nice Treaty should be broadened. In the event, the Treaty remained relatively narrowly focused, although following the 2000 Feira European Council, it also dealt with 'enhanced cooperation'. Difficult constitutional questions, including the status of the Charter of Fundamental Rights, the form of which had been agreed prior to Nice, were deferred until the 2004 IGC. The Treaty of Nice then might well be described as dealing with the leftovers of the ToA but going no further.

1.7.1 **Changes to the TEU: enhanced cooperation**

The main changes to CFSP and JHA pillars relate to the provisions on closer cooperation, now called in what seems like a symbolic change, 'enhanced cooperation'. Article 43 TEU, which introduced closer cooperation, has been replaced by a revised version of that provision and new Articles 43a and 43b. Significantly, following Nice, enhanced cooperation may take place with only eight Member States. Under the ToA version 'a majority of Member States' was required. Although eight out of fifteen Member States would constitute a majority of Member States at that time, post-enlargement this is no longer the case. In a EU of 25 members (or perhaps more), the number of participating Member States required to make a majority has increased. Article 43 EC following Nice is less strict in other aspects too, particularly as regards the level of impact 'enhanced co-operation' is permitted to have on non-participating Member States. Article 43(1)(f) in its original form required that any closer cooperation:

> does not affect the competences, rights, obligations and interests of those Member States which do not participate therein,

whilst the post-Nice version requires that the competences, rights and obligations of such Member States be respected. Similarly post-Nice, the *acquis communautaire* is to be 'respected' rather than to be unaffected by the cooperation, as had been the requirement following ToA. In both instances, it will be easier to satisfy the tests in the post-Nice version of Article 43 than it would have been under the version inserted by ToA. It would seem that the intention is to make the enhanced cooperation provisions more workable.

1.7.2 Changes to the EC pillar

As already noted, certain institutional changes were included in Nice: these are discussed further in Chapter 2. Changes were also made to the court structure, significantly strengthening the role of the Court of First Instance which gained the right to hear some preliminary rulings procedures. (See Part II.) The closer cooperation provisions in Article 11 EC have been amended and renamed 'enhanced cooperation' in line with the amendments to Article 43 EC. Further, co-decision and qualified majority voting are extended to a wider range of substantive provisions. Certain sensitive areas, such as taxation, still remain outside qualified majority voting.

1.7.3 Status of the Treaty of Nice

Although it may not have had the great ambitions of TEU, Nice ran into difficulties when the Member States sought the approval of the treaty within their own legal orders. Surprisingly, perhaps, the Irish voted 'no' to the Nice Treaty in June 2001. This was an embarrassing result, as the institutional rebalancing contained in Nice was viewed as the necessary precursor to further enlargement, which was already being negotiated. It was only in October 2002 that a second Irish referendum accepted the Treaty of Nice. Ireland finally lodged its instrument of ratification on 18 December 2002. As provided in the Nice Treaty, it came into force on 1 February 2003.

1.8 Treaty establishing a Constitution for Europe

Although the Declaration on the Future of Europe attached to the Treaty of Nice identified specific issues that would need to be addressed—the delimitation of powers between the EU and the Member States; the simplification of the treaties; and the role of the national parliaments within the EU—it also called for 'a wider and deeper debate about the future of the European Union'. The Laeken Declaration confirmed the issues to be addressed by the next round of treaty negotiations. It confirmed the points identified in the Nice Declaration and emphasised the importance of bringing Europe closer to its citizens. In doing so, however, it raised the possibility of reorganising the treaties so as to introduce a constitutional text for the EU. Such a text would be important for setting down the future characteristics of the Union; indeed the fact that the word 'constitutional' has been introduced is seen by some as significant. Unusually by comparison with the intergovernmental nature of previous treaty revisions, the Laeken Declaration provided for the establishment of a Convention on the Future of Europe. The Convention's function was to identify and discuss the relevant issues before drawing up a final document containing the possible options for the Union's future development to form a starting point for the IGC's discussions.

The resulting treaty, the Treaty establishing a Constitution for Europe (the Constitution), was signed on 29 October 2004. The status of the treaty is in doubt as not all Member States have ratified it. Significantly, referenda held in France and The

Netherlands produced a 'no' vote, and the governments of both countries have accepted this outcome. Nonetheless, the 'Constitution' is not yet dead. Although two Member States have voted against ratifying the Constitution and according to its terms, the Treaty cannot therefore come into force, 13 Member States have ratified it. The European Council in June 2005 adopted a Declaration which agreed that the ratification process should continue, although the November 2006 deadline should be extended. In the remaining states, it seems that the process of ratification has stalled somewhat, the difficulties occasioned by the two 'no' votes perhaps being seized opportunistically by domestic politicians as a means of avoiding difficult debates within the domestic arena. The Union has entered a period of reflection to consider how to proceed and in particular how to proceed with the Treaty. Should the Constitution be revived, it is not clear even whether it will remain in its current form. Given its uncertain status, this edition will not deal with the changes proposed by the Treaty in any great detail, though a brief overview follows and specific important points will be identified where appropriate throughout the book. References to the Constitution are to the document signed by the Member States in 2004.

Despite the grand title, the Constitution can be seen as reordering, clarifying and simplifying, and making existing principles express rather than adding much that is totally new. Despite the attempt to make the Treaty underpinning the Union more accessible, standing at nearly 500 pages long and comprising approximately 155,000 words, the Constitution is hardly a light read. To make navigation around this tome easier, it is laid out in seven parts. Part I, which is untitled, deals with the general principles underlying the Union. The Charter of Fundamental Rights follows as Part II. Part III, the longest section of the treaty, comprises the policies and functioning of the Union, and includes much of the former EC Treaty and TEU. Title IV concerns relations between the Union and remaining colonial dependencies. Title V is more general in scope as it covers external relations of the EU generally, bringing together the previously disparate elements currently found in both the EC Treaty and the TEU. Title VI covers institutions, finance and 'enhanced cooperation'. The Constitution concludes with a brief set of provisions in Title VII, General and Final Provisions, which deals with issues such as official languages, territorial scope and how the Constitution may be revised. The structure of the Constitution is reflected in the numbering. Each article is identified by a roman numeral which identifies the part in which it is located, as well as an Arabic number identifying it within that part.

Although the Constitution may be a consolidating act, it will introduce some changes, some of which, though small, are significant. Crucially, when implemented, it will repeal all existing treaties and the current pillar structure, thus removing the distinction between Community and Union. It also identifies the powers, or competence, of the Union and the Member States expressly (discussed in Chapters 3 and 15), as well as formally incorporating the doctrine of primacy of Union law (discussed in Chapter 4). Some changes are made to the operation of the institutions, mainly to improve efficiency of decision-making (see Chapter 2) and to contain the size of the institutions with the increased size of the Union. Particular controversy surrounded the introduction of a formal president of the council as well as a foreign minister. Some limited areas of Union competence are added and the scope of some areas amended. Thus we see references to space, energy, humanitarian aid and territorial cohesion. Although these areas were not hitherto mentioned in the treaties, their introduction seems to reflect existing Union practice. Similarly, areas such as sport have been the subject of declarations attached to treaties, if not part of the formal Union competence. Article I–44 deals with enhanced co-operation. A minimum of one-third of the Member States must participate, a lower percentage than currently, but enhanced cooperation is expressed to be used only as a last resort and within the framework of Union non-exclusive competence. Finally, there are changes to the types of Union legislation and their terminology, discussed further in Chapter 3.

How do we assess the impact of the Constitution? On the one hand it formally introduces the notion of constitution, with all its implications of statehood. On the other, the word 'constitution' has been used in the context of the Community and the Union for some considerable time: the ECJ in its judgment in *Parti Ecologiste 'Les Verts'* v *European Parliament* (case 294/83) referred to the EC Treaty as a constitutional document and the debates about statehood of the Union arose in the context of European citizenship, introduced by TEU. In terms of the text itself, the Constitution does not constitute a huge turning point. As with many of the previous treaties, it is a reaction to the current concerns afflicting the EU. In this case, the triggers seem to have been the need to 'tidy up' the Union's procedures in the face of the expansion in membership and, importantly, to try to deal with the increased public disaffection with the EU. Thus we see an increased emphasis on democracy, participation, the rights of individuals and the values of the Union. Vaclav Havel, President of the Czech Republic, sought a 'concise, clearly formulated and universally understandable constitution [which] would simply make it easier for the citizens of an integrating Europe to recognize what the European Union stands for; to understand it better; and, consequently, to identify with it'. Whether this aim has been achieved is altogether another matter.

1.9 Theories of integration

Although the development of the Union is usually described as a linear progression towards a specified goal, it has also been argued that the integration process has actually fallen into different phases with key characteristics. These phases may even suggest that, despite the rhetoric of an 'ever closer Union', the end goal of the Union is not well defined or even necessarily agreed upon. Different theories have been put forward to describe and explain these different phases, though the degree to which it is possible to describe each such phase only by reference to an individual theory is debatable. The main schools of thought follow.

1.9.1 Functionalism

Functionalism was a theory which was popular during the Community's early years. As its name implies, it is based on identifying specific, discrete economic areas, usually those perceived as 'non-contentious', in which Member States are encouraged to cooperate. Technocrats (technical experts in the relevant field) would manage these fields in the interests of the Community as a whole. Unlike politicians, they would not be influenced by the need to retain power. Instead, technocrats were perceived as making rational choices. Functionalism can be used to describe the European Coal and Steel Community prior to its demise.

1.9.2 Neofunctionalism

What is now the European Community is much broader than the ECSC. Neofunctionalism developed as a way of describing this endeavour. It has similarities to functionalism in that it too is based on cooperation in specific areas. Neofunctionalism argues, however, that those involved in the process became key players to whom allegiance may be transferred. Integration in non-contentious areas spills over into other, more sensitive areas. The process results in a diminution of natural governmental power and a matching increase in the power of the technocratic level to deal with sensitive issues.

1.9.3 Intergovernmentalism

Both of the above theories can be described as forms of supranationalism. Supranationalism argues that power is located above the nation state. This view is challenged by intergovernmentalism, which assumes that the central actors are the States themselves, which essentially act to protect their own interests and power base.

The EC Treaty can be seen as containing elements that illustrate a supranational aspect, but also intergovernmental elements. Intergovernmentalism can be seen in the Luxembourg Accords, in which the then Member States agreed that one Member State could effectively veto a measure in its national interest. The sections of the Union Treaty which deal with justice and home affairs and common foreign and security policy vest most power in the Council, made up of representatives of the Member States' Governments. Agreement in these spheres was by agreement of all Member States. In contrast, the powers of the institutions are unusual in their scope and their independence from the Member States (see further Chapter 2). The use of qualified majority voting in Council (see Chapter 3) introduces the possibility of Member States being outvoted with the consequence that a Member State may be obliged to implement policies with which it might not agree. This is not easily compatible with a view of Member States each acting in their own interest unless membership of the Community itself is taken into account.

1.9.4 Multi-level governance

To some extent the discussion in academic writing about the tension between supranationalism and intergovernmentalism has been replaced during the 1990s with writings on the subject of multi-level governance. Multi-level governance seeks to explain how the Union is governed rather than focusing on the nature of the integration process. Theories in this school of thought allow a broader range of actors to appear in the discussion of EU governance. This results in a picture which is not just based on a conception of the EU as driven by the Member States or by the actions of the EU institutions.

1.10 Conflicting attitudes towards the Union

It should be noted that the frequency of Treaty revision has increased dramatically during the 1990s. While the EEC Treaty survived from 1957 to the SEA of 1986 relatively unchanged, since then there have been three Treaty revisions that have been brought into force: TEU, ToA and Nice, as well as the proposed revisions contained in the Constitution. The significance of this development is unclear. One might suggest that it reflects the political changes occurring during the 1990s, particularly in Europe. Alternatively, the change could reflect the dissatisfaction of the Member States (and their population) with the current EU. The difference between the European Communities and the other two pillars created by the TEU and, unless the Constitution comes into force, largely retained is illustrative of the conflicting attitudes held by Member States and individuals towards the Community (and now the Union) since its inception, as exemplified by the divergent views expressed by politicians. Although academic literature may now focus on the way the EU operates, within political debate tensions remain as to the nature of the EU and its future. These tensions seemed particularly apparent during the negotiation and ratification of the TEU, although as noted at 1.9.3, this issue is not new, nor has it gone away. The problem is that there are two main competing visions of Europe: the intergovernmental and the federal. In *Brunner* v *European Union Treaty* [1994] 1 CMLR 57 Germany's power to ratify the TEU was challenged as being contrary to the German constitution. It was argued that in transferring further powers and competence to the EC institutions, the TEU was seeking to create a Euro-State. The German Constitutional Court found, it is submitted correctly, that the EC was a federation of States not a Euro-State. Nevertheless, the loss of autonomy of action of the Member States consequent on membership of the EC has certainly been considerable. This has increased during the life of the EC as more and more powers have been transferred to the Community in the SEA, the TEU and the ToA, and even Nice. This process has been emphasised by the increased use of both qmv and co-decision. Some integrationists approve of this as part of the process of achieving an 'ever closer union'. Others fear the loss of sovereignty and see the EC as having grown beyond the loose association of States within a free trade area that the EC was intended to be.

Sometimes these differing views of the EU result in Member States being characterised as either Euro-sceptic or pro-Europe, but a degree of caution must be exercised about such generalisations. There is a difference between political rhetoric and legal reality. Out of the group of 15 Member States, it is perhaps surprising that Italy and France, both original Member States, had a much less impressive record of compliance than Denmark, which is often perceived as more Euro-sceptic. According to the 2004 Commission *Review on Implementation of Community Law* (COM (2005) 570), all the EU15 states had a much less impressive implementation record than the new Member States, though this may be due to the pressures of proving compliance with the Copenhagen Criteria and acceding to the EU, than evidence of a long-term political intention to ensure prompt implementation of all Community legislation. Furthermore, there is a tendency for Member States' representatives to put national interest – or national political pressures – over the Community interest. This is not just the case with France (see its ban on British beef in defiance of the Community position) or the UK (veto on introduction of Community tax on interest income, thought to threaten the UK bond market), but with all Member States (see the impact of the Greek position on the accession of Turkey; Portugal on the diversion of Community funding to new Member States).

With the introduction of monetary union, the transfer of further competence to the EC and the proposed expansion in membership the question, 'Where next?' assumes a new significance as Member States try to fight for their own view on the future of Europe. The ToA, re-emphasised by Nice, has sought to solve the problem by the principle of 'flexibility'; but the danger is that a flexible Europe could become a fragmented Europe. Arguably, any risk of fragmentation could increase with further expansion, as the Union will have not just more voices, but a greater variety of interests to satisfy.

1.11 The future: a period of reflection

With the future of the Constitution uncertain, there has been debate amongst the institutions and national politicians about where to go next. The EU entered a one-year period of reflection to enable further debates to take place within the various Member States on how best to proceed. As the European Parliament noted in its December 2005 Resolution, the discussions have so far focused on the context of the Treaty, rather than the actual legal text, thus reaffirming the idea that the development of the Union has resulted from responses to external pressures rather than developing in a legal vacuum according to a grand plan laid down in advance. Equally, there is a gap between the legal form of the Constitution and the concerns expressed about it, which reflect rather more general concerns about the nature of Europe. Whether the period of reflection will solve the difficulties is not yet known. So far, it is equally unclear whether the Constitution is dead or whether it will arise, either as it is or in some similar guise.

A Commission communication suggests that the Member States re-affirm their commitment to the EU by a solemn political declaration to commemorate the fiftieth anniversary of the Community in 2007. It also suggests that another institutional takes place in 2008. This communication will be the subject of discussion by the European Council in June 2006.

In view of the disputes and reservations within the Union about its future, the continuing enthusiasm for membership may seem surprising, but it cannot be denied that the EU has achieved a great deal. It is an important market. The figures for the EU15 in 2001 show that the Union was responsible for just under 20 per cent of world trade in goods and approximately 25 per cent of trade in services. Especially in view of its expansion in membership, it thus constitutes a trading block which has the potential significantly to influence world affairs. Membership of the EU gives states the opportunity to be part of this. Also, for some countries, because of the criteria for membership, belonging will indicate that they have achieved democratic respectability in the eyes of other nations. Last, but by no means least, during the past fifty years the EC has enjoyed an era of unprecedented peace, and the expansion of peace, stability, freedom and prosperity has been an underlying aim of the eastward enlargement of the Union. It is easy to overlook the fact that one of the underlying objectives of the European communities was, in the words of the preamble to the ECSC Treaty:

to substitute for age-old rivalries the merging of their essential interests; to create . . . the basis for a broader and deeper community among peoples long divided by bloody conflicts.

FURTHER READING

Birkinshaw, P., 'A Constitution for the EU?' (2004) 10(1) EPL 57.

—, 'Constitutions, Constitutionalism and the State' (2005) 11(1) EPL 31.

Bradley, K., 'Institutional Design in the Treaty of Nice' (2001) 38 *CML Rev* 1095.

Church, C. H. and Phinnemore, D., *Understanding the European Constitution: An Introduction to the EU Constitutional Treaty* (Routledge, 2006).

Craig, P., 'Constitutions, Constitutionalism and the European Union' (2001) 7(2) *European Law Review* 125.

Curtin, D., 'The Constitutional Structure of the Union: A Europe of Bits and Pieces' (1993) 30 CML Rev 17.

Curtin, D. and Decker, I., 'The EU as a "layered" International Organisation: Institutional Unity in Disguise' in Craig, P. and de Burca, G. (eds), *The Evolution of EU Law* (Oxford University Press, 1999).

De Burca, G., 'The Institutional Development of the EC: A Constitutional Analysis' in Craig, P. and de Burca, G. (eds), *The Evolution of EU Law* (Oxford University Press, 1999).

Delacourt, C., 'The *Acquis Communautaire*: Has the Concept had its Day?' (2001) 38 CML Rev 829.

de Witte, B., 'The Closest Thing to a Constitutional Conversation in Euorpe: The Semi-Permanent Treaty Revision Process' in Beaumont, P., Lyons, C. and Walker, N. (eds), *Convergence and Divergence in European Public Law* (Hart Publishing, 2002).

Douglas-Scott, S., 'In Search of Union Citizenship' (1998) 18 YEL 29.

Edwards, D., 'The Impact of the Single Market' (1987) 24 CML Rev 19.

Ehlermann, C. D., 'Differentiation, Flexibility, Closer Cooperation: The New Provisions of the Amsterdam Treaty' (1998) 4 *ELJ* 246.

Gormley, L., 'Reflection on the Architecture of the EU after the Treaty of Amsterdam' in O'Keeffe, D. and Twomey, P. (eds), *Legal Issues of the Amsterdam Treaty* (Hart Publishing, 1999).

Harmser, R., 'A European Union of Variable Geometry' (1994) 45 *NILQ* 109.

Lasok, P., 'The European Constitution—New Wine or Old?' (2005) 37 *Bracton Law Journal* 15.

Meyring, B., 'Intergovernmentalism and Supranationality: Two Stereotypes of a Complex Reality' (1997) 22 *EL Rev* 221.

Schilling, T., 'The Autonomy of the Community Legal Order: An Analysis of Possible Foundations' (1996) 37 *Harv Int'l LJ* 307.

Shaw, J., Magnette, P., Hoffmann, L. and Bausili, A. V. (eds), *The Convention on the Future of Europe: Working Towards an EU Constitution* (Federal Trust for Education and Research, 2003).

Usher, J., 'Variable Geometry or Concentric Circles: Patterns for the European Union' (1997) 46 *ICLQ* 243.

Weiler, J. H. H., 'The Transformation of Europe' (1991) 100 *Yale LJ* 2403.

Weiler, J. H. H. and Haltern, U. R., 'Response: The Autonomy of the Community Legal Order – Through the Looking Glass' (1996) 37 *Harv Int'l LJ* 411.

2

Institutions of the EC: composition and powers

2.1 Introduction

One of the defining features of the Community and, to a certain extent the Union, is the scope and level of power given to its institutions. This chapter outlines the composition and powers of the institutions and the relationship between them. Where appropriate, the main changes that would be introduced by the Treaty establishing a Constitution for Europe ('the Constitution'), should it come into force, will be outlined.

The relationship between the institutions is important, because it is the different powers ascribed to the institutions and the way they have to work together that provide the 'checks and balances' within the Community legal order. It is the institutional balance that prevents one institutional actor from becoming too powerful, rather than the more traditional notion of 'separation of the powers'. It is clear that the powers of the respective institutions have evolved over time. The institutional balance is not a static notion.

A preliminary question, however, is 'What are the institutions?'

The principal institutions set up by the original EEC Treaty (now Article 7 (ex 4) EC) to carry out the Community's tasks comprised:

(a) the Assembly or Parliament,

(b) the Council,

(c) the Commission, and

(d) the Court of Justice.

In addition, Article 7 (ex 4) provided for the setting up of a Court of Auditors and an Economic and Social Committee, and the Merger Treaty 1965 (Article 4) for the creation of a Committee of Permanent Representatives of the Member States (COREPER). Following the SEA, the Court of First Instance was set up in October 1988 (Decision 88/591 [1989] OJ C215/1). Under the TEU the Court of Auditors was added to the institutions listed in Article 7, and the various treaties, including the Constitution, as well as ECJ case law, have affected its evolution. Both COREPER and the Committee of the Regions are now based on Article 7(2) EC. In addition, a European Investment Bank has been created (Article 9 (ex 4b) EC), and provision made for setting up of the European System of Central Banks (ESCB) and a European Central Bank (ECB) (Article 8 (ex 4a) EC).

This chapter focuses on the institutions that have general roles in the Community and so will not deal with bodies like the ECB, whose function is more specific. It should also be noted that the TEU provides for institutional unity within the Union. The same institutions have roles not only within the EC but within the other two pillars. Save for noting that the institutions' roles, especially those of the Commission and the Parliament, are very different with respect to JHA and CFSP, this chapter does not deal with the institutions' functions under the other two pillars. Should the Treaty establishing a Constitution for Europe enter into force (see Chapter 1), the three-pillar structure would be abandoned and there would be a single Union; however, the provisions on JHA (to be renamed 'Area of Freedom, Security and Justice') and CFSP would continue to apply different rules from the remainder of the EU's activities. The core institutional framework would also be reduced to the Parliament, European Council, Council of Ministers, the Commission and the Court of Justice (Article I–19(1)). The remaining institutions would be relegated to a group of 'other union institutions and advisory bodies' (Part I, Title IV, Chapter II).

2.2 Parliament (Articles 189–201 (ex 137–44) EC)

2.2.1 Appointment

As created by the Treaty of Rome in 1957, the European Parliament, called in that treaty the Assembly (but since called by the SEA the Parliament), was not a democratic body, although the Treaty provided for the eventual introduction of direct elections. It consisted of representatives of Member States who were required to be members of a national parliament. The introduction of direct elections, which occurred in 1979, resulted in increased democracy and increased concentration and expertise, since members are responsible to their electorate, and, as anyone is now eligible to stand, many are no longer subject to the rigorous demands of the 'dual mandate' at home and in Europe. MEPs are elected for five years. A perennial complaint is that, despite the introduction of direct elections, the uniform system of election envisaged by Article 190(3) (ex 138(3)) EC has not yet been introduced. It should be noted that recent elections have revealed a low voter turnout, which may cast doubt on the claims of the European Parliament to legitimacy on the basis of the direct election of its members.

2.2.2 Composition

Following enlargement in 2004, Parliament consists of 732 members, with Germany having 99, France, Great Britain and Italy each having 78 representatives, Poland and Spain 54, The Netherlands 27, Belgium, the Czech Republic, Greece, Hungary and Portugal 24, Sweden 19, Austria 18, Denmark, Finland and Slovakia 14, Ireland and Lithuania 13, Latvia 9, Slovenia 7, Cyprus, Estonia and Luxembourg 6, and Malta 5. The Treaty of Nice fixed the maximum number of MEPs at 732 (Article 189 EC). Article 190(2) EC specifies the number of representatives. The division of MEPs among the Member States has always been subject to criticism: Germany has fewest representatives per head of population, whilst Luxembourg has a disproportionately high number of representatives given its size. The post-Nice position may also be seen as unfair in some regards: for example, the Czech Republic and Hungary are, arguably, under-represented. Again, this may cast doubt on the representative nature of democracy in the European Parliament.

Members meet in plenary sessions of approximately one week per month in Strasbourg, although the majority of Parliament's Committee meetings, where much important work is done, are held in Brussels. The rest take place in Strasbourg or, occasionally, Luxembourg. Members, who are drawn from 75 political parties, sit in 11 broad, multi-national political groupings, the largest being the Socialist group; they are required to vote 'on an individual and personal basis' and 'they shall not be bound by any instructions and shall not receive a binding mandate' (Act Concerning Direct Elections, Article 4(1)). Although the fact that MEPs do not sit in national groupings might indicate that the European Parliament has supra-national characteristics, it should not be forgotten that MEPs are still elected within national systems along national party lines. The European Parliament does not have what might be termed a 'European political consciousness'. Article 191 EC, however, contains an expression of the importance of political parties at the European level for the formation of 'a European awareness' and the expression of 'the political will of the citizens of the Union'. The Treaty of Nice has supplemented this provision by the insertion of a second paragraph which gives the Council the power to lay down regulations governing such parties and their funding. This was done with Regulation 2004/2003 on the regulations governing political parties at European level and the rules regarding their funding ([2003] OJ L297/1), which provides the criteria for allocating funding, with the main role given to the European Parliament. A first report by the European Parliament was adapted on 23 March 2006, but came too late to be considered here.

2.2.3 Functions

As befitted a non-elected body, the original Parliament had few powers. Its functions were advisory and supervisory. It was not intended as a legislative body. Following the introduction of direct elections, Parliament has played an increasingly important consultative role in the legislative process and has been given the final say over certain aspects of the budget. Budgetary procedure will be discussed further below. The TEU, ToA and Nice have further and substantially increased its powers, so that it is no longer limited to the merely consultative but may be said to have a legislative role. The Constitution, were it to enter into force, would consolidate this role.

In its advisory role, Parliament was originally required by the Treaty to be consulted by the Council of Ministers where legislation is proposed in a number of specific (and important) areas, e.g., Articles 52, 83 and 308 (ex 63, 87 and 235 EC respectively), but contrast Article 40 (ex 49) (workers). In these areas the Council must seek, and is obliged to consider, Parliament's opinion, although there is no obligation on the Council to follow it. This is an essential procedural requirement. Legislation has been successfully challenged when, although the Parliament had been consulted on an initial draft of the legislation, it was not consulted following substantial amendment to the draft (*Parliament* v *Council* (case C–21/94) (road taxes); by contrast *Germany* v *Council* (case C–280/93) (banana quotas) was unsuccessful. In *Roquette Frères SA* v *Council* (case 138/79) and *Maizena GmbH* v *Council* (case 139/79) a regulation of the Council was annulled because, although Parliament's opinion had been sought, the regulation had been passed by the Council before that opinion had been obtained. Nonetheless, in *Parliament v Council* (case C–65/93), where the Parliament's opinion was clearly required as a matter of some urgency, the Council made all efforts to obtain that opinion in time. In failing to meet the deadline, the Parliament, according to the Court, had failed in its duty of cooperation. The Court, as a consequence, refused to annul the regulation. How far the Parliament's duty of cooperation extends is not clear. The Advocate-General in this case was clearly unhappy about the effect such a decision would have on the institutional balance and thought that any changes to it would be more appropriately dealt with by treaty amendment.

The requirement for consultation and cooperation by Parliament, and consequently Parliament's influence, was strengthened by the introduction of conciliation procedures in 1977 (Joint Declaration of the European Parliament, the Council and the Commission, [1975] OJ C89/1) and the cooperation procedures introduced by the SEA. The SEA also greatly extended the range of matters on which Parliament had to be consulted. The SEA also gave Parliament the power of (final) assent in respect of the admission of new members and the conclusion of association agreements with non-member countries. The TEU gave Parliament certain rights to be consulted in respect of the JHA and CFSP provisions. What was then Article K.6 (now Article 34) TEU provided that Parliament was to be consulted on the principal aspects of activities within JHA provisions. This provision also ensured that the Parliament's views were duly to be taken into consideration. Similar provisions existed in respect of the CFSP provisions (Article 21 (ex J.7) TEU). Parliament's right to be consulted and informed has increased under the ToA and Nice, but it still has no real powers over the second and third pillars of the TEU. Although there would no longer be separate pillars if the Constitution were to enter into force, Parliament's role would remain confined to a consultative role (see Articles I–40(8) and I–41(8) of the Constitution re CFSP, and Articles III–263, III–266(3) and III–269(3) for FSJ; note also the consent rules, e.g., in Articles III–270(2)(d) and III–271(1), requiring Parliament's consent in adopting measures relating to judicial cooperation in criminal matters).

As well as a right to be *consulted*, and to participate in *conciliation* and *cooperation* procedures, the TEU introduced for Parliament, in a new Article 251 (ex 189b) EC, a right of *co-decision* with the Council in certain defined areas. Thus, under this procedure, the European Parliament now has a significant power of veto in matters subject to the new procedures. The co-decision procedure was to apply in a number of areas previously governed by the less onerous cooperation procedures (e.g., Articles 40, 44, 46 and 94 (ex 49, 54(2), 56(2), 100a) EC) and in some new spheres of activity (e.g., health, consumer protection). In other areas, the consultation or cooperation procedures (the latter now laid down in Article 252 (ex 189c) EC) were to continue to apply. In cases of doubt it will be necessary to consult the Treaty to ascertain which procedure is applicable, although the ToA and Nice have greatly extended the areas to which co-decision applies with the result that the cooperation procedures in future will largely disappear. Should the Consitution come into effect, there would be an 'ordinary legislative procedure', which is, in essence, the present co-decision procedure (see Article III–396 of the Constitution). This would form the default legislative procedure in the Treaty. These procedures will be examined further in Chapter 3. Despite the increase in areas in which the co-decision procedure is used already, the European Parliament is still limited to a subordinate role in certain key areas, such as agriculture, and in the JHA and CFSP pillars, a position which would not change under the Constitution.

Parliament was also given a new power of initiative by the TEU. Under Article 192 (ex 138b) EC it may, acting by a majority of its members, request the Commission to submit any appropriate proposals on matters on which it considers that a Community act is required for the purpose of implementing the Treaty. It has been suggested that, provided Parliament stays within the guidelines set out in its rules of procedure, these requests are likely to be considered sympathetically by the Commission. To date, Parliament has exercised these rights sparingly.

Although the European Parliament's powers have been increased, there are weaknesses in the ways it fulfils its responsibilities. The European Parliament does not have great expertise in highly technical areas. Further, under Article 192 it may *request* policy initiatives; it does not have the *right* of policy initiative. This would remain the case if the Constitution were to come into effect in its present form.

In its supervisory role, Parliament exercises direct political control over the Commission. Commissioners must reply orally or in writing to its questions. The Commission must publish a general report which is discussed in Parliament in open session. Parliament meets members of the Commission in committees, and in practice, though this is not required by law, members of Parliament are consulted by the Commission at the pre-legislative stage. Parliament also has the power to dismiss the Commission, by passing a vote of censure (Article 201 (ex 144) EC). Such a motion must be carried by a two-thirds majority of the votes cast, which must represent a majority of the members of Parliament. A particular weakness of this sanction is the fact that the existing Commissioners will remain in office until their replacements are appointed. There is nothing to prevent the Member States from suggesting the same Commissioners be reappointed. Nonetheless, it was the Parliament's dissatisfaction with the conduct of the Commission that resulted in the Commissioners resigning in 1999. Some, but not all, of the Commissioners were re-appointed. Prior to Maastricht, Parliament had no say in the appointment of new Commissioners. This has now been remedied; under Article 214(2) (ex 158(2)) EC, Parliament must be consulted on the nomination of the President and the appointment of Commissioners and the Commission as a whole has to be approved by Parliament. Parliament approves the appointment of the President individually and then the President and the other Commissioners together as a group. This procedure would, in essence, remain under the Constitution (see Article I–27).

The Council is not subject to the control of Parliament, but is subject to extensive supervision. Parliament reports on the activities of the Council three times a year, and the President of the Council must present an address to Parliament at the beginning of every year. This is followed by a general debate. The incoming President also presents a survey of the previous six months' presidency, and the chairman of the conference of foreign ministers reports to Parliament once a year on the progress of European political cooperation. Under the Constitution, there would be a new role of 'European Council President' (see Article I–22), who would be required to report to Parliament after each meeting of the European

Council. Unlike proceedings in the Council and the Commission, proceedings in Parliament are published in the *Official Journal* (see the discussion on transparency in Chapter 3).

Parliament also has standing to challenge the legality of acts adopted by the other institutions in accordance with Article 230 (ex 173) EC (see Chapter 11). It is through such challenges that Parliament enforces its rights and seeks to ensure that the correct treaty base is used for legislative measures. This is important because the treaty base affects the degree of parliamentary involvement in the legislative process. Judicial review under Article 230 EC has been used vigorously for these purposes. In passing, it should be noted that the Parliament's power in this regard was extended under the Treaty of Nice and it now also has the power to request advisory opinions under Article 300(6) from the European Court of Justice.

To broaden Parliament's role it was given power under the TEU to set up a temporary committee of inquiry to investigate alleged contraventions or maladministration in the implementation of Community law (except where the alleged facts are being examined before a court or subject to legal proceedings) (Article 193 (ex 138c) EC) and has been required to appoint an Ombudsman to receive and enquire into complaints of maladministration in the activities of the EC institutions or bodies (with the exception of the Court of Justice and the Court of First Instance acting in their judicial capacity) (Article 195 (ex 138e) EC). At the end of an investigation, the Ombudsman is under an obligation to produce a report to the Parliament and to the institution under investigation. The original complainant is also notified of the result. The Ombudsman has also to produce an annual report to Parliament. In addition, any natural or legal person residing or having its registered office in a Member State is to be given the right to address a petition to the European Parliament on a matter which comes within the Community's fields of activity, and which affects him, her or it directly (Article 194 (ex 138d) EC). These provisions would remain essentially unaltered, should the Constitution become effective in its present form (see Articles III–334 and III–335).

One area of the Parliament's activities which is sometimes overlooked is the work that it does in promoting human rights. We will see when looking at the role of general principles of community law (Chapter 6) that the Parliament was instrumental in persuading the other institutions to recognise the importance of human rights and, in particular, the European Convention on the Protection of Human Rights. The Parliament is not concerned only with human rights protection within the Union. The European Parliament also established a subcommittee to identify urgent cases of human rights abuse throughout the world, and the facts surrounding each case. In appropriate circumstances it will put forward resolutions on specific cases to the whole Parliament. The passing of such resolutions can raise the profile of certain issues and can therefore play a useful role in generating pressure to remedy the problem. The subcommittee also produces an annual report and the degree of reaction that it provokes in countries criticised by it is indicative of its influence.

2.3 Council (Articles 202–210 (ex 145–154) EC)

2.3.1 Appointment

The Council, following the TEU now called 'The Council of the European Union', consists of representatives of the Member States, one from each Member State, who must be 'at ministerial level, authorised to commit the government of that Member State' (Article 203 (ex 146) EC). Ministerial representatives tend not to be appointed specifically for their role within the Council; appointment is a consequence of their appointment within the domestic system. Although ministerial representatives may be accountable as part of an individual Member State's government through that Member State's parliamentary system, there is no body, at European or national level, to hold the Council itself accountable.

2.3.2 Composition

The Council is not a fixed body. Although it is limited to one voting delegate from each State, membership may fluctuate depending on the topic under discussion. For example, where matters of agriculture are at stake, the Ministers of Agriculture will normally participate; if the matters relate to general economic policy the Chancellors may be present; where high-level policy matters are to be discussed, the Council may consist of Heads of State.

Where Heads of State come together in a specially constituted body, acting on matters of both EC law and political cooperation, the body is termed the European Council. Although it had been in existence since 1974 it was not recognised in the EC Treaty until the Single European Act. Article 2 SEA provided:

> The European Council shall bring together Heads of State or of government of the Member States and the President of the Commission of the European Communities. They shall be assisted by a Minister for Foreign Affairs and by a member of the Commission. They shall meet at least twice a year.

This provision has been further amplified by Article 4 (ex D) TEU.

Specific configurations based on subject matter have been identified. This varying membership has led to criticism that the Council of Ministers lacks coherency: there is no one who is responsible for co-ordinating policies. It also means that the role of bodies assisting the Council, notably COREPER (discussed further at 2.3.6) is crucial in the legislative process. It has been suggested that to improve coherency the different configurations of the Council should be reduced.

The Constitution, should it enter into force, would not impose a restriction on the number of different configurations. Two improvements would be made, however: there would be a 'General Affairs Council' responsible for ensuring consistency in the work of the different Council configurations (Article I–24(1)). Moreover, the European Council would be given the power to specify, by qualified majority, the various configurations of the Council of Ministers (Article I–24(4)). The one exception is a 'Foreign Affairs Council', which would have a formal basis in Article I–24(3).

Under the Constitution, there would be a more formal separation between the European Council (Article I–21) and the Council of Ministers (as it would be called again; see Article I–23). The European Council would comprise the Heads of State or Government for the Member States, together with the President of the European Council and the President of the Commission. The Union's Minister for Foreign Affairs would also participate.

2.3.3 Functions

The Council's task is 'to ensure that the objectives set out in this Treaty are attained' (Article 202 (ex 145) EC). To this end it 'shall . . . ensure coordination of the general economic policies of the Member States; have power to take decisions . . . and confer on the Commission, in the acts which the Council adopts, powers for the implementation of those rules which the Council lays down'. The degree to which ministers can comply with this requirement and satisfy their domestic obligations is, however, debatable.

Since the Council has the final power of decision on most secondary legislation some control by the Member States is thus assured. However, in most cases it can only act on the basis of a proposal from the Commission. Furthermore, other institutions are involved in the decision-making process to an increasing degree. Nonetheless, since legislation (even under the co-decision procedure) cannot be enacted without the consent of the Council, its methods of voting are crucial. The Treaty (Article 205 (ex 148) EC as amended) provides that voting may be by a simple majority (which is rare), by qualified majority or by unanimity. Under the Constitution, voting by qualified majority would be the default position for the Council of Ministers, except where the Constitution provides that a different majority would be required (Article I–23(3)). The European Council (see 2.3.2), however, would generally be required to act by consensus (Article I–21(4)).

2.3.4 The emergence of qualified majority voting

It is generally the case today that most decisions by the Council are taken by qualified majority voting. However, this has not always been the case. The existence of qualified majority voting is one of the more unusual, and perhaps controversial, aspects of EC law – whenever a new area is opened up to qualified majority voting, objections are raised against 'giving up the veto' in respect of that area. Yet, there are good reasons for having this form of majority.

Historically, some more sensitive areas of the Treaty were required to be implemented only by unanimous vote (e.g., Article 94 (ex 100) EC on the approximation of laws). It was, however, intended that once the period of adjustment to membership, known as the transitional period, provided by the Treaty had expired, Member States would be required to move towards qualified majority voting. This did not happen. A crisis in the Council in 1962 resulted, at the insistence of the French, in the Luxembourg Accords (1966). Under the Accords, where vital national interests are at stake, States may insist on a unanimous vote. The Accords noted 'a divergence of views on what should be done in the event of a failure to reach agreement'. It has been suggested that this approach is partly a reaction against the judicial activism of the time.

The Luxembourg Accords did not have the force of law, but they were followed in practice, with the result that in many cases the Council sought unanimity where the Treaty would not have required it. In only one case, in 1982, was a measure passed by the Council by qualified majority vote against the wishes of the UK Government, in a situation in which it was suggested that the UK was abusing its veto by attempting to force the Council's hand in a matter unrelated to the measure under discussion.

Qualified majority voting is a system of weighted voting. Clearly, from the Community standpoint it makes for more rapid and effective decision-making than unanimity as the consent of all parties is not required. It is, however, controversial because it runs contrary to the idea that a nation State is a sovereign entity and the government (or ruler) of that entity has freedom to choose which policies to implement within that State. With qualified majority voting (and also with simple majority voting) a Member State could be put in the position of being under a Treaty obligation to put in place a policy for which it had not voted.

Perhaps the most significant innovation of the SEA was to increase the number of areas in which voting was to be by qualified majority. The majority of legislation required to complete the internal market was enacted by qualified majority. Only fiscal measures, measures relating to the free movement of persons and to the rights and interests of employed persons (Article 95(2) (ex 100a(2)) and measures relating to professional training and standards (Article 47(2) (ex 57(2)) now require a unanimous vote. The TEU, ToA and Nice all further increased the scope for qualified majority voting, introducing qualified majority voting into Article 175 (ex 130s) (environment), Article 141(3) (ex 119(3)) (equal pay) and Article 100 (ex 103) (difficulties in economic situation), respectively. Many more sensitive areas however remain subject to unanimous approval. The Constitution would broaden the use of qualified majority voting further still, but there would remain some areas where unanimity would continue to be required. Member States have so far been prepared to accede to a qualified majority vote in the areas in which it has been required, although in some cases they have challenged the appropriateness of the legal basis of a measure demanding such a vote.

Furthermore, the procedure has been reinforced in the ToA in respect of the new 'flexibility' provisions of both the EC and EU Treaties (new Articles 11 EC and 43 TEU, as amended by Nice).

A difficulty with qualified majority voting is to determine the respective strength of each Member State's vote, an issue which gains in complexity whenever new countries join the existing Member States. When Finland, Sweden and Austria joined in 1995, concern was expressed that the number of votes required to block a proposal would increase. Eventually, the Ioannina Compromise (1994) was agreed with the result that the blocking minority increased to 71 per cent of the new total, but if States carrying together 23 to 25 votes intended to vote against the proposal then negotiations would continue in an attempt to satisfy their concerns.

The Ioannina Compromise raised concerns that the attitudes of Member States had not changed since the Luxembourg Accords. A contrary view has also been suggested. Although clearly there are difficulties, the Ioannina Compromise does represent some progress because under its terms the Member States are committed to trying to come to some form of compromise acceptable to all. Contrast this with the Luxembourg Accords, where Member States merely agreed to disagree.

Further attempts were made to improve the system of qualified majority voting in the ToA, and then by the Treaty of Nice. The current position (in Article 205(2) EC) is that a minimum of 232 votes (out of a total of 321) must be in favour of a proposal for it to be adopted (72.3 per cent of the share, a slight increase from 71 per cent prior to the 2004 enlargement), provided that a majority of Member States have voted in favour too (a two-thirds majority may be required where the vote is not based on a proposal by the Commission). But even then, a Member State may request confirmation that the votes in favour represent at least 62 per cent of the total population of the Union; where that is not the case, the vote will still fail (Article 205(4)).

The distribution of votes in Council is as follows:

Germany, France, Italy, United Kingdom	29
Spain, Poland	27
Netherlands	13
Belgium, Czech Republic, Greece, Hungary, Portugal	12
Austria, Sweden	10
Denmark, Ireland, Lithuania, Slovakia, Finland	7
Cyprus, Estonia, Latvia, Luxembourg, Slovenia	4
Malta	3
TOTAL	**321**

The Constitution, if it becomes effective, would retain the above distribution of votes until 31 October 2009. For further accessions before that date, the weighting would have to be recalculated. Thereafter, Article I–25 of the Constitution would move away from a numerical distribution of votes, and re-define a qualified majority as at least 55 per cent of the members of the Council making up at least 15 in number and representing at least 65 per cent of the population of the Union. Moreover, a blocking minority would have to comprise at least four Council members, or the qualified majority would be deemed to have been attained. Where the Council is not acting on a proposal from the Commission, the qualified majority would be at least 72 per cent of the members of the Council, representing at least 65 per cent of the Union's population. The intention is clearly to simplify the concept of a 'qualified majority', but only practical experience would demonstrate if that would be the effect of this provision.

2.3.5 COREPER

Since the Council is not a permanent body, meeting only a few days a month, and its members have full-time responsibilities at home, either as ministers or civil servants (civil servants have no power to vote), much of its work has been taken over by the Committee of Permanent Representatives (COREPER) (see Article 207 (ex 151) EC). COREPER is a permanent and full-time body, also consisting of representatives of Member States, whose main task is to scrutinise and sift proposals coming from the Commission prior to a final decision being made by the Council. COREPER is assisted in turn by a number of working groups, similarly represented, operating at different levels and in specialised areas. This sifting process, from working group to COREPER to Council, enables the more straightforward issues to be decided at the appropriate level, leaving the Council to focus on the more difficult or controversial decisions. Indeed, the amendments inserted by the ToA expressly recognise the power of COREPER to make procedural decisions where provided for by the Council's Rules of Procedure (see new Article 107(1) EC). Although COREPER and the working groups might be crucial in ensuring the Council can operate as a decision making body, their use is problematic in terms of transparency and accountability. The Constitution would retain the function of COREPER (Article III–344) (see also Chapter 3).

2.4 Commission (Articles 211–219 (ex 155–163) EC)

2.4.1. Appointment

The Commissioners themselves are nominated by individual Member States, and agreed amongst the Member States. Since the TEU, they are appointed for a period of five years (Article 214 (ex 158) EC), and may be reappointed. Following the entry into force of Nice, voting on this point will be by qualified majority voting. Since TEU, the Parliament has been given an increasing role in the appointment process (see 2.2.3), lending the Commissioners and especially the President of the Com-mission, a greater degree of legitimacy. At the moment, all the Member States have one Commissioner (Article 213(1), amended as of 1 January 2005). Although Commissioners are not supposed to represent the national interest of the Member State of origin, it is felt that Member States accept policies more readily where they have a voice in the discussions forming that policy. With each wave of enlarge-ment, the Commission has adhered to the principle of one Commissioner per Member State. Continuing with this would have made the Commission unwieldy and would also have made it difficult for it to continue to function as it currently does. The Treaty of Nice accepts that it will no longer work on the basis that each Member State will have a Commissioner. According to a Protocol adopted at Nice, once there are 27 Commissioners, the Council will determine the number of Commissioners and the mechanism by which they are to be selected. Some form of rotation is envisaged based on the principle of 'equality' and reflecting 'satisfactorily the demographic and geographical range of all the Member States'.

2.4.2 Composition

The present Commission consists of 25 members (one from each Member State), chosen on the grounds of their general competence and 'whose independence is beyond doubt' (Article 213 (ex 157) EC). Although appointees of the Member States, they must, in the performance of their duties, 'neither seek nor take instruc-tions from any government or from any other body' (Article 213(2) (ex 157(2)) EC). The Commission is headed by a President appointed from among the Commissioners.

The Commission is divided into directorates-general, each one responsible for certain aspects of Community policy (e.g., D/G competition), and headed by a director-general. Commissioners are given responsibility for particular directorates (a 'portfolio'). Portfolios vary considerably in size and prestige. Although Commissioners are supposed to be generally competent, whether they have any particular expertise in the portfolio allocated to them is a matter of luck rather than judgement, as individual Member States seek to ensure that its commissioner has the most prestigious portfolio possible. One might argue that, as a result, the interests (or prestige) of individual Member States takes priority over the interests of the Community.

The position of enlargement to 27 Member States has already been noted (see 2.4.1, above). However, should the Constitution come into effect, the first Commission appointed under the Constitution would, once again, include a member from each of the Member States (Article III–26(5)). Once the term of office of that Commission has expired, the number of commissioners would be reduced to two-thirds of the number of Member States, unless the European Council unanimously decided to change that number (Article III–26(6)). The new Union Minister for Foreign Affairs (see 2.10.2, below) would be a member of the Commission, and would take up the place of one national from a Member State.

2.4.3 Management powers of the Commission President

In addition to the changes noted at 2.4.1 relating to appointment, the Nice Treaty gives more power to the President regarding the management of the Commissioners (Article 217), although these changes substantially reflect changes introduced by the working rules of the Prodi Commission (OJ [2000] L308/26). In particular, Prodi suggested that the portfolios of the commissioners should be allocated on a more rational basis rather than as a matter of horse trading between the various Member States. Although the Commission acts collectively, Article 217(4) as inserted by Nice allows individual commissioners to be impugned, again reflecting the Prodi working practice. The Constitution, if it were to enter into force, would confirm the management powers of the Commission President (Article III–350).

2.4.4 Functions

The functions of the Commission are threefold. First, it acts as initiator or 'motor' of Community action. It has described itself as 'the driving force behind European integration' ((2000) COM 34), although some commentators have criticised this view of the Commission as having a unitary goal, since its policies are fragmented and sometimes conflict with each other. Nonetheless, all important decisions made by the Council must be made on the basis of proposals from the Commission (subject to the Council's power to 'request the Commission to undertake any studies which the Council considers desirable for the attainment of the common objectives, and to submit to it any appropriate proposals' (Article 208 (ex 152) EC) and the Parliament's powers to request the Commission to submit proposals (Article 192 (ex 138b) EC). Using the EC Treaty as its brief, the Commission may formulate proposals on any matter provided for under the Treaty, either where the power is specifically granted or under the more general power provided by Article 308 (ex 235) EC. Clearly, as long as a policy of unanimous voting was pursued by the Council the Commission's power of initiative was limited to what was politically acceptable; measures must of necessity be diluted for common consumption.

Nevertheless, although the Council may limit the Commission's power of initiative, the importance of this power should not be underestimated. The power of initiative allows the Commission to frame the terms of the debate in Council and Parliament through the way it drafts the proposals. Furthermore, the Commission has responsibilities which also give it control: it sets the legislative timetable for the year; and it formulates more general policy guidance through its white papers.

Secondly, the Commission acts as the Community watchdog: it has been described as the guardian of the treaties. Member States are obliged under Article 10 (ex 5) EC to: 'take all appropriate measures . . . to ensure fulfilment of the obligations arising out of this Treaty or resulting from action taken by the institutions of the Community. . . . They shall abstain from any measure which could jeopardise the attainment of the objectives of this Treaty.' It is the Commission's task to seek out and bring to an end any infringements of EC law by Member States, if necessary by proceedings under Article 226 (ex 169) EC (see Chapter 10) before the ECJ. (See also similar provisions for the enforcement of the law relating to State aids, Article 88 (ex 93) EC.) The Commission has complete discretion in this matter (see *Alfons Lütticke GmbH* v *Commission* (case 48/65) noted in Chapter 11).

Thirdly, the Commission functions as the executive of the Community. Once a policy decision has been taken by the Council, the detailed implementation of that policy, often requiring further legislation, falls to the Commission, acting under powers delegated by the Council. In exercising its powers of implementation the Commission is subject to the supervision of a range of advisory, management and regulatory committees, comprising national civil servants and appointed by the Council for that purpose. This process is referred to as 'comitology'. It has been suggested that this system, together with the Council's power under Article 202 (ex 145) (3rd indent) to reserve the right 'to exercise directly implementing powers itself' alone, or on the advice of its committees, tends to undermine the Commission's authority. Comitology has also been criticised for adding to the lack of transparency over democratic accountability in the decision-making process (see Chapter 3).

The Commission has in addition 'its (own) power of decision' (Article 211 (ex 155) EC). Regulations enacted, for example in the field of agriculture, to implement Community rules may provide for decisions of an executive nature to be taken by the Commission alone.

Finally, in pursuit of the Community's external policies, the Commission is required to act as negotiator, leaving agreements to be concluded by the Council (Articles 300 and 133) (ex 228 and 113) EC). Certain agreements can only be concluded after the assent of the European Parliament has been obtained (Article 300(3)) (ex 228(3)). It has been suggested that the role of the Council under the FSP provisions may in time overshadow this aspect of the Commission's role.

The functions of the Commission would essentially remain the same if the Constitution enters into force, although there have been changes to the wording of the relevant provisions to reflect the general changes that would be introduced (see, e.g., Article I–26(1)).

2.5 Economic and Social Committee (Articles 257–262 (ex 193–198) EC)

The Economic and Social Committee plays a consultative role in the Community decision-making process. Its members are appointed by the Council in their personal capacity, and represent a variety of sectional interests such as farmers, workers, trade unionists, or merely members of the general public. Where consultation is provided for by the Treaty this is an essential procedural requirement: such consultation must also be referred to in any resulting legislation. The Committee may also be consulted by the Council and the Commission whenever they consider it appropriate. In addition, it is entitled to advise the Community institutions on its own initiative on all questions affecting Community law. The Constitution would re-enact this position (see Articles I–32(1) and Articles III–389 to III–392).

2.6 Committee of the regions

This committee was established by the TEU to represent regional interests, and to act (like the Economic and Social Committee) in an advisory capacity in specified circumstances, as provided by the EC Treaty (e.g., Article 149(4) (ex 126(4)) education; 151(5) (ex 128(5)) culture; 161 (ex 130d) and 162 (ex 130e) regional development). Its current membership is 317 (post-enlargement). The Treaty of Nice introduced a limit of 350 on its total membership (see Article 263, as amended by Nice). Although the committee is supposed to represent the regions, Member States take a different approach to whether representatives should be determined regionally or centrally. The committee does not represent one particular set of interests and so its members may be pursuing divergent if not conflicting goals. In any event its powers are weak: the Treaty only requires that it be consulted and, unlike the Parliament, it cannot rely on the judicial review mechanism in Article 230 to ensure its powers are respected.

2.7 Budgetary procedures

These are laid down by Article 272 (ex 203) EC. As might be expected, the Commission is responsible for drawing up a preliminary draft budget. The Commission thus sets the parameters, and fixes the 'maximum rate of increase' for 'non-compulsory items' of expenditure, which neither the Council nor the Parliament is free to exceed. The preliminary draft is forwarded to the Council, which establishes the draft budget and forwards it to Parliament. At this stage Parliament may approve the budget within 45 days, in which case it stands adopted. Alternatively, Parliament may suggest 'modifications' or 'amendments'. 'Modifications' may be proposed to items of 'compulsory' expenditure – expenditure already accounted for by Community rules, principally the amount (approximately half) allocated to the common agricultural policy. 'Amendments' refer to non-compulsory expenditure, principally concerned with regional or social policy. In this case the draft is returned to the Council and Parliament's 'modifications' may then be rejected by the Council acting by a qualified majority. Its 'amendments' too may be subject to 'modification' by the Council within a 15-day time-limit. However, on return to Parliament that body may reject the Council's 'modifications' within a 15-day time-limit, acting by a majority of its members and three-fifths of the votes cast. Parliament may then adopt the budget.

Thus Parliament is responsible for adopting the budget and has the final say over 'non-compulsory' expenditure. It also has one further weapon. If it is not satisfied with the budget overall it may reject it, and in 1979 and 1984 it did not hesitate to do so. Should the Constitution come into effect, the conciliation procedure could be invoked if the Parliament did not accept the proposed budget, although the Commission would retain the ability to amend the draft budget until the Committee was convened (Article III–404).

2.8 Court of Auditors

The Court of Auditors was established in 1975 under the Budgetary Powers Treaty ([1977] OJ L359/1). Article 247 EC provides that the Court of Auditors comprises one member from each of the Member States. Appointment is by the Council of Ministers after consultation with Parliament. Following Nice, the term of office is six years. Its function is to exercise control and supervision over the implementation of the budget. Its creation represents an important step forward in the accountability of the institutions, particularly the Commission. Its annual report is published in the *Official Journal*. As a sign of its importance it was added to the list of Community institutions in Article 7 (ex 4) of the EC Treaty by the TEU (although it would be relegated from this position under the Constitution). This change may be seen as purely symbolic. A more concrete change is the requirement that it must provide both the Parliament and the Council with a statement of assurance as to the reliability of the Community accounts and the legality of the underlying transactions (Article 248 (ex 188c(1)) EC) which, following the ToA, will be published in the *Official Journal*. Article 248 EC also requires the Court of Auditors to report any cases of irregularity. It is, however, limited in its effectiveness because there seems to be no one conception amongst the Member States of what it is intended to do. Secondly, there is no one body to respond to the Court of Auditors' reports to ensure that the Community is getting value for the money it spends. This is worrying in a time where there is increased public concern about the amounts of public spending and potential fraud within the Community. Indeed, the Court of Auditors has refused to sign off the budget for the past 11 years, although in what was the most recent instance at the time of writing, 'significant improvements' in budgetary controls compared to previous years were noticed.

2.9 Court of Justice (Articles 220–245 (ex 164–168) EC)

2.9.1 Appointment

There is currently one judge from each Member State (Article 220), chosen 'by common accord of the governments of the Member States' (Article 233 EC). The Constitution would maintain the position that there would be one judge from each Member State for the Court of Justice, and at least one from each Member State for the 'General Court' (the current CFI) (Article I–29). The inclusion of judges from all the Member States allows the national legal traditions to be reflected (Articles 235 and 255 EC). The judges have a variety of backgrounds within the legal sphere, but are not appointed to represent the political interests of their 'home' Member State. All must be 'persons whose independence is beyond doubt' (Article 223 (ex 167) EC).

Judges are appointed for a six-year term, as are the judges of the Court of First Instance (CFI). They are eligible for reappointment, but there is no express guarantee that they could not be removed during their term. Appointments are staggered so that not all judges are replaced at the same time. In practice, some of the judges and advocates-general have had a long term of office: Jacobs, a former British Advocate-General, was at the Court from 1988–2006.

The judges of the ECJ are assisted by eight Advocates-General. Should the Constitution come into force, a seven-strong panel drawn from former members of the Court, national supreme courts and 'lawyers of recognised compentence' would give their opinion on candidates for appointment as judges or advocates-general before the Member States would make their appointments (Article III–357).

2.9.2 Composition

There are currently 25 judges and eight Advocates-General. Although it could sit with all 25 members, given its increasing workload, the court may sit in chambers of three or five judges, or a Grand Chamber of 11 judges (Article 16 of the Statute of the Court of Justice, based on Article 221 EC, as amended by the Treaty of Nice). The ECJ will now only sit with all members in the small instances specified in Article 16 of its Statute. Whereas a Member State could previously request a hearing before a full court, it will now only be possible to insist on a hearing before the Grand Chamber.

The ECJ may face further reform due to the pressures of enlargement. More Member States mean more judges, more different languages and a wider range of legal traditions. It remains to be seen how the Court will cope with these pressures in terms of working method and how much the changes introduced by Nice will ameliorate problems of delay. The ECJ has commented that enlargement would mean the ECJ 'would cross the invisible boundary between a collegiate court and a deliberative assembly'. The use of chambers or a devolved system of justice, however, may cause problems in ensuring uniformity between the different chambers, especially given the different legal traditions in which each judge will be grounded.

All cases before the ECJ are allocated a number, the last two digits of which refer to the year in which the action was started. Since the setting up of the CFI in 1988, all ECJ cases start with the letter 'C'. Cases with the suffix 'P' are appeals from the CFI, and those followed by 'R' are applications for interim relief.

2.9.3 Functions

The task of the ECJ is to 'ensure that in the interpretation and application of this Treaty the law is observed' (Article 220 (ex 164) EC). It is the supreme authority on all matters of Community law, and in this capacity may be required to decide matters of constitutional law (see, e.g., Chapters 4 and 6), administrative law (see Chapters 11–13), social law (Chapters 20–5) and economic law (Chapters 14–19, 26–31) in matters brought directly before it or on application from national courts. Its jurisdiction is principally over the acts of the institutions and Member States within the Communities' sphere of activity. It thus does not have jurisdiction over the actions of the European Council (*Roujansky v Council* (case T–584/93) and Article 46 (ex L) TEU excluded the ECJ's jurisidiction as regards the majority of the TEU provisions (see also *Grau Gomis* (case C–167/94)). The ECJ's jurisdiction in relation to instruments made under the JHA has been extended under the ToA: new Article 35 TEU provides that the ECJ may have jurisdiction in this area subject to the agreement of the Member States (discussed further below).

An Advocate-General's function is to assist the Court by presenting his 'submissions' – a detailed analysis of all the relevant issues of fact and law together with his recommendations to the Court. Under the new Statute of the Court, Article 20 permits the Court to decide not to have a submission from the Advocate-General if the case raises no new point of law. This possibility has already been used extensively.

Although the Advocate-General's recommendations are not always followed, where they are they are useful as a means of ascertaining the reasoning behind the Court's decision. The judgment itself, which is a single collegiate decision, is, to English eyes, terse, cryptic, with little indication of the reasoning on which it is based. Even where the Advocate-General's recommendations are not followed they may still be invoked as persuasive authority in a subsequent case.

In its practices and procedures the ECJ draws on continental models; in developing the substantive law it draws on principles and traditions from all the Member States. Although the ECJ seeks to achieve consistency in its judgments, its precedents are not binding in the English sense; it always remains free to depart from previous decisions in the light of new facts. An example of the Court expressly, and somewhat abruptly, departing from previous jurisprudence on the scope of Article 28 (ex 30) can be found in the infamous case of *Keck* (case C–267/91), in which the ECJ stated 'contrary to what has previously been decided . . .'. This judgment has been the subject of some criticism, as the ECJ never precisely identified which previous case law it overturned. (See further Chapter 18.)

As the EC Treaty is a framework treaty the ECJ has been extremely influential in 'filling the gaps', and in doing so has created law in bold, and, to those accustomed to English methods of interpretation, often surprising ways. As Lord Diplock pointed out in *R v Henn* [1981] AC 850:

> The European Court, in contrast to English courts, applies teleological rather than histori-
> cal methods to the interpretation of the Treaties and other Community legislation. It

seeks to give effect to what it conceives to be the spirit rather than the letter of the Treaties; sometimes, indeed, to an English judge, it may seem to the exclusion of the letter. It views the Communities as living and expanding organisms and the interpretation of the provisions of the Treaties as changing to match their growth.

The Court has on occasion been criticised for its activism. Others have argued that such boldness was necessary to carry the Community forward at a time, during the 1970s and early 1980s, when progress was blocked by political inertia. Whether in response to criticism, or as a result of the increased dynamism of the other institutions following the SEA, more recent judgments of the Court show signs of a new conservatism, although in certain areas, for example the imposition of penalties on the Member States for non-compliances with EC law under Article 228, it continues to surprise (see, e.g., *Commission v France* (case C–304/02); see Chapter 10). It has been this dynamism, or the consequences thereof, which led to the suggestion that the jurisdiction of the Court be limited by the 1996 IGC. This suggestion was not taken up in the ToA. Indeed following the ToA, it is possible that the ECJ's jurisdiction can be extended. Prior to the ToA, it had no power to rule on matters under the TEU. Following the ToA, it has the power to rule on decisions made under JHA provisions of the TEU, subject to agreement by individual Member States. Also, the transfer of competence over some of the JHA provisions to the EC Treaty will bring more policy areas under the ECJ's jurisdiction: it is here, however, that we find some limitations creeping in. Within these policy areas, only the courts of last instance may make a reference to the ECJ (new Article 68 EC), compared with the usual 'any court or tribunal' empowered to refer under Article 234 (ex 177) EC in respect of all other areas of the EC Treaty (see Chapter 9). Furthermore, there are significant exceptions to the jurisdiction of the ECJ where a measure concerns national security (new Article 68(2) EC). These are worrying developments as they undermine the homogeneity of the ECJ's jurisdiction and reduce the scope for the protection of individuals.

2.9.4 Court of First Instance

In 1986 the SEA provided for the setting up of a new Court of First Instance (CFI). Approval for this court was obtained in October 1988 ([1989] OJ C215/1). The court commenced proceedings on 1 September 1989. There are now 15 judges who, as in the ECJ, may sit in chambers. Its jurisdiction includes disputes between the Community and its servants ('staff cases'), and applications for judicial review and damages by 'natural and legal persons', under Articles 230 and 232, respectively). There is a right of appeal on matters of law from this court to the ECJ. An applicant cannot appeal against a decision of the ECJ unless new facts come to light (*ISAE/VP v Commission* (case C–130/91); see further Chapters 7 and 11).

The CFI's jurisdiction can be extended now that the Treaty of Nice has entered into force. Crucially, it will have jurisdiction to hear preliminary references 'in specific areas laid down by the Statute [of the Court]' (Article 225(3) as amended by Nice), although to date, no areas have been allocated to the CFI. Article 225a, introduced by Nice, creates the possibility for some areas, such as staff cases, that are currently the responsibility of the CFI, to be dealt with by judicial panel (Article

225a EC). The Civil Service Tribunal was set up by Council decision in November 2004 (2004/752/EC, Euratom, [2004] OJ L333/7) and is a judicial panel attached to the CFI. Until the Tribunal has established its own rules of procedure, it will continue to operate under the CFI's rules. It has, in essence, been set up to deal with staff cases between the Community and its officials.

Under the Constitution, the present position of the courts would, in essence, remain. However, the Court of First Instance would, perhaps confusingly, be renamed the 'General Court'. This may reflect the intention to deal with a greater number of cases which are not raising difficult new issues of law at first instance, and reserving the ECJ itself for more complex cases.

2.10 Treaty establishing a Constitution for Europe

In the preceding sections, we have already set out the impact of the Constitution on the institutions of the EC/EU, should the Constitution enter into force. In addition, there would be two further significant developments: the creation of the separate office of 'European Council President', and the establishment of a 'Union Minister for Foreign Affairs'. Both developments sparked considerable controversy, because the existence of a political figurehead and of a foreign minister might be seen as a further step towards a European state. However, on closer examination, these fears are overstated, and both positions would be a development of existing roles.

2.10.1 Council President

Article I–22 would establish a European Council President, elected by the European Council, for a period of two-and-a-half years, renewable once. The Council President would not be a current Head of State or Government, or be entitled to hold any other national office (Article I–22(3)). He or she would be responsible for chairing the European Council and managing its work, and represent the Union externally on matters falling within the CFSP.

2.10.2 Union Minister for Foreign Affairs

The Minister for Foreign Affairs would also be elected by the Council, and would preside over the Foreign Affairs Council (Article I–28), i.e., the configuration of the Council involving the national ministers responsible for foreign affairs. He or she would also be responsible for conducting the CFSP, as well as the common security and defence policy. The Minister would be one of the Commission's vice-presidents, and would be responsible for coordinating external actions within the Commission.

2.11 Conclusions

The current institutional structure of the Communities was established for a system with a more limited membership; originally there were only six Member States.

Since 1957 membership of the Communities (and then the Union) has more than quadrupled and significant policy areas, such as monetary union, have been added to the Community's remit and there is also the impact of the introduction of the Union itself and the issues included in the other two 'pillars' (FSP and JHA). Prior to the ToA, it was generally accepted that the current institutional structure was unable to function effectively in the modern Union and that institutional problems would only be exacerbated by further enlargement. Obviously, expanding the Community's competence itself increases the number of tasks the Community institutions have to perform, but increased membership brings further problems. It may be more difficult to reach agreement within the institutions: not only is it more difficult to reach agreement between a greater number of representatives, but with eastward expansion the Member States reflect a greater diversity of interests, traditions and languages. In addition to the sheer weight of numbers, there will be a risk of fragmentation as the Union becomes less cohesive. The current Member States were aware of this problem even before the ToA, resulting in a Protocol being annexed to the ToA regarding proposed institutional reform. Although this document envisaged a two-stage approach to reform, to commence negotiations with more than 10 candidate countries, it was decided to commence full-scale institutional reform foreseen by the second stage of the ToA Protocol. The result was the Treaty of Nice. To what extent has it dealt with institutional problems identified prior to and immediately after the ToA?

In contrast to the TEU, Nice was not a treaty aimed at creating a momentus constitutional change to the EU structures. Instead, it aimed to revise the way the institutions worked, to prepare the Union for enlargement. On one level the treaty can be seen as successful: difficult points of principle, such as the composition of the Commission and the issue of qualified majority voting in Council, were agreed. Given the tension between the large and small nations, it is commendable that a balance between these different interests was found. On the other hand, one could argue that many changes to the internal workings of the institutions, such as the strengthening of the role of the President in the Commission, added little, if anything, to the revised working practices already in place following the reviews of 1999. Although points of principle have been agreed, many difficulties, such as the rotation of Commissioners, remain. Implementing these decisions may give rise to problems. Nice may have taken steps to prevent all the institutions turning into 'deliberative assemblies' but some issues relating to efficiency, such as the need for multiple translations, the six-monthly rotating presidency of the Council and democracy (discussed further in Chapter 3) were not resolved.

The Constitution would change the institutional structure to an extent, but it would not produce a complete overhaul. The main institutions would remain, although their organisation and voting arrangements would be streamlined. Perhaps the most signficant development would be the departure of the 'one Commissioner per Member State' approach, although the Council would retain a power to override the Treaty by agreeing to maintain that principle beyond the expiry of the first Commission's term of office after the Constitution has come into effect. It remains to be seen whether these provisions will appear in a new Treaty, whichever form it might take.

FURTHER READING

Arnull, A., 'The European Court and Judicial Objectivity: a Reply to Professor Hartley' (1996) 112 LQR 411.

—, 'Taming the Beast? The Treaty of Amsterdam and the Court of Justice' in O'Keeffe, D. and Twomey, P. (eds), *Legal Issues of the Amsterdam Treaty* (Hart Publishing, 1999).

Bradley, K., 'The European Parliament and Treaty Reform: Building Blocks and Stumbling Blocks' in O'Keeffe, D. and Twomey, P. (eds), *Legal Issues of the Amsterdam Treaty* (Hart Publishing, 1999).

Capelletti, M., *The Judicial Process in Comparative Perspective* (Clarendon Press, 1989).

Dashwood, A. and Johnson, A., 'The Institutions of the Enlarged EU under the Regime of the Constitutional Treaty' (2004) 41 CML Rev 1481.

Dehousse, R., 'European Institutional Architecture after Amsterdam: Parliamentary System or Regulatory Structure?' (1998) 35 CML Rev 595.

Dinan, D., 'Governance and Institutions: A New Constitution and a New Commission' (2005) 43 *JCMS Supp* 37–54.

European Parliament, 'Co-Governing After Maastricht' Working Paper POLI 104/rev EN.

Fennelly, N., 'The Area of "Freedom, Security and Justice" and the European Court of Justice – A Personal View' (2000) 29 ICLQ 1.

Harden, I. and Donnelly, K., 'The Court of Auditors and Financial Control and Accountability in the European Community' [1995] EPL 599.

Hartley, T., 'Constitutional and Institutional Aspects of the Maastricht Treaty' (1993) 42 ICLQ 213.

—, 'Federalism, Courts and Legal Systems: The Emerging Constitutions of the European Community' (1986) 34 Am J Comp L 229.

Hartley, T.C., 'The European Court, Judicial Objectivity and the Constitution of the European Union' (1996) 112 LQR 95.

Laffan, B., 'Becoming a "Living Institution": The Evolution of the European Court of Aduitors' (1999) 37 JCMS 252.

Lang, J.T., 'Checks and Balances in the European Union: The Institutional Structure and the "Community Method"' (2006) 12 *European Public Law* 127–154.

Lefevre, S., 'Rules of Procedure do Matter: The Legal Status of the Institutions' Power of Self-Organisation' (2005) 30 *European Law Review* 802–820.

Petersen, J., and Bomberg, E., *Decision-Making with European Union* (MacMillan, 1999).

Rasmussen, H., 'Between Self-Restraint and Activism: A Judicial Policy for the European Court' (1988) 13 EL Rev 28.

Skiadis, D.V., 'European Court of Auditors and European Investment Bank: An Uneasy Relationship' (1999) 5 EPL 215.

Slynn, G., 'The Court of Justice of the European Communities' (1984) 33 ICLQ 409.

Tridimas, T., 'The Court of Justice and Judicial Activism' (1996) 21 EL Rev 199.

Usher, J., 'Institutional aspects of the Constitutional Treaty – which way does it go?' (2005) 37 *Bracton Law Journal* 30.

3

Scope of the EC Treaty: laws and law-making
in the Community

3.1 Introduction

The purpose of this chapter is to outline the main tasks of the Community and the
mechanisms by which the Community and the institutions carry out those tasks.
This chapter looks at the provisions setting down the general objectives of the
Community and their relationship to more specific policy areas. It then goes on to
consider matters such as treaty base for legislative action, legislative procedures and
subsidiarity, before looking at difficulties in this area. It also develops a couple of
points touched on in Chapter 2: the institutional balance and the democratic legitimacy – or lack of it – of the European Union. Note that the main focus of this
chapter is the law-making powers of the institutions as they relate to the current EC
Treaty; the separate systems under the second and third pillars, such as justice and
home affairs, will not be discussed directly. The main changes that would be introduced by the Constitution should it come into force are briefly discussed where
relevant.

3.2 Scope of the EC Treaty

Although primarily an economic treaty, concerned with creating a single market in
Europe, the original EEC Treaty extended far beyond the traditional free-trading
agreement such as we find in GATT and EFTA, to cover a wide range of matters only
peripherally economic, and expressly included a number of purely social goals. The
Single European Act (SEA) further extended the scope of Community competence
into new areas which had hitherto been dealt with only on a piecemeal basis. It also
provided a formal framework for political cooperation by Member States which was
absent from the original Treaty. At Maastricht, and to a lesser extent in Amsterdam
and Nice, this led to a further and significant extension of Community (and Union)
goals. The Constitution, should it come into force, will not extend Union competence significantly, though it will remove the structural distinction between
Community and Union competence.

Although some provisions do not require further implementation, the EC Treaty
is essentially a 'framework' treaty (*traité cadre*). It sets out as broad general principles
the aims to be achieved, leaving its institutions, where necessary, to fill the gaps by
means of secondary legislation.

The general aims of the Treaty, as variously amended, are set out in Article 2:

> The Community shall have as its task, by establishing a common market and an economic and monetary union and by implementing policies or activities referred to in Articles 3 and 4, to promote throughout the Community a harmonious, balanced and sustainable development of economic activities, *a high level of employment and of social protection*, equality between men and women, sustainable and non-inflationary growth, a high degree of competitiveness and convergence of economic performance, *a high level of protection and improvement of the quality of the environment*, the raising of the standard of living and quality of life, and economic and social cohesion and solidarity among Member States.

Article 3 provides:

> For the purposes set out in Article 2, the activities of the Community shall include, as provided by this Treaty and in accordance with the timetable set out therein:
> (a) the prohibition as between Member States, of customs duties and quantitative restrictions on the import and export of goods, and of all other measures having equivalent effect;
> (b) a common commercial policy;
> (c) an internal market characterised by the abolition, as between Member States, of obstacles to the free movement of goods, persons, services and capital;
> (d) measures concerning the entry and movement of persons as provided for in Title IV;
> (e) a common policy in the sphere of agriculture and fisheries;
> (f) a common policy in the sphere of transport;
> (g) a system ensuring that competition in the common market is not distorted;
> (h) the approximation of the laws of the Member States to the extent required for the functioning of the common market;
> (i) the promotion of coordination between employment policies of the Member States with a view to enhancing their effectiveness by developing a coordinated strategy for employment;
> (j) a policy in the social sphere comprising the creation of a European Social Fund;
> (k) the strengthening of economic and social cohesion;
> (l) a policy in the sphere of the environment;
> (m) the strengthening of the competitiveness of Community industry;
> (n) the promotion of research and technology development;
> (o) encouragement for the establishment and development of trans- European networks;
> (p) a contribution to the attainment of a high level of health protection;
> (q) a contribution to education and training of quality and to the flowering of the cultures of the Member States;
> (r) a policy in the sphere of development cooperation;
> (s) the association of the overseas countries and territories in order to increase trade and promote jointly economic and social development;
> (t) a contribution to the strengthening of consumer protection;
> (u) measures in the spheres of energy, civil protection and tourism.

Article 4 (ex 3a), introduced by the TEU, sets out the Community's policies in the field of economic and monetary union, including the creation of the single currency.

Although Article 3 was greatly extended by the TEU, it must be noted that Article 3(a)–(h), (j) and (s) as currently numbered were all present in the original EEC Treaty, albeit differently numbered and with some differences in wording. The remaining provisions were new to Article 3, but most of the activities listed had already been subject to some Community legislation, even before the SEA, and a number of these (Article 3(k), (l), (n)) had been incorporated into the Treaty by the SEA, if not in Article 3. Their incorporation into Article 3 thus merely reflected, and gave greater legitimacy to, existing practice. Only the provision for economic and monetary union in Article 4 (ex 3A) represented a genuine new departure for the EC. The ToA further amended Articles 2 and 3 EC, reflecting the increased emphasis to be put on both employment and environmental concerns (see italicised provisions of Article 2).

These provisions would be revised were the Constitution to come into force, as that treaty re-orders and rephrases the objectives and general principles of the Union (see 3.2.2 below). Although the internal market (rather than common market) is mentioned in Part I, it comes further down the list of objectives than it does currently in the EC Treaty. Article I–3 specifies that the Union's aim is to 'promote peace, its values and the well-being of its peoples'. Article I–3(2) provides that the 'Union shall offer its citizens an area of freedom, security and justice without internal frontiers, and an internal market where competition is free and undistorted'. Article I–3(3) lists the more specific tasks of the Union. Again there are differences between the current format and that proposed by the Constitution. Notably, the provision commences by referring to Europe's sustainable development and, although there are references to a competitive economy, the provision also makes clear that one of the elements on which this development is to be based is a social market economy, not just a market economy, a point implicit in the current EC Treaty.

3.2.1 Relationship between Articles 2 and 3 EC and other Treaty Articles

Articles 2 and 3 describe the main objectives of the Community and identify the means by which they are to be attained. They do not themselves impose specific legal obligations on the Member States. The detailed obligations are spelled out in specific provisions in subsequent parts of the Treaty. Articles 2 and 3 nonetheless have interpretive value; they may be used to clarify the scope of the more precise treaty provisions. A similar relationship may be discerned between Parts I and III of the Constitution.

3.2.2 General principles

In addition to the goals and tasks enunciated in Articles 2 and 3, the EC Treaty contains other provisions laying down principles underlying the Community. This list of principles has been expanded by the successive Treaty amendments. The EC Treaty always did contain a provision prohibiting discrimination on the grounds of nationality (current Article 12 EC) and the principle of cooperation by the Member States (Article 10 EC). The SEA introduced the notion of the internal market. The TEU introduced concepts as varied as the introduction of monetary union as a goal of the Community (Article 4 EC) and the principle of subsidiarity (Article 5 EC). The ToA continued this trend by highlighting the importance of environmental protection (new Article 6), introducing closer cooperation (Article 11) and a provision on the importance of services of general economic interest (Article 16). As noted in Chapter 1, the principle of non-discrimination has been extended by the ToA with the insertion of a new article (new Article 13 EC) to cover discrimination on grounds of sex, race and ethnic origin, religion or belief, disability, age or sexual orientation. Unlike the provision on discrimination on grounds of nationality, the Treaty does not expressly state that such discrimination is prohibited; instead it merely permits the Member States, acting unanimously, to take action to combat such discrimination. For example, a directive prohibiting discrimination on grounds of race has already been enacted (Directive 2000/43/EC OJ L180/22 2000). As has been suggested, these principles vary considerably in subject matter and in form, so some, such as Articles 6, 12 and 13, may have a greater impact on the interpretation of provisions comprising the Community policies than others. The Constitution, should it come into force, would consolidate the general principles of the Community with those contained in the TEU, such as the principle of respect for human rights. The principles identified in Part I of the Constitution include some further principles, such as the supremacy of Union law, which were part of the jurisprudence of the ECJ but not expressly mentioned in the EC Treaty (see further below and Chapter 4).

3.2.3 Community policies

We have already noted the introduction of provisions relating to monetary union (Chapter 1). In addition, and as a supplement to the activities listed in Article 3, the EC Treaty provided for the harmonisation of indirect taxation (Articles 90–93 (ex 95–99) EC).

Central to the creation of both the common and the internal market are the four freedoms: the free movement of goods, services, persons and capital (Article 14(2) EC). These are elaborated in Titles 1 and 3 of Part III to the Treaty. A more detailed discussion of these freedoms forms Part Three of this book.

The EC Treaty also provided for action in the field of social policy, requiring Member States to promote improved working conditions and living standards (Article 136 (ex 117)) and to harmonise conditions of health and safety (Article 138 (ex 118a)) for workers, and to observe a principle of equal pay for equal work for men and women (Article 139 (ex 119)). A Protocol on Social Policy was attached to the TEU. It further committed all Member States except the UK to a range of actions designed to protect the interests of workers. The social policy provisions in the EC Treaty were substantially amended as the ToA incorporated this Protocol on Social Policy into the main body of the Treaty (new Articles 136–145 EC), replacing and augmenting the existing provisions. This had the advantage of removing the potential for disputes over the borderline between social measures permissible under the EC Treaty and those which, hitherto, should have been made under the Protocol. In addition, following the ToA, the EC Treaty also includes a new chapter on employment (new Articles 125–130 EC). These provisions are not aimed at giving individuals rights to a job; rather, they aim at coordinating the Member States' employment policies so as to reduce unemployment. These policies may be seen as a form of economic management, an approach which is reinforced by these provisions' location within the Treaty, which is between monetary union and common commercial policy, rather than next to social policy.

Following the ToA, the Treaty also incorporated new measures (new Part III Title IV, Articles 61–69 EC) to attain the free movement of individuals within the EC (see Chapter 24). These have been broadly based on the measures taken under the 1990 Schengen Agreement on the abolition of frontier controls between the signatory States, an agreement outside the Union framework but which most of the EU Member States have joined. A protocol annexed to the ToA stated that on ratification of the ToA, the Schengen *acquis* (that is, all binding decisions made under the Schengen Agreement) would apply to the Member States and that these decisions would be treated as though they were measures made in accordance with procedures of the EC Treaty. The UK and Ireland have opted out of this chapter of the Treaty (although either of them may opt in to individual measures), and consequently the Schengen *acquis* and measures made under the new chapter in the EC Treaty will not necessarily apply to them. Denmark has also expressed reservations about these provisions. Although the inequalities and the uncertainties concerning the scope of the social policy provisions of the EC Treaty will have been removed by the ToA, new but similar problems will replace them in relation to the free movement of persons.

It should be noted that although Community competence has been expanded, the level of Community activity in different policy areas varies. Articles 94 and 95 (discussed below at 3.3.1 and in Chapter 15) authorise the institutions to take harmonising action in the area of the common and internal market. Article 47 also authorises this for the mutual recognition of qualifications and the cross-border provision of services. In other areas, Community action is constrained. Article 152, for example, which relates to public health, expresses Community action as complementing, rather than replacing, national action. Community involvement tends to be limited in this way on flanking policy areas. Should the Constitution come into force, the fact that the Union's power to act in certain fields is constrained, and that it has different powers in different areas, would be recognised in the clause dealing with Union competence (see further below at 3.5.5).

3.2.4 External competence

To enable the Community to carry out its policies towards third countries, the EC Treaty provides that 'The Community shall have legal personality' (Article 281 (ex 210) EC). Note that the Union currently does not enjoy legal personality, although this will change should the Constitution come into force. Article 300 (ex 228) EC empowers the Commission to negotiate, and the Council to conclude (in most cases following consultation with Parliament) agreements between the Community and one or more States or an international organisation. The EC Treaty also contains a provision (Article 310 (ex 238) EC) allowing the Community to conclude association agreements. Many agreements have been concluded in the field of trade and aid under these provisions.

Article 133 (ex 113) EC also allows the Commission, under the guidance of the Council, to enter into negotiations to make agreements necessary to implement the Common Commercial Policy. It was on this basis that representation for Member States at GATT meetings was developed. The line between Community competence and that of the Member States is not, however, clear-cut as *Opinion 1/94* shows. The Court in this opinion determined that not all the issues covered by the WTO fall within Community competence and therefore not only must the EC be a member of the WTO, but so must the Member States. This may lead to difficulties in the administration of the WTO as far as the Member States are concerned, as their membership, to a certain extent, is duplicated. By contrast, the negotiation of the Lugano Convention dealing with conflicts of national jurisdiction and enforcement of judgments in civil and commercial matters was held to fall within the exclusive competence of the Community. The ECJ in its opinion on Community competence in this area (*Opinion 1/03*) emphasised that the Lugano Convention would affect the uniform and consistent application of Community rules.

Article I–3(4) Constitution specifically refers to the Union's external competence, stating that 'in its relations with the wider world, the Union shall uphold and promote its values and interests', specifically contributing to 'peace, security and sustainable development of the earth, solidarity and mutual respect among peoples, free and fair trade, eradication of poverty and protection of human rights'. Whether these aims would limit the Union's external competence, should the treaty come into force, is far from clear. Given that the Union's activities should already take at least some of these concerns into account, arguably there would not be much difference in substantive approach. A more detailed discussion of the Union's external policies falls outside the scope of this book.

3.3 Basis for legislative action

Such then, in outline, is the framework provided by the EC Treaty. The three main institutions of the Community – the Commission, the Council and the European Parliament – are empowered to legislate (subject to review by the European Courts) on any of the matters within this framework. Many of the Treaty provisions, for example, the articles relating to free movement of goods and workers (Articles 25, 28 and 39 (ex 12, 30 and 48) respectively) contain obligations which are sufficiently precise to be applicable as they stand (see further Chapter 5). Others provide for, and often require, further measures of implementation before they can take full legal effect.

3.3.1 Broad provisions for action

Article 94 (ex 100) EC provides for the 'approximation' (i.e., harmonisation) of such laws as directly affect the establishment or functioning of the common market by unanimous vote. Article 95 (ex 100a) makes similar provision for measures which have as their object the establishing or functioning of the internal market, in most cases, by qualified majority vote (see Article 95(4) and Chapter 15). Both these provisions are broad and their precise extent and relationship to each other and to other Treaty provisions is sometimes open to discussion (see further Chapter 15 and discussion of Tobacco Advertising directive case (*Germany* v *Parliament and Council* (case C–376/98)).

Even where the institutions are not specifically empowered to act, Article 308 (ex 235) provides:

> If action by the Community should prove necessary to attain, in the course of the operation of the common market, one of the objectives of the Community and this Treaty has not provided the necessary powers, the Council shall, acting unanimously on a proposal from the Commission and after consulting the European Parliament, take the appropriate measures.

This blanket power has been used as a basis for legislation on matters of regional or social policy (e.g., equal treatment for men and women) which fell within the broad aims of the Community, as expressed in the preamble, but which were not spelt out specifically in the Treaty. Many of these matters have now been incorporated expressly into the EC Treaty by subsequent Treaty amendments. Although this provision is potentially wide, concerns about its use to extend Treaty competence by the back door are limited by the fact that the consent of all Member States to any proposed measure is required under Article 308. This point does not, however, recognise that Article 308 permits the European Parliament a very limited role; it also excludes the national parliaments. Both sets of institutions have a much more limited role than that they would have if Community competence was to be expanded by formal Treaty amendment. Given the breadth of Articles 94 and 95, recourse to Article 308 seems to have become less frequent. The expansion of express Community competence by various treaties and the related political tensions (discussed at 3.3.2) render it less likely that Article 308 (ex 235) EC will be used as extensively as hitherto. During the deliberations on the Future of Europe it was suggested that Article 308 be removed to prevent further 'competence creep', that is, an expansion of the Union's competence. Although the 'flexibility clause' (Article I–17), as it came to be known, survived, national parliaments were given an increased role in determining the circumstances in which this provision could be used. Should the Constitution come into force, under Article I–17(2) the Commission would be required to solicit the views of national parliaments on the compliance with the principle of subsidiarity (discussed at 3.5) of any measure put forward under this provision.

3.3.2 Implied powers

The Court has also determined that the Community has implied powers, so that when powers which are not specifically enumerated in the Treaty are required to achieve a Community goal, the Community is deemed to have the necessary powers. There are two possible formulations of this doctrine. The narrow approach states that the existence of a power implies the existence of any other power that is reasonably necessary for the exercise of the original power. This was the approach taken by the Court in *Fédération Charbonnière de Belgique* v *High Authority* (case 8/55). A wider approach was taken in *Germany* v *Commission* (cases 281, 283–5 & 287/85) where the powers of the Commission arising out of original Article 118 (which has been amended significantly and renumbered as 137 EC by the ToA) were the subject of dispute. The article provided the Commission with a task, that of promoting close cooperation between Member States in the social field, but did not give the Commission any specific legislative powers. Germany therefore argued that the proposed legislative act of the Commission was outside the Treaty. The Court commented that to avoid rendering provisions such as the then Article 118 totally ineffective, the powers necessary for carrying out the task must be inferred. This is a significant decision because there are many instances where the Commission has been allocated a task but not been given legislative power.

It is not just internally that the Court has deduced Community competence. Following *Commission* v *Council* (case 22/70) (the *ERTA* case) and *Opinion 1/76* it was thought that the EC would have implied powers to act in the international sphere in relation to matters with respect to which the EC has power to act within the Union under the EC Treaty. In addition, the *ERTA* case appeared to suggest that the competence of the Community, in this regard, was exclusive: Member States were precluded from acting. The degree, however, to which this is still the case is now unclear following *Opinion 1/94*, in which the Court held that, although the EC had exclusive competence under Article 113 (now Article 133) to act in some spheres, with respect to other areas (such as intellectual property) the Member States also have competence. In more and more spheres the Court has acknowledged that Member States and the Community have concurrent competence (e.g., *Commission* v *Council* (case C–25/94) (FAO Fishery Agreement), but c.f. the approach in the *Lugano Convention* case: *Opinion 1/03*). Following the German Constitutional Court's decision in *Brunner* v *European Union Treaty* [1994] 1 CMLR 57 (see further below at 3.4 and Chapter 4), it is likely that the national courts will keep a watchful eye on all Community activities in the internal and external field to ensure that the Community institutions do not exceed their powers.

3.4 Expansion of Community competence

The degree to which the framework provided by the Treaty has been filled in will form the subject-matter of later chapters of this book. Suffice it to say that all the main areas of activity outlined above, in both the internal and external fields, have been subject to some measures of implementation. In some cases, such as agriculture and competition policy, implementation has been extensive. In others, such as the free movement of capital, transport, and freedom to provide services, progress was, initially, slow. As a result of the SEA there was substantial progress, although some barriers to trade still exist, as well as in the 'new' areas of health and safety, environmental and consumer protection and research and technological development. The TEU ensured continuing activity in these fields as well as in the newer field of education and training, culture and the development of trans-European networks and tourism. As noted above, the changes introduced by the ToA, especially to Articles 2 and 3, indicate an increased emphasis to be placed on environmental and employment policies.

From the foregoing outline two matters will be clear:

(a) The framework provided by the Treaty, both originally and as amended by subsequent treaties (SEA, TEU, ToA and Nice), is extremely broad, embracing many areas of economic and social activity which had hitherto been within the sole competence of Member States.

(b) Within that framework there is almost unlimited (though not uncontrolled) scope for legislation by the Community institutions.

Since, under Article 10 (ex 5) of the EC Treaty, Member States are required to 'take all appropriate measures, whether general or particular, to ensure fulfilment of the obligations arising out of this Treaty or resulting from action taken by the institutions of the Community' and 'shall abstain from any measure which could jeopardise the attainment of the objectives of this Treaty' perhaps it is not surprising that Lord Denning MR was moved to say, in *H.P. Bulmer Ltd* v *J. Bollinger SA* [1974] Ch 401: 'the Treaty is like an incoming tide. It flows into the estuaries and up the rivers. It cannot be held back.'

It is no doubt to stem that tide that the principle of subsidiarity was incorporated as a general principle into the EC Treaty by the TEU, in Article 5 (ex 3b) EC. It is with subsidiarity in mind that the German Constitutional Court delivered its landmark judgment in *Brunner* v *European Union Treaty* [1994] 1 CMLR 57. In upholding the powers of the German Parliament to ratify the Maastricht Treaty, it sounded a number of warnings about the extent of the powers of the Community and its institutions. Any further transfer of powers to Community level will need express democratic approval to be binding. As it commented in the judgment (at para. 33):

> because the principle of limited powers is adhered to, no power to extend its powers is conferred on the European Union, and the claiming of further functions and powers by the European Union and the Communities is made dependent on supplementation and amendment of the Treaty and is therefore subject to the affirmative decision of the national parliaments.

The Member States' status as 'masters of the treaty' would to some extent be reinforced in the Constitution. The Constitution makes express the principle of primacy of Union law, but primacy is limited to the Union operating within the sphere of competence conferred on it by the Member States. The use of the word 'conferred' seems to suggest that the relationship between the Member States and the Union is one of delegated powers (see Articles I–6, I–11(1) and (2)).

3.5 Competence and subsidiarity

3.5.1 Principle of attributed powers

Subsidiarity is, following the Maastricht Treaty, a well-known word. Its meaning is, however, not clear. The first paragraph of Article 5 EC is not contentious: it merely restates what was common ground, that the Community can only act within the powers conferred on it by the Treaty. Although the Constitution would introduce some changes with regard to Union competence, the principle of subsidiarity would remain in broadly similar terms (Article I–11(3) Constitution).

3.5.2 **Principle of subsidiarity**

The difficulties start with the second paragraph of current Article 5 EC. This states that:

> In areas which do not fall within its exclusive competence, the Community shall take action, in accordance with the principle of subsidiarity, only if and insofar as the object-ives of the proposed action cannot be sufficiently achieved by the Member States and can therefore, by reason of the scale or effects of the proposed action, be better achieved by the Community.

Clearly, subsidiarity will not apply where the Community has exclusive com-petence. Therefore, to determine whether subsidiarity applies, we must distinguish between areas where the Community has exclusive competence and areas where it does not. The boundary between exclusive Community competence and shared competence has not been clear: there are no provisions in the EC Treaty or TEU which identify the exclusive (or non-exclusive) powers of the Community (or the Union). Although the ToA has a protocol on subsidiarity annexed to it, the protocol does not clarify where the boundary of exclusive Community competence lies. This issue was discussed by the Convention on the Future of Europe, and a group of provisions has been included in the Constitution that would address the issue of Union competence in its various types. These articles are discussed below at 3.5.5.

3.5.3 **Test for the exercise of concurrent powers**

Looking now at the principle of subsidiarity itself, it can be seen that the idea in the second paragraph of Article 5 can be broken down into two further blocks:

(a) that no Community action should be taken unless the action cannot be sufficiently achieved by the Member States; and

(b) that because of the proposed scale or effects of the measure, the Community can better achieve the end result desired.

This test raises several issues: it is a test of comparative efficiency ('Commission Communication to the Council and the European Parliament', Bull EC 10–1992, 116) which might, in the context of achieving goals such as common trading rules throughout the Union, be seen to favour action at Community level. How this fits in with the definition of subsidiarity given in the preamble to the TEU (which, there-fore, is of interpretative value) is not clear, as that version states that the principle of subsidiarity requires that decision-making should be made as close to the citizen as possible. Further, when will 'sufficiently' be satisfied? Will these questions relate to the scale or the effect of the proposed action? Although the protocol annexed to the ToA is aimed at clarifying the meaning of subsidiarity it does not answer these questions. It puts forward three criteria which reflect the two-stage test above:

(a) the issue has transnational aspects which cannot be satisfactorily regulated by other Member States;

(b) actions by Member States alone would conflict with requirements of the Treaty such as the internal market provisions;

(c) action at Community level would produce clear benefits by reason of its scale or effects.

It is submitted that these criteria do no more than restate the problem; indeed they may even add to the difficulties because it is not even clear whether these criteria are cumulative or alternative. These problems could lead to litigation to obtain clarification of these points. Some writers have suggested that, in any event, these issues are not appropriately decided by the Court because of their political nature. In view of the fact that a number of cases have already raised this issue (e.g., *UK* v *Council* (case C–84/94) and *Germany* v *Parliament* (case C–233/94)), it seems that the Court has not, so far, refused jurisdiction and is now unlikely to do so. Note also that annexed to the Constitution is a protocol on subsidiarity and proportionality; this seems more focused on ensuring the implementation of the principles than in clarifying the meaning of either subsidiarity or proportionality.

3.5.4 Principle of proportionality

The final element of subsidiarity is that contained in the third paragraph of Article 5. It states:

> Any action by the Community shall not go beyond what is necessary to achieve the objective of this Treaty.

This requirement, an expression of the proportionality principle which permeates EC law, and which is re-stated in the Constitution, may have an impact on the type of action proposed by the Community. Rather than adopting an approach which prescribes the obligations of the Member States in minute detail, this would require the Community simply to provide the outline, leaving the Member States to fill in the detail. This would follow the 'new' approach to harmonisation already adopted by the institutions to ensure the completion of the internal market. Article 149 (ex 126) EC, for example, also embodies this approach which requires the Community to support and supplement Member State action rather than prescribing rules with which Member States must comply.

3.5.5 Impact of the Constitution: different types of Union competence

We have seen that the distinction between exclusive and concurrent competence is key to the operation of subsidiarity but that there has been little clarity about the scope of the two groups of competence. The Commission has tended to take a broad view; individual Member States a narrower view. The Constitution addresses the matter, though whether it would solve all the problems in this area is unlikely. It identifies three main categories of competence: exclusive Union competence; competence shared between the Union and the Member States; and supporting, coordinating and supplementing competence. Additionally there are specific provisions dealing with the coordination of economic and employment policies and the common foreign and security policy. One can thus suggest that although the three-pillar system under which CFSP was kept separate from other policies will be abolished by the Constitution coming into force, CFSP would still be identified as a special case (even if the legislative procedures and acts available for action in this area are the same as in other policy areas). There is no category of exclusive Member State competence, although the Constitution also makes express the point that competences not conferred upon the Union remain with the Member States.

The Constitution then goes on to identify the policy areas which fall within two of the three categories of competence. Thus exclusive competence comprises the customs union; the establishment of the competition rules necessary for the functioning of the internal market; monetary policy, for the Member States whose currency is currently the Euro; the conservation of marine biological resources under the common fisheries policy (presumably this means more than the conservation of fish stocks); and common commercial policy. Additionally, the Union would have exclusive competence for the conclusion of international agreements where such an agreement is provided for in a Union legislative act, or is necessary to enable the Union to exercise its internal competence. The wording of the Constitution in this regard has clear links to the jurisprudential position discussed at 3.2.4. The coordination competence concerns action in the areas of the protection and improvement of human health; industry; culture; tourism; education, youth, sport and vocational training; civil protection; and administrative cooperation. Shared or joint competence is not listed exclusively, probably because it seems the intention of the Treaty is that this category of competence would be the default or fall-back position. The Constitution gives examples of shared competence, which includes the internal market and the area of freedom, security and justice. Interestingly, the Union has not been granted exclusive competence in areas relating to the creation of the internal market, for example, in free movement of goods, persons and services, although the Commission had argued for this position, presumably because of the potential breadth of internal market measures. Although these provisions have the advantage of relative brevity and simplicity, the real test would be likely to arise in the application of the provisions and the determination in individual cases of where the boundaries lie between the different types of competence. Note also that the Constitution specifies that the scope of the Union's respective competences is to be determined by the provisions specific to each area in Part III of the Constitution, that is the provisions which, *inter alia*, reflect the substantive provisions of the EC Treaty. It may be that the Constitution would not solve difficult boundary problems; it would merely relocate them to a different part of the Treaty.

3.6 Law-making process

As we have seen in Chapter 2, the legislative process involves three out of the five institutions: the Commission as initiator, the Council and the Parliament. The relative importance of the Parliament's role varies according to the nature of the legislation and whether the legislation is to be made according to the consultation, the cooperation or the co-decision procedure.

3.6.1 Consultation procedure

This procedure requires that the Council consult the European Parliament before it adopts an act. Parliament's views must be considered but have no binding effect on the Council (see *Roquette Frères SA* v *Council* (case 138/79) discussed in Chapter 2). Indeed, the Council need give no reasons for its disregard of the Parliament's views. Until the SEA, consultation was the usual form of legislative process. It is still used in some areas, such as agriculture, and it has also been introduced into new areas in the TEU, ToA and even by Nice. Examples of these areas are economic and social cohesion (Article 159 EC) and economic and monetary policy (Articles 104 (14), 107 (6) and 117 EC). Some of these 'new' areas, such as Article 13 EC regarding non-discrimination, have now been amended so that they fall under the co-decision procedures.

3.6.2 Cooperation procedure (Article 252 (ex 189c) EC)

This requires that the European Parliament be given the opportunity to propose amendments to the draft legislation.

First, the proposal is sent to both the Parliament and the Council. The Council agrees a common position on the proposal, after taking into account the opinion of the Parliament. Parliament then has a second opportunity to consider the draft proposal. It may agree with the common position of the Council. If this is the case, the Council may adopt the common position acting by qualified majority vote.

Alternatively, Parliament may propose amendments to the common position or reject it. Either way, the proposal is then returned to the Commission, to re-examine. The Commission produces a new draft adopting all, some, or none of Parliament's proposed amendments. The document is then sent to the Council. If the Council wishes to adopt the proposal in its new form, it may do so by qualified majority vote. If, however, it wishes to amend the proposal further (or even adopt the original agreed common position), it needs to act by unanimity. Although the Council ultimately has the final say, it can only overrule Parliament (and the Commission) if it acts unanimously. This procedure, which gave only limited powers to the Parliament, was criticised. The Council could still overrule Parliament; all Parliament could do, in the absence of agreement, was hinder the legislative process. Nonetheless, the procedure did result in changes in the way in which institutions operate, stimulating a greater dialogue, for example, between the Parliament on the one hand and the Commission and the Council on the other.

The cooperation procedure was introduced in limited but important areas, such as the single market provisions. TEU expanded the areas in which it was used, mainly by virtue of the introduction of new areas of Community competence. Post-ToA and Nice, however, the cooperation has virtually disappeared, being virtually limited to certain aspects of monetary policy (e.g., Article 102).

3.6.3 Co-decision procedure (Article 251 (ex 189b) EC)

This procedure, which was introduced by the TEU and amended by ToA, improved the bargaining power of Parliament. Here, Parliament, as with the cooperation procedure, has two opportunities to view the proposal. If Parliament approves the common position, the act is adopted (usually by qualified majority vote in the Council). Parliament may reject the common position or propose amendments. The document is re-examined by the Commission, which may include or reject any or all of the Parliament's amendments in a new draft. The Council may accept the new form of document acting by qualified majority. If it wished to accept some of the Parliament's proposals which the Commission, in re-examining the document, has rejected then it may do so, but only by acting unanimously (Article 251(3)).

If the Council does not adopt the new form of the proposal then the Conciliation Committee, made up of the members of the Council or their representatives and an equal number of representatives of the Parliament, meets to try to reach a compromise. If the Conciliation Committee approves a joint text, it is then sent to the Council and the Parliament. Both institutions must approve the text for it to be adopted; either (or both) may reject it.

Although the Council's common position may be affirmed, ultimately Parliament may veto a piece of legislation. It is also more difficult to ignore the Commission's views on the form of the amended proposal; if it wishes to do so, the Council must act unanimously. In giving the Parliament more power, the procedure might be seen as improving the democratic credentials of the Community, but post-TEU the procedure was not only long-winded and complex, it also only applied within specified policy areas.

The amendments introduced by the ToA went some way to improving this situation. The list of areas in which co-decision may be used have been increased; indeed, the cooperation procedure has virtually ceased to exist, a process taken further by Nice. Should the Constitution come into force more areas will be dealt with by co-decision, re-named the ordinary legislative procedure. Perhaps more importantly, the co-decision procedure was streamlined by the ToA and in such a way as to tilt the balance of power a little more in the direction of the Parliament. Prior to the ToA, in the event of the Parliament rejecting the Council's common position entirely at its second reading, the Conciliation Committee was convened at that stage to try to reach a solution. Now, in such an event, the act shall be deemed not to be adopted. The power of the Council to reaffirm its common position in the absence of agreement in the Conciliation Committee (albeit subject to rejection by Parliament), originally granted under TEU, was removed by the ToA. If the institutions fail to reach an agreement through the Conciliation Committee, the proposed legislation will fall.

Although co-decision now seems to have given the Parliament real power within the legislative process, it is not without its critics. Even after the ToA changes, the procedure is complex. Co-decision, especially when the Conciliation Committee procedure is activated, adds to the length and complexity of the legislative process. The proceedings of the Conciliation Committee are not open to the public, which leads to questions as to how transparent and democratic the process actually is.

3.6.4 Assent

The assent procedure was also introduced by the SEA. As the name suggests, a measure to be adopted by the assent procedure may only be so adopted if the Parliament gives its consent. This procedure gives the Parliament considerable power and is used only in limited circumstances such as external relations

(Article 300 EC); and post-Nice, with the finding regarding the right to reject association agreements of a serious and persistent breach of fundamental rights by a Member State (Article 7 TEU). The disadvantage with this procedure is that there is no mechanism by which the Council and Parliament might resolve their differences: the only option for Parliament is to agree or block the proposal entirely.

3.6.5 Delegation

As noted in Chapter 2, Article 202 EC gives the Council the power to delegate 'powers for the implementation of the rules which the Council lays down' which Article 211 EC requires the Commission to so exercise. On one level this is relatively unproblematic. Many legal systems allow the delegation of powers to prevent the entire legislative process from being clogged up with matters of detail; such delegation also permits issues to be dealt with by experts. The current system often involves supervision of the Commission decisions in these areas by committees of national experts. This system is referred to as comitology (see Comitology Decision 1999/468/EC, [1999] OJ L184). The Commission has not appeared particularly happy with such oversight, suggesting in its White Paper on Governance (COM (2001) 428 final) that comitology committees should be removed. The difficulty is that the Community practice is not transparent and is problematic from a democratic perspective. Nonetheless, dispensing with the comitology committees, which allow some level of supervision by the Member States, albeit themselves unelected and non-accountable, would arguably remove whatever level of national or Council-based oversight there currently is. Despite these difficulties, the ECJ has confirmed that delegation to the Committee is permissible if the matter is one of implementation rather than determining general policy (Case 25/70 *Koster*). Some of the difficulties about transparency and access were alleviated by reforms in 1999 which, *inter alia*, allowed for greater involvement by the European Parliament and, as we shall see below at 3.9.2, comitology committees are subject to the right of access to documents.

The Council may delegate powers to itself, to Member States, and to outside agencies. In such agencies, the Court has reviewed the permitted scope of the delegation closely, presumably to ensure that the institutional balance in the Community legal order is not affected. Delegation in these circumstances raises similar problems regarding democracy to delegation to the Commission.

3.6.6 Matters of procedure

In each case where the institutions have the power to enact legislation, the Treaty specifies the type of legislation to be made and which sort of procedures must be used. The Treaty provision itself, or the procedure chosen, will specify whether the Council must act unanimously, by qualified majority voting or by simple majority voting. A failure to abide by these procedural requirements may give rise to an action for the annulment of the measure. The various combinations arising out of the possible permutations of the different voting procedures in Council, types of Community act and degrees of involvement of Parliament make the legislative process very complex. Despite attempts to do so, the various treaties have done little to improve this situation. In addition to encouraging challenges to the correct legal base or procedural requirements likely, this complexity has been criticised as making the Community legal order impenetrable to the average lay person.

There are further restrictions on the making of Community acts. As noted at 3.5.1, the institutions can only act within the scope of the powers conferred on them. Community acts must make their legal basis within the Treaty clear. They must 'state the reasons on which they are based and shall refer to any proposals or opinions which were required to be obtained pursuant to this Treaty' (Article 253 (ex 190) EC). This is done in the preamble to the legislation. It is an essential procedural requirement. Any act which does not comply will be subject to annulment (see Chapter 11, Article 230 (ex 173) EC, Chapter 9, Article 234 (ex 177) EC). Further, the freedom of the institutions to legislate is now counterbalanced by the notion of subsidiarity (Article 5 EC) (see 3.5.2). According to the protocol on subsidiarity annexed to the Constitution, draft legislative acts should contain a detailed statement making it possible to appraise compliance with the principles of subsidiarity and proportionality.

3.7 Legislative acts

The legislative powers of the Community institutions are laid down in Article 249 (ex 189) EC:

> In order to carry out their task the Council and the Commission shall, in accordance with the provisions of this Treaty, make regulations, issue directives, take decisions, make recommendations or deliver opinions.

Article 249 EC was amended by the TEU to take into account Parliament's power of co-decision. Note that the other two pillars of the Union used different legal instruments to give effect to policy decisions. For example, under CFSP we see references to common positions and joint actions; under the JHA we see not only common positions but also framework decisions and conventions. Should the Constitution come into force, the abolition of the pillar system will mean that in principle the types of legal act in use will be common to all areas of policy.

The measures in Article 249, described as 'acts', are defined as follows:

> A regulation shall have general application. It shall be binding in its entirety and directly applicable in all Member States.
> A directive shall be binding, as to the result to be achieved, upon each Member State to which it is addressed, but shall leave to the national authorities the choice of form and methods.
> A decision shall be binding in its entirety upon those to whom it is addressed.
> Recommendations and opinions shall have no binding force.

There is a division between binding and non-binding acts. Only the first three are binding. Non-binding acts can be seen as a form of soft law. Article 249 is open to criticism because, beyond this basic division, it does not provide a clear definition of each of the types of act. Nor does it distinguish between legislation and administrative acts, which most Member States' legal systems do. To a certain extent, it has fallen to the ECJ to fill in some of the detail.

3.7.1 Regulations

The principal feature of a regulation is its general application: it is a normative rather than an individual act, designed to apply to situations in the abstract. The ECJ has held that 'the Regulation, being of an essentially normative character, is applicable not to a limited identifiable number of persons but rather to categories of persons envisaged both in the abstract and as a whole' (joined cases 16 and 17/62 *Confédération Nationale des Producteurs de Fruits et Légumes* v *Council*). Since it is 'binding in its entirety and directly applicable in all Member States' it does not require further implementation to take effect. It may give rise to rights and obligations for States and individuals as it stands. Indeed, it has been held (*Leonesio* v *Ministero dell' Agricoltura e delle Foreste* (case 93/71)) that the rights bestowed by a regulation cannot be subjected, at the national level, to implementing provisions diverging from those laid down by the regulation itself.

3.7.2 Directives

A directive is binding 'as to the result to be achieved, upon each Member State to which it is addressed', but allows States a discretion as to the form and method of implementation. Thus it is a measure intended to be addressed to, and binding on *States*, either individually or collectively, but apparently requiring implementation by States before it can be fully effective in law. Indeed it seems that Member States are obliged to enact implementing measures rather than rely on the fact that pre-existing law or administrative practice complied with the requirements of the directive.

3.7.3 Decisions

A decision is an individual act designed to be addressed to a specified person or persons. As a 'binding' act it has the force of law and does not therefore require implementation in order to take effect. Decisions may be addressed to States or individuals.

3.7.4 Recommendations and opinions

Since they have no binding force, they are ineffective in law, although clearly of persuasive authority (see *Grimaldi* (case C–322/88) noted in Chapter 5).

3.7.5 Acts *sui generis*

Article 249 does not provide an exhaustive list of legal acts and the Court has recognised acts not identified by Article 249. These are usually described as *sui generis* acts and include rules relating to the internal management of the Community, such as rules of procedure.

3.7.6 **Boundary between different types of act**

The line between these acts is not as clear-cut as Article 249 would suggest. It was held in *Confédération Nationale des Producteurs de Fruits et Légumes v Council* (cases 16 & 17/62) that the true nature of an act is determined not by its form but by its content and object. The label attached to the measure is not decisive, and in the case of *International Fruit Co. NV v Commission (No. 1)* (cases 41–4/70) what was termed a regulation was found to comprise a 'bundle of decisions'. Measures have been found to be hybrid; to contain some parts in the nature of a regulation, and other parts in the nature of decisions (see Advocate-General Warner's submissions in *NTN Toyo Bearing Co. Ltd v Council* (case 113/77)). In ascertaining the true nature of the act, the essential distinction seems to be between a regulation, which is normative, applicable not to a limited identifiable number of designees but rather to categories of persons envisaged both in the abstract and as a whole, and a decision, which concerns designated persons individually (*Confédération Nationale des Producteurs de Fruits et Légumes v Council*). The nature of a directive has not been called into question, but considerable controversy has arisen over its effects. These will be discussed in Chapter 5.

It should be noted that, from time to time, it has been suggested that the issue of the Community's legal acts should be revisited to re-order the Community's legislative activity in a more coherent way and to identify more clearly the differences between the different types of legal act. This is often referred to as creating or revising the hierarchy of norms. Declaration No. 16 attached to the TEU indicated that the Member States were prepared to consider the question of the hierarchy of norms, at the 1996 IGC, although neither the ToA nor Nice have dealt with the issues. The matter was finally dealt with by the Convention on the Future of Europe. The provisions in the Constitution are discussed below at 3.7.9.

3.7.7 **Publication**

With regard to publication, Article 254 (ex 191) EC provides:

1. Regulations, directives and decisions adopted in accordance with the procedure referred to in Article 251 [ex 189b] shall be signed by the President of the European Parliament and by the President of the Council and shall be published in the *Official Journal* of the Community. They shall enter into force on the date specified in them or, in the absence thereof, on the twentieth day following that of their publication.
2. Regulations of the Council and of the Commission, as well as directives of those institutions which are addressed to all Member States shall be published in the *Official Journal* of the Community. They shall enter into force on the date specified in them or, in the absence thereof, on the twentieth day following that of their publication.
3. Other directives and decisions shall be notified to those to whom they are addressed and shall take effect upon such notification.

The majority of EC legislation must be published in the *Official Journal*.

3.7.8 Soft law

In addition to the above types of law specified in Article 249 (ex 189) EC, the Commission has, in recent years, used new ways of developing policy, for example, by issuing guidelines (for example, in the State aid field, see Chapter 30). In the area of competition law, the Commission has issued notices. A notice provides guidance on the Commission's policy in particular fields but is non-binding. Therein lies the difficulty: while these documents are often of great importance and are relied on by individuals, as non-binding instruments they are not open to challenge before the CFI, although they have been challenged before national courts. Their creation is informal and ad hoc and not subject to the rules laid down in the Treaty for the enactment of other forms of Community legislation. It is difficult to hold the policy-makers to account and this has further implications for democracy.

Despite possible problems with informal approaches to law-making, a further move towards the use of soft law methods can be seen following the conclusions of the Lisbon Council Summit (European Council 2002). There the European Council formally established its Open Method of Co-ordination (OMC). This is a method of rule-making which allows for the agreement of policy guidelines through exchanges of information on best practice, benchmarking, monitoring, target-setting and peer review. This approach potentially allows discretion on best practice to be exercised by national regulatory bodies. It has the disadvantage of other soft law methods: OMC allows the democratic structures of the European Parliament to be bypassed, increasing concerns about any democratic deficit in policy-making.

3.7.9 Impact of the Constitution

The Constitution sought to simplify Union legislation, in regard to both the types of legislation and the uses to which they should be put, and their legislative procedures. In introducing the changes contained in the Constitution, the drafters had in mind not just the need for clarity but also concerns about democracy and the separation of powers, and in particular the boundary between legislative acts and administrative acts. The relevant provisions are found in Article I–32 and Article I–36. Article I–32 introduces two categories of acts: legislative and non-legislative. The drafters seem thus to be seeking to distinguish between primary and delegated legislation, an approach which would generally be welcomed, although as some commentators have noted, the distinction between the two is not always easy to make. Within the category of legislative acts, there would be two types of act: European laws and European framework law. European laws correspond to regulations under the current system and European framework laws to directives. Note, however, that Article-32(1) defines European framework laws in different terms from those used in respect of directives. It provides that Member States are entirely free to choose the form by which the specified end results might be achieved. Arguably this would emphasise a greater degree of Member State discretion than currently obtains, though, given that it would still be the responsibility of the ECJ to police the boundary between ends and means (see, e.g., discussion on enforcement, Chapter 10), the degree to which there would be any change in practice should the Constitution come into force is questionable.

There are three types of non-legislative act specified in Article I–32: the European regulation; the European decision; and the recommendation or opinion. European regulations are non-legislative acts of general application for the implementation of legislative acts and certain specified provisions of the Constitution. Effectively European regulations would be a secondary form of European laws and European framework laws, as the circumstances require. European decisions are described as being binding in their entirety, and when the decision is addressed to a specific person (or group of persons), it would be binding only on them. Recommendations and opinions would not have binding force. Note that although the acts are described as non-legislative, this label is misleading. Effectively these acts would constitute delegated legislation. Articles I–34–36 deal with the way in which non-legislative acts may be made. Of particular note is Article I–35, which provides that European laws and framework laws may delegate to the Commission the power to enact delegated regulations to 'supplement or amend certain non-essential elements of the European law or framework law', although there are limits on the scope of such delegation. Nonetheless, some commentators have voiced concerns that this provision would alter the inter-institutional balance by giving the Commission significant power to make policy choices, with little input from the Council and the European Parliament, and removing the comitology procedures and committees. Furthermore, the degree of control that would remain with the Council and the Parliament is not clear, and could in practice be weak.

Article I–36 provides for another category of act—implementing acts. As well as requiring Member States to adopt all measures of national law necessary to implement Community law, it empowers the Commission to take implementing action. Implementing acts can take the form of implementing regulations or implementing decisions (Article I–36(4)). Article I–36(3) specifies that the European laws are to lay down in advance rules and general principles for the mechanisms of general control by Member States over such implementing acts.

3.8 Sources of EC law

The sources of EC law comprise the following:

(a) The EC Treaty and Protocols, as amended by the succeeding Treaties: Merger Treaty 1965; Acts of Accession 1972 (UK, Ireland, Denmark), 1979 (Greece), 1985 (Spain, Portugal), 1995 (Austria, Finland, Sweden); Budgetary Treaties 1970, 1975; Single European Act 1986; Treaty on European Union 1992; Treaty of Amsterdam 1998; Treaty of Nice 2001; and Treaty of Accession 2003. Should the Constitution come into force, the treaties constituting the Community and Union will be replaced by the Constitution.

(b) EC secondary legislation in the form of regulations, directives and decisions. Recommendations and opinions are of persuasive force only. Should the Constitution come into force, existing laws will retain their legal status; future laws would be of the types specified in the Constitution.

(c) Such international agreements as are entered into by Community institutions on behalf of the Community pursuant to their powers under the EC Treaty. These agreements may result from accession by the Community to existing agreements, such as GATT, or from new agreements such as the Lomé Convention. Conventions entered into by *Member States*, on the other hand, even though entered into pursuant to the EC Treaty, Article 293 (ex 220) EC, cannot be considered as forming part of Community law. Despite the apparent clarity of the provision, there has been some erosion of this principle. Note that some international human rights treaties have been found to inspire principles of Community law (see further Chapter 6). Further, the Commission has suggested that the UN Convention on the International Sale of Goods, to which some but not all Member States are parties, should be viewed as Community law.

(d) Judicial legislation. This comprises the entire jurisprudence of the European Courts, embracing not only decisions, but general principles and even expressions of opinion, provided they concern matters of *Community law* and now, to a limited extent, some aspects of Union law. The importance and the extent of the Court of Justice's contribution to the corpus of EC law will become apparent in the course of this book. This jurisprudence on the interpretation of treaty provisions will remain good law should the Constitution come into force in respect of the interpretation of the comparable provisions of the Constitution.

As a matter of international law, the law arising from all these sources is binding on Member States which are obliged under Article 10 (ex 5) EC, to 'take all appropriate measures, whether general or particular, to ensure fulfilment' of all these obligations. Special provision was made for certain provisions of the EC Treaty to apply to countries linked to Member States by particular association agreements (Article 229 and Annex II (ex 227 and Annex IV)).

Since the UK is dualist in its approach to international law, that is, it does not regard international law as part of its domestic legal system unless it is incorporated by an Act of Parliament, EC law did not become binding in the UK as a matter of *internal* law until incorporated by the European Communities Act 1972.

3.9 Problems in the law-making process

Prior to the 1996 IGC leading to the ToA, a reflection group was established to consider the issues that needed addressing. Its reports revealed that the central issues which the IGC had to tackle were democracy, transparency and, as already discussed in Chapter 2, efficiency. We will look mainly at the first two of these issues, identifying the problem as presented at the IGC and then assessing what not only the ToA has done to improve the position, but also the impact of the Nice Treaty. The significance of the Constitution will be briefly reviewed where relevant.

3.9.1 Democracy

The EC decision-making process has often been criticised for its lack of democratic legitimacy. This is frequently referred to as the 'democratic deficit'. Before we go on to look at some specific issues, some general points may be made. The problem of democratic legitimacy has bedevilled the Community (and the Union) for some time. One of the reasons for the introduction of European citizenship, it seems, was a desire to create a greater connection between individuals and the Community/ Union. This developed the direct link between individual and Community introduced with direct elections to the Parliament (recognised in the Constitution at Article I–46(2)). Nonetheless, concerns remained, and the democratic legitimacy of the Union is one of the central themes of the Constitution. Not only is one of the Union's values expressed to be a respect for democracy (Article I–2), which is not new, but a separate title, Title VI, in Part I of the Constitution is entitled 'The democratic Life of the Union', emphasising the significance of democracy within the Union order. In particular, Article I–46(1) states that 'the functioning of the Union shall be founded on representative democracy', though the obligation on the institutions is stated to be to involve citizens by 'appropriate means' (Article I–47(1)), without specifying those means. The issues to be addressed are whether the Constitution adds anything new and the effect of new provisions; are they merely words with little impact?

One of the main concerns is the lack of democratic accountability of the institutions. The Commission is not elected at all, the Commissioners being political appointments by individual Member States. As we have seen in Chapter 2, however, changes have been made to increase the European Parliament's control over the appointment process. Although the Council of Ministers usually constitutes members of the national parliaments, those members tend not to have been elected for the purpose of serving as a member of the Council of Ministers. As noted in Chapter 2, any control is therefore indirect and only over the individual members rather than the Council as a body. The Belgian people will only have control over the Belgian ministers but not, for example, the Danish ministers. Ministers can avoid taking responsibility for a decision by passing it on to ministers of the other Member States. The quality of democratic control will rest with each of the national parliaments, so its standard may well vary throughout the Union.

Another concern is the use of non-elected bodies in the decision-making process. There are many of these, for example, ECOSOC and the Committee of the Regions. These fulfil an advisory role only. Of more concern here is COREPER, which plays an important role in filtering out the non-contentious issues. It has been argued that in so doing, although technically the final decision is the Council's, in effect COREPER is functioning as a decision-making body. In deciding whether issues are contentious or not, COREPER frames the terms of the debate in Council, potentially having the effect of discouraging debate on certain issues. The role of COREPER is likely to remain strong.

The only directly elected body, the Parliament, has historically been the weakest of the institutions involved in the decision-making process. Admittedly, the TEU improved the position by increasing the control of Parliament over the Commission, introducing the Ombudsman and introducing the co-decision procedure. This latter, however, operated only in limited areas. We have seen that the ToA and Nice increased the areas in which co-decision is used and that the ToA amended the procedure so as to limit further the Council's power under this procedure. Both of these moves can be seen as improving the democratic legitimacy of the Community, though, of course, problems have been noted regarding the operation of the conciliation committee. The Constitution would bring a further shift in the areas in which co-decision is be used. Significantly, the co-decision procedure is also renamed by the Constitution: 'ordinary legislative procedure'. This change in terminology re-emphasises the fact that it is this procedure, which requires the greatest level of involvement of the European Parliament, that should be the normal or default form of law-making in the Union.

Further increases in powers relate to the appointment of the Commission (discussed in Chapter 2). Although the Parliament's powers in the second and third pillars remain limited, the transfer of the powers formerly contained in the TEU or the Schengen Agreement to the Community also brings issues which were dealt with in an intergovernmental and therefore undemocratic manner within the comparatively democratic system of the EC. The incorporation of Schengen brings its own problems, however. The protocol incorporating the Schengen *acquis* gives the force of law to decisions made under Schengen. Not only does the protocol not identify a full list of such texts, but also some of these decisions were made, following the old Schengen procedures, in secret by unelected bureaucrats rather than by politicians. This gives rise to concerns about the democratic accountability of the people who made these decisions; it also raises questions about respect for the rule of law within the Union. Comitology, as noted at 3.6.5 and in Chapter 2, continues to give rise to similar concerns. Similarly, the changes to the articles relating to COREPER confirmed that it may make procedural decisions, although it remains unaccountable. The ECJ has no jurisdiction to review acts of COREPER. Furthermore, its jurisdiction in relation to the new free movement of persons provision is limited and is subject to an exception in the interests of 'national security'. We have seen that the Constitution proposes changes in this area, providing at least a constitutional framework for the exercise of delegated powers even if there are some concerns about where the boundary between legislative and executive acts lies.

One might suggest that the national parliaments could compensate for some of the European Parliament's weaknesses. There are difficulties with this suggestion. The main problem is that, at the level of individual pieces of legislation, national parliaments became involved in the process too late to have any real impact on the outcome, and the level of control exercised by the individual national parliaments may vary significantly between Member States. The problems in this context were apparent even at the time of the TEU: a declaration (No. 13) which was attached to that treaty emphasised the importance of giving a greater role to the national parliaments. The ToA took this point up with a Protocol, which provided that draft legislation must be circulated to each national parliament at least six weeks before it can be considered by the Council. The position was still clearly unsatisfactory and the role of the national parliaments continued to be a subject of debate in the Convention on the Future of Europe. As noted in the discussion of subsidiarity, the Constitution envisages a greater role for the involvement of national parliaments prior to the enactment of European legislation. Although we might still comment that there could be variation in the level of oversight, with national parliaments perhaps having neither the time nor the inclination to review Union legislation thoroughly, at least in the Constitution's framework national parliaments would have the possibility of having a voice in the legislative process.

3.9.2 Transparency

The complexity of the legislative procedures means that decision- making is not transparent. Consequently, it is difficult for individuals to become involved in the process and to hold the decision-makers accountable. The suggestion was to sim-plify these procedures, without altering the institutional balance. Similarly, improvements could be made in the way documents are drafted and made available. A Council resolution on plain language was passed in 1993 ([1993] OJ C166), but the position did not improve much. ECOSOC subsequently made an own-initiative resolution on plain language, requesting that the Commission make attempts actually to comply with the 1993 Council resolution on the same subject, arguably to as little effect. The Commission has also been aware of the concern, producing annual reports on 'Better Lawmaking' together with various initiatives on simplifying legislation in specific areas. In this context, subsidiarity and pro-portionality may also have a role to play in determining the scope and style of legislation. The need to take action was re-emphasised by the *White Paper on Gov-ernance* (COM (2001) 428 final). We have seen that the Constitution would intro-duce new types of legislation. In some ways it seems that the position would be more complex, with the possible introduction of distinctions between legislative and non-legislative acts, as well as the distinction between delegated and imple-menting acts. Access to the legislative process by the individual seems unchanged. Further, whether these changes would solve problems relating to questions of indi-vidual substantive pieces of law is another question entirely.

The availability of documents is another part of the overall problem revolving round the way the decision-making process, particularly at Council level, operates. The complaint is that, because the Council operated behind closed doors, it was not possible for the citizen to identify who is agreeing to which proposals or the basis on which this is done. The counter-argument that has always been raised is that if Council meetings were completely open to the public gaze, it would make it dif-ficult for the Ministers to reach decisions as many of the compromises made are politically sensitive. However, some changes have been made.

In 1993, a Code of Conduct regarding public access to Council and Commission documents was published (93/730/EC; see also Council Decision 93/731/EC, [1993] OJ L340). The significance of this was emphasised by *Carvel v Council* (case T–194/94). This case relied on the Code of Practice to seek the annulment of a Council decision refusing to reveal Council meeting minutes to the applicant. The CFI held that although the Code might permit the withholding of documents when certain specified interests would be threatened by their disclosure, this is not automatic. The rights of citizens to see documents must be balanced against the other inter-ests. In this case the Council had *automatically* refused to reveal the minutes on the basis that all minutes are confidential. Since there was no attempt to take the claims of the applicant into account, the Council was therefore held to be in breach of the Code. Although this did not mean that citizens have an automatic right to see all documents, it was a step forward in that the Council has to consider whether it is proper to refuse access, arguably changing the attitude of ministers towards the release of non-controversial information. In addition, the Council agreed, amongst other points, that the outcome of votes on legislative acts should be made public, that debates on issues of public significance will be broadcast; and that access to the minutes of meetings will be facilitated (Bull 5–1995, 1.9.5). Subsequent case law has made it clear that exceptions to the rights are to be construed narrowly, a point made expressly in *WWF* (case T–105/95), and clarified certain points not covered by Council Decision 93/731 and Commission Decision 94/90. For example, in *Rothmans* (case T–188/97), the CFI held that comitology committees were covered by the right of access to documents. Further, institutions should consider whether partial access to documents is possible where full disclosure is not (*Mattila* (case C–353/01P).

Again, there has been some progress in attempting to ensure transparency of following the ToA, but equally, some difficulties arise. Looking at the progress first, the streamlining of the co-decision procedure and the virtual removal of the cooperation procedure (this remains in monetary policy areas only) makes the legislative process simpler and, as a consequence, more transparent. A declaration annexed to the Amsterdam Treaty re-emphasises the points made in the Council resolution on plain language referred to above. It goes on to state that the institutions ought to establish by common accord guidelines for improving the drafting of Community legislation. Whether such guidelines will have much impact in practice is another question, although the declaration also obliges the institutions to take the internal organisational measures necessary to make sure the guidelines are properly carried out. Clarifying and codifying Community legislation will, it is to be hoped, improve transparency. Additionally, we have already noted the impact of other initiatives regarding the approach to drafting and legislation in relation to the types of legal act available should the Constitution come into force, and the use of soft law.

Article 255 EC provides that 'any citizen, and any natural or legal person residing or having its registered office in a Member State, shall have a right of access to European Parliament, Council and Commission documents'. Thus, all the institutions must amend their own rules of procedure to allow access to documents. Access to Council documents is particularly important. Article 207 EC provides that, within the limits set down by the needs of efficient decision-making, documents involved in the legislative process should be accessible to the public and that, in any event, the results of the vote, explanations of the vote together with any statements in the minutes, shall be made public. Although it does not clarify what the needs of 'efficient decision-making' are, it is still to be hoped that this provision will increase the accountability of the ministers in the Council to their national parliaments, as individuals will be able to identify how the individual representatives of the Member States voted. The right to access documents is, however, subject to limitation in the public or private interest (Article 255(2) EC).

Article 255(2) EC specified that a legal instrument was to be enacted under the co-decision procedure to give effect to the principle in Article 255(1). Regulation 1049/2001 on Access to Information was finally adopted on 30 May 2001 after a troubled negotiation period, which included the proposal by the Commission of a draft regulation without any public consultation and the amendment of the Council's earlier decision on access to documents by the introduction of further categories of mandatory public interest exception.

Nonetheless, agreement on a form of regulation has been reached, even if there is some dissent on an assessment of its usefulness. Article 2(3) of the regulation provides that public access will apply to all documents *held* by an institution and not just those which it drafted. This principle applies not just to the EC, but also to the other two pillars. Article 11 obliged the institutions to draw up a public register of documents by 3 June 2002. Article 4 contains a list of exceptions, comprising nine different categories divided into three groups.

The first group consists of public security; defence and military matters; international relations; financial, economic or monetary policy of the Community or a Member State; privacy and integrity of an individual (especially regarding personal data). Article 4(1) specifies that the appropriate test for determining whether access should be allowed to documents in any of these categories is whether public access would undermine the protection of the public interest. Article 9 provides for extra protection of the public interest in relation to 'sensitive documents' dealing with issues falling in Article 4(1)(a).

The second group of concerns comprises the commercial interests of private persons; court proceedings and legal advice; and inspections, investigations and audits. The test here is whether public access would undermine the protection of one of these interests themselves.

Finally, Article 4(3) provides that documents relating to a matter on which a decision has not yet been taken 'shall be refused if the disclosure of the document would seriously undermine the institution's decision-making process, unless there is an overriding public interest in disclosure'. It is still too early to tell what impact this regulation will have in practice.

The Constitution also emphasises transparency as part of its title on democracy. The institutions in general are under an obligation to 'conduct their work as openly as possible'. Although we might suggest that the use of the proviso, 'as possible', undercuts the obligation considerably, Article I–50(2) specifies that the European Parliament should meet in public, as should the Council when considering and voting on a draft legislative act. Article I–50(3) embodies the right of access to information introduced by Article 255.

3.9.3 Efficiency

The institutions have also been criticised for being inefficient, especially as regards the time-consuming need to reach unanimity. This problem can only get worse with enlargement of the Union. Qualified majority voting was extended to new policy areas by both ToA and Nice. The Constitution continues this trend. Notwithstanding this development, difficulties remain. Notably, the Community law-making processes remain extremely complex, inevitably taking considerable time to reach agreement. This is compounded by the need to work in all official languages. The number of languages has risen and will rise again with enlargement and, although it is likely that not all documents will be translated into all languages, all legally binding documents of general application, as the situation currently stands, will be. In addition to problems relating to efficiency, the need to translate into all official languages increases the risk of small differences in meaning of key terms between the different language versions. (See also Chapter 9.)

3.10 **Conclusions**

The Community has the competence to make law in a broad range of areas, albeit constrained by a procedural framework. It is perhaps this breadth of scope that has led to concern about the law-making procedures. As a result of this successive treaty revisions have amended the law-making procedures, which has affected the institutional balance. Over the years, the role of the European Parliament has increased, arguably increasing the Community's democratic credentials as a result.

Nonetheless, problems with the efficiency, democratic accountability and transparency of the procedures remain, as a glance at the issues dealt with by the Convention on the Future of Europe and the resulting Constitution illustrate. The role of national parliaments has found express form and there has been an attempt to clarify if not simplify the types of Union law. There are, however, other concerns: in particular, the vexed question of the proper scope of Community competence. There are two main aspects to this issue. The first is the identification of exclusive and concurrent competence, particularly important in the context of subsidiarity. The second is the question of how 'complementary competence' – those additional areas of Community competence in which the Community's role is to support the activities of Member States – should be dealt with. Although the Constitution attempts to deal with these, even if it comes into force, it is unlikely to solve all these difficulties that have dogged the Community for some period, especially given the fact that the Community (and Union) legal order has changed and continues to change over time. It is to be hoped, however, that some of these problems will be ameliorated.

FURTHER READING

Bradley, K. St Clair, 'Comitology and the Law: through a Glass Darkly' (1992) 29 CML Rev 693.

Craig, P., 'The Hierarchy of Norms' in Tridimas, T. and Nebbia, P. (eds), *European Law for the Twenty-first Century* (Hart Publishing, 2004).

Curtin, D., 'The Constitutional Structure of the Union: a Europe of Bits and Pieces' (1993) 30 CML Rev 170.

Dashwood, A., 'The Limits of European Community Powers' (1996) 21 EL Rev 113.

—, 'States in the European Union' (1998) 23 EL Rev 201.

De Burca, G., 'The Quest for Legitimacy in the European Union' (1996) 59 MLR 349.

Dryberg, P., 'Current Issues in the Debate on Public Access to Documents' (1999) 24 EL Rev 3.

Emilou, N., 'Subsidiarity; an Effective Barrier Against Enterprises of Ambition' (1992) 29 CML Rev 383.

Koopmans, T., 'The Role of Law in the Next Stage of European Integration' (1986) 35 ICLQ 925.

Lane, R., 'New Competences and the Maastricht Treaty' (1993) 30 CML Rev 939.

Lenaerts, K. and Verhoeven, A., 'Towards a Legal Framewok for Executive Rule-Making in the EU' (2000) 37 CML Rev 645.

Mancini, G. F., 'The Making of a Constitution for Europe' (1989) 26 CML Rev 594.

Obradovic, D., 'Repatriation of Powers in the European Community' (1997) 34 CML Rev 59.

O'Keeffe, D. and Twomey, P. (eds), *Legal Issues of the Maastricht Treaty* (Wiley Chancery Law, 1994).

Peers, S., 'Justice and Home Affairs: Decision-making after Amsterdam' (2000) 23 EL Rev 183.

Rasmussen, H., *On Law and Policy-making in the European Communities* (1986) Nijhoff Publications, 1986.

Scott, J. and Trubeck, D., 'Mind the Gap: Law and New Approaches to Governance in the European Union' (2002) 8 ELJ 1.

Swaine, E. T., 'Subsidiarity and Self Interest: Federalism at the European Court of Justice' (2000) 41 Harv Int'l LJ 1.

Usher, J., 'Variable Geometry or Concentric Circles: Patterns for the European Union' (1997) 4620ICLQ 243.

Zuleeg, M., 'Cohesion and Democracy in the US and EC' (1997) 45 Am J Comp L 505.

4

Principle of supremacy of EC law

4.1 Introduction

The wide scope of the EC Treaty, covering a number of areas normally reserved to national law alone, coupled with the extended application by the ECJ of the principle of direct effects (discussed in Chapter 5), led inevitably to a situation of conflict between national and EC law. In such a case, which law was to prevail? The way in which that conflict was resolved was of crucial importance to the Community legal order; it was a constitutional problem of some magnitude for Member States. After considering the position in traditional international law, this chapter will review the development of the ECJ's case law on this point and identify the problems from the perspective of the national courts. Finally, we will consider the potential impact of the Constitution, should that treaty come into force.

4.2 The problem of priorities

The EC Treaty is silent on the issue of which law should in the case of conflict take priority, and always has been. Perhaps this was a diplomatic omission; perhaps it was not thought necessary to make the matter explicit, since the extent to which Community law might be directly effective was not envisaged at the time of signing the Treaty. In the absence of guidance, the matter was left to be decided by the courts of Member States, assisted by the ECJ in its jurisdiction under Article 234 (ex 177) EC (see Chapter 9). As with the concept of direct effects, the Court has proved extremely influential in developing the law.

The question of priorities between directly effective international law and domestic law is normally seen as a matter of national law, to be determined according to the constitutional rules of the State concerned. It will depend on a number of factors. Primarily it will depend on the terms on which international law has been incorporated into domestic law. This in turn will depend on whether the State is monist or dualist in its approach to international law. If monist, it will be received automatically into national law from the moment of its ratification, without the need for further measures of incorporation. If dualist, international law will not become binding internally, as part of domestic law, until it is incorporated by a domestic statute. In the EC, France, for example, is monist; Germany, Belgium, Italy and the UK are dualist. But whether received automatically, by process of 'adoption', or incorporated by statute, by way of 'transformation', the incorporation of international law does not itself settle the question of priorities. The status accorded to international law will depend, in the case of each State, on the extent to which that State has provided for this, either in its constitution, where it has a written constitution, or, where it has no written constitution, in its statute of incorporation.

There is wide variation in the way in which, and the extent to which, Member States of the Union have provided for this question of priorities. Where States have a written constitution, there will be express provision for this issue. At the time of their accession, it ranged from the whole-hearted acceptance of international law of the Dutch constitution (Article 66), which accords supremacy to *all* forms of international law, whether prior or subsequent to domestic law, to Article 55 of the French constitution, which, at that time, provided that treaties or agreements duly ratified 'have authority superior to that of laws' (thus leaving open the question of secondary legislation), to Article 24 of the German constitution (Grundgesetz (GG)), which provided, rather loosely, that the State 'may transfer sovereign powers' to international organisations (although Article 23 GG has been introduced to deal specifically with the EU); or Article 11 of the Italian constitution whereby the State 'consents, on conditions of reciprocity with other States, to limitations of sovereignty necessary for an arrangement which may ensure peace and justice between the nations'. (Under the principle of reciprocity, if one party to an agreement breaches his obligations, the other contracting parties may regard themselves as entitled to be relieved of theirs.)

A State which does not have a written constitution, and which is dualist, such as the UK, must provide for priorities in the statute of incorporation itself. This statute will have the same status as any other statute. As such it will be vulnerable to the doctrine of implied repeal, or *'lex posterior derogat priori'*, whereby any inconsistency between an earlier and a later statute is resolved in favour of the latter. The later statute is deemed to have impliedly repealed the earlier one (see *Ellen Street Estates Ltd* v *Minister of Health* [1934] 1 KB 590). On a strict application of this doctrine, any provision of a domestic statute passed subsequent to the statute incorporating EC law, in the British case the European Communities Act 1972, which was inconsistent with EC law, would take priority. (See further 4.4.1.)

Given the differences from State to State it is clear that if national courts were to apply their own constitutional rules to the question of priorities between domestic law and EC law, there would be no uniformity of application, and the primacy of EC law could not be guaranteed throughout the Community. This was the principal reason advanced by Advocate-General Roemer in *Van Gend en Loos* (case 26/62) for denying the direct effects of what was then Article 12 EEC (now 25 EC). Not only would this weaken the effect of Community law, it would undermine solidarity among the Member States, and in the end threaten the Community itself. It is no doubt reasons such as these which led the ECJ to develop its own constitutional rules to deal with the problem, in particular the principle of supremacy, or primacy, of EC law.

4.3 The Court of Justice's contribution

4.3.1 Development of the principle of supremacy

The first cautious statement of the principle of supremacy of EC law came in the case of *Van Gend en Loos* (case 26/62). The principal question in the case was the question of the direct effects of Article 25 (ex 12) EC. The conflict, assuming that that article were found directly effective, was between Article 25 and an *earlier* Dutch law. Under Dutch law, if Article 25 were directly effective it would, under the Dutch constitution, take precedence over domestic law. So the questions referred to the ECJ under Article 234 did not raise the issue of sovereignty directly. Nevertheless, in addition to declaring that what is now Article 25 was directly effective, the Court went on to say that:

> the Community constitutes a new legal order in international law, for whose benefit the States have limited their sovereign rights, albeit within limited fields.

Although the main emphasis of the judgment relates to the doctrine of direct effect, it is also significant because, by referring to the 'new legal order', the ECJ indicated that the Community was not just a 'normal' international law organisation. In particular, the Community had a more independent status as well as, arguably, greater impact on the national legal systems of the Member States.

The conflict in *Costa* v *ENEL* (case 6/64) posed a more difficult problem for the Italian courts. This case too involved an alleged conflict between a number of Treaty provisions and an Italian statute nationalising the electricity company of which the defendant, Signor Costa, was a shareholder, but here the Italian law was later in time than the Treaty provision. On being brought before the Milan *tribunale* for refusing to pay his bill (the princely sum of L1,925, or approximately £1.10), Signor Costa argued that the company was in breach of EC law. The defendants argued '*lex posterior*'; the Italian Act nationalising the electricity company was later in time than the Italian Ratification Act, the Act incorporating EC law, and therefore took priority. The Italian court referred this question of priorities to the ECJ. It also referred the matter to its own constitutional court. This time the principle of supremacy was clearly affirmed by the Court. It cited *Van Gend*; the States had 'limited their sovereign rights'. It went further. It looked to the Treaty and noted that Article 249 (ex 189) indicated that there had been a transfer of powers to the Community institutions; Article 10 (ex 5) underlined States' commitment to observe Community law. The Court concluded:

> The reception, within the laws of each Member State, of provisions having a Community source, and more particularly of the terms and of the spirit of the Treaty, has as a corollary the impossibility, for the Member State, to give preference to a unilateral and *subsequent* measure against a legal order accepted by them on a basis of reciprocity . . .
>
> Such a measure cannot be inconsistent with that legal system. The executive force of Community law cannot vary from one State to another in deference to subsequent domestic laws, without jeopardizing the attainment of the objectives of the Treaty . . .

The obligations undertaken under the Treaty establishing the Community would not be unconditional, but merely contingent, if they could be called into question by subsequent legislative acts of the signatories . . .

It follows from all these observations that the law stemming from the Treaty, an independent source of law, could not, because of its special and original nature, be over-ridden by domestic legal provisions, however framed, without being deprived of its char-acter as Community law and without the legal basis of the Community itself being called into question.

The transfer, by Member States, from their national orders in favour of the Community order of the rights and obligations arising from the Treaty, carries with it a clear limita-tion of their sovereign right upon which a *subsequent* unilateral law, incompatible with the aims of the Community, cannot prevail. (Emphasis added.)

The reasoning used by the ECJ is worthy of note as, in developing its argument, the ECJ uses a teleological – or purposive – approach that is not tied in particularly closely to the actual wording of the Treaty. The ECJ's substantive arguments can be divided into two main groups:

(a) those relating to the *nature* of the Community; and

(b) those relating to the *purposes* of the Community.

The first category comprises the ECJ's assertion about the independent nature of the new Community legal order and the mechanism by which this legal order was created: the permanent limitation of Member States' sovereign rights. There is no express basis in the Treaty for either of these points. The other arguments, referring to the aims of the Treaty, are more practical. They look to the purpose of the Community and the need to ensure that those goals are not undermined. These arguments are based on the need to make Community law effective.

In the case of *Internationale Handelsgesellschaft mbH* (case 11/70) the Court went even further. Here, the conflict was between not a Treaty provision and a domestic statute, but between an EC regulation and provisions of the German constitution. The claimant argued that the regulation infringed, *inter alia*, the principle of pro-portionality enshrined in the German constitution and sought to nullify the regu-lation on those grounds. Normally, any ordinary law in breach of the constitution is invalid, since the constitution is superior in the hierarchy of legal rules to statute law. EC law had been incorporated into German law by statute, the Act of Ratifica-tion. There was no provision in the constitution that the constitution could be overridden by EC law. Article 24 GG merely provided for 'the transfer of sovereign powers to intergovernmental institutions'. So the question before the German administrative court (Verwaltungsgericht, Frankfurt) was: If there were a conflict between the regulation and the German constitution, which law should prevail? As in *Costa*, the German judge referred the question to the ECJ and his own federal constitutional court (Bundesverfassungsgericht).

The ruling from the ECJ was in the strongest terms. The legality of a Community act cannot be judged in the light of national law:

the law born from the Treaty [cannot] have the courts opposing to it rules of national law *of any nature whatever* . . . the validity of a Community instrument or its effect within a Member State cannot be affected by allegations that it strikes at either the fundamental rights as formulated in that State's constitution or the principles of a national consti-tutional structure. (Emphasis added.)

Underlying this judgment one can see concerns similar to those expressed in *Costa*: the need to ensure the effectiveness of Community law, whatever the cost to the national legal order. If the Court's ruling seems harsh in the light of the importance of the rights protected in a State's constitution, many of which are regarded as fundamental human rights, it is worth adding that the Court went on to say that respect for such rights was one of the principal aims of the Community and as such it was part of its own (albeit unwritten) law (see Chapter 6).

The principle of supremacy of Community law applies not only to internal domestic laws, but also to obligations entered into with third countries, that is, countries outside the EU. In the *ERTA* case (case 22/70) the ECJ held, in the context of a challenge to an international road transport agreement to which the Com-munity was a party, that once the Community, in implementing a common policy, lays down common rules, Member States no longer have the right, individually or collectively, to contract obligations towards non-Member States affecting these common rules. And where the Community concludes a treaty in pursuance of a common policy, this excludes the possibility of a concurrent authority on the part of the Member States. This means that where a State attempts to exercise concur-rent authority it will be overridden to the extent that it conflicts with Community law. This principle does not, however, appear to apply to Member States' pre-accession agreements with third countries. Where such agreements are 'not com-patible' with the EC Treaty, Member States are required to 'take all appropriate steps to eliminate the incompatibilities established' (Article 307 (ex 234) EC). In *R* v *Secretary of State for the Home Department, ex parte Evans Medical Ltd* (case C–324/93), the Court conceded that provisions of such an agreement contrary to Community law may continue to be applied where the performance of that agreement may still be required by non-Member States which are parties to it. The Court has, however, urged national courts to give effect to such provisions only to the extent that it is necessary to meet the demands of that agreement (*Minne* (case C–13/93)). Thus, subject to this exception, as far as the ECJ is concerned *all* EC law, whatever its nature, must take priority over *all* conflicting domestic law, whether it be prior or subsequent to Community law. Given the fact that the Court was approaching the matter *tabula rasa*, there being no provision in the Treaty to this effect, on what basis did the Court justify its position?

All these cases show a common theme in the ECJ's approach: the need to ensure the effectiveness of Community law. The position can be summarised as follows. The Court's reasoning is pragmatic, based on the purpose, the general aims and spirit of the Treaty. States freely signed the Treaty; they agreed to take all appropriate measures to comply with EC law (Article 10 EC); the Treaty created its own institu-tions, and gave those institutions power to make laws binding on Member States (Article 249 EC). They agreed to set up an institutionalised form of control by the Commission (under Article 226 (ex 169), see Chapter 11) and the Court. The Com-munity would not survive if States were free to act unilaterally in breach of their obligations. If the aims of the Community are to be achieved, there must be uni-formity of application. This will not occur unless all States accord priority to EC law.

4.3.2 Problems for the national courts

The reasoning is convincing. Nonetheless national courts were understandably reluctant to disregard their own constitutional rules and the Italian and German constitutional courts in *Costa v ENEL* ([1964] CMLR 425 at p. 430) and *Internationale Handelsgesellschaft mbH (Solange I)* ([1974] 2 CMLR 540), adhering to their own traditional view, refused to acknowledge the absolute supremacy of EC law.

There were other problems too for national courts – problems of application. Even if the principle of primacy of EC law were accepted in theory, what was a national judge to do in practice when faced with a conflict? No English judge can declare a statute void or unlawful (subject to limited powers in respect of the Human Rights Act); in most countries with a written constitution only the constitutional court has power to declare a domestic law invalid for breach of the constitution, if it has such a power at all. Must the national judge wait for the offending national law to be repealed or legally annulled before he can give precedence to EC law?

The ECJ suggested a solution to this problem in *Simmenthal SpA* (case 106/77). This case involved a conflict between a Treaty provision, the then Article 30 (now 28) EC on the free movement of goods, and an Italian law passed *subsequent* to the Italian Act incorporating EC law, a similar clash to the one in *Costa v ENEL* (case 6/ 64). Following *Costa*, the Italian constitutional court had revised its view and declared that it would be prepared to declare any national law conflicting with EC law invalid. When the problem arose in *Simmenthal* the Italian judge, the Pretore di Susa, was perplexed. Should he apply EC law at once to the case before him, or should he wait until his own constitutional court had declared the national law invalid? He referred this question to the ECJ. The Court's reply was predictable:

> any recognition that national legislative measures which encroach upon the field within which the Community exercises its legislative power or which are otherwise incompatible with the provisions of Community law had any legal effect would amount to a corresponding denial of the effectiveness of obligations undertaken unconditionally and irrevocably by Member States pursuant to the Treaty and would thus imperil the very foundations of the Community (para. 18).
>
> . . . a national court which is called upon . . . to apply provisions of Community law is under a duty to give full effect to those provisions, if necessary refusing . . . to apply any conflicting provision of national legislation, even if adopted subsequently, and it is not necessary for the court to request or await the prior setting aside of such provision by legislative or other constitutional means (para. 24).

The reasoning behind the judgment is clear. Unless Community law is given priority over conflicting national law at once, from the moment of its entry into force, there can be no uniformity of application throughout the Community. Community law will be ineffective. According to the ECJ, national judges faced with a conflict between national law, whatever its nature, and Community law, must ignore, must shut their eyes to national law; they need not, indeed must not, wait for the law to be changed. Any incompatible national law is automatically inapplicable.

The principles expressed in *Simmenthal SpA* were applied by the Court in *R v Secretary of State for Transport, ex parte Factortame Ltd* (case C–213/89), in the context of a claim before the English courts by a group of Spanish fishermen for an interim injunction to prevent the application of certain sections of the Merchant Shipping Act 1988, which denied them the right to register their boats in the UK, and which the claimants alleged were in breach of EC law. The question of the 'legality' of the British provisions under Community law had yet to be decided, following a separate reference to the ECJ. The British courts were being asked to give primacy to a *putative* Community right over an allegedly conflicting national law, and to grant an interim injunction against the Crown, something which they considered they were not permitted to do under national law. Following a reference by the House of Lords asking whether they were obliged to grant the relief in question as a matter of Community law, the ECJ pointed out that national courts were obliged, by Article 10 EC, to ensure the legal protection which persons derive from the direct effect of provisions of Community law. Moreover:

> The full effectiveness of Community law would be . . . impaired if a rule of national law could prevent a court seised of a dispute governed by Community law from granting interim relief in order to ensure the full effectiveness of the judgment to be given on the existence of the rights claimed under Community law. It follows that a court which in those circumstances would grant interim relief, if it were not for a rule of national law, is obliged to set aside that rule (para. 21).

The obligation on Member States to ensure the full effectiveness of Community law requires national courts not only to 'disapply' the offending national law but also to supply a remedy which is not available under national law. It now seems that the obligation to disapply inconsistent national law extends beyond the courts to administrative agencies. In *Larsy* (case C–118/00), reasoning from its judgments in *Simmenthal* and *Factortame* (case C–213/89), the ECJ held that the national social security institution, INASTI, should disapply national laws that precluded effective protection of Larsy's Community law rights (para. 53). (See also *CIF* v *Autorita* (case C–198/01): disapplication of national legislation incompatible with the competition provisions.) The issue of procedural rules and remedies is discussed further in Chapter 8.

A finding that a provision of national law is 'inapplicable' because of its incompatibility with Community law does not, however, result in its annulment, or even prevent its application in situations falling outside the scope of Community law. In *IN. CO. GE. '90* (cases C–10 & 22/97) the Court held that 'it does not follow from *Simmenthal* that a domestic rule which is incompatible with EC law is non-existent'. Similarly in *Arcaro* (case C–168/95) it made it clear that there was 'no method or procedure in Community law allowing national courts to eliminate national provisions contrary to a directive which has not been transposed where that provision may not be relied on before the national court'. In *ICI* v *Colmer* (case C–264/96) the ECJ found a system of tax relief for holding companies with a seat in the EU discriminatory, and therefore contrary to EC law, when applied to subsidiary companies in other Member States, but lawful in a situation where holding companies control subsidiaries in non-Member States. Despite its inapplicability in the former context, the national court was under no obligation to disapply national law in the latter situation, since that lay outside the scope of Community law.

However:

> Where the same legislation must be disapplied as contrary to EC law in a situation covered by Community law it is for the competent body of the Member State concerned to remove that legal uncertainty insofar as it might affect rights deriving from Community rules.

4.3.3 EC rules which do not have direct effect

It may be noted that all the earlier landmark rulings of the Court, up to and including *Simmenthal* (case C–106/77), were expressed in terms of directly effective Community law, that is, rules that gave rise to rights that could be relied on within the national legal system. Until the Court introduced the principle of indirect effects in *von Colson* (case 14/83) (Chapter 5) and the principle of State liability in *Francovich* (cases C–6 & 9/90) (see Chapter 8), it was thought that national courts would only be required to apply, and give priority to, EC law which was directly effective. This proved not to be the case. The obligation on national courts to interpret domestic law to comply with EC directives which are not directly effective (because invoked horizontally), as extended in *Marleasing*, impliedly requires those courts to give priority to EC law. Similarly, although the granting of a remedy in damages against the State under *Francovich* does not require the *application* of Community law, the remedy, based on Member States' obligation to guarantee full and effective protection for individuals' rights under Community law, is premised on the supremacy of EC law. This obligation was held in *Francovich* (at para. 42) to apply to all rights 'which parties enjoy under Community law'. That protection cannot be achieved unless those rights prevail over conflicting provisions of national law. As *Brasserie du Pêcheur* and *R v Secretary of State for Transport, ex parte Factortame* (cases C–46 & 48/93) subsequently made clear, individuals' Community rights, including the right to damages, must prevail over *all* acts of Member States, legislative, executive or judicial, which are contrary to Community law.

4.4 The Member States' response

Although the ECJ might rule that Community law is supreme, this principle requires acceptance by the courts of the Member States if it is to have any real effect. After a shaky start (we have already noted the Italian and German constitutional courts' response in *Costa* and *Internationale Handelsgesellschaft mbH*), the courts of Member States have now broadly accepted the principle of supremacy of EC law *provided they regard it as directly effective*. They have done so in a variety of ways: in some cases by bending and adapting their own constitutional rules; in others by devising new constitutional rules to meet the new situation. The point to note here is that in each system it seems that the national courts have accepted supremacy on the terms of their constitutional system. That is, they have argued for the supremacy of Community law on the basis of national legal provisions, not the provisions of Community law itself. Their acceptance of supremacy is thus, to a certain extent, conditional and there is consequently the potential for conflict on specific issues, as the human rights cases illustrate (see further Chapter 6). Given the expanded membership of the Union, for reasons of space alone, it is not possible to discuss the response of each of the Member States; further, for new Member States, it may well be too soon for any problems to work their way through the judicial system. It would be naive to suggest that the newer Member States would have no difficulties absorbing the doctrine of primacy, as they should have been aware of it on entry. As is illustrated by the case of the UK, whose politicians knew of the doctrine at the time of accession, legal reality is often different from political aspirations, and resolving the difficulties takes some inventiveness as well as good will. What follows is a discussion of the response of the British courts and of the German courts; a full comparative survey of the position of the other Member States must fall outside the scope of what is a book about Community law.

4.4.1 Great Britain

As a dualist State without a written constitution the status of Community law in the UK derives from the European Communities Act 1972. To what extent does that Act enable the British courts to give effect to the principle of supremacy of EC law?

The most important provisions are ss. 2 and 3.

Section 2(1) provides for the direct applicability of EC law in the UK:

> All such rights, powers, liabilities, obligations and restrictions from time to time created or arising by or under the Treaties, and all such remedies and procedures from time to time provided for by or under the Treaties, as in accordance with the Treaties are without further enactment to be given legal effect or used in the United Kingdom shall be recognised and available in law, and be enforced, allowed and followed accordingly; and the expression 'enforceable Community right' and similar expressions shall be read as referring to one to which this subsection applies.

Section 2(2) provides a general power for the further implementation of Community obligations by means of secondary legislation.

This is subject to Sch. 2. Schedule 2 lists the 'forbidden' areas, such as the power to increase taxation, to introduce retrospective measures or to create new criminal offences. These areas apart, s. 2(2) thus allows for ongoing domestic legislation over the whole field of objectives of the Treaty.

Section 2(4) is the section relevant to the question of primacy. It does not expressly say EC law is supreme. Section 2(4) provides (emphasis added):

> The provision that may be made under subsection (2) above includes, subject to schedule 2 to this Act, any such provision (of any such extent) as might be made by Act of Parliament, and *any enactment passed or to be passed*, other than one contained in this part of this Act [i.e., an enactment of a non-Community nature], *shall be construed and have effect subject to the foregoing provisions of this section* [i.e., obligations of a Community nature].

4.4.2 **Effect of the European Communities Act 1972, s. 2(1) and (4)**

4.4.2.1 *Directly effective EC law*

The first question to arise is whether the combined effect of s. 2(1) and (particularly) s. 2(4) of the European Communities Act 1972 is sufficient to enable the British courts to give priority to EC law, on *Simmenthal* (case 106/77) principles, as the ECJ would require. Or does it merely lay down a rule of construction, whereby domestic law must be *construed*, so far as possible, to conform with EC law? The traditional constitutional view is that the doctrine of parliamentary sovereignty, and particularly the principle of implied repeal, makes entrenchment of EC law impossible. Parliament is not free to bind its successors. Therefore priority for EC law cannot be guaranteed, and s. 2(4) can only provide a rule of construction.

An approach based on the jurisprudence of the ECJ, particularly *Simmenthal*, would involve a departure from that view.

There was considerable wavering in the early years on the question of primacy, but in 1979 the Court of Appeal in *Macarthys Ltd* v *Smith* ([1979] ICR 785), a landmark case, took the 'European' view. Cumming-Bruce and Lawton LJJ, invoking the ECJ in *Costa* (case 6/64) and *Simmenthal* (case 106/77), were prepared, on the basis of the European Communities Act 1972, s. 2(4), to give European law 'priority'. Lord Denning MR preferred to use s. 2(4) as a rule of construction and construed the relevant English legislation (Equal Pay Act 1970) to conform with the principle of equal pay for equal work in what was then Article 119 (now, as amended, 141) EC. However, in doing so he took a rather broader view of 'construction' than is usually taken in construing international agreements. In construing the English statutes, he said, 'we are entitled to look to the Treaty as an aid to its construction: and even more, not only as an aid but as an overriding force'. He went on to say that 'If . . . our legislation is deficient – or is inconsistent with Community law . . . then it is our bounden duty to give priority to Community law'.

The current British position is found in the ruling of the House of Lords in *Factortame Ltd* v *Secretary of State for Transport* ([1990] 2 AC 85). Lord Bridge suggested that the combined effect of subsections (1) and (4) of the European Communities Act 1972, s. 2, was 'as if a section were incorporated in Part II [the impugned part] of the Merchant Shipping Act 1988 which in terms enacted that the provisions with respect to registration of British fishing vessels were to be without prejudice to the directly enforceable Community rights of nationals of any Member State of the EEC'. He suggested that if it were to be found that the British Act was in breach of the claimants' directly effective Community rights the latter rights would 'prevail' over the contrary provisions of the 1988 Act.

Subsequently, in applying the ECJ's ruling (in case C–213/89 noted above) that national courts must grant interim relief against the Crown where this was necessary to protect individuals' Community rights, the House of Lords, unanimously, granted that relief (*R* v *Secretary of State for Transport, ex parte Factortame Ltd* [1991] 1 AC 603 at 645). Here clearly no question of 'interpretation' of national law was possible; the House simply gave 'priority' to Community law. In justification, Lord Bridge pointed out that the principle of supremacy of Community law, if it was not always inherent in the Treaty, was 'well established in the jurisprudence of the Court long before the United Kingdom joined the Community. Whatever limitation of its sovereignty Parliament accepted when it enacted the European Communities Act was entirely voluntary'. As a corollary, it seems that the doctrine of implied repeal, discussed at 4.2, has changed. In the context of 'constitutional' acts of Parliament, such as the European Communities Act (and the Human Rights Act), express intention to repeal the act is required. Such acts will not be repealed through inconsistency with a later act. (See *Metric Martyrs* case, *Theburn* v *Sunderland CC* [2003] QB 151, QBD.)

Primacy of Community law, together with obligation imposed by Article 10 EC on national courts to provide effective protection for individuals' Community rights (the 'effectiveness' principle), has resulted in remedies being granted which were not at the time available under national law (see Chapter 8).

4.4.2.2 *The limits of primacy*

Thus the British courts have been willing to accord supremacy to directly effective Community law, either by a (fictional) 'construction' of domestic law, or, where necessary, by applying EC law directly, in priority over national law. As suggested by Lord Bridge in *Factortame*, this appears to rest on the implied intentions of Parliament. However, both Lord Denning in *Macarthys Ltd* v *Smith* and Lord Diplock in *Garland* have made it clear that should Parliament expressly attempt to repudiate its EC obligations the courts would be obliged to give effect to wishes.

> If the time should come when our Parliament deliberately passes an Act – with the intention of repudiating the Treaty or any provision in it – or intentionally of acting inconsistently with it – and says so in express terms – then . . . it would be the duty of our courts to follow the statute of our Parliament (per Lord Denning in *Macarthys Ltd* v *Smith* [1979] ICR 785 at p. 789).

While this is unlikely to happen as long as the UK remains a member of the Community, it was perhaps seen as important that it should remain a theoretical possibility. As Laws, LJ noted in the *Metric Martyrs* case, any changes have been introduced as a matter of English law, not as a direct requirement of Community law. If the British courts have changed in their approach to statutory interpretation in the context of Community law, the principle of parliamentary sovereignty remains intact.

4.4.2.3 *EC law which is not directly effective*

In *Factortame* their Lordships' views on the European Communities Act 1972, s. 2(4), were expressed in the context of a conflict between domestic law and *directly effective* Community law. Is it possible to achieve primacy for EC law for provisions of EC directives which, although sufficiently clear and precise for direct effects, are not directly effective because they are being invoked against a private party? In other words, does s. 2(4) of the Act enable the British courts to follow *von Colson* (case 14/83) and *Marleasing* (case C–106/89) (see Chapter 5) and interpret domestic law to comply with EC law, even when it is not directly effective? In *Duke* v *GEC Reliance Ltd* ([1988] AC 618) the House of Lords thought not. The European Communities Act 1972, s. 2(1) and (4), said Lord Templeman, applied, and only applied, to EC law which was directly effective.

> Section 2(4) of the European Communities Act 1972 does not . . . enable or constrain a British court to distort the meaning of a British statute in order to enforce against an individual a Community Directive which has no direct effect between individuals.

This reasoning may have been understandable on the particular facts of the case. In *Litster* v *Forth Dry Dock & Engineering Co. Ltd* ([1990] 1 AC 546), in the context of a claim against a 'private' party, the House of Lords interpreted certain UK regulations to comply with EC Directive 80/777, suggesting that where legislation had been introduced specifically in order to implement an EC directive, UK courts must interpret domestic law to comply with the directive, if necessary 'supplying the necessary words by implication' in order to achieve a result compatible with EC law. No reference was made to *Duke* v *GEC Reliance Ltd*, nor to the fact that the directive in question was not directly effective.

Thus, in the absence of evidence, such as was adduced in *Duke* v *GEC Reliance Ltd*, that Parliament did not intend to comply with Community law, *Litster* suggests that even where EC law is not directly effective, 'priority' for EC law should be ensured by way of interpretation of national law. However, there is no guarantee that *Litster* will be followed. In *Webb* v *EMO Air Cargo (UK) Ltd* ([1992] 2 All ER 43) Lord Templeman's dicta in *Duke* v *GEC Reliance Ltd* were cited by the Court of Appeal and the House of Lords ([1993] 1 WLR 49). However, following a ruling from the ECJ on the interpretation of Directive 76/207, the House of Lords found that it was possible to construe s. 5(3) of the Sex Discrimination Act 1975 to comply with the Court's ruling without 'distorting' the meaning of the section. The Court of Appeal's decision had been based on a different, if equally legitimate, interpretation of s. 5(3), and past case law. On the other hand, in *R* v *British Coal Corporation, ex parte Vardy* ([1993] ICR 720), Glidewell J found that it was 'not possible' to follow the House of Lords' example in *Litster* and interpret certain provisions of the Trade Union and Labour Relations Act 1992 to comply with EC (Collective Redundancies) Directive 75/129 since they were clearly at odds with the directive. Thus in the absence of ambiguity or evidence that Parliament intended UK law to have the meaning contended for or where there is a clear conflict between domestic and EC law, it seems that the British courts will be reluctant to apply the *von Colson* principle, particularly as extended by the ECJ in *Marleasing*. This appears to have been acknowledged by the ECJ in *Wagner Miret* (case C–334/92). Arguably this approach, which respects the principles of legal certainty and non-retroactivity, is consistent with the principles of EC law expressed by the ECJ in *Officier van Justitie* v *Kolpinghuis Nijmegen* (case 80/86, noted Chapter 5). Where it is not possible for national courts to give indirect effect to Community directives, enforcement of EC law should perhaps be left to the Commission under Article 226, or, now, to an action against the State under *Francovich* (cases C–6 & 9/90), as suggested by the Court in *Dori* (case C–91/92) and *Wagner Miret*. Note, however, the possibility for an action against the State for judicial failure to apply Community law (see Chapter 8)

4.4.2.4 *State liability in damages*

The UK courts have had little difficulty in applying the principle of State liability following the ECJ's rulings in *Francovich* (cases C–6 & 9/90) and *Brasserie du Pécheur* (cases C–46 & 48/93) They have accepted that the State may be liable for *legislative* breaches of Community law. In *R v Secretary of State for Transport, ex parte Factortame Ltd (No. 2)* ([1991] 1 AC 603), the House of Lords demonstrated its willingness to grant an interim injunction to prevent the application of a British statute (allegedly) in breach of EC law in order effectively to protect the claimants' directly effective Community rights. In *R v Secretary of State for Employment, ex parte Equal Opportunities Commission* ([1995] 1 AC 1), the House of Lords, following the 'precedent' set by *Factortame*, was prepared to grant a declaration that certain provisions of the Employment Protection (Consolidation) Act 1978, which imposed a two-year threshold for protection against unfair dismissal and redundancy, were incompatible with the then Article 119 EC (now after amendment, 141). Lord Keith suggested that it was not necessary for the purposes of the case to declare the United Kingdom *in breach* of its obligations under Community law. A declaration establishing the *incompatibility* of domestic law with EC law would be sufficient to establish a State's 'failure' for the purposes of a claim under *Francovich*. It could be argued that as long as incompatibility was established, a formal declaration to that effect would not be necessary.

From these cases it was but a small step for the British courts to accept a principle of liability in damages for legislative breaches of Community law. This step was taken by the Court of Appeal in *R v Secretary of State for the Home Department, ex parte Gallagher* ([1996] 2 CMLR 951). Here Lord Bingham of Cornhill CJ, invoking the ECJ's ruling in *Francovich*, said, at para. 10:

> It is a cardinal principle of Community law that the laws of Member States should provide effective and adequate redress for violations of Community law by Member States where these result in the infringement of specific individual rights conferred by the law of the Community.

However, while accepting that the UK might be liable in principle for a British statute (the Prevention of Terrorism (Temporary Provisions) Act 1989) contrary to EC Directive 64/221 (now repealed and replaced by Directive 2004/38/EC), he rejected the applicant's claim. The applicant had failed to establish the requisite causal link between the alleged breach and the damage sustained. Even without the breach, a breach of the applicant's procedural rights under the directive, the result, the applicant's removal from the UK, would have been the same. Nor was the breach of Community law sufficiently serious to warrant liability. Although the UK's transposition of the directive was wrong, the error did not constitute a 'manifest and grave breach' of EC law.

In applying the ECJ's ruling on the damages claim in *Factortame* (case C–48/93)

([1998] 1 CMLR 1353), the Court of Appeal ([1998] 3 CMLR 192) and the House of Lords ([1999] 3 CMLR 597) accepted the principle of State liability for damage resulting from a British statute, the Merchant Shipping Act 1988, found by the ECJ to be contrary to the then Article 52 (now 43) EC. Basing their reasoning on the Court's rulings in *Francovich* (cases C–6 & 9/90) and *Brasserie du Pêcheur* (cases C–46 & 48/93) they found that the UK's breach constituted a sufficiently serious breach of Community law, for which the UK might be liable in damages, subject to the applicants' establishing the requisite damage and causation.

Following the UK courts' example in *Factortame (No. 5)*, the High Court in a number of cases, for example *Bowden v South West Water Services* ([1999] 3 CMLR 180) and *R v Dept of Social Security, ex parte Scullion* ([1999] 3 CMLR 798), likewise dealt without demur with claims for damages based on *Francovich*. The English courts have had no problem in applying the principle of State liability, even when the breach of Community law is contained in a British statute.

It interesting to note that the courts' decisions in all of these cases were based on the ECJ's jurisprudence: they did not seek to justify their decisions on the basis of the European Communities Act 1972. Had they thought it to be necessary, it is submitted that it would have been possible to do so. The rights recognised and incorporated into domestic law by the European Communities Act 1972, s. 2(1), are sufficiently widely expressed to embrace not only directly effective and indirectly effective Community rights but also rights based on *Francovich*. Furthermore, support for the primacy of all EC rights may be provided by the European Communities Act 1972, s. 3(1), which provides that:

> For the purposes of all legal proceedings any question as to the meaning or effect of any of the Treaties, or as to the validity, meaning or effect of any Community instrument, shall be treated as a question of law (and, if not referred to the European Court, be for determination as such in accordance with the principles laid down by and any relevant decision of the European Court or any court attached thereto).

The relevant decisions of the ECJ for the purposes of State liability, as has been acknowledged by the English High Court and the Court of Appeal, are clearly *Francovich* (cases C–6 & 9/90) and *Brasserie du Pêcheur* (cases C–46 & 48/93).

4.4.3 Germany

The German federal constitutional court modified its original view in *Internationale Handelsgesellschaft (Solange I)* ([1974] 2 CMLR 540). In *Steinike und Weinleg* ([1980] 2 CMLR 531) it suggested that any challenge to the constitutionality under German law of EC law could only be brought by way of challenge to the German Act of Ratification itself, and in October 1986, in *Application of Wünsche Handelsgesellschaft (Solange II)* ([1987] 3 CMLR 225), its position in *Internationale Handelsgesellschaft* was finally reversed. As long as EC law itself ensured the effective protection of fundamental rights, a ruling from the ECJ under Article 234 would not, the court held, be subject to review. Similarly, in *Re Kloppenberg* ([1988] 3 CMLR 1), in the context of a successful challenge to the Bundesfinanzhof's decision on the direct effect of directives (see *Re VAT Directives* [1982] 1 CMLR 527, noted in Chapter 5), it affirmed the principle of the supremacy of Community law in the strongest terms.

In 1992, as in France, the constitution was amended to provide specifically for the transfer of sovereign powers to the EU (see new Article 23 GG).

However, the case of *Brunner* v *The European Union Treaty* ([1994] 1 CMLR 57) indicates that the German federal constitutional court (Bundesverfassungsgericht), while respecting the supremacy of Community law in matters within the sphere of Community competence, will itself reserve the right:

(a) to ensure the protection of fundamental human rights guaranteed under the German constitution; and

(b) to decide whether the Union institutions have acted within their powers under the EC and EU Treaties.

The case involved a challenge to the German Federal Parliament's power to ratify the TEU. It was argued that the transfer via the proposed Act of Ratification of further powers and competences to the European Union would threaten human rights and democratic principles protected under the German constitution. The Bundesverfassungsgericht found these allegations unfounded. The TEU did not, as was suggested, establish a European State but a federation of States. It equipped the Union only with specific competences and powers in accordance with the principle of limited individual competences and established a principle of subsidiarity for the Union. It would permit no further extension of Community competence under Article 308 (ex 235, see Chapter 3). If the Union institutions or organisations were to develop the Treaty in a way not covered by the Treaty in the form that was the basis for the Act of Accession the resultant legislative instruments would not be binding within the sphere of German sovereignty. If parts of the Community legal order were to breach fundamental rights protected under the German Constitution it would declare those provisions inapplicable. Accordingly, the court would review legal instruments of European institutions and agencies to see whether they remained within the sovereign rights conferred on them or transgressed them. Germany was one of the masters of the Treaty with the intention of long-term membership: but it could ultimately revoke its adherence by a contrary act.

According to the federal constitutional court, German sovereignty remains intact, and that court will itself decide whether the institutions of the Union have acted within their powers under the EC and EU Treaties.

The unequivocal stance of the federal constitutional court in *Brunner* emboldened the German courts to take a stand in a series of cases concerning the Community's banana regime. The regime, which was set up in 1993 by EC Regulation 404/93, and which operated to the serious disadvantage of German importers, was challenged by Germany on the grounds that it breached the Community's international obligations (*inter alia* GATT) and violated vested property rights protected under the German Constitution. Despite strong arguments, acknowledged by Advocate-General Gulmann, that there were 'circumstances which might provide a basis for a finding that the Regulation was invalid' the ECJ found that there was no illegality in the Community's market organisation of bananas (*Germany* v *Council* (case C–280/93); see further Chapter 10).

This case, which was extremely thin in its reasoning, for which it was roundly criticised, even by a former judge of the ECJ (see article by Everling noted below), did little to stem the flood of actions before the German (and not only German) courts seeking to suspend the application of the contested regulation and/or to obtain compensation for damage suffered as a result of its application. Following *Germany* v *Council* the legality of the Banana regulation was again questioned before the Frankfurt administrative court (Verwaltungsgericht), and further questions referred to the ECJ (*Atlanta* (case C–465/93)). While affirming national courts' power to award interim relief, even positive relief in the form of the grant of import licences, pending a ruling from the ECJ on validity, the ECJ confirmed its finding in *Germany* v *Council* on the legality of the regulation, pointing out that in deciding whether or not to grant interim relief national courts were 'obliged to respect what the Community Court has decided on this issue' (*Atlanta* (case C–465/93)). This did not prevent further claims before the German courts raising the issue of the compatibility of the regulation with the German Constitution, and questioning its applicability in Germany on the basis of *Brunner*. In one case, following rejection of the claimants' application for relief by the Kassel Verwaltungsgerichtshof, which followed the ECJ's ruling in *Germany* v *Council*, the claimants took their case to the federal constitutional court, which ordered a re-examination of the case, basing its decision on Article 19(4) of the German Basic Law. Article 19(4) enshrines the right to effective judicial protection. Significantly the constitutional court did not seek a ruling from the ECJ. On re-examination, the referring court granted the requested interim relief and referred further questions to the ECJ on the interpretation and validity of the regulation. In another case, the federal finance court (Bundesfinanzhof) accepted the finding of the Finanzgericht Hamburg that parts of the Banana regulation might be incompatible with GATT, and suggested that if they were, the German courts might be prevented from applying them following principles established in *Brunner*. Again further questions on the compatibility of the regulation with GATT were referred to the ECJ (*T. Port GmbH & Co.* v *Hauptzollamt Hamburg-Jonas* (cases C–364 & 365/95)).

Although the courts have not openly contradicted the ECJ's judgment in *Germany* v *Council* (case C–280/93) they have been prepared to question its applicability and even refrain from applying it. As Everling pointed out, the German courts 'are deeply concerned about the extremely unjust effects of the Banana Regulation and insufficiency of the judicial control by the ECJ in this case'. So far they have avoided open conflict by awarding provisional relief and submitting further questions to the ECJ in the hope that the Court will reconsider its decision in case C–280/93. It appeared to have done so (albeit to a limited extent) in *T. Port GmbH & Co.* v *Hauptzollamt Hamburg-Jonas* (cases C–364 & 365/95) when it found that certain aspects of the banana regime were invalid for breach of the principle of non-discrimination. However, it has denied national courts' power to award interim relief in the context of the EC institutions' (allegedly unlawful) *failure to act*, holding that any challenge to such a failure could only be brought before the ECJ under Articles 230 and 232 (ex 173 and 175, respectively) (*T. Port GmbH & Co. KG* (case C–68/95). As will be seen in Chapters 11 and 12, this represents a weakness in the system of judicial control of the EC institutions.

The administrative court which had made the reference in *Atlanta* (case C–465/93) was still not satisfied by the ECJ's response and referred the question back to the German constitutional court. It was only in 2000, four years later, that that court delivered its ruling, declaring in a much criticised judgment that the administrative court's application was inadmissible. The constitutional court argued that in *Solange II* and *Brunner* it had found the level of human rights protection in Germany and within the EC legal order to be comparable. To succeed in a challenge against Community law, it would be necessary to show that the level of protection guaranteed by the ECJ fell below the German level of protection. In the case in issue, the referring administrative court had not pointed to any decline in human rights standards since *Solange*. Some commentators have suggested that this ruling constituted evidence of renewed cooperation between the constitutional court and the ECJ. Indeed, some have also suggested that in the light of this judgment and *Alcan* (BVerf G judgment 17 February 2000) that the threat to supremacy suggested by *Brunner* has been dispersed and even that *Brunner* has partially been repealed. Although the immediate threat may be gone, difficult questions about the proper scope of the test for the guarantee of fundamental rights remain.

It seems that as long as Community law does not threaten German constitutional rights or make unwarranted intrusions into areas within the legislative jurisdiction of Member States, the German courts are prepared fully to comply with the principle of primacy of EC law. In applying the ECJ's ruling in *Brasserie du Pêcheur SA v Germany* ([1997] 1 CMLR 971), the German Federal Supreme Court held that, even though there was no basis for the applicants' claim for damages in these circumstances for legislative breaches of Community law under German law, liability in respect of such breaches 'flowed directly from that [Community] law itself'. Nevertheless, although the State might be liable in principle for such breaches, Germany was found on the facts not to be liable, since the breach of Community law which caused the applicants' damage (the prohibition on the use of additives in the manufacture of beer) was, as the ECJ itself had suggested, not sufficiently serious to give rise to liability.

Like the UK courts the German courts have had difficulty with the principle of direct effects, and particularly indirect effects, in the context of the application of EC directives. In *Re v Rehabilitation Centre* ([1992] 2 CMLR 21) the German Federal Supreme Court refused to 'interpret' the German Legal Code against its clear meaning, to comply with EC Equal Treatment Directive 76/207. The court held:

> even an interpretation of statutes by reference to conformity with the constitution reaches its limits when it comes into conflict with the wording and evident intention of the legislature. The position can be no different as regards the interpretation of national law in the light of the wording and purpose of a Directive.

As is suggested in Chapter 5 it is likely that these difficulties and this resistance caused the ECJ to turn to the alternative remedy of State liability in damages in *Francovich v Italy* (case 9/90).

4.5 The Constitution

The Constitution provides, in Article I–6, that:

> The Constitution and law adopted by the institutions of the Union in exercising competences conferred on it shall have primacy over the law of the Member States.

Despite the extensive and well-established jurisprudence on this point, Article I–6 constitutes the first express treaty reference to primacy of Community, and Union, law, causing some consternation in those who would seem not to have included Community law textbooks in their reading. The provision seems straightforward and a protocol attached to the Treaty establishing a Constitution for Europe clarifies that the provision is intended only to codify the existing law. Nonetheless, some commentators have questioned whether Article I–6 is merely a codification. They argue that it implicitly gives the ECJ the power to review matters in *all* areas covered by the Constitution, an extension on its current jurisdiction. Equally, others have pointed out that Article I–6 reaffirms the limitation on the Union's powers, as primacy occurs only within the scope of attributed powers (see Chapter 3). Given the current status of the Constitution and the stated intention of the provision, this debate does not seem the most immediately significant.

4.6 Conclusions

The ECJ, in introducing the notion of supremacy, was instrumental in providing a view of the Community as a body that went beyond what was normal for an international law organisation. In a number of key judgments it identified the Community as an independent legal order, supreme over the national legal systems. One of the mechanisms used to justify this was the effectiveness of Community law, a doctrine that the ECJ has used again and again in different contexts to justify the development of Community law in a particular direction. As has been noted, however, the success of this project cannot be ascribed entirely to the ECJ. To a large part, it has been dependent on the cooperation of the Member States, particularly their courts. In a relatively short space of time the courts of Member States, despite their different constitutional rules and traditions, have adapted to the principle of supremacy of EC law where it is found to be directly effective. Their application of directives, particularly their indirect application, remains uncertain. Their reaction to *Francovich*, as refined in *Brasserie du Pêcheur* (cases C–46 & 48/93) has been positive. Credit for national courts' acceptance of the principle of supremacy of EC law must go to the ECJ, which has supplied persuasive reasons for doing so. However, equal credit must go to the courts of Member States, which have contrived to embrace the principle of primacy of Community law while at the same time insisting that ultimate political and judicial control remains within the Member States. As *Brunner* indicates, the courts of Member States, particularly their supreme courts, will be vigilant, and use all the means at their disposal, to ensure that the EU institutions do not exceed their powers or transgress fundamental constitutional rights, particularly in the new post-Maastricht political climate, with its emphasis on subsidiarity. As Kumm suggests, 'they need to keep a handle on the emergency brake'; but they would disapply a Community act or a ruling from the ECJ only where that act or that ruling was manifestly and gravely erroneous. So far they have stopped short of outright defiance, despite the occasional errors of understanding the scope of Community law. Note, however, that when an individual seeks to rely on Community law rights, the ECJ has not shied away from the ultimate step, a claim for damages against the State in respect of judicial breaches of Community law (see *Kobler* (case C–224/01), discussed Chapter 8).

FURTHER READING

See also the reading list at the end of Chapter 5.

Bebr, G., 'Agreements Concluded by the Community and their Possible Direct Effects: from International Fruit Company to Kupferberg' (1983) 20 CML Rev 35.

Bonnie, A., 'The Constitutionality of Transfers of Sovereignty: The French Approach' (1998) 4 *EPL* 517.

Coppel, J. and O'Neill, A., 'The European Court of Justice: Taking Rights Seriously?' (1992) 29 CML Rev 669.

Craig, P., 'UK Sovereignty after *Factortame*' (1991) 11 YEL 221.

de Noriega, E., 'A Dissident Voice: The Spanish Constitutional Case Law on European Integration' (1999) 5 EPL 269.

De Witte, B., 'Community Law and National Constitutional Values' (1991) 2 LIEI 1.

Elbers, U. and Urban, N., 'The Order of German Federal Constitutional Court of 7 June 2000 and the Kompetenz-Kompetenz in the European Judicial System' (2001) 7 EPL 21.

Everling, U., 'Will Europe Slip on Bananas? The Bananas Judgment of the European Court and National Courts' (1996) 33 CML Rev 401.

Gaja, G., 'New Developments in a Continuing Story: the Relationship between EEC Law and Italian Law' (1990) 27 CML Rev 83.

Green, N., 'Directives, Equity and the Protection of Individual Rights' (1984) 9 EL Rev 295.

Hartley, T., 'International Agreements and the Community Legal System: Some Recent Developments' (1983) 8 EL Rev 383.

Herdegen, M., 'Maastricht and the German Constitutional Court: Constitutional Restraints for an Ever Closer Union' (1994) 31 CML Rev 235.

Hoskins, M., 'Tilting the Balance: Supremacy and National Procedural Rules' (1996) 21 EL Rev 365.

Kumm, M., 'Who is the Arbiter of Constitutionality in Europe?' (1999) 36 CML Rev 351.

Marshall, G., 'Parliamentary Sovereignty – the New Horizons' [1997] PL 1.

Obradovic, D., 'Aspects of European Constitutionalism' (1996) 21 EL Rev 32.

—, 'Repatriation of Powers in the European Community' (1997) 34 CML Rev 59.

Oliver, P., 'The French Constitution and the Treaty of Maastricht' (1994) 43 ICLQ 1.

Peers, S., 'Taking Supremacy Seriously' (1998) 23 EL Rev 146.

Pescatore, P., 'The Doctrine of Direct Effect: an Infant Disease of Community Law' (1983) 8 EL Rev 155.

Peters, A., 'The Bananas Decision 2000 of the German Federal Constitutional Court: Towards Reconciliation with the ECJ as regards Fundamental Rights Protection in Europe' (2000) 43 German Yearbook of International Law 276.

Pollard, D., 'The Conseil d'État is European – Official' (1990) 15 EL Rev 267.

Reich, N., 'Judge-made Europe à la Carte: Some Remarks on Recent Conflicts between European and German Constitutional Law Provoked by the Bananas Litigation' (1996) 7 EJIL 103.

Schermans, H., 'The Scales in Balance: National Constitutional Court v Court of Justice' (1990) 27 CML Rev 97.

Schmid, C., 'All Bark and No Bite: Notes on the Federal Constitutional Court's "Banana Decision" ' (2001) 7 *ELJ* 95.

Steiner, J., 'Coming to Terms with EEC Directives' (1990) 106 LQR 144.

Weiler, J., 'The Community System: the Dual Character of Supranationalism' (1981) 1 YEL 267.

—, 'The Transformation of Europe' (1991) 100 Yale Law Journal 2403.

—, 'The Reformulation of German Constitutionalism' (1997) 35 JCMS 597.

Weiler, J. and Lockhart, N., ' "Taking Rights Seriously" Seriously'? (1995) 32 CML Rev 51 and 579.

Wyatt, D., 'Direct Effects of Community Law, not forgetting Directives' (1983) 8 EL Rev 241.

Zuleeg, M., 'The European Constitution under European Constraints: the German Scenario' (1997) 22 EL Rev 19.

5

Principles of direct applicability and direct effects

5.1 Introduction

It has already been seen that EC law is supreme to national law and that domestic courts are under an obligation to give full effect to EC law (see Chapter 4). With this in mind, the question then arises to what extent individuals can rely on EC law before the national courts, particularly where a Member State has failed to implement a particular measure, or where the implementation is in some way defective and does not provide the full extent of the rights an individual should enjoy by virtue of the relevant EC measure. To deal with this question, and very much in accordance with the principle of supremacy, the ECJ has developed three inter-related doctrines: direct effect, indirect effect and state liability. Taken together, these seek to ensure that individuals are given the greatest possible level of protection before their national courts. This chapter considers the scope of the doctrines of direct and indirect effect, as well as identifying difficulties in the jurisprudence. One particular area in which problems arise is that of ensuring the enforceability of directives. Chapter 8, dealing with remedies in the national courts, will examine the jurisprudence in the field of state liability.

5.2 Doctrine of direct effects

5.2.1 Direct applicability

As was noted in Chapter 4, the European Community Treaties were incorporated into UK law by the European Communities Act 1972. With the passing of this Act all Community law became, in the language of international law, directly applicable, that is, applicable as part of the British internal legal system. Henceforth, 'Any rights or obligations created by the Treaty are to be given legal effect in England without more ado' (per Lord Denning MR in *H.P. Bulmer Ltd* v *J. Bollinger SA* [1974] Ch 401). As directly applicable law, EC law thus became capable of forming the basis of rights and obligations enforceable by individuals before their national courts.

Provisions of international law which are found to be capable of application by national courts *at the suit of individuals* are also termed 'directly applicable'. This ambiguity (the same ambiguity is found in the alternative expression 'self-executing') has given rise to much uncertainty in the context of EC law. For this reason it was suggested by Winter that the term 'directly effective' be used to convey this secondary meaning. Although this term has generally found favour amongst British academic writers, the ECJ as well as the British courts tend to use the two concepts of direct applicability and direct effects interchangeably. However, for purposes of clarity it is proposed to use the term 'directly effective' or 'capable of direct effects' in this secondary meaning, to denote those provisions of EC law which give rise to rights or obligations which individuals may enforce before their national courts.

Not all provisions of directly applicable international law are capable of direct effects. Some provisions are regarded as binding on, and enforceable by States alone; others are too vague to form the basis of rights or obligations for individuals; others are too incomplete and require further measures of implementation before they can be fully effective in law. Whether a particular provision is directly effective is a matter of construction, depending on its language and purpose as well as the terms on which the Treaty has been incorporated into domestic law. Although most States apply similar criteria of clarity and completeness, specific rules and attitudes inevitably differ, and since the application of the criteria often conceals an underlying policy decision, the results are by no means uniform from State to State.

5.2.2 Relevance of direct effect in EC law

The question of the direct effects of Community law is of paramount concern to EC lawyers. If a provision of EC law is directly effective, domestic courts must not only apply it, but, following the principle of primacy of EC law (discussed in Chapter 4), must do so in priority over any conflicting provisions of national law. Since the scope of the EC Treaty is wide, the more generous the approach to the question of direct effects, the greater the potential for conflict.

Which provisions of EC law will then be capable of direct effect?

The EC Treaty merely provides in Article 249 (ex 189) that regulations (but only regulations) are 'directly applicable'. Since, as has been suggested, direct applicability is a necessary pre-condition for direct effects, this would seem to imply that only regulations are capable of direct effects.

This has not proved to be the case. In a series of landmark decisions, the ECJ, principally in its jurisdiction under Article 234 (ex 177) EC to give preliminary rulings on matters of interpretation of EC law on reference from national courts, has extended the principle of direct effects to treaty articles, directives, decisions, and even to provisions of international agreements to which the EC is a party.

5.2.3 Treaty Articles

5.2.3.1 *The starting point: Van Gend en Loos*

The question of the direct effect of a Treaty article was first raised in *Van Gend en Loos v Nederlandse Administratie der Belastingen* (case 26/62). The Dutch administrative tribunal, in a reference under Article 234, asked the ECJ:

> Whether Article 12 of the EEC Treaty [now 25 EC] has an internal effect . . . in other words, whether the nationals of Member States may, on the basis of the Article in question, enforce rights which the judge should protect?

Article 25 (ex 12) EC prohibits States from:

> introducing between themselves any new customs duties on imports or exports or any charges having equivalent effect.

It was argued on behalf of the defendant customs authorities that the obligation in Article 25 was addressed to States and was intended to govern rights and obligations between States. Such obligations were not normally enforceable at the suit of individuals. Moreover the Treaty had expressly provided enforcement procedures under what are now Articles 226 (ex 169) and 227 (ex 170) (see Chapter 10) at the suit of the Commission or Member States, respectively. Advocate-General Roemer suggested that Article 25 was too complex to be enforced by national courts; if such courts were to enforce Article 25 directly there would be no uniformity of application.

Despite these persuasive arguments the ECJ held that Article 25 was directly effective. The Court stated that:

> this Treaty is more than an agreement creating only mutual obligations between the contracting parties . . . Community law . . . not only imposes obligations on individuals but also confers on them legal rights.

These rights would arise:

> not only when an explicit grant is made by the Treaty, but also through obligations imposed, in a clearly defined manner, by the Treaty on individuals as well as on Member States and the Community institutions.
> . . . The text of Article 12 [now 25] sets out a clear and unconditional prohibition, which is not a duty to act but a duty not to act. This duty is imposed without any power in the States to subordinate its application to a positive act of internal law. The prohibition is perfectly suited by its nature to produce direct effects in the legal relations between the Member States and their citizens.

And further:

> The vigilance of individuals interested in protecting their rights creates an effective control additional to that entrusted by Articles 169 to 170 [now 226–227] to the diligence of the Commission and the Member States.

Apart from its desire to enable individuals to invoke the protection of EC law the Court clearly saw the principle of direct effects as a valuable means of ensuring that EC law was enforced uniformly in all Member States, even when States had not themselves complied with their obligations.

5.2.3.2 *Subsequent developments*

It was originally thought that, as the Court suggested in *Van Gend*, only prohibitions such as Article 25 ('standstill' provisions) would qualify for direct effects; this was found in *Alfons Lütticke GmbH* v *Hauptzollamt Saarlouis* (case 57/65) not to be so. The article under consideration in this case was Article 95(1) and (3) (now 90); this article contains a prohibition on States introducing discriminatory taxation; the then Article 95(3) contained a positive obligation that:

> Member States shall, not later than at the beginning of the second stage, repeal or amend any provisions existing when this Treaty enters into force which conflict with the preceding rules.

The ECJ found that the then Article 95(1) was directly effective; what was Article 95(3), which was subject to compliance within a specified time-limit, would, the Court implied, become directly effective once that time-limit had expired.

The Court has subsequently found a large number of Treaty provisions to be directly effective. All the basic principles relating to free movement of goods and persons, competition law, discrimination on the grounds of sex and nationality may now be invoked by individuals before their national courts.

5.2.3.3 *Criteria for direct effect*

In deciding whether a particular provision is directly effective certain criteria are applied: the provision must be sufficiently clear and precise; it must be unconditional, and leave no room for the exercise of discretion in implementation by Member States or Community institutions. The criteria are, however, applied generously, with the result that many provisions which are not particularly clear or precise, especially with regard to their scope and application, have been found to produce direct effects. Even where they are conditional and subject to further implementation they have been held to be directly effective once the date for implementation is past. The Court reasons that while there may be discretion as to the means of implementation, there is no discretion as to ends.

5.2.3.4 *Vertical and horizontal effect of Treaty provisions*

In *Van Gend* the principle of direct effects operated to confer rights on Van Gend exercisable against the Dutch customs authorities. Thus the obligation fell on an organ of the State, to whom Article 25 was addressed. (This is known as a 'vertical' direct effect, reflecting the relationship between individual and State.) But Treaty obligations, even when addressed to States, may fall on individuals too. May they be invoked by individuals against individuals? (This is known as a 'horizontal effect', reflecting the relationship between individual and individual.)

Van Gend implies so, and this was confirmed in *Defrenne* v *Sabena (No. 2)* (case 43/75). Ms Defrenne was an air hostess employed by Sabena, a Belgian airline company. She brought an action against Sabena based on what was then Article 119 of the EEC Treaty (now 141 EC). It provided that:

> Each Member State shall during the first stage ensure and subsequently maintain the application of the principle that men and women should receive equal pay for equal work.

Ms Defrenne claimed, *inter alia*, that in paying their male stewards more than their air hostesses, when they performed identical tasks, Sabena was in breach of the then Article 119. The gist of the questions referred to the ECJ was whether, and in what context, that provision was directly effective. Sabena argued that the Treaty articles so far found directly effective, such as Article 25, concerned the relationship between the State and its subjects, whereas former Article 119 was primarily concerned with relationships between individuals. It was thus not suited to produce direct effects. The Court, following Advocate-General Trabucci, disagreed, holding that:

> the prohibition on discrimination between men and women applies not only to the action of public authorities, but also extends to all agreements which are intended to regulate paid labour collectively, as well as to contracts between individuals.

This same principle was applied in *Walrave* v *Association Union Cycliste Internationale* (case 36/74) to Article 12 (ex 6, originally 7) EC which provides that:

> Within the scope of application of this Treaty, and without prejudice to any special provisions contained therein, any discrimination on grounds of nationality shall be prohibited.

The claimants, Walrave and Koch, sought to invoke Article 12 in order to challenge the rules of the defendant association which they claimed were discriminatory.

The ECJ held that the prohibition of any discrimination on grounds of nationality

> does not only apply to the action of public authorities but extends likewise to rules of any other nature aimed at regulating in a collective manner gainful employment and the provision of services.

To limit the prohibition in question to acts of a public authority would risk creating inequality in their application.

As will become evident in the chapters of this book devoted to the substantive law of the Community, many Treaty provisions have now been successfully invoked vertically and horizontally. The fact of their being addressed to, and imposing obligations on, States has been no bar to their horizontal effect.

5.2.4 Regulations

A regulation is described in Article 249 EC as of 'general application . . . binding in its entirety and directly applicable in all Member States'. It is clearly intended to take immediate effect without the need for further implementation.

Regulations are thus by their very nature apt to produce direct effects. However, even for regulations direct effects are not automatic. There may be cases where a provision in a regulation is conditional, or insufficiently precise, or requires further implementation before it can take full legal effect. But since a regulation is of 'general application', where the criteria for direct effects are satisfied, it may be invoked vertically or horizontally.

In *Antonio Munoz Cia SA* v *Frumar Ltd* (case C–253/00), the ECJ confirmed that regulations by their very nature operate to confer rights on individuals which must be protected by the national courts. In this case, Regulation 2200/96 ([1996] OJ L 297/1) laid down the standards by which grapes are classified. Munoz brought civil proceedings against Frumar who had sold grapes under particular labels which did not comply with the corresponding standard. The relevant provision in the regulation did not confer rights specifically on Munoz, but applied to all operators in the market. A failure by one operator to comply with the provision could have adverse consequences for other operators. The ECJ held that, since the purpose of the regulation was to keep products of unsatisfactory quality off the market, and to ensure the full effectiveness of the regulation, it must be possible for a trader to bring civil proceedings against a competitor to enforce the regulation. This decision is noteworthy for several reasons. As with the early case law on the Treaty articles, it reasons from the need to ensure the effectiveness of Community law. It also confirms that, as directly applicable measures, regulations can apply horizontally between private parties as well as vertically against public bodies. In terms of enforcement, it also seems to suggest that it is not necessary that rights be conferred expressly on the claimant before that individual may rely on the sufficiently clear and unconditional provisions of a regulation. In this, there seems to be the beginning of a divergence between the jurisprudence on regulations and that on directives.

5.2.5 Directives

5.2.5.1 *The problem of the direct effect of directives*

A directive is (Article 249 EC):

> binding, as to the result to be achieved, upon each Member State to which it is addressed, but shall leave to the national authorities the choice of form and methods.

Because directives are not described as 'directly applicable' it was originally thought that they could not produce direct effects. Moreover the obligation in a directive is addressed to States, and gives the State some discretion as to the form and method of implementation; its effect thus appeared to be conditional on the implementation by the State.

5.2.5.2 *The principle of direct effect of directives*

This was not the conclusion reached by the ECJ, which found, in *Grad* v *Finanzamt Traunstein* (case 9/70) that a directive could be directly effective. The claimant in *Grad* was a haulage company seeking to challenge a tax levied by the German authorities which the claimant claimed was in breach of an EC directive and decision. The directive required States to amend their VAT systems to comply with a common EC system and to apply this new VAT system to, *inter alia*, freight transport from the date of the Directive's entry into force. The German government argued that only regulations were directly applicable. Directives and decisions took effect internally only via national implementing measures. As evidence they pointed out that only regulations were required to be published in the *Official*

Journal. The ECJ disagreed. The fact that only regulations were described as directly applicable did not mean that other binding acts were incapable of such effects:

> It would be incompatible with the binding effect attributed to Decisions by Article 189 [now 249] to exclude in principle the possibility that persons affected may invoke the obligation imposed by a Decision . . . the effectiveness of such a measure would be weakened if the nationals of that State could not invoke it in the courts and the national courts could not take it into consideration as part of Community law.

Although expressed in terms of a decision, it was implied in the judgment that the same principle applied in the case of directives. The direct effect of directives was established beyond doubt in a claim based on a free-standing directive in *Van Duyn v Home Office* (case 41/74). Here the claimant sought to invoke Article 3 of Directive 64/221 to challenge the Home Office's refusal to allow her to enter to take up work with the Church of Scientology. Under EC law Member States are allowed to deny EC nationals rights of entry and residence only on the grounds of public policy, public security and public health (see Chapter 23). Article 3 of Directive 64/221 provides that measures taken on the grounds of public policy must be based exclusively on the personal conduct of the person concerned. Despite the lack of clarity as to the scope of the concept of 'personal conduct' the ECJ held that Mrs Van Duyn was entitled to invoke the directive directly before her national court. It suggested that even if the provision in question was not clear the matter could be referred to the ECJ for interpretation under Article 234 EC.

So both directives and decisions may be directly effective. Whether they will in fact be so will depend on whether they satisfy the criteria for direct effects – they must be sufficiently clear and precise, unconditional, leaving no room for discretion in implementation. These conditions were satisfied in *Grad*. Although the directive was not unconditional in that it required action to be taken by the State, and gave a time-limit for implementation, once the time-limit expired the obligation became absolute. At this stage there was no discretion left. *Van Duyn* demonstrates that it is not necessary for a provision to be particularly precise for it to be deemed 'sufficiently' clear. Significantly, the ECJ held in *Riksskatteverket v Soghra Gharehveran* (case C–441/99) that a provision in a directive could be directly effective where it contained a discretionary element if the Member State had already exercised that discretion. The reason for this was that it could then no longer be argued that the Member State still had to take measures to implement the provision.

The reasoning in *Grad* was followed in *Van Duyn* and has been repeated on many occasions to justify the direct effect of directives once the time limit for implementation has expired. A more recent formulation of the test for direct effects, and one that is generally used, is that the provision in question should be 'sufficiently clear and precise and unconditional'.

A directive cannot, however, be directly effective before the time-limit for implementation has expired. It was tried unsuccessfully in the case of *Pubblico Ministero v Ratti* (case 148/78). Mr Ratti, a solvent manufacturer, sought to invoke two EC harmonisation directives on the labelling of dangerous preparations to defend a criminal charge based on his own labelling practices. These practices, he claimed, were not illegal according to the directive. The ECJ held that since the time-limit for the implementation of one of the directives had not expired it was not directly effective. He could, however, rely on the other directive for which the implementation date had passed.

Even when a State has implemented a directive it may still be directly effective. The ECJ held this to be the case in *Verbond van Nederlandse Ondernemingen (VNO) v Inspecteur der Invoerrechten en Accijnzen* (case 51/76), thereby allowing the Federation of Dutch Manufacturers to invoke the Second VAT Directive despite implementation of the provision by the Dutch authorities. The grounds for the decision were that the useful effect of the directive would be weakened if individuals could not invoke it before national courts. By allowing individuals to invoke the directive the Community can ensure that national authorities have kept within the limits of their discretion. Arguably, this principle could apply to enable an individual to invoke a 'parent' directive even before the expiry of the time-limit, where domestic measures have been introduced for the purpose of complying with the directive (see *Officier van Justitie v Kolpinghuis Nijmegen* (case 80/86)). This view gains some support from the case of *Inter-Environment Wallonie ASBL v Region Wallonie* (case C–129/96). Here the ECJ held that even within the implementation period Member States are not entitled to take any measures which could seriously compromise the result required by the directive. This applies irrespective of whether the domestic measure which conflicts with a directive was adopted to implement that directive (case C–14/02 *ATRAL*). In *Mangold* (case C–144/04; see further below), the ECJ strengthened this view. According to its ruling, the obligation on a national court to set aside domestic law in conflict with a directive before its period for implementation has expired appears to be even stronger where the directive in question merely aims to provide a framework for ensuring compliance with a general principle of Community law, such as non-discrimination on the grounds of age (see Chapter 25).

5.2.5.3 *Member States' response*

Initially national courts were reluctant to concede that directives could be directly effective. The Conseil d'État, the supreme French administrative court, in *Minister of the Interior v Cohn-Bendit* ([1980] 1 CMLR 543), refused to follow *Van Duyn v Home Office* and allow the claimant to invoke Directive 64/221. The English Court of Appeal in *O'Brien v Sim-Chem Ltd* ([1980] ICR 429) found the Equal Pay Directive (75/117) not to be directly effective on the grounds that it had purportedly been implemented in the Equal Pay Act 1970 (as amended 1975). *VNO* was apparently not cited before the court. The German federal tax court, the Bundesfinanzhof, in *Re VAT Directives* ([1982] 1 CMLR 527) took the same view on the direct effects of the Sixth VAT Directive, despite the fact that the time-limit for implementation had expired and existing German law appeared to run counter to the directive. The courts' reasoning in all these cases ran on similar lines. Article 249 expressly distinguishes regulations and directives; only regulations are described as 'directly applicable'; directives are intended to take effect within the national order via national implementing measures.

On a strict interpretation of Article 249 EC this is no doubt correct. On the other hand the reasoning advanced by the ECJ is compelling. The obligation in a directive is 'binding "on Member States" as to the result to be achieved'; the useful effects of directives would be weakened if States were free to ignore their obligations and enforcement of EC law were left to direct action by the Commission or Member States under Article 226 or Article 227. Moreover States are obliged under Article 10 to 'take all appropriate measures . . . to ensure fulfilment of the obligations arising out of this Treaty or resulting from action taken by the institutions of the Community'. If they have failed in these obligations why should they not be answerable to individual litigants?

5.2.5.4 *Vertical and horizontal direct effects: a necessary distinction*

The reasoning of the ECJ is persuasive where an individual seeks to invoke a directive against the State on which the obligation to achieve the desired results has been imposed. In cases such as *VNO*, *Van Duyn*, and *Ratti*, the claimant sought to invoke a directive against a public body, an arm of the State. This is known as *vertical* direct effect, reflecting the relationship between the individual and the State. Yet as with Treaty articles, there are a number of directives, impinging on labour, company or consumer law for example, which a claimant may wish to invoke against a private person. Is the Court's reasoning in favour of direct effects adequate as a basis for the enforcement of directives against individuals? This is known as *horizontal* direct effect, reflecting the relationship between individuals.

The arguments for and against horizontal effects are finely balanced. Against horizontal effects is the fact of uncertainty. Prior to the entry into force of the TEU, directives were not required to be published. More compelling, the obligation in a directive is addressed to the State. In *Becker* v *Finanzamt Münster-Innenstadt* (case 8/81) the Court, following *dicta* in *Pubblico Ministero* v *Ratti* (case 148/78), had justified the direct application of the Sixth VAT Directive against the German tax authorities on the grounds that the obligation to implement the directive had been placed on the State. It followed that 'a Member State which has not adopted, within the specified time limit, the implementing measures prescribed in the Directive, cannot raise the objection, as against individuals, that it has not fulfilled the obligations arising from the Directive'. This reasoning is clearly inapplicable in the case of an action against a private person. In favour of horizontal effects is the fact that directives have always in fact been published; that Treaty provisions addressed to, and imposing obligations on, Member States have been held to be horizontally effective; that it would be anomalous, and offend against the principles of equality, if an individual's rights to invoke a directive were to depend on the status, public or private, of the party against whom he wished to invoke it; that the useful effect of Community law would be weakened if individuals were not free to invoke the protection of Community law against *all* parties.

Although a number of references were made in which the issue of the horizontal effects of directives was raised, the ECJ for many years avoided the question, either by declaring that the claimant's action lay outside the scope of the directive, as in *Burton* v *British Railways Board* (case 19/81) (Equal Treatment Directive 76/207) or by falling back on a directly effective Treaty provision, as in *Worringham* v *Lloyds Bank Ltd* (case 69/80) in which the then Article 119 (now 141) was applied instead of Directive 75/117, the Equal Pay Directive.

The nettle was finally grasped in *Marshall* v *Southampton & South West Hampshire Area Health Authority (Teaching)* (case 152/84). Here Mrs Marshall was seeking to challenge the health authority's compulsory retirement age of 65 for men and 60 for women as discriminatory, in breach of the Equal Treatment Directive 76/207. The difference in age was permissible under the Sex Discrimination Act 1975, which expressly excludes 'provisions relating to death or retirement' from its ambit. The Court of Appeal referred two questions to the ECJ:

(a) Was a different retirement age for men and women in breach of Directive 76/207?

(b) If so, was Directive 76/207 to be relied on by Mrs Marshall in the circumstances of the case?

The relevant circumstances were that the area health authority, though a 'public' body, was acting in its capacity as employer.

The question of vertical and horizontal effects was fully argued. The Court, following a strong submission from Advocate-General Slynn, held that the compulsory different retirement age was in breach of Directive 76/207 and could be invoked against a public body such as the health authority. Moreover:

> where a person involved in legal proceedings is able to rely on a Directive as against the State he may do so regardless of the capacity in which the latter is acting, whether employer or public authority.

On the other hand, following the reasoning of *Becker*, since a directive is, according to Article 249, binding only on 'each Member State to which it is addressed':

> It follows that a Directive may not of itself impose obligations on an individual and that a provision of a Directive may not be relied upon as such against such a person.

If this distinction was arbitrary and unfair:

> Such a distinction may easily be avoided if the Member State concerned has correctly implemented the Directive in national law.

So, with *Marshall v Southampton & South West Hampshire Area Health Authority (Teaching)* the issue of the horizontal effect of directives was, it seemed, finally laid to rest (albeit in an *obiter* statement, since the health authority was arguably a public body at the time). By denying their horizontal effect on the basis of Article 249 the Court strengthened the case for their vertical effect. The decision undoubtedly served to gain acceptance for the principle of vertical direct effects by national courts (see, e.g., *R v London Boroughs Transport Committee, ex parte Freight Transport Association Ltd* [1990] 3 CMLR 495). But problems remain, both with respect to vertical and horizontal direct effects.

5.2.5.5 *Vertical direct effects: reliance against public body*

First, the concept of a 'public' body, or an 'agency of the State', against whom a directive may be invoked, is unclear. In *Fratelli Costanzo SPA v Comune di Milano* (case 103/88), in a claim against the Milan Comune based on the Comune's alleged breach of Public Procurement Directive 71/305, the Court held that since the reason for which an individual may rely on the provisions of a directive in proceedings before the national courts is that the obligation is binding on all the authorities of the Member States, where the conditions for direct effect were met, 'all organs of the administration, including decentralised authorities such as municipalities, are obliged to apply these provisions'. The area health authority in *Marshall* was deemed a 'public' body, as was the Royal Ulster Constabulary in *Johnston* v *RUC* (case 222/84). But what of the status of publicly-owned or publicly-run enterprises such as the former British Rail or British Coal? Or semi-public bodies? Are universities 'public' bodies and what is the position of privatised utility companies?

These issues arose for consideration in *Foster* v *British Gas plc* (case C–188/89). In a claim against the British Gas Corporation in respect of different retirement ages for men and women, based on Equal Treatment Directive 76/207, the English Court of Appeal had held that British Gas, a statutory corporation carrying out statutory duties under the Gas Act 1972 at the relevant time, was not a public body against which the directive could be enforced. On appeal the House of Lords sought clarification on this issue from the ECJ. That court refused to accept British Gas's argument that there was a distinction between a nationalised undertaking and a State agency and ruled (at para. 18) that a directive might be relied on against organisations or bodies which were 'subject to the authority or control of the State or had special powers beyond those which result from the normal relations between individuals'. Applying this principle to the specific facts of *Foster* v *British Gas plc* it ruled (at para. 20) that a directive might be invoked against 'a body, whatever its legal form, which has been made responsible, pursuant to a measure adopted by the State, for providing a public service under the control of the State and has for that purpose special powers beyond those which result from the normal rules applicable in relations between individuals'. On this interpretation a nationalised undertaking such as the then British Gas would be a 'public' body against which a directive might be enforced, as the House of Lords subsequently decided in *Foster* v *British Gas plc* ([1991] 2 AC 306).

It may be noted that the principle expressed in para. 18 is wider than that of para. 20, the criteria of 'control' and 'powers' being expressed as alternative, not cumulative; as such it is wide enough to embrace any nationalised undertaking, and even bodies such as universities with a more tenuous public element, but which are subject to *some* State authority or control. However, in *Rolls-Royce plc* v *Doughty* ([1992] ICR 538), the English Court of Appeal, applying the 'formal ruling' of para. 20 of *Foster*, found that Rolls-Royce, a nationalised undertaking at the relevant time, although 'under the control of the State', had not been 'made responsible pursuant to a measure adopted by the State for providing a public service'. The public services which it provided, for example, in the defence of the realm, were provided to the *State* and not to the *public* for the purposes of benefit to the State: nor did the company possess or exercise any special powers of the type enjoyed by British Gas. Mustill LJ suggested that the test provided in para. 18 was 'not an authoritative exposition of the way in which cases like *Foster* should be approached': it simply represented a 'summary of the (Court's) jurisprudence to date'.

There is little evidence to support such a conclusion. The Court has never distinguished between its 'formal' rulings (i.e., on the specific issue raised) and its more general statements of principle. Indeed such general statements often provide a basis for future rulings in different factual situations. A restrictive approach to the Court's rulings, as taken in *Rolls Royce plc* v *Doughty*, is inconsistent with the purpose of the ECJ, namely to ensure the effective implementation of Community law and the protection of individuals' rights under that law by giving the concept of a public body the widest possible scope. This was acknowledged by the Court of Appeal in *National Union of Teachers* v *Governing Body of St Mary's Church of England (Aided) Junior School* ([1997] 3 CMLR 630) when it suggested that the concept of an emanation of the state should be a 'broad one'. The definition provided in para. 20 of *Foster* should not be regarded as a statutory definition: it was, in the words of para. 20, simply *'included among* those bodies against which the provisions of a Directive can be applied'.

The British courts' approach to, and the outcome of the enquiry as to whether a particular body is an 'emanation of the state' for the purpose of enforcement of EC directives is unpredictable. It is not altogether surprising that they fail to take a generous view when the result would be to impose liability on bodies which are in no way responsible for the non-implementation of directives, a factor which was undoubtedly influential in *Rolls-Royce plc* v *Doughty*. But even if national courts were to adopt a generous approach, no matter how generously the concept of a 'public' body is defined, as long as the public/private distinction exists there can be no uniformity in the application of directives as between one State and another. Neither will it remove the anomaly as between individuals. Where a State has failed to fulfil its obligations in regard to directives, whether by non-implementation or inadequate implementation, an individual would, it appeared, following *Marshall*, be powerless to invoke a directive in the context of a 'private' claim.

5.2.5.6 *Horizontal direct effects*

In 1993, in the case of *Dori* v *Recreb Srl* (case C–91/92), the Court was invited to change its mind on the issue of horizontal direct effects in a claim based on EC Directive 85/577 on Door-step Selling, which had not at the time been implemented by the Italian authorities, against a private party. Advocate-General Lenz urged the Court to reconsider its position in *Marshall* and extend the principle of direct effects to allow for the enforcement of directives against *all* parties, public and private, in the interest of the uniform and effective application of Community law. This departure from its previous case law was, he suggested, justified in the light of the completion of the internal market and the entry into force of the Treaty on European Union, in order to meet the legitimate expectations of citizens of the Union seeking to rely on Community law. In the interests of legal certainty such a ruling should however not be retrospective in its effect (on the effect of Article 234 rulings, see Chapter 9).

The Court, no doubt mindful of national courts' past resistance to the principle of direct effects, and the reasons for that resistance, declined to follow the Advocate-General's advice and affirmed its position in *Marshall*: Article 249 distinguished between regulations and directives; the case law establishing vertical direct effects was based on the need to prevent States from taking advantage of their own wrong; to extend this case law and allow directives to be enforced against individuals 'would be to recognise a power to enact obligations for individuals with immediate effect, whereas (the Community) has competence to do so only where it is empowered to adopt Regulations'. This decision was confirmed in subsequent cases, such as *El Corte Inglés SA* v *Rivero* (case C–192/94) and *Arcaro* (case C–168/95).

However, in denying horizontal effects to directives in *Dori*, the Court was at pains to point out that alternative remedies might be available based on principles introduced by the Court prior to *Dori*, namely the principle of indirect effects and the principle of State liability introduced in *Francovich* v *Italy* (cases C–6 & 9/90, see Chapter 8). *Francovich* was also suggested as providing an alternative remedy in *El Corte Inglés SA* v *Rivero*. *Pfeiffer* (joined cases C–397/01 to 403/01) confirmed that directives could not have horizontal direct effect, but it emphasised, in the strongest possible terms, that a court was obliged to interpret domestic law in so far as possible in accordance with a directive (see 5.3, below). In the circumstances of that case, the practical outcome would have been akin to admitting horizontal direct effect, albeit by following the 'indirect effect' route. It must be borne in mind that one of the principal justifications for rejecting 'horizontal direct effect' has been that directives cannot, of themselves, impose obligations on individuals. In two-party situations, this reasoning is straightforward. It is less so in a three-party situation where an individual is seeking to enforce a right under a directive against the Member State where this would have an impact on a third party. This issue arose most recently in *Wells* v *SoS for Transport, Local Government and the Regions* (case C–201/02), where Mrs Wells challenged the government's failure to carry out an environmental impact assessment (as required under Directive 85/337/EEC, [1985] OJ L175/40) when authorising the recommencement of quarrying works. The UK government argued that to accept that the relevant provisions of the directive had direct effect would result in 'inverse direct effect' in that UK government would be obliged to deprive another individual (the quarry owners) of their rights. The ECJ dismissed this, holding that permitting an individual to hold the Member State to its obligations was not linked to the performance of any obligation which would fall on the third party (at para. 58), although there would be consequences for the third party as a result. It would be for the national courts to consider whether to require compliance with the directive in the particular case, or whether to compensate the individual for any harm suffered. In coming to this conclusion, the ECJ relied, in part, on case law developed in the context of Directive 83/189/ EEC on the enforceability of technical standards which have not been notified in accordance with the requirements of that directive. It had been suggested that these cases create something akin to 'incidental' horizontal effect, and it is therefore necessary to examine these in more detail.

5.2.5.7 'Incidental' horizontal effect

There have been cases in which individuals have sought to exploit the principle of direct effects not for the purposes of claiming Community rights denied them under national law, but simply in order to establish the illegality of a national law and thereby prevent its application to them. This may occur in a two-party situation, in which an individual is seeking to invoke a directive, whether as a sword or a shield, against the State. It presents particular problems in a three-cornered situation, in which a successful challenge based on an EC directive by an individual to a domestic law or practice, although directed at action by the State, may adversely affect third parties. In this case the effect of the directive would be felt horizontally. To give the directive direct effects in these cases would seem to

go against the Court's stance on horizontal direct effects in the line of cases beginning with *Dori* v *Recreb Srl*, and the reasoning in these cases. Two cases, with contrasting outcomes, *CIA Security International SA* v *Signalson SA* (case C–194/94) and
Lemmens (case C–226/97), illustrate the difficulty. Both cases involve Directive
83/189 (Directive 83/189 has been replaced and extended, by Directive 98/34
([1998] OJ L204/37; amended by Directive 98/44, OJ L217/18); see 15.3.6). The
directive, which is designed to facilitate the operation of the single market, lays
down procedures for the provision of information by Member States to the Commission in the field of technical standards and regulations. Article 8 prescribes
detailed procedures requiring Member States to notify, and obtain clearance from,
the Commission for any proposed regulatory measures in the areas covered by
the directive. In *CIA Security International SA* v *Signalson SA*, the defendants, CIA
Security, sought to rely on Article 8 of Directive 83/189 as a defence to an
action, brought by Signalson, a competitor, for unfair trading practices in the
marketing of security systems. The defendants claimed that the Belgian regulations
governing security, which the defendants had allegedly breached, had not been
notified as required by the directive: they were therefore inapplicable. Contrary
to its finding in the earlier case of *Enichem Base* v *Comune di Cinsello Balsamo*
(case C–380/87), involving very similar facts and the same directive, the ECJ
accepted this argument, distinguishing *Enichem* on the slenderest of grounds. Thus
the effects of the directive fell horizontally on the claimant, whose actions, based
on national law, failed.

Article 8 of Directive 83/189 was again invoked as a defence in *Lemmens* (case
C–226/97). Lemmens was charged in Belgium with driving above the alcohol limit.
Evidence as to his alcohol level at the relevant time had been provided by a breath
analysis machine. Invoking *CIA Security International SA* v *Signalson SA*, he argued
that the Belgian regulations with which breath analysis machines in Belgium were
required to conform had not been notified to the Commission, as required by
Article 8 of Directive 83/189. He argued that the consequent inapplicability of the
Belgian regulations regarding breath analysis machines impinged on the evidence
obtained by using those machines; it could not be used in a case against him. The
ECJ refused to accept this argument. It looked to the purpose of the directive,
which was designed to protect the interest of free movement of goods. The Court
concluded:

> Although breach of an obligation (contained in the Directive) rendered (domestic)
> regulations inapplicable inasmuch as they hindered the marketing of a product which
> did not conform with its provisions, it did not have the effect of rendering unlawful
> any use of the product which conformed with the unnotified regulations. Thus the
> breach (of Article 8) did not make it impossible for evidence obtained by means of such
> regulations, authorized in accordance with the regulations, to be relied on against an
> individual.

This distinction, between a breach affecting the marketing of a product, as in *CIA
Security International SA* v *Signalson SA*, and one affecting its use, as in *Lemmens*, is
fine, and hardly satisfactory. The decision in *CIA Security International SA* v *Signalson
SA* had been criticised because the burden imposed by the breach (by the State)
of Article 8, the non-application of the State's unfair practice laws, would have

fallen on an individual, in this case the claimant. This was seen as a horizontal application in all but name. In two other cases decided, like *CIA Security International SA* v *Signalson SA*, in 1996, *Ruiz Bernaldez* (case C–129/94) and *Panagis Parfitis* (case C–441/93), individuals were permitted to invoke directives to challenge national law, despite their adverse impact on third parties.

Lemmens, on the other hand, did not involve a third-party situation. The invocation by the defendant of Article 8 of Directive 83/189 did, however, smack of abuse. The refinement introduced in *Lemmens* may thus be seen as an attempt by the ECJ to impose some limits on the principle of direct effects as affected by *CIA Security* and as applied to directives.

The *CIA Security* principle was, however, confirmed and extended to a contractual relationship between two companies in *Unilever Italia SpA* v *Central Food SpA* (case C–443/98). Italy planned to introduce legislation on the geographical origins of various kinds of olive oil and notified this in accordance with Article 8 of the directive after the Commission requested that this be done. The Commission subsequently decided to adopt a Community-wide measure and invoked the 'stand-still' procedure in Article 9 of the directive, which requires a Member State to delay adoption of a technical regulation for 12 months if the Commission intends to legislate in the relevant field. Italy nevertheless adopted its measure before the 12-month period had expired. The dispute leading to the Article 234 reference arose when Unilever supplied Central Foods with olive oil which had not been labelled in accordance with Italian law. Unilever argued that Italian legislation should not be applied because it had been adopted in breach of Article 9 of the directive. Advocate-General Jacobs argued that the *CIA* principle could not affect contractual relations between individuals, primarily because to hold otherwise would infringe the principle of legal certainty. The Court disagreed and held that the national court should refuse to apply the Italian legislation. It noted that there was no reason to treat the dispute relating to unfair competition in *CIA Security* differently from the contractual dispute in *Unilever*. The Court acknowledged the established position that directives cannot have horizontal direct effect, but went on to say that this did not apply in relation to Articles 8 and 9 of Directive 83/189. The Court did not feel that the case law on horizontal direct effect and the case law under Directive 83/189 were in conflict, because the latter directive does not seek to create rights or obligations for individuals.

The initial reaction to *CIA Security* was that the Court appeared to accept that directives could have horizontal direct effect. But after *Unilever*, it is clear that this has not been its intention. However, this area remains one of some uncertainty. The position now seems to be that private parties to a contract for the sale or supply of goods need to investigate whether any relevant technical regulations have been notified in accordance with the directive. There may then be a question of whether the limitation introduced by *Lemmens* comes into play. The end result appears to be the imposition on private parties of rights and obligations of which they could not have been aware – this was the main reason *against* the acceptance of horizontal direct effect in the case of directives. Although the Court in *Unilever* was at pains to restrict this line of cases to Directive 83/189 (and its replacement, Directive 98/34), this is not convincing. Nevertheless, the ECJ has maintained its approach under this Directive (see, e.g., case C–303/04, *Lidl Italia Srl* v *Comune di Stradella*), and it would appear to be best to regard the case law under Directive 98/34 (and its predecessor) as being confined to the context of that and similar directives (see also, e.g., case C–201/94, *R* v *Medicines Control Agency ex parte Smith & Nephew Ltd* in the context of the authorisation of medicinal products under Directive 65/65/EEC (superseded by 1993 measures), permitting the holder of a marketing authorisation to rely on Article 5 of that directive in challenging the grant of an authorisation to a competitor). Such a view should, of course, not be understood as reducing the significance of these cases in the context of an important field of EC law, and *Wells* (case C–201/02) has taken this approach into the field of direct effect generally.

5.2.5.8 *No direct effect to impose criminal liability*

One important limitation to the direct effect principle was confirmed in *Berlusconi and others* (joined cases C–387/02, C–391/02 and C–403/02). Here, Italian company legislation had been amended after proceedings against Mr Berlusconi and others had been commenced to make the submission of incorrect accounting informa-tion a summary offence, rather than an indictable offence. The Italian criminal code provides that a more lenient penalty introduced after proceedings have been commenced but prior to judgment should be imposed, and in the instant cases, proceedings would therefore have to be terminated as the limitation period for summary offences had expired. The ECJ was asked (in Article 234 proceedings) if Article 6 of the First Company Law Directive (68/151/EEC) could be relied upon directly against the defendants. Having observed that the Directive required an appropriate penalty and that it was for the national court to consider whether the revised provisions of Italian law were appropriate, the Court confirmed that it is not permissible to rely on the direct effect of a directive to determine the criminal liability of an individual (paras 73–78). In so holding, the ECJ followed the principles developed in the context of indirect effect (5.3.2, below) and reflects general principles of law (see Chapter 6).

5.2.5.9 *Direct effect of directives: conclusions*

The jurisprudence of the ECJ in this area has matured sufficiently to permit the conclusion that, as a general rule, directives cannot take direct effect in the context of a two-party situation where both parties are individuals. Directives can only be relied upon against a Member State (in a broad sense) by an individual (on limita-tions on the obligations an individual can enforce, see further 8.2.5, *Verholen* (cases C–87/9/90). A directive cannot impose an obligation on an individual of itself; it needs to be implemented to have this consequence. Nevertheless, it is apparent that the clear-cut distinction between vertical and horizontal direct effect in two-party situations becomes blurred when transposed into a tripartite context. The enforcement by an individual of an obligation on the Member State may affect the rights of other individuals, which, according to *Wells* (case C–201/02), is a consequence of applying direct effect, but does not appear to change its vertical nature. The rather specific context of notification and authorisation directives, which may also have an effect on relationships not involving Member States, adds to the uncertainty. But whilst the case law may seem settled, the debate as to whether directives *should* have horizontal direct effect is one that is unlikely to go away soon.

5.2.6 **Decisions**

A decision is 'binding in its entirety upon those to whom it is addressed' (Article 249 EC).

Decisions may be addressed to Member States, singly or collectively, or individuals. Although, like directives, they are not described as 'directly applicable', they may, as was established in *Grad* v *Finanzamt Traustein* (case 9/70), be directly effective provided the criteria for direct effects are satisfied. The direct application of decisions does not pose the same theoretical problems as directives, since they will only be invoked against the addressee of the decision. If the obligation has been addressed to him and is 'binding in its entirety', there seems no reason why it should not be invoked against him. Although it has not so far arisen it might be permissible for an individual to invoke a decision against a 'public' party who is not the addressee of the decision, but not against a 'private' (third) party, for the same reasons as apply in the case of directives.

5.2.7 **Recommendations and opinions**

Since recommendations and opinions have no binding force it would appear that they cannot be invoked by individuals, directly or indirectly, before national courts. However, in *Grimaldi* v *Fonds des Maladies Professionnelles* (case C–322/88), in the context of a claim by a migrant worker for benefit in respect of occupational diseases, in which he sought to invoke a Commission recommendation concerning the conditions for granting such benefit, the ECJ held that national courts were 'bound to take Community recommendations into consideration in deciding disputes submitted to them, in particular where they clarify the interpretation of national provisions adopted in order to implement them or where they are designed to supplement binding EEC measures'. Such a view is open to question. It may be argued that recommendations, as non-binding measures, can at the most only be taken into account in order to resolve ambiguities in domestic law.

5.2.8 **International agreements to which the EC is a party**

There are three types of international agreements capable of being invoked in the context of EC law arising from the Community's powers under Articles 281, 300, 133 and 310 (ex 210, 228, 113 and 238 EC, respectively; see Chapter 3). First, agreements concluded by the Community institutions falling within the treaty-making jurisdiction of the EC; secondly, 'hybrid' agreements, such as the WTO agreements, in which the subject matter lies partly within the jurisdiction of Member States and partly within that of the EC; and thirdly, agreements concluded prior to the EC Treaty, such as GATT, which the EC has assumed as being within its jurisdiction, by way of succession. There is no indication in the EC Treaty that such agreements may be directly effective.

The ECJ's case law on the direct effect of these agreements has not been wholly consistent. It purports to apply similar principles to those which it applies in matters of 'internal' law. A provision of an association agreement will be directly effective when 'having regard to its wording and the purpose and nature of the agreement itself, the provision contains a clear and precise obligation which is not subject, in its implementation or effects, to the adoption of any subsequent meas-ure'. Applying these principles in some cases, such as *International Fruit Co. NV v Produktschap voor Groenten en Fruit (No. 3)* (cases 21 & 22/72), the Court, in response to an enquiry as to the direct effects of Article XI of GATT, held, following an examination of the agreement as a whole, that the Article was not directly effective. In others, such as *Bresciani* (case 87/75) and *Kupferberg* (case 104/81), Article 2(1) of the Yaoundé Convention and Article 21 of the EC–Portugal trade agreement were examined respectively on their individual merits and found to be directly effective. The reasons for these differences are at not at first sight obvious, particularly since the provisions in all three cases were almost identical in wording to EC Treaty articles already found directly effective. The suggested reason (see Hartley (1983) 8 EL Rev 383) for this inconsistency is the conflict between the ECJ's desire to provide an effective means of enforcement of international agreements against Member States and the lack of a solid legal basis on which to do so. The Court justifies divergencies in interpretation by reference to the scope and purpose of the agreement in question, which are clearly different from, and less ambitious than, those of the EC Treaty (*Opinion 1/91* (on the draft EEA Treaty)). As a result, the criteria for direct effects tend to be applied more strictly in the context of international agreements entered into by the EC.

Since the *International Fruit Co.* cases the Court has maintained consistently that GATT rules cannot be relied upon to challenge the lawfulness of a Community act except in the special case where the Community provisions have been adopted to implement obligations entered into within the framework of GATT. Because GATT rules are not unconditional, and are characterised by 'great flexibility', direct effects cannot be inferred from the 'spirit, general scheme and wording of the Treaty'. This principle was held in *Germany v Council* (case C–280/93) to apply not only to claims by individuals but also to actions brought by Member States. As a result the opportunity to challenge Community law for infringement of GATT rules is ser-iously curtailed. Despite strong arguments in favour of the direct applicability of WTO provisions from Advocate-General Tesauro in *T Hermes International v FH Marketing Choice BV* (case C–53/96), the Court has not been willing to change its mind. It appears that there is near-unanimous political opposition to the direct application of WTO.

However, where the agreement or legislation issued under the agreement confers clear rights on *individuals* the ECJ has not hesitated to find direct effects (e.g., *Sevince* (case C–192/89); *Bahia Kziber* (case C–18/90)).

Thus, paradoxically, an individual in a dualist State such as the UK will be in a stronger position than he would normally be *vis-à-vis* international law, which is not as a rule incorporated into domestic law.

5.2.9 Exclusions from the principle of direct effects

In extending the jurisdiction of the ECJ to matters within the third (JHA) pillar of the TEU to encompass decisions and framework decisions in the field of political and judicial cooperation in criminal matters taken under Title VI TEU, the ToA expressly denied direct effects to these provisions (Article 34(2) TEU). Similarly, although areas within the third pillar of the TEU, relating to visas, asylum, immi-gration and judicial cooperation in civil matters, were incorporated into the EC

Treaty (new Title IV), the ToA excluded the ECJ's jurisdiction to rule on any measure or decision taken pursuant to Article 62(1) 'relating to the maintenance of law and order and the safeguarding of internal security' (Article 68(2) EC), thus access to the ECJ via a claim before their national court was denied to individuals in areas in which they may be significantly and adversely affected. As noted in Chapter 2, should the Treaty establishing the Constitution come into force, the ECJ's jurisdiction in respect of the corresponding provisions would remain limited, or excluded altogether.

Although not an express exclusion from the principle of direct effects, a situation in which an individual was not be able to rely on Community law arose in the case of *Rechberger and Greindle* v *Austria* (case C–140/97). The case, a claim based on *Francovich*, concerned Austria's alleged breaches of Directive 90/134 on package travel both before Austria's accession, under the EEA Agreement, and, following accession, under the EC Treaty. The ECJ held that where the obligation to implement the directive arose under the EEA Agreement, it had no jurisdiction to rule on whether a Member State was liable under that agreement prior to its accession to the European Union (see also *Ulla-Brith Andersson* v *Swedish State* (case C–321/97)).

5.3 **Principle of indirect effects**

Although the ECJ has not shown willing to allow horizontal direct effect of directives, it has developed an alternative tool by which individuals may rely on directives against another individual. This tool is known as the principle of 'indirect effect', which is an interpretative tool to be applied by domestic courts interpreting national legislation which conflicts with a directive in the same area. It is sometimes also called the principle of consistent interpretation.

The principle of indirect effects was introduced in a pair of cases decided shortly before *Marshall, von Colson* v *Land Nordrhein-Westfalen* (case 14/83) and *Harz* v *Deutsche Tradax GmbH* (case 79/83).

Both cases were based on Article 6 of Equal Treatment Directive 76/207. Article 6 provides that:

> Member States shall introduce into their national legal systems such measures as are necessary to enable all persons who consider themselves wronged by failure to apply to them the principle of equal treatment . . . to pursue their claims by judicial process after possible recourse to other competent authorities.

The claimants had applied for jobs with their respective defendants. Both had been rejected. It was found by the German court that the rejection had been based on their sex, but it was justifiable. Under German law they were entitled to compensation only in the form of travelling expenses. This they claimed did not meet the requirements of Article 6. Ms von Colson was claiming against the prison service; Ms Harz against Deutsche Tradax GmbH, a private company. So the vertical/horizontal, public/private anomaly was openly raised and argued in Article 234 proceedings before the ECJ.

The Court's solution was ingenious. Instead of focusing on the vertical or horizontal effects of the directive it turned to Article 10 of the EC Treaty. Article 10 requires States to 'take all appropriate measures' to ensure fulfilment of their Community obligations.

This obligation, the Court said, applies to *all* the authorities of Member States, including the courts. It thus falls on the courts of the Member States to interpret national law in such a way as to ensure that the objectives of the directive are achieved. It was for the German courts to interpret German law in such a way as to ensure an effective remedy as required by Article 6 of the directive. The result of this approach is that although Community law is not applied directly – it is not 'directly effective' – it may still be applied indirectly as domestic law by means of interpretation.

The success of the *von Colson* principle of indirect effect depended on the extent to which national courts perceived themselves as having a discretion, under their own constitutional rules, to interpret domestic law to comply with Community law. Although the courts in the UK showed some reluctance initially to apply this principle, relying on a strict interpretation of s. 2(1) of European Communities Act 1972 as applying only to directly effective Community law (see the House of Lords in *Duke* v *GEC Reliance Ltd* ([1988] AC 618)), the position soon changed (*Litster* v *Forth Dry Dock & Engineering Co. Ltd* ([1990] 1 AC 546). Occasional 'hiccups' still occurred, however, and may still do so today. In *Finnegan* v *Clowney Youth Training Programme Ltd* ([1990] 2 AC 407) the House of Lords had refused to interpret art. 8(4) of the Sex Discrimination (Northern Ireland) Order 1976 (SI 1976/1042) in line with *Marshall*, even though the order had been made after the ECJ's decision in *Marshall*. This was because that provision was enacted in terms identical to the parallel provision considered in *Duke* v *GEC Reliance Ltd*, and 'must have been intended to' have the same meaning as in that Act. In the light of *Marleasing* (case 106/89, see below), such a decision would be unsustainable now, and today, the UK courts are taking their obligation seriously (see, e.g., *Braymist Ltd* v *Wise Finance Co Ltd* [2002] Ch 273; *Director-General of Fair Trading* v *First National Bank* [2002] 1 AC 481).

5.3.1 The scope of the doctrine: *Marleasing*

The ECJ considered the scope of the 'indirect effect' doctrine in some depth in *Marleasing SA* v *La Comercial Internacional de Alimentación SA* (case C–106/89). In this case, which was referred to the ECJ by the Court of First Instance, Oviedo, the claimant company was seeking a declaration that the contracts setting up the defendant companies were void on the grounds of 'lack of cause', the contracts being a sham transaction carried out in order to defraud their creditors. This was a valid basis for nullity under Spanish law. The defendants argued that this question was now governed by EC Directive 68/151. The purpose of Directive 68/151 was to protect the members of a company and third parties from, *inter alia*, the adverse effects of the doctrine of nullity. Article 11 of the directive provides an exhaustive list of situations in which nullity may be invoked. It does not include 'lack of cause'. The directive should have been in force in Spain from the date of accession in 1986, but it had not been implemented. The Spanish judge sought a ruling from the ECJ on whether, in these circumstances, Article 11 of the directive was directly effective.

The ECJ reiterated the view it expressed in *Marshall* that a directive cannot of itself 'impose obligations on private parties'. It reaffirmed its position in *von Colson* that national courts must *as far as possible* interpret national law in the light of the wording and purpose of the directive in order to achieve the result pursued by the directive (para. 8). And it added that this obligation applied *whether the national provisions in question were adopted before or after the directive*. It concluded by ruling specifically, and without qualification, that national courts were 'required' to interpret domestic law in such a way as to ensure that the objectives of the directive were achieved (para. 13).

Given that in *Marleasing* no legislation had been passed, either before or after the issuing of the directive, to comply with the directive, and given the ECJ's sugges- tion that the Spanish court must nonetheless strive to interpret domestic law to comply with the directive, it seems that, according to the ECJ, it is not necessary to the application of the *von Colson* principle that the relevant national measure should have been introduced for the purpose of complying with the directive, nor even that a national measure should have been specifically introduced at all.

5.3.2 **The limits of *Marleasing***

The strict line taken in *Marleasing* was modified in *Wagner Miret* v *Fondo de Garantira Salaria* (case C–334/92), in a claim against a private party based on Directive 80/987. This directive is an employee protection measure designed, *inter alia*, to guarantee employees arrears of pay in the event of their employer's insolvency. Citing its ruling in *Marleasing* the Court suggested that, in interpreting national law to conform with the objectives of a directive, national courts must *presume* that the State intended to comply with Community law. They must strive '*as far as possible*' to interpret domestic law to achieve the result pursued by the directive. But if the provisions of domestic law cannot be interpreted in such a way (as was found to be the case in *Wagner Miret*) the State may be obliged to make good the claimant's loss on the principles of State liability laid down in *Francovich* v *Italy* (cases 6 & 9/90).

Wagner Miret thus represents a tacit acknowledgment on the part of the Court that national courts will not always feel able to 'construe' domestic law to comply with an EC directive, particularly when the provisions of domestic law are clearly at odds with an EC directive, and there is no evidence that the national legislature intended national law to comply with its provisions, or with a ruling on its provi- sions by the ECJ. This limitation proved useful for courts which were unwilling to follow *Marleasing*. Thus, in *R* v *British Coal Corporation, ex parte Vardy* ([1993] ICR 720), a case decided after, but without reference to, *Marleasing*, the English High Court adverted to the House of Lords judgment in *Litster* but found that it was 'not possible' to interpret a particular provision of the Trade Union and Labour Rela- tions Act 1992 to produce the same meaning as was required by the relevant EC directive (see also *Re Hartlebury Printers Ltd* [1993] 1 All ER 470 at p. 478b, ChD).

Thus the indirect application of EC directives by national courts cannot be guar- anteed. Some reluctance on the part of national courts to comply with the *von Colson* principle, particularly as applied in *Marleasing*, is hardly surprising. It may be argued that in extending the principle of indirect effect in this way the ECJ is attempting to give horizontal effect to directives by the back door, and impose obligations, addressed to Member States, on private parties, contrary to their understanding of domestic law. Where such is the case, as the House of Lords remarked in *Duke* v *GEC Reliance Ltd* (see also *Finnegan* v *Clowney Youth Training Programme Ltd*), this could be 'most unfair'. Indeed, the dividing line between giving 'horizontal direct effect' to a directive and merely relying on the interpretative obligation under the doctrine of 'indirect effect' can be a very fine and technical one in the circumstances of a particular case, as evidenced by *Mangold* (case C–144/04). This case involved an interpretation of the notion of 'working time' in the context of the Working Time Directive (93/104/EC [1993] OJ L307/18). German case law had developed a distinction between duty time, on-call time and stand-by time, with only the first being regarded as 'working time'. Emergency workers employed by the German Red Cross had challenged a provision in their collective labour agreement which, they argued, extended their working time beyond the prescribed 48-hour limit. The Court suggested that this agreement may be in breach of the directive, but that the claimants could not rely on the directive itself as against their employer. Having re-stated the basic principle that national law must be interpreted in accordance with the Treaty, in particular where this has been enacted to implement a directive, the Court went on to say that this obligation was not restricted to the provisions themselves, but extended to 'national law as a whole in order to assess to what extent it may be applied so as not to produce a result contrary to that sought by the directive' (para. 115). A national court must do 'whatever lies within its jurisdiction' to ensure compliance with EC law. The ECJ did not go so far as to state expressly that existing case law might have to be reviewed to ensure such compliance, but the force of its reasoning appears to point in that direction. On the facts of the case, the outcome would be very close to allowing the individuals to invoke the direct effect of the directive against their employer.

The case of *Kolpinghuis Nijmegen* (case 80/86) may offer a limitation to the 'indirect effect' doctrine, which might also meet the objection that this might result in 'horizontal effect' by the back door. Here, in the context of criminal proceedings against Kolpinghuis for breach of EC Directive 80/777 on water purity, which at the relevant time had not been implemented by the Dutch authorities, the Court held that national courts' obligation to interpret domestic law to comply with EC law was 'limited by the general principles of law which form part of Community law [see Chapter 6] and in particular the principles of legal certainty and non-retroactivity'. Although expressed in the context of criminal liability, to which these principles were 'especially applicable', it was not suggested that the limitation should be confined to such situations. Where an interpretation of domestic law would run counter to the legitimate expectations of individuals *a fortiori* where the State is seeking to invoke a directive against an individual to determine or aggravate his criminal liability, as was the case in *Arcaro* (case C–168/95, see further below), the doctrine will not apply. Where domestic legislation has been introduced to comply with a Community directive, it is legitimate to expect that domestic law will be interpreted in conformity with Community law, provided that it is capable of such an interpretation (cf. *Mangold*, case C–144/04, above). Where legislation has not been introduced with a view to compliance domestic law may still be interpreted in the light of the aims of the directive as long as the domestic provision is reasonably capable of the meaning contended for. But in either case an interpretation which conflicts with the clear words and intentions of domestic law is unlikely to be acceptable to national courts. This has been acknowledged by the Court in *Wagner Miret* (case C–334/92) and *Arcaro* (case C–168/95).

Arcaro (Case C–168/95) could also be seen as introducing further limitations on the scope of indirect effect. There, the ECJ held that the 'obligation of the national court to refer to the content of the directive when interpreting the relevant rules of its own national law *reaches a limit where such an interpretation leads to the imposition on an individual of an obligation laid down by a directive which has not been transposed* or, more especially, where it has the effect of determining or aggravating, on the basis of the directive and in the absence of a law enacted for its implementation, the liability in criminal law of persons who act in contravention of that directive's provisions'. The Court has subsequently affirmed that the obligation to interpret domestic law in accordance with EC law cannot result in criminal liability independent of a national law adopted to implement an EC measure, particularly in light of the principle of non-retroactivity of criminal penalties in Article 7 of the European Convention on Human Rights (case C–60/02 *Criminal Proceedings against X ('Rolex')*). This reasoning has also been applied in the context of direct effect (see *Berlusconi and others* (joined cases C–387/02, C–391/02 and C–403/02)).

The phrase 'imposition on an individual of an obligation' in *Arcaro* could be interpreted to mean that indirect effect could never require national law to be interpreted so as to impose obligations on individuals not apparent on the face of the relevant national provisions. It is submitted, however, that the ECJ's view in *Arcaro* is limited to the context of criminal proceedings, and that the application of the doctrine of indirect effect can result in the imposition of civil liability not found in domestic law (see also Advocate-General Jacobs in *Centrosteel Srl* v *Adipol GmbH* (case C–456/98), paras 31–35).

This seems to be the result of *Oceano Grupo Editorial* v *Rocio Murciano Quintero* (case C–240/98). Here, Oceano had brought a claim in a Barcelona court for payment under a contract of sale for encyclopaedias. The contract contained a term which gave jurisdiction to the Barcelona court rather than a court located near the consumer's home. That court had doubts regarding the fairness of the jurisdiction clause. The Unfair Contract Terms Directive (93/13/EEC) requires that public bodies be able to take steps to prevent the continued use of unfair terms. It also contains a list of unfair terms, including a jurisdiction clause, but this only became effective in Spanish law *after* Oceano's claim arose. Spanish law did contain a general prohibition on unfair terms which could have encompassed the jurisdiction clause, but the scope of the relevant Spanish law was unclear. The question arose whether the Barcelona court should interpret Spanish legislation in accordance with the Unfair Contract Terms Directive. The ECJ reaffirmed the established position that a

> national court is obliged, when it applies national law provisions predating or postdating [a directive], to interpret those provisions, so far as possible, in the light of the wording of the directive' (para. 32).

The Court went on to say that in light of the emphasis on public enforcement in the Unfair Contract Terms Directive, the national court may be required to decline of its own motion the jurisdiction conferred on it by an unfair term. As a consequence, Oceano would be deprived of a right which it might otherwise have enjoyed under existing Spanish law. This latter consideration should not prevent the national court from interpreting domestic law in light of the directive. In terms of the scope of the doctrine of indirect effect, it would be nonsensical to distinguish between cases which involve the imposition of obligations and those which concern restrictions on rights. Often, in a relationship between individuals, one individual's right is an obligation placed on another individual. The reasoning in *Arcaro* is best confined to the narrow context of criminal penalties.

It may therefore be stated that the doctrine of indirect effect continues to be significant. However, there will be circumstances when it will not be possible to apply it. In such a situation, as the Court suggested in *Wagner Miret*, it will be necessary to pursue the alternative remedy of a claim in damages against the State under the principles laid down in *Francovich* v *Italy* (cases C–6 & 9/90, see Chapter 8). It may be significant that in *El Corte Inglés SA* v *Rivero* (case C–192/94) the Court, in following the *Dori* ruling that a directive could not be invoked directly against private parties, did not suggest a remedy based on indirect effect, as it had in *Dori*, but focused only on the possibility of a claim against the State under *Francovich*.

5.3.3 Indirect effect in other contexts

The discussion has, so far, concentrated on the application of this principle in the context of directives. However, in *Maria Pupino* (case C–105/03), the ECJ held that the obligation to interpret national law in accordance with European rules can extend to framework decisions adopted under Article 34(2) TEU, and that a national court is required to interpret domestic law, in so far as possible, in accordance with the wording and purpose of a corresponding framework decision. The decision is controversial, because it extends the notion of indirect effect into the domain of criminal law, an area in respect of which the Community has no competence to act and seems also to circumvent the limitation on the direct effect of JHA provisions noted at 5.2.9.

5.4 Conclusions

The principle of direct effects, together with its twin principle of supremacy of EC law, discussed in Chapter 4, has played a crucial part in securing the application and integration of Community law within national legal systems. By giving individuals and national courts a role in the enforcement of Community law it has ensured that EC law is applied, and Community rights enforced, even though Member States have failed, deliberately or inadvertently, to bring national law and practice into line with Community law. Thus, as the Court suggested in *Van Gend* (case 26/62), the principle of direct effects has provided a means of control over Member States additional to that entrusted to the Commission under Article 226 and Member States under Article 227 (see further Chapter 10). But there is no doubt that the ECJ has extended the concept of direct effects well beyond its apparent scope as envisaged by the EC Treaty. Furthermore, although the criteria applied by the ECJ for assessing the question of direct effects appear straightforward, in reality they have in the past been applied loosely, and any provision which is justiciable has, until recently, been found to be directly effective, no matter what difficulties may be faced by national courts in its application, or what impact it may have on the parties, public or private, against whom it is enforced. Thus the principle of direct effects created problems for national courts, particularly in its application to directives.

In recent years there have been signs that the ECJ, having, with a few exceptions, won acceptance from Member States of the principle of direct effects, or at least in the case of directives of vertical effects, had become aware of the problems faced by national courts and was prepared to apply the principles of direct and indirect effect with greater caution. Its more cautious approach to the question of standing, demonstrated in *Lemmens* (case C–226/97), has been noted above. In *Comitato di Coordinamento per la Difesa della Cava* v *Regione Lombardia* (case C–236/92), the Court found that Article 4 of Directive 75/442 on the Disposal of Waste, which required States to 'take the necessary measures to ensure that waste is disposed of without endangering human health and without harming the environment', was not unconditional or sufficiently precise to be relied on by individuals before their national courts. It 'merely indicated a programme to be followed and provided a framework for action' by the Member States. The Court suggested that in order to be directly effective the obligation imposed by the directive must be 'set out in unequivocal terms'. In *R* v *Secretary of State for Social Security, ex parte Sutton* (case C–66/95) the Court refused to admit a claim for the award of interest on arrears of social security benefit on the basis of Article 6 of EC Directive 79/7 on Equal Treatment for Men and Women in Social Security, although in *Marshall (No. 2)* (case C–271/91) it had upheld a claim for compensation for discriminatory treatment based on an identically worded Article 6 of Equal Treatment Directive 76/207. The Court's attempts to distinguish between the two claims ('amounts payable by way of social security are not compensatory') were unconvincing. In *El Corte Inglés SA* v *Rivero* (case C–192/94) it found the then Article 129a (now 153) of the EC Treaty requiring the Community to take action to achieve a high level of consumer protection insufficiently clear and precise and unconditional to be relied on as between individuals. This may be contrasted with its earlier approach to the former Article 128 EC, which required the Community institutions to lay down general principles for the implementation of a vocational training policy, which was found, albeit together with the non-discrimination principle of (the then) Article 7 EEC, to be directly effective (see *Gravier* v *City of Liège* (case 293/83), discussed in Chapter 23). Thus, a directive may be denied direct effects on the grounds that:

(a) the right or interest claimed in the directive is not sufficiently clear, precise and unconditional; or

(b) the individual seeking to invoke the directive did not have a direct interest in the provisions invoked (*Verholen*, cases C–87–9/90); or

(c) the obligation allegedly breached was not intended for the benefit of the individual seeking to invoke its provisions (*Lemmens*).

In the area of indirect effects, in *Dori* v *Recreb Srl* (case C–91/92), the ECJ, following its lead in *Marshall* (case 152/84), declared unequivocally that directives could not be invoked horizontally. This view was endorsed in *El Corte Inglés SA* v *Rivero, Arcaro* (case C–168/95) and, most recently, in *Pfeiffer* (joined cases C–397/01 to C–403/01).

In *Wagner Miret* (case C–334/92) the ECJ acknowledged that national courts might not feel able to give indirect effect to Community directives by means of 'interpretation' of domestic law. This was also approved in *Arcaro*. In almost all of these cases, decided after *Francovich*, the Court pointed out the possibility of an alternative remedy based on *Francovich*, discussed in Chapter 8.

FURTHER READING

Amstutz, M., 'In-between Worlds: *Marleasing* and the Emergence of Interlegality in Legal Reasoning' (2005) 11 *European Law Journal* 766.

Bebr, G., 'Agreements concluded by the Community and their possible direct effects; from International Fruit Company to Kupferberg' (1983) 20 CML Rev 35.

Caranta, R., 'Learning from our Neighbours: Public Law Remedies Homogenisation from Bottom Up' (1997) MJ 220.

Coppel, J., 'Rights, Duties and the end of *Marshall*' (1994) 57 MLR 859.

Craig, P., 'Directives: Direct Effect, Indirect Effect and the Construction of National Legislation' (1997) 22 EL Rev 519.

—, 'Once more unto the Breach: The Community, the State and Damages Liability' (1997) 113 LQR 67.

Curtin, D., 'The Province of Government; Delimiting the Direct Effect of Directives' (1990) 15 EL Rev 195.

—, 'The Effectiveness of Judicial Protection of Individual Rights' (1990) 27 CML Rev 209.

de Burca, G., 'Giving Effect to European Community Directives' (1992) 55 MLR 215.

Green, N., 'Directives, Equity and the Protection of Individual Rights' (1984) 9 EL Rev 295.

Hartley, T., 'International Agreements and the Community Legal System; Some Recent Developments' (1983) 8 EL Rev 383.

Lackoff, K. and Nyssens, H., 'Direct Effect of Directives in Triangular Situations' (1998) 23 EL Rev 397.

Lenz, M., 'Horizontal what? Back to basics' (2000) 25 EL Rev 502.

Lewis, C., and Moore, S., 'Duties, Directives and Damages in European Community Law' [1993] PL 151.

Mastoianni, R., 'On the Distinction between Vertical and Horizontal Direct Effects of Community Directives: What Role for the Principle of Equality?' (1999) 5 EPL 417.

Prechal, S., 'Remedies after *Marshall*' (1990) 27 CML Rev 451.

—, *Directives in European Community Law*, 2nd edition (Oxford University Press, 2005), ch. 9.

Ross, M., 'Beyond *Francovich*' (1993) 56 MLR 55.

Ruffert, M., 'Rights and Remedies: European Community Law: a Comparative View' (1997) 34 CML Rev 307.

Steiner, J., 'Coming to Terms with EEC Directives' (1990) 106 LQR 144.

Szyczak, E., 'Making Europe more Relevant to its Citizens' (1996) 21 EL Rev 351.

Van Gerven, W., 'The Horizontal Effect of Directive Provisions Revisited: the Reality of Catch-words', Institute of European Public Law Lecture Series, University of Hull (1993).

Winter, T. A., 'Direct Applicability and Direct Effects' (1972) 9 CML Rev 425.

Wyatt, D., 'Direct Effects of Community Law, not forgetting Directives' (1983) 8 EL Rev 241.

6

General principles of law

6.1 Introduction

6.1.1 The relevance of general principles

After the concept of direct effects and the principle of supremacy of EC law the third major contribution of the ECJ has been the introduction of general principles of law into the corpus of EC law. Although primarily relevant to the question of remedies and enforcement of EC law, a discussion of the role of general principles of law is appropriate at this stage in view of their fundamental importance in the jurisprudence of the ECJ.

General principles of law are relevant in the context of EC law in a number of ways. First, they may be invoked as an aid to interpretation: EC law, including domestic law implementing EC law obligations, must be interpreted in such a way as not to conflict with general principles of law. Secondly, general principles of law may be invoked by both States and individuals to challenge Community action, either to annul or invalidate acts of the institutions (under Articles 230, 241, 234 and 236 (ex 173, 184, 177 and 179) EC), or to challenge inaction on the part of these institutions (under Articles 232 or 236 (ex 175 and 179) EC). Thirdly, as a logical consequence of its second role, but less generally acknowledged, general principles may also be invoked as a means of challenging action by a Member State, whether in the form of a legal or an administrative act, where the action is performed in the context of a right or obligation arising from *Community* law (see *Klensch* (cases 201 & 202/85); *Wachauf* v *Germany* (case 5/88); *Lageder* v *Amministrazione delle Finanze dello Stato* (case C–31/91); but *cf. R* v *Ministry of Agriculture, Fisheries and Food, ex parte Bostock* (case C–2/93)). The degree to which general principles of law affect actions by Member States will be discussed in more detail later in this chapter. General principles of law may be invoked to support a claim for damages against the Community (under Article 288(2) (ex 215(2))) (see Chapter 13). These reasons are all practical reasons, based in the arena of legal action. There are other reasons, too, which relate to how the Community and Union is seen; what sort of values it has. The jurisprudence in this area expands the rights of individuals beyond the economic rights found in the original Treaty. In parallel with the concept of citizenship, the protection of such rights suggests the

Union itself has greater links with the individuals and is, itself, obtaining greater legitimacy.

This area has become a steadily evolving aspect of Community law. This chapter examines the general historical development of the Court's jurisprudence to explain how general principles have been received into Community law. It will be seen that general principles, in particular fundamental rights, are invoked with increasing frequency before the European courts. Some of these general principles are examined in more detail. However, this chapter does not provide a full survey of the substantive rights which are now recognised in Community law. Such a discussion is beyond the scope of this book and readers should refer to the specialist texts which are now available.

6.1.2 Fundamental principles

General principles of law are not to be confused with the fundamental principles of Community law, as expressed in the EC Treaty, for example, the principles of free movement of goods and persons, of non-discrimination on the grounds of sex (Article 141 (ex 119, as amended) EC) or nationality (Article 12 (ex 6) EC), although there may be some overlap or commonality between the two. General principles of law constitute the 'unwritten' law of the Community.

6.2 Rationale for the introduction of general principles of law

The legal basis for the incorporation of general principles into Community law is slim, resting precariously on three articles. Article 230 gives the ECJ power to review the legality of Community acts on the basis of, *inter alia*, 'infringement of this Treaty', or '*any rule of law relating to its application*'. Article 288(2), which governs Community liability in tort, provides that liability is to be determined '*in accordance with the general principles common to the laws of the Member States*'. And Article 220, governing the role of the ECJ, provides that the Court 'shall ensure that in the interpretation and application of this Treaty *the law* is observed'.

In the absence of any indication as to the scope or content of these general principles, it has been left to the ECJ to put flesh on the bones provided by the Treaty. This function the Court has amply fulfilled, to the extent that general principles now form an important element of Community law.

One of the reasons for what has been described as the Court's 'naked law-making' in this area is best illustrated by the case of *Internationale Handelsgesellschaft mbH* (case 11/70). There the German courts were faced with a conflict between an EC regulation requiring the forfeiture of deposits by exporters if export was not completed within an agreed time, and a number of principles of the German constitution, in particular, the principle of proportionality. It is in the nature of constitutional law that it embodies a State's most sacred and fundamental principles. Although these principles were of particular importance, for obvious reasons, in post-war Germany, other Member States of the Community also had written constitutions embodying similar principles and rights. Clearly it would not have done for EC law to conflict with such principles. Indeed, as the German constitutional court made clear ([1974] 2 CMLR 540), were such a conflict to exist, national constitutional law would take precedence over EC law. This would have jeopardised not only the principle of primacy of EC law but also the uniformity of application so necessary to the success of the new legal order. So while the ECJ asserted the principle of primacy of EC law in *Internationale Handelsgesellschaft*, it was quick to point out that respect for fundamental rights was in any case part of EC law.

Another reason now given to justify the need for general principles is that the Community's powers have expanded to such a degree that some check on the exercise of the institutions' powers is needed. Furthermore, the expansion of Community competence means that the institutions' powers are now more likely to operate in policy areas in which human rights have an influence. Although those who wish to see sovereignty retained by the nation State may originally have been pleased to see the limitation of the EC institutions' powers, the development of human rights jurisprudence in this context can be seen as a double-edged sword, giving the ECJ increased power to impugn both acts of the Community institutions and implementing measures taken by Member States on grounds of infringement of general principles.

6.3 Development of general principles

6.3.1 Fundamental human rights

The Court's first tentative recognition of fundamental human rights as part of EC law was prior to *Internationale Handelsgesellschaft*, in the case of *Stauder* v *City of Ulm* (case 29/69). Here the applicant was claiming entitlement to cheap butter provided under a Community scheme to persons in receipt of welfare benefits. He was required under German law to divulge his name and address on the coupon which he had to present to obtain the butter. He challenged this law as representing a violation of his fundamental human rights (namely, equality of treatment). The ECJ, on reference from the German court on the validity of the relevant Community decision, held that, on a proper interpretation, the Community measure did not require the recipient's name to appear on the coupon. This interpretation, the Court held, contained nothing capable of prejudicing the fundamental human rights enshrined in the general principles of Community law and protected by the Court.

The ECJ went further in *Internationale Handelsgesellschaft*. There it asserted that respect for fundamental rights forms an integral part of the general principles of law protected by the Court – such rights are inspired by the constitutional traditions common to the Member States. One point to note here is that the ECJ is not comparing EC law with *national* law but with the principles of *international* law which are embodied in varying degrees in the national constitutions of Member States. A failure to make the distinction between general principles of international law (even if embodied in national laws) which the Community legal order respects and national law proper could erode the doctrine of supremacy of Community law *vis-à-vis* national laws.

The *International Handelsgesellschaft* judgment can be taken as implying that only rights arising from traditions *common to* Member States can constitute part of EC law (a 'minimalist' approach). It may be argued that if the problem of conflict between Community law and national law is to be avoided in *all* Member States it is necessary for *any* human right upheld in the constitution of *any* Member State to be protected under EC law (a 'maximalist' approach). In *Hoechst* v *Commission* (cases 46/87, 227/88), in the context of a claim based on the fundamental right to the inviolability of the home, the Court, following a comprehensive review by Advocate-General Mischo of the laws of all the Member States on this question, distinguished between this right as applied to the 'private dwelling of physical persons', which was common to all Member States (and which would by implication be protected as part of Community law), and the protection offered to commercial premises against intervention by public authorities, which was subject to 'significant differences' in different Member States. In the latter case the only common protection, provided under various forms, was protection against arbitrary or disproportionate intervention on the part of public authorities. Similarly, but dealing with administrative law, in *Australian Mining & Smelting Europe Ltd* v *Commission* (case 155/79), in considering the principle of professional privilege, the Court found that the scope of protection for confidentiality for written communications between lawyers and their clients varied from State to State; only privilege as between independent (as opposed to in-house) lawyers and their clients was generally accepted, and would be upheld as a general principle of Community law.

These cases suggest that where certain rights are protected to differing degrees and in different ways in Member States, the Court will look for some *common* underlying principle to uphold as part of Community law. Even if a particular right protected in a Member State is not universally protected, where there is an apparent conflict between that right and EC law, the Court will strive to interpret Community law so as to ensure that the substance of that right is not infringed. An exception to this approach can be seen in *Society for the Protection of the Unborn Child* v *Grogan* (case 159/90). This case concerned the officers of a students' union who provided information in Ireland about the availability of legal abortion in the UK. SPUC brought an action alleging that this was contrary to the Irish constitution. The officers' defence was based on the freedom to provide services within the Community and on the freedom of expression contained in the ECHR which also forms part of Community law as a general principle (see further below). The ECJ evaded this issue. Since the students' union did not have an economic link with the clinics whose services they advertised, the provision of information about the clinics was not an economic activity within the Treaty. As the issues fell outside the scope of EC law, the officers could not rely on either the provisions on freedom to provide services in the Treaty or on general principles of law. (See further Chapter 22.)

6.3.2 Role of international human rights treaties

Following *Internationale Handelsgesellschaft* the scope for human rights protection was further extended in the case of *J. Nold KG* v *Commission* (case 4/73). In this case J. Nold KG, a coal wholesaler, was seeking to challenge a decision taken under the ECSC as being in breach of the company's fundamental right to the free pursuit of business activity. While the Court did not find for the company on the merits of the case, it asserted its commitment to fundamental rights in the strongest terms. As well as stating that fundamental rights form an integral part of the general principles of law, the observance of which it ensures, it went on to say:

> In safeguarding these rights, the Court is bound to draw inspiration from constitutional traditions common to the Member States, and it cannot therefore uphold measures which are incompatible with fundamental rights recognised and protected by the constitutions of those States.
> • Similarly, international treaties for the protection of human rights on which the Member States have collaborated or of which they are signatories, can supply guidelines which should be followed within the framework of Community law.

The reasons for this inclusion of principles of certain international treaties as part of EC law are clearly the same as those upholding fundamental constitutional rights; it is the one certain way to guarantee the avoidance of conflict.

In this context, the most important international treaty concerned with the protection of human rights is the European Convention for the Protection of Human Rights and Fundamental Freedoms 1950 (ECHR), to which all Member States are now signatories. The Court has on a number of occasions confirmed its adherence to the rights protected therein, an approach to which the other institutions gave their support (Joint Declaration, [1977] OJ C103/1). In *R v Kirk* (case 63/83), in the context of criminal proceedings against Kirk, the captain of a Danish fishing vessel, for fishing in British waters (a matter subsequently covered by EC regulations), the principle of non-retroactivity of penal measures, enshrined in Article 7 of the ECHR, was invoked by the Court and applied in Captain Kirk's favour. The EC regulation, which would have legitimised the British rules under which Captain Kirk was charged, could not be applied to penalise him retrospectively. (See also *Johnston v Chief Constable of the Royal Ulster Constabulary* (case 222/84) (ECHR, Article 6, right to judicial process); *Hoechst* (cases 46/87, 227/88) contrast substantive ruling in *Roquette Frères* (case C–94/00); *National Panasonic v Commission* (case 136/79) (ECHR Article 8, right to respect for private and family life, home and correspondence – not infringed).)

Thus, it seems that any provision in the ECHR may be invoked, provided it is done in the context of a matter of EC law. In *Kaur v Lord Advocate* ([1980] 3 CMLR 79), an attempt was made to invoke the Convention (Article 8 'respect for family life') by an Indian immigrant seeking to challenge a deportation order made under the Immigration Act 1971. She failed on the grounds that the Convention had not been incorporated into British law. Its alleged incorporation via the European Communities Act 1972 did not enable a party to invoke the Convention before a Scottish court in a matter *wholly unrelated to EC law* (see also *SPUC v Grogan* (case 159/90) and *Kremzow v Austria* (case C–299/95)). In *Mannesmannröhren-Werke AG v Commission* (Case T–112/98), the CFI emphasised that although the ECHR has special significance in defining the scope of fundamental rights recognised by the Community, because it reflects the constitutional traditions common to the Member States, the Court has no jurisdiction to apply the ECHR itself. The CFI therefore rejected arguments based directly on Article 6 ECHR in relation to an application to annul a Commission decision, but allowed the application on other grounds (see 6.6.7, below). The CFI's view with regard to invoking ECHR articles may be technically correct, but it sits somewhat uneasily with other judgments both by the CFI and the ECJ in which the courts appeared more willing to refer directly to ECHR provisions, and even to the jurisprudence of the European Court of Human Rights itself (see, e.g., *Roquette Frères* (case C–94/00); *Orfanopoulos* (case C–482/01), citing *Boultif* v *Switzerland* concerning right to family life; *Connolly* v *Commission* (case C–274/99P): civil servants' freedom of expression under Article 10 ECHR).

Other international treaties concerned with human rights referred to by the Court as constituting a possible source of general principles are the European Social Charter (1971) and Convention 111 of the International Labour Organisation (1958) (*Defrenne* v *Sabena (No. 3)* (case 149/77)). In *Ministère Public* v *Levy* (case C–158/91) the Court suggested that a Member State might even be obliged to apply a national law which conflicted with a ruling of its own on the interpretation of EC Directive 76/207 where this was necessary to ensure compliance with an international convention (in this case ILO Convention 89, 1948) concluded prior to that State's entry into the EC.

6.3.3 Relationship between different legal systems protecting human rights

6.3.3.1 *Relationship with national constitutions*

We saw at the beginning of this chapter that one of the central reasons for the introduction of fundamental rights into EC law was the resistance of some of the constitutional courts to giving effect to Community rules which conflicted with national constitutional principles. The ECJ's tactics to incorporate these principles and stave off rebellion were undoubtedly successful as exemplified by the *Wünsche* case ([1987] 3 CMLR 225), in which the German constitutional court resiled from its position in *Internationale Handelsgesellschaft* ([1974] 2 CMLR 540) (see Chapter 4). This does not, however, mean that the ECJ can rest on its laurels in this regard. The Italian constitutional court in *Fragd* (*SpA Fragd* v *Amministrazione delle Finanze* Decision No. 232 of 21 April 1989) reaffirmed its right to test Community rules against national constitutional rules and stated that Community rules which, in its view, were incompatible with the Italian constitution would not be applied. Similarly, the German constitutional courts have reasserted the right to challenge Community legislation which is inconsistent with the German constitution (see, e.g., *Brunner* v *European Union Treaty* [1994] 1 CMLR 57; *M GmbH* v *Bundesregierung* (case 2 BvQ 3/89) [1990] 1 CMLR 570 (an earlier tobacco advertising case) and the bananas cases – *Germany* v *Council (Re Banana Regime)* (case C–280/93), *Germany* v *Council (Bananas II)* (case C–122/95) and *T. Port GmbH* v *Hauptzollamt Hamburg-Jonas* (cases C–364 & 365/95) – discussed further in Chapter 4). Although the supremacy of Community law *vis-à-vis* national law might not be threatened by the possibility of its review in accordance with provisions of national constitutions embodying general principles of international law, its uniformity and the supremacy of the ECJ might well be eroded if national courts seek themselves to interpret these broad and flexible principles, rather than referring for a Community ruling on these matters from the ECJ. Equally, a failure on the part of national courts to recognise fundamental principles, in conjunction with a failure to refer, may have a similar effect.

6.3.3.2 *Accession to the ECHR*

Deferring to the ECJ does, however, concentrate a significant degree of power in that court, against whose rulings there is no appeal. One suggested safeguard for fundamental rights would be for the Community to accede to the ECHR. Questions of human rights and, in particular, interpretation of the ECHR, could then be taken to the European Court of Human Rights (ECtHR), a court which specialises in these issues. This would minimise the risk of the ECJ misinterpreting the ECHR and avoid the possibility of two conflicting lines of case law developing (e.g., *Orkem* (case 374/ 87) and *Funke* v *France* (case SA 256A)). The ECJ, however, has ruled that accession to the ECHR would not be within the present powers of the Community: Treaty amendment would be required before the Community could take this step (*Opinion 2/94* on the *Accession by the Community to the European Convention on Human Rights*).

This was one of the issues discussed by the Convention on the Future of Europe preparing for the 2004 IGC. The Treaty establishing a Constitution would not only incorporate the EU Charter of Fundamental Rights (a separate document, not to be confused with the ECHR) into the Constitution (see further below), but also include an article in Part I which provides that the Union 'shall accede to the European Convention for the Protection of Human Rights and Fundamental Freedoms'. A further declaration provides for cooperation between the ECHR and the ECJ. The Constitution is not in force, and even if it were, the details of timing and other practicalities of accession remain to be worked out. Yet, this is a significant step forward. It also follows the line established by recent Treaty amendments, which have seen a progressive raising of the profile of human rights protection within the Community and, indeed, the Union.

6.3.3.3 *Enforcing respect for the ECHR within the EU structure*

The TEU had included in the Union general provisions a reference to the ECHR to the effect that, 'The Union shall respect fundamental rights, as guaranteed by the European Convention for the Protection of Human Rights and Fundamental Freedoms . . . and as they result from the constitutional tradition common to the Member States, as general principles of Community law' (Article 6(2) (ex F(2) TEU)). Should the Constitution come into force, the provision will be reformulated as 'Fundamental Rights, as guaranteed by the European Convention for the Protection of Human Rights and Fundamental Freedoms and as they result from the constitutional traditions common to the Member States, shall constitute general principles of the Union's law' (Article I–9(3)).

Note that the scope of protection awarded is confined to the Union treaties. The courts are not empowered to review decisions of the UN, including the Security Council, even in the light of Community law or the fundamental rights recognised by Community law (*Ahmed Ali Yusuf and Others* v *Council of the European Union* (cases T–306 & 315/01)). The CFI based this decision on the fact that, according to its interpretation of the requirements of international law, the obligations of the Member States of the United Nations prevail over any other obligation. The Community, although not itself a member of the UN, must, in the CFI's opinion, be bound by the obligations flowing from the Charter of the United Nations. Nonetheless, the

CFI reserved the rights of the Community courts to check the lawfulness of the Council Regulation (which implemented the UN Security Council Resolution and was under challenge in this case), and therefore implicitly the underlying resolution, by reference to the higher rules of international law (*jus cogens*), from which neither the Member States nor the bodies of the Union should, under international law, be able to derogate. This includes provisions intended to secure universal protection of fundamental human rights. On the facts, the CFI found the application unfounded.

Additionally, Article 6(1) (ex F(1)) TEU stated that the Union was founded on respect for 'liberty, democracy and respect for human rights'. However, by Article L TEU, as it then was (now amended and re-numbered as Article 46 TEU), the ECJ's jurisdiction as regards the general Union provisions was excluded. The ToA amended Article 46 TEU to give the ECJ express competence in respect of Article 6(2) TEU with regard to action of the institutions 'insofar as the ECJ has jurisdiction either under the treaties establishing the Communities or under the TEU'. This would seem to be little more than a confirmation of the existing position, at least as far as the EC Treaty is concerned, though it might have some significance in respect of the ECJ's (limited) jurisdiction regarding JHA.

The ToA also inserted a new Article 7 into the TEU. This provided that where there has been a persistent and serious breach of a principle mentioned in new Article 6(1) TEU, the Council may suspend certain of the rights of the offending Member State, including its voting rights. Were this provision to be used, it could have serious consequences for the Member State in question; such a Member State would lose its opportunity to influence the content of Community legislation by which it would be bound, even in sensitive areas where otherwise it could have vetoed legislation. On this viewpoint, one might suggest that the need to comply with fundamental principles is being taken seriously indeed. It is likely, though, that this provision will be used only rarely given the severity of the breach needed to trigger the procedure which itself is long-winded, requiring unanimity (excluding the offending Member State) in the first instance. Given the potential consequences for Member States, however, the complexity of the procedure is perhaps appropriate. Nonetheless, it does detract from the effectiveness of the procedures. Should the Constitution come into force, this procedure will be rephrased in Article I–59.

6.4 Relationship between the EC/EU and the ECHR in the protection of human rights: view from the ECHR

All Member States of the EU have signed the ECHR, and in most Member States, the Convention has been incorporated into domestic law. (It was incorporated in the UK by the Human Rights Act 1998, which came into force in October 2000.) When it is so incorporated, the Convention's provisions may be invoked before the domestic courts in order to challenge *national* rules or procedures which infringe the rights protected by the Convention. Even without the Convention being incorporated into domestic law, the Member States are bound by its terms and individuals, after they have exhausted national remedies, have a right of appeal under the Convention to the European Court of Human Rights.

The ECJ has done a great deal to ensure the protection of human rights within the context of the application of Community law, whether by Community institutions or by Member States. But, as the ECHR has not so far been incorporated into *Community* law, its scope has been limited and the relationship between the ECHR and the Union legal system is somewhat unclear. The difficulties are illustrated by the decision of the ECtHR in the *Matthews* case (ECtHR judgment, 18 February 1999).

Matthews concerned the rights of UK nationals resident in Gibraltar to vote in European Parliamentary elections. They were excluded from participating in the elections as a result of the 1979 agreement between the Member States which established direct elections in respect of the European Parliament. The applicants argued that this was contrary to Protocol 1, Article 3 of the ECHR, which provides that signatory States to the Convention are under an obligation 'to hold free elections at reasonable intervals by secret ballot, under conditions which will ensure the free expression of the opinion of the people in the choice of the legislature'. The British government argued that not only was Community law not within the jurisdiction of the ECHR (as the Community had not acceded to the Convention), but also that the UK Government could not be held responsible for joint acts of the Member States. The European Court of Human Rights found, however, that there had been a violation of the Convention.

The Court held that States which are party to the ECHR retain residual obligations in respect of the rights protected by the Convention, even as regards areas of law-making which had been transferred to the Union. Such a transfer of power is permissible, provided Convention rights continue to be secured within the Community framework. In this context the Court of Human Rights noted the ECJ's jurisprudence in which the ECJ recognised and protected Convention rights. In this case, however, the existence of the direct elections was based on a *sui generis* international instrument entered into by the UK and the other Member States which could not be challenged before the ECJ, as it was not a normal Community act. Furthermore, the TEU, which extended the European Parliament's powers to include the right to co-decision thereby increasing the Parliament's claim to be considered a legislature and taking it within the terms of Protocol 1, Article 3 of the ECHR, was equally an act which could not be challenged before the ECJ. There could therefore be no protection of Convention rights in this regard by the ECJ. Arguing that the Convention is intended to guarantee rights that are not theoretical or illusory, the Court of Human Rights held that:

> The United Kingdom, together with all other parties to the Maastricht Treaty, is responsible *ratione materiae* under Article 1 of the Convention and, in particular, under Article 3 of Protocol 1, for the consequences of that Treaty (para. 33).

It may be noted that it is implicit in the reasoning in this judgment that the EU is regarded by the Court of Human Rights as being the creature of the Member States, which remain fundamentally responsible for the Community's actions – and for those of the Union. This corresponds with the conception of the EU expressed by some of the Member States' constitutional courts (e.g., see the German constitutional court's reasoning in *Brunner* [1994] 1 CMLR 57).

Arguably, this judgment opens the way for the Member States to be held jointly responsible for those Community (or Union) acts that currently fall outside the jurisdiction of the ECJ, sealing lacunae in the protection offered to individual human rights within the Community legal order. The difficulty is, of course, that in this case only the UK was the defendant. The British government is dependent on the cooperation of the other Member States to enable it to fulfil its own obligations under the ECHR. It is possible that a case could be brought under the ECHR against all Member States jointly. (See, e.g., *Société Guerin Automobiles* (Application No. 51717/99), inadmissible on other grounds; *DSR Senator Lines*, (Application No. 56672/00) (Grand Chamber), dismissed as the applicant could not claim on the facts to be a victim, though note third-party representations, including that of the ICJ.) Although this would not obviate the need for cooperation to remedy any violation found, it would avoid the situation where one Member State alone was carrying the responsibility for Union measures that were the choice of all (or most) Member States.

The implication that the Court of Human Rights will step in only where there is no effective means of securing human rights protection within an existing international body (i.e., that the ECJ has primary responsibility for these issues in the EU) is underlined by its approach in another case involving another European supranational organisation, Euratom (*Waite and Kennedy* v *Germany*, ECtHR judgment, 18 February 1999). There the Court emphasised the necessity for an independent review board which is capable of protecting fundamental rights to exist within the organisational structure. More recently, we can see this approach in *Bosphorus Airways* v *Ireland* (ECtHR judgment, 30 June 2005 (GC)), which concerned alleged human rights violations resulting from Community secondary legislation which the ECJ had upheld. There the European Court of Human Rights held that it would not interfere provided the rights protection awarded by the ECJ was equal to that under the ECHR, noting that in this context, 'equal' means equivalent or comparable rather than identical (para. 155). It should be noted that in a concurring judgment, one of the ECtHR judges did make the point that, although there have been reviews of ECJ jurisprudence, they have looked at the level of protection in a general or formal way, rather than looking at the substance of a right in an individual case (Concurring Opinion of Judge Ress, para. 2), highlighting a potential weakness in the system of protection awarded to individuals.

6.5 The EU Charter of Fundamental Rights

6.5.1 Background

We have already seen that there has been a debate about whether the EC/EU should accede to the European Convention on Human Rights. In 1999, the Cologne European Council set up a Convention, under the chairmanship of Roman Herzog (a former German Federal President), to produce a draft Union charter as an alternative mechanism to ensure the protection of fundamental rights. This was completed in time for the 2000 European Council meeting at Nice, where the European institutions solemnly proclaimed the charter (published at [2000] OJ

C364/1 – hereinafter EUCFR). At the present time, the EUCFR does not have legal effect. The Constitution, which has not been ratified, would incorporate the Charter as Part II and Article I–9(1) specifies that 'the Union shall recognize the rights, freedoms and principles set out in the Charter of Fundamental Rights'. Nonetheless the scope of the rights granted is as limited as it was under the Charter. Further provisions clarify that the incorporation of the Charter does not create any new rights or extend the Union's competence.

Despite some contention about the status and impact of the Charter, the ECJ has already mentioned the EUCFR in a number of judgments by way of reference in confirming that the European legal order recognises particular fundamental rights (see, e.g., *R v SoS ex parte BAT* (Case C–491/01), where the Court observed that 'the right to property, . . . is recognised to be a fundamental human right in the Community legal order, protected by the first subparagraph of Article 1 of the First Protocol to the European Convention on Human Rights ("ECHR") and *enshrined in Article 17 of the Charter of Fundamental Rights of the European Union*' (para. 144, emphasis added). See also *Jego-Quere et Cie v Commission* (Case T–177/01 para. 42; see further Chapter 11 and *Mannesmannröhren-Werke AG v Commission* (case T–112/98) paras 15 and 76). However, there has been no judgment to date in which the ECJ has *based* its judgment on the EUCFR.

6.5.2 Scope

By virtue of Article 51(1) EUCFR, its provisions are addressed to the institutions and bodies of the Union and to the Member States only when they are implementing Union law. As far as the institutions and bodies of the Union are concerned, due regard is to be had to the principle of subsidiarity. It is not entirely clear what the significance of this reference is, other than perhaps to confirm that the Union must always act in accordance with the principle of subsidiarity. With regard to the Member States, Article 51(1) EUCFR confirms existing case law which held that there is only an obligation on the Member States to respect fundamental rights under EU law when they are acting in the context of Community law (see *Karlsson and others* (case C–292/97), para. 37). Outside this context, Member States are, of course, obliged to respect fundamental rights under the ECHR (see above, on 'residual obligations').

Article 52(1) EUCFR provides that limitations on the exercise of the rights and freedoms guaranteed by the EUCFR must be provided by law. Any such limitations must be proportionate and are only permitted if they are necessary and genuinely meet objectives recognised by the EU. In this, there are similarities to the approach taken with regard to the derogation provisions in the ECHR. Article 52(2) EUCFR further confirms that those rights which derive from the treaties are subject to the conditions and limitations that apply to the corresponding treaty provisions.

6.5.3 Substance

The EUCFR is divided into six substantive chapters.

Chapter I, Dignity, includes:

(a) human dignity;

(b) the right to life;

(c) the right to the integrity of the person, and

(d) prohibitions on torture, inhuman or degrading treatment or punishment, slavery and forced labour.

Chapter II, Freedoms, provides for:

(a) right to liberty and security;

(b) respect for private and family life;

(c) protection of personal data;

(d) right to marry and found a family;

(e) freedom of:

  (i) thought, conscience and religion;

  (ii) expression and information;

  (iii) assembly and association;

  (iv) the arts and sciences;

  (v) a right to education;

  (vi) choice in an occupation and a right to engage in work;

  (vii) ability to conduct a business, right to property, right to asylum, and protection in the event of removal, expulsion or deportation.

Chapter III, Equality, guarantees:

(a) equality before the law, non-discrimination, cultural, religious and linguistic diversity;

(b) equality between men and women;

(c) the rights of the child and the elderly; and

(d) the integration of persons with disabilities.

The solidarity rights in chapter IV are:

(a) the workers' right to information and consultation with the right of collective bargaining and action;

(b) right of access to placement services;

(c) protection in the event of unjustified dismissal;

(d) fair and just working conditions;

(e) prohibition of child labour and protection of young people at work;

(f) family and professional life;

(g) social security and social assistance;

(h) health care;

(i) access to services of general economic interest;

(j) environmental protection; and

(k) consumer protection.

Chapter V provides for citizenship rights (see also Chapter 24), which are the right to:

(a) vote and stand as candidate at elections to the European Parliament and at municipal elections;

(b) good administration;

(c) access to documents;

(d) access to the Ombudsman;

(e) petition the European Parliament;

(f) have freedom of movement and residence; and

(g) diplomatic and consular protection.

Finally, chapter VI, Justice, guarantees a right to:

(a) effective remedy and to a fair trial;

(b) presumption of innocence and right of defence;

(c) principles of legality and proportionality of criminal offences and penalties; and

(d) not to be tried or punished twice in criminal proceedings for the same criminal offence.

The preceding enumeration of all the rights contained in the EUCFR demonstrates that the Charter consists of a mixture of human rights found in the ECHR, rights derived from other international conventions and provisions of the EC Treaty. The Council of the European Union has published a booklet which explains the origin of each of the rights contained in the EUCFR (see 'Further Reading' at the end of this chapter).

6.5.4 Overlap between the Charter and the ECHR

Article 52(3) deals with the complex problem of overlap between the ECHR and the EUCFR. It specifies that those rights in the EUCFR which correspond with ECHR rights must be given the same meaning and scope as the ECHR rights. EU law may provide more generous protection, but not a lower level of protection than guaranteed under the ECHR and other international instruments (Article 53).

At present, the question of overlap is not a cause for concern, because the EUCFR has no legal status. However, if the Constitution comes into force, it will be necessary to determine to what extent the ECJ has jurisdiction to enforce the Charter. Presumably, Article 51 would mean that the EUCFR rights are not free-standing rights, but are only relevant in matters of European law. In that case, the position would probably not be any different from the current situation.

If, however, certain EUCFR rights (such as those based on the ECHR) are regarded as free-standing rights, then the ECJ may be in danger of 'competing' with the European Court of Human Rights. The ECJ would be obliged to interpret EUCFR rights in accordance with the ECHR, but a difficulty may arise if the ECJ interprets an ECHR-based right in one way and the Court of Human Rights subsequently takes a different view. Member States may then face a conflict between complying with their obligations under European law, in particular the doctrine of supremacy (see Chapter 4) and under the ECHR, respectively. It is submitted that in such a case, the ECHR should prevail. This seems to be the current position under the ECJ's case law. In *Roquette Frères* (case C–94/00), the question arose whether business premises could be protected under Article 8 ECHR against 'dawn raids' by the Commission under Regulation 17 (now replaced by Regulation 1/2003; see Chapter 29). In its earlier decision in *Hoechst* (case C–46/87), the ECJ had held that Article 8 required no such protection. However, subsequent ECHR case law has extended the scope of Article 8 to cover business premises. In *Roquette*, the ECJ held that the case law under the ECHR must be taken into account in applying the *Hoechst* decision. The ECJ therefore appears to recognise that ECHR case law can have an impact on the scope of fundamental rights guaranteed by Community law.

6.5.5 Conclusion on EUCFR

Currently, the EUCFR has only declaratory status and it remains to be seen whether it will become legally binding. If this were to happen, some thought would need to be given to the relationship between the ECHR and the EUCFR and the role of the ECJ in interpreting the fundamental rights contained in the EUCFR. The potential accession of the EU to the ECHR, which would be possible if the Constitution became effective in its current form, would acknowledge the supremacy of the Convention and the ECtHR.

The general principles of Community law have been expanded through the case law of the ECJ to cover a wide variety of rights and principles developed from many sources. We will now look at some specific examples of those rights. The following is not, however, an exhaustive list, and there may be degrees of overlap between the categories mentioned.

6.6 Rules of administrative justice

6.6.1 Proportionality

This was the principle invoked in *Internationale Handelsgesellschaft mbH* (case 11/70). It is now enshrined in Article 5 (ex 3b) EC (see 6.8 below). The principle, applied in the context of administrative law, requires that the means used to achieve a given end must be no more than that which is appropriate and necessary to achieve that end. The test thus puts the burden on an administrative authority to justify its actions and requires some consideration of possible alternatives. In this respect it is a more rigorous test than one based on reasonableness.

The principle has been invoked on many occasions as a basis of challenge to EC secondary legislation, often successfully (e.g., *Werner A. Bock KG v Commission* (case 62/70); *Bela-Mühle Josef Bergmann KG v Grows-Farm GmbH & Co. KG* (case 114/76). It was applied in *R v Intervention Board for Agricultural Produce, ex parte E.D. & F. Man (Sugar) Ltd* (case 181/84) in the context of a claim by E.D. & F. Man (Sugar) Ltd before the English Divisional Court, on facts very similar to *Internationale Handelsgesellschaft*. Here the claimant, E.D. & F. Man (Sugar) Ltd, was seeking repayment of a security of £1,670,370 forfeited when it failed to comply with an obligation to submit licence applications to the Board within a specified time-limit. Due to an oversight they were a few hours late. The claimant's claim rested on the alleged illegality of the EC regulations governing the common organisation of the sugar market. The regulations appeared to require the full forfeiture of the deposit (lodged by the exporter at the time of the initial offer to export) in the event of a breach of both a *primary* obligation to export goods as agreed with the Commission and a *secondary* obligation to submit a licence application following the initial offer within a specified time-limit. The ECJ held, on a reference from the Divisional Court on the validity of the regulations, that to require the same forfeiture for breach of the secondary obligation as for the primary obligation was disproportionate, and to the extent that the regulation required such forfeiture, it was invalid. As a result of this ruling, the claimant was held entitled in the Divisional Court to a declaration that the forfeiture of its security was unlawful: a significant victory for the claimant.

The proportionality principle has also been applied in the context of the EC Treaty, for example, in the application of the provisions relating to freedom of movement for goods and persons. Under these provisions States are allowed some scope for derogation from the principle of free movement, but derogations must be 'justified' on one of the grounds provided (Articles 30 (ex 36) and 39(3) (ex 48(3))). This has been interpreted by the ECJ as meaning that the measure must be *no more than is necessary* to achieve the desired objective (see Chapters 18–19 (goods), 20–24 (persons)).

In *Watson* (case 118/75) the proportionality principle was invoked in the sphere of the free movement of persons to challenge the legality of certain action by the Italian authorities. One of the defendants, Ms Watson, was claiming rights of residence in Italy. The right of free movement of workers expressed in Article 39 EC is regarded as a fundamental Community right, subject only to 'limitations' which are 'justified' on the grounds of public policy, public security or public health (Article 39(3)). The Italian authorities sought to invoke this derogation to expel Ms Watson from Italy. The reason for the defendants' expulsion was that they had failed to comply with certain administrative procedures, required under Italian law, to record and monitor their movements in Italy. The ECJ, on reference from the Italian court, held that, while States were entitled to impose penalties for noncompliance with their administrative formalities, these must not be disproportionate; and they must never provide a ground for deportation. Here, it is worth noting, it is a Member State's action which was deemed to be illegal for breach of the proportionality principle. Likewise, in *Wijsenbeek* (case C–378/97) the ECJ held that, although Member States were still entitled to check the documentation of EC nationals moving from one Member State to another, any penalties imposed on those whose documentation was unsatisfactory must be proportionate: in this case, imprisonment for failure to carry a passport was disproportionate. (See further Chapter 24.)

Similarly, in the context of goods, in a case brought against Germany in respect of its beer purity laws (case 178/84), a German law imposing an absolute ban on additives was found in breach of EC law (Article 28 EC) and not 'justified' on public health grounds under Article 30. Since the same (public health) objective could have been achieved by other less restrictive means, the ban was not 'necessary'; it was disproportionate.

More recently, however, there seems to have been a refinement of the principle of proportionality. In the case of *Südzucker Mannheim/Ochsenfurt AG* v *Hauptzollamt Mannheim* (case C–161/96) the ECJ confirmed the distinction between primary and secondary (or administrative) obligations made in *R* v *Intervention Board for Agricultural Produce* (case 181/84). The breach of a secondary obligation should not be punished as severely as a breach of a primary obligation. On the facts of the case, the ECJ held that a failure to comply with customs formalities by not producing an export licence was a breach of a primary and not a secondary obligation. The ECJ stated that the production of the export licence was necessary to ensure compliance with export requirements and thus the production of the export licence was part of the primary obligation. On this reasoning, it may be difficult to distinguish between primary and secondary obligations.

Further, the ECJ has held that, where an institution has significant discretion in the implementation of policies, such as in CAP, the ECJ may only interfere if the 'measure is manifestly inappropriate having regard to the objectives which the competent institution is seeking to pursue' (*Germany* v *Council (Re Banana Regime)* (case C–280/93), para. 90). The same is also true of actions of Member States where they have a broad discretion in the implementation of Community policy (see *R* v *Minister of Agriculture, Fisheries and Food, ex parte National Federation of Fishermen's Organisations* (case C–44/94)). In these circumstances, the distinction between proportionality and *Wednesbury* reasonableness is not great.

6.6.2 Legal certainty

The principle of legal certainty was invoked by the Court of Justice in *Defrenne* v *Sabena (No. 2)* (case 43/75). The principle, which is one of the widest generality, has been applied in more specific terms as:

(a) the principle of legitimate expectations;

(b) the principle of non-retroactivity.

The principle of legitimate expectations, derived from German law, means that, in the absence of an overriding matter of public interest, Community measures must not violate the legitimate expectations of the parties concerned. A legitimate expectation is one which might be held by a reasonable person as to matters likely to occur in the normal course of his affairs. It does not extend to anticipated windfalls or speculative profits. In *Efisol SA* v *Commission* (case T–336/94) the CFI commented that an individual would have no legitimate expectations of a particular state of affairs existing where a 'prudent and discriminating' trader would have foreseen the development in question. Furthermore, in *Germany* v *Council (Re Banana Regime)* (case C–280/93), the ECJ held that no trader may have a legitimate expectation that an existing Community regime will be maintained. In that the principle requires the encouragement of a reasonable expectation, a reliance on that expectation, and some loss resulting from the breach of that expectation, it is similar to the principle of estoppel in English law.

The principle was applied in *August Töpfer & Co. GmbH* v *Commission* (case 112/77) (see Chapter 11). August Töpfer & Co. GmbH was an exporter which had applied for, and been granted, a number of export licences for sugar. Under Community law, as part of the common organisation of the sugar market, certain refunds were to be payable on export, the amount of the refunds being fixed in advance. If the value of the refund fell, due to currency fluctuations, the licence holder could apply to have his licence cancelled. This scheme was suddenly altered by an EC regulation, and the right to cancellation withdrawn, being substituted by provision for compensation. This operated to Töpfer's disadvantage, and it sought to have the regulation annulled, for breach, *inter alia*, of the principle of legitimate expectations. Although it did not succeed on the merits, the principle of legitimate expectations was upheld by the Court. (See also *CNTA SA v Commission* (case 74/74), monetary compensation scheme ended suddenly and without warning: Chapter 13.) In *Opel Austria GmbH v Council* (case T–115/94) the Court held that the principle of legitimate expectations was the corollary of the principle of good faith in public international law. Thus, where the Community had entered into an obligation and the date of entry into force of that obligation is known to traders, such traders may use the principle of legitimate expectations to challenge measures contrary to any provision of the international agreement having direct effect.

The principle of non-retroactivity, applied to Community secondary legislation, precludes a measure from taking effect before its publication. Retrospective application will only be permitted in exceptional circumstances, where it is necessary to achieve particular objectives and will not breach individuals' legitimate expectations. Such measures must also contain a statement of the reasons justifying the retroactive effect (*Diversinte SA v Administración Principal de Aduanos e Impuestos Especiales de la Junqueros* (case C–260/91)).

In *R v Kirk* (case 63/83) the principle of non-retroactivity of penal provisions (activated in this case by a Community regulation) was invoked successfully. However, retroactivity may be acceptable where the retroactive operation of the rule in question improves an individual's position (see, for example, *Road Air BV v Inspecteur der Invoerrechten en Accijnzen* (case C–310/95)).

This principle also has relevance in the context of national courts' obligation to interpret domestic law to comply with Community law when it is not directly effective (the *Von Colson* principle, see Chapter 5). In *Pretore di Salò v Persons Unknown* (case 14/86) in a reference from the Salò magistrates' court on the compatibility of certain Italian laws with EEC Water Purity Directive 78/659, which had been invoked against the defendants in criminal proceedings, the Court held that:

> A Directive cannot of itself have the effect of determining or aggravating the liability in criminal law of persons who act in contravention of the provisions of the Directive.

The Court went further in *Officier van Justitie v Kolpinghuis Nijmegen* (case 80/86). Here, in response to a question concerning the scope of national courts' obligation of interpretation under the *von Colson* principle, the Court held that that obligation was 'limited by the general principles of law which form part of Community law and in particular the principles of legal certainty and non-retroactivity'. Thus national courts are not required to interpret domestic law to comply with EC law in violation of these principles. This would appear to apply even where the EC law in question has direct effects, at least where criminal proceedings are in issue (see *Berlusconi* (joined cases C–387/02, C–391/02 and C–403/02), discussed in Chapter 5).

Problems also arise over the temporal effects of ECJ rulings under Article 234 (ex 177). In *Defrenne v Sabena (No. 2)* (case 43/75) the Court held that, given the exceptional circumstances, 'important considerations of legal certainty' required that its ruling on the direct effects of the then Article 119 (now 141) should apply prospectively only. It could not be relied on to support claims concerning pay periods prior to the date of judgment, except as regards workers who had already brought legal proceedings or made an equivalent claim. However, in *Ariete SpA* (case 811/79) and *Meridionale Industria Salumi Srl* (cases 66, 127 & 128/79) the Court affirmed that *Defrenne* was an exceptional case. In a 'normal' case a ruling from the ECJ was retroactive; the Court merely declared the law as it always was. This view was approved in *Barra* (case 309/85). However, in *Blaizot* (case 24/86), a case decided the same day as *Barra*, 'important considerations of legal certainty' again led the Court to limit the effects of its judgment on the lines of *Defrenne*. It came to the same conclusion in *Barber* v *Guardian Royal Exchange Assurance Group* (case 262/88). These cases indicate that in exceptional cases, where the Court introduces some new principle, or where the judgment may have serious effects as regards the past, the Court will be prepared to limit the effects of its rulings. *Kolpinghuis Nijmegen* may now be invoked to support such a view. Nevertheless, the Court did not limit the effect of its judgment in *Francovich* (cases C–6 & 9/90) contrary to Advocate-General Mischo's advice, despite the unexpectedness of the ruling and its 'extremely serious financial consequences' for Member States. Nor did it do so in *Marshall (No. 2)* (case C–271/91) when it declared that national courts were obliged, by Article 5 of Directive 76/207 and their general obligation under Article 10 (ex 5) EC to ensure that the objectives of the directives might be achieved, to provide full compensation to persons suffering loss as a result of infringements of the directive, a matter which could not have been deduced either from the ECJ's case law or from the actual wording of the directive (see further Chapter 25).

The question of the temporal effect of a ruling from the ECJ under Article 234 EC was considered by the Italian constitutional court in *Fragd (SpA Fragd* v *Amministrazione delle Finanze* Decision No. 232 of 21 April 1989) in the light of another general principle. Although the point did not arise out of the reference in question, the Italian court considered the effect that a ruling under Article 234 holding a Community measure void should have on the referring court if the ECJ had held that the ruling would apply for future cases only, excluding the judgment in which it was given. The Italian constitutional court suggested that in the light of the right to judicial protection given under the Italian constitution, such a holding should have effect in the case in which the reference was made. A finding of invalidity with purely prospective effect would offend against this principle and would therefore be unacceptable.

6.6.3 Procedural rights

Where a person's rights are likely to be affected by EC law, EC secondary legislation normally provides for procedural safeguards (e.g., Regulation 1/2003, competition law, Chapter 29; Directive 2004/38/EC, free movement of workers, Chapter 20). However, where such provision does not exist, or where there are lacunae, general principles of law may be invoked to fill those gaps.

6.6.4 **Natural justice: the right to a hearing**

The right to natural justice, and in particular the right to a fair hearing, was invoked, this time from English law, in *Transocean Marine Paint Association* v *Commission* (case 17/74) by Advocate-General Warner. The case, which arose in the context of EC competition law (see Chapter 29), was an action for annulment of the Commission's decision, addressed to the claimant association, that their agreements were in breach of EC law. The Court, following Advocate-General Warner's submissions, asserted a general rule that a person whose interests are perceptibly affected by a decision taken by a public authority must be given the opportunity to make his views known. Since the Commission had failed to comply with this obligation its decision was annulled. The principle was affirmed in *Hoffman-La Roche & Co. AG* v *Commission* (case 85/76), in which the Court held that observance of the right to be heard is, in all proceedings in which sanctions, in particular fines and periodic payments, may be imposed, a fundamental principle of Community law which must be respected even if the proceedings in question are administrative proceedings.

Another aspect of the right to a fair hearing is the notion of 'equality of arms'. This is exemplified in a series of cases against the Commission following a Commission investigation into alleged anti-competitive behaviour on the part of ICI and another company, Solvay. In the *Solvay* case (case T–30/91) the Court stated that the principle of equality of arms presupposed that both the Commission and the defendant company had equal knowledge of the files used in the proceeding. That was not the case here, as the Commission had not informed Solvay of the existence of certain documents. The Commission argued that this did not affect the proceedings because the documents would not be used in the company's defence. The Court took the view that this point was not for the Commission to decide, as this would give the Commission more power *vis-à-vis* the defendant company because it had full knowledge of the file whereas the defendant did not. Equally, in the *ICI* cases (T–36 & 37/91) the Commission's refusal to grant ICI access to the file was deemed to infringe the rights of the defence.

There are, however, limits to the rights of the defence: in *Descom Scales Manufacturing Co. Ltd* v *Council* (case T–171/94), the ECJ held that the rights of the defence do not require the Commission to provide a written record of every stage of the investigation detailing information which needed still to be verified. In this case, the Commission had notified the defendant company of the position although it had not provided a written record and the ECJ held that this was sufficient.

The right to a hearing within Article 6 ECHR also includes the right to a hearing within a reasonable period of time. The ECJ, basing its reasoning on Article 6 ECHR, thus held that, in respect of a case that had been pending before the CFI for five years and six months, the CFI had been in violation of its obligation to dispose of cases within a reasonable time (*Baustahlgewerbe* v *Commission* (case C–185/95 P)).

6.6.5 **The duty to give reasons**

The duty was affirmed in *Union Nationale des Entraîneurs et Cadres Techniques Professionels du Football (UNECTEF)* v *Heylens* (case 222/86). In this case, M. Heylens, a

Belgian and a professional football trainer, was the defendant in a criminal action brought by the French football trainers' union, UNECTEF, as a result of his practising in Lille as a professional trainer without the necessary French diploma, or any qualifications recognised by the French government as equivalent. M. Heylens held a Belgian football trainers' diploma, but his application for recognition of this diploma by the French authorities had been rejected on the basis of an adverse opinion from a special committee, which gave no reasons for its decision. The ECJ, on a reference from the Tribunal de Grande Instance, Lille, held that the right of free-movement of workers, granted by Article 39 EC, required that a decision refusing to recognise the equivalence of a qualification issued in another Member State should be subject to legal redress which would enable the legality of that decision to be established with regard to Community law, and that the person concerned should be informed of the reasons upon which the decision was based.

Similarly in *Al-Jubail Fertiliser Company (SAMAD)* v *Council* (case C–49/88) in the context of a challenge to a Council regulation imposing antidumping duties on the import of products manufactured by the applicants, the Court held that since the applicants had a right to a fair hearing the Community institutions were under a duty to supply them with all the information which would enable them effectively to defend their interests. Moreover if the information is supplied orally, as it may be, the Commission must be able to prove that it was in fact supplied.

6.6.6 The right to due process

As a corollary to the right to be informed of the reasons for a decision is the right, alluded to in *UNECTEF* v *Heylens* (case 222/86), to legal redress to enable such decisions and reasons to be challenged. This right was established in *Johnston* v *Chief Constable of the Royal Ulster Constabulary* (case 222/84). The case arose from a refusal by the RUC (now the Police Service of Northern Ireland) to renew its contracts with women members of the RUC Reserve. This decision had been taken as a result of a policy decision taken in 1980 that henceforth full-time RUC Reserve members engaged on general police duties should be fully armed. For some years women had not been issued with firearms nor trained in their use. Ms Johnston, who had been a full-time member of the Reserve for some years and wished to renew her contract, challenged the decision as discriminatory, in breach of EC Directive 76/207, which provides for equal treatment for men and women in all matters relating to employment. Although the measure was admittedly discriminatory, since it was taken solely on the grounds of sex, the Chief Constable claimed that it was justified, arguing from the 'public policy and public security' derogation of Articles 30 (goods, see Chapter 19) and 39 (workers, see Chapter 23), and from Article 297, which provides for the taking of measures in the event of, *inter alia*, 'serious internal disturbances affecting the maintenance of law and order'. As evidence that these grounds were made out the Chief Constable produced before the industrial tribunal a certificate issued by the Secretary of State certifying that the act refusing to offer Ms Johnston further employment in the RUC Reserve was done for the purpose of safeguarding national security and safeguarding public order. Under Article 53(2) of the Sex Discrimination (Northern Ireland) Order 1976 (SI 1976/1042) a certificate that an act was done for that purpose was 'conclusive evidence' that it was so done. A number of questions were referred to the ECJ by the industrial tribunal on the scope of the public order derogation and the compatibility of the Chief Constable's decision with Directive 76/207. The question of the Secretary of State's certificate and the possibility of judicial review were not directly raised. Nevertheless this was the first matter seized upon by the Court. The Court considered the requirement of judicial control, provided by Article 6 of Directive 76/207, which requires States to enable persons who 'consider themselves wronged' to 'pursue their claims by judicial process after possible recourse to the competent authorities'. This provision, the Court said, reflected:

> a general principle of law which underlies the constitutional traditions common to the Member States. That principle is also laid down in Articles 6 and 13 of the European Convention for the Protection of Human Rights and Fundamental Freedoms . . . .
>
> It is for the Member States to ensure effective judicial control as regards compliance with the applicable provisions of Community law and of national legislation intended to give effect to the rights for which the Directive provides.

The Court went on to say that Article 53(2) of the Sex Discrimination (Northern Ireland) Order 1976, in requiring the Secretary of State's certificate to be treated as conclusive evidence that the conditions for derogation are fulfilled, allowed the competent authority to deprive an individual of the possibility of asserting by judicial process the rights conferred by the directive. Such a provision was contrary to the principle of effective judicial control laid down in Article 6 of the directive. A similar approach has, in fact, been taken by the European Court of Human Rights in relation to such certificates issued in relation to a variety of substantive issues (e.g., *Tinnelly and Others* v *UK*, ECHR judgment, 10 July 1998).

Although the ECJ's decision was taken in the context of a right provided by the directive it is submitted that the right to effective judicial control enshrined in the European Convention on Human Rights and endorsed in this case could be invoked in any case in which a person's Community rights have been infringed. The case of *UNECTEF* v *Heylens* (case 222/86) would serve to support this proposition. Further, the CFI has held that the Commission, in exercising its competition policy powers, must give reasons sufficient to allow the Court's review of the Commission's decision-making process, if that decision is challenged (e.g., *Ufex* v *Commission* (case C–119/97P)).

Thus general principles of law act as a curb not only on the institutions of the Community but also on Member States, which are required, in the context of EC law, to accommodate these principles alongside existing remedies and procedures within their own domestic systems of administrative law and may result eventually in some modification in national law itself. There are, in any event, problems in determining the boundaries between matters of purely national law and matters of Community law (see 6.9 below).

6.6.7 Right to protection against self-incrimination

The right to a fair trial and the presumption of innocence of 'persons charged with a criminal offence' contained in Article 6 ECHR are undoubtedly rights which will be protected as general principles of law under Community law. However, in *Orkem* (case 374/87) and *Solvay* (case 27/88) the ECJ held that the right under Article 6 not to give evidence against oneself applied only to persons charged with an offence in criminal proceedings; it was not a principle which could be relied on in relation to infringements in the economic sphere, in order to resist a demand for information such as may be made by the EC Commission to establish a breach of EC competition law (see Chapter 29). This view was placed in doubt following a ruling from the Court of Human Rights in the case of *Funke* v *France* (case SA 256A) ([1993] 1 CMLR 897) and has been the subject of some academic criticism.

Funke involved a claim, for breach of Article 6 ECHR, in respect of a demand by the French customs' authorities for information designed to obtain evidence of currency and capital transfer offences. Following the applicant's refusal to hand over such information fines and penalties were imposed. The European Court of Human Rights held that such action, undertaken as a 'fishing expedition' in order to obtain documents which, if found, might produce evidence for a prosecution, infringed the right, protected by Article 6(1) ECHR, of anyone charged with a criminal offence (within the autonomous meaning of that phrase in Article 6 ECHR), to remain silent and not incriminate himself. It appears that Article 6, according to its 'autonomous meaning', is wide enough to apply to investigations conducted under the Commission's search and seizure powers under EC competition law, and that *Orkem* and *Solvay* may no longer be regarded as good law. This view, assimilating administrative penalties to criminal penalties, appears to have been taken by the ECJ in *Otto BV* v *Postbank NV* (case C–60/92). Moreover, in *Mannesmannröhren-Werke AG* v *Commission* (case T–112/98), also a case involving a request for information about an investigation into anti-competitive agreements, the CFI held that although Article 6 ECHR could not be invoked directly before the Court, Community law offered 'protection equivalent to that guaranteed by Article 6 of the Convention' (para. 77). A party subject to a Commission investigation could not be required to answer questions which might involve an admission of involvement in an anti-competitive agreement, although it would have to respond to requests for general information.

6.7 Equality

The principle of equality means, in its broadest sense, that persons in similar situations are not to be treated differently unless the difference in treatment is objectively justified. This, of course, gives rise to the question of what are similar situations. Discrimination can only exist within a framework in which it is possible to draw comparisons, for example, the framework of race, sex, nationality, colour, religion. The equality principle will not apply in situations which are deemed to be 'objectively different' (see *Les Assurances du Crédit SA* v *Council* (case C–63/89) – public export credit insurance operations different from other export credit insurance operations). What situations are regarded as comparable, subject to the equality principle, is clearly a matter of political judgement. The EC Treaty expressly prohibits discrimination on the grounds of nationality (Article 12 (ex 6) EC) and, to a limited extent, sex (Article 141 (ex 119) EC provides for equal *pay* for men and women for equal work). In the field of agricultural policy, Article 34(3) (ex 40(3)) prohibits 'discrimination between producers or consumers within the Community'.

The ToA introduced further provisions, giving the EC powers to regulate against discrimination on grounds of race, religion, sexual orientation or disability (Article 13 EC). Directive 2000/43/EC ([2000] OJ L180, p. 22) has been adopted to combat discrimination, both direct and indirect, on grounds of racial or ethnic origin, in relation to employment matters, social protection, education, and access to public goods and services. Directive 2000/78/EC [2000] OJ L303, p. 16) has been adopted to combat discrimination on the grounds of religion or belief, disability, age or sexual orientation with regard to employment and occupation. These directives are discussed further in Chapter 25.

However, a general principle of equality is clearly wider in scope than these provisions. In the first isoglucose case, *Royal Scholten-Honig (Holdings) Ltd* v *Intervention Board for Agricultural Produce* (cases 103 & 145/77), the claimants, who were glucose producers, together with other glucose producers, sought to challenge the legality of a system of production subsidies whereby sugar producers were receiving subsidies financed in part by levies on the production of glucose. Since glucose and sugar producers were in competition with each other the claimants argued that the regulations implementing the system were discriminatory, i.e., in breach of the general principle of equality, and therefore invalid. The ECJ, on a reference on the validity of the regulations from the English court, agreed. The regulations were held invalid. (See also *Ruckdeschel* (case 117/76); *Pont-à-Mousson* (cases 124/76 & 20/77).)

Similarly, the principle of equality was invoked in the case of *Airola* (case 21/74) to challenge a rule which was discriminatory on grounds of sex (but not pay), and in *Prais* (case 130/75) to challenge alleged discrimination on the grounds of religion. Neither case at the time fell within the more specific provisions of Community law, although would now fall within the scope of Directive 2000/78/EC (see above).

6.8 Subsidiarity

The principle of subsidiarity in its original philosophical meaning, as expressed by Pope Pius XI (Encyclical letter, 1931), that:

> It is an injustice, a grave evil and disturbance of right order for a larger and higher association to arrogate to itself functions which can be performed efficiently by smaller and lower societies

was invoked in the Community context during the 1980s when the Community's competence was about to be extended under the Single European Act. It was incorporated into that Act, in rather different form, in respect of environmental measures, in the then Article 130r (now 174) EC, and introduced into the EC Treaty in Article 5 (ex 3b) by the TEU. Article 5 EC requires the Community to act:

> only if and so far as the objectives of the proposed action cannot be sufficiently achieved by the Member States, and can therefore, by reason of the scale or the effects of the proposed action, be better achieved by the Community.

As expressed in Article 5 EC, subsidiarity appears to be a test of comparative efficiency; as such it lacks its original philosophical meaning, concerned with fostering social responsibility. This latter meaning has however been retained in Article 1 (ex A) TEU, which provides that decisions of the European Union 'be taken as closely as possible to the people'. Although it has not been incorporated into the EC Treaty it is submitted that this version of the principle of subsidiarity could be invoked as a general principle of law if not as a basis to challenge EC law at least as an aid to the interpretation of Article 5 EC (see Chapter 3). The principle of subsidiarity in its narrow form in Article 5 has, on occasion, been referred to as a ground for challenge of EC legislation (*R v Secretary of State for Health, ex parte British American Tobacco and others* (case C–491/01); *R v SoS for Health ex parte Swedish Match* (case C–210/03)), but this has never succeeded.

6.9 General principles applied to national legislation

It has been suggested that general principles of law, incorporated by the ECJ as part of Community law, also affect certain acts of the Member States. These fall into three broad categories:

(a) when EC rights are enforced within national courts;

(b) when the rules of a Member State are in (permitted) derogation from a fundamental principle of Community law, such as free movement of goods (Articles 25 and 28 EC) or persons (Articles 39 and 49); and

(c) when the Member State is acting as an agent of the Community in implementing Community law (e.g., *Klensch* v *Secrétaire d'État à l'Agriculture et à la Viticulture* (cases 201 & 202/85)).

6.9.1 Enforcement of Community law in national courts

The ECJ has repeatedly held that, in enforcing Community rights, national courts must respect procedural rights guaranteed in international law; for example, individuals must have a right of access to the appropriate court and the right to a fair hearing (see, e.g., *Johnston* v *RUC* (case 222/84) and *UNECTEF* v *Heylens* (case 222/86)). This applies, however, only where the rights which the individual seeks to enforce are derived from *Community* sources: Ms Johnston relied on the Equal Treatment Directive (Directive 76/207); M. Heylens on the right of freedom of movement for workers enshrined in Article 39 EC. In *Konstantinidis* (case C–168/91), a case concerning the rules governing the transliteration of Greek names, the ECJ handed down a judgment which did not follow the Opinion of the Advocate-General. The Advocate-General suggested that such rules, which resulted in a change in a person's name as a result of the way the transliteration was carried out, could constitute an interference with the rights protected by Article 8 ECHR. Although the ECJ agreed that this could be the case, it held that such rules would only be contrary to EC law where their application causes such inconvenience as to interfere with a person's right to free movement.

The constraints implied by this case seem to have been undermined. *Carlos*

Garcia Avello (case C–148/02) concerned a Spanish national's right to register his children's names in the Spanish style in Belgium, where they were born. The case is based not on free movement rights, but on European citizenship, a factor which both the European Commission and the Advocate-General agree allows a broader scope to EC protection of human rights. The ECJ agreed with the outcome without expressly considering human rights. The decision seems to limit the notion of the internal situation seen in *Kaur* (discussed above) and *Uecker and Jacquet* (joined cases C–64/96 & C–65/96, discussed in Chapter 24) and to extend the scope of circumstances in which the ECJ would be required to respect ECHR rights (see 6.9.4). A similar extension can be seen in *Chen* (case C–200/02), in which a baby holding Irish nationality but born in the UK was deemed to have rights to have her mother, a Chinese national, remain in the UK with her (see further Chapter 24).

The extension of human rights protection is not limited to circumstances in which citizenship is in issue, but arises in the context of any of the Treaty freedoms. In *Karner* (case C–71/02), a case concerning advertising on the Internet, the ECJ held that the national rules complained of were not selling arrangements and therefore they would not fall within Article 28 EC (see Chapter 18). In this aspect, the case is different from the preceding cases, as those cases concerned situations where the national legislation fell within the relevant Treaty provision. Despite the fact that the situation seemed to lie outside the prohibition in Article 28 (thus rendering a consideration of a derogation, discussed at 6.9.2, unnecessary), the ECJ then went on to give the national court 'guidance as to interpretation necessary to enable it to assess the compatibility of that legislation with the fundamental rights whose observance the Court ensures' (para. 49). According to the ECJ, in this case the national legislation fell within the scope of application of EC law (see further below 6.9.4).

Finally, any penalties imposed by national judicial bodies must be proportionate (e.g., *Watson and Belmann* (case 118/75)).

6.9.2 Derogation from fundamental principles

Most Treaty rules provide for some derogation in order to protect important public interests (e.g., Articles 30 and 39(3)). The ECJ has insisted that any derogation from the fundamental principles of Community law must be narrowly construed. When Member States do derogate, their rules may be reviewed in the light of general principles, as the question of whether the derogation is within permitted limits is one of Community law. Most, if not all, derogations are subject to the principle of proportionality (e.g., *Watson* (case 118/75)). The *ERT* case (*Elliniki Radiophonia Tileorassi AE* v *Dimotiki Etairia Pliroforissis* (case C–260/89)) concerned the establishment by the Greek government of a monopoly broadcaster. The ECJ held that this would be contrary to Article 49 (ex 59) regarding the freedom to provide services. Although the Treaty provides for derogation from Article 49 in Articles 46 and 55 (ex 56 and 66), any justification provided for by Community law must be interpreted in the light of fundamental rights, in this case the principle of freedom of expression embodied in Article 10 ECHR. Similarly, in *Vereinigte Familiapress Zeitungsverlags- und vertriebs GmbH* v *Heinrich Bauer Verlag* (case C–368/95), the need to ensure plurality of the media (based on Article 10 ECHR) was accepted as a possible reason justifying a measure (the prohibition of prize games and lotteries in magazines) which would otherwise breach Article 28 EC. More recently, in

Schmidberger (C–112/00), Advocate-General Jacobs argued that the right to freedom of expression and assembly permits a derogation from the free movement of goods (Article 28 EC)) in a context where the main transit route across the Alps was blocked for a period of 28 hours on a single occasion and steps were taken to ensure that the disruption to the free movement of goods was not excessive. The ECJ came to the same end conclusion, noting the wide margin of discretion given to the national authorities in striking a balance between fundamental rights and Treaty obligations (and contrast *Commission v France* (case C–265/95)). (See also on Article 8 ECHR *Mary Carpenter v SoS for the Home Department* (case C–60/00).)

One issue in this context is whether fundamental human rights should properly be seen as a derogation from Treaty freedoms, perhaps falling within the scope of the public policy objection, or whether they should be seen as operating to limit Treaty freedoms at an earlier point in the legal analysis. In *Omega Spielhallen* (case C–36/02), human dignity was seen as forming part of the public policy grounds of derogation. In her opinion in this case, Advocate-General Stickx-Hackl emphasised, the importance of the protection of human dignity, and suggested that public policy should be interpreted in the light of the Community law requirement that human dignity should be protected. Nonetheless, this still leaves human rights protection with the status of an exception to EC Treaty freedoms rather than constraining the scope of those rights in the first palce.

6.9.3 State acting as agent

When Member States implement Community rules, either by legislative act or as administrators for the Community, they must not infringe fundamental rights. National rules may be challenged on this basis: for example, in *Commission v Germany* (case 249/86), the Commission challenged Germany's rules enforcing Regulation 1612/86 which permitted the family of a migrant worker to install themselves with the worker in a host country provided that the worker has housing available for the family of a standard comparable with that of similarly employed national workers. Germany enforced this in such a way as to make the residence permit of the family conditional on the existence of appropriate housing for the duration of the stay. The ECJ interpreted the regulation as requiring this only in respect of the beginning of their period of residence. Since the regulation had to be interpreted in the light of Article 8 ECHR concerning respect for family life, a fundamental principle recognised by Community law, German law was incompatible with Community law. When Member States are implementing obligations contained in Community law, they must do so without offending against any fundamental rights recognised by the Community. In *Wachauf v Germany* (case 5/88)) the ECJ held that:

> Since those requirements are also binding on the Member States when they implement Community rules, the Member States must, as far as possible, apply those rules in accordance with those requirements (para. 19).

6.9.4 Scope of Community law

In all three situations listed above, general principles have an impact because the situations fall *within the scope* of Community law. The ECJ has no power to examine the compatibility with the ECHR of national rules which do not fall therein (*Cinéthèque SA* v *Fédération Nationale des Cinémas Françaises* (cases 60 & 61/84), noting the different approach of Advocate-General and Court, and contrast *Karner* (case C–71/02)). The problem lies in defining the boundary between Community law and purely domestic law, as can be seen in, for example, *Karner*. The scope of Community law could be construed very widely, as evidenced by the approach of the Advocate-General in *Konstantinidis* v *Stadt Altensteig-Standesamt* (case C–168/91). As noted above, he suggested that, as the applicant had exercised his right of free movement under Article 43 (ex 52) EC, national provisions affecting him fell within the scope of Community law; therefore he was entitled to the protection of his human rights by the ECJ. The Court has not expressly gone this far although some of the citizenship cases can be seen in this light (see *Garcia Avello* (case C–148/02), *Carpenter* (case C–60/00), *Chen* (case C–200/02)).

One particular problem area is where an individual seeks to extend the nature of the fundamental principles recognised in his or her home state by reference to rights protected in other Member States and recognised as such by the ECJ. This can be illustrated by contrasting two cases which arose out of similar circumstances: *Wachauf* v *Germany* (case 5/88) and *R* v *Ministry of Agriculture, Fisheries and Food, ex parte Bostock* (case C–2/93).

Wachauf was a tenant farmer who, upon the expiry of his tenancy, requested compensation arising out of the loss of 'reference quantities' on the discontinuance of milk production. When this was refused, he claimed that this was an infringement of his right to private property, protected under the German constitution. The German authorities claimed that the rules they applied were required by the Community regulation, but the ECJ held that on its proper interpretation the regulation required no such thing: although the regulation did not itself provide the right to compensation, equally it did not preclude it. The discretion thereby given to the Member States by the regulation should be exercised in accordance with fundamental rights, thus, in practice meaning that the applicant should receive the compensation.

Bostock, similarly, had been a tenant farmer. Following *Wachauf* (case 5/88) he argued that he too should be entitled to compensation for the value of the reference quantities on the expiry of his lease. Unlike the situation in Germany, though, this right was not protected by British law at the time when Bostock's lease ended. Bostock therefore sought to challenge that British law on the basis that the provisions breached general principles of non-discrimination and unjust enrichment. Despite its approach in *Wachauf*, the ECJ ruled that the right to property protected by the Community legal order did not include the right to dispose of the 'reference quantities' for profit. The ECJ held that the question of unjust enrichment, as part of the legal relations between lessor and lessee, was a matter for national law and therefore fell outside the scope of Community law.

It is difficult to reconcile these two cases if one accepts that general principles accepted by the ECJ should apply across the EU. From recent case law we can still see differences in the approach to the scope of rights deemed worthy of protection. In *Omega Spielhallen* (case C–36/02), the German authorities sought to prevent a laserdome game operating on the basis that a game based on shooting people infringed respect for human dignity; no such problem arose in the UK where the game operator originated. One clear message seems to be that there are limits to the circumstances when general principles will operate and that a challenge to national acts for breach of a general principle is likely to be successful only when national authorities are giving effect to clear obligations of *Community* law. In matters falling within the discretion of Member States, national authorities are not required to recognise general principles not protected by that State's national laws.

6.10 Conclusions

This chapter illustrates the importance of general principles of law in the judicial protection of individual rights. Member States' commitment to fundamental human rights has now been acknowledged in Article 6 TEU. Nonetheless, certain points should be noted.

The fact that a particular principle is upheld by the ECJ and appears to be breached does not automatically lead to a decision in favour of the claimant. Fundamental rights are not absolute rights. As the Court pointed out in *J. Nold KG v Commission* (case 4/73), rights of this nature are always subject to limitations laid down in the public interest, and, in the Community context, limits justified by the overall objectives of the Community (e.g., *O'Dwyer v Council* (cases T–466, 469, 473–4 & 477/93)). The pursuit of these objectives can result in some hard decisions (e.g., *Dowling v Ireland* (case C–85/90)), although the Court has held that it may not constitute a 'disproportionate and intolerable interference, impairing the very substance of those rights' (*Wachauf* (case 5/88) at para. 18). This principle was applied in *Germany v Commission (Re Banana Regime)* (case C–280/93), para. 78, another harsh decision.

Thus, where the objectives are seen from the Community standpoint to be essential, individual rights must yield to the common good. In *J. Nold KG v Commission* the system set up under an ECSC provision whereby Nold, as a small-scale wholesaler, would be deprived of the opportunity, previously enjoyed, to buy direct from the producer, to its commercial disadvantage, was held to be necessary in the light of the system's overall economic objectives. 'The disadvantages claimed by the applicant', held the Court, 'are in fact the result of economic change and not of the contested Decision'.

A similar example is provided in *Walter Rau Lebensmittelwerke v Commission* (case 279, 280, 285 & 286/84). Here the claimants were a group of margarine producers. They were seeking damages for losses suffered as a result of the Commission's 'Christmas butter' policy. This was an attempt to reduce the 'butter mountain' (surplus stocks acquired as a result of the Community's system of intervention buying under the common agricultural policy (CAP)) by selling butter stocks at greatly reduced prices to certain groups of the population over the Christmas period. As a basis for their claim the claimants alleged that the regulations implementing the Christmas butter policy were in breach of the principles of equality and proportionality. Since margarine and butter are clearly in competition with each other it might have been imagined that, following the first isoglucose cases (e.g., *Royal Scholten-Honig Holdings Ltd v Intervention Board for Agricultural Produce* (cases 103 & 145/77), they had a good chance of success. But they failed. The Court held that the measure must be assessed with regard to the general objectives of the organisation of the butter market:

> taking into consideration the objective differences which characterised the legal mech-
> anisms and the economic conditions of the market concerned, the producers of milk and
> butter on the one hand and the producers of oils and fats and margarine manufacturers
> on the other, are not in comparable situations.

The measures were no more than was necessary to achieve the desired objective.

This latitude shown to the Community institutions, particularly where they are exercising discretionary powers in pursuit of common Community policies (most notably the CAP) does not always extend to Member States in their implementation of Community law. Where Member States are permitted a certain discretion in implementation (and Member States have little discretion as regards the ends to be achieved), the Court will not substitute its own evaluation for that of the Member State: it will restrict itself solely to the question of whether there was a patent error in the Member State's action (*R v Minister of Agriculture, Fisheries and Food, ex parte National Federation of Fishermen's Organisations* (case C–44/94)). Otherwise, general principles of law are strictly enforced. Thus under the guise of the protection of individual rights general principles of law also serve as a useful (and concealed) instrument of policy.

The adoption of the Charter of Fundamental Rights marks a significant further step. Although little more than a summary of the current level of protection recognised by the Community, it may evolve into a legally binding instrument which reaches beyond fundamental human rights to include employment and social rights. Nonetheless difficulties remain with its relationship with the ECHR, a convention to which the Union, it now seems, is intended to accede. Of crucial significance in the successful and equal protection of individuals' rights is the relationship between the European Court of Human Rights and both the CFI and, most importantly, the ECJ. This issue has yet to be fully resolved.

FURTHER READING

Alston, P., *The EU and Human Rights* (OUP, 1999).

Ashiagbor, D., 'Economic and Social Rights in the European Charter of Fundamental Rights' (2004) 1 EHRLR 62.

Canor, I., '*Primus inter pares*. Who is the Ultimate Guardian of Fundamental Rights in Europe?' (2000) 25 EL Rev 57.

Council of the EU, *Charter of Fundamental Rights of the European Union – Explanations relating to the complete text of the Charter* (Office for Official Publications of the European Communities, 2001).

De Burca, G., 'Fundamental Human Rights and the Reach of EC Law' (1993) 13 Oxford J Legal Stud 283.

Jowell, J. and Lester, A., 'Beyond *Wednesbury*: Substantive Principles of Administrative Law' [1987] PL 368.

Knook, A., 'The Court, the Charter, and the Vertical Division of Powers in the European Union' (2005) 42(2) CML Rev 367.

Krogsgaard, L., 'Fundamental Rights in the EC after Maastricht' [1993] LIEI 99.

Liisberg, J., 'Does the EU Charter of Fundamental Rights Threaten the Supremacy of Community Law?' (2001) 38 CML Rev 1171.

Mancini, G. F., 'The Making of a Constitution for Europe' (1989) 26 CML Rev 594.

McGoldrick, D., 'The European Union after Amsterdam: An Organisation with General Human Rights Competence' in O'Keeffe, D. and Twomey, P. (eds), *Legal Issues of the Amsterdam Treaty* (Hart Publishing, 1999).

Mendelson, M., 'The European Court of Justice and Human Rights' (1981) 1 YEL 126.

Ortega, L., 'Fundamental Rights in the European Constitution' (2005) 11(3) EPL 363.

Riley, A., '*Saunders* and the Power to Obtain Information in European Community and United Kingdom Competition Law' (2000) 25 EL Rev 264.

Schermers, H., 'The European Community Bound by Fundamental Human Rights' (1990) 27 CML Rev 249.

Schermers, H., 'The Scales in Balance: National Constitutional Court v Court of Justice' (1990) 27 CML Rev 97.

Schermers, H. G., *The Protection of Human Rights in the European Community* (Zentrum für Europäisches Wirtschaftsrecht, Vorträge und Berichte 36) (1994).

Schwarze, J., 'Tendencies towards a Common Administrative Law in Europe' (1991) 16 EL Rev 3.

Sharpston, E., 'Legitimate Expectations and Economic Reality' (1990) 15 EL Rev 103.

Twomey, P., 'The European Union: Three Pillars without a Human Rights Foundation' in O'Keeffe, D., and Twomey, P. (eds), *Legal Issues of the Maastricht Treaty* (Chancery Publications, 1993).

Usher, J. A., *General Principles of EC Law* (Longmans, 1998).

Weiler, J., 'Eurocracy and Distrust: Some Questions Concerning the Role of the European Court of Justice in the Protection of Fundamental Human Rights within the Legal Order of the European Communities' (1986) 61 Wash L Rev 1103.

Weiler, J. H. H., 'Fundamental Rights and Fundamental Boundaries: on Standards and Values in the Protection of Human Rights' in Neuwahl, N. A., *The European Union and Rights* (1995).

Weiler, J. H. H., and Lockhart, N. J. S., ' "Taking Rights Seriously" Seriously?' (1995) 32 CML Rev 51, 579.

Woods, L., 'Freedom of Expression in the EU' (2006) June, EPL, forthcoming.

PART II

PART II

7

Overview of the jurisdiction of the European Courts

7.1 Introduction

The discussion in Part Three, which by no means covers the whole range of Community law, illustrates the extent to which EC law permeates our lives. In addition to the law stemming from the Treaty, a wealth of secondary legislation has been, and is in the constant process of being, enacted, covering a wide and ever-increasing range of activities. Much of this law is directly effective (see Chapter 5), and will, under the principle of primacy of EC law (see Chapter 4), take precedence over any conflicting rules of national law. It thus forms an important source of *rights* and *obligations* for both States and individuals.

An effective system of enforcement requires that the rights arising under EC law may be enforced against three groups of people:

(a) *The institutions of the Community*, who in their law-making or administrative capacity may have acted or failed to act in breach of EC law.

(b) *Member States*, which in carrying out or failing to carry out their obligations under the Treaty or secondary legislation may have acted in breach of EC law.

(c) *Individuals*, who in failing to comply with their obligations under the Treaty or secondary legislation may have acted in breach of EC law.

The EC Treaty itself provides an extensive range of remedies. It provides, by way of *direct* action before the European Courts (ECJ and CFI), for actions against the institutions of the Community and against Member States. Community secondary legislation may be challenged *indirectly* before the courts of Member States, and questions of validity referred to the ECJ under Article 234 (ex 177) EC (Chapter 9). Chapters 11–13 are concerned primarily with the means whereby States, and sometimes individuals, may challenge the institutions *directly* before the European Courts. The European Courts have no jurisdiction over acts of the European Council (*Roujansky* v *Council* (case T–584/93)). Following the transfer by the ToA (new Article 46 TEU) to the EC Treaty (new Title IV) of matters within the third pillar of the TEU relating to visas, asylum, immigration and judicial cooperation in civil affairs, the ECJ has assumed a limited jurisdiction over these matters (Article 68 EC), as well as over framework decisions and decisions concerning police and judicial cooperation in criminal matters remaining within the third pillar of the TEU, subject to agreement, both as to the jurisdiction itself and its extent, by individual Member States (new Article 35 TEU). The ToA also gave the Court jurisdiction over the new 'flexibility' clauses providing for 'closer cooperation' agreements to be established under the new Articles 11 EC and 40 TEU and, for the first time, express power to rule on the conformity of action of the EC institutions with fundamental human rights in those areas where the Court has jurisdiction under the EU Treaties (new Article 46(1)(d) TEU). Matters within the second pillar of the TEU (Foreign and Security Policy) remain wholly outside the jurisdiction of the ECJ.

7.2 Action before the European Courts

7.2.1 Actions against the institutions of the Community

These comprise actions:

(a) for judicial review, in the form of actions to 'review the legality of acts of the Council and the Commission other than recommendations or opinions' (Article 230 (ex 173), the 'annulment action', and Article 241 (ex 184), the 'plea of illegality'), and an action for 'failure to act' (Article 232 (ex 175));

(b) for damages (Articles 235 and 288(2) (ex 178 and 215(2)); and

(c) in respect of disputes between the Community and its servants ('staff cases' Article 236 (ex 179)).

7.2.1.1 *Significance of judicial review*

There are two ways in which control over the institutions needs to be exercised. First, it is necessary to ensure that the legislation issued by the institutions is valid; i.e., that the institution has the power to issue the act concerned, that it has been passed according to the correct procedures, and exercised for the right purposes. This constitutes a check on the institutions' *activities*. This is provided under Article 230, and, as an adjunct to that Article, Article 241. Article 234 also provides for the possibility of a similar review via the national courts and preliminary ruling mechanism, discussed further below. Secondly, there is a need to check on the institutions' *inactivity* – to ensure that the institutions do not fail to act when they are under a legal duty to do so. This is provided by Article 232.

Judicial review under Articles 230 and 232 requires an examination of three separate questions. First there is the question of *locus standi*: does this applicant have the right, personally, to bring proceedings? Secondly, has he brought his action in time? These two questions relate to admissibility. And thirdly, if the first questions are answered in the affirmative, is he entitled to succeed on the merits?

7.2.1.2 *Jurisdiction of the CFI*

All claims by natural and legal persons under (a) and (b), including the areas introduced in Regulation 139/2004 (control of concentrations between undertakings), Regulation 40/94 (Community trade mark, as amended) and Regulation 2100/94 (Community plant variety rights) are now dealt with by the Court of First Instance (CFI), with a right of appeal to the ECJ (Article 225 (ex 168a) EC). Claims under (c) are now within the jurisdiction of the Civil Service Tribunal, which is attached to the CFI (see 2.9.4). The CFI also has jurisdiction to hear and determine actions brought by natural and legal persons relating to the European Central

Bank (see Council Decisions 93/350 ([1993] OJ L144/21) and 94/149 ([1994] OJ L66/29)).

Following the Treaty of Nice, the jurisdiction of the CFI was changed. It retains the right to hear direct actions, but the amended Article 225 introduces the possibility of some specialist areas being referred to judicial panels, with the CFI hearing appeals from the decisions of those panels. As noted at 2.9.4, the first such panel is the Civil Service Tribunal. The precise boundary between the jurisdiction of these panels, the CFI and the ECJ is to be determined in the Statute of the Court of Justice. As part of the Convention on the Future of Europe and as required by Declaration 12 of the Nice Summit, a proposal was put forward drawing the boundaries between the various judicial bodies to jurisdiction in relation to actions brought under Articles 230 and 232 EC. The Constitution, should it come into force, expressly refers to the possibility of specialist courts.

7.2.1.3 Appeals to the ECJ in judicial review cases

Appeal is limited to points of law and must be based on the grounds of lack of competence of the CFI, breach of procedure before it which adversely affects the interests of the appellant, or infringement of Community law by the CFI (Article 58 of the Statutes of the Court of Justice). An appeal must contain the pleas in law and legal arguments relied on. It must indicate precisely the contested elements of the judgment which the appellant seeks to have set aside and also the legal arguments specifically advanced in support of the appeal. That requirement is not satisfied by an appeal confined to repeating the pleas and arguments previously submitted to the CFI. Such an approach would constitute no more than a re-examination by the ECJ of the application submitted to the CFI. The ECJ has no jurisdiction to do this.

In *John Deere* (case C–7/95P), on appeal from a judgment of the CFI, the ECJ started by referring to Article 255 (ex 168a) EC and what was Article 51 (now 58) of the EC Statute of the Court of Justice, which then stated that an appeal is to be limited to points of law and must be based on the grounds of lack of competence of the CFI, breach of procedure before the CFI which adversely affects the interests of the appellant, or infringement of Community law by the CFI. Furthermore, what remains Article 112(1)(c) in the current version of the Court's Rules of Procedure provided that an appeal must contain the pleas in law and the legal arguments relied on in the appeal; this means that an appeal must indicate *precisely* the contested elements of the judgment which the appellant seeks to have set aside, and also the legal arguments *specifically* advanced in support of the appeal. The ECJ also commented that this requirement, 'is not satisfied by an appeal confined to repeating or reproducing word for word pleas in law and arguments previously submitted to the Court of First Instance, including those based on facts expressly rejected by that court'.

The ECJ also has no jurisdiction to establish facts of examined evidence. The appraisal by the CFI of the evidence does not constitute a point of law which is subject to review by the ECJ, unless the evidence has been fundamentally misconstrued (see *John Deere v Commission* (case C–7/95P) and also *Hilti v Commission* (case C–53/92P), para. 42). After a period when the ECJ seemed to dispose of appeals from the CFI on matters of intellectual property law on the facts, as can be seen in *Baby Dry* (Case C–383/99 P), the ECJ has reverted to this approach. In *DKV Deutsche Krankenversicherung AG v OHIM* (case C–104/00 P), the ECJ held that the CFI has exclusive jurisdiction to find the facts and to appraise them. That assessment of the facts cannot be reviewed unless 'the clear sense of the evidence before it has been distorted' (para. 22). Coming to the same conclusion, the Advocate-General in this case suggested that the role of the ECJ as 'highest interpreter of the law' was to 'lay down principles of general application' (Opinion, para. 59).

These requirements clearly limit the scope for potential appeals; this does not, however, seem to have stopped some applicants from trying, especially in the competition field. Although the ECJ will refuse jurisdiction, these cases still impact on the ECJ's workload as in each case it still has to investigate the issue of the appeal's admissibility.

In addition to appeals made by the parties, where the CFI is hearing an appeal from a judicial panel within the terms of Article 225(2), and the First Advocate General (appointed in accordance with Article 10 of the Court's Rules of Procedure) considers that there is a serious risk of the unity or consistency of Community law being affected by that case, he may propose that the ECJ review the decision of the CFI. That proposal must be made within one month of the delivery of the CFI's judgment and the ECJ then has a further month in which to decide whether or not the decision should be reviewed (Article 62 of the Statute of the Court of Justice).

7.2.2 Actions against Member States

These comprise:

(a) action by the Commission against a Member State for failure 'to fulfil an obligation under this Treaty' (Article 226 (ex 169) EC);

(b) action by a Member State against another Member State for failure 'to fulfil an obligation under this Treaty' (Article 227 (ex 170) EC);

(c) action by the Commission against a Member State, via accelerated procedures similar to those provided under Article 226 (ex 169), for breach of its obligation to notify the Commission under Article 88(2)(b) (ex 93(2)(b)) (State aids) and Article 95(4) (ex 100a(4)) (unilateral restrictions on free movement of goods);

(d) similar accelerated proceedings brought by the Commission under Article 298 (ex 225) where emergency measures taken by Member States under Articles 272 (ex 203) (to protect essential security interests) and 272 (ex 204) (in the event of serious internal disturbances) distort conditions of competition within the Community.

These actions are brought directly before the ECJ. Note that indirect challenges to Member States' actions or inaction can be brought using the preliminary reference procedure. Although the ECJ is involved in such procedures the action is commenced in the national courts and discussed below.

7.2.2.1 *Right to intervene*
Member States and Community institutions have a right to intervene in cases before the Court. This right is also open to any other person establishing an interest in the result of any case submitted to the Court, except in cases between institutions of the Community or between Member States and institutions of the Community.

In *British Coal Corporation* v *Commission* (case T–367/94), a case based on the parallel provisions of the statutes of the ECSC, the Court held that an applicant must establish a 'direct, existing interest in the grant by the Court of the order as sought and not purely an interest in relation to the plea in law advanced'. The fact that representative associations have a right to intervene in order to protect their members in cases raising questions of principle liable to affect those members cannot be relied on in support of an individual application to intervene (see also *Dorsch Consult Ingenieurgesellschaft mbH* v *Council & Commission* (case T–184/95)).

7.2.2.2 Interim relief

Although actions before the Courts do not have suspensory effect the Courts may, 'if [they] consider that the circumstances so require it, order that the application of the contested act be suspended' (Article 242 (ex 185)). They may also order 'any necessary interim measures in any of the above proceedings' (Article 243 (ex 186)). However, action under Article 242 is admissible only if the applicant is challenging that measure 'in proceedings before the Court'. Similarly action under Article 243 will be admitted only if it is made 'by a party to the case before the Court and relates to that case'. Interim measures may not be ordered 'unless there are circumstances giving rise to urgency and factual and legal grounds establishing a prima facie case for the measures applied for'. The urgency of the application will be assessed according to the necessity for such an order in order to prevent serious and irreparable damage. Parties wishing to establish the existence of 'serious and irreparable damage' for the purpose of obtaining the suspension of a Community act must provide documentary evidence both as regards the specific damage suffered or likely to be suffered and the causative link between that damage and the contested act (*Descom Scales Manufacturing Co. Ltd* v *Council* (case C–6/94R), application for suspension of anti-dumping regulation rejected for lack of evidence). Purely financial damage cannot in principle be regarded as irreparable (*Cargill* v *Commission* (case 229/88R)). The interim measures requested must be of such a nature as to prevent the alleged damage (*Commission* v *United Kingdom (Re Merchant Shipping Rules)* (case 246/89R)). In such proceedings relief can be very speedy. In *Commission* v *Ireland (Re Dundalk Water Scheme)* (case 45/87R) an interim injunction was granted *ex parte* within three days of application.

The case of *Antonissen* (case C–393/96 P/R) concerned a claim for an interim award of damages. The case came on appeal to the President of the ECJ from the President of the CFI, who had rejected the applicant's request. The applicant sought provisional damages, pending a final ruling in a claim for compensation against the Community. The applicant, a dairy farmer, had been refused a milk quota on the basis of an allegedly invalid EC regulation. As a result he had received a request for payment of a substantial supplementary levy, threatening to cause him severe financial distress. The President of the ECJ allowed his appeal. He held that if an interim order is justified, prima facie, in law and in fact, and it is urgent, in order to avoid serious and irreparable damage, it must be made before a decision is reached in the main proceedings. An absolute prohibition on obtaining, in interim proceedings, part of the compensation claimed in the main proceedings, and seeking to protect the applicant's interest, would not be compatible with the individual's right to effective judicial protection. Such payment may be necessary to ensure the practical effect of the judgment in the main application. However, before ordering such payment the Court must examine the applicant's assets to assess whether it would be possible to recover any payment by way of advance when the final judgment is delivered. Recourse to such a remedy must be restricted to situations in which the prima facie case is strong and the urgency is undeniable.

7.2.3 Action against individuals

There is no provision in the EC Treaty for direct action before the ECJ *against individuals*. Individuals may, however, be vulnerable to fines and penalties under EC secondary legislation (e.g., Regulation 17/62, now Regulation 1/2003 see Chapter 29), which may be challenged before the CFI. Under Article 229 the ECJ has unlimited jurisdiction in regard to the penalties provided in such regulations.

7.3 Action before national courts

7.3.1 Basic principles

In addition to these direct remedies before the European Courts, questions of infringement of EC law by Community institutions and Member States may also be raised before national courts. In describing regulations as 'directly applicable' (Article 249 (ex 189) EC) and in providing a means whereby national courts might refer questions of interpretation and validity of EC law to the ECJ (Article 234 EC) the Treaty clearly envisaged a role for national courts in the enforcement of EC law. This role has been greatly enlarged by the development by the ECJ of the principle of direct effects and, more recently, the principles of indirect effects and State liability under *Francovich* v *Italy* (cases C–6 & 9/90) (see Chapters 5 and 8). A ruling on the interpretation of Community law may reveal that a national law or practice is inconsistent with Community law; a ruling that a provision of an EC regulation, or a directive or a decision is invalid renders it unenforceable against the individual concerned. In both cases it may provide the basis for a claim in damages.

7.3.2 Significance of actions before national courts

This possibility of an alternative remedy via their national courts is of particular importance for individuals, since they have no *locus standi* to bring a direct action before the ECJ in respect of infringements of EC law by Member States, nor any power to compel the Commission to bring such an action (see *Alfons Lütticke GmbH* v *Commission* (case 48/65), Chapters 11 and 12). Also their *locus standi* in direct actions against the EC institutions for judicial review is limited. Moreover, national courts remain the only forums in which action can be brought *by* individuals in respect of infringements of EC law *against* individuals. EC law may be invoked as a defence to a criminal charge (e.g., *Ratti* (case 148/78)) or to resist payment of a charge exacted, or support a claim for the return of money withheld, in breach of EC law (e.g., *Van Gend en Loos* (case 26/62)). It may provide a basis for an injunction, to prevent or put an end to action in breach of EC law (e.g., *Garden Cottage Foods Ltd* v *Milk Marketing Board* [1982] QB 1114, Court of Appeal; [1984] AC 130,

House of Lords) or a declaration, e.g., that a particular national measure is illegal, being based on an invalid EC regulation (e.g., *Royal Scholten-Honig* v *Intervention Board for Agricultural Produce* (cases 103 & 145/77)). It may also provide the basis for a claim in damages, either on the principles of direct or indirect effect, against parties acting in breach of substantive provisions of EC law, or, under *Francovich* v *Italy* (cases C–6 & 9/90), against the State itself for its failure to comply with its obligation under Article 10 (ex 5) EC to 'take all appropriate measures . . . to ensure fulfilment of the obligations arising out of this Treaty or resulting from action taken by the institutions of the Community'. Thus acts of Member States or of Community institutions which are illegal under EC law may be challenged, and remedies provided. While the illegal acts are not set aside as a result of the action, they cannot be enforced.

7.3.3 **Remedies in national courts**

Where individuals seek to assert their Community rights before national courts or tribunals, they may do so in the context of any proceedings of national law, public or private, in which EC rights are relevant, in pursuit of any remedy, interim or final, available under national law. The issue of remedies is discussed in Chapter 8.

7.3.4 **Jurisdiction of the European Courts to give preliminary rulings**

To assist national courts in their task of enforcing EC law, Article 234 gives the ECJ jurisdiction to give preliminary rulings concerning the interpretation of EC law and the validity of acts of the institutions of the Community at the request of national courts. Originally, only the ECJ had the power to give preliminary rulings, but following Nice, some part of this jurisdiction will fall to the CFI. According to Article 225(3), even within these limits, there will be the possibility of review of the CFI's decisions by the ECJ. Article 225(3) specifies, however, that such review will occur only in exceptional circumstances. The procedure seems not to be an appeals procedure. According to Article 62 of the Statute of the Court of Justice, the decision as to whether review is necessary is to be made by the First Advocate-General of the Court of Justice, not the parties to the case.

Although the ECJ has no power to *decide* the issue before the national court, an interpretation on the matter of Community law involved, or on the validity of the act in question, will normally be sufficient to establish whether an infringement of EC law has occurred. On this basis the national court may then supply the appropriate remedy. As noted above, the Court's jurisdiction to rule on these matters has been extended by the incorporation into the EC Treaty of areas previously governed by the TEU, and by a new jurisdiction over parts of the third pillar (police and judicial cooperation in criminal matters) remaining within the TEU, in provisions analogous to Article 234. Regrettably, these provisions are more limited in scope than Article 234 and, in allowing Member States a choice as to the extent and even the possibility of access to the ECJ, seriously undermine the uniformity of judicial protection for individuals under EU law (see further Chapter 11).

7.4 **Conclusions**

The role played by the ECJ in securing the enforcement of Community law against both EC institutions and Member States cannot be overstated. Recognising and respecting the limitations of the remedies provided under the EC Treaty, it has provided, via the principles of direct effect, indirect effect, and State liability in damages, an extremely effective alternative means of enforcement of Community law by individuals, within the courts of Member States. It has insisted on the effective protection of individuals' Community rights by these courts, even when the rights have not been expressly, or even impliedly, granted to individuals. This principle of effective judicial protection has revealed the deficiencies in national legal systems and extended the scope of legal protection of individuals in matters of Community law. This has spilt, and will continue to spill over into domestic law, raising the standard of judicial protection in matters of purely national law: national courts are rightly reluctant to apply a double standard. This process has resulted in some harmonisation of remedies in the legal systems of Member States.

In contrast, the approach of the ECJ and CFI regarding challenges to the actions of the institutions, especially where the challenge comes from a non-privileged applicant, fails to protect the interests of the individual adequately. As discussed in Chapter 28, the narrow view of *locus standi* for non-privileged applicants taken by the European courts has given rise to some adverse criticism. It has made the possibility of challenging the validity of EC measures via national courts and the preliminary ruling mechanism particularly important. The jurisdiction of the Courts in the context of judicial review remains important, as it is one mechanism by which the institutional balance of the Union is maintained.

FURTHER READING

Albors-Llorens, A., 'Changes in the Jurisdiction of the European Court of Justice under the Treaty of Amsterdam' (1998) 35 CML Rev 1273.

Caranta, R., 'Judicial Protection against Member States: a new Jus Commune takes shape' (1995) 32 CML Rev 679.

Eeckhaut, P. 'The European Courts after Nice' in Andenas and Usher (eds) *The Treaty of Nice and Beyond: Enlargement and Constitutional Reform* (Hart Publishing, 2003).

Fennelly, N., 'The Area of Freedom, Security and Justice and the European Court of Justice' (2000) 46 ICLQ 941.

Garbagnati Ketvel, M-G., 'The Jurisdiction of the European Court of Justice in Respect of the Common Foreign and Security Policy' (2006) 5 ICLQ 77.

Jacque, J. P., and Weiler, J., 'On the Road to European Union: A New Judicial Architecture: An Agenda for the Intergovernmental Conference' (1990) 27 CML Rev 185.

Lang, J.T., 'The Duties of National Authorities under Community Law' (1998) 23 EL Rev 109.

8

State liability and remedies in national courts

8.1 Introduction

The preceding chapters have identified that the ECJ, relying to a significant extent on the need to make EC law effective, extended the possible mechanisms by which individuals could seek access to rights derived from EC law in their national courts. Perhaps the most significant development in this area over the past 25 years has been the creation and development of the principle of State liability under *Francovich* (cases C–6 & 9/90). A logical development of the notion of direct effect, it can enable an individual, before his national court, to seek a remedy for losses suffered as a result of the failure by a Member State to implement, or apply correctly, provisions of EC law.

But State liability is not the only area in respect of which EC law imposes particular obligations on the national legal systems. *Francovich* and subsequent cases are concerned with a failure to give effect to individual rights in domestic law. But even where such rights have been properly enacted, there may be problems. As the ECJ itself noted, however, extending access to substantive rights means nothing unless it is possible, in procedural terms, to access the national court system to obtain a remedy for any violation of those substantive rights. In *Heylens* (case 222/86), the Court stated:

> since free access to employment is a fundamental right which the Treaty confers individually on each worker in the Community, the existence of a remedy of a judicial nature against any decision of a national authority refusing the benefit of that right is essential in order to secure for the individual effective protection for his right (para. 14).

Rules relating to *locus standi*, periods of limitation and quantum of damages can all have an effect on whether it would be possible to bring an action and if any such action would, in practice, be worth bringing before the national courts. The EC Treaty is, however, silent on the issue of such procedural rules and it has fallen to the Court to develop the law in this area.

This chapter first discusses the principle of State liability. It then outlines the ECJ's relevant jurisprudence and identifies how the ECJ has developed the principles of 'equivalence' and 'effectiveness' – key concepts underlying the Court's approach to procedure and remedies – to limit the scope of what might be termed 'national procedural autonomy'. In so doing, we will identify a trend in the ECJ's rulings: first to limit the freedom of national legal systems and then to respect their autonomy.

Against this background, one particular issue should be addressed: to what extent does EC law require the creation of new remedies for EC law rights?

8.2 Principle of State liability under *Francovich* v *Italy*

8.2.1 The *Francovich* ruling

The shortcomings of the principles of direct and indirect effects, particularly in the context of enforcement of directives, as outlined in Chapter 5, led the Court to develop a third and separate principle in *Francovich* v *Italy* (cases C–6 & 9/90), the principle of State liability. Here the claimants, a group of ex-employees, were seeking arrears of wages following their employers' insolvency. Their claim (like that in the subsequent case of *Wagner Miret* (case C–334/92)) was based on Directive 80/987, which required Member States, *inter alia*, to provide for a guarantee fund to ensure the payment of employees' arrears of wages in the event of their employers' insolvency. Since a claim against their former employers would have been fruitless (they being insolvent and 'private' parties), they brought their claim for compensation against the State. There were two aspects to their claim. The first was based on the State's breach of the claimants' (alleged) substantive rights contained in the directive, which they claimed were directly effective. The second was based on the State's primary failure to implement the directive, as it was required to do under Article 249 (ex 189) and Article 10 (ex 5) of the EC Treaty. The Court had already held, in Article 226 (ex 173) proceedings, that Italy was in breach of its Community obligations in failing to implement the directive (*Commission* v *Italy* (case 22/87)).

With regard to the first claim, the Court found that the provisions in question were not sufficiently clear, precise and unconditional to be directly effective. Although the content of the right, and the class of intended beneficiaries, was clear, the State had a discretion as to the appointment of the guarantee institution; it would not necessarily itself be liable under the directive. The claimants were, however, entitled in principle to succeed in their second claim. The Court held that where, as here, a State had failed to implement an EC directive it would be obliged to compensate individuals for damage suffered as a result of its failure to implement the directive if certain conditions were satisfied. That is, where:

(a) the directive involved rights conferred on individuals;
(b) the content of those rights could be identified on the basis of the provisions of the directive, and
(c) there was a causal link between the State's failure and the damage suffered by the persons affected.

The Court's reasoning was based on the Member States' obligation to implement directives under Article 249 and their general obligation under Article 10 EC to 'take all appropriate measures . . . to ensure fulfilment of' their obligations under Community law; on its jurisprudence in *Van Gend en Loos* (case 26/62) and *Costa* v *ENEL* (case 6/64) that certain provisions of EC law are intended to give rise to rights for individuals, and that national courts are obliged to provide effective protection for those rights, as established in *Amministrazione delle Finanze dello Stato* v *Simmenthal SpA* (case 106/77) and *Factortame* (case C–213/89), see further Chapter 4). It concluded that 'a principle of State liability for damage to individuals caused by a breach of Community law for which it is responsible is inherent in the scheme of the Treaty'.

Thus, where the three conditions of *Francovich* are fulfilled, individuals seeking compensation as a result of activities and practices which are inconsistent with EC directives may proceed directly against the State. There will be no need to rely on the principles of direct or indirect effects. Responsibility for the non-implementation of the directive will be placed not on the employer, 'public' or 'private', but squarely on the shoulders of the State, arguably, where it should always have been. Rather than changing the law, it provides compensation for a Member State's failure to do so.

8.2.2 Scope of the principle

The reasoning in *Francovich* is compelling; its implications for Member States, however, remained unclear. Although expressed in terms of a State's liability for the non-implementation of a directive, *Francovich* appeared to lay down a wider principle of liability for all breaches of Community law 'for which the State is responsible'. Would it then apply to legislative or administrative acts and omissions in breach of Treaty articles or other provisions of EC law? Would it be an additional remedy, or available only in the absence of other remedies based on direct or indirect effects? Apart from the three conditions for liability, which are themselves open to interpretation, what other conditions would have to be fulfilled? Would liability be strict or dependent on culpability, even serious culpability, as was the case with actions for damages against Community institutions under Article 288 (2) (ex 215(2)) (see Chapter 13)? In the case of non-implementation of directives, as in *Francovich* itself, the State's failure is clear; *a fortiori* when established by the Court under Article 226. But in cases of faulty or inadequate implementation it is not. The State's 'failure' may only become apparent following an interpretation of the directive by the Court (see, e.g., the sex discrimination cases such as *Marshall* and *Barber*, see Chapter 25). Here the case for imposing liability in damages on the State is less convincing.

8.2.2.1 *Type of action*

Many of these questions were referred to the Court of Justice for interpretation in *Brasserie du Pêcheur SA* v *Germany* and *R* v *Secretary of State for Transport, ex parte Factortame* (cases C–46 & 48/93). The Court held that the principle of State liability is not confined to a failure to implement EC directives; rather, *all* domestic acts and omissions, legislative, executive and judicial, in breach of Community law, can give rise to liability. Provided the conditions for liability are fulfilled it applies to breaches of *all* Community law, whether or not directly effective. However, arguing from the principles applicable to the Community's non-contractual liability under Article 288(2), the Court held that where a State is faced with situations involving choices comparable to those made by Community institutions when they adopt measures pursuant to a Community policy it will be liable only where three conditions are met (see paras 50 and 51 of the judgment):

(a) the rule of law infringed must be intended to confer rights on individuals;

(b) the breach must be sufficiently serious; and

(c) there must be a direct causal link between the breach of the obligation resting on the State and the damage sustained by the injured parties.

The 'decisive test' for whether a breach is sufficiently serious is whether the institution concerned has 'manifestly and gravely exceeded the limits of its discretion' (para. 55). The factors to be taken into account in assessing this question included:

> the clarity and precision of the rule breached, the measure of discretion left by that rule to the national or Community authorities, whether the infringement and the damage caused was intentional or voluntary, whether any error of law was excusable or inexcusable, the fact that the position taken by a Community institution may have contributed towards the omission, and the adoption or retention of national measures or practices contrary to Community law (para. 56).

8.2.2.2 For whose actions is the State liable?

One question left open by *Brasserie de Pêcheur* is for whose action a Member State can be liable. There can be little doubt as to the State's liability for actions taken by the government itself in the context of the obligation to implement EC measures. But what about other parts of the State? In *Haim* v *Kassenzahnartzliche Vereinigung Nordrhein* (case C–424/97) it was established that a legally independent body may be liable under *Francovich*, as well as the Member State itself. *Brasserie de Pêcheur* also suggested that there may be liability for judicial failures, which was controversial. However, in *Köbler* v *Austria* (case C–224/01), the ECJ confirmed that such liability may arise in particular circumstances. The case concerned the refusal by the Austrian Administrative Supreme Court (Verwaltungsgerichtshof) to grant Mr Köbler a 'length of service' increment on the basis that the payment would be a loyalty bonus, for which time spent in similar positions in other Member States could not be taken into account. This was a wrong interpretation of EC law and in direct conflict with an earlier ruling by the ECJ (*Schöning-Kougebetopoulou* (case C–15/96); see Chapter 20), and Mr Köbler therefore brought a new claim under *Francovich* for the failure of the Verwaltungsgerichtshof to apply EC law correctly.

The ECJ stated that, in international law, State liability can arise on the basis of acts by the legislature, executive and judiciary, and that the same must be true of EC law (para. 32). In addition, the principle of effectiveness (see 8.4.2., below) requires that there must be instances when a State will incur liability for actions by its courts which are in breach of EC law (para. 33). However, the ECJ limited this to instances where courts are adjudicating at the last instance (para. 33) and emphasised the mandatory jurisdiction of such a court under Article 234 to request a preliminary ruling on the interpretation of EC law (see Chapter 9). In order to ensure the effective protection of individual's rights under Community law, there has to be a possibility of claiming compensation for damage caused by an infringement of these rights by a court adjudicating at last instance (para. 36). Such an infringement must be manifest, and it is for the national legal system to designate the courts that would hear such claims.

This ruling, it is submitted, follows logically from the basic justification for State liability, and its restrictions to courts of last instance is entirely appropriate, because at that point, there would be no possibility of an appeal against a ruling which infringes an individual's Community rights. In order to avoid opening the flood-gates to claims of State liability, or Article 234 references, in such circumstances, the ECJ is at pains to emphasise that 'State liability for an infringement of Community law by a decision of a national court adjudicating at last instance can be incurred only in the exceptional case where the court has manifestly infringed the applicable law' (para. 53). Whether this will serve as an appropriate brake to such actions remains to be seen.

In coming to its conclusion, the Court had to deal with several fundamental objections. The first was that the principle of *'res judicata'* (finality of judgments) might be undermined by imposing liability on the State for a serious infringement of EC law. The Court, somewhat optimistically, stated that State liability in such circumstances would not affect the finality of the judgment at issue, especially because the parties to the State liability action would be different, and a finding of liability would not result in a revision of the original decision (para. 39). At a technical level, that may be correct, although it cannot be denied that the authority of the ruling in the original case would be undermined. Secondly, there was concern that the independence of the judiciary may be affected, and the authority of the court undermined, by the possibility of a State liability claim. This, too, was given short shrift by the Court, simply denying that there would be 'any particular risk to the independence' of the court concerned (para. 42), and that the possibility of a State liability action might be 'regarded as enhancing the quality of a legal system and . . . the authority of the judiciary' (para. 43). However, the Court did not expand on this in any detail, and its assertion remains somewhat unconvincing. Finally, there was concern as to whether there would be an appropriate domestic court which might hear a claim for State liability. In this regard, the ECJ referred back to established principles according to which it is for national legal systems to determine the appropriate court to hear such claims. That, however, does not solve the difficulties that may arise in practice. Presumably, a Member State found liable before a domestic court has a right of appeal. In the UK, this might produce the rather strange situation whereby the House of Lords might eventually be called upon to hear a case in State liability based on one of its own judgments. Whilst the basic outcome in *Köbler* therefore can be defended at a purely logical level, there are many practical difficulties which remain unresolved by this decision. As a final point, it may be noted that in *Köbler* itself, the ECJ thought that the breach by the Austrian Verwaltungsgerichtshof was not sufficiently serious for a claim in State liability to succeed.

8.2.2.3 *Liability only where measure confers rights*

One of the key requirements of liability under *Francovich/Brasserie de Pêcheur* is that the rule of law infringed must be intended to confer rights on individuals. Consequently, where a directive in issue does not confer rights on individuals, then there can be no claim under *Francovich*. Thus, in *Peter Paul v Germany* (case C–222/02), the failure of the German banking supervisory authority correctly to supervise a bank, which subsequently failed, in accordance with the relevant directive (94/19/EC), did not permit depositors to maintain an action for compensation for lost deposits beyond the maximum threshold of €20,000 provided for in the directive.

This was because the obligation to ensure supervision was not combined with an independent right to compensation for the consequences of any failure in that regard, and the individual rights under this directive were limited to a specified amount of compensation (which had been paid already).

8.2.3 Conditions of liability

For liability to arise it is not necessary for the infringement of Community law to have been established by the Court under Article 226 or 234; nor is it necessary to prove fault on the part of the national institution concerned *going beyond that of a sufficiently serious breach of Community law*. In *Brasserie du Pêcheur* the Court rephrased the three conditions laid down in *Francovich* and incorporated a requirement that the breach be sufficiently serious. Condition (b) of *Francovich* (the content of the right infringed must be sufficiently clear) may now be regarded as contained within the definition of 'sufficiently serious'.

The Court based its decision on its past case law, particularly its reasoning in *Francovich*: States are obliged under Articles 249 and 10 to provide effective protection for individuals' Community rights and ensure the full effect of Community law. As regards its own jurisdiction to rule on the matter of States' liability in damages, challenged by the German government, it reasoned that, since the EC Treaty had failed to provide expressly for the consequences of breaches of Community law, it fell to the Court, pursuant to its duty under Article 220 (ex 164), to ensure that 'in the interpretation and application of this Treaty the law is observed'. The application of the Court's ruling and questions of damages and causation are discussed further below.

Despite the hostility with which this decision was greeted in anti-European quarters, it is submitted that the Court's ruling on the question of, and conditions for, liability is prima facie consistent with existing principles and, provided that the multiple test in para. 56 of what will constitute a 'sufficiently serious' breach is rigorously applied, strikes a fair balance between the interests of the Community in enforcing Community law and the interests of Member States in restricting liability to culpable breaches of Community law.

8.2.3.1 *Meaning of 'sufficiently serious'*

For liability to arise, the institution concerned must have 'manifestly and gravely exceeded the limits of its discretion': the breach must be 'inexcusable'. If there is to be equality of *responsibility* as between the liability of the Community under Article 288(2) EC and Member States under *Francovich*, the criterion of a 'sufficiently serious' breach laid down in *Brasserie du Pêcheur* should be interpreted strictly. The question remaining was whether the Court would apply the 'sufficiently serious' test to *all* claims based on *Francovich*, including claims for damage resulting from breaches of Community law which do *not* involve legislative 'choices' analogous to those made by Community institutions when implementing policy. Alternatively it might continue to 'interpret' Member States' actions as involving such choices, as it did, surprisingly, in *Brasserie du Pêcheur*. To limit the application of the sufficiently serious test to situations in which Member States are involved in 'legislative choices', by analogy with the position of Community institutions under Article 288(2) (see Chapter 13), as was suggested in *Brasserie du*

Pêcheur, would be to ignore the essential difference between the position of Member States, when *implementing* Community law, and that of Community institutions when *making* Community law. Since liability depends on the breach by a Member State of a Community obligation, liability should in all cases depend on whether the breach is sufficiently serious. This is reflected in the multiple test laid down in para. 56.

Given the lack of clarity of much EC law, and that Member States have no 'choice' to act in breach of Community law, it is submitted that the crucial element in para. 56 will often be the clarity and precision of the rule breached, as suggested by Advocate-General Tesauro in *Brasserie du Pêcheur*.

This view obtained some support in *R v Her Majesty's Treasury, ex parte British Telecommunications plc* (case C–392/93), a case decided shortly after *Brasserie du Pêcheur*. The case, brought by BT, concerned the alleged improper implementation of Council Directive 90/351 on public procurement in the water, energy, transport and telecommunication sectors ([1990] OJ L297/1). BT, which claimed to have been financially disadvantaged as a result of this wrongful implementation, was claiming damages based on *Francovich*. The Court, appearing to presume that the other conditions for liability were met, focused on the question whether the alleged breach was sufficiently serious. It applied the test of para. 56 of *Brasserie du Pêcheur*. Although it found that the UK implementing regulations were contrary to the requirements of the directive, it suggested that the relevant provisions of the directive were sufficiently unclear as to render the UK's error excusable. At para. 43 of its judgment the Court said that the article in question (Article 8(1)) was:

> imprecisely worded and was reasonably capable of bearing, as well as the construction applied to it [by the ECJ] the interpretation given to it by the United Kingdom in good faith and on the basis of arguments which are not entirely void of substance. The interpretation, which was also shared by other Member States, was not manifestly contrary to the wording of the Directive or to the objective pursued by it.

This interpretation was, it is submitted, generous to the UK. The Court held that in the context of the transposition of directives, 'a restrictive approach to State liability is justified' for the same reasons as apply to Community liability in respect of legislative measures, namely, 'to ensure that the exercise of legislative functions is not hindered by the prospect of actions for damages whenever the general interest requires the institutions or Member States to adopt measures which may adversely affect individual interests' (para. 40).

The Court adopted a rather different approach in *R v Ministry of Agriculture, Fisheries and Food, ex parte Hedley Lomas (Ireland) Ltd* (case C–5/94). This case concerned a claim for damages by an exporter, Hedley Lomas, for losses suffered as a result of a UK ban on the export of live sheep to Spain. The ban was imposed following complaints from animal welfare groups that Spanish slaughterhouses did not comply with the requirements of Council Directive 74/577 on the stunning of animals before slaughter ([1974] OJ L316/10). The Spanish authorities had implemented the directive, but had made no provision for monitoring compliance or providing sanctions for non-compliance. The UK raised the matter with the Commission, which, following discussion with the Spanish authorities, decided not to take action against Spain under Article 226. Although the UK ban was clearly in breach of Article 29 (ex 34) of the EC Treaty, the UK argued that it was justified on the grounds of the protection of health of animals under Article 30 (ex 36) (for further discussion of the substantive issues see chapter 19). However, the UK provided no evidence that the directive had in fact been breached, either by particular slaughterhouses or generally.

The Court found that the ban was in breach of Article 29, and was not justified under Article 30. The fact that the Spanish authorities had not provided procedures for monitoring compliance with the directive or penalties for non-compliance was irrelevant. 'Member States must rely on trust in each other to carry out inspections in their respective territories' (para. 19). Furthermore, the breach was 'sufficiently serious' to give rise to liability under *Francovich*. The Court suggested (at para. 28) that:

> where, at the time when it committed the infringement, the Member State in question was not called upon to make any legislative choices and had only considerably reduced, or even no, discretion, the mere infringement of Community law may be sufficient to establish the existence of a sufficiently serious breach.

This ruling, delivered two months after *R v Her Majesty's Treasury, ex parte British Telecommunications plc*, was surprising. While a finding that the UK would in principle be liable in damages was justified on the facts, the UK having produced no evidence of breach of the directive constituting a threat to animal health to justify the ban under Article 30, the suggestion that a 'mere infringement' of Community law might be sufficient to create liability where the State is not 'called upon to make any legislative choices' or has 'considerably reduced, or no, discretion' is questionable. While a State may have a choice as to the 'form and method of implementation' of directives, and some discretion under the Treaty to derogate from basic Treaty rules, its discretion is strictly circumscribed, and it has no discretion to act in breach of Community law. The UK had no more 'legislative' discretion in implementing Directive 90/531 in *BT*, indeed possibly less, than it had under Article 30 in *Hedley Lomas*. Indeed, prior to the Court's decision in *Hedley Lomas*, it was thought that a Member State *would* have a discretion to derogate from the prohibition of Article 29 where this was necessary to protect a genuine public interest (see Chapter 19). To pursue the analogy between the Community's liability for 'legislative choices involving choices of economic policy' and Member States' liability under *Francovich*, as the Court has done in all these cases, is to disguise the fact that *the two situations are not similar*. The principal reason for limiting liability under *Francovich* is not because Member States' 'discretion' in implementing Community law must not be fettered, but because the rules of Community law are often not clear. To hold them liable in damages for 'mere infringements' of such rules, thereby introducing a principle akin to strict liability, would not only be politically dangerous, it would be contrary to the principle of legal certainty, itself a respected principle of Community law (for further analysis see Chapter 13).

Nevertheless the principle of liability for a 'mere infringement' of Community law in situations in which Member States are not required to make legislative choices was invoked by the ECJ in *Dillenkofer v Germany* (cases C–178, 179, 188, 189 and 190/94) in a situation in which Germany's failure, on all fours with that of the

Italian government in *Francovich*, was clearly 'inexcusable' and therefore, as the Court acknowledged, 'sufficiently serious' to warrant liability. In neither *Hedley Lomas* nor *Dillenkofer* did the Court attempt to apply the multiple test laid down in para. 56 of *Brasserie du Pêcheur*.

However, in *Denkavit International BV v Bundesamt für Finanzen* (cases C–283, 291 & 292/94), which were cases involving claims for damages resulting from the faulty implementation of a directive decided shortly after *Dillenkofer*, the Court reverted to its approach in *BT*. Following a strong submission from Advocate-General Jacobs it applied the criteria of para. 56 of *Brasserie du Pêcheur* and concluded that, as a result of the lack of clarity and precision of the relevant provisions of the directive, and the lack of clear guidance from the Court's previous case law, Germany's breach of Community law could not be regarded as sufficiently serious to justify liability. Significantly, the Court did not draw a distinction, for the purposes of liability, between acts of Member States involving 'choices of economic policy' and 'mere infringements' of Community law.

In an attempt to rationalise this aspect of State liability, Advocate-General Jacobs in *Sweden v Stockholm Lindöpark AB* (case C–150/99) commented on the origins of the phrase 'sufficiently serious breach'. At paragraph 59 of his opinion, he noted that:

> In French, the Court has always used – originally with regard to liability incurred by the Community – the term 'violation suffisamment caractérisée'. This is now normally translated into English as 'sufficiently serious breach'. However, the underlying meaning of 'caractérisé', which gives rise to its inherent implication of seriousness, includes the notion that the breach (or other conduct) has been clearly established in accordance with its legal definition, in other words, that it is a definite, clear-cut breach. This may help to explain why the term was previously translated as 'sufficiently flagrant violation' and may throw additional light on the choice of factors which the Court has indicated should be taken into consideration when deciding whether a breach is 'sufficiently serious'.

On this reasoning, a clear-cut breach of Community law would be sufficiently serious.

The ECJ's approach to the assessment of the matter of a 'sufficiently serious' breach remains inconsistent. In *Brinkman Tabakfabriken GmH v Skatteministeriet* (case C–319/96), it followed the more moderate line it had taken in *BT* (case C–392/93), and found that the Danish authorities' failure properly to implement Directive 79/30 on taxes other than turnover taxes affecting the consumption of manufactured tobacco was not sufficiently serious to incur liability. The classification adopted by the authorities, which resulted in the applicant having to pay the higher rates of taxes, was not 'manifestly contrary' to the wording and aim of the directive. It was not clear from the directive whether the tobacco rolls imported by the applicant, which had to be wrapped in paper to be smoked, constituted 'cigarette tobacco' or 'cigarettes'. Significantly, both the Commission and the Finnish government supported the classification adopted by the Danish authorities. The question of liability was in fact decided by the Court on the basis of causation. The directive in question had not been implemented in Denmark by legislative decree, although the authorities had given immediate (albeit imperfect) effect to its provisions. There was no direct causal link between that former (legislative) failure and the damage suffered by the applicant. It is implicit in the decisions that, contrary to the view of some commentators, provided that the requirements of a directive are complied with in practice, a failure to implement a directive by legislative means will not necessarily constitute a sufficiently serious breach to warrant liability.

Rechberger and Greindle v *Austria* (case C–140/97) concerned a claim for damages for losses suffered as a result of Austria's alleged imperfect implementation of Directive 90/314, designed to protect consumers in the event of travel organisers' insolvency. The ECJ found that the implementing measures, which failed to provide the level of protection required under the directive, and which set the period for the commencement of claims at a date some months later than the time-limit for implementation of the directive, were 'manifestly' incompatible with the directive, and sufficiently serious to attract liability.

In both *Brinkman* and *Rechberger*, the assessment as to whether the breach was sufficiently serious depended primarily on the clarity and precision of the provisions breached. However, in *Norbrook Laboratories Ltd* v *Minister of Agriculture, Fisheries and Food* (case C–127/95), a case involving a claim for damages for wrongful implementation of EC directives on the authorisation of veterinary products, the ECJ, following an extensive examination of the provisions of the directive allegedly breached, which revealed a number of clear breaches, invoked the *Hedley Lomas/Dillenkofer* mantra: 'Where . . . the Member State was not called upon to make legislative choices, and had considerably reduced, if no discretion, the mere infringement of Community law may be sufficient to establish the existence of a sufficiently serious breach.' It was left to the national court to assess whether the conditions for the award of damages based on *Francovich* were fulfilled.

In *Klaus Konle* v *Austria* (case C–302/97), in a claim for damages for losses suffered as a result of laws of the Tyrol governing land transactions, allegedly contrary to Article 46 (ex 56) and Article 70 of the Act of Accession, the Court, having examined these provisions for their compatibility with Community law, and finding some (but not all) of the laws to be 'precluded' by Community law, left it to the national court 'to apply the criteria to establish the liability of Member States for damage caused to individuals by breaches of Community law in accordance with the guidelines laid down by the Court of Justice'. Thus the national court was required to decide whether Austria's breach of Community law was sufficiently serious. The ECJ took a similar approach in *Haim* v *KLV* (case C–424/97). However, it seems that the *ex parte BT* approach will not be followed where the ECJ has previously interpreted a particular provision of Community law and a Member State has subsequently failed to apply that provision in accordance with the ECJ's interpretation (*Gervais Larsy* v *Institut national d'assurances sociales pour travailleurs indépendants (Inasti)* (case C–118/00)). In that case, it can no longer be said that the Member State has a legislative choice.

If national courts are to assess this crucial question of the seriousness of the breach, as was required in *Klaus Konle* (and as, in principle, given the nature of the ECJ's jurisdiction under Article 234, they should, see Chapter 9), it is essential that these guidelines are clear. The multiple criteria laid down in para. 56 of *Brasserie du Pêcheur* are clear and comprehensive. The *Hedley Lomas* requirement, that in some circumstances a 'mere infringement' of Community law will suffice to establish liability, clouds the issue. It is submitted that if it is to be invoked, it will be applicable only *following* an examination of the Community law allegedly breached under the multiple test in para. 56; for only then will the issue of whether the State has any 'discretion' in the exercise of its legislative powers be resolved. If the aim, and the substance, of the Community obligation allegedly infringed is 'manifest', the State will have no discretion to act in its breach. If it is not, the breach will not be sufficiently serious. The *Hedley Lomas* mantra is, it is submitted, superfluous. Nevertheless, it was invoked in *Haim* v *KLV* alongside the multiple test of para. 56.

In *Sweden* v *Stockholm Lindöpark AB* (case C–150/99), the Court again followed *Hedley Lomas*. Lindöpak had not been entitled to deduct VAT on goods and services used for the purposes of its business activities in breach of the sixth VAT directive (91/680/EEC, [1991] OJ L376/1). Sweden had amended its VAT legislation with effect from 1 January 1997, following which Lindöpak was entitled to deduct VAT. It claimed for a return of VAT payments made between Sweden's accession to the Community on 1 January 1995 and 1 January 1997. The ECJ observed that the right to deduct VAT was capable of being directly effective. Although the question of Member State liability did not strictly speaking arise, the ECJ was nevertheless prepared to indicate whether Sweden had committed a sufficiently serious breach. It noted that:

> given the clear wording of [the directive], the Member State concerned was not in a position to make any legislative choices and had only a considerably reduced, or even no, discretion.

The mere infringement of the directive was therefore enough to create liability. In contrast, in *Schmidberger* v *Austria* (case C–112/00), Advocate-General Jacobs suggested that a breach of Article 28 in that case would not be sufficiently serious. Austria had authorised a 28-hour demonstration which blocked the main transit route across the Alps. Although technically a breach of Article 28, the Advocate-General thought that this had to be balanced against the freedom of expression of the demonstrators (see further Chapter 6). This and the short duration of the disruption would not be a sufficiently serious breach of Community law. The ECJ, having decided that there was no breach of Article 28, declined to deal with this question.

8.2.3.2 *The claimant must prove that damage has been suffered*

It is also important that the claimant is able to establish that he has suffered loss or damage. In *Schmidberger* v *Austria* (case C–112/00), Austria had allowed a public protest to take place on the main motorway across the Alps which closed the motorway for 28 hours. Schmidberger claimed damages for delay to his business of transporting goods from Germany to Italy on the basis that this amounted to a breach of Article 28 (see Chapter 18). Advocate-General Jacobs noted that it was necessary for the claimant to establish loss or damage which is attributable, by a direct causal link, to a sufficiently serious breach of Community law. Importantly, this included a right to claim for lost profit. However, if the claimant is unable to establish the existence of any loss or damage, then there cannot be a claim for State liability. The Advocate-General was willing to accept that it may not be possible to quantify exactly the loss suffered, in which case this may be calculated on an appropriate flat-rate basis. As noted above, the ECJ did not address the question of State liability in its judgment. It is submitted that the reasoning of this Advocate-General is sound.

8.2.4 *Brasserie du Pêcheur* in the English courts

In 1997 the ECJ's ruling in *Brasserie du Pêcheur* and *R v Secretary of State for Transport, ex parte Factortame Ltd* (cases C–46 and 48/93) was applied in the English High Court with a view to ascertaining whether the UK's action in introducing the Merchant Shipping Act 1988 in fact constituted a sufficiently serious breach of Community law (*R v Secretary of State for Transport, ex parte Factortame Ltd (No. 5)* [1998] 1 CMLR 1353). Hobhouse LJ considered the ECJ's case law on State liability and concluded that whether or not a Member State's action involved the exercise of discretion (i.e., 'legislative choices') the same test, requiring proof of a sufficiently serious breach of Community law, applied. That test, requiring a 'manifest and grave disregard of whatever discretion the Member State might possess', was based on the same principles as applied to Community liability under Article 288(2), and was a relatively difficult one to meet. Having reasoned impeccably thus far he concluded that the UK's breach as regards the Merchant Shipping Act 1988 was sufficiently serious to warrant liability and referred the case back to the Divisional Court to decide the question of causation. Two factors in particular were cited by Hobhouse LJ as rendering the breach of Community law (Article 43 (ex 52) EC) sufficiently serious: (a) the UK had introduced the measures in question in primary legislation in order to ensure that the implementation would not be delayed by legal challenge (at the time it was thought that primary legislation could not be challenged, but see now *R v Secretary of State for Transport, ex parte Factortame Ltd* (case C–213/89), noted in Chapter 4); and (b) the Commission had from the start been opposed to the legislation on the grounds that it was (in its opinion) contrary to Community law.

Both the Court of Appeal and the House of Lords agreed with Hobhouse LJ that the UK's breach of Community law was sufficiently serious to warrant liability. Both courts applied the multiple test laid down in para. 56 of *Brasserie du Pêcheur* (cases C–46 and 48/93) (although they suggested that the list was 'not exhaustive') and found that the balance tipped in favour of the respondents. In pressing ahead with its legislation, against the advice of the Commission, despite its clear adverse impact on the respondents, and in a form (statute) which it was thought could not be challenged, the UK Government was clearly taking a 'calculated risk'. Lord Slynn did, however, express the opinion, contrary to the view of Hobhouse LJ and the Court of Appeal, that the considered views of the Commission, although of importance, could not be regarded as conclusive proof as to:

(a) whether there had been a breach of Community law, and

(b) whether the breach was sufficiently serious to justify an award of damages.

Lords Hoffmann and Clyde expressed a similar view; the position taken by the Commission was 'a relevant factor to be taken into account' in deciding whether a breach was sufficiently serious, but it was not conclusive.

Following the House of Lords' decision in *Factortame*, Sullivan J in the English High Court, in assessing the seriousness of the Department of Social Security's breach of Article 7(1) of the Sex Discrimination Directive 79/7 in *R v Department of*

Social Security, ex parte Scullion ([1999] 3 CMLR 798), also applied the multiple test of para. 56 of *Brasserie du Pêcheur*, which he described as the 'global' or 'basket' approach, and decided that, since there the scope of Article 7(1) was not clear at the relevant time, and there was no evidence that the Department had sought legal advice on the matter either from the Commission or from its own legal advisers, the breach was sufficiently serious.

8.2.5 Impact of the principle of State liability under *Francovich*

It remains to be seen whether, or the extent to which, the principle of State liability will have an impact on the principles of direct and indirect effect, particularly in the context of enforcement of directives. If it is necessary to prove in all cases the existence of a sufficiently serious breach – and this is a difficult test to satisfy – there will still be a need for individuals to rely on these principles. Until now, liability under the principles of both direct and indirect effect has been strict (this was confirmed in *Draehmpaehl* v *Urania Immobilienservice OHG* (case C–180/95)); there has been no need to consider whether the alleged breach of Community law is 'sufficiently serious'. For direct effects, the criteria have in the past been loosely applied; sometimes, in the case of indirect effects (and sometimes in the case of direct effects), they have not been applied at all. On the other hand national courts' reluctance to apply these principles in some cases (e.g., *Duke* v *GEC Reliance Ltd*; *Rolls-Royce plc* v *Doughty*) appears to have stemmed in part from the perceived injustice of imposing liability, retrospectively, on parties, public or private, when the precise nature of their obligations under Community law at the relevant time was not clear. The existence of a remedy under *Francovich* could lead to a more rigorous application of the criteria for direct effects, especially following the denial by the Court of the direct effects of the relevant provisions of Directive 80/987 in *Francovich* itself. This latter fact was noted by, and appeared to be influential on, Blackburne J in *Griffin* v *South West Water Services Ltd* ([1995] IRLR 15). In *Three Rivers District Council* v *Bank of England (No. 3)* ([1996] 3 All ER 558), a case involving a claim for damages based on the defendants' breach of statutory duty in failing to supervise the credit institutions in the BCCI affair, Clarke J in the English High Court construed the EC directive which the defendants had allegedly breached, and on which the claimants based their claim, as *not intended to give rise to rights for individuals* and therefore not directly effective. Does this represent an attempt on the part of the Court to limit the direct effect of directives? If so, is it legitimate?

The ECJ's test for direct effects (the provision must be sufficiently clear, precise and unconditional) has never expressly included a requirement that the directive should be intended to give rise to rights for the individual seeking to invoke its provisions. However, the justification for giving direct effect to EC law has always been the need to ensure effective protection for individuals' Community rights. Furthermore, the ECJ has, in a number of recent cases, suggested that an individual's right to invoke a directive may be confined to situations in which he can show a particular interest in that directive. In *Becker* v *Finanzamt Munster-Innenstadt* (case 8/81), in confirming and clarifying the principle of direct effect as applied to directives, the Court held that 'provisions of Directives can be invoked by individuals *insofar as they define rights which individuals are able to assert against the state'*. Drawing on this statement in *Verholen* (cases C–87 to C–89/90), the Court suggested that only a person with a direct interest in the application of the directive could invoke its provisions: this was held in *Verholen* to include a third party who was directly affected by the directive. In *Verholen*, the husband of a woman suffering sex discrimination as regards the granting of a social security benefit, contrary to Directive 79/7, was able to bring a claim based on the directive in respect of disadvantage to himself consequential on the discriminatory treatment of his wife.

In most recent cases in which an individual seeks to invoke a directive directly, the existence of a direct interest is clear. The question of his or her standing has not therefore been in issue. Normally the rights he or she seeks to invoke, be it for example a right to equal treatment, or to employment protection, are contained in the directive. Its provisions are clearly, if not explicitly, designed to benefit persons such as the individual. There are circumstances, however, where this is not so.

As noted in 5.2.5.5, individuals seeking to base their claim on a breach of a directive by the State will now need to establish that the breach interfered with a right or interest intended to be conferred on them. However, where this right or interest can be proved, the problem of adverse horizontal effects in cases involving third-party situations, such as *CIA Security International SA* v *Signalson SA*, *Panagis Parfitis* and *Ruiz Bernaldez*, remains (see 5.2.5.7). Where individuals suffer damage in these situations, their only possible remedy lies in a claim under *Francovich*.

It is worthy of note that in *Three Rivers DC* v *Bank of England (No. 3)* (noted above), Clarke J invoked the same reasoning as he applied to the question of direct effects to the applicants' claim for damages under *Francovich*. He found that the directive allegedly breached contained no right intended to benefit the claimant. If they had no sufficient right or interest for direct effects, they had no claim under *Francovich*, because 'here too it is necessary to establish the same right or interest' (at para. 66). The cases from the ECJ considered above suggest that it too may be moving towards the same approach, thereby achieving some sort of consistency between the rules relating to individual standing in claims based on the principle of direct effect and claims under *Francovich*. This approach was also adopted by Beldam J in the English Court of Appeal in *Bowden* v *South West Water Services* ([1999] 3 CMLR 180). In examining the Environmental Directive 79/903, he found it to confer rights on the claimant for the purposes of a claim for damages based on direct effects and under *Francovich*.

8.3 General principles regarding national procedural rules

8.3.1 Overview of principles

The ECJ has laid down a number of principles which must be observed by national courts in claims involving Community law. It has held consistently that:

> In the absence of Community rules it is for the domestic systems of each Member State to designate the courts having jurisdiction and the procedural conditions governing actions at law intended to ensure the protection of the rights which subjects derive from the direct effects of Community law, it being understood that such conditions cannot be less

favourable than those relating to similar actions of a domestic nature nor render virtually impossible or excessively difficult the exercise of rights conferred by Community law.

(See *Rewe Zentralfinanz* v *Landwirtschaftskammer Saarland* (case 33/76), *Peterbroeck* (case C–312/93), *Van Schijndel* (cases C–430 & C–431/93) and *Wells* (case C–201/02).) This statement may be seen to embody three separate principles:

(a) The principle of national treatment ('it is for the domestic systems of each Member State to designate . . . effects of Community law').

(b) The principle of non-discrimination ('conditions cannot be less favourable than those . . . of a domestic nature').

(c) The principle of effectiveness ('nor render impossible or excessively difficult the exercise of rights conferred').

There is little basis in the Treaty for these principles, although the principle of national procedural autonomy might seem self-evident when cases originate in national courts. An approach which starts from the presumption that national rules will, in principle, be accepted by the ECJ also respects the integrity of the national legal system. These arguments do not justify the principles of non-discrimination and effectiveness, which operate to limit the principle of national procedural autonomy. Article 10, which requires Member States to 'take all appropriate measures . . . to ensure fulfilment of the obligations arising out of this Treaty or resulting from actions taken by the institutions of the Community' could be seen as providing some form of treaty basis for these principles, although this provision does not specifically address the question of procedures or remedies. Nonetheless, although established in early case law, these three principles remain central to the ECJ's jurisprudence in this area.

8.3.2 Equivalence and effectiveness

As the scope of national procedural autonomy depends on them, both of the concepts of non-discrimination (equivalence) and effectiveness deserve further explanation. A preliminary question concerns the relationship between the three principles noted above and the principles of equivalence and effectiveness. Since the national remedy provided for a claim based on domestic law may not be exactly comparable to a claim based on EC law, or, although seemingly comparable, may operate to the detriment of the party relying on EC law, commentators, and even the Court, have tended to merge the first and second principles (that is the principles of national treatment and non-discrimination) into a single principle of *equivalence* discussed at 8.4.3.

As we have seen in 8.3.1, the ECJ referred in a number of cases to the principle that national rules should not 'render impossible or excessively difficult the exercise of the rights conferred'. The Court has not always used this formulation of the effectiveness principle. Another version, enunciated in *Harz* v *Deutsche Tradax GmbH* (case 79/83) requires that the remedies and sanctions provided for breach of Community law must have a real deterrent effect and must be 'such as to guarantee full and effective protection' for individuals' Community rights. It is arguable that the two different formulations give the principle of effectiveness a different scope, the 'impossible or excessively difficult test' being narrower than the requirement for 'full and effective protection' of EC law rights. The differences between the two approaches to effectiveness are discussed further at 8.4.2.

There are a number of difficulties with the approach that the ECJ has adopted. One relates to the fact that procedures and remedies will not be uniform across the Member States, meaning that an individual in one Member State might be able to bring an action or be awarded a certain amount of damages that an individual in another Member State, relying on the same substantive right and factual situation, would not. The second set of problems relate to the scope of equivalence and effectiveness and their impact on the principle of national procedural autonomy.

8.4 Finding the balance between national procedural autonomy and the principles of equivalence and effectiveness

8.4.1 Tension between national procedural autonomy and the principles of equivalence and effectiveness

A number of issues can be seen. First, it may not be easy to assess what is an 'equivalent' national remedy. EC law is *sui generis*. It cuts across the boundaries and classifications of national law. Even where domestic law provides a remedy in the context of a similar claim, for example in restitution, or in the field of employment law, such claims may be dealt with in different courts, subject to different procedures and different limitations as to time or the award of damages. Some potential remedies may be more 'effective' than others. How, then, is equivalence to be assessed? Does the principle of effectiveness require that the most generous treatment be accorded to claims based on EC law? Secondly, there are circumstances in which an equivalent domestic remedy may not exist. EC law is supreme over all national law. Where an individual seeks to invoke his Community rights in order to challenge national law, he may do so against any law, whatever its nature. In most Member States concepts of sovereignty prohibit challenge to the legality of statute or, *a fortiori*, constitutional law. Furthermore, in most Member States there are lacunae, gaps in the legal protection of individuals, arising from traditional privileges and immunities. Sometimes these limitations are justified, sometimes they are not. What remedy or procedure is to be provided by national courts in these circumstances?

The ECJ, in its jurisdiction under Article 234, has provided guidance on these matters. Its approach to the principles of equivalence and effectiveness has developed over the years, from an absolutist, interventionist approach in cases such as *Marshall (No. 2)* (case C–271/91), *Emmott* (case C–208/90) and *Factortame (Nos 1 and 2)*, towards a more 'hands-off' approach, described by Tridimas as a policy of 'selective deference to national rules of procedure'.

8.4.2 **Meaning of 'effectiveness'**

In some circumstances it will be clear that an effective remedy has not been pro-vided. For example, rules that deny access to the courts altogether, such as a rule restricting payment of a duty held by the ECJ to be contrary to EC law to claimants who have brought an action for repayment before the delivery of that judgment, as was the situation in *Barra* v *Belgium* (case 309/85), will clearly be ineffective in protecting the Community rights of persons bringing their claim, based on that judgment, after the date of judgment (see also *Deville* v *Administration des Impôts* (case 240/87)). But there are many situations in which the position is not so clear. Many of the important cases in this area have arisen in the field of sex discrimin-ation legislation. To what extent, however, is that jurisprudence representative of the approach taken by the Court in other policy fields? We will therefore consider the jurisprudence relating to procedural rules in two segments: that relating to sex discrimination legislation and then the more general case law.

8.4.2.1 *Jurisprudence in the field of sex discrimination legislation*

A significant number of cases in this area have arisen in the context of sex dis-crimination legislation, notably – though not exclusively – Directive 76/207, the Equal Treatment Directive. Crucially, Article 6 of that directive requires Member States to provide judicial remedies for those with a substantive claim under the directive. The starting point for this line of jurisprudence was the *Von Colson* case (case 14/83), discussed in Chapter 5. *Von Colson* concerned two women who applied for jobs but who were not appointed. They claimed successfully that they had been discriminated against on the grounds of their gender. The damages in the case were assessed on the basis of the claimants' actual loss, in this case, travelling expenses. The question referred to the ECJ was whether this was sufficient, or, in the words of the ECJ's jurisprudence, 'effective'. The ECJ remarked that:

> if a Member State chooses to penalize breaches of [the prohibition on sex discrimination] by the award of compensation, then in order to ensure that it is effective and that it has a deterrent effect, that compensation must in any event be adequate in relation to the damage sustained and must therefore amount to more than purely nominal compensa-tion such as, for example, the reimbursement only of the expenses incurred in connection with the application (para. 26).

This judgment can be seen to be making a number of points. It re-affirmed that remedies must be effective. This point is linked, as we have seen, to the idea that without adequate recompense from the perspective of the victim, a right has little value. Crucially, the ECJ also looked to the impact of the remedy on the body responsible for the violation of EC law: any compensation must be such as to make the violation of EC law-derived rights much less attractive.

The ECJ developed the effectiveness principle in this field significantly during the early 1990s. *Dekker* (case C–177/88) concerned a claim that the applicant had been discriminated against on the basis that she had not been employed because she was pregnant. Under national law, claims for redress could be subject to a requirement of fault on the part of the defendant, or a claim could be subjected to arguments based on justification; the right to compensation was not absolute even once discrimination had been shown. The ECJ, basing its judgment on *Von Colson*, held that, to be effective, 'any infringement of the prohibition suffices in itself to make the person guilty fully liable' (para. 26). This ruling would seem to have pushed the boundaries of the effectiveness requirement wider than in *Von Colson*. In contrast to *Von Colson*, the damages that would have been awarded under national law in this case were not necessarily only nominal. In the words of the early judgments, it could not to be said that the national rules operated to make the exercise of substantive rights 'impossible in practice'.

In *Marshall (No. 2)* (case C–271/91), two national rules were in issue: a statutory ceiling on the amount of damages that could be awarded for sex discrimination claims and the jurisdictional limitation on the relevant tribunal which meant that it could not award interest on damages. Again, reasoning from *Von Colson*, the ECJ, based on Equal Treatment Directive 76/207, held that where damages were awarded for breaches of individuals' rights under the directive, national courts must provide 'full' compensation, including interest on the award from the date of judgment. A system in which compensation was subject to statutory limits, as provided under the UK Sex Discrimination Act 1975, would not be 'sufficiently effective to achieve the objectives of the Directive'. A principle of full compensation required that 'reparation be commensurate with the loss or damage sustained'. This case was a step forward from *Von Colson*, as the Court describes in more detail the requirements of an effective remedy. Rather than describing the lower end of what would be required, that is more than nominal, the Court imposed a higher test: that the remedy be *full* compensation. This ruling, generally applied, could have had potentially far-reaching consequences.

However, in recent years the Court has been prepared to accept some limits to the principle of full compensation. In *R v Secretary of State for Social Security, ex parte Sutton* (case C–66/95), in a claim based on EC Directive 79/7 on equal treatment for men and women in social security, it accepted a statutory bar on the payment of interest on an award of damages, even though the wording of the directive on which the applicants sought to rely, requiring Member States to ensure that persons alleging discrimination are able to 'pursue their claims by judicial process', was virtually identical to that on which the applicants based their claim in *Marshall (No. 2)* (case C–271/91). *Marshall* was distinguished on the basis that there the award of interest was an 'essential component of compensation for the purpose of ensuring real equality of treatment'. In contrast, *Sutton* 'concerned social security benefits paid by the competent bodies which must . . . examine whether the conditions laid down in the relevant legislation were fulfilled'. The amounts paid 'in no way constituted reparation for loss or damage sustained'. The distinction is fine, and may be seen as an example of the Court's more cautious approach following criticisms of its activism expressed by some Member States in the period leading up to the ToA. The Court in *Sutton* was similarly reserved in its comments on the possibility of recovery of interest on arrears of payment in an alternative claim based on *Francovich*. It enunciated the principles governing state liability in damages but insisted that it was for the national court to assess, in the light of those principles, whether the claimant was entitled to reparation for the loss she had suffered.

However, *Marshall (No. 2)* was followed in *Draehmpaehl v Urania Immobilienservice OHG* (case C–180/95), a case decided on the same day as *Sutton*. Here, in a claim by a man, the Court held that a limit of three months' wages as compensation for sex discrimination as regards access to employment (the job advertisement requested female applicants), and a six-month aggregate limit where several applicants were involved, would not guarantee effective judicial protection for individuals' Community rights. A three-month limit would only be acceptable as reasonable if the employer could prove that the applicants would not have been given the job in the absence of discrimination. Clearly, if the applicant would have been given the job in the absence of discrimination, the limits on compensation in this case would not have been sufficient to compensate for the damage sustained. Although *Marshall (No. 2)* may have been limited, it is not extinct.

A separate line of cases deals with the issue of time limits. In general, the ECJ had rules that a limitation of a 'reasonable' period would not make it 'impossible in practice' to exercise Community law rights. We have seen that this phrase was extended in the context of amount of damages for sex discrimination cases. How would the ECJ approach the question of time limits for sex discrimination? A case arose in respect of Directive 79/7, on equal treatment for men and women in matters of social security, *Emmott* (case C–208/90).

The case concerned a challenge to the Irish authorities' refusal to grant Ms Emmott disability benefit. She claimed that this was discriminatory, in breach of Directive 79/7 on equal treatment for men and women in matters of social security. At the time when her cause of action arose she was unaware that it was directly effective. When she became aware that it was, following a ruling from the Court in *McDermott v Minister for Social Welfare* (case 286/85) she applied to the Minister for her case to be reviewed. Her application was deferred pending a ruling from the ECJ in *Cotter v Minister for Social Welfare* (case C–377/89). When she was finally granted leave to institute proceedings, she was found to be out of time. The Irish judge referred to the ECJ to ascertain whether it was contrary to Community law for the authorities of a Member State to rely on national procedural rules, in particular relating to time limits, in defending claims based on Community directives. The Minister argued that, even though a directive had not been implemented, or properly implemented, the principle of direct effects enabled the individual effectively to assert his Community rights, at least against a 'public' body. The Court disagreed. It held that the principle of direct effects provided only a minimum guarantee: as long as a directive has not been properly implemented the individual is in a state of uncertainty; the individual is unaware of the full extent of his or her rights. Therefore the competent authorities of Member States cannot rely, in an action against them based on the directive, on national procedural rules relating to time limits for bringing proceedings as long as that Member State has not properly implemented that directive into national law.

One important point to note about *Emmott* is that (like *Cotter and McDermott* (case C–377/89)), the ECJ's reasoning is significantly different from that used in the damages cases. Although both sets of jurisprudence are aimed at ensuring the full effectiveness of Community law rights, *Emmott* is based on the principle of estoppel, that is, the State cannot benefit from its own wrongdoing. It has been suggested, notably by Advocate-General Jacobs, that it was because the State was in the wrong and indeed created the problem in *Emmott*, that the ECJ took such an uncompromising stance in that case.

This decision, expressed in the broadest terms, gave rise to some alarm in

Member States. It might be acceptable in a case in which the State's failure to implement a Community directive is clear, or when, as in *Emmott's* case, it was 'excessively difficult', as a result of action by the national authorities, for the claimant to enforce her rights. But it was likely to cause injustice, contrary to the principle of legal certainty, when applied in cases of inadvertent failure on the part of the State and when it exposed public bodies, acting *bona fide* according to their legitimate understanding of the law, to a flood of retrospective claims. It might be years before a directive was found not to have been 'properly' implemented into national law. Nor was it clear whether *Emmott* applied solely to the non- or faulty implementation of directives. The reasoning on which the decision was based might be applied to any breach of Community law, including claims under *Francovich* v *Italy* (cases C–6 & 9/90).

Perhaps recognising that it had gone too far, the Court distinguished *Emmott* in *Steenhorst-Neerings* (case C–338/91). Here it held that a statutory limit on the retrospective payment of invalidity benefit (not in itself a limitation period, although similar in its effect) was not contrary to EC law, being justified by the need to preserve the financial equilibrium of social security funds. There was a difference between national rules fixing time limits for bringing an action, as in *Emmott*, and rules which merely limited the retroactive effect of claims. *Steenhorst-Neerings* was followed, on similar facts, in *Johnson* v *Chief Adjudication Officer* (case C–410/92), in which the benefit in question was non-contributory, therefore posing no threat to the financial balance of social security funds (see also *Alonso-Pérez* v *Bundesanstat für Arbeit* (case C–394/93), three-month ceiling on the retrospective payment of family benefits did not render the exercise of Community rights impossible). It seems that time limits will be set aside only when they render the exercise of Community rights absolutely impossible and that *Emmott* is limited to its facts.

Similar thinking, albeit to different effect, lay behind the Court's ruling in *Magorrian* v *Eastern Health and Social Services Board* (case C–246/96). This case concerned a claim for the retrospective payment of certain pension benefits to which the applicant, a female part-time worker, found she was entitled under Article 119 (now 141) EC following a ruling from the ECJ (see *Fisscher* (case C–128/93), Chapter 25). Her claim, which related to the period from 1976 to 1990, was subject to a two-year limitation period running from the date of commencement of her action. The defendant Board opposed her claim, relying on *Steenhorst-Neerings* and *Johnson*. The Court distinguished these cases. The claim in this case was not, it held, for the retrospective award of certain additional benefits but for the recognition of entitlement to full membership of an occupational scheme through acquisition of MHO status, which confers entitlement to the additional benefits. The two-year limitation rule prevented the entire record of service from 1976 to 1990 being taken into account for the purposes of calculating the additional benefits which would be payable even after the date of the claim. It 'struck at the very essence' of the applicant's rights and would not be permissible under Community law. The ECJ took the same view of the same rule in *Preston* v *Wolverhampton NHS Healthcare Trust* (case C–78/98). Although the ECJ accepts the need for limitation periods, even those imposing a short period of time in which would-be applicants must act, where the rule affects the underlying principle of non-discrimination, the substantive right in issue in these cases, the Court still seems prepared to strike down national measures.

8.4.2.2 *Effectiveness in other circumstances*

The case law in the sex discrimination field has shown that the ECJ has been pre-pared to take an extensive view of what the notion of effectiveness requires, although some of the more far-reaching cases have been limited. Given that in many of the sex discrimination directives, EC law requires that Member States provide a remedy, the question is to what extent the ECJ has taken a similar approach in other circumstances. This can be seen in some consumer protection cases, but again, these involve Community measures which require that Member States must provide remedies (see e.g., *Cofidis* (case C–473/00) concerning Directive 93/13/EEC on unfair consumer contracts). What, however, has been the ECJ's approach to effectiveness where the express provisions of EC law are silent as to the need to provide remedies?

The Court has applied the notion of effectiveness of national remedies outside the scope generally from its early jurisprudence. It is in the early 1990s (as with the sex discrimination jurisprudence) that we see the logic of effectiveness being taken to its limits and in this context *Factortame I* (case C–213/89) is significant. The case concerned a challenge to British primary legislation and the applicants sought an interim injunction against the Crown, suspending the relevant legislation. At that point the English courts had no power to grant the relief sought. The matter was referred to the ECJ, which reasoned from the obligation of Member States under Article 10 EC to ensure the legal protection which derives from Community law, and its judgment in *Simmenthal* (case 106/77) (discussed in Chapter 4). It summarised *Simmenthal* as requiring:

> that any provision of a national legal system and any legislative, administrative or judi-cial practice which might impair the effectiveness of Community law . . . are incompatible with those requirements, which are the very essence of Community law.

The ECJ then held that:

> the full effectiveness of Community law would be just as much impaired if a rule of national law could prevent a court seised of a dispute governed by Community law from granting interim relief in order to ensure the full effectiveness of the judgment to be given on the existence of the rights claimed under Community law (paras 20–21).

The Court here was clearly focusing on the need to ensure that Community law is respected. As with the other cases already mentioned at 8.4.2.1, note that the Court actually uses the word 'effectiveness' rather than the phraseology used in its earliest jurisprudence. There, what was prohibited was that the relevant national rule makes the application of Community law 'impossible or excessively difficult': effectiveness is arguably a harder test for national law to satisfy. National pro-cedural autonomy is not mentioned; indeed the Court's first reference to the role of national legal systems was in the context of the obligation under Article 10 EC to ensure that Community law rights are protected. This could suggest a shift away from the presumption that national rules are the starting point for any discussion of remedies. The issue of equivalence was not discussed: the fact that cases based on domestic law rights would be similarly hindered was not considered. Arguably, the

ECJ at this stage was prioritising the principle of effectiveness over the principle of autonomy. In any event, in this case we see the application of the effectiveness principle creating a form of reverse discrimination, a difference in treatment that the Court did not seem to find objectionable. Other consequences of this ruling for the domestic legal system are discussed at 8.4.2.3.

Factortame I was handed down at roughly the same time as cases such as *Marshall (No. 2)* and might be thought to be part of the high water mark of the effectiveness jurisprudence. In subsequent cases the ECJ has continued to reason from the need to ensure effectiveness, although with less spectacular effects. This point is well illustrated by *Peterbroeck* (case C–312/93) and *Van Schijndel* (cases C–430 and 431/93), both of which concerned the ability of national courts to refer questions to the ECJ on their own motion. *Van Schijndel* concerned a Dutch rule which precluded the national court from referring a question to the ECJ when the parties themselves had not raised the issue of EC law. The question of whether the Dutch rule itself was compatible with the principles of effectiveness and equivalence came before the ECJ. In contrast to its approach in *Factortame I*, the Court commenced by re-stating the concept of national procedural autonomy, subject – as ever – to the requirements of effectiveness and equivalence. Rather than emphasising the effectiveness of EC law as a guiding principle, it returned to its earlier formulation of 'impossible or excessively difficult', albeit with a new twist. In *Van Schijndel*, the Court held that:

> a national procedural provision [which] renders application of Community law impossible or excessively difficult must be analysed by reference to the role of that provision in the procedure, its progress and its special features, viewed as a whole, before the various national instances. In the light of that analysis the basic principles of the domestic judicial system, such as the *protection of the rights of the defence, the principle of legal certainty* and the *proper conduct of procedure must*, where appropriate, *be taken into consideration*.

What is clear from this ruling is that the impact of the national rule must be analysed on the facts of each case, to see whether the exercise of the Community law right is rendered excessively difficult taking into account the demands of natural justice and legal certainty. The courts therefore have to balance competing interests. In *Van Schijndel*, the Court came to the conclusion that the Dutch rule was not incompatible with Community law. In *Peterbroeck* (case C–312/93), which imposed a 60-day time limit beyond which neither party to the case could raise a matter of EC law, the ECJ using identical reasoning to that used in *Van Schijndel*, found on the facts that the exercise of the EC law right had been rendered excessively difficult. In this case it was not the limit of 60 days in itself that was the problem, but the particular circumstances of the case.

Although there are a series of cases on similar points, *Van Schijndel* and *Peterbroeck* illustrate the consequence of the ECJ's 'balancing' approach. On the one hand, it might be suggested that this approach reconciles the tension between the principle of national autonomy and the need to ensure effective protection of EC law rights. The problem is that in emphasising the importance to be given to the particular facts in each case, the ECJ has – despite its emphasis on legal certainty – introduced a significant amount of uncertainty into this area. It is not possible to say that national courts must have the right to refer questions to the ECJ of their own motion or, on the other hand, that they need not. Instead, the answer to whether national rules limiting national courts' rights to refer questions of EC law to the ECJ of their own motion are acceptable is, 'it depends'. By introducing the balancing test, the ECJ has referred the assessment of all the facts back to the national courts, at least in most cases, which adds a further element of uncertainty in this area. This approach was recently confirmed in *Evans* (case C–63/01), a case involving the requirement in the Second Insurance Directive (84/5/EEC) to set up a compensation scheme for injuries caused by an unidentified vehicle. In the UK, this scheme is operated by the Motor Insurers' Bureau (MIB). Evans sought to challenge the procedural arrangements for appealing MIB decisions. Having confirmed its earlier case law, the ECJ stated that the ultimate assessment was for the national courts, although in this case, the Court also confirmed that the directive required only minimum procedural rules, and that the UK's system appeared to be compatible.

8.4.2.3 *The creation of new remedies?*

We have seen the starting point of the Court's jurisprudence being the concept of national procedural autonomy. As the ECJ confirmed in *Rewe-Handelsgesellschaft Nord mbH* (case 158/80), a Member State is not required to create new remedies for Community law rights, subject always to the principles of equivalence and effectiveness. It is the consequences of the application of effectiveness that gives rise to problems here, in a number of ways.

The first point to note is that in some instances the Court has seen the remedy as forming part of the substantive right. In cases involving repayment of charges levied in breach of Community law, the Court has held that repayment of the sums is a consequence of, and an adjunct to, the right not to pay customs duties. If there was no right to repayment, the substantive right itself would be undermined. This in practice requires a specific form of remedy to be available as a matter of EC law, although the procedural elements of such a claim will fall to be determined by national law, subject always to the principles of equivalence and effectiveness. Although the Court has not phrased this idea in terms of effectiveness itself, in other circumstances it has recognised that judicial remedies are, in principle, necessary to secure effective protection for the individual's rights.

We have also seen that in developing the notion of effectiveness, the ECJ has required that national rules which impede the effectiveness of Community law should be disapplied. In this context, there is a fine line between the disapplication of rules and the creation of new remedies. The *Factortame I* (case C–213/89) case is a good example. In that case, national rules precluded the granting of interim relief by injunction against the Crown. The ECJ held that the national courts should set aside this rule. The consequence was that the English courts were required to apply what was admittedly an existing remedy, but in an entirely novel situation. *Factortame I* had other consequences. The immediate result of the application of the ruling was that EC-derived rights would be treated more favourably than those based in domestic law. The English courts recognised that it is difficult to justify a difference in available remedies in similar situations based on whether the applicant's claim was based on EC law or not. When, in a subsequent case (*M v Home Office*), the possibility of an injunction against the Crown was raised, the House of

Lords agreed that in principle such injunctions were available, despite the fact that the rights in question were based on English law, not EC law.

One might have argued that the *Factortame I* ruling was an isolated case, and, in the light of the ECJ's more cautious approach to the principle of effectiveness, it was not to be seen as suggesting that the 'no new remedies' principle had been eliminated entirely. *Francovich* (case C–6 and 9/90) and more recent cases, however, suggest that it has again been eroded. The Court in *Francovich* (cases C–6 & 9/90) introduced the notion of State liability. It can be seen as another enforcement mechanism for EC law rights, and is discussed above at 8.2. As will be seen there, *Francovich* created substantive rights for individuals in certain circumstances, with national legal systems again to provide the procedural framework within which individuals can exercise those rights. Although the ECJ has provided some guidance as to the requirements to be satisfied regarding a successful claim under state liability, the remainder of the cause of action will also be determined within the national legal system. All elements determined by the national legal system are subject to the requirements of effectiveness and equivalence. The end result is that a cause of action and remedy is to be provided as a matter of EC law, requiring Member States to provide remedies should their national legal system not already provide them in those circumstances.

Palmisani v *INPS* (case C–261/95) concerned a claim for damages for losses suffered as a result of the belated transposition of Directive 80/987 on the protection of employees in the event of their employers' insolvency. INPS was the agency responsible for managing the fund set up to guarantee employees' arrears of wages as required by the directive. Following the ECJ's ruling in *Francovich* (cases C–6 & 9/90), the directive had finally been implemented in Italy by legislative decree. Under the decree, claims for compensation from INPS were limited to not more than one year from the date of entry into force of the decree. The claimant's claim, having been brought outside this period, had been rejected by the Italian court. He argued before the ECJ that the one-year limitation period was unlawful, being contrary to the requirement of equivalence and effectiveness. More recently, *Metallgesellschaft & Hoechst* v *Inland Revenue* (case C–410/98) concerned a British ruling which imposed advance corporation tax on subsidiary companies whose parents were not UK resident, a discriminatory rule. The applicants challenged the imposition of the tax, claiming the interest they would have earned had they not been subject to the advance taxation. It was far from clear under English law that restitution would be available in these circumstances (see discussion at 8.5.4). The Court ruled that it was the premature levying of the tax that created the lack of equality contrary to Article 43 EC. To protect the rights to equality guaranteed by the freedom of establishment, the lost interest could be claimed by way of restitution. The Court went further and, reasoning from *Marshall II* (paras 24–32), held that interest on the sum claimed was also due.

This case is significant in two main respects. The first is that the ECJ did not seem unduly concerned with whether the remedy claimed would have been available under national law or not. This disregard is hard to square with an approach that is based on respect for national procedural autonomy and the notion that Member States would not be required to create new remedies. In this judgment the Court is returning to the approach that can be found in the 'repayment' cases mentioned earlier: that is, the Court has reasoned from the importance of the substantive

EC law right in issue. In *Metallgesellschaft & Hoechst*, this was the principle of non-discrimination lying at the heart of the freedom of establishment in Article 43 (ex 52). The Court in *Metallgesellschaft & Hoechst* therefore seemed less concerned with assessing the effectiveness of national remedies and more with ensuring the effectiveness of the EC law right itself.

One might argue that *Metallgesellschaft & Hoechst* constitutes nothing more than a recent example of the early case law. The Court has however also looked to the substance of the EC law rights in other circumstances, not concerned with repayment. In *Courage* (case C–353/99), the ECJ held that a right of action in damages against another private party for breach of Article 81 (ex 85) must, in principle, be available. In reaching this conclusion, the Court argued that:

> [t]he full effectiveness of Article 85 [now 81] of the Treaty and, in particular, that practical effect of the prohibition laid down in Article 85(1) [now 81(1)] would be put at risk if it were not open to any individual to claim damages for loss caused to him by a contract or by conduct liable to restrict or distort competition (para. 26).

Similar trends to those identified in *Metallgesellschaft & Hoechst* can be seen here. Again there is an emphasis on the effectiveness of the substantive right which requires a cause of action to be provided, irrespective of the provisions of the national legal system. In this case, the Court emphasised the centrality of the competition provisions within the Treaty and *Courage* might therefore be limited to competition cases or to other areas which are central to the Community project on competition law (see further Chapters 26–29). Nonetheless, in the light of these cases, it is difficult to maintain that EC law does not in some circumstances require that new remedies be provided. This was confirmed further by the decision in *Antonio Munoz Cia SA* v *Frumar Ltd* (case C–253/00), involving Regulation 2200/96 ([1996] OJ L297/1) on the standards for the classification of grapes. Munoz brought civil proceedings against Frumar who had sold grapes under particular labels which did not comply with the relevant standard. Although the regulation did not confer rights on individuals such as Munoz, but applied to all operators in the market, it was accepted that failing to comply with the regulation could have adverse consequences for other operators. Referring to the principle of effectiveness, the Court held that a trader must be able to bring civil proceedings against a competitor to ensure that the regulation is enforced effectively (assuming that the provisions in issue are directly applicable). This rather generous view seems to cement the position in *Courage* v *Crehan*, and it is now the case that, insofar as a provision of EC law is directly applicable (as opposed to directly effective – see Chapter 5), it is open to be invoked in civil proceedings even though the provision itself does not confer rights on an individual (see also Betlem (2004) 64 *Cambridge Law Journal* 126).

8.4.3 Principle of 'equivalence'

Whilst much of the earlier case law considered in some detail the requirements of effectiveness, less attention was paid to the notion of 'equivalence'.

Clearly, a rule which discriminates, directly or indirectly, against claimants relying on EC law will be contrary to Community law. Such was the case in *Criminal Proceedings against Bickel and another* (case C–274/96). Here, rules of the Trento-Alto region of Italy, which provided that the German language was to have the same status as Italian in relations between *citizens of that area* and the judicial and administrative authorities, but which did not extend to persons of Austrian and German nationality and residence, were held to be discriminatory in their effect, contrary to Article 12 EC. Since then, the ECJ has had to consider more directly the question of equivalence.

On the question of equivalence in *Palmisani*, the applicant pointed to other, more generous limitation rules governing claims for damages and to the 'manifest difference' between (for example) the five-year limitation period for reparation in general claims for non-contractual liability and the one-year period allowed for claims based on *Francovich*. The Court held that to ascertain comparability, 'the essential characteristics of the domestic system of reference must be examined'. Prior to the passing of the legislative decree there was no remedy in Italy for such a claim: 'If the domestic system [was] incapable of serving as a basis for a claim under *Francovich* no other relevant comparisons [could] be made.' The Member State must therefore make reparation for the consequences of the loss or damage caused to the claimant on the basis of national rules of liability, provided that they satisfy the requirement of effectiveness.

In *Edis* (case C–231/96), national time limits were again the subject of challenge. This case concerned a shorter time limit imposed for claims for the recovery of payments made regarding charges which had not actually been due, when compared with the time limits for payments made for other sums paid but not due. The applicant had made payments for charges that had not been due; it claimed that the principle of equivalence meant that the longer of the two periods should be applied, as the charges had their basis in EC law. The matter was referred to the ECJ, which began by reiterating the principle that procedural rules must apply without distinction to actions originating in Community law and those based on national law. The Court continued, however, to make the point that this principle of equivalence did not mean that national legal systems could not distinguish between different types of action, such as making a distinction, as in this case, between rules regarding challenges to charges and levies and those relating to the recovery of sums paid in other circumstances, unless the less favourable rules applied only for actions based on Community law. The ECJ concluded that the principle of equivalence could not 'be interpreted as obliging a Member State to extend its most favourable rules governing recovery under national law to all actions for repayment of charges or dues levied in breach of Community law'. (para. 36.)

The Court continued:

> Community law does not in principle preclude the legislation of a Member State from laying down, alongside a limitation period applicable under the ordinary law to actions between individuals for the recovery of sums paid but not due, special detailed rules governing claims and legal proceedings to challenge the imposition of charges and other levies. The position would only be different if those detailed rules applied solely to actions based on community law for the repayment of such charges and levies (para. 37).

National rules are thus permitted to distinguish between different circumstances such as whether public bodies are parties to the action.

This passage in *EDIS* was cited verbatim in a similar claim for repayment of the

Italian registration charge in *IN.CO.GE '90* (cases C–10 & 22/97). Here the Court held that 'any reclassification of the legal relationship between the tax authorities and certain companies in that state . . . in such circumstances . . . is a matter for national law'.

Similarly, in *Criminal Proceedings against Nunes* (case C–186/98) the Court upheld the right of a Member State to impose criminal penalties for the improper use of the European Social Fund, even though the regulation governing misuse of such funds provided only for civil remedies. The Court held that where a Community regulation failed to provide specifically for any penalty for an infringement of Community law, Article 10 of the EC Treaty required Member States to take all measures necessary to ensure the application and effectiveness of that law. The choice of penalties remained at Member States' discretion, provided that the penalty chosen complied with the principle of equivalence, and was 'effective, proportionate and dissuasive'.

The Court has had further opportunity to consider equivalence in a number of cases subsequently. In *Levez* v *TH Jennings (Harlow Pools) Ltd* (case C–326/96), in a claim for damages in respect of sex discrimination brought under Article 141 EC and Directive 75/117, the Court was asked to consider a two-year time limit on arrears of payment of damages under the UK Equal Pay Act in the light of the principles of equivalence and effectiveness. It was argued that the claim, brought before an industrial tribunal, could have been brought before a county court, by analogy with claims for unlawful deductions from wages or unlawful discrimination in terms of employment on grounds of race or disability, which were subject to more generous limitation rules. The Court held that it was 'for national courts to ascertain whether the procedural rules intended to safeguard rights derived from Community law were safeguarded under national law and complied with the principle of equivalence'. A rule of national law would be deemed equivalent 'where the purpose and cause of action are similar'. However, citing the earlier case of *EDIS* v *Ministero delle Finanze* (case C–231/96), it held that 'that principle is not to be interpreted as requiring Member States to extend their most favourable rules to all actions brought . . . in the field of employment law'. In assessing equivalence, the national court must consider 'the purpose and essential characteristics of allegedly similar domestic actions'. It must review the different procedures as a whole and weigh the relative advantages and disadvantages of each. On the facts it was found that the two-year period could not be enforced against the applicant, since, having been misled by her employer, she had no way of determining whether she was being discriminated against, or to what extent: 'To allow her employer to rely on the two-year rule would be to deprive his employee of the means provided by the Directive of enforcing the principle of equal pay before the court.' Thus, *in these particular circumstances* the remedy provided was ineffective. In applying the ECJ's ruling in *Levez*, the Employment Appeal Tribunal ([1999] 3 CMLR 715) found that the two-year limitation period provided under the Equal Pay Act did not satisfy the requirement of equivalence, since it had been introduced in order to give effect to Britain's EC obligations and it applied only to equal pay claims based on sex discrimination. This is, it is submitted, a somewhat stricter line than that taken by the ECJ in *Palmisani*.

The House of Lords referred further questions to the ECJ on how to identify a 'similar' cause of action in *Preston* (case C–78/98). The ECJ re-emphasised the general balancing approach which it had taken in the effectiveness cases of *Peterbroeck* (case C–312/93) and *Van Schijndel* (cases C–430 and 431/93; see above at 8.4.2.3). It commented that the relevant national rules must be considered in their general context and concluded, in terms very similar to those used in *Van Schijndel*, that 'the national court must verify objectively, in the abstract, whether the rules at issue are similar taking into account the role played by those rules in the procedure as whole, as well as the operation of that procedure and special feature of those rules' (para. 63).

8.5 Impact of EC law on national remedies

Although EC law does not in principle prescribe specific remedies and procedures to be adopted by national courts in actions based on EC law, the obligation to ensure that national remedies are effective, or sufficiently effective, to protect individuals' Community rights has on occasions required the modification of national law, even the provision of new remedies. These will now be considered, bearing in mind that some of the earlier cases might be decided differently today.

8.5.1 Interim relief

In *R v Secretary of State for Transport, ex parte Factortame Ltd* (case C–213/89) the Court held that English courts were obliged to provide interim injunctions against the Crown where there was no other means of protecting individuals' Community rights, even though, as the House of Lords had found in that case ([1990] 2 AC 85), no such remedy was available as a matter of national law. Following the ECJ's ruling, the House of Lords granted the requested relief ([1991] 1 AC 603 at 645). In *Zuckerfabrik Süderdithmarschen AG* (cases C–143/88, 92/89) the ECJ laid down *Community* criteria for the granting of interim relief pending a ruling from the ECJ under Article 234 on the validity of a Community act, based on the principles applicable to the exercise of its own jurisdiction to grant such relief under Articles 242 and 243 (ex 185 and 186) EC. Relief should be granted only if the facts and legal circumstances are such as to persuade the court that:

(a) serious doubts exist about the validity of the Community measures on which the contested administrative decision is based;

(b) in cases of urgency, and

(c) to avoid serious and irreparable damage to the party seeking the relief.

Given that the granting of interim relief pending a ruling on the *validity* of Community law involved a new situation for national courts, and that the suspension of a Community act would have serious implications for the Community legal order, it is not surprising that the Court provided a common Community solution here. However, although it might have been desirable, in the interests of the coherence of legal remedies, to require national courts to apply the same criteria in a claim for interim relief pending a ruling on the *interpretation* of Community law, the Court is not now likely to do so. Thus, in this context, national procedural rules will continue to apply. It may be noted that in *R v Secretary of State for Health, ex parte Imperial Tobacco Ltd* (*The Times*, 16 November 1999, QBD) Turner J. considered it unnecessary to apply the criteria provided by the ECJ *in Zucherfabrik Süderdith-marschen AG* in a claim for an interim injunction to prevent the enactment of domestic regulations banning tobacco advertising pending a ruling from the ECJ on the validity of the directive on which the regulations were based. He preferred to apply the domestic criteria applicable to claims for interim relief, thereby 'avoiding the problem of the applicant having to prove that the damage that he would suffer in the absence of the grant of suspensory relief would be irreparable'. However, his justification, on the facts perhaps acceptable, was that in this case the date for implementation of the directive, 30 July 2001, had not yet been passed; thus an interim injunction would not have the effect of suspending the application of an *existing* EC obligation.

Zuckerfabrik Süderdithmarschen AG concerned the granting of *suspensory* meas-ures pending a ruling on the validity of a Community measure under Article 234. In *Atlanta Fruchthandelsgesellschaft mbH* (case C–465/93) the Court held, in the context of a claim for interim relief in the form of a grant of licences to import bananas from third countries pending a ruling on the validity of a Council regulation setting up a common banana regime, that the principles laid down in *Zuckerfabrik Süderdithmarschen AG* also applied to the grant of *positive* measures. It was not possible to make a distinction between an order designed to preserve an existing position and an order intended to create a new legal position. In decid-ing whether to grant such relief, national courts must respect existing decisions from the ECJ on the matter in question whether under Article 234 or Article 230; they must take into account the Community interest, particularly the damage which the non-application of a Community regulation may cause to an estab-lished Community regime. National courts may also consider the repercussions which an interim order may entail on important individual interests and even on national interests, economic and social. If the grant of interim relief represents a financial risk for the Community the national court must be in a position to require the applicant to provide adequate guarantees, such as the deposit of money or other security. The decision whether or not to grant interim relief is a difficult one, not to be taken lightly, particularly when it involves the suspen-sion of a normative act, a Community regulation, as was the case in *Atlanta Fruchthandelsgesellschaft mbH*.

Zuckerfabrik Süderdithmarschen AG and *Atlanta Fruchthandelsgesellschaft mbH* con-cerned the national courts' powers to grant interim relief pending a ruling from the ECJ on the validity of a Community act, a regulation. In the more recent case of *T. Port GmbH & Co. KG v Bundesanstalt für Landwirtschaft und Ernährung* (case C–68/95), the CFI refused to take the next logical step when it held that national courts had no power to order interim measures pending a decision on the EC institutions' *failure to act*. Indeed the national courts had no jurisdiction to refer questions con-cerning such alleged failures to the ECJ. Judicial review of alleged failures on the part of the institutions could only be carried out by the Community courts. Given the limited access of individuals to the Community courts under Article 232 EC this decision appears to have left a gap in the judicial protection of individuals (see further Chapter 12).

8.5.2 **Challenge to statutory provisions**

Claims based on Community law will often involve a challenge to legislative acts or omissions. In many cases the challenge is indirect, ancillary to the principal action based on Community law. If the national court finds the provisions of a national statute incompatible with Community law, it may grant the remedy requested and simply 'disapply' them, on the principles established in *Simmenthal SpA (No. 2)* (case 106/77, see Chapter 4). The case of *R v Secretary of State for Employment, ex parte Equal Opportunities Commission* concerned a direct challenge to a domestic statute, something which is clearly not permitted in British law. The Equal Opportunities Commission applied for a declaration that certain provisions of the Employment Protection (Consolidation) Act 1978 were contrary to Community sex discrimination law and an order of mandamus requiring the Secretary of State to rectify the breach. A majority of the Court of Appeal thought that it would be 'wrong and unconstitutional for the Courts to grant a declaration or mandamus in an attempt to enforce obligations of Community law which, if they existed, did so only in international law' ([1993] 1 WLR 872). The House of Lords disagreed, and granted a declaration that the provisions in question were *incompatible* with EC law (the claim for mandamus was not pursued) ([1995] 1 AC 1). There was no need to declare that the UK or the Secretary of State were in *breach* of their obligations under Community law. A declaration of incompatibility would suffice for the purposes sought by the EOC and was capable of being granted consistently with the precedent afforded by *Factortame (No. 2)* [1991] AC 603.

8.5.3 **Damages**

As the case law discussed above illustrates, national rules limiting the amount of damages that may be awarded will not always be successful. The approach taken in *Marshall II* requiring 'full' compensation can be seen in other areas, such as the state liability cases, such as *Bonifaci* (cases C–94 and 95/95). Applying this principle in *Brasserie du Pêcheur*, cases C–46 & 48/93) the ECJ held that a 'total exclusion' of loss of profit as a head of damage would not be permissible. Even an award of exemplary damages 'could not be ruled out' if such damages could be awarded pursuant to a similar claim or action founded on domestic law (para. 89).

The case law is not entirely clear, however, as the Court has sought to distinguish the approach to whether interest should be awarded by reference to the nature of the right at stake, as the sex discrimination cases illustrate. Article 6 of the Equal Treament Directive (76/207/EEC) was amended by Directive 2002/73/EC, and now limits the cases in which an upper limit on the amount of damages could be imposed in advance. This is, of course, of no help in other areas and the problem remains regarding the principles to be applied in determining whether limitations on damages and interest on damages are 'effective' for the purposes of EC law. In *Evans* (case 63/01), a case under the Second Insurance Directive, the ECJ held that compensation awarded under the rules implementing Article 1(4) of Directive 84/5/EEC 'must take account of the effluxion of time until actual payment of the sums awarded in order to guarantee adequate compensation for the victims', which suggests that the obligation to award interest may extend to other areas of EC law.

8.5.4 **Restitution**

There have been many claims before national courts for the return of money paid in breach of Community law. The EC Treaty prohibits the imposition of customs duties or charges having equivalent effect, and discriminatory taxation (see Chapter 17). These charges are normally levied by national authorities. As early as 1960 the ECJ held, in the context of a claim for sums levied in breach of the ECSC Treaty, that once a Member State had been found to have breached Community law it must take the necessary measures to make good the lawful effects of the breach, making restitution for sums wrongfully levied as a result of that breach (*Humblet v Belgium* (case 6/60)). There is now a consistent line of authority to this effect (see, e.g., *Express Dairy Foods Ltd* v *Intervention Board for Agricultural Produce* (case 130/79)). Prior to the House of Lords' decision in *Woolwich Equitable Building Society* v *Inland Revenue Commissioners* ([1993] AC 70), it was thought that there was no general right under English law to the recovery of money paid under a mistake of law. Since sums paid in breach of Community law would normally be paid under a mistake of law, such a rule would not have been 'sufficiently effective' to protect individuals' Community rights. This factor undoubtedly coloured the House of Lords' finding in *Woolwich Equitable Building Society* v *Inland Revenue Commissioners*, in the context of a claim based on domestic law, that money paid under a mistake of law was in certain circumstances recoverable as a matter of British law. 'It would be strange,' said Lord Goff, 'if the right of the citizen to recover overpaid taxes were to be more restricted under domestic law than European law.' The ruling in *Metallgesellschaft & Hoechst* would seem to have confirmed this position.

8.5.5 **Time-limits**

In *Express Dairy Foods Ltd* v *Intervention Board for Agricultural Produce* (case 130/79) the Court suggested that a 'reasonable' period of limitation would not make it 'impossible in practice' for national courts effectively to protect individuals' Community rights. This principle, consistently invoked, was put in doubt by the Court's decision in *Emmott* v *Minister for Social Welfare* (case C–208/90), decided in 1991. Subsequent case law has retreated from the approach in *Emmott*. In *Palmisani*, on the question of the effectiveness of the remedy provided, with its one-year limitation rule, the Court held that although in principle reparation must be commensurate with the loss or damage sustained (see *Marshall (No. 2)* (case C–271/91) and *Brasserie du Pêcheur* (cases C–46 & 48/93)), 'reparation cannot always be ensured by the retroactive and proper application in full of the measures implementing the Directive'. The setting of 'reasonable' limitation periods was permitted under EC law. A one-year limitation period such as the one in question 'cannot be regarded as making it excessively difficult or *a fortiori* impossible to lodge a claim for compensation'. Thus the one-year limitation period would not be incompatible with EC law.

In *Preston* v *Wolverhampton NHS Healthcare Trust* (case C–78/98), the ECJ found a six-month bar on proceedings (following termination of employment) acceptable under EC law. In *Fantask A/S* v *Industriministeriet* (case C–188/95) the ECJ accepted a Danish statutory five-year limitation period for the recovery of debts, running from the date on which the debt became payable, in the context of a challenge to the

Ministry's refusal to reimburse company registration charges levied from the applicant in breach of EC Directive 69/335. The Court held (at para. 48) that it had:

> acknowledged, in the interests of legal certainty, which protects the taxpayer and the authorities concerned, that the setting of reasonable limitation periods for bringing proceedings [was] compatible with Community law. Such periods cannot be regarded as rendering impossible or excessively difficult the exercise of rights conferred by Community law, even if the expiry of those periods necessarily entails the dismissal, in whole or in part, of the action brought.

This paragraph was cited by the Court in *Levez* (case C–326/96) and *EDIS* (case C–231/96).

The five-year limitation period was re-examined in *Fantask* and found to be neither discriminatory nor unreasonable. Distinguishing *Emmott*, the Court held that *Emmott* was 'justified on the particular facts of the case, in which the time bar had the result of *depriving the applicant of any opportunity whatsoever* to rely on her right to equal treatment under the Community Directive'.

It seems that reasonable limitation rules will be acceptable, since they do not render the exercise of Community rights impossible or excessively difficult; but where they 'deprive the applicant of any opportunity whatsoever' to rely on her rights, or 'strike at the very essence of those rights', or where the applicant has been misled as to her Community rights, as in *Levez*, they will not be permitted. These principles have been re-affirmed by the ECJ in recent case law. In *Grundig Italiana SpA* v *Ministero delle Finanze* (case C–255/00), the ECJ had to deal with the national rules which shortened the period within which claims for sums paid but not due could be recovered. Crucially, the ECJ confirmed that such changes could be made, referring again to the 'practically impossible' test, but then went on to hold that such a change requires transitional arrangements to deal with the situation where such a change of time limits would have the effect of retroactively depriving individuals of rights to repayment, or of allowing such claimants too short a period in which to assert their rights. Rather than leaving this matter for the national court to assess, the ECJ determined that the 90-day transitional period allowed by the national legislation was too short to allow 'normally diligent tax payers [to] familiarise themselves with the new regime and commence proceedings in circumstances which do not compromise their chances of success' (para. 40). This is a slightly more stringent approach to assessing national rules than that taken about other aspects of time limits since *Emmott*, as the ECJ did not require that there be a total bar to the exercise of the rights before the national rule be set aside. This aspect of the ruling, however, concerned only one aspect of the issue of time limits, that of the transitional arrangements. In contrast, in *Recheio-Cash & Carry SA* (case C–30/02), a 90-day limitation period for launching a claim for the repayment of charges levied in breach of Community law was held to be compatible with the principle of effectiveness. This case concerned the limitation period itself, rather than transitional arrangements, so issues about allowing time for acclimatisation to a new system do not arise. Nonetheless, it is noteworthy that the Court did not refer to *Grundig Italiana* in its judgment.

The trend of case law since *Emmott* indicates that the Court will be slow to regard Member States' limitation rules as unreasonable. Nevertheless, the acceptance of reasonable limitation rules will inevitably operate to modify the principle of full compensation, as occurred in *Fantask* (case C–188/95), in which the applicant sought, unsuccessfully, to recover company registration charges levied in breach of Community law over a nine-year period, from 1983 to 1992. The precise limits of what will be regarded as reasonable remain unclear.

8.5.6 State liability

The principle of State liability, discussed above at 8.2, remains a hybrid, part national, part Community law. This has created problems for national courts. Prior to *Brasserie du Pêcheur* it was assumed, following *Francovich*, that a claim for damages against the State must be brought on the same basis, and according to the same rules, as the 'equivalent' claim based on national law. However, although the claim in English law would clearly be in the nature of a tort it was not clear which tort was appropriate. The nearest 'equivalent' actions available against a public authority, the torts of misfeasance in public office, of breach of statutory duty, or of negligence, were, as the Court found in *Brasserie du Pêcheur*, too restrictive to provide effective protection for individuals' Community rights under *Francovich*. A similar problem had arisen in the context of claims for damages based on the principle of direct effects (see, e.g., *Garden Cottage Foods Ltd* v *Milk Marketing Board* [1984] AC 130 (HL); *Bourgoin SA* v *Ministry of Agriculture, Fisheries and Food* [1986] QB 716 (CA)). English law admitted no claim for damages in respect of legislative or judicial acts. The only way in which individuals' rights under *Francovich* might be effectively protected was either by 'modifying' (i.e., reinterpreting) the existing national remedies of misfeasance or breach of statutory duty (negligence having been rejected as clearly inappropriate), resulting in the possibility of a different standard of liability, depending on whether the claim was based on national or Community law, or by admitting that the Community principle of State liability was a new principle calling for the creation of a new *sui generis* '*Francovich*' tort.

In applying the ECJ's ruling in *R* v *Secretary of State for Transport, ex parte Factortame Ltd (No. 5)* ([1998] 1 CMLR 1353) Hobhouse LJ in the English High Court adopted a compromise position. He examined the question of breach, and the seriousness of the breach, according to the principles laid down by the ECJ in *Brasserie du Pêcheur*. He concluded that 'whilst it could be said that the cause of action was *sui generis*, it was of the character of a breach of statutory duty'. He could find no similarity between the applicants' claim in respect of the UK's breach of its Community obligations and a claim in respect of tortious misfeasance. If the English courts were to follow his lead and treat claims based on *Francovich* as breaches of statutory duty, they would do so on the understanding that such claims could be subject to different principles, and a different approach to interpretation, from those which apply to similar claims based on domestic law. Given that the ECJ has now laid down a number of precise conditions for State liability, it is submitted that it would be better to acknowledge the unique nature of such a claim, based on the breach of a higher legal norm, and treat it as a *sui generis* tort. This now appears to have occurred. Both the Court of Appeal and the House of Lords in *Factortame (No. 5)* dealt with the matter of liability simply by applying the principles of Community law laid down by the ECJ in *Brasserie du Pêcheur*. Likewise, shortly after the final decision in *Factortame (No. 5)*, Sullivan J in the English High Court, in assessing the seriousness of the public authorities' breach of Directive 79/7 in *R v Department of Social Security, ex parte Scullion* ([1999] 3 CMLR 798), adopted the 'basket' or 'global' approach laid down by the ECJ in para. 56 of *Brasserie du Pêcheur* (cases C–46 & 48/93) see 8.2, above) and made no attempt to fit a claim for damages based on *Francovich* into the straight-jacket of the English law of torts.

However, regrettably, as noted above, the rules governing State liability laid down in *Brasserie du Pêcheur* were not comprehensive. It was left to national courts to decide, according to the principles applicable to equivalent claims based on national law, whether the Community law breached was intended to benefit persons such as the applicant (condition (a)); whether there existed the appropriate direct causal link between the State's breach and the applicant's damage (condition (c), which was raised, but not decided, in *Schmidberger* (case C–112/00)); and whether the damage suffered was of a kind in respect of which damages might be awarded.

In *Three Rivers District Council v Bank of England* ([1996] 3 All ER 558), a case decided shortly before *Factortame (No. 5)*, the English High Court was faced with a claim for damages based on breach of statutory duty for the Bank's failure to supervise the credit institutions (notably BCCI), resulting in damage to the investors. The applicant investors argued that the failure was in breach of EC Banking Directive 77/780. Their claim was based on the direct effects of the directive or, in the alternative, *Francovich*. Clarke J, applying the English approach to construction in claims based on breach of statutory duty, found that the directive in question was not intended to give rise to rights to individuals. Nor, for the same reason, did the applicants have a claim under *Francovich*. Whether their claim was based on the direct effects of Directive 77/780 or on *Francovich*, the applicants must establish the relevant Community rights required to be protected. The result required by the directive did not extend to the compensation of savers for any breach of the duties imposed by the directive. On appeal to the House of Lords, the appellants argued their claim for damages under the English tort of misfeasance in public office, as well as on Community law. Again they failed (*The Times*, 19 May 2000). The House found that the respondents did not have the requisite intention or recklessness for liability in misfeasance; nor were the obligations in the directive allegedly breached sufficiently well defined to give rise to rights for individuals.

Like Clarke J in the High Court in the *Three Rivers* case, the English Court of Appeal in *Bowden* v *South West Water Services* ([1999] 3 CMLR 180), focused on the first condition of *Francovich*, whether the Community law allegedly breached was intended to confer rights on the applicant. It construed Environmental Directive 79/903 as intended to benefit persons such as the claimant, whose living as a fisherman had been affected by the defendant's alleged failure properly to implement the directive, and allowed his claim to proceed. It is submitted that an applicant who has suffered damage as a result of alleged breaches of Community law should not be turned away because of an over-restrictive approach to the question of individual rights, a notoriously slippery and subjective concept. Liability can always be restricted or excluded, where this is justified, under the second or third conditions of *Francovich*, on the basis of the seriousness of the breach or the directness of the damage.

It is a matter for regret that the ECJ, in laying down common Community rules concerning the nature of the breach required to give rise to liability, failed to provide some common rules or guidelines covering *all* aspects of liability, as, particularly in the area of non-contractual liability, the rules relating to breach and damage and causation are interrelated, and operate together as control mechanisms restricting or extending liability according to perceived requirements of policy. While the overall result may not differ greatly from State to State the individual elements vary considerably. As long as the principle of national treatment applies in any of these areas there will be inequality in the application of the principle of State liability from State to State. There will also be uncertainty, as national rules are vulnerable to attack as being ineffective, or insufficiently effective, to protect individuals' rights. However, given the ECJ's unequivocal affirmation of the principle of national treatment in recent years, further judicial development of common Community rules appears unlikely.

Although a principle of State liability for executive acts, and judicial remedies in respect of such acts, already exists in all Member States, these claims will now also be subject to the rules laid down in *Brasserie du Pêcheur*. As with legislative acts, existing national remedies may need to be modified to ensure that they are effective in protecting individuals' rights; alternatively (and preferably) claims may be brought under a new *Francovich* tort.

A principle of liability for judicial acts in breach of Community law, as laid down in *Brasserie du Pêcheur*, clearly breaks new constitutional ground in most if not all Member States. If available in theory, it is unlikely to be applied freely in practice. If only for reasons of polity, neither the ECJ nor a national court is likely to find a judicial breach of Community law sufficiently serious to warrant liability.

8.6 Conclusions

The principle of 'State liability' provides individuals with a strong tool before their national courts to secure the enforcement of their rights under Community law. Although controversial, the decision in *Köbler* v *Austria* strengthens this further. However, as the case law on State liability has shown, *Francovich* is not a universal panacea. To succeed in a claim for damages the applicant must establish that the law infringed was intended to confer rights on individuals and that the breach is sufficiently serious (as well as the requisite damage and causation). In cases of non-implementation of directives, as in *Francovich* or *Dillenkofer*, where there is no doubt about the nature of the Community obligation, the breach is likely to be sufficiently serious. However, where the Community obligation allegedly breached is less clear, the breach may well be found to be excusable. As far as other remedies before national courts are concerned, the law in this area divides the responsibility for procedural rules and remedies between European and national law. The underlying principle is that in the absence of harmonizing measures the national legal system should apply, subject to the EC law rules of equivalence and effectiveness. There seems to be little difference in the ECJ's approach to cases where EC law has specifically required that a remedy be provided and those areas where there is no such express requirement. The case law identified above shows clear parallels in the approach taken by the ECJ, both in its expansive phase and when it has become more cautious. The division between national rule and those of EC law reflects the division between the ECJ and the national courts shown in Article 234. There the national courts have the responsibility for hearing the case, determining the facts and making a ruling in the light of EC law requirements as interpreted by the ECJ.

The balance between the two court systems has not been static, reflecting different approaches by the ECJ. The cases of the early years show deference to the autonomy of the national legal systems. A more expansive approach to the requirements of 'effectiveness' can be seen immediately prior to the TEU. The problem with an approach which emphasises the need for remedies to be 'effective', rather than looking for equivalence, is that EC rights could end up being treated more favourably than rights deriving from national law. It seems as though the ECJ recognised this difficulty, or a least recognised that some concerns were being expressed as, subsequently, the ECJ has adopted an approach which seeks to balance the two extremes. In *Dorsch Consult* (case C–54/96) it held:

> It is for the legal system of each Member State to determine which court or tribunal has jurisdiction to hear disputes involving individual rights derived from Community law ... It is not for the Court of Justice to involve itself in the resolution of questions of jurisdiction to which the classification of certain legal situations may give rise in the national legal system.

While in earlier judgments the Court was prepared to prescribe specific Community rules and express its views on the adequacy or effectiveness of particular domestic remedies or procedures, more recently it has emphasised that:

> it is for national courts to ascertain whether the procedural rules intended to secure that the rights derived from Community law are safeguarded under national law and comply with the principle of equivalence (*Levez* v *Jennings (Harlow Pools) Ltd* (case C–326/96)).

This latter approach clearly recognises the importance of the national legal systems in providing the legal framework within which EC law operates and which fall to the national courts to assess. The principles of EC law do not mean that national rules will automatically fail. Nor does the new approach, however, mean that the national courts will not be required to disapply national rules or create new remedies, as can be seen from even recent examples. In each case, it will be a matter for the facts: the precise scope of the rules in question and their interplay with the substantive EC law rights.

This view is borne out in the case of *Adidas AG* (case C–223/98), decided in 1999. The case concerned the implementation by the Swedish authorities of EC Regulation 3295/94, designed to prevent trade in counterfeit goods. Under the regulation implementation was left expressly to the national authorities. Following the seizure of counterfeit goods by the Swedish customs the owner of the original product sought to take action to enforce his rights against the consignee of these goods. The Swedish authorities, bound by their national confidentiality rules, refused to reveal his identity. In a reference for interpretation of the regulation under Article 234 the Court found that the system laid down by the regulation depended directly for its effective application on the information supplied to the holder of the right. If the identity of the consignee could not be disclosed to him it was in practice impossible for him to proceed with his case. The regulation could not therefore be understood as precluding disclosure to the holder of the right of the information which he needs.

The result of the ECJ's approach is that there will be some differences in the ways and circumstances in which individuals may enforce their rights under EC law throughout the Union. The Court has been criticised for a piecemeal and reactive approach to the question of procedures and remedies, although given the sensitivity of the area such an incremental approach is hardly surprising. Indeed, there are those who far from criticising the ECJ, have recognised that it has had to tread a difficult line between excessive judicial activism and the need to ensure that EC law rights are protected effectively. It seems clear that legislative action in this area is necessary should more thorough changes be introduced. Despite judicial suggestions that such action is desirable, if not necessary, there has been little response from the political institutions. It may be that the Member States have chosen not to legislate in this area; that agreement is difficult to reach because of the sensitivity and complexity of the issues involved; or, simply, that the question of harmonisation in this area has simply not had a sufficiently high priority to bring it on to the legislative agenda. For the time being, then, it seems that procedural matters will continue to be decided on the principle of national procedural autonomy balanced by concepts of equivalence and effectiveness.

FURTHER READING

Accetto, M. and Zleptnig, S., 'The principle of effectiveness: rethinking its role in Community Law' (2005) 11 *EPL* 375.

Albors-Llorens, A., 'Changes in the Jurisdiction of the European Court of Justice under the Treaty of Amsterdam' (1998) 35 CML Rev 1273.

Anagnostaras, G., 'The Principle of State Liability for Judicial Breaches: the Impact of European Community Law' (2001) EPL 281.

Betlem, G., 'Torts, A European Ius Commune And The Private Enforcement Of Community Law' (2004) 64 CLJ 126.

Biondi, A., 'The ECJ and certain national procedural limitations: not such a tough relationship' (1999) 36 CML Rev 1271.

Cabral, P. and Chaves, M.C., 'Member State Liability for Decisions of National Courts Adjudicating at Last Instance' (2006) *Maastricht Journal of European and Comparative Law* 109–126.

Caranta, R., 'Judicial Protection against Member States: a new Jus Commune takes shape' (1995) 32 CML Rev 679.

—, 'Learning from our Neighbours: Public Law Remedies Homogenization from Bottom Up' (1997) MJ 220.

Case notes on C–224/01 *Köbler* v *Republik Österreich* [2005] ERPL 419.

Coppell, J., 'Domestic Limitations on Recovery for Breach of EC Law' (1998) ILJ 259.

Craig, P., '*Francovich*, Remedies and the Scope of Damages Liability' (1993) 109 LQR 595.

—, 'Once more unto the Breach: the Community, the State and Damages Liability' (1997) 113 LQR 67.

Dougan, M., 'Cutting your Losses in the Enforcement Deficit: A Community Right to the Recovery of Unlawfully Levied Charges?' (1998) 1 CYELS 233.

Fennelly, N., 'The Area of Freedom, Security and Justice and the European Court of Justice' (2000) 46 ICLQ 941.

Gravells, N., 'Disapplying an Act of Parliament: Constitutional Enormity or Community Law Right?' [1989] PL 568.

Himsworth, C., 'Things Fall Apart: the Harmonisation of Community Judicial Protection Revisited' (1997) 22 EL Rev 291.

Hoskins, M., 'Tilting the Balance: Supremacy and National Procedural Rules' (1996) 21 EL Rev 365.

Kilpatrick, C., Novitz, T. and Skidmore, P. (eds), 'The Future of Remedies in Europe' (Hart Publishing, 2000).

Lang, J. T., 'The Duties of National Courts under Community Constitutional Law' (1997) 22 EL Rev 3.

—, 'The Duties of National Authorities under Community Law' (1998) 23 EL Rev 109.

Oliver, P., 'Enforcing Community Rights in English Courts' (1987) 50 MLR 881.

Prechal, S., 'Community Law in National Courts: The lessons from *Van Schijndel*' (1998) 35 CML Rev 681.

—, 'Member State Liability and Direct Effect: What's the Difference after all?' (2006) 17 EBL Rev 299–316.

Ross, M., 'Refining Effective Enjoyment' (1990) 15 EL Rev 476.

—, 'Beyond *Francovich*' (1993) 56 MLR 55.

Snyder, F., 'The Effectiveness of European Community Law' (1993) 56 MLR 19.

Steiner, J., 'How to Make the Action Fit the Case: Domestic Remedies for Breach of EEC Law' (1987) 12 EL Rev 102.

—, 'From Direct Effects to *Francovich*: Shifting Means of Enforcement of Community Law' (1993) 18 EL Rev 3.

—, 'The Limits of State Liability for Breach of European Community Law' [1998] EPL 69.

Vajda, C., 'Liability for Breach of Community Law: A Survey of the ECJ Cases Post *Factortame*' (2006) 17 EBL Rev 257–268.

Van den Berg, R. and Schafer, H. B., 'State Liability for Infringements of the EC Treaty' (1998) 23 EL Rev 552.

Van Gerven, W., 'Bridging the Gap between Community and National Law: Towards a Principle of Homogeneity of Legal Remedies' (1995) 32 CML Rev 679.

Woods, L. and Smith, F., 'Causation in *Francovich*: The Neglected Problem' (1997) 46 ICLQ 925.

9

The preliminary rulings procedure

9.1 Introduction

The preliminary rulings procedure is important for a number of reasons relating not only to the substantive development of EC law, but also to the relationship between EC law and national law. A glance through the preceding chapters of this book will reveal that the majority of cases cited, and almost all the major principles established by the ECJ, were decided in the context of a reference to that court for a preliminary ruling under Article 234 (ex 177) EC. Cases such as *Van Gend en Loos* (case 26/62), *Costa v ENEL* (case 6/64) and *Defrenne v Sabena (No. 2)* (case 43/75), concerned with questions of interpretation of EC law, enabled the ECJ to develop the crucial concepts of direct effects and the supremacy of EC law. *Internationale Handelsgesellschaft mbH* (case 11/70); *Stauder v City of Ulm* (case 29/69) and *Royal Scholten-Honig (Holdings) Ltd* (cases 103 & 145/77) (see Chapter 6), which raised questions of the validity of EC law, led the way to the incorporation of general principles of law into EC law. The principle of State liability in damages was laid down in *Francovich* (cases C–6, 9/90) in preliminary ruling proceedings. In all areas of EC law, the Article 234 procedure has played a major role in developing the substantive law. The procedure accounts for over 50 per cent of all cases heard by the ECJ. This percentage has of course increased as the CFI has taken over responsibility for judicial review actions (Chapters 11 and 12) and actions for damages (Chapter 13). Nonetheless, the preliminary rulings procedure plays a central part in the development and enforcement of EC law.

If the procedure has been valuable from the point of view of the Community, as a means of developing and clarifying the law, it has been equally valuable to the individual, since it has provided him or her with a means of access to the ECJ when other, direct avenues have been closed. In this way the individual has been able indirectly to challenge action by Member States (e.g., *Van Gend en Loos* – import charge levied in breach of the then Article 12 (now 25)) or by Community institutions (e.g., *Royal Scholten-Honig* – EC regulation invalid for breach of principle of equality) before the ECJ and obtain an appropriate remedy from his national court (see Chapter 8).

The importance of the Article 234 procedure, both in absolute terms and relative to other remedies, has been greatly increased by the development by the ECJ of the concept of direct effects. Where originally only 'directly applicable' regulations might have been expected to be invoked before national courts, these courts may now be required to apply treaty articles, decisions and even directives. Even where EC law is not directly effective it may be invoked before national courts on the principles of indirect effects or State liability under *Francovich*. As a result, national courts now play a major role in the enforcement of EC law. As we will see, the cooperative relationship between the ECJ and the national courts has been a key factor in the success of the preliminary rulings procedure.

Although the preliminary rulings procedure has assumed such an importance in the ways outlined above, its primary and original purpose was to ensure, by means of authoritative rulings on the interpretation and validity of EC law, the correct and uniform application of EC law by the courts of Member States. In assessing its effectiveness, and the attitudes of national courts and the ECJ towards its use, this function, as well as its importance both for individuals and for the Community, should be borne in mind.

9.2 The procedure

Article 234 EC provides that:

> The Court of Justice shall have jurisdiction to give preliminary rulings concerning:
> (a) the interpretation of this Treaty;
> (b) the validity and interpretation of acts of the institutions of the Community;
> (c) the interpretation of the statutes of bodies established by an act of the Council, where those statutes so provide.
> Where such a question is raised before any court or tribunal of a Member State, that court or tribunal may, if it considers that a decision on the question is necessary to enable it to give judgment, request the Court of Justice to give a ruling thereon.
> Where any such question is raised in a case pending before a court or tribunal of a Member State, against whose decisions there is no judicial remedy under national law, that court or tribunal shall bring the matter before the Court of Justice.

Since the TEU, Article 234 is not the only preliminary reference mechanism. Maastricht introduced the possibility for preliminary references within the JHA pillar by virtue of Article 35 TEU. With Amsterdam and the introduction of the new title into the EC Treaty came a separate preliminary rulings mechanism in Article 68 EC for questions relating to that title. The majority of this chapter is devoted to Article 234; Articles 68 EC and 36 TEU will be discussed briefly below at 9.9.

The Treaty of Nice amended Article 225 (ex 168) EC on the jurisdiction of the Court of First Instance to enable it to deal with preliminary rulings under Article 234 'in specific areas laid down by the Statute [of the Court of Justice]' (Article 225(3)). So far, the CFI has not been allocated any specific areas and has therefore yet to give a preliminary ruling (see Statute of the Court of Justice, November 2005 version). (On the relationship between the CFI and ECJ, see also Chapter 7.)

9.2.1 Nature of the preliminary rulings procedure

The preliminary rulings procedure is not an appeals procedure. An appeals procedure implies a hierarchy between the different types of court, some courts being higher and having more authority than those lower down the judicial architecture.

Typically, appeal courts can overrule the decisions of lower courts. The decision whether or not to appeal lies, in the first place, in the hands of the parties, although in some instances leave to appeal from certain courts is required. In contrast, the preliminary rulings procedure merely provides a means whereby national courts, when questions of EC law arise, may apply to the ECJ for a preliminary ruling on matters of interpretation or validity prior to themselves applying the law. In principle, it is a matter for the national courts to decide whether or not to make a reference. (See further 9.6.7.) It is an example of shared jurisdiction, depending for its success on mutual cooperation. As Advocate-General Lagrange said in *De Geus en Uitdenbogerd* v *Robert Bosch GmbH* (case 13/61), the first case to reach the ECJ on an application under the preliminary rulings procedure:

> Applied judiciously – one is tempted to say loyally – the provisions of Article 177 [now 234] must lead to a real and fruitful collaboration between the municipal courts and the Court of Justice of the Communities with mutual regard for their respective jurisdiction.

To assess how this collaboration operates, in principle and in practice, it is necessary to examine the procedure from the point of view of: (a) the ECJ, and (b) national courts.

9.3 Jurisdiction of the Court of Justice

The jurisdiction of the ECJ is twofold. It has jurisdiction to give preliminary rulings concerning:

(a) interpretation, and

(b) validity.

9.3.1 Interpretation

In its interpretative role, the Court may rule on the interpretation of the Treaty, of acts of the institutions, and of statutes of bodies established by an act of the Council, where those statutes so provide. Its jurisdiction with regard to interpretation is thus very wide. 'Interpretation of the Treaty' includes the EC Treaty and all treaties amending or supplementing it. It did not, however, pursuant to original Article L TEU, have jurisdiction to interpret Articles A–F, J and K TEU (save for Article K. 3(2)(c)(3)) (*Grau Gomis* (case C–167/94)), effectively excluding a number of the common provisions of the TEU, together with the JHA and CFSP pillars. As noted in Chapter 2, the ToA amended the original Article L, now 46 TEU, to give the ECJ jurisdiction in relation to the JHA Pillar of the TEU (subject to the requirement in new Article 35 TEU that Member States must, by declaration, accept the ECJ's jurisdiction) and the TEU provisions on closer cooperation (now Articles 43–45 TEU). These changes will be discussed further below.

'Acts of the institutions' is a broad concept. It covers not only binding acts in the form of regulations, directives and decisions, but even non-binding acts such as recommendations and opinions, since they may be relevant to the interpretation of domestic implementing measures. On the same reasoning the Court has held that an act need not be directly effective to be subject to interpretation under Article 234 (*Mazzalai* (case 111/75)), nor need the party concerned have relied on the act before his national court: that court can raise it before the ECJ of its own motion (*Verholen* (cases 87, 88 & 89/90)). The Court has also given rulings on the interpretation of international treaties entered into by the Community, on the basis that these constitute 'acts of the institutions' (see *R. & V. Haegeman Sprl v Belgium* (case 181/73)). This includes 'mixed agreements', such as the WTO agreement, where interpretation relates to obligations undertaken by the Community (*Hermes* (case C–53/96), noted (1999) 36 CML Rev 663). However, the Court has held in the context of a claim based on the Statute of the European School, that it has no jurisdiction to rule on agreements which, although linked with the Community and to the functioning of its institutions, have been set up by agreement *between Member States* and not on the basis of the Treaty or EC secondary legislation (*Hurd* v *Jones* (case 44/84) – headmaster of European School unable to invoke Statute against HM Tax Inspectorate).

9.3.2 Validity

Here the Court's jurisdiction is confined to acts of the institutions. It has been suggested, by extension of the reasoning in *R. & V. Haegeman Sprl v Belgian State*, that 'acts of the institutions' would include international agreements entered into by the Community. Here, however, the ruling would be binding only on the Community members; it would be ineffective against third-party signatories. The grounds for invalidity are the same as in an action for annulment under Article 230 (ex 173) (see Chapter 11).

As with interpretation, Article 46 TEU excludes the majority of the TEU from the ECJ's jurisdiction. Although the ECJ has not had to consider the limits to its jurisdiction under Article 46 TEU in respect of references for a preliminary ruling, it has had to consider these matters in the context of a judicial review action (*Commission* v *Council (Airport transit visas)* (case C–170/96)). The case concerned the appropriate Treaty base for airport transit visas, the Council arguing that the then Article K.3 TEU (which has been significantly amended by the ToA) was the appropriate base, the Commission (and the Parliament) considering that the then Article 100c EC (repealed by the ToA), which dealt with visas, was more appropriate. The Council claimed that the ECJ had no jurisdiction to hear the case as the then Article L TEU in its original form (now Article 46), applied to exclude the ECJ's jurisdiction. The ECJ emphasised that that provision was subject to Article 47 (ex M) TEU, which provides that nothing in the TEU shall affect the EC Treaty, a phrase which the ECJ has interpreted to include the *acquis* (i.e., the entire body of EC law). The ECJ from this basis argued that it had the duty to review measures made under TEU provisions to ensure that they did not erode Community law. Presumably, it would take a similar approach were a similar question to arise under an Article 234 EC reference on validity. This boundary would seem now be of less significance as the ToA, in amending Article 46 TEU, permitted the ECJ jurisdiction to interpret and review the validity of certain acts and agreements made under the JHA pillar, should the Member States agree thereto (see Article 35 TEU).

One important question in relation to the ECJ's jurisdiction under Article 234 and correspondingly the national courts' right to refer was identified in *T. Port GmbH & Co. KG v Bundesanstalt für Landwirtschaft und Ernährung* (case C–68/95). There the ECJ held that the preliminary ruling procedure did not give the Member States' courts the power to refer questions concerning an EC institution's alleged failure to act. Any such claim would have to be brought under Article 232 (ex 175) EC (see Chapter 12).

9.4 Scope of the Court's jurisdiction

9.4.1 Matters of Community law

The Court is only empowered to give rulings on matters of Community law (and, as noted, limited aspects of the JHA). It has no jurisdiction to interpret domestic law, nor to pass judgment on the compatibility of domestic law with EC law. The Court has frequently been asked such questions (e.g., *Van Gend en Loos* (case 26/62); *Costa v ENEL* (case 6/64) *Netherlands v Ten Kate Holding BV* (case C–511/03)), since it is often the central problem before the national court. But as the Court said in *Costa v ENEL:* 'a decision should be given by the Court not upon the validity of an Italian law in relation to the Treaty, but only upon the interpretation of the above-mentioned [Treaty] Articles in the context of the points of law stated by the Giudice Conciliatore'. Where the Court is asked to rule on such a matter it will merely reformulate the question and return an abstract interpretation on the point of EC law involved.

9.4.2 Interpretation, not application

The Court maintains a similarly strict dividing line in principle between inter-pretation and application. It has no jurisdiction to rule on the application of Community law by national courts. However, since the application of Community law often raises problems for national courts, the Court, in its concern to provide national courts with 'practical' or 'worthwhile' rulings, will sometimes, when interpreting Community law, also offer unequivocal guidance as to its application (see e.g., *Stoke-on-Trent City Council v B & Q* (case C–169/91); *R v Her Majesty's Treasury, ex parte British Telecommunications plc* (case C–392/93); *Arsenal Football Club v Reed* (case C–206/01)).

9.4.3 Non-interference

The Court maintains a strict policy of non-interference over matters of what to refer, when to refer and how to refer. Such matters are left entirely to the discretion of the national judge. As the Court said in *De Geus en Uitdenbogerd v Robert Bosch GmbH* (case 13/61), its jurisdiction depends 'solely on the existence of a request from the national court'. However, it has no jurisdiction to give a ruling when, at the time when it is made, the procedure before the court making it has already been terminated (*Pardini* (case 338/85); *Grogan* (case C–159/90)). In contrast, the Court does have jurisdiction where a court is involved in preparatory inquiries in criminal proceedings which may or may not lead to a formal prosecution, where the question of EC law may determine whether the inquiries will continue (case C–60/02, *Criminal proceedings against X ('Rolex')*).

No formal requirements are imposed on the framing of the questions. Where the questions are inappropriately phrased the Court will merely reformulate the questions, answering what it sees as the relevant issues. It may interpret what it regards as the relevant issues even if they are not raised by the referring court (e.g., *OTO SpA v Ministero delle Finanze* (case C–130/92)). Nor will it question the timing of a reference. However, since 'it is necessary for the national court to define the legal context in which the interpretation requested should be placed', the Court has suggested that it might be convenient for the facts of the case to be established and for questions of purely national law to be settled at the time when the reference is made, in order to enable the Court to take cognisance of all the features of fact and law which may be relevant to the interpretation of Community law which it is called upon to give (*Irish Creamery Milk Suppliers Association v Ireland* (cases 36 & 71/80); approved in *Pretore di Salò* (case 14/86)). In *Telemarsicabruzzo SpA v Circostel* (cases C–320, 321, 322/90) it rejected an application for a ruling from an Italian magistrates' court on the grounds that the reference had provided no background factual information and only fragmentary observations on the case. The ECJ has since reaffirmed this approach in several cases (e.g., *Pretore di Genova v Banchero* (case C–157/92); *Monin Automobiles v France* (case C–386/92)). The ECJ has held, however, that the need for detailed factual background to a case is less pressing when the questions referred by the national court relate to technical points (*Vaneetveld v Le Foyer SA* (case C316/93)) or where the facts are clear, for example, because of a previous reference (*Crispoltoni v Fattoria Autonoma Tabacchi* (cases C–133, 300 & 362/92)). The concern seems to be that not only must the ECJ know enough to give a useful ruling in the context, but that there is also enough information for affected parties to be able to make representations. This, according to the ECJ, is especially relevant in competition cases (*Deliege* (case C–191/97), paras 30 and 36). (See further Chapter 29.) The Court has issued an 'Information Note on references from national courts for a preliminary ruling' ([2005] OJ C143/1, replacing guidance issued in 1996), consolidating its rulings in these cases. The circumstances in which the ECJ will decline jurisdiction are discussed further below.

9.4.4 Limitations in practice

The above limitations of the Court's jurisdiction are more apparent than real. The line between matters of Community law and matters of national law, between interpretation and application are more easily drawn in theory than in practice. An interpretation of EC law may leave little room for doubt as to the legality of a national law and little choice to the national judge in matters of application if he is to comply with his duty to give priority to EC law. The Court has on occasions, albeit in abstract terms, suggested that a particular national law is incompatible with EC law (e.g., *R v Secretary of State for Transport, ex parte Factortame Ltd* (case C–221/89); *Johnston v RUC* (case 222/84)). The Court may even offer specific guidance as to the application of its ruling. In the *BT* case (case C–392/93), for example, the ECJ commented:

> Whilst it is in principle for the national courts to verify whether or not the conditions of State liability for a breach of Community law are fulfilled, in the present case the Court has all the necessary information to assess whether the facts amount to a sufficiently serious breach of Community law.

The Court then went on to hold that there had been no breach. Further, in rephrasing and regrouping the questions the Court is able to select the issues which it regards as significant, without apparently interfering with the discretion of the national judge.

It may be argued that some encroachment by the ECJ on to the territory of national courts' jurisdiction is necessary to ensure the correct and uniform application of Community law. However, its very freedom of manoeuvre in preliminary rulings proceedings, combined with its teleological approach to interpretation, have resulted on occasions in the Court overstepping the line, laying down broad general (and sometimes unexpected) principles, with far-reaching consequences, in response to *particular* questions from national courts (e.g., *Barber* (case 262/88); *Marshall (No. 2)* (case C–271/91)). This has not been conducive to legal certainty. Such activism has not gone without criticism, as calculated to invite 'rebellion', even 'defiance' by national courts.

The potential difficulties arising from the ECJ overstepping the boundary between its role of interpreting EC law and the national courts' role of applying that ruling to the facts can be seen in the case of *Arsenal Football Club* v *Reed* ([2002] All ER (D) 180 (Dec)). The case before the national court concerned the action commenced by Arsenal to prevent Reed from continuing to sell souvenirs which carried its name and logos. The national court referred a number of questions to the ECJ on the interpretation of the Trade Mark Directive (see case C–206/01). The main issue was whether trade mark protection extended only to the circumstances in which the sign was used as a trade mark or whether an infringement would occur irrespective of how the marks were used. The ECJ handed down a judgment in the following terms:

> In a situation which is not covered by Article 6(1) of the First Council Directive 89/104/EEC of 21 December 1988 to approximate the laws of the Member States relating to trade marks, where a third party uses in the course of trade a sign which is identical to a validly registered trade mark on goods which are identical to those for which it is registered, the trade mark proprietor of the mark is entitled, in circumstances such as those in the present case, to rely on Article 5(1)(a) of that directive to prevent that use. It is immaterial that, in the context of that use, the sign is perceived as a badge of support for or loyalty or affiliation to the trade mark proprietor.

The phrase 'in circumstances such as those in the present case' would seem to give the national court little freedom in its determination of the case for which the preliminary ruling was originally made. In the *Arsenal* case, however, the referring court accepted the argument of the defendant's counsel to the effect that in the course of its judgment and in particular by tying the operative part of its judgment to the facts of the case, the ECJ had made a determination of fact which in some aspects was inconsistent with the finding of fact made by the national court. On this basis, the national court commented:

> If this is so, the ECJ has exceeded its jurisdiction and I am not bound by its final conclusion. I must apply its guidance on the law to the facts as found at the trial (para. 27).

It further remarked:

> The courts of this country cannot challenge rulings of the ECJ within its areas of competence. There is no advantage to be gained by appearing to do so. Furthermore national courts do not make references to the ECJ with the intention of ignoring the result. On the other hand, no matter how tempting it may be to find an easy way out, the High Court has no power to cede to the ECJ a jurisdiction it does not have (para. 28).

Although the court has phrased this in terms of the limits of jurisdiction, rather than an overt defiance, the assertion by the national court of the limits of the ECJ's jurisdiction was itself a form of rebellion. The High Court before which the *Arsenal case* was heard did point out that there was the possibility of an appeal to the Court of Appeal, which might make a different finding on the facts and thereby remove this discrepancy. This is what happened subsequently (see [2003] 2 CMLR 25), when the Court of Appeal held that the ECJ's reference to the facts was *not* at variance with those of the trial judge, but that there was a difference in legal reasoning. The trial judge had therefore been wrong to disagree with the ECJ in this case, although the Court of Appeal did confirm the principle on which the first instance decision was based.

9.4.5 Restrictions on the type of reference

Although the ECJ has in a few, albeit increasing number of cases refused its jurisdiction, it has generally, despite a constantly growing workload, encouraged national courts to refer. We have already seen that the ECJ will refuse jurisdiction when the referring court has not included enough information to enable the ECJ to give a ruling on the question referred (at 9.4.3; see e.g., *Telemarsicabruzzo SpA* v *Circostel* (cases C–320, 321, 322/90)).

9.4.5.1 *Artificiality of proceedings*

Another example of an exception to this open-door policy in the early years occurred in the cases of *Foglia* v *Novello (No. 1)* (case 104/79) and *Foglia* v *Novello (No. 2)* (case 244/80). Here for the first time the Court refused its jurisdiction to give a ruling in both a first and a second application in the same case. The questions, which were referred by an Italian judge, concerned the legality under EC law of an import duty imposed by the French on the import of wine from Italy. It arose in the context of litigation between two Italian parties. Foglia, a wine producer, had agreed to sell wine to Mrs Novello, an exporter. In making their contract the parties agreed that Foglia should not bear the cost of any duties levied by the French in breach of EC law. When duties were charged and eventually paid by Foglia, he sought to recover the money from Mrs Novello. In his action before the Italian court for recovery of the money that court sought a preliminary ruling on the legality under EC law of the duties imposed by the French. The ECJ refused its jurisdiction. The proceedings, it claimed, had been artificially created in order to question the legality of the French law; they were not 'genuine'.

The parties were no more successful the second time. In a somewhat peremptory judgment the Court declared that the function of Article 234 was to contribute to the administration of justice in the Member States; not to give advisory opinions on general or hypothetical questions.

The ECJ's decision has been criticised. Although the proceedings were to some extent artificial, in that the duty should ideally have been challenged at source, by the party from whom it was levied, the Italian judge called upon to decide the case was faced with a genuine problem, central to which was the issue of EC law. If, in his discretion, he sought guidance from the ECJ in this matter, surely it was not for that Court to deny it. The principles expressed in *Foglia* v *Novello* were, however, applied in *Meilicke* v *ADV/ORGA AG* (case C–83/91). Here the Court refused to answer a lengthy and complex series of questions relating *inter alia*, to the interpret-ation of the second Company Law Directive. The dispute between the parties centred on a disagreement as to the interpretation of certain provisions of German company law. It appeared that the EC directive was being invoked in order to prove the theories of one of the parties (a legal scholar). The Court held that it had no jurisdiction to give advisory opinions on hypothetical questions submitted by national courts (contrast *Mangold* (case C–144/04, discussed in Chapter 5), which also appeared to have been raised to prove an argument made by one of the parties (cf. para. 32), but a contract forming the basis of the dispute and the Article 234 reference had been performed – thereby causing the ECJ to reject the German Government's claim that the case was artificial).

It has been suggested that political considerations and national rivalries played their part in the *Foglia* decision (the Court held it 'must display special vigilance when . . . a question is referred to it with a view to permitting the national court to decide whether the legislation of another Member State is in accordance with Community law': *Foglia* v *Novello (No. 2)*). This assessment is supported by the more recent case of *Bacardi-Martini SAS* v *Newcastle United Football Company Ltd* (case C–318/00). Bacardi entered into a contract for advertising time on an electronic revolving display system during a match between Newcastle and Metz, a French football club. The match was to be televised live in the United Kingdom and France. Although the advertising deal was in compliance with English law, it contravened French law and Newcastle therefore pulled out of the advertising agreement. Bacardi brought an action against Newcastle, claiming that it could not rely on the French law to justify its actions, as the French law was incompatible with Article 49 (ex 59) on the freedom to provide services. The High Court made a reference on this point. When discussing the question of admissibility, the ECJ referred to *Foglia* and the special need for vigilance when the law of another Member State was in issue; it then reviewed whether the national court had made it clear why an answer was necessary. The ECJ concluded:

> In those circumstances, the conclusion must be that the Court does not have the material before it to show that it is necessary to rule on the compatibility with the Treaty of legislation of a Member State other than that of the court making the reference (para. 53).

From this case, it seems that although a national court is not precluded from referring questions relating to the national laws of other Member States, the ECJ will review the justification for the reference more stringently than it would otherwise do.

9.4.5.2 *Internal situations*

Another area in which the ECJ has sometimes limited references has been when the subject matter of the case is 'internal' and does not involve Community law directly. This issue came before the Court in *Dzodzi v Belgium* (cases C–297/88 and C–197/89). Here the Court was prepared to provide a ruling on the interpretation of EC social security law in a purely 'internal' matter, for the purpose of clarifying provisions of Belgian law invoked by a Togolese national. The Court held that it was 'exclusively for national courts which were dealing with a case to assess, with regard to the specific features of each case, both the need for a preliminary ruling in order to enable it to give judgment, and the relevance of the question'. Following *Dzodzi*, in *Leur Bloem* (case C–28/95), the ECJ held that it has jurisdiction to interpret provisions of Community law where the facts of the case lie outside these provisions but are applicable to the case because the national law governing the main dispute has transposed the Community rule to a non-Community context ('spontaneous harmonisation'). This is subject to the proviso that national law does not expressly prohibit it (*Kleinwort Benson* (case C–346/93)). Similarly, the ECJ has accepted references for a preliminary ruling in circumstances where a national provision is tied into a Community rule in order to avoid non-discrimination even in purely internal situations (case C–300/01, *Salzmann* – internal situation affected by rules on free movement of capital in Article 56 (ex 73b) EC).

The lines of reasoning established in *Foglia* and *Meilicke* on the one hand and *Dzodzi, Leur Bloem, Kleinwort Benson* and *Salzmann* on the other have been followed by others in which the ECJ declined jurisdiction either on the basis that the questions referred were not relevant to the dispute before the national court (e.g., *Dias* v *Director da Alfândega do Porto* (case C–343/90); *Corsica Ferries Italia Srl* v *Corpo dei Piloti del Porto di Genova* (case C–18/93)) or because the matter was purely internal, although recent case law seems to have conflated these two points (see e.g., *Banque internationale pour l'Afrique occidentale SA (BIAO)* v *Finanzamt für Großunternehmen in Hamburg* (case C–306/99), para. 89).

9.4.5.3 *Ruling 'objectively required'*

Another potential limitation on the ECJ's willingness to accept references can be seen in *Monin Automobiles – Maison du Deux-Roues* (case C–428/93). There the ECJ suggested that the questions referred must be 'objectively required' by the national court as 'necessary to enable that court to give judgment' in the proceedings before it as required under Article 234(2). This case concerned a company which was in the process of being wound up. The company argued that it should not be finally wound up until certain questions relating to EC law had been answered. Conversely, the company's creditors thought that the company had been artificially kept in existence for too long already and should be wound up immediately. The national court referred the EC law questions to determine the strength of the company's argument. The ECJ held that, although there was a connection between the questions and the dispute, answers to the question would not be *applied* in the case. The ECJ therefore declined jurisdiction.

It is submitted that these cases should not be construed as constituting a restrictive approach on the part of the ECJ towards applications under Article 234. Admittedly, the ECJ has declined jurisdiction in a number of cases, but, looking at the facts of these cases, and of *Telemarsicabruzzo SpA* v *Circostel* (cases C–320–2/90) and similar cases, it can be argued that rejection was justified in the circumstances. This point is reinforced if we contrast the above cases with *Leclerc-Siplec* v *TF1 Publicité SA* (case C–412/93), which, in effect, concerned a challenge to French law. The Commission suggested that, in the light of the *Foglia* cases, there was no dispute before the national court because the parties were agreed about the outcome and that, therefore, the ECJ did not have jurisdiction to answer the question. The ECJ disagreed, holding that the parties' agreement did not render the dispute less real and that the question needed an answer because, without it, the referring court could not deal with the dispute before it. Furthermore, in *Leur-Bloem* (case C–28/95) the ECJ despite the opinion of the Advocate-General to the contrary, distinguished *Kleinwort Benson* and returned to its more generous approach in *Dzodzi*. Whether the ECJ should, in the light of increasing workload, the more established nature of the Community legal order and imminent further enlargement, impose greater controls on the cases referred to it is discussed further below.

9.4.6 Challenges to validity: relationship with Article 230

The Court's decision in *TWD Textilwerke GmbH* v *Germany* (case C–188/92) has given rise to concern. Here the Court refused to give a ruling on the validity of a Commission decision, addressed to the German Government, demanding the recovery from the applicants of State aid granted by the government in breach of EC law. Its refusal was based on the fact that the applicants, having been informed by the government of the Commission's decision, and advised of their right to challenge it under Article 230, had failed to do so within the two-month limitation period. Having allowed this period to expire the Court held that the applicants could not, in the interests of legal certainty, be permitted to attack the decision under Article 234. This decision, wholly out of line with its previous jurisprudence, which has been to encourage challenges to validity under Article 234 rather than (the more restrictive) Article 230, has caused concern, as calculated to drive parties, perhaps prematurely, into action under Article 230, for fear of being denied a later opportunity to challenge Community legislation under Article 234 (see further, Chapter 11).

However, the ECJ has since mitigated some of the effects of its judgment in *TWD*. In *R* v *Intervention Board for Agriculture, ex parte Accrington Beef Co. Ltd* (case C–241/95), the parties had not sought to bring an action for annulment within the time limits set out in the then Article 230. Nonetheless, the ECJ was prepared to hear the preliminary ruling reference because it was not clear, as the parties were seeking to challenge a regulation, that they would have had standing to bring an action under Article 230 (see also *Atzeui and others* (cases C–346 and 529/03), discussed at 11.4.3.4). In addition it may be noted that while a national court is able to interpret Community law without recourse to the Court under Article 234, it has no power to declare a Community law invalid (*Zuckerfabrik Süderdithmarschen AG* v *Hauptzollamt Itzehoe* (cases C–143/88, C–92/89)).

9.5 'Court or tribunal'

Jurisdiction to refer to the ECJ under Article 234 is conferred on 'any court or tribunal'. With rare exceptions (e.g., *Nordsee Deutsche Hochseefischerei GmbH* (case 102/81) to be discussed below; *Corbiau v Administration des Contributions* (case C–24/92) (a fiscal authority is not a court or tribunal); *Victoria Film A/S v Riksskattenverkert* (case C–134/97) (a court exercising its administrative duties is not a court or tribunal)) this has been interpreted in the widest sense. Whether a particular body qualifies as a court or tribunal within Article 234 is a matter of *Community* law. The ECJ is generally accepted as having set down a number of criteria by which a 'court or tribunal' might be identified. The early case law identified five criteria:

(a) statutory origin;

(b) permanence;

(c) *inter partes* procedure;

(d) compulsory jurisdiction; and

(e) the application of rules of law.

(See also *Dorsch Consult v Bundesbaugesellschaft Berlin* (case C–54/96), para. 23). Subsequent decisions, such as *Preto di Salo v Persons Unknown* (case 14/86), made it clear than the independence of the body would also be a factor.

In *Broekmeulen* (case 246/80) the Court was faced with a reference from the appeal committee of the Dutch professional medical body. One of the questions referred was whether the appeal committee was a 'court or tribunal' within what is now Article 234. The Court held that it was

> in the practical absence of an effective means of redress before the ordinary courts, in a matter concerning the application of Community law, the appeal committee, which performs its duties with the approval of the public authorities and operates with their assistance, and whose decisions are accepted following contentious proceedings and are in fact recognised as final, must be deemed to be a court of a Member State for the purpose of Article 177 [now 234].

It was imperative to ensure the proper functioning of Community law that the ECJ should have the opportunity of ruling on issues of interpretation and validity.

More recently, the ECJ has held that an individual immigration officer, an Immigration Adjudicator, could make a reference (*El-Yassini v Secretary of State for the Home Department* (case C–416/96)). In this case, the office of Immigration Adjudicator was a permanent office, established by statute which gives the officer in question the power to hear and determine disputes in accordance with rules set down by statute. The ECJ further agreed with the Advocate-General, who had emphasised the *inter partes* nature of the procedure (para. 20) and the fact that the adjudicators are required to give reasons for their decisions.

The ECJ has since been criticised by the Advocate-General in *de Coster* (case C–17/00) for an approach to the interpretation of a 'court or tribunal' that is confused, especially as regards the criteria of whether the body is established by law, the independent nature of the body and the need for *inter partes* procedure, as well as the requirement that the body's decision be of a judicial nature. Although in cases such as *Criminal Proceedings against X* (cases C–74 and 129/95), in which the ECJ declared it did not have jurisdiction because the prosecutor making the reference was not independent, and *Dorsch Consult* (case C–54/96), in which the Court emphasised the need for the referring body to carry out its responsibilities 'independently' (para. 35), in other instances, such as *El-Yassini*, the ECJ has not stringently assessed the requirement of independence. Another such example is *Gabalfrisa* v *AEAT* (cases C–110–147/98). There the ECJ held that the Spanish Economic-Administrative Courts, which do not form part of the judiciary but are part of the Ministry of Economic Affairs and Finance, fell within Article 234. The ECJ accepted that the separation of functions between the departments of the Ministry responsible for tax collection and the Economic-Administrative Courts, which ruled on complaints lodged against the collection departments, was sufficient to ensure independence, despite the Opinion of Advocate-General Saggio in that case to the contrary.

In *de Coster* the Court, contrary to the view of the Advocate General, accepted the reference. It noted that the body in question was 'a permanent body, established by law, that it gives legal rulings and that the jurisdiction thereby invested in it concerning local tax proceedings is compulsory' (para. 12). It also commented that the criterion that the procedure be *inter partes* was not absolute. In the subsequent *Schmid* case (case C–516/99), however, the ECJ went to great lengths to distinguish the Fifth Appeal Chamber for the Regional Finance Authority, the referring body in *Schmid*, from the bodies found to fall within the definition of a 'court or tribunal' in *Dorsch Consult* and *Gabalfrisa*, which the Advocate General in *de Coster* had criticised. Like the bodies in those cases, the appeal chamber was linked in organisational terms to the body whose decisions it reviewed. The ECJ held that the appeal chamber was not independent. In *Synetairismos Farmakopoion Aitolias & Akarnanias* v *GlaxoSmithKline plc* (Case C–53/03), the ECJ held that the Greek competition tribunal was subject to control by the relevant government department and therefore not sufficiently independent to be regarded as a 'court or tribunal' for the purposes of Article 234. Whether these cases indicate that the ECJ has taken the comments of the Advocate General in *de Coster* into account, or rather reflects the fact that some administrative bodies simply cannot be seen as independent is debatable.

Moreover, the ECJ has emphasised the importance of the *inter partes* nature of proceedings (see, e.g., *El Yassini* (case C–416/96)), although there have been cases, such as *Dorsch Consult* which concerned undefended proceedings, where this criterion has seemed less central to the determination of the question as to whether a body constitutes a 'court or tribunal'. Confusion has also arisen with regard to assessing the nature of the decision made. In *Victoria Film* (case C–134/97) the referring body was held not to be a court because its function was not to settle any dispute but to give advisory opinions. In *Pretore di Salà* v *Persons Unknown* (case 14/86), the ECJ held that this applied to any court acting in the general context of a duty to act, independently and in accordance with the law, upon cases in which the law has conferred jurisdiction upon it, even though its functions may not be of a judicial nature. Thus, the name of the body is irrelevant.

9.5.1 Can arbitrators be a 'court or tribunal'?

The position of arbitrators has always given rise to problems in this context. The Court took a narrow view of a 'court or tribunal' in the early case of *Nordsee Deutsche Hochseefischerei GmbH* (case 102/81). The case arose from a joint shipbuilding project which involved the pooling of EC aid. The parties agreed that in the event of a dispute they would refer their differences to an independent arbitrator. Their agreement excluded the possibility of recourse to the ordinary courts. They fell into disagreement and a number of questions involving the interpretation of certain EC regulations were raised before the arbitrator. He sought a ruling from the ECJ as to, *inter alia*, whether he was a 'court or tribunal' within the meaning of Article 234. The Court held that he was not. According to the Court, the key issue was the nature of the arbitration. Here the public authorities of Member States were not involved in the decision to opt for arbitration, nor were they called upon to intervene automatically before the arbitrator. If questions of Community law were raised before such a body, the ordinary courts might be called upon to give them assistance, or to review the decision; it would be for *them* to refer questions of interpretation or validity of Community law to the ECJ.

The Court's decision ignored the fact that in this case recourse to the courts was excluded, and the arbitrator was thus required to interpret a difficult point of Community law, of central importance in the proceedings, unaided.

Since in *Nordsee Deutsche Hochseefischerei GmbH* there was no effective means of redress before the ordinary courts and the decisions of the arbitrator were accepted following contentious proceedings and recognised as final it seems that the only factor distinguishing it from *Broekmeulen* was the element of *public* participation or control. This, it seems, will be essential. Certainly, in subsequent cases, such as *Danfoss* (case 109/88), the ECJ has focused on the compulsory nature of an arbitrator's jurisdiction, by contrast to the position in *Nordsee*, when the parties agreed to refer their dispute to arbitration.

The position was confirmed in *Denuit* v *Transorient* (C–125/04) involving a dispute under the Package Travel Directive (90/314/EEC) before the arbitration panel of the Belgian Travel Dispute Committee. Having confirmed its case law, the ECJ rejected the reference on the basis that the panel was not a 'court or tribunal', because the parties were 'under no obligation, in law or in fact, to refer their disputes to arbitration' (at para. 16). No regard was had to the fact that, in a consumer situation, arbitration may be the only formal procedure which may practically be available to a consumer because of the comparatively high cost of court action; a matter which surprises in view of the increasing emphasis on out-of-court procedures in consumer cases.

9.5.2 'Court or tribunal': evaluation

In general, the ECJ's approach to the definition of 'court or tribunal' for the purposes of Article 234 (and presumably Articles 68 EC and 35 TEU) has been generous. This approach would seem to have been driven by the need to ensure correct and uniform interpretation of the Treaty. One might argue that access to justice from the perspective of the parties would also argue in favour of such a broad definition, especially when the referring body did not meet the criterion of independence.

Against this, however, a number of other factors should be weighed. One of the significant problems in the current jurisprudence is a lack of certainty as to where the ECJ will draw the line between a 'court or tribunal' for the purposes of the EC Treaty and other bodies. The current approach, which (usually) takes a broad view of the bodies permitted to refer means that the ECJ receives more references. An approach which encourages references was understandable during the early years of the Community when both the substantive law and the relationship between the ECJ and national courts needed to be consolidated, but what of the position now? It has been suggested that although there is much to be said for encouraging national courts, now more experienced in the application of EC law, to decide matters for themselves, there is no justification for a position whereby access to the ECJ is totally excluded. The Advocate-General in *de Coster*, however, commented that:

> [o]ne well thought out and well-founded decision resolves more problems that a large number of hasty judgments which do not go deeply into the reasoning and do not address the questions submitted to them.

Essentially, it seems that the ECJ is a victim of its own success, with longer delays in dealing with references, delays themselves that do not assist in the proper administration of justice. The Advocate-General suggested that the ECJ should tighten its definition of 'court or tribunal', with the likely consequence that the relationship between the national courts and the ECJ (and CFI, post-Nice) would change. The national courts from this perspective would need to take greater responsibility for Community law.

9.6 Jurisdiction of the national courts to refer

Although any court or tribunal may refer questions to the ECJ under Article 234, a distinction must be drawn between those courts or tribunals which have a discretion to refer ('permissive' jurisdiction) and those for which referral is mandatory ('mandatory' jurisdiction). Under Article 234(3), where a question concerning interpretation is raised 'in a case pending before a court or tribunal of a Member State, *against whose decisions there is no judicial remedy under national law*, that court or tribunal *shall* bring the matter before the Court of Justice' (emphasis added). For all courts other than those within Article 234(3) referral is discretionary. Note that special rules apply to cases falling within the new Title IV to the EC Treaty, introduced by the ToA. These are discussed below. (See also Chapter 24.)

9.6.1 Mandatory jurisdiction

The purpose of Article 234(3) must be seen in the light of the function of Article 234 as a whole, which is to prevent a body of national case law not in accordance with the rules of Community law from coming into existence in any Member State (*Hoffman-La Roche AG* v *Centrafarm Vertiebsgesellschaft Pharmazeutischer Erzeugnisse mbH* (case 107/76)). To this end Article 234(3) seeks to ensure that, when matters of EC law arise, there is an obligation to refer to the ECJ at some stage in the proceedings. This purpose should be kept in mind when questions of interpretation of Article 234(3) arise.

The scope of Article 234(3) is not entirely clear. While it obviously applies to courts or tribunals whose decisions are *never* subject to appeal (the 'abstract theory'), such as the House of Lords in England, or the Conseil d'État in France, it is less clear whether it applies also to courts whose decisions *in the case in question* are not subject to appeal (the 'concrete theory'), such as the Italian magistrates' court (*guidice conciliatore*) in *Costa* v *ENEL* (case 6/64) (no right of appeal because sum of money involved too small). When leave to appeal from the Court of Appeal (or, in certain criminal matters, from the High Court) to the House of Lords is refused, or when the High Court refuses leave for judicial review from a tribunal decision, do these courts become courts 'against whose decisions there is no judicial remedy under national law'?

The judgment of the ECJ in *Costa* v *ENEL* was seen, albeit *obiter*, to support the wider, 'concrete' theory. In that case, in the context of a reference from the Italian magistrates' court, from which there was no appeal due to the small amount of money involved, the Court said, with reference to the then Article 177(3) (now 234(3)): 'By the terms of this Article . . . national courts against whose decisions, *as in the present case*, there is no judicial remedy, *must* refer the matter to the Court of Justice' (emphasis added). Taking into account the function of Article 234(3) and particularly its importance for the individual, this would have seemed to be the better view.

It has been suggested that where the right of appeal or judicial review depends on the granting of leave, a lower court or tribunal from which a reference under Article 234 is sought must *either* grant leave or refer to the ECJ. Where this is not done, and leave depends on permission from a superior 'final' court, that latter court should be obliged to grant the requested leave. Any other course would frustrate the purpose of Article 234 and amount to a denial of the individual's Community rights.

The issue has finally been resolved by the ECJ. In *Lyckeshog* (case C–99/00), the question was referred of whether national courts are 'final' courts for the purposes of Article 234(3) if leave to appeal from their judgment is required. The ECJ noted that the function of the obligation on courts against whose decisions there was no judicial remedy to refer questions to the ECJ was to prevent a body of national case law coming into being that was inconsistent with the requirements of Community law. Despite this finding, the ECJ went on to hold that decisions of courts which could be challenged did not fall within this category of court. The ECJ argued that 'the fact that examination of the merits of such appeals is subject to a prior declaration of admissibility by the supreme court does not have the effect of depriving the parties of a judicial remedy' (para. 16). In coming to this conclusion, the ECJ assumed that 'uncertainty as to the interpetation of the law applicable, including Community law, may give rise to review, at last instance, by the supreme court' (para. 17). It would seem, as some have suggested, that the ECJ has been influenced by the recurring possibilities for review of the ECJ's jurisdiction which the repeated Treaty amendments constitute and the consequent threat of its jurisdiction's curtailment. Nonetheless, in terms of access to justice this ruling is somewhat worrying, as it presupposes that litigants have the time and the money to litigate through to the last possible court before being able to obtain a reference to the ECJ.

9.6.2 Discretionary or 'permissive' jurisdiction

Courts or tribunals which do not fall within Article 234(3) enjoy, according to the ECJ, an unfettered discretion in the matter of referrals. A court or tribunal at any level is free, 'if it considers that a decision on the question is necessary to enable it to give judgment', to refer to the ECJ in any kind of proceedings, including interim proceedings (*Hoffman-La Roche AG* v *Centrafarm Vertriebsgesellschaft Pharmazeutischer Erzeugnisse mbH* (case 107/76)), at any stage in the proceedings. In *De Geus en Uitdenbogerd* v *Robert Bosch GmbH* (case 13/61) the Court held that national courts have jurisdiction to refer whether or not an appeal is pending; the ECJ is not even concerned to discover whether the decision of the national judge has acquired the force of *res judicata*. However, following *Pardini* (case 338/85) and *Grogan* (case C–159/90), if proceedings have been terminated and the Court is aware of this fact, it may refuse jurisdiction on the grounds that its ruling is not necessary to enable the national court to give judgment.

9.6.2.1 *Referral where there is previous ruling*

Even if the ECJ has already ruled on a similar question, national courts are not precluded from requesting a further ruling. This point was made in *Da Costa en Schaake NV* (cases 28–30/62). There the Court held, in the context of a reference for interpretation of a question substantially the same as that referred in *Van Gend en Loos*, that the Court should retain a legal right to depart from its previous judgments. It may recognise its errors in the light of new facts. It ruled in similar terms in the context of a request concerning the effect of a prior ruling of validity in *International Chemical Corporation SpA* v *Amministrazione delle Finanze dello Stato* (case 66/80). Here it held that while national courts could assume from a prior declaration of invalidity that the regulation was invalid, they should not be deprived of an opportunity to refer the same issue if they have a 'real interest' in making a further reference.

9.6.2.2 *Impact of national rules of precedent*

This discretion to refer is in no way affected by national rules of precedent within the Member State. This important principle was established in the case of *Rheinmühlen-Düsseldorf* (case 146/73). In this case, which concerned an attempt by a German cereal exporter to obtain an export rebate under Community law, the German federal tax court (the Bundesfinanzhof), hearing the case on appeal from the Hessian tax court (Hessische Finanzgericht), had quashed the Hessian court's judgment and remitted the case to that court for a decision on certain issues of fact. The Hessian court was not satisfied with the Bundesfinanzhof's ruling since questions of Community law were involved. It sought a ruling from the ECJ on the interpretation of the Community law, and also on the question of whether it was permissible for a lower court to refer in this way when its own superior court had already set aside its earlier judgment on appeal. On an appeal by Rheinmühlen-Düsseldorf to the Bundesfinanzhof challenging the Hessian court's right to refer to the ECJ, the Bundesfinanzhof itself referred certain questions to the Court of

Justice. The principal question, raised in both cases, was whether Article 234 gave national courts an unfettered right to refer or whether that right is subject to national provisions whereby lower courts are bound by the judgments of superior courts.

The Court's reply was in the strongest terms. The object of the preliminary rulings procedure, the Court held, was to ensure that in all circumstances the law was the same in all Member States. No provision of domestic law can take away the power provided by Article 234. The lower court must be free to make a reference if it considers that the superior court's ruling could lead it to give judgment contrary to Community law. It would only be otherwise if the question put by the lower court were substantially the same. The ECJ's view may be compared with that of Wood J in the Employment Appeal Tribunal in *Enderby* v *Frenchay Health Authority* ([1991] ICR 382). Here he suggested that lower English Courts were bound even in matters of Community law by decisions of their superior courts; thus they should not make references to the ECJ but should leave it to the House of Lords, *a fortiori* when the House has decided on a particular issue that British law does not conflict with EC law. Wood J's observations are clearly at odds with Community law. It appears that *Rheinmühlen-Düsseldorf* was not cited before the tribunal. A reference to the ECJ was subsequently made in this case by the Court of Appeal ([1992] IRLR 15) resulting in a ruling (case C–127/92) and a decision on an important issue of equal pay for work of equal value contrary to that of Wood J and in the claimant's favour.

If national courts have the widest discretion in matters of referral, when, and on what basis, should they exercise this discretion? Two aspects of this problem may be considered.

First, the national judge must consider that a decision on a question of Community law is '*necessary* to enable it to give judgment'; then, if it is necessary, he must decide whether, in his discretion, he should refer.

Guidelines on both these matters have been supplied by the ECJ and by national courts. It is submitted that as the ultimate arbiter on matters of Community law only the ECJ's rulings are fully authoritative on this point.

9.6.3 When will a decision be necessary?

The ECJ was asked to consider this matter in *CILFIT Srl* (case 283/81). The reference was from the Italian Supreme Court, the Cassazione, and concerned national courts' mandatory jurisdiction under Article 234(3). On a literal reading of Article 234(2) and (3) it would appear that the question of whether 'a decision on a matter of Community law if necessary' only applies to the national courts' discretionary jurisdiction under Article 234(2). However, in *CILFIT* the ECJ held that:

> it followed from the relationship between Article 177(2) and (3) [now 234(2) and (3)] that the courts or tribunals referred to in Article 177(3) [now 234(3)] have the same discretion as any other national court or tribunal to ascertain whether a decision on a question of Community law is necessary to enable them to give judgment.

There would be no need to refer if:

(a) the question of EC law is irrelevant; or

(b) the provision has already been interpreted by the ECJ, even though the questions at issue are not strictly identical; or

(c) the correct application is so obvious as to leave no scope for reasonable doubt. This matter must be assessed in the light of the specific characteristics of Community law, the particular difficulties to which its interpretation gives rise, and the risk of divergences in judicial decisions within the Community.

These guidelines may be compared with Lord Denning's in *H.P. Bulmer Ltd* v *J. Bollinger SA* ([1974] Ch 401), Court of Appeal. He suggested that a decision would only be 'necessary' if it was 'conclusive' to the judgment. Even then it would not be necessary if:

(a) the ECJ had already given judgment on the question, or

(b) the matter was reasonably clear and free from doubt.

Although the criteria in both cases are similar, the first and third *CILFIT Srl* criteria are clearly stricter; it would be easier under Lord Denning's guidelines to decide that a decision was not 'necessary'. The issues at stake in the former case have proved to be both important and difficult, and were only finally resolved by the ECJ in the cases of *Brown* (case 197/86) and *Lair* (case 39/86) (for full discussion of the issues see Chapter 20).

9.6.4 *Acte clair*

Criteria (b) and (c) of *CILFIT Srl* (case 238/81) and (a) and (b) of *H.P. Bulmer Ltd* v *J. Bollinger SA* ([1974] Ch 401) could be described as versions of *acte clair*. *Acte clair* is a doctrine originating in French administrative law, whereby if the meaning of a provision is clear no 'question' of interpretation arises. The doctrine was introduced in the context of interpretation of treaties, in order to strengthen the powers of the Conseil d'État *vis-à-vis* the executive. If doubts existed concerning the interpretation of a treaty, the courts were obliged to refer to the government. If the provision was found to be *acte clair*, there was no need to refer. The utility of the doctrine, in that context, is clear.

The doctrine was first invoked in the sphere of EC law by Advocate-General Lagrange in *Da Costa en Schaake NV* (cases 28–30/62), in the context of a reference on a question of interpretation almost identical to a matter already decided by the Court in *Van Gend en Loos* (case 26/62). Like *CILFIT Srl*, it arose in a case concerning the court's mandatory jurisdiction under Article 234(3). While asserting that Article 234(3) 'unqualifiedly' required national courts to submit to the ECJ 'every question of interpretation raised before the court', the Court added that this would not be necessary if the question was materially identical with a question which had already been the subject of a preliminary ruling in a similar case.

This case has been taken as an endorsement by the Court of *acte clair*, albeit interpreted in a very narrow sense. The principle was approved in *CILFIT Srl*.

Acte clair was applied in a much wider sense, in very different circumstances, in the French case of *Re Société des Pétroles Shell-Berre* ([1964] CMLR 462). This case involved a number of difficult questions of French and EC competition law. These questions had not been subject to prior rulings under Article 234. Nevertheless the Conseil d'État, led by the Commissaire du Gouvernement, Madame Questiaux, took the view that only if the judge is not competent to determine the meaning of an act is he faced with a 'question of interpretation' and decided that there was no doubt as to the meaning and so there was no need to refer.

The dangers of *acte clair* were revealed in the Court of Appeal in the case of *R v Henn* ([1978] 1 WLR 1031). There Lord Widgery suggested that it was clear from the case law of the Court of Justice that a ban on the import of pornographic books was not a quantitative restriction within Article 28 (ex 30) of the EC Treaty. A subsequent referral on this matter by the House of Lords revealed that it undoubtedly was. Lord Diplock, giving judgment in the House of Lords ([1981] AC 850), warned English judges not to be too ready to hold that because the meaning of an English text seemed plain to them no question of interpretation was involved: the ECJ and the English courts have very different styles of interpretation and may ascribe different meanings to the same provision. He did, however, approve a version of *acte clair* consistent with that of the ECJ in *Da Costa en Schaake NV* and *CILFIT Srl* in *Garland v British Rail Engineering Ltd* ([1983] 2 AC 751) when he suggested that where there was a 'considerable and consistent line of case law' from the ECJ the answer would be 'too obvious and inevitable' to be capable of giving rise to what could properly be called a question within the meaning of Article 234.

Although most of the above cases arose in the context of Article 234(3) they have been discussed at this stage because they may equally be invoked in the context of national courts' discretionary jurisdiction, and they demonstrate that *acte clair* can be applied both in a narrow sense, as in *Da Costa en Schaake NV* ('provision materially identical') and *CILFIT Srl* ('so clear as to leave no room for doubt, taking into account', etc.) and in a looser, more subjective sense, as in *H.P. Bulmer Ltd v J. Bollinger SA* ('reasonably clear and free from doubt') and *Shell-Berre* ('no doubt'). Although a loose interpretation does not have such serious consequences in the context of a court's discretionary jurisdiction as in its mandatory jurisdiction, a narrow interpretation is preferable if the pitfalls of *R v Inner London Education Authority, ex parte Hinde* ([1985] 1 CMLR 716) and *R v Henn* are to be avoided. Where a disappointed party does not have the means or the stamina to appeal it may result in a misapplication of EC law.

9.6.5 Exercise of discretion

If courts within the area of discretionary jurisdiction consider, applying the *CILFIT* criteria, that a decision from the ECJ is necessary, how should they exercise their discretion?

On the question of timing, the ECJ has suggested that the facts of the case should be established and questions of purely national law settled before a reference is made (*Irish Creamery Milk Suppliers Association v Ireland* (cases 36 & 71/80)). This would avoid precipitate referrals, and enable the Court to take cognisance of all the features of fact and law which may be relevant to the issue of Community law on which it is asked to rule. A similar point was made by Lord Denning MR in *H.P. Bulmer Ltd v J. Bollinger SA* ([1974] Ch 401) ('decide the facts first') and approved by the House of Lords in *R v Henn* ([1981] AC 850). However, Lord Diplock did concede in *R v Henn* that in an urgent, e.g., interim matter, where important financial interests are concerned, it might be necessary to refer *before* all the facts were found.

With regard to other factors, Lord Denning suggested in *H.P. Bulmer Ltd v*

J. Bollinger SA that time, cost, workload of the ECJ and the wishes of the parties should be taken into account by national courts in the exercise of their discretion. Factors such as time and cost need to be treated with care, weighing the fact, as did Bingham J in *Commissioners of Customs and Excise v Samex ApS* ([1983] 3 CMLR 194), that deferring a referral may in the end increase the time and cost to the parties: there may be cases where it is appropriate to refer at an early stage. The more difficult and uncertain the issue of EC law, the greater the likelihood of appeal, requiring, in the end, a referral to the ECJ under Article 234(3).

The workload of the ECJ is an increasing problem and no doubt a reason for some modification in recent years of its open-door policy. However, whereas it may justify non-referral in a straightforward case, it should not prevent referral where the point of EC law is difficult or novel. The *CILFIT* criteria should operate to prevent unnecessary referrals.

The wishes of the parties also need to be treated with caution. If the point of EC law is relevant (which under *CILFIT* it must be) and difficult or uncertain, clearly *one* of the parties' interests will be better served by a referral. As Templeman LJ said in the Court of Appeal in *Polydor Ltd v Harlequin Record Shops Ltd* ([1980] 2 CMLR 413) when he chose to refer a difficult point of EC law in proceedings for an interim injunction, 'it is the right of the plaintiff [claimant] to go to the European Court'. Furthermore, the ECJ has held that the question of referral is one for the national court and that a party to the proceedings in the context of which the reference is made cannot challenge a decision to refer, even if that party thinks that the national court's findings of fact are inaccurate (*SAT Fluggesellschaft mbH v European Organization for the Safety of Air Navigation* (case C–364/92)).

Another factor which might point to an early referral, advanced by Ormrod LJ in *Polydor Ltd v Harlequin Record Shops Ltd* is the wider implications of the ruling. In *Polydor Ltd v Harlequin Record Shops Ltd* there were a number of similar cases pending. The issue, which was a difficult one, concerned the protection of British copyright law in the context of an international agreement between the EC and Portugal, and affected not merely the parties to the case but the record industry as a whole.

Finally, in *R v Henn* Lord Diplock suggested that in a criminal trial on indictment it might be better for the question to be decided by the national judge and reviewed if necessary through the hierarchy of the national courts. Although this statement could be invoked to counter spurious defences based on EC law, and unnecessary referrals, it is submitted that where a claim is genuinely based on EC law, and a ruling from the ECJ would be conclusive of the case, delay would serve no purpose. The time and cost of the proceedings would only be increased.

Where matters of validity are concerned special considerations apply. Although a national court may find a Community act to be valid, it has no power to make a finding of invalidity. Thus, despite the apparent permissive words of Article 234(2), where a court has serious doubts as to the validity of the act in question, provided that a decision on the question of EC law is 'necessary', a referral to the ECJ should be made. A national court may, however, grant an interim injunction based on the (alleged) invalidity of Community law. These matters, hinted at in *Foto-Frost v Hauptzollamt Lübeck-Ost* (case 314/85), have now been confirmed in *Zuckerfabrik Süderdithmarschen AG v Hauptzollamt Itzehoe* (cases C–143/88 and C–92/89).

9.6.6 **Exercise of mandatory jurisdiction**

Where a court or tribunal falls within Article 234(3), this creates, as the ECJ pointed out in *Da Costa en Schaake* (cases 28–30/62), an absolute obligation to refer. However, as the Court suggested in *CILFIT*, this obligation only arises if the court 'considers that a decision on the question is necessary to enable it to give judgment' (Article 234).

While it is clearly not necessary for 'final' courts to refer questions of Community law in every case, a lax approach by such courts towards their need to refer, resulting in non-referral, may lead to an incorrect application of Community law and, for the individual concerned, a denial of justice. Since *Köbler* (case C–224/01), 'final' courts choosing not to make a reference run the risk of incurring liability under *Francovich* should they get the point of EC law significantly wrong (see 8.2.2.2).

9.6.6.1 *'Acte claire'*

The doctrine of *acte clair* is crucial in this context. Under this doctrine, if the court is satisfied that the answer to the question of Community law, whether concerning interpretation or validity, is clear, then no decision on the question is 'necessary'. The judge is thus relieved of his obligation to refer.

As noted, the application of *acte clair* prevented the French Conseil d'État in *Shell-Berre* from referring to the ECJ when the matter of EC law seemed, to many eyes, far from clear. What seemed clear to Lord Widgery in *R* v *Henn* turned out to be incorrect. Moreover, the doctrine, depending as it does on a subjective assessment as to what is clear, can all too easily be used as a means of avoiding referral. This appears to have occurred in *Minister of the Interior* v *Cohn-Bendit* ([1980] 1 CMLR 543). In this case, heard by the French Conseil d'État, the supreme administrative court, Cohn-Bendit sought to invoke an EC directive to challenge a deportation order made by the French authorities. Certain provisions of the directive had already been declared by the ECJ to be directly effective (*Van Duyn* v *Home Office* (case 41/74); see Chapter 5). Despite urgings from the Commissaire du Gouvernement, M. Genevois, that in such a situation the Conseil d'État must either follow *Van Duyn* and apply the directive or seek a ruling from the Court under Article 234(3), the Conseil d'État declined to do either. In its opinion, the law was clear. The directive was not directly effective.

The role of *acte clair* in EC law was clarified by the ECJ in *CILFIT Srl* (case 283/81) in the context of a question from the Italian Cassazione (Supreme Court) concerning its obligation under Article 234(3), namely, did that article create an absolute obligation to refer, or was referral conditional on a prior finding of a reasonable interpretative doubt? From the Court's response, that there was no need to refer if the matter was (a) irrelevant, (b) materially identical to a question already the subject of a preliminary ruling, or (c) so obvious as to leave no scope for reasonable doubt, the second and third criteria may be taken as endorsing a version, albeit a narrow one, of *acte clair*. On the second criterion, which was a reiteration of its position in *Da Costa en Schaake*, the Court held that the questions at issue need not be identical, as long as the Court has already dealt with the point in question. Of particular importance to its third criterion is the Court's rider that, in deciding whether a matter was free from doubt, account must be taken of the specific characteristics of Community law, its particular difficulties, and the risk of divergence in judicial interpretation. Thus, if *acte clair* is to be invoked in the context of EC law, it must be on the basis of the criteria supplied by *CILFIT Srl*.

9.6.6.2 *Previous decision deals with the point*

However, the *CILFIT* criteria are not foolproof and have been criticised as providing national courts with an excuse not to refer, undermining the very purpose of Article 234(3). In *R v Secretary of State for the Home Department, ex parte Sandhu* (*The Times*, 10 May 1985), the House of Lords was faced with a request for a ruling on the interpretation of certain provisions of Regulation 1612/68 (concerning rights of residence of members of the family of workers), in the context of a claim by an Indian, the divorced husband of an EC national, threatened with deportation from the UK as a result of his divorce. The *CILFIT* criteria were cited, as was *Diatta v Land Berlin* (case 267/83), a case dealing with the rights of residence of a *separated* wife living apart from her husband, which was decided in the wife's favour. The House of Lords applied the second *CILFIT* criterion, found that the matter had already been interpreted in *Diatta*, and, on the basis of certain statements delivered *obiter* in *Diatta*, decided not to refer. On their Lordships' interpretation Mr Sandhu was not entitled to remain in the UK. Thus a loophole in the *CILFIT* criteria was exploited with disastrous results for Mr Sandhu. (For further discussion, see Chapter 20.)

The existence of a previous decision may not negate a national court's obligation to refer under Article 234(3) where the matter involves the legality of an EC measure, an issue considered in *Gaston Schul v Minister van Landbouw* (case C–461/03). This case involved a question as to the validity of Articles 4(1) and (2) of Commission Regulation 1423/95 on import rules for products in the sugar sector ([1995] OJ L141/16). The provisions corresponded with those in another regulation (1484/95) which had been declared invalid by the ECJ in an earlier decision (*Kloosterbooer Rotterdam*, case C–317/99). The Dutch court in *Gaston* therefore asked whether it was still subject to the mandatory rule in Article 234(3). The ECJ held that questions of validity differed from questions of interpretation, and a reference should always be made, even where there is an earlier ruling dealing with corresponding provisions in another measure (para. 25). The possible time delay was not a justification for changing the position that questions of invalidity are only for the ECJ to decide upon (para. 23).

9.6.6.3 *Avoiding relevance of EC law issue*

A court may avoid its obligations under Article 234(3) by deciding the case before it without considering the possibility of referral (see, e.g., *Mees v Belgium* [1988] 3 CMLR 137, Belgian Conseil d'État). In *Wellcome Foundation Ltd v Secretary of State for Social Services* ([1988] 1 WLR 635) the House of Lords, in considering the factors to be taken into account by a licensing authority in issuing a licence to parallel import a trade-mark medicine, thought it 'highly undesirable to embark on considerations of Community law which might have necessitated a referral to the Court of Justice under Article 177 [now 234]'.

In contrast, the German Federal Constitutional Court has emphasised national courts' duty to refer under Article 234(3), according to the *CILFIT* criteria, in the strongest terms. In quashing the German Bundesfinanzhof's decision on the direct effects of directives in *Re VAT Directives* ([1982] 1 CMLR 527), *Kloppenburg* v *Finanzamt Leer* ([1989] 1 CMLR 873) (see Chapter 5), it held that a court subject to Article 234(3) which deliberately departs from the case law of the ECJ and fails to make a reference under that Article is acting in breach of Article 101 of the German constitution. The principle of *acte clair* could not operate where there existed a ruling from the ECJ to the contrary (*Re VAT exemption* [1989] 1 CMLR 113). In *Re Patented Feedingstuffs* ([1989] 2 CMLR 902), the same court declared that it would review an 'arbitrary' refusal by a court subject to Article 234(3) to refer to the ECJ. A refusal would be arbitrary:

(a) where the national court gave no consideration at all to a reference in spite of the accepted relevance of Community law to the judgment and the court's doubt as to the correct answer;

(b) where the law consciously departs in its judgment from the case law of the ECJ on the relevant questions, and nevertheless does not make a reference or a fresh reference; and

(c) where there is not yet a decisive judgment of the ECJ on point, or such judgments may not have provided an exhaustive answer to the relevant questions or there is a more than remote possibility of the ECJ developing its case law further, and the national court exceeds to an indefensible extent the scope of its necessary judicial discretion, as where there may be contrary views of the relevant question of Community law which should obviously be given preference over the view of the national court.

It is suggested that these principles, applied in good faith, would ensure that a reference to the ECJ will be made in the appropriate case. Although a decision of a domestic court rather than of the ECJ, these principles should prove useful to the courts from all the Member States.

9.6.7 National courts' ability to refer of their own motion

Another possible limitation on the ability of the national courts to refer questions to the ECJ concerns the degree to which national courts are free to refer an issue of Community law of their own motion. In *R* v *Secretary of State for the Environment, ex parte Greenpeace Ltd* ([1994] 4 All ER 352), the English High Court took the approach that since the parties did not request a preliminary rulings reference, then, despite the fact that national rules expressly permit the court to refer of its own motion, the court should not make a reference. It is submitted that this approach is unduly restrictive. It ignores the underlying purpose of Article 234, which is to ensure correct and uniform interpretation of EC law throughout the Community, and it undermines the effectiveness of the Community law remedies (see Chapter 8). Although the ECJ has not discussed this point directly, it has itself assumed jurisdiction to rule on questions not referred (*OTO SpA* v *Ministero delle Finanze* (case C–130/92)) and it has more recently touched on these questions indirectly in *Peterbroeck Van Campenhout & Cie SCS* v *Belgium* (case C–312/93) and *van Schijndel* v *Stichting Pensioenfonds voor Fysiotherapeuten* (cases C–430 & 431/93). Unlike the British example cited above, the last two cases involved applications to amend pleadings to include a new point of Community law. In *Peterbroeck* the ECJ held that because the claimant had, in the circumstances, not had the opportunity of amending its pleadings before the time limit for so doing had expired, the effectiveness of Community law would preclude the application of national pro- cedural rules preventing the court from considering an issue of Community law. In *Van Schijndel* the applicants sought to introduce the Community law point on appeal. The ECJ held that if one could include new points of national law on appeal, one could not treat Community rules less favourably, but the national court was otherwise not obliged to raise the issue of its own motion in civil cases where the Community law point was beyond the existing ambit of the dispute. In civil litigation, both parties to the dispute have the opportunity to define the issues relevant to their dispute, and to allow the introduction of new issues might endanger legal certainty and procedural fairness. Thus one may conclude that Community law does not *prevent* national courts from raising issues of their own motion and, where it is desirable to ensure effective protection of individuals' rights, it should be done, provided that both parties have an opportunity to put forward their cases.

9.7 Effect of a ruling

Clearly a ruling from the ECJ under Article 234 is binding in the individual case although the English High Court in *Arsenal* v *Reed* had taken a narrow view of what this obligation means.

Given Member States' obligation under Article 10 (ex 5) EC to 'take all appropri- ate measures . . . to ensure fulfilment of the obligations arising out of this Treaty or resulting from action taken by the institutions of the Community' the ruling should also be applied in all subsequent cases. This does not preclude national courts from seeking a further ruling on the same issue should they have a 'real inter- est' in making a reference (*Da Costa en Schaake* (cases 28–30/62) – interpretation; *International Chemical Corporation SpA* (case 66/80) – validity).

9.7.1 References involving interpretation

The question of the temporal effect of a ruling, whether it should take effect retro- actively ('*ex tunc*', i.e., from the moment of entry into force of the provision subject to the ruling) or only from the date of judgment ('*ex nunc*') is less clear. In *Defrenne* v *Sabena (No. 2)* (case 43/75) the Court was prepared to limit the effect of the then Article 119 (now 141) to future cases (including *Defrenne* itself) and claims lodged prior to the date of judgment. 'Important considerations of legal certainty' the Court held, 'affecting all the interests involved, both public and private, make it impos- sible to reopen the question as regards the past'. The Court was clearly swayed by the arguments of the British and Irish Governments that a retrospective application of the equal pay principle would have serious economic repercussions on parties (i.e., employers) who had been led to believe they were acting within the law.

However, in *Ariete SpA* (case 811/79) and *Salumi Srl* (cases 66, 127 & 128/79) the Court made it clear that *Defrenne* was to be an exceptional case. As a general rule an interpretation under Article 234 of a rule of Community law 'clarifies and defines where necessary the meaning and scope of that rule as it must be or ought to be understood and applied *from the time of its coming into force*' (emphasis added). A ruling under that article must therefore be applied to legal relationships arising prior to the date of the judgment provided that the conditions for its application by the national court are satisfied. 'It is only exceptionally', the Court said 'that the Court may, in the application of the principle of legal certainty inherent in the Community legal order and in taking into account the serious effects which its judgments might have as regards the past, on legal relationships established in good faith, be moved to restrict for any person concerned the opportunity of rely-ing on the provision as thus interpreted with a view to calling into question those legal relationships.'

Moreover, 'such a restriction may be allowed *only* in the actual judgment ruling upon the interpretation sought' and 'it is for the Court of Justice *alone* to decide on the temporal restrictions as regards the effects of the interpretation which it gives'.

These principles were applied in *Blaizot* (case 24/86) and *Barra* (case 309/85). Both cases involved a claim for reimbursement of the Belgian minerval, based on *Gravier* (case 293/83, see Chapter 20). In both cases the claims were in respect of periods prior to the ECJ's ruling in *Gravier*. In *Barra* it was not disputed that the course for which the minerval had been charged was vocational; but *Blaizot's* course, a university course in veterinary medicine, was, the defendant university argued, not vocational, not within the scope of the *Gravier* ruling.

Since *Barra's* case fell squarely within *Gravier* and the Court had imposed no temporal limits on the effect of its judgment in *Gravier* itself, that ruling was held to apply retrospectively in *Barra's* favour. *Blaizot*, on the other hand, raised new issues. In deciding that university education could, and a course in veterinary science did, constitute vocational training the Court, clearly conscious of the impact of such a ruling on Belgian universities if applied retroactively, decided that 'important con-siderations of legal certainty' required that the effects of its ruling should be limited on the same lines as *Defrenne*, that is, to future cases and those lodged prior to judgment.

Unless the Court can be persuaded to change its mind and reconsider the ques-tion of the temporal effect of a prior ruling in a subsequent case when *no* new issues are raised, the question of the temporal effect will need to be considered in every case in which a retrospective application may give rise to serious repercussions as regards the past. Yet it is in the nature of this kind of ruling that it, and therefore its consequences, are unpredictable. Should a party wish, subsequently, to limit the effects of an earlier ruling, it will be necessary to ensure, as in *Blaizot*, that some new issue of EC law is raised.

In *Barber v Guardian Royal Exchange Assurance Group* (case C–262/88) the Court was again persuaded by 'overriding considerations of legal certainty' to limit the effects of its ruling that employers' contracted-out pension schemes fell within the then Article 119 (now 141) EC. Unfortunately the precise scope of the non-retroactivity principle that 'Article 119 [now 141] may not be relied upon in order to *claim entitlement* to a pension with effect prior to that of this judgment (except in the case of workers . . . who have initiated proceedings before this date or raised an equivalent claim under the applicable national law)' was disputed as being unclear. This lack of specificity, a characteristic of the Court's style of judgment, can create problems in the context of rulings on interpretation under Article 234. The Court's judgments can on occasions be too Delphic, leaving too much to be decided by national courts. It has taken a Protocol to the Maastricht Treaty and further cases to spell out the precise scope of the *Barber* ruling (see Chapter 25). Only now are the *full* implications of the Court's rulings in *Francovich* (cases C–6, 9/90) and *Marshall (No. 2)* (case C–271/91) being revealed.

Despite its commitment to the principle of legal certainty the Court has chosen not to limit the effect of its rulings in a number of cases in which it has introduced new and unexpected principles with significant consequences for Member States and even (in the case of Treaty articles) for individuals. It did not limit the effects of its judgment in *Francovich* despite Advocate-General Mischo's warnings as to the 'extremely serious' financial consequences for Member States if the judgment were not so limited: nor did it do so when it laid down a principle of full compensation for breach of a directly effective directive in *Marshall (No. 2)*. Where a ruling is likely to result in serious consequences, whether for States or 'public' or private bodies, for example employers, Member States would be advised to take advantage of their opportunity to intervene in Article 234 proceedings as they are entitled to do, to argue against retroactivity, as they did successfully in *Defrenne* and *Barber*. Other 'interested parties' may also apply to intervene.

The effects of the ECJ's strict approach to retroactivity may be mitigated by its more recent approach to Member States' procedural rules. In a number of cases (*IN CO GE* '90 (cases C–10 & 22/97) and *EDIS* (case C–231/96)), it has held that the principle of retroactivity should not prevent the application of detailed procedural rules (in these cases relating to limitation of actions) governing legal proceedings under national law, provided that these national rules do not make it 'impossible or excessively difficult' for individuals to exercise their Community rights (see further Chapter 8).

The impact of an interpretation on previous rulings by domestic administrative authorities which conflict with the ECJ's ruling was considered in *Kühne & Heitz NV v Productschap voor Pluimvee en Eieren* (case C–453/00). The case involved a claim for reimbursement of export refunds made by a Dutch administrative authority against Kühne. The latter's objection had been rejected by a court and the claim had therefore become a final decision by the administrative authority. The ECJ then delivered a ruling (*Voogd Vleesimport en-export* (case C–151/93)) which rendered the previous Dutch decision incorrect. Kühne therefore requested a reopening of the administrative procedure. The ECJ held that there was an obligation on administrative authorities to comply with an interpretation given by the Court in respect of all legal relationships, because the effect of a ruling is to clarify and define the meaning of a European rule 'as it ought to have been understood and applied from the time of its coming into force' (para. 21). This was subject to the principle of legal certainty, requiring finality of administrative decisions once a reasonable time-limit for legal remedies had expired or those remedies had been exhausted (para. 24); in such circumstances, there was no obligation to reopen previous decisions which had become final. However, on the facts of the case, the Dutch authority could reopen its decision, and the ECJ held that in such a situation, where a decision had become final and was based on a misinterpretation of EC law adopted without a preliminary ruling, and the matter had been raised without delay after the ECJ's intepretation, the administrative authority should review its decision.

9.7.2 References as to validity

The cases considered above relate to rulings on interpretation. Where matters of validity are concerned, the Court's approach is more flexible. It has assimilated the effects of a ruling of invalidity to those of a successful annulment action, as a result of which the illegal act is declared void. However, arguing from Article 231(2) (ex 174(2)), which enables the Court, in a successful annulment action, to limit the effects of a regulation which it has declared void (see Chapter 11), the Court has limited the effects of a finding of invalidity in a number of cases, sometimes holding the ruling to be purely prospective (i.e., for the future only, *excluding* the present case, e.g., *Roquette Frères* v *France* (case 145/79); policy doubted in *Roquette Frères SA* v *Hauptzollamt Geldern* (case C–228/92, see Chapter 11). The Court has not so far insisted that the effect of a ruling of invalidity can only be limited in the case in which the ruling itself is given.

The Court is more likely to be prepared to limit the effects of a ruling on validity than one on interpretation. Where matters of validity are concerned parties will have relied legitimately on the provision in question. A retrospective application of a ruling of invalidity may produce serious economic repercussions: thus it may not be desirable to reopen matters as regards the past. On the other hand too free a use of prospective rulings in matters of interpretation would seriously threaten the objectivity of the law, its application to all persons and all situations. Moreover, as the Court no doubt appreciates, a knowledge on the part of Member States and individuals that the law as interpreted may not be applied retrospectively could foster a dangerous spirit of non-compliance.

9.8 Interim measures

A national court may be requested to order interim measures pending a ruling from the ECJ under Article 234, either on interpretation or validity. *R* v *Secretary of State for Transport, ex parte Factortame Ltd* (case C–213/89) established that a national court must grant interim relief pending a ruling on the interpretation of Community law where this is necessary to protect individuals' directly effective Community rights, even where such a remedy is not available as a matter of national law. As a result of this ruling the House of Lords was prepared to grant an interim injunction against the Crown, preventing the application of the Merchant Shipping Act 1988. In *Zuckerfabrik* (cases C–143/88 & 92/89) the Court confirmed that national courts may also be obliged to grant interim relief pending a ruling from the ECJ on the validity of Community law, and set out the criteria to be applied by national courts in the exercise of their discretion as to whether or not to do so. It may be deduced from the terms of the Court's judgment that these criteria should be applied in all applications for interim relief, whether relating to matters of interpretation or validity. National courts' powers to grant interim relief pending a ruling under Article 234 have been held to include positive as well as suspensory measures (*Atlanta*

Fruchthandelsgesellschaft mbH v *Bundesamt für Ernährung und Forstwirtschaft* (case C–465/93)) (see further Chapter 8).

9.9 Extension of jurisdiction after the Treaty of Amsterdam

Although there had been suggestions that the ECJ's jurisdiction under the preliminary ruling procedure should be curtailed, the ToA increased the areas on which the ECJ may, in principle, rule. JHA and closer cooperation procedures of the TEU may now fall within its ambit. Additionally, the new Title IV in Part Three of the EC Treaty (on visas, asylum, immigration and other policies relating to free movement of persons), the subject matter of which was, prior to the ToA, mainly dealt with by the JHA pillar and therefore outside the ECJ's competence, now fall within the ECJ's jurisdiction (Article 68 EC). This has benefits in ensuring a respect for the rule of law and for access to justice.

Praise for the developments in the ToA cannot be unqualified, however; the provisions indeed raise some concerns. As noted earlier, the ECJ will have jurisdiction in relation to the JHA provisions of the TEU only in respect of 'framework decisions and decisions' and conventions established under the JHA, and only insofar as each Member State accepts its jurisdiction (Article 35 TEU). Even then, the Member States may not necessarily accept the ECJ's jurisdiction to the same degree. The Member States have the option of limiting the rights of the national courts to refer a question to the ECJ to courts against whose decision there is no judicial remedy under national law. This 'flexible' approach to jurisdiction will, at least, lead to confusion, but may also be criticised for the uncertainties and inequalities it introduces into the system: individuals' rights of access to the ECJ will vary depending on the Member State in which the action is brought. One may still comment that this is better than the previous position under the TEU, where there was no such access. The courts of some Member States are availing themselves of the possibility to refer questions in the field of Justice and Home Affairs, and the ECJ has handed judgments in this area on the Convention implementing the Schengen Agreement (see *Hüseyin Gözütok* and *Klaus Brügge* (cases C–187 and 385/01)).

The new provisions in Title IV of the EC Treaty have been subjected to a different regime as regards the jurisdiction of the ECJ. Although a preliminary ruling procedure will, in principle, apply to these provisions, there are certain differences from Article 234. Notably, only the courts against whose decisions there is no judicial remedy are required to ('shall') make a reference 'if they consider it necessary' to do so. Furthermore, the ECJ will not have jurisdiction in relation to measures taken under new Article 62(1) EC (concerning the crossing of external borders) relating to 'the maintenance of law and order and safeguarding of internal security'.

The new provisions create holes in the judicial protection offered; unlike the JHA Pillar of the TEU, the ECJ's jurisdiction under Article 234 prior to the ToA applied to the whole of the EC Treaty. The ToA amendments undermine the homogeneity and generality of access to the ECJ. Many important references under Article 234 came from the lower courts: now these courts will, in this new area, be precluded from making references. Consequently, individuals seeking a European ruling will be forced to litigate through their national appeal structure. The provision also creates uncertainty: when will circumstances necessitating the maintenance of law and order or safeguarding internal security arise? Indeed, who decides this question? It affects, in particular, those most in need of protection: an asylum seeker, for example, may not be in a position to exhaust national remedies. Even if he does, he may then find he falls outside the ECJ's jurisdiction. The new approach, accepted with reluctance by the Commission on the insistence of Member States, hardly matches up with a Union which claims to be based on the rule of law and respect for human rights.

9.10 Nice and the impact of enlargement

The current system governing preliminary rulings is under stress as, despite the *acte clair* doctrine, the number of references made to the ECJ remains high. With enlargement, the backlog can only get worse. There will probably be an increased number of referrals as an enlarged geographic jurisdiction will lead to a greater number of people (and courts) covered by EC law. The very fact that the new Member States are still new to the EC legal system could mean that they are likely to create initially a disproportionate number of references. This arises from two linked points. The first is that there are more likely to be questions arising in the new Member States as their legal systems adjust to the Community legal order. Further, their courts are less likely to have the experience and confidence to deal with many EC law questions without guidance from the ECJ, especially given that many of the new Member States are relatively new to democracy and a market economy. The Treaty of Nice addressed this problem by providing in Article 225(3) that the CFI is to have jurisdiction to hear preliminary references in areas specified in the Statute of the Court. As a safety mechanism, the same paragraph further provides that where a 'case requires a decision of principle likely to affect the unity or consistency of Community law' the CFI 'may refer the case to the Court of Justice for a ruling'. Additionally, decisions of the CFI on preliminary references may be subject to review by the ECJ. This possibility is stated to be available 'exceptionally' and 'where there is a serious risk of the unity or consistency of Community law being affected'. In the November 2005 version of the Statute, no areas were allocated to the CFI under Article 225(3).

Once the power in Article 225(3) is exercised, the restriction of access to the ECJ may cut down that Court's workload and, subject to the CFI not being swamped by the cases diverted to it, may reduce the backlog in cases – especially the preliminary references. In any event, this would constitute a significant change in the judicial architecture within the European Union.

9.11 Impact of the Treaty establishing a Constitution for Europe

The corresponding provision to Article 234 in the European Constitution is Article III–369, which reproduces the current Article 234 with some modifications. Thus, the ECJ would have jurisdictions with regard to (a) the interpretation of the Constitution and (b) the validity and interpretation of acts of the institutions, bodies, offices and agencies of the Union. The current Article 234(c) is not reproduced, but this may already be inherent in the new paragraphs (a) and (b) of Article III–369. Perhaps the most obvious change to the present position is that the ECJ would be able to rule on the interpretation of all the provisions of the Constitution, and the present anomaly regarding Title IV of the EC Treaty (see 9.9, above) would be removed. Indeed, the new provision on preliminary rulings contains an additional paragraph, requiring the ECJ to act 'with the minimum of delay' where a request for a preliminary ruling is made with regard to a person in custody (Article III–369, final sentence). However, matters relating to the CFSP would continue to fall outside the scope of the ECJ's jurisdiction (Article III–376).

9.12 Conclusions

The success of the preliminary rulings procedure depends on a fruitful collaboration between the ECJ (and, at some point, the CFI) and the courts of Member States. Generally speaking both sides have played their part in this collaboration. The ECJ has rarely refused its jurisdiction or attempted to interfere with national courts' discretion in matters of referral and application of EC law. National courts have generally been ready to refer; cases in which they have unreasonably refused to do so are rare. Equally rare are the cases in which the ECJ has exceeded the bounds of its jurisdiction without justification.

However, this very separation of powers, the principal strength of Article 234, is responsible for some of its weaknesses. The decision whether to refer and what to refer rests entirely with the national judge. No matter how important referral may be to the individual concerned (e.g., *Sandhu*) he cannot compel referral; he can only seek to persuade. And although the ECJ will extract the essential matters of EC law from the questions referred it can only give judgment in the context of the questions referred (see *Hessische Knappschaft* v *Maison Singer et Fils* (case 44/65)). Thus, it is essential for national courts to ask the right questions. As the relevance of the questions can only be assessed in the light of the factual and legal circumstances of the case in hand, these details must also be supplied. A failure to fulfil both these requirements may result in a wasted referral or a misapplication of EC law. Given the increasing pressures on the ECJ, wasted references and the drafting of sloppy questions can also be seen as a waste of the limited judicial resources at the Community level.

As the body of case law from the ECJ has developed and national courts have acquired greater confidence and expertise in applying EC law and ascertaining its relevance to the case before them, there should be less need to resort to Article 234. The initial question, of whether a decision on a question of EC law is 'necessary', has become crucial. As we have seen *CILFIT Srl* (case 283/81) has supplied guidelines to enable national courts to answer this question. Where a lower court is in doubt as to whether a referral is necessary the matter may be left to be decided on appeal. On the other hand, where a final court has the slightest doubt as to whether a decision is necessary it should always refer, bearing in mind the purpose of Article

234(3) and its particular importance for the individual litigant. These courts would do well to follow the lead provided by the German Constitutional Court. They will be more likely to do so if they are confident that the ECJ will not abuse its power in these proceedings by interpreting EC law too freely and failing to pay sufficient regard to 'important considerations of legal certainty'.

The significance of the ECJ's rulings and the Article 234 procedure has been well recognised by courts, commentators and Member States. The restrictions currently placed on its new jurisdiction, however, indicate not only that these areas are sensitive, but that the Member States wished to limit the opportunities for the ECJ to deliver one of its more far-reaching judgments in these areas. One point seems certain: the creation of a new approach to references to the ECJ indicates that both the Court and the procedure have been victims of their own success, and the occasional excess.

FURTHER READING

Alexander, W., 'The Temporal Effects of Preliminary Rulings' (1988) 8 YEL 11.

Anderson, D., 'The Admissibility of Preliminary References' (1994) 14 YEL 179.

Anagnostaras, G., 'Preliminary Problems and Jurisdiction Uncertainties: The Admissibility of Questions Referred by Bodies Performing Quasi-Judicial Functions' (2005) 30 EL Rev 878–890.

Barnard, C. and Sharpston, E., 'The Changing Face of Article 177 References' (1997) 34 CML Rev 1113.

Bebr, G., 'Arbitration Tribunals and Article 177' (1985) 22 CML Rev 498.

—, 'The Reinforcement of the Constitutional Review of Community Acts under Article 177 EEC' (1988) 25 CML Rev 684.

Gray, C., 'Advisory Opinions and the European Court of Justice' (1983) 8 EL Rev 24.

Koopmans, T., 'The Future of the Court of Justice of the European Communities' (1991) 11 YEL 15.

Maher, I., 'National Courts as European Community Courts' (1994) 14 LS 226.

Nascimbene, B., 'Community Courts in the Area of Judicial Cooperation' (2005) 54 ICLQ 489–497.

O'Keeffe, D., 'Appeals against an Order to Refer under Article 177 of the EEC Treaty' (1984) 9 EL Rev 87.

—, 'Is the Spirit of Article 177 under Attack? Preliminary References and Admissibility' (1998) 23 ELR 509.

'Quis Custodiet the European Court of Justice?' Editorial (1993) 30 CML Rev 905.

Rasmussen, H., 'The European Court's Acte Clair Strategy in CILFIT' (1984) 9 CML Rev 242.

—, 'Between Self-Restraint and Activism; a Judicial Policy for the European Court' (1988) 13 EL Rev 28.

Toth, A., 'The Authority of Judgments of the European Court of Justice: Binding Force and Legal Effects' (1984) 4 YEL 1.

Tridimas, T., 'The Court of Justice and Judicial Activism' (1996) 21 EL Rev 199.

Waelbroeck, M., 'May the Court of Justice Limit the Retrospective Operation of its Judgments?' (1981) 1 YEL 115.

Watson, J., 'Experience and Problems in Applying Article 177 EEC' (1986) 23 CML Rev 207.

10

Enforcement actions

10.1 Introduction

We have already seen that it is vital for the success of the Community that Member States comply with their obligations under the EC Treaty (Article 10 (ex 5) EC). Member States should ensure not only that they implement Community legislation by the due date, but also that they comply with decisions made by the Commission (e.g., in the field of state aid), and judgments of the Court of Justice (e.g., on the interpretation of particular provisions of Community law under an Article 234 (ex 177) reference). There is a danger that this obligation would be ineffective were there no mechanism by which Member States that infringe Community law could be pursued. Indeed, the Commission would find it much more difficult to fulfil one of its main objectives, which is to ensure compliance with Treaty obligations (Article 211 (ex 155) EC), if it did not have strong tools to support it in this task. The inclusion of provisions whereby a Member State may be brought before the ECJ for non-compliance with its obligations under EC law, and may even be fined for continued non-compliance, is important not just in terms of the effective implementation of EC law. It also illustrates certain supranational elements in the Union structure.

10.2 Outline of enforcement mechanism

The principal mechanism provided by the Treaty to pursue infringements of EC law by Member States is the direct action before the ECJ under Article 226 (ex 169) EC, which provides:

> If the Commission considers that a Member State has failed to fulfil an obligation under this Treaty, it shall deliver a reasoned opinion on the matter after giving the State concerned the opportunity to submit its observations.
>
> If the State concerned does not comply with the opinion within the period laid down by the Commission the latter may bring the matter before the Court of Justice.

A second procedure, in similar terms, provides for action by Member States under Article 227 (ex 170) EC.

Also, 'in derogation from the provisions of Articles 226 and 227', the Commission is empowered to bring a Member State before the Court under Article 88(2) (ex 93(2)) (infringement of Community rules on State aid provision, see Chapter 30), Article 95(9) (ex 100a(4)), para. 3 (improper use of derogation procedure provided by Article 95(4) (ex 100a(4)), para. 1, see Chapter 15) and Article 298 (ex 225) (measures taken to protect essential security interests or to prevent serious internal disturbances, see Chapter 19).

The Commission's power under Article 226 applies to the whole of the EC Treaty (Article 46 TEU). In contrast to the position as regards the preliminary reference procedure (see Chapter 9), this power, bringing with it the possibility of the ECJ's jurisdiction, has not been limited in regard to the new Title IV in the EC Treaty introduced by the ToA. Conversely, although the ECJ's jurisdiction to interpret the provisions of the JHA remaining within the TEU has been introduced by the ToA, the Commission has not been given the power to bring a Member State which has failed in its obligations under these provisions before the ECJ.

Article 226 was not designed as a punitive measure. Until the passing of the TEU (1992) no sanction was provided against Member States found by the ECJ in breach of their obligations; they were merely required 'to take the necessary measures to comply with the judgment of the Court of Justice' (original Article 171 EC). Although normally no time limit was prescribed for Member States' compliance the Court had held (*Commission v Italy* (case 69/86)) that implementation of a judgment must be undertaken immediately and must be completed within the shortest possible time. Where a State failed to comply with these obligations the Commission could only seek to enforce the judgment by further proceedings for breach of original Article 171 (now 228(1) EC). While few such actions were taken in the early days of the Community, their number increased alarmingly in the course of the 1980s. As a result Article 228 (ex 171) was amended by the TEU to allow the Commission, subject to the Court's approval, to impose fines and penalties on Member States which had failed to comply with a judgment against them in Article 226 proceedings. The Commission now takes decisions under this provision, and while most of these have not necessitated a fine being imposed by the ECJ, there have been a number of high-profile cases in recent years (see 10.7 below) which have.

10.3 Purpose of enforcement actions

The purpose of Article 226 EC is threefold. First, and primarily, it seeks to *ensure compliance* by Member States with their Community obligations. Secondly, it provides a valuable non-contentious *procedure for the resolution of disputes* between the Commission and Member States over matters of Community law: at least one-third of all Article 226 EC proceedings are settled at the preliminary informal stage. And finally, where cases do reach the ECJ they serve not only to bring particular breaches of EC law to light but also to *clarify* the law for the benefit of all Member States.

It is no doubt on account of the latter function that the Court has held that even if a State has complied with its obligations prior to the hearing before the Court, the Commission is entitled to judgment; it is not necessary for the Commission to show the existence of a 'legal interest' (*Commission v Italy (Re Ban on Pork Imports)* (case 7/61)). It is in the general interest of the Community to obtain a declaration of any failure to fulfil obligations under the Treaty, because this may assist other Member States in ensuring that they comply with Community law (*Commission* v *France* (case C–333/99), para. 23).

10.4 Member States' failure to fulfil an obligation

10.4.1 Member States as defendants

Although national governments appear before the Court as defendants in an Article 226 action, proceedings are brought against the *State*. Thus they may be brought in respect of a failure on the part of *any* agency of that State, executive, legislative or judicial. The responsibility of the State is engaged 'whatever the organ of the State whose action or inaction constitutes a failure, even if it concerns an institution which is constitutionally independent' (*Commission* v *Belgium* (case 77/69)). So far no action has been taken in response to a judicial failure. Although national courts have on occasion clearly acted in breach of their obligations (e.g., *Minister of the Interior* v *Cohn-Bendit* [1980] 1 CMLR 543 – French Conseil d'État failed to comply with its obligation under Article 234(3), see Chapter 9) and action in respect of such infringements could have been undertaken in theory (per Advocate-General Warner in *Meyer-Burckhardt* v *Commission* (case 9/75)), the Commission, no doubt agreeing with Advocate-General Warner that such action should not be lightly undertaken, prefers to publicise national courts' failures in its annual reports on the monitoring and application of Community law. Considerations of diplomacy could not, however, prevent an action before a domestic court against a national judicial failure based on *Francovich* v *Italy* (case C–6 & 9/90), which was confirmed by the ECJ in *Köbler* v *Austria* (case C–224/01) (see Chapter 8). Also, a failure by domestic courts or administrative authorities may be based on a problem with the legislation which these bodies have to apply. In *Commission* v *Italy* (case C–129/00), Italian legislation on the repayment of tax levied in breach of Community law was ambiguous with regard to the burden of proof in establishing whether the costs incurred as a result of having paid such a tax had been passed on to third parties. Some court judgments imposed that burden on the person who had paid the tax in a manner contrary to Community law. The ECJ confirmed that an action could be brought under Article 226 EC in these circumstances, and noted that a provision open to judicial constructions which could be interpreted both in line with, and contrary to, Community law was not sufficiently clear. The ECJ concluded that Italy had been in breach for failing to amend the legislation to remove the ambiguity. An issue not raised before the Court was the obligation of the domestic courts to interpret legislation in accordance with Community law under the doctrine of indirect effect (see Chapter 5), which would have made it necessary to consider the availability of an Article 226 action for incorrect judicial application of Community law head-on. It now seems that in a situation such as this, the non-compliance will be found in the legislation itself, rather than the domestic courts' failure to interpret this correctly. It remains to be seen what would happen if a domestic court were to make an error of law in applying a directly applicable provision of Community law.

10.4.2 Meaning of 'failure'

A State's 'failure' may be in respect of any binding obligation arising from Community law. This would cover obligations arising from the EC Treaty and its amending and supplementing treaties; from international agreements entered into by the Community and third countries where the obligation lies within the sphere of Community competence; from EC regulations, directives and decisions; and even from general principles of law recognised as part of Community law where the breach of these principles occurs within the context of an obligation of EC law (see Chapter 6). 'Failure' can include any wrongful act or omission, ranging from a failure to notify an implementation measure, to partial implementation, to faulty implementation, to non-implementation of Community law, or simple maintaining in force national laws or practices incompatible with EC law. As the case of *Commission* v *France* (case C–265/95) also makes clear, the failure to fulfil an obligation may also arise in circumstances where the State has failed to take action to prevent other bodies from breaching EC law. In this case, the French authorities' failure to take action in the face of blockades of imported products was found, following an Article 226 action by the Commission, to be a breach of Article 28 (ex 30) in conjunction with Article 10 (see further Chapter 18, and discussion at 10.6.2).

10.5 Procedure

Notices of Member States' failures may come as a result of the Commission's own enquiries, from (increasing) complaints from the public, or from the European Parliament. The Commission's 22nd Annual Report on Monitoring the Application of Community Law for 2004 (COM (2005) 570, 5 November 2005) showed that the number of complaints from the public increased from the 2003 figure to 1,146, although the 2004 figure includes both the group of 15 Member States and the 10 new countries that joined in 2004. With regard to the group of 15, there was a decrease in 2004 from 1,290 complaints to 1,080. The Commission itself detected a total of 328 cases, of which 285 were from the group of 15 Member States (an increase on 2003). Complaints now constitute more than one-third of the total number of cases.

The sensitive nature of an action under Article 226 is reflected in its procedure. It follows a number of stages. The initial stages, both formal and informal, between the Commission and the Member State, are designed to achieve compliance by persuasion. Only if this fails is it necessary to proceed to the final, judicial stage before the ECJ.

10.5.1 Informal proceedings

The Commission begins informally with a notification to the State concerned of its alleged failure, to which the State will respond. At least one-third of complaints are settled at this stage. Where they are not the Commission may proceed to the next, formal stage.

10.5.2 Formal proceedings: first stage

10.5.2.1 *Formal notice*

The Commission opens proceedings by letters of formal notice, inviting the Member State concerned to submit its observations. In order that the State has a full opportunity to put its case, the Commission must first inform the State of its grounds of complaint. The complaint need not at this stage be fully reasoned, but the State must be informed of *all* the charges which may be raised in an action before the Court. In *Commission* v *Italy (Re Payment of Export Rebates)* (case 31/69) the Commission alleged that Italy was in breach of its EC obligations in failing to pay certain export rebates to its farmers, required under EC regulations; in opening the proceedings the Commission charged Italy with breaches up to 1967, but failed to mention a number of breaches committed after that date. When the matter came before the Court, the Court refused to consider the later breaches. The Court said that the Member States must be given an adequate and realistic opportunity to make observations on the alleged breach of Treaty obligations. In deciding whether a State has had such an opportunity the Court may take into account communications made by the Commission during the informal stage.

The Commission must send a letter of formal notice which is identified as relating to Article 226 proceedings. It seems that a formal letter sent under a different measure will not suffice. In *Commission* v *France* (case C–230/99), France had notified the Commission under Directive 83/189/EEC (see 15.3.6) of a draft order concerning rubber materials. The Commission felt that, if implemented, the order would affect the free movement of goods and delivered a detailed opinion under the directive, setting out its objections to the proposed French order. France rejected the Commission's opinion and adopted the order. The Commission subsequently sent a reasoned opinion pursuant to Article 226 (10.5.2.2, below). The Court ruled that the enforcement action was inadmissible because the Commission had failed to follow the correct procedure by not sending a formal notice before submitting its reasoned opinion. Moreover, a formal notice must allege a prior failure by the Member State to whom it is addressed to comply with Community law, which could not be the case here as the opinion sent under Directive 83/189/EEC related to a draft measure. The ECJ took the view that it would violate the principle of legal certainty should the function of the opinion change, i.e., from notification under Directive 83/189/EEC to a letter of formal notice, depending on whether the Member State amended its proposed legislation in accordance with the opinion.

10.5.2.2 *Reasoned opinion*

Following the submission of the State's observations to the Commission, the Commission issues a 'reasoned opinion'. Half of the cases which continue past the informal stage are resolved without the need for the Commission to issue this 'opinion'. The reasoned opinion will record the infringement and require the State to take action to end it, normally within a specified time-limit. Although it cannot introduce issues not mentioned in the formal notice, this does not mean that the reasoned opinion and the formal notice have to be exactly the same. In particular, the Commission may limit the scope of the enquiry (*Commission* v *Italy* (case C–279/94)). Further, although the opinion must be 'reasoned' it need not set out the Commission's case in full. In the case of *Commisson* v *Italy (Re Ban on Pork Imports)* (case 7/61) the Court held, in response to the Italian government's claim that the Commission's reasoned opinion was inadequate, that the reasoned opinion need only contain a coherent statement of the reasons which had convinced the Commission that the Italian Government had failed to fulfil its obligations. No formalism was required. The only purpose of the reasoned opinion was to specify the point of view of the Commission in order to inform the government concerned, and, possibly, the Court. The reasoning behind the decision is clear. If the State refuses to accept the Commission's opinion, it may proceed to the second stage before the Court. It will then be for the Court to weigh in detail the merits of the case on both sides.

10.5.2.3 *Challenging a reasoned opinion*

In *Commission* v *Germany* (case C–191/95) Germany challenged the admissibility of Article 226 proceedings on a number of grounds. The first of these related to the Commission's decision to issue the reasoned opinion for breach of the principle of collegiality. Germany argued that the Commissioners themselves at the time did not have all the facts to enable them to make such a decision; furthermore they had not seen the draft reasoned opinion. The ECJ held that the decision to issue a reasoned opinion could not be described as a measure of administration or management and could not be delegated by the Commissioners themselves to their officers. Nonetheless, this does not mean that the Commissioners have to agree the wording of the reasoned opinion; it is sufficient if they have the information on which the decision to send a reasoned opinion is based.

The ECJ has held (*Alfons Lütticke GmbH* v *Commission* (case 48/65)) that the reasoned opinion is merely a step in the proceedings; it is not a binding act capable of annulment under Article 230 (ex 173) (Chapter 11). While the defendant State may choose to impugn the Commission's opinion in proceedings under Article 226 before the Court, where the Member State complies with the opinion, a third party, possibly adversely affected by the Commission's opinion, has no equivalent right. However, in *Amministrazione della Finanze dello Stato* v *Essevi SpA* (cases 142 & 143/80) the Court held that the Commission has no power in Article 226 proceedings to determine conclusively the rights and duties of a Member State. These may only be determined, and their conduct appraised, by a judgment of the Court. The Commission may not, in the opinion which it is obliged to deliver under Article 226, exempt a Member State from compliance with its obligations under the Treaty or prevent individuals from relying, in legal proceedings, on the rights conferred on them by the Treaty to contest any legislative or administrative measure of a Member State which may be incompatible with Community law. Thus, a third party, dissatisfied with the Commission's opinion, could raise the issue of the legality of the Member State's action indirectly before his national court and seek a referral on the relevant questions of interpretation to the ECJ under Article 234. This was done in *Essevi SpA* in a domestic action for the recovery of taxes levied allegedly in breach of Article 90 (ex 95).

The same principle would apply where the Commission has decided in its discretion not to institute or pursue Article 226 proceedings. In *Alfons Lütticke GmbH* v *Commission* (case 48/65), Alfons Lütticke GmbH had complained to the Commission that its own (German) Government was acting in breach of EC law by introducing a levy on imported powdered milk. As an importer of powdered milk the levy affected it adversely. It asked the Commission to take action under Article 226 against Germany. The Commission refused. Germany had since withdrawn the levy and the Commission decided in its discretion not to take action. It was a political compromise. Lütticke, on the other hand, wished to establish the infringement in order to recover for losses suffered while the German law was in force. Since Article 226 gave the Commission a discretion in the matter there was no way in which its refusal to bring proceedings could be challenged either under Article 230 (annulment action) or Article 232 (ex 175) (failure to act) (see Chapters 11 and 12). However, in a parallel action before its national courts in *Alfons Lütticke GmbH* v *Hauptzollamt Saarlouis* (case 57/65), it succeeded in obtaining a ruling under Article 234 from the ECJ on the direct effects of Article 90, the article which it alleged the German Government had breached. Since the article was found directly effective, it could be applied in the company's favour.

10.5.2.4 *Time-limits*

While there are no time-limits in respect of the stages leading up to the reasoned opinion, thereby giving both parties time for negotiation, the Commission will normally impose in its reasoned opinion a time-limit for compliance. A Member State will not be deemed in breach of its obligations until that time-limit has expired. Where the Commission does not impose a time-limit the Court has held that a reasonable time must be allowed. A State cannot be relieved of its obligations merely because no time-limit has been imposed (*Commission* v *Italy (Re Premiums for Reducing Dairy Production)* (case 39/72)). The Commission has a complete discretion in the matter of time-limit, subject to the possibility of review by the Court. The Court may dismiss an action under Article 226 on the grounds of inadequate time-limit. An action by the Commission against Belgium for its failure adequately to implement the *Gravier* Decision (case 293/83) was dismissed on the grounds that the compliance period of 15 days prescribed by the Commission in its reasoned opinion did not give Belgium sufficient time to respond to its complaints, either before or after the issuing of its reasoned opinion (*Commission* v *Belgium (Re University Fees)* (case 293/85)). On the other hand, in *Commission* v *Belgium* (case 85/85) a compliance period of 15 days was held to be reasonable in the light of the extensive information provided by the Commission at the informal stage.

10.5.3 **Formal proceedings: second stage**

If a Member State fails to comply with the Commission's reasoned opinion within the specified time-limit, proceedings move to the final, judicial stage before the Court. The Court will examine the situation as it prevailed when the time-limit set in the reasoned opinion expired and will not take account of any subsequent changes (*Commission* v *France* (case C–147/00)). However, the action taken before the Court must be based on the same grounds as stated in the reasoned opinion and may not introduce new grounds (cases C–35/96, *Commission* v *Italy* and C–439/99, *Commission* v *Italy*). It is possible to limit the subject matter of the proceedings (case C–203/03, *Commission* v *Austria*), or to rephrase the grounds for complaint as long as this does not change its substance (case C–305/03, *Commission* v *UK*). Moreover, if the Member State concerned amends its legislation in order to comply with EC law, but does so incompletely, the Commission may withdraw its action in part but continue it with regard to the domestic provisions that are not in compliance (*Commission* v *France* (case C–177/04)).

Again, the initiative rests with the Commission, which '*may* bring the matter before the Court of Justice' (Article 226). No time-limits are imposed on the Commission in commencing the second stage; however, this position seems to be qualified by a requirement that the length of the pre-litigation procedure must not have adversely affected the rights of defence of the Member State concerned (*Commission* v *France* (case C–333/99), para. 25). Here the Commission is obliged to set out the subject matter of the dispute, the submissions and a brief statement of the grounds on which the application is based. With regard to the latter it is not enough simply to refer to all the reasons set out in the letter of formal notice and the reasoned opinion (*Commission* v *Germany* (case C–43/90)).

The judicial stage is not a review procedure, although at this stage the legality of the Commission's reasoned opinion may be reviewed (*Commission* v *Belgium* (case 293/85)). Here the Court, exercising plenary jurisdiction in contentious proceedings, conducts a full enquiry into the merits of the case and decides the matter *de novo*. Interested Member States (but not individuals: *Commission* v *Italy (Re Import of Foreign Motor Vehicles)* (case 154/85R)) are entitled to intervene in the proceedings. The Commission is entitled to request, and the Court to order, interim measures (e.g., *Commission* v *UK (Re Merchant Shipping Rules)* (case 246/89R); *Commission* v *Ireland (Re Dundalk Water Scheme)* (case 45/87R), see Chapter 25). Application for interim relief may, however, only be made 'by a party to the case before the Court' and where it 'relates to' that case.

10.6 Defences

Many defences to an action under Article 226 have been attempted; few have succeeded. The best defence is clearly to deny the obligation. It may be conditional, for example, on a time-limit which has not expired. Member States may also argue about the substantive scope of the obligation they are alleged to have breached, suggesting that their actions fall within the proper scope of the relevant obligation. Where a breach of secondary legislation is alleged, the legislation may be attacked for illegality. Otherwise, the traditional defences of international law offer little hope of success.

10.6.1 Reciprocity

The defence of *reciprocity*, an accepted principle of international law, even entrenched in some Member States' constitutions (e.g., France, Article 55), whereby in the event of a breach of his obligations by one party the other party is likewise relieved of his, was rejected by the Court in *Commission* v *Luxembourg and Belgium (Re Import of Powdered Milk Products)* (cases 90 & 91/63). Here the governments argued that their alleged breach of Article 25 (ex 12) of the EC Treaty would have been legal but for the Commission's failure to introduce certain measures which they were authorised to enact. This argument, based on reciprocity, the Court held, was not applicable in the context of Community law. The Community was a new legal order; it was not limited to creating reciprocal obligations. Community law governed not only the powers, rights and obligations of Member States, but also the *procedures* necessary for finding and sanctioning all violations that might occur.

The defence of reciprocity was also rejected in the context of a failure by another Member State to comply with a similar obligation; it made no difference that Article 226 (ex 169) proceedings had not been instituted against that State in respect of a similar breach (*Commission* v *France (Re Restrictions on Imports of Lamb)* (case 232/78); *Steinike und Weinlig* (case 78/76)).

10.6.2 **Necessity and** *force majeure*

Similar reasoning to that advanced in *Commission* v *Luxembourg and Belgium* led to the rejection of a defence of *necessity* in *Commission* v *Italy (Re Ban on Pork Imports)* (case 7/61). The Treaty provided, in Article 226 for procedures to be followed in cases of emergency. This precluded unilateral action on the part of Member States.

A defence based on *force majeure* was rejected in *Commission* v *Italy (Re Transport Statistics)* (case 101/84). Here Italy was charged with non-implementation of a Community directive; the reason for its non-implementation was that the data-processing centre involved in the implementation of the directive had been bombed. The Court held that while this might amount to *force majeure*, which could provide an excuse for non-implementation, a delay of four-and-a-half years, as in this case, was inexcusable. As the Court said, 'time will erode the validity of the excuse'.

The concept of *force majeure* was considered in the case of *McNicholl* v *Ministry of Agriculture* (case 296/86), not in Article 226 proceedings, but in order to challenge via the preliminary rulings procedure the forfeiture of a deposit for failing to comply with an export undertaking as required by Community law. The Court held that:

> whilst the concept of *force majeure* does not presuppose an absolute impossibility of performance, it nevertheless requires that non-performance of the act in question be due to circumstances beyond the control of persons pleading *force majeure*, that the circumstances be abnormal and unforeseeable and that the consequences could not have been avoided through the exercise of all due care.

This definition should be equally applicable in Article 226 proceedings. Where it is clear that the fulfilment of a Community obligation will be impossible, a Member State should alert the Commission at the earliest opportunity in order to ascertain whether a compromise arrangement can be made (*Commission* v *Italy* (case C–349/93)).

The ECJ faced a situation of civil disorder, by French farmers blocking imports of agricultural produce, contrary to Article 28 EC, in *Commission* v *France* (case C–265/95). Here, despite complaints by the Commission, the French authorities had failed to take any significant action to prevent the demonstrations, arguing that more determined action might lead to more serious breaches of public order or even to social conflict. The ECJ refused to accept these arguments. 'Apprehension of internal difficulties could not justify a failure by a Member State to apply Community law correctly. . . . It was for a Member State to guarantee the full scope and effect of that law, to ensure its proper implementation, unless the State could show that action by it could have consequences for public order with which it could not cope.' The government had failed to adduce any evidence of the latter. Although a serious threat to public order might justify non-intervention by the police, that argument could only be adduced with regard to a specific incident, and not, as in the case in question, in a general way, covering all the incidents cited.

10.6.3 Constitutional difficulties

Another defence, frequently raised and consistently rejected by the Court, is based on *constitutional, institutional or administrative difficulties* within a Member State. As the Court held in *Commission v Italy* (case 28/81), a Member State cannot plead the provisions, practices or circumstances existing in its own legal system in order to justify a failure to comply with obligations resulting from Community directives. The same reasoning would apply to a failure to comply with any other Community obligations (e.g., *Commission v Italy (Re Premiums for Reducing Dairy Production)* (case 39/72 – regulation).

Similarly in *Commission v United Kingdom (Re Tachographs)* (case 128/78) the Court refused to accept an argument based on *political* (i.e., trade union) difficulties, submitted as justification for a failure to implement a Community regulation on the installation of tachographs.

10.6.4 Factual application

Another popular but equally unsuccessful defence rests on the argument that while Community law may not be applied *de jure, administrative practices ensure that EC law is in fact applied*. This argument was advanced in *Commission v France (Re French Merchant Seamen)* (case 167/73), in an action based on the French Code Maritime. The code was clearly discriminatory, since it required a ratio of three Frenchmen to one foreigner in certain jobs. The French government's argument that the code was not enforced in practice was unsuccessful. Enforcement by administrative practices, the Court held, is not enough. The maintenance of national laws contrary to EC law gives rise to an ambiguous state of affairs, and leaves citizens of a Member State in a state of uncertainty (see also *Commission v Ireland* (case C–381/92)).

Similar reasons led to the rejection of another argument in the same case based on the *direct effects* of Community law. If the Community law in question, in this case what was then Article 7 of the EEC Treaty (now Article 12 (ex 6) EC), were directly effective, argued the French, this would be enough to ensure that the State fulfilled its obligations. The Court did not agree (see also *Commission v Belgium (Re Type Approval Directives)* (case 102/79)).

The Court took a (seemingly) more moderate line in *Commission v Germany (Re Nursing Directives)* (case 29/84). Here it conceded that a defence based on direct effects might succeed if the State's administrative practices guaranteed that the directives would be applied fully and ensured that the legal position was clear and that all persons concerned were fully aware of their rights. These requirements were not, however, found to be satisfied in this case. It is submitted that they will rarely be satisfied. This seems to be borne out in the case of *Commission* v *Italy* (case 168/85), in which the Court held that the right of citizens to plead directly applicable provisions of the Treaty before national courts is only a minimum guarantee and insufficient in itself to ensure full and complete application of the Treaty.

10.6.5 **Domestic law is in compliance**

A variation on the defence of 'factual application' is either that existing domestic law already adequately implements the corresponding EC rule, or that the legislation that has been adopted to give effect to an EC rule will be interpreted by the courts in accordance with it (in line with the principle of 'indirect effect'; see Chapter 5). The ECJ has accepted that existing domestic law can be sufficient to give effect to an EC Directive, even where the words of the domestic measure depart from the text of the Directive itself. Provided that the general legal context ensures the full application of a directive in a sufficiently clear and precise manner, a Member State will be deemed to have fulfilled its obligations (see, e.g., *Commission* v *Germany* (case 29/84), para. 23; *Commission* v *Germany* (case C–217/99), para. 31, and *Commission* v *Spain* (case C–58/02), para. 26). In *Commission* v *Spain* (case C–58/02), Spain sought to rely on its existing criminal code provisions on the violation of intellectual property rights as being equivalent to the requirements of the Directive on conditional access services (98/84/EC, [1998] OJ L320/54), but this was rejected by the court (see also *Commission* v *Italy* (case C–372/99) and *Commission* v *Netherlands* (case C–144/99), discussed in Chapter 15).

Where legislation has been adopted to give effect to an EC obligation, but the wording of that legislation differs from the EC text, there is an obvious risk that domestic law may not comply with EC law. However, the mere fact that a different wording has been chosen may not be conclusive evidence of a failure to comply with EC law if there is no corroborating evidence such as court judgments (see, in particular, *Commission* v *United Kingdom* (case C–300/95), discussed further in Chapter 15).

10.6.6 **Treaty derogation**

Where there is a derogation from a Treaty obligation in the Treaty itself, provided the terms of that derogation are satisfied then it goes without saying that an Article 226 EC action would be unsuccessful. In *R* v *Chief Constable of Sussex, ex parte International Trader's Ferry Ltd* ([1999] 1 CMLR 1320) the House of Lords was asked to consider whether a failure by the Sussex constabulary adequately to police animal rights protestors seeking to obstruct the export of live cattle from local ports was in breach of Community law. Faced with mounting and unsustainable costs, the Chief Constable had decided to reduce policing from five to three days per week. Although that failure might constitute a barrier to exports, in breach of Article 29 (ex 34), it was argued that the breach was justified under Article 30 (ex 36), on public policy grounds. Given that there was no likelihood of obtaining funds from the government, and that the police had a continuing obligation to protect the general public against crime and disorder, the restrictions on policing were neither unreasonable nor disproportionate. This argument was accepted by the House of Lords. The question is, would it have been accepted by the ECJ?

In *Commission* v *France* (case C–265/95), the Court conceded in principle, it is submitted correctly, that the need to preserve public order is, in an appropriate situation, a valid defence. Given the competing demands of public order in *R v Chief Constable of Sussex* and the necessity, in the face of finite public funds, to strike a balance between them, it may be argued that the House of Lords was right in concluding that the Chief Constable's Decision, taken conscientiously, to reduce policing at the ports was justified, albeit on public policy or public order grounds rather than simply on the grounds of cost, and was not disproportionate.

10.7 Consequences of a ruling and of a failure to comply

10.7.1 Obligations following a ruling under Article 226 EC

If the Court finds that the Member State has failed to fulfil its obligations under the EC Treaty the Member State is 'required to take the necessary measures to comply with the judgment of the Court of Justice' (Article 228 (ex 171) EC). Until the Maastricht Treaty the only sanction against a State which had failed to comply with a ruling from the Court under Article 226 was a second action under that Article for failure to comply with its obligations under Article 228. The number of such repeat actions had been steadily increasing. Although the ECJ had provided individuals with a means of enforcement of their Community rights via the principles of direct and indirect effects and State liability under *Francovich* (cases 6, 9/90), these remedies were uncertain and unequal in their application, and provided a remedy only in the individual case. Following its clarification in *Brasserie du Pêcheur* (cases C–46 & 48/93), a remedy under *Francovich* will only be available in circumstances where the State has 'manifestly and gravely' acted or failed to act in breach of EC law. A State will not be liable in damages for 'excusable' failures. Although excusable failures may be established in actions based on direct effects or indirect effects, in which liability has hitherto been strict, or under Articles 226 and 227, success in such actions will not *of itself* guarantee that States rectify their breaches of Community law.

10.7.2 Penalty payments for continuing failure to comply

At Maastricht a further weapon was added to the Court's armoury. Article 228(2) now provides as follows:

> If the Commission considers that the Member State concerned has not taken such measures [to comply with the Court's judgment under Article 226] it shall, after giving the State an opportunity to submit its observations, issue a reasoned opinion specifying the points on which the Member State concerned has not complied with the judgment of the Court of Justice.
>
> If the Member State concerned fails to take the necessary measures to comply with the Court's judgment within the time limit laid down by the Commission, the latter may bring the case before the Court of Justice. In so doing it shall specify the amount of the lump sum or penalty payment to be paid by the Member State concerned which it considers appropriate in the circumstances.

> If the Court of Justice finds that the Member State concerned has not complied with its judgment it may impose a lump sum or penalty payment on it.

In its 2004 Report, the Commission stated that a there were 73 cases under consideration for which the Article 228 procedure had been opened. The worst offender was France, with 17 cases under consideration, followed by Italy (12 cases).

There is no Treaty limit to the level of fines that may be imposed by the Court, although the Commission is required to propose a fine when it commences proceedings. Initially it was not clear how the Commission was going to calculate the fines, and it was only in November 1997 (four years after this provision came into effect) that the Commission published guidance on calculating the penalty payments (COM (97) 299). A new notice was issued in December 2005 (SEC (2005) 1658), which applies to all Article 228 cases started after 1 January 2006.

In the past, the Commission requested periodic penalty payments rather than a lump sum. This may have been the result of an ambiguity in Article 228(2) authorising the ECJ to impose 'a lump sum *or* penalty payment' (emphasis added). In *Commission* v *France* (case C–304/02), the ECJ held that the word 'or' should be understood in a cumulative rather than an alternative sense, and that it would be possible to impose both a lump sum and penalty payment. The lump sum would reflect the failure of the Member State to comply with the earlier judgment (particularly where there has been a long delay), whereas the penalty payment would act as an incentive to the Member State to bring the infringement to an end as soon as possible (para. 81). Consequently, the Commission has changed its practice and will now request a lump sum penalty as well as a periodic payment. The lump sum is intended to penalise the continuation of the infringement between the dates of the judgment in the Article 226 proceedings and of the Article 228 proceedings, whereas the penalty payment is to cover each day of delay after the judgment under Article 228 EC.

In considering what sort of financial penalty to ask for, the Commission will take into account the seriousness of the infringement, its duration and the need for deterrence to prevent future infringements (para. 6). The Notice then spells out the approach the Commission adopts in calculating the penalty payment. It starts from a standard flat rate amount currently set at €600 per day. This amount is multiplied by a 'seriousness coefficient' ranging from 1 to 20. This is followed by a 'duration coefficient' which increases that sum by a multiplier of between 1 and 3 (at a rate of 0.10 per month from the date of the Article 226 judgment). That sum is then multiplied by a further factor specific to each Member State based on its GDP and number of votes in Council (although should the Constitution come into effect, weighted votes in Council would be abolished).

As far as the lump sum is concerned, a minimum sum for each Member State is specified in the Notice. This will be requested unless a sum calculated by multiplying a daily amount by the number of days the infringement persists exceeds that amount. The 'daily amount' is calculated in the same way as the daily penalty payment. The number of days will be the period between the first judgment (under Article 226 EC) and the judgment under Article 228 EC. In this regard, it should be noted that the Commission does have a degree of discretion as to the timing of launching Article 228 proceedings, which may affect the duration of the period on the basis of which the lump sum is calculated. It remains to be seen whether this fact could form the basis for a claim of discriminatory treatment by the Commission against a particular Member State, or whether the time it takes the Commission to take action under Article 228 reflects the nature and seriousness of the infringement.

The combination of lump sum and penalty payments could therefore result in the imposition of considerable fines, which may act as a strong deterrent. The Court of Justice has made it clear that it is not bound by the Commission guidance, although it regards it as 'a useful point of reference' (*Commission* v *Greece* (case C–387/97), paras 89–90; *Commission* v *Spain* (case C–278/01), para. 41; *Commission* v *France* (case C–304/02), para. 103), and it has, so far, calculated the penalty on the basis of the criteria specified by the Commission (although not always applying the same factors). It has made it clear that the Commission can propose a penalty, but that the ultimate decision is for the Court, and that the Court may depart from the criteria stated in the Notice, e.g., by adopting a duration coefficient that exceeds the maximum of 3 (*Commission* v *France* (case C–177/04), para. 71).

For the first few years after Maastricht, there were no actions involving the imposition of fines. In 1996 and 1997, the first fines were proposed, and the first case in which a penalty was imposed was *Commission* v *Greece* (case C–387/97). In this case, Greece was found to have failed to comply with an earlier judgment in Article 226 proceedings (case C–45/91). The Court therefore exercised its powers under Article 228(2) and imposed a penalty of €20,000 for each day of delay in ensuring compliance with the earlier judgment. Ultimately, Greece paid €5.4 million in penalties before it finally complied with the judgment in March 2001 (19th Annual Report on Monitoring the Application of Community Law (COM (2002) 324 final, p. 14).

Since then, there have been several further cases (e.g., *Commission* v *Spain* (case C–278/01); *Commission* v *France* (case C–304/02); *Commission* v *France* (case C–177/ 04)) and others are pending (e.g., *Commission* v *Italy* (case C–119/04), Advocate-General's opinion delivered on 26 January 2006). In *Commission* v *Spain*, Spain had failed to comply with the Bathing Water Directive (76/160/EEC [1976] OJ L31/1) even after an adverse judgment under Article 226 (see *Commission* v *Spain* (case C–92/96)). Having found that Spain continued to be in breach, the ECJ addressed the question of penalty payments. A difficulty with imposing a daily payment was that the nature the obligation imposed by the directive (improvements to the quality of bathing waters) meant that compliance could only be established on an annual basis once the water had been analysed and a report submitted. The ECJ accepted that it would be unfair to impose a daily fine at the same level up to the point when a report confirming compliance was received, because Spain may in fact have complied sooner. The court therefore imposed a penalty payment which would only be payable annually, and be calculated on the basis of the percentage of Spanish bathing waters not in compliance with the Directive. This decision is important in that it creates a balance between ensuring that the fine achieves its objective of securing compliance and the need to avoid penalising a Member State which has already complied.

The more recent decision, *Commission* v *France* (case C–304/02), seems to herald a much stricter approach by the ECJ in dealing with Article 228 EC cases, at least in circumstances where the infringement in question has persisted for a significant time after the initial judgment in Article 226 proceedings. The case involved the failure by France fully to comply with control measures for fishing activities, in respect of which the ECJ had given judgment in 1991 (*Commission* v *France* (case C–64/88)). Despite repeated inspections, a reasoned opinion by the Commission in April 1996, and a supplementary opinion in June 2000, France still failed to comply fully with the earlier judgment. The ECJ therefore held that France had failed to fulfil its obligations under Article 228 EC. The Commission had suggested the imposition of penalty payments rather than a lump sum. The ECJ, clearly irritated by the fact that France had not complied more than a decade after the first judgment, raised of its own motion the possibility of imposing a lump sum in addition to penalty payments (para. 75). Having concluded that it would be possible to impose both penalty payments and a lump sum (paras 76–86), the Court then had to consider whether it was appropriate for it to depart from the Commission's suggestions as to penalty. Some Member States expressed concerns that the Court exercising a discretion of this kind would conflict with the principles of legal certainty, predictability, transparency and equal treatment. Moreover, it was argued that the ECJ could not go beyond the parties' claims, and the defaulting Member State would need to be able adequately to defend itself. The ECJ rejected those concerns, primarily because of the special nature of Article 228 proceedings to bring about a cessation of an infringement. The ECJ thereby reserved the right to determine the type of penalty and level of payment that it regards as the most appropriate to the infringement at issue. In this case, it held that a penalty payment, to be imposed on a half-year basis, was appropriate; however, because France had remained in default for a long period since the judgment in Article 226 proceedings, it was 'essential to order payment of a lump sum' (para. 114). There can be little doubt that the imposition of a lump sum as well as penalty payments reflected the ECJ's view that the degree of non-compliance in the particular case was severe, and the failure of France to put matters right sooner bordered on contempt. This judgment sends a strong message to the Member State to respond more rapidly to a finding of non-compliance in Article 226 proceedings, and it also sees the ECJ flexing its muscles in an area where hitherto a finding of non-compliance may have been little more than a minor embarrassment.

As noted above, in the wake of *Commission* v *France* (case C–304/02), the Commission has amended its guidelines and will now always ask for a lump sum to cover the continuation of the infringement, as well as a penalty payment to bring the Member State into line. It remains to be seen how the ECJ will handle subsequent cases. In *Commission* v *Italy* (case C–119/04), which involves an infringement which started in 1995 and in respect of which the court passed judgment against Italy in 2001 (*Commission* v *Italy* (case C–212/99)), Advocate-General Mauduro proposed that the Court should not exercise its discretion to impose a lump sum in addition to the penalty payments suggested by the Commission because whilst the period since the Article 226 judgment was 'substantial', it was 'not in the same league as the exceedingly long period' (para. 49) in *Commission* v *France* (case C–304/ 02). In *Commission* v *France* (case C–177/04), the infringement that remained following amendments made after the Article 226 proceedings (*Commission* v *France* (case C–52/00), see chapter 15) was not particularly serious, which may have influenced the ECJ in deciding not to impose a lump sum, despite the fact that the infringement had carried on for over 17 years.

10.8 Action by Member States (Article 227 (ex 170) EC)

In addition to enforcement actions brought by the Commission, there may be situations in which one Member State has reason to complain about an infringement of Community law by another Member State. In such circumstances, it should be enough for the complaint to be submitted to the Commission, but if the Commission fails to act, then a Member State may wish to bring infringement proceedings itself. This possibility is provided for in Article 227 (ex 170) EC, which states:

> A Member State which considers that another Member State has failed to fulfil an obligation under this Treaty may bring the matter before the Court of Justice.
>
> Before a Member State brings an action against another Member State for an alleged infringement of an obligation under this Treaty, it shall bring the matter before the Commission.
>
> The Commission shall deliver a reasoned opinion after each of the States concerned has been given the opportunity to submit its own case and its observations on the other party's case both orally and in writing.
>
> If the Commission has not delivered an opinion within three months of the date on which the matter was brought before it, the absence of such opinion shall not prevent the matter from being brought before the Court of Justice.

The procedure is thus similar to that of Article 226 EC save that it is initiated by a Member State which, if the Commission fails to deliver a reasoned opinion within three months, is entitled to bring the matter before the ECJ. In addition, both parties are entitled to state their case and comment on the other's case both orally and in writing.

It has been suggested that since Article 227(1) gives Member States a general right to bring proceedings, the issuing of a reasoned opinion cannot preclude the complainant State from bringing proceedings before the Court if it is dissatisfied with the opinion or if it wishes to obtain a final judgment from the Court. This latter occurred in *France* v *United Kingdom (Re Fishing Net Mesh Sizes)* (case 141/78).

The procedure provided under Article 227 has rarely been used; Member States seem cautious about bringing an action under this provision because, since no Member State has a perfect record for the implementation of Community law, there is a danger that a defendant State might bring a retaliatory action against its prosecutor. It is likely to be deemed more politic to bring the alleged infringement to the attention of the Commission, leaving the Commission to act under Article 226. Nonetheless, the Article 227 procedure was used in *Belgium* v *Spain* (case C–388/95), concerning the rules regarding the application of the wine denomination, Rioja. It is interesting to note that the dispute brought in other Member States, which intervened in favour of one side or the other, revealing a split in opinion between the main wine growing States and others. The ECJ found in favour of Spain.

In case of dispute between Member States, the Treaty also provides a further, voluntary procedure. Under Article 239 (ex 182) EC, States may agree to submit to the ECJ any dispute relating to the subject matter of the Treaty.

10.9 Impact of the proposed Constitution

Although the future of the Treaty establishing a Constitution for Europe is uncertain at this time (see Chapter 1), the changes that were proposed merit brief consideration. Articles 226–228 EC would become Articles III–360 to III–362 of the Constitution. They would be identical in substance to the current provisions, with one addition: a new sub-paragraph (3) would be added to Article III–362 (current 228 EC) which would permit the Commission to ask for a fine in proceedings under Article III–360 (current 226 EC) where a Member State has failed to notify the measure transposing a 'European framework law' (currently known as 'directives') to the Commission. If the ECJ decides that a fine should be paid, it may not exceed the amount specified by the Commission.

This provision is remarkable, because it would enable the Commission to request a fine (lump sum or penalty payment) in the context of what are currently Article 226 EC proceedings. This would change the purely declaratory nature of these proceedings. However, it must be emphasised that this procedure could only be used for a failure to *notify*. If a Member State has notified transposition measures, but has incorrectly implemented a 'framework law', then the Commission can only request a fine after having first obtained judgment under Article III–360 (current 226 EC) and having taken further action under Article III–362 (current 228 EC).

The Constitution would abolish the current three-pillar structure, and the ECJ's powers under Articles III–360 to III–362 would cover all of the Constitution. However, Article III–376 would remove the CFSP (in particular, Article I–40 and I–41) from the ECJ's jurisdiction. Although the Court would have jurisdiction in respect of the Area of Freedom, Security and Justice, this would not extend to actions by the law-enforcement agencies of the Member States (Article III–377).

10.10 Special enforcement procedures: State aid, breach of Article 95(4) (ex 100a(4)) procedures and measures to prevent serious internal disturbances

These procedures, which apply only within the areas specified, operate 'in derogation from the provisions of Articles 226 and 227'. There are certain essential differences between these procedures and Articles 226 and 227. In the case of Article 88(2) (ex 93(2)) the Commission, after giving the parties concerned an opportunity to submit their comments, issues a *decision* requiring the Member State concerned to alter or abolish the disputed aid within a specified time-limit. If the State concerned does not comply with the decision within the prescribed time, the Commission or any other interested State may bring the matter to the ECJ. Since a *decision*, unlike a reasoned opinion, is a binding act it will be subject to challenge under Article 230 (ex 173) EC (*Commission v Belgium* (case 156/77); see Chapter 11).

Article 298 (ex 225) EC provides an accelerated procedure whereby the Commission can, without preliminaries, bring a Member State directly before the ECJ if it considers that that State is making improper use of its powers provided under Articles 296 and 297 (ex 223 and 224) EC. Under these provisions Member States are empowered to take emergency measures to protect essential security interests (Article 296) or in the event of serious internal disturbances, war or threat of war, or for the purposes of maintaining peace and international security (Article 297). A ruling of the Court under Article 298 is given in camera.

Article 95(9) also provides for an accelerated procedure whereby the Commission and any Member State may bring a State before the Court if it considers that a Member State has made improper use of the powers of derogation provided for in Article 95(4) in deciding 'to maintain national provisions on grounds of major needs referred to in Article 30, or relating to the protection of the environment or the working environment', or in Article 95(5) (see also Chapter 15).

10.11 Conclusions

The compliance of the Member States with their Community obligations is crucial in ensuring the success of the Community. Without the enforcement procedure provided in Article 226 EC, it seems that there would be a much lower level of compliance. The procedure itself seems to work tolerably well, although the Commission has on occasion been slow to proceed to the second stage of the formal procedure. The possibility of imposing penalty payments appears to have encouraged Member States to put a stop to continuous infringements more quickly than would otherwise have been the case. Yet, there is still a general problem with most Member States as far as complying with Community law is concerned, and there is a steady stream of cases under Article 226.

The case law which is developing under Article 228 EC seems to be marking the start of a new period of activism by the ECJ, at least with regard to persistent failures to comply with EC law. The Court appears to have lost its patience with countries that disregard judgments under Article 226 EC and has given a very strong indication that penalties under Article 228 should be punitive, as well as remedial. The Commission has responded by changing its practice, as confirmed in the 2005 Guidelines.

The recent enlargement of the Community may increase the Commission's workload in this area significantly if it is to fulfil its role as 'guardian of the treaties' adequately. Early indications are that the countries which joined in 2004 generally managed to ensure that their national legal systems had implemented the *acquis communautaire*, although there have already been some instances of inconsistent application, and failures to comply outright.

FURTHER READING

Commission's Annual Reports on the Monitoring and Application of Community Law (published at http://europa.eu.int/comm/secretariat_general/sgb/droit_com/index_m).

Hilson, C., 'Legality Review of Member State Discretion und Directives' in Tridimas, T. and Nebbia, P. (eds), *European Law for the 21st Century* (Hart Publishing, 2004).

Timmermans, C., 'Use of the Infringement Procedure in Cases of Judicial Errors', in de Zwaan, J. W., Jans, J. H. and Nelissen, F. A. (eds), *The European Union – An Ongoing Process of Integration* (The Hague: TMC Asser Press, 2004).

Wenneras, P., 'A New Dawn for Commission Enforcement under Articles 226 and 228 EC: General and Persistent (GAP) Infringements, Lump Sums and Penalty Payments' (2006) 43 CML Rev 31–62.

11

Direct action for annulment

11.1 Introduction

One of the fundamental means by which the actions of any legislature can be controlled is the process of judicial review. This enables a court to consider whether a legally binding measure violates procedural or substantive rules of law and should therefore be rendered inapplicable. Binding acts of the Community institutions are subject to review through a number of routes (see Chapter 7), and the most direct way of review is to challenge the legality of a particular measure. Article 230 (ex 173) EC provides the mechanism for a direct challenge to the legality of Community acts. A further means of challenge is provided by Article 241 (ex 184) EC, which permits a claim *incidental* to a main action that a regulation should not be applicable.

This chapter examines the operation of the Article 230 procedure in detail. There are four main elements: the types of act that are subject to review; the bodies that may bring an action for review; the time within which an action may be brought; and the grounds on which such an action may be based. We will consider each of these aspects in turn.

It will be seen that the most controversial aspect of this provision concerns the limited extent to which individuals are able to bring a challenge under Article 230. There have been many calls for reform, and recent case law of the Court of First Instance (CFI) and the Court of Justice (ECJ) revealed the existence of conflicting views as to the extent to which individuals can rely on the procedure in Article 230 to have a measure annulled, although, as will be seen, the ECJ has reasserted the established, restrictive, view. We will return to this point in detail below, having examined the basic framework in Article 230. Despite many calls for European institutions and law-making to come closer to the citizen, it seems that the limitations in this area currently remain. Another limiting aspect of the judicial review procedure is the strict time-limit. The interrelationships between Article 230 and other mechanisms for review are thus important. We shall see how the ECJ has limited the scope of avoiding time-limits in Article 230 by recourse to Article 234 and examine the operation of the indirect review mechanism found in Article 241.

11.2 Overview of provisions

11.2.1 Judicial review

Article 230 EC provides:

> The Court of Justice shall review the legality of acts adopted jointly by the European Parliament and the Council, of acts of the Council, of the Commission and of the [European Central Bank], other than recommendations and opinions, and of acts of the European Parliament intended to produce legal effects *vis-à-vis* third parties.
>
> It shall for this purpose have jurisdiction in actions brought by a Member State, the European Parliament, the Council or the Commission on grounds of lack of competence, infringement of an essential procedural requirement, infringement of this Treaty or of any rule of law relating to its application, or misuse of powers.
>
> The Court shall have jurisdiction under the same conditions in actions brought by the Court of Auditors and by the European Central Bank for the purpose of protecting their prerogatives.
>
> Any natural or legal person may, under the same conditions, institute proceedings against a decision addressed to that person or against a decision which, although in the form of a regulation or a decision addressed to another person, is of direct and individual concern to the former.
>
> The proceedings provided for in this Article shall be instituted within two months of the publication of the measure, or of its notification to the plaintiff, or, in the absence thereof, of the day on which it came to the knowledge of the latter, as the case may be.

The equivalent provision in the Constitution is found in Article III–265. With the exception of a couple of amendments, this provision, on its entry into force, would not change the current position much. The changes are more in the way of updating and reflecting the existing practice than anything else. The crucial exception to note is the change to the wording of the position of individuals seeking to challenge acts not addressed to them (see below, 11.4.3.5).

11.2.2 Indirect challenge

Article 241 (ex 184) EC provides:

> Notwithstanding the expiry of the period laid down in the fifth paragraph of Article 230, any party may, in proceedings in which a Regulation adopted jointly by the European Parliament and the Council, or a Regulation of the Council or of the Commission is in issue, plead the grounds specified in the second paragraph of Article 230, in order to invoke before the Court of Justice the inapplicability of that Regulation.

As with the other judicial review actions, Article 241 has been amended to reflect the ability of the European Parliament and the European Central Bank to adopt binding acts.

11.3 Judicial review: reviewable acts

11.3.1 Acts that may be challenged

Reviewable acts, defined as acts 'other than recommendations and opinions', are not confined, as they might appear to be, to regulations, directives or decisions. The Court has held that they include all measures taken by the institutions designed to have legal effect, whatever their nature or form (*Commission* v *Council (Re European Road Transport Agreement)* (case 22/70)). The measure in this case was a Council resolution setting out the position to be taken by the Council in the preparation of the road transport agreement. The Commission sought to challenge this resolution, since it considered that the matter lay outside the Council's sphere of competence. Applying the above test, the action was declared admissible.

Similarly in *Re Noordwijk's Cement Accord* (cases 8–11/66), the act challenged was a registered letter sent by the Commission to the applicant in the context of EC competition policy, to the effect that the companies' immunity from fines was at an end. The letter was not called a 'decision'. Nevertheless it was held that since it produced legal effects for the companies concerned and brought about a change in their legal position it was an act capable of annulment under Article 230 (see also *BEUC* v *Commission* (case T–37/92)). In *France* v *Commission* (*Re Pension Funds Communication*) (case C–57/95) the ECJ held that a communication, which was phrased in imperative language, was intended to have legal effects and could be challenged. In *Infront WM AG* v *Commission* (case T–33/01), the applicant sought to challenge a Commission letter to the United Kingdom Government, indicating that the Commission had no objection to measures taken, in accordance with Article 3a Television without Frontiers Directive (Directive 89/552/EEC, as amended), by the UK to ensure the broadcast of football World Cup finals on free-to-air television. In defence, it was argued that the letter was not a decision, but was analogous to a definition of position of intention not to take action under Article 226 proceedings, which is not susceptible of review (see, e.g., *Dumez* v *Commission* (case T–126/95)). Further, the legal effects stemmed from the underlying national law, not the Commission letter, which did not change the legal position. The CFI disagreed and held the letter was susceptible of review as it concluded the verification procedure which the Commission is obliged to carry out under the Television without Frontiers Directive. It therefore triggers the mutual recognition system in the Directive, according to which other Member States are obliged to prevent broadcasters established under their respective jurisdictions from avoiding national regulation about access to television content.

Not all letters issued by the Commission will necessarily be capable of challenge. The *max.mobil* case (case T–54/99, *max.mobil* v *Commission*, on appeal case C–141/02P) illustrates the difficulty of determining whether a decision by an institution is capable of being reviewed. The underlying complaint concerned the telecommunications market in Austria. Max.mobil complained to the Commission, asking it to take action under Article 86. The Commission, referring to its existing policy in this area, declined to do so and wrote to max.mobil to this effect. Max.mobil sought to challenge this letter; the Commission argued that it was of an informative nature only. The CFI agreed with max.mobil, suggesting that on the basis of previous case law (notably case C–107/95P *Bilanzbuchhalter*, discussed in Chapter 12), an individual had the right to have a diligent and impartial treatment of the complaint; thus the Commission must consider the matter before coming to its decision. The letter, in the view of the CFI, was therefore a decision on this basis which was subject to review. The ECJ disagreed. It argued that '[t]he fact that max.mobil has a direct and individual interest in the annulment of the Commission's decision to refuse to act on its complaint is not such as to confer on it the right to challenge that decision' (para. 70). It concluded that the letter to max.mobil was of an informative nature only. Such an approach does limit the protection awarded by Article 230, and is particularly worrying given the ease with which a challenge to inaction can be ended. It is equally difficult to reconcile the approach here with that taken by the CFI in *Air France* (case T–3/93).

In *Air France* v *Commission* (case T–3/93) a mere statement by a Commission spokesman, not published but reported by the press agencies, that a proposed acquisition of Dan-Air by British Airways lay outside the scope of the Commission's competence under Regulation 4064/89, was held to be capable of annulment, since it confirmed the Commission's position 'beyond all doubt'. The fact that the statement was not addressed to a particular person and was given orally was not relevant: it was the content and legal effect of the measure which were crucial. (See also cases regarding the European Parliament at 11.3.2.) It may be that one way of reconciling these cases is to note that the more broad approach to the notion of a decision is taken by the CFI, the ECJ seemingly taking a narrower approach.

Both courts have held, in contrast to the case law discussed above, that preliminary measures, designed simply to pave the way for a final decision, are not reviewable (see *Nashua Corporation* v *Commission* (cases C–133, 150/87)). In *Dysan Magnetics Ltd* v *Commission* (case T–134/95), the opening by the Commission of a dumping investigation, a purely preparatory measure which preceded the adoption of definitive anti-dumping duties, and which did not have an immediate and irreversible effect on the legal situation of concerned undertakings, was held not to be open to challenge under Article 230. In *Philip Morris International and others* v *Commission* (cases T–377/00, T–379/00, T–380/00, T–260/01 and T–272/01), the Commission's decision to commence proceedings against various tobacco manufacturers in an American court was challenged by the defendants to that action, but the CFI held that the action was inadmissible because the decision to commence proceedings had no binding legal effects on the applicants. The legal effects, if any, would derive from the decision of the American court.

This principle, that it is the true nature and effect of a measure rather than its label which determines whether it may be reviewed under Article 230, is very important, since this provision is subject to a strict two-month time-limit. If the measure is not recognised as a binding act and challenged in time, the action will be declared inadmissible, whatever its merits (e.g., *Commission* v *Belgium* (case 156/77) – no success under Article 241 because the original act (a letter) was not attacked in time; see below).

The Constitution amends this provision to give the ECJ power to review the legality of 'European laws and framework laws', in line with the changes to the types of legislation the Union institution may enact (see Chapter 3 and 11.3.4).

11.3.2 Acts of Parliament

Although only acts of the Council and the Commission were expressed to be capable of challenge under the original Article 173, the Court had, prior to the passing of the TEU, admitted challenges to acts of the European Parliament having legal force with regard to third parties (see *Luxembourg* v *Parliament* (case 230/81); *Partie Ecologiste ('Les Verts')* v *Parliament* (case 294/83)). This was justified on the grounds that Parliament had over the years acquired powers to issue such acts. In *Luxembourg* v *Parliament*, Luxembourg was seeking to challenge Parliament's resolution to move its seat from Luxembourg to Strasbourg and Brussels. In *'Les Verts'* v *Parliament* the Green Party sought to challenge a decision of the Bureau of Parliament on the allocation of campaign funds for the 1984 European elections. Clearly Parliament's acts in these cases produced significant legal effects for both applicants (cf. *Les Verts* v *Parliament* (case 190/84)).

Contrast these cases with *Le Pen* (case T–353/00, under appeal, case C–208/03 P). It concerned the question of a declaration of the President of the Parliament, and turned on the issue of whether the declaration had legal effects. In earlier cases (*Council* v *Parliament* (case 34/86) and *Council* v *European Parliament* (case C–284/90)), the ECJ had held that a declaration could have legal effects. The *Le Pen* case was different. The declaration here consisted of a recognition of the legal position in France, rather than creating legal effects of its own. Thus, when looking at acts giving rise to legal effects, it is not sufficient that the act be of the type that could give rise to legal effects, but it must itself give rise to such effects.

The principles established in cases such as *'Les Verts'* have now been incorporated into Article 230 EC. Also, reflecting Parliament's powers of co-decision granted under the TEU, Article 230 now provides for challenge to acts adopted 'jointly by Parliament and the Council' under Article 251 (ex 189(b)) EC.

11.3.3 Acts of other bodies

Article 230 also now specifies that acts of the European Central Bank may be challenged. It seems that the acts of other bodies may also be challenged though, in order to be capable of challenge, the measure must proceed from a Community institution empowered under the Treaty to enact binding measures. Thus in *Commission* v *Council* (case C–25/94), a decision by the Committee of Permanent Representatives (COREPER), and in *Parliament* v *Council* (case C–181/91), a decision of the *Member States meeting in Council* (but not of the *Council* as such), could not be challenged. The Constitution recognises this. Should it come into force, the relevant provision, Article III–270, provides that the Court may review 'the legality of acts of bodies, offices or agencies of the Union intended to produce legal effects *vis-à-vis* third parties'.

11.3.4 Review under TEU

The ECJ's jurisdiction under Article 230 EC is, of course, limited to Community acts. This does not mean that the actions of the Union will completely escape the ECJ's review. The ECJ has already held that it has the power to review actions taken under the JHA pillar of the TEU to ensure that such measures have been properly adopted thereunder and are not diluting the Community *acquis* (*Commission* v *Council (Air Transport Arrangements)* (case C–170/96)).

Following the ToA, Article 35 TEU provides for judicial review of actions taken under the JHA pillar, albeit limited in terms of the measures which may be challenged (framework decisions and decisions) and the grounds of challenge. Furthermore, only the Commission and the Council can bring an action under these provisions. Parliament and 'natural or legal persons' have no *locus standi* to challenge action in this area. The Court will be responsible for policing this boundary.

Note that the Constitution, should it come into force, would abolish the three-pillar structure. In principle, the exclusion from the Court's jurisdiction of certain areas based on the pillar system itself would also go. However, Articles III–376 and III–377 limit the Court's jurisdiction regarding Articles I–40 and I–41, that is CFSP.

11.4 *Locus standi*: who may bring an action?

The question of *locus standi* (or standing), that is, of who should be entitled to challenge the legality of a particular measure, is controversial. On the one hand, it may be desirable to provide for broad *locus standi* to ensure that the legislature is subjected to adequate control. On the other hand, it is equally desirable to ensure that somebody who is wholly unconnected with the adoption or effects of a legally binding act is not in a position to challenge its validity, as this would otherwise admit too many challenges, with an adverse effect on legal certainty, as well as the Court's workload. There are strict *locus standi* requirements in Article 230. Applicants are divided into privileged and non-privileged applicants, with the Court of Auditors and the Central Bank occupying a semi-privileged position. The main controversy in recent years has been over the restricted interpretation given by the Court to the *locus standi* rules on non-privileged applicants. This part examines these rules in more detail.

11.4.1 Privileged applicants

Member States, the Parliament, the Council and the Commission are entitled to challenge *any* binding act under Article 230. A 'Member State' for the purposes of this article does not include governments of regions or of autonomous communities (*Region Wallonie* v *Commission* (case C–95/97)). However, regional authorities may intervene, if they have legal personality under their domestic law, as a non-privileged applicant. As such, they must satisfy the requirements of direct and individual concern (*Comunidad Autonoma de Cantabria* v *Council* (case T–238/97)) (see further below). It is arguable that regional authorities should have semi-privileged status to protect their prerogatives, but this has not been given serious consideration by the Community.

11.4.1.1 *The changing nature of Parliament's standing*

Although Parliament is now a privileged applicant, this was not always so, despite the fact that Parliament has always had *locus standi* to bring an action against another Community institution for a failure to act (Article 232 (ex 175); Chapter 12). It had sometimes been suggested that, because of the parallels between Articles 232 and 230 EC, the Parliament's standing under Article 230 should match that under Article 232 EC. In *Parliament v Council (Comitology)* (case 302/87), however, the Court held that there was 'no necessary link' between the actions under Article 230 and 232, respectively. This seemed to rule out any right of Parliament to challenge the validity of measures adopted by the Commission and Council. Nonetheless, in *Parliament v Council (Chernobyl)* (case C–70/88), the Court held that Parliament *did* have standing to challenge acts of the Commission or the Council under the precursor of Article 230 where this was necessary to protect its prerogative powers. Parliament was therefore entitled to challenge a Council decision which had allegedly been taken in breach of an obligation to consult Parliament (see also *Parliament v Council* (case C–65/90)).

At the IGC in Maastricht in 1992, the Heads of State decided not to grant Parliament a *general* right to challenge acts of the Council or the Commission, and, despite suggestions that it should, the position did not change at Amsterdam either. Article 230 was revised by the TEU to include Parliament's right of challenge to the extent that this was necessary to protect its prerogatives, reflecting the approach in the Court's jurisprudence. The Court had adopted a strict interpretation of this requirement. In *Parliament v Council (Re aid to Bangladesh)* (cases C–181 & 248/91), Parliament could not challenge the Commission's handling of aid to Bangladesh because no prerogative power of Parliament had been infringed. (See also *Parliament v Commission (Re legislation on organic production* (case C–156/93)). Moreover, where Parliament's prerogatives were in issue, the Court insisted on strict compliance with form. In *Parliament v Council (Re European Development Fund)* (case C–316/91), Parliament challenged an act of Council as enacted on the wrong legal basis, not requiring consultation with Parliament. The allegedly correct basis required consultation, but the Court held that there had been no breach of Parliament's prerogatives because Parliament had, in fact, been consulted.

It was not until the Treaty of Nice came into force in early 2003 that Parliament finally assumed the full status of privileged applicant. Arguably, as the only democratically elected EC institution, with an express role in *supervising* Community activities, this is a welcome development. However, as Douglas-Scott notes, parliamentary procedure is not designed for litigation and it may seem a little strange that Parliament has the power of challenge, particularly in view of the diverse political interests it represents. It is submitted that the rather unique legislative procedure in Community law and the nature of the Community itself merit this form of control.

11.4.1.2 *Other bodies*

Should the Constitution come into force in its current form, Article III–270 extends the semi-privileged position noted in relation to the Court of Auditors and the ECB to include the Committee of the Regions (Article III–265(3)).

11.4.2 **Non-privileged applicants**

Compared with Member States and Community institutions, the *locus standi* of individuals under Article 230 is much more limited. A 'natural or legal person' is entitled only to challenge:

(a) a decision addressed to *himself or herself,* or

(b) a decision, in the form of a regulation or a decision addressed to another person, which is of direct and individual concern to himself or herself.

A 'natural or legal person' includes a State which is not a Member State of the EC (*Gibraltar* v *Council* (case C–298/89)) as well as autonomous regions of a Member State (see 11.4.1).

All claims by natural or legal persons are now brought before the CFI with a right of appeal to the ECJ on points of law only (see Chapter 7).

No problem exists where the decision is addressed to the applicant, with one minor exception (to be discussed in Chapter 12). Provided the applicant brings the action within the two-month time-limit his or her claim will be admissible. Many such decisions have been successfully challenged (e.g., in competition law).

Where the decision is addressed to another person, problems arise. 'Another person' has been held to include a Member State (*Plaumann & Co.* v *Commission* (case 25/62)). Despite dicta by the ECJ in *Plaumann*, that the provisions of the Treaty concerning the right to seek a legal remedy ought not to be interpreted strictly, the Court, and now the CFI, has adopted a very restrictive approach towards the individual seeking to challenge acts addressed to another person, although there has been some relaxation of the rules in recent years.

11.4.2.1 *Trade associations*

Although the Court has been unwilling to entertain actions by trade or other associations under Article 230, maintaining that 'defence of a common interest is not enough to establish admissibility', the CFI held in *Associazione Italiana Tecnico Economica del Cemento (AITEC)* v *Commission* (cases T–447–9/93) that a trade association would be permitted to bring an action against a decision addressed to 'another person' where it represented the individual interests of some of its members whilst at the same time protecting the interests of the section as a whole. The CFI noted that 'in these circumstances collective action brings procedural advantages'. As a result Italian and British associations of cement producers were able to challenge a Commission decision addressed to the Greek Government approving the grant of State aid to a Greek producer, Heracles, and succeeded in obtaining its annulment. Likewise a trade union and a works council, as 'recognised representatives' of employees affected by a proposed merger under Merger Regulation 4064/89, were held entitled to challenge a Commission decision approving Nestlé's takeover of Perrier SA (see *Comité Central d'Entreprise de la Société Générale des Grandes Sources* v *Commission* (case T–96/92) and *Aktionsgemeinschaft Recht und Eigentum eV* v *Commission* (case T–114/00) – association formed to protect the collective interests of its members had *locus standi* to challenge a Commission decision not to instigate the formal procedure under Article 88(2) EC, on behalf of those members who would have been parties concerned within the meaning of Article 88(2) EC (see Chapter 30)). In *Federolio* v *Commission* (case T–122/96), the CFI identified three situations when an association would be granted *locus standi*:

(a) the trade association has been expressly granted procedural rights;

(b) it represents the individuals or undertakings which themselves have standing; or

(c) the trade association itself is affected – for example if its right to negotiate is affected.

This will still leave many associations or pressure groups without *locus standi* (see, for example, *Stichtling Greenpeace Council* v *Commission* (case C–585/93), the subject of an unsuccessful appeal (case C–321/95 P)). Perhaps this is not surprising, given the stringency of the test applied to individuals.

11.4.3 Challenging decisions addressed to another person

For a claim by a 'natural or legal person' against a decision addressed to 'another person' to be admissible, three criteria must be satisfied:

(a) the measure must be equivalent to a decision;

(b) it must be of direct concern to himself or herself; and

(c) it must be of individual concern to himself or herself.

Since *all* of these criteria must be fulfilled the question of admissibility may be decided, and the application rejected, on the basis of any one of them. In the order in which it examines the above requirements, and in its approach to all three criteria, the Court has not been consistent. Further, it now seems that the CFI is requiring an individual seeking to challenge a decision to show a legal interest in bringing the proceedings as an additional test. In *Schmitz-GothaFahrzeugwerke* v *Commission* (case T–167/01), the CFI held that showing a legal interest in bringing the challenge is an essential and fundamental pre-requisite for any legal proceedings and without it, the court will not proceed to examine the questions of whether the decision is of direct and individual concern (*Olivieri* v *Commission* (case T–236/99)). It seems in this regard that the burden of proof lies on the applicant (*Sniace SA* (case T–141/03), paras 31–32). Given the strictness with which both courts have interpreted these requirements, the extent to which this makes it more difficult for individuals to challenge acts, or whether the difficulty is merely being re-phrased is questionable. In *Infront* (case T–33/01), the applicant was found to have an interest but was then also found to satisfy the test for standing.

11.4.3.1 *The measure must be, as far as the applicant is concerned, a decision*

Since many of the Commission's policies, for example in the highly regulated field of agriculture, are implemented by directly applicable regulations, often with wide-ranging and adverse effects on individuals (e.g., withdrawal of subsidies, imposition of levies), many cases have arisen in which individual applicants have sought to challenge regulations. Although it would have been open to the Court to interpret Article 230(2) to enable them to do so provided that the applicant could prove 'direct and individual concern', the Court was originally insistent that a natural or legal person could not challenge a 'true' regulation. For this reason in *Koninklijke Scholten-Honig NV* v *Council and Commission* (case 101/76) the applicant glucose producers' attempt to challenge certain regulations requiring glucose producers to pay levies on the production of glucose, for the benefit of sugar producers, was held, despite the merits of the case, to be inadmissible. (See also *Calpak SpA* v *Commission* (cases 789 & 790/79) – attempt (failed) by Italian pear processors to challenge a regulation fixing production aids for pear processors; *Alusuisse* (case 307/81).)

However, whether a measure is, as far as the applicant is concerned, a 'true' regulation or not involves a very subtle enquiry, a fact underlying the decision of the ECJ in *R v Intervention Board for Agricultural Produce, ex parte Accrington Beef Co. Ltd* (case C–241/95). There, the ECJ acknowledged that an individual seeking to challenge a regulation could not be sure whether or not he would have *locus standi* under Article 230. In *Confédération Nationale des Producteurs de Fruits et Légumes* v *Council* (cases 16 & 17/62) the Court held that to determine the legal nature of an act it is necessary to consider the nature and content of an act rather than its form. It is the substance, not the label, which is crucial. A true regulation is a measure of general application, i.e., normative; it applies to objectively determined situations and produces legal effects on categories of persons viewed abstractly and in their entirety. On the other hand the essential feature of a decision, which is defined as 'binding upon those to whom it is addressed' (Article 249 (ex 189)) arises from the limitation of the persons to whom it is addressed; a decision concerns designated persons individually.

In *International Fruit NV v Commission (No. 1)* (cases 41–4/70) the applicants, a group of fruit importers, were held entitled to challenge a Community 'regulation' laying down the quantity of import licences to be issued for a certain period. The quantity of licences was calculated on the basis of applications from, *inter alia*, the applicants, received during the preceding week; thus it applied to a finite number of people and was issued in response to their applications. Although it appeared to be a general measure it was found in fact to be a disguised bundle of decisions addressed to each applicant (see also *Roquette Frères SA v Council* (case 138/79)).

The ECJ has also suggested that a measure may be 'hybrid' in nature, i.e., it may be a measure of general application which is, nonetheless, in the nature of a decision for certain 'designated individuals'. In the *Japanese ball-bearings* cases (cases 113 & 118–21/77) four major Japanese producers of ball-bearings were held entitled to challenge an EC anti-dumping regulation. Although the measure was of general application some of its articles specifically referred to the applicants. For them, it was in the nature of a decision. In *Allied Corporation v Commission* (cases 239 & 275/82) some of the applicant companies seeking to annul an anti-dumping regulation were charged with illegal dumping in the regulation itself. The ECJ held that although measures involving anti-dumping duties were:

> as regards their nature and scope, of a legislative character, inasmuch as they apply to all traders concerned taken as a whole, the provision may nonetheless be of direct and individual concern to those producers and exporters who are charged with practising dumping.

On this basis the applicant producers' and exporters' claims were held to be admissible.

In *Timex Corporation v Council* (case 264/82) the applicant company, which succeeded in establishing *locus standi* to challenge another anti-dumping regulation, was this time a complainant which, through its national trade association, had brought certain illegal dumping practices (concerning Russian watches and watch movements) to the Commission's attention. The regulation had been issued as a result of enquiries following Timex's complaints. The ECJ held that although the measure was legislative (i.e., normative) in nature, it was a decision of direct and individual concern to Timex since it had been issued in response to Timex's complaint and the company had given evidence to the Commission during the anti-dumping proceedings.

It may be noted that in *Allied*, in admitting that the measures challenged were legislative in character, i.e., 'true' regulations, the ECJ did not consider the question whether they were in the nature of a decision to the applicants. It appeared to be sufficient that the applicants had established direct and individual concern. This approach, although not followed in *Timex*, has since been adopted in a number of cases, principally, but not exclusively, in the context of challenge to regulations imposing anti-dumping duties. Under EC anti-dumping rules such duties, which are normally levied on importation of the product concerned, can only be imposed by regulation. Such regulations may adversely affect undertakings such as producers and exporters situated outside the Union who have no opportunity to challenge the measures in an action before the courts of Member States. The Court has admitted a number of challenges to regulations by producers or exporters who were able to establish that they were identified in the measures adopted by the Commission or the Council (as in *Timex*) or were concerned in the Commission's preliminary investigations (see *Nashua Corporation* v *Commission* (cases C–133, 150/87), *Neotype* v *Commission* (case C–305/86)): also by importers whose retail prices for the goods in question or whose business dealings with the manufacturer of those goods played a part in establishing the existence of dumping (*Enital* v *Commission* (case C–304/86); *Gestetner Holdings plc* v *Commission* (case C–156/87)). Such claims were admissible because (as well as the applicants being directly concerned) the factors cited above were deemed to constitute individual concern. In *Extramet Industrie SA* v *Council* (case C–358/89), the ECJ went further and admitted a challenge to a 'true' regulation by an *independent* importer whose retail prices and business dealings in the goods in question were *not* taken into account in establishing the existence of dumping, simply because he was able to establish individual (as well as direct) concern.

Also, outside the area of anti-dumping, in *Sofrimport* v *Commission* (case C–152/88), the ECJ allowed an applicant importer to challenge a regulation suspending imports into the EC of apples from certain third countries solely on the basis of direct and individual concern; the Court did not avert to the question of whether the measure was in the nature of a decision as regards the applicant.

In *Codorniu SA* v *Council* (case C–309/89) the principal producer of quality sparkling wine in Spain, and holder of graphic trade-mark rights in the title 'Gran Cremant di Codorniu' was allowed to challenge EC regulations on the description of sparkling wines in which the word 'cremant' was to be reserved for certain quality sparkling wines produced in France and Luxembourg. Although the measures in question were legislative measures applicable to traders in general they were of individual concern to the applicant.

These cases suggest that in the context of a challenge to a regulation, where the applicant can prove direct and (particularly) individual concern the Court may no longer require proof that the measure constitutes a decision as far as he is concerned. This approach, although prima facie contrary to the literal wording of Article 230 EC and the Court's earlier case law is, as Advocate-General Jacobs pointed out in *Extramet*, consistent with the general scheme and purpose of the article and necessary to ensure effective judicial protection for those (such as manufacturers and exporters in countries outside the EC) who may be seriously affected by regulations but who lack alternative or adequate means by which to challenge them. Since the concept of individual concern is very strictly interpreted by the Court it may be argued that it is sufficient in itself (together with the concept of direct concern) to restrict access to judicial review of regulations by natural or legal persons. Moreover, since as will be seen the two questions of (a) whether a measure, although called a regulation, is in fact in the nature of a decision to the applicant and (b) whether it is of individual concern to the applicant often involve the same enquiry: thus where the latter criterion is met, the need to prove the former becomes superfluous.

There have been few examples of challenge by natural or legal persons to directives. Since directives are addressed to Member States it might have been thought that they are closer to a decision than to a regulation, and as such, more likely to be challengeable. However in *Gibraltar* v *Council* (case C–298/89) the Court refused to admit a challenge to an EC directive by the government of Gibraltar (found to be a natural or legal person) on the grounds that directives, being 'normally a form of indirect regulatory or legislative measure' were not open to challenge by such persons. Since the directive in question, although affecting the applicants by excluding them from its territorial scope, applied to 'objectively determined situations' the applicants' claim was inadmissible. Here, however, unlike the applicants mentioned above who succeeded in establishing *locus standi* to challenge regulations, the applicants were unable to prove individual concern. In *Salamander and others* v *European Parliament and Council* (joined cases T–172 and T–175–177/98), concerning a challenge to the Tobacco Advertising Directive (Directive 98/43/EC), the CFI seemed to suggest that a directive could in principle be capable of challenge by individuals provided they could show direct and individual concern. In this case, however, the applicants were unable to show direct concern.

By contrast to the position taken in *Gibraltar* v *Council* in relation to directives, where the measure in question is described as a decision, provided it has a specific addressee, the Court presumes it to be a decision, even though, as in the case of a decision addressed to a Member State, it may lay down normative rules.

11.4.3.2 *The measure must be of direct concern to the applicant*

A measure will be of direct concern to the applicant if it leaves the Member State no real discretion in implementation. Often the Commission will issue a decision to a State requiring, or authorising, the State to act in a particular manner. Whether the individual affected by such action may challenge the Community decision will depend on whether the action affecting the applicant was within the area of the Member State's discretion or not. In *Eridania* v *Commission* (cases 10 & 18/68) an Italian sugar-refining company sought to challenge three Commission decisions granting aid to its competitors. Its action under Article 230 was declared inadmissible. Although the Commission's decisions had authorised the granting of aid, and indeed named the companies concerned, those decisions were not of direct concern to the applicants, since the decision regarding the *allocation* of the aid had been made by the Italian Government. This was a matter within the government's discretion. Where the matter of which the applicant complains lies within the discretion of the State the appropriate challenge is to the national authority responsible for the relevant decision.

The question of whether a particular Community decision leaves room for discretion on the part of a Member State is susceptible to different interpretations. Interpreted broadly, as in *Plaumann & Co.* v *Commission* (case 25/62) and *SA Alcan Aluminium Raeren* v *Commission* (case 69/69), it could mean that where the Commission merely *permits* or *authorises* a Member State to act the State still retains a discretion as to whether to act or not. In *Alcan* the Court agreed with Advocate-General Roemer's suggestion in *Plaumann* that even where the Commission *refuses* permission to act, the State, in its discretion, may choose to act in disregard of this refusal and face the consequences of an action under Article 226 (ex 169). On the other hand, interpreting the question of discretion narrowly, as in the *Japanese ball-bearings* case (cases 113 & 118–21/77), it could be said that where implementation of a Community decision is *automatic* or a *foregone conclusion*, as can be presumed where permission or authorisation is sought, no real discretion exists on the part of the State, and the measure will be of direct concern to the applicant.

A number of cases in which the applicant has succeeded in establishing *locus standi*, such as *Alfred Toepfer KG* v *Commission* (cases 106 & 107/63) and *Werner A. Bock KG* v *Commission* (case 62/70) have involved decisions of confirmation (*Toepfer*) or authorisation (*Bock*). In these cases it seems to have been presumed that the measures were of direct concern to the applicants. In the subsequent case of *AE Piraiki-Patraiki* v *Commission* (case 11/82), in the context of a Commission decision authorising the French to impose a quota system on imports of Greek yarn, Advocate-General VerLoren van Themaat suggested that a Community measure would be of direct concern if its legal effects on interested parties and their identity could 'with certainty or with a high degree of probability be inferred'. The Court considered that the possibility that the French Government would not take advantage of the Commission's decision was 'purely theoretical'. Thus the more recent dicta and the practice of the Court indicate that the more generous attitude to questions of direct concern – at least as far as the involvement of Member States is concerned – will be preferred to the restrictive approach of *Plaumann* and *Alcan*. Nonetheless on the question of direct concern *Plaumann* and *Alcan* still remain a trap for the unwary (see Commission's view in *Spijker Kwasten BV* v *Commission* (case 231/82)).

Decisions need not, of course, be addressed to Member States. Where decisions have been addressed to natural or legal persons, the CFI has often taken a narrow view of when these decisions could be said to affect other persons directly. The Commission's decision to approve Nestlé's takeover of Perrier in *Comité Central d'Entreprise de la Société Générale des Grandes Sources* v *Commission* (case T–96/92) was found not to be of direct concern to the applicant employee representative bodies. Any disadvantage suffered by employees following the merger would result from action by the merged undertaking itself, subject to the protection provided for employees in these circumstances under national and Community law. It did not result directly from the Commission's decision. The applicants were only directly concerned by the decision to the extent that their procedural rights, granted to 'recognised representatives' under the Merger Regulation, might have been infringed. More recently, a supplier under a contract with the Ukraine, which received financial aid from the Community, was held not to be directly affected by a Commission decision that its contracts did not satisfy the Community's criteria for release of payments to the Ukraine (*Richco Commodities Ltd v Commission* (case T–509/93)). The CFI pointed out that there was no legal relationship between the supplier and the Commission. The fact that the contract was expressed to be conditional on payment of the aid was irrelevant; standing under Article 230 cannot be dependent on decisions made in commercial negotiations. This ruling may now be open to question. In a series of cases on appeal from the CFI regarding the same point, the ECJ has held the individual to be directly concerned (see, e.g., *Glencore Grain Ltd v Commission* (case C–403 & 404/96)). By contrast, in *Infront* (case T–33/01), the CFI held that the decision of the Commission approving UK arrangements in relation to the broadcasting of sporting events directly affected Infront as it was the holder of exclusive broadcasting rights to the football World Cup.

11.4.3.3 *The measure must be of individual concern to the applicant*

The concept of individual concern has been construed very restrictively by the ECJ (and CFI). Because it operates to exclude so many cases it is often the first criterion to be examined, as it was in *Plaumann & Co. v Commission* (case 25/62). Plaumann & Co. were importers of clementines who sought to annul a Commission decision, addressed to the German Government, refusing the government permission to reduce its customs duties on clementines imported from outside the EC. Plaumann & Co. claimed that as a large-scale importer of such clementines they were 'individually concerned'. The Court disagreed. The importing of clementines, the Court held, was an activity which could be carried out by anyone at any time. There was nothing in the decision to distinguish Plaumann & Co. from any other importer of clementines. In order to establish individual concern, the applicant must prove that the decision affects him or her because of:

> certain characteristics which are peculiarly relevant to him, or by reason of circumstances in which he is differentiated from all other persons, and not by the mere fact that he belongs to a class of persons who are affected.

The '*Plaumann*' test has become the classic test for individual concern. It was most recently confirmed in *Union de Pequenos Agricultores v Council* (case C–50/00; see 11.4.3.5 below). It is, however, more easily stated than applied, since it does not specify *what* characteristics 'peculiarly relevant to him' the applicant must prove to establish individual concern or what circumstances will differentiate him from all other persons.

It will *not* be sufficient to prove that his business interests have been adversely affected, as was clearly the case in *Plaumann & Co. v Commission. Nor* is it sufficient that they were affected in a different way, or more seriously, than other similar traders. These arguments were rejected in *Eridania* (cases 10 & 18/68), and in *Calpak* (cases 789 & 790/79), in which the applicant pear processors claimed that the Commission's mode of calculation of pear processing aids operated particularly unfairly on itself as a private company as compared with other pear producers such as public companies and cooperatives.

Equally is it not sufficient that the applicant's identity is known to, or ascertainable by, the Commission when the measure is passed. In *UNICME v Council* (case 123/77) an association of Italian motorcycle importers was seeking to annul a Commission regulation, authorising the Italian Government to impose temporary quotas on motorcycles imported from Japan. The measure was in retaliation for the imposition by the Japanese of a quota on the import of Italian ski boots. Members of the association were the only persons concerned and they were all concerned. They were ascertainable and many had already applied for import licences. Their application was held inadmissable. The Court found it unnecessary to consider whether the contested measure was a true regulation, as it was not of direct or individual concern to the applicants. It 'would only affect the interests of the applicants when their request for a licence was refused'. 'The possibility of determining more or less precisely the number or even the identity of the persons to whom the measure applies by no means implies that it must be regarded as being of individual concern to them.' While the former statement may be open to question as a ground for denying direct and individual concern, since it could be applied to *any* act addressed to a third party, such as the decisions in *Bock* and *International Fruit Co. NV*, which were found to be of individual concern, the latter recurs consistently in the Court's case law on individual concern.

Will a measure be deemed of individual concern if a causal connection can be proved between a particular measure and the applicant's own case? This was not found to be the case in *Spijker Kwasten BV v Commission* (case 231/82). Here the Commission issued a decision, at the request of the Dutch Government, enabling the government to ban the import of Chinese brushes for a six-month period, from July to 31 December 1982. Prior to the above request being made the applicant had applied for a licence to import such brushes. There was no doubt a causal link between its application and the Dutch government's request. The request and the Commission's decision were prompted by its application. Moreover the company was the only importer of these brushes in Holland, and the only one likely to want to import them during the six-month period in question. Yet it was held not to be individually concerned. The measure, the Court held, was of general application. There was nothing to stop others applying for licences during that same period.

This case also confirmed a point established earlier in *Glucoseries Réunies v Commission* (case 1/64), that the fact that the applicant (in this case the sole producer of glucose in Belgium and the principal exporter of glucose in France) is the *only* person likely to be affected by the measure is not a characteristic peculiarly relevant to him such as to give rise to individual concern, as long as there is a theoretical possibility that others can enter the field and be affected by the same measure.

What characteristic peculiarly relevant to him must the applicant then prove in order to establish individual concern?

(a) *Measure referable specifically to applicant's situation and affecting a closed class*
Although there is no single satisfactory test a common thread runs through most of the cases in which individual concern has been held to exist. In almost every case the measure which the applicant seeks to challenge, although addressed to another person, is referable specifically to his situation. Moreover, not only does it affect him as though he were the person addressed, but it affects him either *alone* or as a member of a fixed and *closed* class; no one else is capable of entering the field and being affected by the same measure.

For example, the measure may have been issued in response to a licence or tender application. In *Alfred Toepfer KG v Commission* (cases 106 & 107/63) Toepfer had, amongst others, requested a licence from the German Government to import cereals from France. The Commission's decision, made at the request of the German Government, was a confirmation of the government's measure refusing to grant the import certificate. The only persons affected by the decision were those who had already applied for licences. They were individually concerned.

Similarly in *Werner A. Bock KG v Commission* (case 62/70), the firm of Bock had applied for a permit to import a consignment of Chinese mushrooms, for which it already had a firm offer. As Chinese mushrooms at the time were in free circulation in the EC, the German Government, if it wished to prohibit their import into Germany, needed authority from the Commission to do so. Following Bock's application, the German Government, on 11 September, applied to the Commission for that authority, which the Commission granted by a decision on 15 September. The Court held that Bock was individually concerned; the decision was passed in response to its application. (See also *Simmenthal SpA v Commission* (case 92/78) – decision issued in response to claimant's tender.)

A similar connection existed in *Philip Morris Holland BV v Commission* (case 730/79). Here the decision in question, which was addressed to the Dutch Government, requested the government to refrain from granting State aid to the applicant tobacco company, Philip Morris. The Court assumed without argument that the company was individually concerned. In *Consorzio Gruppo di Azione Locale 'Murgia Messapica' v Commission* (case T–465/93) the applicant consortium had applied for grants from the Community Leader programme: they were found to be individually concerned by the Commission's decision addressed to the Italian authorities rejecting their application for aid.

International Fruit Co. NV v Commission (No. 1) (cases 41–4/70) concerned a Commission 'regulation', controlling the issue of import licences for apples from non-Member States. The regulation was issued by the Commission on the basis of applications received during the preceding week, following an assessment of the overall situation. It applied *only* to those who had applied for licences during that week. It was held to be of individual concern to the applicants. On the same reasoning the measure was found not to be a true regulation at all, but a bundle of decisions.

However, even a 'true' regulation can be of individual concern to *some* individuals, as it can be in the nature of a decision to some individuals, if it is referable expressly or impliedly to their particular situation, either alone or as a member of a known and *closed* class (*Japanese ball-bearing case* (cases 113 & 118–21/77); *Allied Corporation v Commission* (cases 239 & 275/82); *CAM SA v Commission* (case 100/74), overruling *Compagnie Française Commerciale et Financière SA v Commission* (case 64/69)). Likewise in *Codorniu SA v Council* (case C–309/89) the applicant producers of sparkling wine were differentiated from all other producers of sparkling wine because they were prevented by the regulation from exercising their registered trade-mark right in 'Gran Cremant di Codorniu'. *Sofrimport SARL v Commission* (case C–152/88) also concerned a successful challenge of this nature. The applicants, who were fruit importers, were seeking to annul a number of Commission regulations suspending the issue of import licences for apples from Chile and fixing quantities of such imports from third countries. Under one of the regulations

(2702/72) the Commission was required under Article 3 to take into account, when exercising its powers under the regulations, the 'special position of products in transit' when the regulations come into force. The applicants had goods in transit when the contested regulations came into force. The ECJ held that they were individually concerned. 'Such persons constituted a restricted group *which could not be extended* after the contested measure took effect.'

The reason why the applicant in *Spijker Kwasten* (case 231/82) failed to establish individual concern was that, although there was a causal link between its licence application and the Commission's decision, the latter measure allowing the Dutch authorities to introduce a quota was deliberately designed to take effect for the period *subsequent* to that for which the applicant had applied for licences. The applications it had already lodged were not affected by the measure: it applied only to future transactions: thus there was a theoretical possibility that other traders could be equally affected.

(b) *Measure issued as a result of proceedings initiated by applicant or in which the applicant has played a legitimate part*

A rather different situation in which the necessary link has been held to exist between the applicant and the challenged act to constitute individual concern, is when the act is not 'directed at' him but issued as a result of proceedings in which the applicant has played a legitimate part. In *Metro-SB-Grossmärkte GmbH & Co. KG* v *Commission* (case 26/76) the applicant was seeking to challenge a decision issued to another firm, SABA, in the context of EC competition policy. The decision was issued following a complaint by Metro under Article 3 of Regulation 17/62 (now repealed, see Chapter 29) that SABA was acting in breach of Article 81 (ex 85). The Court held, on the question of admissibility, that since persons with a legitimate interest were entitled, under Article 3 of Regulation 17/62, to request the Commission to investigate the infringement they should be allowed to institute Article 230 proceedings in order to protect that interest. Thus Metro was individually concerned.

On similar reasoning, in *Timex Corporation* v *Council* (case 264/82), Timex was deemed to be individually concerned and permitted to challenge an anti-dumping regulation; the company had initiated the complaint (as it was entitled to do under a further anti-dumping regulation) and had given evidence in the proceedings. (See also *COFAZ* v *Commission* (case 169/84) – applicants individually concerned in Commission decision concerning State aids; they had initiated the complaint and taken part in the proceedings; see also *FEDIOL* v *Commission* (case 191/82); *Associazione Italiana Tecnico Economica del Cemento* v *Commission* (cases T–447–9/ 93); *Comité Central d'Entreprise de la Société Générale des Grandes Sources* v *Commission* (case T–96/92) – applicants were 'recognised representatives of employers' under Regulation 4064/89).)

(c) *Anti-dumping cases*

It has been noted above that in considering whether the measure challenged is in the nature of a decision to the applicant, the Court appears to have moved towards a more liberal approach, particularly in the context of a challenge to anti-dumping duties, even when they are imposed in 'true' regulations. It has also relaxed its approach to the question of individual concern in this area. Where the applicant is a complainant or has been concerned in the preliminary investigations he will be individually concerned on the principles outlined above. But he will also be deemed to be individually concerned where his retail prices or business dealings have been used as a basis for establishing the existence of dumping (see *Enital* (case C–304/86)). However, in the absence of these factors the ECJ was not in its earlier case law prepared to find individual concern. In *Allied*, independent importers (as opposed to manufacturers and exporters) who had not been involved in the preliminary proceedings and who were affected simply as members of a class failed to establish individual concern. However, in *Extramet* (case C–358/89) the ECJ, departing from its previous case law, was prepared to concede that an independent importer, who was not involved in the original proceedings and whose retail prices or dealings with manufacturers or exporters of the goods in question were not taken into account by the Commission in establishing the exist- ence of dumping was individually concerned in a regulation imposing definitive anti-dumping duties on imports of calcium metal from the People's Republic of China and the Soviet Union. The ECJ held that:

> the recognition of the right of certain categories of traders to bring an action for the annulment of certain anti-dumping Regulations cannot prevent other traders from also claiming to be individually concerned by reason of certain attributes which are peculiar to them and which differentiate them from all other persons.

The relevant attributes, satisfied in *Extramet*, were:

(i) they were the largest importer of the product forming the subject-matter of the anti-dumping measure and were the end users of the product;

(ii) their business activities depended to a very large extent on the imports in question and were seriously affected by the contested regulation;

(iii) there was a limited number of manufacturers of the product concerned and the importers had difficulty in obtaining supplies from the sole Community producer, who was its main competitor for the processed product (pure calcium for use in the metallurgy industry).

The judgment in *Extramet* extended, but did little to clarify the law in this dif- ficult area; it did however indicate a possible trend towards a more liberal approach to the question of individual concern where the number of affected applicants is limited and the effect of the measure on the applicant severe. The principles stated were not expressly confined to anti-dumping cases.

(d) *Other situations*
In addition to the categories of cases outlined above in which individual concern may be found two further exceptional cases must be mentioned. In *Partie Écologiste 'Les Verts' v Parliament* (case 294/83) the ECJ found that the Green Party was indi- vidually concerned in Parliament's decision, taken in 1983, allocating funds for the European election campaign of 1984, even though the decision affected all the political parties, actual and potential, seeking election in 1984. The Green Party was only affected as a member of an indeterminate class. However, the Court's decision on this matter was clearly (and expressly) based on policy. It reasoned that the political parties represented on the Bureau making the decision on the allocation of funds had themselves benefited from the allocation, and there was no way in which

rival groupings might challenge this allocation in advance of the elections. The case was admissible and the applicants succeeded in their claim for annulment. As has been noted, the Court took a more restrictive view in the subsequent case of *Les Verts* v *Parliament* (case 190/84).

AE Piraiki-Patraiki v *Commission* (case 11/82) concerned rather different facts. The applicants were a group of Greek manufacturers and exporters of cotton yarn, who sought to challenge a Commission decision addressed to the French Government authorising the latter to impose a quota system on the import of Greek cotton yarn. As the decision applied generally and there were no factors linking it directly with the applicants' particular situation, one might have imagined that individual concern would be lacking. This was not found to be the case. The Court found that for those who, prior to the decision, had entered into contracts to be performed subsequently, the decision was of individual concern. The Court's decision was firmly based on Article 13(3) of the Act of Accession 1979, which imposes a duty on the Commission to consider those whose contracts may be affected by their measures. The Commission's decision was held not to be of individual concern to manufacturers and exporters whose existing contracts were not affected by the measure.

In that the Act of Accession expressly required the Commission to take into account those manufacturers and exporters whose contracts might be affected by its measures the decision is consistent with *Sofrimport* (case C–152/88). Nevertheless, while such a class is closed it is potentially very wide. Thus *AE Piraiki-Patraiki* must be seen as a case resting on its own special facts, and not as giving rise to a general claim for individual concern based on interference with the applicants' existing contracts. EC legislation will frequently interfere with existing business contracts: this will not of itself be sufficient to constitute individual concern.

11.4.3.4 *Can the restrictive interpretation of* locus standi *for individuals still be justified?*

There is no doubt that it is fear of opening floodgates, together with a desire not unduly to hamper the institutions in their task of implementing Community policies, problems common to all administrative law systems, which has led the courts to interpret Article 230, particularly Article 230(2) concerning the *locus standi* of individuals, restrictively. In closing the door to an application under this article the courts have often adverted to the possibility of alternative means of challenge to the validity of Community law under Article 234, in an action before the applicant's national court (e.g., *Spijker Kwasten BV* v *Commission* (case 231/82); *UNICME* (case 123/77)). Any binding Community act can be challenged in preliminary rulings proceedings (see Chapter 9). It has been suggested that this roundabout approach to matters of validity (which can only be decided authoritatively by the ECJ) is prompted by a desire to filter out unnecessary claims and ensure that only the claims of genuine merit reach the ECJ. One such claim was *Royal Scholten-Honig (Holdings) Ltd* v *Intervention Board for Agricultural Produce* (cases 103 & 145/77) in which the claimant finally succeeded in obtaining a declaration of invalidity on a reference under Article 234 having failed to establish *locus standi* in an action under Article 230 (*Koninklijke Scholten-Honig NV* v *Council and Commission* (case 101/76)) on the grounds that the disputed measure was a true regulation. Thus where there is an appropriate issue of national law which a 'natural or legal person' may raise before his national court, to which he may attach a challenge to the validity of Community law, *a fortiori* where there may be difficulty in establishing individual concern, the safer course would be to raise the issue of invalidity before his national court and press for an early reference to the ECJ under Article 234. Where he has no claim under national law, and thus no alternative remedy, and is able to establish direct and individual concern, the courts' recent case law suggests that an application under Article 230 may be admissible even if the applicant seeks to challenge a true regulation.

The above comments, based on the ECJ's past jurisprudence, have now to be considered in the light of *TWD Textilwerke Deggendorf GmbH* v *Germany* (case C–188/92), decided in 1994. Here the ECJ refused to exercise its jurisdiction under Article 234 to declare on the validity of a Commission Decision, addressed to the German Government, requiring the government to recover State aids paid to the applicant in breach of the then Articles 92 and 93 (now 87 and 88) EC. The German Government had informed the applicants of the existence of the decision and of their right to challenge it under Article 230, but the applicants took no action under this article. Instead they sought to challenge the decision later, in the context of domestic proceedings for recovery of the aid wrongfully paid. When the German judge referred to the ECJ for a ruling on the validity of the Commission's decision the ECJ refused its jurisdiction on the grounds that the applicants could and should have challenged the decision directly under Article 230. Since they had been informed of the decision and of their right to challenge it they could not circumvent the two-month limitation period of that Article by resorting to action under Article 234.

The implications of this decision are disturbing. Although the applicants were aware of the decision as soon as it was received and clearly would have had *locus standi* to challenge it under Article 230, as being directly and individually concerned, it was not addressed to them. Nor had they been informed of its existence officially, by the Commission. Can and should a notification and advice to act by a national government be deemed sufficient notice of a party's rights and obligations, when he is not the addressee of the decision, such as to require that he move immediately to action under Article 230, or forfeit his right of challenge? Can this be deemed effective judicial protection for individuals' Community rights? Although the *TWD* ruling has been applied subsequently (for example, *Wiljo NV* v *Belgium* (case C–178/95)), the ECJ has also recognised the difficulties for an applicant unsure of his *locus standi*. In *R* v *Intervention Board for Agricultural Produce, ex parte Accrington Beef Co. Ltd* (case C–241/95) the ECJ held that a preliminary rulings reference challenging the validity of a regulation was admissible despite the applicant's failure to bring a claim under Article 230 within the time limit, since it was not clear that the applicants would have had standing for a judicial review application. More recently, an Article 234 reference which came before the ECJ in a case based on the same facts as those in which a judicial review action had been summarily dismissed by the CFI was held to be admissible (*Atzeni and Others* (joined cases C–346 and 529/03)). The CFI had dismissed the judicial review action for being out of time without considering the *locus standi* of Atzeni *et al*. When the matter came before the ECJ via Article 234, the ECJ had to consider whether *TWD* applied. It emphasised that the *locus standi* of the applicants was not clear: they had not been mentioned in the decision addressed, in this case, to the Italian

Government; nor had the government informed them of the decision and of the possibility of reviewing it.

Given the difficulties of establishing clear rules in relation to *locus standi* for Article 230, the extent of this ruling is not clear, although it seems that the ECJ is limiting *TWD* to its facts. Nonetheless, the approach in *TWD* will undoubtedly continue to create uncertainty, and encourage pre-emptive and possibly inappropriate action under that article by parties fearing rejection in preliminary rulings.

11.4.3.5 *A false dawn* – Jego-Quere *(case T–177/01)* v Union de Pequenos Agricultores *(case C–50/00)*

Despite the frequent criticism of the restrictive interpretation given to direct and individual concern, the ECJ has adhered to the view originally taken in *Plaumann*. However, a strong Advocate-General's opinion in *Union de Pequenos Agricultores (UPA)* v *Council* (case C–50/00) and the judgment by the Court of First Instance in *Jego-Quere et Cie* v *Commission* (case T–177/01) appeared to herald a more liberal attitude to the interpretation of individual concern.

In *UPA*, a trade association challenged a Commission regulation (1638/98), but this application had been dismissed by the CFI because UPA could not demonstrate individual concern. Moreover, the CFI pointed out that UPA could have brought an action under national law and then asked for a reference to be made under Article 234 to question the legality of the regulation in question. UPA's argument that the restrictive interpretation of individual concern meant that there was no effective legal protection for individuals was rejected. On appeal, Advocate-General Jacobs was unconvinced by the CFI's reasons for dismissing the application and reviewed extensively the arguments put forward for the restrictive interpretation of individual concern. He observed that a direct challenge under Article 230 would be more appropriate than the procedure under Article 234, and that the restrictive approach taken to individual applicants was 'anomalous' in the light of the Court's case law on other aspects of judicial review (para. 37). The difficulty with the Article 234 route is that it requires an action before a national court which is not itself entitled to annul the contested measure. Instead, the national court has to consider whether there is sufficient doubt as to its legality for a reference for a preliminary ruling to be made under Article 234. Moreover, not all Community measures could give rise to an action before a national court; consequently, such measures could not be challenged through the Article 234 route at all.

In relation to the test for individual concern itself, Jacobs argued that there was no reason why this should entail a requirement that an individual applicant was differentiated in some way for all others affected by the measure. If a measure adversely affects a large number of individuals and causes widespread harm, then this is a strong reason for accepting challenges by one or more of those individuals (para. 59). Accordingly, the test of individual concern should be satisfied if a Community measure, by reason of an individual's particular circumstances, has, or is liable to have, a substantial adverse effect on his interests (para. 60, and see paras 61–99 for a detailed justification).

The Advocate-General's opinion in *UPA* found favour with the CFI in *Jego-Quere* (case T–177/01), which was decided between the delivery of the Advocate-General's opinion and the judgment in *UPA*. In *Jego-Quere*, the applicant was found not to have individual concern within the meaning of the established *Plaumann* line of reasoning. In *Jego-Quere* the only possibility for the claimant to challenge the contested regulation was by violating the rules it laid down and then claiming their illegality by way of defence in national proceedings. Nonetheless, the CFI held (rightly, it is submitted), that individuals cannot be required to breach the law to gain access to justice (para. 45). Accordingly, and largely in line with Advocate-General Jacob's opinion in *UPA*, the CFI proposed a revised test for individual concern. According to this, a

> person is to be regarded as individually concerned by a Community measure of general application that concerns him directly if the measure in question affects his legal position in a manner which is both definite and immediate, by restricting his rights or imposing obligations on him (para. 51).

Although this judgment was welcomed by commentators throughout the Community, it appears to have been rather short-lived. When the ECJ handed down its judgment in *UPA*, it re-affirmed the *Plaumann* jurisprudence on individual concern, and emphasised that there was a complete system of judicial protection in place at the Community level. It was for the Member States to ensure that they provide a system which ensures respect for the right to effective judicial protection and which would allow individuals to use the Article 234 route to challenge the validity of Community measures. The Court barely mentioned the Advocate-General's opinion, and completely ignored the decision in *Jego-Quere*. When it heard the appeal from the CFI's decision in *Jego-Quere* (case C–263/02), the ECJ reiterated this reasoning. Despite the continued concerns of Advocate-General Jacobs, the ECJ overturned the decision of the CFI.

These judgments are a serious blow to those who favoured a more liberal interpretation of the test for individual concern, in particular because *UPA* was decided by an extended Court. It seems that, for the time being, the established interpretation of individual concern will continue to apply. It is now unlikely that there will be a change, and an amendment to the Treaty will be required to counter the effects of the *Plaumann* judgment.

This point has been evident for some time. In a report issued in May 1995 for the IGC in 1996 on possible revisions of the provisions relating to the judicial system, the ECJ pointed out the limitations of direct action for annulment for natural or legal persons. It questioned whether the right to bring an action under this provision, which individuals enjoy only with regard to acts of direct and individual concern to them, was sufficient to guarantee for them effective protection against possible infringements of their fundamental rights from the legislative activity of the Community. Unfortunately, no action was taken at Amsterdam, nor at Nice, to guarantee that protection. The Constitution does change the position, though it does not adopt the solution proposed by Advocate-General Jacobs. Instead Article III–365(4) provides that

> Any natural or legal person may . . . institute proceedings against an act addressed to that person or which is of direct and individual concern to him or her, and against a regulatory act which is of direct concern to him or her and does not entail implementing measures.

Note that this provision changes, and potentially enlarges, the categories of acts which might be challenged by an individual. Crucially, as far as regulatory acts are concerned, the requirement of individual concern has been deleted.

11.4.3.6 *Admissibility and interim relief*

In an action for interim relief in a claim based on invalidity of a Community measure, the court will not usually examine the question of admissibility, so as not to prejudice the substance of the case. However, where there is a contention that the claim is 'manifestly inadmissible', the judges hearing the application for interim relief must investigate whether there is a prima facie case for finding that the main application is inadmissible.

11.5 **Time limits**

An applicant, whether an individual, a Member State or a Community institution, must bring a claim for annulment within two months of:

(a) the publication of the measure, or

(b) its notification to the claimant, or, in the absence thereof,

(c) the day on which it came to the knowledge of the latter, as the case may be (Article 230(3).

The Rules of Procedure of the Court of Justice, as amended, provide that time runs from receipt by the person concerned of notification of the measure or, where the measure is published, from the end of the fourteenth day after its publication in the *Official Journal*.

Since regulations and, following the TEU, directives and decisions adopted under the co-decision procedure of Article 251 EC and directives of the Council and the Commission addressed to all Member States are required to be published, time will run for them from the date of their entry into force, which will be either the date specified in the provisions or on the twentieth day following that of their publication (Article 254(1) and (2) (ex 191(1) and (2)) EC). Other directives and decisions 'shall be notified to those to whom they are addressed and shall take effect upon such notification' (Article 254 (ex 191(3))). In the case of a measure addressed to a person other than the applicant, time will run from the date of the applicant's knowledge. This has been held to require 'precise knowledge' of both the contents of the measure in question and the grounds on which it is based. This is necessary to ensure that the applicant is able to exercise his right to initiate proceedings. Thus a summary of the measure will not suffice (*Commission* v *Socurte* (case C–143/95 P)). Once he is aware of the existence of the measure he must, however, ask for a full text within a reasonable period (*Consorzio Gruppo di Azione Locale 'Murgia Messapica'* v *Commission* (case T–465/93)).

The 'date of knowledge' is the date on which the applicant became aware of the precise content of the measure. It is not the date on which he realised it could be challenged. Hence the importance of recognising an act as a measure capable of annulment.

The limitation period may be extended to take into account the distance between the ECJ at Luxembourg and the applicant's place of residence. In the UK 10 days are allowed. It may also be extended if the party concerned proves the existence of unforeseeable circumstances or *force majeure*. In *Bayer AG* v *Commission* (case C–195/91 P) the ECJ held that in order to establish such grounds the applicant must show 'abnormal difficulties, independent of the will of the person concerned, and apparently inevitable, even if all due care is taken'. Likewise, the concept of 'excusable error', justifying derogation from time-limits, can concern only 'exceptional circumstances' in which the conduct of the EC institution has given rise to a pardonable confusion on the part of the party concerned. The applicant cannot rely on his or her own organisation's internal malfunctioning as an excuse for an error.

11.5.1 **Expiry of time-limit**

Once the two-month time-limit has expired a claimant cannot seek to challenge a measure by the back door, either by invoking Article 241 (*exception d'illégalité*, see *Commission* v *Belgium* (case 156/77)) or by alleging a failure to act when the institution concerned refuses by decision to amend or withdraw the disputed measure (see *Eridania* v *Commission* (cases 10 & 18/68)) or take the requested action (*Irish Cement Ltd* v *Commission* (cases 166/86, 220/86), see Chapter 12). Time-limits will not be allowed to run afresh when the addressee objects to the EC institution's initial reasoning and that institution (normally the Commission) merely confirms its original decision (*Control Union Gesellschaft für Warenkontrolle mbH* v *Commission* (case C–250/90)).

An indirect challenge using the preliminary rulings procedure before the applicant's national court will not be subject to the two-month limit. In actions before national courts national rules of limitation apply, provided they are adequate to ensure the effective protection of individuals' Community rights (see Chapter 8). However, following *TWD Textilwerke Deggendorf GmbH* v *Germany* (case C–188/92) it is possible that an individual who has *locus standi* under Article 230 will not be allowed to circumvent the time-limit imposed by that Article by challenging legislation outside those limits under Article 234. If this is the case access to the Court under Article 234 should only be denied when the applicant's *locus standi* under Article 230 is unequivocally clear.

11.6 **The merits**

Once the Court has decided that the claim is admissible, the case will be decided on the merits. Article 230 provides four grounds for annulment, drawn directly from French administrative law. These are:

(a) lack of competence
(b) infringement of an essential procedural requirement
(c) infringement of the Treaty or any rule of law relating to its application
(d) misuse of powers.

These categories are not mutually exclusive, and often more than one ground is cited in a given case. Nonetheless, in making an application, the applicant must identify clearly the facts and basic legal arguments of the case. In particular, the applicant should not rely on 'catch-all' references to documents annexed to the application. The CFI has held that it is not for the Court to seek out and identify the grounds in which the application is based (see, e.g., *Cipeke – Comércio e Indústria de Papel Lda* v *Commission* (case T–84/96), paras 29–4). However, it is not clear how this statement relates to the idea that the Court can consider an infringement of an essential procedural requirement of its own motion (see *Socurte – Sociedade de Curtumes a Sul do Tejo Lda* v *Commission* (case T–432–434/93), para. 63). It seems, however, that the principle has gained acceptance. More recently, in *Laboratoires Servier* v *Commission* (case T–147/00, on appeal case C–156/03P), the CFI annulled a Commission decision withdrawing marketing authorisation for certain medicinal products. It did so on its own motion, observing that the lack of competence of an institution which has adopted an act constitutes a ground of annulment for reasons of public policy, which must be raised by the court. The ECJ confirmed this approach in the appeal against the CFI's decision. (See also *Strabag Benelux* v *Council* (case T–183/00, under appeal case C–186/030; and *Henkel* v *OHIM-LHS (UK)* (case T–308/01).)

11.6.1 Lack of competence

This is the equivalent to the English doctrine of substantive *ultra vires*. The institution responsible for adopting the measure in question must have the legal authority to do so. This may derive from the EC Treaty or from secondary legislation. In the *ERTA* case (case 22/70) the Commission challenged the Council's power to participate in the shaping of the road transport agreement, since under the Treaty (Article 300 (ex 228)) it is the Commission which is empowered to negotiate international agreements and the Council whose duty it is to conclude them. On the facts the Court found that the Council had not exceeded its powers. On a number of occasions Community law has been challenged as having been enacted under the wrong legal basis (see *Parliament* v *Council* (case C–295/90)). Clearly the choice of legal basis will be important, as it will determine the appropriate procedure to be followed and the vote required for the adoption of legislation (see Chapters 2 and 3).

The Court allows the institutions some latitude in their choice of legal base and their scope for action under that base. In *Germany* v *Commission* (case C–359/92) it held that Article 95 (ex 100a), which provides for the approximation of the provisions laid down by law, regulation or administrative action in Member States which have as their object the establishing and functioning of the internal market (see Chapter 15) was to be interpreted as 'encompassing the Council's power to lay down measures relating to a specific class of products and, if necessary, individual measures concerning those products'. Germany's challenge to Article 9 of Council Directive 92/59 on product safety, based on former Article 100a (new 95), which empowered the Commission to adopt decisions requiring Member States to take temporary measures in the event of a serious and immediate risk to the health and safety of consumers, failed. In *Portugal* v *Council* (case C–268/94), the Portuguese Government sought the annulment of a decision on the basis that the wrong treaty base had been used. The decision referred to what were then Articles 113 and 130y (now 120 and 181) EC, dealing with commercial policy, which only required that the decision be adopted by qualified majority vote. The Portuguese Government claimed that the agreement to which the decision related contained provisions aimed at protecting democracy and human rights in India, and should have been made under former Article 235 (now 308) EC, which would have required unanimity. The ECJ held that on the facts of the case the provisions of the then Article 130y (now 181) were broad enough to encompass the complained-of clauses, and that to rule otherwise would be to deprive the specific clauses of their substance.

The Court is stricter in its approach to questions concerning the allocation of competence between the EC institutions (see, e.g., *France, Netherlands and Spain* v *Commission* (case C–327/91)), and, as noted earlier, the ECJ's decisions have protected the procedural rights of the European Parliament (see, e.g., *Parliament* v *Council (Re European Development Fund)* (case C–316/91)).

11.6.2 Infringement of an essential procedural requirement

This is equivalent to procedural *ultra vires* in English law. Institutions, when enacting binding measures, must follow the correct procedures. These procedures may be laid down in the EC Treaty or secondary legislation. For example, Article 253 (ex 190) of the EC Treaty requires that all secondary legislation must state the reasons on which it is based, and must refer to proposals and opinions which were required to be obtained. The Court has held that reasons must not be too vague or inconsistent; they must be coherent; they must mention figures and essential facts on which they rely. They must be adequate to indicate the conscientiousness of the decision, and detailed enough to be scrutinised by the Court (*Germany* v *Commission (Re Tariff Quotas on Wine)* (case 24/62) – Commission decision annulled; too vague, no facts and figures). The purpose of the requirement to give reasons is to enable those concerned to defend their rights and to enable the Court to exercise its supervisory jurisdiction. However, the Court will not annul an act for an insignificant defect. Nor will it annul an act on this ground unless the claimant can prove that, but for this defect, the result would have been different (*Distillers Co. Ltd* v *Commission* (case 30/78)).

In *Roquette Frères SA* v *Council* (case 138/79) and *Maizena GmbH* v *Council* (case 139/79) a Council regulation was annulled on the grounds of the Council's failure to consult Parliament, as it was required to do under Article 37 (ex 43(2)) EC. Although the Council had consulted Parliament, it was held not to have given Parliament sufficient time to express an opinion on the measure in question. Where no time limit is imposed it is presumed that Parliament must be given a reasonable time in which to express its opinion. In *Infront* (case T–33/01), the letter to the UK Government was signed by a Director-General of the Commission who had not consulted the College of Commissioners. The letter was therefore annulled for failure to follow proper procedures.

11.6.3 Infringement of the Treaty or any rule of law relating to its application

Clearly, when an act is invalid for lack of competence or for an infringement of an essential procedural requirement, this may involve an infringement of the Treaty, but this ground of annulment is wider since it extends to *any* Treaty provision. In

Adams v *Commission (No. 1)* (case 145/83), an action for non-contractual liability (see Chapter 13), the Commission was found to have acted in breach of its duty of confidentiality under Article 287 (ex 214).

Infringement of any rule of law relating to the Treaty's application is wider again, and certainly wider than any comparable rule of English law. This is where general principles of law, discussed at length in Chapter 6, are relevant. A measure can be annulled if it is in breach not only of any general principle of law approved by the Court (e.g., equality, proportionality) but of any principle common to the constitutions of Member States (*Internationale Handelsgesellschaft mbH* (case 11/70)) and even principles of international treaties in the field of human rights on which Member States have collaborated (*J. Nold KG* v *Commission* (case 4/73)). In *Royal Scholten-Honig (Holdings) Ltd* v *Intervention Board for Agricultural Produce* (cases 103 & 145/77) a Community regulation was held invalid for breach of the principle of equality. In *Transocean Marine Paint Association* v *Commission* (case 17/74) (see Chapter 6) part of a decision was annulled for breach of the principle of natural justice. In *August Töpfer & Co. GmbH* v *Commission* (case 112/77) a decision was annulled for breach of the principle of legal certainty, for infringement of the applicant's legitimate expectations. Although the Court will not lightly set aside legislation for breach of this principle and will expect businessmen to anticipate and guard against foreseeable developments, within the bounds of 'normal' economic risks, this is a ground of some potential (see *Amylum* v *Council* (case 108/81); *Mulder* v *Council* (case C–104/89)). Note, however, that a trader is unlikely to have legitimate expectations that do not accord with existing Community rules (see, for example, *Efisol SA* (case T–336/94)). Thus, it is difficult to argue that a requirement to pay back illegally granted State aid would be in breach of legitimate expectations. In *Opel Austria GmbH* v *Council* (case T–115/94), the CFI held that the principle of legitimate expectations within the EC was the corollary of the principle of good faith in public international law. Where Community institutions have deposited their instruments of approval of an international agreement and the date of the entry into force of that agreement is known, any measures contrary to provisions of such agreements having direct effect, will be in breach of legitimate expectations. In *Racke* (case C–162/96), the ECJ held that the ECJ's jurisdiction to review the validity of a Community act could not be limited as regards the grounds on which it could find a measure invalid. In this case, it held that a Community measure, a regulation, could be held to be invalid were it contrary to international law.

Although it has not yet been done successfully, legislation could in principle be challenged for breach of the principle of subsidiarity, either as a general principle or as now expressed in Article 5 (ex 3b) EC (see Chapters 3 and 6). The German Government raised the question of subsidiarity, albeit in a different context, in *Germany* v *Parliament* (case C–233/94). It sought to challenge Directive 94/19, arguing that there had been a breach of the duty to state reasons for the legislation as required by the then Article 190, in that the directive did not explain how it complied with the principle of subsidiarity set out in Article 5 EC. The ECJ rejected this argument, stating that the necessary information could be inferred from the recitals to the directive.

Because of the breadth of the concept of 'any rule of law relating to the [treaty's] application', the acts of the EC institutions are vulnerable to attack on this ground. Thus the ECJ has held that where the Community legislature has a discretion to act in a complex economic situation, such as the implementation of the Community's agricultural policy, both as regards the nature and scope of the measures to be taken and the finding of basic facts, the Court, in reviewing the exercise of such a power, 'must confine itself to examining whether it contains a manifest error or constitutes a misuse of power or whether the authority in question did not clearly exceed the bounds of its discretion' (*Commission* v *Council* (case C–122/94)). The ECJ's approach to the Community's liability in damages for legislative measures involving choices of economic policy, which the CFI adopts also, reflects a similar concern not to fetter the discretion of the EC institutions when they are implementing Community policy. In this context the Court may be accused of occasionally going too far to protect the Community institutions (see *Germany* v *Council* (case C–280/93), see Chapters 6 and 13).

11.6.4 Misuse of power

This concept stems from the French *'détournement de pouvoir'*. It means, broadly, the use of a power for purposes other than those for which it was granted, for example, where powers granted to help one group (e.g., producers) are used to benefit another (e.g., distributors) (see *Simmenthal SpA* v *Commission* case 92/78)). It has been defined by the ECJ as 'the adoption by a Community institution of a measure with the exclusive or main purpose of achieving an end other than that stated or evading a procedure specifically prescribed by the Treaty for dealing with the circumstances of the case' (*Parliament* v *Commission* (case C–156/93)). The concept is not confined to abuses of power, nor is an ulterior or improper motive essential; an improper or illegitimate use of power is all that is required. However, this provision has been narrowly interpreted. In *Fédération Charbonnière de Belgique* v *High Authority* (case 8/55), in interpreting the comparable provision (Article 33) of the ECSC Treaty, the Court held that a measure will not be annulled for misuse of power if the improper use had no effect on its substance; nor will it be annulled if the authority had acted from mixed motives, proper and improper, as long as the proper purpose was dominant. It is thus a difficult ground to establish.

The case of *Werner A. Bock KG* v *Commission* (case 62/70) was considered, but not decided, on this ground. Although there was no clear collusion between the German Government and the Commission over the issuing of the decision, there were definite signs of collaboration. The case was eventually decided, and the decision annulled, for breach of the principle of proportionality. The Commission's action was more than was necessary in the circumstances, since the quantities of mushrooms at stake were so small as to be insignificant.

There is much overlap between the above grounds. The Court rarely examines each one precisely and is often vague as to which ground forms the basis of its decision. *BEUC* v *Commission* (case T–37/92) concerned the Commission's decision not to investigate the agreement between the British Society of Motor Manufacturers and the Japanese Government limiting imports of Japanese cars to 11 per cent of total UK sales. This decision was prima facie contrary to Article 81, but was justified by the Commission, *inter alia*, because the agreement was permitted as a matter of UK policy. The CFI annulled the decision simply on the ground that it constituted an 'error of law'. Despite the Court's lack of precision in these matters it is wise to plead as many grounds as seem applicable.

The grounds apply equally to an examination of the validity of a measure on reference from national courts under Article 234. They also apply to an enquiry into the validity of regulations under Article 241 (below) and to an application for damages under Article 288(2) (ex 215(2)) (Chapter 13) where the action is based on an illegal act of the institutions.

11.7 **Consequences of a successful action**

If an annulment action under Article 230 is successful the act will be declared void under Article 231 (ex 174). A measure may be declared void in part only, provided that the offending part can be effectively severed. Under Article 231(2), however, the Court may, following a successful action for annulment, 'state which of the effects of the Regulation which it has declared void shall be considered as definitive'. This has been done in the interests of legal certainty, to avoid upsetting past transactions based on a regulation, a normative act. In *Roquette Frères SA v France* (case 145/79) a declaration of invalidity of a Community regulation was held to be purely prospective in its effects. The wisdom of such a ruling has since been doubted, on the grounds that such a limitation would deprive the applicant of his right to effective judicial protection (*Roquette Frères SA v Hauptzollamt Geldern* (case C–228/92)). However, in *Parliament v Council* (case C–360/93) the ECJ annulled two Council decisions and, on the basis of Article 231(2) ordered that *all* the effects of the annulled decisions must be maintained in force. In *R v Ministry of Agriculture, Fisheries and Food, ex parte H. and R. Ecroyd Holdings Ltd* (case C–127/94) the ECJ held that, in a complex field, an individual may not rely on a ruling of invalidity, even in a situation arising *after* that ruling, until replacement legislation has been introduced. Nonetheless, it should be noted that in a subsequent case involving Ecroyd (*Ecroyd v Commission* (case T–220/97)), the CFI held that should a court find a measure invalid, it is not enough to repeal that measure; the position of the complainants must also be addressed so that they do not continue to suffer loss. A successful action for damages under Article 288(2) could arise in these circumstances, as indeed it did in this case.

A slightly different point arose in *Commission v AssiDoman Kraft Products AB* (case C–310/97P). The case concerned certain fines imposed on a number of undertakings for breach of the competition rules. Some of the undertakings appealed against the Commission's decisions, resulting in the partial annulment of the Commission's decision and the reduction of the fines imposed on the appellant undertakings. Several other companies, which had also been fined but which had not been party to the appeal, then requested that the Commission reconsider their position in the light of the annulment ruling. The Commission refused, as it argued that the companies involved in the competition proceedings had each been addressed individually and therefore a finding of invalidity as regards a decision addressed to one company did not affect a similar decision addressed to another. The applicant companies sought to challenge before the European courts on the basis that the Commission was obliged to reconsider by virtue of Article 233 (ex 176). The matter finally came before the ECJ, the CFI having found in the companies' favour. The ECJ overturned the CFI's ruling, holding that the scope of

Article 233 was limited in two ways. First, a ruling for annulment could not go further than the applicant requested, and thus the matter tried by the Community courts could relate only to aspects of the decision which affected the applicants. The ECJ then held that although the operative part of the judgment and its reasoning were binding *erga omnes*, this 'cannot entail annulment of an act not challenged before the Community judicature but alleged to be vitiated by the same illegality' (para. 54). The applicants in this case could not of course challenge the original Commission decision to fine them because the time limits for bringing a challenge had long expired. Although one might argue that the companies in this case could have challenged the Commission's decision earlier, the ruling in this case does lead to the anomalous position that some companies are treated less favourably than others in an equivalent situation.

11.8 Scope of indirect review under Article 241 EC

11.8.1 Scope

Although Article 241 entitles 'any party' to attack a regulation 'notwithstanding the expiry' of the time-limit laid down in Article 230, it is not designed to provide a means of escaping the restrictions either of time or *locus standi* laid down in Article 230. No action can be brought *directly* against a regulation under Article 241. As the Court held in *Milchwerke Heinz Wöhrmann & Sohn KG v Commission* (cases 31 & 33/62), in the context of an action brought under Article 241 to annul three Commission decisions, a plea under Article 241 can be raised as an *incidental* matter *only* in the course of legal proceedings based on other provisions of the Treaty. In *Wöhrmann* the action was brought *solely* under Article 241, since the time-limit within which the decisions should have been challenged under Article 230 had elapsed. Thus, the application was rejected. (See also *Commission v Belgium* (case 156/77) and, more recently, *Comité des Salines de France v Commission* (case T–154/94).)

The purpose of Article 241 is to allow a party to question the legality of a general act on which a subsequent act (e.g., a decision), or failure to act, is based. A decision is often, indeed normally, based on some general authorising act. Although a decision, in principle subject to challenge under Article 230, may in itself be unimpeachable, it may be based on a general act that is not. A non-privileged applicant has no *locus standi* to challenge a general act under Article 230. Even a privileged applicant under Article 230 may not be aware of the illegality of the general act until affected by some subsequent act issuing from that 'tainted' source. By this time the two months within which the original act should have been challenged may have elapsed. Article 241 provides a means whereby this underlying act may be challenged *indirectly*, free of time-limit, before the ECJ in proceedings in which it is 'in issue', in much the same way as questions concerning the validity of EC law may be raised indirectly in the context of domestic proceedings before national courts.

11.8.2 Proceedings in which Article 241 may be invoked

In theory Article 241 may be invoked in the context of any proceedings brought directly before the ECJ in which it is relevant. This interpretation should be treated with caution. In *Hessische Knappschaft v Maison Singer et Fils* (case 44/65) the Court was not prepared to consider a claim under Article 241 in the context of a reference from a national court under Article 234. However, in that case the parties had attempted to raise the plea of illegality as a new issue; it had not been raised in the reference by the national court. Their attempt to raise it before the ECJ was thus seen by the Court as an interference with the national court's discretion, and, as such, unacceptable. Nevertheless, it would not be necessary to invoke Article 241 before a national court since these courts are free to refer to the ECJ under Article 234 questions of validity of *any* Community act, and are not constrained by the time-limit applicable to a direct challenge under Article 230, subject, of course to the impact of *TWD*. This point seems to have been made in *Nachi Europe GmBH v Hauptzollamt Krefeld* (case C–239/99). The Court held that Article 241 could not be invoked in the context of a preliminary reference under Article 234, because this is not regarded as a main action before the Court of Justice (para. 34). To hold otherwise would be to provide a duplicate means of challenge as Article 234 already provides for a challenge to the validity of the measure on which a domestic court has requested a ruling.

The main context in which Article 241 is likely to be invoked is to support a challenge under Article 230 to the validity of a measure based on the original, allegedly invalid, act. If the underlying act, challenged under Article 241, is found invalid, it will be declared 'inapplicable' and the subsequent act, affecting the claimant, will be void. Thus the principal object of the exercise will be achieved.

Article 241 may also be relevant to an action under Article 232 for failure to act, where the failure (e.g., to issue a decision to the claimant) is based on an invalid general act (see *SNUPAT v High Authority* (cases 32 & 33/58), action under the equivalent provision of the former ECSC Treaty, Article 35). It may also, in theory, be invoked to support an action for damages under Articles 235 and 288(2) EC, or arising out of contract under Article 238 (which gives the court 'jurisdiction to give judgment pursuant to any arbitration clause contained in a contract concluded by or on behalf of the Community') or in appeals against penalties under Article 229 EC. It is submitted that Article 241 may also be invoked as a defence to an action against a Member State under Article 226 (but see *Commission v Belgium* (case 156/77)).

A legitimate challenge under Article 241 may be brought by the applicant or the defendant. There must, however, always be a 'direct judicial link' between the act (or failure to act) affecting the applicant and the general underlying measure subject to challenge (*Italy v Council* (case 32/65)).

As Article 241 is only a complementary remedy it is essential to its success that the time-limit and *locus standi* requirements imposed in the principal action before the Court are observed. Article 241 does not provide a means of evading these limits (see *Wöhrmann* (cases 31 & 33/62); *Commission v Belgium* (case 156/77)). Indeed, the Court recently ruled that a private claimant could not rely on Article 241 EC where it would have been able to bring a challenge under Article 230 EC but failed to do so within the time-limit (*Nachi Europe GmBH v Hauptzollamt*

Krefeld (case C–239/99)). In this we might see parallels with the ECJ's approach under *TWD*.

11.8.3 **Reviewable acts**

Although Article 241 is expressed to apply only to regulations, the Court, in keeping with its approach in Article 230, has held that Article 241 applies to any general act having binding force. In *Simmenthal SpA* v *Commission* (case 92/78) the claimant, a meat processing company, was seeking to annul, under Article 230, a decision addressed to the Italian Government, in which the company was directly and individually concerned. The basis of its claim for annulment was that the 'parent' measure, a general notice of invitation to tender, on which the decision was based, was invalid. The Court held that since the notice was a general act, which, although not in the form of a regulation, produced similar effects, it could be challenged under Article 241. The challenge was successful and resulted in the annulment of the decision affecting the claimant.

11.8.3.1 *Is the scope for challenge under Article 241 limited to general measures?*

The principal reason for making an 'exception' for regulations would appear to be to enable individuals, who are unable to challenge general acts under Article 230, to do so when they seek, legitimately, to rely on their invalidity in the context of other proceedings before the Court. A secondary reason would be that, since a regulation is 'of general application' and is not addressed to anyone, its invalidity may not be apparent to the claimant until a subsequent individual measure, based on the general measure, brings it to his attention. Both reasons, i.e., lack of opportunity to challenge and absence of notification, would justify extending the scope of Article 241 to enable an individual to challenge, indirectly, any 'parent' act which was not addressed to him or in which he was not directly and individually concerned. The second reason would provide grounds for allowing a privileged applicant to challenge indirectly any 'parent' act which was not addressed to the applicant. This matter has yet to be decided by the Court.

11.8.4 *Locus standi*

Although *locus standi* under Article 241 appears to apply to 'any party', doubts have been expressed as to whether it extends to privileged applicants. It is argued that since Member States and institutions are entitled to seek annulment of *any* act under Article 230, to allow them to invoke Article 241 would be to enable them to challenge acts which they should have challenged, within the time-limit, under Article 230. However, Advocate-General Roemer in *Italy* v *Council* (case 32/65) took the view that a Member State *should* have *locus standi* under Article 241, since the wording of the provision was in no way restrictive, and the illegality of the general provision might not become apparent until it was applied subsequently in a particular case. The Court did not comment on the matter, since it found that the regulations in issue were not relevant to the case, but its silence could be read as consent. Advocate-General Roemer's reasoning is persuasive. Moreover,

Article 241 can never be used *merely* to circumvent time-limit; it can only be invoked as an incidental issue, when the claimant is affected by some subsequent act (or failure) arising from the original general act. This provides ample safeguard against abuse.

This point is illustrated by *Commission* v *Belgium* (case 156/77). Here Article 241 was raised as a defence to an enforcement action against Belgium for infringement of Community law relating to State aids. The Belgians had failed to comply with a Commission decision of May 1976, addressed to the Belgian Government, requiring the Belgians to abolish certain State aids within a three-month period; nor had they attempted to challenge that decision. In proceedings brought by the Commission in December 1977 for non-compliance with the decision the Belgian Government argued, invoking Article 241, that the decision was invalid. The claim was held inadmissible. The Court found that the Belgians' claim was in essence a claim for the annulment of the decision of May 1976. They had been free to contest this decision under Article 230, but had failed to do so within the time-limit. They could not allow this limit to elapse and then challenge the decision's legality under Article 241.

This case, it is submitted, does not decide that Article 241 can never be raised in enforcement proceedings against Member States. The Belgians' claim under the then Article 184 was rejected on different and wholly legitimate grounds. They were not invoking the article as a collateral issue; their defence was based *solely* on the legality of a decision addressed to them which they had failed to challenge in time.

11.8.5 Grounds of review

The grounds on which regulations may be challenged under Article 241 are the same as those provided under Article 230 (see *Simmenthal SpA* v *Commission* (case 92/78)).

11.8.6 Consequences of a successful challenge

Where an action under Article 241 is successful, the regulation is declared 'inapplicable'. Since there is no time-limit within which acts may be challenged under the article, it is not, for reasons of legal certainty, void, but voidable. However, a declaration of inapplicability will render a subsequent act, based on that act, void. Thus, although action under Article 241 is an 'incidental matter', it will be conclusive of the principal action before the Court. A declaration of inapplicability under this article may also be invoked to prevent the application of the invalid act in a subsequent case.

11.9 Conclusions

The procedure in Article 230 is an important cog of the judicial review machinery, but it is not without shortcomings. The time-limits can impose significant constraints and we have seen that other possible routes to challenge Community acts have been interpreted so as not to undermine this limitation. The greatest criticism has been of the restrictive test for individual concern, and the attitude to trade associations and pressure groups is also rather restrictive. Although there have been attempts to broaden the test to provide for more effective judicial protection, it seems that, for the time being, the *status quo* will prevail. It is arguable that too broad a rule could open the floodgates, but that does not have to be the inevitable consequence of a more relaxed approach to non-privileged standing. Moreover, if a particular measure has adversely affected a large number of people, then fairness demands that they be given the opportunity to challenge the measure in question. In any event, it must be remembered that to be given *locus standi* is not tantamount to succeeding on the substance, and an individual who may have standing could still lose on the merits. Although the Constitution could ease the situation somewhat, its scope will still be subject to interpretation by the CFI and ECJ, which could transfer the interpretation of direct concern into the requirements for standing under the Constitution. Nonetheless, the change in itself could be seen as a signal that the political institutions feel that the current test for standing is too restrictive.

FURTHER READING

Arnull, A., 'Private Applicants and the Action for Annulment under Article 173 of the EC Treaty' (1995) 32 CMLR 7.

—, 'Private Applicants and the Action for Annulment since *Cordoniu*', (2001) 38 CML Rev 7.

Bradley, K. St Clair, 'Sense and Sensibility: *Parliament* v *Council* Continuing' (1991) 16 EL Rev 245.

Craig, P., 'Legality, Standing and Substantive Review in Community Law' (1994) 14 Oxford J Legal Stud 507.

Enchelmeier, S., 'No-One Slips Through the Net? Latest Developments, and Non-Developments, in the European Court of Justice's Jurisprudence on Art. 230(4) EC' (2005) 24 YEL 173.

Greaves, R., '*Locus Standi* under Article 173 EEC when Seeking Annulment of a Regulation' (1986) 11 EL Rev 119.

Harding, C., 'The Private Interest in Challenging Community Action' (1980) 5 EL Rev 345.

Harlow, C., 'Towards a Theory of Access for the European Court of Justice' (1992) 12 YEL 213.

Neuwahl, N. A. E. M., 'Article 173 Paragraph 4 EC: Past, Present and Possible Future' (1996) 21 EL Rev 17.

Ragolle, F., 'Access to Justice for Private Applicants in the Community Legal Order: Recent (R)evolutions' (2003) 40 CML Rev 90.

Rasmussen, H., 'Why is Article 173 Interpreted against Private Plaintiffs?' (1980) 5 EL Rev 112.

Van Nuffel, P. 'What's in a Member State? Central and Decentralised Authorities before the Community Courts' (2001) 38 CML Rev 871.

12

Action for failure to act

12.1 Introduction

If the institutions of the Community are to operate according to the rule of law, as they are obliged to do under Article 7 (ex 4) of the EC Treaty, they must be answerable not only for their actions but for their failure to act in breach of EC law. This is provided for by Article 232 (ex 175), as follows:

> Should the European Parliament, the Council or the Commission, in infringement of this Treaty, fail to act, the Member States and the other institutions of the Community may bring an action before the Court of Justice to have the infringement established.
>
> The action shall be admissible only if the institution concerned has first been called upon to act. If, within two months of being so called upon, the institution concerned has not defined its position, the action may be brought within a further period of two months.
>
> Any natural or legal person may, under the conditions laid down in the preceding paragraphs, complain to the Court of Justice that an institution of the Community has failed to address to that person any act other than a recommendation or an opinion.
>
> The Court of Justice shall have jurisdiction under the same conditions in actions or proceedings brought by the European Central Bank in the areas falling within the latter's field of competence and in actions or proceedings brought against the latter.

Actions brought by a natural or legal person under Article 232 EC now fall within the jurisdiction of the CFI, although appeal on points of law may be made to the ECJ (see Chapter 7).

Articles 232 and 230 (ex 173) are essentially complementary remedies. As the ECJ held in *Chevalley* v *Commission* (case 15/70) when confronted with the applicant's uncertainty as to whether Articles 232 or 230 was the appropriate form of action, it is not necessary to characterise the proceedings as being under one or the other article, since both articles merely prescribe one and the same method of recourse. They represent two aspects of the same legal remedy. For this reason it has been suggested that any inconsistency between the two provisions should be resolved by applying the same principles to both. This is known as the 'unity principle'. This is all the more important in the light of the Court's interpretation of Article 232, which may result in an action, begun under that article, being concluded under Article 230. It should be noted that this principle will not extend to the more limited provisions for annulment of measures taken under the JHA pillar of the TEU (Article 35 TEU); moreover, the latter does not provide for an action for failure to act in respect of measures in this area. Nonetheless, in cases arising under the EC Treaty, the unity principle, or the coherence between the two provisions, remains a relevant factor referred to by the CFI (see, e.g., *Gestevision Telecinco* v *Commission* (case T–95/96)).

12.2 **Reviewable omissions**

The institution's failure to act must, first and foremost, be 'in infringement of this Treaty'. Since this would include legislation enacted under the Treaty it would apply to any failure on the part of the institution to act when it was under a legal duty to do so. In *Parliament* v *Council* (case 13/83), in an action by Parliament under Article 232 alleging the Council's failure to implement a Community transport policy, the Court held that 'failure' can cover a failure to take a number of decisions; the nature of the acts which may be requested need not be clearly circumscribed as long as they are sufficiently identified. The failures alleged by Parliament in this case were:

(a) failure to introduce a common transport policy, as required by the then Article 74, and

(b) failure to introduce measures to secure freedom to provide transport services, as required by the then Articles 75, 59, 60 and 61.

The Court held that Parliament was entitled to succeed on the second allegation but not on the first. While the second obligation was complete and legally perfect, and should have been implemented by the Council within the transitional period, the former obligation was insufficiently precise to constitute an enforceable obligation. Prior to the TEU, action under Article 175 (now 232) could be brought only against the Council or the Commission, but now, action may also be brought against the European Parliament. Omissions of the European Central Bank are also subject to review under Article 232. Although the Court of Auditors was awarded the power to bring actions under Article 230 by the ToA, its inaction is not subject to review under Article 232. This is probably a consequence of their limited and non-binding status. It has now been established that the actions of the Ombudsman may give rise to liability under Article 288 (ex 215) EC (see case C–234/02P, *European Ombudsman* v *Lamberts*), and it may therefore also be possible for an individual to complain under Article 232 EC, should the Ombudsman fail to act in response to a complaint.

Although only non-binding acts in the form of recommendations and opinions are expressly excluded in the context of individual action under Article 232, third paragraph, the unity principle would suggest that a failure under Article 232 would only cover a failure to issue a binding act.

12.3 *Locus standi*

12.3.1 **Privileged applicants**

Parliament, is, along with Member States and the other institutions, a 'privileged applicant' under Article 232. Privileged applicants enjoy a right to challenge *any* failure on the part of the Council and the Commission, i.e., an omission to adopt *any* binding act which these institutions have a duty to adopt. Under the TEU, the European Central Bank was given *locus standi* to bring proceedings under Article 232 'in the areas falling within [its] field of competence'.

It should be noted that there is no obligation on a Member State to bring an action under Article 232. This was confirmed by the ECJ in *Netherlands* v *Ten Kate Holding BV* (C–511/03), where a Dutch manufacturer sought to bring an action against the government for failing to take action under Articles 230 and 232 EC. The Court held that neither provision imposed an obligation on a Member State to bring an action, and not doing so would not constitute an infringement of that State's obligations under EC law (and therefore not give rise to a claim in state liability under *Francovich*). However, the ECJ emphasised that EC law did not preclude a domestic rule that would impose liability on the government of a Member State which could have brought an action under Articles 230 or 232 EC, but did not do so. This would be a matter entirely for domestic law on which the ECJ could not express an opinion.

12.3.2 **Individuals**

12.3.2.1 *Measures subject to challenge by individuals*

In comparison with Member States and Community institutions, individuals, as under Article 230, have a limited *locus standi* under Article 232(3). Natural or legal persons may bring proceedings only where the institution complained of has failed to address to that person any act other than a recommendation or an opinion. Since an act which is addressed to a designated person is in substance a decision, this seems to mean that an individual's *locus standi* is limited to a failure on the part of the Council or Commission to adopt what is in essence a *decision* addressed to *himself or herself*. The individual has no express *locus standi* to challenge an omission to address to *another person* a decision of direct and individual concern to himself or herself.

This apparent deficiency has been remedied by the Court. In *Nordgetreide GmbH & Co. KG* v *Commission* (case 42/71), Advocate-General Roemer, invoking the unity principle, suggested that since Articles 230 and 232 constituted part of a coherent system, an individual should have a right to demand a decision *vis-à-vis* a third party in which the individual was directly and individually concerned. In *Bethell* v *Commission* (case 246/81) this right was implied when the Court, in rejecting Lord Bethell's claim as inadmissible, held that he had failed to show that the Commission had failed to adopt, in relation to him, a measure *which he was legally entitled to claim*. In the context of Article 232, the equivalent to a decision of direct and individual concern under Article 230, it was a decision which the applicant is *legally entitled to claim*.

This test was relaxed in *T. Port GmbH & Co. KG* v *Bundesanstalt für Landeswirtschaft und Ernährung* (case C–68/95)). Reasoning from the unity principle and the test of direct and individual concern used for Article 230 actions, the ECJ stated that Article 232(3) could be invoked where an institution has failed to act in respect of a measure which would have concerned the applicant in the same way (para. 59). The CFI has subsequently followed the *T. Port* case in the more recent cases involving challenges to the funding of public service broadcasters (e.g., *Gestevision Telecinco SA* v *Commission* (case T–95/96)), thus suggesting that this approach has now been consolidated into the courts' case law.

Many of the claims under Article 232 (ex 175) prior to *T. Port GmbH* (case C–68/95) failed because the applicant was seeking the adoption of an act which he was not entitled to claim. For example, in *Ladbroke Racing Ltd* v *Commission* (case T–32/93), an individual complainant was held not to have a right to demand action by the Commission under the State aid provisions of the then Article 90(3) (now Article 86(3)). This may be compared with the more recent case of *Bundesverband der Bilanzbuchhalter eV* v *Commission* (case C–107/95 P) in which the ECJ accepted that in limited circumstances, details of which it did not elaborate, an applicant could demand action under Article 86(3) (ex 90(3)) EC, although in *Commission* v *T-Mobile Austria* (case C–141/02P), the ECJ appeared to move away from that view (see paras 68–69). In *Gestevision Telecinco SA* v *Commission* (case T–95/96), the CFI held that an individual could demand that the Commission make a decision at the end of the initial investigatory phase of State aid proceedings under Article 88(3). Further, where the Commission has difficulty in determining whether the funding in issue constitutes State aid or whether it is compatible with the common market, 'the institution has a duty to gather all necessary views and to that end initiate the procedure under 93(2) [now 86(3)]'. In both of these circumstances, Article 232 proceedings could be brought against a failure on the Commission's part to act. It may be that the easing of the test here and in *T. Port* (case C–68/95) will result in an increase in the number of successful actions brought by non-privileged applicants. Arguably, a more generous approach to individuals' *locus standi* under Article 232 EC is justified if individuals are to be denied access to the ECJ to challenge an institution's failure to act under Article 234 (ex 177) EC.

On rather different reasoning in another failed claim in the earlier case of *Eridania* v *Commission* (cases 10 & 18/68), the Court held that the applicants could not invoke Article 232 to obtain a revocation by the Commission of a decision addressed to third parties, as other methods of recourse, namely, Article 230, were provided by the Treaty; to allow parallel recourse via Article 232 would enable applicants to avoid the conditions (i.e., time-limit) laid down by the Treaty.

12.3.2.2 *Challenges with regard to regulations*

It is clear that the act demanded must be in substance a decision. In *Nordgetreide GmbH & Co. KG* v *Commission* (case 42/71) the applicant company was seeking the amendment by the Commission of a regulation. When the Commission rejected its request the company instituted two actions, one for failure to act, under Article 232, and one under Article 230 for annulment of the Commission's decision refusing to act. The action under Article 232 would in any case have failed because, as Advocate-General Roemer pointed out, the company was seeking from the Commission what would have amounted to a normative act; in fact the Court found its claim inadmissible on different grounds (to be discussed below). The claim under Article 230 was also held inadmissible. Although the contested decision was addressed to the applicant, the Court held that a decision refusing to act (a 'negative' decision) would only be open to attack under Article 230 if the *positive* measure being sought were open to attack (see also Advocate-General Gand in *Alfons Lütticke GmbH* v *Commission* (case 48/65)). Since the company was seeking to amend a regulation, this would not be the case. This same reasoning would apply to a refusal by the Commission to issue a decision to another person which the applicants were not entitled to claim. Thus, even though a decision may have been addressed to the applicant, Article 230 cannot be invoked as an adjunct to Article 232 to annul a decision not to act, in order to compel an institution to act *when it has no duty to do so at the behest of the applicant.* Although this has been attempted on a number of occasions, it has always failed (e.g., *Alfons Lütticke GmbH* v *Commission* (case 48/65); *Star Fruit Company SA* v *Commission*; *J* v *Commission* (case T–5/94) – applicants demanding action by the Commission under Article 226 (ex 169) against a Member State; *Bethell* v *Commission* (case 246/81) – applicant seeking to force Commission to take action under Article 85 (ex 89) against Member States' airlines).

12.3.2.3 *Procedural rights*

A case in which the applicant was entitled to demand action from the Commission, but in which its claim was surprisingly held inadmissible, was *Deutscher Komponistenverband* v *Commission* (case 8/71). Here the applicant alleged that the Commission had failed in its obligation under EC competition law (Regulation 17/62, now repealed) to grant it, as a complainant under Article 3 of that regulation, a hearing. Advocate-General Roemer suggested that acts susceptible of action under Article 232 should cover any measures which give rise to legal effects for the applicant; they should then include measures of a procedural nature. The Court disagreed, holding that Article 232(3) only applied to a failure to adopt a decision; it did not cover the promulgation of a formal act. Nevertheless the Court did examine the merits and concluded that since the applicant had had an opportunity to make its submissions in writing there had been no failure on the part of the Commission.

It is submitted that Advocate-General Roemer's view is to be preferred to that of the Court. Since there was no doubt that the applicant was entitled to a hearing any failure to grant it that hearing should have been actionable under Article 232. And if it was refused such a hearing, as it was, it should have been entitled to challenge that refusal under Article 230, as the positive measure requested was one which it was entitled to demand.

This view seems to have been taken by the Court in *FEDIOL* v *Commission* (case 191/82). In this case an EC federation of seed crushers and oil processors was seeking to compel the Commission to take action against alleged dumping practices on the part of Brazil. As undertakings which considered themselves injured or threatened by subsidised imports, the applicants were entitled under Regulation 3017/79 (the principal anti-dumping regulation) to lodge a complaint (Article 5), to be consulted (Article 6), and to receive information (Article 9). In April 1980 they lodged a complaint with the Commission. Following enquiries and negotiations with the Brazilian Government the Commission decided to take no further action. In September 1981 FEDIOL instituted Article 232 proceedings. Following further correspondence between FEDIOL and the Commission the Commission informed FEDIOL by letter in May 1982 that it intended to take no further action against Brazil. FEDIOL then brought Article 230 proceedings to annul that letter. The Court held that since the regulation under which they complained recognised specific rights on the applicants' part they were entitled to a review by the Court of any exercise of power by the Community institutions which might affect these rights. Thus the action was held admissible. Although the applicants could not compel the

Commission to take action against Brazil, that being a matter within the Commission's discretion, they were entitled to a review by the Court of the Commission's letter of May 1982 to ensure that their procedural rights were respected.

This case may be contrasted with the earlier case of *GEMA v Commission* (case 125/78). Here GEMA initiated a complaint to the Commission under Article 3 of Regulation 17/62, alleging a breach by Radio Luxembourg of Articles 81 and 82. In March 1978 the Commission wrote to GEMA saying that it had decided not to pursue the matter. In May 1978 GEMA instituted Article 232 proceedings against this refusal to act. Subsequently, in March 1979 GEMA brought proceedings under Article 230 to annul the letter of March 1978. The action under Article 232 failed because the Commission was held to have defined its position in the letter of March 1978. The action under Article 230 failed on the grounds that, assuming that the letter could be contested, this did not entitle the applicants to a *final decision* on the existence of an infringement under Article 82. In any case the letter had not been challenged in time and the parties' attempts to extend the limit on the grounds of fresh issues based on matters of fact and law failed. In the appeal in *Guérin Automobiles v Commission* (case C–282/95 P), the ECJ confirmed that a letter to a complainant was a definition of a position for the purposes of Article 232, but that it could not be challenged because the letter was a preparatory stage in proceedings. The applicants were entitled under competition procedural rules to make representations, after which the Commission must make a decision which would have legally binding effects. It would be at this stage that an applicant could challenge a failure to act although it still could not force the Commission to take a decision that was favourable to the applicants.

Thus, in all of these cases the parties were only entitled in law to protection by way of review under Articles 232 and 230 to protect their procedural rights. They had no right to compel the Commission to institute proceedings against third parties; that was a matter within the Commission's discretion (see also *Ladbroke Racing Ltd v Commission* (case T–32/93)). Even in *Gestevision*, where the Commission seemed to be under an obligation to investigate the funding to State broadcasters further, this obligation arose out of the need to protect the procedural rights of all involved and did not entitle Gestevision to any particular finding on the question of State aid.

Where an individual does have a right to complain and to request action, as in *FEDIOL, GEMA* and *Guérin*, should the Commission take action and issue a decision to a third party, the complainant will be deemed to be directly and individually concerned, and will be entitled to a full review of the decision under Article 230 EC (*Metro-SB-Grossmärkte GmbH & Co. KG v Commission* (case 26/76); *Timex Corporation v Council* (case 264/82), see Chapter 11; *COFAZ* (case 169/84); *British American Tobacco Co. Ltd v Commission* (cases 142 & 156/84)).

12.4 Procedure

Where the applicant has a right to require an institution to act, and the institution is under a corresponding duty, the applicant must first call upon the institution to act. No time-limit is imposed for the institution's alleged failure, but the Court has held that proceedings must be brought within a reasonable time of the institution's having demonstrated its intention not to act (*Netherlands* v *Commission* (case 59/ 70)—case brought under Article 35 of the ECSC Treaty).

The institution then has two months within which it may either act in accordance with the request, or 'define its position'.

If the institution fails to act or to define its position the claimant has two months within which to bring his case before the ECJ, running from the date on which the institution should have defined its position. These limits are strictly enforced. In *Guérin Automobiles* v *Commission* (case T–195/95) the Commission, responding to a complaint by Guérin concerning an alleged breach by Nissan of Article 81(1) (ex 85(1)), merely sent them a copy of Nissan's response to the complaint. When Guérin subsequently submitted their observations to the Commission in February 1995, the Commission failed to respond. In October 1995 they brought an action before the CFI under Article 232. The Court found the action inadmissible. Even supposing that the letter sent by the applicants in February 1995 could be regarded as an invitation to act in the sense of Article 232, to which the Commission had failed to respond, the application to the CFI should have been introduced within four months of the date on which the letter was sent, as required by that article. Guérin wrote to the Commission again, and then brought another action under Article 232, this time within four months from the date of this letter. Again, the company was unsuccessful, as the Commission had, by the time the matter came before the CFI, defined its position.

It may sometimes be difficult to establish the point at which the institution can be said to have defined its position. In *CEVA and Pharmacia* v *Commission* (cases T–344 and T–345/00), a letter which merely stated that the questions submitted by the applicants were still under consideration by the Commission was not a definition of position, whereas the subsequent adoption of a draft regulation was. The action under Article 232 could not proceed. However, a delay by a Community institution in defining its position which results in loss to an applicant may give rise to liability under Article 288 EC (see Chapter 13).

12.4.1 Effect of definition of position

Article 232 is silent as to what happens if the institution concerned defines its position. Although it was not necessary so to construe this article, the Court held in *Alfons Lütticke GmbH* v *Commission* (case 48/65) that a definition of position brought proceedings under Article 232 to an end. The claimant in this case, it will be remembered, was attempting to persuade the Commission to bring an action under Article 226 against the German Government for its alleged infringement of Article 90. When the Commission refused to act Alfons Lütticke GmbH brought proceedings under Article 232 for failure to act. The Commission defined its position in a letter to Lütticke, again refusing to act, and Lütticke brought proceedings under Article 230 to annul that refusal. The Court, in the briefest of judgments, held that the Commission's refusal was a 'definition of position' which ended its failure to act. The action under Article 232 was therefore inadmissible.

With regard to the action under Article 230, Advocate-General Gand's submissions were again convincing. The applicant would only be entitled to challenge the Commission's refusal to act (the 'negative decision'), he suggested, if it had been entitled to challenge the positive act requested. This it would not, since it had no right to demand action from the Commission *vis-à-vis* the German Government. The Court, on the other hand, chose to treat the Commission's refusal not as a definition of position but as a 'reasoned opinion' under Article 226, which, as a purely preliminary act, was not, the Court held, capable of annulment.

The Court did adopt reasoning similar to that of Advocate-General Gand in *Lütticke* in *Star Fruit Company SA* v *Commission* (case 247/87). Here, as in *Lütticke*, the applicants, a firm of banana importers, were seeking to compel the Commission to institute Article 226 proceedings, this time against France in respect of the French regime regulating banana imports, which they considered was in breach of Article 28 EC (ex 30 EC). They had complained to the Commission and the Commission had acknowledged their request. The applicants subsequently brought Article 232 proceedings against the Commission for their failure to take action against France, and Article 230 proceedings for the annulment of the Commission's letter of acknowledgment. On the claim for failure to act, the Court held that since the Commission was not required to instigate proceedings under Article 226, but on the contrary had a discretionary power, 'individuals were not entitled to require that the institution adopt a particular position'.

On the claim under Article 230, the Court pointed out that by requesting the Commission to set in motion a procedure under Article 226 the applicant was 'in reality requesting the adoption of acts which were not of direct and individual concern to it within the meaning of Article [230], and which in any event it could not challenge by means of an action for annulment'.

12.4.2 Definition of position and Article 230

The Court has, however, consistently followed its position in *Lütticke* and held that, in Article 232 proceedings, a definition of position by the defendant institution ends its failure to act. It is not surprising that so few cases have reached the ECJ and now the CFI under that provision. However, this is not necessarily the end of the road for the applicant. In a *legitimate* case, *where he is entitled to demand action* from the institution concerned, he may challenge the definition of position, as a decision addressed to himself, under Article 230, and provided that he does so in time, his application should be admissible. It is submitted that *Lütticke*, with its special facts (applicant not entitled to demand action), and its judgment cast in terms of Article 226, cannot be invoked to prevent such a challenge. *FEDIOL* (case 191/82) supports this view. Although not described as such, the Commission's letter of May 1982, in which the Commission informed FEDIOL of its decision not to act, and which FEDIOL were held entitled to challenge under Article 230, was undoubtedly a 'definition of position' within Article 232 (see *GEMA* (case 125/78)).

Where an institution defines its position and refuses to act, an applicant who is not entitled to demand that action cannot challenge that refusal under Article 230; and even a legitimate claim under Article 232 is likely to result in an action to review that refusal under Article 230. In the latter case it is therefore essential that a definition of position be recognised as a decision capable of challenge under Article 230, and that it be challenged in time (cf. *GEMA; Irish Cement Ltd*). The extent of the review conducted by the Court under Article 230 will depend on the extent of the applicant's rights. Since the institutions have wide discretionary powers in the pursuit of economic policy objectives, individuals' rights, at least where action *vis-à-vis* third parties are concerned, are likely to be limited, and mainly of a procedural nature. However, as has been demonstrated in *Parliament* v *Council* (case 13/83), Article 232 offers considerable scope for privileged applicants.

In *Parliament* v *Council* (case 13/83) Parliament's case was heard before the ECJ under Article 232, as the Council's 'definition of position' was found to be inadequate. As it neither confirmed nor denied the alleged failure (implementation of transport policy), and failed to reveal the Council's position with regard to the measure which the Council intended to adopt, it was held not to amount to a definition of position at all.

12.5 Consequences of a successful action

Whether the action is admitted before the Court under Article 232, as a failure to act, or under Article 230, as a claim for annulment of a decision not to act, the consequences of a successful action are the same. Under Article 233 (ex 176):

> The institution whose act has been declared void or whose failure to act has been declared contrary to this Treaty shall be required to take the necessary measures to comply with the judgment of the Court of Justice.

The institution will be required by the Court to take action to remedy its failure. It will not necessarily be the action required by the applicant. Should he wish to challenge the institution's implementation of the judgment he could do so under Article 230.

No sanctions beyond the possibility of further action under Article 232 are provided for non-compliance with the Court's judgment. Unlike Article 228, which was amended by the TEU to provide for the imposition of fines and penalties on Member States which fail to comply with a judgment of the Court under Article 226 (see Chapter 10), Article 233 was not amended to provide for similar penalties against EC institutions in respect of their failures established under Article 232. Also, although Article 233(2) provides that the obligation imposed by Article 233(1) 'shall not affect any obligations which may result from the application of the second paragraph of Article 288' (governing the Community's non-contractual liability) the opportunity for individuals to obtain damages from the Community is, as will be seen, extremely limited (see Chapter 13).

12.6 Impact of the proposed Constitution

Should the relevant provisions of the Treaty establishing a Constitution for Europe enter into force, there would be some changes to the scope of the current Article 232 EC. The European Central Bank would be given the same standing as the other institutions. Moreover, the scope of Article III–367 (current Article 232 EC) would extend to 'bodies, offices and agencies of the Union which fail to act'.

Whether this extension would make a significant difference in practice is difficult to predict.

12.7 Conclusions

It has been seen that the procedure under Article 232 complements the Article 230 procedure for directly challenging the validity of acts adopted by the institutions because it seeks to ensure that the institutions act on their powers whenever required. It is just as important to challenge legislation adopted by the institutions where this exceeds their powers as it is to challenge inaction when a positive step was required. Once Article 232 is invoked, the institution concerned must at least define its position. This, in turn, can then be reviewed under Article 230, subject to the requirements on *locus standi* (see Chapter 11). Although a successful Article 232 claim may persuade the institution concerned to take action, this does not mean that the claimant will receive the decision he might prefer. Nevertheless, action by the Community institution would remove the uncertainty that could otherwise prevail if no action were taken at all.

13

Community liability in tort—action for damages

13.1 Introduction

We have already seen that there are various mechanisms in the Treaty by which the acts of the Community institutions can be reviewed. In addition to challenging acts directly and, if the challenge is successful, having these declared inapplicable, it may also be necessary to make good any loss that has been caused as a result of the adoption of a measure which is unlawful. The Treaty contains provisions that provide for the non-contractual liability of the Community in Articles 235 (ex 178) and 288 (ex 215). Although Article 288 is potentially of great utility, in practice its application has been limited by the Court, not necessarily in terms of *locus standi*, but in terms of the test to show a violation of the Community's obligations.

13.2 Scope of non-contractual liability

According to Article 235:

> The Court of Justice shall have jurisdiction in disputes relating to the compensation for damage provided for in the second paragraph of Article 288.

Article 288(2) provides that:

> In the case of non-contractual liability, the Community shall, in accordance with the general principles common to the laws of the Member States, make good any damage caused by its institutions or by its servants in the performance of their duties.

Thus, the Community may be liable for both *'fautes de service'*, i.e., wrongful acts on the part of one of its institutions, and *'fautes personelles'*, wrongful acts on the part of its servants. Provided in both cases that the wrongful acts are committed in the performance of the perpetrator's Community functions, the responsible institution may be sued. Where more than one institution is concerned, or where there is doubt as to which institution is responsible, both (or all) may be sued. In the case of *faute personelle*, the Community is liable on the principle of vicarious liability, albeit interpreted in a slightly narrower sense than that in which it is understood under English law (see *Sayag* v *Leduc* (case 9/69), proceedings under Article 188(2) of the Euratom Treaty, in which it was held that the Community is only liable for those acts of its servants which, by virtue of an internal relationship, are the *necessary* extension of the tasks entrusted to the institutions).

In applying Article 288(2) the Court is required to determine liability 'in accordance with the general principles common to the laws of Member States'. Where the principles of non-contractual liability, which embrace principles concerning the basis of liability (i.e., fault or non-fault), causation and damages are not 'common' to all Member States, the Court has drawn on the principles governing tortious liability in the Member States in order to develop its own specific principles of Community law. The process is thus different from its approach to the incorporation of general principles of law for the purposes of judicial review of Community law (see Chapter 6).

As was the case with actions for failure to act under Article 232 (ex 175), the ToA (Article 35 TEU) failed to provide for an action for damages in respect of measures taken under the JHA pillar of the TEU.

Should the Treaty establishing a Constitution for Europe enter into force, Article 235 EC would be re-enacted as Article III–370, and Article 288 EC as Article III–431. There would be no substantive difference, although the third paragraph of Article 288 would be clarified by imposing liability on the European Central Banks for damage caused by it or its servants.

13.3 *Locus standi*

Unlike the position in the area of judicial review, there are no personal limitations on the right to bring an action under Article 288(2). There is no distinction between privileged and non-privileged applicants. Moreover, a specific and generous limitation period of five years is provided (Article 46 Statute of the Court of Justice), running from the occurrence of the event giving rise to liability. The Court has held that the limitation period cannot begin until all the requirements for liability, particularly damage, have materialised (*Birra Wührer SpA* v *Council* (cases 256, 257, 265 & 267/80 & 5/81)). Where the damage results from a legislative measure, time runs not necessarily from the date of enactment but from the date on which the injury occurs, or at least when the applicant becomes aware of it (see, e.g., *Buhring* v *Council* (case T–246/93)).

These *locus standi* provisions are important, since, as will be seen, it may be possible to obtain a declaration of invalidity in the context of a claim for damages, thereby circumventing the *locus standi* limitations of Article 230 (ex 173) (see *Aktien-Zuckerfabrik Schöppenstedt* v *Council* (case 5/71)). The ECJ did, however, make the point in *Krohn & Co. Import-Export GmbH & Co. KG* v *Commission* (case 175/84) that a claim might not be admissible if the purpose of the Article 288(2) action was purely to attain by another route the remedy provided by Article 230, an approach reaffirmed by the CFI in declaring an action inadmissible in *Cobrecaf SA* v *Commission* (case T–514/93) and reflecting that taken by the ECJ regarding time limits on Article 234 (ex 177) references on the validity of Community acts (*TWD Textilwerk Deggendorf GmbH* v *Germany* (case C–188/92)) (see Chapters 9 and 11).

13.4 Elements of non-contractual liability

The basic elements of non-contractual liability are familiar. They embrace:

(a) unlawful conduct on the part of the institutions,

(b) damage to the claimant, and

(c) a causative link between the two.

(See, most recently, *Medici Grimm KG* v *Council* (case T–364/03), para. 59.)

For liability to arise, all three elements must be proved. The CFI has noted that it is not necessary to deal with these elements in any particular order. If it seems likely that one of them will not be satisfied, the Court can deal with it first and, if appropriate, dismiss the application without discussing the remaining elements (*Elliniki Viomichania Oplon AE (EVO)* v *Council and Commission* (case T–220/96)).

Neither the ECJ nor the CFI has (yet) endorsed a principle of liability without fault in EC law, despite the opportunity to rule specifically on this matter in *Atlanta* (case T–521/93) and *Édouard Dubois et Fils SA* v *Council* (case T–113/96). The ECJ has not, however, ruled out that possibility (see *Compagnie d'Approvisionnement* v *Commission* (cases 9 & 11/71); *Biovilac* v *Commission* (case 59/83)). In *Dorsch Consult* (case T–184/95), the CFI commented, without specifically ruling on the point of whether liability could arise for a lawful act, that a precondition for such liability would in any event be the existence of 'unusual' and 'special' damage, which in this case was not satisfied.

13.5 Wrongful acts or omissions

Although, following continental traditions, non-contractual liability is not divided up into specific 'torts', wrongful acts and omissions may be grouped under three broad categories:

(a) Failures of administration. Community institutions are under a duty of good administration. Failures of administration would include, for example, a failure to adopt satisfactory procedures, a failure to obtain the relevant facts before making the decision, the giving of misleading information, a failure to give the necessary information (e.g., *Odigitria AAE* v *Council* (case T–572/93) – but no liability because of lack of causal link), or a significant delay in acting (*CEVA and Pharmacia* v *Commission* (case T–344 and T–345/00) – failure to act for a period of 19 months constituted a clear and serious breach of the principle of sound administration). As with negligence, the decision taken or advice offered need not be right as long as it is adopted according to the correct procedures and the conclusions reached are reasonable in the light of the information to hand.

(b) Negligent acts by a servant in the performance of his duties. This category would also include a single negligent act. For example, in *Grifoni* v *Euratom* (case C–308/87), a case concerning the Euratom Treaty, Euratom contracted with Mr Grifoni to have the roof of a building repaired. While inspecting the roof, Grifoni fell off. The ECJ held that Euratom was at fault in not providing the necessary guard rails.

(c) The adoption of wrongful (i.e., illegal or invalid) acts having legal effect, or the wrongful failure to adopt a binding act when under a duty to do so.

This chapter focuses principally on the last issue, because this is most closely linked with the remedies considered so far relating to judicial review. However, it is also important to appreciate that, following *Bergaderm* (case C–352/98) (discussed below), the administrative or legislative nature of the act complained about is no longer crucial (paras 46–47).

13.6 Liability for wrongful acts having legal effect

13.6.1 Action taken under the EC Treaty

It is perhaps self-evident that liability cannot arise from action taken under primary legislation, that is, pursuant to the EC treaties themselves. This was confirmed in *Édouard Dubois et Fils SA* v *Council* (case T–113/96). Here the applicant, a customs agent, was seeking damages for losses arising from the completion of the single internal market. Following its completion on 1 January 1993 his business suffered 'an almost total and definitive cessation of its activities as a customs agent', resulting in material damage. He claimed compensation on the basis of strict liability or, alternatively, fault. The CFI held that the agreement to complete the single internal market contained in the SEA, as an agreement between Member States, could not give rise to non-contractual liability on the part of the Community. Articles 235 and 288(2), being also primary Community law, cannot be brought to bear on instruments of an equivalent level where this is not expressly provided for. It was thus unnecessary to answer the question concerning strict liability.

13.6.2 Relationship with judicial review

As regards liability in respect of executive acts, there is some indication in the EC Treaty that damages may be recoverable as a result of unlawful action or a wrongful failure to act on the part of the EC institutions. Article 233(2) (ex 176(2)) provides that the obligation to remedy a failure to act 'shall not affect any obligation which may result from the application of the second paragraph of Article 288'. From this it may be deduced, applying the 'unity' principle (see Chapters 11 and 12), that liability in damages for unlawful legislative acts exists and that liability under Article 288(2) exists as a *separate* remedy from the remedies under Articles 230 and 232 for judicial review.

This was the view taken in *Alfons Lütticke GmbH* v *Commission* (case 4/69). In this case, Lütticke, having failed to establish the Commission's failure to act under Article 232 (see Chapter 12), sought damages from the Commission in a separate action under Article 288(2). The action was held admissible. The Court said that the action for damages provided for under Articles 235 and 288(2) was established as *an independent form of action with a particular purpose to fulfil*. It would be contrary to the independent nature of this action, as well as to the efficacy of the general system of forms of action created by the Treaty, to regard as a ground of inadmissibility the fact that, in certain circumstances, an action for damages might lead to a result similar to that of an action for failure to act under Article 232. Although *Lütticke* failed on the merits (there being no wrongful failure), an important principle was established.

Similarly, *Aktien-Zuckerfabrik Schöppenstedt* v *Council* (case 5/71), the Court held that the claimant company could sue the Council for damages on the basis of an allegedly illegal regulation even though as a 'natural or legal person' they would have no *locus standi* to seek its annulment under Article 230. In *Krohn & Co. Import-Export GmbH & Co. KG* v *Commission* (case 175/84), the Court held that since an action for non-contractual liability was an autonomous form of action, the expiry of the time-limit for challenge under Article 230 did not render an action for damages inadmissible.

The principle expressed initially in *Lütticke* (case 4/69) that action for non-contractual liability is an independent form of action now seems firmly established, and it will not be necessary in a claim for damages based on an illegal act (or failure to act) to bring a prior action for annulment or failure to act, nor even to establish *locus standi* to bring such action.

13.7 Establishing an unlawful act

The problem with an action for non-contractual liability lies not in establishing admissibility but in succeeding on the merits of the case. Originally, the ECJ adopted a very restrictive approach towards Community liability in tort, particularly towards liability resulting from the adoption of wrongful acts (or the wrongful failure to adopt an act). Indeed, there are strong policy reasons for limiting the non-contractual liability of public authorities. These bodies are charged by law to take decisions in the general interest over a wide range of activities. These decisions often involve the exercise of discretion and affect a substantial section of the public. Sometimes the decisions are unlawful. Whilst it is right that such decisions be subject to judicial review, it may be argued that to expose public bodies to liability in damages for unlawful acts in the absence of bad faith or an improper motive or (*quaere*) 'gross' negligence would unduly hamper the administrative process and impose an excessive burden on the public purse, *a fortiori* in a community as large as the EC.

Thus, it is not sufficient for Community liability to arise that the measure in question is unlawful, nor that the institution has unlawfully failed to act. For some time, the test to establish whether there was an unlawful act was the so-called 'Schöppenstedt' formula (from *Aktien-Zuckerfabrik Schöppenstedt* v *Council* (case 5/71)): where the action concerns a legislative measure which involves choices of economic policy the Community incurs no liability unless a sufficiently serious breach of a superior rule of law for the protection of the individual has occurred. A significant body of case law has built up under this formula. However, there had been concern that the approach to Community liability under Article 288 and the development of State liability (see Chapter 8) ought to be following the same principles. This nettle was grasped in *Brasserie du Pêcheur and Factortame* (joined cases C–46/93 and C–46/93; see Chapter 8), where the Court, in the context of a State liability case, stated that the basis of liability under Article 288 and under the State liability principle should be the same, because the protection of individuals' rights cannot vary depending on whether a national authority or a Community authority is responsible for the act or omission which is the subject of complaint. This was firmly established in *Laboratoires Pharmaceutiques Bergaderm SA and Goupil* v *Commission* (case C–352/98 P), a case decided under Article 288.

Before we set out the current position, it will be helpful to examine the approach adopted in this area prior to *Bergaderm*. As was noted above, the *Schöppenstedt* formula contains three essential elements. It requires a legislative measure involving choices of economic policy, a breach of a superior rule of law for the protection of individuals and that the breach is 'sufficiently serious'. These will now be examined in turn.

13.7.1 Development of the *Schöppenstedt* formula: a brief overview

13.7.1.1 *A legislative measure involving choices of economic policy*

Although the term 'legislative act' relates primarily to regulations, it will apply to any binding act which purports to lay down general rules. In *Gibraltar* v *Council* (case C–298/89) the Court suggested, albeit in the context of proceedings under Article 230, that directives 'normally' constitute 'a form of indirect regulatory or legislative measure'. It was accepted in *Odigitria AAE* v *Council* (case T–572/93) that an international agreement dealing with fishing rights would be a legislative act involving economic policy because of its impact on the Community's fisheries policy. The majority of legislative measures will involve choices of economic policy, since the institutions enjoy wide discretionary powers in all areas of activity, and it is possible to construe many measures even of a social nature as economic in the context of the EC Treaty.

Following the ECJ's judgment in *Laboratoires Pharmaceutiques Bergaderm SA and Goupil* v *Commission* (case C–352/98P) (discussed below), it is no longer crucial whether the measure is legislative or individual. Now, the important consideration for determining whether there was a wrongful act giving rise to liability is whether the institution concerned was involved in the exercise of any form of discretion.

13.7.1.2 *A breach of a superior rule of law for the protection of individuals*

Any general principle, such as equality or proportionality, accepted as part of Community law (see Chapter 6) would constitute a superior law for the protection of individuals. Thus, a breach of the principle of legitimate expectations was argued successfully in a claim for damages in *Sofrimport SARL* v *Commission* (case C–152/88, see Chapter 11). Most general principles of *Community* law (e.g., freedom of movement for workers; non-discrimination between producers and consumers (Article 34(2)), agriculture) whether expressed in the EC Treaty or in secondary legislation could likewise form the basis of a claim for damages. In *Firma E. Kampffmeyer* v *Commission* (cases 5, 7 & 13–24/66) a provision in an EC regulation directed at ensuring 'appropriate support for agricultural markets' was construed as intending to benefit, *inter alia*, the interests of individual undertakings such as importers. The claimants, as importers, were thus entitled to claim damages as a result of the Commission's action in breach of these provisions. It seems therefore that as long as the rule of law can be construed as designed in part to benefit a particular class of people it may be deemed to be 'for the protection of individuals'.

The original formulation of the test in *Schöppenstedt* refers to a 'superior rule of law', but the word 'superior' was dropped in more recent cases, referring to general principles such as proportionality simply as a 'rule of law' (see, e.g., *Etablissements Biret* v *Council* (case T–210/00), para. 53). Following *Bergaderm*, the focus is now on a rule intended to confer rights on individuals, in parallel with the rules on State liability.

13.7.1.3 *The breach must be 'sufficiently serious'*

Even under the old formula, a breach of a superior rule of law, including a fundamental rule such as the principle of equality, was not in itself sufficient to give rise to a claim in damages. The claimant must prove that the breach is 'sufficiently serious'. This principle has been very narrowly construed. In *Bayerische HNL Vermehrungsbetriebe GmbH & Co. KG* v *Council* (cases 83 & 94/76, 4 15 & 40/77), the Court suggested that in a legislative field in which one of the chief features is the exercise of a wide discretion, the Community does not incur liability unless the institution concerned has *manifestly and gravely disregarded the limits on the exercise of its power.*

When interpreting this requirement, the Court adopted two broad approaches. In one line of cases, the Court looks at the *effect* of the measure on the applicant, at the nature and extent of the harm to his interests. Thus, in *HNL* v *Council* an action had been brought by a number of animal feed producers for damages for loss suffered as a result of an EC regulation requiring animal feed producers to purchase skimmed milk powder instead of the cheaper and equally effective soya, as a means of disposing of surplus stocks of milk. This regulation had been found by the Court in a prior preliminary ruling proceeding (*Bela-Mühle Josef Bergmann KG* v *Grows-Farm GmbH & Co. KG* (case 114/76); *Granaria BV* v *Hoofdproduktschap voor Akkerbouwprodukten (No. 1)* (case 116/76)) to be in breach of the principles of non-discrimination and proportionality. In deciding whether the breach was sufficiently serious, i.e., whether the Commission had manifestly and gravely disregarded the limits on the exercise of its powers, the Court looked at the effect of the breach. It had affected a wide group of persons (all buyers of protein for the production of animal feed); the difference in price between the skimmed milk and soya had only a limited effect on production costs, insignificant beside other factors such as world prices; and the effect of the regulation on their profits did not exceed the normal level of risk inherent in such activities. The breach was not sufficiently serious (cf. *P. Dumortier Frères SA* v *Council* (cases 64 & 113/76, 167 & 239/78, 27, 28 & 45/79), where the claimants were a small, clearly defined group, and their loss went beyond the risks normally inherent in their business). In *Sofrimport SARL* v *Commission* (case C–152/88), it was suggested that not only must the group affected be small and clearly defined but it must also be closed. In this case, in deciding that the applicant importers were entitled to damages the Court pointed out that undertakings such as the claimants, with goods in transit at the time when the regulations were made, constituted a 'restricted group *which could not be extended* after the contested measures took effect'.

In other instances the court looks at the nature of the breach; in what way, and to what extent, is the institution *culpable*? It seems from the case law that both enquiries are relevant. The breach must be both serious as regards its effect on the applicant *and* inexcusable. Thus, in the 'Isoglucose' cases (*Koninklijke Scholten-Honig NV v Council* (case 143/77); *G.R. Amylum NV v Council* (cases 116 & 124/77)), the claimant glucose producers were seeking damages for losses suffered as a result of a Community regulation which imposed levies on the production of glucose in order to increase consumption of Community sugar. Clearly glucose and sugar were to some extent in competition for a market. The regulation had been found invalid, in breach of the principle of equality, in a prior preliminary ruling reference in *Royal Scholten-Honig (Holdings) Ltd v Intervention Board for Agricultural Produce* (cases 103 & 145/77) (see Chapter 9). The claimants were a small and closed group, and the damage which they suffered as a result of the regulation was described as 'catastrophic'. One firm, the Dutch firm Koninklijke Scholten-Honig NV had been forced into liquidation. Yet they failed to obtain damages. Although the treatment of the glucose producers as compared with that of the sugar producers was 'manifestly unequal', the Court held that the defendants' errors were not of such gravity that their conduct could be regarded as 'verging on the arbitrary'.

The approach that had, therefore, been adopted in a claim for damages resulting from a wrongful act in a field in which the Community institutions exercise a wide discretion, was that it had to be shown that:

(a) the measure has adversely affected a (*quaere* small and) clearly defined group,

(b) its effect goes beyond the normal level of risk inherent in the claimant's business, i.e., is unforeseeable, and

(c) the institution's breach was a serious one, and

(d) was *without justification*.

Whether a particular risk is regarded as foreseeable will be determined according to the standard of the prudent and discriminating trader (see, e.g., *EFISOL SA v Commission* (case T–336/94)).

13.7.2 The modern approach: *Bergaderm* and beyond

In view of the stringent nature of the *Schöppenstedt* formula it is not surprising that very few claimants succeed. The Court had justified its strict approach on the basis of its 'concern to ensure that the legislative function is not hindered by the prospect of actions for damages whenever the general interest requires the institutions . . . to adopt measures which may adversely affect individual interests' (*R v HM Treasury, ex parte BT* (case C–392/93), para. 40). In its anxiety to protect the EC institutions it has applied the restrictive *Schöppenstedt* test in a seemingly indiscriminate manner to claims arising from actions which do not involve legislative choices. For this it has been rightly criticised. As Advocate-General Tesauro pointed out in *Brasserie du Pêcheur* (cases C–46 & 48/93) on the date on which the opinion was approved (26 November 1995), only eight awards of damages against Community institutions had been made. Although there have been a number of successful cases since then, these have tended to arise in the context of administrative failures rather than in circumstances involving economic policy (e.g., *New Europe*

Consulting and Brown v *Commission* (case T–231/97) and *Embassy Limousines* v *European Parliament* (case T–203/96)).

The emergence of the principle of State liability served to highlight the limitations of Article 288(2) and pointed to the need for a broader and more flexible test for liability capable of taking into account the different types of breach and the different situations of EC institutions and Member States.

In relation to State liability, this was provided in *Brasserie du Pêcheur*. Here the Court confirmed the concept of the 'sufficiently serious' breach as the basis for liability, but introduced, in para. 56, a wide range of criteria by which the question of whether the breach was sufficiently serious might be judged. These included 'the clarity and precision of the EC rule breached, the measure of discretion left by that rule to the national or Community authorities, whether the infringement and the damage caused was intentional or voluntary, whether [the] error of law was excusable or inexcusable' (see further Chapter 8). Subsequently, this test has been applied to all breaches of Community law, whether by EC institutions or by Member States. It enabled the Court to decide, in a whole variety of circumstances, whether a breach of Community law, whether committed by an EC institution or by a Member State, was sufficiently serious to attract liability. The ECJ clearly intended this approach to be used in all these circumstances, although it was not until *Bergaderm* that the application to Community liability was confirmed.

The action in *Laboratoires Pharmaceutiques Bergaderm SA and Goupil* v *Commission* (case C–352/98 P) arose out of an amendment to Directive 76/768/EEC ([1976] OJ L262, p. 169) to limit the level of psolaren molecules in sun oils. Bergaderm was no longer able to sell its sun oil and the company was put into liquidation. It brought an action under Article 288(2) EC, claiming that the Commission had committed various wrongful acts (procedural errors, breach of the principle of proportionality and misuse of powers) during the adoption of the Adaptation Directive (which amended Directive 76/768/EEC), which had caused significant financial damages to Bergaderm. The claim was rejected by the CFI (*Laboratoires Pharmaceutiques Bergaderm SA and Goupil* v *Commission* (case T–199/96)). On appeal, the ECJ brought Article 288 and State liability full circle. Having considered the test for State liability in *Brasserie du Pêcheur* (see Chapter 8), the Court held that there would be liability under Article 288 where a rule of law intended to confer rights on individuals had been infringed; the breach had to be sufficiently serious, and there had to be a direct causal link between the breach and the damage caused. With regard to establishing whether a breach was 'sufficiently serious', the Court said that:

> as regards both Community liability under [Article 288] of the Treaty and Member State liability for breaches of Community law, the decisive test for finding that a breach of Community law is sufficiently serious is whether the Member State or the Community institution concerned manifestly and gravely disregarded the limits on its discretion (C–352/98P, para. 43).

This meant that the crucial factor in establishing whether there had been an unlawful act was the degree of discretion available to the institution concerned. The Court also noted that where there is no exercise of discretion, the *Hedley Lomas* (case C–5/94) principle developed in the context of Member State breaches of Community law (see Chapter 8) applies, according to which, if there is considerably reduced, or no, discretion, the mere infringement of Community law may be a sufficiently serious breach.

The new approach, in the wake of *Bergaderm*, therefore marks a departure from *Schöppenstedt* in three main aspects: first, it is no longer necessary to consider whether the rule infringed was a 'superior rule of law'; instead, the rule infringed has to be one intended to confer rights on individuals. Secondly, in establishing whether a breach is sufficiently serious, the criteria listed in para. 56 of *Brasserie de Pêcheur* are now applied, rather than the cases on the effects of the breach and harm to the claimant. Finally, the focus has also shifted away from the question of whether the act complained about was administrative or legislative; instead, what matters now is the degree of discretion for the Community institution.

Although the vast majority of cases involving Article 288 decided after *Bergaderm* have followed this new approach (e.g., *Beamglow Ltd* v *Parliament, Council and Commission* (case T–383/00) *Medici Grimm KG* v *Council* (case T–364/03)), there are some decisions which have been decided squarely on the basis of *Schöppenstedt*. Thus, in *CEVA* v *Commission* (T–344/00), an instance of Commission inaction under Regulation 1308/99, the CFI regarded this as a breach of the principle of sound administration (a higher-ranking rule of law), and imposed liability on that basis. In *Commission* v *Fresh Marine* (case C–472/00), the claimant's case that there had been a breach referred to *Schöppenstedt*, but the ECJ considered the claim purely on the basis of *Bergaderm* (see also, e.g., *Comafrica and Dole Fresh Fruit* v *Commission* (joined cases T–230/97, T–171, 174 & 198/95 and T–225/99)).

13.7.3 Individual acts

It should be noted that the *Bergaderm* approach, as did the '*Schöppenstedt*' formula, does not apply to individual acts which do not involve the exercise of discretion. Since such acts affect only their addressees they do not raise the same floodgate problems, thus it is not necessary to subject them to such stringent criteria. The Court is not always mindful of this point (see Advocate-General Tesauro's criticism of the Court's application of Article 288(2) in *Brasserie du Pêcheur* (cases C–46 & 48/90)). Where an individual act is prima facie unlawful and threatens to cause damage to its addressee, it may be challenged under Article 230. Where he fails to challenge the measure in time he may still bring an independent action under Article 288(2) where damage has occurred as a result of its application (*Krohn* (case 175/84)). To succeed, however, it may not be enough to establish the illegality of the measure. Although there is little authority on this point it is thought that fault must be proved, although what may be deemed to constitute fault in this context remains unclear. In *Grifoni* v *Euratom* (case C–308/87), for example, a failure to provide a guard rail despite clear guidelines requiring their provision provided the basis for community liability.

13.8 Damage

Once it has been established that there was an unlawful act, it is necessary to consider if damage has been caused. This requirement will be considered in this section.

13.8.1 Only specific losses are recoverable

The ECJ (and now the CFI) is as restrictive in its approach to damages as it is to fault. Clearly the Court will award compensation for damage to person or property provided the damage is sufficiently direct. Although it will in principle award damages for economic loss, such losses must be specific, not speculative. Only actual, certain and concrete damages are recoverable (*Société Roquette Frères* v *Commission* (case 26/74). Thus in *Firma E. Kampffmeyer* v *Commission* (cases 5, 7 & 13–24/66) the Court was prepared to award damages for lost profits on contracts which had already been concluded, which applicants had had to cancel as a result of the illegal decision, although these damages were reduced to only 10 per cent of the profits they might have expected to make, on account of the risks involved in the transactions in question. Applicants who had not concluded contracts prior to applying for import permits were awarded no damages at all. In *CNTA SA* v *Commission* (case 74/74) the Court found that the Commission had breached the principle of legitimate expectations when it introduced a regulation, suddenly and without warning, which deprived the claimant of export refunds at a particular rate, fixed in advance. Although the regulation was not in itself invalid, the Commission's mode of introduction of the measure was wrongful. Thus the Commission was liable in principle. However, although CNTA had entered into export contracts on the basis of its legitimate expectations, the Court held that it was only entitled to recover for losses actually suffered, not anticipated profits, and, since currency fluctuations at the time of import had resulted in its suffering no loss on the refunds themselves, it recovered no damages (see also *Firma Gebrüder Dietz* v *Commission* (case 126/76)).

In *CEVA* v *Commission* (T–344/00), the CFI decided to rule that the Community was liable in damages even though it was not, at the time of judgment, possible to quantify the loss suffered by the applicant.

13.8.2 Loss and third parties

Where the loss has been passed on to third parties, or could have been passed on in higher prices, no damages will be recoverable (*Interquell Stärke-Chemie GmbH & Co. KG* v *Council* (cases 261 & 262/78), 'quellmehl' case). In *P. Dumortier Frères SA* v *Council* (cases 64 & 113/76, 167 & 239/78, 27, 28 & 45/79) the claimants satisfied the Court that the losses could not have been passed on without risk of losing valuable markets. An injured party is expected to show reasonable diligence in limiting the extent of his loss; otherwise he must bear the damage himself (*Mulder* (case C–104/89)). In *Antillean Rice Mills NV* v *Commission* (cases T–480 & 483/93), the CFI suggested that since the damage to the applicants was foreseeable they could have taken precautions against it. Since they did not, 'neither the fault nor the damage alleged by the applicants are such as to cause the Community to incur non-contractual liability'.

In *Dorsch Consult* (case T–184/95), the CFI held that the applicant had not shown actual and certain damage. The case concerned a contract for the provision of services in Iraq. The applicants had not been paid for the work done when the UN Security Council imposed a trade embargo on Iraq, which the European Community implemented within the EC. As a response to this, the Iraqi Government froze all property, assets and income from them held at the material time by the governments, undertakings, companies and banks of those States which had adopted 'arbitrary decisions' against Iraq. The applicants claimed that the Community was liable for the damage it had suffered from not being able to obtain payment from Iraq. The CFI pointed out that the applicants had not tried to press for payment, even when the relevant Iraqi law was repealed.

13.8.3 Loss of a chance

In *Farrugia* (case T–230/94) the CFI considered a claim for compensation for the loss of a chance. The applicant claimed that an error on the part of the Commission concerning his nationality had deprived him of the opportunity of a fellowship in the field of research and technological development in the UK. The CFI found that although the Commission had made a mistake the applicant had failed to prove that, in the absence of that mistake, he would have had a 'strong chance' of being awarded the fellowship he sought. This implies that the Court would consider a claim for loss of a chance of success provided that the chance was proved to be sufficiently strong. The Court did not indicate what standard of proof would be necessary to establish a 'strong chance' of success.

13.8.4 Payment of damages in national currency

Damages are payable in the applicant's national currency at the exchange rate applicable on the date of the judgment under Article 288(2). Interest on that sum is payable from the date of judgment (*Dumortier*).

13.9 Causation

The Court is similarly restrictive in its approach to matters of causation. In *Dumortier* it said that the principles common to the laws of Member States cannot be relied on to deduce an obligation to make good every harmful consequence, even a remote one, of unlawful legislation. The damage must be a *sufficiently direct* consequence of the unlawful conduct of the institution concerned.

Thus in *Dumortier* the parties were entitled to recover the refunds which had been unlawfully withheld as a result of the invalid regulation, but not for further alleged losses in the form of reduced sales or for general financial difficulties resulting in the closing of some factories. Even though these difficulties might have been exacerbated by the illegal regulation they were not a sufficiently direct consequence of the unlawful act to render the Community liable (see also *Blackspur DIY Ltd* v *Council* (case T–168/94)). Other factors such as obsolescence and financial stringency were responsible. Similarly, where a party engages in activities designed to replace activities denied or restricted as a result of Community law any operating losses incurred as a result of these activities will be deemed too remote, and not attributed to the Community (*Mulder* (cases C–104/89, C 37/90)).

Elliniki Viomichania Oplon AE (EVO) v *Council and Commission* (case T–220/96), concerned the trade embargo imposed on Iraq following its invasion of Kuwait. The Community had adopted Regulation 2340/90 ([1990] OJ L213, p. 1) to implement the embargo. EVO had supplied ammunition to Iraq, but Iraq failed to pay sums due. It claimed that it could not pay because of two United Nations resolutions which also imposed an embargo on the country. EVO brought an action under Article 288 EC to recover the payment due from Iraq by way of a damages claim against the Community. The CFI rejected the claim both because Iraq had not refused payment because of Regulation 2340/90 but because of the UN resolutions and because the regulation itself did not apply to the particular contracts for which EVO was still owed payment. There was no causal link between the loss suffered and the Community act complained about (see 13.8.2 above and 13.9.2 below for a further claim based on the Iraq embargo in *Dorsch Consult*).

13.9.1 Break in the chain of causation

The ECJ (and now the CFI) has taken the view that the acts of the applicants, and sometimes even their failure to act, will break the chain of causation. Traders are expected to act as prudent business people. For example, in a claim based on misleading information the required causal link will be established only if the information would have caused an error in the mind of a reasonable person (*Compagnie Continentale France* v *Council* (case 169/73); see also *SA Oleifici Mediterranei* v *EEC* (case 26/81) and *Antillean Rice Mills NV* v *Commission* (cases T–480 & 483/93)). In *EFISOL SA* v *Commission* (case T–336/94) the CFI suggested that a legitimate expectation (as to a certain state of affairs) could not arise from conduct on the part of the (Community) administration which was inconsistent with Community rules. Thus it seems that the prudent trader is expected to know if a Community institution misapplies Community rules!

In *International Procurement Services SA* v *Commission* (case T–175/94) the applicant tenderer suffered loss in a contract with the Mozambique Government. Following advice from the Commission the government reduced the payment originally agreed for the supply of steel billets by the applicant. Although the Commission was found to have indirectly influenced the Mozambique government's decision to pay the lower price, the applicant's damage was held by the CFI to derive from two factors: the Mozambique government's refusal to pay the originally agreed price, and the applicant's failure to challenge that refusal in arbitration proceedings, as it was entitled to do. The fact that IPS had taken that course of action because it was 'in urgent need of liquid funds' would not have the effect of attaching responsibility for the damage to the defendants.

13.9.2 Loss must be foreseeable

Where other factors can be seen as contributing to the claimant's loss the damage is normally seen as too remote. The CFI considered the nature of the causal link in *Dorsch Consult* (case T–184/95). There, it commented that the applicant had not succeeded in showing that the adoption by the Iraqi Government of a law freezing the applicants' assets in retaliation for the trade embargo imposed on Iraq was 'an objectively foreseeable consequence, in the normal course of events, of the adoption' of that Community's regulation implementing the embargo. A requirement of foreseeability seems to have been introduced as a precondition to the finding of a causal link.

13.9.3 **Contributory negligence**

The Court does not as a general rule attempt to apportion blame on the basis of contributory negligence. It appears that apportionment is reserved for claims of particular merit. In *Adams* v *Commission (No. 1)* (case 145/83) Adams's damages for the Commission's breach of confidence, which had caused him irreparable financial and emotional damage, were reduced by 50 per cent to take into account Adams's contribution in failing to protect his own interests (see Chapter 29). Similarly, in *Grifoni* v *Euratom* (case C–308/87), although Euratom was clearly at fault in not providing guard rails, equally Grifoni, an experienced contractor, should have known that he had to take some precautions himself. His damages were reduced, also by 50 per cent.

13.10 **Impact of other possible causes of action**

Where the Court rejects a claim for damages, as in the isoglucose cases, it often points out that applicants are not without a remedy. The action must be assessed having regard to the whole system of legal protection of individuals set up by the Treaty. Where a person suffers, or is likely to suffer, damage as a result of an unlawful act he may challenge that measure before his national courts and seek a ruling under Article 234 on its validity. The Court has said that the existence of such an action is by itself of such a nature as to ensure the effective protection of the individuals concerned. Not all would agree with this view. There may be no issue of national law in which to raise questions of EC law. As is borne out in *Koninklijke Scholten-Honig NV* v *Council* (case 143/77), heavy, even irreparable losses may be incurred while proceedings before the national courts are pending. An action before a national court may be successful in obtaining interim relief (see, e.g., *Zuckerfabrik Süderdithmarschen AG* v *Hauptzollamt Itzehoe* (cases C–143/88 & 92/89); *Antonissen* v *Council* (case C–393/96 P/R), noted in Chapter 7), or, in time, a declaration of invalidity: but where damage has occurred a national court cannot award compensation for wrongs attributable to the Community (see *Krohn* (case 175/84), discussed below).

Surely the most appropriate forum in which to challenge Community action (or inaction) would be before the European Courts under Article 230 EC (or Article 232 EC), alongside, or prior to, a claim for damages under Article 228(2). Yet, as has been seen in Chapter 11, the individual has no *locus standi* to challenge or demand genuine legislative measures under these articles. Since the European courts are understandably reluctant to expose the Community to unlimited claims, and, where the exercise of discretion by a Community institution is concerned, to fetter that discretion by the prospect of such exposure, arguably the most effective protection for applicants would be speedy interim relief from the European courts to forestall the application of unlawful measures and prevent damage occurring. Although this may be obtained in an action under Article 288(2) (see *Kampffmeyer* (cases 56–60/74), considered at 13.11), it would seem more logical, in the absence of damage, to proceed under Article 230. Where damage is suffered as a result of lawful action on the part of the Community, perhaps the courts could be persuaded, in exceptional cases, to accept some form of strict liability on the principle of *'égalité devant les charges publiques'*. It cannot be right that a few should bear a disproportionate burden as a result of measures enacted in the interest of the many.

13.11 Relationship between Article 288(2) and other remedies

If a claim for damages for non-contractual liability, particularly a claim based on an unlawful legislative act, is unlikely to succeed for the many reasons outlined above, its value in the overall scheme of remedies available against the Community should not be underrated. Since an action under Article 288(2) is an independent form of action (*Lütticke* (case 4/69); *Schöppenstedt* (case 5/71); *Krohn* (case 175/84)), an action for damages based on invalidity or wrongful failure may be effective in obtaining a declaration of invalidity or failure to act notwithstanding that the applicant has no *locus standi*, either personal or temporal, to challenge that same act (or inaction) in proceedings under Article 230 or Article 232. Moreover, the Court has held (*Kurt Kampffmeyer Mühlenvereinigung KG v Council* (cases 56–60/74)) that where the damage to the claimant is imminent, or likely with a high degree of certainty to occur, the claimant may bring proceedings under Article 288(2)) *before* the damage has occurred. Although he may not be found entitled in principle to damages, he may obtain a declaration of invalidity or unlawful failure to act, including interim relief, in time to prevent the damage occurring.

It is submitted that the Court will admit such actions under Article 288(2) only where a claim for damages is genuine; it will not allow this provision to be used solely as a means of evading the *locus standi* limitations of Articles 230 and 232 (see *Krohn* (case 175/84) and *Cobrecaf SA v Commission* (case T–514/93)).

13.12 Concurrent liability

As Community law is to a large extent implemented by national authorities, there may be cases in which it is unclear whether the cause of action, for example, for the return of money paid under an invalid regulation, or for a wrongful failure on the part of a national body to pay a subsidy to which the applicant feels he is entitled, lies against the national authority, in national courts, according to national law, or against a Community institution, before the CFI, or against both. Motivated no doubt by a desire to reduce its work-load and/or its potential liability, the Court, as illustrated by *Koninklijke Scholten-Honig NV* (case 143/77) (and countless other cases), prefers to direct applicants to seek a remedy before their national courts, leaving questions of validity to be referred to the ECJ, if necessary, under Article 234.

Largely as a result, it is submitted, of this preference, the case law on what might loosely be termed concurrent liability is both confusing and contradictory.

Initially, in cases such as *Firma E. Kampffmeyer* v *Commission* (cases 5, 7 & 13–24/66) and *R. & V. Haegeman Sprl* v *Commission* (case 96/71), the ECJ espoused a doctrine of 'exhaustion of national law remedies'. In *Kampffmeyer* the applicant grain dealers were seeking, before the ECJ:

(a) the return of levies paid to the German authorities, and

(b) compensation for contracts cancelled

as a result of an invalid EC regulation. They had already begun parallel proceedings before the German courts, but those proceedings had been stayed pending the outcome of the Community proceedings. The ECJ held that the German court should first be given the opportunity to decide whether the German authorities were liable. The proceedings were stayed accordingly.

In *Haegeman* the applicant was seeking the annulment of a Commission decision refusing to return levies paid to the German authorities by the applicant as a result of an allegedly invalid regulation. This time, unlike *Kampffmeyer*, the levies had been paid into Community funds, and Haegeman had not instituted parallel proceedings before its national courts. Again the Court refused to admit the action. Haegeman's claim should have been made against the national authorities to whom the refunds were originally paid.

There followed a series of cases in which claims before the ECJ were made

(a) for the return of *sums unlawfully levied* (e.g., *Société Roquette Frères* v *Commission* (case 26/74)), and

(b) seeking payment of *sums unlawfully withheld* (*IBC* v *Commission* (case 46/75); *Lesieur Costelle et Associés SA* v *Commission* (cases 67–85/75)).

These were held to be inadmissible on the grounds that the applicants should have brought their actions before their national courts.

On the other hand in *Compagnie d'Approvisionnement de Transport et de Crédit SA* v *Commission* (cases 9 & 11/71); *Merkur-Aussenhandels GmbH* v *Commission* (case 43/72); *Holtz & Willemsen GmbH* v *Council* (case 153/73); *CNTA SA* v *Commission* (case 74/74) the ECJ was prepared to admit claims seeking payment of *sums unlawfully withheld* without requiring claimants to proceed first before their national courts.

In *Firma Gebrüder Dietz* v *Commission* (case 126/76), and *CNTA* (case 74/74) the applicants were seeking damages for losses suffered as a result of the sudden introduction by the Commission of Monetary Compensatory Amounts in agriculture; they had not brought actions before their national courts. Their claims under Article 288(2) were held admissible.

In the second 'grits' and 'quellmehl' cases, and the 'isoglucose' cases, admitted under Article 288(2), proceedings had already been brought and the invalidity of the measures in question decided, before the applicants' national courts.

From the above cases the following tentative conclusions may be drawn:

(a) A claim for the return of sums unlawfully paid to the relevant national authorities should always be brought before a national court, even though those sums may have been paid into Community funds (*Kampffmeyer, Haegeman; Roquette*; see also more recently *Industrie-en Handelsonderneming Vreugdenhil BV* v *Commission* (case C–282/90)).

(b) A claim for sums unlawfully withheld, even when withheld by a national authority, may be brought *either* before national courts or the CFI. The weight of authority (*Compagnie d'Approvisionnement; Merkur; Holtz & Willemsen; CNTA*) leans towards this view. However, the existence of *IBC* and *Costelle* render it advisable to bring such a claim before a national court, *provided* that no further damages are required from the Community *and* payment of the sums involved was required to be channelled through the national authority.

(c) A claim for unliquidated damages for losses suffered as a result of illegal Community action (e.g., financial losses in *Dietz; CNTA; Dumortier*) can *only* be brought before the European Courts under Article 288(2). In this respect it is submitted that *Kampffmeyer* was wrong. Therefore, if these losses result from sums unlawfully withheld, the appropriate forum for recovery of *both* sums would be at the European level.

Further support for principles (b) and (c) above may also be derived from *Krohn & Co. Import-Export GmbH & Co. KG v Commission* (case 175/84). Krohn & Co. was seeking compensation for financial losses suffered as a result of its national (German) authority's refusal to grant it licences to import manioc from Thailand. In rejecting its application the authorities were acting on mandatory instructions from the Commission. Krohn brought an action before the German courts seeking an annulment of the national authority's decision and an injunction requiring it to issue the licences, and a parallel action before the ECJ for compensation for losses suffered as a result of its action in denying him the licences. The Commission argued that the action under Article 288(2) was inadmissible, since:

(a) the refusal of the licence came from the national authority;

(b) the applicant should have exhausted its remedies before its national court; and

(c) to admit liability would be equivalent to nullifying the Commission's decision, which the applicant had failed to challenge in time.

All three arguments were rejected by the Court. With regard to (a) the Court found that although the refusal emanated from the national authority the unlawful conduct was to be attributed not to the German authorities but to the Community itself. The Commission was the 'true author' of the decision.

With regard to (b) the Court held that while admissibility may be dependent on national rights available to obtain the annulment of a national authority's decision, that would only be the case where national rights of action provide an *effective means of protection* for the individual concerned and are capable of resulting in compensation for the damage alleged.

Clearly, since the alleged 'tort' had been committed by the Community, only the Community would be liable to pay compensation.

The Court's response to (c) has already been noted. An action under Article 288(2) was an autonomous form of action with a particular purpose to fulfil (*Lütticke* (case 4/69)).

Thus in deciding whether action should be brought before a national court or before the European Courts, the appropriate question is whether action before a national court can provide an *effective means of protection* for the claimant's interests. Where he merely seeks the return of money paid, or payment of money unlawfully withheld, or a declaration of invalidity or an injunction to prevent the application of the unlawful act, a *fortiori* when the wrongful act can be laid at the door of the national authorities (see *Société des Grands Moulins des Antilles* v *Commission* (case 99/74); *Krohn*, in which it was held that national courts retain sole jurisdiction to order compensation for damage caused by national institutions), he should proceed before his national courts. Where he seeks damage from the Community for injury suffered as a result of wrongful acts attributable to the Community, his action must be before the CFI (or ECJ). This is a right which cannot be 'exhausted' before a national court. Where remedies are required of both national authorities and the Community, it will be necessary to proceed against both. Clearly he cannot recover twice for the same loss.

13.13 Conclusions

In dealing with claims under Article 288, the European Courts have to balance the conflicting interests of permitting flexibility in decision-making and protecting individuals who may suffer as a result of such action. For a long time, the Court had taken a very restrictive approach to claims brought under Article 288, but it is questionable whether this approach was entirely justified. The alignment of Community liability and State liability through *Brasserie de Pêchuer* and *Bergaderm* has improved this position to an extent, but it remains difficult for individuals seeking damages against the Community to succeed with their claim. Following *Brasserie du Pêcheur*, claims for damages under Article 288(2) should now be approached in the same way as claims under the State liability principle. In situations where the defendant institution is acting pursuant to a wide discretion (which will often be the case in action taken under Article 288), the list of factors to be taken into account in establishing whether a breach is sufficiently serious set out in para. 56 of *Brasserie du Pêcheur* is now relevant. Moreover, it also appears that, following *Bergaderm*, it seems less relevant whether the measure complained of is of general or individual application. But although the applicant may succeed in establishing the existence of a sufficiently serious breach, he may still fail to establish that damage and causation. Although restrictive rules in relation to damage and causation may be justified to protect the Community against extensive liability to commercial undertakings for pure economic loss, it is questionable whether the rules as they currently are offer effective judicial protection for individuals. This has not changed to any significant extent in the wake of recent developments. Despite this somewhat tentative extension of the scope of Article 288, it remains of limited use.

FURTHER READING

Hartley, T.C., *The Foundations of European Community Law*, 5th ed. (OUP, 2003).

Hilson, C., 'The role of discretion in EC law on non-contractual liability' (2005) 42 *CML Rev* 677.

Kuijper, P.J. and Bronckers, M., 'WTO Law in the European Court of Justice' (2005) 42 CML Rev 1313–1355.

Schermers, H., Heukels, T., and Mead, P. (eds), *Non-contractual Liability of the European Communities* (Nijhoff Publications,1988).

Steiner, J., 'The Limits of State Liability for Breach of European Community Law' (1998) EPL 69.

Wils, W., 'Concurrent Liability of the Community and a Member State' (1992) 17 EL Rev 191.

PART III

PART III

14

Introduction to the common market

14.1 Introduction

The creation of the common market is one of the central purposes of the European Community. The specific activities to fulfil this task can be found in Article 3: Article 3(1)(a) refers to the prohibition of customs duties while Article 3(1)(b) refers to the Community's common commercial policy, as well as common policies in certain areas, such as agriculture, fisheries and transport. Article 3(1)(g) specifies that the Community shall introduce a system to ensure that 'competition in the internal market is not distorted', and Article 3(1)(h) provides for 'the approximation of laws of the Member States to the extent required for the functioning of the common market'.

Following the SEA, another term was introduced, that of an 'internal market'. Although often treated as synonymous with the 'common market', it is arguable that there is a difference in scope. Article 14 (ex 7a) describes the internal market as:

> an area without internal frontiers in which the free movement of goods, persons, services and capital is ensured in accordance with the provisions of the Treaty.

These are referred to together as the 'four freedoms'. The common market, in addition to the four freedoms, also deals with common commercial policy – commercial relations with third countries – and competition policy. On this basis, the term common market is slightly wider than internal market. The ECJ has, in practice, not tended to distinguish between the terms. It seems that should the Constitution come into force, the blurring of boundaries between the two concepts would continue: Article I–3 would identify the Union's objectives. Specifically, Article I–3(2) would state that the provision of 'an internal market where competition is free and undistorted' is one such objective. It would not refer to the common market (or single market) at all. Article I–4 would then go on to identify the free movement of goods, persons, services and capital as fundamental freedoms of the Union amongst other objectives of the Union (see also Article III–130). Nonetheless, the 'four freedoms' remain central. This chapter identifies certain common themes affecting those of the four freedoms treated in this book: subsequent chapters look at the detail of these provisions.

14.2 The four freedoms

14.2.1 Free movement of goods

The principle of freedom of movement of goods has been described as a fundamental freedom, the 'corner-stone' of the Community. For many Member States
the opportunity of access for their goods to a single, Community-wide market was,
and remains, a primary reason for membership. The free play of market forces
within that larger market would increase economic efficiency, widen consumer
choice, and enhance the Community's competitiveness in world markets. However, since the principle of freedom of movement was intended to apply to all
goods, including goods imported from outside the Community, it was necessary to
eliminate distortions of competition resulting from different national rules regulating trade with third countries by presenting a common commercial front to the
outside world. To achieve these goals the Treaty sought:

(a) to establish a *customs union* which shall involve (Article 23 (ex 9) EC):
   (i) 'the prohibition between Member States of customs duties on imports
       and exports and of all charges having equivalent effect', and
   (ii) 'the adoption of a common customs tariff in their relations with third
        countries'.
(b) the elimination of quantitative restrictions on imports and exports and all
    measures having equivalent effect (Articles 28 and 29 (ex 30 and 34) EC).
(c) in addition States were required to adjust any State monopolies of a
    commercial character so as to ensure that . . . no discrimination regarding the
    conditions under which goods are procured and marketed exists between
    nationals of Member States (Article 31 (ex 37) EC).

The provisions relating to the free movement of goods apply to both industrial
and agricultural products (save, where agriculture is concerned, as otherwise provided in Articles 33–38 (ex 39–46) EC (Article 32(2) (ex 38(2)), whether originating
in Member States or coming from third countries which are in free circulation in
Member States, even where, in the latter case, the goods have been admitted to the
original State of import under special dispensation from the Commission under
Article 134 (ex 115) EC (*Levy* (case 212/88)). Products coming from third countries
are regarded as in free circulation in a Member State 'if the import formalities have
been complied with and any customs duties or charges having equivalent effect
which are payable have been levied in that Member State, and if they have
not benefited from a total or partial drawback of such duties or charges' (Article 24
(ex 10(1)) EC).

14.2.2 Free movement of people

The basic principles relating to the free movement of persons are contained in
Articles 39–42 (ex 48–51) EC (workers), and Articles 43–48 (ex 52–58) EC (freedom
of establishment). The freedom to provide services is often seen as providing for the
free movement of people although it is identified separately within the four free-

doms (see 14.2.3). These freedoms have been further substantiated by secondary legislation. Although the Euratom Treaty contains its own specific provisions for workers in the industries it covers, EC law relating to the free movement of persons will apply to those workers insofar as their position is not covered by that Treaty. The rules apply throughout the territories of the Member States of the Community.

The basic rights enshrined in these provisions, granted to EU nationals (defined according to the law of each Member State) and companies and firms formed in accordance with the law of one of the Member States (Article 48 (ex 58)), comprise the right freely to leave, or enter and reside in a Member State for the purposes of work or establishment (or the provision of services) and the right to be treated in the host Member State free from discrimination on the grounds of nationality. In *Tilmant* v *Groupement des ASSEDIC de la Région Parisienne* ([1991] 2 CMLR 317) the French Cour de Cassation held, no doubt correctly, that the principle of non-discrimination applied also to workers working outside the EU where the legal relationship of employer and employee is situated in the Community, whether by reason of the place where it is established or by reason of the place where it takes effect.

These basic Community rights are not absolute. Rights of entry and residence are subject to derogation on the grounds of public policy, public security and public health (Articles 39(3)) and 46; Directive 2004/38/EC). Exceptions from the non-discrimination principle are provided for 'employment in the public service' (Article 39(4)) and 'activities connected with the exercise of official authority' (Article 45).

Although the rights contained in the Treaty were originally expressed to be limited to those who are economically active, that is, workers or persons, natural or legal, exercising rights of establishment or providing services in the host State, broad definitions of the relevant terms, in particular the definition of worker, and generous interpretation on the part of the Court, have extended the scope of their protection. Furthermore, secondary legislation enacted in 1968 and 1970 extended these rights to the families of migrant workers. Unlike the worker, members of the family are not required to be nationals of a Member State to claim Community rights. Similar rights were extended to a wider category of persons, firstly by the enactment of three directives (90/364, 90/365, 90/366 (amended and re-enacted as Directive 93/96) [1990] OJ L180) granting rights of entry and residence to retired persons, to persons of independent means and to students (provided they are EU nationals) 'insofar as they do not enjoy these rights under other provisions of Community law' and then by provision for the introduction of citizenship rights under Articles 18 *et seq.* (ex 8a–e), introduced by the TEU. Most recently, these rights have been consolidated and updated by the introduction of another direct-ive, sometimes called the 'Citizenship Directive' (Directive 2004/38/EC). The rights under these provisions have been supported by an extensive interpretation by the ECJ. The Schengen Agreement signed in 1990 (see further below) already allowed for the free movement of EU citizens between its signatory States. Under the ToA all existing Schengen provisions were incorporated into the EC Treaty and apply to most Member States (see further Chapter 24). The Schengen provisions must be interpreted in the light of the protection granted to individuals under EC law, as laid down in a protocol annexed to the ToA (see further case C–503/03 *Commission* v *Spain*)).

These rights were supported by provisions for the enactment of 'flanking' measures to ensure more uniform standards of worker protection (then Articles 117–122, now replaced by Articles 136–145) and by the principle of equal pay for equal work for men and women (then Article 119 EEC, now 141 EC, discussed in Chapter 25), the principal purpose of which was to create a more level playing field within the single internal market. But these ancillary provisions and the ECJ's jurisprudence demonstrate that the Community was from the beginning also concerned with humanitarian goals. As Advocate-General Trabucci commented in *F* v *Belgium* (case 7/75), 'the migrant worker is to be regarded not as a mere source of labour but as a human being' (see also *Defrenne* v *Sabena (No. 2)* (case 43/75)).

This approach has been reinforced by successive Treaty amendments. The TEU (1992) notably extended Article 2 to pledge the Community to a 'high level of employment and of social protection, the raising of the standard of living and quality of life, and economic and social cohesion and solidarity among Member States'. Likewise, the introduction of European citizenship in the TEU (Part 2 of the EC Treaty) emphasised the move away from the notion of the individual as a purely economic actor. This process, emphasising the social aspect of the EU, would continue were the Constitution to come into force.

Citizenship rights, set out in Articles 18–21 EC, comprise the right 'to move and reside freely within the territory of the Member States', the right to stand and vote in municipal and European Parliament elections, and the right to petition the Ombudsman and the European Parliament. The introduction of the concept of citizenship raises questions as to what rights citizens should expect, and has fuelled the debate on whether the Community should do more to protect the individual citizen. This question, for example, was addressed by the Commission in *Modernising and Improving Social Protection in the EU* (COM (97) 102 of 13 March 1997). Despite the opportunity to amend the citizenship provisions that the ToA (1997) provided, nothing was done expressly to expand the rights attaching to citizenship, although it did introduce the so-called area of freedom, security and justice (Article 62(1) EC). More recently, as we have already noted, rights have been given an express form, not only in the Citizenship Directive, but also in the 'Family Reunion Directive' (Directive 2003/86/EC, [2003] OJ L251/12) and the Directive on Third Country Nationals who are Long-term Residents (Directive 2003/109/EC). Thus, when considering the provisions relating to the free movement of persons and to provisions on social policy in general, it is important to remember the dual imperatives, economic and social, affecting the development of these provisions and their interpretation.

14.2.3 Freedom to provide services

The freedom to provide services is found in Articles 49–55 EC. In this book the freedom to provide services is treated as part of the free movement of people. When someone provides a service, it may also involve that person moving, even if temporarily, to the Member State where the service is received. However, it should be noted that services themselves can move, without necessarily requiring that a person also moves to provide the service. Examples of this principle can be seen in sectors such as broadcasting, or insurance. Nonetheless, the same provisions of Article 49 EC *et seq.* apply in this context as apply in relation to the provision of services where a person moves, although it may be that a difference in the way the provisions are interpreted can be seen in the two types of circumstance. The fundamental right comprises the freedom to access both the territory and market of other Member States and to be treated on the same basis as the nationals of the host Member State.

14.2.4 Free movement of capital

The provisions on capital and payments, substantially amended by the TEU, are found in Articles 56–60 (ex 73b–73g). In its post-Maastricht form, the central provision bears a resemblance to the approach taken in relation to the free movement of goods. Recent case law suggests that the ECJ's approach has paralleled that taken in respect of the other three freedoms.

It should be noted that the Treaty distinguishes between payments and capital movements between Member States themselves and between Member States and third countries. In the latter situation the Council may, in limited circumstances, take measures limiting the movement of capital and payments from third countries (Article 57(2) (ex 73c(2)), Article 59 (ex 73f), and Article 60 (ex 73g)).

Article 58 (ex 73d) deals with tax, and permitted distinctions based on place of residence, as well as public policy exceptions to the free movement of capital. Despite these provisions, it will be seen in the chapter on establishment (Chapter 21) that Member States' freedom in the field of taxation has been curtailed. Article 58(2) provides that the provisions relating to capital are to operate without prejudice to the operation of restrictions on the freedom of establishment that are compatible with the Treaty. Effectively, this means that a person cannot seek to evade a legitimate restriction on establishment via the capital provisions. It seems, however, that the reverse might be true. The relationship between capital and the other provisions as discussed at 16.5.

Finally, Article 58(3) provides that any national measures taken on the basis of Article 58(1) are 'not to constitute a means of arbitrary discrimination or a disguised restriction on the free movement of capital'. This wording parallels that used in relation to the derogation from the free movement of goods found in Article 30 (see further Chapter 16).

14.3 Common themes in the free movement provisions

Although the terms of the freedoms are each worded slightly differently, certain common elements must be shown before a case for the application of one of the freedoms can be made. In all cases it seems that there must be both an economic element and an inter-state factor to bring the situation within the scope of any of the freedoms. It has also been argued that a convergence can be seen in the approach taken to identifying the trigger for the application of the freedoms.

14.3.1 Economic activity

In the earlier years of the Community, to invoke the non-discrimination principle it was necessary for the migrant claimant to be or have been engaged in some form of economic activity in the host State. In *Walrave* v *Association Union Cycliste Internationale* (case 36/74), in the context of a challenge to the cycling association's rules relating to 'pacemaker' cyclists, which were clearly discriminatory, it was held that the prohibition of discrimination on the grounds of nationality contained in former Article 7 EEC (currently Article 12 (ex 6) EC) does not apply to sports teams which have nothing to do with economic activity. The practice of sport is subject to Community law *only insofar as it constitutes an economic activity* within Article 2 of the Treaty (see further, e.g., *Deliege* (joined cases C–51/96 and C–191/97), discussed in Chapter 22). Just as the rights of free movement are only granted to workers and the self-employed and their families (albeit, as will be seen, very liberally interpreted), to invoke the principle of non-discrimination of Article 12 EC in this context, there must be some economic nexus.

This principle has been considerably eroded over the past three decades, as the European Economic Community has been transformed into the European Union. In *Gravier* v *City of Liège* (case 293/83) and *Cowan* v *French Treasury* (case 186/87) the Court held that students (*Gravier*) and tourists (*Cowan*), temporarily resident in a Member State as recipients of services, were entitled to invoke the then Article 7 EEC (now 12 EC) to claim equality of treatment for certain financial benefits available under national law only to nationals of the host State (see also *Commission* v *Spain* (case C–45/93)). Similarly the directives extending free movement rights to persons of independent means, to retired persons and to students, now consolidated into the Citizenship Directive, also appeared to dilute the need for an economic link. Persons claiming under these directives must be covered by medical insurance and must have sufficient financial resources to avoid becoming a burden on the Member State. This requirement suggests that such persons may not be able to claim publicly-funded welfare benefits on a basis of equality with nationals of the host State. Although European citizenship is not limited to the economically active, it is 'subject to the limitations and conditions laid down in this Treaty and by the measures adopted to give it effect' (Article 18(1) EC). Nonetheless, more recent decisions of the ECJ now suggest that Union citizens who are not economically active but who enjoy or acquire rights to enter and reside in another Member State may invoke the non-discrimination principle to claim rights currently accorded to that State's nationals or to migrant workers and their families, although the precise extent to which they may do so remains unclear (e.g., *Martinez Sala* v *Freistaat Bayern* (case C–85/96); *Trojani* v *Le Centre Public d'Aide Sociale de Bruxelles* (case C–456/02); *Collins* (case C–138/02); *Bidar* (case C–209/03)). Important questions regarding the scope of application of the non-discrimination principle remain to be resolved, either by secondary legislation or by the Court. On the Court's past record it is unlikely that it would tolerate discriminatory treatment of EU migrants and their families or deny *settled* immigrants the right of residence when their resources are exhausted (see, e.g., *Baumbast* (case C–413/99) and Chapter 24).

Although goods are not usually considered in this light, economic considerations can be seen in the definition attributed to them in the ECJ's jurisprudence. Though the terms are used interchangeably, 'goods' and 'products' are not defined in the Treaty. They were interpreted by the ECJ in *Commission* v *Italy (re Export Tax on Art Treasures)* (case 7/68) as anything capable of money valuation and of being the object of commercial transactions. It does not matter whether the individuals are moving goods as part of their business or in their private capacity, provided the items satisfy the definition of goods.

14.3.2 Internal situations

An individual who has never sought to exercise his or her right to freedom of movement will not be able to rely on EC law rights. The matter will be regarded as 'wholly internal' (see, e.g., *R* v *Saunders* (case 175/78); *Ministère Public* v *Gauchard* (case 20/87)). This principle, that EC law has no application to purely internal matters, can operate harshly. In *Morson* v *Netherlands* (cases 35 & 36/82), two mothers from Surinam wished to join their children in The Netherlands. Since they were not entitled to do so under Dutch law they sought to rely on EC law, which permits family members to join EC migrants. In this case the applicants were unsuccessful: since their children had never exercised their right to freedom of movement in the Community there was no factor connecting them with Community law. Equally in *Sloman* (cases C–72 & 73/91) the ECJ held that it was not contrary to Community law to discriminate against migrant workers from third countries (that is, countries outside the EU) in the absence of factors connecting them with Community law. Even in the context of citizenship, some transnational element must be identified (joined cases C–64 and 65/96, *Hecker* and *Jacquet*).

Once again, the impact of this rule has been limited. Once a connecting factor has been established, however, migrants will be able to rely on EC rights on returning to their own Member State (*R* v *Immigration Appeal Tribunal, ex parte Secretary of State for the Home Department* (case C–370/90) see further Chapter 20). Further, in more recent cases involving citizenship, no cross-border movement was involved. The Community link was shown by citizens of one Member State challenging the rules in another Member State (*Garcia Avello* (case C–148/02); *Chen* (case C–200/02)).

A similar approach is taken in relation to goods. Again the Court has limited the circumstances in which an internal situation will be found through the width of the test used to determine when there is an impact on trade. The famous test in *Dassonville* (case 8/74) refers to a measure 'directly or indirectly, actually or potentially' hindering trade being sufficient to trigger Article 28, suggesting that an actual inter-state element is not necessary in a particular case provided the possibility of such an effect can be shown. From the case law it seems possible that cases where a national trader selling or distributing national goods seeking to challenge a rule of the same Member State could fall within Article 28, as happened in *Pistre* (case C–321–324/94, discussed in Chapter 18). Similar approaches can be seen in relation to capital, services and establishment.

14.3.3 Discrimination or access to the market?

Because of the fundamental importance of the principle of free movement of goods the Treaty rules in this area have been strictly enforced, and exceptions, where provided, have been given the narrowest scope. In interpreting the rules the ECJ looks not to the name of a particular national measure, nor to the motive for its introduction, but to its *effect* in the light of the aims of the Treaty; does it create an obstacle to the free movement of goods within the single internal market?

Article 28 is not limited to circumstances in which a Member State has discriminated against imported goods. The provision, as seen by the ECJ, is far wider than that. Interpreted in this way, many national measures, not overtly or intentionally protectionist, designed to achieve the most worthy objectives, have been found to be capable of hindering trade between Member States, prima facie in breach of Community law. Such measures, as will be seen, have nevertheless been permitted by the Court on an *ad hoc* basis where they could be proved to be 'objectively justified' as necessary to safeguard vital interests ('mandatory requirements'), such as the protection of health, or the environment, or the consumer.

A move away from an interpretation based on the need to show discrimination, whether direct or indirect, to one that focuses on the removal of obstacles to free movement can be seen in the context of persons too. The basic right contained in Articles 39, 43 and 49 is that migrant workers should not be discriminated against on grounds of nationality. This is reinforced by Article 12 EC which provides that 'Within the scope of application of this Treaty, and without prejudice to any special provisions contained therein, any discrimination on grounds of nationality shall be prohibited'. This provision has been important in ensuring that the migrant individual and his family, once legally resident in the host Member State, receives parity of treatment with nationals of the host State in respect not only of employment rights but of social rights in general.

The prohibition of discrimination on the grounds of nationality applies to all forms of discrimination, both overt and covert. It will often take the form of a residence or length of residence requirement. In *Sotgiu v Deutsche Bundespost* (case 152/73) the claimant was an Italian national employed by the German post office in Germany. His family lived in Italy. Following the issue of a circular, post office workers separated from their families in Germany were to be paid an increased 'separation' allowance while workers who were living abroad at the time of recruitment would continue to be paid at the same rate. The rule was not overtly discriminatory, since it applied to all workers, regardless of nationality. But clearly its effects could fall more heavily on foreigners. The Court, on a reference from the Bundesarbeitsgericht held that the prohibition of discrimination (expressed here in Article 7(1) of Regulation 1612/68, but equally applicable to Article 12 EC) prohibited all covert forms of discrimination which, by the application of criteria other than nationality nevertheless led to the same result. A residence criterion *could* have a discriminatory effect, prohibited by the Treaty and the regulation. In the *O'Flynn* case (case C–237/94), the ECJ characterised four groups of conditions as potentially discriminatory, even if phrased in nationality neutral terms. The conditions are:

(a) those which affect essentially migrant workers;

(b) those where the great majority of those affected are migrant workers;

(c) those which can be more easily satisfied by national workers than by migrant workers; and

(d) those where there is a risk that they might operate to the particular detriment of migrant workers.

Thus, in the context of the provision of services and establishment (as well as to workers), certain professional rules and codes of practices or even professional qualifications have been found to be indirectly discriminatory. By imposing conditions additional to those required in the worker's home State, and which may be more difficult or burdensome for the migrant worker to satisfy, they create obstacles to the free movement of persons in the same way as indistinctly applicable rules applied to goods (see Chapter 16).

More recent case law such as *Bosman* (case C–415/98) in respect of workers; *Säger* v *Dennemeyer* (case C–76/90) in respect of services; and *Gebhard* (case C–55/94) in respect of establishment, have developed this category of indirectly discriminatory measures. Indeed, they suggest that the Court is phrasing its arguments in terms of obstacles to trade and movement rather than as species of discrimination. In this again, we see parallels to the approach taken in relation to goods, and which can now also be found in the context of capital.

As in the case of goods, such measures may be permitted if they are objectively justified, that is, if they are not disproportionate and pursue legitimate ends. The extent to which these principles applicable to goods can be applied in the context of workers, establishment and services has been raised in a number of cases. (See, for example, the comments of the Advocates-General in *Bosman* (case C–415/93) and *Volker Graf* (case C–190/98) see Chapter 20). Certain differences in approach remain, as illustrated by the case of *Alpine Investments* (case C–384/93) (see further Chapter 22).

14.3.4 Direct effect

Although the free movement provisions are addressed to Member States all the main articles have been found to be directly effective (see Chapter 5) and thus may be invoked by individuals. Whether *all* the Treaty freedoms are horizontally effective is less clear; contrast the position regarding goods and persons.

14.3.5 Need for harmonisation

The Treaty derogations and the grounds for justification accepted by the Court, described as mandatory requirements or reasons of overriding public interest clearly jeopardised the functioning of the single market. Nor was the problem confined to goods; it also applied to the other elements of the internal market. It became clear that if important public interests were to be protected without impairing the functioning of the internal market, action would have to be taken at Community level. Following the publication by the Commission in 1985 of a White Paper on the Completion of the Internal Market Member States agreed to embark on a massive harmonisation programme, designed to provide common standards of protection, to be completed by 31 December 1992. This was enshrined in the Single European Act 1996 (Article 14 EC). To speed up the legislative process, a new Article 95 (ex 100a) was introduced into the EC Treaty, providing for the 'approximation' (i.e., harmonisation) of the 'provisions laid down by law, regulation or administrative action in Member States which have as their object the establishing and functioning of the internal market' (subject to some exceptions in Article 95(2)) by measures to be enacted by qualified majority vote, instead of as heretofore, under Article 94 (ex 100), by unanimity. (See Chapter 15.) This programme, an example of 'positive integration' (as opposed to the 'negative integration' achieved by decisions of the ECJ rendering 'inapplicable' domestic measures contrary to EC law), has been largely successful. Although not all of the Commission's proposals were approved within the deadline, the vast majority of measures, particularly those relating to the free movement of goods, are now in place. By the end of 1994, 89 per cent of Community legislation relating to the internal market had been transposed into national law. Legislative activity has, of course, not ceased with the passing of 1992. Not only has Community competence extended since then, but legislation also needs to be reviewed and updated in the light of changing circumstances. For example, the development of electronic commerce has generated directives on electronic signatures and on contracts concluded via electronic means. The more recent emphasis in the internal market programme is that of simplifying legislation (SLIM), with the aim of increasing transparency and making cross-border transactions easier. The so-called Open Method of Co-ordination (OMC) (discussed in Chapters 3 and 15) can also be seen as part of the attempt to lessen the regulatory burden on businesses.

14.4 Relationship between the freedoms

The Court has held that the freedoms are mutually exclusive. This approach is supported by the terms of the Treaty itself. As noted above, the provisions on capital are expressed to apply without prejudice to the operation of the principles on establishment, and the service provisions are expressed to apply to situations 'insofar as they are not governed by the provisions relating to freedom of movement for goods, capital and persons'. Despite the similarity in approach between the freedoms identified above, it remains necessary to identify the scope of particular freedoms. It seems easy to identify where the boundary between goods and persons might arise, but other circumstances are less clear-cut. The boundary between services and establishment seems in some instances to be one of degree, rather than there being any qualitative difference between the subject matter of the two freedoms. (See further 21.3.2.) More difficulties arise in relation to the boundary between goods and capital, on the one hand, and goods and services on the other.

In *R v Thompson* (case 7/78) goods were held to include collectors' coins in gold and silver, provided they were not coins in circulation as legal tender. The latter are covered by the provisions of the Treaty relating to capital (Article 56 EC, see *Bordessa* (cases C–358 & 416/93)). In *Commission v Ireland Re Dundalk Water Supply* (case 45/87) the concept of goods was held to apply not only to the sale of goods *per se* but to goods and materials supplied in the context of the provision of services. However, where goods are supplied in the context of the provision of services, to fall within the goods provisions of the Treaty, the importation or exportation of the goods in question must be an end in itself. Materials such as advertisements or tickets, supplied simply as an adjunct to a service, for example, a lottery, will fall within the provisions governing services, namely Articles 49 and 50 EC (*Her Majesty's Customs and Excise v Schindler* (case C 275/92), see Chapter 22). The cases involving advertising of goods, especially those concerning broadcast advertising, illustrate the narrow boundary between goods and services (see, e.g., *de Agostini* (joined cases C–34–36/94), discussed further in Chapters 18 and 22). In cases of doubt it is advisable to invoke both goods and services provisions.

14.5 **The social dimension**

In addition to the rights conferred on those seeking to exercise their right to free movement, the Treaty seeks to increase social protection in areas such as employment and education. Where not already included, these goals were explicitly incorporated into the EC Treaty by the TEU (see Article 3(i), (o) and (p)). The purpose of EC *employment* legislation is to harmonise national laws, normally by directive, to provide common standards of protection throughout the Community, in the interest both of the worker and the more effective functioning of the single market. Harmonised standards are intended to create a level playing field, and avoid social dumping. It is thought that disparity between the laws of Member States as regards standards of employment protection will give a competitive advantage to States with lower standards. EC action in the field of *social rights* aims to promote and encourage the well-being of Union citizens, by action in the field of public health, or education, or to benefit the disabled, the deprived ('victims of social exclusion') or the elderly, or victims of disaster. Measures here are designed to stimulate and complement rather than replace national provision, according to the principle of subsidiarity.

Although the TEU re-emphasised the need for increased social protection, both by extending the Community's goals and by introducing a more rounded conception of the individual in the Community, the Member States were by no means in agreement about the extent of the rights to be granted by Community law, particularly in relation to employment legislation. In the field of employment rights 11 of the then 12 Member States (the UK, then under John Major's Conservative government, excepted) signed an Agreement on Social Policy in a protocol attached to the Maastricht Treaty, with a view to 'continuing along the path laid down in the 1989 Social Charter'. The agreement had as its objectives: 'the promotion of employment, improved living and working conditions, proper social protection, dialogue between management and labour, the development of human resources with a view to lasting high employment and the combating of exclusion' (Article 1). The signatory States were required to take implementing measures in respect of these policy areas, but this has turned out to be problematic. Difficult questions arose as to where the boundary between the protocol and the EC Treaty's pre-existing social provisions lay. These difficulties are now, as far as social policy is concerned, at an end. Following the change in UK Government after Labour's election victory in 1997, the UK agreed to have the provisions of the Agreement on Social Policy incorporated into the EC Treaty by the ToA, replacing the social chapter provisions currently there, to give a more extensive set of rights to workers. The few measures agreed under the Agreement were extended to the UK in advance of the ratification of the ToA. However, the new social protection provisions introduced by the ToA (Articles 136–141 EC) are, in keeping with the spirit of the ToA, extremely cautious, and voting will continue to be required to be unanimous in the more sensitive areas (e.g., Article 137(3)). Although there might not have been much direct action under the social policy provisions, workers' protection is also ensured by the general non-discrimination provisions (discussed in Chapter 25).

14.6 Completion of the internal market and the position of third-country nationals

The EC Treaty has always envisaged the possibility of a frontier-free Europe. This was re-emphasised by the insertion by the SEA of Article 14 EC, which provides for 'an area without internal frontiers in which the free movement of goods, persons, services and capital is ensured'. Progress on achieving an internal market in persons, by abolishing the barriers existing at the frontiers of Member States, was slow, partly because of the sensitivity of the area and partly because Member States were not agreed on whether the internal market in persons should include third-country nationals (TCNs) or be limited to EC nationals. The result was that certain Member States concluded an agreement outside the framework of the EC/EU to achieve such an area. Under an agreement signed at Schengen in 1990, five Member States (Germany, France and the Benelux countries, later joined by Italy, Spain, Portugal and Greece) agreed to remove all checks on the movement of people across their borders.

With the changes introduced by the TEU, the Union began to develop, under the Justice and Home Affairs pillar (JHA) of the TEU, the foundations for a policy on TCNs. Although some decisions were made under JHA, progress in this area was slow. The need to reform the JHA was an important issue considered at Amsterdam.

Prior to the ToA, the majority of Member States had signed, if not ratified, the Schengen Agreement. The majority thus agreed at the 1996 IGC in effect to incorporate the terms of the Schengen Agreement into the EC Treaty (the UK and Ireland opting out, and the Danish being undecided). The result was a new Title IV in Part Three of the EC Treaty. Individuals lawfully resident within the EU will be able to travel between Member States which have agreed to Title IV without being stopped at internal borders. Member States are also to develop common immigration and visa policies under these new provisions. (See Chapter 24 for further detail.) These changes, especially the ability to move freely between Member States, will benefit third-country nationals as well as EU citizens, although as noted the relationship between these provisions and the right to free movement of persons as part of the four freedoms might raise some questions.

With the advent of the concept of European citizenship and the development of common immigration and asylum policies, as now envisaged following the ToA, there will be further pressure to extend the rights currently granted to EU workers and their families to all persons legitimately resident in the European Union. Although the concept of citizenship under Article 17 EC comprises only limited political rights, it provides for the granting of rights 'to move and reside freely within the territory of the Member States'. These provisions are already leading to social rights which apply to a more extensive group of EU citizens. It remains to be seen how far TCNs (who are not members of the family of EU nationals) legitimately resident in the Community will be able to claim equality of treatment with EU nationals. So far, the emphasis under JHA as regards TCNs seems to have been directed more at keeping them out of the EU, rather than integrating them into the Community. Nonetheless recent legislative activity (discussed in Chapter 24) does seem to have improved the position somewhat, even if the position of TCNs is not on a par with migrant EU citizens. Thus, even where they are legitimately resident, or indeed have been born in the European Union, TCNs cannot claim the same rights of EU citizenship as EU nationals: nor are they entitled to rights granted to them under the Citizenship Directive.

This point has been raised as particularly problematic for some individuals in the new Member States who have not been granted nationality of those states due to political sensitivities (see discussion in Chapter 20). This point is not unique to these States; many of the EU 15 Member States have established minority communities who escape the full protection of Community law. As Weiler comments:

> It would be ironic that an ethos which rejected the nationalism of the Member States gave birth to a new European nation and European nationalism. . . . We have made little progress if the Us becomes European (instead of German or French or British) and the Them becomes those outside the Community or those inside who do not enjoy the privileges of citizenship.

The following chapters deal with the four freedoms. We then consider competition policy, including State aids. This part of the book also considers certain provisions relating to citizenship and the free movement of third-country nationals as part of the free movement of persons. Finally, we look at sex discrimination, one of the Treaty's key objectives and which was central to the early development of Community law.

FURTHER READING

Barnard, C., 'Fitting the Remaining Pieces into the Goods and Persons Jigsaw?' (2001) 26 EL Rev 35.

Closa, C., 'The Concept of Citizenship in the Treaty on European Union' (1992) 29 CML Rev 1137.

Commission's Annual Report on the Internal Market: from 1993.

Curtin, D., and Meijers, H., 'The Principle of Open Government in Schengen and the European Union: Democratic Retrogression?' (1995) 32 CML Rev 391.

Curtin, D., and O'Keeffe, D. (eds), *Constitutional Adjudication in European Community and National Law* (1992), p. 67.

d'Oliveira, H., 'Expanding External and Shrinking Internal Borders: Europe's Defence Mechanism in the Areas of Free Movement, Immigration and Asylum', in O'Keeffe, D. and Twomey, P. (eds), *Legal Issues of the Maastricht Treaty* (Wiley Chancery Law, 1994), p. 261.

—, 'Nationality and the European Union after Amsterdam' in O'Keeffe, D. and Twomey, P. (eds), *Legal Issues of the Amsterdam Treaty* (Hart Publishing, 1999).

Fitzpatrick, B., 'Community Social Law after Maastricht' (1992) 21 ILJ 199.

Mortelmans, K., 'The Common Market, the Internal Market and the Single Market: What's in a Market?' (1998) 35 CML Rev 101.

O'Higgins, T. F., 'The Family and European Law' (1990) 140 NLJ 1643.

O'Keeffe, D., 'The Free Movement of Persons and the Single Market' (1992) 17 EL Rev 3.

—, 'Union Citizenship' in O'Keeffe, D. and Twomey, P. (eds), *Legal Issues of the Maastricht Treaty* (Wiley Chancery Law, 1994).

Peers, S., 'Towards Equality: Actual and Potential Rights of Third-country Nationals in the European Union' (1996) 33 CML Rev 7.

Pickup, D., 'Reverse Discrimination and Freedom of Movement for Workers' (1989) 23 CML Rev 135.

Shaw, J., 'Twin-track Social Europe – the Inside Track' in O'Keeffe, D. and Twomey, P. (eds), *Legal Issues of the Maastricht Treaty* (1994, Wiley Chancery Law).

Snell, J., 'And Then There Were Two: Products and Citizens in Community Law' in Tridimas and Nebbia (eds) *European Union Law for the Twenty-First Century: Rethinking the New Legal Order* (Hart Publishing, 2004).

Van den Bogaert, S., 'Horizontality: The Court Attacks?' in Barnard and Scott (eds) *The Law of the Single Market: Unpacking the Premises* (Hart Publishing, 2002).

Watson, P., 'The Community Social Charter' (1991) 28 CML Rev 37.

—, 'Social Policy after Maastricht' (1993) 30 CML Rev 481.

Weiler, J. H. H., 'The Transformation of Europe' (1991) 100 Yale LJ 2403.

15

Harmonisation

15.1 Introduction

The objective of creating the internal market requires the removal of barriers to the four freedoms. It will be seen how Articles 28 and 29 strike down domestic rules which could constitute barriers to trade between the Member States. However, these articles do not strike down all such rules because both the Treaty itself (Article 30) and the jurisprudence developed under Article 28 (*Cassis de Dijon, Keck*) recognise that there are public interests that may need to be protected by such domestic rules. A similar approach can be seen with regard to workers, services and establishment, as well as capital. Barriers to trade will therefore remain, as significant differences in the laws of the various Member States still exist, in particular where national laws are aimed at protecting interests recognised by the Community. Although the removal of barriers would undoubtedly improve the workings of the internal market, it would not be enough simply to remove those national rules which affect the free movement of goods, services, persons and capital. Positive steps towards creating standards throughout the Union to protect such interests are also necessary. The creation of such standards would also reduce the potential threat of a 'downward spiral' in standards arising from producers and service providers seeking to move their base to the Member State with the lowest regulatory burden. This process, by which the EC sets down a standard in a particular field which all the domestic legal systems must meet, is known as harmonisation.

This chapter considers the nature of harmonisation, as opposed to other forms of Community action, as well as discussing the different approaches taken by the Community to harmonisation itself. This chapter also reviews the scope of the Community's power to enact harmonising measures in the context of the internal market. In so doing, much of the discussion will relate to measures dealing with trade in goods; similar principles, however, also apply to the other freedoms.

15.2 The nature of harmonisation

15.2.1 Positive and negative harmonisation

The form of harmonisation by which a common standard is introduced through-out the Community is sometimes referred to as 'positive' harmonisation, because new standards are introduced. The removal of existing barriers by the striking down of national laws (e.g., under Articles 28 (ex 30), 39 (ex 48), 43 (ex 52) and 49 (ex 59) EC) is known as 'negative' harmonisation. This chapter focuses on positive harmonisation.

From the beginning, the EC Treaty provided for the creation of common Community rules, not only in the areas marked out for common organisation, such as agriculture, but in all the areas of activity outlined in the Treaty, or falling within the broader objectives of the Community (see Article 308 (ex 235) EC and Chapter 3). A huge body of rules is now in place. Many of these rules, particularly, but not exclusively, those enacted under Articles 94 and 95 (ex 100 and 100a) EC, seek to harmonise national laws, normally by means of directives. Although directives require implementation at national level, and leave national authorities some choice as to 'the form and method of implementation' (Article 249 (ex 189) EC; see Chapter 3), once the period allowed for implementation has expired, Member States are not free to enact or maintain domestic measures inconsistent with their obligations under the directive or with the general purposes of the directive. Where there is a conflict between provisions of national and Community law, Community law must prevail (see Chapter 4). A question that arises once harmonisation has taken place is the extent to which the Member States are free to derogate from their obligations under the Treaty either under the *Cassis* rule of reason or Article 30 (ex 36) EC, or to enact more stringent rules. These issues will be considered below.

Positive harmonisation may be seen to have a number of advantages over negative harmonisation. It seems possible at least in principle, to attain two objectives through the use of harmonising measures: the protection of the public interest objective; and the creation of the internal market. Where negative harmonisation is used, there seems to be a trade-off between the need to protect the public interest (letting the national rule stand) and the creation of the internal market (striking down the national rule). As will be seen, although mutual recognition facilitates the free movement of goods, disparities in national systems remain where 'mandatory requirements' and Treaty derogations operate to save national rules that prima facie constitute a barrier to inter-State trade. Subsequent chapters indicate a similar process in relation to the other freedoms.

There are other possible advantages to positive harmonisation too – one of these can be seen if we consider the way negative and positive harmonisation operate. Negative harmonisation, through a finding that a Treaty freedom has been violated and the national measure cannot be justified, means that the national rule will be struck down; the ECJ cannot create an alternative acceptable rule to replace the offending national measure. It is for this reason that negative harmonisation is said to be deregulatory, as it can only remove rules. In contrast, positive harmonisation re-regulates at the Community level. Although inconsistent national measures will no longer be good law, they will be replaced by the Community standards, reducing the risk of creating a regulatory gap, and in the case of an action against a public body, potentially may be relied on in national courts (see Chapter 5). Further, as noted at 15.1, positive harmonisation could counter the threat of a downward spiral in standards. Positive harmonisation might also be said to respect the division of powers within the Union. Laws and standards are properly made through the democratic process – that is by the involvement of political institutions, rather than by the judicial process. Finally, in theory, the use of directives allows the various Member States to take account of legal principles already in existence within their individual legal systems and to ensure that the requirements of Community law blend in with that system.

15.2.2 Harmonisation and unification

Harmonisation may be contrasted with 'unification'. A process of unification would result in the complete replacement of particular aspects of the legal orders of the Member State with a new order adopted at the European level. For example, although it has not pursued this idea, in its Communication on European Contract Law (COM (2001) 398 final), the Commission considered among other things whether the entire system of contract law of the Member States might be replaced with a new European contract code. Unification would mean that existing legal principles would be replaced with new principles applicable throughout all the Member States. In contrast, although harmonisation may result in the creation of a common set of rules which have the same substantive scope, the implementation of these rules utilises the legal principles and concepts familiar to each particular Member State.

15.2.3 Other forms of Community action

It needs to be remembered that the Community does not focus exclusively on harmonisation. In some fields, such as public health, harmonisation is expressly precluded (see further 15.4.2). Harmonisation is clearly an important aspect of the Community's activities, but there are other means by which Community objectives can be supported, for example through the coordination of national measures – this is the approach taken in relation to social security arrangements. There, Regulation 1408/71 provides the framework for the transfer of social security arrangements between Member States' social security schemes, but does not provide Community standards.

A further form of Community action, which operates independently, but may also be a precursor to a harmonising measure, is the 'Open Method of Policy Co-ordination'. This has a legal basis in Article 137(2)(a) EC in respect of social rights, but the approach was extended by the Lisbon European Council in March 2000 to other policy areas. It does not result in legislation at the European level. The White Paper on European Governance (COM (2001) 428 final) states that this method of coordination can be used to encourage cooperation, exchange best practice and agree common targets and guidelines for the Member States. Progress by the Member States towards reaching these targets is monitored regularly. The Commission generally assumes a coordinating role, and the White Paper emphasised the need to keep the European Parliament informed. This form of Community action may complement legislative action, but can also be used where 'there is little scope for legislative solutions (p. 22)' (see also, e.g., *Strengthening the social dimension of the Lisbon strategy: Streamlining open coordination in the field of social protection* (COM (2003) 261 final)).

15.3 Types of harmonisation

There are several forms of harmonisation. These may be classed according to the degree of freedom left to the Member States to adopt measures that differ from the harmonised rules, either by setting a higher standard, or by maintaining existing lower standards. There is a certain lack of consensus about the number and types of categories of harmonisation; the types discussed in this section are the main forms of harmonisation usually found in EC Law.

15.3.1 Total harmonisation

Total harmonisation leaves the Member States with no scope for further independent action in the field covered by the harmonising measure. As far as the area covered by a total harmonisation directive is concerned, Member States must ensure that their domestic system provides exactly what is required by that directive. It is not possible to introduce a stricter standard. In *Commission* v *United Kingdom*, (*Dim-Dip Lights*) (case 60/86), the compatibility of a requirement introduced by the UK that all new cars should be equipped with dim-dip lights with the relevant directive, Directive 76/759, was decided against the UK because the directive specified exhaustively the types of lights which could be fitted to cars. In its earlier decision in *Prantl* (case 16/83), the ECJ stated that:

> once rules on the common organisation of the market may be regarded as forming a complete system, the Member States no longer have competence in that field unless Community law expressly provides otherwise (para. 6).

Thus if a measure is a total harmonisation measure, Member States will not be free to adopt additional provisions covering the same sector. These principles are not limited to technical rules relating to goods, but apply to all aspects of EC law. Thus, in *Inspire Art* (case C–167/01), Dutch legislation imposing disclosure obligations on branches of foreign companies exceeded the requirements of the Eleventh Company Law Directive (89/666/EC), and was therefore not permitted. That directive was exhaustive and a branch could not be required to disclose information beyond that required by the Directive.

The exclusion of higher domestic standards applies even where this might be of benefit to individuals, such as consumers. In *Commission* v *France* (case C–52/00), the ECJ held that France had incorrectly implemented several provisions of Directive 85/374/EEC (Product Liability Directive [1985] OJ L210/29). Article 9 specifies that liability for property damage would only arise if the damage caused were to exceed €500. France chose not to implement this threshold and put forward two arguments to justify its position. It claimed first that the directive should be interpreted in the light of Article 153 (ex 129a) EC which permits a higher national level of protection than specified in relevant consumer protection directives. Moreover, the Product Liability Directive allowed the Member States to depart from several of the rules it laid down and permission to do likewise in relation to other areas covered by the directive could be inferred. The ECJ rejected France's contention and held that:

> The margin of discretion available to the Member States . . . is *entirely determined by the directive itself* and must be inferred from its wording, purpose and structure (para. 16).

Member States may only derogate from the provisions of a total harmonisation directive in so far as the directive expressly permits. The fact that a directive permits derogation for particular aspects falling within the scope of the directive or leaves certain matters for domestic law does not change its character as a total harmonisation measure (para. 19, case C–52/00).

This position was also adopted in *Sanchez* v *Medicina Asturiana SA* (case C–183/00), again involving Directive 85/374/EEC. The Product Liability Directive establishes a system of strict liability for injury or property damage caused by defective products. Article 13 of the directive preserves the application of other systems of contractual or non-contractual liability *based on other grounds*. Prior to the introduction of the directive Spain had adopted a system of strict liability which it did not repeal when it implemented the directive. The earlier system was more favourable to the claimant. The ECJ held that although Article 13 did not prevent the maintenance of a fault-based system of product liability, it precluded the retention of a more extensive system of liability which uses the same basis as that in the directive (i.e., strict liability).

Both cases illustrate the impact of a total harmonisation measure. Such a directive precludes Member States from adopting or retaining rules which cover the same ground as the directive and which are based on the same legal principles. A total harmonisation measure may permit specific derogations by giving Member States the option whether to implement particular provisions in the directive. Apart from such instances, it will be necessary to identify exactly what the directive provides and which aspects of the relevant field it regulates, i.e., it is necessary to identify the 'occupied field'.

However, areas which lie outside the field of a total harmonisation directive can still be regulated by the Member States. This will be subject to the requirement to comply with the Treaty, which, in practice, means the provisions on the four freedoms. For example, in *Inspire Art* (case C–167/01), mentioned above, the Dutch legislation on branches of foreign companies also introduced several obligations on such branches that went beyond disclosure obligations, including the requirement to have a minimum share capital. The Directive on branches (89/666/EEC) only dealt with disclosure obligations, and any additional requirements which had to be met by branches of foreign companies were within the domain of the Member States. The minimum capital requirement could therefore be imposed unless it conflicted with the freedom of establishment (Article 43 EC). The ECJ first considered whether this requirement was caught by Article 43, and having found that it was, considered whether it could be justified on objective grounds, applying the *Säger* v *Dennemeyer* (case C–76/90) test. On the facts, the minimum capital requirement was not justified and therefore incompatible with the Treaty.

15.3.2 Derogation from a total harmonisation measure

The general rule is that once a common Community organisation for a particular product has been set up, Member States are no longer entitled to maintain in force provisions or adopt practices which are incompatible with the scheme of common organisation or which jeopardise its aims or functioning (see also *Tasca* (case 65/75)). In each case it is necessary to examine the harmonising measure to ascertain whether the field is occupied. If so, any national measure conflicting with the common provision will be illegal. If not, national measures are permissible provided they do not impair the effective functioning of the common organisation or run counter to Article 28 EC. In this case derogation may still be permissible under Article 30 (ex 36) EC.

It was originally thought that, once the Community had legislated in a particular field, States were no longer free to enact legislation in that field or resort to Article 30 EC (the 'strict', 'total', or 'classic' pre-emption theory). This view derived support from the Court's ruling in *Tedeschi* v *Denkavit Commerciale Srl* (case 5/77). Here in the context of a dispute concerning a Community directive regulating the use of food additives, the Court held that where in the application of the then Article 100 (now 94), Community directives provide for harmonisation of the measures necessary to the free movement of goods, recourse to Article 30 was no longer justified. The Court appeared to take the same view in a case involving Solvents Directive (73/173) in *Ratti* (case 148/78). However, in both cases, the directives contained 'market access' clauses, expressly prohibiting domestic restrictions on imports which complied with the requirements of the directives, and, more importantly, provided safeguard procedures (requiring notification to, and approval by, the Commission) should Member States need to adopt 'protective measures' in the public interest.

Where EC legislation did not provide such procedures, it subsequently appeared to be possible for States to take emergency action based on what is now Article 30, provided a genuine justification could be proved. In *van Bennekom* (case 227/82) the Court held (at para. 35):

> It is only when Community directives . . . make provision for the *full* harmonisation of all the measures needed to ensure the protection of [in this case] human and animal life and *institute Community procedures to monitor compliance therewith* that recourse to Article 36 [now 30] ceases to be justified (emphasis added).

(See also *van der Veldt* (case C–17/93).) *Van Bennekom* seems to have suggested a double test for the exclusion of Member State competence. Not only must there be total harmonisation in the field, but monitoring procedures should be included in the relevant EC legislation.

This view was modified in *R* v *Ministry of Agriculture, Fisheries and Food, ex parte Hedley Lomas (Ireland) Ltd* (case C–5/94), in a move towards a narrower view of Member State competence. The case concerned a claim for damages against the UK for losses resulting from a ban on the export of live sheep to Spain on the grounds that Spain had failed to comply with Council Directive 74/557. The directive, an animal welfare measure, required Member States to provide for the stunning of animals before slaughter. It did not expressly require Member States to monitor its implementation or provide penalties for non-compliance. The directive was implemented by the Spanish authorities but without providing for monitoring procedures or penalties for non-compliance. Although the ban was clearly contrary to Article 29, the UK argued that it was justified under Article 30 as a measure designed for the protection of the health of animals. The Court found that it was not. The UK had failed to adduce any evidence that Spanish slaughterhouses were not fulfilling their obligations under the directive.

This finding was no doubt correct on the facts: the necessity for a ban was not proved, and it was in any case disproportionate. Also, to the extent that the direct-ive provided for harmonisation of the measures necessary to achieve the *specific objective* required by the UK Government (i.e., the stunning of animals before slaughter), the matter was covered by Community law. However, since Community law failed to prescribe procedures to monitor compliance, Member States might have thought they were entitled to resort to Article 30 EC when there was evidence that the directive had been breached, as had been suggested in *van Bennekom* (case 227/82). In *Hedley Lomas* the Court found otherwise:

> recourse to Article 36 [now 30] is no longer possible where Community directives provide for harmonisation of the measures necessary to achieve the *specific objective which would be furthered by reliance upon this provision*.
>
>   This exclusion of recourse to Article 36 [now 30] cannot be affected by the fact that . . . the directive does not lay down any Community procedure for monitoring compliance nor any penalties in the event of breach of its provisions. . . . Member States are obliged, in accordance with the first paragraph of Article 5 [now 10] and the third paragraph of Article 189 [now 249] of the Treaty, to take all measures necessary to guarantee the application and effectiveness of Community law. . . . In this regard, the Member States must rely on trust in each other to carry out inspections on their respective territories (paras 18 and 19, emphasis added).

This ruling was clearly designed to prevent Member States from taking reciprocal action contrary to the Treaty in the face of alleged breaches of Community law *to protect an interest which is already protected by Community rules*. However, it does not mean that States are powerless to protect such an interest in the face of a breach of those rules. They may persuade the Commission to act under Article 226 (ex 169) EC. If the Commission refuses to act, they may themselves take action under Article 227 (ex 170) EC, if necessary seeking interim relief. Arguably they may now claim damages on the basis of *Francovich* v *Italy* (cases 6 & 9/90) (see Chapter 8). But they will not be allowed to act unilaterally in breach of Articles 28 or 29 EC on the basis of Article 30. This is consistent with the Court's rejection of the defence of reciprocity in actions under Article 226 EC (see Chapter 10).

15.3.3 **The Community's power to re-legislate**

Although it is clear that Member States have no power of action once a total har-monisation measure has been adopted, the Community itself is able to amend existing harmonisation measures and thereby to re-legislate in an area in which it has previously adopted harmonising measures. In *R v Secretary of State for Health, ex parte British American Tobacco and others* (case C–491/01), it was argued that Directive 2001/37/EC ([2001] OJ L194/26) on the manufacture, presentation and sale of tobacco products was void because it *inter alia* amended Directive 90/239/EEC ([1990] OJ L137/36) on the maximum yield of tar of cigarettes. Both directives had been adopted on the basis of Article 95. The applicants' contention was that Directive 90/239/EEC had already established a fully harmonised regime on the yield of tar of cigarettes and that the Community could therefore not legislate afresh, at least not in the absence of new scientific evidence. The ECJ held (at para. 77) that although the *Member States* were no longer able to introduce a rule in this area, the *Community* was nevertheless able to amend earlier legislation to safeguard the general interests recognised by the Treaty. The Court went on to hold that:

> It follows that, even where a provision of Community law guarantees the removal of all obstacles to trade in the area it harmonises, that fact cannot make it impossible for the Community legislature to adapt that provision in step with other considerations (para. 78).

Such adaptation may be the result of new developments based on scientific facts (para. 79), but may also follow from 'other considerations, such as the increased importance given to the social and political aspects of the anti-smoking campaign' (para. 80). The Community has a general power to re-legislate, but can only exercise this power if there are scientific or other reasons for doing so.

15.3.4 Minimum harmonisation

There was a trend, commencing with the SEA, and particularly since Maastricht, towards minimum harmonisation, although in more recent times, the focus seems to be turning away from this form of harmonisation in favour of maximum harmonisation (see, e.g, Directive 2005/29/EC on Unfair Commercial Practices).

In a minimum harmonisation measure, the EC will set down a minimum standard with which all the Member States must comply. Beyond this minimum level, Member States are free to set their own standards, subject to the requirements of the EC Treaty. The main objective of minimum harmonisation is not to specify an absolute standard which must be met by all the Member States, but rather to reduce the differences that exist by narrowing the freedom given to the Member States to regulate particular aspects within their territory. Importantly, minimum harmonisation 'does not limit Community action to the lowest common denominator, or even to the lowest level of protection established by the various Member States' (*Commission v UK* (case C–84/94), para. 56). It simply indicates that there is a degree of freedom left to the Member States to exceed the standard set by such a measure.

Minimum harmonisation can only be of limited assistance in creating a level playing field. It may be useful to the extent that it sets a minimum standard below which none of the Member States may fall, but it still leaves room for divergence in standards between Member States. Minimum harmonisation does no more than to shift the boundaries of what is permissible, in that Member States are no longer free to maintain standards lower than those in a minimum harmonisation directive, but standards higher than those in such a directive can be maintained. Sometimes, the level of protection contained in a minimum harmonisation directive is high, in which case there would be only very limited scope for the Member States to adopt additional rules. In many instances, however, there will still be a considerable degree of variation between the Member States in respect of the area subject to minimum harmonisation because, with lower standards identifying the base level of protection, Member States will enjoy relative freedom to impose stricter standards. An added dimension to this problem is introduced when directives include optional provisions which Member States are permitted, but not obliged to, implement.

Arguably, minimum harmonisation and optional provisions undermine the purpose of harmonisation, because the continuing freedom to set standards above the base-line identified by the harmonising measure still subjects individuals and businesses to the possibility of divergent rules throughout the Community. These differences may impose extra burdens on producers, if applied to imported as well as domestic products, and are likely to create barriers to the internal market. If they do so, actually or potentially, will they be permitted to apply only to domestically produced goods, or may they be applied to all goods? If applicable only to domestic production, domestic producers will be disadvantaged. If applicable to all goods, when, and in what circumstances, will they be permitted?

15.3.5 **Minimum harmonisation and reverse discrimination**

In the case of a minimum harmonisation measure, it may be easier for the Member States to derogate from the harmonised standard than it is in the case of total harmonisation. Indeed, it is inherent in the concept of minimum harmonisation that Member States *will* introduce or retain rules which go beyond what is required of such a directive. However, it is clear that Member States cannot fall below the minimum standard introduced by a directive, and even where national legislation sets a higher standard than the relevant directive, the national measure has to comply with the Treaty.

Confusingly, EC harmonisation measures do not follow a single pattern. Some minimum harmonisation directives contain a 'market access' clause, whereas others do not. A market access clause specifies that Member States may not prevent the import of products which comply with the minimum standard, but do not meet the higher standard imposed by the particular Member State. Such a provision was at issue in *R v Secretary of State for Health, ex parte Gallaher Ltd* (case C–11/92). The question was whether domestic producers could invoke a market access clause to challenge national rules which applied only to domestic production (reverse discrimination). The case concerned a challenge by three leading UK cigarette producers to UK regulations implementing Tobacco Directive 89/622. The directive required Member States to provide *inter alia* for health warnings on cigarettes to cover 'at least' 4 per cent of the packet (Article 4(4)). It also contained a market access clause. Member States were not to prohibit or restrict the sale of products which complied with the directive (Article 8(1)). The UK regulations provided for more extensive health warnings than required by the terms of the directive, to cover six per cent of the packet, but these requirements were applicable only to domestic production. The ECJ held that this was permitted.

If *Gallaher* is followed (and always depending on the wording of the directive), where there is minimum harmonisation and a market access clause, EC law will permit reverse discrimination, as it has done in other areas. Such a proposition was confirmed in *R* v *Minister of Agriculture, Fisheries and Food, ex parte Compassion in World Farming Ltd* (case C–1/96). Here a British animal welfare group was seeking to prevent the export of live calves to other Member States which permitted the rearing of calves in crates, a practice prohibited by the UK (and a Council of Europe Convention). EC Directive 91/629, a harmonisation measure relating to the health of animals, laid down minimum common standards for the protection of live calves, but specifically allowed Member States to apply, within their own territory, stricter rules. In this way, as the ECJ pointed out, the directive aimed to strike a balance between the interests of animal protection and the smooth functioning of the organisation of the market in calves and derived products. It followed that:

> a Member State cannot rely on Article 36 [now 30] of the Treaty in order to restrict the export of calves to other Member States for reasons relating to the protection of the health of animals, which constitutes the specific objective of the harmonisation undertaken by the directive.

In reaching this conclusion, paras 18 and 19 of *Hedley Lomas*, quoted above, which referred to a total harmonisation directive, were invoked. Although there might be questions in a given case as to the specific objective of the harmonisation, it can be seen that the ECJ has unequivocally held that where a Community directive providing for minimum standards of harmonisation allows Member States to maintain stricter standards these can only be applied in their own territory to the State's own products. A similar approach is now being taken in the fields of services and establishment (see Chapters 21 and 22).

Gallaher has been criticised as tending to undermine competition in the internal market and discourage experiment and diversity. It is argued that Member States are unlikely to enact legislation in the interest of higher standards where this will result in a competitive disadvantage for domestic products. However, in the light of the principle of subsidiarity, a system permitting reverse discrimination may be a more practical way of regulating Member States' freedom to supplement Community provision than *ad hoc* assessment by the Court under Article 30 EC or the rule of reason. Higher standards may even prove more attractive to consumers.

As noted, some other directives contain no market access clause. In such a case, domestic measures over and above those required by the directive which restrict interstate trade will be permissible provided they are justified under the rule of reason or Article 30. Where the directive provides procedures for derogation, or, in the case of measures enacted under Article 95 EC, under Article 95(4), those procedures must be followed (see below).

15.3.6 Technical harmonisation and the 'new approach'

Originally, Member States had the power to lay down the performance objectives and design specifications, or 'technical standards', for goods manufactured and sold in their territory. Goods which did not comply with such technical standards could not be sold in that Member State. As seen in other chapters dealing with the four freedoms, some of these rules could be struck down as barriers to trade under Articles 28 and 29, but others would be accepted as necessary by the ECJ. Such a divergence in technical standards can lead to competitive distortions in much the same way as differences between national measures in other fields. That is why the Community has had a specific programme for the harmonisation of such technical standards, often referred to as 'technical harmonisation'.

In the field of technical harmonisation, the Community initially adopted a sector-by-sector approach to adopt very detailed technical specifications. In 1985, when it had become apparent that the slow progress would make it very difficult to complete the internal market, the Council adopted a resolution on the 'New Approach to Technical Harmonisation' ([1985] OJ C136). The EC will now lay down so-called 'essential safety requirements' for a particular sector, but leave it to the European standardisation bodies, such as CEN, to work out the detailed technical rules by which compliance with the requirements can be demonstrated. Compliance with a European standard creates a presumption that products comply with the essential safety requirements, although it is not compulsory to follow these standards. Compliance with European standards is indicated by the CE marking on the product. Producers can opt to comply with other standards (such as those created by ISO, the International Standards Organisation) or not to comply with a technical standard at all, but they must nevertheless satisfy the procedures for assessing conformity which will be set out in the relevant directive which specifies the essential safety requirements for a particular sector. In addition to sector-specific measures, the EC also adopted the Directive on General Product Safety (Directive 2001/95) which imposes a general requirement that all goods put on the internal market must be safe. Compliance with this general safety requirement can be demonstrated in the same manner as with sector-specific measures by complying with relevant European or national standards.

In addition, Directive 98/34/EC (which replaces Directive 83/189) lays down a procedure for the provision of information in the field of technical standards and regulations which applies when a Member States adopts a new technical regulation. Such a measure must be notified to the Commission before it is adopted to ensure that its impact on the free movement of goods is minimised and that both the Commission and the other Member States are aware of the measure and given an opportunity to propose amendments to it. Given the fact that non-notified national measures may not be relied on (see the discussion in Chapter 5), the scope of the directive – particularly the meaning of 'technical standards' – has gained in significance.

15.3.7 Other types of harmonisation

Some harmonisation measures are limited to the cross-border context. If goods are sold across borders, the goods must comply with the harmonised standards used. For those who operate exclusively within the territory of one Member State, there is no need to comply with the Community standard. Sometimes, producers who do not operate across borders may be given the option of whether to comply with the Community or domestic standards. This may be of benefit to a producer who may intend to trade across borders in the future. Slot describes these two related forms as 'optional' and 'partial' harmonisation, respectively. Optional harmonisation allows a producer to select whether to follow the harmonised or the national rules. Partial harmonisation requires a producer to adopt the Community standard if he wishes to engage in cross-border trade. These forms of harmonisation may be less intrusive than other types but seem to be less frequently used.

15.3.8 The 'country of origin' principle

First espoused by the Court of Justice in *Cassis de Dijon* (case 120/78) in the context of 'negative harmonisation', the 'mutual recognition' principle has become a stalwart of EC law. In essence, the principle requires any Member State to admit on to its territory goods or services which are marketed lawfully in the originating Member State. It will thus rarely be possible to prevent the free circulation of goods within the internal market once these are sold lawfully in one Member State, although derogations remain possible (see further Chapter 18). It is a difficult principle to apply, although the Commission has published an interpretative communication on facilitating the access of products to the markets of other Member States: the practical application of mutual recognition ([2003] OJ C265/2) in the context of the EC/Turkey agreement.

A variation of the 'country of origin' principle is occasionally used in legislation which also harmonises some parts of the relevant laws of the Member States (see, e.g., Article 2 of the Television without Frontiers Directive (89/552/EEC [1989] OJ L298/23; also Art. 3(1) of the Electronic Commerce Directive (2000/31/EC; [2000] OJ L178/1). Under this principle, an operator in the internal market is only subject to regulation in his home Member State, and another Member State may not restrict that operator's activities in the host territory. Crucially, no derogations seem permissible, except where expressly provided for (see Article 2a Television without Frontiers Directive). For a trader seeking to sell goods or services in another Member State, this approach can be attractive, because it is only necessary to comply with the specific requirements imposed in the home country. However, it also gives rise to concerns about a 'race to the bottom', particularly where there is a significant variation in the level of regulation between the Member States (see further discussion in Chapters 21 and 22). Such concerns could be met by combining this principle with a maximum harmonisation measure, as all Member States' standards would then be the same. Even then the principle may be rejected (see, e.g., the recent Directive on Unfair Commercial Practices (2005/29/EC), the first proposal of which included a country of origin clause which was removed during the legislative process; see also the debate about a directive on services (see Chapter 22), especially where there are concerns about the level of protection conferred by the directive in question.

It is clear, however, that the country of origin principle has a role to play in the harmonisation landscape in that it can complement measures harmonising some aspects of domestic law. It may also be a bargaining tool in the legislative process to secure agreement on a harmonising measure, although, as more recent examples show, it can also have the opposite effect.

15.4 Article 95 and harmonisation

Much of the EC's harmonising legislation centres on the internal market, and it is therefore appropriate to consider the key provision in this regard, Article 95 EC, in some detail. This is particularly important because the ECJ has attempted to lay down clear limits within which this provision may be utilised for the adoption of legislation. It may be noted in passing that, should the Constitution enter into force in its present form, Article 95 EC would be re-enacted as Article III–172, with minor linguistic alterations.

Before the adoption of the SEA, harmonisation measures were often adopted on the basis of Article 94. This provision enables the adoption of harmonising directives which directly affect the establishment or functioning of the common market. Article 94 requires unanimity within the Council, and requires only that the Parliament be consulted. The unanimity requirement was blamed for the slow progress in completing the common market.

The SEA introduced what has become the most significant provision for the EC's harmonisation programme: Article 95. Article 95(1) states that:

> By way of derogation from Article 94 and save where otherwise provided in this Treaty, the following provisions shall apply for the achievement of the objectives set out in Article 14. The Council shall, acting in accordance with the procedure referred to in Article 251 and after consulting the Economic and Social Committee, adopt the measures for the approximation of the provisions laid down by law, regulation or administrative action in Member States which have as their object the establishment and functioning of the internal market.

In contrast to Article 94, there is no requirement for unanimity. Moreover (since TEU) Parliament is actively involved in the legislative process through the use of the co-decision procedure.

Article 95 can form the basis for two types of measures: those which have the object of establishing the internal market, and those which relate to the functioning of the internal market. The objective of Article 95 is to reduce or remove altogether competitive disadvantages caused by the higher cost of having to comply with rules which are stricter in some Member States than in others. In addition, it may extend to cover harmonising measures which affect goods irrespective of their ultimate destination, including goods manufactured exclusively for export, if there is a risk that their re-import could undermine the harmonising measure (in *R* v *Secretary of State for Health, ex parte British American Tobacco and others* (case C–491/01) at para. 82, and see para. 166 of Advocate-General Geelhoed's opinion in the same case).

It must be noted that not all measures which may be significant for the internal market will be based on this provision. For example, the directives in the company law field are generally adopted on the basis of Article 44, especially Article 44(2)(g), although they are clearly of relevance to the internal market (e.g., Directive 2005/56/EC on cross-border mergers of limited liability companies [2005] OJ L310/1). However, such measures pursue a different objective and are not necessarily concerned with the establishment or functioning of the internal market as such, although sometimes the dividing line can be a fine one (cf. Directive 68/151/EEC, adopted before Article 95 was introduced, and concerned, *inter alia*, with the protection of third parties dealing with companies, which seeks to introduce equivalent safeguards throughout the EC).

15.4.1 The extent of the Community's power to legislate under Article 95

Article 95 has formed the basis of numerous directives. The Community has used its powers under Article 95 extensively. It seemed that the scope of legislation on the basis of this article was very broad. The extent of the Community's powers under this article was clarified in *Germany* v *Parliament and Council* (case C–376/98), when the ECJ annulled Directive 98/43/EC on Tobacco Advertising and Sponsorship. The Court emphasised that Article 95 could form the basis only for measures which are intended to improve the conditions for the establishment and functioning of the internal market, but that it did not give a general power to the Community legislature to regulate the internal market (para. 83). Such a general power would conflict with Article 5 EC, which provides that the Community must act within its powers (see further Chapter 3). The Court went on to say that:

> a measure adopted on the basis of Article 100a [now 95] of the Treaty must *genuinely* have as its object the improvement of the conditions for the establishment and functioning of the internal market (para. 84, emphasis added).

It has often been the case that Article 95 was used not only to harmonise existing divergences to facilitate the functioning of the internal market, but also to prevent the emergence of *future* obstacles to trade which could be caused by the diffuse development of the national legal systems. The Court confirmed that Article 95 could still be used for that purpose provided that 'the emergence of such obstacles [is] likely and the measure in question [is] designed to prevent them' (para. 86; see also *R* v *Secretary of State for Health, ex parte Swedish Match* (case C–210/03), para. 31). However, a 'mere finding of disparities between national rules and of the abstract risk of obstacles to the exercise of fundamental freedoms or of distortions of competition' (para. 84) would be insufficient to justify Community action. If a particular measure is aimed at eliminating distortions of competition, the Court has to be satisfied that this distortion is 'appreciable', because the powers of the Community legislature would otherwise be 'practically unlimited' (para. 107, and see also *Commission* v *Council, Titanium Dioxide* (case C–300/89) and *R* v *Secretary of State for Health, ex parte Alliance for Natural Health* (joined cases C–154/04 and 155/04). The holding in *Tobacco Advertising* confirms the views of Advocate-General Fennelly, who observed that:

> the pursuit of equal conditions of competition does not give *carte blanche* to the Community legislator to harmonise any national rules that meet the eye . . . it would risk transferring general Member State regulatory competence to the Community if recourse to Article 100a [now 95] . . . were not subject to some *test of the reality of the link between such measures and internal market objectives* (Opinion, case C–376/98, para. 89).

A measure could not be justified on the basis of Article 95 if its effect on the harmonisation of competitive conditions was 'merely incidental' (para. 91). In *Germany* v *Parliament and Council* (case C–376/98), the directive prohibited outright advertising of, and sponsorship by, tobacco products. The ECJ held that Article 95 was an inappropriate legal basis for the directive because it not only failed to improve competition but sought to eliminate it altogether.

There is therefore a burden on the Community legislator to identify obstacles to the functioning of the internal market before adopting harmonising legislation on the basis of Article 95. It is necessary to establish first of all that disparate national laws actually constitute a barrier to free movement or distort competition, and then that Community action contributes to the establishment and functioning of the internal market and goes no further. This may require a detailed analysis of the competitive conditions prevailing in a particular sector to establish whether an identified obstacle to free movement or competition is appreciable such as to justify Community action.

15.4.2 Article 95 and 'flanking policies'

A further question is to what extent Article 95 can be used as a legal basis to harmonise areas in which the Community does not have a direct competence to harmonise, or where there is more than one potential legal basis for a particular measure. In *Germany* v *Parliament and Council*, it was argued that the directive sought to harmonise public health legislation. Under Article 152(4) (ex 129(4)), the Community is expressly precluded from harmonising legislation in this area. The ECJ emphasised that other Treaty articles may not be used to circumvent an express exclusion of harmonisation such as the one laid down in Article 152(4), but this did not rule out the possibility that harmonising measures adopted on the basis of other Treaty provisions could have an impact on the protection of human health (para. 78). In *R* v *Secretary of State for Health, ex parte British American Tobacco and others* (C–491/01), Advocate-General Geelhoed emphasised that it must be possible to adopt harmonising measures under Article 95 to the extent that national measures within the field of public health create barriers to trade, but it is also clear that there is no independent power to harmonise public health legislation (see paras 112–114). The ECJ confirmed that as long as a directive 'genuinely has as its object the improvement of the conditions for the functioning of the internal market', it would be possible to adopt it on the basis of Article 95 'and it is no bar that the protection of public health was a decisive factor in the choices involved in the harmonising measures' (para. 76).

On this basis, the Community has a degree of competence to harmonise all areas in which divergent national laws may adversely affect the operation of the internal market, but cannot adopt measures that have the effect of harmonising excluded areas beyond what is necessary to eliminate distortions of competition. This seems to be a very fine distinction to make and will require the Community legislator to be even more careful in adopting legislation on the basis of Article 95.

An additional problem with 'flanking policies' may arise where a measure could be adopted on the basis of two or more Treaty provisions. For example, in *ex parte BAT*, the directive had been adopted on the basis of both Article 95 and Article 133. It was argued that this combined legal basis was inappropriate. The ECJ observed that if a measure simultaneously pursues a number of objectives without one or more being secondary to a main objective, multiple legal bases may be acceptable. However, the Court regarded this as 'exceptional' and the general position is that:

> If examination of a Community act shows that it has a twofold purpose . . . and if one of these if identifiable as main or predominant, whereas the other is merely incidental, the act must be founded on a sole legal basis, that is, the one required by the main or predominant purpose (para. 94).

In the case, all the relevant provisions could have been adopted on the basis of Article 95, and the additional use of Article 133 was not permissible. This in itself did not mean that the directive was invalid, however, because it only formed a 'purely formal defect' (see also *R v Secretary of State for Health, ex parte Swedish Match* (case C–210/03), para. 44). However, if the use of multiple legal bases gives rise to an irregularity in the procedure used for the adoption of the directive concerned, the position would be different (see also *Titanium Dioxide*, case C–300/89, paras 17–21). In *ex parte BAT*, the relevant legal bases were Article 95 and 133. In contrast to Article 95, which requires use of the co-decision procedure, Article 133 simply requires a decision by qualified majority in the Council, without any involvement by Parliament. The ECJ did not regard this as a procedural irregularity, because both articles required a decision by qualified majority and the co-decision procedure had, in fact, been followed. That case differed from *Titanium Dioxide*, where one of the conflicting legal bases required a unanimous decision. Although this view appears attractive, the ECJ sidestepped the argument that use of the co-decision procedure under Article 133 was contrary to the separation of powers in the Treaty by holding that Article 133 was not required for the adoption of the directive.

15.4.3 Derogation under Article 95

Where derogation may legitimately be sought from harmonisation measures enacted under Article 95(1), this will now be governed by Articles 95(4) and 95(5). Article 95(4), first introduced by the SEA in 1986, provides that where harmonising legislation has been passed by qualified majority, Member States who deem it necessary to *maintain* national provisions on grounds of major needs referred to in Article 30, or relating to the protection of the environment or the working environment' must notify the Commission and state the grounds for maintaining these rules. Similarly, Article 95(5) requires notification to the Commission if a Member State deems it necessary, after the adoption of a harmonising measure, to *introduce* national measures based on new scientific evidence relating to the protection of the environment or the working environment on grounds of a problem specific to that Member State (note that Article 95(5) does not refer to Article 30 as a ground for introducing new measures).

The Commission may then approve or reject the national provisions after having verified that they do not constitute a means of 'arbitrary discrimination or disguised restriction on trade between Member States', nor an obstacle to the functioning of the internal market (Article 95(6)). There is no obligation on the Commission to give the Member State who made the notification, nor any other Member State, the right to make representations (*Denmark* v *Commission* (case C–3/00)).

The Commission must decide within six months, although this period may be extended by a further six months if the matter is complex and there is no danger to human health. If the Commission fails to act within that time, the national measure is deemed to have been approved (for an example, see *Germany* v *Commission* (case C–512/99)). The Commission has issued guidelines setting out the procedures for submitting notifications under Articles 95(4) and (5) by the Member States and explaining how the Commission will handle such notifications (COM (2002) 760 final). The Commission or any other Member State may bring the matter before the ECJ if it considers that a State is making improper use of these powers.

Although expressed to apply only where harmonisation measures have been enacted by qualified majority, it has been suggested that the same procedure should be available where legislation has been passed unanimously; the Article 95(4)/(5) procedure is not in terms limited to States which have not agreed to the measure in question, and some scope for derogation should be available to meet emergencies not foreseen at the time when the legislation was passed. Moreover, in an emergency, arguably it should not be necessary for a State to obtain *prior* approval for its actions from the Commission, provided that the need for action is genuine and urgent and the Commission is notified at the earliest possible time (for a recent example, see *Land Oberösterreich* v *Commission* (case T–366/03)).

15.5 The impact of harmonisation on domestic law

The general obligation of the Member States to ensure compliance with EC law has already been discussed. Generally, it is necessary to implement directives and to ensure that they are fully given effect in domestic legislation. For some Member States, the adoption of a directive, even a minimum harmonisation measure, may result in significant changes to domestic law whereas the same measure may have a very limited impact in others. An example is Directive 99/44/EC on the sale of consumer goods, which triggered a complete reform to the German law of obligations and significantly improved the position of German consumers. In contrast, the directive's impact in the United Kingdom was far less severe and resulted in few changes to the substance of English law.

It is, however, appropriate to highlight particular aspects of this obligation which arise in the context of harmonisation. It is usually the case that harmonisation is to be achieved through the adoption of directives. These need to be implemented into the legal orders of the Member States. Directives are 'binding as to the result to be achieved' (Article 249 EC), but the Member States are free to choose how to implement the rules in a directive. It seems, therefore, that a Member State is not required to reproduce the text of a directive verbatim in the implementing legislation, as long as it can demonstrate that national law complies with the directive. However, the more detailed and technical the provisions of a directive, the narrower will be the scope for a Member State to depart from its wording. Moreover, a directive which takes a total harmonisation approach may have to be transposed by closely following its wording to avoid the risk of incorrectly implementing it (see, e.g., the difficulties caused by Directive 2005/29/EC on Unfair Commercial Practices, a total harmonisation measure with, potentially, a very wide reach into domestic consumer laws).

If a directive is not transposed at all, or only incompletely, someone seeking to rely on the directive may be able to use on the doctrine of direct effect (see Chapter 5). Similarly, if domestic legislation is worded differently from the corresponding provisions in a directive, the doctrine of indirect effect requires that domestic legislation should be interpreted to conform with the directive (see Chapter 5). However, recent cases suggest that the Commission and the ECJ distinguish between two different types of domestic legislation. Where a Member State introduces specific legislation to implement a directive, the use of a (slightly) different wording may be acceptable, provided that the domestic courts would interpret such legislation in accordance with the directive. In contrast, it does not seem acceptable for a Member State to rely on existing legislation and argue that it could be interpreted in line with the directive (and, indeed, should be so interpreted: see *Ratti*), particularly where direct rights are at stake and where the retention of existing rules could conflict with the principle of effectiveness (see also Chapter 8). This position is reflected in a number of cases involving consumer protection measures.

In *Commission* v *United Kingdom* (case C–300/95), the Commission brought infringement proceedings against the United Kingdom for a failure correctly to implement Article 4(1)(e) of Directive 85/374/EEC (Product Liability Directive). The UK Government had chosen a wording that differed from that in the directive, although it did not conflict directly with it. The ECJ rejected the Commission's application, because there was insufficient evidence that the UK had failed to give full effect to the requirements of Article 4(1)(e). In particular, there was no case law at the time on the application of the directive and therefore no evidence that the implementing legislation would lead to results different from those required by the directive. There was nothing to suggest that the domestic courts would fail to interpret the implementing legislation in accordance with the directive. *Commission* v *UK* suggests that Member States have some leeway in implementing the provisions of a directive and that greater evidence, such as court decisions, is required before it is possible to say that there is a failure correctly to implement a directive. As a result, the courts in the United Kingdom have adopted an approach whereby cases brought under the relevant domestic legislation are, in effect, dealt with by applying the corresponding directive itself (see *A and others* v *The National Blood Authority* [2001] 3 All ER 289 (High Court); also *Director-General of Fair Trading* v *First National Bank* [2002] 1 AC 481 (House of Lords)).

The principle in *Commission* v *UK* was accepted in *Commission* v *Italy* (C–372/99). The Commission claimed that Italy had failed to ensure that terms recommended by trade association in standard contracts could be challenged when the term had not actually been used in a consumer contract (as per Article 7(3) of the Unfair Contract Terms Directive 93/13/EEC). The Italian implementing legislation was ambiguous and capable of interpretation contrary to the objective pursued by the directive. The ECJ noted that the possibility of ensuring compliance with a directive through case law, even where there is case law in line with the directive, did not suffice where the legislation itself was insufficiently clear, or contradictory. Accepting compliance through case law would not be in accordance with the principle of legal certainty. Moreover, Italian case law was neither unanimous nor sufficiently well established to guarantee an interpretation in line with the Unfair Contract Terms Directive.

Therefore, this approach may not be sufficient to satisfy the Member States' obligations where the domestic legislation does not clearly and precisely reflect the position under the relevant directive. In *Commission v Netherlands* (case C–144/99), the ECJ held that the Netherlands had failed fully to implement Directive 93/13/EEC on Unfair Contract Terms. The Commission was particularly concerned about the implementation of Article 4(2) (an exception from the fairness requirement for core contract terms) and Article 5 (a 'plain and intelligible language' requirement) of the directive. The Netherlands argued that there was no need expressly to implement particular parts of a directive if existing national rules already fulfilled the requirements of that directive. Moreover, taking the lead from *Commission v United Kingdom* (case C–300/95), compliance with the directive would be ensured by the courts which would interpret existing legislation in accordance with the directive, as required by the EC case law on indirect effect. The ECJ disagreed. It held that the legal position under national law must be sufficiently clear and precise so that individuals are made fully aware of their rights (para. 17). It had not been demonstrated that the Dutch courts consistently interpreted the legislation in line with the directive (para. 20). Finally, even where it is settled in the case law of a Member State that provisions of national law *are* interpreted in line with a directive, this does not ensure the clarity and precision to meet the requirement of legal certainty. This is particularly relevant in the context of consumer protection (para. 21).

Commission v Netherlands appears to mark a significant tightening of the requirement to implement directives into domestic law. It seems to depart from the position accepted in *Commission v United Kingdom* and could be seen as throwing some doubt on whether that ruling remains good law. It may be possible to distinguish the two decisions on the basis that the conflict in *Commission v Netherlands* was between a directive and a national provision already in place, whereas in *Commission v United Kingdom*, the national measure had been adopted to comply with the directive. Moreover, in *Commission v UK*, there were no cases under the national measure. However, in *Commission v Italy*, the implementing measures were ambiguous and case law interpreting these was not unanimous. In those circumstances even new national measures may not be treated as correctly implementing a directive.

Member States may not enjoy as great a choice as suggested by Article 249 in implementing harmonisation directives. In particular, where individual rights are affected, it now seems that domestic legislation must be clear and precise to allow individuals to ascertain the scope of their rights from the legislation. A significant factor underlying this development may be the greater involvement of the Parliament in the legislative process. It has become a common feature of the co-decision procedure that Parliament and the Council will disagree over details in the wording of particular provisions in a draft directive (see for example, the legislative history to Directive 99/44/EC on the sale of consumer goods), and the actual text of the directive has political significance. To permit Member States to deviate from the text of directives which have resulted may be regarded as side-stepping, or even undermining, the legislative procedure.

However, it also seems that, in practice, the fact that a directive is a minimum harmonisation measure may cause a Member State to be less systematic in transposing it into domestic law. A maximum harmonisation measure may necessitate a thorough review of the affected area of domestic law, and a high degree of care in ensuring that the implementing legislation fits into the wider legal framework. This may be less important where a directive permits variations, and domestic rules are often retained on the basis of a minimum clause.

The Commission has become concerned about the long delays in transposing many directives, particularly those affecting the internal market. It has therefore issued a Recommendation to the Member States about procedural matters to be adopted at the national level to ensure a speedy and accurate transposition of these directives ([2005] OJ L98/47). Unfortunately, this document does not contain any substantive guidance on how to transpose directives.

15.6 Conclusions

It has been seen that harmonisation is a fundamental, and perhaps the most significant, aspect of EC law. It is not without problems, however. One of the central difficulties relates to the fact that there is no one type of harmonisation: different approaches leave Member States varying degrees of legislative freedom. Although total harmonisation is necessary in some areas, there has been a minimum harmonisation approach in some areas (such as consumer protection) to create at least a 'lowest common denominator' in the Member States. Nevertheless, as Weatherill comments, the process of minimum harmonisation 'does not solve the specific problem of which market-partitioning national measures are justified and which are not'. National measures which set a standard that exceeds a minimum harmonisation measure are always potentially liable to challenge under provisions guaranteeing free movement. A second problem concerns the scope of the EU's power to enact harmonising measures, especially in relation to Article 95 EC. Despite the fact that harmonisation might seem to solve a number of problems with the operation of the internal market, the EU does not have a general power to regulate trade. The precise scope of Member States' power to legislate and the impact of the four freedoms on that competence will continue to be relevant.

FURTHER READING

Cross, E. D., 'Pre-emption of Member State Law in the European Economic Community: A Framework for Analysis' (1992) 29 CMLR 447–472.

Davies, G., 'Can Selling Arrangements be Harmonised?' (2005) 30 EL Rev 370.

De Sadeleer, N., 'Procedures for Derogations from the Principle of Approximation of Laws under Article 95 EC' (2003) 40 CMLR 889–915.

Dougan, M., 'Minimum Harmonisation and the Internal Market' (2000) 37 CMLR 853–885.

Howells, G., 'Federalism in USA and EC – The Scope for Harmonised Legislative Activity Compared' (2002) ERPL 601–622.

Kurcz, M. B., 'Harmonisation by Means of Directives – Never-Ending Story?' [2001] EBLR 287.

Radeideh, M., *Fair Trading in EC Law* (Groningen: Europa Law Publishing, 2005).

Slot, P. J., 'Harmonisation' (1996) 21 EL Rev 378–397.

Waelbroek, M., 'The Emergent Doctrine of Community Pre-emption', in Sandalow, T. and Stein, E. (eds), *Courts and Free Markets* (Clarendon Press, 1982).

Weatherill, S., *Law and Integration in the European Union* (Clarendon Press, 1995), Ch. 5.

—, 'Why Harmonise?' In Tridimas and Nebbia (eds) *European Union Law for the Twenty-First Century: Rethinking the New Legal Order* (Hart Publishing, 2004).

—, 'Harmonisation: How Much, How Little' [2005] EBLR 533.

—, 'Free Movement of Goods' (2006) 55 ICLQ 457–467.

—, 'Recent Developments in the Law Governing the Free Movement of Goods in the EC's Internal Market' (2006) 2 ERCL 90–111.

—, 'European Private Law and the Constitutional Dimension' in Cafaggi, F. (ed.) *The Institutional Framework of European Private Law* (Oxford University Press, 2006).

Woods, L., *Free Movement of Goods and Services within the European Community* (Ashgate, 2004), ch. 13.

16

Free movement of payments and capital

16.1 Introduction

Originally the free movement of capital was governed by Articles 67–73 EEC and by secondary legislation made under those provisions. Although one of the four freedoms listed in Article 14 EC, its treatment had been somewhat different from the liberal approach taken both in the secondary legislation and by the ECJ regarding the free movement of persons, services and goods. Indeed, by striking contrast to its approach to these freedoms, the ECJ ruled that the original pre-TEU capital provisions did not have direct effect (*Casati* (case 203/80)) and could therefore not be relied on before the domestic courts (see Chapter 5). As noted in the chapter on the preliminary reference procedure (Chapter 9), the fact that individuals can rely on EC rights in national courts has been a significant factor in the development of Community law. The capital provisions, quite apart from being more cautiously drafted, therefore lacked this mechanism for development. The area was sensitive, linked to monetary policy, a fact that was reflected in the drafting of the original provisions dealing with free movement of capital.

The TEU changed the position significantly, as it introduced the provisions for the development of Economic and Monetary Union (EMU) (consideration of which lies outside the scope of this book), and included changes in the provisions relating to capital and payments. What was then Article 73a EC replaced the original system with the then Articles 73b EC–73g EC. Following ToA, these articles were re-numbered Articles 56–60 EC. There are also a number of pieces of secondary legislation aimed at facilitating the free movement of capital. With these changes, the ECJ's approach has also changed, moving towards the approach taken with regard to the other freedoms. As Leo Flynn commented in 2002, 'free movement of capital has ceased to be the runt of the litter amongst the market freedoms'.

16.2 Outline of provisions relating to the free movement of capital

The 'fourth' freedom, capital, can be broken down into two linked elements:

(a) capital; and

(b) payments.

Article 56 prohibits all restrictions on the free movement of capital (Article 56(1) EC) and payments (Article 56(2) EC) whether between Member States or between Member States and third countries. In this, there is a change from the scope of the prohibition contained in the original Article 67 EEC: that provision referred not only to restrictions on the movement of capital but also to 'discrimination based on the nationality or on the place of residence of the parties or on the place where such capital is invested'. Whether this has had any significant impact on the way the ECJ has interpreted the capital provision is debatable (see 16.3.4, below). Article 56 will be re-enacted at Article III–156 should this constitution come into force.

Articles 57–60 contain the exceptions to the general rule. These can be divided into two categories: those that relate to capital movement between Member States (Article 58, see also Articles 119 and 120 (ex 109h and 109i)); and those that relate to movement to third countries (Articles 57, 59 and 60). Article 58 is the provision containing the express exceptions to the free movement of capital. It can be seen as analogous to Articles 30 (goods), 40(3) (workers) and 46 (establishment/services). Nonetheless, there are also some differences, as Article 58 contains some exceptions that are specific to capital: Article 58(1)(a) contains provisions specific to Member States' individual tax regimes. Article 58 also specifically raises the question of the relationship of the free movement of capital with the freedom of establishment (Article 58(2) and (3)). This issue, as well as the relationship between capital and services, is discussed below at 16.5.

16.3 Scope of the free movement of capital

16.3.1 Who can rely on the free movement of capital?

Community nationals may rely on this freedom, as may legal persons. The original Article 67 EEC has merely required residence in the EC for a body to be able to rely on the freedom of capital. The situation is now wider still, Article 56 making no reference to such a requirement. Like the provisions relating to the free movement of goods, and in contrast to those relating to services and people, the capital provisions may be relied on by third-country nationals (TCNs). The situation is the same whether the capital movement is intra-Community, or between a third country and the Community.

16.3.2 Direct effect

In contrast to the position prior to the amendments made by the Maastricht Treaty noted above, the current prohibition *has* been held to be directly effective: see *Bordessa* (cases C–358 and 416/93) and *Sanz de Lera and others* (cases C–163, 165 and 250/94). This is the case whether we are considering prohibitions on restrictions on capital movements between Member States or between Member States and third countries. There is no jurisprudence as yet on whether Article 56 will have horizontal effect (see Chapter 5).

16.3.3 Types of act caught

The ECJ has taken a broad approach to the types of act caught by the prohibition in Article 56 EC. This was the case even before the Maastricht amendments to the capital provisions. In *Brugnoni and Ruffinengo* (case 157/85), decided in 1986, the ECJ accepted that 'restriction' covered more than just legislative acts, and also covered administrative obstacles to free movement. Equally, it seems not to matter in which capacity a government is acting when a potential restriction under Article 56 is in issue. In *Eurobonds* (case C–478/98), a case involving a prohibition on Belgian residents subscribing to securities issued abroad (Eurobonds), the Belgian government argued that it was acting not in its capacity as public authority but on the same terms as a private borrower when it adopted the restriction. The ECJ rejected this argument on the facts of the case, although the status of measures not dependent on public powers remains open.

16.3.4 Meaning of capital

The prohibition operates on both capital movements and those relating to payments. Although this would suggest that the two concepts are different, and indeed early case law, *Luisi and Carbone* (case 286/82), distinguished between the two, since the prohibition operates on both in the same terms, effectively the need to distinguish between the two has been removed. Neither term is defined in Article 56, although Article 57 lists some types of capital, such as direct investments and the provision of financial services. This provision has not, however, been referred to by the ECJ in determining the scope of 'capital'. In terms of defining capital, the ECJ held in *Trummer* (case C–222/97) that Directive 88/361, passed before the changes brought in by TEU, remains relevant in terms of identifying what constitutes capital (see para. 21 of the judgment). An annex to this directive contains an indicative 'nomenclature' (a list of categories), listed under 13 headings (e.g., property investment). As the ECJ made clear, this list is not exhaustive. In *Verkooijen* (case C–35/98), the ECJ ruled that the receipt of dividends from investments abroad, a category not listed in the nomenclature, was inextricable from a capital movement and therefore fell within the scope of Article 56. Potentially the scope of Article 56 *et seq.* is wide, especially as the nomenclature in Directive 88/361 includes not only the capital movement itself but also the underlying transaction (see, e.g., heading VIII 'Financial Loans and Credits'). This approach opens up the possibility of overlap between the free movement of capital and the freedom to provide services (see further 16.5).

16.3.5 Test for application of free movement of capital

The concept of a 'restriction on the free movement of capital' has been interpreted broadly, as with the other freedoms. The prohibition operates to eliminate measures which effectively prevent an individual being able to use a currency of another Member State, such as in *Trummer* (case C–222/97) (prohibition on mortgages in a foreign currency). It also applies to less stringent measures, such as requirements for prior authorisation of currency transactions. The prohibition does not apply just to absolute barriers to free movement, but also to those measures which hinder or dissuade people from exercising free movement rights.

In the other freedoms we have seen a move from a discrimination-based approach to one that looks at hindrances. The change in emphasis in wording, noted in 16.2, between Article 67 EEC and Article 56(1) reflects this trend. Nonetheless, the ECJ has not always distinguished clearly between restrictions and discrimination when handing down its judgments. Thus in the *Portuguese Golden Shares* case (case C–367/98), it was accepted that the Portuguese national rules precluding investors from other states from acquiring more than a specified number of shares in certain newly privatised companies constituted 'unequal treatment of nationals of other Member States and restricts the free movement of capital' (para. 40). This is a case of direct discrimination. Similarly, in *Konle* (case C–302/97), an Austrian rule, which in the interests of planning control exempted Austrian nationals only from having to obtain authorisation before acquiring a plot of land was seen as creating a discriminatory restriction against nationals of other Member States. Even in this case, however, the ECJ linked the existence of discrimination to the creation of a restriction. In other cases the ECJ has used terms such as 'obstacles' or 'liable to dissuade' (*Trummer*). These phrases seem similar to the approach taken in relation to the freedom to provide services (see Chapter 22). In the British *Golden Shares* case, the ECJ noted that even rules which apply without distinction to non-nationals and nationals alike can

> deter investors from other Member States from making such investments and, consequently, affect access to the market. [*Commission* v *UK* (*Golden Shares*) (case C–98/01), para. 47].

It seems the ECJ here is moving away from a discrimination-based approach and looking at the impact on the market. Certainly, in the *Portuguese Golden Shares* case, the ECJ commented that Article 56 'goes beyond the mere elimination of unequal treatment, on grounds of nationality, as between operators on the financial markets' (para. 44).

16.3.5.1 *Requisite impact on the market*

The UK Government in the *Golden Shares* case (case C–98/01) suggested that the principle in *Keck* should apply to Article 56. It argued that the rules in issue had an impact on the market which was too indirect to fall within the scope of the prohibition. The ECJ did not address this point directly. Nonetheless, the implication of the wording in the UK *Golden Shares* case, with its emphasis on access to the market, is that rules that have an impact which is too indirect will not fall within Article 56. This approach indeed had been suggested by the Advocate-General in the earlier case of *ED Srl* (case C–412/97), but again the ECJ did not address the point. Instead, it dealt with the matter under a different provision of the Treaty, as one concerning goods (see further Chapter 18).

16.3.5.2 *Effects-based test*

The purpose behind the national rule is not relevant, although the ECJ will sometimes highlight when there is a protectionist motive (see, e.g., *Verkooijen* (case C–35/98), para. 34, *Reisch* (joined cases C–515, 519–540/99), para. 32). It is the effect that is crucial and, as with the other freedoms, there is no *de minimis* exception.

16.3.6 **Internal situations**

Like the other freedoms, Article 56 may not be relied on in internal situations. It cannot therefore be used to challenge Member States rules regarding, for example, the acquisition of property. It should be noted, however, that the ECJ has given a generous interpretation of when there is no such internal situation. In the case of *Reisch et al.* (cases C–515, 519–540/99), the ECJ held:

> A reference for a preliminary ruling from a national court may be rejected by the Court only if it is quite obvious that the interpretation of Community law sought by that court bears no relation to the actual nature of the case or the subject-matter of the main action (para. 25).

This is potentially a very broad test and one that is uncertain in the scope of its application. It seems that few rules would fall within the 'internal situation'.

16.4 **Exceptions to the free movement of capital**

16.4.1 **Express Treaty derogation**

Member States can restrict free movement of capital and payments on the grounds set out in Article 58.

16.4.1.1 *National taxation systems*

Member States may distinguish between taxpayers who are not in the same situation with regard to their place of residence or with regard to the place where their capital is invested (Article 58(1)(a)).

As noted earlier, this is a specific exception, unique to the free movement of capital provisions. This is restrictively interpreted: although taxation remains within Member States' competence, this power must be exercised within the scope of Community law. In *Petri Manninen* (case C–319/02), the ECJ commented that Article 58(1)(a)

> cannot be interpreted as meaning that any tax legislation making a distinction between taxpayers by reference to the place where they invest their capital is automatically compatible with the Treaty (para. 28),

and in particular noted that Article 58(1)(a) is limited by Article 58(3) (see below). In *Verkooijen* (case C–35/98), the ECJ commented that this provision effectively codified the approach that it had taken in *Schumacker* and *Bachmann* (discussed in Chapter 20), which permits Member States to protect the coherence of their internal taxation system. However, an argument based on the need to safeguard the cohesion of a tax system must be examined in the light of the objective pursued by the tax legislation in question (*De Lasteyrie du Saillant* (case C–9/02), para. 67) to see if such rules are actually necessary. Indeed, the ECJ has consistently held that reduction in tax revenue cannot be regarded as an overriding reason in the public interest which may be relied on to justify a measure which is in principle contrary to a fundamental freedom (see, e.g., *Verkooijen*, para. 59; *X and Y* (case C–436/00), para. 50). Laws may also be justified where the difference in treatment concerns situations which are not objectively comparable or in the interests of the fight against tax avoidance and the effectiveness of fiscal supervision. These will be similarly strictly reviewed.

16.4.1.2 *Anti-avoidance and public policy*

Member States may take action to prevent the avoidance of national regulation; to lay down procedures for the declaration of capital movements for the purposes of administrative or statistical information; or in the interests of public policy or public security (Article 58(1)(b)).

This is a three-pronged exception, which is a mixture of concern for fiscal supervision and a standard public policy exception. The concern for fiscal supervision has links with the issues discussed at 16.4.1.1, above. In the *Eurobonds* case (case C–478/98), the prohibition on the acquisition by Belgian residents of securities of a loan issued abroad was not justified. The ECJ commented that 'a general presumption of tax evasion or tax fraud cannot justify a fiscal measure', especially where the national measure constituted 'an outright prohibition of a fundamental freedom' (para. 45). Note that the reference to 'national regulation' is not necessarily limited to concerns listed in Article 58(1)(b): taxation and the prudential supervision of financial institutions. In *Bordessa* (joined cases C–358/93 and C–416/93), the ECJ held that other types of measure would be permitted where they were aimed at preventing 'illegal activities of comparable seriousness, such as money laundering, drug trafficking or terrorism' (para. 21).

Note that the second element of Article 58(1)(b) is potentially a broad category, although the ECJ will construe all exceptions to Treaty freedoms narrowly. There is also no equivalent provision to this provision in the articles derogating from the other Treaty freedoms. In this instance, therefore, jurisprudence developed in relation to the other Treaty freedoms can probably not be used to derive guidance on the likely scope of this derogation. It seems that some prior *notification* requirements for statistical purposes or to prevent money laundering, for example, may be acceptable, but not prior *authorisation* (see *Sanz de Lera* (cases C–163, 165 and 250/94).

Looking at the third aspect of Article 58(1)(b), note that a similar wording is used here to the exception to the free movement of goods and the exceptions relating to services, workers and establishment (see Chapters 20–22). Likewise, the test adopted is that a sufficiently serious threat to fundamental interest exists and is similar to that used in regard to the other freedoms. (See for example *Association Eglise de Scientology de Paris and Scientology International Reserves Trust* v *the Prime Minister* (case C–54/99); *Commission* v *Belgium* (case C–503/99); *Commission* v *France* (case C–483/99); and the *Golden Shares* cases: *Commission* v *UK* (case C–98/01) and *Commission* v *Spain* (case C–436/00)). See also the prohibition on buying property near military sites, which would be acceptable only if military interests of the Member State would be exposed to real, specific and serious risks which could not be countered by less restrictive means (*Albore* (case C–423/98)).

16.4.1.3 *Impact on establishment*

Restrictions may result in restrictions on the right of establishment and must there-fore be compatible with those provisions (Article 58(2)). (See, e.g., *Algemene Maat-schappij voor Investering* (case C–141/99).) The relationship between establishment and capital is discussed below at 16.5.

16.4.1.4 *Interpreting the derogations*

As the ECJ noted in the *Church of Scientology* case (case C–54/99) derogations from the fundamental principle of the free movement of capital must be interpreted strictly. Their scope cannot be determined unilaterally by individual Member States without any supervision by Community institutions. In any event, any rule falling within any of the above exceptions cannot constitute a means of arbitrary dis-crimination or disguised restriction on the free movement of capital or payments (Article 58(3)). The ECJ has reaffirmed that derogations cannot be applied so as to serve purely economic ends (see also *Portuguese Golden Shares* case (case C–367/98)). As with the other exceptions to Treaty freedoms, it would seem that the crucial question will be proportionality of the Member State's measure, whether the Member State is seeking to justify its measure under express Treaty derogations or in relation to a rule of reason-style argument. More unusually, the ECJ in the *Church of Scientology* case made two more points about the use of derogations. Any person affected by such a restrictive measure had to have access to legal redress: in this, the ECJ is reflecting the general approach to right to a remedy found in Community law (see further Chapter 8). Additionally, such a person had to be

> apprised of the extent of their rights and obligations deriving from Article [56] of the Treaty (para. 22).

Again, this reflects a general principle of Community law. What is interesting is that it is only in respect of the free movement of capital that this point is made express.

16.4.1.5 *Non-Euro Member States*

For Member States which have not joined up to the Euro, there are two further provisions which may be relied on where there are balance of payment difficulties—Articles 119 and 120 EC. Although these empower such Member States to take uni-lateral action (subject only to veto or amendment by the Council acting by qualified majority), the protective measures must cause the least possible disturbance to the common market and must not be wider in scope than is strictly necessary.

16.4.2 **Rule of reason?**

There are more similarities with the other freedoms: Article 56 does not just catch those rules which discriminate directly against capital movements, it also catches rules which indirectly restrict capital movements. With a restriction-based test, it seems that Member States may be able to rely on grounds of overriding public interest to justify a national measure. In *Reisch* (joined cases C–515, 519–540/99), the Court, referring to its previous case law in *Konle* (case C–302/97), summarised the position as follows:

It is not in dispute that those measures, by laying down a procedure of prior notification/ authorisation for the acquisition of immovable property, restrict, by their very purpose, the free movement of capital [see, to that effect, *Konle*, cited above, para. 39].

Such restrictions may nevertheless be permitted if the national rules pursue, in a non-discriminatory way, an objective in the public interest and if they observe the principle of proportionality, that is if the same result could not be achieved by other less restrictive measures (paras 32–33).

This point was re-emphasised in the *Golden Shares* cases (*Commission* v *UK* (C–98/01), *Commission* v *Spain* (C–436/00); see also *Communication of the Commission on Certain Legal Aspect Concerning intra-EU Investment* ([1997] OJ C220/15)). As with the other freedoms, the list of possible public interest justifications, by contrast with the exceptions in Article 58, is open-ended. Thus in *Konle*, town and country planning was accepted as an appropriate overriding requirement in the general interest; similarly, environmental protection and land management concerns have been recognised (*Reisch* (joined cases C–515, 519–540/99)); and the *Golden Shares* cases (*Commission* v *UK* (case C–98/01), *Commission* v *Spain* (case C–436/06)) recognised the importance of undertakings which are involved in the provision of services in the public interest.

There is some lack of clarity around the consequence of whether a national rule is discriminatory or not. In the *Portuguese Golden Shares* case (case C–367/98), the ECJ reiterated the position that overriding requirements of the general interest may be used in relation to rules 'which are applicable to all persons and undertakings pursuing an activity in the territory of the host Member State'; in this it is following the approach already identified in *Reisch* (joined cases C–515, 519–540/99). Nonetheless, in some cases the ECJ has accepted the principle on an overriding reason in the general interest although the rule has been characterised as discriminatory. See, for example, *Svensson and Gustavvson* (case C–484/98), which, at paras 16–19, contains a discussion of overriding reasons in the general interest despite the fact that the ECJ had held, in para. 15 of the same judgment, that there had been discrimination because the rule was based on the place of establishment and that the rule could therefore only be justified by reference to the grounds of derogation set out expressly in the Treaty.

As with the express Treaty derogation, and in common with the other freedoms, any Member State measure must satisfy the test of proportionality. As the ECJ phrased this in *Reisch* (joined cases C–515, 519–540/99), proportionality requires that 'the same result could not be achieved by other less restrictive measures'. In practice it seems that this is a hard test to satisfy: in many cases the requirement of prior authorisation has not been found to be proportionate. It seems that the ECJ is more likely to find a requirement to make a declaration acceptable (see, e.g., *Bordessa* (cases C–358 and 416/93). The ECJ did accept in the Portuguese *Golden Shares* case (case C–367/98) that in some instances prior authorisation might be necessary (here the provision of services in the public interest or strategic services), but even then any such system must be proportionate and use non-discriminatory criteria which would be known in advance to the relevant undertakings. Further, all persons affected by a restrictive measure had to have a legal remedy available to them. On the facts of the case, the Portuguese Government was unsuccessful.

16.5 Relationship with other freedoms

The precise scope of these provisions is not clear: some have suggested that the free movement of capital is ancillary to the other freedoms, for example goods or establishment. Certainly, those provisions may be seen as dependent on the freedom of payments – there would be little incentive to export goods, for example, were it not possible to repatriate the value of those costs. Equally clearly, there is a potential for overlap between the provisions, as the provisions relating to tax harmonisation and the harmonisation of the market for financial services illustrate (see directives on insurance and banking). See also the discussion in cases such as *Trummer* v *Mayer* (case C–222/97) (national prohibition on the creation of a mortgage in a foreign currency), *Svensson and Gustavvson* (case C–484/98), *Safir* v *Skattemyndigheten i Dalamas Lan* (case C–118/96) (taxation of savings where a different tax regime applied according to where the insurance company providing savings scheme was established) and *Konle* v *Austria* (case C–302/97) (authorisation required for acquiring immovable property).

It is not entirely clear whether the capital provisions may be applied in tandem with the provisions relating to establishment or those concerning services, although (despite the wording of the Treaty with regard to Article 49) this would seem to be the case (e.g., *Safir* (case C–118/96). The Advocates-General in *Svensson and Gustavsson* (case C–484/98) and in *Safir* expressed unease with an approach which conflates services and capital. In *Safir*, the Advocate-General suggested that the boundary lay between a direct restriction on capital, which would fall to be considered under Article 56, and the situation where the restriction was indirect, which would be considered as affecting services. In its judgment, the ECJ merely remarked that it was unnecessary to consider the free movement of capital provisions; it is unclear whether this silence on the reasoning of the Advocate-General connotes agreement with his reasoning or not. In the *Italian Recruitment Agencies* case (case C–279/00), the Commission brought an action against Italy in respect of a requirement that undertakings providing temporary workers must lodge a guarantee with a credit establishment having its seat or a branch in Italy. The Commission argued that this rule violated both the freedom to provide services and the free movement of capital. The ECJ analysed this rule both from the perspective of the employment agencies and from that of the banks. The ECJ ruled that the provision was a restriction on capital movement as far as the employment agencies were concerned and a violation of the banks' freedom to provide services within Article 49. It has been suggested that given that there are two sets of circumstances arising from the same rule, there is not a concurrent application of the two freedoms – though arguably the real effect is the same as the concurrent application of such rules.

16.6 Restrictions on free movement of capital between Member States and third countries

Although in principle free movement of capital between Member States and third countries is secured by Article 56 EC, the restrictions on free movement of capital set out in Article 58 apply equally to free movement as regards third countries. This seems to be a less liberalised framework, however, than that relating to intra-Community movements. Additional restrictions may also apply:

(a) Article 56 does not apply to national measures existing on 31 December 1993 – although the Council may act to remove such measures (Article 57; see 16.7 below).

(b) In limited circumstances where serious difficulties in the operation of EMU arise, the Council may take short-term measures restricting capital movements to third countries (Article 59).

(c) In urgent cases, restrictions which form part of economic sanctions may be introduced (Article 60).

16.7 Power to legislate in the field of free movement of capital

Article 57(2) provides that the Council may, by qualified majority and following a proposal by the Commission, legislate on the free movement of capital to or from third countries. There appears to be some tension in this provision. On the one hand, the objective of such action has to be to endeavour to achieve the free movement of capital between Member States and third countries 'to the greatest extent possible'. Nonetheless, the same provision envisages the possibility of a 'step back in Community law' regarding the liberalisation of capital to or from third countries, although this is tempered somewhat by the requirement that any measure constituting a 'step back' must be adopted unanimously.

In contrast to the other freedoms, therefore, there is no all-encompassing competence to adopt legislation to facilitate the free movement of capital (and payments) between Member States. However, where the European legislator has deemed it necessary to adopt legislation dealing with the movement of capital between Member States, it has achieved this by relying on Article 95 EC (e.g., Directive 97/5/EC on cross-border credit transfers [1997] OJ L43/25). For a discussion of the limits of Article 95, see Chapter 15.

16.8 Conclusions

Since 1992 and the TEU, the number of cases decided under the free movement of capital provisions has increased significantly, and the jurisprudence on this freedom has developed correspondingly. The ECJ seems to have been willing to borrow principles from the other freedoms and apply them to the capital case law, resulting in certain parallels between all the freedoms. The result is that the approach to the free movement of capital has been liberalised, with potentially far-reaching effects on Member States' internal policies, particularly their taxation systems, as recent cases show. Problem areas do remain, particularly with regard to the ECJ's approach to the relationship between the different freedoms. Despite the increasing parallelism, it must be recognised that certain provisions remain unique to the free movement of capital, and that there may be circumstances in which the difference between the freedoms remains important.

FURTHER READING

Flynn, L., 'Coming of Age: The Free Movement of Capital Case Law 1993–2002' (2002) 39 CML Rev 773–805.

Mitroyanni, J., 'Exploring the Free Movement of Capital in Direct Taxation' (2005) 8(1) EC Tax Journal 1.

O'Brien, M., 'Company Taxation, State Aid and Fundamental Freedoms: Is the Next Step Enhanced Cooperation?' (2005) 30(2) EL Rev 209.

Oliver, P. and Bache, J-P., 'Free Movement of Capital between the Member States: Recent Developments' (1989) 26 CML Rev 61.

Peers, S., 'Free Movement of Capital: Learning Lessons or Slipping on Spilt Milk' in Barnard and Scott (eds) *The Law of the Single Market: Unpacking the Premises* (Hart Publishing, 2002).

Usher, J., 'Capital Movements and the Treaty on European Union' (1992) 12 YEL 35.

Wattel, P. J., 'Red Herrings in Direct Tax Cases before the ECJ' (2004) 31(2), Legal Issues of Economic Integration 81–95.

17

Customs union

17.1 Introduction

As we have seen in Chapters 3 and 14, the main mechanism for attaining the Community's goals is through the creation of a common market. Central to the common market is the free movement of goods, which aims to ensure that imported goods are not disadvantaged by extra costs of whatever nature. The most obvious way in which extra costs can be imposed on imports is by subjecting them to additional duties, such as customs duties, or by imposing a separate (and disadvantageous) taxation system on them. There are a number of relevant provisions in the Treaty to deal with this problem: notably Article 23 and Article 90. The articles in the EC Treaty go further than prohibiting such charges; they aim to create a customs union, which requires all Member States take a common approach to the import of goods from third countries. The EC Treaty, therefore, contains provisions for a Common Customs Tariff (Articles 26–27 (ex 18–29).) Allied to these provisions are Articles 3(b) and 131–134 (ex 110–115) EC, which provide for the establishment of a common commercial policy towards third countries.

This chapter discusses the provisions establishing the Common Customs Tariff, the prohibition on customs duties and on discriminatory taxation. In doing so, several key points should be noted. First the prohibition on customs duties is one of the central features of the customs union. It has been interpreted broadly as a result, and any exceptions to the prohibition are strictly limited. The provisions on customs duties are linked to those on discriminatory taxation – the prohibition on discriminatory taxation serves to prevent Member States from circumventing the prohibition on customs duties by discriminating against imports via their internal taxation system. It is because of this link that the discriminatory taxation provisions are dealt with here, as part of the free movement of goods, despite the fact that within the Treaty they are located in a separate section dealing with taxation. Despite their common function, in some ways the taxation provisions are more problematic than those relating to customs duties. Taxation in general still remains part of the Member States' competence; further, in determining the scope of 'similar' products, the ECJ has a certain degree of interpretive freedom. Although Article 90 does not require Member States to adopt any particular system of taxation, the rulings of the ECJ under Article 90 have had an impact on Member States' policy choices. Article 90 jurisprudence is, to some degree, therefore contentious.

17.2 **Common customs tariff**

As part of its common commercial policy, and to ensure equal treatment in all Member States for goods imported into the EC from third countries, thereby enabling *all* goods in circulation within the Community to benefit equally from the free movement provisions, the Treaty provided for the introduction of the common customs tariff (CCT), sometimes known as the common external tariff (CET). The CCT applies to all products imported into the Community from outside the EC, erecting a single tariff wall which no individual State is free to breach.

The operation of the CCT is governed by Articles 26–27 EC and is enacted by directly applicable regulations. Under the CCT goods are classified according to a common nomenclature, and are subject to common Community rules as to value and origin. Products are divided into lists, the classifications being derived from the Brussels Convention on Nomenclature for the Classification of Goods. The lists, and the applicable tariff rates, are set out in Annexe I to the EC Treaty. The CCT is published by the Commission and is regularly updated. The Council, acting by qualified majority on a proposal from the Commission, is empowered to alter or suspend duties within certain limits (Article 26 (ex 28)). Once goods are imported into the Community, that is, when they have complied with import formalities and paid the relevant customs duties, the free movement provisions of the Treaty apply. Even where goods are imported into a Member State under a special tariff quota the ECJ has held that a State cannot deny the application of the free movement provisions to the import and export of such goods within the Community unless the Commission has, under Article 134 (ex 115) EC, authorised derogation in order to avoid a deflection of trade or economic difficulties in one or more Member States (see *Criel, nee Donckerwolcke* (case 41/76) and note by J. Usher (1986) 11 EL Rev 210).

The Commission, subject to the Council's approval, has a central role in establishing and administering the CCT. In carrying out its task it is required to balance a number of (often conflicting) economic needs set out in Article 27 (ex 29), in the light of the general aims of the Community. Although the Commission has an important role in the administration of the CCT, there is no such body as a Community customs service. The Community is dependent on the customs officers of the various Member States to implement the CCT. Duties raised under the CCT are payable to the Community and form part of the Community's 'own resources'.

17.3 **Prohibition between Member States of customs duties on imports and exports and of all charges of equivalent effect**

This is governed by Articles 23 and 25. Article 25 is the 'standstill' provision, prohibiting the introduction between Member States of any new customs duties on imports and exports or any charges having equivalent effect.

Article 23 states:

> 1. The Community shall be based upon a customs union which shall cover all trade in goods and which shall involve the prohibition between Member States of customs duties on imports and exports and of all charges having equivalent effect, and the adoption of a common customs tariff in the relations with third countries.
> 2. The provisions of Article 25 and of Chapter 2 of the Title shall apply to products originating in Member States and to products coming from third countries which are in free circulation in Member States.

These provisions will be found at Article III–151 should the Constitution in its current form come into force.

17.3.1 Scope of the prohibition

The prohibition applies to all duties, whether applied directly or indirectly. In *Van Gend en Loos* (case 26/62) the product in question had been reclassified under Dutch law, with the result that it became subject to a higher rate of duty. The ECJ held that this would constitute a breach of Article 25. Article 25 has also been held to apply to a charge on imports and exports into a *region* of a Member State, not only insofar as it is levied on goods entering that region from other Member States, but also when it is levied on goods entering that region from another part of the same State (*Simitzi* v *Kos* (cases C–485 & 486/93), re *ad valorem* municipality tax imposed on imports into and exports from the Dodecanese (Greece)). This obligation was held to derive from the 'absolute nature' of the prohibition of all customs duties applicable to goods moving between Member States. This also applies to additional charges levied on goods imported into a region which originated from a third country (*Société Cadi Surgélés* v *Ministre des Finances* (case C–126/94)), and to charges levied on goods *exported* from a region, irrespective of whether their final destination is within the same Member State, or abroad (*Carbonati Apuani Srol* v *Comune di Carrara* (case C–72/03)).

   If the meaning of 'custom duties' is clear, what are 'charges having equivalent effect' to a customs duty? It was held by the ECJ in the case of *Sociaal Fonds voor de Diamantarbeiders* (cases 2 & 3/69), in the context of a challenge to a 'tax' imposed on imported diamonds, that it included any pecuniary charge, however slight, imposed on goods by reason of the fact that they cross frontiers. The charge need not be levied at the frontier; it can be imposed at any stage of production or marketing; but provided it is levied *by reason of importation* it will breach Article 25 (*Steinike und Weinleg* v *Germany* (case 78/76)).

17.3.2 Distinction between customs duties and taxes

A charge of equivalent effect to a customs duty may come in many guises, and is often disguised as a 'tax'. Since genuine taxes fall to be considered under Article 90 EC, it is necessary at the outset to distinguish between a charge, falling within Articles 23 and 25, and a genuine tax. A genuine tax was defined in *Commission v France (Re Levy on Reprographic Machines)* (case 90/79) as one relating 'to a general system of internal dues applied systematically to categories of products in accordance with objective criteria irrespective of the origin of the products'. To ascertain whether a 'tax' is genuine it must be examined to see whether it fits into an overall system of taxation or whether it has been superimposed on the system with a particular purpose in mind. Provided the tax is genuine, it may be imposed on imports even where the importing State produces no identical or similar product (*Commission* v *France*). In such a case it will not breach Article 25 but may be examined for its compatibility with Article 90.

17.3.3 An effects-based test

To breach Article 25, a charge need not be introduced for protectionist reasons. It was pointed out in the *Sociaal Fonds* case that no diamond-mining industry existed in Belgium, and the proceeds of the charge were used for a most worthy purpose, to provide a social fund for workers in the diamond industry. These factors were held by the ECJ to be irrelevant. Such duties are forbidden independently of the purpose for which they are levied and the destination of the charge. In reaching its decision the Court looked at the effect of the measure: any pecuniary charge imposed on goods by reason of the fact that they cross frontiers is an obstacle to the free movement of goods.

A similar conclusion was reached by the ECJ in *Commission* v *Luxembourg (Re Import on Gingerbread)* (cases 2 & 3/62) in the context of a compensatory 'tax' on imported gingerbread. The governments claimed the 'tax' was introduced merely to compensate for the competitive disadvantage resulting from a high rate of domestic tax on rye, an ingredient of gingerbread. The purpose of the prohibition on measures of equivalent effect to customs duties, the Court held, was to prohibit not only measures ostensibly clothed with the classic nature of a customs duty but also those which, presented under other names or introduced by the indirect means of other procedures, would lead to the same discriminatory or protective *results* as customs duties. If compensatory 'taxes' of this type were allowed, States would be able to make up for all sorts of taxes at home by imposing a so-called balancing charge on imports. This would ensure that imported goods would lose any competitive advantage they might have as against the equivalent domestic product and thereby frustrate the objectives of the single market.

17.3.4 Limitations on the prohibition

Even when the charge is levied to benefit the importer it may still breach Article 25. In *Commission* v *Italy (Re Statistical Levy)* (case 24/68) a levy, applied to all imports and exports, regardless of source, the proceeds of which were used to finance an export statistical service for the benefit of importers and exporters, was found to be in breach of Articles 23–25 EC. The ECJ held that the advantage to importers was so general and uncertain that it could not be considered a payment for service rendered (see also *W. Cadsky SpA* (case 63/74), in relation to charges on the *export* of goods).

This implies that a charge levied for a service rendered to the importer and which is not too general and uncertain would be permissible. This principle has, however, been given the narrowest possible scope. The ECJ has held that where an inspection service is imposed in the general interest, for example, for health or safety purposes, or quality control, this cannot be regarded as a service rendered to the importer or exporter to justify the imposition of a charge *(Rewe-Zentralfinanz eGmbH* v *Land-wirtschaftskammer Westfalen-Lippe* (case 39/73)). This principle applies regardless of the nature of the agency, public or private, providing the service, and whether or not the charge is borne by virtue of a unilateral measure adopted by the authorities or as a result of a series of private contracts (*Édouard Dubois et Fils SA* v *Garonor Exploitation SA* (case C–16/94)). Even when such inspections are expressly *permitted* under EC law, as in *Commission* v *Belgium (Re Health Inspection Service)* (case 314/82), the Court held that a charge for such a service cannot be regarded as a service rendered for the benefit of the importer. It is only when such services are mandatory, as part of a common Community regime, or arising from an international agreement into which the EC has entered (*Bakker Hillegom* (case C–111/89)), that Member States are entitled to recover the cost, and no more than the cost, of the service (*Bauhuis* v *Netherlands* (case 46/76)).

Unless a service is required under Community law, it appears that only a service which gives a tangible benefit to the importer, or the imported goods, for example, a finishing or packaging service, will be regarded as sufficient to justify a charge, and even then it will not be permissible if the 'service' is one imposed on the importer in the general interest. Where a genuine service is provided for the benefit of the importer the ECJ has held that the charge must not exceed the value or the cost of the service (*Rewe-Zentralfinanz eGmbH* (case 39/73)), or a sum proportionate to the service provided (*Commission* v *Denmark* (case 158/82)). A charge based on the value of the goods is not permissible (*Ford España SA* v *Spain* (case 170/88)). In *Donner* (case 39/82) the Court suggested that a charge by the Dutch Post Office for dealing with the payment of VAT on imported books on behalf of the claimant might be regarded as a payment for services rendered but left the national court to decide whether on the facts it was, and if so whether it was proportionate.

Where a charge is imposed only upon domestically produced goods, the ECJ appears to take a more lenient view. In *Apple & Pear Development Council* v *K. J. Lewis Ltd* (case 222/82) a number of growers challenged a compulsory levy imposed on growers of apples and pears in the UK. The proceeds of the levy went to finance the Apple and Pear Development Council, a semi-public body whose functions included research, the compilation of statistics, provision of information, publicity and promotion. The ECJ held that since the levy did not apply to imported products there was no breach of Articles 23–25. The charge would only be illegal if it served to finance activities which were incompatible with EC law.

17.3.5 Non-discriminatory charges

All the cases considered so far have concerned unilateral charges, charges imposed only upon imported or exported products and not on the comparable domestic product (or vice versa). Clearly such charges undermine the principle of free trade and free competition within the common market. What about a non-discriminatory charge, applied to a particular product regardless of source? Will this be capable of infringing Articles 23 and 25 EC? This calls for a more subtle enquiry into:

(a) the nature of the charge and its mode of calculation, and

(b) the destination of the charge, i.e., who receives the benefit.

Three situations may be considered:

(a) If the charge is identical in every respect and levied as part of a general system of taxation it will not fall within Article 25 and will be treated as a fiscal measure, and examined for its compatibility with Article 90 (prohibition on discriminatory taxation).

(b) If the same charge is levied on a particular product, regardless of source, it will nonetheless breach Article 25 if the charge on the imported or exported product is not imposed in the same way and determined according to the same criteria as apply to the domestic product. This point was made by the ECJ in *Marimex SpA v Italian Minister of Finance (No. 2)* (case 29/72) in the context of a challenge to a 'veterinary inspection tax' imposed on imported meat, live and dead, to ensure that it conformed to Italian health standards. Similar domestic products were subject to corresponding inspections which were also 'taxed', but they were conducted by different bodies according to different criteria. The ECJ held that such a tax on imports would be in breach of the then Article 9 (now 23).

(c) Even if the charge is levied at the same rate and according to identical criteria it may still breach Articles 23 and 25 if the proceeds of the charge are applied to benefit the domestic product *exclusively*. This point was first made in *Capolongo v Azienda Agricola Maya* (case 77/72). In this case the Italians had introduced a charge on imported egg boxes, as part of an overall charge on cellulose products, the aim being to finance the production of paper and cardboard in Italy. Although the charge was imposed on all egg boxes, domestic and imported, the Court held it was in breach of the then Article 13 (deleted by ToA). Although applied to domestic and imported goods alike, it was discriminatory if it was intended exclusively to support activities which specifically benefited the domestic product.

The scope of *Capolongo* was restricted in the subsequent case of *Fratelli Cucchi v Avez SpA* (case 77/76). Here a dispute arose concerning the legality of a levy on imported sugar. Domestically produced sugar was subject to the same levy. The proceeds of the levy went to finance the sugar industry, to benefit two groups, the beet producers and the sugar-processing industry. The ECJ held that such a charge would be of equivalent effect to a customs duty if three conditions were fulfilled:

(a) if it has the *sole* purpose of financing activities for the specific advantage of the domestic product;

(b) if the taxed domestic product and the domestic product to benefit are the same; and

(c) if the charges imposed on the domestic product are made up *in full*.

If these conditions are not fulfilled the charge will not breach Article 25 EC. However, where the same tax, levied on domestic and imported products alike, gives only *partial* benefit to the domestic product, it may be deemed a discriminatory tax, in breach of Article 90 EC (*Commission v Italy* (*Re Reimbursement of Sugar Storage Costs*) (case 73/79); *Cooperative Co-Frutta* (case 193/85)). A grant to a particular industry may be adjudged a State aid in breach of Article 87 (ex 92) EC.

17.3.6 Derogation from prohibition on customs duties

The rules concerning charges of equivalent effect to a customs duty are strictly applied by the ECJ. Indeed, in its anxiety to ensure that no pecuniary restriction, however small, shall create obstacles to trade, particularly to imports, the Court is even prepared to countenance a degree of reverse discrimination, since Member

States are required themselves to finance measures such as health inspections which may be fully justified in the public interest (see *Rewe-Zentralfinanz eGmbH* (case 39/73)). Nor does the Treaty or the Court provide for any derogation in this field. In *Commission v Italy (Re Export Tax on Art Treasures)* (case 7/68) the Italians argued that the tax was justified to protect their artistic heritage. Under Article 30 (ex 36) States are entitled to derogate from the prohibition on imposing quantitative restrictions on imports (Article 28 EC) or exports (Article 29 EC), or measures of equivalent effect, on the grounds of *inter alia*, 'the protection of national treasures possessing artistic, historic or archaeological value'. The Court held that the then Article 36 (now 30) could never be invoked to justify a charge (see also *Marimex SpA* (case 29/72)). The only way for a Member State to defend a charge is to argue either that it does not fall within the definition of customs duty by virtue of it being part of an internal system of taxation, in which case it will be assessed by reference to Article 90; or that the charge is required by Community law in accordance with the principles in *Bauhuis* (case 46/76) (see 17.3.4 above).

17.3.7 Enforcing Articles 23–25

Since Articles 23 and 25 are directly effective, any sums paid under an illegal charge are recoverable. This might, in certain circumstances, require the relevant domestic bodies to reconsider a previous decision once it has become clear that charges should not have been made (*Kühne & Neitz NV v Productschap voor Pluimvee and Eieren* (case C–453/00)). Although repayment must be sought within the framework, and according to the rules, of national law, conditions must not be so framed as to render it excessively difficult or impossible in practice to exercise the rights conferred by Community law (*SpA San Giorgio* (case 199/82) – see further Chapter 8). The principle of unjust enrichment may be invoked to deny a claim for repayment where the charge has been incorporated into the price of goods and passed on to purchasers *(SpA San Giorgio, Weber's Wine World* (case C–147/01)). However, national authorities may not impose the burden of proving that a charge has *not* been passed on to those persons seeking reimbursement, nor may restrictive or onerous evidential requirements (such as documentary evidence alone) be imposed. Member States are not entitled to presume that illegal taxes have been passed on (*Commission v Italy Re Repayment of Illegal Taxes* (case 104/86)). In *Just* v *Danish Ministry for Fiscal Affairs* (case 68/79), in a claim based on Article 90, the Court held that national courts may take into account damage suffered by the person liable to pay the charge by reason of the restrictive effect of the charge on imports from other Member States. This principle should also apply to damage suffered as a result of a charge in breach of Article 25 EC.

17.4 Prohibition of discriminatory taxation

17.4.1 Meaning of taxation

As noted above, the Court draws a distinction between a charge having equivalent effect to a customs duty and a genuine tax. A genuine tax is a measure relating to a system of internal dues applied systematically to categories of products in accordance with objective criteria irrespective of the origin of the products (*Commission* v *France (Re Levy on Reprographic Machines)* (case 90/79)). Even what may appear a genuine tax may be treated as a charge if it is earmarked to benefit only the domestic product subject to the tax (see *Fratelli Cucchi* v *Avez SpA* (case 77/76)). However, the fact that it is levied by a body other than the State, or is collected for its own benefit and is a charge which is special or appropriate for a specific purpose, cannot prevent it from falling within the field of application of Article 90 (*Ianelli & Volpi* v *Meroni* (case 74/76)).

Since the line between a charge and a genuine tax may be hard to draw, and since the Court has held (*Fratelli Cucchi* v *Avez SpA*) that the prohibition of customs duties and charges having equivalent effect and of discriminatory internal taxation are mutually exclusive, it is safer in case of doubt to invoke both Article 25 and Article 90 and leave the Court to define the boundaries.

17.4.2 Scope of Article 90

A 'genuine' tax must comply with Article 90. It provides that:

> No Member State shall impose, directly or indirectly, on the products of other Member States any internal taxation of any kind in excess of that imposed directly or indirectly on similar domestic products.
>
> Furthermore, no Member State shall impose on the products of other Member States any internal taxation of such a nature as to afford indirect protection to other products.

While States are free to decide on the rate of taxation to be applied to a particular product and discriminate between different types of product (for example *Outokumpu Oy* (case C–213/96), different sources of fuel) (subject to certain overriding provisions of EC law (see further below)), they are not free to apply rates which discriminate, directly or indirectly, as between domestic and imported products which are similar or which afford indirect protection to the former. To do so would give a competitive advantage to the less highly taxed product and thereby distort competition within the single market. As the Court has held in a number of cases, a Member State's internal taxation system will be compatible with the requirements of Article 90 only if it is shown to be structured so as to exclude any possibility of having a discriminatory effect (see, e.g., *Haahr Petroleum Ltd* v *Åbenrå Havn* (case C–90/94), para. 34).

There are a number of aspects to Article 90. The issue of discriminatory taxation is clearly central to any discussion (see 17.4.3). The meaning of 'products from other Member States' is discussed in more detail at 17.4.4. Note, also, that Article 90 contains two prohibitions:

(a) Article 90(1) which deals with 'similar' products;
(b) Article 90(2) which concerns goods which, although not exactly similar, are still in competition with each other.

The difference between the two provisions may be slight and therefore difficult to identify with precision. Indeed, in early case law the ECJ did not always bother to distinguish between Article 90(1) and 90(2), holding that Article 90 could be applied as a whole (see, e.g., *Commission* v *France (Spirits)* (case 168/78), para. 13). The problem of adopting a 'global' approach to Article 90 is that it blurs the distinction between paragraphs (1) and (2) in terms of the consequences of a finding of a violation for Member States. A Member State is obliged to *equalise* the taxes on domestic and imported products when the Court has found a violation of Article 90(1). In contrast, when there has been a violation of Article 90(2), the Member State is required to remove the protective effect of the offending national rules. Such a requirement does not necessarily entail equalisation of the tax burdens on the goods in question; i.e., the tax on imported products need not be identical to that on domestic products. It seems that in later cases the ECJ has made greater efforts to distinguish between Article 90(1) and 90(2). In the *John Walker* case (case 243/84), concerning whether liqueur fruit wine was comparable to whiskey, the ECJ found that the two products were not 'similar' for the purposes of Article 90(1), therefore the national rules would be assessed by reference to Article 90(2). The notion of similarity is discussed further below at 17.4.5.

17.4.3 Discriminatory measures

A measure will be indirectly discriminatory if, although applicable to all goods, regardless of origin, it falls more heavily on the imported product. For example in *Humblot* v *Directeur des Services Fiscaux* (case 112/84) a French car tax, calculated according to the power rating of the car, which imposed a disproportionately heavy burden on the more powerful cars, *all of which were imported*, was found to breach Article 90. There was no apparent justification for the excessive difference between the rates charged on the different categories of car. It should be noted that a taxation system should not be discriminatory '*solely* because *only* imported products, in particular those from other Member States, come within the most highly taxed category' (case 132/88 *Commission* v *Greece*, para. 18, emphasis added). Differentiating between products on objective grounds, which is permissible, can lead to imports and domestic products being treated differently because of the specific characteristics of the two categories of goods. Objective grounds for differentiation in treatment are considered at 17.4.6.

The Court has held that internal tax may be imposed on imported products even if there is no domestic production of a similar or competing product as long as it applies to the product as a class, irrespective of origin *(Fink-Frucht GmbH* (case 27/67), applied in *Commission* v *France* (case 90/79)). However, if in this case the 'tax' is set at such a level as to compromise the free circulation of trade within the Community it cannot be deemed part of a general system of taxation (*Commission* v *Denmark* (case 47/88)). It may, however, fall within other provisions of the Treaty.

In assessing the question of discrimination, it is necessary to take into account not only the rate of direct and indirect internal taxation on domestic and imported products, but also the basis of assessment and the detailed rules for its collection. Where differences result in the imported product being taxed, *at the same stage of production or marketing*, more heavily than the similar domestic product, Article 90 is infringed (*Ianelli & Volpi* v *Meroni*). It may also be necessary to have regard to taxation levied at earlier stages of manufacture and marketing, particularly to ensure that goods are not taxed twice (*FOR* v *VKS* (case 54/72)). The Court insists on strict equality, rather than broad equivalence, to ensure 'transparency'. It has even applied Article 90 to penalties. In *Commission* v *France* (case 276/91) a provision of the French customs code, which provided for more severe penalties for VAT offences in relation to imported goods than for similar offences related to domestic transactions, was found to breach Article 90. Although some difference in treatment might be justified for administrative reasons, in that VAT offences committed outside the importing State were not as easily discoverable as those committed in the home State, this could not justify a manifest disproportion in the severity of the two categories of offences. It has been suggested that this decision, no doubt correct as to its result, would have been better based on Article 28, or Article 12, the general prohibition of discrimination on the grounds of nationality.

17.4.4 **Products from other Member States**

Although Article 90 is expressed as applying to the 'products of other Member States', the Court has held (*Cooperative Co-Frutta SLR* v *Amministrazione delle Finanze dello Stato* (case 193/85)), arguing from *Criel, nee Donckerwolcke* v *Procureur de la République* (case 41/76), that the prohibition of discriminatory taxation must apply, by analogy with the free movement of goods provisions, to goods from third countries in free circulation within the Member States. Similarly, although the reference to 'products of other Member States' would seem to imply that Article 90 only applies to taxes which discriminate against imports, the Court has held that in order to guarantee the neutrality of national systems of taxation, Article 90 will also apply to exports (*Statenskontrol* v *Larsen* (case 142/77)).

17.4.5 **'Similar' products**

It is clear that products need not be identical to fall within Article 90. What then is a 'similar' product? In the course of a number of judgments, mostly infringement proceedings against Member States under Article 226 (ex 169) EC (see Chapter 10), in respect of allegedly discriminatory taxation of alcoholic drinks (e.g., *Commission* v *France (Spirits)* (case 168/78)), the Court has held that 'similar' must be interpreted widely. In assessing the question of similarity, classification of the product under the same heading in the CCT will weigh heavily, but it is not conclusive. The important factor is whether the products 'have similar characteristics and meet the same needs from the point of view of consumers . . . not according to whether they are strictly identical but whether their use is similar or comparable' (*Commission* v *Denmark* (case 106/84)). The concept of similarity is thus analogous to that of the relevant product market in EC competition law (see Chapter 28).

To decide if the products meet the same consumer needs the Court has held (*Commission* v *UK (Re Excise Duties on Wine)* (case 170/78)) that it is necessary to look not only at the present state of the market but also at possible developments, i.e., the possibility of substituting one product for another. Taxation policy must not be allowed to crystallise consumer habits. In *Commission* v *Italy (Bananas)* (case 184/85), the ECJ had to determine whether bananas were 'similar' fruit for the purposes of Article 90(1). In making its assessment, the Court took into account the objective characteristics of bananas and other fruit, including the extent to which they could satisfy the same consumer need. In this case, the ECJ held that bananas were not similar to other fruit (although the national rules in the issue might fall within Article 90(2)).

17.4.6 Objective grounds for differentiation

Different rates of taxation may, however, be applied to what appear to be 'similar' products provided they are based on objective criteria, designed to achieve economic policy objectives which are compatible with EC law, and are applied in such a way as to avoid discrimination against imports or afford indirect protection to domestic products. This reasoning was applied in *Commission* v *France* (case 196/85) in the context of infringement proceedings for a system of differential taxation in which certain wines known as natural sweet wines or liqueur wines, production of which is 'traditional or customary', attracted more favourable tax rates than ordinary wine. The purpose of the special rate was to bolster the economy in areas largely dependent on the production of these wines, to compensate for the relatively rigorous conditions under which they are produced. The Court found the economic policy objectives pursued by the French to be justified. Such rules, it said, may not be regarded as contrary to Community law merely because they may be applied in a discriminatory manner if it is not proved that they have in fact been applied in such a manner. Clearly in this case it felt that neither discrimination nor protectionist motives had been proved (see also *Chemial Farmaceutici SpA* v *DAF SpA* (case 140/79)). Where a system involving different rates of taxation, although prima facie objectively justified, in effect discriminates against the imported product or affords indirect protection to domestic products, it will not be permissible (*Bobie* v *HZA Aachen Nord* (case 127/75)). This principle can be seen in operation in *Commission* v *Greece* (case C–375/95), which concerned a Greek rule which provided that a reduced rate of tax would apply to cars using 'anti-pollution' technology. According to the Greek government, this reduced rate was not available to imports because the testing of each import to verify that it satisfied the relevant criteria was not practicable. The ECJ responded that such consideration could not justify discriminatory taxation (see also *Outokumpu Oy* (case C–213/96)). Reverse discrimination on the other hand will be permitted (*Peureux* v *Directeur des Services Fiscaux* (case 86/78)).

17.4.7 Taxation affording indirect protection to domestic products

Internal taxation will be contrary to Article 90 if it affords indirect protection to domestic products. Article 90(2) is intended to cover 'all forms of indirect tax protection in the case of products which, without being similar within the meaning of Article 95(1) (now 90(1)), are nevertheless in competition, even partial, indirect or potential competition, with each other' (*Cooperative Co-Frutta SRL* (case 193/85)). It is wider than Article 90(1), and wider than the concept of the relevant product market in EC competition law. This may be demonstrated by comparing *Cooperative Co-Frutta* with the case of *United Brands* v *Commission* (case 27/76, see Chapter 28). In *Co-Frutta* a consumer tax, imposed on both domestic and imported bananas but which in practice applied almost exclusively to imported products (domestic production being extremely small), and which was not applied to other fresh (principally home produced) fruit was found to afford indirect protection to domestic production, in breach of Article 90(2). In *United Brands* on the other hand bananas were found to constitute a separate product market; the relevant product market did not include other fresh fruit. Clearly a more generous approach to the question of competition is justified in the context of Article 90(2), to safeguard the Community against fiscal protectionism on the part of Member States.

Since Article 90(2) does not depend on 'similarity' between the domestic and imported products, it will be necessary, in a claim based on this article, to demonstrate that the domestic and imported products, while not being similar, are in fact in competition with each other, and that the effect of the impugned tax regime is to afford indirect protection to the domestic product (*Commission* v *UK* (case 170/78)). This is the case concerning British rules which subjected some wines to a rate of taxation approximately five times that applied to beer. In determining whether wine and beer were in fact in competition with each other, the Court held that 'to a certain extent at least, the two beverages were capable of meeting identical needs' (para. 8). It would seem that product substitutability is the basis on which the ECJ will determine whether products are in competition. Further, as seems to be the case for determining similarity, consumer preferences will not be determinative because they are 'essentially variable in time and space' (para. 8).

Once it has been determined that certain products are in competition, the next question is whether there is a 'protective effect'. In *Commission* v *Belgium* (case 356/85), national rules were in issue. Wine, an imported product, was taxed at 25 per cent, whereas beer, a domestic product, was taxed at 19 per cent. The ECJ rejected the argument that the legislation provided a protective effect in favour of beer. The Court based its reasoning on the insignificant impact of the difference in tax rates on price. The Court's approach in this case did not require complex market analysis but seems, rather, to have depended on a 'common sense' assessment of the impact of the tax differential. On the other side of the coin, the Court has taken an equally common sense view of whether there is likely to be an impact, rather than requiring a detailed statistical analysis of the point. Statistics have, however, been used to show that apparently neutral rules do in fact discriminate.

17.5 Harmonisation of indirect taxation

Although the Community has the power to harmonise laws relating to indirect taxation to the extent that it is necessary to ensure the establishment and functioning of the internal market (Articles 93 and 94 (ex 99 and 100)) and has made considerable progress in this area in the case of VAT, excise duties and corporation tax, Member States have understandably been reluctant to cede competence to the Community outside these areas. Proposals to approximate rates of indirect taxation within broad tax bands, introduced under the internal market programme, have not so far met with success. Since different tax regimes clearly have an adverse impact on the functioning of the internal market by distorting the 'normal' flow of trade and competition within the Community the Commission has expressed its intention to continue to seek progress in this area. However, since fiscal measures remain subject to a requirement of unanimity, as an exception to the principle of qualified majority voting introduced by Article 95 (ex 100a), which remains even after Nice, it is likely that progress will be slow; a position unlikely to change under the Constitution. As Weatherill and Beaumont suggested, 'tax equalisation is not a serious prospect and is in any event scarcely conceivable in the absence of a single currency'. This position may, of course, now change with the advent of the Euro. Indeed, a communication from the Commission to the Council European Parliament and ECOSOC on Tax Policy (COM (2001) 260 final) suggests that the Commission is attempting to move matters forward in this area. This can be seen in the consolidation of the existing regimes dealing with, for example, VAT (see Regulation 1777/2005). More contentions issues arise where direct taxation has an impact on other policies, as has been seen in cases involving the free movement of persons and the freedom to provide services. Taxation also has an impact in the context of other areas, such as employment, the environment, public health, not to mention monetary union, for all of which the Community has competence. Nonetheless, legislative progress may well be slow, given the sensitivity of the issues involved and the fact that the need for unanimity remains.

17.6 Conclusions

The creation of the customs union is one of the fundamental elements of the Community project. In view of this, the Court's broad interpretation of the relevant prohibitions is not surprising. Given the international law trade context, in which overt protectionism is frowned on, the ECJ's approach to customs duties and measures having equivalence caused, in general, little comment. The provisions relating to taxation are the subject of greater discussion, touching as they do on an area of competence central to Member States' sovereignty. The breadth of some of the judgments has impinged on Member States' freedom to pursue other policy objectives, such as protection of the environment. It is somewhat ironic that increasingly, these objectives are recognised as worthy of a high level of protection by the Treaty. A further irony for the Member States lies in the fact that, in failing to agree to harmonising legislation in all but limited fields of indirect taxation, they have effectively put the development of taxation policy in the hands of the ECJ. This may result in decisions that have a greater impact on national taxation policies than any harmonised legislation.

FURTHER READING

Barents, R., 'Recent Case Law on the Prohibition of Fiscal Discrimination under Article 95' (1986) 23 CML Rev 641.

Danusso, M. and Denton, R., 'Does the European Court of Justice Look for a Protectionist Motive under Article 95?' (1991) 1 LIEI 67.

Easson, A., 'Fiscal Discrimination: New Perspectives on Article 95 of the EC Treaty' (1981) 18 CML Rev 521.

Grabitz, E. and Zacher, C., 'Scope for Action by Member States for the Improvement of Environmental Protection under EEC Law: the Example of Environmental Taxes and Subsidies' (1989) 26 CML Rev 423.

Schwartze, J., 'The Member States' Discretionary Powers under the Tax Provisions of the EEC Treaty' in J. Schwartze (ed.), *Discretionary Powers of the Member States in the Field of Economic Policies and their Limits under the EEC Treaty* (Baden-Baden: Nomos, 1988).

Tryfonidou, A., '*Carbonati Apuani Srl v Comune di Carrara*: Should We Reverse "Reverse Discrimination"?' (2005) 16 King's College Law Journal 373–381.

18

Free movement of goods

18.1 Introduction

The rules relating to the abolition of measures having equivalent effect to quantitative restrictions have been central to the development of the single market. The abolition of customs duties and charges of equivalent effect and prohibition on discriminatory taxation would not have been sufficient to guarantee the free movement of goods within the common market. In addition to pecuniary restrictions there are other barriers to trade of a non-pecuniary nature, usually in the form of administrative rules and practices, protectionist and otherwise, equally capable of hindering the free flow of goods from State to State. Articles 28 and 29 (ex 30–34) EC are designed to eliminate these barriers.

The significance of these rules is based on the breadth of the circumstances in which they can come into play. The prohibition on measures having equivalent effect do not just apply to rules that apply at the border, or which intend to discriminate against imports (or exports). They apply in a much wider ranger of circumstances, catching national rules that may have been enacted for non-trade related reasons, such as worker protection, consumer protection or protection of the environment, and which apply to domestic goods as well as to imports or exports. Given this, the central question is, 'Where does the proper scope of Article 28 end?' As we shall see below, this question has given rise to a considerable amount of case law and academic criticism. Given the supremacy of Community law, the issue is important as the scope of Articles 28 and 29 may limit the powers of each of the Member States to regulate trade-related matters. As a result, there is a tension between integration and national regulatory competence.

Running parallel to this issue is another concern: that of the de-regulatory effect of the Treaty freedoms. The effect of using Articles 28 and 29 is to strike down national legislation, thereby removing the rules regulating trade. This is sometimes called negative harmonisation. The difficulty is that that national rule may have been enacted for a good reason. The ECJ is therefore left with the task of balancing trade concerns with other concerns, as permitted by the Treaty derogation (Article 30, discussed in Chapter 19) and through the rule of reason (see 18.6.5). Given that the ECJ may not be the best body to assess such questions, it is sometimes suggested that the use of positive harmonisation, which involves the political institutions in the determination of agreed standards (see Chapter 15), should be preferred.

A further obstacle to the free movement of goods may be caused by the existence of what is referred to in the EC Treaty as a 'State monopoly of a commercial character'. Such monopolies exist where a Member State has restricted the right to sell particular goods to one body. State monopolies are clearly capable of obstructing the free movement of goods as their position in a particular market enables such monopolies to control the flow of goods in and out of the Member State, as well as the conditions under which trade in such goods takes place. Although a separate provision, Article 31 (ex 37), deals with state monopolies, it is dealt with here because of the broad similarity of the potential effect on trade. When considering Article 31 and state monopolies, the relationship between this provision and competition provisions, notably State aid (Chapter 30) as well as Article 86 EC, should also be borne in mind. All these provisions seek to deal with State behaviour which has the effect of distorting, or reinforcing the distortion of, competition.

18.2 Outline of provisions

18.2.1 Quantitative restrictions

As will be apparent, Articles 28 and 29 EC cover a much wider range of measures than Articles 23 (ex 9) and 25 (ex 12), but unlike these latter articles provision is made for derogation under Article 30 (ex 36).

The principal provisions are:

(a) Article 28 (ex 30), which prohibits quantitative restrictions, and all measures having equivalent effect, on *imports*.

(b) Article 29 (ex 34), which contains a similar prohibition on *exports*.

The prohibition is twofold, embracing:

(a) quantitative restrictions, and

(b) measures of equivalent effect to quantitative restrictions.

Original Articles 31–33, which provided for the gradual abolition of import restrictions during the transitional period, were deleted by the ToA. Should the Constitution come into force in its current format, Article 28 and 29 will be consolidated. Article III–153 provides:

> Quantitative restrictions on imports and exports and all measures having equivalent effect shall be prohibited between Member States.

Article 30 (ex 36) provides that the prohibitions in Articles 28 and 30 will not apply to restrictions on imports and exports which are *justified* on a number of specified grounds (see Chapter 19).

Even where a particular activity falls within other provisions of the Treaty, such as the 'services' provisions, it may still fall foul of Article 28 (ex 30) (*Commission v Ireland (Re Dundalk Water Supply)* (case 45/87); requirement that pipes required under a contract for the supply of services must comply with Irish specifications held in breach of Article 28 (ex 30)). The relationship between the four freedoms, together with the definition of 'goods', is discussed further in Chapter 14.

18.2.2 **State monopolies**

Article 31(1) (ex 37) EC states that:

> Member States shall adjust any State monopolies of a commercial character so as to ensure that no discrimination regarding the conditions under which goods are procured and marketed exists between nationals of Member States.

It will be re-enacted in the Constituion as Article III–155 in its current form.

Member States must also refrain from introducing any new measure which is contrary to Article 31(1) or which restricts the scope of Articles 25, 28 or 29 (ex 12, 30 and 34) (Article 31(2)). This does not mean that no new monopolies may be created, but rather that if such monopolies are formed, they must be compatible with the provisions on the free movement of goods. There is no specific provision derogating from Article 31; Article 30 cannot be used in this context.

There is special emphasis, in respect of state monopolies designed to make it easier to dispose of agricultural products, on safeguarding the employment and standard of living of the agricultural producers (Article 31(3)).

Should the Constitution come into force in its current form, this provision will be found at Article III–155.

18.3 **Whose actions are caught?**

These articles are addressed to, and relate to, measures taken by Member States. Despite their wording, there are two senses in which Articles 28 and 29 do not just apply to Member States.

First, the institutions are likewise bound by the terms of the Treaty, including these provisions. Community institutions may derogate from the provisions of Articles 28 and 29 where they are expressly authorised to do so by other provisions of the Treaty, for example in implementing the common agricultural policy (Articles 33–38 (ex 39–46) EC) (*Rewe Zentrale AG v Direktor der Landwirtschaftskammer Rheinland* (case 37/83)).

Secondly, 'measures taken by Member States' have been interpreted in the widest sense. They include the actions of all forms of government, whether central, regional or local and extend to the activities of any public body, legislative, executive or judicial, or even semi-public body, such as a quango, exercising powers derived from public law (e.g., *Apple & Pear Development Council v K. J. Lewis Ltd* (case 222/82)). In *R v Royal Pharmaceutical Society of Great Britain* (cases 266, 267/87) the Court held that measures adopted by professional bodies, such as the Royal Pharmaceutical Society, on which national legislation has conferred regulatory or disciplinary powers were 'measures taken by Member States' subject to Article 28. In determining whether the actions of a body fall within the scope of Article 28, the ECJ will consider the body's functions, statutory basis, management and funding; its legal form will not be determinative. In the *Quality Labels* case (*Commission v Germany* (case C–325/00)), the fact that a body which awarded quality labels to German products was established as a private limited company did not take its actions outside Article 28, despite the fact that the German Government could not directly influence its actions. The ECJ noted that it was financed by a public body itself financed by compulsory contributions, its functions were determined, albeit broadly, by statute and it was subject to the supervision of the public body from which it derived its funding.

One question is whether these provisions have horizontal direct effect, a question that gained importance with the ECJ's ruling in *Angonese* (see Chapter 20). Given the nature of Article 31, it is unlikely that this is a question that has much relevance for this provision. Although there had been some debate on the horizontality of Articles 28 and 29, it seems that these provisions are limited to the actions of public bodies, however broadly seen (see, e.g., *Sapod-Audic* (case C–159/00). This does not mean that individuals are completely free to act in breach of these articles. In *Commission* v *France* (case C–265/95), it became clear that the Member States' duties were more far-reaching than may have previously been thought. The problem in this case did not concern actions by the French State but rather its failure to take action to prevent private individuals from impeding the cross-border flow of goods. According to the Commission, the French government should have taken action to stop the blockade of imported agricultural produce and demonstrations in which property was damaged. The ECJ agreed, stressing the fundamental nature of Article 28 and then referring to Article 10 (ex 5) EC which puts Member States under an obligation 'to take all necessary and appropriate measures' to ensure that Community fundamental freedoms are respected in their territory. This ruling makes it clear that Member States' obligations extend to positive measures as well as refraining from taking action incompatible with the EC Treaty. The precise extent of this obligation remains uncertain, although *Schmidberger* (case C–112/00) (discussed below) provides further guidance. In the *Angry Farmers* case, the ECJ emphasised the duration and severity of the incidents in France and the passivity of the French authorities in this case. Note also that a Member State is only obliged to take 'necessary and proportionate' measures. Member States thus still retain some discretion in determining, for example, their policing policy, and would certainly not be obliged to quell every public demonstration. The question then is when does the Member State's obligation arise?

In *R* v *Chief Constable of Sussex, ex parte International Trader's Ferry Ltd* ([1997] 3 WLR 132 [1999] 1 CMLR 1320) a similar argument to that advanced by the ECJ in *Commission* v *France* was accepted by the English courts in relation to Articles 29 and 10 EC. In the English case, the authorities had taken some action, providing policing of demonstrations by animal rights protestors against the export of live animals on three days a week, but this was not enough to eliminate the effects of the demonstrations on the export of live animals by the applicant. The House of Lords found for the authorities, but would the UK be seen as being in breach of its obligations had the question been referred to the ECJ? Certainly a majority of their Lordships suggested that, were the case to turn on the question of whether the Chief Constable's decision as to the appropriate level of policing constituted a measure having equivalent effect or not, that question should be referred. The view was expressed that, given the wide discretion in the field of internal security which Member States enjoy, the positive obligations imposed on a Member State by Article 10 in conjunction with Article 29 would not be sufficiently precise to be directly effective. These issues were not decisively resolved, as their Lordships held the Chief Constable's decision to limit policing of Shoreham Harbour to be justified under Article 30 on the grounds of public policy, in the sense of the need to maintain law and order. The Chief Constable's decision, given the resources available, was not disproportionate. It is submitted that this ruling was, on the facts, correct. (This case is discussed further below and in Chapters 8 and 19.) The question of the extent of Member States' obligations to take measures becomes ever more important in the light of the possibility of a claim for damages under the doctrine of State liability in respect of public authorities' liability for omissions (see Chapter 8), an issue that was raised but not decided in *Schmidberger* (case C–112/00).

After the *Angry Farmers* case, a regulation, the so-called 'rapid intervention mechanism', was enacted to deal with obstacles to trade which originate in the action or inaction of the Member States (Regulation 2679/98 ([1998] OJ L337/8)). In defining 'inaction' the regulation tracks the wording of the *Angry Farmers* case. The regulation gives the Commission the power to intervene in such circumstances, providing the Commission with the possibility of taking a Member State before the ECJ should obstacles covered by the regulation continue in existence. The regulation defines in Article 1 the notion of an 'obstacle' requiring action. It lists three cumulative requirements:

(a) the serious disruption of the free movement of goods;

(b) serious loss to individuals affected; and

(c) the necessity of immediate State action.

This definition would seem to take one-off actions outside the scope of the regulation. Such an approach would seem in line with the *Angry Farmers* case, which emphasised the severity and duration of the French farmers' action. In the more recent *Schmidberger* case (case C–112/00), the Advocate-General suggested that a one day motorway blockade held in accordance with the relevant Member State's laws should trigger the application of Articles 28 and 29 where relevant, a view the Court followed. In the ECJ's reasoning the severity of the disruption would be relevant for justification rather than the application of Article 28 or 29 in the first place. Seemingly, there is now a divergence between the Treaty jurisprudence and specific secondary legislation.

18.4 Types of act caught by Articles 28 and 29

Articles 28 and 29 refer to measures, which clearly include national legislative acts. It seems from the ECJ's case law that a 'measure' for the purpose of Article 28 is wider than that. It would seem to include administrative acts, as the *Franking Machine* case (case 21/84) shows. Although a discriminatory law had been repealed, the administrative practice had not changed, the authorities showing a 'systematically unfavourable' attitude towards the approval of imported products. A measure does not need to be a binding act. This was expressly provided by the Commission in the preamble to its Directive 70/50, and confirmed by the ECJ in *Commission v Ireland (Re 'Buy Irish' Campaign)* (case 249/81). In this case certain activities of the Irish Goods Council, a government-sponsored body charged with promoting Irish goods by, *inter alia*, advertising, principally on the basis of their Irish origin, were held to be in breach of the then Article 30 (now 28). Even though no binding measures were involved, the Board's actions were capable of influencing the behaviour of traders and thereby frustrating the aims of the Community. As we have already seen, it seems as though omissions can also constitute 'measures'.

18.5 Prohibition on quantitative restrictions

These were interpreted in *Riseria Luigi Geddo* v *Ente Nazionale Risi* (case 2/73) as any measures which amount to a total or partial restraint on imports, exports or goods in transit. They would clearly include a ban, as was found to be the case in *Commission* v *Italy (Re Ban on Pork Imports)* (case 7/61) and *R* v *Henn* (case 34/79) (ban on import of pornographic materials). They would also include a quota system, as in *Salgoil SpA* v *Italian Ministry for Foreign Trade* (case 13/68). The *Ditlev Bluhme* case (case C–67/97) confirms that a ban on imports operates as a quantitative restriction even if the prohibition extends to part only of a Member State's territory. This case concerned the Danish prohibition on the import onto the island of Læsø of live domestic bees or reproductive material for them, the aim of which was to protect the Læsø brown bee. This, the ECJ held, was a quantitative restriction although it applied only to a small part of Denmark.

A covert quota system might operate by means of an import (or export) licence requirement. A licensing system might in itself amount to a quantitative restriction, or, alternatively, a measure of equivalent effect to a quantitative restriction. It was held in *International Fruit Co. NV* v *Produktschap voor Groenten en Fruit* (cases 51–4/71) that even if the granting of a licence were a pure formality the requirement of such a licence to import would amount to a breach of Article 28. In that case it was deemed to be a measure of equivalent effect to a quantitative restriction.

18.6 Prohibition on measures having equivalent effect to quantitative restrictions

The concept of measures having equivalent effect to quantitative restrictions (MEQR) is altogether wider in scope than that of quantitative restrictions. Perhaps to the surprise of Member States, it has been interpreted very generously by both the Commission and the ECJ, to include not merely overtly protective measures or measures applicable only to imports or exports ('distinctly applicable' measures), but measures applicable to imports (or exports) and domestic goods alike ('indistinctly applicable' measures), often introduced (seemingly) for the most worthy purpose. Such measures have included regulatory measures designed to enforce minimum standards, for example, of size, weight, quality, price or content, to tests and inspections or certification requirements to ensure that goods conform to these standards, to any activity capable of influencing the behaviour of traders such as promoting goods by reason of their national origin, as was the case in *Apple & Pear Development Council* v *K.J. Lewis Ltd* (case 222/82) and *Commission* v *Ireland (Re 'Buy*

Irish' Campaign) (case 249/81). Even if not designed to be protectionist, such measures, by imposing extra burdens on imported products, already required to comply with different standards in their home State, or simply by prejudicing consumer choice, clearly give domestic products an advantage over imported goods, thereby distorting competition in the single market.

18.6.1 Definition of MEQR

To offer States guidance as to the meaning and scope of 'measures having equivalent effect' to quantitative restrictions, the Commission passed Directive 70/50. Although passed under the then Article 33(7) (which itself was deleted by the ToA) and therefore applicable only to measures to be abolished during the transitional period, it has been suggested that the directive may still serve to provide non-binding guidelines to the interpretation of Article 28. Having noted this possibility, it should equally be noted that the ECJ has not tended to refer to Directive 70/50 of late, referring instead to its own established case law. Article 2(3) of the directive provides a non-exhaustive list of measures capable of having equivalent effect to quantitative restrictions. These are divided into:

(a) 'measures, *other than those applicable equally to domestic or imported products'*, i.e., 'distinctly applicable' measures, 'which hinder imports which could otherwise take place, including measures which make importation more difficult or costly than the disposal of domestic production' (Article 2(1)), and

(b) measures *'which are equally applicable to domestic and imported products'*, i.e., 'indistinctly applicable' measures (Article 3). These measures are only contrary to Article 28 'where the restrictive effect of such measures on the free movement of goods exceeds the effects intrinsic to trade rules', that is where 'the restrictive effects on the free movement of goods are out of proportion to their purpose', or where 'the same objective cannot be attained by other measures which are less of a hindrance to trade' (Article 3).

Thus, indistinctly applicable rules appear to be acceptable provided that they comply with the principle of proportionality.

The ECJ, in 1974, in the case of *Procureur du Roi* v *Dassonville* (case 8/74), introduced its own definition of measures having equivalent effect to quantitative restrictions. This definition, now known as the *'Dassonville* formula', has since been applied consistently, almost verbatim, by the ECJ. According to the formula:

> All trading rules enacted by Member States which are capable of hindering, directly or indirectly, actually or potentially, intra-Community trade are to be considered as measures having an effect equivalent to quantitative restrictions.

It is not necessary to show an actual hindrance to trade between Member States as long as the measure is capable of such effects. Unlike the competition provisions of Articles 81 and 82 (ex 85 and 86), which require an *'appreciable effect'* on trade and competition between Member States, the ECJ has in the past held that Article 28 is not subject to a *de minimis* rule (*van de Haar* (case 177/82)). It does, however, require proof of a *hindrance* to trade.

18.6.2 Internal situations

A measure which is not capable of hindering trade between Member States, which merely affects the flow of trade *within* a Member State, will not breach Article 28 (ex 30). In *Oebel* (case 155/80) a Belgian law banning the production and delivery to consumers and retail outlets of bakery products during the night hours, designed to protect workers in small and medium-sized bakeries, was held not to breach Article 28 because, although delivery of imported products through some outlets was precluded, 'trade within the Community remained possible at all times' (see also *Blesgen* (case 75/81)). In *Quietlynn Ltd* v *Southend Borough Council* (case C–23/89) a licensing requirement for the sale of sex appliances by sex shops was held not to breach Article 28, since the goods in question, which included imported goods, 'could be marketed through other channels'. However, the case law of the Court has not been consistent on this point. In *Torfaen Borough Council* v *B & Q plc* (case 145/88) the Court found that a ban on Sunday trading in England and Wales under the Shops Act 1950, the effect of which was to restrict the volume of imports to the shops trading in breach of the rules, was prima facie contrary to Article 28, even though alternative outlets for the sale of these goods existed during the working week (see also *Conforma* (case C–312/89) and *Marchandise* (case C–332/89)). Following a change in the Court's approach in recent years, these latter cases involving Sunday trading would be decided on a different basis today (see *Keck* (cases C–267 & 268/91) and subsequent cases to be discussed below). The ECJ discussed the question of whether a national measure had an effect on intra-Community trade in *Pistre* (joined cases C–321–4/94) which concerned a French rule limiting the marketing of products with the designation of 'montagne' to those originating in certain areas in France. The ECJ held that this rule had a Community dimension. In the ECJ's view, it did not matter that all the relevant facts arose in France; it was sufficient that the rule could affect intra-Community trade. It would seem clear from this case, and other similar cases, that the question of internal situation is very closely linked to the question of whether there is hindrance to intra-Community trade (see also 18.6.9). This connection can be seen from the ECJ's more recent re-statement of the position in *Karner* (case C–71/02):

> That principle has been upheld by the Court not only in cases where the national rule in question gave rise to direct discrimination against goods imported from other Member States (*Pistre and Others*, paragraph 44), but also in situations where the national rule applied without distinction to national and imported products and was thus likely to constitute a potential impediment to intra-Community trade covered by Article 28 EC (see, to that effect, case C–448/98, *Guimont*, paras 21 and 22) (para. 20).

18.6.3 Reverse discrimination

A measure falling within the *Dassonville* formula but which operates solely to the disadvantage of domestic production will not fall foul of Community law. The ban in *Oebel* on the production of bakery products during the night, which prevented Belgian bakers from benefiting from the early morning trade in adjacent Member States, was found not to breach Articles 12, 28 or 29 EC. The Court held that it was not contrary to the principle of non-discrimination on grounds of nationality for States to apply national rules where other States apply less strict rules to similar products.

The ECJ took the same view of a Dutch regulation concerning the permitted ingredients of cheese, which was only applicable to cheese produced in Holland (*Jongeneel Kaas BV* v *Netherlands* (case 237/82)) and of a French law requiring French retailers to adhere to a minimum selling price for books, provided it was not applied to books which, having been exported, were reimported into France (*Association des Centres Distributeurs Édouard Leclerc* v '*Au Blé Vert' Sàrl* (case 229/ 83)). In this respect, as in other areas (e.g., free movement of workers), the Court is prepared to accept a measure of reverse discrimination. While Member States must be compelled, in the interests of the single market, not to discriminate against, or in any way prejudice, imports, it seems that they may be safely left to act themselves in order to protect their own interests. There is now a consistent line of authority from the ECJ to this effect.

18.6.4 Early application of *Dassonville*

The measure in issue in *Dassonville* was a requirement, under Belgian law, that imported goods should carry a certificate of origin issued by the State in which the goods were manufactured. Dassonville imported a consignment of Scotch whisky from France. Since the seller was unable to supply the required certificate he attached a home-made certificate of origin to the goods and appeared before the Belgian court on a forgery charge. In his defence, he claimed that the Belgian regulation was contrary to EC law. On a reference from the Belgian court, the ECJ, applying the *Dassonville* formula, found the measure was capable of breaching Article 28.

In the cases of *Tasca* (case 65/75) and *van Tiggele* (case 82/77) the *Dassonville* test was applied in the context of a domestic law imposing maximum and minimum selling prices, respectively. The laws were indistinctly applicable. In both cases the issue of Article 28 arose in criminal proceedings against the defendants for breach of these laws. Tasca was accused in Italy of selling sugar above the permitted national maximum price; van Tiggele in Holland of selling gin below the national minimum price. Both pleaded that the measures were in breach of EC law. Applying the *Dassonville* test the ECJ found that both measures were capable of breaching Article 28. Regarding the maximum price, the Court held a maximum price does not in itself constitute a measure equivalent in effect to a quantitative restriction. It becomes so when fixed at a level such that the sale of imported products becomes if not impossible more difficult. The maximum price in *Tasca* could have that effect, in that importers of more highly priced goods might have to cut their profit margins or even be forced to sell at a loss. In *van Tiggele* the minimum price also acted as a hindrance to imports, since it would prevent the (possibly) lower price of imported goods from being reflected in the retail selling price. The Court suggested, however, that a prohibition on selling below cost price, or a minimum profit margin, would be acceptable, since it would have no adverse effect on trade between Member States (principle applied in *Commission* v *Italy (Re Fixing of Trading Margins)* (case 78/82)).

In applying the *Dassonville* formula in these three cases, the Court did not distinguish between distinctly and indistinctly applicable measures, and ignored the proportionality test laid down for the latter in Directive 70/50. The breadth of the formula, especially when applied 'mechanically', looking to the *effect* of the measure on intra-Community trade rather than to the question of *hindrance*, bore harshly on Member States, particularly where the measure was indistinctly applicable and might be justified as in the public interest.

18.6.5 Indistinctly applicable measures: the *Cassis de Dijon* test

Perhaps taking heed of criticisms arising from its application of the *Dassonville* formula in these last three cases discussed above, the Court took a decisive step in the case of *'Cassis de Dijon' (Rewe-Zentral AG v Bundesmonopolverwaltung für Branntwein* (case 120/78) and paved the way for a distinction between distinctly and indistinctly applicable measures. The question before the ECJ in *Cassis* concerned the legality under EC law of a German law laying down a minimum alcohol level of 25 per cent for certain spirits, which included cassis, a blackcurrant-flavoured liqueur. German cassis complied with this minimum, but French cassis, with an alcohol content of 15–20 per cent, did not. Thus although the German regulation was indistinctly applicable, the result of the measure was effectively to ban French cassis from the German market. A number of German importers contested the measure, and the German court referred a number of questions to the ECJ.

18.6.5.1 *Rule of reason*

The ECJ applied the *Dassonville* formula, but, developing a suggestion of the Court in *Dassonville* that State measures falling within the formula might be acceptable where the restrictions on intra-Community trade were 'reasonable', went on to state that:

> Obstacles to movement within the Community resulting from disparities between the national laws relating to the marketing of the products in question must be accepted insofar as those provisions may be recognised as being necessary in order to satisfy mandatory requirements relating in particular to the effectiveness of fiscal supervision, the protection of public health, the fairness of commercial transactions and the defence of the consumer.

This principle ('the first *Cassis* principle'), that certain measures, though within the *Dassonville* formula, will not breach Article 28 if they are necessary to satisfy mandatory requirements, has come to be known as the 'rule of reason', a concept borrowed from American anti-trust law, which also occasionally appears in the context of EC competition law (see Chapter 26).

Prior to *Cassis*, it was assumed that any measure falling within the *Dassonville* formula would breach Article 28 and could be justified only on the grounds provided by Article 30. Since *Cassis*, at least where indistinctly applicable measures are concerned, courts may apply a rule of reason to Article 28. If the measure is necessary in order to protect mandatory requirements, it will not breach Article 28 at all. Distinctly applicable measures on the other hand will normally breach Article 28, but may be justified under Article 30.

This distinction is significant, since the mandatory requirements permitted under *Cassis* are wider than the grounds provided under Article 30, and, unlike Article 30, are non-exhaustive. In *Oebel* (case 155/80) it was not disputed that the improvement of working conditions could constitute a mandatory requirement, although it was not necessary to the judgment, since the Court found the rules in any case compatible with Article 28. In *Cinéthèque SA* (cases 60 & 61/84) Advocate-General Slynn suggested – in the context of a non-discriminatory French law prohibiting the marketing of videograms of films within 12 months of first showing, designed to protect the cinema industry – that cultural activities could constitute a mandatory requirement. Without expressly endorsing that statement the Court found that the rule, designed to encourage the creation of cinematographic works, was justified on *Cassis* principles and did not breach Article 28. In *Commission* v *Denmark (Re disposable Beer Cans)* (case 302/86) the protection of the environment was held to constitute a mandatory requirement, and in *Torfaen Borough Council* v *B & Q plc* (case 145/88) measures such as the English and Welsh Sunday trading rules, designed to protect 'national or regional socio-cultural characteristics' were held to be justifiable under the rule of reason. More recently, in the *Vereinigte Familiapress* case (case C–368/95), the ECJ held that diversity of the press could constitute a mandatory requirement. The ECJ has, however, refused to contemplate a justification based on purely economic grounds (see, e.g., *Duphar BV* v *Netherlands* (case 238/82) and, more recently, *Decker* (case C–120/95)).

It should be noted that the rule of reason as laid down in *Cassis* was not in terms confined to indistinctly applicable measures. Although shortly after *Cassis* in *Gilli* (case 788/79) (Italian cider vinegar case) the Court suggested (para. 14) that the principle applied only where national rules apply *without discrimination* to both domestic and imported products, it has not insisted on this distinction, and, perhaps because the line between the two is not always clear, has not infrequently considered the question of justification of indistinctly applicable measures not on *Cassis* principles but under Article 30 (see *Sandoz BV* (case 174/82)). There appear to be two possible reasons for this approach: in some cases the Court is merely responding to questions submitted by national courts under Article 234 (ex 177); in others, where the 'mandatory requirement' falls under one of the specific heads of derogation provided by Article 30, the Court may prefer to rely on the express provisions of that article (see, e.g., *Commission* v *Germany (Re German Sausages)* (case 274/87) (health justification) and *Ditlev Bluhme* (case C–67/97) (protection of biodiversity and the environment/health and life of animals)).

In applying the rule of reason to the facts in *Cassis* the Court found that the German law was in breach of Article 28. Although the measure fell within the categories suggested, being allegedly enacted in the interests of public health (to prevent increased consumption resulting from lowering the alcoholic content of cassis) and the fairness of commercial transactions (to avoid giving the weak imported cassis an unfair advantage over its stronger, hence more expensive, German rival), the measure was not *necessary* to achieve these ends. Other means, such as labelling, which would have been less of a hindrance to trade, could have been used to achieve the same ends. Thus the word 'necessary' has been interpreted to mean no more than is necessary, i.e., subject to the principle of proportionality. With *Cassis* the ECJ appears finally to have fallen in line with Directive 70/50, albeit adding a 'mandatory requirement' test to the principle of proportionality.

18.6.5.2 *Mutual recognition and proportionality*

The Court established a second important principle in *Cassis* ('the second *Cassis* principle'). It suggested that there was no valid reason why 'provided that [goods] have been lawfully produced and marketed in one of the Member States, [they] should not be introduced into any other Member State' (para. 14).

Is this principle, known as the principle of 'mutual recognition', not in conflict with its *first* principle, the rule of reason? It is submitted that it is not. It merely gives rise to a presumption that goods which have been lawfully marketed in another State will comply with the 'mandatory requirements' of the importing State. This can be rebutted by evidence that further measures are *necessary* to protect the interest concerned.

That presumption will however be hard to rebut; the burden of proving that a measure is necessary is a heavy one, particularly when, although justifiable in principle, it clearly operates as a hindrance to intra-Community trade.

In *Prantl* (case 16/83) Article 28 was invoked in the context of criminal proceedings against Prantl for breach of a German law designed to prevent unfair competition. He had imported wine from Italy in bulbous-shaped bottles which closely resembled a German bottle known as a '*Bocksbeutel*'. The *Bocksbeutel* was protected under German law as denoting a quality wine from a particular region of Germany. The Italian bottle was a bottle traditional to Italy. Although the measure was arguably justifiable under *Cassis* in the interests of fair trading ('the fairness of commercial transactions') and consumer protection, the Court held that as long as the Italian wine was in accord with fair and traditional practice in its State of origin there was no justification for its exclusion from Germany (but see now *Deutsche Renault AG v Audi AG* (case C–317/91), noted in Chapter 31).

Similarly in *Miro BV* (case 182/84) it was held that a generic name such as '*jenever*', reserved in Holland for gin with a minimum alcohol content of 35 per cent, could not be restricted to one national variety provided the imported product, in this case Belgian *jenever*, with a 30 per cent alcohol content, had been lawfully produced and marketed in the exporting State. This was despite the fact that Dutch *jenever* was subject to a higher rate of tax because of its high alcohol content and would be at a competitive disadvantage *vis-à-vis* the imported product. (See also *Ministère Public v Deserbais* (case 286/86) re minimum fat content for Edam cheese.)

Although, where a domestic measure is challenged before a national court it is for the national court to apply the proportionality principle, the ECJ has often, in interpreting Community law at the request of national courts, offered guidance as to the specific application of that principle. In doing so it has applied the principle rigorously, excluding all measures that go beyond what is strictly necessary to achieve the desired end. In *Walter Rau Lebensmittelwerke v De Smedt PVBA* (case 261/81) a Belgian law requiring margarine to be packed in cube-shaped boxes, allegedly introduced in the interests of consumers, to enable them to distinguish margarine from butter, was held to be in breach of Article 28. The same objective could have been achieved by other means, such as labelling, which would be less of a hindrance to trade. Similar arguments have been used successfully to challenge national rules, allegedly in the interest of public health and consumer protection, concerning the permitted ingredients of pasta (*Drei Glöcken* (case 407/85)) and sausages (*Commission v Germany* (case 274/87)). In *Schutzverband gegen Unwesen in der Wirtschaft v Rocher* (case C–126/91) a German law prohibiting 'eye-catching' price comparisons in advertisements, designed to prevent consumers from being misled, was held to be disproportionate on the grounds that such advertisements were forbidden *whether they misled the public or not*. It was implied that a ban on *misleading* price comparisons would have been acceptable.

Where a defence is based on the rule of reason the genuineness of the justification proffered by Member States as well as the proportionality of the measure adopted will be closely scrutinised by the Court in the light of existing knowledge. This occurred in *Commission* v *Germany* (case 178/84). The case involved a challenge to the German beer purity laws. According to these laws, only beer brewed from specific approved ingredients could be designated 'beer'. The law also imposed an absolute ban on the use of additives. The Court examined the evidence scrupulously, and found that, having regard to the results of international scientific research, in particular the work of the FAO (Food and Agriculture Organisation) and WHO (World Health Organisation), and to eating habits in the Member State of importation, that the additives used did not constitute a danger to public health and met a real need, in particular a technological need. Although the drinking habits of the German population might have justified a selective exclusion of certain additives the exclusion of all additives was found on the evidence to be disproportionate.

By comparison, in the earlier case of *Sandoz BV* (case 174/82) the existing state of scientific knowledge was not such as to undermine a justification for a measure prohibiting, on public health grounds, the use of certain vitamin additives in food without prior authority. Provided the national authorities could prove a 'real need' for the measure, it would be permitted under Article 30.

18.6.5.3 *Impact of Cassis* on rules of origin and quality

The extent to which Member States are now limited, in the interests of the single market, in their ability to introduce indistinctly applicable and seemingly justifiable measures is illustrated by the case of *Commission* v *UK (Re Origin Marking of Retail Goods)* (case 207/83). Here the Commission claimed that a British regulation requiring certain goods (e.g., clothing, textiles) sold retail to indicate their country of origin was in breach of Article 28. The British government argued that the measure was justified on *Cassis* principles in the interest of consumers, who regarded the origin of goods as an indication of their quality. The Court refused to accept this argument. It held that the regulation merely enabled consumers to assert their prejudices, thereby slowing down the economic interpenetration of the Community. The quality of goods could as well be indicated on the goods themselves or their packaging, and the protection of consumers sufficiently guaranteed by rules which enabled the use of false indications of origin to be prohibited. Whilst manufacturers remained free to indicate their own national origin it was not necessary to compel them to do so. The regulation was in breach of Article 28.

This judgment, initially surprising, demonstrates the Commission's and the Court's overriding concern to promote market integration by striking down national rules which tend to compartmentalise the market, particularly along national lines. In a single market, based on free competition, products must be allowed to compete on their merits, not on the basis of national origin. (See also *Apple & Pear Development Council* v *Lewis* (case 222/82); *Commission* v *Ireland (Re 'Buy*

Irish' Campaign) (case 249/81) and Chapters 26–30 on competition law.) There has, however, more recently been some softening of the rules in respect of local or regional designations of origin of goods.

In *Exportur SA v LOR SA et Confiserie du Tech* (case C–3/91) the Court held that rules protecting indications of provenance and designations of origin laid down by a bilateral Convention between Member States were permissible under Community law provided that the protected designations had not acquired a generic connotation in their country of origin. A regulation has now been enacted (Regulation 1107/96 ([1996] OJ L 148/1, as amended) under the procedure set down in Article 17, Regulation 2081/92 ([1992] OJ L 208/1) providing for the protection of designations of origin and geographic indications for in excess of 300 named products, such as Stilton cheese and Hereford beef. This regulation protects registered designations of origin against all use, including 'evocations'. An evocation is a designation so evocative of the protected designation that, when a consumer is confronted with the product, the image that is triggered in the consumer's mind is that of the product the designation of which is protected. Thus, a soft cheese manufactured in Germany and called 'Cambozola' is an evocation of 'Gorgonzola' (*Conzorzio per la Tutela del Formaggio Gorgonzola v Käserei Champignon Hormeister GmbH & Co. KG, Eduard Bracharz GmbH* (case C–87/97)). There are limitations to the protection granted. For example, since Cambozola had been made and registered as a trademark long before the introduction of the regulation, the ECJ also held that notwithstanding the prima facie prohibition of the use of the evocation, the trade mark 'Cambozola' could still be used were its initial registration to have been made in good faith and its continued use not likely to deceive the public. Community law will not, however, allow Member States to protect generic names, such as Cheddar cheese, which are not tied to a particular geographical area.

The principles of *Miro BV* (case 182/84) and *Ministère Public v Deserbais* (case 286/86) (discussed at 18.6.5.2) remain good law.

18.6.6 Over-extension of Article 28

Although the rule of reason has allowed States some latitude to enact or maintain indistinctly applicable measures that are capable of hindering trade between Member States to protect important national interests, while ensuring that such measures are subject to judicial control as to their proportionality, the rule has not been without its problems. These have arisen from a tendency to a lax, 'mechanical' application of the *Dassonville* formula, requiring measures which might affect the volume of imports overall, but with little potential to *hinder* imports, to be justified under the rule of reason. Defence lawyers in Member States have been quick to exploit the 'Eurodefence' of Article 28 to charges involving a wide range of regulatory offences. Examples of such defences include challenges to Dutch laws restricting the use of free gifts for promotional purposes (*Oosthoek's Uitgeversmaatschappij BV* (case 286/81)); to French laws prohibiting the door-to-door selling of educational materials (*Buet v Ministère Public* (case 382/87)); to English laws requiring the licensing of sex shops for the sale of sexual appliances (*Quietlynn Ltd v Southend Borough Council* (case C–23/89)); to laws prohibiting 'eye-catching' price comparisons as in *Rocher* (case C–126/91); and a number of cases such as *Torfaen Borough Council v B & Q plc* (case 145/88) pleading the illegality under Article 28 of national rules limiting Sunday trading. In all of these cases the legality of these measures under EC law was ultimately upheld, sometimes (e.g., *Quietlynn*), on the grounds that Article 28 was not applicable at all, more often following the application of the rule of reason. As was noted above, the case law has not been consistent here. Moreover, as the Sunday trading cases demonstrate, national courts face great difficulties in applying a rule of reason, particularly when there exist a number of possible justifications for the measure challenged and its harmful effect on trade between *Member States* (as opposed to between particular undertakings) is minimal. In these circumstances a national judge may be reluctant to entertain a challenge to domestic legislation, duly enacted by Parliament, based on its lack of proportionality (see e.g., Hoffmann J in *Stoke-on-Trent City Council* v *B & Q plc* [1991] Ch 48).

These problems surfaced in the Sunday trading cases. In *Torfaen Borough Council* v *B & Q plc*, the ECJ had held that the rules in question, which prohibited large multiple shops such as the defendant's from opening on Sunday, might be justified to ensure that working hours be arranged to accord with 'national or regional socio-cultural characteristics', and directed the referring magistrates' court to examine the rules in the light of their proportionality. Unfortunately the precise grounds of justification permitted to protect such socio-cultural characteristics were not spelt out; nor was any guidance offered on the question of proportionality. Different British courts in different cases came to different conclusions. Courts which concluded that the socio-cultural purpose of the rules was to protect workers who did not want to work on Sunday not surprisingly concluded that the rules were disproportionate (e.g., *B & Q Ltd* v *Shrewsbury & Atcham Borough Council* [1990] 3 CMLR 535); those which saw the rules as designed to 'preserve the traditional character of the British Sunday' legitimately concluded otherwise: the rules were not more than was necessary to achieve that end (e.g., *Wellingborough Borough Council* v *Payless DIY Ltd* [1990] 1 CMLR 773). Despite a clear ruling from the Court in two cases subsequent to *Torfaen Borough Council* v *B & Q plc* (*Conforama* (case C–312/89); *Marchandise* (case C–332/89)) that similar rules would be permissible under the rule of reason, the question of the legality of the English Sunday trading rules was only decided conclusively when the ECJ, following a reference from the House of Lords in *Stoke-on-Trent City Council* v *B & Q plc* (case C–169/91), applying the (first) *Cassis* principle, found that the rules were justified and not disproportionate.

Whether as a result of these problems and the uncertainty surrounding the scope of Article 28 in the case of non-discriminatory national rules with a minimal impact (in terms of hindrance) on intra-Community trade, resulting in some exploitation of Community rules, or of a new post-Maastricht commitment to the principle of subsidiarity, the Court, in *Keck and Mithouard* (cases C–267 & 268/91), signalled an important change of direction.

18.6.7 *Keck* and *Mithouard*

These cases concerned the legality under EC law of a French law prohibiting the resale of goods in an unaltered state at prices lower than their actual purchase price, in the interests of fair trading, to prevent 'predatory pricing' (see Chapter 28). Keck and Mithouard, who had been prosecuted for breach of this law, claimed that it was incompatible with EC law. Although Article 28 was not expressly invoked, the reference being made for interpretation of Articles 3 and 12, the Court, to provide the French court with a 'useful' reply, focused on Article 28, which was clearly the relevant article. It cited the *Dassonville* test. It pointed out that legislation such as the French law in question:

> may restrict the volume of sales, and hence the volume of sales of products from other Member States, insofar as it deprives traders of a method of sales promotion. But the question remains whether such a possibility is sufficient to characterise the legislation in question as a measure having equivalent effect to a quantitative restriction on imports.

It went on to suggest:

> in view of the increasing tendency of traders to invoke Article 30 [now 28] of the Treaty as a means of challenging any rules whose effect is to limit their commercial freedom even where such rules are not aimed at products of other Member States, the Court considers it necessary to re-examine and clarify its case law on this matter.

Citing the (first) *Cassis de Dijon* principle it drew a distinction between rules which lay down 'requirements to be met' by goods, such as those relating to designation, size, weight, composition, presentation, labelling and packaging, and rules relating to 'selling arrangements'. Rules governing 'requirements to be met' falling within the *Dassonville* formula remained subject to the (first) *Cassis* principle. However, 'contrary to what [had] previously been decided':

> the application to products from other Member States of national provisions restricting or prohibiting certain selling arrangements is not such as to hinder, directly or indirectly, actually or potentially, trade between Member States within the meaning of the *Dassonville* judgment, provided that those provisions apply to all affected traders operating within the national territory and provided that they affect in the same manner, in law and in fact, the marketing of domestic products and of those from other Member States.
>
> Where these conditions are fulfilled, the application of such rules to the sale of products from another Member State meeting the requirements laid down by that State is not by nature such as to prevent their access to the market or to impede access any more than it impedes the access of domestic products. Such rules therefore fall outside the scope of Article 30 [now 28] of the Treaty.

This new approach to Article 28 was affirmed, on the same grounds, shortly after *Keck*, in *Hünermund* (case C–292/92) in the context of a challenge to a rule of the Baden-Württemberg pharmacists' ruling body, prohibiting pharmacists from advertising, outside pharmacy premises, pharmaceutical products which they are authorised to sell. Without applying the *Cassis* test the rule was held not to breach Article 28. It adopted the same approach, invoking the principle laid down in *Keck* relating to 'selling arrangements', in *Commission* v *Greece* (case C–391/92) and *Belgapom* (case C–63/94). Here it found that rules which required processed milk for infants to be sold only in pharmacies (*Commission* v *Greece*) and rules prohibiting sales yielding very low profit margins (*Belgapom*) were permissible under Article 28 without resort to the rule of reason. Similarly in *Banchero* (case C–387/93), in a case involving an ingenious 'Euro-defence' to a smuggling charge, the Court found that Italian rules reserving the retail sale of tobacco to authorised distributors were compatible *per se* with Article 28 even though the retailers were authorised to trade by a national body holding a monopoly over tobacco production in Italy. It was important to the judgment that the system did not impede access to the national market and showed no evidence of discrimination: the monopoly did not intervene in the procurement choices of retailers. (See *Franzen* (case C–189/95), discussed below.)

By contrast with these cases involving 'selling arrangements', measures constituting 'requirements to be met', such as a Dutch law prohibiting dealings in gold and silver products not bearing a Dutch, Belgian or Luxembourg hallmark (*Houtwipper* (case C–293/93)) and German rules requiring the labelling of the contents of certain foods additional to that which was required under Community law (*Commission* v *Germany* (case C–51/94) were examined, as *Keck* suggested, under the rule of reason and found not to be justified.

18.6.8 **Weaknesses of the *Keck* approach**

The full scope of the Court's ruling in *Keck*, and the extent to which it has supplanted the need for the application of a rule of reason in the case of indistinctly applicable measures, remains to be seen. *Keck* can be viewed as a return to an approach based on discrimination. The move towards a more 'formalistic' approach towards Article 28 initiated in *Keck* has been both criticised as 'lacking in principle' and acclaimed for its 'tendency to cut back on unnecessary intrusions into the laws of the Member States in cases where access to the relevant national market is not at stake' (see the articles by Reich and Roth respectively, listed in the further reading). Roth argues, persuasively, that the focus of Article 28 should be on access to the (national) market, its purpose to promote interstate trade in goods, not to ensure commercial freedom as such. It is arguable that the more recent post-*Keck* cases see the ECJ responding to some of these criticisms and, at least, considering questions such as the impact of a measure on access to the market (see 18.6.9). Perhaps a more appropriate way to view *Keck* is, as the Advocate-General in *Volker Graf* (case C–190/98) suggested, to consider the view that selling arrangements are harmless in internal market terms as a rebuttable presumption rather than as a rule. Even now, more than a decade after the decision, the jury seems still to be out on *Keck*.

18.6.8.1 *Meaning of 'selling arrangement'*

There is no doubt that the 'formalistic' approach introduced in *Keck* creates uncertainty. The ambit of the phrase 'certain selling arrangements' is unclear. We can see from the cases above that some aspects of marketing (e.g., advertising claims on packaging) (*Mars: Verein gegen Unwesen In Handel und Gewerbe Köln eV* v *Mars GmbH* (case C–470/93; and *Clinique: Verband Sozialer Wettbewerb eV* v *Clinique Laboratoires SNC et Estee Lauder Cosmetics GmbH*. (case C–315/92)) can fall within the notion of a product requirement, whereas other restrictions as to place and time of sale seem to be 'selling arrangements'. The ECJ summed the position up in *Morellato* (case C–416/00), that 'the need to alter packaging or the labelling of imported products prevents such requirements from constituting selling arrangements' (para. 29). This case concerned the requirement to pre-package bread made from partially baked dough, but finished off on-site, such packaging to contain certain information. Here the ECJ held that the prior packaging did not mean it was necessary to alter the product. The rules therefore concerned selling arrangements and would be acceptable provided they applied equally in law and in fact (see 18.6.8.2).

It seems that a requirement to package will also constitute a product requirement (*Schwarz* (case C–366/04)). Austrian law required chewing gum to be packaged if it was to be dispensed via certain types of vending machine, whereas other Member States, specifically Germany, did not impose this requirement. Those manufacturers of gum established in a State where there was no such requirement would therefore have to go to the extra expense of packaging the gum to distribute in Austria. Without considering the question of a selling arrangement, the ECJ went on to assess and accept the question of justification under Article 30. The Advocate-General adopted the same approach as the court in *Morellato*, and found the requirement to be a product requirement (para 29).

One particular problem area in this context is that of advertising. One might argue that it falls within the ambit of 'selling arrangement' rather than 'requirements to be met'; indeed in *Leclerc-Siplec* (case C–412/93) the ECJ held that legislation which prohibits television advertising in a particular sector concerns selling arrangements for the products in that particular sector. Therefore, as the ECJ suggested in *Komsummentombudsmannen* v *De Agostini* (joined cases C–34–6/95), even an outright ban on the advertising of certain products – here toys – will not fall within the then Article 30 provided always that such measures apply to domestically produced and imported products equally in law and in fact.

The boundary between the two situations – sales promotion/advertising constituting a 'selling arrangement' on the one hand and product characteristics (including packaging) on the other – will not always be easy to identify. With the development of new television services, such as television shopping and 'infomercials', it will become increasingly difficult to identify where broadcasting (a service) ends and selling arrangements start.

There are in any event circumstances when advertising and mechanisms for increasing volume of sales will not fall within 'selling arrangements'. One example of this occurred in *Vereinigte Familiapress Zeitungsverlags- und Vertriebs GmbH* v *Heinrich Bauer Verlag* (case C–368/95), which concerned the Austrian prohibition on prize draws or competitions in periodicals. Although the ECJ accepted that publishers would include such games in publications with the hope of increasing circulation, this was not enough to bring the rule within *Keck*: the prohibition concerned the content of a magazine and therefore was a requirement to be met. Since it was an indistinctly applicable measure, it could, however, be justified under the *Cassis* rule of reason.

18.6.8.2 *Non-discrimination in Keck*

It is not clear the extent to which the *Keck* assumption that selling arrangements should fall outside Article 28 is being undercut by the requirement that any such selling arrangements should apply equally in law and, crucially, in fact. This point was raised in *De Agostini* (joined cases C–34–36/95). In this case, the prohibition applied to all adverts, whether they related to imported products or not. It therefore did operate equally in law. The difficult question of whether it operated equally in fact was left by the ECJ to the national court, although the ECJ did note that in some circumstances the only practicable way to break into a new market will be through such advertising. Implicitly, this suggests that it would be difficult for such a rule to apply equally in practice.

The ECJ itself undertook the assessment of the equal operation of the selling arrangement in law and in fact in *Schutzverband gegen unlauteren Wettbewerb* v *TK-Heimdienst Sass GmbH* (case C–254/98). Under Austrian legislation bakers, butchers and grocers may offer goods for sale on rounds from door to door, provided such sales are made by traders who have a permanent establishment in that district or in a municipality adjacent to it and the sales relate to the type of goods sold at that establishment. This rule became the subject of proceedings and the question as to whether the rule was compatible with Article 28 was referred. The ECJ found that the rules constituted a selling arrangement; it then went on to consider whether the rules applied equally in law and in fact. The fact that traders established in one part of Austria would also be affected in respect of home delivery services in other areas of Austria does not change this assessment. What was important is that 'the national legislation impedes access to the market of the Member State of importation for products from other Member States more than it impedes access for domestic products'. Whereas the application of equality in law seems to be based on the notion of discrimination, the approach to equality in fact seems to bring us back to questions about access to the market, characteristic of pre-*Keck* jurisprudence.

The problem of the equal application of selling arrangements arose again in the context of Swedish rules limiting the advertising of alcoholic beverages to publications directed to point of sale and the trade press. In *Gourmet International Products* (case C–405/98), a publisher challenged these rules on the basis that they were contrary to Articles 28 and 49 EC. In its judgment, the ECJ re-stated the test in *Keck,* and following *Tk-Heimdienst* closely, re-iterated a test based on access to the market (para 18).

It then noted that *De Agostini* accepted the possibility that a prohibition might have a greater impact on imports than on domestic products. The Court concluded:

> Even without its being necessary to carry out a precise analysis of the facts characteristic of the Swedish situation, which it is for the national court to do, the Court is able to conclude that, in the case of products like alcoholic beverages, the consumption of which is linked to traditional social practices and to local habits and customs, a prohibition of all advertising directed at consumers in the form of advertisements in the press, on the radio and on television, the direct mailing of unsolicited material or the placing of posters on the public highway is liable to impede access to the market by products from other Member States more than it impedes access by domestic products, with which consumers are instantly more familiar (para. 21).

The ECJ in this case seems to give the national court very little scope but to follow the ECJ's view that the national rules here do not apply equally in fact. The consequence is that the rule will fall to be assessed under the rule of reason and Article 28, as it would have been pre-*Keck*. It should be noted that the ECJ is not stating that all advertising will necessarily fall within Article 28; it clearly seeks to limit the impact of its judgment by linking the type of product to 'traditional social practices'. Nonetheless, both *Gourmet International Products* and *TK Heimdienst* suggest that the selling arrangement/product requirement distinction proposed in *Keck* will not always answer the question of whether a measure falls outside the scope of Article 28 or not. The problem, as the ECJ seems to be recognising, is that even selling arrangements may have an impact on trade.

The current problem is what degree of impact, actual or potential, is required before a selling arrangement does not operate equally in fact. In *Deutscher Apothek-erverband eV* v *0800 DocMorris* (case C–322/01), the ECJ noted in respect of a prohibition on the mail order sale of medicinal products that, despite the fact that it limited the ability of German pharmacies to gain access to the entire German market, '[a] prohibition which has greater impact on pharmacies established outside the German territory could impede access to the market for products from other Member States more than it impedes access for domestic products' (para. 74). On this basis the selling arrangement did not apply equally in fact and therefore triggered an analysis under Article 28. The wording the ECJ uses in this case is broad. Although very similar to the test used in *TK-Heimdienst* and *Gourmet*, it seems not to require an actual impact, but suggests that a potential effect would suffice. It is hard to square this approach—or, indeed, that in *TK-Heimdienst* and *Gourmet*—with that in the *Greek Pharmacies* case (*Commission* v *Greece* (case C–391/92)), handed down shortly after *Keck*. The boundary of Article 28 seems to have moved, becoming more broadly drawn again.

There seems some uncertainty as to where the actual boundary does now lie. *Karner* concerned the Austrian prohibition on misleading advertising in relation to the sale of goods via auction. In this case, the auction catalogue, including the (misleading) statement that the goods in issue were from an insolvent estate, was advertised on the Internet. By contrast to *de Agostini*, in the Court's opinion, the national provision in this case did not constitute a total prohibition on all forms of advertising. Consequently, although the Court accepted that the prohibition could affect the total number of sales, it did not affect the marketing of products originating from other Member States more than it affects the marketing of products from the host Member State (para. 42). Crucially, the ECJ pointed to lack of evidence from those seeking to benefit from Article 28 as to the impact of the national rule. This approach which implicitly requires an actual impact, does not seem entirely on all fours with the approach in *DocMorris*. It may well be that the different rules did have a differential impact on the facts, justifying a difference in treatment. Nonetheless, any unifying principles on which these judgments are based remain unclear. Furthermore, given that many selling arrangements may not operate equally in fact, the *Keck* solution to the over-extension of Article 28 (ex 30) will be of limited utility.

18.6.9 Alternative solutions

It is submitted that a more principled approach, focusing on the question of whether a measure impedes access to a national market, subject to a *de minimis* rule, would provide a more workable rule. A test of 'substantial' hindrance was suggested by Advocate-General Jacobs in *Leclerc-Siplec* (case C–412/93), although the Court chose to apply *Keck*. An approach which considers the impact of a measure, however, seems to have been favoured by the ECJ in a number of cases recently. We have seen that in cases such as *TK-Heimdienst* and *Gourmet International Products*, the ECJ has focused on the importers' ease of access to the markets of other Member

States, rather than on the issue of whether a rule is a selling arrangement or not. In *DocMorris*, we also find references to ease of access to the market in the context of assessing whether the selling arrangement applies equally in fact. Indeed, in *Gourmet International Products*, the phrasing of the judgment is not in terms of discrimination but of access to the market.

On the other side of the coin the ECJ has also emphasised that the impact of national rules must not be too remote from inter-state trade. In *BASF AG v Präsident des Deutschen Patentamts* (case C–44/98), BASF tried to challenge a German law which, as permitted by the European Patent Convention, required patents that were granted by the European Patent Office in respect of Germany to be translated, at the patent proprietor's cost, into German. BASF argued that because of high translation costs, patent proprietors would be forced into choosing the countries in which to have patent protection as they would not be able to afford the translation costs for the entire Community. This, in turn, would affect patent proprietors' decisions about the Member States in which the patented product would be marketed, thus partitioning the internal market contrary to Article 28. In *ED Srl v Fenocchio* (case C–412/97), ED argued that Italian rules which precluded the obtaining of summary judgments against debtors who resided outside Italy would dissuade those resident in Italy from contracting with those who resided elsewhere, as debt recovery would be more difficult in respect of non-Italian residents. On this basis, it was argued that the rule should be regarded as incompatible with Article 29 as it would discourage exports. In both cases the ECJ gave these convoluted arguments short shrift, holding in both instances that the effect on Community law was too uncertain and indirect to constitute a measure having equivalent effect. A similar approach has also been used in the context of freedom of establishment (see Chapter 21). These cases are unlikely to constitute a significant shift in the ECJ's approach to the scope of Article 28 in which access to markets is clearly impeded. (Contrast *Schutzverband gegen unlauteren Wettbewerb v TK-Heimdienst Sass GmbH* (case C–254/98) in which the Austrian government unsuccessfully tried to argue that the impact of the legislation there would be too uncertain.)

The ECJ's approach in *BASF* and *ED Srl* was similar to that in the earlier case of *DIP SpA* (cases C–140–2/94), although with a different result. *DIP SpA* concerned a challenge to an Italian law permitting the opening of new shops in particular areas only on receipt of a licence, to be issued by municipal authorities on the recommendation of a local committee. The committee, which represented a variety of interest groups, made its recommendations according to specific criteria. Perhaps because the rule did not fall clearly within the category of either 'requirements to be met' or 'selling arrangements' the Court did not apply the *Keck* formulae. Instead it looked at the effect of the measure, and found its restrictive effect 'too uncertain and too indirect' for the obligation which it imposed to be regarded as hindering trade between Member States. It was thus compatible with Article 28. *Decker* (case C–120/95) is another case in which the ECJ did not consider the *Keck* formula, instead looking at the impact of the rules. The case concerned national rules which required an individual to obtain prior authorisation before incurring medical expenses in another Member State if the individual wanted those expenses reimbursed under health insurance cover. Here, the cost was related to the purchase of spectacles. In this case, the ECJ simply applied the *Dassonville* test and held that these rules 'must be categorised as a barrier to the free movement of goods, since they encourage insured persons to purchase those products in Luxembourg rather than in other Member States' (para. 36) and that the rules were not justified under the public health exception. (See also reasoning in *Schwarz* (case C–366/04).)

18.6.10 Continued need for a rule of reason

Whether the Court continues to apply *Dassonville*, as it did in *Decker*, or to operate on the basis of the distinction drawn in *Keck* or focuses on the question of hindrance to imports, subject to the application of a *de minimis* rule, as it appeared to do in *DIP SpA*, there will still be a need in many cases for courts to apply a rule of reason, since national regulatory rules more often than not constitute a real hindrance to imports. The *Cassis* judgment thus remains of supreme importance in the application of Article 28 to indistinctly applicable rules. Its twin principles formed the basis for the Commission's new approach to the freeing of the internal market within the 31 December 1992 deadline, outlined in its White Paper of 1985. Relying on the principle of mutual recognition, the presumption that goods lawfully marketed in one State are to be freely admitted into other Member States, the Commission proposed to concentrate its efforts on harmonisation measures designed to provide *essential* guarantees to safeguard the 'mandatory requirements' of Member States (see Chapter 15). The Court in *Keck* and subsequent cases appears to be prepared to give more latitude to Member States in the enactment of indistinctly applicable measures which do not in fact impede access to national markets. If it seemed necessary in 1984, in *van de Haar* (case 177/82), to reject a *de minimis* rule, in the interests of the (burgeoning) single market, arguably that market is now sufficiently established for the Court to permit national rules where their burden on imports and exports is minimal, thereby bringing the rules in relation to goods into line with EC competition law (see Chapter 27).

18.7 Prohibition, as between Member States, of quantitative restrictions on exports and of all measures having equivalent effect (Article 29)

All the principles relating to imports under Article 28 will also apply to exports under Article 29, including, as seems to have been accepted by the English courts in *R v Chief Constable of Sussex, ex parte International Trader's Ferry Limited* ([1996] QB 197 (QBD), [1997] 3 WLR 132 (CA), [1999] 1 CMLR 1320), the possibility of Member States being under positive obligations by virtue of Article 29 in conjunction with Article 10, with one important exception. Measures which are *indistinctly applicable* will not breach Article 29 merely because they are capable of hindering, directly or indirectly, actually or potentially, intra-Community trade. The *Dassonville* test does not apply. To breach Article 29 such measures must have as their specific object or effect the restriction of patterns of exports and thereby the establishment of a difference in treatment between the domestic trade of a Member State and its export trade in such a way as to provide a particular advantage for national production or for the domestic market of the State in question, at the expense of the production or of the trade of other Member States. In other words, they must be overtly or covertly protectionist.

This principle was established in *P.B. Groenveld BV* (case 15/79). Here, a national law prohibiting the large-scale manufacture of horsemeat sausages and limiting the sale of such sausages by small specialist butchers to consumers only, designed to safeguard exports of such products to countries which prohibit the sale of horse-flesh, was found, applying the above test, not to breach Article 29, although, as Advocate-General Capotorti pointed out, it presented an almost insuperable obstacle to exports. The Court's judgment represented a clear departure from the opinion of the Advocate-General. He had approached the matter along the lines of Article 28; he applied the *Dassonville* test, and *Cassis*, and found that the measure was not justified since other, less restrictive measures, such as labelling, could have been used to achieve the same ends.

In *Oebel* (case 155/80) the restriction on night working and delivery hours for bakery products, although undoubtedly a barrier to exports, since it precluded Belgian bakers from selling bread in adjacent Member States in time for breakfast, was found, following *P. B. Groenveld BV*, not to breach Article 29.

On the other hand measures which are *distinctly applicable* and which discriminate against exports *will* normally breach Article 29. In *Bouhelier* (case 53/76) the requirement in France of an export licence, following a quality inspection, for watches destined for export was held to breach Article 29 since the same inspection and licences were not required for watches sold on the domestic market.

The principles of both *P.B. Groenveld BV* and *Bouhelier* were applied in *Jongeneel Kaas BV* (case 237/82). Here Dutch rules, indistinctly applicable, regulating the quality and content of cheese produced in The Netherlands were found not to breach Article 29, even though domestic producers were thereby at a competitive disadvantage *vis-à-vis* producers from other States not bound by the same standard of quality, since they did not fall within the *P.B. Groenveld BV* criteria, whereas a distinctly applicable rule requiring inspection documents for exports alone was, following *Bouhelier*, in breach of Article 29. This approach has been reiterated more recently, for example in *Ravil* (case C–469/00).

The Court's tolerance towards indistinctly applicable, non-protective restrictions on exports introduced in *P.B. Groenveld BV* is in line with the Court's attitude, noted above, towards reverse discrimination. Clearly where there is no danger of protectionism the Court can afford to take a more lenient view. Restrictions on imports, on the other hand, will always raise a suspicion of protectionism.

Since only protective or discriminatory measures will breach Article 29 it was usually thought that a rule of reason will not be applied and justification can only be sought under Article 30. In the recent case of *Schmidberger* (case C–112/00), the ECJ discussed the justification for a 'measure' within Article 29 in conjunction with that for a MEQR within Article 28. This suggests that similar principles should be used in assessing derogations from Article 28 and 29. The ECJ did not, however, address the point directly.

18.8 State monopolies

18.8.1 Meaning of 'monopoly'

The bodies subject to Article 31 are those through which 'a Member State, in law or in fact, either directly or indirectly, supervises, determines or appreciably influences imports or exports between Member States' (Article 31(1), para. 2).

To qualify as a monopoly it is not necessary to exert total control of the market in particular goods. It is sufficient if the bodies concerned have as their object transactions regarding a commercial product which could be traded between Member States, if they play an *effective* part in such trade (*Costa* v *ENEL* (case 6/64).

It seems that State monopolies must be used for the pursuit of a public interest aim; therefore, the object of Article 31 EC is to reconcile the desire of a Member State to do so with the need to maintain the common market (*Harry Franzen* (case C–189/95)). It is not clear whether monopolies which do not pursue a public interest aim are compatible with the provisions on the free movement of goods, although it is arguable that state restrictions on granting a monopoly to a body could be characterised as 'selling arrangements' under *Keck* and *Mithouard* (contrast the approach in the *Infant Milk case* and *DocMorris*).

A State monopoly within the scope of Article 31 may also exist where an exclusive right to export or import particular goods is given to one body (*Manghera* (case C–59/75). However, Article 31 does not apply where retailers in a Member State need to be authorised to sell a product, such as tobacco (*Banchero* (case C–387/ 93)). This is subject to the proviso that the State does not interfere with the *supply* of the goods to be sold and leaves the retailers free to choose the source of the product.

18.8.2 Prohibition on discrimination on grounds of nationality

Article 31 prohibits discrimination on the grounds of nationality in the operation of the State monopoly. The aim of Article 31 is not to abolish monopolies *per se*, but rather to ensure that they do not operate in a discriminatory manner. The overriding objective is to ensure that obstructions to the free movement of goods and distortions of competition within the Community as a result of such a monopoly are kept to a minimum. In *SA des Grandes Distilleries Peureux* (case 119/78), rules regarding the French monopoly for the distillation of raw materials were held to be discriminatory and contrary to Article 31(1) EC because they prohibited the use of raw materials imported from another Member State. In contrast, in *Harry Franzen* (case C–189/95), Swedish provisions on the existence and operation of the monopoly retailer of alcoholic beverages were found to be compatible with Article 31. The existence of this monopoly was not of concern, provided that it was set up in such a way that it was not more difficult for suppliers from other Member States to sell alcohol in Sweden.

More recently another Swedish monopoly, one concerning the retail sale of medicinal preparations, has been successfully challenged (*Hanner* (case C–438/ 02)). The Court reiterated its position that Article 31 does not require the abolition of State monopolies; it controls the way they operate. In this instance, the contract establishing the monopoly did not provide for either a purchasing plan or a system of calls for tender which would provide an opportunity for producers of products that are not selected by the monopoly to find out why and, possibly, to challenge the decision. Here, the State monopoly had absolutely free choice as to the products it would stock. The ECJ held that the agreement did not therefore ensure that discrimination was ruled out. On this basis the State monopoly's system for selecting the products to stock is liable to place products from other Member States at a disadvantage. It was therefore, in principle, contrary to Community law.

18.9 Relationship with other Treaty provisions

18.9.1 Article 28

Article 31 is part of Title I, Chapter 2 of the EC Treaty on prohibitions of quantitative restrictions between Member States. It is as noted complementary to Articles 28 and 29 EC. However, in contrast to Articles 28 and 29, Article 31 does not benefit from the equivalent of the Article 30 derogation (see Chapter 19), and it may therefore be important to identify whether a particular provision is subject to the free movement provisions or the State monopoly provision.

It has been held that Article 31 only applies to activities that are intrinsically connected with the specific business of the monopoly (*SA des Grandes Distilleries Peureux* (case 119/78)). However, related activities may be subject to Article 28 EC. In *Franzen*, it was argued that the Swedish alcohol monopoly was contrary to both Articles 28 and 31. The ECJ drew a distinction between those provisions which related to the existence and operation of the monopoly itself, which would be subject to Article 31, and provisions which were separable from the operation of the monopoly but which had a bearing on it. The latter would be subject to assessment under Article 28 EC. The provisions at issue in *Franzen* concerned both the monopoly itself and the requirement for importers of alcohol to hold a licence. The monopoly itself was not contrary to Article 31, but the requirement of an import licence fell foul of Article 28 and could not be justified under Article 30.

18.9.2 Other provisions

Article 31 only applies to State monopolies in the provision of goods. It does not apply to services. However, if a State monopoly exists in the provision of services, and operates in a discriminatory manner, then it may be caught by the general prohibition against discrimination on grounds of nationality in Article 12 (ex 6) EC. It may also be subject to the provisions on the free movement of services (Articles 49–56 EC (ex 59–66)), or Article 82 (ex 86) EC, which prohibits the abuse of a dominant position. To the extent that there is a comparable provision regarding services, this is Article 86(2), which deals with the provision of services of general economic interest (see also Chapter 30).

18.10 **Conclusions**

This chapter illustrates the importance of the jurisprudence defining the scope of the prohibition on measures having an equivalent effect to quantitative restriction. The key question is the relationship between free movement and national regulatory competence. This question is affected by the scope of the derogation principles (Chapter 19) and by positive harmonisation measures (Chapter 15). In addition to these provisions, there is also Article 31. Although there is very little jurisprudence on Article 31, it nevertheless fulfils an important function in ensuring that the free movement of goods in the common market is not restricted any more than is justifiable.

As far as this chapter is concerned, the central problem relates to how to determine the scope of Article 28. The ECJ's case law has not always been consistent and it seems that during the development of the Community different approaches have been taken ranging from tests based on discrimination, access to the market and the more formalistic approach under *Keck*. Behind all of these runs the underlying questions of how much regulation of trade (and trade-related matters) is desirable and who gets to choose the form of that regulation. With the single market, if not actually completed, being in a more developed phase than when *Dassonville*, *Cassis de Dijon*, and even *Keck*, were handed down, one remaining question is whether the internal market should tolerate more regulation and greater divergence or less.

FURTHER READING

Arnull, A., 'What Shall We Do on Sunday?' (1991) 16 EL Rev 112.

Barents, R., 'New Developments in Measures Having Equivalent Effect' (1981) 18 CML Rev 271.

Diamond, P., 'Dishonourable Defences: the Use of Injunctions and the EEC Treaty: Case Study of the Shops Act 1950' (1991) 54 MLR 72.

Gormley, L., 'Actually or Potentially, Directly or Indirectly? Obstacles to the Free Movement of Goods' (1989) 9 YEL 197.

Krämer, L., 'Environmental Protection and Article 30 EEC Treaty' (1993) 30 CML Rev 111.

Mortelmans, K., 'Article 30 of the EEC Treaty and Legislation Relating to Market Circumstances: Time to Consider a New Definition?' (1991) 28 CML Rev 115.

Oliver, P., 'Measures of Equivalent Effect: a Reappraisal' (1982) 19 CML Rev 217.

Quinn, M. and McGowan, N., 'Can Article 30 Impose Obligations on Individuals?' (1987) 12 EL Rev 163.

Reich, N., 'The November Revolution: *Keck, Meng, Audi* Revisited' (1994) 31 CML Rev 459.

Roth, W. H., Casenote on *Keck* and *Hünermund* (1994) 31 CML Rev 845.

—, 'Export of Goods and Services within the Single Market: Reflections on the Scope of Articles 29 and 49 EC' in Tridimas and Nebbia (eds) *European Union Law for the Twenty-First Century: Rethinking the New Legal Order* (Hart Publishing, 2004).

Steiner, J., 'Drawing the Line: Uses and Abuses of Article 30 EEC' (1992) 29 CML Rev 749.

Weatherill, S., 'After *Keck*: Some Thoughts on how to Clarify the Clarification' (1996) 33 CML Rev 885.

Weatherill, S., 'Recent developments in the law governing the free movement of goods in the EC's internal market' (2006) 2 ERCL 90.

White, E., 'In Search of Limits to Article 30 of the EEC Treaty' (1989) 26 CML Rev 235.

Wils, W. P. J., 'The Search for the Rule in Article 30: Much Ado about Nothing?' (1993) 18 EL Rev 475.

Woods, L., *Free Movement of Goods and Services in the European Community* (Ashgate, 2004), Chs 4–6.

19

Derogation from the free movement of goods

19.1 Introduction

The previous chapter has explored and emphasised the width of the fundamental principle of the free movement of goods. Article 30 EC contains the Treaty exception to this principle. The balance between principle and exception reveals tensions at two, linked, points. The first is substantive: the balancing of different policy interests, which can be characterised as trade versus non-trade interests. The second relates to competence, that is the freedom of Member States to put into place policies and the extent to which the EC policy of free movement of goods constrains that freedom. It will be seen that, although to some degree the scope of Article 30 will be affected by the arguments brought by the Member States to justify specific national rules in sets of circumstances pertaining to individual Member States, for example national conceptions of morality, the ECJ has ensured that final review of the scope of Article 30 remains at the Community level. Two general points can be made about the ECJ's approach. As with other freedoms, the ECJ has held that any derogation from a Treaty freedom must be interpreted narrowly. This has an effect not only on the substantive scope of the heads of derogation found in Article 30, but also in terms of the application of those grounds to the national rules. The ECJ has developed the notion of proportionality, found in other areas of Community law (see Chapter 6), to ensure that where a legitimate interest exists, Member States do not try to use it to hide measures that are essentially restrictions on trade.

19.2 Outline of Article 30

The principal provision for derogation from Articles 28 and 29 (ex 30–34) EC is Article 30 (ex 36) EC, which provides:

> The provisions of Articles 28 and 29 shall not preclude prohibitions or restrictions on imports, exports or goods in transit justified on grounds of public morality, public policy or public security; the protection of health and life of humans, animals or plants; the protection of national treasures possessing artistic, historic or archaeological value; or the protection of industrial and commercial property. Such prohibitions or restrictions shall not, however, constitute a means of arbitrary discrimination or a disguised restriction on trade between Member States.

Should the Constitution come into force, it will be re-enacted as Article III–154.

19.2.1 **Relationship with the 'rule of reason' under** *Cassis de Dijon*

Since indistinctly applicable measures restricting imports from Member States will now be subject to the rule of reason under *Cassis* (case 120/78) (Chapter 18), it will normally only be necessary to apply Article 30 EC to distinctly applicable measures in breach of Articles 28 and 29 EC. However, where indistinctly applicable measures are clearly discriminatory in their effect on imports or fall within one of the heads of derogation of Article 30 EC, the Court may consider the question of justification under Article 30 EC. (See *R* v *Royal Pharmaceutical Society of Great Britain* (cases 266, 267/87); *Commission* v *UK (Re UHT Milk)* (case 124/81) to be discussed later.) Distinctly applicable measures, on the other hand, can never be justified under *Cassis*.

This was tried in *Commission* v *Ireland (Re Restrictions on Importation of Souvenirs)* (case 113/80). Here the Irish government sought to justify, on *Cassis* principles, an Order requiring that imported souvenirs be marked 'foreign', or with their country of origin, arguing that the measure was necessary in the interests of consumers and fair trading – to enable consumers to distinguish the 'genuine' (home-produced) souvenirs from the (imported) 'fakes'. The Court held that since the measure applied only to imported souvenirs it could not be judged on *Cassis* principles. It could only be justified on the grounds provided by the then Article 36 (now 30). Since that article created an exception to the principle of free movement of goods it could not be extended to situations other than those specifically laid down. The measure could not be justified in the interests of consumer protection.

The ECJ has on occasion seemed to bend the definition of what might be seen as a discriminatory measure to allow a national measure, particularly those aimed at environmental protection, to be justified following *Cassis* on grounds not set out in Article 30 (see e.g., *Commission* v *Belgium* (*Walloon Waste*) (case C–2/90)). Advocate-General Jacobs in the case of *PreussenElektra* (*PreussenElektra AG* v *Schleswag AG* (case C–379/98)) criticised the *Walloon Waste* case and suggested that the ECJ should abandon the distinction between distinctly and indistinctly applicable measures and allow even discriminatory measures to be capable of justification by reference to mandatory requirements, at least where environmental protection is concerned. The ECJ, however, disregarded the suggestions of the Advocate-General, and came to the conclusion that the national rules, which were aimed at encouraging the use of electricity produced from renewable energy sources, did not contravene Article 28 in the first place. As a consequence, not only has the ECJ's approach to determining whether there is a discriminatory or indistinctly applicable measure not been consistent, but it seems reluctant to address the issue of whether the distinction should stay.

19.3 **Proportionality and disguised restriction on trade**

Although the grounds listed in Article 30 EC appear extensive they have been narrowly construed. The Court has held on many occasions that the purpose of this article is not to reserve certain matters to the exclusive jurisdiction of the Member States; it merely allows national legislation to derogate from the principle of free movement of goods to the extent to which this is and remains justified to achieve the objectives set out there (*Commission* v *Germany (Re Health Control on Imported Meat)* (case 153/78)). A measure is 'justified' if it is necessary, and no more than is necessary, to achieve the desired result (the proportionality principle). Moreover, Article 30 EC cannot be relied on to justify rules or practices which, though beneficial, are designed primarily to lighten the administrative burden or reduce public expenditure, unless in the absence of such rules or practices the burden or expenditure would exceed the limits of what can reasonably be required (*Officier van Justitie* v *de Peijper* (case 104/75)).

As well as being necessary, measures must comply with the second sentence of Article 30; they must not 'constitute a means of arbitrary discrimination or a disguised restriction on trade between Member States'. Discrimination will be regarded as arbitrary if it is not justified on objective grounds. The enquiry under Article 30 is very similar to that conducted in applying the rule of reason (see 18.6.5.1) and, as with the application of that rule, the presumption in favour of goods lawfully marketed in one of the Member States of the Community means that a State seeking to rebut that presumption must itself prove that the conditions for the application of Article 30 are satisfied.

19.4 Grounds for derogation

19.4.1 Public morality

The public morality ground was considered in two English cases, *R* v *Henn* (case 34/79) and *Conegate Ltd* v *Customs and Excise Commissioners* (case 121/85). In *R* v *Henn*, the then Article 36 (now 30) was invoked to justify a ban on the import of pornographic materials. To a certain extent the ban was discriminatory, since not all pornographic material of the kind subject to the ban was illegal in the UK. In the UK it was illegal only if likely to 'deprave or corrupt', whereas under UK customs legislation, import was prohibited if the goods were 'indecent or obscene'. On a reference from the House of Lords, the ECJ found that the ban was in breach of the then Article 30 but was justified under former Article 36 (now 30). Although it was discriminatory, the discrimination was not arbitrary; nor was it a disguised restriction on trade between Member States; there was no lawful trade in such goods in the UK. The measure was genuinely applied for the protection of public morality, not for the protection of national products. It was for each State to determine in accordance with its own scale of values the requirements of public morality in its territory.

The ECJ took a stricter view in *Conegate Ltd* v *Customs and Excise Commissioners*. Here Article 30 was invoked to justify the seizure by HM Customs and Excise of a number of inflatable rubber dolls euphemistically described as 'love dolls' together with other exotic and erotic articles imported from Germany, on the grounds that they were 'indecent and obscene'. The importers claimed the seizure was in breach of Article 28, and, since there was no ban on the manufacture and sale of such items in the UK (the sale was merely restricted), it was discriminatory. Their argument succeeded before the ECJ. The Court held that the seizure was not justified under Article 30, since, unlike *R* v *Henn*, there was no general prohibition on the manufacture and marketing of such goods in the UK; nor had the State adopted serious and effective measures to prevent the distribution of such goods in its territory. (Similar reasoning has been applied in the sphere of free movement of persons, see Chapter 23.)

19.4.2 Public policy

This ground, potentially wide, has been strictly construed, and has rarely succeeded as a basis for derogation under Article 30 EC. However, in *R* v *Thompson* (case 7/78) a restriction on the import and export of gold collectors' coins was held to be justified on the grounds of public policy, since the need to protect the right to mint coinage was one of the fundamental interests of the State.

A similar principle has been applied to the public policy exception to the principle of freedom of movement of persons (see *Rutili* v *Ministre de l'Intérieure* (case 36/75) and Chapter 23). More recently, however, it seems that the test developed under the free movement of people in the case of *Bouchereau* is being used across the four freedoms. Thus the ECJ will seek to identify if there is a sufficiently serious threat to one of the fundamental interests of society in issue. Unsurprisingly, the Court has repeatedly stated that public policy cannot provide a clause of general safeguard (*Commission* v *Italy (Re Ban on Pork Imports)* (case 7/61)) and can never be invoked to serve purely economic ends (*Commission* v *Italy* (case 95/81)). In *R* v *Secretary of State for the Home Department, ex parte Evans Medical Ltd* (case C–324/93) it found that a prohibition against the importation into the UK without a licence of the drug diamorphine could not be justified by the need to maintain the economic viability of the sole licensed manufacturer of the drug in the UK, although it might be permitted on public health grounds to ensure that a country has reliable supplies for essential medical purposes.

The interrelationship between public funding, in which economic considerations might play a part, and public policy underlay the debate in *R* v *Chief Constable of Sussex, ex parte International Trader's Ferry Ltd* ([1997] 3 WLR 132, CA, [1999] 1 CMLR 1320 HL). The case arose in the context of widespread demonstrations by animal rights supporters against the transporting of live animals for slaughter. Demonstrations were centred in docks and airports around the UK. Extensive and expensive policing had been in force to ensure that the traffic in these animals, which was lawful, might not be prevented. The action arose from the Chief Constable's decision to restrict his force's services in policing demonstrations at particular ports to three days a week, in order to save resources. As a result, International Trader's Ferry Ltd was prevented by the protesters from transporting loads on the days on which policing had been withdrawn. The company sued the Chief Constable for the resultant losses under both English and EC law. The House of Lords' decision, confirming the legality of the Chief Constable's decision to withdraw policing of animal rights demonstrators on public policy grounds, was firmly based on the need to protect public order. Financial factors, such as the need to balance scarce resources, were relevant only to the reasonableness and proportionality of the Chief Constable's decision.

This case which, it is submitted, is on its facts correct, may be compared with *Commission* v *France* (case C–265/95). Here, in the context of widespread public demonstrations in France to prevent foreign produce from reaching local markets, the ECJ found that the French authorities, in failing to take any significant action against these demonstrations, despite repeated requests from the Commission, had failed in their obligations under the EC Treaty. Since they had adduced no evidence justifying this failure, they could not rely on the public policy derogation under Article 30.

The cases about public protest illustrate another aspect of the public policy exception. In *Schmidberger* (case C–112/00), which concerned protests about the environmental impact of excessive road transport, the ECJ accepted that the need to protect human rights fell within public policy.

Even where a public policy justification appears to be legitimate, as in *Campus Oil Ltd* (case 72/83) (see below), in which Advocate-General Slynn was prepared to accept a public policy justification, the Court has in the past preferred to base its judgment on other grounds. It seems that public policy will be an exception of last resort.

Public policy cannot be invoked on the grounds that the activity which the impugned national measure seeks to curb carries criminal sanctions (*Prantl* (case 16/83)). Indeed, in many cases, as in *Prantl* itself, Article 28 EC has proved a valid defence to a criminal charge.

19.4.3 Public security

This ground was successfully invoked in *Campus Oil Ltd* (case 72/83) to justify an Irish order requiring importers of petroleum oils to buy up to 35 per cent of their requirements of petroleum products from the Irish National Petroleum Co. (INPC), at prices to be fixed by the minister. The measure was clearly discriminatory and protective. The Irish government argued that it was justified, on public policy and public security grounds, to maintain a viable national refinery which would meet essential needs in times of crisis. The Court found it in breach of Article 28 but, contrary to the view of the Commission, justifiable on public security grounds, since its purpose was to maintain the continuity of essential oil supplies. Petroleum products, the Court held, are of fundamental importance to the country's existence, since they are needed not only for the economy, but for the country's institutions, its vital services, and the survival of its inhabitants. The Court stressed that purely economic objectives would not provide justification under Article 30, but provided the measure was justified on other grounds the fact that it might secure economic objectives did not exclude the application of that article. As to whether the measures were necessary, the Court held that a compulsory purchase requirement would be justified only if the output of the INPC refinery could not be freely disposed of at competitive prices, and the compulsory prices only if they were competitive in the market concerned; if not the financial loss must be borne by the State, subject to the application of Articles 87 and 88 (ex 92 and 93) (prohibition on State aids, see Chapter 30).

The reasoning in *Campus Oil* (case 72/83) was much criticised and has not been successfully argued since. In *Cullet* (case 231/83), which concerned similar rules, the Advocate-General went to some lengths to distinguish the case from *Campus Oil*. In another case involving oil refineries, the ECJ found the national rules in issue disproportionate (*Commission v Greece* (case 347/88)).

19.4.4 **Protection of the health and life of humans, animals and plants**

Discriminatory measures for which justification may be sought on health grounds may include bans, tests and inspections of imports to ensure that domestic standards are met, and licensing or documentary requirements to provide evidence of this fact. To succeed on this ground it is necessary to prove a real health risk (see also *Duphar BV* (case 238/82)). This will not be the case where the exporting State maintains equivalent standards and those standards are adequate to meet that risk. In *Commission v UK (Re UHT Milk)* (case 124/81) the Court found that a requirement that UHT milk should be marketed only by approved dairies or distributors (allegedly to ensure that milk was free from bacterial or viral infections) which necessitated the repacking and retreating of imported milk, was not justified, since there was evidence that milk in all Member States was of similar quality and subject to equivalent controls. (Although the measure was prima facie indistinctly applicable the Court considered it to be discriminatory in effect and examined it for its compatibility with Article 30.) (See also *Decker* (case C–120/95) regarding the need to maintain the quality of medical products.)

In contrast, in *Rewe-Zentralfinanz eGmbH* (case 4/75) a plant health inspection applied only to imported apples, designed to control a pest called San José scale, which was clearly in breach of Article 28, was found to be justified on health grounds, since the imported apples constituted a real risk which was not present in domestic apples. Although discriminatory, the discrimination was not arbitrary. (Although the inspection was justified it will be remembered from Chapter 17 that the charge for the inspection was not, since Article 30 is not available to justify a charge: *Rewe-Zentralfinanze GmbH* (case 39/73).)

More recently in *Ditlev Bluhme* (case C–67/97), a prohibition on the import onto the island of Læsø of Danish domestic bees and reproductive material for them was held to be justified under Article 30. The aim of the measure was to protect an indigenous population that was in danger of disappearance as a result of cross-breeding with other bee species. The ECJ held that by seeking to protect biodiversity through ensuring the survival of a distinct indigenous species, the measures protect the life of those animals.

The health justification has often failed on proportionality grounds, or because it constitutes 'arbitrary discrimination or a disguised restriction on trade between Member States'. In the *UHT Milk* case (case 124/81), in addition to the marketing restrictions, UHT milk coming into the UK required a specific import licence. The Court found both requirements disproportionate; it was not necessary to market the products in that way, and the information gleaned from processing the licensing applications could have been obtained by other less restrictive means, for example, by declarations from importers, accompanied if necessary by the appropriate certificates. For similar reasons in *Commission v UK (Re Imports of Poultry Meat)* (case 40/82) a specific import licence requirement for poultry and eggs, allegedly designed to prevent the spread of Newcastle disease, was found not to be justified. Yet in *Commission v Ireland (Re Protection of Animal Health)* (case 74/82), which also concerned Newcastle disease, a similar import licence requirement was permitted under Article 30 on account of the exceptionally high health standards of Irish poultry, a standard which was not matched by British flocks. The Court said it was necessary in each case to weigh the inconvenience caused by the administrative and financial burden against the dangers and risks to animal health. Thus it may be difficult to predict when a specific import licence requirement will or will not be justified.

In the first Newcastle disease case, *Commission* v *UK* (case 40/82) the same licensing system was found to result in a total ban on imports from six Member States. The Court found that the measure did not form part of a seriously considered health policy and operated as a disguised restriction on trade between Member States.

Similar protectionist motives were discovered in *Commission* v *France (Re Italian Table Wines)* (case 42/82). Here the Court found excessive delays in customs clearance of wine imported from Italy into France, pending analysis of the wine to ensure it complied with French quality standards. While it conceded that some analysis in the form of random checks, resulting in minor delays, might be justified, the measures taken by the French, which involved systematic checks greatly in excess of those made on domestically produced wine, were both discriminatory and disproportionate.

Cases concerning pharmaceuticals and other medicinal products have shown a greater leniency on the part of the Court, especially when there is no evidence of a protectionist motive. In *R* v *Royal Pharmaceutical Society of Great Britain* (cases 266, 267/87) the Court found that the rules of the Society prohibiting the substitution by pharmacists of other equivalent drugs for proprietary brands prescribed by doctors, although clearly discriminatory in the effect on imports, were justified to maintain patients' confidence and to avoid the 'anxiety factor' associated with product substitution (see also *Lucien Ortscheit GmbH* v *Eurim-Pharm Arzneimittel GmbH* (case C–320/93)).

Although there have been a number of harmonising directives in the field of pharmaceuticals and similar products, the area is not exhaustively regulated at EC level. There is still then room for the Treaty derogation (see *DocMorris* (case C–322/01), discussed in Chapter 18), which concerned, *inter alia*, the sale via mail order of prescription goods. The ECJ accepted that Article 30 could apply to such a restriction given the risks attaching to such products, the need to ensure the patient understands how to use them and the need to ensure that prescriptions reach their intended recipient (para. 119).

Another argument was put forward in *DocMorris* (case C–322/01), that the German system to which the Dutch mail order suppliers were not subject, obliged pharmacies to stock a range of drugs at certain prices. The control of prices was necessary to ensure the functioning of part of the German health system. This is a different kind of public health argument, one that is linked to the provision of a public service (see also Chapters 22 and 23). Nonetheless the ECJ has accepted the argument, at least in principle, here and in other cases. Thus in *DocMorris*, the ECJ held:

> Although aims of a purely economic nature cannot justify restricting the fundamental freedom to provide services, it is not impossible that the risk of seriously undermining the financial balance of the social security system may constitute an overriding general-interest reason capable of justifying a restriction of that kind (see *Kohll*, para. 41; *Vanbraekel*, para. 47; *Smits and Peerbooms*, para. 72; and case C–358/99 *Müller-Fauré and Van Riet* [2003] ECR I–4509, paras 72 and 73). Moreover, a national market for prescription medicines could be characterised by non-commercial factors, with the result that

national legislation fixing the prices at which certain medicinal products are sold should, in so far as it forms an integral part of the national health system, be maintained (para. 122).

Crucially in *DocMorris*, the German Government had not put forward any arguments on this point and so the ECJ dismissed the point for that reason.

In cases where it is unclear whether a product or additive is safe (and there is no Community legislation on the point), it is possible for individual Member States to restrict the sales of such products, provided that there is a swift and accessible authorisation procedure available.

The prohibition in the Danish bee case (*Ditlev Bluhme* (case C–67/97)) was also found to be proportionate. In that case, as well as there being no protectionist motive, the ECJ highlighted the fact that the measures formed the basis of a mechanism recognised in international law for the protection of species – the establishment of a conservation area.

19.4.5 Protection of national treasures possessing artistic, historic or archaeological value

So far these grounds have not been used to provide a basis for derogation under Article 30, but it was suggested in *Commission* v *Italy (Re Export Tax on Art Treasures)* (case 7/68) that a desire to prevent art treasures leaving the country would have justified a quantitative restriction, even though it could not justify a charge. It is thought that it would normally apply to restrictions on exports. There is also now a directive governing the export of cultural property (Directive 93/7/EC) to complement the already existing regulation (Regulation 3911/92/EEC), which deals with the export of cultural goods from Member States to third countries.

19.4.6 Protection of industrial and commercial property

The exception provided by Article 30 for industrial and commercial property has perhaps been one of the most litigated heads of derogation. It is noteworthy in three main respects. First it constitutes the grant of a derogation in respect of actions of private individuals, the intellectual property rights holders; the national law granting the intellectual property rights is not under challenge as a result of Article 295 (ex 222) EC. It provides that:

This Treaty shall in no way prejudice the rules in Member States governing the system of property ownership.

Given this basis, it should not be surprising that a number of challenges to the rights of intellectual property holders have also arisen under competition law. The ECJ has attempted to develop a parallel approach.

Secondly, the nature of intellectual property rights is such that they often operate (or can be used) to partition the market; they thus run counter to the basic notion of the internal market. The ECJ has thus had to reconcile these competing notions. It has done so by developing two main doctrines. The first of these is the idea that there is a difference between the existence of the right and its exercise. Whilst the former is protected, the latter is subject to review to ensure that protection claimed by holders of property rights does not exceed the central area protected by the property rights, its 'specific subject matter'. Further, the Court has applied the doctrine of exhaustion to limit the scope of intellectual property rights. The owner of the right can control the first marketing of the product, but cannot control its marketing and distribution thereafter.

The third significant point is that the doctrine of proportionality, which is central in the assessment of the acceptability of derogations under other grounds and, indeed, in respect of the rule of reason, does not tend to arise here, or at least not expressly. It may be that the limitations imposed by the specific subject matter of the right operate to fulfil the same function, or that the exercise of rights beyond those limitations implicitly constitutes a disguised restriction on trade.

In the light of the vast body of cases, the parallels with intellectual property rights cases under the competition provisions and the dissimilarities with those under Article 30, this chapter will not deal with the case law on intellectual property rights. Instead, they will be discussed together with the relevant competition law cases in a separate chapter, Chapter 31.

19.5 Derogation provisions other than Article 30 EC

In addition to the rule of reason and Article 30 EC there are further specific provisions of the Treaty allowing for derogation from the principles of Articles 28 and 29 EC, mainly in the field of economic and commercial policy; hence the Court's refusal to allow Article 30 to justify purely economic measures. These comprise:

(a) measures to meet *short-term economic difficulties* ('conjunctural policy') (Article 99 (ex 103) EC),

(b) measures to meet *balance of payment difficulties* (Articles 108–111 (ex 107, 108 and 109) EC), and most important of all,

(c) measures to meet:

   (i) *deflections of trade* which might obstruct the execution of Community commercial policy, or

   (ii) *economic difficulties in any Member State* resulting from the implementation of commercial policy (Article 134 (ex 115) (see *Criel, nee Donckerwolcke* v *Procureur de la République* (case 41/6)).

Article 134 EC applies only in the context of the common commercial policy, i.e., to goods originating from third countries which are in free circulation within the EC, and is necessary, since deflections of trade or economic difficulties may well arise as a result of differences in regimes between Member States, permitted under the Community's common commercial policy.

Measures taken under the above articles are required to be taken either by the Commission or the Council (on a proposal from the Commission), or, if taken by

Member States, subject to authorisation or approval by the Commission. They are subject to strict Community control. As with measures taken under Article 30, they must comply with the proportionality principle.

Derogation is also permitted *in the interests of national security* (Articles 296–7 (ex 223 and 224) EC). Under Article 296, a State 'may take such measures as it considers necessary for the protection of the essential interests of its security which are connected with the production of or trade in arms, munitions and war material', provided that such measures do not adversely affect competition within the common market regarding products which are not intended for military purposes. Under Article 297 EC, States may consult with each other and take steps to counteract measures taken by a Member State in the event of war or the threat of war or serious internal disturbances, or to carry out obligations undertaken for the purpose of maintaining peace or international security. Should the Commission or a Member State consider that a State is making improper use of its powers under Articles 296 and 297 they may bring that State before the Court under Article 298 EC. It would seem that for these provisions, as for Article 30, where there is a Community measure covering the specific subject, a Member State cannot rely on the derogation provided in the Treaty itself. In *R v HM Treasury, ex parte Centro-Com Srl* (case C–124/5), for example, the UK sought, on the basis of the UN sanctions against Serbia and Montenegro, to prevent the payments of sums held in a London bank account by a Montenegrin to an Italian company. The ECJ, however, pointed out that this issue was dealt with by an EC regulation and that the UK could thus not rely on the national security exception in the then Article 224 (now 297) EC.

19.6 **Conclusions**

In the area of the derogation from free movement, the ECJ has sought to reconcile the tension between the needs of the internal market and those of the individual Member States, a task that is not always easy to accomplish. The approach of the ECJ has interpreted the scope of the derogation provisions narrowly. Although the ECJ has shown some willingness to accept a Member State's assessment of when a public interest issue arises, as can be seen in the sphere of public policy, public health and even as regards the existence of intellectual property rights, it has stringently assessed whether any national measures are necessary or whether such measures constitute a disguised restriction on trade. In this context the principle of proportionality has been central. Some relatively recent case law, such as *Preussen-Elektra* in the environmental field, suggest that in policy areas in which the EC itself has interests – such as the protection of the environment (see Article 6 EC, discussed in Chapter 2) – then the ECJ may be prepared to more generous. This case law is as yet tentative and may well be limited to environmental concerns. For the rest, it seems that the internal market and trade concerns continue to be high priorities, a state of affairs which means that the protection offered through Community legislation (Chapter 15) remains important.

FURTHER READING

Alexander, W., 'IP and the Free Movement of Goods – 1996 Caselaw of the ECJ' [1998] 29 IIC 16.

Castillo de la Torre, F., 'Trade Marks and Free Movement of Pharmaceuticals in the European Community: To Partition or not to Partition' [1997] 6 EIPR 304.

Roberts, G., Casenote on *Gallaher* (1994) 31 CML Rev 165.

Weatherill, S., 'Regulating the Internal Market: Result Orientation in the House of Lords' (1992) 17 EL Rev 299.

Weatherill, S., Casenote on *Gallaher* (1994) 19 EL Rev 55.

Woods, L., *Free Movement of Goods and Services in the EC* (Ashgate, 2004) Ch. 7.

20

Free movement of workers

20.1 Introduction

The free movement of workers is one of the four freedoms forming the foundations of the common market. As such, it has been interpreted broadly. The free movement right can be seen to comprise three elements. The first is the right to move to another Member State and to live there. This is a prerequisite to the second right, which is to access the job market in the host Member State. This has the most immediate economic aspect. Finally, but importantly in terms of removing disadvantages to the worker arising from the exercise of the right of free movement, there are ancillary rights. These range from the right of workers to move family members with them through to many social rights. They aim to ensure that the migrant and his or her family integrate into the host Member State.

As well as having an economic function, allowing the movement of factors of production, the free movement of workers has also been interpreted in the light of the fact that workers are people, not just inanimate objects. Indeed, it has been suggested that free movement, as well as constituting an economic freedom, has the status of a fundamental right. The personal aspect to the freedom of workers has lead to a particularly broad interpretation, especially of ancillary rights. This is a key theme of the Article 39 EC jurisprudence. One further distinguishing feature of this area of law is the significant quantity of secondary legislation which has been enacted to delineate more precisely the scope of an individual's rights. In discussing the scope of the free movement of workers, this chapter considers the terms of the secondary legislation, as well as Article 39 EC itself.

Although broad, the scope of Article 39 is not unlimited. In this, the definition of 'worker' has been key in identifying who may benefit from the rights granted and who does not. The limitations imposed by the economic aspect of 'worker' have been ameliorated, if not eradicated, by the ECJ's approach to citizenship. Although this chapter will identify cases in which the ECJ has relied on citizenship in conjunction with the provisions relating to workers, further discussion of citizenship itself can be found in Chapter 24.

20.2 Fundamental Community rights

The principal Treaty provision governing the free movement of workers is Article 39 (ex 48) EC:

1. Freedom of movement for workers shall be secured within the Community.

2. Such freedom of movement shall entail the abolition of any discrimination based on nationality between workers of the Member States as regards employment, remuneration and other conditions of work and employment.

3. It shall entail the right, subject to limitations justified on grounds of public policy, public security or public health:

   (a) to accept offers of employment actually made;

   (b) to move freely within the territory of Member States for this purpose;

   (c) to stay in a Member State for the purpose of employment in accordance with the provisions governing the employment of nationals of that State laid down by law, regulation or administrative action;

   (d) to remain in the territory of a Member State after having been employed in that State, subject to conditions which shall be embodied in implementing regulations to be drawn up by the Commission.

4. The provisions of this Article shall not apply to employment in the public service.

The Constitution, should it come into force in its current format, would amend the wording of the provisions relating to workers, albeit slightly. It seems the intention is to reflect the fact that these rights are now fully in force and are not conditional. Notably Article III–133(1) would simply provide that '[w]orkers shall have the right to move freely within the Union' and paragraph (2) is phrased as a prohibition on discrimination.

All the above rights may be denied to a worker, whether temporary or long-term, and to a member of his family, on the grounds of public policy, public security and public health (see Chapter 23).

As required under Articles 39(3)(d) (ex 43(3)(d)) and 40 (ex 49), secondary legislation was introduced to give further substance to the above principles. The principal measures, adopted in the late 1960s and in force for more than 35 years, were:

(a) Directive 68/360, governing rights of entry and residence.

(b) Regulation 1612/68, governing access to, and conditions of, employment.

(c) Regulation 1251/70, governing rights to remain in the territory of a Member State after having been employed there.

(d) Directive 64/221, governing Member States' right to derogate from the free movement provisions on the grounds of public policy, public security or public health.

Directive 2004/38/EC updates and consolidates these measures (see further below). Specifically, Directives 68/360/EEC and 64/221 have been repealed and Regulation 1612/68 has been amended by this directive, Articles 10 and 11 being repealed. The rights conferred by Regulation 1251/70 have been extended, that regulation being replaced by the provisions in Directive 2004/38/EC (see also Chapter 24). One effect of this change is that some rights which were provided by regulation, those relating to migrant workers' families, will now be protected by a directive. As we have seen in Chapter 3, there are different legal consequences from the choice of type of legal measure, regulations being directly applicable and directives being binding on those to whom they are addressed. Given that the doctrine of direct effect (Chapter 5) cannot be relied on in horizontal situations in respect of directives, the use of the directive rather than a regulation may have consequences for the enforceability of these rights should it be necessary to rely on them against private individuals (e.g. refusal to give employment to a migrant worker's family member on grounds of nationality – see former Article 11 Regulation 1612/68). Rights of access to the territory (formerly found in Article 10 Regulation 1612/68) will only be relied on against public bodies and should not therefore cause problems in this regard. We may question whether a measure of such central importance as this directive would not have better been adopted as a regulation, thereby minimising the risks of incomplete implementation.

These measures, as the Court held in *Procureur du Roi* v *Royer* (case 48/75), merely determine the scope and detailed rules for the exercise of rights conferred directly by the Treaty. Article 39 may thus be relied on by individuals in their national courts. Clearly, an individual may enforce the rights contained in Article 39 against public bodies. Further, as the ECJ, drawing on its previous case law (*Walrave* (case 36/74), see Chapter 22 and *Bosman* (case C–415/93) discussed further below), recently stated in its judgment in *Angonese* v *Cassa di Risparmio di Bolzano SpA* (case C–281/98), 'limiting application of the prohibition of discrimination based on nationality to acts of a public authority risks creating inequality in its application' (para. 33). Therefore the prohibition on discrimination set out in Article 39 applies to private persons as well as to public bodies (para. 36).

20.3 **Personal scope**

The rights granted under Article 39 and the secondary legislation implementing it are granted to workers and their families. They may also be relied upon by the employers of migrant workers. The fact of employment usually provides the requisite economic nexus to bring these provisions into play. The families' rights derive from their relationship with the worker. The worker must be a national of one of the Member States. Nationality is determined according to the domestic law of the Member State concerned.

Where a state has acceded to the EC but is still subject to transitional arrangements, a national of that State may claim rights as a 'favoured EC national' only insofar as that status ensues from the transitional provisions, unless he has been lawfully employed in the territory of one of the old Member States (*Lopes da Veiga* (case 9/88)).

Transitional restrictions apply to eight of the 10 new Member States, Cyprus and Malta having been excepted. The provisions provide for restrictions on what is termed a two-year plus a further three-plus-two basis. Until May 2006, EU 15 Member States (i.e., the pre–2004 members) would apply their respective national rules to migrant workers from new Member States. Note that the special rules apply to free movement of workers, not establishment and services. At this point, the Commission must report on migration patterns and the EU 15 Member States will be required to define their position on the matter. Thereafter, any Member States which experienced serious and unexpected disturbances of the labour markets would be allowed to apply safeguard measures for three years. This follows the pattern of previous enlargement, where similar safeguard measures have been available but, in practice, never used. From 1 May 2009, the EU 15 Member States will be called on to open up their respective labour markets, subject to the possibility of seeking safeguard measures to address serious and unexpected disturbances of the labour market. Full free movement rules will apply across the current new Member States as from 1 May 2011. Not all of the EU 15 Member States are applying the restrictions (see, e.g., the position of the UK). The new Member States Hungary, Poland and Slovenia invoked reciprocity and imposed restrictions *vis-à-vis* the EU 15 Member States. New Member States are obliged to respect free movement of workers as amongst themselves.

These arrangements have been criticised both as a matter of principle and for practical reasons. The restrictions run counter to the notion of free movement and equality of citizenship enshrined in the EU Treaties. They are also complex, especially given the way different Member States have chosen to apply them.

A non-EC national may not rely on the free movement rights contained in Article 39 unless he or she is a member of a migrant worker's family. The position of third-country nationals falls to be dealt with in Part IV of the EC Treaty (Articles 61–69 EC), introduced by the ToA (discussed in Chapter 24). Finally, to bring Community law into play, the worker must have exercised his or her rights to move (see, e.g., case C–244/98 *D'Hoop*, discussed at 20.3.3).

20.3.1 Workers

As the ECJ held in *Levin* v *Staatssecretaris van Justitie* (case 53/81), the concept of 'worker' is a Community concept, not dependent for its meaning on the laws of Member States. There are two aspects to the definition of worker: a formal aspect and an economic aspect. The formal aspect questions whether an individual is employed, rather than self-employed; while the economic test looks at the nature, duration and quality of the work. *Lawrie-Blum* v *Land Baden-Württemberg* (case 66/85), concerned a trainee teacher. The German Government contended that, as a trainee, Lawrie-Blum did not fall within the definition of 'worker'. The ECJ rejected this argument and in doing so laid down a three-stage test for a worker in its formal aspect. It suggested that the 'essential characteristic' of a worker is that (i) during a certain period of time; (ii) he performs services for and under the direction of another; (iii) in return for remuneration. Note that remuneration need not be in the form of cash, but could also be benefits in kind (see *Steymann* (case 196/87), below).

The term 'worker' has been generously construed. In *Hoekstra* v *BBDA* (case 75/63) the Court held that it extended not merely to the present worker, but to one who, having lost his job, is capable of taking another. As will be seen, Directive 2004/38/EC, replacing the equivalent provision in Directive 68/360, expressly provides that a worker's right of residence cannot be withdrawn merely because he is temporarily incapable of work, either as a result of illness or accident or involuntary unemployment). The ECJ considered the meaning of 'involuntary unemployment' in relation to a fixed-term contract in the case of *Ninni-Orasche* (case C–413/01). The ECJ noted that in some sectors workers might have no choice but to accept fixed-term contracts; becoming unemployed on the cessation of such contract could not therefore be considered to be a choice of the worker. It was not therefore voluntary unemployment. If a worker is not genuinely seeking work, once the employment relationship has ended the person concerned loses his or her status as a worker. As we shall see below, some rights acquired whilst a worker do not expire immediately on the termination of the worker status. An individual may also have rights under other provisions of the Treaty, such as the citizenship provisions (see Chapter 24), or under specific secondary legislation, such as the right to remain (see below).

Looking at the economic, or qualitative, aspect in *Levin* (case 53/81), the ECJ held, that the term 'worker' applied even to those who worked to a limited extent (i.e., part-time), provided that the work was 'real' work, and not nominal or minimal. The rights only attach to those who perform or wish to perform an activity of an economic nature. The Court went on to say that this principle applied whether the worker was self-supporting or whether he wished to make do with less than the national minimum income. It was able to side-step the problem of the part-time worker who relies on public funds for his support.

This issue was squarely faced in *Kempf* v *Staatssecretaris van Justitie* (case 139/85). Kempf was a German, a part-time music teacher working in The Netherlands from 1981 to 1982. During this time he was in receipt of Dutch supplementary benefit, both sickness benefit and general assistance. In November 1981 he applied for a Dutch residence permit. He was refused on the grounds that he was not a 'favoured EC citizen', since his income from his work was not sufficient to meet his needs. He challenged that decision before the Dutch courts. The Raad van State referred to the ECJ the question whether a part-time worker such as Kempf, whose income was below subsistence level and who did not have sufficient means of support, was a 'worker' entitled to benefit under Community law. The Court replied that he was. Freedom of movement of workers was, it held, one of the fundamental freedoms and must, as such, be defined broadly; a person who pursued a genuine and effective activity as an employed person, even on a part-time basis, could not be excluded from the scope of Community rules merely because he sought to supplement his income, which was lower than the means of subsistence, by other lawful means of subsistence. It was irrelevant whether the income was supplemented out of a private income or from public funds. The boldness of this judgment will be more apparent when the full extent of the rights flowing from the status of 'worker' or 'favoured Community citizen' is appreciated.

The Court has, however, held that the duration of the activity concerned was a factor which might be taken into account in assessing whether the employment was effective and genuine or so limited as to be marginal or ancillary (*Raulin* (case C–357/89), see further 20.3.2).

Following *Kempf*, in *Steymann* v *Staatssecretaris van Justitie* (case 196/87) the Court held that the claimant's occupation as part of a religious community, entitling him to his 'keep' and pocket money, but not to formal wages, constituted a genuine and effective activity where commercial activity is an inherent part of membership of that community. In contrast, in *Bettray* v *Staatssecretaris van Justitie* (case 344/87) paid activity provided by the State as part of a drug rehabilitation programme under its social employment law was held by the Court not to represent 'real and genuine economic activity'. To give rise to the status of 'worker', the work performed must fulfil, or derive from, some *economic* purpose. It has been suggested, however, that the principle of *Bettray* does not apply to 'ordinary' sheltered employment.

The undertaking in *Bettray* existed solely for the purpose of rehabilitation and re-education of the persons employed therein.

The question of whether an individual who works and receives benefits in kind at a minimal level was raised in *Trojani* (*Trojani* v *Le Centre Public d'Aide Sociale de Bruxelles* (case C–445/02)). In this case, the ECJ reiterated the points made in its earlier case law. The determination of whether someone is a worker is a question of fact to be assessed by objective criteria. In this case, the applicant was carrying out jobs for approximately 30 hours per week for the Salvation Army as part of a personal reintegration programme. In return, he received benefits in kind. The ECJ made two points. The ECJ then identified that the key question in determining whether Trojani was a worker or not was whether his activities formed part of the 'normal labour market'. Secondly, this was a question of fact over which the national court has exclusive jurisdiction. The ECJ consequently did not come to a final determination on the facts. Although the final result in this case is therefore not clear, the principle remains that rehabilitation does not constitute work for the purposes of Article 39. It may well be, however, that this issue has lost much of its significance with the introduction of citizenship (see Chapter 24).

20.3.2 **Workers and students**

The position of people who migrate and then become students has given rise to difficulties. The status of students as workers was raised in *Brown* (case 197/86) and *Lair* (case 39/86). In both these cases the parties, having obtained a place at university, Brown at Cambridge, to study engineering, and Lair at the University of Hanover, to study languages, were claiming maintenance grants from the UK and German authorities, respectively. Although Brown had dual French/English nationality, he and his family had for many years been domiciled in France; Lair was a Frenchwoman. Prior to taking up his place at Cambridge, Brown had obtained university sponsorship from, and worked for, Ferranti in Scotland. The job lasted for eight months. Lair had worked intermittently in Germany for over five years, with spells of involuntary unemployment. Both parties were refused a grant and sought to challenge that refusal on the basis of, *inter alia*, Regulation 1612/68, Articles 7(2) and 7(3) (their claim based on the original Article 7 of the EEC Treaty (now Article 12 (ex 6) EC) and 'vocational training' will be discussed in Chapter 21, in the context of *Gravier* (case 293/83)).

The crucial question was whether Brown and Lair were 'workers', and therefore entitled to claim the grants under Article 7, Regulation 1612/68. Brown had come to the UK primarily to prepare for his engineering studies at Cambridge and his work experience formed part of this preparation; he had obtained his place at Cambridge prior to taking up work in the UK. Lair on the other hand had undoubtedly come to Germany many years before, intending to work. The Court, which delivered judgments in both cases on the same day, held that the concept of worker must have a Community meaning. Nevertheless, in Brown's case, although he might be regarded as a worker, he was not entitled to claim the grant as a social advantage because he had acquired the status of worker exclusively as a result of his having been accepted for admission to university. The employment was merely ancillary to the studies to be financed by the grant. With regard to Lair's claim, the Court draw a distinction between a claim by a migrant worker who was *in*voluntarily unemployed, who, if legitimately resident, was entitled to the same treatment as regards reinstatement or re-employment as national workers, and one who gave up his work in order to undertake further training in the host Member State. In the latter case, he or she might only claim a grant for such a course if there was some link between the studies to be pursued and his previous work activity.

The Court chose to base its decision in both cases on fine factual distinctions rather than on the 'genuineness' of the claimant's status as a worker, although it did add in *Lair*, in response to the expressed worries of Member States as to the possibility of abuse, that 'insofar as a worker has entered a Member State for the sole purpose of enjoying, after a very short period of work activity, the benefit of the student assistance system in that State, it should be observed that such abuses are not covered by the Community provisions (i.e., Article 7(2) and 7(3)) in question' (para. 43). It is regrettable that in its concern to appease the anxiety of Member States it chose in *Lair* to limit the scope of Article 7(2) by denying a right to 'social advantages' in the form of grants to migrant workers who have not become unemployed but who genuinely want to improve their prospects by retraining in a *new* field of activity. In an era of rapid technological and economic change, flexibility in the workforce is surely to be encouraged.

In *Raulin* (case C–357/89), in a claim by a French national for a grant to pursue a full-time course in the plastic arts in the Netherlands, following 60 hours work as a waitress there, the Court followed *Brown* and *Lair*, adding only that in assessing whether the work undertaken was 'effective and genuine' for the purpose of acquiring the status of worker, both the length of time of employment and all the activities undertaken in the host State might be taken into account, but not the activities conducted elsewhere in the Community. This approach might be criticised, not least because of its tendency to partition the national markets.

The situation of someone who works for a short period and then becomes a student was considered again in *Ninni-Orache* (case C–413/01). The applicant was an Italian national who married an Austrian and moved to Austria. After about two years, she took up a fixed-term contract as a waitress and cashier, working for only a couple of months. She also completed a distance learning diploma in bookkeeping and commerce. She then tried to get a job relying on her diploma but was unsuccessful, so she started studying Romance languages at Klagenfurt University. The case concerned her claim for financial assistance from the Austrian Government. The assessment of her status as a worker was thus again linked to the issue of continuing rights. The ECJ reiterated its approach in *Lair* and *Raulin*, that is, a worker who ceases to work retains some rights to social assistance provided there is continuity between the previous occupational activity and the studies pursued. Following its previous case law, the ECJ also noted that this limitation was not imposed on those who are involuntarily unemployed. In this case, the ECJ emphasised that the determination of whether someone is a 'worker' is based on objective criteria and should take into account circumstances as a whole.

If Ninni-Orache was a worker, could she then claim the right to student support? Here the issue of whether the 'continuity' requirement found in *Lair* and *Raulin* applies is key. As we have seen, a fixed-term contract expiring does not necessarily mean a person has become voluntarily unemployed. This assessment may vary on facts. Some of the factors the ECJ dismissed in relation to the determination of whether the economic aspect of 'worker' was satisfied might be relevant in identifying if a worker has become voluntarily unemployed or not. This was a matter for the national court to assess. Motivation for moving is not a relevant factor in determining whether someone is a worker in the first place, but seems to become relevant where an individual stops work and seeks to rely on continuing rights. Nonetheless, the approach here might seem to be taking a more generous line than that adopted in *Raulin*. (See also *Ioannidis* (case C–258/04), the ECJ assumed a migrant who had completed a paid training course in another Member State was a worker.)

The real significance of the *Lair* and *Brown* line of case law is its impact on students' rights to social advantages to which workers are normally entitled (Article 7(2) Regulation 1612/68, see below). Under *Lair* and *Brown* it seems that even students who have worked prior to becoming a student and who continue to work during their studies may not be considered a 'full' worker. They have some of the workers' rights, such as access to the territory and, presumably the job market (to the extent consistent with their studies), but not the full range of social rights. Whilst the case law can be seen as a separate strand of cases relating specifically to students, the cases might, of course, be seen as part of the case law on continuing rights. Since continuing rights remain after a person ceases to be a worker, it could be argued that this justifies a slightly more restrictive view of the scope of the rights available to individuals in such circumstances. Note that Article 7(3)(d) Directive 2004/38/EC specifies that an individual will retain the status of a worker if 'he/she embarks on vocational training. Unless he/she is involuntarily unemployed, the retention of the status of worker shall require the training to be related to the previous employment.' Further, the rights of students to travel to other Member States to study is dealt with by specific secondary legislation (Council Directive 93/96/EC, now replaced by Directive 2004/38/EC). As with many other issues in this area, the position of the individual may well have been improved by the introduction of European citizenship (see, e.g., *Grzelczyck* (case C–184/99) and *Bidar* (case C–209/03), discussed in Chapter 24).

20.3.3 Families

It is in the context of determining family rights that the changes introduced by Directive 2004/38/EC can be seen. In some respects the fundamental position has not changed. The rights of family members are parasitic on those of the worker. As noted in the general section, a worker must migrate before he or she, or any family members can benefit from the rights granted. If, for example, a child of an EC national moved to another Member State to study but her parents remained in the Member State of origin, the child cannot rely on the rights granted to migrant workers' families. The child would not constitute a worker; the parents have not migrated (*D'Hoop*, case C–244/98). Of course, migrant EC nationals in these circumstances may be able to rely on other Community law rights. The changes can, however, be seen in the definition of family member, as Directive 2004/38 not only incorporates judicial developments in this area, but fills in lacunae in protection left by the ECJ's jurisprudence.

Families were defined in Regulation 1612/68 (Article 10(1)) as a worker's 'spouse and their descendants who are under the age of 21 years or are dependants', and 'dependent relatives in the ascending line of the worker and his spouse'. Under Directive 2004/38/EC, Article 10 (as well as Article 11) of Regulation 1612/68 are repealed. Article 10(1) is replaced by Article 2(1)(2), which states:

'Family member' means:

(a) the spouse;

(b) the partner with whom the Union citizen has contracted a registered partnership, on the basis of the legislation of a Member State, if the legislation of the host Member State treats registered partnerships as equivalent to marriage and in accordance with the conditions laid down in the relevant legislation of the host Member State;

(c) the direct descendants who are under the age of 21 or are dependants and those of the spouse or partner as defined in point (b);

(d) the dependent direct relatives in the ascending line as defined in point (b).

Article 3 identifies the beneficiaries of the rights specified in the directive. In addition to Union citizens and their family members, Article 3(2) recommends that Member States facilitate the entry of two other groups of people:

(a) any other family members, irrespective of their nationality, not falling under the definition in point 2 of Article 2 who, in the country from which they have come, are dependents or members of the household of the Union citizen having the primary right of residence, or where serious health grounds strictly require the personal care of the family member by the Union citizen;

(b) the partner with whom the citizen has a durable relationship, duly attested.

20.3.3.1 'Spouse' and 'partner'

We can see that the definition in Article 2(2) includes both the category of a worker's spouse and that of a worker's partner. In this, the article is broader than the drafting of Article 10 Regulation 1612/68, but in fact reflects the jurisprudence of the ECJ, based on the principle of non-discrimination. In *Netherlands v Reed* (case 59/85) the ECJ was asked whether the term 'spouse' included a cohabitee. The case concerned Ms Reed's right to reside in Holland with her English cohabitee of five years' standing, who was working in Holland. Ms Reed, who was also English, was not herself a worker. The Court held that in the present state of Community law the term 'spouse' referred to marital relationships only. This did not mean that Ms Reed was not entitled to remain in Holland. As her cohabitee was a worker in Holland, and since aliens with stable relationships with *Dutch* nationals were entitled in similar circumstances to reside in Holland, it would be discriminatory, in breach of what is now Article 12 (ex 6) EC and 39 (also Article 7(2), Regulation 1612/68), not to accord him the same treatment as national workers. Ms Reed was not entitled to remain as a 'spouse', but she was entitled to remain on account of her cohabitee's rights not to be discriminated against under EC law.

'Cohabitee' in the *Reed* sense seems to equate to 'partner' in the context of Article 2(1). There are two points to note. First, non-marital partnerships within the meaning of Article 2 are limited to those which are registered; other partnerships are dealt with under Article 3(2). Secondly, the directive is based on the principle of non-discrimination based on a comparison with how a registered partnership is treated under the national regime of the host Member State. This was the approach taken in *Reed*. The approach in Reed was criticised because it did not introduce equality across the Union; different Member States could treat non-married couples differently. The new directive has not addressed this point. Nonetheless, this line of reasoning may have the benefit of assisting same-sex couples in Member States where they may register their unions.

Since the rights of partners are to some degree limited, the precise extent of the notion of spouse still has significance; the case law from Regulation 1612/68 is probably still good law in this regard. Another question which arises is whether a divorced spouse is entitled to claim rights as a 'spouse' under EC law. This can be seen as a question about the meaning of the term 'spouse', or as a question of whether someone who was a spouse has residual rights after he or she ceases to be a spouse. In *Diatta v Land Berlin* (case 267/83) the Court held that a separated spouse (in this case a Senegalese national), who intended to obtain a divorce and who was living apart from her husband, a worker in Germany, did not lose her rights of residence in Germany merely because she did not live under the same roof as her husband. The marital relationship is not dissolved, the Court held, when spouses live separately. As the matter came before the Court on a reference for interpretation under Article 234 (ex 177), it was not necessary for the Court to decide on the effect of divorce on a spouse's rights. The problem for a divorced spouse is particularly acute where the spouse is not a national of a Member State, as in *Diatta*. A spouse who has EC nationality can always become a worker in her own right, and, after *Kempf* (case 139/85), even for a spouse with family responsibilities this should not prove too daunting a prospect.

The position of the divorced spouse where there are children seems now to have been addressed by the ECJ in *Baumbast and R* (case C–413/99), concerning two separate cases referred by the British Immigration Appeal Tribunal. In one of the cases, *R*, a migrant EC national divorced a United States citizen but remained in the host Member State. The non-EC national, the mother, was the principal carer for the children who had the right to remain (see below). On this basis the ECJ determined that the mother also had the right to remain as a corollary of the children's rights. The fact that she was not an EC national and was divorced from the migrant EC worker made no difference.

It is important to note, however, that this case did not address the position of the divorced spouse in her own right; her position was considered as an adjunct of her children's rights. The position of the divorced spouse without children remained unclear. The matter has now, somewhat inelegantly, been addressed by Directive 2004/38/EC. Article 13 provides both EU nationals and third-country nationals with some protection in the event of divorce, annulment or termination of registered partnerships. The precise phraseology and scope of Article 13 should be noted. There is a drafting point: the right is granted to family members. This approach assumes that for the purposes of EC law, family members remain family members even after divorce or termination of a civil partnership. Otherwise the protection would have no force whatsoever, terminating at the end of the relationship, that is, at the precise point it was supposed to start operating. The position for family members who are not EC nationals is more limited. To claim the benefit of the continuing rights under Article 13, the third-country national must satisfy one of four tests. The four possibilities are:

(a) prior to initiation of the divorce or annulment proceedings or termination of the registered partnership, the marriage or registered partnership has lasted at least three years, including one in the host Member State;

(b) by agreement between the spouses or partners or by court order, the person who is not an EC national has custody of the Union citizen's children;

(c) this is warranted by particularly difficult circumstances, such as having been the victim of domestic violence during the subsistence of the marriage or registered partnership; or

(d) by agreement between the parties or by court order, the spouse or partner who is not an EC national has the right of access to a minor child, provided that the court has ruled that the access must be in the host Member State, for as long as is required.

Note that the protection granted by Article 13 does not appear to extend to partnerships which are not registered, nor does it apply to other family members falling within Article 3(2)(a). Presumably a *Reed*-style argument could be used to gain equivalence of protection where the host Member State granted rights to remain to those who have not registered their partnership or who were family members within the sense of Article 3(2)(a).

20.3.3.2 *Dependants and descendants*

For the children of the marriage, or the worker's dependent relatives, problems should not have arisen. Even after divorce they will remain members of the worker's family. They will now benefit from the rights granted by Article 13 (see above). Problems may have arisen for a spouse's dependent relatives. If they, like the spouse, are not EC nationals, they too risk losing their status as 'favoured Community citizens' on the separation or divorce of their relative.

Although families are expressed in terms of 'descendants' it would be in keeping with the ECJ's approach to take a broad view of the rights of children of the family. It would not be likely to deny favoured EC citizen status to children who had been treated as children of the family (i.e. children of the Union citizen and the third-country national) even though they were not, strictly speaking, descendants of the Union citizen. In *Baumbast and R* (case C–413/99), the ECJ confirmed that descendants within Article 10(1) Regulation 1612/68 extended 'both to the descendants of that worker and to those of his spouse. To give a restrictive meaning to that provision to the effect that only the children common to the migrant worker and his spouse have the right to install themselves with them would run counter to the aim of Regulation 1612/68' (para. 57). This ruling now finds its expression in Article 2(2)(c) Directive 2004/38/EC and the same approach has been taken with respect to relatives in the ascending line. All such persons would be able, in principle, to claim the continuing rights granted under Article 13 Directive 2004/38/EC.

A family member threatened with the loss of EC rights, perhaps because he or she did not satisfy the tests in Article 13(2), could invoke the principle of respect for the right to family life expressed in Article 8 of the European Convention of Human Rights, which in the context of the application of Community law must be respected by the authorities of Member States (see *Commission* v *Germany* (case 249/86) and *Carpenter* (case C–60/00), discussed in Chapters 21 and 22, respectively; see also Chapter 6).

20.3.4 **Rights on return**

The position of migrants returning to their country of origin arose in the case of *R v Immigration Appeal Tribunal, ex parte Secretary of State for the Home Department* (case C–370/90). Mr Singh was an Indian who had married a British national in 1982. He and his wife subsequently went to work in Germany, returning in 1985 to open a business in the UK. Their marriage broke down in 1988. Following the issue of a *decree nisi* but before the decree became absolute, that is before the divorce was finalised, the UK authorities sought to deport Mr Singh. His appeal against the deportation order was successful. Since the divorce was not yet a legal fact, the case still concerned the position of spouses and the rights that spouses could claim under EC law. The question of the effect of the subsequent divorce was not an issue before the Court (although the fact of divorce was known). The ECJ held that, as the spouse of an EC national who had exercised her rights to work in Germany, Singh was entitled on their return to claim his rights as a spouse under EC law. *Singh*, at the time, was considered significant for its approach regarding genuine marriages; the full significance of the right to return had yet to be recognised.

Thus the *Singh* case illustrated that migrant workers could rely on at least some rights as against their Member State on return. The scope of this right was somewhat uncertain, but was more recently raised before the ECJ in *Akrich* (case C–109/01), yet another referral from the British Immigration Appeals Tribunal. *Akrich* concerned a Moroccan who was refused entry into the UK. He subsequently married a UK national. She moved to Ireland to work for a short period and he entered Ireland, relying on EC law-derived rights. The couple then tried to return to the UK on the basis of the *Singh* judgment. It transpired that the purpose of the sojourn in Ireland had been for the purpose of bringing the couple within Community law, so seeking to evade British immigration controls. This case therefore raises concerns about the abuse of Community law. Were *Akrich's* argument to be accepted, it would introduce the possibility that no Member State would have any control over immigration into the EU in such cases.

The Advocate-General in his opinion did not address the issue of abuse of Community law directly, but in his view, the couple should not be able to rely on Community law rights in these circumstances. He described the right in issue in *Singh* as a form of right that would continue to subsist after the expiry of the worker's migrant status; it is therefore limited (see further below, and cases such as *Meints* (case C–57/96) and *Leclere and Deaconescu* (case C–43/99)). The Advocate-General also noted that the situation in *Singh* was different from that in issue in a number of respects. Crucially, Akrich had not been permitted to enter any Member State under national law. The Advocate-General commented 'Singh does not create a right in favour of that national of a non-Member State to enter the territory of the European Union' (para. 134). The ECJ also found in favour of the UK Government, arguing that, as Akrich could not lawfully reside with his wife in the UK, there was no disincentive in her not having her husband with her if she moved to another Member State, that is, the prohibition could not 'constitute less favourable treatment than that which they enjoyed before the citizen made use of the opportunities afforded by the Treaty as regards free movement of persons' (para. 53). The ECJ confirmed the point it had made in earlier jurisprudence, that the motives of persons seeking to exercise their rights of free movement are not relevant when assessing whether or not they benefit from those rights (paras 55–56), though the position might be different in the context of marriages of convenience. *Akrich* does suggest that there is a difference in the treatment of third-country family members depending on whether they are moving with a migrant worker from one Member State to another, or whether the third-country national enters the host Member State directly to join the migrant worker. The ECJ made a number of statements regarding the scope of EC law, notably that Regulation 1612/68 concerned only movement *within* the Community and not initial access to the territory of the Union. The ECJ then added that to benefit from the rights granted, the spouse of a citizen had to be 'lawfully resident in a Member State when he moves to another Member State to which the citizen of the Union is migrating or has migrated' (para. 49).

Although it is submitted that the *Singh* ruling should be limited, the reasoning of both the ECJ and the Advocate-General in *Akrich* is problematic. The precise scope of the ruling is not clear and does not sit easily with other cases, such as *MRAX* (case C–459/99) (discussed below). *MRAX* did not distinguish between the role of national and Community law in determining the right of access to Union territory. Neither did it make the distinction between legal and illegal immigrants, a distinction central in *Akrich*. It has been suggested that the solution which best reconciles the case law is one which sees *Akrich* as confined to similar factual situations, where a third-country national has been illegally resident in a Member State and is using Community law to avoid attempts to deport him, and does not affect all third-country nationals wishing to enter directly into the host Member State. It is debatable whether this interpretation deals with all the questions arising from *Akrich*. Nonetheless, the reasoning in *Akrich* has another value in that it highlights the tensions in this area and consequent difficulties in identifying the proper boundary to workers' rights. It is likely that case law, developed piecemeal, may result in a jurisprudence that has many such tensions: secondary legislation would seem to be needed to ensure an appropriate balance between the rights of the individual to a family life and the concerns of the Member States over immigration. Note that the new directive has a provision, Article 35, entitled 'abuse of rights' which provides that Member States 'may adopt the necessary measures to refuse, terminate or withdraw any right conferred by this Directive in the case of abuse of rights or fraud, such as marriages of convenience'. Any such measures would have to comply with the principle of proportionality. The Community has recently agreed a number of directives dealing with the position of TCNs: Family Reunification Directive (Directive 2003/86/EC, [2003] OJ L251/12), a Directive on the Status on Long-Term Residents (Directive 2003/109/EC) and the proposed directive on the Right of Entry for those seeking Work or Self-Employment (COM (2001) 386), which may solve some of the problems in this area. (See further Chapter 24.)

20.4 **Test for the application of Article 39**

Much of the early jurisprudence was based on a test of discrimination. This is not surprising as the terms of Article 39(2) refer expressly to the abolition of discrimination on the grounds of nationality. Article 39 is in this context a specific form of the general prohibition on discrimination on the grounds of nationality found in Article 12 EC. From the wording of Article 39(2), this requirement would seem to be a minimum. Certainly the ECJ has adopted a very broad approach to the issue of discrimination, including covert or indirect discrimination, such as residence requirements. More recent case jurisprudence indicates that the ECJ is moving towards a test similar to the *Bilka Kaufhaus* test as applied to cases of indirect sex discrimination (see Chapter 25) and the first *Cassis* principle applied to indistinctly applicable measures affecting goods (see Chapter 16). A similar trend can be seen in the context of the rules relating to services and establishment (see Chapters 21 and 22). This approach as regards workers was clarified in the *Bosman* case (case C–415/93), which raised the question of whether former Article 48 (now 39) would apply to rules which were not overtly discriminatory but which still had an adverse impact on individuals' ability to exercise their free movement rights.

The case centred on Belgian football transfer rules, which accorded with international football rules. These rules provided that a club which sought to engage a player must pay a specified, sometimes considerable sum to the player's existing club. The rules applied irrespective of the nationality of the player and whether the player was going to be playing for a Belgian team or not. Further, there were limits on how many non-nationals a club could employ. In Bosman's case, he was signed up to play for a Belgian team and the rules effectively stopped him from moving to play for a French team. After a lengthy legal dispute, the matter was referred to the ECJ. Bosman argued that the rules were, *inter alia*, contrary to Article 39. The ECJ held that, although the rules were not discriminatory, they still 'directly affect[ed] players' access to the employment market in other Member States and are thus capable of impeding freedom of movement of workers'. In principle, the rules were incompatible with Article 39 unless they pursued a legitimate aim compatible with the Treaty, were justified by pressing reasons of public interest and were proportionate. In *Bosman*, therefore, the ECJ was not concerned with discrimination but with the question of whether cross-border access to the job market of each Member State was safeguarded. In this approach we clearly see parallels to that taken by the ECJ in relation to the free movement of goods and 'indistinctly applicable' measures.

The *Bosman* ruling, like the *Dassonville* and *Cassis de Dijon* judgments as regards free movement of goods, could potentially affect many national rules. The ECJ took the opportunity to refine the scope of *Bosman*, and consequently the scope of Article 39 as regards non-discriminatory rules which nonetheless might affect the functioning of the internal market, in *Volker Graf* v *Filzmoser Maschinenbau* (case C–190/98). The rules challenged in this case concerned Austrian employment legislation which required employers to make certain payments to employees on the termination of an employment contract, when the employee was not leaving the job voluntarily. Graf handed in his notice to go to work in Germany. He claimed the payments, but Filzmoser Maschinenbau refused to make the payments as Graf was leaving voluntarily. He argued that the rules which excluded him from receiving the payments were likely adversely to affect those who sought to move from Austria to another Member State more than those who were leaving employment but staying in Austria. Arguing from the ECJ's approach in *Bosman*, Graf claimed that the Austrian rules were incompatible with what is now Article 39 EC. The question as to whether this was incompatible with the requirements of the free movement of workers was referred. The ECJ confirmed that Article 39 not only applies to discriminatory rules but also to rules which, although they are expressed to apply without distinction, impede the exercise of free movement rights. It went on to say, however, that for such rules to constitute an obstacle prohibited under Article 39, the provisions 'must affect access of the workers to the labour market'. In this case, the entitlement was only contingent on certain events happening – basically the unfair dismissal of an employee – and therefore any effect on the internal market of this sort of rule was too uncertain and indirect to fall within the prohibition. Thus, although the ECJ's test of measures affecting access to the host market would seem on the face of it to be very broad, the latter part of the judgment clearly focuses on the need for an obstacle to accessing that market to exist. A similar approach can be seen, as regards goods, in *Dip Spa* (cases C–140–2/94) (discussed in Chapter 18), though it does not seem to be evolving in relation to establishment and services. Nonetheless it should be noted that in many cases concerning personal rights, such as social rights, the ECJ still uses a test based on discrimination (see, e.g. *Ioannidis* (case C–258/04)).

20.5 Material scope

20.5.1 Rights of entry and residence (Directive 2004/38/EC)

These rights are now regulated by Directive 2004/38/EC as part of the citizenship package, replacing Directive 68/360: they comprise, for the worker and his family (as defined above: Directive 2004/38/EC Article 2(2)), the right:

(a) To leave their home State for another Member State (Directive 2004/38/EC, Article 4).

(b) To enter the territory of another Member State on production of a valid identity card or passport' (Article 5(1)). Entry visas (or their equivalent) may not be demanded except for members of the family who are not nationals of a Member State in accordance with Regulation 539/2001 or, in some instances, national law. Where a person has a residence card within the meaning of Article 10 Directive 2004/38/EC, they shall be exempt from any visa requirement. Member States are required to accord to such persons every facility for obtaining the necessary visas (Article 5(2)). According to *MRAX* (case C–459/99), although Article 3(2) Directive 68/360 made the right of entry conditional on the holding of the visa, the rights of the Member State in respect of this condition are limited indeed. Such a visa should be issued without delay and, as far as possible, at the place of entry into the Member State. These requirements are now found in Article 5(2) Directive 2004/38/EC. The ECJ further held in *MRAX* that, where a third-country national is able to prove his or her identity and provide evidence of a marriage, it would be disproportionate to send a third-country national back to his or her state of origin in the absence of evidence that he or she represents a risk to public policy, public security or public health. Article 5(4) Directive 2004/38/EC incorporates these requirements, additionally specifying that a Member State must give such persons a reasonable opportunity of obtaining the necessary documents or of having them sent or otherwise proving that they are covered by the right of free movement and residence.

(c) A worker need only register when he or she is resident for more than three months; in such cases the obligation to apply occurs only when the Member State runs a registration scheme. To obtain a registration certificate a worker needs to provide:

(i) a valid identity card or passport, and

(ii) a confirmation of engagement from the employer or a certificate of employment (Article 8(3));

and, for members of the family who are Union citizens (Article 9(5)):

(i) their documents of entry,

(ii) a document proving their relationship with the worker, and where relevant documents testifying to their dependent status (Article 3(2)(a)) or proof of a durable relationship (see Article 3(2)(b)).

For family members who are not Union citizens, Article 9 provides for a separate procedure. Member States are required to issue such family members with a residence card within six months of the date of application. To obtain a residence card a family member must show:

(a) a valid passport;

(b) documentary evidence of their relationship with the worker;

(c) in the case of relatives identified in Article 2(2)(c) or (d), and Article 3(2)(a) and (b) proof that the conditions specified in the respective provisions are satisfied (see 20.3.3).

The residence permit must be valid throughout the territory of the Member State which issued it; it must be valid for at least five years from the date of issue or for the envisaged period of residence of the Union citizen; and it must be automatically renewable (Article 11). Temporary absences, as detailed in Article 11(2), do not affect the validity of the residence card. Workers and Union citizens have the right to reside for as long as they satisfy the conditions in Article 7. This may be described as the right to 'settled' or 'lawful' residence.

The right of residence may not be withdrawn from a worker solely on the grounds that he is no longer in employment, either because he is temporarily incapable of work as a result of illness or accident, or because he is involuntarily unemployed (Article 7(3)).

These provisions are generous, and, in their previous format, have been even more generously interpreted by ECJ. In *Procureur du Roi* v *Royer* (case 48/75) the Court held that the right of entry granted at that time by Article 3 of Directive 68/360 included the right to enter *in search of work*. In *R* v *Immigration Appeal Tribunal, ex parte Antonissen* (case C–292/89), the ECJ was asked to rule on the legality of English immigration rules which permit the deportation of migrants after six months if they have failed to find employment. The Court held that there was 'no necessary link' between the right to unemployment benefit under Regulation 1408/71, discussed below, and the right to stay in a Member State for the purpose of seeking work. A Member State could, however, deport an EC migrant if he had not found employment after six months unless he provided evidence that he was continuing to seek employment and that he has a genuine chance of being engaged. Significantly the Court chose not to impose a specific time-limit. More recently, it was held that Belgian legislation which, in effect, excluded those seeking work after three months was in contravention of Community law (*Commission* v *Belgium* (case C–344/95)). Thus, it seems that, at the least, those genuinely seeking work are entitled to stay in the host Member State for longer than three months. These rights have been incorporated in Article 14(4) Directive 2004/38/EC. Following the introduction of European citizenship, such persons may have additional rights (see Chapter 24).

Under Directive 2004/38/EC migrant Union citizens fulfilling the terms of Article 7 do not even need to have a residence permit, though they may need to register in accordance with host Member State rules. A worker's right to reside in the State where he is employed is not dependent on his possession of a certificate of registration. Neither a worker nor his family can be deported because the identity card or passport on which they entered the host Member State has expired (Article 15(2), Directive 2004/38/EC). As long as the worker is a worker, he will be entitled to reside in the host Member State without formalities. And, as long as he is entitled to stay, his family will also be entitled to stay. In *MRAX* (case C–459/99) the ECJ confirmed that a Member State is not permitted to refuse a residence permit to a family member, who is able to prove his or her identity and the existence of a marriage to a migrant EC worker, purely on the grounds that he or she entered the host Member State illegally (see also *Commission* v *Spain* (case C–503/03) on the relationship between Community law and the Schengen system with regard to TCNs who are family members, discussed in Chapters 23 and 24). Nor can that Member State expel such a third-country national on the grounds that his or her visa expired before he or she applied for a residence permit. A residence permit may not be refused on these grounds either.

A Member State is, however, entitled to demand that migrant workers and their families comply with its administrative formalities on immigration, as is recognised in Directive 2004/38/EC, Articles 8 and 9, and can even impose penalties in the form of fines for non-compliance, provided that the penalties are not disproportionate. In *Messner* (case C–265/88) a time-limit of three days from crossing the frontier in which aliens were required to register their presence with the Italian police, sanctioned by criminal penalties, was found to be unreasonable. A failure to comply with such formalities can never be a ground for deportation (see also *Watson* (case 118/75); *Commission* v *Belgium* (case 321/87)).

Although the directive specifically provides that a right of residence does not end if the worker becomes incapable of work through illness or accident or involuntary unemployment, Article 7(3)(b) implies that that right will be lost if he is *voluntarily* unemployed, where the worker has only been working for a period of less than a year.

Since the rights of the family are 'parasitic', in that they depend on their relationship with the worker, their rights of residence will be coterminous with his, unless the family members are EC citizens who qualify in their own right, or have acquired the right to remain as his survivors under Articles 12–14.

The question of whether a worker or a member of his family is entitled to 'settled' residence in a Member State is of fundamental importance because, as will be seen, their right to equal treatment in the host State, and all that that involves, has been held to flow not so much from the claimant's status as a worker, although it originates there, as from the worker's, and his family's, 'lawful residence' in a Member State (see 20.5.4.2.), though once again the introduction of citizenship may have extended the Union citizen's rights.

20.5.2 Access to employment; equality of treatment (Regulation 1612/68)

Regulation 1612/68 was passed to implement Articles 39(2) and 39(3)(a) and (b) of the EC Treaty. As stated in the preamble to Regulation 1612/68, the attainment of the objective of freedom of movement for workers requires, in addition to rights of entry and residence, 'the abolition of any discrimination based on nationality between workers of the Member States as regards employment, remuneration and other conditions of work and employment' (first recital). It also requires, in order that the right of freedom of movement may be exercised 'in freedom and dignity', equality of treatment in 'all matters relating to the actual pursuit of activities as employed persons' and that 'obstacles to the mobility of workers shall be eliminated, in particular as regards the worker's right to be joined by his family and the conditions for the integration of that family into the host country' (fifth recital). The ECJ has drawn heavily on this preamble in interpreting this regulation and other measures in this field.

Regulation 1612/68 is divided into several parts. Part I, which is of principal concern here, is entitled 'Employment and workers' families'. Title I, 'Eligibility for employment' covers a worker's rights of access to employment; Title II, 'Employment and equality of treatment', covers his right to equality of treatment not only in all matters relating to employment, but also to 'social advantages', including matters of housing. Title III, 'Workers' families' deals with families' rights and has been amended by Directive 2004/38/EC. The remaining parts of the regulation provide for the setting up of machinery and institutions for the clearance and coordination of vacancies and applications for employment.

20.5.3 Eligibility for employment (Articles 1–6)

Any national of a Member State has the right to take up activity as an employed person, and pursue such activity, in the territory of another Member State under the same conditions as nationals of that state (Article 1).

A Member State may not discriminate, overtly or covertly, against non-nationals, by limiting applications and offers of employment (Article 3(1)), or by prescribing special recruitment procedures or limiting advertising or in any other way impeding recruitment of non-resident workers (Article 3(2)). Member States must not restrict by number or percentage the number of foreign nationals to be employed in any activity or area of activity (Article 4; see *Commission v France (Re French Merchant Seamen)* (case 167/73) – ratio of three French to one non-French imposed under Code du Travail Maritime 1926 on crew of French merchant ships held in breach of EC law).

Member States must offer non-national applicants the same assistance in seeking employment as are available to nationals (Article 5).

States are, however, entitled to permit the imposition on non-nationals of conditions 'relating to linguistic knowledge required by reason of the nature of the post to be filled' (Article 3(1)). In *Groener* v *Minister for Education* (case 379/87) the ECJ held that a requirement of Irish law that teachers in vocational schools in Ireland should be proficient in the Irish language would be permissible under Article 3(1) in view of the clear policy of national law to maintain and promote the use of the Irish language as a means of expressing national identity and culture. The Irish language was the national language and the first official language of Ireland. Such a requirement must not, however, be disproportionate to the object-ives pursued. A similar approach to the non-discrimination Treaty provision of Article 39(2) was taken, albeit with a different result, in *Spotti* v *Freistaat Bayern* (case C–272/92), in the context of a challenge to a German law permitting contracts of limited duration for foreign language teaching assistants. The Court held that such contracts, prima facie in breach of Article 39(2), would only be permitted if they were objectively justified. Since the principal justification for the rules was that they ensured up-to-date tuition it is not surprising that the Court found them not to be justified (see also *Alluè* v *Università degli Studi di Venezia* (cases C–259, 331 & 332/91); *Commission* v *Luxembourg* (case C–111/91)). The burden of proving justification for discriminatory rules will always be heavy: the rules must be designed to achieve legitimate ends, and must be both appropriate and necessary to achieve those ends.

An employer may require a non-national to undergo a vocational test provided he expressly requests this when making his offer of employment (Article 6(2)). These provisions may not however be used as a means of covert discrimination.

20.5.4 Employment and equality of treatment (Articles 7–9)

These rights are expressly granted to workers. However, as will be seen, some of these rights have now been extended to benefit the families of workers.

20.5.4.1 *Conditions of work*

Article 7(1) provides that:

> A worker who is a national of a Member State may not, in the territory of another Member State, be treated differently from national workers by reason of his nationality in respect of any conditions of employment and work, in particular as regards remuner-ation, dismissal, and should he become unemployed, reinstatement or re-employment.

This article covers all forms of discrimination, direct and indirect. In *Ugliola* (case 15/69) a condition whereby a German employer took into account, for the purposes of calculating seniority, employees' periods of national service *in Germany*, thereby prejudicing an employee such as Ugliola, who was required to perform his national service in Italy, was held unlawful under this article. Similarly in *Sotgiu* v *Deutsche Bundespost* (case 152/73) the German post office's decision to pay increased separation allowances only to workers living away from home in Germany, was held to be *capable* of breaching Article 7(1). More recently, in *Schöning-Kougebetopoulou* v *Freie und Hansestadt Hamburg* (case C–15/96), the ECJ held that a collective wage agreement which provided for promotion on grounds of seniority after eight years' employment in any given group, excluding periods of comparable employment in the public service of another Member State, was contrary to the Treaty. The terms of the agreement manifestly worked to the disadvantage of migrant workers as they are less likely, or it is harder for them, to satisfy the eight-year rule.

20.5.4.2 *Social and tax advantages*

Article 7(2) packs perhaps the largest punch of all EC secondary legislation in this area. It entitles the migrant worker to 'the same social and tax advantages as national workers'. The term 'social advantages' has been interpreted in the widest sense.

(a) *Social advantages*

In *Fiorini* v *SNCF* (case 32/75) the Court was faced with a claim by an Italian lady living in France, the widow of an Italian who had worked in France, for a special fare reduction card issued by the French railways to parents of large families. Her husband had claimed it while he was alive. She had been refused the card on the grounds that she was not of French nationality. She claimed discrimination in breach of Article 12 and Article 7(2) of Regulation 1612/68. The French tribunal took the view that Article 7(2) was not applicable, since it was concerned only with advantages granted to citizens within the ambit of work or by virtue of work as employed persons. This would limit the advantages that could be claimed by a worker to those directly linked to his or her employment. The ECJ took a different view. It held that, although certain provisions of Article 7(1) refer to relationships deriving from the contract of employment, there are others which have nothing to do with such relationships. Article 7(2) covers all social and tax advantages, whether or not attached to contracts of employment. Moreover, these rights continue even if the advantages are sought after the worker's death to benefit the family remaining. Since the family had a right under Community law (what was then Regulation 1251/70) to remain in France, they were entitled under Article 7(2) to equal 'social advantages'.

Subsequently, in *Even* (case 207/78), the Court held, following *Fiorini*, that the social advantages covered by Article 7(2) were 'those which, whether or not linked to a contract of employment, are generally granted to national workers primarily because of their objective status as workers *or by virtue of the mere fact of their residence on national territory*' (emphasis added). This formula, the '*Even*' formula, has since been applied in a number of cases in the context of claims by both workers and the members of their families to a wide range of social benefits.

In *Reina* v *Landeskreditbank Baden-Württemberg* (case 65/81) an Italian couple living in Germany, the husband being a worker in Germany, invoked Article 7(2) to claim a special childbirth loan, State-financed, from the defendant bank. The loan was payable under German law only to German nationals living in Germany. The bank argued that the loan was not a 'social advantage' within Article 7(2), since the loan was granted not as a social right, but rather in the field of political rights, for demographic purposes, i.e., to increase the birth rate in Germany. Granting of the loan was, moreover, discretionary. It argued also that the difference in treatment was justified on account of the practical difficulties of recovering loans from workers who return to their own countries. Despite these persuasive arguments the ECJ found that since the loan was granted by reason of the claimant's objective status as a worker or by virtue of the mere fact of residence it was a 'social advantage' within Article 7(2). Social advantages covered not only benefits granted as of right but also those granted on a discretionary basis.

In *Castelli* v *ONPTS* (case 261/83), on similar reasoning, an Italian mother, who, on being widowed, went to live with her son in Belgium (the son having been a worker and retired there), was held entitled to claim a guaranteed income (not a social security benefit) paid to all old people in Belgium. Since she had a right under Article 10 of Regulation 1612/68 to install herself with her son, she was entitled to the same social and tax advantages as Belgian workers and ex-workers. The Court again applied the *Even* formula; the old-age benefit was one granted to national workers primarily because of their objective status as workers or by virtue of their residence of national territory. The reasoning seems to be that if dependants were not paid benefits, this could constitute an obstacle to the free movement of workers (see, e.g., *Deak* (case 94/84)).

The same reasoning was applied in *Hoeckx* (case 249/83), and *Scrivner* (case 122/84), to claims in Belgium for a minimum income allowance, the 'minimex', by a member of the family of a worker and an unemployed worker, respectively. (See also *Frascogna* (case 256/86); *Deak* (case 94/84), 'tiding over' allowance paid to young job-seekers a 'social advantage'; *Schmid* (case 310/91), allowance for handicapped child of a retired worker; *Commission* v *Luxembourg* (case 111/91), childbirth allowance.) Similarly in *Matteucci* v *Communauté Française de Belgique* (case 235/87) a scholarship to study abroad arising under a reciprocal arrangement between Belgium and Germany was held to constitute a social advantage to which the child of an Italian, established as a worker in Belgium, was entitled. (See also *Meeusen* (case C–337/97).)

There are limits to the possibility of treating migrant workers exactly the same as nationals of the host State. The ECJ recognised in *Kaba* (case C–466/00) that the worker's status is conditional upon that individual continuing to satisfy the test of being a worker. In *Kaba* this conditionality justified a difference between the period that must elapse before the spouse of a person present and settled in the UK under English could apply for indefinite leave to remain (12 months) and that in respect of the spouse of a migrant EC national (four years).

Further, the benefit claimed must constitute a social advantage for the State's own nationals. In *Belgium* v *Taghavi* (case C–243/91) the Iranian wife of an Italian national residing as a worker in Belgium was held not to be entitled to a benefit for handicapped persons, described as a 'personal' right and not a social security benefit, on the grounds that the benefit was not available to spouses of *Belgian* nationals who were not themselves EC nationals.

In this area, as with discrimination in other areas, indirect discrimination may be permitted as 'objectively justified' if the legislation pursues a legitimate end and the measure is no more than is necessary to achieve that end. (For an example of the ECJ's reasoning see *O'Flynn* v *Adjudication Officer* (case C–237/94).)

Despite the breadth of the *Even* test, not all State support falls within Article 7(2). We shall see below that social security is excluded. Even outside the field of social security there are still some limitations on the *Even* test. In *Baldinger* (case C–386/02) the payment in issue was a monthly grant to former prisoners of war, subject to the condition that the recipient is an Austrian national. The applicant was a former Austrian national, who had been a prisoner of war in the former USSR from 1945 to

1947, but who had become a Swedish national, losing his Austrian nationality, in 1967. He sought to claim equality of treatment. The ECJ rejected his argument. The payment was made to compensate citizens for the hardships they had endured for their country. It was not granted to individuals either because of their status as a worker or because of their lawful residence in a Member State and therefore did not fall within Article 7(2). The payment also had nothing to do with conditions of employment, remuneration or working conditions. It therefore could not fall within Article 39(2) EC either.

The right to equal social advantages cannot be claimed by all EC nationals and their families who are lawfully resident in the host State. An important limitation was placed on Article 7(2) in *Centre Public d'Aide Sociale de Courcelles* v *Lebon* (case 316/85), in the context of a claim by a French national, Ms Lebon, for the Belgian minimex. She was living in Belgium and her claim was based, *inter alia*, on the fact that she was looking for work in Belgium. The ECJ held that the right to equality of treatment in the field of social and tax advantages granted by Article 7(2) enured for the benefit only of workers and not for nationals of Member States who migrate in search of employment.

In *Lebon*, for the first time, the Court drew a distinction between those who are lawfully entitled to 'settled' residence as a result of obtaining employment, and those who are permitted temporary rights of residence in order to search for work. Only the former will be entitled to equality of treatment in respect of all social advantages. Likewise, EC nationals (and their families) who move within the Community to receive services will not be entitled to full equality of treatment as regards social benefits provided by the host State. Collins (*Collins* v *Secretary of State for Work and Pensions* (case C–138/02)) sought to challenge the distinction between those seeking work and those actually working on the basis of the ECJ's ruling in *Martinez Sala* (case C–85/96) (see further Chapter 24) in which the Court held that a person seeking work should be considered a worker for the purposes of Regulation 1612/68 (para. 32). The ECJ reiterated its previous jurisprudence to the effect that the notion of 'worker' for the purposes of the Treaty must be interpreted broadly. Nonetheless the ECJ has consistently drawn a distinction between the situation where a person has entered a Member State but not yet worked and a person who is not currently working but has worked (see, e.g., *Lair* (case 39/86) discussed above, paras 32–33). The former group enjoy equality of treatment as regards access to work whilst the second group may claim the same social and tax advantages. In confirming that '[t]he concept of "worker" is thus not used in a uniform manner', the ECJ reaffirmed its approach in *Lebon* as to workers. Nonetheless, the ECJ accepted in *Collins* that discrimination within the scope of the Treaty was not permissible unless justified, discussed below at 20.5.4.7, which has the effect of undermining the *Lebon* distinction it seemed to have started off by accepting.

As we have seen, a second important limitation was placed on Article 7(2) in the cases of *Brown* (case 197/86), and *Lair* (case 39/86), also as a result of the claimants' status.

(b) *Continuing rights*

In some circumstances, a former migrant worker who ceases to be a worker will continue to retain the benefit of his or her former status, without any condition that he or she resides in the competent Member State. In a number of cases, the ECJ has held that such benefits are those 'the payment of which is dependent on the prior existence of an employment relationship which has come to an end and is intrinsically linked to the recipients' objective status as workers' (case C–43/99, *Leclere and Deaconescu* v *Caisse nationale des prestations familiales*, para. 57; see also case C–57/96, *Meints*, para. 41). This means that a person who is no longer a worker, even if he still receives some benefits, such as invalidity pension, by virtue of his former worker status, can claim new rights, such as childbirth rights for his family members, which have no links with his former employment (*Leclere and Deaconescu*).

This reasoning was relied on in *Collins* (case C–138/02). Collins was born in the United States of America and as well as possessing American nationality, had Irish nationality. He spent ten months working in the UK in 1980–81, before returning to the USA. He did not return to the UK until 1998, when he tried to find employment in the social services sector. During his job search, he tried to claim job seeker's allowance, based on the fact that he had been a worker and migrant workers are entitled to certain rights linked to that status even when no longer employed. Even accepting that the level of work carried out by Collins made him a worker, he was not entitled to job seeker's allowance as no link could be established between that work and the search for another job 17 years later (para. 28). Given the length of Collins's absence, his position was comparable with that of someone searching for work for the first time. The consequences of the reasoning in *Collins* are not clear; it seems to be introducing (or clarifying) a limitation on the circumstances in which a worker can claim continuing rights, in that the ECJ required that there be a link between the original work and the search for another job, though the nature of that link is uncertain. Note, however, that in *Collins*, the ECJ also held that migrant EC nationals enjoy equality of treatment in their search for a job under Article 39 EC itself (see below).

(c) *Tax advantages*

Although migrant workers are entitled under Article 7(2) of Regulation 1612/68 to the same tax advantages as nationals of the host State, this is an area where a measure such as a residence requirement, which is covertly discretionary, may be objectively justified, or where the situations of the national worker and the migrant worker will not be regarded as comparable. Such may be the case, as was conceded in *Schumacker* (case C–279/93) where the worker's residence and principal place of work (and therefore of income) is in another Member State, in which the taxing authorities are better able to take into account his personal and family circumstances (see also *Wielockx* v *Inspector der Directe Belstingen* (case C–80/94)). In *Bachmann* v *Belgium* (case C–204/90) the Court found that a Belgian rule, which allowed the deduction from income tax of contributions to health and life insurance policies only if they were paid in Belgium, although indirectly indiscriminatory, was justified as necessary to ensure the coherence of the tax system. Under this system, tax deductions in respect of insurance contributions could be offset by taxes levied from insurers in Belgium. This would not be possible where insurance was effected in another Member State. This case may be contrasted with *Asscher* (case C–107/94), a case involving the right of establishment where differential taxation rates were found to be indirectly discriminatory but unjustified. This case can be seen as an example of the ECJ seeking to limit the circumstances in which a

Member State may rely on the coherence of the tax system justification. (See more recently, e.g., *Verkooijen* (case C–35/98) – rebates for income tax limited to residents – unjustified.) As in other areas involving indirect discrimination, the Court will in each case scrutinise the justification offered and ensure that the measures adopted are not disproportionate.

20.5.4.3 *Access to training in vocational schools and retraining centres*

Article 7(3) entitles workers to access, under the same conditions as national workers, to training in vocational schools and retraining centres.

Although Article 7(3) is expressed in terms of access, it seems likely that the ECJ will take a broad view of what is meant by access. In *Casagrande v Landeshauptstadt München* (case 9/74) the Court held, in the context of a claim by a child, under Article 12 of Regulation 1612/68, that the right to be *admitted* to the host State's educational, apprenticeship and vocational training courses included not only admission but 'general measures to facilitate attendance', which in Casagrande's case, included a grant. Since grants and loans would now appear to be included in the category of 'social advantages' under Article 7(2) there is perhaps no need for special pleading for their inclusion in Article 7(3). This was the view taken by the Court in *Brown* and *Lair*. In a claim for a university maintenance grant based on Article 7(2) and 7(3), the Court opted for a restrictive interpretation of Article 7(3), holding that the term 'vocational school' applied only to institutions offering sandwich or apprenticeship courses, whilst pointing out that the claim could constitute a 'social advantage' under Article 7(2). Article 7(2) and 7(3) were not mutually exclusive.

20.5.4.4 *Collective and individual agreements*

Article 7(4) deals with collective and individual agreements relating to eligibility for work, as well as terms and conditions of work, remuneration and conditions of dismissal. Any such conditions shall be null and void insofar as they are discriminatory in respect of workers from other Member States. In *Merida* (case C–400/02), a collective agreement applicable to civilians employed by foreign armed forces in Germany was in issue. It provided for 'interim assistance' to workers where their contract has been terminated. The payment was subject to the deduction of the German income tax. Merida was a French national. Due to a taxation treaty between France and Germany, Merida's tax should have been calculated on the basis of his country of residence, at that time France, rather than in Germany at the German rate. He brought an action arguing that this was contrary to Article 39 EC and Article 7(4) Regulation 1612/68. Although the terms of Article 7(4) do not refer to the possibility of justification, the ECJ did note the possibility that indirectly discriminatory measures (such as this one) could be justified in the public interest provided it was proportionate to its aim. Despite accepting this possibility in principle, the ECJ rejected the German Government's justifications based on simplified administration and limitation of financial charges.

20.5.4.5 *Trade union rights; rights of representation and management*

Under Article 8 of Regulation 1612/68 a migrant worker is entitled to equality of treatment as regards 'membership of trade unions and the exercise of rights attaching thereto, including the right to vote and to be eligible for the administration and management of bodies governed by public law and from holding office governed by public law'.

20.5.4.6 Housing

A migrant worker is entitled to enjoy 'all the rights and benefits accorded to national workers in matters of housing, including ownership of the housing he needs' (Article 9; see *Commission* v *Greece* (case 305/87), restrictions on foreigners' right to acquire property held unlawful). The right extends to public and private housing. It is submitted that all statutory protection in this field must apply equally to 'favoured EC citizens', i.e., those who are lawfully resident. These rights would also constitute 'social advantages' under Article 7(2).

20.5.4.7 Article 39 and workers' rights

Note that the rights contained in Regulation 1612/68 are an expression of the rights granted to workers by Article 39 and do not replace them. It is possible to bring an action under Article 39, as Collins did (*Collins* (case C–138/02)). Despite being unsuccessful in his claims under Article 7(2) Regulation 1612/68, the ECJ accepted that he could argue that there had been discrimination under Article 39(2). The UK Government had rejected his application for job seeker's allowance as he was not habitually resident in the UK. This constituted indirect discrimination in the context of access to employment, but was on the circumstances justified. Although unsuccessful on the facts, the fact that the ECJ accepted that the principle of non-discrimination might apply to job seekers could have the effect of undermining the significance of the distinction in *Lebon* between those who move for work and those who move to seek work (see discussion at 20.5.4.2(a)). The *Collins* style of reasoning was applied in *Ioannidis* (case C–258/04), in which the ECJ re-emphasised that nationals of a Member State seeking employment in another Member State fall within the scope of the EC Treaty and therefore enjoy the right to equal treatment. (Note the position under the Citizenship Directive, Article 24(2).)

20.5.4.8 Impact of Directive 2004/38/EC

We suggested above that Directive 2004/38/EC mainly consolidates the existing case law, at least as regards workers' rights. At first glance Directive 2004/38/EC might seem to change the position somewhat, as it has abolished the possibility of requiring a residence permit in respect of migrant EU citizens and has consolidated all the different rights of residence into one piece of legislation (discussed further Chapter 24). At Article 24(1) it states that, 'all Union citizens residing on the basis of this Directive in the territory of the host Member State shall enjoy equality of treatment with the nationals of that Member State within the scope of the Treaty'. This right is subject to any express provisions to the contrary and Article 24(2) contains limitations applying to those who are not economically active. It excludes social assistance during the first three months of residence, as well as social assistance whilst a migrant is seeking work. It might be tempting to suggest that the categorisation of a citizen's status, based on the now repealed Directive 68/360/EEC, of lawfully resident, which was tied into having a job, is now redundant. This is not the case. Although Member States may not require migrants to apply for a residence permit, Directive 2004/38/EC still contains conditions which migrants must satisfy to gain the right of residence, that is, to be lawfully resident. Further,

Directive 2004/38/EC also still distinguishes between the different categories of migrant citizens in terms of the requirements to be satisfied before the migrant can claim the right of residence and the other rights that they can claim (Article 24(2)). Thus, although we might have to move away from an assessment based on the old question of whether someone has a residence permit, the question of whether someone has a job (or is established) still has relevance for the assessment of legal residence under the Directive, as well as the general right to equality of treatment (Article 24). How well this approach in the directive sits with the ECJ's approach under Article 39(2) in *Collins*, is debatable.

Further, the changes do not mean that Article 7(2) can now be claimed by all Union nationals; Regulation 1612/68 still applies just to workers. On the other hand, EC nationals claiming rights of establishment should be able to claim equal social advantages. Originally this would have been an argument made under Article 12 (ex 6) EC by analogy with Article 7(2) of Regulation 1612/68 (see Chapter 21), but may now be covered by Article 24 Directive 2004/38/EC.

20.5.5 Rights of workers' families (Articles 23–24 Directive 2004/38/EC, Article 12 Regulation 1612/68)

20.5.5.1 *Residence*

The meaning of 'family' is discussed at 20.3.3. Members of a worker's family have a right to install themselves with the migrant worker (who must be an EC national), irrespective of their nationality (Article 3).

In addition to the family members defined in Article 2(2) Directive 2004/38/EC who have the right to join the migrant worker, Member States are required to facilitate the admission of any member of the family not falling within the definition in Article 2(2) if they, 'in the country from which they have come are dependent on the worker . . . or members of the household of the Union citizen having the primary right of residence' (Article 3(2)(a) Directive 2004/38/EC). This seems to be a rephrasing of the provisions contained in the now repealed Article 10(2) Regulation 1612/68. Article 3(2) extends the categories of person whose admission Member States are required to facilitate in two ways. Article 3(2)(a) also includes those 'where serious health grounds strictly require the personal care of the family member by the Union citizen'. Article 3(2)(b) includes 'the partner with whom the Union citizen has a durable relationship, duly attested'. Children of this relationship are not directly mentioned, though if they are the children of the Union citizen, they would in any event have fallen within the definition of 'family member'. Article 3(2) also puts the onus of proof on the Member State seeking to reject such family members, rather than requiring them to prove that they should be admitted.

Once admitted and installed it is submitted that such members attain the status of favoured EC citizens. In *Lebon* (case 316/85) the Court held, in the context of a claim for the Belgian minimex by the adult child of a retired French worker living in Belgium, that the status of dependency resulted from a purely factual situation, i.e., support provided by the worker; it did not depend on objective factors indicative of a need for support. Certainly, Article 24 Directive 2004/38/EC extends the principle of equality of treatment to family members who are not nationals of a

Member State and who have the right of residence or permanent residence (see 20.5.5.4). Family members who are nationals of a Member State are covered by the directive in their own right, as migrant EU nationals.

However, *Lebon* also established that once a worker's children reach the age of 21 they will cease to be 'members of the family' unless they are still dependent on the worker. They will lose their rights as favoured Community citizens until they themselves become 'workers'. The High-level Panel Report on the Free Movement of Workers (1997) has suggested that the upper age limit be removed, although no action has been taken; indeed the age limit of 21 remains for those described as children of the Union citizen and his or her spouse or partner.

Article 10(3) Regulation 1612/68 requires that, in order that the family may install themselves with the worker, the worker must have available for his family 'housing considered as normal for national workers in the region where he is employed'. The Court interpreted this requirement narrowly (*Commission* v *Germany* (case 249/86)) and the terms of Article 10(3) have not been carried over into Directive 2004/38/EC.

20.5.5.2 *Employment*

Article 11 of Regulation 1612/68 has been repealed. It has been replaced by Article 23 which provides, in somewhat broader terms:

> Irrespective of nationality, the family members of a Union citizen who have the right of residence or the right of permanent residence in a Member State shall be entitled to take up employment or self-employment there.

As we have seen in the jurisprudence in relation to old Article 11 (*Gül* (case 131/85)), as long as the family member has the qualifications and diplomas necessary for the pursuit of the occupation in question in accordance with the legislation of the host State, and observed the specific rules governing the pursuit of that occupation, he was entitled under Article 11 (and now under Article 23), as the spouse of an EC worker, to practise his profession in that State, even though he did not have EC nationality. In the case of a spouse seeking to practise a profession it will be necessary to establish whether the spouse's qualifications are recognised as equivalent, which in Gül's case they were. (For a fuller discussion of this matter see Chapter 21.) It might be of significance in this context that the provisions are now contained in a directive rather than a regulation should a Member State fail to transpose the provisions. A private employer might discriminate against a TCN either directly on grounds of nationality, or on grounds of qualification. Directives do not have horizontal direct effect and it might be therefore difficult to enforce rights in such a case (though note the possibility of indirect effect – see further Chapter 5).

In *Diatta* (case 267/83) the Court held that a spouse's right under Article 11 to take up employment in the host State gave her the right to install herself in that State even under a separate roof from her husband, since it might be necessary to live apart from her husband to exercise her right to work. These principles would seem to apply to rights under Article 23. Article 11 in *Diatta* was held not to give rise to a right of a residence for the spouse independent of the migrant worker's rights. The position of the family members' rights of residence have been strengthened and clarified by Articles 12 (retention of right in the case of death or departure of

Union citizen), 13 (retention of right after divorce, annulment or termination of registered partnership) and Article 16 *et seq.* (right of permanent residence).

20.5.5.3 *Children: access to educational apprenticeship or vocational training courses*

As was mentioned in the context of workers' rights under Article 7(3), the case of *Casagrande* (case 9/74) established that Article 12 entitled children not merely to admission to such courses but also to general measures to facilitate attendance, including grants. This right has been held to extend to a grant to study abroad provided it is available to nationals of the host State (case C–308/89)). In *Commission v Belgium* (case 42/87) the Court held that the children of migrant EC workers are entitled to full national treatment as regards *all* forms of State education, even if the working parent has retired or died in that State. The Court went further in *Moritz v Netherlands Minister for Education* (case 390/87). This case involved a claim for an educational allowance from the Dutch authorities by the child of a migrant worker, a German, who had left Holland and returned to his native country. His son sought to return to Holland to complete his studies there since he could not do so in Germany, there being no coordination of school-leaving certification as between the two countries. The Court held that in such a case, having regard to the need to ensure the integration of migrant workers in the host State, and the need for continuity in their children's education, a child was not to be regarded as having lost its status as a 'child of the family' benefiting from the provisions of Regulation 1612/68 merely because his family had moved back to its State of origin. It may be presumed that his rights under Regulation 1612/68 would cease when the course was concluded. A similarly generous approach was taken in *Gaal* (case C–7/94). Here it held that a child of a (deceased) migrant worker, a Belgian national (legitimately) living in Germany, who was over the age of 21 and not dependent on his remaining parent, was entitled to claim equality with nationals under Article 12 in order to obtain finance for studies in Scotland from the German authorities. The Court held that the definition of family in Article 10 could not be invoked to limit financial assistance to students by age or dependency. The generous interpretation of Article 12 of Regulation 1612/68 has continued. In *Baumbast and R* (case C–413/99), Article 12 was interpreted not just to give the children of a migrant worker the right to stay in the host Member State to study, but also to give the parent with responsibility for their care the right to remain also, irrespective of their nationality or whether the responsible parent was married to a resident migrant worker.

Despite the fact that Article 12 does not give a spouse the right to equal access to educational, apprenticeship or vocational training courses, a spouse was successful in claiming such a right in *Forcheri v Belgium* (case 152/82). Mrs Forcheri was the wife of an Italian working as a Community official in Brussels. She applied for admission to a social work training course in Brussels. She was accepted, but required to pay a special fee, the '*minerval*', required of all students who were not Belgian nationals. She claimed that the fee was discriminatory, in breach of then Articles 7 (now 12 (ex 6) EC) and 48 EEC (now 39 EC) and Article 12 of Regulation 1612/68. The ECJ, drawing support from the fifth recital in the preamble to Regulation 1612/68, held that to require of a national of another Member State, *lawfully established* in the first Member State, an enrolment fee which is not required of its own nationals constitutes discrimination by reason of nationality which is prohibited by what is now Article 12 EC.

In Mrs Forcheri's case, the right was deemed to arise not from Article 12 of Regulation 1612/68, from which she was clearly excluded, but from the general prohibition on discrimination in the Treaty (now Article 12 EC). Her position as a favoured EC citizen, as the spouse of a worker, brought her 'within the scope of application of this Treaty'.

In the light of subsequent developments in the ECJ's jurisprudence, it would now be permitted to base such a claim for fees levied at the lower, Belgian rate on Article 7(2), as a social advantage.

It should always be borne in mind, as was made clear in *Lebon* (case 316/85), that members of the worker's family are only *indirect* beneficiaries of the right to equal treatment accorded to the worker under Article 7(2) of Regulation 1612/68; social advantages can only be granted to members of the family under Article 7(2) as advantages to the *worker*. This is a subtle distinction, but an important one. Even though Article 24 Directive 2004/38/EC also gives family members rights to equal treatment (see below), this right is dependent on the status of being a family member of a migrant EU national. Thus, the distinction remains.

20.5.5.4 *Equal treatment and other rights*

Article 24 Directive 2004/38/EC provides that migrant Union citizens 'shall enjoy equal treatment' with the nationals of the host Member State. This right is expressly extended to TCNs. The rights of EU nationals who are family members would seem to be covered by the fact that such persons would have their own independent rights under the directive. There are limitations. Article 24(2) specifies that a host Member State is not required to provide social assistance during the first three months of residence or a longer period if the right to reside of the Union citizen, on whom the family's right to reside is dependent, is granted under Article 14(4)(b), that is, job seekers.

There is the potential for an anomaly arising from the fact that family members who are EU nationals claim their own rights. It seems from the terms of Article 24 that such individuals would only gain *full* equal treatment if they themselves were economically active, and thus would not be able to claim rights to assistance as a student or job seeker's allowance, which TCNs would seem, via the rights of the working migrant EU national on whom they are dependent for their status, entitled. Presumably in such a situation it is possible for the worker still to claim rights in respect of his or her family under Article 7(2), and the introduction of Directive 2004/38 would not operate to preclude such a possibility. (See, e.g., *Castelli* (case 261/83) and *Hoeckx* (case 249/83) as well as *Collins* (case C–138/02) in relation to Article 39(2) EC and the cases based on citizenship (see Chapter 24).)

20.5.6 **Social security**

In addition to 'social advantages' in Regulation 1612/68 Article 7(2), the Treaty also makes provision for the coordination of social security. Under the laws of Member States, both eligibility for benefit and the amount of benefit paid may depend on the number and extent of contributions made to the institution responsible for social security in the relevant state. Eligibility may also be conditional on the claimant's residence in the State responsible for payment and benefits.

It was to meet these problems that Article 42 (ex 51) of the EC Treaty provided for measures to be adopted in the field of social security to secure for migrant workers and their dependants the implementation of two fundamental principles:

(a) aggregation, for the purpose of acquiring and retaining the right to benefit and of calculating the amount of benefit, of all periods taken into account under the laws of the several countries;

(b) payment of benefits to persons resident in the territories of Member States.

To this end, Regulation 1408/71 was passed, replacing the earlier Regulation 3/58. Regulation 1408/71 was implemented and supplemented by Regulation 574/72. Initially applying only to workers and their families these regulations were amended to include the self-employed by Regulations 1390/81 and 3795/81. These regulations are to be amended by Regulation 883/2004, due to come into force at the end of 2006 (see below).

The aim of EC legislation on social security is not to harmonise Member States' social security legislation but to *coordinate* their provision to secure the objectives of Article 42; to ensure that claimants' contributions in different Member States are *aggregated* for the purpose outlined in Article 42(a) of the EC Treaty, and that persons entitled to benefits may *collect* them wherever they are resident in the Community. The system is designed to abolish as far as possible the territorial limitations on the application of the different social security schemes within the Community (*Hessische Knappschaft* v *Maison Singer et Fils* (case 44/65)). However, in securing these objectives, clearly Member States' social security laws will be modified.

Regulation 1408/71, as supplemented by Regulation 574/72, is long and complex. It is not possible in a book of this nature to examine each substantive provision in detail. Instead it is proposed to examine its general scope, both in terms of the *persons* and the *kind of benefits* covered, and the *principles* on which the detailed provisions are based.

The complexity of Regulations 1408/71 and 574/72, and the difficulty of reconciling the autonomous systems of Member States with the demands of Community law, have inevitably resulted in loopholes and anomalies, some remedied by the Court, some beyond the power of the ECJ to resolve. Where this has occurred regulations amending Regulations 1408/71 and 574/72 have been passed. The principal amending regulations are Regulation 2001/83 ([1983] OJ L230/6), and Regulation 1248/92 ([1992] OJ L136/7) as well as Regulation 883/2004.

20.5.6.1 *Personal scope*

Regulation 1408/71 covers the same groups as are covered by the other legislation relating to free movement of persons: workers, the self-employed and their families and survivors. The workers and self-employed must be nationals of one of the Member States. It also covers survivors who are EC nationals irrespective of the nationality of the worker, and stateless persons and refugees (Article 2). However, the definition of the employed and self-employed is different, being the fact of being or having been insured under any form of social security scheme. As long as the employed or self-employed person is covered by some national scheme for insured persons in one of the Member States he will be covered by the regulation, even, it seems, if he is or has been working outside the Community (see *Laborero* (cases 82 & 103/86) – claimants working in Belgian Congo).

Also in contrast with other legislation relating to workers, these provisions may apply to persons who move as recipients of services (e.g., *Kohll* (case C–158/96)). In *Hessische Knappschaft* v *Maison Singer et Fils* (case 44/65) a German worker was killed in a road accident while on holiday in France. His dependants were paid by the German social security authorities who then sought to sue the driver of the vehicle responsible for the accident in France. To do so they needed to rely on their rights of subrogation under Regulation 3/58 (now Regulation 1408/71, Article 93(1)). It was argued that the rights arising under the then Article 51 (now 42) of the EC Treaty were such as to promote freedom of movement for workers *as* workers, not *qua* holidaymakers. The Court disagreed, holding that nothing in the then Article 51 required that the concept of worker be limited solely to migrant workers *sensu stricto*, or to workers required to move for the purpose of their employment.

The definition of family member is also different, being defined in Article 1(f) as 'any person defined or recognised as a member of the family or designated as a member of the household by the legislation under which benefits are provided', and 'where . . . the said legislations regard as a member of the family or a member of the household only a person living under the same roof as the worker, this condition shall be considered satisfied if the worker in question is mainly dependent on that worker'.

Both families' and survivors' benefits under EC social security legislation derive from the worker's insurance, unless they are or have been themselves insured under the appropriate scheme. The Court has not infrequently made exceptions to this principle (e.g., *F* v *Belgium* to be discussed later in this chapter). In its earlier case law, the ECJ distinguished between social security benefits which were granted as a personal right and those acquired solely through the claimant's status as a member of the family of a worker. Only the latter could be claimed, on a basis of equality with national claimants, under Regulation 1408/71 (*Kermaschek* (case 40/76)). However, in *Bestuur van de Sociale Verzekeringsbank* v *Cabanis-Issarte* (case C–308/93), the ECJ departed from *Kermaschek*. Here it held that the claimant, a French woman who had lived with her French husband in Holland while he worked there, and who had never herself been a worker, could, on their return to France following his retirement, invoke the non-discrimination principle of Article 3 of Regulation 1408/71 in order to claim equality of contribution to a Dutch voluntary personal pension scheme to which she had contributed while she was living in the Netherlands. To maintain a distinction between rights in person and derived rights would, the Court held, 'undermine the fundamental Community law requirement that its rules should be applied uniformly, by making their applicability to individuals depend on whether the national law relating to the benefits question treats the rights concerned as rights in person or derived rights, in the light of the specific features of the domestic social security scheme'.

Cabanis-Issarte and *Kermaschek* concerned rights which were undisputedly social security rights. Social benefits which are not strictly speaking social security rights covered by Regulation 1408/71 should now be claimed alternatively or additionally under Regulation 1612/68, Article 7(2), as a 'social advantage'. This seems to accord with the Court's jurisprudence dating from the mid-1970s and *Fiorini* (case 32/75).

20.5.6.2 *Principles*

The general principles underlying Regulation 1408/71 are stated in the preamble; they are laid down in more detailed form in the regulation itself. Most of these principles are designed to secure one further overriding goal, that the migrant worker and his family should suffer no disadvantage as a result of moving within the Community.

(a) *Non-discrimination on grounds of nationality*

This is perhaps the most important principle. It has certainly been the most frequently invoked. Article 3(1) of Regulation 1408/71 provides that:

> Subject to the special provisions of this Regulation, persons resident in the territory of one of the Member States to whom this Regulation applies shall be subject to the same obligations and enjoy the same benefits under the legislation of any Member State as the nationals of that State.

Article 3(1) applies to all forms of discrimination, direct and indirect. Discrimination will often take the form of a residence or length of residence requirement. A benefit covered by the regulation cannot be refused in breach of Article 3. Unlike other areas of EC law it appears that in its social security rules reverse discrimination is not permitted. The Court held in *Kenny* v *Insurance Officer* (case 1/78):

> it is for the national legislation to lay down the conditions for the acquisition, retention, loss or suspension of the right to social security benefits so long as those conditions apply without discrimination to *the nationals of the Member State concerned* and to those of other Member States (para. 16, emphasis added).

(b) *Payment regardless of residence*

This principle derives from Article 42(b) of the EC Treaty. Article 10(1) of Regulation 1408/71 provides that certain types of benefit are payable even if the recipient no longer resides in the competent Member State. It will be noted that this principle, known as the 'exportability' principle, is not expressed to apply to *all* social security benefits; sickness benefits and family benefits, for example, are subject to special provision in Regulation 1408/71 and Regulation 574/72. Article 10 is expressed to apply only 'save as otherwise provided'.

(c) *No overlapping of benefits*

Article 12(1) of Regulation 1408/71 provides that:

> This Regulation can neither confer nor maintain the right to several benefits of the same kind for one and the same period of compulsory insurance.

In *Schmidt* v *Rijksdienst voor Pensioenen* (case C–98/94) the Court held that benefits will be of the 'same kind' when the purpose and object as well as the basis on which they are calculated and the conditions for granting them are identical. On the other hand characteristics which are purely formal are not relevant criteria for the classification of benefits. Benefits calculated or produced on the basis of periods of employment of two different persons cannot be treated as benefits of the same kind. Thus in *Schmidt* a retirement pension for a divorcee, designed to ensure for that person adequate means of support, was not of the same kind as a personal retirement pension.

Where a worker has contributed to social security schemes in two or more Member States, he may have become entitled to benefit in respect of the same contingency from more than one State. Article 12 operates to prevent him receiving double benefit. However, since entitlement is subject to the single State principle (see below), and the 'competent' State is determined according to Community law, Article 12 could result in the claimant receiving a lesser sum from the competent State than that to which he would be entitled under the law of another State. Where this occurs the Court has held he is entitled to receive the difference between the smaller and the larger sum, the difference payable by the competent institution in the more 'generous' State. 'A worker cannot be deprived of more favourable allowances by substituting the benefits available from one Member State for the benefits due from another Member State' (see e.g., *Baldi* (case 1/88), family allowances; *Di Felice* (case 128/88), retirement pension; *Georges* (case 24/88), family allowances).

Article 12(1) does not apply to benefits in respect of invalidity, old age, death (pensions) or occupational disease, for which there is special provision for apportionment amongst Member States (Article 12(1)).

(d) *Aggregation*
This principle, derived from Article 42(a) EC, is spelt out specifically with regard to each type of benefit covered. It means that the competent Member State, when calculating the right to benefits, is obliged to take into account insurance periods or periods of residence spent in other Member States.

(e) *The single State principle*
This is provided by Article 13, which states as a general rule that:

> A worker to whom this Regulation applies shall be subject to the legislation of a single Member State only.

(f) *No disadvantage*
As noted above, the Court has held that a worker may not be allowed to suffer disadvantage as a result of the application of Community rules. EC rules against overlapping cannot result in a loss of advantages for a migrant worker. Where the worker is doubly entitled, he or she may choose the more advantageous benefit (*Iacobelli* v *I.N.A.M.I.* (case C–275/91)). The worker cannot as a result of moving from one Member State to another be put in a worse position than workers who have not availed themselves of their right of free movement (*Masgio* (case C–10/90)).

The Court has been forced to acknowledge that some disadvantage to migrant workers cannot be cured by the application of this principle. This is the inevitable result of the fact that Article 42 (ex 51) is not designed to create a common social security scheme but simply to coordinate national social security schemes (see *McLachlan* v *CNAVTS* (case C–146/93)).

20.5.6.3 *Material scope*

Article 4(1) of Regulation 1408/71 provides that:

> This Regulation shall apply to all legislation concerning the following branches of social security, reflecting the nine official categories recognised by the ILO:
>
> (a) sickness and maternity benefits;
> (b) invalidity benefits, including those intended for the maintenance or improvement of working capacity;
> (c) old-age benefits;
> (d) survivors' benefits;
> (e) benefits in respect of accidents at work and occupational diseases;
> (f) death grants;
> (g) unemployment benefits;
> (h) family benefits.

Article 4(2) provides that the regulation shall apply 'to all general and special social security schemes, whether contributory or non-contributory'.

However, the regulation does *not* apply to 'social and medical assistance, to benefit schemes for victims of war or its consequences, or to special schemes for civil servants and persons treated as such' (Article 4(4)).

As the term 'social assistance' is not a term of art, it is not defined in Regulation 1408/71, and will be subject to different interpretations in different Member States. Interpretation has been left to the ECJ, largely on reference from national courts seised with the problem. Not surprisingly, the Court has given the term the narrowest scope.

In a series of cases, starting with *Frilli* v *Belgium* (case 1/72), the Court, in assessing whether a particular benefit, which may look like social assistance, qualifies as social security, has applied a 'double function' test. Some kinds of benefit, the Court reasons, perform a double function; they are akin to social assistance, since need is the essential criterion, and eligibility is not dependent on employment; yet they are akin to social security since they confer on the beneficiary a legally defined position. Since such difficulties must not be allowed to prejudice the rights of workers, such benefits must be deemed to be social security benefits, and assimilated where possible to the social security benefits listed in Article 4(1). Applying this test in *Frilli*, a non-contributory guaranteed minimum income, unrelated to insurance, payable in Belgium to Belgian citizens or those resident for a minimum period of five years, was assimilated to the old age pension and deemed to be social security; as such it could not be denied to Frilli in breach of Regulation 1408/71, Article 3. Similarly in *Callemeyn* v *Belgium* (case 187/73) a special payment to the handicapped, unrelated to either employment or contributions (the claimant being the wife of a migrant worker), refused by the Belgian authorities on the grounds of her nationality, was assimilated to invalidity benefit and held, applying the same test, to constitute social security.

In *F* v *Belgium* (case 7/75) the claimant was the 14-year old handicapped son of an Italian worker in Belgium. He had been refused a special grant for handicapped persons, again because he could not fulfil the (Belgian) nationality or (15-year) residence requirement. Prima facie the benefit was social assistance; it was not a 'family' benefit, nor a workers' invalidity benefit; it was not related to contributions and was available to the whole (handicapped) population. Nevertheless, applying the double function test the Court found it to be social security within Regulation 1408/71. Further, a dependent person such as Mr and Mrs F's son was entitled to equality of treatment as long as his parents were resident in a Member State. Even when he ceased to be a minor his right to equality of treatment would not cease. The migrant worker, as Advocate-General Trabucchi suggested, must be treated not just as a source of labour but as a human being.

These cases were followed by many others (e.g., *Inzirillo* (case 63/76); *Vigier* (case 70/80); *Piscitello* (case 139/82)) in which benefits of extremely dubious status as social security benefits were upheld as such. The only criterion by which a claim might still be excluded as constituting 'social assistance', applied by the Court in *Fossi* (case 79/76) and *Tinelli* (case 144/78), was if the benefit involved a discretion-ary assessment of need or personal circumstances. Needless to say this test did not serve to exclude many claims (*Fossi* and *Tinelli* were claiming as 'victims of war' and thus fell within Regulation 1408/71, Article 4(4)).

Perhaps sensing that it had gone too far, the Court switched its approach in the 1980s. Instead of stretching Regulation 1408/71 to encompass 'social assistance'-type claims the Court chose an alternative route, treating the benefits as 'social advantages' under Article 7(2) of Regulation 1612/68, the scope of which was expanded following the introduction of the 'lawful residence' test in *Even* (case 207/78) (see 20.5.4.2).

Regulation 1408/71 will, of course, continue to apply, and apply alone, to 'genu-ine' social security benefits, and, if a claimant wishes to 'export' a benefit this can only be achieved under the specific provisions of that regulation. A claimant who wishes to invoke the aggregation principle will likewise have to show that his claim falls within Regulation 1408/71.

From the above cases it is clear that the ECJ will use all the means at its disposal to ensure that migrant workers and their families are in no way disadvantaged as a result of moving within the Community. To achieve its ends the Court will not be deterred by apparent shortcomings in EC legislation.

20.5.6.4 *Regulation 883/2004*

Despite the ECJ's extensive interpretation, there were lacunae in protection awarded to migrant individuals such as those who were not economically active. The institutions agreed a regulation to amend the current system, updating and streamlining it, but also filling in some of these gaps in protection. At the forefront of the changes was a concern to ensure that migration should be made easier by removing the risk of loss of benefits. From a starting point of European citizenship, Regulation 883/2004 applies to non-economically active persons. Healthcare benefits have been aligned; restrictions on the export of special, non-contributory benefits are to be based on transparent and objective criteria; and the possibility of exporting a job seeker's allowance has been increased from three months to six months.

20.5.7 Rights to remain in the territory of a Member State after having been employed in that State (Regulation 1251/70, now replaced by Directive 2004/38/EC)

These provisions implement Article 39(3)(d) (ex 48(3)(d) EC. As stated in the pre-amble to Regulation 1251/70, 'the right of residence acquired by workers in active employment has as a corollary the right ... to remain in the territory of a Member State after having been employed in that State' (first recital); moreover, 'the exercise by the worker of the right to remain entails that such right shall be extended to members of his family; [and], in the case of the death of the worker during his working life, maintenance of the right of residence of the members of his family must also be recognised' (seventh recital). Regulation 1251/70 has been replaced by provisions in Directive 2004/38/EC. Rather than distinguish between the rights of workers and of their families, the directive deals with the rights of Union citizens together. Rights of third-country nationals who are family members for the purposes of the directive are dealt with additionally.

Chapter IV provides for a right of permanent residence. Article 16 provides the basic rules for eligibility: Union citizens who have resided legally for a continuous period of five years in the host Member State have a right to claim permanent residence there. Article 16(2) extends this right to family members who have legally resided with a Union citizen in the host Member State, again for a period of five years. Continuity of residence is specified not to be affected by temporary absences as detailed in Article 16(3). Once acquired, the right of permanent residence can only be lost through absence from the host Member State for a period exceeding two consecutive years (Article 16(4)).

Article 17 provides special rules for those who reach retirement age as well as those who become permanently incapable of working and frontier workers. In the case of each of these workers, the requirement of a five-year period of legal resi-dence is not a precondition for the right to claim permanent residence. In the case of retirement, a three-year period of continuous residence is required together with the requirement that the worker must have been working in the host Member State for at least the preceding 12 months. In the case of permanent incapacity to work, no condition as to length of residence is imposed where such incapacity is the result of an accident at work or the result of an occupational disease entitling the person concerned to benefit payable by the host Member State. Those workers who work in another Member State whilst residing in the host Member State gain the right to claim permanent residence after three years of continuous employment.

Additionally, as we have already noted, Article 12 and 13 deal with the retention of the right of residence by family members in the case of death or departure of the Union citizen or of divorce, annulment of marriage or termination of registered partnership, respectively.

Although these provisions are generous, there is a decision of the ECJ on the calculation of the residence requirement dealing with the equivalent provisions in Regulation 1251/70. In *Givane* (case C–257/00), a worker who died had lived in the UK for more than the then required period of two years. He had, however, left the UK for a period in excess of the three months allowed under the previous regime. He then returned to the UK, bringing his family with him. Although the Advocate-General suggested the requirements for the family's right to remain were satisfied, the ECJ disagreed. The purpose of the provision was to allow those who are integrated into the host Member State to remain there, a purpose which would not be satisfied were the residence period not to be satisfied immediately prior to the worker's death. This narrow judgment is somewhat surprising given the ECJ's history of a broad interpretation of individuals' rights. It remains to be seen whether this approach is carried over to the rights to remain specified in Directive 2004/38/EC.

20.6 'Employment in the public service'

In the field of employment rights, Member States are entitled under Article 39(4) EC to deny or restrict access to 'employment in the public service' on the basis of a worker's nationality. Given the potential breadth of this provision, it is not surprising that it has been exploited by Member States nor that the ECJ has given it the narrowest scope.

The German post office sought to rely on this exclusion in *Sotgiu* v *Deutsche Bundespost* (case 152/73) to counter Sotgiu's allegations that the post office's rules granting extra allowances to workers living apart from their families in Germany were discriminatory. On a reference from the Bundesarbeitsgericht the ECJ held that the exception provided by the then Article 48(4) (now 39(4)) did not apply to all employment in the public service. It applied only to 'certain activities' in the public service, connected with the exercise of official authority. Moreover, it applied only to conditions of *access*; it did not permit discriminatory conditions of employment once access had been granted.

The matter was further clarified in *Commission* v *Belgium (Re Public Employees)* (case 149/79). This was an infringement action against Belgium for breach of the then Article 48 (now 39). Under Belgian law, posts in the 'public service' could be limited to Belgian nationals. This was applied to all kinds of posts: unskilled workers, railwaymen, nurses, plumbers, electricians and architects, employed by both central and local government. The city of Brussels (seat of the EC Commission!) was one of the chief offenders. The Belgian Government (supported by France and Germany intervening) argued that all these jobs were 'in the public service' within Article 39(4). The ECJ disagreed. The concept of public service was a Community concept; it applied only to the exercise of official authority, and was intended to apply only to employees *safeguarding the general interests of the State*. The fact that higher levels of a post might involve the exercise of official authority would not justify assimilating the junior levels to that status. Belgium was in breach of EC law.

Similar proceedings were brought, and upheld, against France in *Commission* v *France (Re French Nurses)* (case 307/84) against a French law limiting the appointment of nurses in public hospitals to French nationals.

When a particular job will involve 'the exercise of official authority' is not altogether clear. It certainly does not apply to civil servants generally. In *Lawrie-Blum* v *Land Baden-Württemberg* (case 66/85) the Court held that access to certain posts could not be limited by reason of the fact that in a given Member State persons appointed to such posts have the status of civil servants. To make the application of Article 39(4) dependent on the legal nature of the relationship between the employer and the administration would enable Member States to determine at will the posts covered by the exception laid down in that provision. To constitute employment in the public service, employees must be charged with the exercise of powers conferred by public law or must be responsible for *safeguarding the general interests of the State*. In *Bleis* v *Ministère de l'Education Nationale* (case C–4/91) the Court held that the concept of public service 'presumes on the part of those occupying such posts the existence of a special relationship of allegiance to the State and reciprocity of rights and duties which form the foundation of the bond of nationality'. This approach by the ECJ might be termed a 'functional' approach to the determination of whether the 'exercise of official authority' is involved, as it considers the responsibilities of each job individually.

On these criteria it seems that the derogation provided by Article 39(4) will be of limited use, confined to occupations such as the judiciary and the higher echelons of the civil service, the armed forces and the police. Article 39(4) needs to be viewed in conjunction with Article 45 (ex 55), which provides that the freedom of establishment permitted under EC law 'shall not apply, so far as any given Member State is concerned, to activities which in that State are connected, even occasionally, with the exercise of official authority'. Despite the difference in wording, identical principles will apply to the interpretation of both provisions.

Since most of the posts in the above cases may not be denied to non-nationals, access to these posts by way of examination or training must be open, on equal terms, to workers (or their families) who are non-nationals. Thus in *Lawrie-Blum* (case 66/85) a practical training scheme for teachers, organised in Baden-Württemberg within the framework of the civil service, was not within Article 39(4) and could not be confined to German nationals.

In view of the widespread practice among Member States of excluding non-nationals from a wide range of occupations in the public service on the basis of Article 39(4) the Commission published a Notice in 1988 ([1998] OJ C72/2) identifying certain sectors of employment which it considered to be for the most part 'sufficiently remote from the specific activities of the public sphere as defined by the European Court that they would only in rare cases be covered by the exception of Article 48(4) [now 39(4)]'. These comprise:

(a) public health care services,

(b) teaching in State educational establishments,

(c) research for non-military purposes in public establishments, and

(d) public bodies responsible for administering commercial services.

The Commission has brought Article 226 (ex 169) EC actions against certain Member States for failure to take action following the communication (for example, *Commission* v *Belgium* (case C–173/94); *Commission* v *Greece* (case C–290/94); *Commission* v *Luxembourg* (case C–473/93)). In its judgments given on the same day, the ECJ confirmed the Commission's approach of identifying types of work which would rarely fall within Article 39(4) EC. In these circumstances, it is still open to the national authorities to show, on a functional basis, that specified jobs within such sections do fall within the public service exception. It has been suggested that the review should result in the opening up of many posts which in many Member States are currently reserved for nationals, representing a 'tremendous leap forward in the attainment of a true community-wide labour market' (see Watson, in Chapters 22 and 23). In the light of the case law, it seems that this has yet to happen.

20.7 Derogation on grounds of public policy, public security or public health

The rights of entry and residence and the right of permanent residence granted by the Treaty to migrant workers and their families are not absolute. States remain free to deny these rights to migrant workers or their families on grounds of 'public policy, public security or public health'. Because of the importance of this principle and the fact that Directive 64/221, now replaced by the relevant provisions in Directive 2004/38/EC, passed to implement the principle, applies to all categories of migrant workers, employed and self-employed, it will be dealt with separately in Chapter 23.

20.8 Conclusions

The ECJ has played a significant role in the development of the free movement of workers, interpreting both the concept of worker and the rights granted to workers broadly. In doing so, it has emphasised the personal aspect of the worker and in many instances taken into account the requirements of fundamental rights. The scope of protection offered is not perfect, however, with limitations affecting in particular students and those who no longer are workers. Against this background, the rights contained in the citizenship provisions may well be important in completing the network of protection offered to migrant individuals.

FURTHER READING

Daniele, L., 'Restrictions to the Free Movement of Persons' (1997) 22 EL Rev 191.

Hartley, T., 'Free Movement of Students in European Community Law' (1989) *Cahiers de Droit Européen*.

O'Keeffe, D., 'Judicial Interpretation of the Public Exception to the Free Movement of Workers' in Curtin, D. and O'Keeffe, D. (eds), *Constitutional Adjudication in European Community Law and National Law* (Butterworths Ireland, 1992), p. 89.

Peers, S., 'Social Advantages and Discrimination in Employment Caselaw Confirmed' (1997) 22 EL Rev 157.

Shuibhue, N., 'Free Movement of Persons and the Wholly Internal Rule: Time to Move On? (2002) 39 CML Rev 731.

Steiner, J., 'The Right to Welfare: Equality and Equity under Community Law' (1985) 10 EL Rev 21.

Stalford, H., 'Concepts of Family under EU Law – Lessons from the ECHR' (2002) *International Journal of Law, Policy and the Family* 410.

Watson, P., 'Free Movement of Workers: a One way Ticket?' (1993) 22 ILJ 68.

Woods, L., 'Family Rights in the EU – Disadvantaging the Disadvantaged?' (1999) 11 Child & Family Law Quarterly 17.

21

Freedom of establishment

21.1 Introduction

The freedoms granted to workers under Article 39 (ex 48) were also granted by the
Treaty to the self-employed in the form of a right of establishment (Articles 43–48
(ex 52–58) EC) and a right to provide services (Articles 49–55 (ex 59–66) EC). This
chapter discusses establishment; the following chapter considers services. Similar
themes as were found in relation to Article 39 underpin both these freedoms, in
particular a broad interpretation of the rights. Similarly, there has been a move
from a discrimination-based test for the application of the article to one based on
the notion of an obstacle to the exercise of the right. As we have seen in Chapter 14,
there has been a tendency to develop case law across the freedoms in parallel.
We might question the extent to which this is wholly appropriate. Whereas the
case law concerning workers necessarily deals with individuals, it should be noted
that there is a dichotomy in the treatment of establishment. The role of citizenship, so significant in relation to workers, can also apply to cases brought under
Article 43 where the applicant is an individual. The fact that freedom of establishment can be seen as part of the free movement of individuals is illustrated by the
fact that the new directive on the free movement of people, discussed in Chapter
20, also applies to establishment. In addition to benefiting individuals, however,
the rights of establishment may be exercised by companies. The personal element,
so important in the context of the individual, may not always be relevant here. We
should therefore distinguish between those barriers to the freedom of establishment that arise in a personal context and those that are found in the commercial
context.

After it defines the scope of establishment and distinguishes between the rights
to establishment and to provide services, this chapter outlines the development of
the different aspects of the right of establishment and the test used to determine
when Article 43 comes into play. In particular, it considers the difference between
rules which operate to deter individuals and companies from moving in the first
place, those that affect access to the market, and the rules that come into play when
running a business. This chapter focuses in particular on certain problem areas,
such as qualifications and the abuse of Community law rights to evade national
regulation, as well as the position regarding companies.

21.2 **Scope of provision**

21.2.1 **Establishment**

Article 43 (ex 52) in its original form provided:

> Within the framework of the provisions set out below, restrictions on the freedom of establishment of nationals of a Member State in the territory of another Member State shall be abolished. Such progressive abolition shall also apply to restrictions on the setting up of agencies, branches or subsidiaries by nationals of any Member State established in the territory of any Member State.
>
> Freedom of establishment shall include the right to take up and pursue activities as self-employed persons and to set up and manage undertakings, in particular companies and firms within the meaning of the second paragraph of Article 58 [now 48], under the conditions laid down for its own nationals by the law of the country where such establishment is effected, subject to the provisions of the Chapter relating to capital [Chapter 4 EC].

This provision is replicated in the Constitution, should it come into force, in Article III–137.

21.2.2 **Enforcing the rights**

Since the right of establishment provided under Article 43 *et seq.* appeared to be conditional on the issuing of directives under Article 47(1) and (2) (ex 57(1) and (2)), it was thought that these rights could not be invoked by individuals until such directives had been passed. This matter was tested in *Reyners* v *Belgium* (case 2/74). Reyners was a Dutchman, born, educated and resident in Belgium, and a doctor of Belgian law. He was refused admission to the Belgian Bar as he was not of Belgian nationality. He challenged this decision, claiming that it was in breach of the then Article 52 (now 43). The Belgian Government argued that this article was not directly effective, since it depended for its effect on the issuing of directives under what is now Article 47. On a reference for interpretation from the Belgian Conseil d'État on this point, the ECJ held that Article 43 was directly effective from the end of the transitional period. The provisions of Article 47 were complementary to Article 43; they were not a necessary precondition. The purpose of Article 47 was merely to facilitate the increase of freedom of establishment; that article, together with Article 12 (ex 6 EC, originally 7 EEC), required that the actual conditions imposed could not be stricter than those imposed on the State's own nationals. Article 43 was thus directly effective.

The principle is binding on all competent authorities as well as legally recognised professional bodies (*Steinhauser* v *City of Biarritz* (case 197/84), see below). Following *Angonese* (see Chapter 20), it is possible that Article 43 will apply as against private parties.

21.2.3 **Limitations**

The right of establishment is subject to derogation on the grounds of 'public policy, public security or public health' (Article 46 (ex 56) EC). Under this article, Member

States 'may provide for special treatment for foreign nationals'. This was originally implemented in terms of 'measures concerning the movement and residence of foreign nationals' by Directive 64/221, but has been replaced by the new codification directive, Directive 2004/38/EC, Articles 27 *et seq.* (see Chapter 23).

Freedom of establishment is expressed not to apply to 'activities which in that State are connected, even occasionally, with the exercise of official authority' (Articles 46 (ex 55) EC). This derogation has been considered in some detail in Chapter 20 in the context of Article 39(4) (ex 48(4)) relating to workers. The principles applicable to workers will apply equally to the establishment provisions. As in the case of workers, the derogation has been given the narrowest scope.

21.3 Meaning of establishment

21.3.1 General

A right of establishment is a right to install oneself, to 'set up shop' in another Member State, permanently or semi-permanently, whether as an individual, a partnership or a company, for the purpose of performing a particular economic activity there. The concept of establishment has been held to be 'a broad one, allowing a Community national to participate on a stable and continuous basis in the economic life of a Member State other than his own' (*Gebhard* v *Consiglio dell'Ordine degli Avvocati e Procuratori di Milano* (case C–55/94)). In the German insurance case (*Commission* v *Germany (Re Insurance Services)* (case 205/84)) the Court suggested that an enterprise would fall within the concept of 'establishment' even if its presence is not in the form of a branch or agency but consists merely of an office managed by the enterprise's own staff or by a person who is independent but is authorised to act on a permanent basis for the enterprise. Thus, in the case of *Gambelli* (case C–243/01), the ECJ commented:

> Where a company established in a Member State . . . pursues the activity of collecting bets through the intermediary of an organisation of agencies established in another Member State (such as the defendants in the main proceedings), any restrictions on the activities of those agencies constitute obstacles to the freedom of establishment (para 46).

21.3.2 Distinction between establishment and services

The relationship between the freedoms is dealt with in general terms in Chapter 14. The relationship between establishment and services should, however, be considered further. The difference between the right of establishment and the right to provide services is one of degree rather than of kind. Both apply to business or professional activity pursued for 'profit' or 'remuneration'. The key distinction seems to be the strength of the connection between the right holder and the host Member State. Whereas establishment suggests some degree of continuity or permanence, the right to provide services connotes the provision of services in one Member State, on a temporary or spasmodic basis, by a person established in another Member State. In the latter case it is not necessary to reside, even temporarily, in the Member State in which the service is provided. The temporary nature of the activities in question should be determined in the light not only of the duration of the service but of its regularity, periodicity and continuity (*Gebhard* (case C–55/94)). Applying these principles in *Gebhard*, the Court found that the setting up of chambers in Italy by a German barrister, a practising member of the Stuttgart Bar, fell within the concept of establishment. A person could be established, within the meaning of the Treaty, in more than one Member State, in particular, in the case of companies, through the setting up of branches or subsidiaries, and, in the case of members of the professions, by establishing a second professional base. The Court suggested that the Treaty provisions relating to workers, establishment and services were mutually exclusive. Therefore, in case of doubt, all should be pleaded. However, in view of the fine line between 'establishment' and 'provision of services', and the fact that the general principles applicable to both are the same (as they are to workers, see *Royer* (case 48/75) discussed in Chapter 20), too much emphasis should not be placed on the difference between the two. Despite dicta by the Court purporting to distinguish between the two, interpretation of both provisions appears to be moving towards convergence. *Gebhard* is significant in this respect.

21.3.3 **Elements of establishment**

Inherent in the above discussions, we can see that certain elements need to be shown to bring the freedom of establishment into play. The first is self-employed activity. The cases on workers discussed in Chapter 20 discuss the definition of employment. We can therefore identify self-employment by a process of elimination. The ECJ identified the criteria for self-employed activity in *Jany* (case C–268/99) starting from this premise. Although the case concerned the Europe Agreements, the principles can nonetheless be applied here as the same concepts as found in the EC Treaty were under consideration. The question before the ECJ was whether women working as window prostitutes in Amsterdam could claim the benefit of the freedom of establishment. The question was crucial for the women in *Jany*, as the association agreements did not give the right to take up employment. The ECJ held that establishment required:

- the provision of a service;
- outside any relationship of subordination concerning the choice of that activity, working conditions and conditions of remuneration;
- under that person's own responsibility; and
- in return for remuneration paid to that person directly and in full (para. 71).

The ECJ rejected the Dutch Government's argument that, given the subordinate relationship of a prostitute to her pimp, she was in an employment relationship; the ECJ pointed out that the Dutch Government had adduced no evidence on the point and furthermore disagreed with the assumption that a relationship of dependency could be equated to an employment relationship. In assessing whether a person is carrying out such activities, it does not matter that he or she is undergoing professional training (*Morgenbesser* (case C–313/01)).

The second element of establishment is that the activity must fall within the economic sphere. When we look at the definition of companies, we can see that Article 48(2) expressly excludes those companies which are non-profit making. This does not mean that the business must make a profit but that it is intended to. Charitable work seems to be excluded. The ECJ has also borrowed jurisprudence from both the workers and services spheres to determine that work or service performed is genuine and effective and not such as to be regarded as purely marginal and ancillary (see, e.g., *Deliège* (joined cases C–51/96 and C–191/97) paras 53 and 54, discussed in Chapter 22) (*Jany*, para. 33).

There must also be a cross-border element. In *Nino* (joined cases C–54, 91/88 and 14/89), Italian law made it an offence to practise as a doctor without proper authorisation. Nino, and others charged with her, were Italian nationals who qualified as biotherapists and pranotherapists, activities which fell within the definition of doctor, while residing in Italy and who were charged as a result of treatment administered solely within the territory of that Member State. The ECJ held that Article 43 did not apply to this situation as it was purely internal.

Nonetheless the requirement of a cross-border element seems quite easy to satisfy. This can occur when an individual moves, or when a company moves, or sets up a branch, agency or subsidiary in another Member State. Establishment rights may be exercised against home and host Member State. In *Marks and Spencer* (case C–446/03) a British law precluded a parent company from deducting losses made by its subsidiaries in other Member States, though it could deduct losses made by subsidiaries in the UK. The effect of this rule was to deter companies established in the UK from establishing subsidiaries in other Member States. Thus a UK rule was challenged by a UK company; the cross-border element was provided by the impact on its choices about whether to set up subsidiaries in other Member States.

A right may also be relied on when those who have exercised their rights of free movement seek to return to their state of origin. In *Knoors* (case 115/78), a Dutch national moved to Belgium where he worked as a plumber. He returned to the Netherlands and relied on his experience in Belgium when he sought to have his qualifications recognised by the Dutch authorities.

21.4 Beneficiaries of the right

The right of establishment and the right to provide services are accorded under the Treaty to EC nationals and to companies formed according to the law of one of the Member States. Article 48 EC specifies:

> Companies formed in accordance with the law of a Member State and having their registered office, central administration or principal place of business within the Community shall be treated in the same way as natural persons who are nationals of Member States.

A company's 'nationality' is determined by reference to the Member State in which it has its seat (*Commission v France* (tax credits) (case 270/83)). Where the central management or principal place of business lies outside the Community the company's activities must have an 'effective and continuous link with the economy of a Member State, excluding the possibility that this link might depend on nationality, particularly the nationality of the partners or the members of the managing or supervisory bodies, or of persons holding the capital stock' ('General programme for the abolition of restrictions on freedom to provide services', *Common Market Reporter,* para. 1546; JO 1962, 32). This link is the price exacted for valuable access to the Community market. A brief overview of the position as regards companies and the particular difficulties arising in that context is given below at 21.10.

The position of third-country nationals is considered in Chapter 24.

21.5 Fundamental Community rights

If we look at the text of Article 43, we can see two linked elements to the right of establishment: the right to establish, that is, the right to move to another country; and the right to carry on business there. As with the jurisprudence on workers, a third aspect to the right has developed, at least in relation to the exercise of Article 43 by individuals, which provides for social and ancillary rights.

21.5.1 Right to move and to reside

In addition to the Treaty, secondary legislation clarifies the rights of entry and residence to self-employed Union citizens. Following the enactment of the new directive, Directive 2004/38/EC, these exist in identical terms to those applicable to workers, as the provisions are expressed to apply to migrant EU citizens. The legislation replaces Directive 73/148 dealing with rights of entry and residence (see 20.5.1) and Directive 75/34 (right to remain permanently in a Member State after having been self-employed there, see 20.5.7). Those who establish themselves have, like workers, the right to leave their Member State of origin and enter and reside on the territory of another Member State (Article 7(1) Directive 2004/38/EC) and may acquire the right of permanent residence in that Member State (Article 16 Directive 2004/38/EC). The rights of family members are likewise dealt with by Directive 2004/38/EC and are the same as those for the family members of workers (see Chapter 20).

The rights of legal persons are not covered by this legislation. This fact does not affect the existence of their rights; legal persons may rely on the Treaty directly. We have seen the *Marks and Spencer* case, in which a national rule which could have the effect of stopping a company from establishing itself, via the incorporation of a subsidiary, in another Member State, was contrary to Article 43. The national rule in this case could be seen as a form of exit tax. (Contrast the position in *Daily Mail* (case 81/87), discussed at 21.10.) Similarly, national rules, which require particular legal formalities to be complied with (such as a minimum share capital), could equally deter the formation of a subsidiary. In *Sevic Systems* (case C–411/03), German rules which prevented the registration of an entity following a cross-border merger fell foul of Article 43 EC. Requirements in the Netherlands concerning the nationality of a board of directors were also held to be contrary to Article 43 (*Commission* v

Netherlands (case C–299/02)). Particular difficulties which arise in relation to companies and the establishment of subsidiaries and branch offices and the possible abuse of Community law rights are discussed below (2.10).

21.5.2 Right of access to the market

Central to the rights in Article 43 is the right to carry on business in another Member State, whether as a primary business (that is, moving and setting up your business entirely within the host Member State), or as a secondary establishment (that is, maintaining an establishment in one Member State and having other offices, whatever their legal form, in other Member States). Article 43 EC applies not just to the market, but also to the terms under which business may be carried on. For example, the recognition of qualifications might be seen as affecting the right to enter a profession or business, codes of conduct tend to control the way businesses are run. The central element of these rights is to be subject to the same conditions as apply to nationals of the host Member State.

Article 43, EC, together with Article 12 (ex 6) EC, may be invoked to challenge a national rule, whether in the form of a nationality or a residence requirement, which is discriminatory. For example, in an enforcement case against Italy (*Commission* v *Italy* (Freedom of Establishment) (case 168/85)), the ECJ confirmed that rules which required Italian nationality as a precondition for the exercise of certain activities – operation of pharmacies and journalism – were contrary to Article 43. This principle applies to both direct and indirect discrimination. The scope of carrying on business is broad as can be seen in *Steinhauser* v *City of Biarritz* (case 197/84). Steinhauser, a German, was a professional artist resident in Biarritz. He applied to the Biarritz authorities to rent a *'crampotte'*, a fisherman's hut of a type used locally for the exhibition and sale of works of art. He was refused on the grounds of his nationality; under the city's regulations *crampottes* could only be rented by persons of French nationality. He challenged that decision, and the ECJ held that freedom of establishment provided under the then Article 52 (now 43) related not only to the taking up of an activity as a self-employed person but also the pursuit of that activity in the widest sense to include, *inter alia*, the right to rent premises, to tender, and to qualify for licences and concessions. More recently, in *Hayes* v *Kronenberger GmbH* (case C–323/95), the requirement for non-national claimants to pay an amount into court as security for costs was held to be in breach of Article 12 EC as nationals of that Member State would not have to do so. The breadth of the potential scope of Article 43 was reiterated recently in *Sevic Systems* (case C–411/03). There, the ECJ held that 'the right of establishment covers all measures which permit or even merely facilitate access to another Member State and the pursuit of an economic activity in that State' (para. 18).

21.5.3 Social and other ancillary rights

In Chapter 20, the huge significance of the ECJ's jurisprudence relating to social rights under Regulation 1612/68 both for the worker and the worker's family was discussed. Regulation 1612/68 (now amended by Directive 2004/38/EC), being expressed in terms of the situation of employment, had no parallel for the self-employed, hence the special importance in this area of the principle of non-discrimination on the grounds of nationality. Where the self-employed or their families are 'lawfully resident' in a Member State, Article 12 EC (ex 6, originally 7 EEC) may, in certain circumstances, be invoked to ensure that they receive equal treatment in the form of 'social' or any other advantages with nationals of the host Member State. For example, in *Commission* v *Italy (re Housing Aid)* (case 63/86) the EC held that a cheap mortgage facility, available under Italian law only to Italian nationals, was in breach of the then Article 7 EEC (now Article 12 (ex 6) EC), even where such provision was an aspect of social law, and thus (it was implied) should be available on a basis of equality in Italy to EC nationals providing services *as long as the nature of the services provided was such as to require a permanent dwelling there*. To a certain extent the significance of the distinction between workers and the self-employed has diminished with the entry into force of Directive 2004/38/EC. Article 24 of Directive 2004/38/EC, which applies to all citizens of the Union and any family members, provides for equal treatment with host Member State nationals, subject to some limited exceptions for social assistance and maintenance grants for studies.

21.6 Test for the application of Article 43

The right of establishment has been described by the ECJ as one of the 'fundamental Community rights'. The principle on which these rights, including the right of establishment, are based is the principle of non-discrimination on grounds of nationality, whether arising from legislation, regulation or administrative practice. As we shall see, the jurisprudence of the ECJ has extended the circumstances to which Article 43 applies to those in which indirect discrimination occurs and, arguably, to circumstances in which non-discriminatory rules operate to create a barrier to the exercise of the right of establishment. There are thus parallels between the development of the right to establishment and the free movement of goods (Chapter 18) as well as the freedom to provide services (Chapter 22) and the free movement of capital (Chapter 16).

21.6.1 Discrimination: personal and professional

Community law on establishment, although concerned with the same rights and based on the same principles as the law relating to workers, also has much in common with the law concerning the free movement of goods. The provisions have a twofold purpose: to the extent that they confer on EC nationals who are self-employed *personal* rights, in the form of a right to enter and reside in a Member State and pursue activities, on a temporary or permanent basis, free from discrimination on the grounds of nationality, their purpose is akin to that of Article 39 EC; inasmuch as they seek to achieve freedom of establishment in a single, Community-wide market and pertain to the practice of a particular profession their goals are economic, more like those of Article 28 EC. While infringements of the former 'personal' rights normally take the form of discrimination on the grounds of nationality, which can rarely be justified, measures which interfere with the functioning of the single market by impeding the free movement of services and freedom of establishment will not necessarily be discriminatory. Where they apply equally to all persons who establish themselves or provide services in a particular Member State and are designed to protect some public interest, they may more readily be justified. This distinction between discriminatory and non-discriminatory measures and, implicitly, the difference in approach between personal and professional rights, are discussed in the following sections.

21.6.2 A discrimination-based test

The early case law of the ECJ on Article 43 tended to focus on personal rights and broad principles of discrimination on the grounds of nationality. In *Reyners* (case 2/74), the applicant was a Dutch national residing in Belgium. He had the necessary Belgian qualification in law for admission as an avocat, but was refused admission purely because he did not have Belgian nationality. The concept of discrimination was extended to include measures which discriminated indirectly against non-nationals such as the residence requirement in *Sotgiu* (case 152/73), which the Court had suggested might be 'objectively justified'. Direct discrimination could only be justified under Article 46 EC. This provision, expressed in terms of *personal* rights, allowing Member States to provide for 'special treatment' for foreign nationals, was very strictly construed.

21.6.3 Measures which apply 'without distinction'

It was thought initially that national regulatory rules and professional practices which were not discriminatory, which applied 'without distinction' to all persons established in a particular Member State, and which clearly served a useful purpose, could not be challenged under the Treaty (e.g., *Koestler* (case 15/78)). Although national regulatory rules might create barriers to the free movement of services and freedom of establishment they could only be removed by harmonisation, as provided under Articles 46 and 47 EC. Since harmonisation proved slow to achieve, some of these measures came to be challenged as 'discriminatory' and it was suggested that they would be permissible provided they could be objectively justified (see, e.g., *van Binsbergen* (case 33/74), albeit in the context of services, Chapter 22).

Although the approach to the freedom to provide services had adopted an approach based on whether or not there was a barrier to the cross-border provision of services rather than the existence of discrimination (indirect or direct), in the case of *Säger* v *Dennemeyer and Co. Ltd* (case C–76/90), as we shall see in Chapter 22, the scope of the ruling was not clear. In particular, did the approach extend to establishment? Arguably, the principles established in *Säger* v *Dennemeyer* appeared to apply only to the provision of services. Paragraph 13, suggested that:

> a Member State may not make the provision of services in its territory subject to the conditions required for establishment . . . and thereby deprive of all practical effectiveness the provisions of the Treaty whose object is, primarily, to provide services.

This implied that persons who established themselves in a Member State must comply with the conditions laid down in that State for its own nationals. Following *Gebhard* v *Consiglio dell'Ordine degli Avvocati e Procuratori di Milano* (case C–55/94) this appears not now to be the case. *Gebhard* involved a challenge by a German lawyer, a member of the Stuttgart Bar, to a decision by the Milan Bar Council prohibiting him from practising from chambers set up in Italy under the title 'avvocato'. He claimed the rules of the Milan Bar breached the then Articles 59 and/ or 52 (now 49 and 43).

The Court held that the possibility for a national of a Member State to exercise his right of establishment, and the conditions for the exercise of that right, had to be determined in the light of the activities which he intended to pursue on the territory of the host Member State. Where an activity was not subject to any rules in the host State, a national of another Member State was entitled to establish himself on the territory of the first State and pursue his activities there. On the other hand, 'Where the taking up and pursuit of a particular activity was subject to certain conditions in the host State a national of another Member State intending to pursue that activity must in principle comply with them'. However:

> National measures which hinder or make less attractive the exercise of fundamental freedoms guaranteed by the Treaty must fulfil four conditions: they must be applied in a non-discriminatory manner; they must be justified by imperative requirements in the general interest; they must be suitable for securing the attainment of the objective which they pursue; they must not go beyond what is necessary in order to attain it.

Member States must take into account the equivalence of diplomas and if necessary proceed to a comparison of the knowledge and qualifications required by their national rules and those of the person concerned. It was left to the national court to decide whether the rules in question were in fact justified.

Gebhard brought the rules relating to establishment broadly into line with those relating to services. It is worthy of note that conditions which simply 'hinder or make less attractive' the fundamental freedoms provided by Article 43 EC will now require justification. Note, however, that the ECJ did not use exactly the same wording in *Gebhard* as it did in *Säger* v *Dennemeyer*. The *Gebhard* test is, on a strict interpretation of the wording, less demanding than the 'prohibit or otherwise impede' threshold introduced in *Säger* v *Dennemeyer*. Whether this test is now to be applied to both establishment and services is not clear. In *Gebhard* the ECJ noted that both constitute 'fundamental freedoms provided by the Treaty'. It would thus make sense that the same test is applied to both articles. Nonetheless in subsequent case law on Article 49 EC, the ECJ has in the main applied the *Säger* test and has not adopted that set out in *Gebhard*. In the more recent *Caixa Bank France* (case C–442/ 02), the ECJ adopted a slightly different test in respect of the freedom of establishment, stating that measures which 'prohibit, impede or render less attractive' the exercise of freedom of establishment are restrictions for the purposes of Article 43. This seems to blend the *Säger* and *Gebhard* tests, arguably requiring very little in the way of an impediment to freedom of establishment. Whether there is any difference between the approaches under Article 43 and 49 in the end result in practice is, in any event, debatable. Indeed, since the emphasis in both cases is on justification for the rules in terms of the *activity undertaken* rather than on the burden imposed on the 'guest' undertaking, it is possible that the result in both cases would be the same, that is, the national rule will be found to have triggered the application of either Article 43 or Article 49.

Following *Caixa Bank* (case C–442/02), amongst other cases, it will be very easy to trigger Article 43. In *Caixa Bank*, a French rule prohibited a certain type of account from being marketed in France. The ECJ argued that the rule hindered subsidiaries of foreign banks by depriving them of the possibility of 'competing more effectively' against established banks because the established banks 'have an extensive network of branches and therefore greater opportunities . . . for raising capital from the public' (para. 13). Implicitly the ECJ seems to suggest that the incoming companies need to be allowed to provide a greater range of services to give them a competitive edge. In this, the ECJ departed from the Opinion of the Advocate-General who noted that the effect of the national measures in question would merely be to 'reduce the economic attractiveness' of carrying on the activity regulated. According to the Advocate-General, such an interpretation would upset the balance of powers between the regulatory powers of the Member States and the Community. He noted that the Community does not have general regulatory powers, such power falling to the Member States subject to the overriding prohibition on discrimination and obstacles to establishment. Further, the impact of such an approach would be de-regulatory as it would enable economic operators to oppose any national measure because that measure could 'in the final analysis narrow profit margins'. As the Advocate-General suggested, this would result in a view of the Treaty freedoms which operated 'not in order to create an internal market in which conditions are similar to those of a single market and where operators can move freely, but in order to establish a market without rules' (*Caixa Bank*, Opinion, paras 58–63). Nonetheless, this is precisely the route the ECJ has seemed to take. As, in the final analysis, any regulatory rule has the effect of making a business less desirable or profitable than if those rules were not in place, the consequence seems to be that any attempt at regulation is capable of being challenged on this approach.

In this, however, the ECJ seems to be just following its previous jurisprudence. In *Pfeiffer Grosshandel* (case C–255/97), the ECJ held that, in principle, Austrian rules to safeguard trade names against the risk of confusion fell within Article 43. The case concerned a prohibition on a subsidiary of a German company using a trade name already used in Germany by the parent company but which was similar to the trade name of an Austrian competitor. The ECJ held that the Austrian rule required the applicants to 'adjust the presentation of the business they operate according to the place of establishment' (para. 20) and therefore fell within Article 43. Note that the rules in question do not directly relate to the establishment or operation of a business, but to its name, emphasising the width of circumstances in which Article 43 can apply (note similarly the earlier case of *Konstantinidis* (case C–168/91)).

The trend as regards Article 43 EC therefore seems to be towards a *Dassonville*-type test applied in all circumstances when Article 43 is relevant. Certainly, it seems that the ECJ is taking the *Gebhard* approach in circumstances other than those relating to professional conduct or qualifications, as we can see from *Caixa Bank* and *Pfeiffer Grosshandel*. In *Sodemare SA v Regione Lombardia* (case C–70/95) the ECJ adopted a comparable approach, although, on the facts, it found that the rules were justified. Thus, the Italian authorities were entitled to limit the involvement of the private sector in old people's homes to non-profit-making bodies. Ironically this is occurring at a time when the ECJ in *Keck* (cases C–267 & 268/91) and subsequent cases appears to be adopting a more lenient approach to some indistinctly applicable rules in the context of claims concerning goods under Article 28 EC (see *De Agostini* (cases C–34–6/98) and Chapter 18). Indeed, the Advocate-General in *Caixa Bank* considered the possibility of limiting Article 43 in a way similar to that adopted in *Keck* and in *Graf* (case C–190/98) in relation to workers (discussed in Chapter 20); requiring that those measures which have an effect which is too uncertain and indirect should not be caught by Article 43. It is striking that the ECJ did not even consider this possibility, thus possibly opening a rift between the case law in this regard on establishment with that concerning goods and workers.

21.7 A rule of reason?

The right of establishment provided under Article 43 EC is not absolute. Apart from the express derogations of Articles 45 and 46 EC, it is subject to one important limitation. The right to equality of opportunity provided by Articles 43(2) can only be exercised 'under the conditions laid down for its own nationals by the law of the country where such establishment is effected' (Article 43(2) EC).

The difficulty for non-nationals seeking to establish themselves or provide services in another Member State is that they may not be able to satisfy the conditions laid down in that Member State for the practice of the particular trade or profession which they wish to exercise. The relevant conditions are those prescribed by trade or professional bodies, normally reinforced by law, relating to:

(a) the education and training required for qualification for the job, and

(b) rules of professional conduct.

Both of these vary greatly in scope and content and quality from Member State to Member State. The need to comply with these conditions thus provided a potent barrier to freedom of movement for the self-employed; it also hindered the free movement of workers, since they too may wish to work as employees in a trade or profession which is subject to regulation at national level.

These types of rule were likely to be caught by Article 43, even prior to *Gebhard*. Equally, striking such measures down would be unlikely to be in the public interest. The ECJ seemed aware of the problem even in the relatively early jurisprudence and, as we have seen in *Gebhard*, discussed above, introduced what might be called a 'rule of reason'. Thus, national rules which aim at a legitimate objective will not be struck down under Article 43 if they satisfy a four-stage test:

(1) they apply in a non-discriminatory manner;

(2) they are justified by overriding reasons in the general interest;

(3) they are suitable for obtaining that objective; and

(4) they do not go beyond what is necessary to attain that objective.

This test, or the last three elements of it, is sometimes referred to as a proportionality test. It is important to emphasise that it is a cumulative test; all elements must be satisfied for a national rule which falls within the *Gebhard* test to be protected.

Although the possible categories of justification are not closed (by contrast to those listed in the Treaty), the scope of this rule is limited in practice by the rigour of the proportionality review.

Some national rules, particularly those relating to conduct of professions and qualifications, might survive the application of Article 43 in the interests of protecting the public from unqualified practitioners. The disadvantage is, of course, that the European market could remain segmented. The answer to this particular problem, as we have seen in Chapter 15, is to replace national regulations with European rules, otherwise known as harmonisation.

The other difficulty in this area concerns the boundary between the discriminatory and non-discriminatory measures. It has been suggested that the ECJ has not always been clear as to whether measures are discriminatory or not, a problem that may be exacerbated by the use of an obstacle-based test rather than one that looks at the notion of discrimination, whether direct or indirect. In *Marks and Spencer*, for example, the measure could be categorised as discriminatory, as different rules applied depending on place of establishment. Nonetheless, the ECJ went on to consider the possible justifications for the rule and did not limit itself to the grounds set out in the express Treaty provisions derogating from the right of free movement. In this, we can see reflections of the difficulties encountered by the ECJ in a number of cases concerning the free movement of goods, specifically in relation to rules designed to protect the environment. In both cases, there have been suggestions from the Advocates-General that the distinction between discriminatory and non-discriminatory rules should be abandoned, but to no avail. Of course, the tax cases involving companies can be problematic because of the uncertainties surrounding the determination of the seat of the company (see 21.10). Analyses based on place of residence, which the ECJ has tended to view as indirect discrimination in the context of individuals (see 21.5.2) become more complex in this context (cf. *RBS* (case C–311/97), *Lankhorst-Hohorst GmbH* (case C–240/00); see also *Danner* (case C–136/00).

21.8 Harmonisation

21.8.1 The early period

The Treaty provided for the abolition of existing restrictions on freedom of establishment (and freedom to provide services) to be achieved in progressive stages during a transitional period. During the first stage the Council, acting on a proposal from the Commission, was to draw up a general programme on the abolition of restrictions on freedom of establishment (former Article 53, which was deleted by the ToA) and on the freedom to provide services (Article 52 (ex 63) EC). In addition these institutions were required, during the first stage, to 'issue Directives for the mutual recognition of diplomas, certificates and other evidence of formal qualifications' (Article 47(1) (ex 57(1) EC) and to 'issue Directives for the coordination of the provisions laid down by law, regulation or administrative action in Member States concerning the taking up and pursuit of activities as self-employed persons' (Article 47 (ex 57(2))).

The general programmes were adopted in 1961 (JO 1962, 36, 32). Although not binding, they provide valuable guidelines in the interpretation of the Treaty, and have been invoked on a number of occasions by the ECJ (e.g., *Steinhauser* (case 197/84)). The issuing of directives under Article 47(1) and (2) proved a more difficult task. National professional bodies were understandably reluctant to compromise on long-established principles and practices, and although many directives passed in areas ranging from wholesaling to hairdressing to medicine, progress was slow. Notably, the Architects' Directive alone took 17 years to pass.

21.8.2 Mutual recognition

Because of the problems outlined above, and because progress on harmonisation for the purpose of mutual recognition of qualifications had been so slow, the Community decided on a new approach. Instead of attempting to harmonise by profession, known as the sectoral or 'vertical' aproach, the Commission adopted a general or 'horizontal' approach, based not on harmonisation but on the mutual recognition of qualifications. This applied not just to individual professions but to all areas of activity for which a higher education diploma was required. Directive 89/48 ([1989] OJ L19/16), based on these principles, was approved in December 1988. The Council then agreed a second directive, to supplement the first, this time dealing with secondary education (Council Directive 92/51/EEC ([1992] OJ L209/25). This directive was also based on the principle of mutual recognition. Both directives have been amended a number of times since they were first enacted, but the basic principles remain, and are discussed below.

21.8.3 Other harmonising measures

It should be noted that the area of qualifications and access to professions are not the only ones resulting in Community measures. Article 47(2) deals with access to professions. It also empowers the institutions to take measures to ensure the coordination of national laws relating to the taking up and pursuit of activities as self-employed persons. This is discussed further in Chapter 22 and in the general chapter on harmonisation.

21.9 Professional qualifications

21.9.1 Jurisprudence of the ECJ

We have seen that professional qualifications in particular have given rise to barriers to the free movement of self-employed persons and that the legislative process for directives in this area was initially slow. It fell to the ECJ to cover the gap in protection offered. A starting point was holding that both Articles 43 and 49 had direct effect. Further, even though directives have not been passed ensuring mutual recognition of diplomas, certificates and other evidence of formal qualifications in a particular trade or profession, the EC has repeatedly held that it is discriminatory, in breach of Article 43, as well as Articles 49 and 50, together with Article 12 EC to refuse permission to practise to a person whose qualifications have been recognised as equivalent to those required in the State in which he seeks to practise.

In *Thieffry* v *Conseil de l'Ordre des Advocats à la Cour de Paris* (case 71/76) the Court held that the French Bar Council could not refuse to allow Thieffry, a Belgian national with a Belgian law degree, to undertake practical training for the French bar, as his Belgian degree had been recognised by the University of Paris and he had acquired a qualifying certificate in France for the profession of *avocat*. Similarly, in *Patrick* v *Ministre des Affaires Culturelles* (case 11/77) the Court held that Patrick, an Englishman, who had trained as an architect in England, was entitled to invoke Articles 43 and 12 to practise architecture in France, since, although no diplomatic convention ensuring recognition had been agreed, as was required by French law, and no EC directives relating to architects had at that time been passed, his English qualifications had been recognised as equivalent to the corresponding French degree under a Ministerial Decree of 1964.

Where a directive has been issued for the mutual recognition or harmonization of qualifications in a particular profession that profession may no longer insist on compliance with its own requirements by persons who have qualified in another Member State according to the terms of the directive. In *Broekmeulen* (case 246/80) the Dutch General Practitioners' Committee was unable to refuse Broekmeulen permission to practise as a GP in Holland even though he had qualified as a GP in Belgium, where it was not necessary to complete the three years' specialised training required for GPs in Holland. The EC Directive 75/362 relating to training for GPs did not require GPs to undergo training additional to their original (three-year) qualification. Parties may not, however, claim freedom of establishment under Article 43 EC (or freedom to provide services under Article 49) in reliance on a directive issued under Article 47 until the period provided for its implementation has expired (*Auer* (case 136/78), or, *a fortiori*, where they do not fall within the terms of the directive (*Dreessen* v *Conseil National de l'Ordre des Architectes* (case C–447/93)).

Until relatively recently, where qualifications obtained in a particular Member State have *not* been subject to harmonisation or recognised in another Member State, it would not have been discriminatory, and therefore not prima facie in breach of EC law, for a State or a professional body to refuse a person possessing these qualifications permission to practise. In *Arantis* v *Land Berlin* (case C–164/94), however, the ECJ held that where a profession was not regulated by an EC directive, the then Articles 6 and 52 (now 12 and 43) EC required the authorities in a host Member State to take into account an individual's qualifications and other relevant experience acquired in the home State. In doing so, the ECJ extended its ruling in *Vlassopoulou* (case C–340/89), which is discussed below in relation to regulated professions, to unregulated professions. In both *Arantis* and *Vlassapoulou* (and arguably *Thieffry*), we can see the ECJ adopting an approach that is based on the idea of mutual recognition, that is, a recognition that in principle the training and experience gained throughout all Member States should be acceptable in other Member States and should therefore be taken into account when assessing an individual's qualifications and experience. What is acceptable in one Member State, broadly speaking, is acceptable in all. This will have a significant effect in blocking any gaps in the protection afforded to those with EC qualifications which are not covered by an EC directive.

21.9.2 **The directives**

The Mutual Recognition Diplomas Directive applies only to regulated professional activities, although it is sufficient if they are regulated in only one State in the Community. It does not attempt to modify the rules applicable to particular professions in individual Member States, nor does it apply to professions which were already subject to separate directives providing for the mutual recognition of diplomas. Like other harmonisation directives concerning qualifications it will apply to workers as well as the self-employed.

Although the concept of a regulated activity might seem clear, it has not been unproblematic. In *Arantis* (case C–164/94), the ECJ defined the term as meaning that the professional activity in question is governed by laws, regulations or administrative provisions that create a system under which that professional activity is expressly reserved for those who fulfil certain conditions and access is prohibited to those who do not fulfil them. It now seems that the profession must be a separate activity from other professions. This can be seen in *Morgenbesser* (case C–313/01), who sought to rely on her French diploma in law to be registered as a practicante in Italy. Although the ECJ accepted that there was a system which denied precluded persons not fulfilling certain criteria from acting as practicante, the ECJ also noted that the activities carried out as a practicante formed the practical part of the training to become an avvocato. The activity of practicante could not therefore be considered as a separate regulated activity within Directive 89/48.

The starting point for the principle of mutual recognition is a higher education diploma awarded on completion of professional education and training of at least three years' duration, or the equivalent period part-time. Where, in the host State, the taking up and pursuit of a regulated profession is subject to the possession of a diploma, the competent authority of that State may not refuse to authorise a national of a Member State to take up and pursue that profession on the same conditions as apply to its own nationals, provided the applicant holds a diploma required in another State for the pursuit of the profession in question, *or* has pursued that profession for at least two years in a State which does not regulate that profession (Article 3). Although this gives an individual holding a diploma certain rights, the operation of mutual recognition is not automatic (*Morgenbesser* (case C–313/01), para. 44); Member States may review the qualifications and, indeed, subsequent articles in the directive provide exceptions to the general principle of mutual recognition.

Where the applicant's education and training is at least one year shorter than that which is required by the host State, or where there is a shortfall in the period of supervised practice required by the host State, the applicant may be required to provide *evidence of professional experience*. This may not exceed the shortfall in supervised practice, nor twice the shortfall in duration of education and training, required by the host State; in any event, it may not exceed four years (Article 4(1)(a)).

The host State may also require an *adaptation period* not exceeding three years:

(a) where matters covered by the applicant's education and training differ substantially from those covered by that of the State; or

(b) where the activities regulated in the host State are not regulated in the applicant's State of origin; or

(c) where the profession regulated in the host State comprises activities which are not pursued in the State from which the applicant originates,

provided, in the latter two situations, the difference corresponds to *specific* education and training required in the host State and covers matters which differ *substantially* from those covered by the evidence of formal qualification (Article 4(1)(b)).

Instead of the adaptation period the applicant may opt for an aptitude test. However, for professions whose practice requires precise knowledge of national law and in which the giving of advice on national law is an essential and constant aspect of that activity, a State may stipulate either an adaptation period or an aptitude test (Article 4(1)(b)).

The requirements of periods of professional experience *and* adaptation cannot be applied cumulatively. The total period cannot exceed four years.

In addition, the host Member State may allow an applicant to undertake in the host State, on a basis of equivalence, that part of his training which consists of supervised professional practice (Article 5).

Member States were required to implement the Directive by 4 January 1991. Provisions which are sufficiently clear, precise and unconditional, were directly effective from that date, at least against a 'public' body, an agency of the State (see Chapter 5). Since professional bodies normally operate subject to statutory authorisation and control, it is submitted that this factor should constitute a sufficiently 'public' element for the purposes of the enforcement of the directive. The directive thus represented a significant breakthrough, removing many of the existing and substantial barriers to the free movement of the employed and the self-employed.

Directive 89/48 was supplemented by Directive 92/51, which applies the same principle of mutual recognition to diplomas and certificates awarded after a post secondary education course of at least one year's duration, whether or not they are complemented by professional training and experience. There is now a third general directive, Directive 99/42/EC, which extends the mutual recognition principle to industrial and professional sectors which had previously been covered by vertical directives. Note that the training of lawyers remains subject to specific legislation: specifically the Lawyers' Directive, Directive 98/5/EC. The effect of the directives is that the training of industrial and professional activities is not regulated at Community level. Instead, the directives focus on the assessment of the 'qualified' individual. Although this has removed highly complex and contentious negotiations at the legislative level, there is a disadvantage. As with the position under Directive 89/48, the right is not to automatic recognition of an individual's professional status, but the right of that individual to have his or her case considered by the competent authorities of the host Member State.

Even in areas not covered, or not yet covered, by these directives, the Court has held that professional bodies of a Member State, in deciding whether to allow persons who do not satisfy their own State's professional requirements, must take into account the applicant's qualification and compare them with the 'home' requirements, in order to assess whether they are in fact equivalent. Applicants are entitled to be given reasons for decisions, and must have an opportunity to challenge them in judicial proceedings (*Vlassopoulou* v *Ministerium für Justiz* (case C–340/89)). There is now a consistent line of authority to this effect.

A person who has qualified in a non-Member State cannot invoke either the directives or the Community principle of mutual recognition even though the qualification is recognised in a *particular* Member State and the person has been practising the profession *within that State*: the only entitlement is to practise *in that State* (*Tawil-Albertini* v *Ministre des Affaires Sociales* (case C–154/93)). However, if a Member State chooses to recognise such a qualification, it must take into account practical training or professional experience obtained in other Member States in order to determine whether the requisite national training period has been fulfilled (*Haim* v *Kassenzahnärtzliche Vereinigung Nordrhein* (cases C–319/92; C–424/97)). The Council issued a recommendation encouraging Member States to recognise diplomas and other evidence of formal qualifications obtained by Community nationals in non-Member States ([1989] OJ L19/24). *Haim* can be seen as imposing on Member States the obligation to undertake a *Vlassapoulou* style comparison of experience in such circumstances. *Hocsman* (case C–238/98) extended the scope of this obligation. Crucially in *Hocsman*, the ECJ stated that Member States were under an obligation to take into account the qualifications obtained elsewhere, as well as any practical experience. This means that the conditional nature of the obligation found in *Haim*, the obligation only arising where a Member State had recognised a qualification, has effectively been removed.

21.10 Establishment and companies

21.10.1 General

Despite the apparent simplicity of Article 48, in practice it has been rather difficult for companies to move around the Union. Companies are entities created by domestic law and only have legal capacity in accordance with these rules. Moving into another jurisdiction might therefore require a company to be wound up in its state of origin, and re-formed in the host Member State. Although Article 293 EC provides a legal basis for the Member States to agree a mechanism for the transfer of companies between them, the only attempt to do so (in 1968) was unsuccessful. Note, therefore, the potential impact that Article 43, which can in principle apply here, might have on the rules of the Member States regarding company formation.

The main problem is that the Member States apply different rules for identifying which legal system is applicable to a company. There are two main approaches to this issue. One possibility is to use the 'incorporation' doctrine, according to which the location of the company's registered office determines the applicable law. On this theory, the applicable law will be that of the country of incorporation. The second theory is the 'real seat' doctrine (or siege reel). Applying the real seat doctrine, a company is subject to the law of the jurisdiction where its head office or central management is based, and this requires that the company's registered office needs to be located in the same jurisdiction. Quite clearly, the different theories will have an impact on the company law applicable, and therefore will affect the procedures and regulations with which a company will need to comply when running its business. The ECJ has been given a number of opportunities to consider the compatibility of these doctrines with EC law, specifically Article 43, but has not been consistent.

In *R v HM Treasury and Commissioners of Inland Revenue, ex parte Daily Mail and General Trust PLC* (case 81/87), a company incorporated under the laws of England and Wales sought to move its central management to the Netherlands, whilst retaining its status as a British company. The Treasury demanded that certain transactions had to occur before it would permit the move. The company argued that this was a restriction on its right of establishment under Article 43. The ECJ held that there was no right under Article 43 for a company to move its head office to another Member State, and the home Member State could impose conditions on a company seeking to leave its jurisdiction.

Daily Mail would seem to suggest that, contrary to the position as regards individuals (discussed at 21.5.1), some restrictions on the movements of companies would not be affected by Article 43 EC. *Daily Mail* has been criticised and it now seems that while Article 43 does not give a company the unrestricted right to maintain its head office in one Member State whilst remaining incorporated under the laws of another, obstacles to its freedom to move aspects of its business through the establishment of a branch, subsidiary or agency will be prohibited by Article 43 unless justified. In *X & Y* (case C–436/00), a Swedish rule which limited certain tax concessions to companies with subsidiaries in Sweden was held to fall foul of Article 43 (see also *Marks & Spencer* (case C–446/03)).

21.10.2 Regulatory competition: identifying the nationality of a company

We have seen in the examples given at 21.5.1 of rules which impede companies' freedom of establishment that there are significant differences in the Member States' individual approaches to company formation and regulation. It might be easier for someone (whether natural or legal) who wishes to trade in one Member State to establish a company in another Member State and rely on the right to secondary establishment contained in Article 43 in order to set up business in the original, target Member State. The question is whether this is a legitimate use of freedom of establishment, or whether it constitutes an abuse of Community law. Early case law in relation to services (discussed in Chapter 22) which arose when individuals and companies were formally established in one Member State but provided services to another constituted an abuse. Indeed in *TV 10* (case C–23/93), in which a company established itself in one Member State and broadcast into another Member State, the Netherlands, hoping to avoid the Dutch limitations on broadcast advertising, the ECJ adopted a broad interpretation of the concept of establishment and decided that the company involved was actually established in the Netherlands. On this basis, the Dutch rules were applicable to the broadcaster. The ECJ here seems to be identifying establishment by reference to a form of the 'real seat' doctrine. Should the same principles be applied to the establishment of a business as to the regulation of its business activities?

In *Centros*, a private limited company registered in the UK but with two Danish shareholders sought to establish a branch in Denmark. At the time, the company had not traded in the UK. In light of the Danish connection (and the lack of any British business activity), the Danish registrar refused to register the branch because he regarded Centros as a Danish company. Crucially, Centros had failed to comply with a minimum capital rule imposed under Danish law but with no equivalent under the English system. The ECJ held that this was a breach of Article 43 EC which could not be justified. The ECJ held:

> the fact that a national of a Member State who wishes to set up a company chooses to form it in the Member State whose rules of company law seem to him the least restrictive and to set up branches in other Member States cannot, in itself, constitute an abuse of the right of establishment. The right to form a company in accordance with the law of a Member State and to set up branches in other Member States is inherent in the exercise, in a single market, of the freedom of establishment guaranteed by the Treaty (para. 27).

Setting up a company in one Member State and then exercising the right to set up a secondary establishment was not an abuse of the right of establishment, even though it had the effect of circumventing incorporation requirements in the host Member State. The decision was interpreted as holding that in EC law, the jurisdiction where the registered office was based would be the law applicable to the company. Consequently, the 'real seat' doctrine might be incompatible with Article 43 EC.

A similar issue arose in *Überseering BV v Nordic Construction Company Baumanagement GmBH* (case C–208/00). There, a Dutch company owned by German shareholders sought to take legal action in the German courts. German law determined a company's legal capacity by reference to its real seat. Since the company had moved its centre of administration to Germany the German courts found its real seat to be in Germany. Überseering was formally incorporated in the Netherlands, and so complied with that State's rules of incorporation rather than German rules. As the company did not comply with German rules the German court held that it was not properly incorporated and therefore did not have the capacity to take legal action. The ECJ held that because the company had been validly incorporated in the Netherlands, and had not lost this status, the German court's refusal to recognise its legal capacity fell within Article 43 and was not on the facts justified. We might suggest that there are similarities here with the *Daily Mail* case. The ECJ distinguished the two cases on the facts (implicitly reaffirming *Daily Mail*). Whilst the *Daily Mail* had sought to rely on Article 43 against its state of incorporation when it sought to emigrate, *Überseering* concerned the rights of an immigrating company against the host Member State. According to the ECJ '[t]he requirement of reincorporation of the same company in Germany is therefore tantamount to outright negation of freedom of establishment' (paras 80–81). In its consideration of justification, the ECJ also seemed to suggest that although restrictions on establishment might be open to justification, outright prohibition on secondary establishment never could. Articles 43 and 48 EC therefore require a host Member State to recognise the legal capacity of a company under the law of its State of incorporation. This seems to be yet another blow to the 'real seat' doctrine.

Most recently, in *Chamber of Commerce Amsterdam v Inspire Art Ltd* (case C–167/01), Dutch law sought to impose a number of restrictions on companies incorporated in a Member State other than the Netherlands, but which were predominantly or exclusively active in the Netherlands. Inspire Art was incorporated under the laws of England and Wales, but had a Dutch sole director. It established a branch in

Amsterdam without complying with the Dutch formalities for 'formally foreign' companies and the competent Dutch authorities brought an action against Inspire Art as a consequence. The ECJ held that insofar as Dutch law gave effect to certain company law directives, the rules were compatible with Article 43 EC, unless foreign companies were treated differently with regard to penalties for non-compliance. Any rules going beyond the directives had to be compatible with the EC Treaty. The additional Dutch rules were caught by Article 43 EC and not justifiable on the facts, and therefore infringed EC law. Once again, the ECJ seems to have favoured the incorporation doctrine over the real seat theory. It should be noted, however, that in these cases the ECJ has refrained from addressing the question directly. It thus remains unclear whether the ECJ intends to eradicate the real seat doctrine in favour of the incorporation theory or not. This allows a certain room for manoeuvre in assessing the precise scope and impact of the jurisprudence. What remains clear is that Member States will not be able to impose restrictions on companies formed elsewhere, even 'pseudo-foreign' companies without very good (and proportionate) reason.

21.11 Conclusions

The scope of Article 43 is broad, covering a wide range of areas from the purely professional, such as access to economic activity, to the personal, such as family rights of residence. Central to the law in this area is the change from a discrimination-based approach for determining when there has been a violation of Article 43, to one based on hindrance or disincentive. Recent case law has confirmed the ease with which Article 43 can be triggered and this approach, which broadly mirrors that taken in relation to goods, applies across all aspects of the freedom of establishment. Company law has proved to raise particular problems, given both the national nature of company laws and the way in which companies (or groups of companies) can reside in more than one Member State at a time. Perhaps of particular significance is the impact of the ECJ's jurisprudence on Member States' tax systems, still formally an area of exclusive Member State competence.

FURTHER READING

See also reading for Chapters 20, 22 and 24.

Daniele, L., 'Non-discriminatory Restrictions to the Free Movement of Persons' (1997) 22 EL Rev 191.

Drury, R., 'The "Delaware syndrome": European fears and reactions' (2005) Nov. JBL 709.

Edward, D., 'Establishment and Services: an Analysis of the Insurance Cases' (1987) 12 EL Rev 231.

Edwards, V., EC Company Law (OUP, 1999).

Lonbay, J., 'Education and Law: the Community Context' (1989) 14 EL Rev 363.

Looijestijn-Clearie, A., '*Centros Ltd* – A Complete U-Turn in the Right of Establishment for Companies?' (2000) 49 ICLQ 621.

O'Brien, M., 'Company Taxation, State Aid and Fundamental Freedoms: Is the Next Step Enhanced Co-operation?' (2005) 30(2) EL Rev 209.

Roth, W-H., 'From *Centros* to *Veberseering*: Free Movement of Companies, Private International Law and Community Law' (2003) 52 ICLQ 177.

22

Freedom to provide services; freedom to
receive services

22.1 Introduction

We have seen in Chapter 21 that in many situations there are similarities between
the freedom of establishment (Article 43 (ex 52)) and the freedom to provide services (Article 49 (ex 59)). Similar themes as were found in relation to Article 43, as
well as to Article 39, underpin the freedom to provide services. In general the rights
have been interpreted widely. We can also see parallels in the development of the
case law, notably a move from a discrimination-based test for the application of
Article 49 to one focusing on access to the market, or on questions of obstacles to
trade. A central question in this regard concerns the extent to which Member States
must take into account home Member State regulation when seeking to regulate
cross-border service providers. This case law then raises issues about regulatory
competition and the deregulatory impact of the freedom to provides services, as
with the other freedoms. As is the case with establishment, the right to provide
(and receive) services may be exercised by companies. In this there is a dichotomy
in the case law between the ancillary rights supported by citizenship and the
business rights of companies; again, this is a theme common to the jurisprudence
on establishment.

Although services and establishment are often considered together, the scope
of services is wider than just being a temporary form of establishment. Article 49
comes into play not just when people move to provide services, but also when they
move to receive them. This line of case law, while providing still further rights for
the migrant individual, has had a great impact on the scope of the Member States
to organise certain sectors of public services. Equally, services may be provided
cross-border without anyone physically moving. In this context there are perhaps
closer parallels between the free movement of goods and the freedom to provide
services than there are between establishment and services. Services in this context
may be provided in more than one Member State simultaneously, raising questions
not only about which Member State should have the right or responsibility to
regulate the service provider, but also about the dangers of abuse of Community
law rights to avoid national regulation.

This chapter looks at services and specifically the issues that are particularly
relevant to the services (as opposed to the establishment) sector. After it defines the
scope of services, it outlines the development of the right and the test used to
determine when Article 49 comes into play. It then looks at the particular problem
areas, right to receive (public) services and the abuse of Community law rights to
evade national regulation.

22.2 Scope of the freedom to provide services

22.2.1 The Freedom to provide services

Articles 49 (and 50(3), as amended by the ToA, provide:

> Within the framework of the provisions set out below, restrictions on freedom to provide services within the Community shall be prohibited in respect of nationals of Member States who are established in a State of the Community other than that of the person for whom the services are intended (Article 49).
>
> Without prejudice to the provisions of the Chapter relating to the right of establishment [Chapter 2], the person providing a service may, in order to do so, temporarily pursue his activity in the State where the service is provided, under the same conditions as are imposed by that State on its own nationals (Article 50(3)).

The provision is essentially replicated in Article III–144 of the Constitution.

22.2.2 Enforcing the rights

As we have seen with the right of establishment, it was originally thought that the right to provide services provided under Article 49 was conditional on the issuing of directives under Article 47(1) and (2) (ex 57(1) and (2)). The direct effect of Article 49 was doubted until the ECJ in *van Binsbergen* (case 33/74), applying a similar line of reasoning to that in *Reyners* (case 2/74, discussed at Chapter 21), confirmed that the enactment of directives was not a precondition to the exercise of the freedom to provide services by individuals.

Article 49 seems to apply horizontally as well as vertically. Thus Article 49 affects public bodies as well as legally recognised professional bodies: *Walrave v Association Union Cycliste Internationale* (case 36/74). Following *Angonese* (see Chapter 20), it now seems that Article 49 will apply as against private parties.

22.2.3 Limitations

The freedom to provide services, like the free movement of workers and the freedom of establishment, is subject to derogation on the grounds of 'public policy, public security or public health' (Article 55 EC, applying Article 46 EC to services). Under these articles Member States 'may provide for special treatment for foreign nationals'. This is implemented in terms of 'measures concerning the movement and residence of foreign nationals'. These terms were originally fleshed out in respect of individuals by Directive 64/221, now repealed and replaced by Directive 2004/38/EC, Articles 27–33 (see Chapter 23). The position of legal entities will be dealt with under the Treaty provision itself. In both situations, the doctrine of proportionality has been key in limiting the scope of Member States' actions.

The freedom to provide services is expressed not to apply to 'activities which in that State are connected, even occasionally, with the exercise of official authority' (Article 55 EC applying Article 45 to services). This derogation has been considered in some detail in the context of Article 39(4) (ex 48(4)) relating to workers.

Although phrased in slightly different language from Article 39(4), the principles applicable to workers will apply equally to the services provisions. As in the case of workers, the derogation has been given the narrowest scope.

22.3 Definition of services

22.3.1 General

'Services' are defined as those 'normally provided for remuneration, insofar as they are not governed by the provisions relating to freedom of movement for goods, capital and persons' (Article 50(1) (ex 60(1)) EC). Services in the field of transport are 'governed by the provisions of the Title [Part Two, Title IV] relating to transport' (Article 51 (ex 61) EC). The liberalisation of banking and insurance services connected with movements of capital was to be effected 'step by step with the progressive liberalisation of movement of capital' although the ToA removed the word 'progressive' from this article. Article 50 EC provides a non-exhaustive list of examples of services. There are a number of key elements in identifying a service for the purposes of Article 49 EC.

22.3.2 Types of activity caught

Although Article 50 provides a list of services that are definitely caught by Article 49, *Society for the Protection of Unborn Children Ltd* v *Grogan* (case C–159/90), discussed below, illustrates that no area of economic activity in principle falls outside the Treaty, no matter what its moral, cultural or ethical status. Article 49 will, in theory, only apply if none of the other freedoms do, that is, it is a catch-all or fall-back provision, and provided the service does not fall within the Treaty provisions dealing with transport.

Because of the special nature of services, lending themselves to promotion and even provision via modern 'distance' methods of communication, a service can be deemed to 'move' within the Community without either the provider or the recipient moving across national borders. Thus, Article 49 can be used to regulate either the provider, or the service itself. In *Alpine Investments BV* v *Minister van Financiën* (case C–384/93) a Dutch prohibition on 'cold calling' (the soliciting of business by telephone), by providers of financial advice established in The Netherlands, was held to constitute a barrier to the free provision of services contrary to the then Article 59 (now 49) EC (although it was found on the facts to be justified). Restrictions on cross-border advertising relating to the distribution of goods will be dealt with under the free movement of goods provisions of Article 28 (ex 30) (*Leclerc-Siplec* v *TF1 Publicité SA* (case C–412/93), decided on *Keck* principles, see Chapter 18) although in some instances service-related issues might also arise. The broad scope of the right means that it can be relied on against both host and home Member State and, as *Alpine Investments* shows, in an 'export' situation as well as when the services are being imported.

Finally, the right to provide services includes the right to receive (*Luisi and Carbonne* (cases 286/82 and 26/83)). This aspect of the rights is discussed further below at 22.10.

22.3.3 **Economic activity**

To be caught by Article 49, the activity must be an economic activity. In *Deliège* (joined cases C–51/96 and C–191/97), the ECJ borrowed the tests from *Levin* (case 53/81) and *Steymann* (case 196/87) in relation to workers (see Chapter 20) to clarify the concept of economic activity. The test derived is that the services performed must be genuine and effective and not marginal and ancillary. In *Deliège*, we can see that the ECJ has found this requirement to be satisfied quite easily. *Deliège* concerned the case of an amateur athlete. In considering whether or not economic activity was involved, the ECJ argued:

> that sporting activities and, in particular, a high-ranking athlete's participation in an international competition are capable of involving the provision of a number of separate, but closely related, services which may fall within the scope of Article 59 [now 49] of the Treaty even if some of those services are not paid for by those for whom they are performed.

In developing its earlier jurisprudence on television broadcasting (see case 352/85 *Bond van Adverteerders and Others* v *Netherlands State*, para. 16), the ECJ seems almost to be saying that there is money involved somewhere, so Article 49 must be engaged. Note that it also seems that it does not matter whether remuneration is found in the particular case under consideration, provided the type of service is such that it is usually provided for remuneration (see, e.g., *Freskot* (case C–355/00), para. 54, but note the difficulties with public services discussed at 22.10.4). Further, it does not matter whether an activity is profitable or not if there is an intention to 'make a cash profit' (*ANOMAR* (case C–6/01), para. 47).

Although the ECJ has repeatedly held that the basic Treaty freedoms must be interpreted widely, there are limits. In *Society for the Protection of Unborn Children Ltd* v *Grogan* (case C–159/90), the provision of information, contrary to the Irish constitution, about abortion clinics in other Member States by officers of a students' union was held not to receive the protection of Article 49. Although abortion (when legal in the Member State in which the procedure took place) could constitute a service within the Treaty, the link between the provision of an information service about the clinics and the clinics themselves was too tenuous to be considered a restriction on the freedom to provide services; specifically it lacked an economic aspect as the students' unions was providing this as a free service and did not receive payment from the clinics. Some have suggested that this judgment is an isolated decision and that the ECJ's reasoning in this case was motivated by a desire to avoid a sensitive political issue. The Irish position as regards abortion was formalised by a Protocol annexed to the TEU.

22.3.4 **Cross-border element**

As with the other freedoms, Article 49 does not apply to purely internal situations (see, e.g., *Jägerskiöld* (case C–97/98), which concerned access to fishing rights). Nonetheless, it sometimes seems that this requirement can be easy to satisfy, as *de Coster* (case C–17/00) illustrates. That case concerned a tax on the installation of satellite dishes. Although the complainant had not exercised his right to free movement, nor were the satellite dishes necessarily imported, the ECJ assumed a cross-border element because the dishes could receive satellite television signals which, as they are inherently transnational, might be from another Member State (see also Deliège).

22.4 Beneficiaries of the right

The right to provide services is accorded under the Treaty to EC nationals and to companies formed according to the law of one of the Member States. The position of companies is discussed further in Chapter 21. To benefit from the freedom to provide services, an EC national (or company) must be established in a Member State. There is thus a double requirement of nationality (of one of the Member States of the Union) and residence.

22.5 Fundamental Community rights

We can sub-divide the right to free movement of services into three groups of rights: the right to move to another Member State and to stay there; the right of access to the market, that is the right to provide (or receive) services; and ancillary or social rights. Whereas all three aspects are significant in relation to individuals, and have been developed in line with the development of citizenship rights, the last category seems of less significance in respect of legal persons.

In addition to the rights that may be derived directly from the Treaty, secondary legislation has been enacted which fleshes out the rights of individuals in this regard. Recently, the legislation as regards individuals has been consolidated in Directive 2004/38/EC, which repeals much of the previous legislation.

22.5.1 Right to move

The right to move and to reside is discussed in relation to the free movement of workers (Chapter 20). Note that in relation to services, the right to remain in the host Member State is coterminous with the provision of the services (this point is no longer expressed – contrast Directive 73/148, Article 4(2)). Nonetheless, given that there is no necessary maximum duration for the provision of a service, service providers (and recipients) together with their families might derive continuing rights of residence under Article 14 (effectively the right to remain if the service provider/recipient has sufficient resources), or the right of permanent residence under Chapter IV of Directive 2004/38/EC (see Chapter 20). The same principles apply in relation to those seeking to receive services. The right to move does not arise in circumstances in which the services themselves move, such as in the case of cross-border broadcasting.

22.5.2 Right of access to the market

Central to the rights in Article 49 is the right to carry on business in another Member State. The core element is equal treatment, that is, to be subject to the same conditions as apply to nationals of the host Member State.

Article 49 EC, together with Article 12 (ex 6) EC, may be invoked to challenge a national rule which is in some way discriminatory. Nationality requirements are clearly discriminatory and can be justified only under the terms of Article 56. It is not clear whether the ECJ considers residence requirements to be directly or indirectly discriminatory. As the ECJ has argued, a residence requirement 'is liable to operate mainly to the detriment of nationals of other Member States, since non-residents are in the majority of cases foreigners' (see, e.g., *Commission v Italy* (museum entry) (case C–388/01), para. 14). In the earlier case of *Gouda* (case C–288/89), the ECJ held that Article 49 catches 'discrimination against a person providing services on the grounds of his nationality or the fact that he is established in a Member State other than one in which the service is provided' (para. 10). The distinction is significant because direct discrimination can be justified only under the terms of the express treaty derogation (*Gouda*, para. 11). Article 49 in any event applies to both direct and indirect discrimination. We should also note the impact of the ECJ's jurisprudence, arguably extending Article 49 to non-discriminatory national measures which still form a barrier to the national market (see discussion at 22.6).

Article 49 addresses discrimination arising not only in the taking up of an activity (access to the profession), but in pursuit of that activity (rules relating to the running of a business). Cases concerning the recognition of qualifications (discussed in more detail in Chapter 21) relate to the taking up of an activity. By contrast, *Van Binsbergen* was a case relating to the Dutch rule which required representatives before tribunals to be resident in the Netherlands. *Gouda* concerned Dutch rules limiting the carrying of advertising on television channels. Both these cases dealt with regulations on the running of a business. This latter category of restrictions must be viewed in the widest sense. As well as including restrictions on those providing services, it can include those measures designed to discourage those who want to travel to receive services. In *Bent Vestergaard* (case C–55/98), for example, Danish tax rules discriminated between professional training courses held in Denmark and those held abroad. The Danish tax authorities allowed the expenses incurred in respect of Danish courses to be deducted from the tax bill; those incurred in respect of overseas trips were not so deductible.

22.5.3 Social and other ancillary rights

In Chapter 20, the huge significance of the ECJ's jurisprudence relating to social rights under Regulation 1612/68 for both the worker and the worker's family was discussed. Regulation 1612/68, being expressed in terms of the situation of employment, has no parallel for the self-employed, hence the special importance in this area of the principle of non-discrimination on the grounds of nationality. Where the self-employed or their families are 'lawfully resident' in a Member State, Article 12 (ex 6, originally 7) may, in certain circumstances, be invoked to ensure that they receive equal treatment in the form of 'social' or any other advantages with nationals of the host Member State.

Certainly this would apply to persons or businesses established in the host Member State (discussed in Chapter 21). In the case of the provider of services, the matter is less clear. While he or she is undoubtedly able to claim full equality as regards access to, and conditions of, work within the host Member State it was less certain that he or she can claim for himself and his family benefits in the form of social assistance, especially when they are ongoing, such as may be claimed as social advantages under Article 7(2) of Regulation 1612/68. It could be argued that these should be claimed from the Member State in which the applicant is permanently established. Nonetheless, Article 24 of Directive 2004/88/EC does extend the principal of equal treatment to all migrant EU nationals, subject to some limitations regarding student grants and social assistance during the first three months of residence. Of course, the impact of citizenship rights may be felt here (see Chapters 20 and 24), as well as the impact of fundamental rights, as we can see in the case of *Carpenter* (case C–60/00).

The issue under discussion in *Carpenter* (case C–60/00) was the scope of the family rights of a service provider. Under secondary legislation, a service provider moving to another Member State to provide services may take family members with him for the duration of the provision of services. *Carpenter*, however, concerned the right of an individual established in his state of origin, who provided services in other Member States, to rely on these rights as against the state of origin. This would be a new departure in the case law. The rationale underlying the right for migrants to have their family members accompany them is the removal of a disincentive to free movement. This argument does not apply in the Carpenters' situation: the exercise of the right to have family members with the service provider did not coincide with the exercise of the right to provide services. On the contrary, the right to provide services actually operates to split the family unit. Nonetheless, the ECJ held that Mr Carpenter could rely on his Community law rights as against his state of origin, and that any derogation from these rights must be assessed in the light of the right to family life contained in Article 8 ECHR. This judgment opens up the possibility of service providers having a much broader range of rights ancillary to the provision of services than might have earlier been thought, though the existence of the human rights in this area may well have encouraged the ECJ's generous view.

Note also the impact of the right to receive services both on the rights of the individual who migrates and on the provision of public services by Member States (see 22.10).

22.6 Test for the application of Article 49

The right to provide services has been described by the ECJ as one of the 'fundamental Community rights'. As we noted at 22.5.2, the central principle on which the right to provide services is based is the principle of non-discrimination on grounds of nationality, whether arising from legislation, regulation or administrative practice.

22.6.1 Discrimination: personal and professional

Community law on services, although concerned with the same rights and based on the same principles as the law relating to workers, also has much in common with the law concerning the free movement of goods. We can see this double nature of the rights arising in relation to establishment, but it is particularly clear in the context of services given the number of ways in which the freedom to provide services may be exercised. Insofar as an EC national moves to provide a service, Article 49 confers *personal* rights, in the form of a right to enter and, to a certain extent, reside in a Member State and pursue activities on a temporary basis, free from discrimination on the grounds of nationality. Here we can see similarities to the function of Article 39 EC. Services may also be exercised by companies and services may also be provided at a distance. Inasmuch as Article 49 seeks to achieve the free movement of services in a single, Community-wide market and pertain to the practice of a particular profession their goals are economic, more like those of Article 28 (ex 30) EC.

We might argue that there is a distinction in the type of infringement that occurs in relation to these two aspects of Article 49, or in the ECJ's analytical approach to resolving the respective types of case before it. While infringements of the former 'personal' rights tend to be seen in terms of discrimination, measures which interfere with the functioning of the single market by impeding the free movement of services will not necessarily be discriminatory; the case law here has similarities to the 'indistinctly applicable' line of cases found in relation to goods. Discriminatory measures can be justified only by reference to the express Treaty derogations. Where measures apply equally to all persons who establish themselves or provide services in a particular Member State and are designed to protect some public interest, they may more readily be justified.

22.6.2 A discrimination-based test

The early case law of the ECJ on Articles 49 and 50 tended to focus on personal rights and broad principles of discrimination on the grounds of nationality. The concept of discrimination was extended to include measures which discriminated indirectly against non-nationals such as the residence requirement in *van Binsbergen* (case 33/74), which the Court had suggested might be 'objectively justified'. Direct discrimination, as established in *Bond van Adverteerders* v *Netherlands* (case 352/85), could only be justified under Articles 45 and 55 EC. These provisions, expressed in terms of *personal* rights, allowing Member States to provide for 'special treatment' for foreign nationals, were very strictly construed.

22.6.3 Measures which apply 'without distinction'

It was thought initially that national regulatory rules and professional practices which were not discriminatory, which applied 'without distinction' to all persons providing services or established in a particular Member State, and which clearly served a useful purpose, could not be challenged under the Treaty (e.g., *Koestler* (case 15/78)). The rights granted to EC nationals under Articles 49 and 50 EC were to provide services in other Member States 'under the same conditions' as applied to the State's own nationals. Although national regulatory rules might create barriers to the free movement of services and freedom of establishment they could only be removed by harmonisation, as provided under Articles 46 and 47 (ex 56 and 57) EC. Since harmonisation proved slow to achieve, some of these measures came to be challenged as 'discriminatory' and it was suggested that they would be permissible provided they could be objectively justified (see, e.g., *van Binsbergen* (case 33/74); *Commission* v *Germany, re Insurance Services* (case 205/84)).

For example, in *Commission* v *Germany*, the rules required, *inter alia*, that a person providing direct insurance must be established and authorised to practise in the State in which the service is provided. The Court held that the then Articles 59 and 60 (now 49 and 50) require the removal not only of all discrimination based on nationality but also *all restrictions on his freedom to provide services imposed by reason of the fact that he is established in a Member State other than that in which the services are provided.*

The case law was, however, slow to develop and the principles were unclear. It was not until 1991 with *Säger* v *Dennemeyer and Co. Ltd* (case C–76/90) that the Court established a coherent approach to indistinctly applicable rules in the field of services parallel to that pioneered in the sphere of goods in the 1970s in *Dassonville* (case 8/74) and *Cassis de Dijon* (case 120/78). In doing so it undoubtedly opened up the possibility for further claims under Article 49 (ex 59), and with it, as with any easing of the rules, some abuse (see, e.g., *TV 10 SA* v *Commissariaat voor de Media* (case C–23/93)).

22.6.4 A new approach

Säger v *Dennemeyer* concerned a specialist in patent renewal services, Dennemeyer, who was based in the UK. He provided these services in Germany, without the licence which German law requires for persons attending to the legal affairs of third parties. Such licences were not normally granted to patent renewal agents. Dennemeyer's right to provide such services in Germany was challenged by Säger, a German patent agent operating in Germany. Dennemeyer argued that the German rules were a hindrance to the freedom of movement of services, contrary to Articles 49 and 50(3). A number of questions were referred to the Court. As Advocate-General Jacobs pointed out, while it was clear that Article 49 applied to discriminatory rules, it was not yet clear whether it applied to rules which were applicable to all providers of services, whether established in the Member State in which the service was provided or not. The principles laid down in *van Binsbergen* and the insurance cases had proceeded on the basis that the rules in question were discriminatory. While it was not unreasonable to expect compliance with the rules of the Member State by any person established in that State, there was less justification for demanding compliance by those providing services there. In these circumstances he suggested an approach based on the Court's jurisprudence on Article 28 (ex 30) in relation to indistinctly applicable rules.

The Court endorsed his suggestion. While asserting that:

> Article 59 [now 49] requires not only the abolition of all discrimination against a person providing services on the ground of his nationality but also the abolition of any

restriction, even if applied without distinction to national providers of services and to those of other Member States, when it is liable to prohibit or otherwise impede the activities of a provider of services established in another Member State where he lawfully provides similar services (para. 12)

it held that:

Having regard to the particular characteristics of certain specific provisions of services, specific requirements imposed on the provider cannot be regarded as incompatible with the Treaty.

However:

The freedom to provide services may be limited only by rules which are justified by imperative reasons relating to the public interest and which apply to all persons and undertakings pursuing an activity in the State of destination insofar as that interest is not protected by rules to which the person providing the service is subject in the State in which he is established. In particular, these requirements must be objectively necessary in order to ensure compliance with professional rules and must not exceed what is necessary to attain those objectives.

It may be noted that, to establish a prima facie breach of Article 49, the rule challenged must be 'liable to prohibit or otherwise impede' the provision of services. This is a stricter test than the *Dassonville* test applied to goods. On the other hand, the criteria relating to justification, embracing the principles of proportionality and mutual recognition, are substantially the same as the twin principles laid down in *Cassis*, albeit lacking examples as to what will constitute 'imperative reasons relating to the public interest'.

The principles laid down in *Säger* v *Dennemeyer and Co. Ltd* have been followed in a succession of cases in which national or professional rules likely to 'prohibit or otherwise impede' the free provision of services have been tested for their compatibility with Article 49 (ex 59). Thus in *Commission* v *France* (case C–154/89) a requirement of French law that tourist guides must obtain a licence by examination, although justifiable in principle in the interest of consumers as contributing to a 'proper appreciation of places and things of interest', was found to be disproportionate. The licence requirement went further than was necessary in order to protect this interest. In *Vander Elst* v *Office des Migrations Internationales* (case C–43/93) the requirement of a French work permit for third-country nationals seeking to work in France was held not to be justified by 'overriding reasons in the general interest' (to regulate access to the national labour market), since these workers were already in possession of a work permit obtained in Belgium. On the other hand, in *Ramrath* v *Ministre de la Justice* (case C–106/91) rules governing the conditions for the provision of auditing services in Luxembourg were found on the facts to be justified and not disproportionate. Similarly in *Alpine Investments BV* v *Minister van Financiën* (case C–384/93) a Dutch prohibition on 'cold calling' by providers of financial advice established in the Netherlands was found to be justified in order to protect consumers and the reputation of the Netherlands' security market and was not disproportionate. In each case the measure in question and its alleged justification were tested on their merits.

In the more recent case of *Kohll* (case C–158/96 – prior authorisation of medical expenses by home State required), the ECJ citing *Commission v France* (case C–381/93) applied a slightly different test from that used in *Säger*. It held that what is now Article 49 (ex 59) 'precludes the application of any national rules which have the effect of making the provision of services between Member States *more difficult* than the provision of services purely within one Member State' (para. 33, authors' emphasis). It is not clear whether the use of this test will become generalised within Article 49 case law: although this version of the test was found in cases involving transport, it seems to be becoming more widely used (see, e.g., *Leichtle* (case C–8/02), reimbursement of expenditure for health cure). In some cases the ECJ seems to be avoiding the issue entirely, using neither of these formulations. For example, in *Gambelli* (case C–243/01), the ECJ merely remarked: 'It is appropriate to inquire whether Article 49 precludes legislation such as that in issue in the main proceedings which, although it does not discriminate on grounds of nationality, restricts the freedom to provide services' (para. 69). This is a yet more stringent approach than *Säger* or *Kohll*. It is, in the final analysis, not obvious what difference in practice the use of the different tests would make. In any event, as with other services cases, the measure in question must be examined to identify if it is objectively justified.

In all these cases except *Vander Elst* (which, involving third-country workers and social security, respectively, may be regarded as 'special') and *Kohll* (which concerned the right to move to receive services in another Member State and is therefore also special), the rules applied equally to all providers of services in the Member State in question, that is, they were 'indistinctly applicable'. Although some of the measures could have been described as 'discriminatory' to the extent that they imposed an extra burden on non-national providers, the Court did not approach the matter as one of discrimination. It is submitted that this is a more satisfactory approach to indistinctly applicable measures than one based on the slippery (and often artificial) concept of discrimination. Only distinctly applicable or overtly discriminatory measures should now breach Article 49 *per se*, capable of justification only under Article 46.

Whether a common test is now to be applied to both establishment and services, if not across all the Treaty freedoms, is not clear. In *Gebhard* (case C–55/94), the ECJ noted that both constitute 'fundamental freedoms provided by the Treaty'. It would thus make sense that the same test is applied to both articles. Despite the fact that the ECJ has not always applied the same test in case law on Article 49 EC, equally it has not adopted the *Gebhard* test used in relation to establishment. In any event, the Court has turned its back on an earlier suggestion from Advocate-General Jacobs (delivered in the context of claims based on Articles 49 and 28, see *Alpine Investments* (case C–384/93) and *Leclerc-Siplec* (case C–412/93)) that the Court adopt a *de minimis* rule, and that only rules which 'substantially impede' the freedom to provide services should be deemed prima facie in breach of Community law. As with establishment, the approach adopted by the ECJ seems to mirror that found in *Dassonville*. The contrast with the goods case law is notable. There, the ECJ sought in *Keck* (cases C–267 & 268/91) and subsequent cases to limit the scope of Article 28 in relation to indistinctly applicable rules (see *De Agostini* (cases C–34–6/98)) and exclude challenges to rules that had an uncertain and indirect impact on trade (see further Chapter 18). In *Alpine Investments*, the ECJ seemed to reject the need for a *Keck*-style approach to services, though the precise scope of the ruling in that context has been the subject of some debate. So far, the ECJ has not accepted a *Keck*-style argument in the services context.

Clearly, the approach in *Säger* would cover rules relating directly to access to the professional activity. It now seems that this approach has a more general application. It was only with *Her Majesty's Customs and Excise* v *Schindler* (case C–275/92) that the Court unequivocally adopted the *Säger* (case C–76/90) line of reasoning to indistinctly applicable measures outside the sphere of professional qualifications and rules. The case arose when HM Customs confiscated invitations and application forms sent by Schindler from the Netherlands, inviting participation in a lottery organised by the German Länder. Schindler, who acted on behalf of the organisers, sought to prevent the invitations being confiscated under UK legislation. He claimed that the UK rules infringed his freedom to provide services, contrary to the then Articles 59 and 60 (now 49 and 50). This time the Court followed the Advocate-General's advice. It found that the organisation of lotteries such as the one in question constituted an economic activity within Article 49. Although it was applicable without distinction to British as well as non-British lotteries, it was likely to 'prohibit or otherwise impede' the provision of lottery services. It was, however, justified by 'overriding considerations of public interest', in this case the protection of consumers and the maintenance of order in society, and it was not disproportionate, since such activities involved a high risk of crime and fraud. Unlike Advocate-General Gulman the Court did not consider the relevance or scope of the then Article 56 (now 46). One might question the extent to which this self-same approach is appropriate in regard to ancillary rights; *Carpenter* (discussed at 22.5.3) suggests a broad interpretation, although in such a context the broad rights of a citizen may render the use of indistinctly applicable tests irrelevant.

22.7 A rule of reason for services?

The freedom to provide services provided under Article 49 is not absolute. Apart from the express derogations of Articles 45, 46 and 55 EC, they are subject to one important limitation. The right to equality of opportunity provided by the Treaty can only be exercised 'under the same conditions as are imposed by that State on its own nationals' (Article 50(3) EC).

The difficulty for non-nationals seeking to provide services in another Member State is that they may not be able to satisfy the conditions laid down in that Member State for the practice of the particular trade or profession which they wish to exercise. The relevant conditions are those prescribed by trade or professional bodies, normally reinforced by law, relating to:

(a) the education and training required for qualification for the job, and

(b) rules of professional conduct.

Both of these vary greatly in scope and content and quality from Member State to Member State. The need to comply with these conditions thus provided a potent barrier to freedom of movement for the self-employed; it also hindered the free movement of workers, since they too may wish to work as employees in a trade or profession which is subject to regulation at national level.

These types of rule are likely to be caught by Article 49, even prior to *Säger* v *Dennemeyer*. Equally, striking such measures down would be unlikely to be in the public interest. The ECJ seemed aware of the problem even in the relatively early jurisprudence. In *van Binsbergen* (case 33/74) it was acknowledged, in the context of a challenge to a residence requirement imposed by the Dutch Bar on those seeking to provide certain legal services in Holland, that specific requirements imposed on a person providing services would not infringe Articles 49 and 50 where they have as their purpose the application of professional rules justified by the general good – in particular, rules relating to organisation, ethics, qualifications, supervision and liability, which are binding on any person established in the territory of the Member State in which the service is provided. The person providing the service cannot take advantage of his right to provide services to avoid the professional rules of conduct which would be applied to him if he were established in that State.

Professional rules which inhibit the free provision of services would only be permissible if they were:

(a) non-discriminatory,

(b) objectively justified, and

(c) not disproportionate.

These principles were subsequently applied in *Webb* (case 279/80) in the context of the provision of manpower services. The Court added in *Webb* that, in ascertaining whether its own rules are justified, the host Member State must take into account the justifications and safeguards already provided by the applicant in order to pursue the activity in question in his State of establishment (approved in *Commission* v *Germany (Re Lawyers' Services)* (case 427/85)).

The principles expressed in *van Binsbergen* and *Webb* were refined and developed in 1986 in the 'insurance' cases (*Commission* v *Germany (Re Insurance Services)* (case 205/84), *Commission* v *Ireland (Re Co-insurance Services)* (case 206/84), *Commission* v *France* (case 220/83), *Commission* v *Denmark (Re Insurance Services)* (case 252/83)). These actions were based on alleged infringements of Articles 49 and 50 (ex 59 and 60) and Directive 78/473 (insurance directive) by the defendant Member States in their rules regulating the provision of insurance services. The rules and the breaches alleged in each State were similar.

Effectively, the imposition of the rules of the host Member State meant that cross-border services providers were subject to regulation more than once. Because of this, the Court held that not *all* the legislation applicable to nationals or those engaged in permanent activities could be applied to the *temporary* activities of enterprises established in another Member State. It could be applied only if three criteria were satisfied:

(a) it is justified by imperative reasons relating to the public interest;

(b) the public interest is not already protected by the rules of the State of establishment; and

(c) the same result cannot be obtained by less restrictive means.

Thus, in the field of services, the Court moved towards a test for professional rules not unlike the *Cassis de Dijon* (case 120/78) test applied to goods (see Chapter 18). As with that test, it is likely that the criteria will be strictly applied to ensure that each rule is necessary and genuinely justified. If not, it will breach Articles 49 and 50. In *Commission* v *Germany* the Court found that the establishment requirement was not justified; indeed, it was the very negation of the freedom to provide services and would only be permissible if indispensable. The authorisation requirement, on the other hand, at least as related to the rules concerning technical reserves, might be justified for the protection of policyholders and insured persons. The Commission's action failed in this respect. Applying the same approach in *Commission* v *Luxembourg* (case C–351/90) the Court found that a 'single surgery' rule applied in Luxembourg, the effect of which was to prohibit doctors, dentists and veterinary surgeons established outside Luxembourg from opening surgeries in Luxembourg, was not justified, as was argued, in the interest of good professional practice (to ensure proximity to patients). Such a general prohibition (which in any case was applied more strictly to professionals established in other Member States) was found to be 'unduly restrictive', 'too absolute and too general'. It should be noted that there seems thus to be a necessary distinction between the necessity and proportionality assessments under services by comparison with establishment (and possibly workers), as the presumption of home Member State control is greater in the context of the provision of services which are often seen as temporary; double regulation is less easily justified.

22.8 Harmonisation and the principle of home country regulation

22.8.1 General

We have seen in the context of establishment the development of both the case law and legislation relating to qualifications. Those principles apply also to the field of services, as they do to workers. It should be noted that the area of qualifications and access to professions are not the only ones resulting in Community measures. Article 47(2) deals with access to professions. It also empowers the institutions to take measures to ensure the coordination of national laws relating to the taking up and pursuit of activities as self-employed persons. Article 55 extends this provision to services. A broad range of directives have been enacted under this provision, such as the Television without Frontiers Directive (Directive 89/552/EEC ([1989] OJ L298/23), as amended). In the *Tobacco Advertising Directive* case (*Germany* v *Parliament and Council* (case C–376/98)), the Advocate-General likened the scope of Article 47(2) to that of Article 95, albeit more limited in scope (para. 63). Similar legislative techniques can be seen in evidence in these directives to those enacted under Article 95. The approach is based on the following principles:

(a) the harmonisation of *essential* safeguards and standards applicable to activities as a whole; and

(b) within that framework, acceptance of the standards of other Member States on a basis of mutual trust and recognition, on the principle of home country control and supervision.

Essential to the effective functioning of these principles would be the concept of the single licence known as home country regulation. This would allow an institution licensed in one Member State to offer its services to another Member State, either by establishing a branch or agency in that State or by supplying its services there. The Television without Frontiers Directive, for example, is a minimum harmonisation directive which operates on the country of origin principle. Although television signals may be received in more than one Member State, only one Member State has responsibility for regulation, the Member State in which the broadcaster is established. (The problems with this approach are discussed below at 22.9.)

22.8.2 The proposed Services Directive

Despite the efforts of the ECJ to develop a broad-based test for the application of Article 49 and the harmonising directives already existing, the Commission concluded that there still existed significant barriers to entry for the cross-border provision of services. To this end, it has proposed that a general Services Directive be enacted, based on the principle of home country regulation, administrative cooperation and administrative simplification. The proposed directive also contained a number of specific derogation principles to temper the potentially deregulatory impact of the directive, as well as excluding some sectors of the service industry, such as gambling and gas and water supply, from its scope. The Services Directive has proved to be controversial. Among the criticisms, it seems clear that some Member States are concerned about the impact of the proposed directive on the provision of public services. The European Parliament, in expressing concern about the relationship between the directive and services of general economic interest (that is, services that are in the public interest), commented that within the EU legal order trade liberalisation is not an end in itself, nor was it to be benefited at the expense of other tasks of the Union. Others consider that the interrelationship between the general Services Directive and the subject-specific directives has been dealt with inadequately. To take an example, consider cross-border radio services. These are not covered by any specific directives at the moment and would therefore fall to be covered under the general Services Directive (if it is ever agreed). To what extent would Member States be free to take measures to protect freedom of expression, cultural diversity and pluralism, which the ECJ in its case law has accepted constitute acceptable public interest objectives, under the services directive? With such fundamental issues (as yet) unresolved, it seems unlikely that the directive will gain broad acceptance. Certainly at the time of writing, although the Council had approved the draft directive, the European Parliament, after intensive lobbying, had voted to remove the country of origin principle. The future of the directive remains uncertain.

22.8.3 Relationship between directives and other provisions

Where directives have been passed harmonising or recognising national rules the provisions of the directive will be conclusive on the matter. However, in each case it will be necessary to decide whether the rule in question has been covered by the directive. This is not always as simple as it might seem. For example, the Television without Frontiers Directive (89/552/EEC, as amended by 97/36/EC), currently under revision for a second time, covers only television broadcasting. In these days of 'web-casting' and watching television on mobile phones, the question must arise, 'What is broadcasting?' The scope of the Television without Frontiers Directive was considered in *De Agostini* (joined cases C–34–36/95, discussed in Chapter 18), in which the Advocate-General and the ECJ came to different conclusions about the scope of the directive in relation to television advertising. In *Commission* v *Germany* (case 205/84) the Insurance Directive was found to be designed to ensure that undertakings were solvent; it did not attempt to harmonise national rules concerning technical reserves. Given the potential impact of the general Services Directive, the precise boundaries between directives might become of more significance.

Harmonisation is discussed in more detail in Chapter 15 and the points made in relation to directives made under Article 95 can, in general, be transposed to those made under Article 47(2).

22.9 Home country regulation and abuse of the freedom to provide services

There has been a concern that the exercise of free movement rights in certain contexts may give rise to a dilution of national standards as businesses establish themselves in the Member State with the most favourable regime and then rely on Article 49 to trade in Member States with more stringent regulatory regimes. In this there are certain commonalities with the problems arising in the field of establishment, particularly with regard to companies setting up branch offices or subsidiaries, discussed in Chapter 21. We might suggest that the difficulty felt in services is in some ways more acute, as Member States' freedom to regulate incoming services is constrained by the need to take into account home country regulation; such host Member State regulation is more likely to be assessed as unnecessary or disproportionate.

As with the other freedoms, the ECJ made it clear that Community law may not be used (or abused) in order to undermine the legitimate rules and standards of Member States. Thus the ECJ has held that establishing oneself in one Member State for the purposes of evading host Member State rules is unacceptable (see, e.g., *van Binsbergen* (case 33/74)). A similar approach can be seen in respect of services regulated by harmonising legislation. For example, in *van de Bijl* v *Staatssecretaris van Economische Zaken* (case 130/88), the Court was asked to rule on a claim by a Dutch decorator, based on EC Directive 64/427, which provided, *inter alia*, for the mutual recognition of qualifications for self-employed persons in small craft industries. Under Directive 64/427 States were required to accept a certification of competence and work experience provided by the appropriate authorities of another Member State in respect of work performed in that State. It was suggested in van de Bijl's case that the certificate issued by the UK authorities, which the Dutch authorities had refused to accept as a basis for registration in Holland, was based on questionable evidence. The Court held that the host (i.e., Dutch) State was entitled to take steps (e.g., verification of evidence) to prevent the relevant Community rules being used for the purpose of circumventing the rules relating to particular occupations applicable to its national.

This line of case law does raise difficult questions of what is considered to be abuse. Are we concerned with the intentions of the parties seeking to rely on the right to provide services, or merely with its impact on the host Member State? If we are looking at intention, is it required that the parties sought to rely on the freedom to provide services *always* with the view to exploit the Treaty freedoms, or is it sufficient that the rights holders start *at some point* intending to evade Community law? The case law in this area has not been clear or consistent. Even apart from this difficult question, how is such intention to be proved? Advocate-General Lenz highlighted this problem in the context of broadcasting. If we argue that a broadcaster established in Luxembourg but staffed in the main by Dutch people, broadcasting in Dutch, to the Netherlands is intending to evade national law and thus abuse Community law rights purely by reference to nationality and language criteria, we are not only undermining the right of those people to exercise rights under Article 39 and 43 to go to Luxembourg in the first place, but arguably we are indulging in a form of nationality discrimination.

Problems with a perceived downward spiral of standards may also arise when policy areas have been harmonised by directive. Minimum harmonisation (discussed in Chapter 15, and see also 22.8.1 regarding harmonisation in the services sector) allows Member States to set different standards, higher than those set out in the directive in question. These rules must of course be compatible with general Treaty objectives. The difficulty in this context arises when there is a market access clause. This will mean that a Member State may require those established within its jurisdiction to comply with the higher standards but cannot impose these requirements on those established elsewhere in the Community. This is often referred to as negative or reverse discrimination. As is the case with goods (see Chapter 18), this is permissible under Community law. It is also open to abuse, but it would seem that the same general rules apply here as to the Treaty articles. The ECJ, in some cases, seems to have avoided this difficulty by re-characterising the legal issue in question, so as to allow the host Member State some control. In *de Agostini* (joined cases C–34–6/95), the question of broadcasting aimed at children in Sweden would seem to fall under the Television without Frontiers Directive (89/552, as subsequently amended by 97/36), which contained a market access clause. The broadcaster was established in the UK, which does not prohibit such broadcasts. On this assessment, given the market access clause and the rules of the Member State in which the broadcaster was established, the Swedish could do nothing to stop the broadcasts. The ECJ, however, took the view that the advertisements should be seen as relating to the sale of the goods they were advertising rather than the service of broadcasting, thereby removing regulation away from the British and allowing the Swedes to maintain their rules (provided such rules operate equally in law and in fact). (See also Chapter 18.)

This area of law is problematic. It highlights the ever-present tension between the need to create and to facilitate the functioning of the internal market and the competence of the Member States and their legitimate concerns. As with the pre-*Keck* case law on the scope of Article 28, the Court seems to be encountering some difficulty in distinguishing between legitimate exploitation of rules and their abuse. It is indeed unfortunate that the ECJ has not developed a unified principle to deal with cases in this area.

22.10 Freedom to receive services

22.10.1 General

The freedom provided by Articles 49 and 50 is expressed in terms of the freedom to *provide* services. It was subsequently extended by the ECJ to embrace the freedom to *receive* services.

The point was originally raised in *Watson* (case 118/75), where the Commission suggested that the freedom to move within the Community to receive services was the necessary corollary to the freedom to provide services. This was approved by the Court in *Luisi* v *Ministero del Tesoro* (case 286/82) in the context of criminal proceedings in Italy against Luisi and Carbone for breach of Italian currency regulations. They were accused of taking foreign currency out of the country in excess of the maximum permitted under Italian law. They had taken the money out for the purposes of tourism and medical treatment. The question referred to the ECJ was whether payment for such services represented movements of capital, within the then Articles 67–73 of the EC Treaty (provisions deleted by the ToA), or payments for the provision of services; if the latter, was it governed by the then Articles 59–66 (now 49–55)?

Advocate-General Mancini, arguing from *Watson* (case 118/75) suggested that Article 49 was concerned with the receipt of services as well as their provision. In support of this view he cited the general programme for the abolition of restrictions on the freedom to provide services (*Common Market Reporter*, para. 1545, JO 1962, 32), Directive 64/221, which expressly referred in Article 1(1) to 'freedom of movement for employed or self-employed persons or the *recipients* of services' and Directive 73/148, Article 1(1)(b), which required Member States to abolish restrictions on the movement and residence of 'nationals of Member States wishing to go to another Member State as *recipients* of services'.

The Court, following Advocate-General Mancini, found the money to be payment for services and held that freedom to provide services, as provided by Article 49, includes the freedom, for recipients of services, to go to another Member State, without restriction, in order to receive a service there. Recipients of services were held to include tourists, persons receiving medical treatment and persons travelling for the purposes of education and business.

Thus, the right to enter and remain in another Member State for the purpose of receiving services has been established. In *Commission* v *Netherlands (Re Entry into Dutch Territory)* (case C–68/89) the Court held that nationals of one EC State were entitled to enter another Member State simply on production of a valid identity card or passport. National immigration authorities were not entitled to question EC nationals seeking to enter a Member State except in order to query the validity of the identity card or passport. On the other hand, when applying for a residence permit national authorities may require proof of the applicant's status as a provider or recipient of services. Recipients of services are entitled to residence for the period during which the service is provided. Any restrictions on these freedoms will prima facie breach Articles 49 and 50, subject to limitation on the grounds of public policy, public security and public health (Articles 46 and 55 EC). The question remains whether the recipient of services, by reason of his status or his right of residence, can invoke these provisions, together with Article 12 (ex 6) EC, to claim equality of treatment with nationals of the host State. A number of services, such as education and medicine, are publicly funded and provided not so much as a commercial activity but as a public service. Are these to be available to nationals of the Member States on the same basis as to the States' own citizens?

22.10.2 Education: vocational training

This matter was considered in the context of educational services in *Gravier* v *City of Liège* (case 293/83). The applicant in this case was a young French woman who had applied to and been accepted by the Liège Académie des Beaux-Arts for a four-year course in the art of strip cartoons. As a foreign student she was charged a special fee, known as a *'minerval'*, for the course. This was not payable by Belgian citizens, whether or not they lived or paid taxes in Belgium, nor by EC nationals working in Belgium, or members of their families. She brought an action before the Belgian Courts, claiming the fee was discriminatory. Her case rested on two arguments.

First, she suggested that the *minerval* constituted an obstacle to her freedom of movement to receive services as established in *Luisi* v *Ministero del Tesoro* (case 286/82) in breach of Article 49. Her second argument was based on the vocational nature of the course. Vocational education fell within the scope of the Treaty; as a matter covered by EC law it was discriminatory, in breach of Article 12 (ex 6 EC, originally 7 EEC), to charge higher prices to EC nationals who were not Belgian citizens or resident in Belgium. This argument was based primarily on *Forcheri's* case (case 152/82, see Chapter 20). Here Ms Forcheri, the wife of an Italian working in Brussels, had succeeded in challenging the higher fees demanded of her as a non-national, to attend a social work course in Brussels. Although her success was based primarily on her lawful residence in Belgium as the wife of an EC worker, which brought her 'within the scope and application of this Treaty' and Article 12 EC, it rested in part on the fact that the course for which she subscribed was vocational. Vocational training, the Court held, was one of the matters covered by Community law; covered in general terms by the then Article 128 EEC ('The Council shall, acting on a proposal from the Commission and after consulting the Economic and Social Committee, lay down general principles for implementing a common vocational training policy', amended by TEU), and specifically, at least for workers and their children, in Regulation 1612/68 (Articles 7(3) and 12, see Chapter 20). Therefore provision of vocational training was subject to Article 12 EC.

The ECJ, following Advocate-General Sir Gordon Slynn, found in Ms Gravier's favour on this second ground. Access to vocational training was a matter covered by Community law; moreover, it was an essential element in promoting freedom of movement for persons throughout the Community. The Court expressly dissociated itself from the wider issues involved, discussed at length by Sir Gordon Slynn, concerning the organisation and financing of such courses, and confined its judgment merely to conditions of access to a course affecting foreign students alone, and relating to a particular kind of course, namely vocational education. However, its definition of vocational education was very wide. It was held to include all forms of teaching which prepares for and leads directly to a particular profession, trade or employment, or which provides the necessary skills for such profession, trade or employment, even if the programme of instruction includes an element of general education.

The decision in *Gravier* caused considerable concern amongst Member States. This decision, with its wide definition of vocational training, meant that many courses, including perhaps university courses, often entailing substantial contributions from public funds (the Belgians pointed out that the *minerval* itself only covered 50 per cent of the cost of the education provided), would have to be offered on equal terms to all EC nationals. Moreover, the precise scope of the term 'vocational training' was unclear. Subsequent cases have provided some answers to these questions.

In *Blaizot* v *University of Liège* (case 24/86), in the context of a claim by university students of veterinary science for reimbursement of the *minerval*, based on *Gravier*, the Court applied the *Gravier* definition of vocational training and held that university education could constitute vocational training:

> not only where the final exam directly provides the required qualification but also insofar as the studies provide specific training (i.e., where the student needs the knowledge so acquired for the pursuit of his trade or profession), even if no legislative or administrative provisions make the acquisition of such knowledge a prerequisite.

In general, university courses would meet these criteria. The only exception would be courses designed for persons seeking to 'improve their general knowledge rather than prepare themselves for an occupation'. Even where, as in veterinary or medical science, the training comprises two stages, the second representing the practical stage, the first, academic stage must be regarded as vocational. The two stages must be viewed as a single unit.

Similar reasoning informed the Court's decision in *Belgium* v *Humbel* (case 263/86). This case concerned a claim by the Belgian authorities for the payment of the *minerval* in respect of *secondary* education received in Belgium by the son of a French national living in Luxembourg. Although the course as a whole appeared to be vocational, the fees giving rise to the dispute concerned one year within that course of general education. The Court held that such a course of general education must none the less be treated as 'vocational' if it forms an integral part of an overall programme of vocational education.

Finally, on the same day as the decision in *Humbel*, the Court, in a case brought by the Commission against Belgium (*Commission* v *Belgium* (case 42/87)) challenging its rules on access to higher education, revised in the light of *Gravier*, allowing access, *inter alia*, to only 2 per cent of 'outsiders', held that inasmuch as the rules related to vocational training they were in breach of what is now Article 12 EC.

On the basis of these cases, where educational courses are concerned, provided they are found *overall* to be vocational, according to the generous interpretation provided by the Court, EC nationals who are neither migrant workers nor the children of migrant workers living in the State in which the education is provided may claim equal access under equal conditions to nationals of the home State, even if the courses are financed or subsidised by the State as a matter of social policy.

Gravier was indeed a landmark case, an example of the Court in activist mood. The legal basis for the decision, resting on (what was at the time) Article 128 EEC, is slender. While Article 128 EEC may have provided a sufficient legal basis for the issuing of directives in the field of vocational training (as the Court found in *UK* v *Commission* (case 56/88)), it may be doubted that it was sufficiently clear, precise and unconditional to give rise to direct effects.

Article 128 EEC was replaced in the Maastricht Treaty by Article 127 (now 150) EC, which requires the Community to implement a vocational training policy which will 'support and supplement the action of Member States while fully respecting the responsibility of the Member States for the content and organisation of vocational training'. This article represents one of several specific examples of the subsidiarity principle introduced by the TEU. The TEU also introduced a specific provision relating to education, Article 149 EC (ex 126), although the precise relationship between Article 149 and Article 150 is not clear. Despite the limitation of the Community to a supporting role in action under Article 149 and 150 and the change in wording of the relevant provisions compared to the text in *Gravier* and *Blaizot*, the ECJ has applied these cases in the context of equal access to Austrian higher education institutions (*Commission* v *Austria* (recognition of qualifications) (case C–147/03)). Imposing discriminatory treatment, in this case the requirement on those who did not do their secondary education in Austria to undertake extra tests to prove their academic status, is contrary to Articles 12, 149 and 150 EC. In coming to this conclusion, the ECJ relied not only on the terms of Article 149(2) EC, which seeks to encourage student mobility, but, significantly, on European citizenship. The ECJ reaffirmed the fundamental nature of European citizenship which enables 'those who find themselves in the same situation to enjoy the same treatment irrespective of their nationality' (*Commission* v *Austria* (recognition of qualifications), para. 45, see further Chapter 24).

22.10.3 Scholarships and grants

The Court in *Gravier* (case 293/83) refrained from considering whether the right of EC nationals to vocational training carried with it a right to grants and scholarships from the host State to enable them to take up these courses. Advocate-General Sir Gordon Slynn was clearly of the opinion that such a right was not included in the right to receive services. In this same context the Belgian, Danish and British Governments regarded such a result as unthinkable in view of the differences which exist between the number of students moving, for educational purposes, into different Member States. The matter was resolved in *Brown* and *Lair* (cases 197/86, 39/86: for detailed discussion of these cases see Chapter 20). Both *Brown* and *Lair* involved claims for maintenance grants for university courses. In both cases their entitlement to the grants as 'workers', or the 'children of migrant workers', was doubtful. So they sought also to rely on *Gravier*, arguing that the course in question constituted vocational training, to which the then Article 7 EEC (now Article 12 EC) applied. Thus they were entitled to be treated on a footing of equality with nationals.

The Court, no doubt anxious to quell the anxieties of Member States on this issue, disagreed. Although university courses (following *Blaizot*) were capable of constituting vocational training, to which they were entitled to equal access in respect of fees, Article 12 EC did not apply to maintenance grants. Assistance in the form of maintenance grants, the Court held, fell outside the scope of the EC Treaty. It was a matter of educational policy, and, as such, had not been entrusted to the Community institutions; it was also a matter of social policy, which fell within the competence of Member States insofar as it was not covered by the provisions of the EC Treaty.

Whilst there is little logic in the distinction between fees, which relate to conditions of access to vocational training, and maintenance grants, which do not, it is clear that the judgments in *Brown* and *Lair* reflected the Court's desire, on grounds of policy, to call a halt to the development of a Community educational policy by means of judicial decision. The judgments were greeted with relief by Member States. *Grzelczyck* (case C–184/99) and other cases in this area suggest that issue may have to be revisited in the light of changes to the Treaty, notably the introduction of European citizenship. As a migrant student, Grzelczyck was not entitled to State assistance under Article 7(2) Regulation 1612/68. As a migrant European citizen however, he might be so entitled (see further Chapter 24).

The specific right of students to residence lasting for the duration of their course of studies was enacted in Directive 90/366 (Article 2) ([1990] OJ L180/30), as reintroduced in 1993 following its annulment by the Court. Families' rights are confined to spouses and dependent children. The Directive expressly provided that it 'shall not establish any entitlement to the payment of maintenance grants by the host Member State on the part of students benefiting from the right of residence (Article 3). This directive has been repealed and replaced by Directive 2004/38/EC (see further Chapters 14, 20 and 24), though the requirement to be self-sufficient in general terms remains.

22.10.4 Scope of the equality principle: impact on public services

One further question, raised but not answered in *Gravier* (case 293/83), was whether the equality principle could be applied as an adjunct to the right, established in *Luisi* (case 286/82) to move within the Community to *receive* services under what was then Article 59 (now 49). In considering the question in *Gravier*, Advocate-General Sir Gordon Slynn suggested that in the sphere of education a distinction should be drawn between education which was provided by private finance, with a view to profit, and education as a public service, financed wholly or partly by the State, as an aspect of social policy. Similar reasoning was adopted by the Court in *Humbel* (case 263/86). Here, the claimant, a French youth, living with his family in Luxembourg, sought to resist the payment of the *minerval* in respect of his secondary education in Belgium on the basis of his right to receive services under Article 49. The Court pointed out that Article 49 applies to 'services provided for remuneration'. The essential characteristic of remuneration is that it 'constitutes the countervailing financial advantage for the services in question and is normally fixed between the supplier and the recipient of the services' (para. 17). This characteristic is not present in the case of a course of study provided in the framework of a national educational system. In providing such a system the State is fulfilling its duty to its people in the social, cultural, or educational field. These principles were affirmed by the Court in *Wirth* v *Landeshaupt Hannover* (case C–109/92).

Apart from the area of vocational training (access and fees) which is governed by *Gravier*, services such as health and education provided by the State for the benefit of its citizens, and not for commercial reasons, with a view to profit, cannot be claimed on a basis of equality by EC nationals who have temporary residence as recipients of services but do not enjoy 'lawful residence' on a 'settled' or permanent basis as 'favoured Community citizens', that is, those who are or have been, employed and self-employed migrants and their families (see Chapter 20) in the State providing the services. Note, however, the potential impact in this context of the reasoning of the ECJ in *Commission v Austria* (recognition of qualifications) (case C–147/03) based on European citizenship. There the emphasis was not on the nature of the service provided, but on the claimant's status as a citizen entitled to equality of treatment.

The equality principle was applied to benefit a recipient of services in rather different circumstances in *Cowan* v *French Treasury* (case 186/87). Here the claimant, an English citizen on holiday in Paris, was claiming compensation for personal injuries sustained as a result of a mugging in the Paris Metro. Under French law compensation in respect of such injuries was provided out of public funds and payable only to French nationals. Cowan claimed that since he was claiming as a tourist, exercising his freedom to receive services, this rule was in breach of Article 12 EC. The ECJ held that as a recipient of services he was entitled to equal protection against, and compensation for, the risks of assault. This right was a corollary of his right to receive services. Since the judgment was expressed in narrow, specific terms, it remains to be seen what rights are to be regarded as a 'corollary' to the right to receive services.

In *Commission* v *Spain* (case C–45/93) the Court found that in charging discriminatory entrance fees to national museums (lower fees being charged for Spanish citizens and residents and EC nationals under 21 years) Spain was acting in breach of Article 12 EC and Article 49 EC. The freedom to provide services recognised by Article 49 included the freedom for recipients of services, including tourists, to go to another Member State to enjoy those services under the same conditions as nationals. As visiting museums was one of the determining reasons why tourists decide to go to another Member State, any discrimination with regard to admission would influence some persons' decisions to visit the country. The fact that a museum service was a public service financed by the State was not raised by the Spanish Government and was not considered by the Court. In subsequent cases concerning discriminatory terms of access to facilities such as museums, the ECJ has not addressed the point whether, relying instead on its reasoning in *Commission* v *Spain* (see, e.g., *Commission* v *Italy* (case C–388/01)).

In a rather different context, in *Hubbard* v *Hamburger* (case C–20/92), a provision of German law requiring a national of another Member State who, in the capacity of executor of a will, had brought proceedings before one of its courts, to lodge security for costs, something which was not required of German nationals, was held to constitute discrimination on grounds of nationality, prohibited by Articles 49 and 50 EC. Although in this case both the provider (the executor) and the recipient (the beneficiary) of services were established outside German territory (in the UK), the rule was clearly a barrier to the free provision (or receipt) of services.

22.10.5 **Cross-border medical care**

In a number of the successful cases, the discrimination principle was used in conjunction with the recipient being in the host Member State for business or for tourist purposes: in either situation contributing to the host Member State's economy. What would be the situation if an individual moved for the purposes of receiving publicly provided services in the host Member State? It is here that the ECJ drew the line in the education cases, as education should not be considered services for the purposes of Article 49. Would the Court take the same view with regard to other public services, such as medical care?

Kohll (case C–158/96) concerned the Luxembourgoise requirement that, if an individual wanted to be able to reclaim the cost of medical treatment outside Luxembourg from the medical insurance company, then prior authorisation granted only in limited circumstances would be required. Kohll sought to challenge this rule on the basis of what was then Article 59 (now 49). The Luxembourg Government argued that the rule complied with Article 22 of Regulation 1408/71 concerning social security. The ECJ agreed that in principle it is for Member States to organise their own social security systems, including the right or duty to be insured with a social security scheme and the benefits available under any such scheme, it held that in doing so Member States must comply with Community law, including the right to provide and receive services. The ECJ held that the orthodontist's treatment in Germany in issue in this case was to be considered 'services' for the purposes of the EC Treaty as the treatment was provided for remuneration and constituted a professional activity. Thus the Luxembourg social security rules regarding medical treatment had to be considered in the light of Article 49. They were found to constitute a barrier to the freedom to provide services and were not objectively justified either for the protection of the financial equilibrium of the social security system or for reasons of national health.

This judgment (and *Decker* (case C–120/95), handed down the same day concerning the provision of spectacles and therefore considered under Article 28 (ex 30); see Chapter 18), which caused some concern among many Member States, raised many questions about the scope of the Treaty freedoms in the context of public health care and the congruence between the case law regarding medical care and the existing case law on public services.

In this context it should be noted that the *Kohll* situation is different from the cases on education. In those cases, the host Member State bore the cost of the individuals moving to receive services; here, the cost is repatriated. Concern arose as to whether the *Kohll* approach would be adopted in regard to healthcare systems which operate by providing the service free rather than by reimbursing the cost. This question was referred to the ECJ in the cases of *Geraets-Smits* v *Stichting Ziekenfonds* and *H.T.M. Peerbooms* v *Stichting CZ Groep Zorgverzekeringen* (case C–157/99). The Advocate-General in this case adopted the reasoning in *Humbel* and *Wirth* (discussed at 22.10.4) to suggest that the provision of healthcare in such systems does not fall within Article 50 EC, constituting instead part of the Member State's obligation towards its population (para. 47). The ECJ, however, followed its approach in *Kohll* and held that medical care fell within the scope of Article 49, although certain restrictions could be justified on public policy grounds, such as the need to protect public health by ensuring an appropriate distribution of hospitals, adequately equipped and staffed, so as to meet the needs of the population.

On one level, it can be said that the judgment avoids distinguishing between the health care systems of the different Member States as to whether they fall within Article 49 or not on the basis of how they are funded. This judgment does, however, mean that there is a split in the jurisprudence between education and health, which seems hard to justify. The alternative interpretation would be that the *Humbel* and *Wirth* line of cases should no longer be viewed as good law. Certainly the ECJ does not seem to be changing its approach to healthcare, as an increasingly long line of cases illustrates (see, e.g., *Leichtle* (case C–8/02) and *R, on the application of Watts* v *Bedford Primarcy Care Trust and Secretary of State for Health* (case C–372/04). Accepting this viewpoint would bring education, as well as public health, well within the Treaty and even the four freedoms, eroding Member State competence. These judgments are therefore hugely significant, as public service has been at the heart of Member State competence and follows the political choices of each of the Member States. Clearly these judgments will have a huge impact on the way the Member States provide public healthcare and possibly other public services.

22.11 Conclusions

The scope of Article 49 is broad, covering a wide range of areas from the purely professional, such as access to economic activity (*van Binsbergen*), to the personal, such as family rights of residence (*Carpenter*). Central to the law in this area is the change from a discrimination-based approach for determining when there has been a violation of Article 49, to one based on hindrance or disincentive. This approach, which broadly mirrors that taken in relation to goods, seems to apply across all aspects of the freedom, including the right to receive services. It is perhaps this last development that is of specific significance. It erodes exclusive Member State competence in the provision of public service, and by doing so provides the right, in principle, for European citizens to receive such services throughout Europe. The jurisprudence of the ECJ in this area may be seen as providing some substantive rights for European citizens in addition to those specified in the Treaty.

FURTHER READING

See also reading for Chapters 20, 21 and 24.

Art J., 'Legislative Lacunae; the Court of Justice and Freedom to Provide Services', in Curtin, D. and O'Keeffe, D. (eds), *Constitutional Adjudication in European Community Law and National Law* (Butterworths Ireland, 1992), p. 121.

Cabral, P., 'Cross-Border Medical Care in the European Union – Bringing Down a First Wall' (1999) 24 EL Rev 387.

Daniele, L., 'Non-discriminatory Restrictions to the Free Movement of Persons' (1997) 22 EL Rev 191.

Lonbay, J., 'Education and Law: the Community Context' (1989) 14 EL Rev 363.

Mei, A. P., 'Cross-Border Access to Medical Care within the European Union – Some Reflections on the Judgments in *Decker* and *Kohll*' [1998] *Maastricht Journal of European and Comparative Law* 277.

Roth, W-H., 'The European Court of Justice's Case Law on Freedom to Provide Services: Is *Keck* Relevant?' in Andenas and Roth (eds) *Services and Free Movement in EU Law* (OUP, 2002).

Van der Woude, M. and Meade, P., 'Free Movement of the Tourist in Community Law' (1988) 25 CML Rev 117.

Van Nuffel, P., 'Patients' Free Movement Rights and Cross-Border Access to Healthcare' (2005) 12(3) Maastricht J 253.

Woods, L., *Free Movement of Goods and Services in the EC* (Ashgate, 2004) Chs 9–11.

23

Free movement of persons: limitation on grounds of public policy, public security or public health

23.1 Introduction

The last few chapters have shown that the ECJ has interpreted the Treaty freedoms applying to persons widely. Nonetheless, as is the case with goods, there are some circumstances where other interests must be balanced against the right to free movement and non-discrimination on the grounds of nationality. We have seen that non-discriminatory measures may be justified on public interest grounds during the application of the Treaty freedom itself. There are specific exceptions to the non-discrimination principle in terms of access to jobs and to professions, as regards linguistic capability (see Article 2(2), Regulation 1612/68) and as regards public services (Article 39(4) as regards workers, Article 45 as regards services and establishment). Beyond these specific and limited provisions, the Treaty permits a Member State to derogate from the Treaty freedoms on the grounds of public policy, public security and public health (Articles 39(3) and 46 EC). As with other derogation provisions, these articles have been interpreted narrowly.

One distinctive feature in this area is that the institutions enacted a directive, Directive 64/221, to delineate the scope of the derogation more clearly in relation to individuals. This directive has now been repealed and replaced by Chapter VI of the Citizenship Directive (Directive 2004/38/EC). Most of the case law relates to Directive 64/221, rather than the underlying Treaty provisions, even though the directive does not apply in all circumstances. The Citizenship Directive, although not phrased in exactly the same terms as Directive 64/221, draws on it and the relevant jurisprudence heavily. It seems likely that the Citizenship Directive will be interpreted along the same lines as Directive 64/221.

A further significant feature is that any derogation needs to be interpreted in the light of individuals' fundamental rights. The ECJ even in its early jurisprudence recognised this. Over the years, the ECJ has, when considering the basis for exceptions to free movement and assessing their proportionality, taken into account the impact of human rights; not only the right to family life but also procedural rights. Additionally, the law in this area increasingly seems to be affected by the notion of European citizenship, as is most recently emphasised by the enactment of the Citizenship Directive, which is based on the concept of citizens' rights.

23.2 Scope of Directive 2004/38/EC and its relationship with Treaty provisions

The exception provided by Articles 39(3) and 46 (ex 48(3) and 56) EC was originally implemented in Directive 64/221 to give substance to the rather vague and potentially catch-all provisions of the Treaty. It allowed for 'special measures concerning the movement and residence of foreign nationals which are justified on the grounds of public policy, public security and public health'. This general principle has been re-stated in Directive 2004/38/EC. Article 27(1) provides that 'Member States may restrict the freedom of movement and residence of Union citizens and their family members, irrespective of nationality, on grounds of public policy, public security or public health'. Although the focal point of the provision remains the same, two points could be made about the changed wording. First, it is more honest, identifying that we are talking about the limitation of individuals' rights (contrast 'special measures concerning'). Secondly, the reference to 'foreign nationals', which distinguished between the nationals of one Member State and another, has been replaced by the reference to 'European citizens', as defined in the Directive.

There are two aspects contained in this section of Directive 2004/38/EC. First it lays down the principles on which a State may refuse entry or residence to those who would otherwise be eligible, on the grounds of public policy, public security or public health; and secondly it lays down procedural safeguards which must be followed by the relevant authorities when they are seeking to exclude non-nationals on one of the permitted grounds.

23.2.1 'Restrictions'

Directive 64/221 applied to 'measures' taken by Member States. 'Measures' taken on the grounds of public policy, public security or public health were defined in *R v Bouchereau* (case 30/77) as any action affecting the rights of persons coming within the field of application of Article 39 EC to enter and reside freely in a Member State on the same conditions as apply to nationals of the host State. This description would still seem to be good law despite the change in terminology to 'restriction'.

23.2.2 Who benefits?

The directive applies to European citizens and their family members; their status as employed or self-employed or otherwise satisfying tests of economic sufficiency is irrelevant. It applies, however, only to restrictions on the *movement* and *residence* of *natural* persons. It does not allow for discrimination as regards access to or conditions of employment, nor does it apply to legal persons. The former will be subject to the derogation provided under Article 2(2) of Regulation 1612/68 (linguistic knowledge) or Articles 39(4) (public services) or 45 (activities connected with official authority); discrimination as regards the latter will be governed by Articles 46 and 50 EC.

Interpretations of the concept of public policy delivered under Directive 64/221, and now Directive 2004/38/EC, which relate to the personal factors justifying discrimination, will not necessarily be appropriate to the public policy exception applicable to undertakings under Article 46 EC. This has not always been recognised by the Court, which has tended to interpret Article 46 by reference to cases decided under Directive 64/221 (see, e.g., Advocate-General Mancini's opinion and the Court's judgment in *Bond van Adverteerders* (case 352/85) noted in Chapter 22). Similar problems have arisen in the context of individuals' rights to receive health care in other Member States in which the Member State has sought to raise public health, that is the provision of a public healthcare system, as a justification. This is a different aspect of public health from that envisaged in ether Directive 64/221 or Directive 2004/38/EC. Nonetheless, it is possible for the underlying Treaty provisions to be relied on where the situation falls outside the scope of the directive, as cross-border medical care cases illustrate (case C–157/99, *Geraets-Smits and Peerboom*, discussed in Chapter 22; DocMorris (case C–322/01), discussed in Chapter 19).

Directive 64/221 did not apply to third-country nationals (TCNs) (save those of EEA countries), except to the extent that they formed part of a migrant EC national's family. In principle this has not changed with the introduction of Directive 2004/38/EC. We will see in Chapter 24 the steps that the institutions have taken to protect the rights of TCNs, especially those that are long-term residents in the EU.

23.2.3 Enforcement

Directive 64/221 provided a source of substantive and procedural rights for individuals, since all its main provisions were directly effective. It seems safe to assume that the relevant provisions in Directive 2004/38/EC will also be directly effective. The underlying Treaty provisions are also capable of being relied on directly.

23.3 Substantive grounds for derogation

23.3.1 Public policy

While public security and public health are reasonably self-explanatory, the meaning and scope of the public policy derogation was originally less clear. In *Van Duyn* v *Home Office* (case 41/74) the Court held, on a reference from the English High Court, that the concept of public policy must be interpreted strictly; its scope cannot be determined unilaterally by Member States without being subject to control by the institutions of the Community. However, the Court conceded that the concept of public policy must vary from State to State; States must have an area of discretion within the limits defined by the Treaty.

As the European integration project progressed, Member States' individual areas of discretion became narrower, a process which is likely to continue. The Court took a rather stricter view in *Rutili* v *Ministre de l'Intérieur* (case 36/75), in the context of an action by Rutili, an Italian and a noted political agitator, to annul a decision from the Minister which restricted his activities to certain regions of France. The Court held that restrictions cannot be imposed on the right of a national of a Member State to enter the territory of another Member State, to stay there and to move within it, unless his presence constitutes a *genuine and sufficiently serious threat to public policy* ('*une menace réelle et suffisamment grave pour l'ordre public*'). This principle, the Court added, was an embodiment of the principles contained in the European Convention on Human Rights that no restrictions in the interests of national security or public safety shall be placed on the rights secured by Articles 8 to 11 of the Convention other than such as are *necessary* for the protection of those interests in a democratic society. All restrictions are subject to the proportionality principle.

The concept was narrowed even further in *R v Bouchereau* (case 30/77) where the Court added that the concept of public policy must always presuppose a genuine and sufficiently serious threat to the requirements of public policy *affecting one of the fundamental interests of society*. This case law has now been embodied in Directive 2004/38/EC. Article 27(2) states that the conduct of the individual which forms the basis of a public policy derogation 'must represent a genuine, present and sufficiently serious threat affecting one of the fundamental interests of society'. This test introduces the requirement that there must be a present, or current threat, rather than a threat that has ceased to be (see, e.g., *Calfa*, discussed below) or that might arise in the future.

Directive 2004/38/EC, like Directive 64/221, lays down a number of circumstances in which measures taken on the grounds of public policy or public security will *not* be justified:

(a) They 'shall not be invoked to serve economic ends' (Article 27(1)). Here the Directive makes explicit what was found to be implicit in cases under the derogating Treaty provisions, such as Article 30 (ex 36) EC, in the context of goods. To allow an economic justification would clearly run counter to the fundamental aims of the Treaty.

(b) 'Previous criminal convictions shall not *in themselves* constitute grounds for the taking of such measures' (Article 27(2), emphasis added). Thus under certain circumstances past criminal convictions may constitute sufficient grounds, but they will not necessarily do so. (See *R v Bouchereau* (case 30/77) and *Donatella Calfa* (case C–348/96), discussed below.) Certainly automatic deportation would seem unacceptable (see Opinion of Advocate-General in *Commission* v *Germany* (case C–441/02)). Article 27(3) allows a host Member State to check the criminal record of a migrant EU citizen for the purposes of assessing whether an individual might constitute a threat, but the provision specifically states that a Member State cannot make such checks automatically.

(c) The expiry of the identity card or passport used by the person concerned to enter the host country and to obtain a residence permit does not justify expulsion from the host Member State (Article 15(2)). As was noted in *Procureur du Roi* v *Royer* (case 48/75), the right of residence does not depend on the possession of a residence permit, it merely provides proof of such a right, which derives from the Treaty itself. The same principle applies to identity cards and passports. As was established in *Watson* (case 118/75), a State may impose penalties for failure to comply with administrative formalities, provided the penalties are not disproportionate, but a failure to comply with such formalities can never provide grounds for deportation. (See also *Wijsenbeek* (case C–378/97), discussed in Chapter 24.)

It seems that the test for the use of the public policy derogation used in respect of cases under the directive has also been applied in the context of Article 46 EC. For example, in *Commission* v *UK* (Open Skies) (case C–466/98), concerning the refusal to grant an operating licence to an airline on the basis that it constituted a threat to public policy, the ECJ applied the *Bouchereau* test. A similar tendency can be seen in relation to the other freedoms.

23.3.2 Public security

Although public security has long been identified as a separate head of derogation, there has been little specific discussion of this term; it tends to be considered with public policy. According to Article 27(2), and in the same way as for public policy, measures to protect public security must be based on the individual conduct of the person concerned. Individual conduct is discussed below at 23.4. The limitations identified at 23.3.1(a)–(c) in relation to public policy apply also to public security. As we shall see below (at 23.5.2.3), Directive 2004/38/EC has introduced a distinction between public policy and public security, but has given no guidance on determining the boundaries between the two categories.

23.3.3 Public health

Article 29(1) specifies that the only diseases justifying measures restricting freedom of movement are those 'with epidemic potential as defined by the relevant instruments of the World Health Organisation', as well as other infectious diseases or contagious parasitic diseases provided they are the subject of protection provisions applying to nationals of the host Member State. This is a narrower list than applied under the previous directive. In its Communication (COM (1999) 372), the Commission made the point that all the Community institutions have clearly stated that the free movement of persons with HIV/AIDS must be safeguarded. Diseases occurring after a three-month period from the date of arrival cannot constitute grounds for expulsion. There is therefore a distinction between the public health justification for expulsion and those based on public policy or public security, in that the latter two categories can be relied on at any point during the migrant's stay in the host Member State; reliance on the public health derogation is limited in time. Again, the host Member State has the right to investigate migrants, this time by requesting an individual to undergo a free medical examination. Such an examination cannot be required as a matter of course.

Note that the scope of public health under the Treaty provisions is somewhat broader than the terms of Directive 2004/38/EC, being developed in parallel with the derogation in relation to goods, Article 30 (see, e.g., *Kohll* (case C–158/96)).

23.4 Personal conduct

Measures taken on the grounds of public policy or public security must be based *exclusively* on the *personal conduct* of the individual concerned (Article 27(2)). This provision reflects the terms of Directive 64/221, Article 3(1), which it replaced.

To justify exclusion, the personal conduct does not have to be illegal. In *Van Duyn v Home Office* (case 41/74) the claimant Ms Van Duyn, a Dutch national, was refused entry into the UK on the grounds of public policy. She was seeking to enter the UK to take up employment with the Church of Scientology. The practice of scientology was not illegal in the UK but it was regarded as socially undesirable. The refusal was claimed to be on the basis of her personal conduct. Two questions were referred, *inter alia,* to the ECJ. First, can membership of an organisation count as 'personal conduct' within the meaning of Article 3(1) Directive 64/221? Secondly, if it can, must such conduct be illegal in order to provide grounds for exclusion on public policy grounds?

In reply to the first question, the Court distinguished between past and present association; past association cannot count as personal conduct; present association, being a voluntary act of the person concerned, can.

With regard to the second question, the Court held that the conduct does not have to be illegal to justify exclusion of non-nationals, as long as the State has made it clear that it considers the activities in question to be 'socially harmful', and has taken administrative measures to counteract the activities. *Van Duyn* must now be read in the light of the more restrictive test advanced in *R* v *Bouchereau* (case 30/77); the activities in question must be sufficiently socially harmful to pose a genuine and sufficiently serious threat to the requirements of public policy affecting one of the fundamental interests of society.

The kind of evidence needed to prove that a particular activity is considered by the State to be sufficiently harmful to justify exclusion on the grounds of public policy was considered by the ECJ, in the context of many questions referred by the Liège District Court, in the case of *Adoui and Cornuaille* v *Belgium* (cases 115 & 116/81). Here two prostitutes were appealing against the Belgian authorities' refusal to grant them a residence permit in Belgium, where they were seeking to practise their arts. The Court held that Member States could not deny residence to non-nationals by reason of conduct which, when attributable to a State's own nationals, did not give rise to repressive measures or other genuine and effective measures to combat such conduct. Evidence of measures of this nature will have to be adduced to prove that the public policy justification is genuine.

Article 27(2) Directive 2004/38/EC, replicating Article 3(2) Directive 64/221/EEC, expressly provides that previous criminal convictions shall not in themselves constitute grounds for measures taken on public policy grounds. The same principle applies to current criminal convictions. In *Bonsignore* v *Oberstadtdirektor of the City of Cologne* (case 67/74), Bonsignore, an Italian worker living in Germany, bought a pistol in breach of German firearms law, and accidentally shot his brother. The action against his brother carried no punishment, but he was fined for unlawful possession of a firearm, and his deportation was ordered. The German authorities argued that his deportation was necessary as a general preventive measure, to deter other immigrants from committing similar offences. The ECJ rejected this argument, holding that the concept of personal conduct expresses the requirement that a deportation order may only be made for breaches of the peace and public security which might be committed by the individual concerned. Thus deportation could not be based on reasons of a general preventive nature. This principle now finds expression in Directive 2004/38/EC. The second paragraph of Article 27(2) provides that justifications which 'are isolated from the particulars of the case or that rely on considerations of general prevention shall not be accepted'.

It should be noted that certain circumstances do permit Member States to take general preventative measures, notably measures connected with gatherings attended by large numbers of people, especially when the people come from different Member States. In its Communication, the Commission suggests examples of such events: large sports events, rock concerts and political demonstrations.

The conduct in *R v Bouchereau* (case 30/77) was more serious than in *Bonsignore*. Mr Bouchereau was a French national who took up employment in the UK in 1975. In June 1976 he was found guilty of unlawful possession of drugs. He had already pleaded guilty to a similar offence in January 1976, and had received a 12-month conditional discharge. In June 1976 the court (Marlborough Street Magistrates) wished to make a deportation order against him. He claimed this was contrary to what was then Article 48 (now Article 39) and Directive 64/221. One of the questions referred to the ECJ concerned Article 3(2) of Directive 64/221 and 'previous criminal convictions'. If they could not 'in themselves' constitute grounds for exclusion, when could they be taken into account? Were they relevant only insofar as they manifested a propensity to act in such a manner, contrary to public policy or public security? The Court held that the existence of previous convictions could only be taken into account as evidence of personal conduct constituting a *present* threat to the requirements of public policy, as showing a propensity to act in the same way again. However, past conduct alone *could* constitute a threat to the requirements of public policy. Thus, it would depend on the gravity of the conduct, past or present, whether it would in fact constitute a present threat to the requirements of public policy.

This point was re-emphasised in *Donatella Calfa* (case C–348/96), concerning a Greek rule which automatically required the expulsion of non-nationals who had been convicted of certain offences, for life. Calfa was an Italian tourist who was convicted of offences relating to the possession of drugs. She appealed against her sentence on the basis that it was incompatible with her right to receive services under what is now Article 49 (ex 59). The ECJ held that her expulsion could only be based on personal conduct *besides* the commission of the offence. It seems that national authorities must thus look at the individual's conduct in addition to that which gave rise to the criminal offence. In any event, all rules must be proportionate, which an automatic life ban is not. Given the wording of Directive 2004/38/EC, it would seem this approach still applies.

The ECJ has also more recently held that Article 3 of Directive 64/221 precludes a national practice whereby national courts cannot take into account changes in factual circumstances when reviewing a decision to deport, especially where there has been a lengthy delay. The requirements of personal conduct and 'present threat' are not satisfied (*Oliveri* (case C–493/01)). Interestingly, this case was brought as a matter of interpretation of Article 3 of Directive 64/221, rather than under the procedural provisions (discussed at 23.6.3). Given the new directive also refers to personal conduct and incorporates the test of a present threat, a similar interpretation would apply to that provision too.

The requirement of 'personal conduct' has implications for the Schengen implementation system (see further Chapter 24). The Commission brought an action against Spain (*Commission v Spain* (case C–503/03)) for refusing entry to two third-country nationals, both of whom were married to migrant EU nationals. Spain refused entry automatically on the basis of information in the Schengen Information System entered by the German authorities. The ECJ held that in the case of a migrant EU national's family member, a Member State must check the threat posed by the individual in the light of the *Bouchereau* test.

Since a denial of residence must be based exclusively on personal conduct, it follows that a worker who is entitled to residence cannot be refused entry or deported merely because the worker is involuntarily unemployed or unable to work through incapacity, even if the worker becomes a charge on public funds (see *Lubbersen* v *Secretary of State for the Home Department* [1984] 3 CMLR 77, Immigration Appeal Tribunal). The same applies to the worker's family. This accords with what was Directive 68/360 (see now Article 7(3) Directive 2004/38/EC and discussion in Chapter 20).

23.5 Types of measure

The original directive was silent as to the type of 'measure' that individual Member States would be permitted to take against foreign nationals. There are a range of options, for example registration requirements, though it would seem the most likely would be refusal of entry or expulsion. Case law has developed limitations in respect of both geographical and temporal considerations, driven by the concept of proportionality and, more recently, citizenship.

23.5.1 Partial restrictions

It was originally thought following the *Rutilli* decision (case 36/75) that the derogation operated only to justify a total ban on residence in a Member State rather than partial restrictions on the right of residence. Unsurprisingly, this ruling came in for a certain amount of criticism as an unnecessary restriction on Articles 39(3) and 46 of the EC Treaty. The derogation exists precisely in order to enable Member States to discriminate against non-nationals on limited and specific grounds. As the ECJ pointed out in *Van Duyn* (case 41/74), it is a principle of international law that States cannot deny rights of residence to their own nationals. To require a total ban where a partial ban would suffice is surely to impose on non-nationals greater restrictions than are necessary to protect the particular interest concerned. This issue was revisited in *Olazabal* (case C–100/01) in which the ECJ reviewed its ruling in *Rutilli*. In contrast to Olazabal, who had been convicted of offences related to terrorism, Rutilli was subject to restrictions because of political and trades union activities. In *Rutilli*, the national referring court had not been sure that national law allowed the adoption of the national measure in question. In *Olazabal*, the national court was clear that Olazabal's activities were of such a serious nature that they justified his deportation. The ECJ concluded that a Member State would not be precluded from imposing limitations on the right to residence within the territory of that Member State provided that:

(a) such action is justified by reasons of public order or public security based on the individual's conduct;

(b) the only alternative course of action, given the seriousness of that conduct would consist of a measure prohibiting the individual from residing in the whole of the national territory; and

(c) the conduct which the Member State concerned wishes to prevent gives rise, in the case of its own nationals, to genuine and effective measures designed to combat it (para. 45).

23.5.2 Expulsion

There are two main problems in this area: expulsion in addition to a criminal penalty; and life-long bans. Case law has sought to limit the Member States' power in such circumstances by use of the doctrine of proportionality and by reading the relevant provisions in the light of the requirements of citizenship. Directive 2004/38/EC incorporates this approach.

23.5.2.1 *Expulsion in addition to a criminal penalty*

Bonsignore indicates that deportation cannot be required in addition to a criminal penalty as a matter of course; this would offend against the requirement of personal conduct and, as in the case of *Calfa*, proportionality. Additionally, there are procedural rights concerning the requirement of temporal proximity between the decision to deport and the deportation itself (23.3.3). These concerns now find their expression in Article 33.

23.5.2.2 *Permanent exclusion*

If a Member State has grounds for restricting the right of free movement, this does not mean that it can permanently exclude someone. Such an approach could, as we have seen in *Calfa*, be disproportionate. Article 27(2) now specifies that any measures shall be proportionate. Article 32 now gives the right to apply for the lifting of an exclusion order where there has been a material change in circumstances.

23.5.2.3 *Protection against expulsion*

An innovation introduced by Directive 2004/38/EC is Article 28 which imposes limitations on a Member State's freedom to expel an EC national. Article 28(1) provides that in deciding whether or not to expel an individual, a Member State must take into account factors such as how long the individual has resided on its territory, the age of the person concerned, state of health, family and economic situation as well as the links with the country of origin. These conditions are the types of consideration that the ECJ has highlighted as being required by respect for family life under Article 8 ECHR (see case C–482/01, *Orfanopoulos*, citing *Boultif* v *Switzerland*). Many of these factors reflect a graduated level of protection awarded to migrants, based on their level of integration into the host Member State, which we will also see in Chapter 24 regarding citizenship rights.

Article 28 then goes on to identify three specific circumstances: the position of those who have a right of permanent residence (Article 28(2)); those who have resided in the host Member State for the previous ten years (Article 28(3)(a)); and minors (Article 28(3)(b)). For those falling within the scope of Article 28(2), Member States may only take an expulsion decision on serious grounds of public policy or public security. For the other two categories, an expulsion decision may only be made on 'imperative grounds of public security'; seemingly public policy will not justify such a decision.

23.6 Procedural rights

Directive 2004/38/EC provides extensive procedural safeguards for parties seeking to assert rights of entry or residence in Member States, based on the provisions in Directive 64/221. The rights in Directive 64/221 were directly effective, and it is highly likely that the equivalent provisions in Directive 2004/38/EC are also directly effective. In the light of this, any decision issued in violation of these rights may be challenged as contrary to EC law.

23.6.1 Temporary residence

Directive 64/221 specified that 'a person awaiting a decision to grant or refuse a first residence permit in a Member State must be allowed to remain temporarily in that State pending that decision. The decision must be taken as soon as possible and not more than six months from the date of application' (Article 5(1)). Given that Union citizens no longer have to apply for a residence permit, there is no equivalent provision in Directive 2004/38/EC. Instead, Article 30(3) requires the Member State to specify the time-limit within which a person must leave the territory, which save in cases of emergency (duly substantiated) may not be less than one month, and Article 31(2) provides that, where an individual appeals and applies for a suspension of the removal order, such a person will not be required to remove themselves from the territory whilst the matter is pending, save in limited, specified circumstances. By contrast to Directive 64/221 (Article 7), there are no specific time-limits contained in Directive 2004/38/EC.

23.6.2 Reasons for decisions

The person concerned shall be informed in writing of any decision made under Article 27, in a manner so that he or she is able to understand not only the decision but its implications. Further, the person must be informed, precisely and in full, of the grounds of public policy, public security or public health upon which the decision taken in his or her case is based, unless this is contrary to the interests of the security of the State (Article 30). Any notification must inform the person of where, when and how an appeal may be lodged (Article 30(3)).

In developing the provisions of Directive 64/221, Directive 2004/38/EC seems to be incorporating the jurisprudence of the ECJ in cases such as *Rutili*. The Court held in *Rutili* (case 36/75) that the authority making the decision must give the applicant a precise and comprehensive statement of the ground for the decision, to enable the applicant to take effective steps to prepare his or her defence. The Commission in its Communication made the point that the duty to give reasons applies also to decisions regarding the applications for visas by family members who are third-country nationals.

23.6.3 Remedies: rights of defence

Directive 2004/38/EC amends the format of the rights of the defence. Directive 94/221 provided for a right of access to remedies by comparison with the position of nationals of the host Member State (Article 8), but then also provided a minimum guarantee, that a decision to deport must be reviewed by a competent authority (Article 9). A certain amount of case law arose about the scope and interrelationship of the two provisions, which may be of historic interest only given the changes introduced by the Citizenship Directive. Article 31 of the Citizenship Directive provides:

> The persons concerned shall have access to judicial and, where appropriate, administrative redress procedures in the host Member State to appeal against or seek review of any decision taken against them on the grounds of public policy, public security or public health.

Interestingly, the phraseology represents a change, in that individuals under the new system are given a right of access to a judicial remedy and possibly an administrative remedy. The matter is not one of comparison, as under former Article 8, nor of merely showing that a competent authority has reviewed the decision.

Although the terms of the two sets of provisions are different, a number of points from the case law on the old system might well be applicable to the new. Note that neither system specified the precise nature of the remedies to be available; this is consonant with the principle of national procedural autonomy (see Chapter 8). The ECJ noted, in relation to Article 9, Directive 64/221, that the provisions incorporated the minimum requirements of natural justice. According to the ECJ, they therefore called for a broad interpretation. Whether a review of the case law truly reveals a high level of protection or not, this principle would seem to apply to Article 31, Directive 2004/38.

In *Royer* (case 48/75), the ECJ held that Member States could not execute a deportation order without giving the migrant the chance to avail himself of the right to the remedy granted under Article 8, Directive 64/221. The substance of Directive 2004/38/EC reflects this. Not only should a Member State not normally allow less than a month for an individual to leave (Article 30(3)), but Article 31(2) allows for an individual to remain on the territory pending the outcome of the appeal, subject to certain specified exceptions (see also Article 31(4)).

There were two aspects to the case law on Article 9, Directive 64/221: the class of people to whom it applied; and the scope of the rights granted.

The ECJ had to consider the question of the beneficiaries of procedural rights in *MRAX* (case C–459/99). In this case the Belgian Government argued that Article 9 did not apply to the third country nationals who were members of a migrant workers family, but who had entered the host Member State illegally. Given the importance of Directive 64/221, and particularly these procedural articles, for guaranteeing the rights set out in Article 6 and 13 ECHR, however, the ECJ held that the illegality of their original entry to the host Member State could not deprive these individuals of the protection granted by Article 9. As the ECJ pointed out, to require an individual to be in possession of a valid identity document or visa would rob the procedural guarantees of much of their effectiveness. A similar argument could be made in respect of the guarantees in Articles 30 and 31, Directive 2004/38.

As regards the scope of the rights, the ECJ seems also to have been influenced by the need to ensure a fair trial and the right to an effective remedy contained in the ECHR, which are surely still relevant under the new system. Under Article 9, Directive 64/221, as the Court pointed out in *Rutili* (case 36/75), the person concerned must at the very least be able to exercise his or her rights of defence before a competent authority, which must not be the same as that which adopted the measure which restricted the person's freedom. Principles of independence must inform an assessment of the appropriateness of bodies providing redress under Article 31, Directive 2004/38; see further below.

In *R v Secretary of State for the Home Department, ex parte Santillo* (case 131/79), Santillo, an Italian, had been convicted in the UK of a number of crimes of violence including rape, buggery and indecent assault. He was sentenced to eight years in gaol, with a recommendation for deportation at the end of his sentence. Nearly five years later the Home Secretary made a deportation order against him. He applied for judicial review to quash this decision. Two issues were raised in the proceedings. First, whether the trial judge's recommendation was an 'opinion from a competent authority', as required by Article 9(1), Directive 64/221; and secondly, if so, whether a lapse of time between the issuing of this 'opinion' and the making of the order could deprive the judge's recommendation of its status as an 'opinion' under Article 9(1). The ECJ, on a reference for interpretation from the English High Court, held that the trial judge's recommendation did amount to an 'opinion' within Article 9(1); but that the safeguard provided by Article 9 could only be a real one if that opinion were sufficiently proximate in time to the decision recommending deportation, to ensure that the factors justifying deportation still existed at the time when the order was made. A change of heart or political climate could mean that the public policy justification had ceased to exist. This safeguard has been enacted by Article 33(2), Directive 2004/38, which provides that where an expulsion order is enforced more than two years after it was issued, the Member State is under an obligation to check that the individual concerned is 'currently and genuinely a threat to public policy or public security' and to assess whether there has been any 'material change' in circumstances since the expulsion order was issued.

Like its predecessor, the Citizenship Directive gives no definition of what appropriate remedies might be. Jurisprudence in respect of Article 9(2), Directive 64/221 was considered in *R v Secretary of State for the Home Department, ex parte Gallagher* (case C–175/94), with particular reference to what could constitute a competent authority and the scope of the information regarding the appeal body that was required to be given to the applicant. Gallagher had been convicted in Ireland for the possession of rifles for unlawful purposes. He subsequently went to the UK and took up employment there. He was arrested and deported. On arrival in Ireland he challenged the deportation decision as unlawful, and was interviewed in Dublin. His interviewer gave no name and no information concerning the grounds for his expulsion. At his request his case was reconsidered by the Home Secretary, but the deportation decision was not reversed. The ECJ found that the matter fell within Article 9(2), but did not specify how the competent authority should be appointed, nor what its composition should be. It was nonetheless essential that it should be independent of the authority empowered to take the measure concerning deportation, and that the person concerned should be able to submit his or her defence. There was no need to notify the claimant of the identity of the authority as long as the national court was in a position to determine whether it was impartial. These questions were left to the national court to decide. Although one might suggest the level of protection awarded in *Gallagher* was low and perhaps driven by political sensitivities, the underlying principles regarding independence and impartiality as touchstones for determining whether procedural safeguards have been satisfied must remain. Article 31(3) further specifies the scope of the jurisdiction of the appeal bodies. It provides that 'the redress procedures shall allow for an examination of the legality of the decision, as well as of the facts and circumstances on which the proposed measure is based. They shall ensure that the decision is not disproportionate, particularly in view of the requirements laid down in Article 28' (discussed at 23.5.2.3).

It seems, following *R* v *Secretary of State for the Home Department, ex parte Shingara* (cases C–65 & 111/95), that where an individual who has been refused admission to a Member State, reapplies for admission to a country after a reasonable length of time (in *Shingara* approximately three years), the procedural safeguards in Articles 8 and 9, Directive 64/221 would apply anew to that reapplication. Individuals expressly have the right to apply to have exclusion orders lifted under Article 32. It is submitted that following the *Shingara* reasoning, they too would benefit from procedural rights, although Article 32(2) states that such persons do not have the right of entry to the territory of a Member State while their application is being considered.

23.7 Conclusions

It can be seen that derogation from the free movement of people has common themes with the derogation from the free movement of goods. Both sets of derogation are interpreted narrowly, with Member States' actions being closely scrutinised. In this context the interpretation of personal conduct has been of great significance in limiting general actions by Member States against groups of EU migrants on the basis of their nationality. Another important aspect of the case law in this area has been the Court's interpretation of the procedural guarantees contained in the second part of the directive, which is clearly linked with the guarantees to a fair trial contained in the ECHR (on fundamental rights in the EU, see Chapter 6). Since *Donatella Calfa*, it now seems likely that the scope of the derogations will also have to be understood in the light of the impact of European citizenship, again constraining Member States' freedom in this area. In this respect the terms of the new directive do not represent a break with past practice, but rather constitute a codification of that jurisprudence.

FURTHER READING

Connor, T. C., 'Migrant Community Nationals: Remedies for Refusal of Entry by Member States' (1998) 28 EL Rev 157.

Furse, M. and Nash, S., 'Free Movement, Criminal Law and Fundamental Rights in the European Community' [1997] JR 148.

Hall, S., 'The European Convention on Human Rights and Public Policy Exceptions to the Free Movement of Workers under the EEC Treaty' (1991) 16 EL Rev 466.

Handoll, J., *Free Movement of Persons in the European Union* (J. Wiley and Son, 1995), Ch. 7.

O'Keeffe, D., 'Practical Difficulties in the Application of Article 48 of the EEC Treaty' (1982) 19 CML Rev 35.

Van Overbeek, P. M., 'Aids/HIV Infection and the Free Movement of Persons in the European Economic Community' (1990) 27 CML Rev 791.

Woods, L., *Free Movement of Goods and Services within the European Community* (Ashgate, 2004), Ch. 12.

24

Completion of the internal market: extending free movement rights – citizenship and third-country nationals

24.1 Introduction

The EC Treaty has always contained provisions granting free movement rights to workers and those seeking to establish themselves or provide (or receive) services. As the preceding chapters show, these rights, although broadly interpreted by the ECJ, have previously been aimed primarily at those who are economically active and are EC nationals, although special rules apply to their families. Even following the SEA, which introduced a number of changes including Article 14 EC (ex 7a), the EC Treaty did not create an internal market allowing the free movement of persons throughout the Community, as not all EC nationals would enjoy all free movement rights under the Treaty. The position of 'third-country nationals' (TCNs) was even more restricted as, unless they were family members of an EU national, they would fall outside the protection of EC law. Another difficulty, as far as the creation of the internal market was concerned, was the fact that the Member States continued to maintain some form of border or passport control. Thus, even when EU nationals sought to exercise their rights of free movement under the Treaty, they would still have to stop at borders between Member States to show their identification. The emphasis on border control arises because there are strong links between the creation of an area without internal frontiers and a common immigration policy. As Member States scale down or eliminate their own controls on immigration, stringent external control, particularly as regards TCNs, needs to exist to replace national controls before an area without internal borders would be acceptable to the Member States.

Following a legislative initiative in the early 1990s, which introduced residence rights for the students (Directive 93/96), ex-employed and self-employed persons (Directive 90/365) and other people who could support themselves (Directive 90/364) (the Residence Directive), there have been Treaty amendments which have extended the right to free movement. Thus, recent treaties have changed the position as regards both the need for an economic nexus between the EU national and the host Member State, and the exclusion, except to the extent that TCNs are an EU national's family members, of TCNs from basic Community rights. The TEU introduced the idea of European citizenship, and one of the primary citizenship rights is the right of free movement throughout the Community. The ToA took a further step towards creating an area without passport controls by introducing a new title to the EC Treaty, Title IV (Articles 61–69 EC), which deals with visas, asylum, immigration and other policies relating to the free movement of persons. Further secondary legislation, dealing with the position of TCNs, was enacted under these new provisions. The cumulative effect of these changes take the Community further towards the completion of the internal market as regards persons.

The new provisions do, however, raise certain questions. One issue is who can claim the benefit of the rights? To what extent are the citizenship rights constrained by requirements of migration and economic self-sufficiency, as the rights granted by Articles 39, 43 and 49 were? There may in this context be difficult issues regarding the relationship between the original free movement rights (workers, establishment and services) and the new rights, particularly as regards the operation of any derogation from these rights. Further, what is the nature of the rights that may be claimed? Are they purely free movement rights, or are ancillary and social rights under a general principle of non-discrimination part of the citizenship package? Essentially, these questions can be reduced to one central issue: to what extent are citizenship rights something new, in addition to those rights granted by the traditional freedom rights? This chapter explores these questions and considered the impact of new secondary legislation, both as regards EU citizens and TCNs.

24.2 The citizen's right of free movement

24.2.1 Overview of provision

Article 18 (ex 8a) EC provides:

> 1. Every citizen of the Union shall have the right to move and reside freely within the territory of the Member States, subject to the limitations and conditions laid down in this Treaty and by the measures adopted to give it effect.

A second paragraph gives the Community institutions the power to enact legislation to facilitate the exercise of the rights granted using the co-decision procedure. The Treaty of Nice has added a further paragraph:

> (3) Paragraph 2 shall not apply to provisions on passports, identity cards, residence permits or any other such document or to provisions on social security or social protection.

Should the Constitution in its current form come into force, the provisions relating to citizenship will be found in Article I–10. The wording is slightly different, but with the possible exception of the deletion of Article 18(3), the changes seem cosmetic. Title V of Part II of the Constitutional Treaty sets out the rights of citizens in more detail.

Note that Article 18 grants two rights: the right to move and the right to reside. Although the ECJ's jurisprudence has long recognised that the corollary of the right to move and to work (whether as an employed or self-employed person) implied the right to reside in the host Member State, Article 18 constitutes the first express Treaty recognition of this right.

It was not originally clear whether Article 18 had direct effect. Many Member States, such as the UK, suggested it did not, whereas the Commission believed that it did. It should be noted that the mere fact that secondary legislation is envisaged in a policy area, as here, does not automatically preclude the Treaty provision itself from having direct effect, as the ECJ itself ruled in the context of freedom of establishment and freedom to provide services (see *Reyners* (case 2/74); *van Binsbergen* (case 33/74) discussed in Chapter 22). The ECJ for some time avoided ruling on whether Article 18 has direct effect, despite a number of references on this point, dealing with the references on other grounds (e.g., *Wijsenbeek* (case C–378/97)). The ECJ has, however, since confirmed that Article 18 does have direct effect (see, e.g., case C–224/98 *D'Hoop*).

24.2.2 Who benefits from the right?

The rights in Article 18 are granted to all European citizens. Article 17 (ex 8) defines European citizens as: 'Every person holding the nationality of a Member State'. On the face of it, the requirement merely to show nationality of a Member State means Article 18 is broader than the pre-existing free movement right contained in Articles 39, 43 and 49 EC, as there is no need to show any economic activity on the part of the individual seeking to move from one Member State to another. Conversely, the rights contained in Article 18 are constrained by 'the limitations and conditions laid down in this Treaty and by the measures adopted to give it effect'. It was not at all clear what the consequence of this proviso would be on the determination of who could claim citizens' rights, and whether limitations on individuals based on whether they had migrated and whether they had been economically active would be imported into Article 18. This view would mean that Article 18 continues to exclude those who would not have been able to rely on the original free movement rights. Certainly, this would seem to have been the view of some of the English courts shortly after the introduction of citizenship. In *R v Secretary of State for the Home Department, ex parte Vitale* ([1996] All ER (EC) 461), for example, Vitale sought entry to the UK although he did not have a job and was not looking for one. The English courts rejected his claim to entry into the UK on the basis that he was not a worker. They did not accept that he might have a right of entry as a European citizen. Although the ECJ might have started from this position, it would seem that its attitude towards citizenship has evolved, taking a broader view of citizenship which does not limit it to the economically active (see e.g., *Chen* (case C–200/02)). In the citizenship cases we are perhaps seeing the ECJ in activist mode again.

24.2.2.1 *Relationship with other free movement rights*

In general, the relationship between the rights in Article 18 and the original free movement rights is not clear. As noted, some commentators suggested that the rights in Article 18 are no more than a re-statement and consolidation of the pre-existing situation, given the enactment of three directives to allow the free movement of students, the retired and other persons (Directives 93/96, 90/365 and 90/364, respectively), especially since the right in Article 18 is 'subject to the limitations and conditions laid down in this Treaty'.

In *Wijsenbeek* (case C–378/97), the ECJ had to consider whether the introduction of European citizenship rendered border controls illegal. In this case the ECJ held that Member States were still entitled to check the identity documents (in this case the passport) of EU nationals travelling between Member States, despite the fact that all EU nationals are now European citizens. The ECJ then went on to hold, however, that any penalties for failure to comply with such rules must be proportionate in the light of European citizenship and the right to move from one Member State to another. In this, the ECJ made a distinction between the right to move between Member States and the ability to do so without having to prove one's identity or nationality. Thus, this ruling would suggest that citizenship on its own is not enough to create an area without internal frontiers even if it is a lot easier, as an EU national, to cross those borders.

The ECJ has now ruled that the right of residence is subject to the limitations contained in the various pieces of secondary legislation already enacted in this area (discussed at 24.3 and Chapter 20). It has also held that where the more specific provisions, for example Article 39, apply there is no need to interpret Article 18 (see case C–92/01, *Stylianakis v Elliniko Dimosio*, regarding the relationship between Article 18 and Article 49 EC; case C–193/94, *Skanavi and Chryssanthakopoulos* regarding establishment; and case C–100/01, *Oteiza Olazabal*, regarding workers). Some lack of clarity remains. In some of these cases where free movement provisions could apply, the ECJ does not refer to citizenship at all (see, e.g., case C–92/01, *Stylianakis v Elliniko Dimosio*). In others, although the question is determined on the basis of one of the four freedoms, the interpretation of that freedom is affected by the notion of citizenship (see, e.g., case C–100/01, *Oteiza Olazabal*; case C–274/96, *Bickel and Franz*), which the ECJ has held to be a fundamental status of EU nationals (see, e.g., case C–184/99, *Grzelczyck*, para. 31).

24.2.2.2 *Nationality requirement*

As a Protocol to the TEU made clear, it is for each Member State to decide for itself who is to be considered a national of that Member State. Thus, Member States may only require that an individual provide appropriate identity documents and may not criticise the decision of another Member State to recognise an individual as having the nationality of that Member State. This approach pre-dates the introduction of European citizenship. In *Micheletti* (case C–369/90), for example, the ECJ held that the Spanish could not challenge the claim of Micheletti – who had the nationality of both Italy and Argentina – to be Italian on the grounds that the Spanish did not recognise the concept of dual nationality. According to the ECJ, the important point was whether the Italians recognised his claim (see post-TEU *Stephen Saldanha and MTS Securities Corporation v Hiross Holding AG* (case C–122/96)). On this basis, the viewpoint of the Member State is determinative, as can be seen in *Kaur*. The English High Court referred certain questions to the ECJ concerning the extent of the freedom of Member States to define citizenship and, in particular, the limitations imposed on this freedom by the need to respect individuals' fundamental rights (*R v Secretary of State for the Home Department, ex parte Manjit Kaur* (case C–192/99)). The ECJ avoided answering the specific questions on the impact of fundamental human rights, but confirmed that the scope of European citizenship, as far as British subjects were concerned, was determined by the relevant British declarations on this subject.

Leaving the determination of citizenship to the Member States may have a number of consequences. In contrast to the definition of 'workers' (see Chapter 20), the notion of European citizen would seem not to be a Community (or Union) concept. The fact that the Member States themselves take radically different approaches to the question of determining nationality may introduce inequalities as to the type of person who benefits from citizenship rights across the Union. The decision of one Member State on this point can have a significant impact on the composition of Union citizens as a whole, but, despite the fact that this decision may consequently affect other Member States, it is a decision that the other Member States cannot influence at all. As the *Chen* case (case C–200/02) (discussed below) illustrates, the patchwork of different national approaches to nationality can have some strange, unintended effects which can be manipulated to an individual's advantage. As *Chen* also illustrates, Member States cannot challenge another Member State's choice about refusing or restricting citizenship/nationality. This may have particular consequences for the new accession states, many of which have not granted citizenship on the Russian population who are nonetheless legally resident within their territory, and many of whom have been born in territory that now forms part of the EU. As a result of a national decision, these people are denied European citizenship, with consequences for free movement rights. In many ways, however, their position is the same as that of other TCNs who are integrated into a Member State. Thus EU treatment of such individuals seems, with the recent accessions, to be of ever more significance.

One final point to note about who may claim full citizenship rights and, in particular, the rights of free movement and residence is that the new Member States are, on the whole, subject to transitional provisions which, rather unevenly, limit the right of free movement (see Chapter 20).

24.2.2.3 *Migrancy*

It might seem self-evident that a provision granting free movement rights implies migrancy. As we have seen in the case of workers, however, social rights, including the right of family reunion, might also be implied (see below). If such rights form part of the citizenship package, can they be claimed as against a citizen's home Member State? From the early case law, it seems that purely internal situations remain outside the scope of Community law (joined cases C–64 and 65/96, *Hecker and Jacquet*; cf. Opinion in case C–148/02, *Avello*).

In *D'Hoop*, the would-be claimant of a job seeker's allowance, who had done her schooling in another Member State although her parents had not moved from their State of origin, was held not to fall within Article 39 (see Chapter 20). The ECJ held that 'the situations falling within the scope of Community law include those involving the exercise of the fundamental freedoms guaranteed by the Treaty, in particular those involving the freedom to move and reside within the territory of the Member States as conferred by Article 8a of the EC Treaty (now, after amendment, Article 18 EC)' (para. 29). In this the ECJ seemingly rejected the argument of the British Government that movement itself was not enough to bring an individual within the scope of Community law and that instead an individual must pursue an activity which falls within the scope of the Treaty, such as studying for a vocational course. It seems, however, that if an individual has not exercised any free movement rights, he or she will not fall within the scope of Community law.

Note that the cross-border element can easily be satisfied. This point is illustrated by the somewhat unusual facts in the case of *Chen* (case C–200/02). The case concerned a Chinese couple who travelled to the United Kingdom when Mrs Chen was six months' pregnant. She gave birth to a daughter, Catherine, in Belfast and both mother and daughter then moved to Cardiff. Catherine did not acquire British citizenship, as birth in the territory of the United Kingdom itself no longer confers British nationality. The operation of Irish nationality laws meant that Catherine did acquire Irish nationality, as any person born on the island of Ireland is an Irish citizen from birth if not entitled to citizenship of any other country. Catherine lost the right to Chinese nationality by virtue of being born in Northern Ireland. None of the parties was entitled to reside in the United Kingdom under British law, but Catherine was not entitled to reside in China. The parties were not dependent on the British State to survive and it was unlikely that they would be so dependent. Nonetheless, the Secretary of State refused Mrs Chen and Catherine long-term residence permits. The British and Irish governments argued that Catherine could not exercise Community law rights because she had not moved from one Member State to another; she had only ever lived in the UK. The ECJ rejected this argument. Relying on *Garcia Avello* (case C–148/02), the ECJ held that the situation of a national of one Member State who has only ever lived in the host Member State cannot be assimilated to a purely internal situation (para. 19). Further, the ability to exercise free movement rights is not circumscribed by the need to acquire legal capacity; children may exercise Community free movement rights.

24.2.3 **Material scope of rights**

24.2.3.1 *Right of free movement*
Article 18 clearly gives the right to free movement; this is the right of transit. It is not unlimited as we have already seen in the case of *Wijsenbeek* (case C–378/97) in which the ECJ held that the right of free movement is different from the obligation to prove one's identity as an EU national. Equally, the right to free movement is subject to the derogations laid down in the Treaty, as can been seen in *ex parte Yiadom* (case C–357/98). In this case, the UK authorities were able to refuse a suspected Dutch people smuggler the right to enter the UK on grounds of public policy. The exercise of such a derogation is subject always to the principle of subsidiarity. The Commission Communication on Directive 64/221/EEC makes it clear that in the Commission's opinion, citizenship rights are subject to limitations for reasons of public policy, public security or public health, as provided in that directive. Nonetheless, in interpreting this directive, and now the relevant provisions of Directive 2004/38, Member States must take into account the existence and nature of citizenship and limit any action to what is strictly necessary and proportional.

24.2.3.2 *Right of residence*
We noted at 24.1 that the right to residence had been widened beyond the scope of the economically active by the enactment of three directives concerning students, retired persons and those of independent means, respectively. The introduction of the concept of citizenship potentially changed the position again, as citizenship, and the right of residence granted to citizens, was not expressly limited to certain categories of person. Instead, it was available to all, a point the ECJ recognised in *Baumbast* (case C–413/99), when it held that the right was conferred on every citizen of the Union irrespective of whether he or she was engaged in an economic activity. In *Baumbast*, the migrant Union citizen did not comply with the formal

requirements of the Residence Directive – to be insured against medical emergencies – but was not a financial burden on the host Member State. According to the ECJ, Article 18(1) had to be read in accordance with the limitations imposed by the Residence Directives, but that these limits themselves had to be understood in the light of the principle of proportionality, and the UK's refusal to renew his residence permit on the facts of this case was disproportionate. *Baumbast* can thus also be seen as authority for the proposition, seen in other cases (see, e.g., *Kaba* (case C–356/98)), that Article 18(1) rights are not unconditional. In *Trojani* (case C–456/02, see Chapter 20 and below), the ECJ held that, contrary to the position in *Baumbast*, a claimant who is carrying out minimal economic activities, and is dependent on the host State, does not derive a right to reside on the territory where the claimant does not have sufficient resources (para. 36). Nonetheless, such a person may be able to rely on general principles of non-discrimination (para. 39).

24.2.3.3 *Social and ancillary rights*

The real impact of citizenship can be seen when considered in conjunction with the concept of discrimination. In *Martinez Sala* (case C–85/96), the ECJ held that a national of one Member State resident in another could rely on the non-discrimination principle in Article 12 EC on matters falling within the scope of the EC Treaty. On one reading this case can be seen narrowly; Martinez Sala had been a migrant worker and therefore came within the scope of Community law on that basis. Alternatively, we could see *Martinez Sala* as the basis of the argument that a lawfully resident migrant European citizen may not be discriminated against by the host Member State on matters falling within the scope of EC law. *Martinez Sala* therefore starts the process of decoupling the acquisition of rights from the requirement to be economically active. The ECJ affirmed this approach in *Baumbast*. There it held that

> The Treaty on European Union does not require that citizens of the Union pursue a professional or trade activity, whether as an employed or self-employed person, in order to enjoy the rights provided in Part Two of the EC Treaty, on citizenship of the Union.

The scope of this ruling has been elaborated in subsequent judgments, perhaps one of the most noteworthy of which is *Grzelczyk* (case C–184/99). It will be remembered from Chapters 20 and 22 that the position of students seeking maintenance grants had caused concern in the Member States. The ECJ ruled in *Brown* (case 197/86, para. 18) that assistance given to students for maintenance and training fell outside the non-discrimination principle currently found in Article 12 EC. *Grzelczyk* concerned a migrant student who, in his third year of studies, applied for such social assistance and was turned down as permitted by *Brown* on the basis of his nationality. The ECJ expressly noted that the nature of the Community has changed since *Brown*, notably with the introduction of citizenship. The ECJ therefore reasoned that:

> the fact that a Union citizen pursues university studies in a Member State other than the State of which he is a national cannot, of itself, deprive him of the possibility of relying on the prohibition of all discrimination on grounds of nationality laid down in Article 6 [now 12] of the Treaty (para. 36).

This judgment effectively overruled the principle in *Brown*: where a Member State does not require its own nationals to be workers to claim certain benefits, it cannot require that a migrant EC national fall within the scope of Regulation 1612/68 to claim the same benefit.

There is a change here in the reasoning of the ECJ. Whereas in *Martinez Sala* the benefit did fall within the scope of Regulation 1612/68, here the right to claim equality is based on the fact that the claimant has moved. On another level, the consequences may be more limited, given the terms of Article 1 of the Students Directive (now replaced by Directive 2004/38/EC) which requires students to be self-supporting. Nonetheless, although Member States may withdraw the right of residence where a student does not have sufficient resources, such a withdrawal may not be automatic. The reasoning here seems to create a circular position; although lawfully resident migrants are entitled to claim some benefits on the basis of non-discrimination, actually claiming those benefits might be proof that they are an unreasonable burden on the host State. The difficulties can be seen in *Trojani v Le Centre Public d'Aide Sociale de Bruxelles* (case C–456/02). Where the migrant is lawfully resident, and Trojani had been issued with a residence permit, the fact that the migrant could not claim the right of residence under Article 18 or Directive 90/364, as was the position here, does not affect the migrant's right to equality of treatment within the scope of the Treaty (para. 40). Lawful residence thus entitles the migrant to social assistance on the same terms as the national of the host Member State. The ECJ, however, expressly pointed out that a Member State could withdraw the residence permit.

One further point about the ECJ's reasoning in these cases should be noted, as we can see from the case of *Collins* (case C–138/02, discussed also in Chapter 20). Collins entered the UK to try to find a job and claimed job seeker's allowance, which he was refused. The ECJ stated that citizens lawfully resident in the territory of a host Member State can rely on Article [12] of the Treaty in all situations which fall within the scope *ratione materiae* of Community law.

> Citizenship of the Union is destined to be the fundamental status of nationals of the Member States, enabling those who find themselves in the same situation to enjoy the same treatment in law irrespective of their nationality, subject to such exceptions as are expressly provided for (para. 61).

The reasoning does reveal, however, a tension. On the one hand, citizenship is a fundamental status, but on the other hand the rights that come with it can seemingly be exercised only by those who are lawfully resident (or as in *Trojani*, have a residence permit), whether the right is claimed under EC law or national law. This suggests that, despite the grand terminology, the ECJ has not adopted a full citizenship model where Community migrants are placed on a completely equal footing unless Community law expressly provides otherwise. An alternative view is that the ECJ has adopted a graduated approach. The longer a migrant has been in the host Member State, the more integrated he or she is, the greater his or her rights. *Martinez Sala* had been resident in Germany for a considerable period and had contributed to host State funds; *Grzelczyck*, with a relatively short stay in the host Member State is entitled to limited social assistance. In *Collins*, the ECJ accepted the principle that Collins could be entitled to claim job seeker's allowance, but then also held that the right could be restricted if objectively justified, *inter alia*, by a wish on the part of the host Member State to ensure that there is a genuine link between an applicant and a social advantage (para. 67). In *Bidar* (case C–209/03), which concerned a legally resident student's claim for state support, the ECJ emphasised the link between the host Member State and the migrant, making it possible for a Member State to impose prerequisites on the right of a claimant. In coming to its conclusion in *Bidar*, the ECJ seems implicitly to have overruled *Lair* (case 39/86) (discussed in Chapter 22). *Ioannidis* (case C–258/04) concerned a claim for a job seeker's allowance (the same allowance as in *D'Hoop*) by a Greek person who had studied in Belgium but then moved to France for a relatively short period and then returned to Belgium. Here, the ECJ reaffirmed that a Member State may wish to ensure that there is a real link between the applicant and the geographic employment market concerned. The condition imposed in this case, that the applicant must have completed his secondary education in the Member State, was not acceptable. It was not necessarily representative of a real and effective degree of connection, and therefore went beyond what was necessary to obtain the objective. In general, it might be argued that those with a stronger temporal link have greater rights. One might suggest that a graduated approach is in line with that adopted in the Citizenship Directive, discussed below at 24.3.

The prohibition of discrimination is not limited to claims concerning financial assistance. *Bickel and Franz* (case C–274/96), an early citizenship case, concerned the right to have court proceedings carried out in a language the migrant can understand. In *Garcia Avello* (case C–148/02), the issue under discussion was the right of a family to register their children's names in Belgium in the Spanish manner. *Chen* (case C–200/02), discussed above, gave a dependent child the right to have her mother reside with her. *Pusa* (case C–224/02) concerned a tax prepayment scheme in one Member State of origin to ensure repayment of a debt, which did not take account of the tax paid on the income in another Member State.

In this context, note that we have been considering discrimination based on nationality. Since the enactment of Directive 2000/43 on Discrimination Based on Ethnic Origin ([2000] OJ L180/22), discrimination based on ethnic origin is also prohibited.

24.2.3.4 *Discrimination, obstacles to free movement and justification*

It seems that, as with other areas, the discrimination prohibited by citizenship applies to both direct discrimination and indirect discrimination. *Garcia Avello* can be seen as concerning rules discriminating against those who had a second nationality. In *Collins*, for example, the job seeker's allowance was refused because the UK had not been Collins's habitual residence, a condition which is harder for nationals to satisfy than non-nationals. As *Collins* also illustrates, such rules may be permissible if objectively justified in addition to the express Treaty derogations and those provisions found in Directive 2004/38/EC (replacing Directive 64/221/EEC).

Given the developments in the context of Articles 39, 43 and 49 towards a restriction-based test (see Chapters 20–22), an obvious question would be whether the ECJ will adopt such an approach in relation to citizenship. Although the case law is not entirely clear, it seems that there are suggestions that the ECJ is moving in this direction. In *D'Hoop* (case C–224/98), the Belgian rules, which required an individual to have completed his or her secondary education in Belgium to claim the 'tideover' allowance whilst finding employment, are likely to affect non-nationals more than nationals. They could thus be viewed as indirectly discriminatory. The ECJ did not expressly phrase its judgment in terms of indirect discrimination, however. It referred to rules which placed those who exercised their right of free movement 'at a disadvantage'. A similar approach can be seen in *Pusa*, in which the ECJ based its reasoning on *D'Hoop*. Both cases are unusual in the sense that they concern the rights of returning migrants against their state of origin. Should this approach become more general, the potential scope of the non-discrimination principle is wide indeed, even taking into account that the rules in *Pusa* and *D'Hoop* were capable in principle of being objectively justified.

24.3 Rights of free movement under the Citizenship Directive (Directive 2004/38/EC)

Although the ECJ has interpreted citizenship in the light of existing secondary legislation, the Treaty specifically provides that secondary legislation may be made under Article 18. The Commission put forward a proposal to consolidate the existing legislation in the area, suggesting the enactment of a directive of the citizens' rights to free movement (COM (2001) 257, [2001] OJ C270 E/150) in accordance with the Presidency Conclusion of the Nice European Council, December 2000. The Citizenship Directive has duly been enacted (though not just on the basis of Article 18).

   The basic principle is that European citizens moving from one Member State to another should be able to do so on similar terms to nationals of a Member State moving around or changing their place of residence or job in their own country, with any additional requirements arising from the fact that an individual is a non-national being kept to a minimum. Significantly, the requirement to apply for a residence card has been replaced with the possibility of registering with the local authorities in Member States which require their own citizens to register. This will effectively abolish the need for a residence card for all migrant EU nationals.

   This does not mean that there are no conditions for the acquisition of the right of residence. After three months, migrant EU nationals must fall into one of several categories, which broadly reflect the legal position before the enactment of the directive. Individuals can be employed or self-employed and need not be self-sufficient. The other categories reflect the groups in the Residence Directive, the Retired Persons Directive and the Residency Directive and are subject, like them, to economic sufficiency conditions. It is likely that the conditions in the Citizenship Directive will be interpreted in a manner similar to those in the residency directives, that is subject to the imperatives of citizenship (see *Baumbast*).

   The directive also introduces what is effectively a permanent right of residence, to be acquired after five years' continuous residence in the host Member State (Article 14). Crucially, this provision will mean that Member States will no longer be able to deprive such individuals of their right of residence, even on the basis of public order or public security, though this right is, broadly speaking, subject to continued residence in the host Member State. The definition of family has been strengthened, broadly following the jurisprudence of the ECJ in this area (Article 2, discussed in Chapter 20). The directive also deals specifically with the retention of residence rights following a divorce or death, although greater conditions are imposed on the retention of such rights in the case of family members who are not EU citizens (see further Chapter 20).

24.4 Impact of the ToA: the new free movement rights

24.4.1 The position prior to ToA

As well as introducing European citizenship, the TEU created the Justice and Home Affairs (JHA) pillar of the Union, which dealt with, amongst other issues, asylum policy, rules regarding the crossing of borders (either between Member States or with third countries) and immigration and treatment of TCNs. As this took place within the JHA pillar, which operated on an intergovernmental basis, the intention was for Member States to coordinate their policies and to adopt common positions or conventions. Any such decisions were to be decided on a unanimous basis between the Member States, with the EC institutions occupying only a peripheral role. The Commission was described in the original Article K.4 TEU as being 'fully associated' with the work under the JHA pillar (whatever that might mean), and the Parliament was merely to be kept informed. Thus, the JHA did not have the impetus towards law-making that the EC does, either in terms of the type of measure which could be enacted within its purview, or as regards its decision-making processes. Although progress was consequently slow, some agreements were reached, such as the Recommendation on harmonising means of combating illegal immigration ([1996] OJ C–5/1) and the Recommendation on the combating of illegal employment of third-country nationals ([1996] OJ C–304/1). A proposed Convention on the Admission of Third Country Nationals was never adopted, however.

As a general proposition, TCNs in their own right did not fall within the scope of the EC Treaty (though they might fall within Union competence under JHA). The position of some TCNs would be dealt with under agreements into which the EC had entered, such as the EEA Agreement and the various cooperation agreements, such as the Europe Agreements entered into with a number of Eastern European states as part of the process towards accession and enlargement. The terms of these agreements were not exactly the same, and therefore TCNs' status would vary in accordance with the terms of the agreement, if any, that applied to them, although many of these provisions were held to be directly effective (e.g., *Pokrzeptowicz-Meyer* (case C–162/00) concerning Article 37 Polish Europe Agreement; *Deutscher Handballbund* v *Kolpak* (case C–438/00) transferring *Bosman* reasoning to the Slovakia Europe Agreement). The only EC provision which dealt expressly with their position was the former Article 100c EC (which was deleted by the ToA), which provided for the adoption of a common visa policy. This in itself created the possibility of overlap with the provisions in the JHA, potentially resulting in disputes as to the appropriate treaty base for action. Other attempts to extend the EC competence to cover TCNs were limited and tended to view these individuals in a somewhat inhuman light (see, e.g., *Vander Elst* v *Office des Migrations Internationales* (case C–43/93) discussed in Chapters 14 and 22). Any attempt to progress towards an internal market which included TCNs was blocked through political difficulties, in particular divergences in views as to whether the internal market was intended to benefit only the nationals of the Member States or not.

With regard to EU nationals, the difficulties experienced in completing the internal market, and indeed the different views of what this concept entailed, led to some Member States forming a separate agreement outside the Community framework. This was the Schengen Agreement 1985, which subsequently led to an implementing Convention in 1990. Schengen aimed to remove passport controls between Member States and to strengthen controls at the external borders. An Executive Committee was set up to take any detailed decisions necessary to implement the Schengen Agreement. The Agreement was eventually signed by the majority of Member States (and also some non-Member States), although implementation of the Convention was patchy, with political problems being exacerbated by technical difficulties. One particular problem was that travel between Member States was now possible on the Schengen basis (i.e., without frontier controls) for Schengen State nationals, or on the EC basis (with passport controls) for those Member States which had not signed up. This came perilously close to institutionalising discrimination between nationals of the two groups of Member States.

24.4.2 Changes introduced by Amsterdam

The ToA in effect moved the immigration, free movement and asylum element of the JHA pillar into a new Title IV of the EC Treaty (Articles 61–69 EC) and deleted the former Article 100c EC. Not all Member States have agreed to the new section of the Treaty; the UK, Ireland and Denmark have all refused to sign up to its provisions. The position of these Member States is dealt with through protocols attached to the ToA. It remained possible for those Member States who did not participate in Part IV of the Treaty to opt in to some of the measures adopted on an *ad hoc* basis. Both Ireland and the UK have opted in to some of these measures (e.g. Decision 2000/365, [2000] OJ L131/43, regarding the UK; and Decision 2002/192, [2002] OJ L64/20 regarding Ireland).

The new Article 61 EC provides that the Council is to adopt measures aimed at 'ensuring the free movement of persons in accordance with Article 14, in conjunction with directly related flanking measures with respect to external border controls, asylum and immigration'. The two following articles, Articles 62 and 63, provide more detail on the measures to be taken, dealing with internal and external borders as well as asylum seekers. Article 61 also provides for the possibility of measures being taken 'to prevent and combat crime', although any such measures must be compatible with the provisions in the JHA pillar (Article 31(e) TEU), which deal with similar issues. A detailed discussion of the asylum provisions and those relating to crime prevention and judicial cooperation are outside the scope of this work: the remainder of the chapter will focus on the creation of an area without internal frontiers, which concerns Articles 62 and 63. In all the areas covered by Article 61 EC, however, the Council has to take legislative action within five years. Failure to do so could, in principle, open the way for an action under Article 232 (ex 175) EC for failure to act (see Chapter 12). The Council and Commission adopted an action plan (3 December 1998) which laid down a timetable of measures to be adopted to achieve the objectives specified in this title within a five-year period, including the establishment of a high-level working group on asylum and immigration. The Commission also put forward a number of proposals, including the Family Reunification Directive, which became the first legal instrument adopted by the Community in respect of legal immigration (see further below).

The principal provisions relevant to the present chapter are Articles 62 and 63. Article 62 can be broken down into three distinct areas:

(a) the creation of the internal market in persons (Article 62(1));

(b) the standards and procedures to be followed by Member States in respect of persons crossing external borders, including rules on uniform visa policy in respect of stays of no more than three months (Article 62(2)); and

(c) the granting to TCNs of the right to travel within the territory of the Member States for up to three months (Article 62(3)).

In achieving the above-mentioned aims of Article 61, this title of the Treaty relies heavily on the approach adopted under the Schengen Agreement. A Protocol attached to the EC Treaty, as amended by the ToA, states that from the coming into force of the ToA, the Schengen *acquis* shall immediately apply to the Member States who have not opted out of this section of the Treaty. The Schengen *acquis* is described as including the Schengen Agreement and Convention together with decisions and declarations adopted under Schengen. The decisions made will be divided between the new Title IV in the EC 'pillar' and the remaining JHA provisions as appropriate, depending on the decision's subject-matter. Unfortunately, as many of these decisions were not made by transparent legal process, it is hard to identify a complete list of the decisions making up the Schengen *acquis*. Nonetheless, the Member States (all 15 of them) managed to identify the relevant decisions, defined in a Council Decision of 20 May 1999. At the same time, the Council divided these measures between the EC provisions and the JHA, so that each decision was retrospectively awarded an appropriate treaty base. The decisions on the removal of internal frontiers, the right to circulate for nationals of third countries, control of external borders and visa policy are now based within the EC Treaty. Future measures will, of course, be made in accordance with the procedures set out in the EC Treaty and a number of measures have now been enacted concerning

(a) standards and procedures to be applied to those crossing external borders under Article 62(2)(a) (see, e.g., Regulation 789/2001, [2001] OJ L116/2);

(b) visas for third-country nationals in respect of visits of no more than three months under Article 62(2)(b)(i) (Regulation 539/2001, as amended, [2001] OJ L81/1, which does not apply to the UK and Ireland);

(c) procedures and conditions for issuing visas under Article 62(2)(b)(ii) (e.g., Council Regulation 415/2003 ([2003] OJ L64/1), which does not apply to the UK and Ireland); and

(d) a uniform format for visas under Article 62(2)(b)(iii) (see, e.g., Regulation 334/2002 ([2002] OJ L53/7), which applies to the UK but not Ireland).

These all constitute a follow-on from the Schengen approach.

Article 63 deals not only with asylum seekers and displaced persons, but also with immigration policy, defined to include conditions of entry to the EU and residence therein (Article 63(3)(a)), and the determination of the terms and conditions under which TCNs legally resident in one Member State may reside in another (Article 63(4)). Although Article 63, like Article 62, is subject in general to a five-year time limit within which to act, the last paragraph of Article 63 provides that 'measures to be adopted pursuant to points 2(b), 3(a) and 4 shall not be subject to the five-year limitation period referred to above'. Legislation has also been enacted on the basis of Article 63, such as Council Directive 2004/81/EC on residence permits issued to third-country nationals who are victims of trafficking in human beings or who have been the subject of an action to facilitate illegal immigration, who cooperate with the competent authorities ([2004] OJ L261/19) and Directive 2003/109/EC concerning the status of third-country nationals who are long-term residents ([2004] OJ L16/44).

24.4.3 **The Constitution**

Part III of the Constitution deals with the policies and functioning of the Union. Much of this part is taken from the previous treaties, with some tidying up of the language. Chapter IV deals with the area of freedom, security and justice. As it brings together the provisions that govern EU activities under both the EC Treaty and the TEU, it introduces more substantial changes to the provisions than is perhaps seen in other policy areas, such as the four freedoms. Nonetheless, although many of the provisions are new, at least in form, they draw heavily on the existing provisions. Given the status of the Constitution, we will not look in detail at the provisions, but merely note that the substantive provisions under which the EU may take action are found in section 2. The most notable change is that, on the whole, qualified majority voting and the ordinary legislative procedure are to be used. Note also that opt-outs in this area would remain.

24.4.4 **Who benefits from the creation of the area without internal frontiers?**

Unlike the other provisions of the EC Treaty, it would seem that at least some of the provisions in this title apply to everyone, whether they be a national of a Member State who has signed up to this title of the EC Treaty or not. Article 62(1) EC specifically states that measures for eliminating controls on persons crossing borders between Member States shall benefit all individuals, 'be they citizens of the Union or nationals of third countries'. Other provisions, such as those relating to visas, are specifically aimed at the position of TCNs, defined as 'any person who is not a citizen of the Union within the meaning of Article 17(1) of the Treaty' (Article 2(a) Directive 2003/109/EC, Article 2(a) Directive 2004/81/EC).

24.4.5 **Scope of Articles 62 and 63**

A preliminary question is whether these are provisions that are capable of having direct effect. The ECJ has not yet had the opportunity to comment on this issue. The nature of the articles' objectives – the establishment of common policies and the enactment of legislation – means that these articles are unlikely to give rise to rights on which individuals may rely, rendering the possibility of Articles 62 or 63 having direct effect unlikely. The fact that the Treaty envisages the Council having a space of five years in which to take action may mean in any event that, until that time, the obligations in these provisions could not be unconditional.

The Tampere European Council in 1999 suggested that legally resident TCNs should be put on a footing as similar to that of the nationals of the Member States as possible. In addition to the Family Reunification Directive (Directive 2003/86/EC, [2003] OJ L251/12) noted above, a number of other proposals were tabled, such as the proposed Directive on the Status on Long-Term Residents (COM (2001) 127), now Directive 2003/109/EC, and that on the Right of Entry for those seeking Work or Self-Employment (COM (2001) 386). According to the Commission, these proposals form part of a broader effort on immigration that has been taking place for some years (for example the proposed amendment to Regulation 1408/71 to cover third-country nationals, see Chapter 20). Only a brief summary of the directives' main aims will be provided here. Note that neither the Family Reunification Directive nor the Directive on Long-term Residents applies to the UK, Ireland or Denmark.

The Directive on the Status of Long-Term Residents was aimed at those TCNs legally resident in the relevant Member State (Article 3(1)). The directive provides that Member States should grant long-term residence status to those TCNs who have resided legally for five years; the issue of legal residence in the first place is one for the individual Member States, subject to the relevant provisions of international law. Periods of residence for temporary or seasonal employment or for diplomatic purposes do not count for the calculation of the five-year period and only half the periods of residence for study purposes may be taken into account. Temporary absences are permissible. The majority of the Member States agreed that acquisition of the long-term residency status should be conditional on complying with any relevant laws on integration into the Member State of residence; Article 5(2) thus permits but does not require Member States to make this a condition of acquiring long-term status. Long-term status is subject to the TCN having both sickness insurance and 'stable and regular resources which are sufficient to maintain himself/herself and the members of his/her family without recourse to the social assistance system of the Member State concerned' (Article 5(1)). Although there are similarities to the position of the non-working migrant EU national in this, note that the prohibition on recourse to the social assistance system seems absolute. Although acquisition of long-term status is expressed to be permanent, it may be lost if the acquisition of the status was fraudulent, if there is an expulsion measure (within the terms of Article 12), or in the event of a 12 month absence (or longer) from the territory of the Community. The directive also regulates and facilitates the free movement from one Member State to another of TCNs who are long-term residents of the first Member State (Article 14 et seq.).

The aim of the Right of Entry Directive is to provide a clear framework for entry to the EU and residence there for those falling within its terms and it is intended to take into account the terms of the Directive on Long-Term Residency. Given that there is little similarity between the rules of the Member States in this area, the central aim of the directive is to provide harmonised standards as to the criteria for admitting TCNs, based on an economic needs test, and to provide the TCNs with at least some rights, which, in common with the other directives whether concerning TCNs or EU nationals, increase with the length of stay. This directive has not yet been agreed.

The Directive on Family Reunification aims to determine the conditions under which the family members of a lawfully resident TCN can also enter that Member State by specifying that a TCN residing lawfully in a Member State and holding a residence permit valid for a year or more and with a reasonable prospect of obtaining permanent residence can apply for family reunification. The directive identifies the family members who may benefit from this right. These include the spouse; the minor children of the resident TCN and of his or her spouse, or minor children where the resident TCN has custody and those children are dependent on him or her. The directive permits the Member States to authorise the entry of other categories of close relatives, such as adult unmarried children or the unmarried partner of the legally resident TCN. In making this distinction between family members who must be admitted and those who may be admitted, the directive parallels the approach taken with regard to migrant EC nationals, though the list of those family members who must be admitted is shorter than in the case of the EU national. Special provisions apply to children over 12 who arrive independently of the rest of the family, as well as to children aged 15 or more. The right of admission is subject to the requirement that there be adequate housing, as well as conditions relating to income and sickness insurance. Note that these conditions differ from those applied to migrant EU nationals in that the condition regarding housing, which used to apply to EU nationals, has been removed by the Citizenship Directive and economic sufficiency is required only in respect of non-workers.

Finally, note that the non-discrimination directives, notably the Race Directive, in principle apply to TCNs in the EU, though the Race Directive specifically excludes conditions of entry and residence of TCNs from its ambit.

24.4.6 **Assessment of the Treaty provisions**

It is likely that reaction to the new Treaty provisions will be mixed. On the one hand, the Community has assumed responsibility for a new area of law, hitherto outside Community competence. It is to be hoped that with this will come more efficient, transparent decision-making which is subject to some judicial scrutiny. On the other hand, there are some serious difficulties with these provisions. For the first five years at least, Council decision-making within this title will require unanimity which might be difficult to attain. The involvement of the other institutions, especially the Parliament, is limited to consultation, giving rise to concerns about democratic accountability.

Although the ECJ does have jurisdiction within the new Title IV of the Treaty, this is subject to special arrangements undermining the development and homogeneity of Community law both in this area and generally. Any measure or decision based on Article 62(1) concerning internal law and order or national security falls outside the ECJ's competence (Article 68(2) EC). Article 62(1) includes measures which are aimed at ensuring the free movement of persons within the internal market. Quite apart from difficulties determining the scope of the exception in Article 68(2), there is a question as to how this will relate (as far as EU nationals and their families are concerned) to the grounds of derogation from the original free movement rights under Articles 39 (ex 48), 43 (ex 52) and 49 (ex 59) and Directive 64/221/EEC, all of which do fall within the jurisdiction of the ECJ. Those who are workers, seeking to establish themselves or to provide services, will presumably be able to rely on a number of treaty provisions to move between Member States. In addition to Articles 39, 43 or 49, such individuals will be able to rely on Article 18 and the rights in the new title. Should a Member State wish to refuse an individual entry under the establishment, services or free movement of workers provisions, it can do so only for reasons of public policy, public security and health, which are being defined increasingly narrowly. The derogation by Member States from the original free movement provisions is subject to judicial scrutiny by the ECJ. Although these grounds for derogation are not exactly the same areas listed in Article 68(2), there will be some overlap between the two, for example in the case of criminals or terrorists. In this instance, the individual may find that there are EC rules which the ECJ has jurisdiction to apply under the original freedom of movement provisions at the same time as a Member State may try to claim that the issue is outside the ECJ's jurisdiction because of the operation of Article 68(2) EC. Although the matter has not yet been decided, a commonsense approach must be to look at the most specific rules (i.e., the original free movement rules) first and use the new provisions as a fall-back where appropriate. This would give the maximum opportunity for judicial scrutiny by the ECJ in this area and limit Article 68(2) to situations involving TCNs and in which there is a real need to take account of concerns for internal security. Homogeneity of EC law is also undermined by limited access to the ECJ under Article 234 (ex 177) introduced by Article 68 and the opt-outs. The adverse impact on EC law would be minimised were the proposed circumscribed approach to Article 68(2) taken.

Overlap may well occur in other areas too. The Treaty itself foresees that there is some connection between this new title of the Treaty and the JHA pillar of the TEU. Thus, the ECJ may well be called on – as it was in *Commission v Council (Air Transport Arrangements)* (case C–170/96), a case concerning the appropriate legal basis for action harmonising Member States' policies on airport transit visas – to determine the boundaries between the two treaties. In this case the Member States had taken joint action under former Article K.3 TEU (now as amended Article 31 TEU), whereas the Commission argued (unsuccessfully) that the appropriate basis for action should have been former Article 100c EC (now deleted by ToA). Although the precise scope of the relevant provisions in that case has changed, there is still considerable room for confusion as to where the boundary between Title IV to the EC Treaty and the JHA 'pillar' of the TEU properly lies. It may be that these issues will become of historic interest should the Constitution come into force.

One final concern relates to the incorporation of the Schengen *acquis* into the Union structure. The decisions made by a non-elected and unaccountable committee in relative secrecy have been turned into binding Community law. This surely offends against the principles, such as democracy and respect for the rule of law, upon which the Community is built. Nonetheless, as Curtin commented in regard to the changes introduced in this area by the ToA:

> By virtue of this move and of the fact that the 'single institutional framework' will henceforth be used, a quantum leap takes place in terms of democratic accountability and judicial control. The leap is from none to some. The result may be imperfect but it is definitely a move in the right direction.

24.5 **Conclusions**

The Community free movement rights started with a focus on movement of the economically active, with a concern not to allow movement for the benefit of social rights. The areas of law discussed in this chapter illustrate very clearly that the Community and the Union have moved away from this position, especially as regards the nationals of the Member States. For them, and their family members, the ECJ in particular has interpreted their rights broadly. Following the Tampere Conclusions, and the enactment of a number of directives specifically addressing the position of TCNs, it seems as if the Union is making some inroads into the conception of Fortress Europe. Some caution should be sounded here. The provisions covered in this chapter focus on those legally resident and those seeking to enter in search of economic activity; perhaps examining the case of the asylum seekers might lead to a slightly different assessment. As the Advocate-General in *Akrich* noted, there is an increasing distance between the standards applied to movement between Member States and the standards applied to allow entry in the first place. It should also be noted that the Member States have been just as keen, if not keener, to identify measures to repatriate the illegal immigrants. One final question is the impact the current concerns over terrorism following the events of 11 September 2001 will have on the position of migrants, particularly TCNs.

FURTHER READING

Curtin, D. and Meijers H., 'The Principle of Open Government in Schengen and the EU' (1995) 32 CMLR 391.

Guild, E. 'Between Persecution and Protection: Refugees and the New European Asylum Policy' (2000) 3 *Cambridge Yearbook of European Legal Studies* 169.

Guild, E., *Immigration Law in the European Community* (Kluwer Law International, 2001).

Hailbronner, K., 'Union Citizenship and Access to Social Benefits' (2005) 42 CML Rev 1245.

Kuijper, P. J., 'Some Legal Problems Associated with the Communitization of Policy on Visas, Asylum and Immigration under the Treaty of Amsterdam and Incorporation of Schengen *Acquis*' (2000) 37 CML Rev 345.

Peers, S., 'Challenging the Validity of EC Immigration and Asylum Law' (2003) 17 *Immigration, Asylum and Nationality Law* 25.

Reich, N., 'Citizenship and Free Movement in an Enlarged EU' (2005) 11 ELJ 675.

Schutte, J., 'Schengen: its Meaning for the Free Movement of Persons in Europe' (1991) 29 CML Rev 549.

Simpson, G., 'Asylum and Immigration in the European Union after the Treaty of Amsterdam' (1999) 5 EPL 91.

White, R., 'Free Movement, Equal Treatment, and Citizenship of the Union' (2005) 54 ICLQ 885.

25

Discrimination

25.1 Introduction

The general principle of non-discrimination on the ground of nationality under-pins much of EC law, as we have seen in the discussion of workers (see Chapter 20). This chapter will examine the many attempts that have been made to combat discrimination. Central to this discussion is the extensive body of legislation and ECJ jurisprudence in the field of equal treatment between men and women. More recently, however, the EC has broadened its focus to deal with discrimination in other areas, including age, race, religious belief and sexual orientation. A brief discussion of these aspects of EC policy lie within this chapter, though it remains to be seen if these provisions will have the impact of the sex discrimination provisions. The main focus of this chapter remains the law on sex discrimination.

Provisions on sex discrimination, or gender discrimination (as it is now called by the EC), have been part of the Treaty since its beginning. They are significant for three main reasons. The prohibition of discrimination on grounds of national-ity has been central to the development of the law in a number of areas (see Chapter 6). The prohibition on sex discrimination was of similar importance, and has seemingly increased in significance. Article 2 EC now includes the promotion of equality between men and women as one of the tasks of the Community, and Article 13 EC includes a general power for the Community to act to combat discrimination on various grounds, including sex. Recent years have also seen the Community attempt to integrate sex equality issues into all its policies and actions (see, e.g., Report on Equal Opportunities for Women and Men (COM (2003) 98 final)).

Additionally, it constitutes an illustration of the interplay, and even conflict, between policy areas. It has been described as one of the 'foundations of the Com-munity', designed, according to the ECJ in *Defrenne v Sabena (No. 2)* (case 43/75), apropos the then Article 119 (now 141), to achieve a 'double objective', economic and social. Its social goal is to achieve 'social progress', the 'improvement of the living and working conditions of their peoples', as required by the Treaty (pre-amble, 2nd and 3rd Recital). It can also be seen as ensuring there are no distortions in competition throughout the Community. Businesses in a Member State which had legislation aimed at ensuring equal treatment could be at a disadvantage in terms of, for example, wage costs compared with businesses established in another Member State without similar legislation. It was, indeed, on this basis that the sex discrimination provisions were included in the original Treaty. It now seems, however, that the economic aim is secondary to the social aim of these provisions.

No doubt because of this double objective, EC law on sex discrimination, unlike the fundamental Treaty provisions relating to goods and workers, is not limited in its application to migrant workers. Its application may be, and invariably is, 'wholly internal'. It is, however, confined strictly within the economic context; it was not designed to settle questions concerned with the organisation of the family, or to alter the division of responsibility between parents. Nor is the prohibition on discrimination absolute; a difference in treatment as between men and women may be permitted if it falls within the specified exceptions set out in the directives or, in the case of indirect discrimination, where it is 'objectively justified'.

Finally, the law in this area is significant because it shows the interrelationship between judicial and political actions. The *Barber* case (case C–262/88) was a broad and unexpected ruling; it led to the Member States seeking to clarify (and limit) its scope in a Protocol to the Treaty. Equally, some judgments which have shown the limits of sex equality, such as *P v S* and *D v Council* (C–125/99P) regarding sexual orientation and *Kalanke* concerning positive discrimination (discussed below), may have provided the spur for Community legislative action.

At the time of writing, the Council had just adopted a common position (see (2006) OJ C–126E/33) on a recast Equal Treatment Directive, which will replace a number of separate directives and incorporate the main decisions of the European Court of Justice, as well as strengthening the provisions on enforcement. This new Directive, due for adoption in the summer of 2006, would not enter into force until late 2008 at the earliest and, for this edition, this chapter retains its existing structure.

25.2 Overview of provisions

Even before the ToA, EC law on sex discrimination was extensive and comprised:

(a) Article 119 of the EC Treaty, which laid down a general principle of *equal pay for equal work* for men and women (now, after amendment, Article 141).

(b) Directive 75/117, which implements the principle of equal pay in more specific terms, to include equal pay for work of *equal value*.

(c) Directive 76/207 (as amended by Directive 2002/73/EC), which provides for *equal treatment* for men and women in the context of employment.

(d) Directive 79/7, which applies the equal treatment principle to matters of social security.

(e) Directive 86/378, which extends the equal treatment principle to occupational pension schemes.

(f) Directive 86/613, which provides for equal treatment in self-employment.

The ToA incorporated into the main body of the EC Treaty, as Chapter 1 of new Title XI of the Treaty, the provisions of the Protocol on the Social Chapter, which had been annexed by the TEU to the EC Treaty, some of which also have a bearing on sex discrimination. The incorporation of the terms of the Protocol on the Social Chapter not only means that legislation enacted under these provisions now extends to the UK (which had hitherto opted out of the extended social policy provisions) as well as to the other Member States, but that the social protection provisions contained within the EC Treaty will be extended significantly. The prohibition on sex discrimination, now amended and renumbered as Article 141 EC (ex 119), remains central.

Linked closely to the question of sex discrimination are a number of issues: the position of part-time workers, the majority of whom are women, and the impact of pregnancy and maternity on the working woman. The Community has enacted certain directives in these areas. Despite this legislative activity, the case law of the ECJ in this area remains important. Less directly connected with employment but still concerned with sex discrimination is Directive 2004/113 on equal treatment in access to goods and services.

In view of the extensive jurisprudence that has evolved in this area, the Commission put forward a proposal to adopt a consolidating directive (COM (2004) 279 final). It aims to recast existing directives 75/117, 76/207 (as amended by 2002/73), 86/378 (as amended by 96/97) and 97/80 in a single measure, and to modernise the text by incorporating some of the well-established ECJ case law. The Council adopted a Common Position on 10 March 2006 (based on the Commission's amended proposal (COM (2005) 380 final)), and the second reading in Parliament was expected in July 2006. At the time of writing, this area was set to undergo a major review, but for this edition, the discussion proceeds on the basis of the existing directives and case law, although, where appropriate, reference will be made to any significant changes which would be introduced by the new Directive, assuming it comes into force in the form accepted by the Common Position. This process reflects the approach adopted elsewhere (e.g., the Citizenship Directive), i.e., the recasting of older legislation in light of ECJ case law and subsequent developments, and is generally to be welcomed.

Since Article 141 EC and, to a more limited extent, the directives on sex discrimination have been declared directly effective (see Chapter 5), EC law has been invoked on a number of occasions by individuals seeking to challenge allegedly discriminatory practices which are nonetheless permissible under domestic law. Domestic implementation of EC law has frequently been found inadequate. Furthermore, the case law in this area has had a significant impact on each Member State's national procedures and remedies (discussed in Chapter 8).

The chapter concludes by looking at Directives 2004/43 and 2000/78 regarding equal treatment irrespective of race or ethnic origin, and religion, respectively. There is little case law on these directives and the discussion is therefore, at this stage, brief.

25.3 Equal pay for equal work: Article 141 EC

Prior to the ToA, the then Article 119 provided:

> Each Member State shall during the first stage ensure and subsequently maintain the application of the principle that men and women should receive equal pay for equal work.

> For the purpose of this Article, 'pay' means the ordinary basic or minimum wage or salary and any other consideration, whether in cash or in kind, which the worker receives, directly or indirectly, in respect of his employment from his employer.

This article, now Article 141, was amended by the ToA. Article 141(1) now provides that:

> Each Member State shall ensure that the principle of equal pay for male and female workers for equal work or work of equal value is applied.

The remaining paragraphs provide that

> 2. For the purpose of this article, 'pay' means the ordinary basic or minimum wage or salary and any other consideration, whether in cash or in kind, which the worker receives directly or indirectly, in respect of his employment, from his employer.
>   Equal pay without discrimination based on sex means:
> (a) that pay for the same work at piece rates shall be calculated on the basis of the same unit of measurement;
> (b) that pay for work at time rates shall be the same for the same job.
> 3. The Council, acting in accordance with the procedure referred to in Article 251, and after consulting the Economic and Social Committee, shall adopt measures to ensure the application of the principle of equal opportunities and equal treatment of men and women in matters of employment and occupation, including the principle of equal pay for equal work or work of equal value.
> 4. With a view to ensuring full equality in practice between men and women in working life, the principle of equal treatment shall not prevent any Member State from maintaining or adopting measures providing for specific advantages in order to make it easier for the underrepresented sex to pursue a vocational activity or to prevent or compensate for disadvantages in professional careers.

Article 141(3) provides a specific legal basis for the adoption of measures to give effect to the principle of equal opportunities and equal treatment.

The fourth paragraph, which permits positive discrimination, was introduced by the ToA, and was given further effect in amending Directive 76/207/EEC by inserting a new Article 2(6). This will be discussed further below (25.9.7.3).

Should the Treaty establishing a Constitution for Europe enter into force, Article 141 EC would become Article III–214 of the Constitution. The wording of this new provision would be identical to the current one, with two exceptions: (i) the words 'male' and 'female' in paragraph (1) would be interposed; and paragraph (3) would be amended to reflect the legislative measures which the Union would be entitled to adopt (see Chapter 3). However, there would be no substantive change and the law discussed in this chapter would continue to apply.

25.3.1 Reach of the basic principle

The principle enshrined in Article 141, and reflected in the secondary legislation noted above, is of fundamental importance. Consequently, EC legislation which conflicts with this principle could be struck down on grounds of illegality, except where there is an objective justification for the EC measure (*Rinke* v *Ärztekammer Hamburg* (case C–25/02)).

25.3.2 Meaning of 'worker'

Article 141 refers to male and female 'workers'. In *Allonby* (case C–256/01), the ECJ noted that there was no single definition of this concept in Community law, but that this varied according to the context in which it was used. At the same time, the concept must be given a Community meaning. The Court chose to adopt the *Lawrie-Blum* (case 66/85) definition of 'a person who, for a certain period of time, performs services under the direction of another person in return for which he receives remuneration', which included a person who was self-employed where the status as self-employed was notional and disguised an employment relationship. In *Allonby*, the claimant was a part-time lecturer at Accrington & Rossendale College who had been made redundant and then immediately re-employed through ELS, an agency supplying lecturing staff. If her self-employed status was regarded as notional, she would be able to rely on Article 141 to challenge the validity of a domestic requirement of being under a contract of employment as a condition for access to a pension scheme for teachers (see also 25.4.2 below). A person will also be regarded as a worker where she is a part-time employee working to need, i.e., only the hours requested by her employer (*Wippel* v *Peek & Cloppenburg* (case C–313/02).

25.4 Pay

25.4.1 What constitutes pay?

If the concept of pay is generously defined in Article 141, it has been even more generously construed. It was applied in *Garland* v *British Rail Engineering Ltd* (case 12/81) to cover the grant of special travel facilities to ex-employees after retirement, even though the benefit was received following termination of employment and was not granted pursuant to any contractual entitlement. The Court held that the argument that the facilities are not related to a contractual obligation is immaterial. The legal nature of the facilities is not important for the purposes of the application of Article 141 provided that they are granted in respect of the applicant's employment. On similar reasoning in *Worringham* v *Lloyds Bank Ltd* (case 69/80) a supplementary payment made by employers to male employees under the age of 25, for the purpose of contribution to the employees' occupational pension scheme, was held to be pay. Sums which are included in the calculation of the gross salary payable to the employee and which directly determine the calculation of other advantages linked to the salary, such as redundancy payments, unemployment benefits, family allowances and credit facilities, form part of the worker's pay. Since the payment was not made to female employees under the age of 25 the scheme was in breach of Article 141.

Questions about the scope of 'pay' for the purposes of Article 141 continue to arise. In *Hill and Stapleton* (case C–143/95), a pay scale which discriminated between full- and part-time workers regarding the calculation of annual pay increments was considered to fall within Article 141, as the scale determined the progression of the workers' pay. *Abdoulage* v *Regie Nationale des Usines Renault* (case C–218/98) concerned a measure which provided that women going on maternity leave, as well as continuing to receive full pay, should also receive a lump sum of FFR 7,500. The ECJ agreed that the lump sum could be considered to fall within pay for the purposes of Article 141. In *R* v *Secretary of State for Employment, ex parte Seymour-Smith* (case C–167/99) the ECJ held that redundancy payments also constituted pay.

However, in *Wippel* v *Peek & Cloppenburg* (case C–313/02), the Court noted that a framework contract within which the actual hours worked could be varied was not within the scope of Article 141 (or Directive 75/117), as the fact that the contract might have financial consequences was insufficient for it to give rise to questions about 'pay'. It was, however, within Directive 76/207 (see further below).

25.4.2 Pensions and social security benefits

The precise extent to which employers' contributions to pensions and other social security benefits fall within the scope of Article 141 has been much litigated.

Worringham v *Lloyds Bank Ltd* (above) was followed in *Bilka-Kaufhaus GmbH* v *Weber von Hartz* (case 170/84) in the context of a claim by a female part-time worker, Ms Weber, who was seeking to challenge her employer's occupational pension scheme. The scheme was non-contributory, financed solely by the employer. Under the scheme part-timers were entitled to benefit only if they had worked with the firm for at least 15 out of a total of 20 years. No such limitation was imposed on full-timers. Ms Weber alleged that the scheme was indirectly discriminatory, in breach of Article 141, since the majority of part-time workers were women. The Court agreed that it was *capable* of falling within the provision, as the scheme was contractual, not statutory, in origin; it originated from an agreement made between Bilka and the works council representing the employees, and the benefits were financed solely by the employer as a supplement to existing social security schemes. The benefit constituted consideration paid by the employer to the employee for his employment.

The reasoning in *Bilka-Kaufhaus GmbH* (case 170/84) seemed to imply that benefits paid by an employer pursuant to or in lieu of a *statutory* scheme might not constitute pay. In *Defrenne* v *Belgium (No. 1)* (case 80/70) the Court had held that although payment in the nature of social security benefits was not excluded in principle from the concept of pay, it was not possible to include in this concept, as defined in Article 141, social security schemes and benefits, especially retirement pensions, which were directly settled by law without reference to any element of consultation within the undertaking or industry concerned, and which covered without exception all workers in general. Thus although Ms Defrenne (an air hostess) was entitled to invoke the then Article 119 (now, after amendment, 141) against her employer to claim equal pay to that of her male counterparts (cabin stewards) (*Defrenne* v *Sabena (No. 2)* (case 43/75)), she was unable to challenge a Belgian law requiring different contributions for male and female employees, made by the employer, to a social security scheme directly imposed by law. Such benefits are, the Court held, 'no more emoluments paid directly by the employer than are roads, canals, or water drains'.

However, the ambit of statutory social security schemes excluded from Article 141 in *Defrenne* has been whittled down by subsequent decisions of the Court. In *Liefting* (case 23/83) a statutory pension scheme applicable to a *particular group* of workers, namely civil servants, was found to be within its scope. The Court held that sums which public authorities are required to pay, though not in themselves pay, become pay if they are included in calculating their employees' gross pay used in the calculation of other salary benefits. If, as a result, the salary-related benefits are not the same for men as for women, Article 141 is infringed.

Article 141 was again held applicable to a statutory social security benefit in *Rinner-Kühn* v *FWW Spezial Gebäudereinigung GmbH & Co KG* (case 171/88). The case concerned a claim by a part-time worker, an office cleaner, against her employer, involving a challenge to German legislation permitting employers to exclude part-time workers (defined as persons working 10 hours or less a week) from entitlement to sick pay. Prima facie the claim appeared analogous to the statutory social security scheme held in *Defrenne* to be outside the scope of the then Article 119 (now, after amendment, 141). Nevertheless, the Court found that the continued payment of wages to a worker in the event of illness fell within the definition of pay; therefore national legislation such as the legislation in question, which *allowed* employers to maintain a global difference in pay between the two categories of workers (one of which was predominantly female), must be regarded as contrary to the objectives pursued in Article 141. Being indirectly discriminatory, it would be acceptable only if objectively justified.

25.4.3 'A benefit received by reason of the existence of the employment relationship' (*Barber*)

In *Barber* v *Guardian Royal Exchange Assurance Group* (case C–262/88), the Court found, in a claim by a group of male employees who were seeking to challenge payments made by their employer under a contracted-out pension scheme, which operated as a substitute for the statutory social security scheme, and under a statutory redundancy scheme, both of which were payable at different ages for men (65) and women (60), that such payments also constituted 'pay' since the worker received these benefits, albeit indirectly, from his employer for his employment.

> Although it is true that many advantages granted by an employer also reflect considerations of social policy, the fact that a benefit is in the nature of pay cannot be called into question where the worker is entitled to receive the benefit in question from his employer *by reason of the existence of the employment relationship* (para. 18).

This point was re-emphasised in *Beune* (case C–7/93), which concerned civil service pensions. The Court held that, even where the pension scheme was affected by considerations of social policy, State organisation, ethics or budgetary concerns (factors usually indicative of a social security scheme), the pension scheme of a public employer would still constitute pay where (a) it concerned only a certain category of workers rather than general categories; (b) it was directly related to the period of service; and (c) it was calculated by reference to the employee's last salary (para. 45; see also *Schönheit* v *Stadt Frankfurt* (case C–4/02)).

As was suggested in *Barber*, the only statutory social security schemes which appear now to fall outside Article 141 are statutory social security pension schemes provided for workers in general as a matter of social policy and funded from the public purse. The precise ambit of the statutory social schemes outside Article 141 is, despite numerous cases on this issue, still unclear.

While the application of Article 141 in a clear case of discrimination in respect of employers' *contribution* to an occupational pension scheme, as in *Worringham* v *Lloyds Bank Ltd* (case 69/80), causes few problems, its extension in *Barber* to the *award* of pensions hitherto tied to a permitted difference in pension age for men and women, in which actuarial factors also play a part, has created problems and led to great complexity.

Because the ruling in *Barber* was likely seriously to affect the financial balance of contracted-out pension schemes, contributions and calculations for which had been based on different retirement ages for men and women, and because, as the Court conceded, both Member States and the parties concerned were reasonably entitled to consider that this provision did not apply to pensions paid under contracted-out pension schemes, the Court held that its ruling as regards such schemes could not be applied retrospectively. Article 141 might not be relied on to claim entitlement to a pension with effect prior to the date of judgment, except in the case of workers, or those claiming under them, who had before that date initiated legal proceedings or raised an equivalent claim under the applicable national law (para. 45). Following dispute over the scope of this ruling, as to whether Article 141 applies to all claims for *pensions arising* after the date of judgment or only to claims based on *benefits earned* after this date, the matter was finally resolved by a protocol issued at Maastricht in favour of the latter, more restrictive view. According to the Protocol:

> For the purposes of Article 119 [now 141] of [the Treaty establishing the European Community], benefits under occupational social security schemes shall not be considered as remuneration if and insofar as they are attributable to periods of employment prior to 17 May 1990, except in the case of workers or those claiming under them who have before that date initiated legal proceedings or introduced an equivalent claim under the applicable national law.

This interpretation of *Barber* has since been applied by the Court in many cases including *Ten Oever* (case C–109/91, survivors' benefit); *Coloroll Pension Trustees Ltd* v *Russell* (case C–200/91); *Moroni* (case C–110/91, supplementary pension scheme, early retirement); *Neath* v *Hugh Steeper Ltd* (case C–152/91, supplementary pension scheme, early retirement); and *Defreyn* (case C–166/99, additional pre-retirement payment). However, in *Vroege* (case C–57/93), and *Fisscher* (case C–128/93) the Court held that the limit on retrospectivity of its ruling in *Barber* did not apply where it should have been clear to the employer that the terms fell within Article 141. In these cases, the provisions related to *access* to pension schemes, which, following *Bilka-Kaufhaus* (case 170/84), should be considered pay. Provided the female employees were prepared to pay the requisite contributions to a pension scheme for any period between *Defrenne* and *Barber*, employers were also obliged to make the relevant employer's contributions to such schemes retrospectively. This principle was affirmed in *Preston* and *Fletcher* (case C–78/98), and the non-retroactivity in

Barber, as reinforced by the Protocol, was affirmed in *Schönheit* v *Stadt Frankfurt* (joined cases C 4 & 5/02)).

Further problems arising from the application of Article 141 to the award of occupational pensions are illustrated in *Neath* v *Hugh Steeper Ltd* (case C–152/91). The case concerned a contracted-out pension scheme in which men were treated less favourably than women in respect of early retirement and lump-sum payments in lieu of pension payments. Neath claimed that, following *Barber*, this was con- trary to Article 141. The Court, however, distinguished between the *accrual of the right* to receive benefits and the *funding* of those benefits. Both the pension payments themselves and the employees' contributions to a pension scheme fell within 'pay', therefore neither should distinguish between the sexes. The funding arrangements established by the employer, however, fall outside the scope of Article 141 because the purpose of those arrangements is to ensure that there are adequate resources to make the pension payments when due. An employer, when calculating its contribution to funding, may therefore rely on actuarial factors which, for example, take into account differing average life expect- ancies of the sexes and thus may make different payments in respect of men and women (para. 22). A corollary to this argument is that capital sum or transfer benefits such as lump-sum payments that are based on the method and amount of funding also do not fall within Article 141 (para. 33). *Neath* was a retreat from the position in *Barber*, and has made the boundaries between pay and pensions even less certain than they seemed before.

The Court's judgment in *Neath* does not affect a further principle established in *Barber*, that, in order to comply with Article 141, it is not enough that the overall package of remuneration received by men and women be equal. Each element of the consideration paid to both sexes must be equal. The system of pay must be 'transparent', in order that clear comparisons as between men and women may be made.

25.4.4 Significance of a broad definition of pay

This broad interpretation of pay to include benefits relating in the widest sense to retirement or even death (provided they are not social security benefits *sensu stricto*) is important, since it provides an opportunity for individuals to challenge as 'pay' matters, relating for example to different retirement ages for men and women, which might otherwise fall under the Equal Treatment Directive (Directive 76/207) (see further below) and Occupational Pensions Directive (Directive 86/378) and even Directive 79/7 on Equal Treatment in Matters of Social Security (discussed in greater detail below). In doing so the Court can often sidestep the limitations of these directives, as well as the problems of horizontal direct effect.

The recast version of the Equal Treatment Directive will adopt the broad notion of pay, which will be defined as 'the ordinary basic or minimum wage or salary and any other consideration whether in cash or in kind, which the worker receives directly or indirectly, in respect of his/her employment from his/her employer'.

25.5 Discrimination

Discrimination, in breach of Article 141, can be direct or indirect.

25.5.1 Direct discrimination

Direct discrimination occurs when men and women are treated differently by virtue of their sex. In these cases, a difference in pay can never be justified. However, a difference in treatment as between men and women, even doing the same work or of equal value, will not necessarily constitute discrimination. In *Birds Eye Walls Ltd* v *Roberts* (case C–132/92) the Court found that a bridging pension, paid *ex gratia* to employees compelled on the grounds of ill health to take early retirement, and calculated to bridge the gap between the sum received under their occupational pension scheme and the State pension they would receive on reaching the statutory age of retirement, although less for the applicant woman than it would have been for a man, was not discriminatory on the grounds of sex. The mechanisms used for calculating the bridging pension were sexually neutral; the applicant's lower bridging pension corresponded to her lower input into the State pension scheme, *for which she had freely opted*. The applicant and the men with whom she sought to compare herself were not in comparable situations. For similar reasons different rates of pay may be awarded according to employees' qualifications, provided they are relevant to the job undertaken.

In *Hlozek* v *Roche Austria* (case C–19/02), a social plan to deal with the impact of a merger included provision of a bridging allowance for employees whose employment was terminated, provided they had reached the age of 55 (men) or 50 (women) and were not yet entitled to a pension. Mr Hlozek was made redundant at the age of 54 and was therefore unable to benefit. The Court held that the bridging allowance was 'pay' for the purposes of Article 141, but that there was no breach of that provision because the allowance was linked to the different retirement ages.

The Court has also accepted that when Member States seek to amend national laws to achieve parity between the sexes, economic considerations may result in both sexes being treated at the level of the disadvantaged group, rather than improving the position of the disadvantaged group to the level of the advantaged group. In *de Weerd* (case C–343/92, discussed below), the Court commented that Member States, in order to control public spending, may remove benefits from certain categories of persons, provided that this was not done in a discriminatory manner. In *Smith* v *Avdel Systems Ltd* (case C–408/92) the ECJ was faced with a claim based on the changes made to pension schemes following *Barber*. The Court held that where discrimination is found, the disadvantaged class should, in the absence of domestic measures rectifying the position, be treated in the same way as the advantaged class. This did not, however, prevent the Member State from introducing measures which 'levelled down' benefits: in this case raising the statutory retirement age to 65. Sex equality, it would seem, does not always benefit women.

In view of the central importance of the notion of 'direct discrimination', the EC has started to incorporate a definition in its most recent directives. The recast Equal Treatment Directive will define this as 'where one person is treated less favourably on grounds of sex than another is, has been, or would be treated in a comparable situation' (Article 2(1)(a)).

25.5.2 Indirect discrimination

Indirect discrimination occurs where rules which seemingly apply to both sexes, adversely affect a significant proportion of one sex more than the other. Unlike direct discrimination, indirect discrimination may be 'objectively justified'. The recast Equal Treatment Directive will incorporate a definition of 'indirect discrimination' as 'where an apparently neutral provision, criterion or practice would put persons of one sex at a particular disadvantage compared with persons of the other sex, unless that provision, criterion or practice is objectively justified by a legitimate aim, and the means of achieving that aim are appropriate and necessary' (Article 2(2)(b)). This definition presents, in very general terms, the substance of the indirect discrimination concept as it has been developed by the ECJ, and a discussion of this case law will help to flesh out the meaning further.

In *Jenkins* v *Kingsgate (Clothing Productions) Ltd* (case 96/80) the ECJ was asked whether a difference in pay (in this case 10 per cent) between part-time and full-time workers could constitute discrimination when the category of part-time workers was exclusively or predominantly female (only one, exceptional male was employed part-time). The Court held that such a difference would not infringe Article 141 provided that the difference in pay was 'objectively justified' and in no way related to discrimination based on sex. However, such inequality of pay would breach this provision where, having regard to the difficulties encountered by women in arranging to work the minimum (full-time) number of hours a week, the pay policy of the undertaking cannot be explained by factors other than discrimination based on sex.

In *Bilka-Kaufhaus GmbH* v *Weber von Harz* (case 170/84) the Court was faced again with a claim by a part-time worker, this time challenging her employer's occupational pension scheme, which discriminated overtly against part-time workers. Here both full- and part-time workforces comprised both men and women, but of the men employed (28 per cent of the total workforce), only 10 per cent worked part-time, as against 27.7 per cent of the female work-force. Overall, male part-time workers comprised only 2.8 per cent of the total workforce. The disadvantage suffered by part-timers thus fell disproportionately on the women. The ECJ was asked whether such a scheme might breach Article 141. Citing paragraph 13 of the judgment in *Jenkins* v *Kingsgate (Clothing Productions) Ltd* almost verbatim, the Court held (at para. 29) that if it was found that a considerably smaller percentage of men than of women worked part-time, and if the difference in treatment could not be explained by any other factor than sex, the exclusion of part-time workers from the occupational scheme would be contrary to Article 141. The difference in treatment would, however, be permissible if it were explained by objectively justified factors which were unrelated to discrimination based on sex. It would be for the employer to prove, and for national courts to decide, on the facts, whether the difference in treatment was in fact objectively justified.

Although many circumstances where part-time employees have been disadvantaged have been found to constitute indirect discrimination by virtue of the larger number of female part-time workers, not all claims succeed: there is a boundary between being paid less because of working less and being discriminated against. In *Stadt Lengerich* v *Helmig* (cases C–399/92 *et al.*) part-time workers alleged indirect discrimination because they did not receive overtime payments for working in excess of their normal working hours. Overtime only became payable when they worked longer than the full-time workers' normal hours. The ECJ held that this was not discrimination because part-timers and those who worked full-time received payment on the same basis for the hours worked. By contrast, *Kuratorium für Dialyse und Nierentransplantation eV* v *Lewark* (case C–457/93) dealt with a part-time worker who took part in a training course arranged within full-time working hours but in excess of her normal working hours. She was compensated for the loss of her normal part-time wages but did not receive payment for all the hours she spent at the course. The Court held that this was discrimination because the overall pay she received for the course was less per hour than that received by her full-time colleagues.

The position of part-time workers is now dealt with by Directive 97/81 ([1998] OJ L14/9), which aims to implement the Framework Agreement reached between general cross-industry organisations (Article 1). The directive was due to be implemented by the Member States in 2000, with a slightly later implementation date of 7 April 2000 for the UK. In particular, the directive provides that part-time workers are not to be treated in a less favourable manner than comparable full-time workers, save where differences in treatment are justified on objective grounds. The directive specifically notes that the principle of *pro rata temporis* may be applied, but this would not generally justify paying a part-time worker a lesser hourly rate than that paid to a comparable full-time worker. In this, there seems to be a convergence between the case law and the approach taken by the legislation.

25.5.3 Discrimination and difference in treatment

Having identified a difference in treatment, is the difference automatically discriminatory? In *Enderby* v *Frenchay Health Authority* (case 127/92) the ECJ commented that a difference in treatment between men and women would give rise to a presumption that discrimination existed. It would then fall to the employer to try to justify the difference in treatment. In the *Royal Copenhagen* case (case C–400/93), however, both men and women worked on a piecework basis under which their wages consisted of a fixed base payment plus a variable amount determined by reference to the work produced. The Court held that here a difference in pay between groups did not necessarily raise an inference of discrimination: the difference in pay might reflect differences in output. The national court must decide if the difference results from differences in output or from unacceptable differences in the amount the worker is paid per item. The Court's approach in this case is clearly more cautious than in *Enderby* as it moves away from the position that a purely statistical difference between groups of men and women creates a presumption of discrimination. It is arguable that in *Royal Copenhagen* the Court is mixing together questions which should be asked when determining justification of indirect discrimination with those that determine discrimination in the first place.

A similarly cautious approach can be discerned in *Angestellten Betriebsrat der Wiener Gebietskrankenkasse* v *Wiener Gebietskrankenkasse* (case C–309/97). The case concerned the difference in pay between two groups of psychotherapists. One group had been trained as doctors; the other, predominantly female group, which received lower pay, comprised graduate psychologists. This group argued, following *Enderby*, that as they were involved in the same work as the doctors they should be on the same pay scale. The ECJ rejected this argument, accepting instead the argument that the difference in training could mean that the two groups of psychotherapists would be required to perform different duties and therefore could not be said to be performing the same work. Thus the approach in *Enderby* was not so much overruled as side-stepped in this case, the ECJ turning the issue into one of equal work rather than discrimination.

It is clear, however, from both *Jenkins* and *Bilka-Kaufhaus GmbH* that the fact that the group adversely affected by a particular measure comprises both sexes does not prevent that measure being discriminatory on the grounds of sex, as long as it affects one sex to *a disproportionate extent*. If this were not so, as Nicholls LJ pointed out in the Court of Appeal in *Pickstone* v *Freemans plc* ([1989] AC 66), as long as there is a man there doing the same work, 'which in some cases might be wholly fortuitous or even, possibly, a situation contrived by an unscrupulous employer', the woman cannot make the comparison, even if the difference in pay is attributable solely to grounds of sex. The criteria to identify when disproportionate discrimination occurs have not been precisely delineated. Further, the question of whether discrimination exists might vary over time as statistical evidence and working patterns changed (*R* v *Secretary of State for Employment, ex parte Seymour-Smith* ([1995] ICR 889)). Thus a regulation which disadvantages part-time workers will be discriminatory only for as long as a disproportionate number of workers are of one sex. Ultimately, unless one sex is disproportionately affected, a claim under Article 141 of discrimination *based on sex* will not succeed.

25.5.4 Pregnancy

Clearly, pregnancy may have an adverse impact on a woman's pay which, since only women become pregnant, is not easily categorised as direct or indirect discrimination. The difficulties pregnant women encounter have given rise to a specific jurisprudence on pregnancy, discussed later (25.10.2).

25.6 Objective justification

25.6.1 General criteria

As noted above, differences in pay (or treatment) which discriminate indirectly against women or men will be permissible if they are objectively justified. Guidelines as to what might constitute objective justification were laid down in *Bilka-Kaufhaus GmbH* v *Weber von Harz* (case 170/84). There the Court held that in order to prove that a measure is objectively justified the employer must prove that the measures giving rise to the difference in treatment:

(a) correspond to a 'genuine need of the enterprise',

(b) are suitable for obtaining the objective pursued by the enterprise, and

(c) are necessary for that purpose.

These principles, reminiscent of *Cassis de Dijon* (see Chapter 18), have been consistently applied by the Court. Requirements (b) and (c) together represent the familiar proportionality principle. What factors, then, will be regarded by the Court as providing 'objective justification' meeting a 'genuine need of the enterprise'?

25.6.2 Arguments based on economic factors and market forces

Jenkins v *Kingsgate (Clothing Productions) Ltd* (case 96/80) and *Bilka-Kaufhaus GmbH* (case 170/84) suggest that economic factors would prove acceptable justification. In *Bilka-Kaufhaus GmbH* the defendants argued that part-time workers were less economic; they were less ready to work on Saturdays and in the evening; that it was necessary to pay more to attract full-timers. Justification on these grounds was not disputed in principle. Whether it would in fact be accepted would depend on whether the need for the difference in pay could be proved, and if so whether the proportionality principle were satisfied. In applying this ruling the German court found that it was not.

Although the Court has been sympathetic to the Member States' concern to control budgetary expenditure (e.g., limitations imposed in *Barber* (case C–262/88); *Steenhorst-Neerings* (case C–338/91)), a *purely* economic justification of discrimination is unlikely to be successful. In *de Weerd* (case C–343/92) concerning Directive 79/7, the Court stated that to allow budgetary considerations to justify discrimination between men and women would be tantamount to agreeing that the fundamental principle of equality could vary over time and throughout the Community depending on the state of the Member States' public finances (paras 35 and 36) (see also *R* v *Secretary of State for Health, ex parte Richardson* (case C–137/94), and *Schönheit* v *Stadt Frankfurt* (case C–4/02)).

25.6.3 Administrative convenience

In *Kirsammer-Hack* v *Sidal* (case C–189/91), in a claim based on Equal Treatment Directive (76/207), the Court was prepared to concede that an exclusion from employment protection provided under German legislation for employees of firms comprising fewer than five employees, excluding employees working less than 10 hours a week or 45 hours per month, even if indirectly discriminatory against women, would be objectively justified on the grounds of the need to lighten the administrative, financial and legal burdens on small enterprises, acknowledged by the Community in the then Article 118a EC and its directives on health and safety of workers.

25.6.4 Social policy objectives

In *Rinner-Kühn* (case 171/88) the Court suggested that a justification based on a 'genuine objective of social policy' might be acceptable, provided that the means selected were appropriate and necessary to the attainment of that objective. However, it firmly rejected an argument that the difference in treatment as regards sick pay between part- and full-time workers was justified on the grounds that part-timers were not integrated into the business in the same way as full-time workers. 'These considerations', the Court said, 'only represent generalised statements concerning certain categories of workers and do not admit the conclusion of objective justification unrelated to any discrimination on the grounds of sex'. Since women form the majority of the part-time workforce, it is they, as the Commission pointed out in *Rinner-Kuhn*, who are most vulnerable and in need of protection; thus a social policy objective resulting in discrimination against part-time workers is unlikely to be seen as valid justification. A justification on the grounds of social policy has, however, been accepted in a number of social security cases not involving part-time workers (e.g., *Teuling* (case 30/85); *Commission* v *Belgium* (case C–229/89)).

25.6.5 Proportionality

It is likely that, as with the *Cassis de Dijon* principle applied to the free movement of goods (see Chapter 18), the Court will seek to ensure that the proportionality principle is rigorously applied, and will not hesitate to pass judgment on whether a purported 'objective justification' is suitable and necessary to achieve its desired and legitimate end. This can be seen in many decisions, such as *Schönheit* v *Stadt Frankfurt* (cases C–4 & 5/02), where a restriction on public expenditure was rejected as a possible justification.

25.7 Equal work

Equal work has been defined in Directive 75/117 as the 'same work' or 'work to which equal value has been attributed'.

25.7.1 Same work

In *Macarthys Ltd* v *Smith* (case 129/79) Advocate-General Capotorti suggested that 'same work' is not confined to identical work; it should include jobs which display a high degree of similarity the one to the other, even if there is not total identity between them. Since 'similar' work will shade into work 'of equal value', which is also subject to the equality principle, a precise definition of 'same' work is unnecessary.

25.7.2 Work of equal value

This concept was introduced into EC law by Directive 75/117. However, since the Court has held (*Jenkins* v *Kingsgate (Clothing Productions) Ltd* (case 96/80)) that Directive 75/117 is merely confined to restating the principle of equal pay as set out in Article 141, and in no way alters its content and scope, a claim for equal pay for work of equal value may be brought under Article 141 as well as under Directive 75/117. Article 141, as amended by ToA, specifically refers to work of equal value. Indeed, a claim under Article 141 is advisable since it avoids possible problems over the direct effects of the directive. The concept of work of equal value will be further discussed in the context of Directive 75/117.

Any comparisons made for the purpose of deciding whether a man and a woman are engaged on the same work, or work of equal value, must be confined to parallels which may be drawn on the basis of concrete appraisals of the work actually performed by employees of different sex within the same establishment or service (*Macarthys Ltd* v *Smith* (case 129/79)). Comparisons cannot be made with the 'hypothetical male'. Further, comparisons must be made with groups picked on an objective basis and not those chosen solely with the aim of maximising the final amount received by the complainants. For example, in *Royal Copenhagen* (case C–400/93) the applicants sought to compare three groups each with different average pay. The lowest-paid group (female) sought to be upgraded first to the pay rate of the middle, male group and then to argue that the discrimination between the middle group (still mainly male) and the highest group (female) was also unjustified sex discrimination, thus raising all workers in the compared groups to that of the highest-paid group. The ECJ took the view that choosing comparator groups to allow 'leap-frogging' was not acceptable. In *Wippel* v *Peek and Cloppenburg* (case C–313/02), a part-time employee working only when needed by her employer could not compare her position with that of a full-time employee working regular hours.

Comparisons are, however, not necessarily limited to the same establishment or service. In *Defrenne* v *Sabena (No. 2)* (case 43/75), the ECJ held that the then Article 119 (now, after amendment, 141) applied to discrimination which has its origin in legislative provisions ('general' social security provision excepted) or in collective labour agreements and which may be detected on a purely legal analysis of the situation. Moreover, where the employer is the same the fact that the pay of different groups of workers has been determined under separate collective bargaining agreements does not necessarily prevent the application of Article 141 (see *Enderby* v *Frenchay Health Authority* (case C–127/92); compare with *Royal Copenhagen* (case C–400/93) and *Angestellten Betriebsrat der Wiener Gebietskrankenkasse* v *Wiener Gebietskrankenkasse* (case C–309/97)).

In the absence of collective agreements or job evaluation schemes affecting undertakings or industries at a national level, it is submitted that comparisons cannot be made *across* undertakings or industries. In *Lawrence* (case C–320/00), the local council, which had employed people directly to carry out cleaning and catering jobs, put these services out to competitive tender. During the tendering period, the women involved in these jobs won a case against the council arguing that their work was equal to work carried out by men for jobs such as gardening, refuse collection and sewage treatment. Thereafter, the women still employed by the council had their wages increased. The contractor who obtained the contract with the council for the cleaning and catering services then re-employed some of the former council workers, but paid them less than they had been paid by the council. The women employed by the contractor then brought a claim on the basis of Article 141 arguing that they were entitled to equal pay with male comparators employed by the council, regardless of whether the appellants had been originally employed by the council or were so employed at present. The ECJ, however, held that where the differences identified in the pay conditions of workers of different sex performing equal work or work of equal value cannot be attributed to a single source, Article 141(1) does not apply. In *Allonby* (case C–256/01), decided under Article 141, the ECJ held that a female lecturer whose contract had not been renewed, but who had been re-employed by the college through an agency, could not compare her situation to that of a male lecturer directly employed by the college.

As is clear from *Macarthys Ltd* v *Smith* comparisons are not limited to men and women engaged in contemporaneous employment. Nor is it necessary that the employment should be in the same Member State.

25.8 Equal pay for work of equal value (Directive 75/117)

25.8.1 Scope of the Directive

As has been noted, Directive 75/117, which was based on Article 119 (now 141), was introduced merely to implement and supplement that Article. Article 1 provides:

> The principle of equal pay for men and women outlined in Article 119 of the Treaty, hereinafter called 'principle of equal pay', means, for the same work or for work to which equal value is attributed, the elimination of all discrimination on grounds of sex with regard to all aspects and conditions of remuneration.
>
> In particular, where a job classification system is used for determining pay, it must be based on the same criteria for both men and women and so drawn up as to exclude any discrimination on grounds of sex.

Article 2 requires Member States to:

> introduce into their national legal systems such measures as are necessary to enable all employees who consider themselves wronged by failure to apply the principle of equal pay to pursue their claims by judicial process after possible recourse to other competent authorities.

In addition, Article 6 requires Member States, in accordance with their national circumstances and legal systems, to:

> take the measures necessary to ensure that the principle of equal pay is applied. They shall see that effective means are available to take care that this principle is observed.

25.8.2 Assessment comparability

In *Commission* v *United Kingdom (Re Equal Pay for Equal Work)* (case 61/81) the UK was found to have failed, in breach of Directive 75/117 (Articles 1 and 6), to provide a means whereby claims of equal value might be assessed in the absence of a job evaluation scheme having been implemented by the employer.

Neither Articles 1 or 6 of Directive 75/117 nor *Commission* v *United Kingdom* (case 61/81) require that a claim to equal value must be assessed pursuant to a job evaluation study; indeed, the Court pointed out in *Commission* v *United Kingdom* that a system of job classification is only one of several possible methods for determining pay for work to which equal value is attributed. All that seems to be required under

EC law is that where a prima facie claim to equal value exists, either as a result of a job evaluation study, as in *O'Brien* v *Sim-Chem Ltd* ([1980] ICR 573, House of Lords), or otherwise, an assessment must be made, if necessary in adversarial proceedings, by a body with the requisite power to decide whether work has the same value, after obtaining such information as may be needed.

It is regrettable that the Court in *Commission* v *United Kingdom* did not spell out in greater detail the scope of Member States' obligations in this field. Clearly some comparability must exist before a legitimate claim to equal value can arise. But how 'like' must two different jobs be for them to be deemed to be comparable? And if they are 'broadly' comparable, how, and in what detail, are they to be assessed in order to decide whether they are equal value? Will a 'felt fair' order of jobs, depending on the general level of expectation as to the value of the job, be adequate, as the Employment Appeal Tribunal suggested in *Bromley* v *H & J Quick Ltd* ([1987] IRLR 456), or should not, as the Court of Appeal decided, a full analytical study be made? If such a study is undertaken, what criteria are to be applied? Clearly the answers to all these questions, and the solutions adopted, will vary from State to State, as will their cost to the State. Moreover, a finding of equal value will have serious repercussions on costs, both for the individual concerned and possibly for an entire industry. This in turn will affect its competitiveness within the common market. Unless the rules relating to the application of the principle of equal value are determined and applied in a uniform manner throughout the Community they are likely to defeat the very 'economic objectives' which they were designed, in part, to achieve.

Where a job classification scheme is devised as a means of determining comparability, some general guidance as to its content was provided by the ECJ in *Rummler* v *Dato-Druck GmbH* (case 237/85). Here a woman packer, classified under wage group III under a job evaluation scheme implemented by her employers, and not, as she considered appropriate, under group IV, was seeking to challenge the criteria on which the scheme was based. These criteria included the muscular effort, fatigue and physical hardship attached to the job. She claimed this was discriminatory. The ECJ held that a job classification scheme based on the strength required to carry out the work or the degree of physical hardship which the work entailed was not in breach of Directive 75/117 as long as:

(a) the system as a whole precluded discrimination on grounds of sex; and
(b) the criteria employed were objectively justified. To be objectively justified they must:
  (i) be appropriate to the tasks to be carried out, and
  (ii) correspond to a genuine need of the undertaking.

In addition, the classification scheme as a whole, if not to be discriminatory, must take into account the criteria for which each sex has a particular aptitude. Criteria based exclusively on the values of one sex contain, the Court suggested, 'a risk of discrimination'.

The principles of *Rummler* v *Dato-Druck* were extended significantly in *Handels- og Kontorfunktion ærernes Forbund i Danmark* v *Dansk Arbejdsgiverforening for Danfoss* (case 109/88), in the context of a challenge by the Danish Employees' Union to the criteria agreed by the Danish Employers Association and applied by the firm of

Danfoss. These included, *inter alia*, the criteria of 'flexibility' and 'seniority'. While the minimum pay for each grade was the same for men and women, it was found that the average pay *within* each grade was lower for women than for men. The applicants alleged that the criteria were indirectly discriminatory. The ECJ held that where the application of neutral criteria, such as the criterion of quality (one element of 'flexibility'), was shown to *result* in systematic discrimination against female workers, this could only be because the employer applied it in an abusive manner. The criteria applied must be 'of importance for the specific duties entrusted to the workers concerned'. In *Brunnhofer* (case C–381/99) a female employee claimed she was being discriminated against in comparison to a male employee who was classified as being in the same job category. Although the basic wages were the same, both were paid, as part of their original contractual arrangements, a monthly allowance. Brunnhofer was paid a smaller allowance than her male counterpart. The ECJ held the fact that both employees were in the same job classification was not conclusive as to whether they were doing equal jobs: instead, the national court should look for more precise evidence regarding the activities the employees actually carry out. The ECJ continued, however, to state that the personal qualities of individual employees and the way in which they carried out their work could not be used to justify a pay differential which existed in the original contractual arrangements. This holding does not mean that such factors cannot be taken into account to justify differences in employees' career development, with a consequent effect on future pay.

25.8.3 Burden of proof

Where a pay system is characterised by a 'total lack of "transparency" ', that is, when the criteria for determining pay increments are not explicit, and where a female worker establishes, by comparison with a relatively large number of employees, that the average pay of female workers is lower than that of male workers, the onus is on the employer to prove that the criteria employed are justified. Moreover, in view of the greater difficulties faced by women in organising their time in a flexible manner, the criterion of adaptability (another element of 'flexibility'), which was prima facie capable of justification, would also require proof of justification from the employer. The criterion of seniority was found by the Court to be sufficiently transparent not to require justification by the employer. Thus, where the criteria employed are not transparent, or where they operate to the patent disadvantage of women, the employer must carry the burden of justification. The issue was discussed in *Brunnhofer* (case C–387/99). Citing *Danfoss* (109/88, para. 54), the ECJ held that the burden of proof would shift to the employer to show there was no discrimination where the employer's system of payment was not transparent. In *Brunnhofer*, the inequality applied to a specific element of the total pay, an additional monthly allowance. In these circumstances the burden of proof remains with the claimant. Note that the question of burden of proof in sex discrimination cases will, in most Member States, now be dealt with under the Burden of Proof Directive (Directive 97/80) (for a recent application of *Brunnhofer* in the UK context, see *Sharp* v *Caledonia Group Services Ltd* [2006] ICR 218).

25.8.4 **Compliance**

Finally, under Article 4 of Directive 75/117, States are required to ensure that provisions of collective agreements, wage scales, wage agreements or individual contracts of employment contrary to the principle of equal value 'shall be, or may be declared, null and void or may be amended'.

States must also, under Article 5, ensure full protection for employees against dismissal as a reaction to a complaint or to legal proceedings 'aimed at enforcing compliance with the principle of equal pay'.

Since the provisions of Directive 75/117 merely define the scope and substance of Article 141 EC they may be invoked, vertically or horizontally, in the context of a claim under that Article. As *Defrenne* v *Sabena (No. 2)* (case 43/75) established, Article 141 is effective against *all* parties. Following *Marshall* v *Southampton and South West Hampshire Area Health Authority (Teaching)* (case 152/84), Directive 75/117, as a directive, will not *in itself* be horizontally effective (see Chapter 5).

25.9 **Principle of equal treatment for men and women (Directive 76/207)**

25.9.1 **Scope of the Directive**

Directive 76/207, which is based not on Article 141 of the EC Treaty but on the institutions' general powers under Article 308 (ex 235), lays down the principle of equal treatment for men and women in Article 1(1):

> as regards access to employment, including promotion, and to vocational training and as regards working conditions and, on the conditions referred to in paragraph 2, social security.

'Working conditions' are defined to include 'conditions governing dismissal' (Article 5).

Article 1, paragraph 2, provides for further action to implement the principle of equal treatment in matters of social security. This has now been achieved with Directives 79/7 (statutory schemes) and 86/378 (occupational schemes).

The Directive was amended by Directive 2002/73/EC ([2002] OJ L269/15), adopted on the basis of the new Article 141(3) EC. The amendment introduces definitions of 'direct discrimination', 'indirect discrimination', 'harassment' and 'sexual harassment' (new Article 2(2) of Directive 76/207). These changes were due to have been brought into force with effect from October 2005.

The principle of equal treatment is defined in Article 2 as meaning that:

> there shall be no discrimination whatsoever on grounds of sex either directly or indirectly by reference in particular to marital or family status.

A new Article 2(2) expands on this by defining 'direct discrimination' as a situation 'where one person is treated less favourably on grounds of sex than another is, has been or would be treated in a comparable situation', and 'indirect discrimination' as 'where an apparently neutral provision, criterion or practice would put persons of one sex at a particular disadvantage compared with person of the other sex' unless objectively justified.

Furthermore, a new Article 2(3) now provides that harassment and sexual harassment, as defined in Article 2(2), are to be regarded as discrimination within the scope of the Directive, as is an instruction to discriminate against persons on the ground of sex (new Article 2(4)).

Derogation from the equal treatment principle is provided under Article 2(5)–(8) (discussed at 25.9.7).

25.9.2 Meaning of 'sex'

For the purposes of this Directive, 'sex' has been held to have a wide meaning, not limited to issues of gender discrimination. In *P v S* (case C–13/94), P's contract of employment was terminated because of P's proposed sex change. The question referred to the ECJ related to Article 5 of the directive: did the directive preclude dismissal of a transsexual for a reason related to his or her gender reassignment? The Court held that the meaning of the directive, in view of the fundamental principle of equality which it represented, could not be interpreted so as to limit the protection to discrimination on grounds of gender. In the light of the broad terms of this judgment, the ECJ's more recent ruling in *Grant v South-West Trains Ltd* (case C–249/96) seems a somewhat surprising retreat. The case concerned a claim by a female employee with a female partner for rail benefits to which married couples were entitled. The ECJ rejected this, stating that the reference to 'sex discrimination' was not a reference to gender orientation. This limited view of sex discrimination was confirmed in *D v Council* (case C–125/99P). The state of protection in the ECJ's jurisprudence with regard to discrimination on grounds of sexual orientation might not seem promising. The meaning of 'sex' has, however, been raised again. *K.B. v The National Health Service Pensions Agency and the Secretary of State for Health* (case C–117/01) concerns the right of transsexuals to marry and consequently to claim a survivor's pension. The argument was that a rule which precluded transsexuals from marrying was discriminatory contrary to the Equal Treatment Directive. The case directly focuses on the tension between the approach in *P v S* and that in *Grant*. The ECJ noted that the domestic rule that prevented a transsexual from marrying had been found incompatible with Article 12 of the ECHR (in *Goodwin v United Kingdom*), and that, in such circumstances, Article 141 precludes domestic legislation which prevents a couple of whom one partner is a transsexual from marrying. In so holding, the ECJ managed to find in favour of the claimant, but it side-stepped the question whether the principle established in *P v S* applied in circumstances such as these. It may be noted that the approach adopted by the ECJ in *P v S* will be reflected in a recital to the recast Equal Treatment Directive.

25.9.3 Retirement and pensions

The principal context in which the Equal Treatment Directive has been invoked in the UK has been to challenge different retirement ages as between men and women, since both the Equal Pay Act 1970 and the Sex Discrimination Act 1975 excluded from their scope 'provisions in relation to death or retirement'. Directive 76/207 contains no such exclusion, but Directive 79/7, Article 7(1), governing equal treatment in matters of social security, allows Member States to exclude from the scope of the equal treatment principle 'the determination of pensionable age for the purposes of granting old-age and retirement pensions and the possible consequences thereof for other benefits'. Directive 86/378 (Article 9) provided a parallel exclusion in respect of occupational pension schemes. It was therefore thought, it is submitted with some justification, that different retirement ages for men and women were permissible under EC law, especially since they were tied to the statutory pensionable age, which in the UK was 60 for women and 65 for men.

The scope of these provisions was considered by the Court in *Burton* v *British Railways Board* (case 19/81) in the context of a challenge by a railway worker, Mr Burton, to a voluntary redundancy scheme operated by British Rail. Under the scheme women were entitled to apply for voluntary redundancy at 55, and men at 60. Mr Burton, who, at 58, wished to take early retirement, alleged that the scheme was discriminatory. On reference from the Employment Appeal Tribunal for an interpretation on the scope and application of Directive 76/207 the ECJ held that the Directive applied in principle to conditions of access to voluntary redundancy schemes. Moreover, the word 'dismissal', brought within the equality principle by Article 5, must be widely construed to cover termination of the employment relationship, even as part of a redundancy scheme. However, since in this case the ages for voluntary retirement were calculated by reference to, and tied to, the statutory retirement age (60 for women, 65 for men), Article 7 of Directive 79/7, which permitted States to exclude from the equal treatment principle 'the determination of pensionable age', applied. His claim under Directive 76/207 failed.

Undeterred by *Burton* v *British Railways Board*, the applicant in *Marshall* v *Southampton and South West Hampshire Area Health Authority (Teaching)* (case 152/84) brought a similar claim under Directive 76/207. Ms Marshall, an employee of the AHA, was seeking to challenge its compulsory retirement policy, under which women employees were required to retire at 60, and men at 65. On a reference from the Employment Appeal Tribunal, the ECJ, following *Burton* v *British Railways Board*, interpreted the retirement scheme as a 'condition governing dismissal' within Article 5 of Directive 76/207. However, distinguishing *Burton*, on the slenderest grounds (benefits *tied to* a national scheme which lays down a different minimum pensionable age for men and women) the Court found that her case was *not* within the exclusion of Article 7 of Directive 79/7. This article allowed Member States to exclude from the equal treatment principle the determination of pensionable age *'for the purposes of granting old-age and retirement pensions and the possible consequences thereof for other benefits'*. Where pensionable age was being determined *for other purposes*, e.g., as in *Marshall*, for the purpose of *retirement*, the equal treatment principle would apply.

The ECJ took the same line, on the same reasoning, in *Roberts* v *Tate & Lyle Industries Ltd* (case 151/84). This time the applicant failed in her challenge to her employer's compulsory early retirement scheme. Although the scheme entitled those retiring to an accelerated pension under the firm's occupational pension scheme, it was held to fall within the scope of Directive 76/207 as a condition governing dismissal, and not Directive 79/7. However, in this case it was not discriminatory, since the age for retirement was fixed at 55 for both men and women (see also *Beets-Proper* v *F. van Landschot Bankiers NV* (case 262/84)).

Member States' power under Article 7 of Directive 79/7 to exclude from the equal treatment principle 'the determination of pensionable age' has, in view of the fundamental importance of the principle of equal treatment, been given the narrowest scope. It seems it will only apply where the difference in age is *for the purpose* of the granting of old-age and retirement *pensions* and the possible consequences thereof for other benefits 'falling within the statutory [or occupational] social security schemes' (*Marshall*, para. 35, see further below). Moreover, the exclusion from the equal treatment principle only applies to the determination of pensionable age for the purposes of granting *statutory* social security pensions. Despite the express exclusion in respect of the 'determination of pensionable age for the purposes of granting old-age or retirement pensions' as regards *occupational* pension schemes, contained in Directive 86/378, the Court held in *Barber* (case C–262/88) that the setting of different retirement ages for men and women for the granting of such pensions was in breach of Article 119 (now 141), since the difference in age *resulted* in a difference in pay. On similar reasoning different ages of access to statutory redundancy benefit for men and women were also held in breach of the then Article 119. *Burton* v *British Railways Board* (case 19/81) appears to have been distinguished out of existence. As was noted above, a difference in the employer's contribution to funded, defined-benefit schemes, affecting the transfer of pension rights and lump sum payments to employees was held in *Neath* v *Hugh Steeper Ltd* (case C–152/91) to fall outside Article 119 (now 141); it may thus be presumed that it will also fall outside Directive 76/207. In *Vergani* (case 207/04), a provision to encourage voluntary redundancy by providing reduced tax on redundancy payments for men who retired after the age of 55 and women who retired after the age of 50 fell foul of Directive 76/207.

25.9.4 Social assistance

Although the main discussion about the scope of the Equal Treatment Directive has concerned equal retirement ages and pensions, that is not the only area where its boundaries are unclear. *Meyers* v *Adjudication Officer* (case C–116/94) concerned family credit, which, at first glance, might fall within social security, Directive 79/7. Ms Meyers, however, brought an action under the Equal Treatment Directive claiming that rules precluding her from deducting child-minding expenses from her income and thus preventing her from claiming family credit were indirectly discriminatory because the rules had a disproportionate adverse effect on single mothers. The Court held that since family credit provided a top-up income to low-income workers and therefore provided both assistance and an incentive for them to accept work, the scheme fell within the Equal Treatment Directive as it concerned both 'access to employment' and 'conditions of employment'. It would seem that the case was not brought under Directive 79/7 following *Jackson* v *Chief Adjudication Officer* (cases C–63 & 64/91) (discussed in more detail below), which held that supplementary benefits did not fall within the terms of that directive.

25.9.5 **Other cases**

Article 2(1) of Directive 76/207 has been held, in the absence of objective justi-fication, to preclude a domestic rule which authorised part-time work for older employees only where they have worked full-time for at least three out of the five years before applying for a change to part-time status, where the vast majority of part-time workers are women and therefore much more likely to fall outside the scope of this rule (*Steinicke* v *Bundesanstalt für Arbeit* (case C–77/02)).

In *Gomez*, a collective agreement between workforce and employer provided for a specific period of annual leave, which overlapped with Gomez's maternity leave. The Court held that an annual leave entitlement was within the scope of (now deleted) Article 5(1) of the Directive, and that the claimant was entitled to take her annual leave at a different time (*Gomez* v *Contintental Industrias* (case C–342/01)). The Court noted that it would generally be the case that a claimant should be entitled to take annual leave at a time different from the maternity leave period.

In *Nikoloudi* v *OTE* (case C–196/02), the post of part-time cleaner was reserved to females, but this was not, in itself, discrimination against women. However, the fact that part-time workers were excluded from appointment to established staff was contrary to Directive 76/207 and meant that this arrangement did constitute direct discrimination.

25.9.6 **Enforcement**

Like Directive 75/117, Directive 76/207, as amended, requires States to 'take the necessary measures to ensure that any laws, regulations and administrative provi-sions contrary to the principle of equal treatment be abolished' (Article 3(2)(a)) and 'any provisions contrary to the principle of equal treatment . . . in collective agreements, individual contracts of employment, internal rules of undertakings or in rules governing the independent occupations and professions shall be, or may be declared, null and void or are amended' (Article 3(2)(b)). The enforcement provisions were strengthened by Directive 2002/73/EC with the insertion of sev-eral new provisions regarding, *inter alia*, real and effective compensation, chal-lenges by associations or organisations with a legitimate interest in ensuring compliance with the Directive, as well as the creation of a body for the promotion of equal treatment. The detail of these provisions is presently beyond the scope of this book. It should be noted that these provisions would be included in the recast Equal Treatment Directive which was due to be adopted by the summer of 2006.

25.9.7 **Derogation from the equal treatment principle (Articles 2(6), 2(7) and 2(8) of Directive 76/207))**

Article 2(6) permits Member States with regard to access to employment and related training, to provide that 'a difference of treatment which is based on a characteristic relating to sex' is not discriminatory where because of 'the nature of the particular occupational activities concerned or of the context in which they are carried out, such a characteristic constitutes a genuine and determining occupational requirement'. Article 2(7) makes Directive 76/207 without prejudice to provisions on the protection of women during pregnancy and maternity leave. In addition, Article 2(8) provides some scope for positive discrimination, by allowing for 'measures within the meaning of Article 141(4) of the Treaty with a view to ensuring full equality in practice between men and women'. These articles provide for derogation from the equal treatment principle in the case of *direct* discrimination, based on the sex of the worker. The provisions replace earlier derogations contained in what was Articles 2(2)–(4) of Directive 76/207. They are designed to reflect both key developments in the ECJ's jurisprudence, and the changes made to Article 141 after the ToA. The provisions have only been in force for a very short time, and no ECJ case law on these revised provisions was available at the time of writing. The discussion below is based on the case law that evolved under the previous exceptions, and this will continue to offer guidance on the interpretation of the recast derogation provisions.

25.9.7.1 *Sex as a determining factor (Article 2(6) formerly in Article 2(2))*

The former Article 2(2) provided for a derogation in respect of 'activities . . . for which . . . the sex of the worker constitutes a determining factor'. This was considered by the ECJ in the Commission's second action against the UK (*Commission* v *United Kingdom (Re Equal Treatment for Men and Women)* (case 165/82)) for failure to comply with the Equal Treatment Directive. One of the failures alleged was the exemption from the equal treatment principle, provided under the Sex Discrimination Act 1975, for employment in a private household (s. 6(3)(a)) and for firms employing less than six staff (s. 6(3)(b)). The UK argued that these provisions were justifiable under the former Article 2(2) of Directive 76/207. The Court disagreed. Whilst exemption under the former Article 2(2) might be available in the *individual* case under such circumstances, where the sex of the worker was a determining factor, the former Article 2(2) did not justify a blanket exclusion. It did, however, provide a valid defence to a charge against the UK in respect of its restriction, under the Sex Discrimination Act 1975, s. 20, on male access to the profession of midwifery. The Court found that this was an activity for which the sex of the worker was a determining factor.

In *Stoeckel* (case C–345/89) a general ban on night work for women, provided for under German law, allegedly to protect women, was held by the Court not permissible under the former Article 2(2). However, in *Ministère Public* v *Levy* (case C–158/91) faced with a question of the compatibility of *Stoeckel* with French law imposing restrictions on night work in industry for women, designed to give effect to a provision of the ILO 1948, the Court suggested that national courts must not apply provisions of national law contrary to Article 5 of Directive 76/207 (now deleted) 'unless the application of national law is necessary to ensure compliance with international obligations' resulting from a convention concluded with third countries 'before the entry into force of the EC Treaty'. (See also *Office Nationale de l'Emploi* v *Minne* (case C–13/93) and *Habermann-Beltermann* (case C–421/92).) The point came before the ECJ again in the case of *Commission* v *Italy* (case C–207/96). In this case, Italy prohibited women from working overnight in accordance with the ILO Convention. Italy had, however, following the ECJ's previous ruling, denounced the Convention. The ECJ thus held that it could not rely on the Convention and that the prohibition was contrary to EC law.

The former Article 2(2) was also raised as a defence in the case of *Johnston* v *Chief Constable of the Royal Ulster Constabulary* (case 222/84) (see Chapter 6). This action was brought by a female member of the Royal Ulster Constabulary (RUC) against a decision by the RUC refusing to renew her contract of employment. The RUC had decided as a matter of policy not to employ women as full-time members of the RUC reserve, since they were not trained in the use of firearms nor permitted to use them. In proceedings before the ECJ concerning the interpretation of Directive 76/207, and in particular the scope for derogation from the equal treatment principle available under EC law, the RUC argued, by analogy with what was Article 48(3) (now 39(3)) EC (see Chapter 20), that in view of the political situation in Northern Ireland derogation was justified on public safety or public security grounds; it was also justified under the former Article 2(2) of Directive 76/207. To allow women to carry and use firearms, the RUC claimed, increased the risk of their becoming targets for assassination. The Court held that there was no general public safety exception to the equal treatment principle available under the EC Treaty. A claim for exemption could *only* be examined in the light of the provisions of Directive 76/207. With regard to the former Article 2(2), the Court held that:

(a) The derogation provided under Article 2(2) could be applied only to specific *duties*, not to activities in general. Nonetheless, it was permissible to take into account the *context* in which the activity takes place.

(b) Where derogation is justified in the light of (a) the situation must be reviewed periodically to ensure that the justification still exists.

(c) Derogation must be subject to the principle of proportionality.

It was for national courts to decide whether these conditions are satisfied.

Similar principles were applied, if somewhat leniently, in *Commission* v *France* (case 318/86). The Commission's action was in respect of recruitment practices in the French civil service, in particular the prison service and the police. Under the system in force men and women were subject to different recruitment procedures, with a fixed percentage of posts being allocated according to sex. The complaint concerning the prison service centred on access to the post of head warder (in male prisons), which was not accessible to women. The complaint regarding the police concerned recruitment to certain police corps generally.

In the case of the prison service the Court found that it was justifiable to discriminate on the grounds of the former Article 2(2) in respect of the post of *warder*. Since professional experience acquired as a warder was desirable for the performance of the duties of a prison governor (a post for which head warders were eligible), and since it was desirable to provide promotion opportunities for those in the lower (warders') posts, it was acceptable to treat the *head* warder's post in the same way. The recruitment practices were justified under the former Article 2(2). The recruitment practices of the police, on the other hand, were not permissible under the former Article 2(2). The exclusion provided by the former Article 2(2), the Court held, allows exceptions to the non discrimination principle only in relation to specific *activities*, and these exceptions must be sufficiently transparent to permit effective scrutiny. The fact that certain police functions cannot be performed by men and women does not justify discriminatory treatment in admission to the police force in general.

The scope of the former Article 2(2) also came under consideration in *Sirdar* v *The Army Board* (case C–273/97). The army board refused to transfer a female chef (who would otherwise be made redundant) to the Royal Marines because of her sex. She argued that this was contrary to the approach set down in *Johnston*. The ECJ, however, took a different view. It confirmed that Member States have a discretion regarding measures necessary for ensuring public security, although it further noted that any derogation from fundamental Treaty rights (such as equality) must be narrowly construed and be proportionate to its aims. In this case, the ECJ focused on the special nature of the Marines, who are, in effect, front-line troops and in respect of whom an absolute rule provides that *all* Marines must be combat ready, irrespective of their normal role. It seems that it was the particularly dangerous nature of the Marines' role that, according to the ECJ, justified the UK's Decision that the Marines should remain exclusively male. By contrast, in *Kreil* v *Germany* (case C–285/98) a German rule of more general ambit which precluded women from occupying posts which would involve the use of firearms constituted sex discrimination, even taking into account Member States' discretion regarding the organisation of their armed forces. *Kreil* cannot be interpreted to mean that Member States cannot organise their compulsory national service to apply to men alone, provided women have access to the armed forces where they choose to enlist (case C–186/01, *Dory*). Arguably, then, these rulings continue the approach to the former Article 2(2) which requires a *specific* assessment of the *specific* duties to be performed in individual cases.

In the light of the above case law, the derogation was recast, and the new Article 2(6), set out above, reflects the very strict interpretation given to the former Article 2(2).

25.9.7.2 *Pregnancy and maternity (Article 2(7))*

Former Article 2(3) of Directive 76/207 permitted 'provisions concerning the protection of women, particularly as regards pregnancy and maternity'. Pregnancy and maternity leave can, potentially, have a detrimental impact on the pay and career progression of women, who will be away from work for a period of time. In *Herrero* v *Imsalud* (case C–294/04), Ms Herrero, who had already been employed by Imsalud, was successful in applying for a new post whilst she was on maternity leave. She was able to defer taking up that post, but she challenged a rule whereby her seniority would only be calculated from the date she took up her post, rather than the date of appointment. The Court held that this situation was within the scope of Directive 76/207, and that it precluded a rule which excluded maternity leave from calculating the period of seniority. It followed the earlier decision in *Land Brandenburg* v *Sass* (case C–284/02), a case involving a woman from the former East Germany who had taken the then statutory period of 20 weeks, of which only eight weeks were taken into account by way of allowance in calculating her length of service. This meant that she was moved to a higher pay grade 12 weeks later than a comparable male worker, which was held to fall outside the derogation in Article 2(3) of the Directive.

In *Johnston* v *Chief Constable of the RUC*, the RUC also sought to justify its action under Article 2(3), as 'concerning the protection of women, particularly as regards pregnancy and maternity'. The Court found that the risks to policewomen arising from the situation in Northern Ireland were not within the scope of Article 2(3). Article 2(3) was intended to protect women's biological condition.

This interpretation of Article 2(3) had been supplied in *Hofmann* v *Barmer Ersatzkasse* (case 184/83) in response to a claim by a father to six months' leave following the birth of his child to look after the child while the mother went back to work. German law, which granted such leave only to the mother, was, he claimed, discriminatory, in breach of Directive 76/207. The Court disagreed. Special provision for maternity leave was, the Court held, permissible under Article 2(3), which was concerned to protect two types of female need. It protected:

(a) the biological condition of women during and after pregnancy; and

(b) the relationship between mother and child during the period following pregnancy and birth.

Directive 76/207 was not intended to cover matters relating to the organisation of the family or to change the division of responsibility between parents.

A second case brought by the Commission against France (*Commission* v *France* (case 312/86)) related to special privileges in the form of, *inter alia*, extended maternity leave, lower retirement age, extra time off to allow for children's illness and holidays, and extra allowances to meet the cost of nursery schools and child minders, awarded under French law to married women. The French sought to justify these privileges under Article 2(3) and 2(4). The Court, citing *Hofmann*, found that such measures fell outside the limits of Article 2(3); nor was there any indication that the rights claimed corresponded to the situation envisaged under Article 2(4). If such privileges are to be justified, they can only be justified on objective grounds *unrelated to sex*, such as the need to assist persons who carry primary responsibility for the welfare of the family, and particularly of children. As the Court pointed out in *Commission* v *France*, such responsibility may be undertaken by men. (See also case C–366/99, *Griesmar*. As an example of the application of 'neutral' criteria, see *Teuling* (case 30/85), which is discussed later in this chapter.)

Contrast *Commission* v *France* with *Abdoulage* v *Regie Nationale des Usines Renault* (case C–218/98), albeit a case based on Article 141 rather than the Equal Treatment Directive. In *Abdoulage* a group of men sought to challenge the payment of a lump sum, in addition to their maternity pay, to women going on pregnancy leave. The men argued that a recent father was not entitled to the same amount and that the measure discriminated against men. The ECJ held the payment of the lump sum to be compatible with Community law as it was intended to compensate woman for the problems inherent in having to take time off work for maternity leave, and which are consequently specific to women.

The precise extent to which, and circumstances in which, a dismissal or refusal to employ a woman for reasons connected with pregnancy and childbirth will breach Directive 76/207 remains unclear, although it seems that the ECJ has become increasingly unsympathetic to employers. In *Dekker* v *VJV-Centrum* (case C–177/88) the defendant employer had withdrawn his offer of employment to the claimant when he discovered she was pregnant. He argued that his action was justified; her absence during maternity leave would not on the facts be covered by insurance, and he could not afford to pay for a replacement worker. The ECJ held that a refusal to employ a woman on the grounds of pregnancy constituted direct discrimination on the grounds of sex; as such it could not be justified on the basis of financial detriment to the employer.

The effect of this ruling was undermined in the Court's judgment in *Handels- og Kontorfunktion ærernes Forbund i Danmark* v *Dansk Arbejdsgiverforening* (*Hertz*) (case C–179/88) delivered on the same day. This case concerned a claim by a female employee against dismissal on the grounds of her extended absence from work as a result of illness which, though connected with pregnancy and childbirth, was suffered some time *after* the end of her maternity leave. The Court held that in this case there was no need to distinguish between illness resulting from pregnancy and maternity and any other illness such as might be suffered by a man. The dismissal was thus not directly discriminatory and could be justified. The reason for the distinction between *Dekker* and *Hertz*, suggested in *Hertz*, lay in Article 2(3) of Directive 76/207 which provides for measures concerning the protection of women, particularly as regards pregnancy and maternity.

Hertz was seized upon by the English Court of Appeal in *Webb* v *EMO Air Cargo (UK) Ltd* ([1992] 2 All ER 43), in the context of a claim at first sight closer to *Dekker*, for discrimination on the grounds of pregnancy. The claimant had been engaged to replace another employee who had become pregnant. Two weeks after accepting the post she discovered she too was pregnant. When she informed the employer of this fact she was dismissed. Glidewell LJ, following counsel for the employer's advice, chose to read *Dekker* and *Hertz* together. Dismissal on the grounds of pregnancy might under *some* circumstances constitute direct discrimination. But on these facts, where the claimant had been employed specifically to replace another pregnant worker, the situation should rather be compared with that of a man in a similar situation, for example, a man with an arthritic hip, who found, shortly after taking up employment, that he was soon to be called for a hip replacement operation necessitating a long absence from work. Since an employer would have been justified in dismissing a man under these circumstances, the claimant's dismissal was not discriminatory on the grounds of sex.

Following the applicant's appeal to the House of Lords questions as to the legality of dismissal on the grounds of pregnancy in these particular circumstances were referred by that court to the ECJ ([1992] 4 All ER 929) and the dismissal was found to be illegal (case C–32/93). In this ruling, the Advocate-General and the ECJ rejected the idea that a pregnant woman should be compared with a sick man (see also *Habermann-Beltermann* (case C–421/92)).

The ECJ's judgment raises some questions, not the least of which concerns where the boundary lies between being dismissed for pregnancy which is unacceptable; and being dismissed for being ill, albeit because of pregnancy, which, provided it occurs outside the normal maternity leave, is acceptable (see *Hertz*). In *Handels-og Kontorfunktion ærernes Forbund i Danmark acting on behalf of Larsson* v *Dansk Handel & Service acting on behalf of Føtex Supermarket A/S* (case C–400/95), the ECJ held that a woman could be dismissed for absences other than maternity leave caused by pregnancy-related illnesses occurring both prior to and after the birth of the child, and in *North Western Health Board* v *McKenna* (case C–191/03), the Court held that where a female worker had been absent due to pregnancy-related illness before her maternity leave, her pay could be reduced if a man who had been absent for the same period would be treated in the same way The decision in *Larsson* should be contrasted with *Brown* v *Rentokil* (case C–394/96), where it was held that a woman could not be dismissed at any time during her pregnancy for absences arising from pregnancy-related illnesses. The Pregnancy Directive (Directive 92/85, [1992] OJ

L348/1) prohibits the dismissal of workers during the period from the beginning of their pregnancy to the end of their maternity leave, save in exceptional circumstances unconnected with their pregnancy. Pregnancy-related illnesses would seem not to justify dismissal during this time. The position after the end of the woman's maternity leave as regards such illnesses is not, however, dealt with expressly and some uncertainty as to the level of protection in this context remains.

Another question arising in *Webb* concerned whether availability for work constitutes a fundamental condition of the employment contract. The ECJ rejected this contention, but on the basis that the time that the woman would be unavailable for work constitutes only a small proportion of the contract time in an indefinite contract. This did, however, undermine the position of women on short-term contracts. Could they be dismissed on the basis that their pregnancy constitutes too large a proportion of the contract? These issues were clarified in the cases of *Teledenmark* (case C–109/00), *Jiménez Melgar* (case C–438/99) and *Busch* (case C–320/01). In *Teledenmark*, a woman was employed on a six months' fixed term contract, two of which were spent on a training course. After commencing employment, she notified her employer that she was pregnant, whereupon she was dismissed. The employer argued that she could not perform a substantial part of her duties and further that, in not mentioning her pregnancy before she was employed, she had violated the principle of good faith. The ECJ rejected these arguments:

> Since the dismissal of a worker on account of pregnancy constitutes direct discrimination on grounds of sex, whatever the nature and extent of economic loss incurred by the company as a result of her absence, because of pregnancy, whether the contract was concluded for a fixed term of for an infinite period has no bearing on the discriminatory character of the dismissal. In either case, the employee's inability to perform her contract of employment is due to pregnancy (para. 31).

The ruling was applied in *Jiménez Melgar*, which concerned a refusal to renew a fixed-term contract. In *Busch*, the ECJ, basing its judgment on *Teledenmark*, confirmed that a woman was under no duty to tell an employer that she is pregnant prior to accepting a job offer or returning to work.

This case law seems to reflect, if not go further than, the terms of the Pregnancy Directive. The directive provides core maternity rights including periods of maternity leave and protection from dismissal during such leave, whether the worker is on a short-term or indefinite contract, and will thus protect workers in this position. The Pregnancy Directive does not, though, deal with the position of the woman who is not appointed because she is pregnant. Presumably, this could still fall within the Equal Treatment Directive following *Dekker*. Certainly, the ECJ held in *Mahlburg v Land Mecklenburg-Vorpommern* (case C–207/98), that a hospital could not refuse to appoint a pregnant woman to a permanent post as a theatre nurse on the basis that she would not be able to carry out her duties while she was pregnant. In this case German legislation prohibited expectant mothers from being exposed to chemicals with which the applicant would have come into contact as part of her job. This demonstrates that where a permanent post is in issue, temporary absence or incapacity (even from the commencement date of the appointment) will not be a legitimate ground for refusal of employment.

The Pregnancy Directive also specifies that women on maternity leave are entitled to an 'adequate allowance'. Ironically, this provision weakened the applicants' arguments in *Gillespie* v *Northern Health and Social Services Board* (case C–342/93) that equal pay requires full pay. The ECJ followed the directive (although the actual situation in *Gillespie* predated it) holding that maternity pay did not need to be full pay, provided it was adequate. The Court also held, however, that maternity pay must take account of any pay increases during the maternity leave or during the period with reference to which the maternity pay is calculated (see also *Alabaster* v *Woolwich plc* (case C–147/02)). The ECJ has also ruled on the impact of maternity leave (in conjunction with sick leave) on a woman's entitlement to be considered for a 'merit increase' (*Caisse Nationale D'Assurance Vieillesse des Travailleurs Salaries (NAVTS)* v *Thibault* (case C–136/95)). As far as the applicant was concerned, the difficulty arose because she did not satisfy the prerequisite of six months' work because of the time she had had off, and was therefore ineligible for the pay rise. The ECJ agreed that this was contrary to the requirements of the Equal Treatment Directive. It stated that if a woman continued to be bound by her contract of employment, she should not be deprived of benefits which apply to men and other women by virtue of the employment relationship. The ECJ, in so holding, emphasised that the Equal Treatment Directive was intended to promote substantive equality. (See also *Gillespie* (case C–342/93).) Whether this desire to safeguard substantive equality is respected in all the ECJ's judgments relating to pregnancy issues is, however, another matter. The precise scope of the rights under the Pregnancy Directive will no doubt continue to be the subject of further litigation.

In the recast version in the new Article 2(7), many of these decisions are now incorporated into the text of the Directive itself. Thus, it is made clear, in the second paragraph to Article 2(7), that a woman is entitled to return to her job, or an equivalent post, after the end of her maternity leave, on no less favourable terms and conditions. The previous case law will continue to be relevant in interpreting this broad statement.

25.9.7.3 *Positive discrimination (Article 2(8))*

The third exception to the principle of equal treatment is that of positive discrimination, which permits schemes to enable women to compete equally with men. Article 2(8) of the Equal Treatment Directive provides that:

> Member States may maintain or adopt measures within the meaning of Article 141(4) of the Treaty with a view to ensuring full equality in practice between men and women.

Article 2(8) therefore now corresponds with the new Article 141(4), inserted by the ToA.

The earlier version of this derogation in the former Article 2(4) expressed the Directive to be without prejudice to measures 'to promote equal opportunity for men and women, in particular by removing existing inequalities which affect women's opportunities'.

The Court had seen this as another derogation from the principle of equal treatment, rather than a means of achieving that goal and had, therefore, regrettably, construed the provision narrowly. In *Kalanke* v *Freie Hansestadt Bremen* (case

C–450/93), the ECJ held that a rule requiring the appointment of the female candidate when applicants were equally qualified and there was an under-representation of women at the level of the position for which the applicants were applying did not fall within the former Article 2(4). The Court stated that the purpose of the provision was to allow measures intended to eliminate or reduce actual instances of inequality so as to allow women to compete equally. In giving women 'absolute and unconditional' priority, the system overstepped the limits in the former Article 2(4).

This somewhat harsh decision caused outcry in certain quarters, including suggestions that the former Article 2(4) be broadened to allow positive discrimination. However, *Kalanke* is now largely of historical value only. As already noted, the ToA amended Article 141 so as to strengthen the provision for positive discrimination with the addition of a new para. (4), which provides that:

> With a view to ensuring full equality in practice between men and women in working life, the principle of equal treatment shall not prevent any Member State from maintaining or adopting measures providing for specific advantages in order to make it easier for the under-represented sex to pursue a vocational activity or to prevent or compensate for disadvantages in professional careers.

The ECJ started to interpret the former Article 2(4) in the light of this change even prior to the entry into force of the ToA (*Marschall* (case C–409/95). See also *Badeck* (case C–158/97, decided after the ToA came into force). It seems that the crucial difference between these two cases and *Kalanke* is the existence of what the ECJ has termed a 'saving clause'. This means that the legislation which provides for the preferential treatment of women is not automatic, instead containing a clause that permits the appointment of a man if other societal reasons specific to that man apply. One example of such a factor is a policy designed to ensure the appointment of appropriately qualified handicapped people. (Compare *Abrahamsson and Anderson* v *Fogalqvist* (case C–407/98).) In *Lommers* (case C–476/99), the ECJ had to consider whether right of access to subsidised nursery places to female employees was acceptable. The ECJ noted that the former Article 2(4) authorises measures relating to access to employment which give a specific advantage to women to allow them to compete on an equal footing with men. The Court noted that the absence of suitable and affordable nursery facilities leads to parents, mainly women, giving up their jobs. The ECJ concluded that such measures would fall within the scope of the former Article 2(4). Nonetheless, any such measure must be proportional. A measure which excludes fathers from all possibility of access to such facilities would be disproportionate. Rules that exceptionally permit fathers who take care of their children would, however, be permissible. The same general approach seems to be taken here as was taken in *Badeck* and *Marschall*.

Interestingly, the ECJ in its judgment noted that measures such as those in this case, 'might nevertheless also help to perpetuate a traditional division of roles between men and women' (para. 41). While there is undoubtedly a risk of stereotyping arising from positive discrimination measures such as this, the alternative may perpetuate a real existing disadvantage. The existence of these conflicting concerns suggests that it is not appropriate to state that all positive discrimination should be viewed as 'good' or 'bad', but that such measures should be assessed individually.

The above cases involving exemption from the equal treatment principle all concern direct discrimination. Where the discrimination is indirect the same principles apply as apply in the field of pay; a difference in treatment as between one group of workers and another which *affects* one sex disproportionately will require objective justification. Here the justification need not be brought within Article 2 of Directive 76/207, since the difference in treatment for which justification is required is not between men and women, but between one group of workers (e.g., part-timers) and another (e.g., full-timers). Following *Danfoss* (case 109/88) the onus of proving justification is likely to fall on the employer. *Kirsammer-Hack* v *Sidal* (case C–189/91) provides an example of a successful defence of objective justification to a claim of indirect discrimination, based on the need to protect small undertakings against excessive administrative, financial and legal burdens.

25.10 **Principle of equal treatment in matters of social security (Directive 79/7)**

Directive 79/7, which implements the principle of equal treatment for men and women in matters of social security, became directly effective once the date for its implementation by Member States had expired, on 23 December 1984 (see *Netherlands* v *Federatie Nederlandse Vakbeweging* (case 71/85); *McDermott* v *Minister for Social Welfare* (case 286/85); *Clarke* v *Chief Adjudication Officer* (case 384/85)). No extension of time is permitted for transitional arrangements (*Dik* v *College van Burgemeester en Wethouders* (case 80/87)). Since Directive 79/7 applies only to *statutory* social security schemes its effects must inevitably be vertical. Also, since Directive 79/7 merely implements the principle of equal treatment in the field of social security expressed in Directive 76/207 (Article 1(1)) there is, as *Burton* v *British Railways Board* (case 19/81) illustrates, some overlap between the two directives. There is also considerable uncertainty as to where the boundary between Article 141 EC and Directive 79/7 lies (*Beune* (case C–7/93)).

25.10.1 **Personal and material scope**

Directive 79/7 applies to the working population, defined broadly to include 'self-employed persons, workers and self-employed persons whose activity is interrupted by illness, accident or involuntary unemployment and persons seeking employment', and to 'retired or invalided workers and self-employed persons' (Article 2). In *Drake* v *Chief Adjudication Officer* (case 150/85) the Court held that the term 'working population' must be defined broadly, to include persons who have been working but whose work has been interrupted. Thus Mrs Drake, who had given up work to look after her invalid mother, was entitled to claim a right to equal treatment under Directive 79/7. Directive 79/7 may also be invoked by the spouse of a person falling within Article 2, provided that the benefit claimed is within the scope of the directive; 'others too may have an interest in seeing the principle of non-discrimination respected on behalf of the person protected' (*Verholen* (cases

C–87, 88 and 89/90)). However, Article 2 cannot be invoked by persons who have not been employed and are not seeking work, or by those who have worked but whose work has not been interrupted by one of the risks referred to in Article 3(1) (*Achterberg-te Riele and Others* v *Sociale Verzekeringsbank* (cases 48, 106, 107/88)). This approach was followed in *Johnson* v *Chief Adjudication Officer* (case C–31/90), in which the ECJ held that a woman who had voluntarily given up work to care for her children would not be within the scope of the directive unless she was looking for work when one of the risks outlined in the directive occurred.

The principle of equal treatment under Directive 79/7 applies to:

(a) statutory schemes providing protection against sickness, invalidity, old age, accidents at work or occupational diseases and unemployment; and

(b) social assistance, insofar as it is intended to supplement or replace these schemes (Article 3(1)).

In *Drake* the Court held that the benefits covered by the directive must constitute whole or part of a statutory scheme providing protection against one of the specified risks or a form of social assistance having the same objective. It appears that the statutory scheme must be one for workers in general, and not one, as in *Liefting* (case 23/83), relating to persons employed by the State. A contracted-out scheme operating as a substitute for the statutory scheme will be treated as an occupational pension scheme, within Directive 86/378 (*Newstead* v *Department of Transport* (case 192/85)).

In an uncharacteristically restrictive interpretation the Court, contrary to Advocate-General Tesauro's recommendations, in *R* v *Secretary of State for Social Security, ex parte Smithson* (case C–243/90), denied the claimant's right to equality of treatment in respect of housing benefit under Directive 79/7 on the grounds that it was not within the scope of the directive. Although eligibility for the benefit, and the amount of benefit, was ascertained, *inter alia*, by reference to a (discriminatory) invalidity pension, the benefit was not 'directly and effectively' linked to the protection provided against one of the risks specified in Article 3(1); a similarly restrictive approach was adopted in *Jackson* v *Chief Adjudication Officer* (cases C–63, 64/91). Here, in a claim by two single mothers, one engaged in vocational training, one in part-time work, in respect of supplementary allowance and income support, the Court held that these benefits, which might be granted in a variety of situations to persons whose means were insufficient to meet their needs, did not relate to any of the risks listed in Article 3(1). Nor did they fall within Directive 76/207. Although the benefits in question might affect the single parent's ability to undertake vocational training or part-time employment, they did not relate to the subject matter of the Directive, which was *access* to employment, including vocational training and promotion and working conditions.

The Court's attitude in these cases stands in stark contrast to its previous approach to the 'social assistance' exemption in Social Security Regulation 1408/71 and to the concept of 'social advantage' under Regulation 1612/68 (see Chapter 20). *Jackson* v *Chief Adjudication Officer* may also be contrasted with *Meyers* v *Adjudication Officer* (case C–116/94). In *Meyers*, the ECJ held that family credit, by enabling a single mother to go out to work, concerned access to employment and therefore fell within the ambit of the Equal Treatment Directive 76/207. *R* v *Secretary of State for Health, ex parte Richardson* (case C–137/94) concerned UK regulations dealing with exemptions from prescription charges which were linked to retirement age and were therefore discriminatory. The ECJ held that such rules fell within Article 3(1) because they formed part of the statutory scheme providing protection against one of the risks covered by the directive, namely, sickness. These cases indicate that the ECJ may have had second thoughts about its earlier case law. Nonetheless, there must still be some links with the risks listed in Article 3(1): in *Atkins* v *Wrekin District Council* (case C–228/94) concessionary travel passes awarded to old age pensioners were held not to fall within the terms of the directive.

Survivors' benefits, and family benefits not granted by way of increases to the benefits covered by the directive, are excluded from Directive 79/7 (Article 3(2)).

Provided that the benefit in question is covered by Directive 79/7, the fact that it may be payable under national legislation to a third party does not take it outside the scope of the directive. Otherwise, as the Court pointed out in *Drake*, it would be possible, by making formal changes to existing benefits covered by the directive, to remove them from its scope. On this reasoning Mrs Drake was held entitled herself to invoke Directive 79/7 in respect of an invalidity allowance payable on behalf of her mother.

25.10.2 Scope of the equal treatment principle

The principle of equal treatment means, according to Directive 79/7, Article 4(1), that:

> there shall be no discrimination whatsoever on grounds of sex either directly, or indirectly by reference in particular to marital or family status, in particular as concerns:
> — the scope of [social security] schemes and the conditions of access thereto,
> — the obligation to contribute and the calculation of contributions,
> — the calculation of benefits including increases due in respect of a spouse and for dependants, and
> — the conditions governing the duration and retention of entitlement to benefits.

In *Drake* an invalidity allowance payable to a married man, but not to a married woman, was found in breach of Article 4(1).

Where a provision is indirectly discriminatory, it may be found to be objectively justified (see the earlier discussion on objective justification). In *Teuling* (case 30/85) an invalidity benefit, the amount of which was determined by marital status and either the (low) income derived from the spouse's occupation or the existence of a dependent child, designed to compensate for the 'greater burden' borne by persons in these categories, although indirectly discriminatory against women, was held to be objectively justified (see also *Commission* v *Belgium* (case C–229/89)). Such benefits, sexually neutral and designed to meet objective needs such as the need to support dependants, happen to benefit men more than women because the former are still, if to a diminishing degree, more likely to be responsible for dependants. Similarly, benefits to aid the long-term unemployed are acceptable because they are designed for gender-neutral policy purposes which, although they may benefit men more than women, are still justified (*Posthuma-van Damme* v *Bestuur van de Bedrijfsvereniging voor Detailhandel, Ambachten en Huisvrouwen* (case C–280/94)). In this case the ECJ also emphasised the wide margin of discretion Member States have in choosing their social policies.

Supplementary benefits payable for a spouse or persons deemed to be dependent on the claimant are payable under Article 4(1) irrespective of the sex of the claimant. This applies even if it results in double payment, for example, payment to both spouses for the same dependants. In response to the Irish Government's argument in *Cotter* v *Minister for Social Welfare* (case C–377/89) that this would result in unjust enrichment the Court held that a defence based on this principle would enable the authorities to use their own unlawful conduct as a ground for depriving Article 4(1) of the Directive of its full effect.

In *Ruzius-Wilbrink* (case 102/88) the ECJ held that the principle of equal treatment expressed in Article 4(1) was capable of being applied to part-time workers. The claim concerned invalidity benefits provided under the Dutch social security system. Under the scheme the amount payable to part-timers was linked to the claimant's previous income; full-time workers, regardless of the size of their previous income, were entitled to a guaranteed 'minimum subsistence income'. The claimant, who had been a part-time worker, claimed that the system was indirectly discriminatory against women, since the part-time workforce in the Netherlands contained a much smaller percentage of men than women. The Court held that in these circumstances the difference in treatment would breach Article 4(1) of Directive 79/7 unless it could be justified by objective factors unrelated to sex. The fact that it would be unfair, as was argued by the Netherlands Social Insurance Board, to grant part-time workers an allowance higher than the wages they had previously received in employment was held not to amount to objective justification, since in a substantial number of cases the amount granted to those entitled to a minimum subsistence income was also higher than their previous income.

The principle of equal treatment is 'without prejudice to the provisions relating to the protection of women on the grounds of maternity' (Article 4(2)). These provisions are likely to be interpreted according to the same principles as apply to Article 2(3) of Directive 76/207.

25.10.3 Exclusions

Article 7(1) expressly allows Member States to exclude certain matters from the scope of the equal treatment principle. These are:

(a) the determination of pensionable age for the purposes of old-age and retirement pensions and possible consequences thereof for other benefits;

(b) benefits or entitlements granted to persons who have brought up children;

(c) wives' derived old-age or invalidity benefits, and

(d) increases granted in respect of dependent wives related to long-term invalidity, old age, accidents at work and occupational disease benefits.

Article 7 must now be read in the light of the Court's case law under Directive 76/207, and in particular *Marshall* (case 152/84), *Roberts* (case 151/84) and *Beets-Proper* (case 262/84). The exemption for the determination of pensionable age will apply *only* for the purposes of old-age and retirement pensions and possible consequences thereof for other social security benefits. In *R* v *Secretary of State for Social Security, ex parte Equal Opportunities Commission* (case C–9/91), in an action brought by the EOC for a declaration that the British Social Security Act 1965, in maintaining different periods of contribution by men and women towards social security benefits, the men's being longer, tied to the difference in pensionable age, was in breach of Directive 79/7, the Court held that the derogation provided by Article 7(1)(a) applied to any forms of discrimination 'necessarily linked' to the different statutory pensionable age. This would include the maintenance of different contribution periods for male and female workers. Such a scheme reflected the purpose of the derogation, which was to:

> allow Member States to maintain temporarily the advantages accorded to women with respect to retirement in order to enable them progressively to adapt their pension systems ... without disrupting the complex financial equilibrium of those systems, the importance of which could not be ignored.

The scope of Article 7(1)(a) was further tested in *Secretary of State for Social Security v Thomas* (case C–328/91) in a claim by a number of women for severe disablement allowances and invalid care allowances. Under British law these benefits were not payable to those who had reached pensionable age (60 for women, 65 for men) unless at that age they were already in receipt of the benefits. The applicants had not received these benefits before attaining pensionable age, nor had they, on reaching that age, been in receipt of an old age pension. They argued that the tying of benefits to pensionable age (save in the case of those already in receipt of benefits) was discriminatory, particularly since they were entitled, following *Marshall*, to continue working until the age of 65. The central question was whether the benefits in question fell within the exception provided by Article 7(1)(a).

Citing *R v Secretary of State for Social Security, ex parte Equal Opportunities Commission* (case C–9/91), that the permitted derogation of Article 7(1)(a), as regards the 'possible consequences thereof for other benefits' was confined to 'forms of discrimination existing under other benefit schemes which are *necessarily and objectively* linked to the difference in retirement age', the Court held that discrimination in respect of other benefits would only be necessary 'to avoid disrupting the complex financial equilibrium of the social security system or to ensure consistency between retirement pension schemes and other benefit schemes' (para. 12). Since the benefits in question were non-contributory there was no question in this case of disruption of the financial equilibrium of the UK social security system; nor was discrimination necessary to avoid inconsistency between different benefit schemes. Since, as the UK had argued, the benefits were intended to replace income in the event of materialisation of the risk, the principle of consistency required that they should be available in cases such as the applicants', where claimants were unable to work and were not in receipt of an old age pension. In any event, national rules against overlapping would prevent double recovery by those in receipt of a pension.

By contrast, in *Secretary of State for Social Security v Graham* (case C–92/94), a case concerning discrimination in respect of contributory invalidity pensions, the ECJ held that the difference in treatment was necessarily and objectively linked to the permitted difference in retirement ages for men and women. To interfere with the ability to set retirement ages would encroach on the rights of the Member States under Article 7(1)(a) and would also introduce inconsistencies in the treatment of able-bodied women who had retired at 60 and their disabled counterparts. Although the Court identified the purpose of the provisions as replacing income from employment, it did not conclude that, as women are entitled to remain in employment until 65 (*Marshall* (case 152/84)), they should be entitled to a replacement income for that period should they be prevented by illness from being able to work. This somewhat circumspect decision may well have been driven, in part, by the need to allay Member States' fears about the reduced scope for exemption under Article 7(1)(a). The ECJ in general has taken a very restrictive view of Article 7(1)(a)'s scope, as it does of all derogations from fundamental Community rights. *Graham* therefore indicates a slightly broader approach, but whether it will constitute the basis of a new approach is another question. In *Taylor* (case C–382/98), which concerned winter fuel payments, the ECJ took an approach similar to that in the *Equal Opportunities* case (case C–9/91). (See also case C–104/98, *Buchner*.) By contrast, in *Hepple* (case C–196/98), which concerned a reduced earnings allowance, the ECJ held that the scheme fell within Article 7(1)(a), and therefore unequal age conditions linked to different pensionable ages for men and women could be imposed. Although the difference in treatment was not necessary to maintain the financial equilibrium of the scheme – as had been the case in *Thomas* and *Graham* – the ECJ accepted that the rules were designed to achieve a coherence between the allowance and the pension scheme and were objectively necessary for that purpose. It is equally uncertain whether the other exceptions will be narrowly or generously construed.

States are required under Article 7(2) periodically to examine matters excluded under Article 7(1) to ascertain whether they are still justified.

25.11 Principle of equal treatment in occupational pension schemes (Directive 86/378)

25.11.1 Relationship with equal pay

Directive 86/378, which is complementary to Directive 79/7, implements the equal treatment principle in the field of occupational, as opposed to statutory, pension schemes. It has, following *Barber*, been amended by Directive 96/97. The original Directive was subject to a three-year implementation period, which expired on 31 July 1989 (Article 12). However, under Article 8, States were given until 1 January 1993 to take 'all necessary steps to ensure that the provisions of occupational [pension] schemes contrary to the principle of equal treatment are revised'. This implies that while States might be liable for failure to implement the directive from 1 August 1989, it did not become *fully* effective until January 1993. Although that point might be of historic interest only, it should be noted that where the difference in treatment arises from the employer's contribution, direct or indirect, to the pension scheme, by way of consideration paid by the employer to the employee in respect of his employment, as in *Worringham* v *Lloyds Bank Ltd* (case

69/80), *Bilka-Kaufhaus GmbH* v *Weber von Harz* (case 170/84) and *Barber* (case 262/88), it may fall to be treated under Article 141 as 'pay', subject to the temporal limitations of *Barber* and the substantive limits imposed by *Neath* v *Hugh Steeper Ltd* (case C–152/91). Following *Bilka-Kaufhaus* such benefits can even be claimed by part-time workers where the discriminatory effects fall disproportionately on one sex, provided that the difference in treatment is not objectively justified. Where the matter falls within Article 141 any problems concerning the direct effects of the directive will be avoided.

25.11.2 Scope of the Directive

With a few important exceptions Directive 86/378 is enacted in near-identical terms to Directive 79/7. It applies to occupational schemes 'not governed by Directive 79/7 whose purpose is to provide workers . . . with benefits intended to supplement the benefits provided by statutory social security schemes or to replace them' (Article 2). It applies to the same categories of persons (Article 3) in respect of the same risks (Article 4). Directive 86/378, however, contains no exclusions for survivors' and family benefits parallel to that of Article 3(2) of Directive 79/7, *provided* these benefits form part of the consideration paid by the employer by reason of the employee's employment (Article 4).

Article 6(1) gives a list of examples of provisions contrary to the equal treatment principle. As noted above, it was amended to reflect the principles contained in *Coloroll* and *Neath*. Article 6(1)(f) prohibits the fixing of different retirement ages for men and women, and Article 6(1)(j) the laying down of different standards or standards applicable only to a specified sex. Article 6(1)(h) disallows 'suspending the retention or acquisition of rights during periods of maternity leave', which has been interpreted to require the continuation of payments to a supplementary occupational pension scheme based on taxable pay, even though maternity pay is not taxable (*Mayer* v *Versorgungsanstalt* (case C–356/03)). Article 6(1)(h) prohibits the setting of different levels of benefit 'except insofar as it may be necessary to take account of actuarial calculation factors which differ according to sex in the case of benefits designated as contribution-defined'. Similarly although different levels of employee contribution are prohibited in principle (Article 6(1)(i)) they *may* be set 'to take account of the different actuarial calculation factors' (Article 9(c)). Thus differences in treatment may be objectively justified. Different levels of employer contribution may also be permitted if they are set 'with a view to making the amount of [contribution-defined] benefits more equal' (Article 6(i)).

25.11.3 Exceptions and derogations

Article 9, like Article 7 of Directive 79/7, enables Member States to exempt from the equal treatment principle the 'determination of pensionable age for the purposes of granting old-age or retirement pensions, and the possible implications for other benefits'. This provision was construed seemingly out of existence in *Barber* (case C–262/88): hence the Court's decision that its ruling on this issue should not be retrospective.

Article 9(b) provides that 'survivors' pensions which do not constitute consideration paid by the employer are exempt from the equal treatment principle until the date on which equality is achieved in statutory schemes, or at the latest, until equality is required by a Directive'. Following *Barber* such benefits, being paid by the employer as a result of the employment relationship, are likely to be construed as consideration and thus will not be exempt under Article 9(b). *Newstead* (case 192/85), which had decided otherwise, thereby excluding the employer's provision for survivors from the equality principle under Article 9(b), is unlikely to be followed. Survivors' pensions which do *not* constitute consideration paid by the employer are also exempt from the equal treatment principle *either* until the date on which equality is achieved in statutory schemes, *or*, at the latest, until equality is required by a directive (Article 9(b)).

25.12 Equal treatment in self-employment (Directive 86/613)

Directive 86/613 is designed to ensure the application of the equal treatment principle 'as between men and women engaged in an activity in a self-employed capacity, or contributing to the pursuit of such an activity, as regards those aspects not covered by Directives 76/207 and 79/7' (Article 1). It is complementary to Directive 76/207.

The directive applies to 'all persons pursuing a gainful activity for their own account . . . including farmers and members of the liberal professions' and to 'their spouses, not being employees or partners, where they habitually . . . participate in the activities of the self-employed worker and perform the same tasks or ancillary tasks' (Article 2).

The principle of equal treatment implies 'the absence of discrimination on the grounds of sex, either directly or indirectly, by reference in particular to marital or family status' (Article 3). This is without prejudice to measures concerning the protection of women during pregnancy and motherhood (preamble, ninth recital).

Under Article 4 Member States are required to take all necessary measures to ensure the elimination of all provisions which are contrary to the principle of equal treatment as defined in Directive 76/207, especially in respect of the establishment, equipment or extension of a business or the launching or extension of any other form of self-employed activity, including financial facilities.

Member States are also required: 'Without prejudice to the specific conditions for access to certain activities which apply equally to both sexes' to take the measures necessary to ensure that the conditions for the formation of a company between spouses are not more restrictive than the conditions for the formation of a company between unmarried persons (Article 5).

Where a contributory social security scheme exists for self-employed workers in a Member State, the States must take the necessary measures to enable those spouses who participate in the activities of the self-employed worker, and who are not protected under the self-employed worker's social security scheme, to join a contributory social security scheme voluntarily (Article 6).

States are required to introduce 'such measures as are necessary to enable all persons who consider themselves wronged by failure to apply the principle of equal treatment in self-employed activities to pursue their claims by judicial process, possibly after recourse to other competent authorities' (Article 9).

Member States were required to bring into force the measures necessary to comply with the directives by 30 June 1989. The date for compliance was extended to 30 June 1991 for States which had to amend their legislation on matrimonial rights and obligations in order to secure the principle of equal treatment in the formation of companies (Article 12). The directive became directly effective as against the State on the expiry of the applicable time-limit. Since the date for implementation has passed it may now be invoked as an aid to interpretation against private parties (*von Colson* (case 14/83) and *Harz* (case 79/83)).

25.13 Remedies

Directive 76/207, Directive 75/117 and the Pregnancy Directive (92/85) all require States to 'introduce into their national legal systems such measures as are necessary to enable all persons who consider themselves wronged by failure to apply the principle of equal treatment . . . to pursue their claims by judicial process after possible recourse to other competent authorities'. Given this obligation, it is unsurprising that the sex discrimination jurisprudence has been central to the development of principles relating to remedies for breach of community law. These matters are discussed in Chapter 8.

25.14 Directive 2004/113/EC: equal treatment of men and women in access to goods and services

The most recent measure to give effect to the principle of equal treatment between men and women is Directive 2004/113/EC on equal treatment between men and women in the access to and supply of goods and services ([2004] OJ L373/37). According to Article 3(1), the directive applies to all persons who provide goods or services to the public and offered outside the area of private and family life. It does not seek to prevent freedom of contract, although it does affect the choice of a contracting partner based on sex (Article 3(2)). The directive also does not deal with employment matters, for which there is, of course, already existing legislation.

Article 4 then gives effect to the general principle of equal treatment, prohibiting both direct and indirect discrimination in this context. A controversial provision during the legislative process was Article 5, which prohibits 'the use of sex as a factor in the calculation of premiums and benefits for the purposes of insurance and related financial services'. There was concern that this would, for example, outlaw the variations in insurance premiums for male and female drivers. To meet such concerns, Article 5(2) allows Member States to decide before December 2007 to permit 'proportionate differences in individuals' premiums and benefits where the use of sex is a determining factor in the assessment of risk based on relevant and accurate actuarial and statistical data'.

This directive is regarded as laying down a minimum standard, and Member States may introduce provisions which are more favourable then the equal treatment principle (Article 7; for minimum harmonisation generally, see Chapter 15).

The remainder of the directive contains provisions on enforcement (Articles 8–11), and on the setting up of a body responsible for promoting and monitoring the equal treatment of all persons (Article 12). The latter provision duplicates provisions found elsewhere, and it seems that entrusting this task to a body generally responsible for equal treatment matters would suffice. Member States are required to implement this directive by 21 December 2007.

It may be noted that the recast Equal Treatment Directive, which would modernise and update the legislation discussed in the preceding sections, does not extend to this most recent directive, which will therefore operate alongside the new general directive.

25.15 Directive 2000/43/EC: equal treatment irrespective of racial or ethnic origin

The ToA enhanced the provisions dealing with discrimination, giving the EC powers to adopt measures against discrimination on grounds of race, religion, sexual orientation or disability (Article 13 EC). Directive 2000/43/EC ([2000] OJ L180, p. 22) has been adopted, on the basis of Article 13 EC, to combat discrimination, both direct and indirect, on grounds of racial or ethnic origin, in relation to employment matters, social protection, education and access to public goods and services. However, the directive allows difference of treatment based on racial or ethnic origin in the context of particular occupational activities, provided that this is legitimate and proportionate (Article 4). It also permits positive action (Article 5). The scope of this provision is somewhat open to doubt as the ECJ has handed down judgments prior to the ToA that limit the scope of Member States' ability to introduce such measures in the field of sex discrimination. Even after the ToA, Member States' freedom to take positive measures in the field of sex discrimination is not unlimited. (See further 25.10.3.)

Directive 2000/43/EC provides a minimum level of protection, and Member States may introduce more stringent standards, but should not use the directive as an excuse to lower existing standards (Article 6). The directive further provides for enforcement and remedies (Articles 7–12), and requires that a body is set up to promote equal treatment without discrimination on grounds of racial or ethnic origin.

25.16 Directive 2000/78/EC: equal treatment in employment and occupation

Directive 2000/78/EC ([2000] OJ L303, p. 16) has been adopted, on the basis of Article 13 EC, to combat discrimination on the grounds of religion or belief, disability, age or sexual orientation with regard to employment and occupation. As with Directive 2000/43/EC, differential treatment is permitted where this is required for the particular activity (Article 4(1)). Moreover, as far as employment with the church or other religious organisations is concerned, difference of treatment based on religious beliefs is also not to be treated as discrimination (Article 4(2)). Article 5 requires that disabled persons are given reasonable accommodation. There are similar enforcement provisions to those in Articles 7–12 of Directive 2000/43/EC. Article 15 recognises the need to achieve a balance of representation of the major religious communities in Northern Ireland both in the police service and in the employment of teachers.

25.17 Conclusions

Recent years have seen an upsurge in the legislative activity in the area of discrimination, with three new major measures taking effect, and further legislation to be adopted shortly. Not only has there been a widening in the substantive scope of the Community's activities, but there has also been a great deal of emphasis on enforcement, reflected initially in Directives 2000/43 and 2000/78, and then in the amendments to Directive 76/207 by Directive 2002/73. The recast Equal Treatment Directive will extend these new enforcement provisions into the remaining parts of the discrimination framework. It is to be welcomed that the legislation in this area is undergoing a major review, taking into account not only the various changes to the Treaty since this legislation was first adopted, but also the jurisprudence by the Court.

In respect of the core area, sex discrimination, it can be seen that the ECJ has interpreted the provisions relating to equal pay and equal treatment broadly, emphasising the personal aspect of the rights over issues relating to distortion of competition. In so doing, the ECJ has not been afraid to make far-reaching decisions. Nonetheless, there are limitations to the scope of Article 141 and some secondary legislation has had its role in clarifying the mechanisms by which individuals' rights might be enforced. Given the development of the law in this area, sex discrimination is an area where the general principles might seem clear, but analysing the precise details of particular situations becomes the work of a specialist.

FURTHER READING

Ahtela, K., 'The Revised Provisions on Sex Discrimination in European Law: A Critical Assessment' (2005) 11 ELJ 58–78.
Arnull, A., 'Out with the Old. . .' (Editorial) (2006) 31 EL Rev 1–2.

Burrows, N. and Robison, M., 'Positive Action for Women in Employment: Time to Align with Europe?' (2006) 33 J. Law & Soc. 24.

Curtin, D., 'Scalping the Community Legislator: Occupational Pensions and *Barber*' (1990) 27 CML Rev 475.

Docksey, C., 'The Principle of Equality between Men and Women: a Fundamental Right under Community Law' (1991) 20 ILJ 258.

Hatzopoulos, V., 'A (more) Social Group: A Political Crossroad or a Legal One-way? Dialogues between Luxembourg and Lisbon' (2005) 42 CML Rev 1599–1635.

Hervey, T. and O'Keeffe, D. (eds), *Sex Equality Law in the European Union* (Wiley, 1996).

Honeyball, S., 'Pregnancy and Sex Discrimination' (2000) 29 ILJ 43.

Howard, E., 'Anti-Race Discrimination Measures in Europe: An Attack on Two Fronts' (2005) 11 ELJ 468–486.

Mancine, G. F. and O'Leary, S., 'The New Frontiers of Sex Equality Law in the European Union' (1999) 24 EL Rev 331.

Neuner, J., 'Protection against Discrimination in European Contract Law' (2006) 2 ERCL 35–50.

Prechel, S., 'Remedies after *Marshall*' (1990) 21 CML Rev 451.

Shaw, J., 'European Community Judicial Method: its Application to Sex Discrimination Law' (1990) 19 ILJ 228.

Whiteford, E., 'Social Policy after Maastricht' (1993) 18 EL Rev 202.

26

Introduction to competition policy

26.1 The structure of EC competition provisions

The competition policy of the Community is based on Article 3(g) EC, requiring: 'a system ensuring that competition in the common market is not distorted', and Articles 81–99 (ex 85–94) EC. The competition provisions can, broadly speaking, be divided into those which focus primarily on the activities of governments and those which deal with the actions of private (and some public) undertakings. The former consist of the rules on State aid (Articles 87–89 (ex 92–94) EC), although the other competition rules may also affect governments' policies. The grant of State aid by a Member State to an undertaking based in its territory may have the effect of distorting competition in the internal market, because an undertaking which would otherwise struggle to compete may find itself in a better position to do so as a result of such financial support. The Treaty provisions prohibit the grant of State aid, but there are several exceptions in recognition of the fact that such aid may be justified in particular circumstances. The rules on State aid are discussed in Chapter 30.

The second group of provisions consists of the rules concerning anti-competitive agreements or concerted practices between undertakings (Article 81 (ex 85)), the prohibition on abuse of a dominant position on the part of individual undertakings or groups of undertakings (Article 82 (ex 86)) and the rules relating to public undertakings granted special or exclusive rights (Article 86 (ex 90) EC).

The following chapters will focus on Article 81 (Chapter 27), Article 82 (Chapter 28), and their enforcement (Chapter 29). The interrelationship between competition rules and intellectual property rights will be considered in Chapter 31, which also examines the overlap with Article 28 (ex 30) in this regard. Although the rules in Article 86 are becoming increasingly important with the dismantling of State monopolies, especially regarding the provision of utilities and other services of general economic interest, this book will look at this provision only insofar as it affects the operation of State aid rules or Article 82. The provisions concerned with the adverse effects on competition of dumping, the exporting of goods to the Community by third countries at prices which are less than the 'comparable' price of the like product on the domestic market, fall outside the scope of this book.

In previous editions of this book, the chapters on competition law were extensive. Competition law was one of the first 'big' areas of EC law, and merited detailed consideration. This subject has become increasingly complex, and has now evolved to such an extent that it is a specialist area of study. In a general book on EU law, it is no longer possible to do full justice to this subject, and the discussion here has been curtailed to what may be regarded as the fundamental aspects of competition law.

26.1.1 The significance of competition policy for the EC

After agriculture, competition policy is perhaps the most highly developed of the Community's common policies, with the greatest impact on undertakings situated both inside and outside the common market. It is an essential complement to the fundamental provisions of the Treaty designed to create the single market. The obligations imposed on Member States to ensure the free movement of goods and services and freedom of establishment within the Community would be of little effect if parties were free to engage in restrictive practices such as concerted price fixing or market sharing which inhibit the free play of market forces within the single market, particularly when such practices tend to partition the market along national lines.

Broadly speaking, the purposes of EC competition policy, which is spelt out in detail in the Commission's annual reports on competition policy, is to encourage economic activity and maximise efficiency by enabling goods and resources to flow freely amongst Member States according to the operation of normal market forces. The concentration of resources resulting from such activity functioning on a Community, rather than a national, scale is intended to increase the competitiveness of European industry in a world market. In addition to this primary goal, and sometimes conflicting with it, Community competition policy seeks to protect and encourage small and medium-sized enterprises so that they too may play their full part in the competitive process.

In order to understand and evaluate the policies pursued by the Commission it is necessary briefly to examine the economic theory underlying competition policy.

26.2 The theory of competition

26.2.1 Perfect competition

The original concept of competition, dating from the eighteenth century, and Adam Smith's *Wealth of Nations* (1776), merely meant the absence of legal restraints on trade. Modern economic theory, however, which stems from the late nineteenth century, and led to the first antitrust legislation, the Sherman Act, in the USA in 1890, is based on the model of 'perfect competition'. This is an idealised concept, based on a number of assumptions. It assumes that there are in the market a large number of buyers and sellers, the latter all producing identical or homogeneous products; that consumers have perfect information, and always act in order to maximise utility; that resources flow freely from one area of economic activity to another, and that there are no impediments to the emergence of new competition ('barriers to entry'); and that business people always maximise profits. A system of 'pure' or 'perfect' competition guarantees the maximum efficiency, the optimum allocation of resources. It is the polar opposite to the monopoly.

26.2.2 Market failures

The 'traditional' view, adopted by the early economists, was that the real world did not correspond to this model of perfect competition. Rival undertakings might choose to cooperate rather than compete. Markets could be divided. Such practices which stood in the way of the achievement of perfect competition, which restricted the freedom of buyers and sellers, must therefore be curtailed. It was necessary to regulate the market in order to bring it closer to the ideal. Intervention was also seen as necessary to keep open opportunities for competitive activity, particularly for small and medium-sized firms, and to preserve real choice for consumers. Early antitrust law, e.g., the Sherman Act (1890, USA), was designed to make capitalism work more effectively.

Antitrust law in western Europe, which only became widespread after the Second World War, was based on this traditional view. The influence of this view was particularly strong in Germany, where concentrations of industrial power in pre-war Germany were seen as having contributed to a concentration of political power. It was this German inheritance, together with the appeal of the traditional view following the Second World War, that shaped EC competition law. French law too, though in much smaller degree, influenced EC law, particularly in its concern to protect the small trader.

26.2.3 The Chicago school

Opposed to the traditional view is the view of the Chicago school of economists. Although implicit in the *laissez-faire* view of the early nineteenth century, it has only recently emerged and has been rapidly gaining ground over the traditional view, particularly in the USA. According to the Chicago school, the real world approximates quite well to the model of perfect competition; even monopolies are not in themselves anti-competitive as long as there are no barriers to entry, i.e., as long as other business people are not prevented from entering the field as competitors. This will only occur if the minimum efficient scale of the operation is such as to make entry virtually impossible. The Chicago school believes that only the minimum intervention is needed, and then only to curb the most blatant forms of anticompetitive activity, as the market will regulate itself.

26.3 EC competition policy

26.3.1 A strict approach

The basic principles of EC competition policy, as adopted in the original EEC Treaty, were drafted in the broadest terms, leaving the Commission, subject to the supervision of the Court, to interpret these provisions and to develop detailed rules. In interpreting the Treaty the Commission was heavily influenced by the traditional school. In the early years, it had been criticised as being excessively interventionist, although in more recent times, its approach has changed fundamentally.

In its concern to strike down all restrictions on competition it has been said that the Commission failed explicitly to distinguish between 'vertical' agreements (agreements between parties at different levels in the chain of distribution, e.g., between manufacturer and his selected dealer, or between dealer and retailer) which carry many economic advantages, and 'horizontal' agreements (agreements between parties at the same level in the economic chain, e.g., cartels between manufacturer and manufacturer, between dealer and dealer), which are potentially much more damaging to competition. Nor did it distinguish sufficiently between *ancillary restraints*, i.e., restraints which are attached to some pro-competitive transaction, and *naked restrictions* on competition, clothed with no desirable transaction at all. While the latter are never justifiable, the former may be judged according to whether they are necessary to make the (desirable) transaction viable. The Commission has since changed its mind on all of these matters, although it has, perhaps, still not thrown off all the shackles of its previous approach.

26.3.2 Market integration versus economic objectives

The Commission was also criticised for subordinating other goals, such as overall economic efficiency, to the supreme goal of market integration. Thus, to protect the single market, *intra-brand* competition (competition between undertakings dealing in the *same* brand, e.g., between rival Ford car dealers) is protected at the expense of *inter-brand* competition (competition between undertakings dealing in *competing* brands, e.g., between Ford dealers (or manufacturers) and Citroën dealers (or manufacturers)). The effect of this may be to reduce the competitiveness of the industry as a whole. These criticisms are less valid today, although the principal prohibition in Article 81(1) continues to be interpreted broadly. The Commission continues to issue exemption to whole categories of agreements which, although in themselves restrictive of competition and prima facie in breach of Article 81(1), are beneficial overall. Over the years, it has steadily extended the scope of these exemptions.

A similar relaxation of the rules is seen in the Commission's approach to Article 82 and merger control. Of late, with the change in economic conditions (slowdown in growth, increased unemployment, increased competition worldwide), mergers have been allowed to proceed which would have been unlikely to have been accepted earlier.

26.3.3 Relationship with other policies

It has also been suggested that by elevating the single market principle above all other considerations, the Commission and the Court (which rarely departs from the view of the Commission in broad matters of policy) have failed to take into account other Community objectives relevant to the application of competition law, such as the need to counter regional or structural imbalances and to safeguard employment and the environment. The increasing integration of the internal market will clearly have regional, social and environmental repercussions which may necessitate the weighing of other wider policy considerations within the context of the application of Community competition rules.

This concern was recognised by the Commission in a statement issued in 1993, in which it stressed the need 'to ensure that the natural and logical linkages between the Community's competition, research, environmental and social policies are fully taken into account in the Commission's approach to competition policy' (ISEC B 21/93). It was acknowledged by the Commission in its *23rd Report on Competition Policy* that the changes brought in by the Maastricht Treaty, such as the need to protect cultural diversity (Article 151 (ex 128) EC) and the environment (Article 174 (ex 130r(2)) EC), now require the Commission to balance more and more competing interests. This factor has been recognised in the State aid provisions, in particular. Further, the Merger Regulation specifically requires the Commission, when considering whether to approve a merger, to take into account social factors such as the impact of the deal on employees' jobs (e.g., *Comité Central d'Entreprise de la Société Générale des Grandes Sources* v *Commission* (case T–96/92); *Comité Central d'Entreprise de la SA Vittel* v *Commission* (case T–12/93)). Concern for the environment was a factor in the favourable Commission Decision on the *Philips/Osram* joint venture ([1994] 5 CMLR 491), in which the Commission took note of the existence of equipment to reduce emissions at the factory in which the joint venture company was to operate. Article 16 EC, introduced by the ToA, which requires Member States providing 'services of general economic interest' to have regard to the 'shared values of the Union as well as their role in promoting social and territorial cohesion', illustrates Member States' concerns regarding the impact of privatisation on the provision of public services. (See also the Protocol on Public Service Broadcasting annexed to the ToA.) Other changes following the ToA, notably the emphasis on environmental policy and concern about high levels of unemployment, also reflect this trend. The Commission has, however, noted that environmental protection programmes could also be used to partition markets or to disguise other anti-competitive practices (see *23rd Report on Competition Policy*). No doubt other policy objectives could also be so used.

These factors and criticisms may be kept in mind when specific cases fall to be examined. Approval or disapproval of Community policies will ultimately depend on one's view of its economic, social and political priorities. No doubt it was essential that market integration should come first during the Community's formative years. Equally, it is not surprising that, as the Community has become more closely integrated, there has been a greater recognition on the part of the Commission and the Court of the need to promote economic efficiency, to enable European industry to compete more effectively in the world market. Indeed the Commission has pointed out the necessity, in a climate of slow economic growth and fierce competition, for distinguishing, in the application of its competition policy, between behaviour which leads to the development and restructuring of European industry and behaviour which holds back that process by partitioning markets and strengthening domestic positions. This recognition of the need to give more weight to economic efficiency is clearly reflected in the Commission's changed attitude both to vertical agreements and horizontal cooperation agreements (see further Chapter 27). For decades, the Commission followed a strict legalistic approach, but in the late 1990s it changed towards a economics-based assessment. As a result, it regards fewer practices as problematic and now focuses on those agreements where the parties have significant market power. This approach, while more in tune with economic analysis, has been criticised by business for being more uncertain and difficult to apply.

26.4 **Enforcement of EC competition law**

For four decades, enforcement of EC competition law had been entrusted to the Commission under Regulation 17/62, giving it exclusive enforcement powers. In view of the maturity of this area, and the increasing membership of the EC, the enforcement was largely devolved to national competition authorities in Regulation 1/2003, which came into force in May 2004. Any decisions still taken by the Commission may, however, be challenged under Article 230 (ex 173) EC (see Chapter 11) and a failure to take such a decision may be challenged under Article 232 (ex 175) EC (see Chapter 12). These matters are now dealt with by the Court of First Instance (CFI) subject to appeal on points of law to the ECJ. Articles 81 and 82 were declared directly effective (*BRT* v *SABAM* (case 127/73)) early in the development of competition policy, and Member States' courts have always been able to apply EC competition law, although they were not empowered to consider exemptions prior to the entry into force of Regulation 1/2003. Under the new enforcement scheme, there will be much more cooperation between both the Commission and national authorities, and the national authorities *inter se*. This is discussed further in Chapter 29.

Unlike the provisions considered so far, a breach of Articles 81 and 82 may give rise to sanctions imposed by the Commission in the form of heavy fines and penalties. This is rare in EC law. Since companies in breach of competition rules may be subject to substantial fines, the European courts have been vigilant in ensuring that the companies' procedural rights are not infringed. For example, in *BASF AG* v *Commission* (cases T–80 et al./89), a decision was impugned because the decision was not properly adopted in all relevant official languages. In the *Soda Ash* cases, the CFI quashed Commission decisions because the companies' right of access to the file had been denied (*Solvay* v *Commission* (cases T–30–2/91); *ICI* v *Commission* (cases T–36 & 37/91)) (see further Chapter 29).

26.5 **Role of the State**

Although the obligations of Articles 81 and 82 are imposed on 'undertakings' and do not prima facie concern the activities of public authorities, Article 86(1) expressly provides that EC competition law applies to 'public undertakings and undertakings to which Member States grant special or exclusive rights', subject to exception for undertakings 'entrusted with the operation of services of general economic interest or having the character of a revenue-producing monopoly' insofar as the application of the rules may 'obstruct the performance of the particular tasks assigned to them' (Article 86(2)). This exception has been strictly construed. Derogation will be permitted only to the extent that it is necessary to the performance of the particular tasks assigned to such undertakings and to the economic equilibrium of the service operated in the general economic interest, for example by providing a set-off between profitable and unprofitable activities (*Corbeau* (case C–320/91) re Belgian postal monopoly). Outside these exempted areas:

> The legal framework within which agreements are made or decisions are taken and the classification (i.e., public or private) given to that framework are irrelevant as far as the applicability of Community rules on competition are concerned (*BNIC* v *Clair* (case 123/83) para. 17).

With the current trend towards privatisation of 'services of general economic interest', in the interests of greater efficiency, it is unlikely that these rules, particularly those governing exemptions, will be relaxed. Even Article 16 EC, which emphasises the importance of public services, states that it operates 'without prejudice' to Articles 73 (public transport), 86 (public undertakings) and 87 (State aid discussed in Chapter 14) and presumably therefore does not disturb the existing case law on these articles (see also the *Green Paper on Services of General Economic Interest* (COM (2003) 270 final – [2003] OJ C76)).

Even where there is no agreement or behaviour on the part of a public (or semi-public) body such as to give rise to liability under Articles 81 and 82, a State may not adopt or maintain in force any measures which deprive these articles of their effectiveness. Any public measure which endorses or encourages action in breach of Articles 81 and 82 will be deemed unlawful (*GB-INNO* v *ATAB* (case 13/77)). Thus a public body, depending on its actions and the measures concerned, may, in the context of anti-competitive action, incur liability under other articles of the Treaty (e.g., Articles 10, 28 and 29 (goods), 49 (services)) *or* Articles 81 and 82. Where doubt exists as to which articles are appropriate, all relevant articles should be pleaded.

A number of areas, such as transport, were originally excluded from EC competition law. As has been noted, there has been scope under Article 86(2) for exemption for public undertakings. The scope of these exclusions has been considerably reduced in recent years, as the Commission has introduced liberalising measures in the field of communications, postal services, transport, energy, insurance and audiovisual media, with a view to further increasing competition in these spheres. Also, to achieve the benefits of free competition within the single market in the important field of public procurement, the Community has issued directives governing the award of public supply and public works contracts, laying down detailed procedures for the advertising (in the *Official Journal*) and award of such contracts, including the payment of damages by authorities acting in breach of these procedures (see Directive 89/665 [1989] OJ L395/33).

26.6 Competition and third countries

In the external sphere the Commission has stepped up its attempts to secure the acceptance and adoption of EC competition policy by the Community's main trading partners by means of bilateral or multilateral negotiation (for example, the revised form of the EU/US Cooperation Agreement has now been adopted ([1995] OJ L94/47, and [1995] OJ L13/38)), with a view to overcoming the adverse effects for EC traders of anti-competitive practices in non-EC markets.

FURTHER READING

Commission's Annual Reports on Competition Policy.

European Competition Law Review.

Flynn, L., 'Competition Policy and Public Services in EC Law after the Maastricht and Amsterdam Treaties' in O'Keeffe, D. and Twomey, P. (eds), *Legal Issues of the Amsterdam Treaties*, (Hart, 1999).

Gerber, D. J., 'The Transformation of European Community Competition Law?' (1994) 35 Harv Int'l LJ 97.

Goyder, D., *EC Competition Law*, 4th edn (Oxford: University Press, 2003).

Hancher, L., 'Community, State and Market' in Craig, P. and De Burca, G. (eds), *The Evolution of EU Law* (Oxford University Press, 1999).

Hofmann, H.C.H., 'Negotiated and Non-Negotiated Administrative Rule Making: The Example of EC Competition Policy' (2006) 43 CML Rev 153–178.

Ross, M., 'Article 16 EC and Services of General Interest: From Derogation to Obligation?' (2000) 25 EL Rev 22.

Wesseling, R., 'Subsidiarity in Community Antitrust Law: Setting the Right Agenda' (1997) 22 EL Rev 35.

Whish, R., *Competition Law*, 5th edn (Butterworths/Oxford University Press, 2003).

27

Anti-competitive agreements, decisions and concerted practices

27.1 Introduction

A common form of anti-competitive behaviour is for businesses in a particular sector to come to an agreement on matters such as pricing, output, and the markets in which they will sell their respective goods. Price-fixing and market-sharing agreements, in particular, have been very common and despite intense competition enforcement around the globe, businesses continue to come to such arrangements. It many cases, businesses that coordinate aspects such as price or output reduce the competitive pressures from other businesses in the same sector. As a result, competition is reduced, which may have the effect of increasing the price of goods or services, which is detrimental to buyers.

In the context of the common market, the danger of market-sharing is perhaps of particular significance. One of the objectives of the Community has been the creation of a market without barriers that transcends national lines. Consequently, businesses will face competition from businesses established in other Member States. It would undermine the aim of establishing the common market, or impede its operation, if businesses from the various Member States were to agree not to compete in each other's respective territories.

The Community was given a strong mandate to pursue anti-competitive practices in the original EC Treaty. Any form of coordination of commercial behaviour is dealt with under Article 81 (ex 85) EC. Traditionally the prohibition was applied on a broad basis. The Commission had a central role in enforcement, which brought with it problems in exempting agreements that were not harmful in competition terms, as well as the solutions to those problems. Since the modernisation process which commenced in the late 1990s (referred to subsequently, where relevant), there has been a shift, with the Commission now focusing its activities on serious cartels, and domestic competition authorities having a stronger role to play.

27.2 The general scheme

Article 81(1), which would be re-enacted in unamended form as Article III–161, should the Constitution enter into force, prohibits:

> all agreements between undertakings, decisions by associations of undertakings and concerted practices which may affect trade between Member States and which have as their object or effect the prevention, restriction or distortion of competition within the common market.

A number of examples of the types of agreements covered by this article are provided in para. (1)(a) to (e). Article 81(2) provides that any agreement or decision in breach of Article 81(2) 'shall be automatically void'. Under Article 81(3), Article 81(1) may, however, be declared 'inapplicable' to agreements or decisions fulfilling a number of specified criteria.

Thus, Article 81(1) provides a very broad base of liability subject to the possibility of exemption under Article 81(3).

The original enforcement mechanism gave the Commission the *sole* power to apply Article 81(3) (Regulation 17/62, Article 9(1)). This approach required that an agreement for which exemption was sought had to be notified to the Commission (Article 4, Regulation 17/62), which would then investigate and decide if there was a breach of Article 81(1) and whether the criteria for exemption in Article 81(3) were satisfied. Under Regulation 1/2003, which took effect from 1 May 2004, agreements will no longer be notified to the Commission. Instead, Article 81 has become directly applicable *in its entirety*. Agreements which meet the criteria in Article 81(3) will be automatically exempt and no decision to that effect will be necessary. The Commission will work in cooperation with Member States' competition authorities in enforcing the competition law provisions, and national authorities and courts will be able to consider whether a particular agreement or concerted practice satisfies the criteria in Article 81(3). Effectively, Article 81(3) will assume the status of a defence to a claim that Article 81(1) has been infringed. This is discussed further in Chapter 29.

The breadth of Article 81(1) and the severity of the consequences of breach caused concern. There was a risk that many desirable, pro-competitive agreements would fall foul of its provisions, which would have required exemption under Article 81(3). In order to ease the operation of Article 81(3), the Commission has, over the years, issued a number of 'notices' and 'block exemptions'. The notices merely provide non-binding guidelines concerning the Commission's policy, principally as to the kinds of agreement which will *not* breach Article 81(1) (e.g., Notice concerning agreements of minor importance, [2001] OJ C368/13). The block exemptions, which are enacted by regulation, apply to agreements which *do* breach Article 81(1) but, because of their beneficial nature, are exempt 'en bloc' on the grounds of Article 81(3). Under Regulation 1/2003, agreements falling outside a notice or block exemption will nevertheless benefit from automatic exemption, provided that the criteria in Article 81(3) are satisfied. However, notices, as non-binding measures, cannot guarantee immunity, and, to obtain the benefit of a block exemption, an agreement must not contain specific anti-competitive clauses listed in the relevant block exemption, even though they may seem to be justifiable. If this is not the case, the competition authorities of the Member States, or the Commission, can find that Article 81(1) has been infringed (see further Chapter 29).

27.3 Elements of an infringement

Article 81(1) contains three essential elements. There must be:

(a) an agreement between undertakings, or a decision by an association of undertakings or a concerted practice,

(b) which may affect trade between Member States, and

(c) which must have as its object or effect the prevention, restriction or distortion of competition within the common market.

27.4 Agreements between undertakings, decisions by associations of undertakings and concerted practices

27.4.1 Undertakings

In the absence of a definition, the word 'undertaking' has been interpreted in the widest possible sense to include any legal or natural person engaged in some form of economic or commercial activity, whether in the provision of goods or services, including cultural or sporting activities (*Bosman* (case C–415/93)), banking (*Züchner v Bayerische Vereinsbank AG* (case 172/80)), insurance (*Verband der Sachversicherer eV v Commission* (case 45/85)) (*13th Report on Competition Policy*) and transport (*Commission v Belgium* (case 156/77)). It is not necessary that the activity be pursued with a view to profit (e.g., *Fédération Française des Sociétés d'Assurance* v *Ministère de l'Agriculture et de la Pêche* (case C–244/94; see also *COAPI Decision* ([1995] 5 CMLR 468) discussed below). In *Re UNITEL* ([1978] 3 CMLR 306) an individual, in the form of an opera singer, was found to be an undertaking! The CFI recently reconsidered the meaning of 'undertaking' in *FENIN v Commission* (case T–319/99). FENIN was a Spanish association of the majority of undertakings marketing medical goods and equipment in Spain. Health bodies (hospitals etc.) in Spain (SNS) purchase their requirements through FENIN. FENIN complained (under Article 82, see Chapter 28) that the SNS bodies were abusing their dominant position by delaying payment for goods obtained through FENIN. This was rejected and FENIN appealed to the CFI, which also rejected the claim, as SNS could not be described as an undertaking. The CFI emphasised that an undertaking must carry on an economic activity, which is characterised by the business of offering goods or services in a particular market, rather than the simple fact of making purchases. Provided that the purpose for which goods purchased are subsequently used is part of an economic activity, then the purchase itself is an economic activity. SNS operated on the principle of solidarity financed by social security contributions and offered a free service to the general public, which is not an economic activity. SNS was therefore not an undertaking. Consequently, it is necessary to establish some economic activity, however marginal, for something to be regarded as an undertaking for the purposes of Community competition law (approach affirmed in the *German Sickness Fund* case; joined cases C–264/01, C–306/01, C–354/01 and C–355/01).

Article 81(1) also applies in the sphere of agriculture (*The Community* v *Milch-förderungs fonds* ([1985] 3 CMLR 101, Commission Decision)), coal and steel, and atomic energy, provided the matter falls outside the scope of existing provision in these areas. It applies to undertakings in the public as well as the private sphere (Article 86(1)) and *Re British Telecom*, Commission Decision 82/861 ([1983] 1 CMLR 457), upheld by ECJ in *Italy* v *Commission* (case 41/83)) but, as regards undertakings falling within Article 86 EC, only insofar as the application of these rules 'does not obstruct the performance, in law or in fact, of the particular tasks assigned to them'.

27.4.2 Agreements

Agreements are not confined to binding agreements or to those which are written down. A 'gentleman's agreement' will suffice. Often, where competition authorities fail to show an agreement, they will be able to prove the existence of concerted practices. In view of the wide scope of 'concerted practices' (27.4.4), the precise extent of the concept of 'agreement' is of less significance.

27.4.3 Decisions by associations of undertakings

The effect of decisions by trade associations may be to coordinate behaviour amongst undertakings with anti-competitive effects, without any need for actual agreement; hence their inclusion in Article 81(1).

This provision has been widely interpreted, and is not confined to binding decisions. It was held in *NV IAZ International Belgium* v *Commission* (case 96/82) that even a non-binding recommendation from a trade association which was normally complied with could constitute a decision within Article 81(1). In *Re the Application of the Publishers' Association* ([1989] 4 CMLR 825) the Association's Code of Conduct was found by the Commission to have the character of a recommendation to its members and customers, and as such was to be considered as a decision of an association of undertakings, despite its non-binding character. As well as the association itself, its members may be liable for fines if they comply, even unwillingly, with a decision in breach of Article 81(1). In *Wouters* (C–319/99), a regulation by the Dutch Bar Association on multi-disciplinary partnerships was held to be a decision by an association of undertakings because it related to the economic activity of its members (barristers) rather than to the public law function which the DBA also fulfilled.

Article 81(1) also applies to decisions by associations of associations (*NV IAZ International Belgium* v *Commission*).

27.4.4 Concerted practices

These are altogether wider than 'agreements' and 'decisions by associations of undertakings'. The concept of a concerted practice was borrowed from US antitrust law; when the original EEC Treaty was signed the competition rules of the Member States contained no rules against such practices. A concerted practice was defined in *Imperial Chemical Industries Ltd* v *Commission* (case 48/69) (Dyestuffs) as a form of cooperation between undertakings which, without having reached the stage where an agreement properly so-called has been concluded, knowingly substitutes practical cooperation between them for the risks of competition.

To constitute a concerted practice, it is not necessary to have a concerted plan. It is enough that each party should have informed the other of the attitude they intended to take so that each could regulate his conduct safe in the knowledge that his competitors would act in the same way. Similarly, in a series of cases, the CFI has held that meeting to exchange information about pricing structures also constitutes a concerted practice as the participants cannot fail to take this information into account when devising their own market strategies (e.g., *Shell International Chemical Co. Ltd* v *Commission* (case T–11/89)). Clearly, such practices can be just as damaging to competition as agreements or decisions by associations, and are much harder to prove.

Imperial Chemical Industries Ltd v *Commission* centred on three uniform price increases covering the same products introduced by a number of leading producers (including ICI) of aniline dyes, almost simultaneously, in 1964, 1965 and 1967. At a meeting in Basle in August 1967 one of the producers announced an 8 per cent increase to take effect from 16 October. Two other producers subsequently announced a similar increase of 8 per cent. The Commission issued a decision that they were engaged in concerted practices in the fixing of price increases, and imposed heavy fines on them (*Re Aniline Dyes Cartel* JO (1969) L195/11, ([1969] CMLR D23)). ICI sought annulment of that decision, arguing that the price increases were merely examples of parallel increases common in oligopolistic situations (an oligopoly exists where the market is dominated by a small number of large independent concerns). The argument failed. The Court held that whilst parallel behaviour does not in itself constitute a concerted practice, it provides strong evidence of such a practice if it leads to conditions of competition which do not correspond to the normal conditions of the market.

This latter aspect of the decision has been criticised. While a finding of concerted practices was acceptable on the facts (the market was found to be divided on national lines; the prior meetings and announcements eliminated all uncertainty between the parties; the increases were general and uniform and covering the same products), it is submitted that a decision based solely on the 'normal conditions of the market' would be incapable of proof, and could render oligopolies highly vulnerable to a charge of concerted practices in the event of quite 'normal' parallel price increases.

Imperial Chemical Industries Ltd v *Commission* concerned the concerted practices of oligopolies. Oligopolies were also examined in *A. Ahlström OY* v *Commission (Re Wood Pulp)* (cases C–89, 104, 114, 116–7 & 125–9/85), in which the ECJ took a more cautious approach. In an action for the annulment of a Commission decision fining a number of the world's leading wood pulp producers, which together held a two-thirds share of the Community market in wood pulp, for concerted practices in announcing quarterly simultaneous and identical price increases, the Court held that these factors did not provide evidence of concerted practices where the system of price announcements represented a 'rational response to the need to limit commercial risk in a long-term market'. It found that the similarity was the result of a high degree of market transparency, and the parallelism of the price increases could be satisfactorily explained by the oligopolistic tendencies of the market. On the other hand, the parties' agreement, at meetings within their trade association, to fix recommended prices and to notify members in advance of any proposed deviation from these prices was held to restrict competition within Article 81(1).

27.4.5 Unilateral action: refusal to supply

Although Article 81(1) appears to require some form of agreement or concertation on the part of two or more undertakings, there are circumstances when what appears to be a unilateral act may be found to breach it.

In *AEG-Telefunken* (case 107/82) the parties had notified their distribution agreements for AEG products and obtained negative clearance from the Commission. AEG was subsequently found in breach of Article 81(1) for having *operated* the agreements in such a way as to restrict competition by systematically refusing to allow dealers into its network who did not comply with the (unofficial) pricing policy apparently observed by existing members. Moreover, since AEG had acted outside the framework of its agreement as notified, notification did not bring it immunity from fines.

Similarly, in *Ford Werke AG* v *Commission* (case 25/84) the Court approved the Commission's refusal to grant clearance for what appeared to be a perfectly acceptable standard distribution agreement because Ford was refusing to supply existing distributors in Germany with right-hand-drive cars for export in England, apparently to maintain an artificial partitioning of the market and thereby different price levels in different Member States. Although there was no clear evidence of concerted action, certainly none of any agreement, the Court held that Ford's decision to cease supplies formed part of the contractual relations between Ford Werke AG and its dealers. Admission to Ford's dealer network implied acceptance by the contracting parties of the policies pursued by Ford. This may be contrasted with the situation in *Volkswagen* (case T–208/01), where a circular issued by VW suggesting a certain level of pricing was held not to constitute an agreement between it and the members of its distribution network. By contrast, in *Bayer* (joined cases C–2/01 and C–3/01), the ECJ noted that the fact that the practical effect of a unilateral decision by a supplier may be equivalent to an export ban does not mean that such a ban was imposed, nor that an agreement about such a ban could be inferred (para. 88).These cases demonstrate that the Commission and the Court, in applying Article 81(1), will take into account the context in which a particular action operates, and will interpret the article against its literal meaning if that is necessary to suppress practices which are against the spirit, even if they seem to be within the letter, of EC competition law. (*AEG–Telefunken* and *Ford Werke* were followed in *Sandoz* [1987] OJ L222/28 and *Tipp-Ex* [1987] OJ L222/1, decision confirmed by the Court: *Tipp-Ex GmbH & Co. KG* v *Commission* (case C–279/87).)

27.5 Public authorities

Where public bodies are concerned, a distinction must be drawn between agreements or concerted practices entered into in the course of commercial activities, which are clearly capable of falling within Article 81(1), and executive measures which merely permit or encourage such action which, although illegal under other provisions of the Treaty such as Articles 28 and 29 (ex 30–34) EC (see e.g., *GB–INNO* v *ATAB* (case 13/77)), will not in themselves breach this article. In *Bodson* v *Pompes Funèbres* (case 30/87) a licensing arrangement, whereby the local authority granted exclusive rights in respect of certain funeral services to the Société des Pompes Funèbres, was held not to constitute an 'agreement between undertakings' within Article 81(1); but had the municipality imposed a certain level of prices on the licensees the Court suggested it would have been subject to EC competition rules.

In the *COAPI Decision* ([1995] 5 CMLR 468), the Commission determined that the Spanish official association of industrial agents fell within the ambit of Article 81, despite COAPI's argument that it was a public service body since it was established by government regulations, as was its scale of charges. The Commission, however, found that the agents were 'undertakings' and that the regulations constituted an agreement completely separate from the Spanish legislation. As the scale of charges, which set a minimum charge to be applied to foreign clients, affected trade between Member States COAPI was in breach of Article 81(1). This decision also makes it clear that associations offering international services with minimum or fixed rates of charges may be caught by Article 81, even if the association and its scale of charges is approved by a Member State.

27.6 Field of application of Article 81(1) EC

27.6.1 Group companies

Article 81(1) applies to agreements or decisions of associations or concerted practices on a vertical level (e.g., between manufacturer and dealer) as well as a horizontal level (e.g., between manufacturer and manufacturer) (*Établissements Consten SA* v *Commission* (cases 56 & 58/64)). The undertakings must, however, be independent of each other. An agreement between a parent and its subsidiary will not breach Article 81(1) unless the subsidiary enjoys full independence of action, the reason being that competition between them cannot be restricted by the agreement, since they were never in competition with each other (e.g., *Viho Europe BV* v *Commission* (case T–102/92)). However, a parent as well as its subsidiary may be liable for acts of the subsidiary *vis-à-vis* third parties in breach of Article 81(1) where the subsidiary has acted as a result of the parent's promptings; and an agreement between parent and (non-independent) subsidiary may fall within Article 82 if it constitutes an abuse of a dominant position (*Béguelin Import Co.* v *GL Import-Export SA* (case 22/71)).

Similarly members of an 'economic unit' comprising bodies with identical interests and subject to common control may be liable under Article 81 or 82 (*Hydrotherm* v *Compact* (case 170/83)). This means that there may be an 'economic unit' where two companies are controlled by the same shareholder, although that fact is not, in itself, sufficient; there must be additional evidence to show that the companies were operated as an economic unit (*Preinsulated Pipes Cartel*, joined cases C–189/02 P, C–202/02 P, C–205/02 P to C–208/02 P and C–213/02 P). The same principles as apply to parents and subsidiaries apply to agreements between principal and agent. However, the Commission will scrutinize the relationship between the parties to ascertain its true nature (see, e.g., *Pittsburg Corning Europe* ([1973] CMLR D2); description of concession agreement as a commercial agency 'mere colouring').

27.6.2 Undertakings outside the Community

An undertaking situated outside the EC may be liable under Article 81(1) provided that the agreements or practices are implemented inside the common market. In *Imperial Chemical Industries Ltd* v *Commission* (case 48/69), ICI (UK) was held liable for the acts of its subsidiary in Holland although the UK was not yet a member of the EC. In *Woodpulp* Commission decision, ([1985] 3 CMLR 474), a number of firms, all from outside the EC, who were not acting through subsidiaries in the EC but who supplied two-thirds of the EC consumption of wood pulp, were fined for concerted practices in breach of Article 81(1) on the grounds that the *effects* of their practices were felt in the Community. Although the Court, in *A. Ahlström & OY* v *Commission* (cases C–89, 104, 114, 116–7, 125–9/85), annulled the decision in part and reduced the fines, since not all the concerted practices were proved, it held that the applicant firms could be liable, even though they were situated outside the EC, as long as their agreement or practices were *implemented* in the Community.

27.7 'Which may affect trade between Member States'

The agreement or decision by associations of undertakings or concerted practice must be one which may affect trade between Member States to breach Article 81(1). In the absence of an effect on inter-State trade any restriction on competition is a matter for national law alone. However, the question of whether trade between Member States may be affected has been broadly interpreted by the Commission and the Court. In *Société Technique Minière* v *Maschinenbau Ulm GmbH* (case 56/65), the Court held that an agreement was capable of affecting trade between Member States if, on the basis of objective legal or factual criteria, it allows one to expect that it will exercise a direct or indirect, actual or potential effect on the flow of trade between Member States. The test is very similar to the *Dassonville* test applied in the context of Article 28 EC, but broader, since it requires simply an *effect* on, not a *hindrance* to, trade between Member States (see Chapter 18). Clearly the most obvious effect on trade between Member States occurs when parties attempt to partition the market along national lines by means of restrictions on 'parallel' imports or exports (i.e., restrictions, usually agreed between manufacturers and appointed dealers, on dealers' powers to import or export goods across internal EC frontiers).

27.7.1 Agreements within a Member State

An effect on trade between Member States can occur even when an agreement takes place wholly within a Member State and appears to concern only trade within that State. This is so particularly in the case of decisions of associations of national agreements which are intended to operate across the whole national market. As the

Court pointed out in *Vereeniging van Cementhandelaren* v *Commission* (case 8/72) – in the context of a challenge to a Commission decision that cement dealers' price-fixing scheme, limited to the Dutch market, infringed Article 81(1) – an agreement extending over the whole of the territory of a Member State by its very nature has the effect of reinforcing the compartmentalisation of markets on a national basis, thereby holding up the economic interpenetration which the Treaty is designed to bring about and protecting domestic production.

The Court has on several occasions held that this provision applies to agreements between undertakings in the same State. For example in *Re Vacuum Interrupters Ltd* ([1977] 1 CMLR D67), a joint venture agreement between three UK manufacturers to design and develop switch-gear apparatus in the UK was held capable of affecting trade between Member States, since in the absence of such agreement they would have attempted to develop the apparatus independently and to market it in other Member States. (See also *Re Italian Flat Glass* [1982] 3 CMLR 366 (agreement between Italian producers and wholesalers of glass representing more than half of the Italian market); *Salonia* v *Poidomani* (case 126/80) (national selective distribution system for newspapers capable of affecting trade between Member States).)

27.7.2 Combined effect of similar agreements

In the case of a domestic agreement between individual traders, it may be necessary to examine the agreement in the context of other similar agreements, to ascertain whether, taken as a whole, they are capable of affecting trade between Member States (*Brasserie de Haecht SA* v *Wilkin (No. 1)* (case 23/67) (Belgian tied-house agreement part of a network of similar agreements)). The question to be asked is whether the agreements taken as a whole make a significant contribution to the sealing-off of national markets from competition from undertakings situated in other Member States (*Delimitis* v *Henninger Bräu* (case C–234/89)).

27.7.3 Actual or potential effect

Since only a *potential* effect of trade need be proved the enquiry is not limited to existing patterns of trade; the Commission is prepared to speculate as to possible future patterns of trade. In *Pronuptia* (case 161/84) the Court accepted the Commission's finding that a franchising agreement between Pronuptia in France (the franchisor) and its franchisee in Germany, which restricted the franchisee's power to operate outside a particular territory, was capable of affecting inter-State trade even though there was no evidence, and indeed it seemed highly unlikely, that the franchisee had any intention of extending its activities to other Member States.

The question of effect on trade between Member States is not concerned with the increase or decrease of trade which might result from an agreement; all that is required to be shown is a deviation (actual or potential) from the 'normal' pattern of trade which might exist between Member States (*Établissements Consten SA* v *Commission* (cases 56 & 58/64)). In assessing this question it is not necessary to examine every clause in the agreement as long as the agreement as a whole is capable of affecting trade between Member States (*Windsurfing International Inc.* v *Commission* (case 193/83)).

27.8 'Which have as their object or effect the prevention, restriction or distortion of competition within the common market'

27.8.1 Application to horizontal and vertical agreements: *Consten*

As with the question of effect on trade between Member States, EC competition law is not concerned with the question of increase in trade between Member States but with whether there is a distortion of the 'normal' competition which should exist within the common market. Moreover, it is concerned not only with 'horizontal' agreements (i.e., between competing manufacturers, or competing wholesalers – the 'classic' cartel), which clearly restrict competition, but also with 'vertical' agreements (i.e., between manufacturer and distributor, between distributor and retailers, parties not competing with each other) which are often economically beneficial, since they streamline the distribution process and concentrate promotional activity, to the eventual benefit of consumers. These principles were established in *Établissements Consten SA v Commission* (cases 56 & 58/64).

This case concerned an exclusive dealership agreement under which Consten was appointed Grundig's sole distributor and granted exclusive rights to Grundig's trade mark, GINT, in France. Consten agreed not to re-export Grundig's products to any other EC country; Grundig agreed to obtain similar assurances from its dealers in other Member States. There was a total ban on parallel imports and exports in Grundig products, reinforced by the GINT trade mark. Consten discovered that another French firm, UNEF, had bought Grundig products from German traders and was selling them in France at prices below those charged by Consten. Consten brought an action against UNEF for infringement of its trade mark; UNEF applied to the Commission for a decision that the Consten-Grundig agreement was in breach of Article 81(1) and the Commission subsequently issued a decision to that effect (*Re Grundig's Agreement* [1964] CMLR 489). In cases 56 & 58/64 the parties sought to annul that decision. The claimants argued that the effect of their agreement was not to reduce trade between Member States but to increase it. The agreement served to concentrate and streamline the distribution of Grundig products in France, and trade in Grundig products had in fact increased. Moreover, Grundig faced lively competition from other rival producers. The Court rejected these arguments. The fact that trade in Grundig products had increased was irrelevant; the agreement might nonetheless affect trade between Member States and harm the object of the Treaty, namely the creation of the single market. Competition law was concerned not only with agreements which restricted competition amongst competing manufacturers (inter-brand competition). The object of the agreement was to eliminate competition in Grundig products at the wholesale level (intra-brand competition). Moreover, the parties could not rely on their trade-mark rights in these circumstances. To use them merely to partition the market constituted an abuse of such rights. However the Court was not prepared, as was the Commission, to declare the whole agreement void. Only the offending clauses were severed.

The decision in *Établissements Consten SA v Commission* has been criticised, but it must be acknowledged that restrictions on intra-brand competition, contained in vertical agreements, while they may carry economic benefits, are often used, as they were in the Consten-Grundig agreement, to partition the market, usually along national lines, in order to insulate the distributor in each State from competition from parallel imports from States where price levels are low. Artificially high price levels may thus be maintained. As will be seen in Chapter 31, industrial property rights have been used to the same purpose.

Because of these dangers the Commission has preferred to maintain the prohibition under Article 81(1) on these agreements, with the possibility of block exemption, although the current block exemption (see below) is very broad indeed.

27.8.2 'Object or effect'

If the object of an agreement is to prevent or restrict or distort competition, for example, a naked price-fixing or market-sharing agreement between competing manufacturers, there is no need to prove its effect. Unless the agreement is clearly incapable of affecting competition, an anti-competitive effect will be presumed. Where the agreement is not designed to restrict competition, for example, a standard distribution agreement, a detailed economic analysis of its effects on the particular market will be necessary before a breach of Article 81(1) can be proved.

The scope of the analysis required was considered in *Société Technique Minière* v *Maschinenbau Ulm GmbH* (case 56/65). The case involved an exclusive distribution agreement between a German manufacturer of heavy earth-moving equipment, Maschinenbau Ulm GmbH (MU), and a French distributor, Société Technique Minière (STM), similar to the Consten-Grundig agreement, but without its undesirable features. It contained no restrictions on parallel imports or exports, and no abusive use of trade marks. STM sought to resile on its agreement, claiming it was in breach of Article 81(1). The ECJ held that in order to ascertain whether an agreement is capable of preventing, restricting or distorting competition a number of factors must be examined, i.e.:

(a) *The nature and quantity of the products concerned* (i.e., the product market, and the parties' combined share in that market). The greater the market share held by the parties, the more damaging its impact on competition.

(b) *The position and size of the parties concerned* (i.e., their position in the market). The bigger they are, in terms of turnover and *relative* market share, the more likely it is that competition will be restricted.

(c) *The isolated nature of the agreement or its position in a series* (see also *Brasserie de Haecht SA* v *Wilkin (No. 1)* (case 23/67)). This is particularly relevant in the case of distribution agreements, which in themselves may appear insignificant, but which often form part of a network of similar agreements.

(d) *The severity of the clauses.* The more severe the clauses the more likely they will be deemed in breach of Article 81(1). However, any clause that is more than is necessary to achieve the desired (beneficial) result will risk infringing Article 81(1) (*L'Oréal NV* v *De Nieuwe AMCK PVBA* (case 31/80)).

(e) *The possibility of other commercial currents acting on the same products* by means of reimports and re-exports (i.e., parallel imports or exports). Thus any agreement which attempts to ban or even limit parallel imports or exports will normally breach Article 81(1): *L. C. Nungesser KG* v *Commission* (case 258/78)).

The agreement between STM and MU was found on the facts not to breach Article 81(1).

The enquiry needed to ascertain whether an agreement has the potential to prevent, restrict or distort competition within the common market is a wide-ranging one, often involving all the factors outlined above, *always* involving the first two. Such is the importance of the question of market definition that the Commission issued a Notice on the Definition of the Relevant Market for the purposes of Community competition law (([1997] OJ C372/5); see Chapter 28). In *European Night Services* v *Commission* (cases T–397/94 and T–375/94), the CFI emphasised that where an agreement does not contain obvious restrictions of competition, it is necessary to consider the actual context within which the agreement functions, with a particular focus on the economic context. In this case, the French, German, British and Dutch railways had decided to form European Night Services to provide overnight passenger rail services between the UK and the continent through the Channel Tunnel. The Commission decided that the agreement was restrictive of competition and only exempted it with stringent conditions. The CFI annulled the decision on the basis that the Commission had failed to demonstrate the restriction of competition within the meaning of Article 81(1) that was caused by the agreement, primarily because the market share of the parties involved was very low. As will be seen, the Commission is equipped with wide investigative powers to undertake this analysis. National courts, on the other hand, particularly those with an accusatorial system such as the UK's, *a fortiori* lower courts (e.g., *Potato Marketing Board* v *Robertsons* ([1983] 1 CMLR 93), Oxford County Court) may have more difficulty in fulfilling this task (see *BEMIM* (cases T–114/92 and 5/93) discussed in Chapter 29).

27.9 The *de minimis* principle

All agreements between business people curtail to some extent each other's freedom of action in the market-place. Clearly not all such agreements are capable of preventing, restricting or distorting competition to any noticeable extent. Always it is a question of size and scale, as the criteria of *Société Technique Minière* v *Maschinenbau Ulm GmbH*, particularly points (a) and (b), indicate, whether in fact they do so. Hence the importance in competition law of the *de minimis* principle.

27.9.1 The decision in *Völk* v *Vervaecke*

The *de minimis* principle was introduced in the case of *Völk* v *Établissements Vervaecke Sprl* (case 5/69), which concerned an exclusive distribution agreement between Völk, a small-scale manufacturer of washing machines in Germany, and Vervaecke, a Dutch distributor of electrical goods. Völk agreed, *inter alia*, to block all sales of his machines into Vervaecke's territory by third parties (i.e., parallel imports). They were seeking absolute territorial protection for Vervaecke in relation to Völk's machines in Belgium and Luxembourg.

On a reference concerning the agreement's legality in the light of EC law, the Court ruled that in order to come within Article 81(1), competition must be affected to a noticeable extent; there must be a sufficient degree of harmfulness. Therefore it was necessary to take into account the position of the parties on the market for the product in question. In this case the effect of Völk–Vervaecke's agreement on the washing machine market in Belgium and Luxembourg was insignificant. (In fact Völk's production of washing machines was between 0.2 and 0.5 per cent of the German market, and his share in the Belgian and Luxembourg market was minute.)

The size of the parties, and even more important, their share in the relevant product market, will be an essential factor in determining liability. However, if the parties are powerful in a particular market (e.g., alcoholic drinks), they cannot rely on the *de minimis* rule for any of their products within that market (e.g., Pimms (No. 1)) even though they may represent a negligible share of the market in other Member States (*Distillers Co. Ltd* v *Commission* (case 30/78)).

27.9.2 Application of the *de minimis* principle

If an agreement falls within the *de minimis* principle, even if it contains the most blatantly anti-competitive clauses (e.g., price-fixing), even if the parties *intend* to restrict competition (clearly the aim of the territorial protection clause in *Völk* v *Vervaecke)* there will be no breach of Article 81(1). Thus, in assessing the question of breach of Article 81(1), some economic and market assessment will have to be made in every case, although agreements which do not have the object of restricting competition will require a more thorough analysis to prove that they are capable of that effect.

The principle of *Völk* v *Vervaecke* can at its best only provide a guideline serving to exclude agreements whose effect on competition is negligible. No figures were suggested as to the size of the market share needed to bring the principle into play. In *Miller International Schallplatten GmbH* v *Commission* (case 19/77) the Court held that a 5 per cent share in the product market did *not* come within the *de minimis* principle.

27.9.3 Commission notices on *de minimis*

Since 1986, the Commission has published a number of notices on agreements of minor importance ([1986] OJ C231/2, amended [1994] OJ C368/20; replaced in 1997 [1997] OJ C372/1). The current *de minimis* notice was issued in 2001 ([2001] OJ C368/13).

The 2001 notice states that agreements between undertakings with a combined market share below a certain threshold will be regarded as *de minimis*. If the aggregate share of the parties to an agreement between competitors does not exceed ten per cent of the relevant markets, it will not fall within Article 81(1). In the case of an agreement between non-competitors, the parties' market share must not exceed 15 per cent to fall within the *de minimis* principle. If it is not possible to classify the agreement as one involving competitors or non-competitors, the lower threshold will apply. However, if more than 30 per cent of the relevant market is covered by parallel agreements, then the market share of the parties to one such agreement must not exceed 5 per cent. However, the *de minimis* notice will not apply if the agreement contains clauses which amount to price fixing, territorial restrictions or output restrictions. The new notice reflects the new approach to competition law enforcement adopted at the Community level, which focuses on harmful anti-competitive agreements, i.e., those involving price-fixing and market sharing.

In *European Night Services*, the CFI observed that even where the thresholds in the notice have been exceeded, the agreement in question may still not be sufficiently appreciable as to give rise to a breach of Article 81(1). Where the threshold is exceeded only marginally, the Commission has to produce clear evidence that the agreement is caught by the prohibition in Article 81(1).

27.10 Agreements capable of preventing, restricting or distorting competition

Examples of agreements likely to breach Article 81(1) are provided in subparagraphs (a) to (e). Any agreement falling within these categories will raise a prima facie case of breach of this article, provided that it does not fall within the *de minimis* principle and that competition within the common market is affected. The Community dimension is essential, but, since it is subject to the same principles as the question of 'effect on trade between Member States', not hard to prove.

Although it is always a question of size and scale whether or not a breach of Article 81(1) has occurred, it is possible from the approach of the Commission and the ECJ to the types of agreement listed in the article to distinguish between 'excusable' and 'inexcusable' restrictions. The inexcusable restrictions will breach the article and are unlikely to obtain exemption under Article 81(3). Excusable restrictions fall into one of two categories. *Either* they are found not to breach Article 81(1) at all, or they are found in breach of the article but eligible for exemption under Article 81(3). The distinction is significant.

27.10.1 Article 81(1)(a): agreements which directly or indirectly fix purchase or selling prices or other trading conditions

27.10.1.1 *Price fixing*

Price-fixing agreements, because of their obvious anti-competitive effects, are almost always inexcusable. The ECJ was, in *Centres-Leclerc* v *'Au Blé Vert' Sàrl* (case 229/83), prepared to accept that French legislation allowing a system of retail price maintenance for books, the prices to be fixed by publishers, was compatible with Article 81(1). The government had claimed that the measure was indispensable to protect books as a cultural medium against the negative effects of fierce price competition and to maintain the existence of specialist bookshops. Evidence was adduced that most Member States operated some form of price maintenance for books. In the absence of common Community provision in the area, clearly a sensitive one, the Court was prepared to let these arguments prevail. However, in *Re the Application of the Publishers Association* ([1989] 4 CMLR 825) the Commission found that the Publishers Association's Code of Conduct, which laid down standard conditions for the sale of books at fixed prices ('net book' prices) and which applied to books sold throughout the UK as well as to exports and reimports, and which provided, *inter alia*, for a system of *collective* price maintenance, was in breach of Article 81(1) and not eligible for exemption under Article 81(3) (ex 85(3)). The CFI (case T–66/89) agreed with the Commission's decision because the agreement restricted competition within the single Community market, *even though it might produce beneficial effects within a national market.* The ECJ, however, overturned this ruling (*Publishers Association v Commission* (case C–360/92P)). The net book agreement was distinguished from the agreement in the Dutch books case (*VBVB v Commission* (cases 43 & 63/82)) to which the CFI had referred. That agreement was held to contravene Article 81(1) as it applied to all books and all publishers and was not capable of exemption under Article 81(3). The net book agreement, by contrast, applied only to some publishers and to those books which fell within the definition of a net book. Furthermore, the ECJ held that the Commission and CFI had failed to appreciate that the benefit to the book trade arising out of the agreement was not restricted to the UK but included the Irish market also, as both countries are primarily English speaking. Shortly after the ECJ's ruling the agreement collapsed.

Minimum prices are regarded in the same light as fixed prices. In *Hennessy/ Henkell* ([1981] 1 CMLR 601, Commission Decision), a clause in an exclusive distribution agreement between Hennessy, the producer, in France, and Henkell, the distributor in Germany, setting maximum and minimum price limits for Hennessy's products, was found by the Commission to be in breach of Article 81(1) and not eligible for exemption under Article 81(3). A similar finding was made and approved by the Court, in the case of recommended prices circulated amongst dealers in *AEG-Telefunken* (case 107/82). However, it was clear in *AEG-Telefunken* that the recommended prices were used to enable the parties to engage in concerted pricing policies. In *Pronuptia v Schillgalis* (case 161/84) the Court ruled that recommended prices issued in the context of a distribution franchising system would not breach Article 81(1) as long as they did not lead to concerted practices and the franchisee remained free to fix his own selling prices. In this area parallel pricing will provide strong evidence of concerted practices, although following *A. Ahlström OY* (cases C–89, 104, 116–17, 125–9/85), it will not be conclusive. In its subsequent Decision on the *Pronuptia* Agreement ([1989] 4 CMLR 355) the Commission found the provision for recommended *maximum* prices to be acceptable.

27.10.1.2 *Other trading conditions*

A manufacturer will often seek to impose trading conditions on his distributors (or retailers) to ensure that the premises are suitable, or that adequate after-sales service is provided. He may insist that his distributor holds minimum stocks or that he engages in specific promotional activities. In return for his efforts, a distributor may seek to safeguard his investment through protection from competition within his particular territory. To what extent are these arrangements compatible with EC law?

The first principle, laid down in *Metro-SB-Grossmärkte GmbH & Co. KG v Commission* (case 26/76), is that selective distribution systems will not breach Article 81(1) provided that dealers are chosen on the basis of objective criteria of a *qualitative* nature relating to the technical qualifications of the dealer and his staff and the suitability of his trading premises, and that such conditions are laid down uniformly and not applied in a discriminatory manner.

In *L'Oréal* (case 31/80) the ECJ followed *Metro*, adding that the qualitative criteria must not go beyond what is necessary. What is regarded as necessary will depend on the nature of the product. In *Re Ideal/Standard Agreement* ([1988] 4 CMLR 627) the Commission found that the characteristics of plumbing fittings were not sufficiently technically advanced to necessitate a selective distribution system in which wholesalers were required to be specialists in the sale of plumbing fittings and sanitary ware and to have a department specialising in the sale of such products. The products were too 'banal' to warrant such a system. With regard to *quantitative* criteria, such as, in *L'Oréal*, requirements that the distributor should guarantee a minimum turnover and hold minimum stocks, these were held to exceed the requirements of a selective distribution system, and were thus in breach of Article 81(1), although it was suggested that they might be exemptible under Article 81(3).

However, in *Pronuptia* v *Schillgalis*, in addition to a number of qualitative restrictions relating to layout, shop fittings, advertising and promotion, the Court did allow, as compatible with Article 81(1), a requirement that the franchisee should buy 80 per cent of its wedding dresses from Pronuptia and the remainder only from suppliers approved by Pronuptia. This requirement, like the qualitative requirements, was found essential in a franchising agreement to protect the know-how and reputation of the franchisor. The Commission confirmed in its decision on *Pronuptia* that certain quantitative restrictions, including an obligation to hold minimum stocks, were permissible as essential to a franchising agreement, at the same time stressing that retail franchising agreements were different in kind from distribution agreements. However, even if a quantitative restriction is not compatible with Article 81(1), it may nevertheless be exempt under Article 81(3), in particular where the block exemption on vertical agreements (Regulation 2790/1999), which does not prohibit quantitative restrictions, applies.

Conditions in the form of import and export restrictions, designed to partition the market and to protect the distributor from (intra-brand) competition within his particular territory, as in *Consten/Grundig*, will always breach Article 81(1) (unless it falls within the *de minimis* exceptions discussed above) and will rarely qualify for exemption under Article 81(3). The hard line taken by the Commission, with the qualified approval of the Court, is illustrated by its attitude to patent licensing agreements. In *L.C. Nungesser KG* v *Commission* (case 258/78), in the context of a licensing agreement assigning plant breeder's rights, the Court drew a distinction between an 'open' exclusive licence (restricting the grantor's right to grant other licences to the licensee's territory or to compete there himself), which was compatible with Article 81(1), and a 'closed' exclusive licence (restricting the rights of third-party importers or licensees in other territories to import into the licensee's territory), which was not. Nor did the latter qualify for exemption under Article 81(3), since the condition was not regarded as indispensable to the agreement. In *Herlitz AG* v *Commission* (case T–66/92), the CFI held that the fact that an export ban had not been implemented did not remove its offensive qualities: the mere existence of such a provision would still have, 'visual and psychological' effect (see also *Parker Ltd* v *Commission* (case T–77/92)). However, in *Pronuptia* there was a suggestion by the Court that a restriction on franchisees' rights to open up on other franchisees' territory, although in breach of Article 81(1), might be justified to protect franchisees' investment in the business. This was confirmed in the *Pronuptia* Decision, and followed in a decision on the *Computerland Europe SA* franchising agreement ([1989] 4 CMLR 259). Thus a degree of territorial protection has been permitted in franchising agreements.

27.10.2 Article 81(1)(b): agreements which control production, markets, technical developments or investments

These agreements, which are normally horizontal agreements, will invariably breach Article 81(1). 'Naked' restrictions of this nature will rarely, if ever, qualify for exemption. However, where the restriction is ancillary to some desirable, pro-competitive agreement, such as a specialisation agreement between small and medium-sized firms, or a research and development agreement, it is likely to qualify for exemption – either block exemption or automatic exemption under Article 81(3). In *Re Vacuum Interrupters Ltd* ([1977] 1 CMLR D67) the parties obtained individual exemption for such an agreement (research and development). (See also *Clima Chapée/Buderus* ([1970] CMLR D7); *ACEC/Berliet* ([1968] CMLR D35).) In *Wouters* (C–309/99), however, a prohibition on multi-disciplinary partnerships issued by the Dutch Bar Association, while capable of being caught by Article 81(1)(b) because it could limit production and technical development, was held not to fall within 81(1) at all because the restriction was necessary for the proper practice of the legal profession.

27.10.3 Article 81(1)(c): agreements to share markets or sources of supply

These too will normally be horizontal agreements in breach of Article 81(1). A market sharing agreement may qualify for exemption if ancillary to some beneficial agreement on the same principles as apply to Article 81(1)(b), provided it does not attempt to establish absolute territorial protection for the product in question in the markets concerned. An agreement to share sources of supply would require exemption, and would be difficult to justify.

27.10.4 Article 81(1)(d): agreements which apply dissimilar conditions to equivalent transactions with other trading parties, thereby placing them at a competitive disadvantage

Concerted discriminatory treatment will always breach Article 81(1) and will rarely if ever be eligible for exemption. However, agreements imposing dissimilar conditions will only breach the Article 81(1) if the transactions are 'equivalent'; there will be no breach if the difference in treatment is objectively justified (see *Metro-SB-Grossmärkte GmbH & Co. KG* v *Commission* (case 26/76)). Thus an agreement to charge different (but not fixed) prices to different customers would be permissible if the prices charged genuinely reflected different (e.g., transport) costs; it would not if they were based on what the market would bear. Similarly, 'quantity' discounts (discounts for bulk purchases), if they genuinely reflect cost savings, are permissible, whilst 'fidelity' or 'loyalty' rebates, which are tied to the volume of business transacted, are not.

27.10.5 Article 81(1)(e): agreements which make the conclusion of contracts subject to acceptance by other parties of supplementary obligations which, by their nature and/or according to commercial usage, have no connection with the subject matter of such contracts

Such agreements, or, rather, such clauses in an agreement, will always breach Article 81(1) and will need to satisfy the criteria for exemption under Article 81(3). However, it is a matter of judgment whether an obligation is deemed to have the requisite connection with the subject matter of the contract. Agreements guaranteeing exclusivity, such as exclusive supply agreements (*Hennessy/Henkell, Pronuptia*) or exclusive licensing agreements (*Nungesser*) are seen as essential to the subject matter of the contract; attempts at territorial protection are not. Trading conditions based on necessary objective qualitative criteria are essential, those based on quantitative criteria are not (*Metro, L'Oréal*), although certain 'essential' quantitative restrictions may be imposed in franchising agreements (*Pronuptia*) at least if expressed in percentage terms. In *Hennessy/Henkell* a clause prohibiting Henkell & Co. from dealing in products competing with Hennessy's was found acceptable as essential to the exclusive distribution agreement; a clause prohibiting them from dealing in any other products at all was not, nor was it justifiable under Article 81(3). 'Non-competition' clauses, i.e., restraint of trade clauses attached on the sale of a business have been found by the Commission to be essential to the main contract, since the know-how and goodwill of a business protected by a non-competition clause are seen to constitute a substantial part of the assets transferred (*Reuter/BASF AG* [1976] 2 CMLR D44; approved by the court in *Remia BV* v *Commission* (case 42/84)). However, the restraints must be no more than is necessary to preserve the value of the bargain. In *Reuter/BASF AG* a non-competition clause of eight years' duration and extending to non-commercial research was found excessive, and not justifiable under Article 81(3), and in *Remia BV* a 10-year restriction on competition was reduced to four.

27.10.6 Other agreements

The above list of agreements capable of preventing, restricting or distorting competition is not exhaustive. In *AEG-Telefunken* (case 107/82) and *Ford Werke AG* (case 25/84) a refusal to supply was found in breach of Article 81(1) where that refusal was made in the context of existing agreements in order to enable anti-competitive practices to continue. In *British American Tobacco (B.A.T.) and Reynolds* v *Commission* (cases 142 and 156/84) the ECJ held for the first time that what is now Article 81(1) applied to mergers. The case arose from a proposed merger between Philip Morris Inc. and Rembrandt Ltd, which would have given Philip Morris a controlling interest in one of its principal competitors, Rothmans Tobacco (Holding) Ltd, in the EC cigarette market. The Commission had been alerted to the proposed merger by the parties' competitors, B.A.T. and Reynolds. Subsequently the agreement was modified by a decision from the Commission reducing Philip Morris's shareholding in Rothmans Ltd, and thereby ensuring that the relationship between them remained competitive. The decision was challenged by B.A.T. and Reynolds. While the decision was upheld by the Court, the Court affirmed that Article 81(1) could apply in principle to mergers. Although the acquisition of an equity interest in a competitor did not in itself restrict competition, it might serve as an instrument to that end.

This decision paved the way for the acceptance by Member States of a regulation on merger control which had been languishing for many years. The final version of the regulation, Regulation 4064/89 (corrected version [1990] OJ L257/13), was adopted in December 1989, after much debate among Member States on the appropriate turnover and market share thresholds required to bring the regulation into operation. It was replaced with a modernised regulation in 2004 (Regulation 139/2004 [2004] OJ L24/1). It requires notification to and approval by the Commission of proposed mergers above certain combined turnover thresholds. Moreover the Merger Regulation applies to 'full-function' joint ventures, which are joint ventures which perform, on a lasting basis, all the functions of an autonomous economic entity (Article 3(4)). Such joint ventures operate in the market in the same way as other undertakings and must have sufficient financial and other resources to be able to operate as a business on a lasting basis (see Commission Notice on Full-Function Joint Ventures, published at [1997] OJ C66 together with other notices on the notion of undertakings concerned, the notion of concentration and the calculation of turnover). However, a joint venture which does not fall within the definition of full-function joint venture will have to be assessed under Article 81, although a block exemption may then be available (see 27.14.2 below). (For further details of the Merger Regulation see Chapter 28.)

27.10.7 Ancillary restrictions

Although neither the Commission nor the Court expressly distinguishes between naked and ancillary restrictions on competition, it is safe to say that naked restrictions in any of the above categories will breach Article 81(1) and will be unlikely to obtain exemption under Article 81(3).

Where ancillary restrictions are concerned, the approach of the Commission and the Court is not entirely consistent. Certain restrictions, contained in exclusive distribution agreements (*Metro-SB-Grossmärkte, L'Oréal, Hennessy/Henkell*), or exclusive licensing agreements (*Nungesser*) or franchising agreements (*Pronuptia, Computerland*), or attached to the sale of a business (*Reuter/BASF, Remia BV*), although apparently falling within the wide words of Article 81(1), have been construed as essential to the main agreement, and as such not in breach of the article at all. Similarly, in *Bayer AG* v *Süllhöfer* (case 65/86) Advocate-General Darmon suggested that a no-challenge clause in a licensing agreement would be acceptable if it was *crucial* to the equilibrium of the licensing agreement, the object and effect of which is not shown to be specifically restrictive of competition. The Court confined itself to stating more narrowly that a no-challenge clause would not breach Article 81(1) where the licence was granted for no consideration or, although granted for consideration, it related to some outdated procedure. Other restrictions in these same types of agreement, although not blatantly anti-competitive, and arguably regarded by one, if not both, of the parties as necessary to the transaction as a whole, have been found in breach of Article 81(1) although possibly exemptible under Article 81(3). In other kinds of agreement, for example, research and development or specialisation agreements, restrictions (e.g., within Article 81(1)(b)) which are clearly justifiable in the context of the agreement as a whole have rarely been regarded by the Commission as acceptable *per se*; they must be capable of exemption under Article 81(3). However, in *Elopak/Metal Box-Odin* ([1990] OJ L209/15), the Commission was prepared to grant negative clearance to a joint venture between Elopak/Metal Box and Odin for the purposes of research and development.

The former approach, where clauses which are to a certain extent restrictive of competition are permitted under Article 81(1) as necessary to the agreement as a whole, is said to be an application of the rule of reason.

27.11 The rule of reason

The concept of 'rule of reason' originated in US antitrust law, where it was applied in interpreting s. 1 of the Sherman Act 1890. This section, which condemns every contract in restraint of trade, does not contain any definition of restraint of trade or any provision for exemption for beneficial agreements on the lines of Article 81(3) EC. It was left to the courts to decide whether or not a restraint of trade had occurred. In 1911 the US Supreme Court held, in *United States* v *American Tobacco* ((1911) 221 US 106 at p. 179) that not every contract in restraint of trade was illegal; it would only be illegal if it was unreasonable in that it operated to the prejudice of the public interest by *unduly* restricting competition. In applying this 'rule of reason', the US courts attempt to balance the pro- and anti-competitive effects of an agreement to assess if a breach of s. 1 has occurred.

The structure of Article 81 is quite different. It was clearly intended that this weighing of the pro- and anti-competitive effects of an agreement was to take place not under Article 81(1) but under Article 81(3). Historically, this required an exemption decision by the Commission under Regulation 17/62. Alternatively, parties could rely on a block exemption. If parties structured their agreements to comply with the exemptions they would be free of risk. Another possible solution lay in the application of a rule of reason. Under the 'European' rule of reason, which is undoubtedly narrower than its US progenitor, only restrictions which constitute an *essential* element of the agreement, without which the agreement would be emptied of its substance, and which pose no real threat to competition or to the functioning of the single market, are deemed compatible with Article 81(1). Non-essential restrictions, or restrictions which might interfere with the functioning of the common market, are left to be decided under Article 81(3). Many of the agreements discussed above (e.g., *Metro-SB-Grossmärkte, L'Oréal, Hennessy/Henkell, Nungesser, Pronuptia, Reuter/BASF AG, Remia BV*) provide examples of both essential and non-essential restrictions. A similar two-tiered approach has already been noted in the Court's interpretation of quantitative restrictions under Articles 28 and 30, although in the case of Article 28 justification under the *Cassis* rule of reason is more explicit (see Chapter 18).

For some time, commentators argued that the Commission and, more particularly, the Court had been moving towards a rule of reason approach, although neither acknowledged the rule as such. Indeed, in *Metropole Television* v *Commission* (case T–112/99), the CFI emphasised that

> the existence of such a rule has not, as such, been confirmed by the Community courts. Quite the contrary, in various judgments the Court of Justice and the Court of First Instance have been at pains to indicate that the existence of a rule of reason in Community law is doubtful . . . (para. 72).

Perhaps the introduction of automatic exemption under Regulation 1/2003 will mean that the question of whether there is a rule of reason approach towards Article 81(1) has less practical relevance, because there will no longer be a need to notify the Commission for negative clearance exemption.

Although in its White Paper on the modernisation of the competition law enforcement mechanism ([1999] OJ C132/1), the Commission mooted the express adoption of a rule of reason approach, it did not proceed with this. Rather than endorsing such a rule, and risking its unequal application by national courts, the Commission has sought to increase legal certainty and encourage agreements which are beneficial overall by issuing notices indicating the types of agreement which will be acceptable under Article 81(1) and introducing or extending block exemptions for those categories of agreement, which, although restrictive of competition, are clearly justified. Where an agreement appears to fall within Article 81(1), is not covered by a notice and has not been subjected to a rule of reason, it would be wise to structure the agreement to fit within a block exemption, or at least to ensure that the agreement meets the requirements of Article 81(3), which is now directly applicable.

27.12 Consequences if agreement is within Article 81(1)

An agreement which is caught by Article 81(1), and not within a block exemption or the criteria in Article 81(3) (see 27.13, below), will be 'automatically void'. Moreover, parties to such an agreement or concerted practice may be fined for their anti-competitive conduct (see Chapter 29).

However, where undertakings in a particular Member State are subject to binding rules which require them to act in a manner which infringes Article 81(1) without any autonomy as to their ability to act, no sanctions may be imposed on them for such conduct. Instead, the national court must disapply the domestic law, and only if the undertakings do not subsequently change their conduct may they be found liable for infringements of Article 81(1) (*Consorzio Industrie Fiammiferi v Autorita Grante della Concorrenza e del Mercato* (case C–198/01).

27.13 Article 81(3): exemption

Under Article 81(3), Article 81(1) may be declared inapplicable to any agreement or category of agreement between undertakings, or any decision or category of decision by associations of undertakings which contributes to improving the production or distribution of goods or to promoting technical or economic progress, while allowing consumers a fair share of the resulting benefit, and which does not:

(a) impose on the undertakings concerned restrictions which are not indispensable to the attainment of these objectives;

(b) afford such undertakings the possibility of eliminating competition in respect of a substantial part of the products in question.

In the past, the Commission had to grant an individual exemption under Article 81(3). This is no longer the case today, although the cases discussed below all arose under the old system. They are still relevant because they provide guidance as to the approach that might be taken by the domestic courts and authorities in applying this provision under the new enforcement system (see Chapter 29).

To quality for an exemption under Article 81(3) the agreement or decision must satisfy four essential criteria.

27.13.1 It must contribute to improving the production or distribution of goods or to promoting technical or economic progress

The agreement as a whole must show positive benefits. These are expressed in the alternative, although the more benefits that are proved the greater the likelihood of exemption. Different kinds of agreement will produce different benefits.

27.13.1.1 *Production*

Benefits in production are most likely to accrue from specialisation agreements. Specialisation enables each party to concentrate its efforts and achieve the benefits of scale; it avoids wasteful duplication. In *Clima Chappée/Buderus* ([1970] CMLR D7) the Commission granted exemption to a specialisation and reciprocal supply agreement between Clima Chappée in France and Buderus in Germany. Both were engaged in the manufacture of air-conditioning and ventilation systems and central-heating apparatus in their own countries. They agreed each to manufacture a certain range of products exclusively, and to supply the other exclusively with these products in the other's own country. Clearly there was some reduction in competition in the common market since they were potential competitors. Nonetheless the gains in production and distribution were clear, and the agreement contributed to both technical and economic progress. The other elements of Article 81(3) too were satisfied. The agreement would result in fair shares for consumers because there was sufficient inter-brand competition to ensure that the parties would pass on the benefit of their agreement to the consumers. Nor had they imposed on each other restrictions which were not indispensable; they were not obliged to purchase the other's products unless they were competitive. And there was no possibility of eliminating competition in respect of a substantial part of the products in question. Even combined, the parties were subject to strong inter-brand competition for the products in question.

27.13.1.2 *Distribution*

Benefits in distribution occur principally through vertical agreements in the form of exclusive supply or dealership or distribution agreements. The benefits result from the streamlining of the distribution process and the concentration of activity on the part of the distributor, whether it be in the provision of publicity, technical expertise, after-sales service, or simply the maintenance of adequate stocks. These factors were important in the *Transocean Marine Paint Association* Decision ([1967] CMLR D9). The agreement here was between a number of small and medium-sized manufacturers and distributors of marine paint from inside and outside the EC. The purpose of their collaboration was to produce and market marine paints to identical standards and to organise the sale of these products on a world-wide basis. They hoped thereby to compete with the giants of the paint world. The paints were sold under a single trade mark, though members were free to add their own name and mark. Markets were to be divided up on national lines, and members were free to sell in each other's territory only on payment of a commission. There was a degree of territorial protection. (Their original plan to prohibit sales on each other's territory was dropped at the request of the Commission.) The advantage claimed for the agreement was the achievement of a world-wide distribution network for the same interchangeable product. Alone, each manufacturer would be too small to offer adequate stocks and expertise.

Exemption was granted. The Commission agreed that the system did improve distribution; it streamlined the service to customers and led to a specialised knowledge of the market. Even the clauses granting limited territorial protection were permitted since they avoided fragmentation of the market, especially important during the launching period. While competition between members was restricted, on an international scale it was greatly increased. The use of the trade mark too was permitted, as it was used to identify the product, not to partition the market.

27.13.1.3 *Technical progress*

Technical progress is most likely to result from specialisation agreements, particularly those concerned with research and development. The *ACEC/Berliet* Decision ([1968] CMLR D35) concerned an agreement between ACEC, who were manufacturers, *inter alia*, of electrical transmission systems for commercial vehicles, and Berliet, who manufactured buses in France. They wished to collaborate to produce a new prototype bus. ACEC was to develop a new transmission system for the bus; Berliet agreed to buy the system only from ACEC; ACEC to supply only Berliet in France and not more than one outlet in any other Member State. ACEC also undertook to give Berliet 'most favoured treatment', and agreed not to reveal to any other manufacturer information acquired from Berliet. Despite these many restrictions the Commission granted them exemption. There were clear gains in production and technical progress.

In *Re Vacuum Interrupters (No. 2)* ([1981] 2 CMLR 217) an agreement in the form of a joint venture between the three leading British companies engaged in the manufacture of switch gear for research and the development of vacuum interrupters was exempted. It was found to lead to benefits on all four fronts, but particularly technical progress (see also *I.C.I./B.P.* [1985] 2 CMLR 330).

27.13.1.4 *Economic progress*

Rather surprisingly economic progress has received scant attention in decisions concerning exemption. It is normally presumed if improvements in production or distribution or technical progress are achieved. However, it did form the basis of a decision granting exemption to an agreement regulating the holding of trade fairs in *Cecimo* ([1969] CMLR D1) on the grounds that it tended to rationalise the operation and avoided wasteful duplication of time and effort.

27.13.2 The agreement must allow consumers a fair share in the resulting benefit

Provided there is sufficient (inter-brand) competition from other producers in the relevant market the improvements achieved will inevitably enure to the benefit of consumers, either in the form of a better product, or a better service, or greater availability of supplies or lower prices. If the parties fail to pass on the benefits to consumers they risk losing out to their competitors. The parties' market share, both in absolute terms and in relation to their competitors, will be crucial. In all the cases considered above where exemption was granted the parties faced lively competition.

27.13.3 The agreement must not impose on the undertakings concerning restrictions which are not indispensable

This is the familiar proportionality principle, the downfall of many an otherwise-exemptible agreement. The Commission will examine each clause in an agreement to see if it is necessary to the agreement as a whole. Fixed prices, even fixed maximum and minimum price limits, as in *Hennessy/Henkell* will rarely be indispensable, nor will clauses seeking absolute territorial protection (*Consten/Grundig* (cases 56 & 58/64), *Hennessy/Henkell, Nungesser* (case 258/78)). Even these restrictions may occasionally be justified. In the *Transocean Marine Paint Association* decision some limited territorial protection in the form of a commission payable by the parallel importer to the appointed distributor in the territory in question was deemed to be necessary to avoid fragmentation of the market during the initial launching period. When the agreement was renewed five years later, when the product was launched and the parties had grown in size and strength, that clause was required to be dropped; it was no longer indispensable. In *Pronuptia* (case 161/84) there was a suggestion by the Court that some territorial protection for the franchisee might be justified. If the agreement is a desirable one, pro-competitive overall, even quite severe restrictions may be deemed indispensable. In *ACEC/Berliet*, ACEC's undertaking not to divulge to any other customer confidential information received from Berliet, even their agreement to give Berliet 'most favoured' (i.e., discriminatory) treatment was considered no more than was necessary to safeguard their investment in the light of the mutual confidence needed and the burden or risk involved in the enterprise.

In the *Carlsberg Beers* agreement ([1985] 1 CMLR 735) a cooperation agreement of 11 years' duration between Carlsberg Brewery Ltd (UK) and Grand Metropolitan plc, whereby Grand Metropolitan agreed to buy 50 per cent of its lager supplies from Carlsberg, was granted exemption. The agreement was necessary to enable Carlsberg to establish itself in the UK market and build up its own independent distribution network.

27.13.4 The agreement must not afford such undertakings the possibility of eliminating competition in respect of a substantial part of the products in question

In all the cases in which exemption has been granted, the parties have been subject to substantial inter-brand competition, whether from producers inside the common market or from outside (e.g., *Re Vacuum Interrupters*, parties faced competition from the Americans and Japanese). It seems that, in the case of new products the market will not be too narrowly defined. In *ACEC/Berliet* the product market, in which the parties were competing, was found to be buses, not buses with special transmission systems. In assessing this question the parties' market share and the structure of the market in which they are competing will be significant.

In *Metropole Television SA (M6) and others v Commission* (cases T–185/00, T–216/00, T–299/00 and T–300/00), the CFI annulled a Commission decision exempting the Eurovision broadcasting agreement because the Commission had been wrong to determine that a sub-licensing scheme to competitors of European Broadcasting Union (EBU) avoided the elimination of competition in that market when the evidence demonstrated that this was not the case.

27.14 Block exemptions

27.14.1 Background

The old-style enforcement system was centralised and required action by the Commission. Because the Commission was unwilling, or felt unable, to apply a rule of reason to many restrictions on competition which were clearly justifiable on the principles outlined above, it chose to solve the twin problems of uncertainty (for business people) and workload (for itself) by means of block exemptions. If an agreement for which it might otherwise have been necessary to seek individual exemption fell within a block exemption, it would no longer need to be notified. Indeed, the block exemptions were passed in order to avoid the need for individual appraisal by the Commission, in the hope that parties would tailor their agreements to fit within their confines. In many cases this became standard practice. These block exemptions, being enacted by regulation, may, and where relevant *must*, be applied by national courts.

Most of the original regulations followed a similar pattern. First, they laid down the kinds of restrictions which were permitted, the 'white' list, the restrictions which are deemed 'essential' to the agreement in question; this was followed by the 'black' list – the kind of clauses which will not be permitted. With the Patent Licensing Regulation the Commission introduced a third category, the 'grey' restrictions. These were subject to a special procedure, known as the 'opposition' procedure. Under this procedure the grey restrictions must be notified to the Commission, but if they were not opposed within a specified period, they were deemed to be exempt. The Commission accepted that these 'old-style' block exemptions were too formalistic and generally failed to take into account the real economic impact of particular agreements. It therefore reviewed all of its block exemptions as they expired and adopted new exemptions which are based on a market-share threshold together with a list of prohibited 'hardcore' restrictions.

In addition the Commission has published detailed guidelines for the assessment of both vertical agreements ([2000] OJ C291/1) and (beneficial) horizontal cooperation agreements (OJ [2001] C3/2). These set out the approach the Commission will adopt when dealing with the types of agreement covered by these notices. Both guidelines reflect a more economics-based approach which focuses on market power (measured as a combination of market share and market concentration) of the parties to an agreement as a key criterion for assessing compatibility of that agreement with Article 81(1). As this is now a highly technical area of law it is not possible in a book of this nature to examine the guidelines and block exemptions in detail. Instead, the general scope of the exemptions, and their limitations, will be considered.

27.14.2 **Vertical agreements**

There is now a single block exemption (Regulation 2790/1999 [1999] OJ L326/21) applying to *vertical restraints* (although special rules continue to apply to some sectors such as petrol distribution). This new block exemption came into force on 1 June 2000. It applies to all agreements containing vertical restraints. It is wider than the previous block exemptions, as it will cover unfinished goods ('intermediate goods') and agreements between multiple parties.

The block exemption, unlike earlier block exemptions in the field, is based on a market share test; where the parties to the agreement have a combined market share of up to 30 per cent, the agreement will enter a 'safe harbour' where the agreement will automatically be exempt from the Article 81(1) prohibition, unless it contains what are described as 'hard-core restrictions'. Market share will be determined by assessing the relevant geographical and product markets. The definition of these markets is discussed further in Chapter 28. Agreements which exceed the safe harbour limit are not necessarily contrary to Article 81 but may need further examination.

The block exemption identifies certain types of clauses which will not be permissible. These are non-compete clauses in excess of five years; clauses which prevent a buyer from manufacturing or selling certain goods after the agreement has terminated (save where innovative products are concerned, in which a one-year prohibition would be acceptable); and 'hard-core restrictions'. Hard-core restrictions include minimum and fixed resale price maintenance; restrictions on resale outside exclusive and selective distribution networks; and restrictions on active or passive selling by members of a selective distribution network.

Although no detailed evidence on how the new regime for vertical restraints works in practice was available at the time of writing, there had been criticism from industry. The legal certainty, which the earlier block exemptions provided, has been sacrificed. In particular, the determination of market share is not an exact science, and industry will be even more reliant on its legal and economic advisers (who are bound to take a cautious view) as to whether it satisfies the market test or not.

In addition to the general exemption for vertical agreements, the Commission recently adopted a new block exemption for vertical agreements in the motor vehicle sector (Regulation 1400/2002, [2002] OJ L203/30). This applies to vertical agreements for the sale or purchase of new cars, spare parts and repair and maintenance services. Generally, the conditions of this exemption are stricter than those in Regulation 2790/1999.

27.14.3 Horizontal agreements

A number of regulations have now been passed granting block exemption to certain categories of agreement, including:

(a) specialisation agreements (Regulation 2658/2000, [2000] OJ L304/3);

(b) research and development agreements (Regulation 2659/2000, [2000] OJ L304/7);

(c) technology transfer agreements (Regulation 772/2004, [2004] OJ L123/11; guidance notice published at [2004] OJ C101/2).

In addition to these general categories, further specific block exemptions have now been agreed (e.g., shipping conferences, certain air transport agreements, insurance).

These block exemptions follow the new, economics-based, approach first adopted by the Commission in the context of vertical agreements (27.14.2, above). In essence, the exemption applies provided that the combined market share of the parties does not exceed a specified threshold (20 per cent for specialisation and technology transfer agreements, 25 per cent for research and development agreements) and the agreement does not include clauses which amount to price-fixing, output-limitation or territorial allocation. In addition, each exemption contains additional provisions relating to the operation of the particular agreements. However, unlike earlier block exemptions, there is no longer a white list and a black list.

As the Commission's 1999 Report on Competition Policy noted, companies need to respond to increasing competitive pressure and changes in the market-place driven by globalisation and the speed of technological progress. In this context, the Commission does not want to discourage horizontal cooperation as it can be a means of sharing risk, saving costs, pooling know-how and consequently facilitating the launch of innovative products. The approach the Commission has adopted is similar to that adopted previously in respect of vertical agreements (see above), consisting as it does of a safe harbour clause for agreements under a certain market share. Although a market share approach for horizontal agreements is likely to run into similar criticisms to those encountered by the block exemption on vertical restraints, action by the Commission in this area must be seen as a positive step, as the reform of the regime for horizontal restraints had long been overdue.

27.15 Conclusions

In recent years, the application of Article 81 has moved from a very rigid, formalistic approach to one that recognises the economic context within which particular agreements operate. The Commission now attempts to base its approach on considerations of market power and market concentration, rather than a simple application of the elements of Article 81(1). Both the new-style block exemptions on vertical agreements and on horizontal cooperation agreements reflect the general assumption that agreements involving parties who do not have a significant degree of market power will not normally be regarded as anti-competitive and can be exempted. At the same time, the *de minimis* threshold below which agreements are deemed not to fall within Article 81(1) at all has also been increased. The Commission's guidelines on vertical agreements and horizontal cooperation agreements, which reflect the experiences of four decades of centralised competition law enforcement, provide vital guidance on the types of agreements which are likely to be caught by Article 81 in future. In essence, only agreements in which the parties involved exercise market power and/or agreements which include hard-core restraints will fall foul of Article 81 and will be pursued vigorously both by the Commission and the national competition law authorities. Although this new approach may be criticised for lacking the legal certainty of the 'old-style' approach, it nevertheless offers a more targeted application of competition rules to agreements and concerted practices which pose a real threat to competition.

Overall, there is now a reasonably settled body of case law that lays down the general principles relating to Article 81, and although there is likely to be a continuous stream of litigation in relation to decisions adopted under this article, it seems that this will be more concerned with factual issues rather than fundamental aspects of the legal rules emanating from Article 81.

FURTHER READING

See reading for Chapters 26 and 28.

Green, N., 'Article 85 in Perspective: Stretching Jurisdiction, Narrowing the Concept of a Restriction and Plugging a Few Gaps' [1988] ECLR 190.

Monti, G., 'Article 81 and Public Policy', (2002) 35 CML Rev 1057.

Nebbia, P., 'Standard Form Contracts between Unfair Terms Control and Competition Law' (2006) 31 EL Rev 102–113.

Odudu, O., *The Boundaries of EC Competition Law: The Scope of Article 81* (Oxford University Press, 2006).

Roitman, D., 'Legal Uncertainty for Vertical Distribution Agreements: The Block Exemption Regulation 2790/1999 (BER) and Related Aspects of the New Regulation 1/2003' (2006) 27 ECLR 261–268.

Steindorff, E., 'Article 85 and the Rule of Reason' (1984) 21 CML Rev 639.

Wesseling, R., 'The Rule of Reason and Competition Law: Various Rules, Various Reasons' in Schrauwen (ed.) *Rule of Reason: Rethinking another Classic of European Legal Doctrine* (Hogenderp Papers 4) (Europe Law Publishing, 2005).

Whish, R. and Sufrin, B., 'Article 85 and the Rule of Reason' (1987) 7 YEL 1.

28

Abuse of a dominant position

28.1 **Introduction**

The previous chapter examined how Article 81 (ex 85) deals with the dangers to competition which may arise when otherwise independent undertakings come together and coordinate their activities. Such collusion can have a serious effect on competition in that it may result in artificially high pricing levels and in limited supply of goods and services to the market. However, it is not always the coordinated action of several undertakings that give rise to concern. Some undertakings enjoy such a strong position in a particular market that they are able to act without any regard for any competitors – they are, to a large extent, immune from competition. Indeed, certain actions of such an undertaking may result in the elimination of competition altogether. It would, of course, be wrong to condemn an undertaking for being a strong player in a particular market in the absence of any anticompetitive practice, but where an undertaking in a strong position uses that position in an abusive manner, serious consequences for competition may follow. That is why Article 82 (ex 86) seeks to deal with such strong undertakings by prohibiting activities which could be regarded as an abuse of the undertaking's dominant position in a particular market.

In December 2005, D/G Competition, the section of the Commission responsible for matters relating to competition policy in its various forms, issued a discussion paper to promote debate about the future priorities in the use of Article 82. In particular, the paper focuses on 'exclusionary abuses', i.e., behaviour which has the effect of keeping actual or potential competitors out of the market and which would therefore ultimately be detrimental to consumers. This document is not intended to lead to any specific legislative changes, but it may result in a change in enforcement practice, e.g., by concentrating resources on particular types of abuse. It also seems that the Commission may adopt a more economics-based approach to Article 82, as it has already done in the context of Article 81 (see Chapter 27). At the time of writing, the consultation was ongoing.

28.2 **Overview of prohibition**

Article 82 EC provides that:

> Any abuse by one or more undertakings of a dominant position within the common market or in a substantial part of it shall be prohibited as incompatible with the common market insofar as it may affect trade between Member States.

The prohibition is followed by a list of examples of abuse considered later in this chapter. The equivalent provision in the Constitution, should it come into effect, would be Article III–162, which is identical. Article 82 is directly effective, and gives rise to rights and obligations for individuals. Provided the matter is seen to have the requisite Community dimension, an individual may challenge behaviour, and obtain remedies, in a situation in which he would have no remedy under national law (see Chapter 29).

Article 82 contains three essential ingredients. There must be:

(a) an undertaking

(b) in a dominant position,

(c) an abuse of that position, and

(d) the abuse must affect trade between Member States.

28.3 **Undertakings**

The term 'undertakings' is subject to the same broad interpretation as is applied to Article 81 EC, and covers the same activities, both public and private. As the Court held in *Italy* v *Commission* (case 41/83), in the context of a challenge to a Commission decision that certain activities of British Telecom were in breach of Article 82, the fact that the enterprise has statutory rule-making powers does not prevent EC competition law from applying to such powers. Similarly, the Commission pointed out in the *Belgian Telemarketing* decision ([1986] 2 CMLR 558) that the fact the dominant (in this case monopoly) position is brought about or encouraged by provisions laid down by law is no bar to the application of Article 82.

As its wording makes clear, the scope of Article 82 is not limited to monopolies or single organisations enjoying substantial market power. It applies also to undertakings within the same corporate or economic group which, when combined, together create a position of dominance. Where parent companies are acting in close conjunction with their subsidiaries they will often be treated as a single undertaking (see *Eurofix & Bauco* v *Hilti AG* [1989] 4 CMLR 677).

Like Article 81, Article 82 applies to undertakings engaged in the provision of goods or services, and can apply to any undertaking in the world as long as the abusive practices take effect inside the common market. The most vulnerable under Article 82 are the large multinationals. The Commission will not hesitate to take into account the economic strength of other members of a group or to fix them with liability if they are implicated in the abusive behaviour. The most obvious example is the case of *Europemballage Corp. and Continental Can Co. Inc.* v *Commission* (case 6/72, discussed below). However, the scope of Article 82 is not limited, as will be seen, to very large undertakings.

28.4 Joint dominance

It was thought originally that Article 82 did not apply to undertakings which were independent of each other, and could not therefore be used to control oligopolies. This has not proved to be the case. In *Re Italian Flat Glass* ([1989] OJ L33/44), the Commission held that three Italian producers of flat glass, who between them held a 79 per cent to 95 per cent share of the Italian market in flat glass, had a *collective* dominant position in these markets and had abused that position. While the decision was annulled in part in *SIV* v *Commission* (cases T–68/89, T 77/89, T 78/89) for lack of proof of dominance, the application of Article 82 to oligopolies was not disputed by the CFI. The potential application of Article 82 to oligopolies has since been affirmed, notably by the ECJ in *Municipality of Almelo* v *Energiededrijf IJsselmij NV* (case C–393/92). In that case, the ECJ stated that a collective dominant position would exist when 'the undertakings in question were linked in such a way that they adopt the same conduct on the market'. In *Irish Sugar* (case T–288/97), the CFI accepted the possibility that Irish Sugar, which produced sugar, and its distributor were together dominant, thus raising the possibility of vertical collective dominance as well as horizontal collective dominance. In *Compagnie Maritime Belge* et al. v *Commission* (case C–395–396P/96), the ECJ noted that it was not necessary to find contractual or other links in law. A finding of collective dominance could be based on 'other connecting factors and would depend on an economic assessment and, in particular, on an assessment of the structure of the market in question' (para. 45). In *Airtours* (case T–342/99), a case under the Merger Regulation, the CFI rejected a suggestion that the mere fact that the same institutional investors were found in three out of the four main tour operators was sufficient to give rise to collective dominance because it was not apparent that these shareholders directly influenced management decisions.

Nevertheless the implications of these decisions for oligopolies are not clear. It remains to be seen whether Article 82 could be invoked to control oligopolistic practices which are not in breach of Article 81(1), but which nevertheless undermine the competitive structure in a particular market. Nonetheless, it seems that Articles 81 and 82 are not mutually exclusive; where doubt exists as to which article is applicable, both should be pleaded.

28.5 The principle of dominance

Dominance was defined in *United Brands Co.* v *Commission* (case 27/76), at para. 65, as:

a position of economic strength enjoyed by an undertaking which enables it to prevent effective competition being maintained on the relevant market by giving it the power to behave to an appreciable extent independently of its competitors, customers, and ultimately of its consumers.

To this the Commission added in *AKZO Chemie BV* ([1986] 3 CMLR 273) at para. 67 that:

The power to exclude effective competition is not ... in all cases coterminous with independence from competitive factors but may also involve the ability to eliminate or seriously weaken existing competitors or to prevent potential competitors from entering the market.

To assess if an undertaking has sufficient economic strength to behave independently of, or even exclude, competitors, it is necessary first to ascertain the relevant market in which competition is said to exist. As the Court pointed out in *Europemballage Corp. and Continental Can Co. Inc. v Commission* (case 6/72), a position can be dominant within the meaning of Article 82 only if it is dominant in a relevant market. The definition of the relevant market requires consideration of three parameters: the relevant product market, the relevant geographical market and the temporal market. The determination of whether an undertaking is in a dominant position will depend on how those parameters are set. The following sections consider these aspects in turn, starting with the relevant product market, which is often the most complex aspect of establishing the relevant market. As a starting point in determining the extent of the relevant market, both in respect of the product market and the geographic market, the Commission, in its Notice on the Definition of the Relevant Market ([1997] OJ C372), suggests a small, but significant and non-transitory increase in prices (SSNIP test) should be postulated and the likely reaction of customers to that change evaluated. The question is, would the consumer switch to readily available substitutes? If such an increase were to result in a loss of profits as consumers switched to alternatives, there would clearly seem to be other suppliers or alternative products in the market. This test would then be reapplied, decreasing the relevant products or areas until there is no such change indicating no competitors.

28.5.1 The relevant product market (RPM)

This is defined by the Commission in its Notice on the Definition of the Relevant Market ([1997] OJ C372) and the Court in terms of product substitution. The relevant product market is one in which products are substantially interchangeable (*Istituto Chemioterapico Italiano SpA v Commission* (cases 6 & 7/73)). It includes identical products, or products considered by consumers to be similar by reason of their characteristics, price or use. Two questions are central to this enquiry:

(a) To what extent is the customer, or importer, or wholesaler, able to buy goods *similar* to those supplied by the dominant firm, or *acceptable as substitutes?* This is known as cross-elasticity of demand, or 'demand-side' substitutability.

(b) To what extent are other firms *able to supply, or capable of producing* acceptable substitutes? This is known as cross-elasticity of supply, or 'supply-side' substitutability.

These questions may be assessed by reference to the characteristics of the product, its price, or the use to which it is to be put. Although the principles are expressed in terms of goods or products they apply equally in the context of services.

28.5.1.1 *End products*

Ascertaining the relevant product market is no easy matter. Its difficulties are illustrated in the case of *Europemballage Corp. and Continental Can Co. Inc.* (case 6/72). This case involved the proposed takeover of a large Dutch packaging firm, Thomassen & Drijver-Vçerblifa NV (TDV) by Europemballage Corporation, a company registered in the USA, held and controlled by another US company, Continental Can Co. Inc. Continental Can was a powerful organisation engaged in packaging operations throughout the world. It held an 86 per cent share in a German packaging company, Schmalbach–Lubeca-Werke AG (SLW), prominent in Germany in the manufacture of, *inter alia*, light metal containers for meat and fish and bottle-sealing machines. Continental Can proposed to transfer its interest in SLW to Europemballage. Thus the whole deal would result in Europemballage and, indirectly, Continental Can, holding significant market power in Europe. The Commission issued a decision that the takeover of TDV by Continental Can via Europemballage constituted a breach of Article 82.

Continental Can, through its holding in SLW, was alleged to be dominant in Germany in three separate product markets:

(a) light metal containers for meat products,

(b) light metal containers for fish products, and

(c) metal closures for glass containers.

The acquisition of TDV by Europemballage would have further increased its dominance in these markets, since it would have removed an important potential competitor to SLW. Continental Can and Europemballage sought to annul the Commission's decision. Although the Court agreed with the Commission in principle that the takeover could constitute an abuse, it found that the Commission had failed to prove the claimants' dominance in the relevant product market. The Commission had failed to explore the question of product substitution. To be regarded as a distinct market, the Court held, the products in question must be individualised not only by the mere fact that they are used for packing certain products, but by particular characteristics of production which make them *specifically suitable for this purpose*. The Commission had also failed to consider the question of substitution on the supply side, i.e., whether other potential competitors might not be able to enter the market by simple adaptation.

The Commission was more thorough in *United Brands Co. v Commission* (case 27/76). In this case the Commission claimed that United Brands, one of the world's largest banana empires, producer of 'Chiquita' bananas, was abusing its dominant position in a number of ways. The question was whether the relevant product market was bananas, branded and unbranded, as the Commission claimed, or fresh fruit, as United Brands claimed. Clearly it was in the Commission's interest to define the market as narrowly, and in the interest of United Brands to define it as widely, as possible. The Commission produced research from the Food and Agriculture Organisation which revealed that the existence of other fruit had very little influence on the price and consumption of bananas. Moreover, bananas occupied a special place in the diet of the very young, the sick, and the old. For them other fruits were not acceptable as substitutes. This time the Court accepted the Commission's view of the relevant product market.

It has been argued that the relevant product market could have been defined even more narrowly, either as branded bananas, or as bananas bought for the old, the sick or the very young, since there was evidence that customers continued to buy branded bananas even when they were considerably more expensive than unbranded bananas, showing little cross-elasticity of demand, while for the old, the sick and the very young, there was practically no cross-elasticity at all.

Another example of a very narrow product market concerned the distribution of tickets for the World Cup football matches held in France ([2000] OJ L5/55), which was the responsibility of a non profit-making organisation set up under French law for the purpose. The dispute concerned the tickets that were to be made available to the general public, as sale was subject to the proviso that those buying the tickets could provide an address in France. In finding that the World Cup tickets constituted a separate product market, the Commission took into account the popularity of football and the fact that one sport cannot be substituted for another. Within the football sphere, the Commission noted the significance of the tournament itself in contrast to other football tournaments, such as national cup finals, and the fact that the tournament does not take place every year. Lastly, it noted the huge demand for tickets, leading the Commission to suggest that even an increase of 10 per cent in the ticket price would have little effect on consumer demand. The Commission then went on to distinguish between the types of tickets available, that is, between those tickets that were sold for particular games so that supporters would know which teams would be playing, and the tickets and passes which were for a number of games but which were sold before it was known which teams were playing in a given match. Further, the Commission determined that, as it was important to take into account the circumstances in which the sale took place, blind sales which took place in 1997 were not substitutable by ticket sales at a later date.

On the question of cross-elasticity, both the Commission and the Court will scrutinize the evidence with care, and will not necessarily agree with the experts. In *Eurofix & Bauco* v *Hilti AG* ([1989] 4 CMLR 677), in the context of a finding of abuse against Hilti, a firm dominant in the market for cartridge strips and nails compatible with Hilti nail guns, the Commission rejected an econometric study produced by Hilti which purported to show significant cross-elasticity between nail guns and power drills, finding that the methodology of the study 'needed further refinement'. Moreover, the findings of the study were inconsistent with the way in which the market operated. The decision in *Hilti* was approved by the Court (*Hilti* v *Commission* (case 98/88)).

28.5.1.2 *Raw materials*

The relevant product market, and the question of substitutability, is not necessarily defined by reference to consumers. In *Istituto Chemioterapico Italiano SpA* v *Commission* (cases 6 & 7/73) the abuse alleged against Commercial Solvents

Corporation (CSC), an American company, and its Italian subsidiary, Istituto Chemicoterapico Italiano SpA (ICI), was a refusal to supply an Italian company, Zoja, with a particular chemical, aminobutanol, which CSC had supplied to Zoja in the past through ICI. The chemical was required for processing into ethambutol, a drug used for the treatment of tuberculosis. CSC had a near monopoly in aminobutanol, which was widely used as the best, and cheapest, for the manufacture of ethambutol. CSC refused to supply Zoja with aminobutanol in order that it might itself manufacture ethambutol in Italy through ICI. However, ethambutol was not the only drug suitable for treating tuberculosis. A number of others existed, based on different raw materials. Thus, there was a substitutable end product. Moreover, ethambutol could be made from other raw materials. So was the relevant product market aminobutanol, CSC's raw material, as the Commission decided – in which case CSC was undoubtedly dominant – or was it raw materials for making ethambutol – in which case CSC was probably not dominant – or was it, as CSC claimed, the end product, a drug for the treatment of tuberculosis – in which case CSC was undoubtedly not dominant? In an action before the Court for annulment of the Commission's decision, CSC argued that what mattered was whether consumers had a choice of drugs for tuberculosis. Article 82 was aimed at abuses which prejudiced the interests of consumers.

The Court disagreed. The article was concerned not only with abuses which prejudiced consumers directly. It was also aimed at abuses which prejudiced consumers indirectly by impairing the competitive structure. The effect of CSC's refusal to supply Zoja was to eliminate one of the principal manufacturers of ethambutol in the common market. Nor was the Court prepared to accept that Zoja could switch to other raw materials for the manufacture of ethambutol. The Court found that it was not feasible for Zoja to adapt its production in this way. Only if other raw materials could be substituted *without difficulty* for aminobutanol could they be regarded as acceptable substitutes. Since they could not the relevant product market was aminobutanol.

The hard line taken in this case illustrates that the Commission and the Court are not concerned merely with the immediate protection of the consumer; they are concerned to protect competition at the manufacturing level and in particular to prevent the smaller firm from suffering at the hands of its more powerful competitors. Similar thinking lay behind the Commission and the Court's approach in *Établissements Consten SA* v *Commission* (cases 56 & 58/64). Both reflect the influence of French and German competition policy on EC law.

28.5.1.3 *Size of RPM*

In the above cases the relevant product market was a substantial one and the parties alleged to be dominant in that market wielded considerable power. But the relevant market, whether in goods or services, can be quite small, and provided an undertaking is dominant in that market it does not need to be generally powerful to fall foul of Article 82 EC. In *Hugin Kassaregister AB* v *Commission* (case 22/78) a Swedish firm, Hugin, which manufactured cash registers, supplying them to Liptons Cash Registers and Business Equipment Ltd in the UK through its British subsidiary, Hugin Cash Registers Ltd, was found to be dominant in the supply of spare parts for Hugin machines to independent repair businesses. (See also *AB Volvo* v *Erik Veng* (case 238/87).) In *British Brass Band Instruments* v *Boosey & Hawkes Interim measures*

([1988] 4 CMLR 67) the relevant product market, in which Boosey & Hawkes held a 90 per cent share, was held to be instruments for *British style* brass bands. The fact that the market, or in this case the sub-market, was defined in narrow terms, did not, the Court said, exclude the application of Article 82. 'The essential question is whether the sub-market is sufficiently distinct in commercial reality.' Similarly, certain activities of a firm which seem quite insignificant may constitute a relevant market in which that firm may be dominant. In *General Motors Continental NV* ([1975] 1 CMLR D20) the issuing of test certificates for second-hand imports of Opel cars, carried out exclusively by General Motors in Belgium, constituted the relevant market, even though in one year (1973) only five cars were involved; and in *British Leyland plc* ([1984] 3 CMLR 92), BL was found to be dominant in the provision of national type-approval certificates for its vehicles since it alone had the right to issue these certificates. The decision was approved by the Court in *British Leyland plc* v *Commisson* (case 226/84).

28.5.2 **The relevant geographical market (RGM)**

28.5.2.1 *Determining the RGM*

To fall within Article 82 an undertaking must be dominant 'within the common market or in a substantial part of it'. Thus, the question of dominance must also be assessed in the context of the relevant geographical market. The relevant geographical market is the one in which the 'objective conditions of competition are the same for all traders' (*United Brands Co.* v *Commission* (case 27/76)). It is the market in which available and acceptable substitutes exist, described, helpfully, by Overbury as 'the area in which consumers are willing to shop around for substitute supplies or in which manufacturers are willing to deliver'. This will depend on the cost and feasibility of transportation as well as consumer habits and preferences.

   Where goods are homogeneous and easily and cheaply transportable, the relevant geographical market may be large. The Commission suggested in the *AKZO Chemie BV* decision ([1986] 3 CMLR 273) that in certain circumstances the whole of the common market may constitute the relevant geographical market. In *Eurofix & Hilti* the whole of the EC was found to constitute the relevant geographical market in the nail cartridge market. Where goods are differentiated, or where consumer tastes are inflexible, or where transportation is difficult or costly, a single State or even part of a State may constitute the relevant market. Where a service is only needed within one particular State, as in *General Motors Continental NV* ([1975] 1 CMLR D20) or *British Leyland plc* v *Commission* (case 226/84) clearly that State will represent the relevant market. As the Court commented in *United Brands,* in order to ascertain whether a particular territory is large enough to amount to a substantial part of the market, the pattern and volume of the production and consumption of the products as well as the habits and economic opportunities of vendors and purchasers (and the users of services) must be considered. In *B&I/Sealink* the Commission decided that a port or airport, even if not itself a substantial part of the common market, may be considered such insofar as reasonable access to the facility is indispensable for the exploitation of a transport route which is substantial for the purposes of Article 82. Sealink's action as port authority in Holyhead in altering its own ferry times, thereby limiting access to the port by B&I's ships, was found to breach Article 82.

In determining the relevant geographical market, the cost of transport is particularly important. When deciding in *Hilti* that the relevant market was the whole of the EC, the Commission took into account the fact that nail cartridges could be transported throughout the Community at relatively little cost. Clearly, geographical markets have been growing and will continue to grow as the barriers to the single internal market are removed.

28.5.2.2 *Application beyond the EC*

In considering the relevant geographical market, the Commission has been criticised for failing adequately to take into account the possibility of countries outside the EC forming part of the relevant market, even though in the case of certain products (e.g., vitamins) a world market may exist. For this reason a firm may be treated as dominant even though it is subject to substantial competition world-wide. However, in *SIV v Commission Re Italian Flat Glass* (cases T–68, 77 & 78/89) the Commission's decision was annulled in part on the grounds, *inter alia*, that the Commission had failed to take into account imports of flat glass from non-Member States.

28.5.3 **The temporal market**

In assessing the question of dominance the temporal aspect of the market should also be considered. It has been suggested that the Commission in *United Brands* should have defined the relevant product market by reference to the particular time of the year (e.g., the winter months), when there was little opportunity for product substitution. The Commission did take the temporal element into account in *Re ABG Oil* ([1977] 2 CMLR D1) in limiting the market for oil to the period of crisis following the OPEC action in the early 1970s.

28.5.4 **Dominance in fact**

Once the relevant market is established, it is necessary to ascertain whether the parties concerned are dominant within that market. An undertaking can be dominant irrespective of whether it is a supplier or a purchaser (*British Airways v Commission* (case T–219/99) – airline dominant in market for purchase of air travel agency services). When will an undertaking be regarded as dominant? The Commission suggested in *United Brands Co.* ([1976] 1 CMLR D28) that:

> Undertakings are in a dominant position when they have the power to behave independently without taking into account, to any substantial extent, their competitors, purchasers and suppliers. Such is the case where an undertaking's market share, either in itself or when combined with its know-how, access to raw materials, capital or other major advantage such as trade-mark ownership, enables it to determine the prices or to control the production or distribution of a significant part of the relevant goods. It is not necessary for the undertaking to have total dominance such as would deprive all other market participants of their commercial freedom, as long as it is strong enough in general terms to devise its own strategy as it wishes, even if there are differences in the extent to which it dominates individual submarkets.

In *Michelin* v *Commission* (case 322/81), the ECJ adopted the test for dominance, which is now usually referred to as:

> A position of economic strength enjoyed by an undertaking which enables it to hinder the maintenance of effective competition on the relevant market by allowing it to *behave to an appreciable extent independently of its competitors and customers*, and ultimately of consumers (para. 30, emphasis added).

See also *Aéroports de Paris* v *Commission* (case T–128/98), para. 47, which refers to 'the power to behave' rather than 'allowing', although there seems to be no significant difference in practice between the terms used).

Thus, the question of dominance requires a wide-ranging economic analysis of the undertaking concerned and of the market in which it operates. There are a range of relevant factors for establishing dominance which will now be considered in turn.

28.5.4.1 *Market share*

This will be of the first importance. In *Istituto Chemioterapico Italiano SpA* (cases 6 & 7/73), CSC (according to the Commisson; this was not found proved by the Court) held a virtual monopoly in aminobutanol. In *Europemballage Corp. and Continental Can Co. Inc.* (case 6/72) SLW, owned by Continental Can, held a 70–80 per cent share in the RPM in Germany. In *Tetra Pak International SA* v *Commission* (case T–83/91) the CFI remarked that a market share of 90 per cent would be regarded as dominant save in exceptional circumstances. But such a high figure is not essential. United Brands held only a 40–45 per cent share in the banana market in a substantial part of Europe. Where the share is less than 50 per cent, the structure of the market will be important, particularly the market share held by the next largest competitor. In *United Brands* (case 27/76) the nearest competitors held 16 per cent and 10 per cent shares in the market. Where the market is highly fragmented the Commission has even suggested that a share of 20–40 per cent could constitute dominance (*10th Report on Competition Policy*). The Court has held that the existence of lively competition does not rule out a dominant position (*United Brands*).

A variation on the market share assessment can be seen in *British Airways* v *Commission* (T–219/99). In this case, BA's dominance as a purchaser in the market for air travel agency services was established on the basis of the number of seats which it was able to offer and therefore the number of tickets it might be able to sell through agencies. Its role was that of purchaser because it was 'buying' the service of the travel agencies for each ticket they sold on BA's behalf. It was irrelevant that there were competitors on some of the air routes, because the market for air transport services was different from that of air travel agency services. This, in turn, produced a market share calculation which demonstrated BA's dominance in the relevant market.

The ECJ, reflecting the view of the Commission, emphasised in *Hoffman La-Roche* (case 85/76) that although a high market share is clearly very important, it is not conclusive, and 'its importance varies from market to market according to the structure of the market'. It is therefore necessary to consider other factors, as well.

28.5.4.2 *The length of time during which a firm has held its position in the RPM*

This point was stressed in *Istituto Chemicoterapico Italiano* and *United Brands*. The firm cannot be dominant unless it is dominant *over time*. Clearly the longer a firm has been dominant, the greater the barriers to entry for potential competitors. Conversely, the greater the number of barriers to entry, the more likely it is that an undertaking may be in a dominant position.

A key factor, particularly in the so-called 'New Economy' (information technology), has been the fact that certain platforms (such as Microsoft) have become the norm and are widely adopted by consumers. This may permit an undertaking to maintain its dominance for a long period of time, and barriers to entry may be high.

28.5.4.3 *Financial and technological resources*

A firm with large financial and technological resources will be in a position to adapt its market strategy in order to meet and drive out competitors. It may indulge in predatory pricing, selling below cost if necessary to undercut rivals (see *AKZO Chemie BV* Decision [1986] 3 CMLR 273); it can maintain demand for its product by heavy advertising, thereby reducing cross-elasticity of demand, as was clearly the case in *United Brands*. Technological resources will enable a firm to keep ahead of potential competitors.

28.5.4.4 *Access to raw materials and outlets*

The greater the degree of vertical integration (i.e., control over businesses up and downstream in the marketing process) the greater a firm's power to act independently. However powerful Zoja may have been as a manufacturer of ethambutol, it was dependent on CSC for its raw materials. CSC, on the other hand, controlled both raw materials and outlets via ICI. United Brands enjoyed an even greater degree of vertical integration. Its empire extended virtually from the plantation to the table. They owned plantations, fleets of refrigerated vessels and refrigerated warehouses in key ports throughout Europe.

28.5.4.5 *Behaviour*

The Commission suggested in *United Brands* that an undertaking's behaviour can in itself provide evidence of dominance. In *United Brands* the firm's discriminatory rebate system was taken, *inter alia*, as an indicium of independence. In *Eurofix & Bauco v Hilti* the Commission regarded Hilti's discriminatory treatment of its customers as 'witness to its ability to act independently and without due regard to other competitors or customers'.

Economists have questioned the validity in economic terms of some of these criteria, and even more so their application by the Commission in particular cases. For example, although United Brands had large financial and technological resources and enjoyed a high degree of vertical integration there was evidence that it faced fierce competition from time to time and its share of the market was falling. Moreover, its banana operations were not showing steady profits. These factors would not seem to indicate a power to behave independently of competitors.

28.5.4.6 *Barriers to entry*

In assessing dominance, it is not enough to examine the allegedly dominant undertaking's position in the existing state of the market; the question of *potential* competition must be assessed. This requires an examination into the whole range of barriers, geographical, financial, technical and temporal, to entry into that market. The Commission's decision in *Continental Can* was annulled for a failure to explore the possibility of product substitution. Both the Commission and the Court have been criticised for giving undue weight to such barriers, and particularly for failing to take a long-term view as to the prospects of market entry. This may result in a finding of dominance when the market is, in the longer term, contestable (see e.g., *Michelin* v *Commission* (case 322/81)).

Common barriers to entry are things such as the superior technology and technical resources of the undertaking which could not be matched easily by others (e.g., *Hoffmann-La Roche*, which was a market leader in innovation. Its ability to generate new technology was an important consideration in establishing dominance). Also, trademarks and brand names owned by the undertaking and its brand identity may make it more difficult for new brands to gain market share (see also 28.6.2.4, below).

28.5.4.7 *Associated markets*

Proof of dominance in a particular market need not always be required. Where two markets are deemed to be associated, and a company is dominant on one of them, proof of dominance on the other does not need to be illustrated. In *Tetra Pak International SA* v *Commission* (case T–83/91) the CFI held that associative links between two product markets could be shown because the key products were the same in both markets and because many of the manufacturers and consumers in the two markets were also the same. Thus, for a company dominant in one market to be in breach of Article 82 EC in respect of an associated market, only abusive behaviour need be shown. The decision of the CFI has been confirmed by the ECJ (*Tetra Pak International SA* v *Commission* (case C–333/94P); see also *British Airways* v *Commission* (case T–219/99)).

28.6 **Abuse**

It is not dominance *per se* but the abuse of a dominant position that brings Article 82 into play. 'Abuse' is not defined in Article 82 itself. In *Hoffmann-la Roche*, the ECJ stated that abuse:

> is an objective concept relating to the *behaviour* of an undertaking in a dominant position which is such as to *influence the structure of a market* where, as a result of the very presence of the undertaking in question, *the degree of competition is weakened* and which, through recourse to *methods different from those which condition normal competition* in products or services on the basis of the transactions of commercial operators, has the effect of *hindering the maintenance of the degree of competition still existing* in the market or the growth of that competition (para. 91, emphasis added).

Examples of abuse are provided by the article. They comprise:

(a) directly or indirectly imposing unfair purchase or selling prices or unfair trading conditions;

(b) limiting production, markets, or technical development to the prejudice of consumers;

(c) applying dissimilar conditions to equivalent transactions with other trading parties, thereby placing them at a competitive disadvantage;

(d) making the conclusion of contracts subject to acceptance by the other parties of supplementary obligations which, by their nature or commercial usage, have no connection with the subject of such contracts.

These are merely examples; the list is not exhaustive.

A glance back to Article 81 will reveal that the kinds of abuse prohibited under Article 82 run in close parallel to the examples of concerted behaviour likely to breach Article 81(1). As far as most forms of behaviour are concerned, the difference between Article 81 and Article 82 is a difference in degree rather than in kind. The existence of a dominant position merely makes the conduct more dangerous; thus there is no possibility of exemption for a breach of Article 82.

Abuses prohibited under Article 82 have been divided into two categories: the exploitative abuses and the anti-competitive abuses. Exploitative abuses occur when an undertaking seeks to take advantage of its position of dominance by imposing oppressive or unfair conditions on its trading partners. Examples of these are provided under (a), (c) and (d) above, and some behaviour under (b). Anti-competitive abuses are those which, while not in themselves unfair or oppressive, are damaging because they reduce or eliminate competition. Such behaviour would arise under paragraph (b) above, and certain practices falling under paragraph (d). Many kinds of behaviour fall into both categories (e.g., *Istituto Chemioterapico Italiano SpA* (cases 6 & 7/73)). The Commission, in its 2005 Discussion Paper, has indicated its desire to focus on what it terms 'exclusionary abuses', i.e., anti-competitive abuses.

For the abusive behaviour to fall within Article 82, it is not necessary that the dominant undertaking reaps financial or commercial benefit from the behaviour the subject of complaint. In the *World Cup* case ([2000] OJ L5/55), the non-profit-making organisation with the responsibility for organising the distribution of tickets put forward the argument that it had not benefited from the limitation it had imposed on ticket sales, an argument the Commission dismissed as irrelevant.

28.6.1 Exploitative abuses

United Brands Co. v *Commission* (case 27/76) provides a number of such abuses.

28.6.1.1 *Unfair prices*

According to the Commission, United Brands Co. was charging excessively high prices for its branded bananas. Although this point was not found proved by the Court, the Court agreed with the Commission on the matter of principle. An excessive price was defined by the Court as one which bears no reasonable relation to the economic value of the product. This test was applied in *General Motors Continental NV* ([1975] 1 CMLR D20) to prices charged by General Motors for its exclusive inspection service for second-hand Opel cars imported into Belgium. The Commission decided that it had charged excessive rates on the service for five Opel cars in 1973. The Court, in annulment proceedings (case 26/75), applying the 'reasonable relation to economic value' test, found that GM's charges were excessive. The charge of abuse was, however, not sustained, as GM had amended its charges and reimbursed the five customers for the excessive charge.

In *British Leyland plc* v *Commission* (case 226/84) the fees charged for the type-approval certificates for left-hand drive cars (when issued) were found to be excessive and discriminatory.

Problems arise over the question of 'economic value'. Deciding the economic value of a product or a service is a complex accounting exercise which leaves ample scope for differences of opinion. Economists would disagree as to what constituted the economic value of a product, and indeed, whether it can be accurately ascertained at all. What uniformity, then, can be hoped for from national courts when called upon to apply Article 82?

28.6.1.2 *Unfair trading conditions*

United Brands was found to be imposing unfair conditions by refusing to allow importers to resell bananas while they were still green. This meant that only wholesalers with the correct storage and ripening facilities were able to handle the bananas. The fact that the consumer might thereby be assured of obtaining a better, more standardised product did not prevent the Commission and the Court from finding that this requirement constituted an abuse. Again we find EC competition law protecting the 'middleman'.

In the *World Cup Decision* ([1999] OJ L5/55), the Commission, citing the ECJ in *Tetra Pak II* (case C–333/94P), held that restrictions which in effect distinguished between different nationalities and which consequently limited the market choice for the consumer, were unfair trading conditions. This type of abuse also runs contrary to the central Community principle of non-discrimination on grounds of nationality.

28.6.1.3 *Discriminatory treatment*

United Brands was charging prices with a difference of, in some cases, more than 100 per cent in different common market countries, not, apparently, according to objective criteria, but according to what the market would bear. This constituted discriminatory treatment. Similarly, *British Leyland* (case 226/84) charged different prices for type-approval certificates for left-hand drive cars, without objective justification.

In *British Airways* v *Commission* (case T–219/99), BA held a dominant position as a purchaser of air travel agency services. It had offered all UK travel agents a performance reward scheme if sales of BA tickets increased. Following a complaint by Virgin Atlantic, the Commission concluded that BA had abused a dominant position. The CFI upheld this finding. One element of the abuse was that it was possible under the scheme that two travel agents with identical sales would receive different rates of commission. BA's scheme therefore had discriminatory effects in the network of travel agents.

28.6.1.4 *Refusal to supply*

United Brands refused to supply one of its most important wholesalers, who had constructed special facilities to store and ripen the bananas, in retaliation for his taking part in an advertising campaign for a competitor. This was found to be an abuse. A refusal to supply which is not retaliatory would fall into the category of anti-competitive abuses, to be discussed next.

28.6.2 Anti-competitive abuse

This kind of abuse is less easy to detect than the exploitative abuse. Here the dominant firm uses its position in such a way as to undermine or even eliminate existing competitors, thereby reinforcing or increasing its dominance. A number of examples may be considered.

28.6.2.1 *Tying in*

A good example of tying-in practices is provided by the case of *Hoffman-La Roche & Co. AG v Commission* (case 85/76). La Roche was the largest pharmaceutical company in the world, with a dominant position in seven separate vitamin markets. The alleged abuses lay in a number of tying-in practices. Customers undertook to buy all or most of their requirements from La Roche ('requirements contracts'); as a reward they were entitled to 'fidelity' rebates (discounts). The agreement also contained 'English' clauses. These provided that if customers found other suppliers offering similar products at cheaper prices they should ask La Roche to 'adjust' their prices. If La Roche failed to respond they were free to buy elsewhere. None of these clauses was oppressive as far as La Roche's customers were concerned. But the Commission (approved by the Court) found the practices to be abusive. The tying-in system limited their customers' freedom to buy from competing suppliers; the English clauses were unacceptable because they enabled La Roche to identify competitors and take pre-emptive action, e.g., by dropping its prices to its competitors' levels, thereby nipping potential rivals in the bud. Similar tying-in practices were condemned in *Hilti*.

28.6.2.2 *Predatory pricing*

This is a strategy whereby prices are reduced, below cost if necessary, in order to drive potential competitors out of the market. In *AKZO Chemie BV* ([1986] 3 CMLR 273), AKZO, a firm dominant world-wide in the production of organic peroxides, was found to be engaged in such practices. However, as the Commission pointed out, it may be necessary to examine a firm's costs and motives in order to ascertain whether its low prices are predatory or merely the result of efficiency. Where low pricing is susceptible of several explanations evidence of an anti-competitive intent may be needed. Indeed, the lowering of prices may even be evidence of weakness. In *Hoffman-La Roche* the Court suggested that the fact that an undertaking is compelled by the pressure of its competitors' price reductions to lower its prices is in general incompatible with that independence which is the hallmark of dominance. The Court, in its first decision on predatory pricing (*AKZO Chemie v Commission* (case 62/86)), agreed with the Commission. There was a distinction, in competition law terms, between lowering prices in order to win new customers and trying to eliminate a competitor. In the case of *AKZO* the firm's 'avowed intention' had been to eliminate one of its competitors.

In the more recent case of *Compagnie Maritime Belge Transports SA v Commission* (case T–24–6 & 28/93), the CFI emphasised the need to show intent. In this case, it was not clear that the dominant undertakings (this was a case involving collective dominance) had actually traded at a loss: certainly the Commission in its investigation did not carry out an analysis of costs and prices. There was, however, evidence to show that the motive behind the practice complained of was to drive the only existing competition out of the market. In this circumstance, the CFI seemed to place the burden on the dominant undertakings to show that their behaviour was not anti-competitive. Although the ECJ reduced the fines imposed in this case on appeal, the Court did confirm this aspect of the CFI's ruling (*Compagnie Maritime Belge Transports v Dafra Lines* (cases C–395–6/96P)). In the case of an allegation of abuse, though, how does the dominant undertaking show that its behaviour was normal in the circumstances? The danger is that normal price competition (for example, the reaction of a dominant undertaking to the news that one of its customers has been offered a lower price by a competitor) may be confused with predatory pricing.

28.6.2.3 *Refusal to supply*

Where supplies (or services) are refused to reduce or eliminate competition, such a refusal will constitute abuse. This appeared to be the case in *Istituto Chemioterapico Italiano SpA* (cases 6 & 7/73) where it was intended that CSC's subsidiary, ICI, would take over production of ethambutol previously undertaken by Zoja (see also *Hugin Kassaregister AB v Commission* (case 22/78)). Boosey & Hawkes' cessation of supplies to BBI was designed deliberately to prevent them entering into the market as competitors. Similarly BL's covert purpose in refusing type-approval to imports of left-hand drive cars was to keep imports out, thus maintaining an artificial partitioning of the market.

However, a refusal to supply either an existing or a new customer will not necessarily be abusive. Arguing from *Metro-SB-Grossmärkte GmbH & Co. KG v Commission* (case 26/76), a refusal may be permissible if it is non-discriminatory and objectively justified. A refusal of supplies, particularly to an existing customer, will require cogent justification, and any signs of an anti-competitive motive will be fatal. In *Radio Telefis Eireann v Commission* (case T–69/89), *British Broadcasting Corporation v Commission* (case T–70/89) and *Independent Television Publications Ltd v Commission* (case T–76/89) the CFI upheld a decision of the Commission which condemned, for the first time, a refusal to supply a party with whom it had no pre-existing commercial relationship. Here the applicant television companies were seeking to exploit their copyright in television programme listings to prevent competitors from publishing television programme guides in competition with their own publications, to the detriment of consumers. The ECJ upheld this decision on appeal (*Radio Telefis Eireann v Commission* (cases C–241 & 242/91P) (*Magill* case)). The ECJ focused on the fact that the television companies were the sole source of the information which is needed to produce weekly listings guides for all channels, that there was a market for such a product and the product was not being produced because of the behaviour of the television companies, and that the television companies were therefore *without objective justification* seeking to reserve a secondary market (television guide publishing) to themselves.

28.6.2.4 *An 'essential facilities' doctrine?*

The *Magill* case and subsequent developments have been interpreted as the development of an 'essential facilities' doctrine. The doctrine concerns undertakings which own or control a facility that is necessary to carry out a particular type of business, but which could not practically be reproduced by a competing entity or a potential competitor. The Commission Notice on access agreements in the telecommunications sector, [1988] OJ C265/3 described an essential facility as:

> a facility or infrastructure which is essential for reaching customers and/or for enabling a competitor to carry on business, and which cannot be replicated by any reasonable means (para. 68).

In the absence of an objective justification, it seems that an essential facility must be made available to a competitor on reasonable terms. For example, in *Rødby Havn* ([1994] OJ L55/52), a Danish port was owned by DSB, a publicly owned port authority, which also operated the only ferry service between there and Germany. Two other companies were interested in running a ferry service on the same route. The Danish Government refused permission to use the port or to build another facility close by. This decision was held to be an abuse within the terms of Article 82 because access to the port, a necessary prerequisite to the provision of the service, was prevented. Similarly, a ferry company controlling access to a port was not permitted to deny access or schedule departures to the detriment of rival companies providing ferry services out of that port without objective justification (*Sealink* [1992] 5 CMLR 255). Where there is no objective justification such behaviour is a prima facie breach of Article 82.

However, in *Oscar Bronner GmbH v Mediaprint* (case C–7/97), the ECJ sought to limit the scope of the doctrine. Bronner published a newspaper which had about 3.6 per cent of the daily market in Austria. Mediaprint's newspapers had a market share of around 44 per cent. Mediaprint had established a nationwide home delivery scheme for its newspapers. Bronner wanted Mediaprint to include its newspaper within that system. Mediaprint did include another newspaper in its scheme, but refused to allow Bronner's newspaper into its network. Bronner claimed that Mediaprint was abusing its dominant position. The ECJ disagreed. It held that four factors were required for a refusal of access to constitute an abuse:

(1) refusal likely to eliminate all competition in the downstream market from the person requiring access;

(2) refusal incapable of objective justification;

(3) access must be indispensable for the other person for carrying on its business; and

(4) no actual or potential substitute for it.

These criteria had not been fulfilled, as Bronner could have set up his own distribution system, albeit at considerable cost.

The essential facilities doctrine must therefore be handled with caution. In the case of intellectual property rights (such as in *Magill*), it could prove to operate against innovation and investment in research and development if companies were ultimately compelled to make available the results of their own efforts and expense. However, in *IMS Health* (C–418/01), the ECJ attempted to readjust the balance between protecting intellectual property rights and innovation, when it held that a refusal to license the use of a particular system for collecting sales data to another undertaking would be an abuse where the undertaking requesting the licence intends to offer new products or services not offered by the IP owner for which there would be demand. Additional relevant factors in determining whether this situation would be an abuse are whether the IP owner would eliminate competition in the market, and whether the refusal could be justified on an objective basis. The criterion of objective justification for the withholding of an essential facility is therefore crucial. (See also Chapter 31 for a more detailed discussion of *IMS Health*.)

28.6.2.5 *Exclusive reservation of activities*

Similar principles to those applicable to a refusal to supply will apply where a dominant undertaking reserves certain activities to itself. This occurred in *Italy* v *Commission* (*Re British Telecommunications* (case 41/83)) where BT reserved for itself exclusive rights to its telex forwarding services, and in *Belgian Telemarketing* (case 311/84), in which a telephone marketing service was channelled exclusively through RTL's agent. The Court pointed out in *Belgian Telemarketing* that there was no 'objective necessity' for its so doing. This implies, in line with *Metro,* that the exclusive reservation of certain activities by a dominant undertaking, whether for itself or for an appointed agent, might be permissible if it were necessary and objectively justified. However the Court was not prepared to accept that the preservation of RTL's image constituted a 'necessity'.

28.6.2.6 *Import and export bans*

In view of the hard line of the Commission and the Court over such restrictions under Article 81 it is no surprise that import and export bans have been held to constitute abuse under Article 82 (*Suiker Unie* v *Commission* (case 40/73)). Apart from when industrial property rights are legitimately exercised to this end (see Chapter 31) it is hard to imagine a situation in which such a ban would not be deemed an abuse.

28.7 Trade between Member States

As with Article 81, there must be some effect on trade between Member States for Article 82 to apply, but such an effect is not hard to establish. The Court held in *British Leyland plc* v *Commission* (case 226/84) that it was not necessary to establish any specific effects, as long as there was evidence that a particular activity *might* affect trade between Member States. A theoretical possibility will be sufficient.

However, in *Hugin Kassaregister AB* v *Commission* (case 22/78) the Court annulled the Commission's decision ([1978] 1 CMLR D19) that Hugin had acted in breach of Article 82. Although it agreed with the Commission on the questions of the relevant product market and abuse, it found that Hugin's refusal to supply Liptons with spares did not affect trade between States. Hugin was a Swedish firm and at that time outside the common market, and Liptons was functioning in London on a purely local scale.

An effect on trade between Member States was held in *Istituto Chemioterapico Italiano SpA* (cases 6 & 7/73) to include repercussions on the competitive structure within the common market. This was approved and followed by the Court in

Bodson v *Pompes Funèbres* (case 30/87) and an effect on trade between Member States found despite the Commission's view that a monopoly in funeral services granted to Pompes Funèbres by the municipality of Charleville-Mèziéres did not affect trade between Member States.

28.8 The Merger Regulation

28.8.1 Article 82 and mergers

Perhaps the most surprising application of Article 82 came in the case of *Continental Can* (*Europemballage Corp. and Continental Can Co. Inc.* v *Commission* (case 6/72)). Here the Commission had applied Article 82 in the context of a proposed merger, namely, the proposed takeover by Continental Can, which owned an 86 per cent share in SLW in Germany, of TDV in Holland, the entire package to be held by Continental Can's subsidiary Europemballage. The Commission issued a decision that the proposed takeover constituted an abuse of their dominant position within the common market (*viz.* Germany). In annulment proceedings Continental Can argued that such action could not be regarded as an abuse. Article 82 was concerned only with behaviour detrimental to consumers. Moreover, it required some causative link between the position of dominance and abuse. Neither Continental Can nor Europemballage had used their power to effect the merger. The Court disagreed. Article 82 the Court said, cannot allow mergers which eliminate competition. Prejudice under that article does not mean affecting consumers directly but also prejudice through interference with the structure of competition itself. Nor was it necessary to prove a causal link between the dominance and the abuse. The mere fact of dominance rendered the proposed takeover an abuse. Although the Court annulled the Commission's decision on the grounds that the relevant product markets had not been fully proved, the principle was established. Following *Continental Can*, in *Tetra Pak* (case T–51/89), the take-over by Tetra Pak of a company holding an exclusive licence to new technology for sterilising milk cartons was held to constitute a breach of Article 82. Although the acquisition of an exclusive licence was not *per se* abusive, Tetra Pak's acquisition of that licence had the practical effect of precluding all competition in the relevant market. The existence of an exemption under the Exclusive Licence Block Exemption Regulation (2349/84) did not release a dominant undertaking from its obligation to comply with Article 82.

Continental Can and Article 82 remained the basis on which the Commission exercised control over mergers until the Court decided for the first time, in *BAT & Reynolds* v *Commission* (cases 142, 156/84), that mergers could also fall within Article 81(1) (see Chapter 27). This widened the scope of the Commission's control, since its jurisdiction no longer depended on the need to prove dominance. *BAT & Reynolds* v *Commission* provided the impetus for the passing of the Merger Regulation, Regulation 4064/89, proposals for which had been circulating for many years. Following a Green Paper in 2001 (COM (2001) 745 final) which identified a number of weaknesses with the Merger Regulation, a revised regulation was adopted in January 2004, which entered into force on 1 May 2004, at the same time as the Enforcement Regulation 1/2003.

28.8.2 **The regulation**

Regulation 139/2004, which came into effect on 1 May 2004, applies to mergers, acquisitions and certain joint ventures, known as 'concentrations' between firms with a combined worldwide turnover of more than €5,000 million, where at least two of the firms have a combined turnover of more than €250 million in the EC but do not earn more than two-thirds of their turnover in a single Member State (Article 1(2)). Article 1(3) provides that where a concentration does not meet these thresholds, it may still have a Community dimension if:

(a) the combined aggregate worldwide turnover of all the undertakings is more than €2,500 million;

(b) in each of at least three Member States, the combined aggregate turnover of all the undertakings is more than €100 million;

(c) in each of at least three Member States considered for (b) above, the aggregate turnover of each of at least two of the undertakings concerned is more than €25 million; and

(d) the aggregate Community-wide turnover of each of at least two of the undertakings concerned is more than €100 million

unless each of the undertakings concerned achieves more than two-thirds of its aggregate Community-wide turnover within one Member State.

A 'concentration' is defined in Article 3(1) as

(a) a merger of two or more previously independent undertakings; or

(b) the acquisition, by one or more persons already controlling at least one undertaking, or by one or more undertakings, whether by purchase of securities or assets, by contract or by any other means, of direct or indirect control of the whole or parts of one or more other undertakings.

'Control' confers the possibility of exercising 'decisive influence' on an undertaking. A joint venture will be concentrative if it performs on a lasting basis all the functions of an autonomous economic entity (Article 3(4)). The Commission issued guidance on the concept of a concentration, calculation of turnover and the definition of a full-function joint venture ([1997] OJ C66) under the old regulation; this had not been replaced at the time of writing.

The principle underlying the regulation is that of the 'one-stop shop'. Concentrations falling within the regulation will be subject to the exclusive jurisdiction of the Commission (Article 21(2)) and must be notified to the Commission (Article 4). A failure to notify may result in a fine of up to 10 per cent of the aggregate turnover of the undertaking(s) concerned (Article 14(2)), whereas supplying incorrect or misleading information may result in fines of up to 1 per cent of aggregate turnover (Article 14(1)). Concentrations falling outside the regulation's thresholds will be subject to control by the relevant national authority. However, a Member State or Member States jointly may ask the Commission to intervene in respect of a concentration falling outside the regulation which will 'significantly affect' competition within its own territory and have an effect on trade between Member States (Article 22(1)). Similarly, the Commission may refer a matter notified to it to the relevant national authority following receipt of notification by the Member State that a concentration may significantly affect competition in a market within that Member State which has the characteristics of a separate market (Article 9). In this context, the Commission has provided guidance on how to deal with the allocation of cases in a Notice on Case Referral in respect of concentrations ([2005] OJ C56/2).

A concentration will be permitted if it would not 'significantly impede effective competition in the common market or in a substantial part of it, in particular as a result of the creation or strengthening of a dominant position' (Article 2(2)/(3)). It is, however, not clear if the test for 'dominance' would be the same as under Article 82. In the Green Paper (COM (2001) 745 final) leading to the reform, an altogether different test was proposed to avoid the links with Article 82, but this has not survived in the final version of the new regulation.

In making its decision, the Commission must take into account, *inter alia*, the 'need to preserve and develop effective competition within the common market', as well as 'the market position of the undertakings concerned and their economic and financial power' (Article 2(1)). The Commission has 25 days in which to decide whether to investigate the matter and four months from the date on which proceedings are initiated in which to reach a final decision (Article 10).

Procedures governing notification and detailed provision in respect of hearings and time-limit are laid down in Regulation 802/2004 ([2004] OJ L133/1).

28.8.3 Residual role for Articles 81 and 82

Since Articles 81 and 82 are directly effective individuals remain free despite the regulation to raise questions concerning *any* concentration, whatever its dimensions, before their national courts. It cannot be guaranteed that concentrations falling outside the Merger Regulation will not be found to breach these articles. This problem apart, the Merger Regulation introduced a welcome degree of certainty in an area likely to be subject to ever-increasing activity as firms both within and outside the Community seek to take advantage of the opportunities offered by the single EC market. In order to increase 'transparency' the Commission publishes a detailed analysis of its decisions under the Merger Control Regulation in its annual reports on Competition Policy.

28.9 Relationship with Article 86(2) (ex 90(2)) EC

Some public undertakings (such as utility companies) defending a claim of alleged abuse under Article 82 may seek to rely on Article 86(2). This provides that undertakings entrusted with the operation of services of general economic interest or which have the character of a revenue-producing monopoly are subject to the rules in the Treaty (including competition rules) unless the performance of the tasks assigned to them would be obstructed by the application of those rules. This exception is subject to the proviso that the 'development of trade must not be affected to such an extent as would be contrary to the interests of the Community'. This provision will be re-enacted by Article III–166.

28.9.1 **When will Article 82 not apply?**

This is a three-stage test. To be able to rely on this exception, not only must the entity show, first, that it is the requisite type of undertaking, but, secondly, that it cannot perform the tasks assigned to it without relying on provisions or behaviour which would normally be in breach of competition provisions, in particular, Article 82. In *Corbeau* (case C–320/91), Corbeau was prevented from running a postal service because the Belgian postal service had a monopoly. Potentially this could have breached Article 82 unless the Belgian postal service could rely on Article 86(2). The ECJ accepted that the Belgian postal service was an undertaking within Article 86(2) and also that a certain amount of restriction of competition was necessary to enable it to remain economically viable. The postal service is required to perform some services which can only be carried out at a loss (for example, delivery to outlying areas) and it funds these activities from profit-making activities. Unrestricted competition would allow other companies to 'cream off' the profitable services without having to carry out the non-profitable activities, leaving the Belgian postal service with the obligation but not the means of paying for it. In *TNT Traco SpA v Poste Italiane SpA* (case C–340/99), therefore, a requirement that economic operators providing an express mail service which fell outside the scope of the universal postal service had to pay the equivalent of the normal postal charges to the universal service provider was compatible with Articles 82 and 86 if the proceeds of such payments were necessary to enable the universal service provider to operate in economically acceptable conditions. Moreover, the universal service provider must be under the same obligation when providing an express mail service which is not part of the universal service.

This does not mean, however, that all competition can be excluded: in deciding if a case falls within Article 86(2), the authorities must identify the extent of restriction necessary to enable the undertaking to perform its tasks, taking into account, 'the economic conditions in which the undertaking operates, the costs which it has to bear and the legislation, particularly concerning the environment, to which it is subject' (*Municipality of Almelo v Energiebedrijf IJsselmij NV* (case C–393/92), para. 49).

28.9.2 **Community interest**

The Community interest must also be taken into account. Although it is not clear precisely what this element of Article 86(2) requires, it will clearly curtail the scope of the exception provided under this article. It has been suggested from the terms of the *Almelo* judgment that, broadly speaking, the same assessment will be made as is made under Article 81(1) (see further Chapter 27), entailing a balancing of the needs of the undertaking with other Community goals. It is not clear what impact Article 16 EC, which obliges Member States to ensure that services of general economic interest 'operate on the basis of principles and conditions which enable them to fulfil their missions', will have, as on the one hand both the Community and Member States are required to take into account the 'shared values of the Union as well as their role in promoting social and territorial cohesion' and, on the other hand, this provision is expressed to be without prejudice to certain Treaty articles including Article 86.

28.10 **Conclusions**

This chapter has considered the scope and application of Article 82. It is obvious that a careful economic assessment of the relevant market in which an undertaking alleged to be dominant operates is necessary to apply Article 82. Such an assessment is a difficult task, and the Commission, in its eagerness to promote the common market, has on occasion been too quick to find that Article 82 has been infringed.

Although abusive behaviour of undertakings in a dominant position is prohibited, it must be recalled that merely being in a strong position is not a problem in itself. It is, however, necessary for major players in a market to be aware of their position because practices which would not fall foul of Article 82 where an undertaking is not dominant will do so where dominance is established. A refusal to deal by a non-dominant undertaking would not be an abuse within Article 82, but it will be so where the undertaking is dominant.

FURTHER READING

Review of Article 82 at: http://europa.eu.int/comm/competition/antitrust/others/article_82_review.html.

Andrews, P., 'Is Meeting Competition a Defence to Predatory Pricing? The Irish Sugar Decision Suggests a New Approach' [1998] ECLR 49.

De Jong, H., 'Unfair and Discriminatory Pricing under Article 86' [1980] ECLR 297.

Eilmansberger, T., 'How to Distinguish Good from Bad Competition under Article 82' (2005) 42 CML Rev 129.

Elland, W., 'The Mergers Control Regulation and its Effect on National Merger Control and the Residual Application of Articles 85 and 86' [1991] ECLR 19.

Fuller Baden, C. W. F. 'Economic Analysis of a Dominant Position: Article 86 of the Treaty' (1979) 4 EL Rev 423.

Korah, V., 'Concept of a Dominant Position within the Meaning of Article 86' (1980) 17 CML Rev 395.

Lang, J. T., 'Defining Legitimate Competition: Companies' Duties to Supply Competitors and Access to Essential Facilities' (1994) 18 Fordham Int'l LJ 437.

Monti, G., 'The Scope of Collective Dominance under Article 82 EC' (2001) 38 CML Rev 131.

Niels, G. and Jenkins, H., 'Reform of Article 82: Where the Link between Dominance and Effects Breaks Down' (2005) 26 ECLR 605–610.

Overbury, C., 'First Experiences of European Merger Control', (1991) European Law Review Competition Law Checklist 1990 p. 79.

Rodger, B. J., 'Market Integration and the Development of European Competition Policy to Meet New Demands. A Study of Oligopolistic Markets and the Concept of a Collective Dominant Position under Article 86 of the Treaty' [1994] 2 LIEI 1.

Soames, T., 'An Analysis of the Principles of Concerted Dominance: A Distinction without a Difference?' [1996] ECLR 24.

Stothers, C., 'Refusal to Supply as Abuse of a Dominant Position: the Essential Facilities Doctrine in the European Union' (2001) 22(7) ECLR 256.

Tillotson, J. and MacCulloch, A., 'EC Competition Rules, Collective Dominance and Maritime Transport' (1997) 21 World Competition (Law and Economics Review, Geneva) No. 1, 57.

Vogelenganz, P., 'Abuse of a Dominant Position in Article 86: the Problem of Causality and some Applications' (1976) 13 CML Rev 61.

Volcker, S., 'Developments in EC Competition Law in 2004: An Overview' (2005) 42 CML Rev 1691.

29

Enforcement of the competition provisions: powers and procedures

29.1 Introduction

Central to the effectiveness of the competition provisions are the rules on enforcement. Without proper enforcement, the substantive competition rules would lose much of their bite. For four decades, Regulation 17/62 gave the Commission a central role in enforcing the competition provisions within the EC Treaty, with significant powers of investigation and the right to impose penalties. During this time, two themes emerged in relation to competition enforcement by the Commission. The first concerned the scope of the Commission's powers. Although the decisions of the Commission may have been subject to judicial review, given their extent and their potential impact on undertakings, including individuals, the need to ensure procedural fairness became ever more important. This point remains central today. Secondly, the previously strongly centralised system meant that D/G Competition was subject to a very high workload, resulting in delays in the decision-making process. A thorough process of reform in a number of aspects of competition law in response to this second point was therefore undertaken. The replacement of the original system of enforcement with a new, decentralised system finally came into place when Regulation 1/2003 ([2003] OJ L1/1) entered into force in May 2004. It is supplemented by Regulation 773/2004 relating to the conduct of proceedings by the Commission pursuant to Articles 81 and 82 of the EC Treaty ([2004] OJ L123/18), as well as a 'Modernisation Package' of Commission notices which provide detailed guidance on the operation of the new system and the interpretation of key concepts (see [2004] OJ C101).

These regulations and notices replace the earlier Regulation 17/62, and this chapter will concentrate on the new system. It should be remembered that the bulk of the *acquis communautaire* in the field of competition law evolved through decisions and cases decided under the previous framework. Readers seeking more detail on the old enforcement system are advised to consult the previous edition of this book.

29.2 Development of competition enforcement

The original enforcement system under Regulation 17/62 required the notification to the Commission of all agreements that fell within Article 81(1) EC, although many of these were relatively harmless in competition terms. Moreover, to obtain an exemption under Article 81(3) EC, a positive decision by the Commission was required. Consequently, the Commission was overwhelmed by the number of notifications, a problem which increased as the Union grew in size. With its resources stretched by the volume of notification, insufficient resources remained to uncover serious breaches of competition rules, such as price-fixing and bid-rigging.

A fundamental overhaul of the competition system was therefore proposed (see the *White Paper on Modernisation* [1999] OJ 132/1). The first major change that was proposed was to remove the Commission's monopoly on granting exemptions under Article 81(3) EC, and, with limited exceptions, the notification procedure. Instead, businesses would have to rely on their own legal and economic advice to assess for themselves if any of their activities infringe Article 81(1) EC and whether these would nevertheless qualify for exemption under Article 81(3) EC. The Commission would retain the possibility of examining particular cases. The national competition authorities and courts would be given the power to apply Article 81 and 82 in full, including Article 81(3). Although this would result in a decentralisation of competition enforcement, the determination of competition policy itself would remain the preserve of the Commission. The Commission would continue to issue guidelines and adopt block-exemptions.

The corollary of these changes would be that there would have to be greater cooperation between the Commission and national competition authorities (and also between national authorities themselves). A cooperation mechanism would include the right of the Commission to intervene in a case pending before a national court or competition authority, and to impose its own decision prior to a decision at national level. In addition, national competition authorities would be obliged to provide information to the Commission on their application of the EC competition rules.

Despite the likely reduction of the burden on business as a result of removing the requirement of notification, these proposals were not welcomed by all the parties affected. UNICE, the confederation of European employers' groups, expressed concern over potential inconsistencies in applying EC competition rules between the Member States. Additionally, the removal of the notification system could result in a loss of certainty for businesses about the legality of their arrangements.

Nevertheless, the Commission pressed ahead with its reform proposals, and these remain largely intact in the final version of the new enforcement regulation, Regulation 1/2003. The Commission has now shifted the focus of its policy towards the detection of serious, hard-core cartels which are commonly regarded as a major problem. In the immediate period before the new system came into force, the Commission had already begun this process of refocusing, and managed to uncover several price-fixing cartels (such as the *Lysine* cartel) and imposed record fines.

A further aspect of the shift of the Commission's resources towards uncovering harmful anti-competitive practices, and cartels in particular, is the adoption by the Commission of a 'leniency' programme under which undertakings who are party to a cartel and disclose this to the Commission or offer full assistance once the Commission has begun an investigation, may be given partial or full immunity from fines (Commission notice on immunity from fines and reduction of fines in cartel cases [2002] OJ C45/3).

In the wake of the ECJ's judgment in *Courage* v *Crehan* (case C–453/99), the

Commission issued a consultation document in December 2005 on whether measures are needed at the Community level to deal with damages actions. This is discussed at 29.8.3, below.

29.3 Powers and duties of the Commission

29.3.1 Scope

As has already been indicated, it is not necessary to notify the Commission in order to obtain a decision that a particular practice is compatible with Articles 81 and 82 EC. Article 1(1) of Regulation 1 states, rather boldly, that 'agreements, decisions and concerted practices caught by Article 81(1) of the Treaty which do not satisfy the conditions of Article 81(3) of the Treaty shall be prohibited, no prior decision to that effect being required' (Article 1(3) contains a similar statement in respect of Article 82 EC). The corollary of this basic prohibition is that an agreement caught by Article 81(1) which *does* satisfy the conditions of Article 81(3) is not prohibited, and no prior decision granting exemption is required (Article 1(2) Regulation 1). Unlike the previous system, it is not necessary to ask the Commission to examine individual agreements to establish whether the criteria for exemption are, in fact, satisfied. Rather, undertakings will have to examine for themselves whether any of their practices conflict with Article 81(1) but are exempt under Article 81(3), thus transferring the workload in making this assessment to the companies involved. This transfer also imposes a certain amount of risk on the companies making the assessment, should their advisors come to the 'wrong' conclusion about the acceptability of their agreements (and this fact comes to competition authorities' attention). Consequently, although the Commission is not involved in this assessment directly, it provides indirect support through its notices and block exemptions, as well as through formal decisions adopted previously and the case law of the courts. In particular, it has issued two documents containing guidelines on the notion of 'effect on trade' ([2004] OJ C101/81) and the application of Article 81(3) ([2004] OJ C101/97).

29.3.2 Role of the Commission and national authorities

Although the Commission no longer deals with notifications, it retains the power to investigate specific anti-competitive practices on its own initiative or in response to complaints received from third parties. As the Commission's focus has now shifted towards investigating harmful anti-competitive practices, such as large price-fixing cartels, it seems likely that the Commission's involvement will be restricted (although it has encouraged complaints to be made). Instead, both national competition authorities (Article 3) and national courts (Article 6) now have the power to apply Articles 81 and 82 EC in full. However, this is subject to the requirement in Article 16 of Regulation 1 that national authorities and courts cannot adopt a decision running counter to a decision adopted by the Commission.

National authorities have the power to require that an infringement is brought to an end, to order interim measures, accept commitments (see below) and to impose fines, periodic penalty payments or any other penalty provided by national law.

Where the Commission does investigate, it may similarly order the termination of an infringement and impose structural or behavioural remedies (Article 7). Under Article 9, where the Commission intends to adopt a formal decision that an infringement should be brought to an end, the undertakings concerned may offer commitments to meet the concerns expressed by the Commission. If these are accepted, the Commission may adopt a decision to that effect and thereby make the commitments binding on the parties. However, if there is a material change in the facts on the basis of which the commitments were accepted, or if the undertakings subsequently fail to honour their commitments, the Commission may re-open its investigation (Article 9(2)). Finally, the Commission retains the power to make a finding of inapplicability if it concludes that Article 81(1) EC or Article 82 EC does not apply at all, or, in the case of Article 81(1) EC, that the conditions of Article 81(3) EC are satisfied (Article 10). However, this power is only exercisable 'where the Community public interest' so requires and where the Commission acts on its own initiative.

The modernised enforcement system is based on the assumption that the relevant principles on the application of the competition rules are now well established, and that the Commission no longer needs to take a central role. However, it has been accepted that 'novel questions' regarding the scope and application of Articles 81 and 82 may still arise. Where undertakings are unable to assess whether a practice they are involved in constitutes an infringement because neither the various guidance notices, nor the *acquis communautaire*, provide an answer, they may seek informal guidance from the Commission in accordance with the Notice on informal guidance relating to novel questions concerning Articles 81 and 82 (2004/C 101/06, [2004] OJ C101/78). If appropriate, the Commission will issue an informal guidance letter, which is without prejudice to any subsequent formal investigation.

29.3.3 **Investigative powers**

Chapter V of the enforcement regulation contains the powers of investigation given to the Commission.

29.3.3.1 *Requests for information*
To carry out its duties, the Commission may ask undertakings and associations of undertakings to provide all necessary information (Article 18 of Regulation 1/2003). This may be done by a simple request or by the adoption of a formal decision. In the case of a request, the Commission should specify the information that is required and specify the time-limit within which it should be provided, as well as highlight its power to impose penalties for providing misleading information (Article 18(2)). If a formal decision is adopted instead, the Commission must additionally refer to the power to impose penalties for failing to comply with the decision, as well as the right to have the decision reviewed by the Court of Justice (under Article 230 EC, see Chapter 11) (Article 18(3)). Generally, owners or the persons authorised to represent the undertakings concerned (usually a board of directors) will be under a duty to supply the information requested. Lawyers who are authorised to provide this information will be responsible if the information supplied is incomplete or misleading (Article 18(4)).

29.3.3.2 *Inquiry into sectors of the economy*

Article 17 of Regulation 1/2003 empowers the Commission to conduct an inquiry into a particular sector of the economy, or into a particular type of agreement that exists across several sectors, where the pattern of trade between Member States, the rigidity of prices or other circumstance suggest that competition within the common market may be restricted or distorted. The Commission can ask the undertakings concerned to supply any relevant information for an assessment under Article 81 or 82 EC to be carried out. It can also exercise the full range of its investigative powers in this context.

29.3.3.3 *Investigations by the Commission*

The Commission has the power to inspect undertakings and associations of under-takings (Article 20 of Regulation 1/2003). This power encompasses the right to enter premises, to examine business records and to take copies of these, as well as interview representatives or staff of the undertakings.

Before an inspection is carried out, written authorisation must be presented by the Commission's officials. Member States should provide the support of a relevant enforcement authority, such as the police, to enable the inspection to be carried out. If required, application for such authorisation should be made to a national court, which is obliged to consider whether the Commission's decision to inspect is genuine. Article 21 empowers the Commission to inspect non-business premises, such as the homes of directors or managers, but this requires the prior authorisation of a national court.

In the context of Regulation 17/62, the Commission's right to conduct so-called 'dawn raids' had repeatedly been challenged. Thus, in *Hoechst* v *Commission* (cases 46/87, 222/88) Hoechst sought to challenge the legality of such a raid, arguing that this breached the fundamental principle of inviolability of the home. Moreover, it was argued that the decision adopted by the Commission to authorise the inspec-tion lacked precision and therefore deprived Hoechst of its right to a fair hearing. The ECJ held that EC law provided protection against arbitrary or disproportionate intervention on the part of public authorities, but on the evidence, there was no breach of these principles. It was for the Commission (subject to control by the national courts) to determine the necessity of an investigation. As far as the lack of precision of the grounds of the Commission's decision was concerned, the Court held that it was not necessary for the Commission to provide 'all the information at its disposal with regard to the alleged infringement or to provide a rigorous classifi-cation of those infringements', as long as it 'clearly indicates the suspicions which it is seeking to verify'. The Commission's statement of reasons in *Hoechst* had been in very general terms, but did contain the essential information required.

In the later decision in *Roquette Freres* v *Directeur General* (case–94/00), in the context of a preliminary reference on the scope of the *Hoechst* judgment in the light of subsequent case law by the European Court of Human Rights, the ECJ modified its position. A national court is required to verify that any coercive meas-ures by the Commission are not arbitrary or disproportionate, but cannot review the justification of those measures beyond what is required for this verification. The Commission must provide a description of the essential features of the sus-pected infringements (at least the relevant market and the nature of competitive restrictions), involvement of the undertaking against which coercive measures are sought, detailed explanations showing the Commission has relevant information and evidence, and as precise as possible an indication of the evidence sought. If this information is not provided to the national court's satisfaction, it must request further information from the Commission. If this is not forthcoming, a national court may reject the assistance sought by the Commission. So in light of this case, it does seem to be necessary for the Commission to provide more concrete information before a national court can be required to sanction the measures applied for by the Commission. Although decided in the context of Regulation 17/62, these judgments are of equal relevance to Regulation 1/2003.

29.3.3.4 *Investigations by national competition authorities*

As well as carrying out investigations itself, the Commission may ask a national competition authority to carry out an inspection on its behalf (Article 22(2) of Regulation 1/2003). In addition, a national authority may carry out an inspection in its own territory on behalf of an authority from another Member State if the latter is already investigating a potential infringement of Articles 81 or 82 EC.

29.3.3.5 *Obligations on undertakings*

Undertakings must comply with the requests for information and must admit Commission officials and those from national authorities to their premises. As already noted, if misleading information is provided, a fine of no more than 1 per cent of the total turnover in the preceding business year may be imposed (Article 23 of Regulation 1/2003). If there is a failure to provide information requested by decision, daily periodic penalty payments of no more than 5 per cent of the average daily turnover in the preceding business year may be imposed.

Although the regulation is silent on the impact of existing case law on self-incrimination, it is submitted that the case law under Regulation 17/62 in this respect will continue to be of relevance. Thus, in *Orkem v Commission* (case 374/87) the Court held that the Commission, although entitled under Article 11 of Regulation 17/62 to compel an undertaking to provide all necessary information relating to facts of which it might have knowledge, could not compel the undertaking to incriminate itself by admitting to infringements of competition rules. To do so would infringe the undertaking's right to a fair hearing, which was a fundamental principle of Community law. It was for the Commission to prove that a breach of Article 81 and 82 had occurred (see also *Solvay & Cie v Commission* (case 27/88) decided on the same day).

This position was confirmed in *Mannesmannröhren-Werke* (case T–112/98), where the CFI ruled that undertakings under investigation are required to cooperate with the Commission and do not enjoy an absolute right of silence. Undertakings do not have to provide answers to the Commission's questions if this might involve an admission on its part of the existence of an infringement. The presumption of innocence requires that the Commission has to prove that there has been anti-competitive conduct. The applicant was therefore entitled to refuse to answer a number of questions by the Commission about discussions held with its competitors.

29.3.4 **Procedural requirements**

Article 33 of Regulation 1/2003 empowers the Commission to adopt implementing provisions regarding the use of its investigatory powers. Regulation 773/2004 relating to the conduct of proceedings by the Commission pursuant to Articles 81 and 82 of the EC Treaty has been adopted to provide clear rules on the initiation of proceedings by the Commission, as well as the handling of complaints about anti-competitive practices and the hearing of the parties concerned. It has already been noted that the Commission can make a finding of inapplicability of Articles 81 or 82 EC to a particular situation (Article 10 of Regulation 1/2003). However, if the Commission has concerns about a practice, it can initiate formal proceedings, and, if it intends to adopt a formal decision, it must first publish a preliminary assessment (cf. Article 9(1) of Regulation 1/2003). At this point, the initiation of proceedings commences (see Article 1 of Regulation 773/2004), and the various procedural rules in Regulation 773/2004 take effect. Under Article 27(1) of Regulation 1/2003, the Commission is required to give the parties under investigation the opportunity of being heard, and more detailed procedural rules on this are found in Articles 11 and 12 of Regulation 773/2004. In essence, the parties to whom a statement of objections has been addressed may request an oral hearing to develop their arguments. They may also be given the right to access the file, although business secrets and other confidential information is excluded from this right, as is correspondence between the Commission and the national competition authorities (Article 15 of Regulation 773/2004).

29.4 **Confidentiality**

Article 28(1) of Regulation 1/2003 states that information collected pursuant to Articles 17 to 22 shall be used only for the purpose for which it was acquired. Moreover, those involved in competition investigations are under a duty not to disclose information acquired during an investigation (Article 28(2)).

The ECJ established in *Dirección General de Defensa de la Competencia* v *Asociación Española de Banca Privada* (case C–67/91), that any information acquired by the Commission, and shared with the national competition authorities, could not be used for a purpose other than the one for which it had been acquired. However, national authorities who receive information from the Commission were not obliged to suffer 'acute amnesia', and such information could be used to assess whether it was appropriate to open *national* procedures.

Similarly, business secrets are protected (Article 27(2)). In *AKZO Chemie BV* v *Commission* (case 53/85), decided under Regulation 17/62, the ECJ held that it was for the Commission to decide whether a particular document contained business secrets. However, before communicating documents allegedly containing business secrets to third parties, the Commission must, by decision, inform the undertaking whose alleged secrets are to be revealed, and give it an opportunity to challenge that decision before the ECJ.

However, a limited exchange of information between the Commission and national authorities is necessary and is authorised to the extent that this is required to comply with Articles 11–15.

29.4.1 Relevance of Article 287 EC

Under Article 287 (ex 214) EC, the Commission is under a general duty 'not to disclose information of the kind covered by the obligation of professional secrecy'. In *Adams* v *Commission (No. 1)* (case 145/83) the applicant, Mr Adams, obtained damages for breach of this duty, in exceptional, and tragic, circumstances. As a senior executive working for Hoffman-La Roche in Switzerland, he had secretly and voluntarily passed to the Commission documents about La Roche's business activities, as a result of which La Roche was eventually fined €300,000 for breach of the then Article 86 (now 82) ((case 85/76), fine reduced to €200,000 by the Court). Adams had asked for his identity to be kept secret. The Commission did not reveal his identity, but in the course of its investigations it passed the documents to La Roche, albeit doctored, and as a result Adam's identity as informer was discovered. La Roche subsequently brought criminal proceedings against Adams, who was found guilty of industrial espionage under Swiss law and sentenced to one year's imprisonment. During this time his wife committed suicide. In his subsequent claim against the Commission for damages the Court held that the Commission's duty of confidentiality under Article 287 EC applied to information supplied even on a voluntary basis. It was in breach of that duty since it had not taken care to prevent his identity becoming known, and had not taken steps to warn Adams when it learned that La Roche was contemplating criminal action against him. However, damages were reduced by 50 per cent on account of Adams's contributory negligence. (He had failed to give the Commission his precise address; failed to warn it that the documents might give a clue to his identity; and had returned to Switzerland knowing that in doing so he risked arrest.) A cautionary tale.

29.5 Sanctions

Generally speaking, the powers to impose fines and other penalties have not changed a great deal from the previous system. Before the Commission can take a final decision regarding an infringement, it must consult the Advisory Committee on Restrictive Practices and Dominant Positions, re-constituted by Article 14 and consisting of representatives from the competition authorities of the Member States. The Commission is obliged to take the Committee's opinion into account and must inform the Committee of the way in which this has been done, but it is not obliged to follow the Committee's opinion.

29.5.1 Fines and penalties

The fines that may be imposed for providing misleading information, or no information at all, have already been noted (29.3.3.5, above). In addition, fines may be imposed if the Commission concludes that there has been a breach of Articles 81 or 82 EC, or if an undertaking contravenes a decision ordering interim measures (see 29.5.3, below), or if an undertaking has failed to comply with a commitment made binding pursuant to Article 9 Regulation 1/2003.

If the Commission decides to impose a fine, it may not exceed 10 per cent of the undertaking's total turnover in the preceding business year (or 10 per cent of the sum of the total turnover for each member in the case of an association of undertakings, and see Article 23(4)) (Article 23(2)). Regard must be had to both the gravity and duration of the infringement (Article 23(3)). Alternatively, the Commission may order periodic penalty payments of no more than 5 per cent of the average daily turnover in the preceding business year.

29.5.2 Other orders

Under Article 7, the Commission may order that an infringement of Article 81 or 82 EC is terminated. It may also impose a wide range of structural or behavioural remedies. In *Radio Telefis Eireann* v *Commission* (cases C–241 & 242/91P) (the *Magill* case) the ECJ held that the Commission had the power under Article 3 of Regulation 17/62 to require positive measures (such as the licensing of intellectual property) from undertakings as well as requiring them to desist from certain behaviour, and it seems likely that this power is preserved under Article 7 of Regulation 1/2003.

29.5.3 Interim measures

The new Enforcement Regulation includes an express power for the Commission to grant interim measures, a change from the previous system. Article 8 of Regulation 1/2003 enacts, to a large extent, the position set out by the ECJ in *Camera Care* v *Commission* (case 792/79R), when the Court confirmed that the Commission had already had a power to order interim measures. The Commission could take interim measures provided they were:

(a) indispensable,

(b) urgent,

(c) to avoid serious or irreparable damage to the party seeking its adoption *or* in a situation which is intolerable to the public interest.

In Article 8, it is now stated that in urgent cases where there is a risk of serious and irreparable damage to competition, the Commission may, on a prima facie finding of infringement, make an order for interim measures (Article 8(1) of Regulation 1/2003). These must be limited to a specified period, but may be renewed if necessary (Article 8(2)).

29.6 Concentrations

As noted in Chapter 28, the Merger Control Regulation 139/2004 disapplies Regulation 1/2003 in respect of *all* concentrations, except in relation to joint ventures without a Community dimension. Concentrations falling within the Merger Regulation will be subject to the powers and procedures laid down in the Merger

Regulation. Note, in this context there is a distinction between full-function and co-operative joint ventures (see Chapter 28).

29.7 Cooperation within the 'Network of Competition Authorities'

It has already been seen that national competition authorities have a much more significant role to play under the new enforcement system. In contrast to the old enforcement system, national authorities will be able to apply Article 81(3) EC and consider whether an agreement meets the criteria for an exemption. It will not, however, be the case that an agreement must be cleared by a national authority before the exemption takes effect; rather, a national authority which has concluded that the criteria in Article 81(3) are *not* satisfied can decide that there has been an infringement of Article 81(1) and may then impose fines or other remedies. In order to assist with the application of the rules on cooperation contained in Regulation 1/2003, the Commission has published a Notice on co-operation with the Network of Competition Authorities (Decision 2004/C 101/03, [2004] OJ C101/43). This contains guidance on the operation of the 'European Competition Network', which comprises all the national competition authorities and the Commission. The Notice elaborates on the division of work, achieving consistency in the application of EC competition rules, and the role of the Advisory Committee.

29.7.1 Powers of the national authorities

Article 5 of Regulation 1/2003 grants national authorities the power to apply Articles 81 and 82 EC to individual cases. To do so, they may:

(a) decide that an infringement be brought to an end;

(b) adopt interim measures;

(c) accept commitments; and

(d) impose fines and periodic penalty payments.

29.7.2 Exchange of information between the Commission and national authorities

Article 11(1) of Regulation 1/2003 imposes a duty of 'close cooperation' on the Commission and the national competition authorities. The Commission is under an obligation to supply the national authorities with copies of the 'most important' documents it has collected when investigating a competition infringement. If a national authority so requests, the Commission must provide other existing documents 'necessary for the assessment of the case' (Article 11(2)).

Moreover, there is a general power given to the Commission and the national competition authorities to exchange information about investigations (Article 12(1)). This power is restricted, however, by a requirement that information exchanged in this manner can only be used for the purposes of applying Articles 81 and 82 EC, and national competition law where this is applied in parallel to Community competition law (Article 12(2)). Information exchanged in this way can only be used to impose sanctions on individuals if the law under which the national authority providing the information operates foresees a similar kind of sanction. However, a receiving national authority may not use the information to impose a custodial sentence (Article 12(3)).

29.7.3 Commission overrides national authorities

If the Commission initiates proceedings for the adoption of a decision, national authorities will be relieved of their competence to apply Articles 81 and 82 EC (Article 11(6) of Regulation 1/2003). If a national authority is already acting on such a case, the Commission must consult with that authority first before initiating proceedings. However, there is no restriction on the Commission's power to initiate proceedings and it may decide to take over from the national authorities if it considers that it is in a better position to investigate an infringement.

The Commission will therefore retain a central coordinating role, although this will be subject to the Advisory Committee which consists of national representatives, which should guarantee greater involvement of the Member States. The Commission will also be available for consultation to the national authorities on the application of Community law to any case.

29.7.4 Obligations on national authorities

If a national authority commences an investigation under Article 81 or 82 EC, it must inform both the Commission and the other national authorities of this. If a national authority proposes to adopt a decision in relation to an infringement, it must notify the Commission and provide it and the other national authorities with relevant documentation (Article 11(3) of Regulation 1/2003). In addition, national authorities may exchange information directly.

To avoid parallel investigations into the same anti-competitive practice, a national authority, as well as the Commission, may suspend its investigation or reject a complaint if this is already under consideration by another national authority (Article 13(1)). However, there does not seem to be an obligation on the national authorities to avoid multiple investigations, although Recital 18 emphasises that the objective of this procedure is that each case is handled by a single authority. Similarly, where a national authority, or the Commission, has received a complaint, it may reject it if the anti-competitive practice has already been dealt with by another authority. The Notice on Co-operation with the Network of Competition Authorities elaborates on how the work should be divided between the members of the European Competition Network.

29.7.5 Cooperation with national courts

Article 15 of Regulation 1/2003 provides that where a national court is dealing with a case involving Articles 81 and 82 EC, it may ask the Commission to provide information relevant to the case. Moreover, a national court may ask the Commission for its opinion on questions concerning the application of the competition rules. Such a 'preliminary reference' may assist in maintaining a uniform approach to competition law enforcement. The Commission may also make written observations to a national court, and, if the court so permits, may make oral submissions, as well. The role of the national courts in the application of the competition rules, and the system of cooperation between the courts and the Commission, is set out in detail in the Notice on the Co-operation between the Commission and the courts of the EU Member States in the application of Articles 81 and 82 EC (2004/C 101/04, [2004] OJ C101/54). This explains how national courts can apply EC competition rules, and contains guidance on how the Commission can assist national courts in this process.

National authorities may also make submissions to a court in their Member State on issues relating to the application of Articles 81 and 82.

Finally, Article 16 of Regulation 1/2003 emphasises that a national court may not prejudge a case under consideration by the Commission, although national courts retain the possibility to make a reference under Article 234 (see Chapter 9).

29.8 The role of individuals

29.8.1 Use of Articles 81 and 82 by individuals

Since Articles 81 and 82 EC are directly effective, vertically and horizontally, individuals are free to invoke these provisions either as a sword or a shield before their national courts. They should thus be able to obtain an injunction to prevent a breach of these Articles, or damages in lieu of an injunction, or a declaration, or the appropriate interim relief. If a definitive tort can be proved damages may be obtained. As shown in *Viho Europe BV* v *Commission* (case T–102/92), however, the individual must adduce sufficient evidence to enable the court, whether national or European, to decide the case. In this case, the CFI refused to consider the claim under the then Article 86 EC (now 82) since the applicant gave no precise particulars on which a claim of abuse of a dominant position might be based.

29.8.2 Regulations 1/2003 and 773/2004

Under the Enforcement Regulation, only those individuals who can show a legitimate interest may bring a complaint about anti-competitive practices before the Commission (Article 7(2) of Regulation 1/2003). Presumably, the Courts and the Commission will continue to give 'legitimate interest' the generous interpretation previously adopted in the context of Article 3(2) of Regulation 17/62. There, the question of 'legitimate interest' had been widely interpreted to include any trader who feels he has been unfairly treated or excluded in breach of these articles. Furthermore, 'legitimate interest' had not been restricted to individuals. An association of individuals could claim a legitimate interest in lodging a complaint provided that it is entitled to represent the interests of its members and the conduct complained of is likely to affect their interests (e.g., *BEUC* v *Commission* (case T–37/92); *BEMIM* v *Commission* (cases T–114/92 & 5/93)).

Chapter IV of Regulation 773/2004 on the conduct of proceedings requires a complainant to use Form C, provided in the Annex to that regulation, to file a complaint. It also contains rules on the involvement of the complainant, and on rejecting complaints. This is supplemented by a Notice on the Handling of Complaints by the Commission under Articles 81 and 82 EC (2004/C 101/05, [2004] OJ C101/65). This sets out the different possible routes by which individuals or undertakings can complain about possible infringements of EC competition rules, and how the Commission will handle complaints.

As already noted, the parties under investigation have an opportunity to be heard under Regulation 773/2004. Individual complainants may also be permitted to speak at an oral hearing at their request (Article 6(2) of Regulation 773/2004). Recital 19 to Regulation 1/2003 states that third parties whose interests may be affected by a decision should be given the opportunity of submitting their observations, and Article 13 of Regulation 773/2004 gives effect to this.

29.8.3 Right to compensation

In *Courage* v *Crehan* (case C–453/99), the ECJ had to consider the question of remedies for those who may have been harmed by an anti-competitive practice. This case arose in the context of beer supply agreements. Crehan was a tenant of a tied house and had to take his supplies of beer from Courage. Crehan complained that Courage charged tied tenants more than independent tenants for their beer, and refused to pay. He also claimed that the beer tie was contrary to Article 81 EC and that he was entitled to damages. The Court of Appeal was faced with the problem that English contract law does not allow a party to an illegal agreement to claim damages from the other party. As Article 81(2) EC renders anti-competitive agreements void, Crehan would be unable to claim damages. It therefore requested a preliminary ruling from the ECJ on whether a person in Crehan's position should be entitled to damages. The Court, having referred to the general principle that national courts must ensure the effective protection of rights conferred on individuals (at para. 25, and see Chapter 8), held that the full effectiveness of Article 81 EC required that an individual must be able to claim damages for loss caused to him by an anti-competitive agreement. It would only be possible to exclude a right to claim damages of a party to an anti-competitive agreement where that party bears a significant responsibility for the distortion of competition. This will usually be so where that party is in an economically stronger position than the other party and has therefore been able to impose his standard terms. This judgment is significant in that it confirms that damages must be available, in principle, as a remedy for anti-competitive practices. However, there may be difficulties in applying the 'significant responsibility' test to the facts of a particular case, because it may be difficult to establish that one party to an anti-competitive agreement had such a responsibility whereas the other party did not.

The decision in *Courage* therefore established that there it must be possible to claim damages for a breach of either Article 81 or 82, but the rules for bringing such actions are a matter for the domestic legal systems. In order to consider whether the right to claim damages for infringements of competition law requires action at the European level, the Commission issued a *Green Paper on Damages Actions for breach of EC antitrust rules* (COM (2005) 672 final, 19 December 2005). This does not contain any specific proposals for action, but raises a string of issues which have to be considered in establishing actions for damages. The Commission intends to consider, at a later stage, whether measures need to be adopted by the Community to support damages actions.

29.9 Conclusions

A strong enforcement mechanism is vital for the operation of Articles 81 and 82 EC (ex 85 and 86). The old-style centralised system, although problematic for creating too heavy a workload for the Commission, has resulted in the creation of a reasonably coherent set of principles. With these firmly established, and the Member States having developed their expertise in the field of competition law, the decentralised approach introduced by Regulation 1/2003 should create a more efficient approach to enforcement. The automatic exemption from the Article 81(1) prohibition, for example, while creating a degree of uncertainty in that the parties concerned will not have a formal confirmation from the Commission that their agreement is covered by Article 81(3), will reduce the burden on the enforcement authorities of dealing with largely benign agreements and should free up resources to pursue harmful anti-competitive practices, such as large price-fixing and market sharing cartels. It is the detection and investigation of such cartels, for example, that could improve competition both in the common market and beyond, and to focus resources on this area is a welcome development.

However, it must not be forgotten that the previous enforcement system operated perilously close to the dividing line between what is and is not acceptable under general principles of EC law, and human rights in particular. On several occasions, the ECJ has had to take note of the case law under the ECHR in limiting the powers of the Commission under Regulation 17. The power to impose fines may appear to be a form of criminal sanction, and the rather blunt assertion in Article 23(5) of Regulation 1 that decisions to impose fines 'shall not be of a criminal nature' may yet be refuted by a judgment by the ECJ.

FURTHER READING

Arp, D. J. and Swaak, C. R. A., 'A Tempting Offer: Immunity from Fines for Cartel Conduct under the European Commission's New Leniency Notice' (2003) 24 ECLR 9.

Brammer, S., 'Concurrent Jurisdiction under Regulation 1/2003 and the Issue of Case Allocation' (2005) 42 CML Rev 1383–1424.

House of Lords Select Committee on the European Union, *Reforming EC Competition Procedures*, 29 February 2000 (House of Lords Paper 33, Session 1999–2000) (London: HMSO, 2000).

Hunnings, N., 'The Stanley Adams Affair: the Biter Bit' (1987) 24 CML Rev 65.

Komninos, P. and Assimakis, P., 'New Prospects for Private Enforcement of EC Competition Law: *Courage* v *Crehan* and the Community Right to Damages' (2002) 35 CML Rev 447.

Nordsjo, A., 'Regulation 1/2003: Power of the Commission to Adopt Interim Measures' (2006) 27 ECLR 299–308.

Reichelt, D., 'To what extent does the co-operation within the European Competition Network protect the rights of undertakings?' (2005) 42 CML Rev 745.

Riley, A., '*Saunders* and the Power to Obtain Information in European Community and United Kingdom Competition Law' (2000) 25 EL Rev 264.

Slot, P. J., 'A view from the mountain: 40 years of developments in EC competition law" (2004) 41 CML Rev 443.

Van Gerven, W., '*Crehan* and the Way Ahead' (2006) 17 EBL Rev 269–274.

30

Restrictions on State aid

30.1 Introduction

State aid, like State monopolies, poses a threat to the free movement of goods, since by conferring a benefit on a particular (normally domestic) undertaking or industry, it distorts competition between Member States and interferes with the functioning of the single market. It should be noted that State aid may also affect the provision of services, such as broadcasting and healthcare. With the completion of the internal market, and the intensification of competition likely to result therefrom, it is even more important that State aid to industry be strictly controlled. Indeed, in a document produced prior to the ToA (CSE (97) 1 final), the Commission identified the need to scrutinise aid as being one of the key actions for the future of the internal market, especially as levels of aid remained high. This concern to scrutinise and control granting of aid remains high, and the Commission has embarked on a process to review, in the light of the Lisbon Agenda, and to streamline the State aid process in the interests of effective implementation of the State aid provisions. In the light of the *Altmark* judgment, the Commission has also produced an action plan to ease the burden of and facilitate the notification procedure.

Even if it poses a threat to the Community interest, State aid represents for Member States a vital instrument of economic and social policy, necessary to the economic health of a region or to whole sectors of the economy, particularly in times of economic difficulty and high unemployment. The regulation of State aid is a sensitive area, requiring a balancing of the interests of Member States and of the Community and recent Treaty amendments re-emphasise the tension between Member States' interests and the creation of the internal market. On the one hand, the industrial provision introduced by the TEU highlights the importance of not distorting competition (Article 157 (ex 130) EC). On the other hand, Article 16 EC highlights the importance of public services and the need to ensure that those who are entrusted with such public services are capable of carrying out their mission. This provision may thus imply that competition concerns are not the only factors to be taken into account but that other considerations, such as social cohesion, also have a value.

The line between State aid, discriminatory taxation and measures equivalent to charges or quantitative restrictions is often a fine one. Therefore, although included under the competition provisions of the Treaty and logically belonging there, State aid should also be considered in conjunction with the provisions relating to the free movement of goods and services.

30.2 Structure of State aid provisions

30.2.1 The framework

The EC Treaty attempts to achieve a balance between Member States and the Community by laying down a broad prohibition on the granting of State aid 'which distorts or threatens to distort competition by favouring certain undertakings or the production of certain goods' insofar as it affects trade between Member States (Article 87(1) (ex 92(1))), subject to express and extensive derogation to protect a number of legitimate economic and social goals (Article 87(2) and (3) (ex 92(2) and (3))). Article 87(2) lays down the categories of aid that *'shall* be compatible with the common market'. These comprise:

(a) aid having a social character, granted to individual consumers, provided that such aid is granted without discrimination related to the origin of the products concerned;

(b) aid to make good the damage caused by natural disasters or exceptional occurrences;

(c) aid granted to the economy of certain areas of the Federal Republic of Germany affected by the division of Germany, insofar as such aid is required in order to compensate for the economic disadvantages caused by that division.

Article 87(3) lists those aids which *may* be compatible with the common market. These comprise:

(a) aid to promote the economic development of areas where the standard of living is abnormally low or where there is serious underemployment;

(b) aid to promote the execution of an important project of common European interest or to remedy a serious disturbance in the economy of a Member State;

(c) aid to facilitate the development of certain economic activities or of certain economic areas, where such aid does not adversely affect trading conditions to an extent contrary to the common interest;

(d) aid to promote culture and heritage conservation where such aid does not affect trading conditions and competition in the Community to an extent that is contrary to the common interest;

(e) such other categories of aid as may be specified by decision of the Council acting by a qualified majority on a proposal by the Commission.

Machinery for the application of Article 87 is provided by Articles 88 (ex 93) and 89 (ex 94). These provisions can be found at Article III–167 *et seq.* in the Constitution. Under Article 88(1) the Commission is required, 'in cooperation with Member States', to 'keep under constant review all systems of aid existing in those States ["existing aid"]'. Under Article 88(3) the Commission must 'be informed, in sufficient time to enable it to submit its comments, of any plans to grant or alter aid ["new aids"]'. New aid may not be put into effect until the review procedure described at 30.2.2 'has resulted in a final decision' (Article 88(3)). It may be difficult to establish whether a particular payment is 'existing' or 'new' aid. This may be particularly relevant where an existing Commission decision authorises aid and a subsequent payment is regarded as falling outside such authorisation. Following *Spain* v *Commission* (case C–36/00), such unauthorised aid should be treated as new aid and must be assessed accordingly. Further, a national amendment to existing aid will mean that that will also be considered as 'new' aid (see, e.g., *Atzeni and Others* (joined cases C–346 and 529/03)).

30.2.2 Procedural aspects

Whether acting in relation to existing aids or in response to plans for new aids, where the Commission considers State aid to be incompatible with the common market, it must act according to the procedure laid down in Article 88(2):

> If, after giving notice to the parties concerned to submit their comments, the Commission finds that aid granted (or proposed) by a State or through State resources is not compatible with the common market having regard to Article 87, or that such aid is being misused, it shall decide that the State concerned shall abolish or alter such aid within a period of time to be determined by the Commission (para. 1).
>
> If the State concerned does not comply with this decision within the prescribed time, the Commission or any other interested State may, in derogation from the provisions of Articles 226 and 227 [ex 169 and 170], refer the matter to the Court of Justice direct (para. 2).

The investigation stage effectively has two stages. The first is a preliminary assessment of new aid under Article 88(3) during which the Commission identifies if there might be a problem with the proposed aid. In such a case the full investigation under Article 88(2) is required; the second stage. In *Commission* v *Germany* (case 84/82), the ECJ held that the Commission must act diligently when informed by a Member State of plans to grant aid under Article 88(3) and must open the Article 88(2) procedure within a reasonable time. If the Commission fails to act within that time, the aid can be put into effect and would then be subject to the rules on existing aid. In *Commission* v *Germany*, it was held that a reasonable period would be two months, drawing on the time limits in Articles 230 and 232 (see also *Austria* v *Commission* (case C–99/98), para. 32)). Member States must provide sufficient information to the Commission for it to be able to carry out an initial assessment under Article 88(3) EC, and if the Commission requests further information, Member States must provide it. The two-month time period within which the Commission has to complete its initial assessment begins to run once sufficient information has been provided by the Member State to carry out the assessment, although the information provided need not be as exhaustive as would be required for a decision to be made under Article 88(2) EC. Whether the Commission has enough information for the purposes of Article 88(3) EC is determined objectively. In *Austria* v *Commission* (case C–99/98), the Commission made five separate requests for additional information, with some delays between each of the requests. The ECJ agreed with Austria's argument that sufficient information had been provided in response to the third request and that the time period had begun at that point. Consequently, the Commission had run out of time to commence a full investigation under Article 88(2) EC. The result of this was that the Austrian aid could no longer be considered as 'new' aid, which could not be implemented until the final decision on its compliance with the Treaty had been made, but had become 'existing aid'. (See now Regulation 659/99, below.)

If the Commission decides that existing aid has to be abolished or amended, it may impose a time limit within which the Member State concerned must act. Where the Commission fails to impose a time limit for the abolition or amendment of existing aid the Court has held that a two-month time limit will normally be appropriate (*Gebrüder Lorenz GmbH* v *Germany* (case 120/73)).

The procedures laid down in Article 88(2) must be followed and procedural guarantees such as the duty to give reasons and the right to a hearing, as general principles of Community law (see Chapter 6), must be observed. The Commission's decision must contain sufficient facts and figures to support its conclusions. Decisions issued in breach of any of these requirements may be annulled (see, e.g., *William Cook* v *Commission* (case C–198/91)). The Court may, however, refuse to annul a decision where the outcome would have been the same in the absence of the irregularity (*Commission* v *France* (case 259/85)).

In exceptional circumstances a Member State may apply to the Council for a decision, which must be unanimous, that in derogation from Article 87 or 89 (ex 92 or 94), an aid which it is granting (existing aid) or intends to grant (new aid) is compatible with the common market. In this case where proceedings have already been initiated by the Commission under Article 88(2) they will be suspended until the Council has made its attitude known (Article 88(2), paras 3 and 4). It may be noted that under Article 87(3)(d) the Council has the power to extend the categories of aid for which dispensation is allowed.

Finally, under Article 89 the Council, acting by qualified majority on a proposal from the Commission, is empowered to make regulations concerning the application of Articles 87 and 88. A regulation was adopted in May 1998 to facilitate the operation of the State aid system (994/98, [1998] OJ L142/1). It provides for the use of a block exemption system for certain categories of aid. A number of exemptions have now been adopted; these are discussed at 14.3.7 below. A second regulation (Regulation 659/99) has also been enacted which codifies the existing procedural practice of the Commission together with the rulings of the ECJ ([1999] OJ L83/1). It also provides for certain enforcement powers for the Commission. These provisions include a requirement on Member States to provide an annual report on all existing aid schemes. Regulation 794/2004 has now been enacted, based on Article 27 Regulation 659/99. It covers the form and content of notifications, introducing a new compulsory notification form, as well as dealing with the form of annual reports. It also covers time-limits and interest rates due on the repayment of illegal aid.

30.2.3 Consequences of aid being granted illegally

The Commission insists on strict compliance by Member States with their obligation under Article 88(3) to inform the Commission of plans to grant or alter aid. Since Member States not infrequently flouted this requirement, or, having notified the Commission, went ahead without giving the Commission time to respond, the Commission, in a practice note issued in November 1983 ([1983] OJ C318/3), expressed its intention to 'use all the measures at its disposal' to ensure compliance by Member States with Article 88(3). Henceforth Member States which had granted aid illegally, i.e., without informing the Commission, or precipitately, would be required to recover such aid from recipients, and, in the agricultural sector, would be refused advance payments from the EAGGF (European Agriculture Guidance and Guarantee Funds). Since then the Commission has taken many decisions requiring the repayment of aid. In July 1990 British Aerospace was required to repay £44.4 million worth of 'sweeteners' it received when acquiring the Rover car group in 1988 (decision successfully challenged on procedural grounds in January 1992: new decision issued in March 1993 (EC Bull 3 1993 1.2.50)).

Recipient businesses are required to make repayments even if the business has changed hands and the new owners have never received aid from the State (*Re aid to ENI Lanerossi* (case C–303/88)). Repayment must be made even if it will cause the recipient of aid to be wound up (*Commission v Belgium* (case 52/84)). Even where the Member State argues that repayment is impossible, this argument cannot be raised without prior warning (*Commission v Italy* (case C–349/93)). The Member State, under its duty of cooperation in Article 10 (ex 5) EC, on encountering difficulties in obtaining repayment should inform the Commission of them, together with suggestions for amendments to the decision requiring repayment so as to solve the problem. Further, in *TWD Textilwerke Deggendorf GmbH v Commission* (cases T–244 & 486/93), the Court of First Instance approved the Commission's stance according to which implementation of a decision approving the payment of lawful aid was conditional on repayment of earlier illegal aid. This decision strengthens the Commission's hand, but weaknesses remain in the system for recovery of aid. Most notably, there is the problem that the recipient of unlawful aid retains the benefit of that aid until the decision is made requiring repayment. The decision-making process can take a considerable time and so the benefit illicitly obtained can be considerable. To counterbalance this benefit, however, the Commission may request the payment of interest running from the date the enterprise received the aid (e.g., *Siemens SA v Commission* (case T–459/93)) (see now Regulation 794/2004). The Commission has also issued a communication to the Member States warning that, in appropriate cases, it will adopt provisional decisions ordering repayment pending completion of the full investigation ([1995] OJ C156/5).

In a number of cases a decision requiring repayment has been challenged on the grounds of breach of the claimant's legitimate expectations. In *RSV Maschinefabrieken & Scheepswerven NV v Commission* (case 223/85) a Commission decision ordering repayment of aid granted to RSV to write off financial losses was annulled at the suit of the recipient, since the decision was issued, without justification for the delay, some 26 months after the aid had been granted. However, in *Commission v Germany* (case C–5/89), the Court, endorsing its decision in *Commission v Germany* (case 94/87), held that save in exceptional circumstances firms in receipt of State aid could not have legitimate expectations concerning the lawfulness of aid unless it had been granted in accordance with the procedures of the then Article 93 (now 88). The diligent recipient of aid would make sure that these procedures had been complied with. This reasoning applies even if there has been significant delay between the granting of the (illegal) aid and the decision that the aid is illegal. Nor could the Member State plead the legitimate expectations of recipients in order to evade its obligation to comply with the Commission's decision requiring the recovery of aid. In *Commission v France* (case C–261/99), the ECJ emphasised that a

Member State must inform the Commission if there are difficulties in recovering illegal aid. However, a Member State cannot bring an action for annulment of the relevant Commission decision to avoid the obligation to recover illegal aid and such aid must be recovered even if the annulment action is still pending.

To ensure 'transparency' the Commission now publishes an annual survey of its aid proceedings in the *Official Journal*, and warns potential recipients of the legal consequences of repayment decisions. It also publishes a section on State aids in its annual report on competition policy. In the light of these practices a defence based on legitimate expectations is only likely to succeed in exceptional circumstances (see, e.g., *RSV* (case 223/85)).

Thus all aids granted by Member States are subject either to the dispensation of the Council, or, more normally, the strict supervision and control of the Commission, with ultimate recourse to the Court, either in annulment proceedings under Article 230 (ex 173) EC (see Chapter 11) or in proceedings under Article 88(2) (ex 93(2)). Note that in a review action, where the Commission has a wide discretion (such as in the assessment of the grounds of exception under Article 92(3)), the ECJ will not substitute its assessment for that of the Commission. It is limited to verifying whether the Commission's assessment of the case is 'vitiated by a manifest error or misuse of powers' (e.g., *Atzeni* (joined cases C–346 and 529/03), para. 84).

30.3 Meaning of State aid

No definition of State aid is given in the Treaty but it has been broadly construed by the Commission and the European courts. State aid has been held to comprise any advantages granted directly or indirectly through State resources. The Commission suggested in its Reports on Competition Policy that four cumulative elements must be shown to satisfy the test for State aid:

(a) the measure must be specific rather than general in nature;

(b) it must grant an advantage to an undertaking;

(c) the aid must come from State resources; and

(d) the advantage must distort competition and have an effect on inter-State trade.

These have been re-stated by the EJC to be: intervention by the State or through state resources; the intervention must be liable to affect trade between Member States; it must confer an advantage on the recipient; and it must distort or threaten to distort competition (*Altmark* (case C–280/00), para. 75; *Pearle and Others* (case C–245/02), para. 32). These cover similar ground to the Commission's criteria, though the ECJ seems to see the requirements of distortion of competition and having an effect on inter-State trade as separate issues. All elements must be shown for the state measure to fall within the definition of aid (see, e.g., *Commission v Belgium* (Tubemeuse) (joined cases C–278–280/92)).

30.3.1 Specificity

For a measure to be classified as State aid, it must assist only certain firms or sectors: general economic policy remains a matter for the Member States. The concept does not include a system of minimum prices, as this is not an advantage granted to favour an undertaking or to benefit certain goods and will normally be applied to all goods irrespective of origin. (The latter will, however, be judged under Article 28 (ex 30) – see *van Tiggele* (case 82/77), discussed in Chapter 18.) State aid also does not include special treatment for small enterprises in the form of exemption from obligations arising from social protection (*Kirsammer-Hack* v *Nurhan Sidal* (case C–189/91)). It follows that, although certain measures of tax or social policy could give a competitive edge to undertakings established in a given Member State (for example, by lower employment costs), they do not fall within the State aid rules.

It is, however, sometimes difficult to identify the boundary between the two categories. In the *Maribel bis/ter case* (*Belgium* v *Commission* (case C–75/97)), for example, the Commission decided that a Belgian law which provided for additional reductions in social security costs constituted aid because it benefited firms most exposed to international competition. Further, for a measure to be considered general, the Member State should have no discretionary power enabling it to vary the application of a measure depending on who was the beneficiary of the measure, even when the criteria to be taken into consideration were objective factors defined by law (*France* v *Commission (Kimberly Clark Sopalin)* (case C–241/94)). Thus, in the *DMT* case (case C–256/97), the ECJ held that the degree of discretion given to the body which had responsibility for chasing up social security payments from employers and employees meant that, although the policy was phrased in general terms, in practice it turned into aid aimed at specific companies, in that they gained a benefit. Thus the same issue can be analysed from different perspectives (see discussion of 'advantage', 30.3.2).

30.3.2 Advantage to a firm

To constitute State aid, a benefit must be conferred. Aid falling within the terms of Article 87(1) may be 'in any form whatsoever'. Thus aid can include, as well as actual payments, preferential tax treatment, preferential interest rates, grants to cover redundancy costs, investment grants and subsidies, financial incentives to privatisation (e.g., British Aerospace), or special prices for land, plant or power (e.g., *Kwkerij Gebroeders van der Kooy* (cases 67, 68 and 70/85) – power company supplying natural gas at special reduced prices to the horticulture industry). In *Syndicat Français de l'Express International* v *La Poste* (case C–39/94), the ECJ defined a State aid as including not only benefits such as subsidies, but also interventions which might mitigate the charges normally included in the budgets of an undertaking and which are therefore of the same character and have the same effect as subsidies. When determining whether State aid exists, the question relates not to the causes or aims of State intervention; instead the test is an objective one, concerned with the effects of such an intervention (see, e.g., *Italy* v *Commission (Re Aid to the Textile Industry)* (case 173/73), *Banco de Credito Industrial SA* v *Ayuntamiento de Valencia* (case C–387/92) and *Ladbroke Racing Ltd* v *Commission* (case T–67/94)).

To constitute State aid, the advantage must be granted for no consideration or countervailing benefit (*Denkavit* (case 61/79)). It will include injections of capital by a public investor which disregard any prospect of profitability (*Re aid to ENI Lanerosse* (case C–303/88)). The Court has also described aid as existing when State support has no objective commercial justification. The test of commercial justification is sometimes referred to as the hypothetical investor test. Its use is not entirely unproblematic, as it does raise the question of what normal investor behaviour would be. If commercial justification does, however, exist then the fact that the support also fulfils a political purpose will not render it 'aid' within Article 87 (*Belgium* v *Commission* (case C–56/93) – special tariff rates to large Dutch industrial producers of ammonia by a company in which The Netherlands Government had a 50 per cent holding justified on commercial grounds).

30.3.3 Public services and services of general economic interest

A controversial question which has occupied the ECJ recently is whether a financial advantage which could be characterised as compensation for a public service obligation should be treated as State aid. Although Article 16 EC, introduced by the ToA, puts greater emphasis on ensuring that services of general economic interest can 'fulfil their missions', this is expressed to be without prejudice to Articles 73, 86 and 87. This provision will be re-enacted, should the Constitution in its current format come into force, as Article III–122. The scope of this article remains uncertain, and, importantly, it does not suggest that public services cannot be subject to Article 87. The jurisprudence of the ECJ has been confused in this respect, as illustrated by two recent cases.

In *Ferring SA* v *Agence centrale des organismes de securite sociale (ACOSS)* (case C–53/00), a pharmaceutical laboratory had been taxed on direct sales to pharmacies, whereas wholesale distributors were not taxed at all. Wholesalers were under a public service obligation to ensure a sufficient supply of pharmaceuticals. Their relief from tax liability on direct sales to pharmacies by other suppliers could be regarded as compensation for the discharge of their public service obligation. Consequently, such differential treatment as regards taxation would not constitute State aid provided that the tax imposed on pharmaceutical laboratories corresponded to the cost actually incurred by wholesale distributors. However, to the extent that the financial advantage resulting from tax relief exceeds the cost incurred, it would constitute State aid within the scope of Article 87(1).

However, in *Altmark Trans GmBH* v *Nahverkehrsgesellschaft Altmark GmBH* (case C–280/00), Advocate-General Leger argued (in a rare second opinion given in the wake of the *Ferring* judgment) in the context of subsidies paid to public transport providers, that the Court should not follow *Ferring*. He proposed that a distinction be drawn between the State as an economic operator who purchases goods or services on its own account and the State as an 'acquirer' of services that are made available directly to the public. In the former situation, there would only be State aid if the price paid exceeded the market price. In the context of public services, however, this approach should not be adopted, and any payments should be regarded as State aid. To do otherwise would result in conflating the question of whether aid is provided and whether the payment in question is compatible with the common market. Consequently, financial advantages granted by a Member State to compensate for the cost of a public service obligation *should* be regarded as

State aid. The argument that the advantage merely compensates for the additional cost incurred by the undertaking in providing the service should be taken into account in establishing whether the aid is compatible with the common market.

It seems that adopting Advocate-General Leger's approach would produce the same substantive outcome in *Ferring* that the tax advantage is not illegal. However, there is an important underlying issue of principle, which is the question of whether *any* form of State financial support to providers of public services should be subject to the State aid rules, or whether there are payments which should be regarded as falling outside the scope of Article 87(1) altogether. If Article 87(1) does apply, then it may be possible to rely either on Article 88, or on Article 86(2), which would enable the disapplication of the competition provisions (see Chapters 26–29 and 31), including Article 87, for services of general economic interest (telecommunications, postal and certain transport services as well as public service broadcasters) if their application would obstruct the performance, in law or in fact, of the particular task assigned to them (see also Chapter 26). However, it is far from clear how exactly these various provisions inter-relate, and clarification in this regard is now urgently needed. The ECJ disagreed with A-G Leger, holding that where a financial measure is compensation for a public services obligation undertaken by the recipient, there is no advantage (and therefore no State Aid), provided that:

(i) the recipient has a clearly defined public service obligation to discharge;

(ii) there is an objective and transparent system, established in advance, for calculating compensation;

(iii) the compensation does not exceed the costs incurred in discharging the obligation, taking account of relevant receipts and a reasonable profit margin; and

(iv) where the provider is not chosen through public procurement procedures, the level of compensation is determined with reference to the costs which a typical undertaking would incur.

All four conditions must be satisfied to take the payment outside the State aid provisions.

It might be argued that the adoption of the *Altmark* test gives the Member States greater scope for providing public services as they see fit, since *Altmark* constitutes a move away from the hypothetical investor test. At another level, as the Commission has noted, it is likely to result in an increased burden for Member States to notify, as few public services have been awarded via a public tender process. Most public service provision will not therefore satisfy the *Altmark* test and will be classified as aid. As a result of the judgment, the Commission has adopted a State aid action plan (see Commission Competition Policy Newsletter (2005) 2, p. 4 *et seq.*), which consists of three main strands: a Commission Decision; a Framework; and a proposed modification of the Transparency Directive. The Commission Decision contains what is effectively a *de minimis* exception for small aid as well as excluding hospitals and social housing from the obligation to notify, in both cases provided there is no over-compensation. This is separate from the *de minimis* exception under the State aid rules generally. The Framework explains how the Commission will assess compatibility with the State aid rules (Communication on Services of General Economic Interest (SGEIs)), which is effectively a codification of the Commission's existing practice under Article 86(2) EC (see further below and

Chapter 26). The modification of the Transparency Directive is to ensure that the public service providers' accounts provide a clear separation of public service costs and costs for commercial services.

30.3.4 Origin of resources

To fall within the State aid rules, the resources benefiting the undertaking must come from State resources, whether directly or indirectly. Aid may be granted through any central or local government body, or any agency subject to the control of the State. No distinction is made between aid granted directly by the State or by public or even private bodies established and operated by it to administer that aid (*Steinike und Weinleg* (case 78/76)). It is not necessary that the aid be paid directly out of public funds as long as the State plays a part in initiating or approving the aid. In *Kwekerij Gebroeders van der Kooy BV* v *Commission* (cases 67, 68 and 70/85), a power company created under private law but controlled by the State through a 50 per cent shareholding, and whose prices were subject to government control, was held to be equivalent to the State for the purpose of establishing State aid. In *Syndicat Français de l'Express (SFEI)* v *La Poste* (case C–39/94), the ECJ held that the provision of logistical or commercial support by a public undertaking (La Poste) to a private subsidiary which was engaged in an activity open to free competition, when that subsidiary gave no counter consideration, constituted aid.

In contrast, in *Firma Sloma Neptun Schiffahrts AG* v *Seebetriebsrat Bodo Ziesemer of Sloman Neptun Schiffahrts AG* (cases C–72 and 73/91), the ECJ held that rules which permitted wages lower than the German minimum to be paid to foreign seamen did not constitute State aid. Although the lower wages costs resulting from the German rules benefited the boat companies, this was not aid for these purposes, as the advantage did not originate from State resources. In a similar vein, *Pearle* (case (C–245/02) clarifies the limits of *Steinike and Weileg*. *Pearle* concerned a trade association's right to raise levies from its members to pay for an advertising campaign. The power to pass byelaws, including that on which the levy was based, was approved by the relevant ministry, as was its general power to organise and develop its sector of activity. *Pearle* challenged the levy on the basis of *Steinike and Weinleg*, arguing that the State's involvement constituted State aid, via its approval of the trade association and its byelaws. The ECJ rejected this argument, stating the requirement of State resources has two elements: direct or indirect use of State resources; and the aid is imputable to the State. Here the financing is not made available though State resources and, given that the advertising was funded by reference to the advantage each member of the association got from the advertising campaign, is no advantage. By contrast, *Steinicke and Weinleg* had involved State subsidy as well as members' contributions. *Steinicke and Weinleg* had also involved the implementation of government policy, thus going to the second element of the test. In *Pearle*, the trade association was implementing its own policy, not that of the government. There was thus no aid.

30.3.5 Distortion of competition

To constitute State aid in breach of Article 87, the benefit must distort or threaten competition by favouring certain undertakings or the production of certain goods.

Given the tendency to use the hypothetical market investor test, i.e., identify whether a firm receives a benefit by reference to what a normal market operator would not do, if an advantage is found then it will, almost by definition, distort competition. Further, in *Vlaams Gewest* v *Commission* (case T–214/95), the CFI held that even small amounts of aid would distort competition for the purposes of this provision. It has been noted that even small amounts of aid can be significant in markets where there are a large number of competitors.

Although the courts have taken this stringent view, the Commission seems to have taken a more generous approach. It issued a Notice on the *de minimis* rule for State aid in 1996 ([1996] OJ C68/9), according to which small amounts of aid would not fall foul of the State aid rules. Furthermore, the Commission, under its powers in Regulation 994/88, has adopted a *de minimis* exception for small amounts of aid, thus giving a legislative basis for its approach to small amounts of aid contained in its Notice, the legal basis for which had been somewhat uncertain. Regulation 69/2001 ([2001] OJ L10/30) applies to all forms of aid, except:

(a) aid given to the transport sector;

(b) activities linked to products listed in Annex I to the EC Treaty;

(c) export activities; and

(d) aid contingent on the use of domestic over imported goods.

It seems that there are plans to update the *de minimis* regulation in 2006.

Aid will not fall within Articles 87(1) and 88(3) EC if the total aid granted to one enterprise does not exceed €100,000 gross over any period of three years (Article 2). Member States must ensure that an enterprise does not receive more than the total *de minimis* amount during any given three-year period (Article 3). To do so, it will be necessary to examine the ownership structure of the enterprises involved. In *Netherlands* v *Commission* (case C–382/99), a case decided under the Notice rather than the regulation, the ECJ upheld the Commission's finding that a Dutch system of granting tax rebates to petrol stations on the Dutch–German border could, in certain circumstances, result in the cumulation of rebates the value of which would exceed €100,000 and that the Dutch system constituted State aid to that extent.

30.3.6 Impact on inter-State trade

Aid must be capable of affecting trade between Member States. Many of the considerations under this heading are similar to those which relate to assessing distortion of competition. State aid will be deemed to affect trade between Member States if the beneficiary of aid competes with enterprises in other Member States, even if it does not export to those States. The argument is that where aid is given in a Member State to an undertaking, the aid might make it harder for a competitor in another Member State to break into the national market. Thus, the courts are focusing on the potential impact rather than any actual quantified impact. Even a small amount of aid may affect trade between Member States if there is strong competition in the relevant sector (*ENI Lanerossi* (case C–303/88), see also *Vlaams Gewest* v *Commission* (case T–214/95)). Again, the introduction of the *de minimis* exception may ease the tension between the Commission's approach and that of the courts.

30.3.7 Exemptions and guidelines

The Commission has issued a number of guidelines regarding the application of the State aid rules, for example the Guidelines on Restructuring Aid, recently amended, and the Guidelines on State Aid for Environmental Protection ([1994] OJ C72/3). As noted above, the Commission also adopted a *de minimis* block exemption. In addition, there are now several other State aid block exemptions in place, which will be summarised in the following paragraphs. These generally favour small and medium-sized enterprises.

Regulation 68/2001 on training aid ([2001] OJ L10/20) exempts from the notification requirement in Article 88 EC training aid given to small and medium-sized enterprises which does not exceed 35 per cent (or 25 per cent if the enterprise is large) of the total cost of training ('aid intensity') if that training is individual or specific to the particular enterprise. For general training which creates transferable skills (such as certificates or degrees), the maximum amount of aid covered by the exemption is 70 per cent (or 50 per cent for large enterprises). However, the maximum amount of aid granted to a particular enterprise must not exceed €100,000.

Regulation 70/2001 on State aid for small and medium-sized enterprises (SMEs) ([2001] OJ L10/33) provides an exemption for various forms of aid to SMEs. Investment aid is covered if it does not exceed 15 per cent (7.5 per cent in the case of a medium-sized enterprise) of the total amount invested or the wage cost of any employment created by a small enterprise, with derogations to these percentages where the investment takes place in an area which qualifies for regional aid (see Article 4(3) of Regulation 70/2001). Aid to support irregular consultancies to SMEs, or costs incurred when participating in trade fairs or exhibitions, may be up to 50 per cent of the total cost involved. However, individual aid is not exempt where either the total cost of the whole project in question exceeds €25 million, or where the total gross aid is not less that €15 million. Regulation 70/2001 has been amended by Regulation 364/2004 so that aid to SMEs includes aid given for research and development.

Regulation 2204/2002 ([2002] OJ L337/3) concerns State aid for employment. This primarily applies to aid given for the creation of employment and the recruitment of disadvantaged and disabled workers. In the case of small enterprises, the aid given must not exceed 15 per cent (7.5 per cent in the case of medium-sized enterprises) of the wage costs of creating employment, although slightly different rules apply if employment is created in areas which qualify for regional aid. As far as the creation of employment for disadvantaged or disabled workers is concerned, aid may be given of up to 50 per cent of the wage costs during the first year after recruitment in the case of disadvantaged workers, and 60 per cent in the case of disabled workers. Additional aid may be given to cover the cost of adapting workplaces and acquiring any specialist equipment that may be required (see Article 6 of Regulation 2204/2002). There are various exclusions from the scope of this exemption in Article 9, including aid targeted at particular sectors, aid to avoid redundancies of existing jobs, or aid to transfer temporary or part-time jobs to permanent full-time jobs. Presumably, this is an attempt to buttress attempts to eradicate discrimination on the basis of disability (on discrimination see Chapter 25).

30.4 **Policy of the Commission**

Whether aid is new or existing, whether it falls allegedly within Article 87(2) and (3), apart from the exceptional case under Articles 87(3)(d) and 88(2), which will be decided by the Council, it is the Commission, subject to final adjudication by the Court, which decides whether it is in fact compatible with Community law. Applicants may thus challenge the Commission's decision that a particular payment or subsidy did (or did not) constitute State aid (see, e.g., *Ladbroke Racing Ltd* v *Commission* (case T–67/94)); or whether it falls within any exception. Clearly if it falls squarely within Article 87(2), it must be allowed. If it falls within the permitted exceptions of Article 87(3)(a) to (c) the Commission has a discretion, both in permitting the exemption and in determining its scope (*Exécutif régional wallon* v *Commission* (case 67/87); modernisation aid granted to Glaverbel (Belgian glass manufacturers) not an important project of common European interest under the then Article 92(3)(b); to constitute the latter must form part of a trans-national European programme).

The exercise of this discretion, as the Court commented in *Philip Morris Holland BV* v *Commission* (case 730/79) involves economic, political and social assessments which must be made in the Community context, the determining factor being the Community interest. As a general rule aid will only be allowed if it promotes recognised Community as opposed to national objectives and does not frustrate progress towards the single market (*20th Report on Competition Policy*). As noted above, the Court will question the exercise of the Commission's discretion only in extreme cases.

In permitting *regional* aid under Article 87(3)(a) (to counter underemployment and to assist development), the Commission looks not to national levels of employment and income but to the standard of the Community as a whole. As a result eligibility for such benefit will depend on the State's position relative to the Community average. The Commission has also, in the interests of transparency, issued guidelines on national regional aid, in which it outlines circumstances in which aid will be considered to be in the Community interest. In so doing, it replaces a significant number of heterogeneous documents previously covering this area.

In allowing *sectoral aid* (e.g., to agriculture, transport, particular industries) under Article 87(3)(c), the Commission's main concern is to prevent the grant of State aid from exacerbating existing problems or from transferring them from one State to another. The Commission will not allow aid which strengthens the power of an undertaking compared with other undertakings competing in intra-Community trade. Thus, in *Philip Morris* the claimant failed to obtain the annulment of a Commission decision refusing to allow the Dutch Government to grant aid to increase the production capacity of a Dutch cigarette manufacturer, who was in competition in Europe with a number of other manufacturers.

Nor will the Commission allow Member States to 'shore up obsolete structures' (*16th General Report*, 1982, 104), to grant relief to rescue firms which are incapable of adjusting to conditions of competition (*15th Report on Competition Policy*, 1981, 103). Aid will only be permitted which will lead to sound economic structures to enable an industry to become competitive, to resolve underlying problems, not to postpone or shift the solution. Thus the recent amendments to the guidelines on restructuring aid have operated to limit the circumstances in which restructuring aid may be granted.

The majority of aids, notably regional and sectoral aids, for example, aids to the textile industry, to shipbuilding and (prior to the TEU) to the film industry, have been granted under Article 87(3)(c) – 'to facilitate the development of certain economic activities or of certain economic areas'. Regional aids, i.e., national as opposed to Community aid granted pursuant to its regional policy, have been subject to progressive coordination since the first formal guidelines were adopted in 1971 (First Resolution on Regional Aids, (1971) JO C111/1).

Exceptions under Article 87(3)(b) must relate to projects of common *European*, as opposed to national interest. Aid has been permitted under this head to enable firms to bring their plant into line with environmental standards (see Commission Guidelines on State Aid for Environmental Protection [2001] OJ C37/3). Article 87(3)(d) providing for the granting of aid to promote culture and heritage conservation, was introduced by the TEU in 1992. The film industry, a former beneficiary under sub-para. (3)(c), has been dealt with since the TEU under this provision. In addition, an amendment to Article 159 (ex 130b) EC, also introduced by the TEU, will require decisions on State aid to take greater account of the need to strengthen economic and social cohesion (see Commission's Report on Competition Policy 1992 and ECOSOC resolution on 24th Report on Competition ([1996] OJ C39/79)).

Since German unification there is no longer any justification for continuing to subsidise areas of East Germany under Article 87(2)(c), although the Commission has recognised that some State aid will be necessary to ease East Germany's transition to a market economy.

General aids as opposed to 'special' aids normally fall outside Article 87. General schemes may exceptionally be permitted for short periods to counter 'a serious disturbance in the economy of a Member State' (Article 87(3)(b)).

The Commission has taken the view that the provisions on State aids apply to aid granted to both private and public undertakings. It has issued directives (Directive 80/723 ([1980] OJ L195/35), amended by Directive 85/43 ([1985] OJ L229/20)) on the transparency of relations between Member States and public undertakings, requiring Member States to ensure that information regarding financial relations between public authorities and Member States be kept at the disposal of the Commission for a five-year period and to supply such information where the Commission 'considers it necessary so to request' (Article 5). In a communication based on these directives issued in 1991 ([1991] OJ C273/2) it expressed its concern at the volume of aid granted by States to public undertakings which had not been notified under the then Article 93(3) (£3.5 billion between 1985 and 1990). It stressed the need for the development of a policy for public undertakings, which had not hitherto been sufficiently subject to State aid disciplines. Aid granted to public undertakings in the manufacturing sector *must* be notified in advance to the Commission. This communication was annulled on procedural grounds in 1993, but, on the Court's recommendation, as noted above, the Commission amended Directive 80/273 to require States to submit an annual report and has reduced the scope of the communication, which now simply describes its policy on aid to public undertakings (EC Bull 7/8 1993 1.2.80). In 1993 the Commission also introduced a system of standard notification of State aids (EC Bull 3 1993 1.2.39). Amendments to these provisions have been incorporated in the Commission's action plan on State aid, introduced following *Altmark* (see above).

30.5 Relationship between State aid and other provisions of the Treaty

30.5.1 Article 28 (ex 30) EC

State aid that is permitted under Article 87 cannot in itself fall within Article 28. To that extent the provisions are mutually exclusive. However, some aspects of State aid, not necessary for the attainment of its object, may be incompatible with other provisions of the Treaty, even though they may not invalidate the aid as a whole (*Ianelli & Volpi SpA* v *Ditta Paola Meroni* (case 74/76)). Therefore, if the aid goes beyond what is necessary to achieve a particular legitimate objective it may infringe Article 28. Similarly, if it is applied to activities which are incompatible with Article 28 (e.g., a 'Buy Irish' campaign sponsored by the Irish Goods Council: *Commission* v *Ireland* (case 249/81)).

30.5.2 Article 31 (ex 37) EC

On the same principle the operations of a State-owned monopoly are not exempt from Article 31 by reason of the fact that they may classify as aids. Even when the activities of a State monopoly are linked with a grant to producers subject to the monopoly they must still comply with the non-discrimination requirements of Article 31 (*Ianelli & Volpi SpA* v *Ditta Paolo Meroni* (case 74/76)).

30.5.3 Article 81 (ex 85) EC

Assessment under Article 88 EC to determine the compatibility of aid with the common market and the exemption from liability under the competition provisions of Article 81(1) provided by Article 81(3) are separate procedures. A favourable determination under one will therefore not preclude an unfavourable decision under the other.

30.5.4 Article 86 (ex 90)

As will be seen in Chapters 25 and 27, this provision prohibits rules contrary to the provisions of the Treaty, especially the competition provisions, being maintained in force in respect of 'public undertakings and those to which Member States have granted special or exclusive rights' (Article 86(1)). Article 86(2), however, provides an exception to this general statement for 'Undertakings entrusted with the operation of services of general economic interest or having the character of a revenue-producing monopoly', which shall be subject to the Treaty rules only insofar as their application 'does not obstruct the performance . . . of the particular tasks assigned to them'. The development of trade, however, must not be affected to such an extent as would be contrary to the interests of the Community (Article 86(2)). This exception in Article 86(2) could overlap with the State aid rules thereby exempting those undertakings falling within Article 86(2) from State aid rules, but the precise limits of the two provisions are currently not clear. Although the question was raised in *Banco de Crédito Industrial SA v Ayuntamiento de Valencia* (case C–387/92), the ECJ did not address the issue. The Commission has, however, made a couple of decisions exempting public service broadcasters such as the BBC on this basis and has issued guidelines on public service broadcasting (see [2001] OJ C320/5). This would indicate that Article 86(2) could be used in relation to State aid, thus providing an additional form of exemption for some cases of aid. As we have seen above, the Commission has now issued a Communication on Services of General Economic Interest, setting out its approach in relation to State aid and Article 86(2).

30.6 Enforcement by individuals

Articles 87 and 89, both being dependent on the exercise of discretion by Community institutions, are not directly effective (*Ianelli & Volpi SpA v Ditta Paola Meroni* (case 74/76)). So, in the absence of a decision from the Commission or ECJ, a national court has no power to decide whether a State aid is compatible with Article 87. However, the procedural obligations of Article 88(3) are directly effective, and as such, as the Commission pointed out in its practice note of 1983, are amenable to assessment by national courts. Thus an individual, provided he has *locus standi* under national law, may challenge in his domestic courts a grant of aid by national authorites in breach of Article 88(3). The Commission issued a Notice on Cooperation between National Courts and the Commission in the State Aid Field ([1995] OJ C312/7). This establishes machinery whereby national courts faced with a potential State aid may seek assistance from the Commission on whether it should be characterised as such. Further, the Commission has also issued guidelines concerning aid in certain sectors, such as the environment ([2001] OJ C37/3) and employment ([1995] OJ C334). Also, as the ECJ noted in *Ianelli & Volpi SpA v Ditta Paolo Meroni*, if Article 87 is invoked before domestic courts in the context of directly effective provisions such as Article 28 and Article 31, questions relating to State aid may, along with other questions, be referred to the ECJ for preliminary ruling.

30.6.1 Challenge to aid granted

The case of *Syndicat Français de l'Express International v La Poste* (case C–39/94) illustrates the subtle relationship between Articles 87 and 88(3). The case concerned a claim for compensation for losses suffered by the applicant, a competitor in the provision of postal services, resulting from alleged State aid granted to La Poste without notification to the Commission, in breach of Article 88(3). The matter had been under consideration by the Commission for two years, following a complaint by SFEI, during which time the Commission had neither adopted a position nor taken a final decision. Hence SFEI's action before the French courts seeking, *inter alia*, compensation in respect of the alleged breach. The French court sought clarification on a number of questions:

(a) whether the recovery of State aid was the only way of guaranteeing the effectiveness of Article 88(3) or whether parties such as the applicant who had suffered loss as a result of the alleged aid could recover compensation in their national court in respect of breaches of that article, and

(b) whether, when the matter is under investigation by the Commission, a national court is under an obligation to declare its lack of jurisdiction, or

(c) if it has declared jurisdiction, it is obliged to stay proceedings until the Commission takes a decision.

The ECJ's reply was unequivocal. The involvement of national courts is the result of the direct effects of Article 88(3). The initiation of procedures before the Commission cannot release national courts from their duty to safeguard the rights of individuals in the event of a breach of the notification requirement. Faced with an alleged breach a national court may have to interpret the concept of aid contained in Article 87 to determine whether a State measure introduced without notification ought to have been subject to that procedure. In doing so it may refer to the ECJ for an interpretation of that article. Where there is a lapse of time it will be for the national court to decide if it is necessary to order interim relief such as the suspension of measures to safeguard the interest of parties. Although the ECJ did not rule specifically on the question of damages it is submitted that where it is necessary to award damages to safeguard individuals' rights under Article 88(3) a national court may do so (for example, the applicants in *Atzeni* (joined cases C–346 and 529/03), discussed above, claimed damages, but were unsuccessful – their claim failed on other grounds). Arguably, it may even, following *Antonissen* (case C–393/96 P(R)), order interim compensation (see further Chapter 7).

In proceedings before national courts, actions by national authorities taken in breach of Article 88(3) cannot be legalised by a subsequent finding by the Commission that the aid is compatible with EC law (*Fédération Nationale du Commerce Extérieur des Produits Alimentaires* v *France* (case C–354/90)). However, a failure to notify the granting of aid does not automatically lead to nullity (*France* v *Commission* (case C–301/87)).

30.6.2 Review of Commission decisions on State aid

Once a decision about State aid has been issued, a recipient or potential recipient may challenge that decision before the ECJ under Article 230 EC; however, where a decision affects a whole industry the Court has held that individual members have no standing to sue, although an organisation created to represent those members, if it took part in the proceedings relating to the granting of aid, may (*Kwekerij Gebruders van der Kooy* (cases 67, 68 & 70/85)). In addition, any interested party who suspects that aid is being granted in breach of Article 87 may complain to the Commission and request the Commission to act, and, provided he acts in time, may challenge any action or inaction on the part of the Commission resulting from his complaint (*Irish Cement Ltd* v *Commission* (case 166/86), see Chapters 11 and 12). It is not just the originator of the complaint who can have standing to bring an action under these articles. The ECJ has held that, because of the lack of transparency and the lack of a role for third parties under Article 88(3), it is not necessary for third parties to show participation in the Commission investigation or to have been substantially effected by the measure to have standing to challenge a Commission decision concerning State aid. A competitor of the recipient of the aid could have standing (*William Cook plc* v *Commission* (case C–198/91); *Matra SA* v *Commission* (case C–225/91R)). In *ASPEC* v *Commission* (case T–435/93), the CFI held that the impact of a decision on the competitive environment of a market together with the small number of producers in that market would give the competing producers sufficient standing to challenge that decision. Moreover, in *Aktionsgemeinschaft Recht und Eigentum eV* v *Commission* (case T–114/00), the CFI held that an association formed to protect the collective interests of its members had *locus standi* under Article 230 EC to bring an action for the annulment of a Commission decision not to instigate the formal procedure under Article 88(2) EC, on behalf of those members who would have been parties concerned within the meaning of Article 88(2) EC and would be individually concerned within the meaning of Article 230 EC.

Any person seeking to challenge a decision concerning State aid, whether to himself or to another party, would be wise, where he has *locus standi*, to proceed quickly under Article 230 since following the decision of the Court in *TWD Textilwerke Deggendorf GmbH* v *Germany* (case C–188/92) there may be difficulties in obtaining relief under the alternative route to annulment provided by Article 234.

Where repayment of aid is ordered, recovery will be governed by the domestic law of the State in question, provided that the rules do not render recovery excessively difficult or impossible in practice (*Commission* v *Germany* (case 94/87)). As noted earlier, interest will be payable from the date on which the unlawful aid was paid. As the Court has decided that undertakings in receipt of State aid must be deemed to be aware of the rules regarding the recovery of illegally granted aid it is unlikely that a person in receipt of such aid can claim damages against the State, either on the basis of tort or under *Francovich* v *Italy* (cases C–6 & 9/90) (see Chapter 8); arguably, in a 'normal' case he could be seen as having caused his own loss.

30.7 Conclusions

State aid continues to result in distortions of the competitive conditions within the Community, especially with the entry of new Member States who are still in the process of adapting their economies to the internal market requirements. It should not be thought, however, that this is an issue just in relation to new Member States. As businesses within the Member States find it more difficult to cope with increased competition, national governments will seek to ensure that 'their' businesses do not fail. To a limited extent, the Commission recognises that aid given in this way may be beneficial for the competitiveness of the Community as a whole in the global marketplace and this is reflected in the various exemptions now adopted under Regulation 994/98. At the same time, however, it is necessary to ensure that the competitive balance between the various Member States is maintained. One important aspect for which clarification is required, especially in a Europe which emphasises social protection, is the extent to which payments to providers of public services are caught by the State aid provisions. Although, following *Altmark*, the Commission has issued a Communication on this point, it should be noted that the tension between competition within the Community and the freedom of Member States to organise public service provision as they see fit remains. Although the State aid provisions seem to catch such activity, other provisions, such as Article 16 EC emphasise the importance of public services and the rights of Member States in this regard. This is a tension that will remain in the Constitution, should it ever come into force reflecting tensions in the objectives of the Union and differing views between Member States.

FURTHER READING

Abbamonte, G. B., 'Competitors' Right to Challenge Illegally Granted Aid and the Problem of the Conflicting Decisions in the Field of Competition Law' [1997] ECLR 87.

Bacon, K. M., 'State Aids and General Measures' (1997) 17 YEL 269.

Commission's Annual Reports on Competition Policy.

Evans, A. and Martin, M., 'Socially Acceptable Distortions of Competition: Community Policy on State Aid' (1991) 16 EL Rev 79.

Gromnicka, E., 'Services of General Economic Interest in the State Aids Regime: Proceduralisation of Political Choices?' (2005) 11(3) EPL 429–461.

Harrison, J. and Woods, L. M., 'Defining European Public Service Broadcasting' (2001) 16 European Journal of Communication 477.

Hellingman, K., 'State Participation as State Aid under Article 92 of the EEC Treaty: the Commission's Guidelines' (1986) 23 CML Rev 111.

Prosser, T., 'Competition Law and Public Services: From Single Market to Citizenship Rights?' 11(4) EPL 543.

Quigley, C., 'The Notion of a State Aid in the EEC' (1988) 13 EL Rev 242.

Rodger, B. J., 'State Aid – A Fully Level Playing Field' [1999] ECLR 251.

Ross, M., 'State Aids and National Courts: Definitions and Other Problems – a Case of Premature Emancipation?' (2000) 37 CMLR 401.

—, 'Article 16 EC and Services of General Interest: From Derogation to Obligation', (2000) 25 Eur LR 22.

Sinnaeve, A., 'Block Exemptions for State Aid: More Scope for State Aid Control by Member States and Competitors' (2001) 38 CML Rev 1479.

Slot Piet, J., 'Procedural Aspects of State Aids: The Guardians of Competition versus the Subsidy Villains' (1990) 27 CML Rev 741.

Slotboom, M. M., 'State Aid in Community Law: A Broad or Narrow Definition?' (1995) 20 EL Rev 289.

Winter, J. A., 'Supervision of State Aid' (1993) 30 CML Rev 311.

—, 'Re(de)fining the Notion of State Aid in Article 87(1) of the EC Treaty' (2004) 41(2) CML Rev 475.

Woods, L., 'The Application of Competition Rules to State Aids for Culture' in *Culture et Marché* (ERA Forum 1/2005).

Intellectual property rights and the internal market

31.1 Introduction

The exercise of intellectual property rights, or industrial and commercial property rights, such as trade marks, patents and copyright, can have a negative impact on the operation of the internal market: it may be used to restrict the free movement of goods between Member States, and it can also result in restrictions of competition. As far as the latter is concerned, it is of course the very purpose of intellectual property rights to give their owner monopoly rights for a certain period of time as a reward for his creative endeavour or the acquired goodwill in his product. Intellectual property rights are therefore necessary to encourage investment of time and money in creative endeavour. A balance has therefore to be struck between recognising intellectual property rights and preventing their use from undermining the internal market objective (including competition policy).

In this chapter, we will consider to what extent it is possible to use intellectual property rights to restrict the free movement of goods by analysing the case law that has developed under Article 30 (ex 36), which contains the derogations from the prohibition against quantitative restrictions or measures having an equivalent effect under Article 28 (ex 30) (see Chapters 18 and 19). We will then examine to what extent competition law under Articles 81 and 82 (ex 85 and 86, respectively) has been applied to control the use of their rights by the owners of intellectual property. It will become apparent that there is a degree of parallelism in the case law developed in these areas.

31.2 Derogation from Article 28: protection of industrial and commercial property

As noted in Chapter 19, Article 30 permits a derogation from Article 28 where this is justified on grounds of the protection of industrial or commercial property. This exception must be read in conjunction with Article 295 (ex 222) EC, which provides that:

> This Treaty shall in no way prejudice the rules in Member States governing the system of property ownership.

Together these provisions would appear to ensure that national laws governing industrial property remain intact. However, since industrial property law by its very nature tends to contribute to a partitioning of the market, usually along national lines, its exercise inevitably restricts the free movement of goods and conflicts with the principle of market integration so fundamental to the Community. As we will see below (31.3), the competition provisions of the Treaty may be invoked to prevent this partitioning, but they are not in themselves sufficient to deal with all the situations in which industrial property law may be used to compartmentalise the market. So the Commission, and more particularly the Court, since the Commission has no power to enforce the free movement of goods provisions against individuals, have solved the problem by the application of Articles 28 and 30. As a result, despite the prima facie protection offered to industrial property rights by Articles 30 and 295 EC, these rights, protected under national law, have undoubtedly been curtailed.

31.2.1 'Specific subject matter' of the right

The scope of Article 30 was considered in *Deutsche Grammophon Gesellschaft mbH* v *Metro–SB–Grossmärkte GmbH & Co. KG* (case 78/70). Here Deutsche Grammophon (DG) were seeking to invoke German copyright law to prevent the defendant wholesalers from selling DG's Polydor records, previously exported to France, in Germany. Since a prohibition on re-import would clearly breach Article 28, the matter fell to be decided under Article 30. Arguing from the second sentence of that Article, that 'prohibitions or restrictions shall not . . . constitute a means of arbitrary discrimination or a disguised restriction on trade between Member States' the Court concluded that the provision permitted prohibitions or restrictions on the free movement of goods only to the extent that they were justified for the protection of the rights that form the *specific subject matter of the property*. The Court drew a distinction between the *existence* of industrial property rights which falls within the specific subject matter of the right and remains unaffected by Community law, and their *exercise*, which may come within the prohibition of the Treaty. The specific subject matter (which overlaps with discussions of the purpose of an intellectual property right) will vary depending on the type of right in issue (e.g., trade marks, see *Hag II*; on copyright see *Magill*, discussed at 31.3.2). If copyright protection is used to prohibit, in one Member State, the marketing of goods brought on to the market by the holder of the rights, or with his consent, in the territory of the other Member State (i.e., to prevent what are known as 'parallel' imports) *solely* because the marketing has not occurred in the domestic market, such a prohibition, maintaining the isolation of the national markets, conflicts with the essential aim of the Treaty, the integration of the national markets into one uniform market. Thus it would constitute an improper *exercise* of the property right in question and would not be justified under Article 30.

31.2.2 Exhaustion

The specific subject matter of the property, to protect which property rights may be legitimately exercised under EC law, was expressed in *Centrafarm BV* v *Sterling Drug Inc.* (case 15/74) and *Centrafarm BV* v *Winthrop BV* (case 16/74), in the context of a claim for infringement of patents and trade marks respectively, as a guarantee that the owner of the trade mark or patent has the exclusive right to use that trade mark or patent, for the purposes of putting into circulation in the EC products protected by the trade mark or patent *for the first time*; either directly, or by the grant of licences to third parties. Once the protected product has been put on the market in a particular Member State by or with the consent of the owner, or by a person economically or legally dependent on him, such as a licensee, a subsidiary, a parent company or an exclusive distributor (but not an assignee of trade-mark rights, see further *IHT* (case C–9/93)), he can no longer rely on national property rights to prevent its import from that State into other Member States. His rights have been exhausted. The ECJ has held that it is not permissible to rely on the right to place goods on the market for the first time to prevent the importation of goods lawfully manufactured in one Member State into the territory of another Member State where the goods have not yet been put into circulation but are in transit in order to be placed on the market of a non-Member State (in this instance, Poland prior to its accession) (*Rioglass* (case C–115/02)).

This doctrine of 'exhaustion of rights' has been applied by the Court to trade marks (*Centrafarm BV* v *Winthrop BV* (case 16/74)), patents (*Centrafarm BV* v *Sterling Drug Inc.* (case 15/74)), industrial designs (*Keurkoop BV* v *Nancy Kean Gifts BV* (case 144/81)) and, subject to some qualification due to its special nature (see *Warner Brothers Inc.* v *Cristiansen* (case 158/86); *Coditel* v *Cine Vog Films* (case 62/79)), copyright (*Musik-Vertrieb Membran GmbH* v *GEMA* (cases 55 & 57/80)). It is thought that plant breeders' rights too would be subject to the principle, since they were held in *L. C. Nungesser KG* v *Commission* (case 258/78) to fall within the concept of industrial and commercial property.

In *Merck & Co. Inc.* v *Stephar BV* (case 187/80), the exhaustion principle was applied where the patent owner had sold his product in Italy, where there existed no system of patent protection. The Court held that having allowed the goods to be sold in Italy, he must accept the consequences as regards free circulation in the Community.

However, where a product has been sold under a compulsory licence, without the consent of the owner, the latter is entitled under Article 30 EC to rely on his property right to prevent the marketing in a third Member State of that product resulting from the exploitation of the compulsory licence, since, not having consented to its use, he is still entitled to enjoy the substance of his exclusive licence (*Pharmon BV* v *Hoechst AG* (case 19/84). See also *Thetford Corp.* v *Fiamma SpA* (case 35/87)). Similarly, where the manufacturing or marketing of a product is lawful in a Member State, *not* through the owner's consent but because of the expiry of the protection period provided for industrial property rights under the law of that Member State, a person with exclusive rights in that product in another Member State may prevent the import of the protected product into the Member State in which he holds these rights (*EMI Electrola GmbH* v *Patricia* (case 341/87), which concerned rights of reproduction and distribution of musical works).

Where a product has been put lawfully on the market in a particular Member State with the owner's consent and the period of protection permitted under national law in that State has *not* expired, its import into another Member State may not be restrained, even though the purpose of an attempt to prevent importation is to prevent parties taking advantage of different price levels in different

Member States, whether the reason for the price differences be government policy, legislation or ordinary market forces (*Centrafarm; GEMA*).

31.2.3 Repackaging

There have been a number of cases involving pharmaceuticals in which importers have sought to take advantage of these price differences and the exhaustion principle, but, because the same product has been marketed in different Member States under different guises, they have needed to repackage or relabel the goods to establish their identity in the Member State of import (see also Commission Communication on parallel imports of proprietary medicinal products for which marketing authorisations have already been granted (COM (2003) 839 final), providing detailed guidance on the implications of the Court's jurisprudence).

The Court has held that persons may rely on trade-mark rights to prevent the import of such goods in order to avoid confusion as to the identity of the product, and to ensure that the consumer can be certain that the trade-marked product has not been subject to interference by a third party. However, it was decided in *Hoffman-La Roche & Co. AG* v *Centrafarm* (case 102/77) that an attempt to prevent the import of the trade-marked goods would constitute a disguised restriction on trade between Member States (bringing it outside Article 30) where:

(a) the marketing system for the products adopted by the owner of the trade-mark rights involves an artificial partitioning of the market; and where

(b) the repackaging cannot adversely affect the condition of the product,

(c) the proprietor receives prior notice of the marketing of the repackaged product, and

(d) it is stated on the new package that the product has been repackaged.

The Court added that these principles were not confined to medical products, a point confirmed by the ECJ in respect of the relabelling of alcoholic drinks in *Frits Loendersloot* (case C–349/95).

Similar reasoning underlay the decision in *Centrafarm BV* v *American Home Products Corporation* (AHPC) (case 3/78) about whether the importer, Centrafarm (again!), could change the name of the product it was seeking to import from the UK into Holland from Serenid D, under which it was marketed in the UK, to Seresta, the name under which a near-identical drug from the same manufacturer (AHPC) was marketed in Holland. The Court held that the proprietor of a trade mark was entitled to rely on his property rights to prevent the unauthorised fixing of trade marks on to the goods. However, while it might be lawful for a manufacturer to use different trade marks in different Member States, where a trade-mark system is used to partition the market along national lines a prohibition on the unauthorised fixing of labels would constitute a disguised restriction on trade between Member States, thereby falling outside Article 30.

The importer in *Pfizer Inc.* v *Eurim-Pharm GmbH* (case 1/81) did its homework. Prior to importing Vibramycin tablets, manufactured by Pfizer Ltd in the UK, into Germany, Eurim-Pharm repackaged the tablets in packets resembling those used for Vibramycin tablets of German manufacture without tampering with the individual tablets; the new packages had windows through which the trade names

'Vibramycin' and 'Pfizer' could be seen. The pack stated that the tablets had been produced by Pfizer Ltd of Great Britain and had been repackaged and imported by Eurim-Pharm. And they had informed the claimant, Pfizer Inc. (USA), the parent company which owned the Vibramycin and Pfizer trade marks in Europe, in advance of what they were intending to do. The Court held that the claimant could not rely on its trade-mark rights and Article 30 to prevent the import of the tablets into Germany under those circumstances. These rulings have been reaffirmed, in the context of the Trade Marks Directive (see further below), in *Merck and Co. Inc.* v *Primecrown Ltd* (cases C–267 & 268/95), *Bristol-Myers Squibb* v *Paranova A/S* (cases C–427, 429 & 436/93), *Pharmacia & Upjohn SA* v *Paranova A/S* (case C–379/97) *Merck, Sharp and Dohme* (case C–443/99) and *Aventis Pharma Deutschland* (case C–43/00). In *Merck, Sharp and Dohme*, however, the ECJ emphasised that the interference with the subject matter of the intellectual property right must be justified by the need to overcome barriers to trade within the EEA, even if the repackaging did no harm to the reputation of the trade-mark owner.

31.2.4 Common origin

The free movement of goods has took precedence, for a while, over national industrial property rights by reason of another doctrine introduced by the Court – the doctrine of common origin, introduced in the case of *Van Zuylen Frères* v *Hag AG* (case 192/73). This doctrine, now discredited, is thought to have applied only to trade-mark rights. The *Van Zuylen* case ('*Hag I*') arose from an attempt by Van Zuylen Frères, who owned the trade mark for Hag coffee in Belgium and Luxembourg, to prevent the import into Luxembourg of 'Hag' decaffeinated coffee made by Hag AG in Germany. The trade mark 'Hag' had been owned originally by a German company, Hag AG, which had operated in Luxembourg and Belgium through its subsidiary company, Hag Belgium. After the Second World War, Hag Belgium was sequestrated and sold to a Belgian family. Its Hag trade mark was eventually transferred to Van Zuylen Frères. Hag AG and Van Zuylen Frères legitimately owned the same mark. Could Van Zuylen Frères invoke their rights to prevent Hag AG from exercising its? There was no question of exhaustion of rights, since Hag AG had clearly not consented to the original transfer of its trade mark. The Court held that they could not. Drawing a distinction between the existence of trade-mark rights and their exercise the Court concluded that it was not possible to rely on a trade mark to prohibit, in one Member State, goods lawfully produced in another Member State under an identified mark which has the same origin.

The ruling in *Van Zuylen Frères* was reconsidered by the Court in a second case, *SA CNL-SUCAL* v *Hag GF AG* (case C–10/89) ('*Hag II*') in a reverse fact situation, Hag (Belgium) having changed hands and Hag (Germany) seeking to restrain import of the former's coffee into Germany. Following its ruling in *Pharmon BV* v *Hoechst AG* (case 19/84), the Court held that in the absence of an element of *consent* on the part of the trade-mark owner to the product being manufactured or marketed in another Member State, the owner was entitled to protect his product against imported goods which could be confused with his but for which he was not responsible. The decision, which was carefully reasoned, was based on the purpose of trade-mark protection, which is to guarantee the identity and origin of the marked products to the consumer and ultimate user, and avoid the possibility of confusion.

As Advocate-General Jacobs had pointed out, the word 'origin' did not refer to historical origin, but to the commercial origin of the goods, as a guarantee of uniform quality. The determining factor, as the Court pointed out (at para. 15), was the absence of consent on the part of the proprietor to the putting into circulation in another Member State of similar products bearing an identical mark or one leading to confusion, manufactured by an undertaking which is legally and economically independent of the proprietor.

Hag II concerned a situation in which a trade-mark right, originally in common ownership, had been divided *involuntarily*, without the consent of the original owner. In *IHT Internationale Heiztechnik GmbH* v *Ideal-Standard GmbH* (case C–9/93), the Court had to decide whether a *voluntary* assignment to an independent undertaking of trade-mark rights in Ideal-Standard products in Germany, originating from a French subsidiary of IHT (USA), would exhaust the rights of the owner of the same trade-mark rights in Germany, which was also a subsidiary of IHT (USA). Would the assignment of such rights by one member of the IHT group, *without the consent of the other*, exhaust the rights of the whole group?

The Court held that it would not. The principle of exhaustion of rights only applied where the owner of the trade mark in the importing State and the owner of the trade mark in the exporting State were the same, or where, even if they are separate persons, they are economically linked, for example, as licensee, or parent company, or subsidiary, or exclusive distributor. It did not apply where trade-mark rights have been assigned to an unrelated enterprise such that the assignor and related enterprises no longer have control.

In the absence of consent, the essential concept for the purposes of exhaustion of rights, replacing the concept of common origin, is unitary control. In the absence of consent, or unitary control, guaranteeing uniform standards, there will be no exhaustion of rights.

31.2.5 'Similar' goods

Where goods have no common origin, but have been manufactured and marketed independently, it has always been possible to invoke trade-mark rights to prevent imports of goods with the same or similar trade marks where this might lead to the confusion of the customer, even though marketing of these goods under their respective marks may be quite lawful and even protected in their country of origin. In *Terrapin (Overseas) Ltd* v *Terranova Industrie C.A. Kapferer & Co.* (case 119/75), a German firm, proprietors of the trade name Terranova, sought to prevent an English company from registering its trade name Terrapin in Germany, since the products of both firms (building materials) were similar, and would, the German company argued, lead to confusion amongst consumers. The ECJ held that Article 30 could be invoked to prevent the import of goods marketed under a name giving rise to confusion where these rights have been acquired by different proprietors under different national laws as long as they do not operate as a means of arbitrary discrimination or disguised restriction on trade between Member States.

A similar situation, involving not trade marks but a registered design, arose in *Keurkoop BV* v *Nancy Keane Gifts BV* (case 144/81). Here Keurkoop BV, the proprietor in Holland of a registered design for a particular style of handbag, sought to prevent the import into Holland of an identical bag, manufactured in France to a design registered in France by a different owner. The ECJ held that it would be entitled under Article 30 to exercise its property rights to prevent the bags being imported from France, since these bags had not been marketed in France by it or with its consent; the rights had arisen independently of each other. The Court did, however, suggest that the matter should be examined to ensure that there was no agreement or concerted practice between the parties concerned which might infringe Article 81.

Keurkoop v *Nancy Keane* was followed in *Consorzio Italiano della Componentistica de Ricambio per Autoveicoli* v *Régie Nationale des Usines Renault* (case 53/87). Here, Renault was held entitled under Article 30 to invoke its registered patent rights in ornamental designs for car body parts to prevent the claimant association's members from manufacturing copies of Renault's parts in Italy, or marketing such parts following their manufacture in other Member States, *without Renault's consent* (see also *AB Volvo* v *Eric Veng* (case 238/87)).

In *Deutsche Renault AG* v *Audi AG* (case C–317/91), Audi was held entitled under Article 30, as the owner of a registered and protected trade mark in Germany, the 'Quattro' mark, to prohibit the use in Germany by a Renault subsidiary established in Germany of the designation 'Espace Quadra' for a four-wheel drive vehicle marketed in France and elsewhere under that name, where the use of the name might cause confusion. It was left to the national court to decide whether the use of the name Espace Quadra would cause confusion, according to the meaning of the term in national (German) trade-mark law. The Court did, however, suggest that Community law 'did not lay down any strict interpretative criterion for the concept of the risk of confusion'. Following this judgment it may be doubted whether *Prantl* (case 16/83, see Chapter 18) remains good law.

The Trade Marks Directive and the Regulation on a Community Trade Mark now provide for the scope of a trade-mark proprietor's rights against infringement (see Trade Marks Directive Article 5, Regulation 40/94/EC Article 9), which includes protection as against similar goods. These provisions, which are central to the law relating to trade marks, have been the subject of judicial interpretation (see, e.g., *Sabel* v *Puma* (case C–251/95); *General Motors* (case C–375/97); *Marca Mode* v *Adidas* (case C–425/98); *Hölterhoff* v *Freiesleben* (case C–2/00; *Davidoff* (case C–292/00); *Arsenal FC plc* v *Matthew Reed* (case C–206/01)). A consideration of this jurisprudence, however, lies outside the scope of this book.

31.2.6 Intellectual property rights and national origin

In these cases, property rights were being invoked to protect the owner's legitimate property in his *product*. Where the owner seeks to invoke his rights to prevent the import of goods solely because the public *may be misled as to their national origin*, the Court has held (*Theodor Kohl KG* v *Ringelhan and Rennett SA* (case 177/83)) that national trade-mark law may not be relied upon in the absence of evidence of unfair competition. Similarly national measures which seek to employ industrial or commercial property rights in order to encourage or protect domestic production at the expense of imports from other Member States will breach Article 28 and will not be permitted under Article 30 (e.g., *Generics UK* v *Smith Kline* (case C–191/90) (re licences of right); *Commission* v *UK* (case C–30/90) (re compulsory patent licences)).

31.2.7 International exhaustion

The principles outlined above will only apply to trade within the Community. Where parties seek to assert their property rights to prevent goods from third countries from entering the Community, the free movement provisions of Articles 28 and 30 do not apply (*EMI Records Ltd* v *CBS United Kingdom Ltd* (case 51/75), *Generics UK Ltd* v *Smith Kline and French* (case C–191/90), *Silhouette International Schmied GmbH & Co. KG* v *Hartlaner Handelsgesellschaft mbH* (case C–355/96) – this last case concerned the Trade Marks Directive, discussed further below). In *Silhouette*, the ECJ held that national rules of an EU Member State providing for exhaustion of trade-mark rights for products put on the market outside the EEA with the consent of the trade-mark proprietor were incompatible with the terms of the Trade Marks Directive. From the wording of Article 7(1), exhaustion would take place only if the goods had been put on the market within the EEA. The Court took the opportunity to refine the scope of this ruling in *Sebago Inc.* v *GB-Unic* (case C–173/98). Sebago was the owner of trade marks for shoes, registered in Benelux. GB-Unic sold some Sebago shoes which had been manufactured in El Salvador and imported into the EU via a supplier in Belgium. Sebago claimed that this violated its rights, as it had not consented to the sale of those shoes in the Community. GB-Unic argued that it is sufficient for consent (thereby triggering the exhaustion doctrine) if the proprietor of the trade mark has consented to the marketing in the EC of similar goods bearing the same trade mark. Having reaffirmed its judgment in *Silhouette*, the ECJ then went on to take a narrow view of consent, stating that consent must relate to the specific goods in respect of which exhaustion was claimed. The question of consent arose again in *Zino Davidoff* v *A & G Imports Ltd* and *Levi Strauss & Co* v *Tesco* (joined cases C–414 to 416/99). The defendants in the case argued that, to fall within *Silhouette* and *Sebago*, a trade-mark proprietor must object to the import of trade-marked goods that had been lawfully marketed outside the EEA; failure to object implied consent. Although the ECJ accepted that consent in the context of international exhaustion could be implied from the circumstances, those circumstances must 'unequivocally demonstrate that the proprietor has renounced his right to oppose placing of the goods on the market within the EEA' (para. 47). In particular, the defendant must prove that the trade-mark proprietor has consented to the marketing of the goods, it is not for the proprietor to prove that it has not so consented. As the ECJ pointed out, to have held otherwise would have meant that consent would have been deemed to be given in the absence of any proof (para. 58), which is a different and more easily satisfied level of consent than implied consent.

The matter of proof came before the ECJ again, albeit in a different context, in the case of *van Doren + Q GmbH* v *lifestyle + sportswear Handelsgesellschaft mbH* (case C–244/00). The defendants in this case argued that they had obtained the goods (manufactured in the United States and subject to an exclusive distribution agreement in Germany) within the EEA and that the doctrine of exhaustion to prevent the trade-mark proprietor from stopping the parallel imports applied. Van Doren, however, alleged that the goods came directly from the United States. The question that was referred was: which party should be subject to the burden of proof and, in particular, whether Article 28 required that the burden of proof be removed from the defendant? The ECJ held that it is generally for the defendant to prove that the conditions for the application of the exhaustion principle exist, but this was qualified: if the defendant shows that there would be a risk of market partitioning if he had to bear the burden of proof, then it would be for the trade-mark owner to demonstrate that the goods in question were originally placed on the market outside the EEA by him or with his consent. A risk of market partitioning would arise because if the defendant had to prove that the goods were placed on the market within the EEA, the trade-mark owner might be able to identify the member of the exclusive or selective distribution network who supplied the defendant, and reduce supplies to that member to prevent further sales to the defendant. However, once the trade-mark owner has established that the goods were first marketed outside the EEA, then it would be for the defendant to prove, in turn, that the trade-mark owner consented to the subsequent marketing of the goods in the EEA.

31.2.8 Free movement of services

The case law discussed so far has been concerned with the free movement of goods, but the free movement of services may similarly be affected by the tension between protecting intellectual property rights and ensuring free movement in the internal market. Although the derogation provision in Article 46 EC does not refer to the protection of industrial property, unlike Article 30, the Court has held that indistinctly applicable measures can justify intellectual property rights which might otherwise conflict with the operation of Article 49 (*Coditel* (case 62/79), *Collins* v *Imtrat* (case C–159/87)). However, in the absence of more specific case law on this point, it is difficult to predict the extent to which the Court would adopt a similar approach to that taken under Article 30 in the field of services.

31.2.9 Harmonisation

Because of the wide disparity in national trade-mark rules and its resulting adverse impact on the internal market, harmonisation at Community level was clearly required. In the field of *trade marks*, Directive 89/104 was passed in 1989 ([1989] OJ L40/1). Its aim was to approximate those aspects of trade-mark law which most directly affect the functioning of the common market, to ensure that the conditions for obtaining and continuing to hold a registered trade-mark right are the same in all Member States. The directive defines trade-mark rights and the rights attached to trade-mark ownership, as well as its limitations. It provides common grounds for refusal of registration, invalidity and loss or exhaustion of rights. The effect of the measure is to broaden the scope of what may be registered as a trade mark and extend the rights conferred by trade-mark registration, thereby reducing the need for reliance on the unpredictable remedy of passing off. However, as the Court pointed out in *IHT* (case C–9/93), the directive does not change the essential character of national trade-mark law, which remains essentially territorial and independent.

The Trade Marks Directive has not been without its critics. One particular area of concern is the scope of the exhaustion doctrine in relation to goods from outside the EU, the case law on which parallels that in relation to similar cases brought under Article 30 (see 31.2.6.) The narrow interpretation of the exhaustion rule in Article 7(c) of the Trade Marks Directive has been the subject of some adverse comment, as, by limiting the scope of the exhaustion doctrine, it allows companies to partition markets and maintain high prices. A report comparing prices between the EU and the USA showed that prices in the USA tend to be between 40–50 per cent of those in the EU.

In the absence of full harmonisation of national trade-mark law, Regulation 90/94 ([1994] OJ L11) was introduced. The regulation provided for the introduction of a Community trade mark, covering all the Member States, to be obtained by a single application. The Commission presented a proposal for amendments to the regulation (COM (2002) 767 final), which was subsequently adopted in Regulation 422/2004 ([2004] OJ L70/1).

The legal protection of designs is now covered by Directive 98/71/EC, which required Member States to harmonise the central elements of their design laws, was agreed in 1998 and came into force in 2001. The Regulation on Community Design was adopted in 2001 (Regulation 6/2002, [2002] OJ L3/1). It introduces Community registered designs and Community unregistered designs as other means of protection for designs. The Commission proposals on 'utility models' (COM (97) 691) have not progressed. The Commission has put forward proposals for a Community patent and a proposal for a Directive on patent protection for inventions related to computer programs, both based on the Green Paper (COM (95) 382).

In the field of *copyright*, eight directives have been agreed. Directive 93/83 provided for the coordination of certain rules relating to copyright and rights relating to copyright applicable to satellite broadcasting ([1993] OJ L246), and Directive 93/98 provided for the harmonisation of the terms of protection of copyright and related rights ([1993] OJ L290). Specific directives apply to copyright in the broadcasting area (e.g., the Lending Rights Directive 92/100/EEC ([1992] OJ L346/61) and the Satellite Broadcasting and Cable Retransmission Directive 93/83/EEC ([1993] OJ L248/15)) and there is a directive on the legal protection of topographies of semiconductor products (Directive 87/54/EEC) and on the legal protection of databases (Directive 96/9). More recently, directives on copyright and the information society (Directive 2001/29); and on the resale right for the benefit of the original author of a work of art (Directive 2001/84) have been agreed. Finally, a directive on measures and procedures to ensure the enforcement of intellectual property rights was adopted in 2004 (Directive 2004/48/EC [2004] OJ L195/16).

31.2.10 Discrimination

It may be noted that any discrimination, direct or indirect, in relation to industrial and commercial property rights will fall foul of Article 12 (ex 6) EC, which prohibits 'any discrimination on the grounds of nationality' (*Collins* v *Imtrat* (cases C–92/92, 328/92)).

31.3 Intellectual property rights and competition law

As the discussion above has demonstrated, the ECJ has drawn a distinction between the *existence* of industrial property rights and their *exercise*. The mere existence of industrial property rights cannot infringe Articles 81 or 82 EC; an improper or abusive exercise of these rights, however, can. The exploitation of industrial or commercial property rights will be improper if these rights are used to defeat Community law on restrictive practices (see, e.g., *Consten* (cases 56 & 58/64; discussed below and in Chapter 27). Any concerted attempt or attempt by a dominant undertaking to use these rights to partition markets, or to maintain artificial price levels, or to impose discriminatory or unfair conditions on trading partners is liable to fall foul of Articles 81 or 82 EC.

31.3.1 Improper exercise of rights

In *Établissements Consten SA* v *Commission* (cases 56 & 58/64) Consten could not rely on its trade-mark rights to prevent parallel imports of Grundig products from other Member States. The purpose of the GINT trade mark was not to protect the owner's legitimate rights in his product, for example, to prevent other goods being passed off as Grundig's, but to partition the market and ensure absolute territorial protection for Grundig products in France. Thus its exercise in the context of Grundig's dealer agreement was in breach of Article 81(1).

The same principle has been applied to patents and copyright. In *Parke, Davis & Co.* v *Probel* (case 24/67) the Court held that an 'improper exploitation' of patent rights in the context of agreements, decisions of undertakings or concerted practices or by firms in a dominant position could breach EC competition law.

In *Re GEMA* ([1971] CMLR D35) the Commission found that GEMA, an authors' rights society holding a dominant position in authors' copyright in Germany, was improperly exploiting its rights in breach of Article 82. GEMA was exploiting its copyrights by discriminatory practices; it was discriminating against nationals from other Member States, who could not become full members; it paid supplementary fees, 'loyalty bonuses', only to some of its members from a fund to which all had contributed, without objective justification. It was imposing unfair conditions on its members, by extending its contractual rights to non-copyright works, and claiming rights to future works. All these practices went beyond what was necessary to protect GEMA's legitimate property rights.

Similarly, in *Windsurfing International Inc.* v *Commission* (case 193/83) WSI, the owner of patent licences in a special sail rig (comprising mast, mast foot, sail and pair of curved booms) for use with windsurfing boards, was seeking in its licensing agreements to impose unnecessary restrictions on its licensees in breach of Article 81(1). For example, licensees were required to exploit the patents (for the rigs) *only* for the manufacture of sailboards using hulls which had been given WSI's prior approval; to pay royalties for rigs made under the patent on the basis of the selling price of the *complete* sailboard; to manufacture only in a specified manufacturing plant; and they were not permitted to challenge the licensed patents. These provisions were all found to constitute improper exploitation.

31.3.2 The specific subject matter of intellectual property rights

In placing limitations on the exercise of industrial property rights, the Commission, supported by the Court, has curtailed the very substance of these rights. These rights can now only be exercised to protect what the Commission regards as the 'specific subject matter' of the property concerned. In this, there are similarities to the approach adopted under Article 30 regarding goods, and under the ECJ's case law regarding services.

The specific subject matter of the property, to protect which industrial property rights may legitimately be exercised, has been narrowly defined. For patents, it is to ensure, to the holder, so as to recompense the creative effort of the inventor, the exclusive right to use an invention (*Centrafarm BV* v *Sterling Drug Inc.* (case 15/74)). Patent rights clearly merit protection if the Community wishes to encourage creative endeavour. Thus while patent licensing agreements have generally been held in breach of Article 81(1) the Commission has been prepared to grant exemption under Article 81(3) (e.g., *Davidson Rubber Co.* [1972] CMLR D52), and it is expected that this view will continue to be taken under the decentralised enforcement system now applicable (see Chapter 29).

The specific subject matter of a trade-mark right is to protect the owner from competitors who would profit, deliberately or accidentally, from the reputation and goodwill attached to the mark by selling goods with the same mark, or one which was sufficiently similar to cause confusion in the mind of the consumer (see, e.g., *Deutsche Renault AG* v *Audi AG* (case C–317/91)). Thus, trade-mark rights cannot be used simply to prevent parallel imports within the EC of the trade-marked product, which may be cheaper than the same product sold in the importing State, even to protect a distributor's investment in a particular territory from 'free riders' (i.e., parallel importers who seek to take advantage of the product's goodwill, built up by the promotional efforts of others). It is only rights *in the product* which are protected.

The specific subject matter or purpose of copyright protection was held in *Radio Telefis Eireann* v *Commission* (case T–69/89) to be to protect the owner's moral rights in the work and ensure a reward for creative endeavour, which entitles the holder to exclusive rights of performance and reproduction of the protected work (para. 71). RTE could not take advantage of its legitimate monopoly in radio and TV broadcasts by refusing to grant licences for the reproduction of its advance programme listings to potential competitors, thereby retaining an 'unlawful monopoly downstream'. Such an exercise of copyright did not correspond to its essential function of copyright protection but pursued an aim 'manifestly contrary to Article [82]'. On appeal (*Radio Telefis Eireann* v *Commission* (cases C–241 & 242/91P)), the ECJ upheld the CFI's judgment, but without ruling explicitly on the purpose of copyright. In *Re GEMA*, the Commission suggested that any conditions embodied in an agreement or practice or imposed by a dominant undertaking which go beyond what is necessary to protect the owners' *existing* property, and certainly any discriminatory treatment, risk infringing Articles 81 or 82.

In *Ministre Public* v *Tournier* (case 395/87), in the context of a reference concerning the compatibility of reciprocal arrangements between copyright management societies with Articles 28, 81 and 86 the Court held that contracts entered into with users would not infringe Article 81 unless the practices at issue exceeded the limits absolutely necessary for the attainment of the legitimate copyright objective of safeguarding the rights and interests of their members *vis-à-vis* users of the protected property, in this case recorded music.

However, in *NDC Health Corporation* v *IMS Health* (case C–481/01 P(R)), the CFI (upheld by the ECJ) emphasised that a refusal to licence intellectual property rights would only then constitute an abuse within Article 82 EC if there are exceptional circumstances in the public interest which required that a licence be granted. The Commission, following a complaint from NDC, had taken the view that IMS Health has a dominant position in the German market for data services on sales and prescriptions of pharmaceuticals. IMS had developed a geographical model of analysis, called a 'brick structure', which is used for making available sales data to IMS customers and which constituted a *de facto* industry standard. The dominance arose because IMS customers had been heavily involved in the development of this 'brick structure' and were therefore dependent on it. Having concluded that IMS's refusal to license the use of their model of analysis meant that there existed a prima facie case for abuse of IMS's dominant position, the Commission ordered IMS to grant a licence by way of interim measure. This decision was suspended by the CFI and an appeal to the ECJ against the suspension failed. The CFI (case T–184/01 R) emphasised that:

> the respect for property rights in general and for intellectual property rights in particular is expressly reflected in Articles 30 and 295 EC. The mere fact that the applicant has invoked and sought to enforce its copyright . . . for economic reasons does not lessen its entitlement to rely upon the exclusive right granted by national law for the very purpose of rewarding innovation (para. 143).

The evidence suggested that the lack of competition which resulted from the refusal to license was not perceptible, but rather that the position of particular competitors had become difficult because they could not use similar technology. This, however, was not enough to find a prima facie infringement of Article 82 (note that the Commission subsequently withdrew its decision).

The decision in *IMS Health*, above, followed a complaint by NDC to the Commission. This had been prompted by a decision by a German court to grant an injunction in favour of IMS to prevent NDC from using a brick structure derived from IMS's structure. The German court referred a number of questions on the interpretation of Article 82 to the ECJ (see *IMS Health* v *NDC Health* (case C–418/01)). The case turned on the application of *Magill* (cases C 241 & 242/91) and *Bronner* (case C–7/97), discussed in chapter 28) to the present situation. The Court confirmed that a refusal to license could not, in itself, be an abuse under Article 82, although the manner in which these rights are exercised could. It therefore held that it would be an abuse by a dominant undertaking which owned an intellectual property right in a brick structure indispensable to the presentation of regional sales data to refuse to grant a licence to another undertaking which also intends to provide such data in the same Member State. This was subject to a number of conditions: first, the undertaking requesting the licence intends to offer new products for which there is potential demand and which are not offered by the owner of the IP rights; secondly, there are no objective justifications for refusing to grant the licences; and finally, the refusal is such as to enable the owner of the IP rights to eliminate all competition on the relevant market.

The upshot of this ruling is that there may be circumstances where Article 82 *does* appear to require a degree of compulsory licensing, at least in circumstances where a refusal to do so would eliminate the possibility of innovation, and where there are no objective justifications for this refusal. The Court in *IMS* did not indicate what sort of objective justifications there might be, and it seems likely that future litigation will turn on this issue. It seems that this will largely be a matter to be resolved before the domestic courts, because the ECJ emphasised that this decision would be for the national courts to take.

It must be emphasised that such protection as is offered to protect the specific subject matter of the property concerned has been significantly reduced by the doctrine of exhaustion of rights discussed above. Any rights claimed in the context of agreements or practices within Articles 81 or 82 EC which are not permitted under this doctrine will risk infringing EC competition law. Furthermore since *Radio Telefis Eireann* v *Commission* (cases C–241 & 242/91P), it is clear that, where exceptional circumstances exist, the holder of an intellectual property right will not be permitted to refuse to license it.

31.3.3 Block exemption and Article 82

The fact that an industrial property right such as an exclusive licence falls within a block exemption cannot protect an undertaking from liability under Article 82 EC if that right is abused, even where the abuse consists only in increasing an already dominant position, thereby eliminating effective competition in a substantial part of the common market (*Tetra Pak* (case T–51/89)).

31.4 Conclusions

The case law of the ECJ, in the context of both the free movement of goods and competition law, represents an uneasy compromise between the single market principle and the need to safeguard legitimate industrial and commercial property rights protected under national law. Other decisions indicate a greater willingness to safeguard the interests of creativity, originality and goodwill protected by intellectual property law, and to encourage and reward the taking of commercial risks. This is evidenced, e.g., by a more generous approach to the question of the permitted *exercise* of property rights protected under national law (e.g., *EMI Electrola* v *Patricia* (case 341/87); *Deutsche Renault AG* v *Audi AG* (case C–317/91)) and by limiting the scope of the exhaustion principle (*Hag II* (case C–10/89); *IHT* (case C–9/93); but cf. *Silhouette* (case 355/96) and *Sebago* (case C–173/98)), although the difficulties with patents, especially pharmaceuticals, remain (e.g., *Merck* v *Primecrown* (cases C–267 & 268/95)). In the area of copyright law the Court has refused to apply the exhaustion principle to the showing of films and hiring of video cassettes (as opposed to their sale), recognising the owners' legitimate claim to benefit from repeated use (*Coditel* v *SA, Ciné Vog Films* (case 62/79); *Warner Brothers Inc.* v *Cristiansen* (case 158/86)).

Community legislation has supplemented the work of the Court and now provides a framework for the protection of industrial property rights in the Community, and steady progress has been made. Member States have clearly recognised industrial and commercial property law as an area in which, under the subsidiarity principle of Article 5 (ex 3b) EC, the objectives 'cannot be sufficiently achieved by the Member States' without endangering the single market and can be 'better achieved by the Community'.

Nevertheless, the Court's restrictive approach to IP rights under both the competition provisions and the doctrine of exhaustion may be criticised for curtailing rather too severely the rights of the owner of IP rights. The desire to promote market integration may have swung the balance too far away from protecting IP rights. The decision in *IMS Health* may be of concern in that it seems to weaken further the rights of IP holders. It seems that the challenge of finding the correct balance between protecting IP rights and promoting the internal market is one that has yet to be resolved in a satisfactory manner.

FURTHER READING

Anderman, S., *EC Competition Law and Intellectual Property Rights* (Oxford University Press, 1998).

Castillo de la Torre, F., 'Trade Marks and Free Movement of Pharmaceuticals in the European Community: To Partition or not to Partition' [1997] 6 EIPR 304.

Stothers, C., 'Who Needs Intellectual Property? Competition Law and Restrictions on Parallel Trade within the European Economic Area' (2005) EIPR 458–466.

Woods, L., *Free Movement of Goods and Services in the EC* (Ashgate, 2004) Ch. 8.

FURTHER READING

PRINCIPAL SOURCES OF EC LAW

Encyclopedia of European Community Law, K.R. Simmonds (general ed.) (London: Sweet & Maxwell, looseleaf). Constitutional Treaties, together with annexes and protocols. Secondary legislation.

Official Journal (L series): Community secondary legislation.

Official Journal (C series): non-binding Community instruments; proposals, notices, opinions, resolutions, reports of proceedings in Parliament and the Court of Justice.

European Commercial Cases.

European Current Law.

European Court Reports: reports of cases from the Court of Justice.

Common Market Law Reports: reports of cases from the Court of Justice and national courts.

Bulletin of the European Union: reports on day-to-day activities of the Communities; supplements on specific topics.

Annual *General Report on the Activities of the European Communities.*

Annual *Report on Competition Policy.*

Halsbury's Laws of England, 4th ed., vols 51 and 52 (D. Vaughan, coordinating ed.) (London: Butterworths, 1986).

Databases:

EUR-LEX – portal to European Union Law (full text)

URL – http://eur-lex.europa.eu/en/index.htm

Prelex – database on inter-institutional procedures allowing access to electronic texts available

URL – http://ec.europa.eu/prelex/apcnet.cfm?CL=en

LexisNexis – commercial database containing European Court reports, European commercial cases, and Commission competition decisions

General introductory

Szyszczak, E., and Cygan, A., *Understanding EU Law* (London: Sweet & Maxwell, 2005)

Selected textbooks in specialised areas

(a) Introductory

Mathijsen, P., *A Guide to European Union Law*, 9th ed. (London: Sweet & Maxwell, 2006)

(b) General textbooks

Craig, P., and De Búrca, G., *EC Law: Text, Cases and Materials*, 3rd ed. (Oxford: Oxford University Press, 2002)

Evans, A., *European Union Law* (Oxford: Hart Publishing, 1998)

Kapteyn, P., and Ver Loren van Themaat, P., *Introduction to the Law of the European Communities*, 3rd ed. by L.W. Gormley (The Hague: Kluwer Law International, 1998)

Weatherill, S., and Beaumont, P., *EU Law*, 3rd ed. (London: Penguin, 1999)

Weatherill, S., *Cases and Materials on EC Law*, 7th ed. (Oxford: Oxford University Press, 2005)

Wyatt, D., and Dashwood, A., *European Union Law*, 5th ed. (London: Sweet & Maxwell, 2006)

(c) Constitutional, institutional and administrative law

Albi, A., *EU Enlargment and the Constitutions of Central and Eastern Europe* (Cambridge: Cambridge University Press, 2005)

Andenas, M., and Usher, W-H., (eds) *The Treaty of Nice and Beyond: Enlargement and Constitutional Reform* (Oxford: Hart Publishing, 2003)

Brown, N., and Jacobs, F., *The Court of Justice of the European Communities*, 5th ed. (London: Sweet & Maxwell, 2000)

Craig, P., and De Búrca, G., (eds) *The Evolution of EU Law* (Oxford: Oxford University Press, 2002)

Curtin, D., (ed) *The EU Constitution: The Best Way Forward?* (The Hague: TMC Asser Press, 2005)

Ellis, E., and Tridimas, T., *Public Law of the European Community: Text, Materials and Commentary* (London: Sweet & Maxwell, 1995)

Hartley, T.C., *The Foundations of European Community Law*, 5th ed. (Oxford: Oxford University Press, 2003).

Hartley, T., *Constitutional Problems of the European Union* (Oxford: Hart Publishing, 1999).

Hopkins, J., *Devolution in Context: Regional, Federal and Devolved Government in the EU* (London: Cavendish, 2002).

Lasok, D., and Bridge, J., *Law and Institutions of the European Union*, 7th ed. (London: Butterworths, 2000).

Lenaerts, K., Van Nuffel, P., and Bray, R., *Constitutional Law of the European Union*, 2nd ed. (London: Sweet & Maxwell, 2004)

Schermers, H.G., and Waelbroeck, D.F., *Judicial Protection in the European Communities*, 5th ed. (London: Kluwer Law & Taxation Publishers, 1992).

Usher, J.A., *EC Institutions and Legislation* (London: Longmans, 1998).

Weiler, J.H.H., *The Constitution of Europe* (Cambridge: Cambridge University Press, 1999).

(d) Substantive law

(i) *Agriculture*

Barents, R., *The Agricultural Law of the EC* (Deventer: Kluwer Law & Taxation, 1994).

O'Rourke, R., *European Food Law*, 2nd ed. (London: Cavendish, 2001).

Usher, J.A., *EC Institutions and Legislation* (London: Longmans, 1998)

(ii) *Civil jurisdiction and enforcement of judgments*

Plender, R., and Wilderspin, M., *European Contracts Convention: the Rome Convention on the Choice of Law for Contracts* (London: Sweet & Maxwell, 2nd ed., 2001)

(iii) *Company law*

Andenas, M., and Kenyan Slade, S., *Financial Market Regulation and Company Law* (London: Sweet & Maxwell, 1993).

Dine, J., *EC Company Law* (Chichester: Jordans, looseleaf).

Drury, R., and Zuereb, P., *Company Laws: a Comparative Approach* (Dartmouth, 1991).

Edwards, V., *EC Company Law* (Oxford: Clarendon Press, 1999).

Maitland-Walker, J., *Guide to European Company Laws*, 2nd ed. (London: Sweet & Maxwell, 1997).

Rider, B., *European Financial Services Law* (The Hague: Kluwer, 1998).

Usher, J., *Law of Money & Financial Services in the EC*, 2nd ed. (Oxford: Oxford University Press, 2000).

(iv)   *Competition law*

Baquero Cruz J., *Between Competition and Free Movement* (Oxford: Hart Publishing, 2002).

Bellamy, C.W., and Child, G.D., *European Community Law of Competition*, 5th ed. (London: Sweet & Maxwell, 2001).

Cook, J., and Kerse, C., *EC Merger Control*, 3rd ed. (London: Sweet & Maxwell, 1999).

Gilstra, D.J. (ed.), *Competition Law in Europe and the USA* (London: Kluwer, 1991).

Gormley, L.W. (ed.), *Current and Future Perspectives on EC Competition Law* (The Hague: Kluwer Law International, 1997).

Goyder, D., *EC Competition Law*, 4th ed. (Oxford: Clarendon Press, 2003).

Grayston (ed) *European Economics and Law: Competition – Trade-Single Market* (London: Cavendish, 1999).

Hancher, L., *EC State Aids*, 2nd ed. (London: Sweet & Maxwell, 1999).

Jones, C., Van der Woude, M., and Lewis, X., *EC Competition Law Handbook* (London: Sweet & Maxwell, annual).

Korah, V., *An Introductory Guide to EC Competition Law and Practice* 7th edition (Oxford: Hart, 2000).

Stanbrook, C., and Bentley, P., *Dumping and Subsidies*, 3rd ed. (The Hague: Kluwer Law International, 1996).

Whish, R., *Competition Law*, 5th ed. (London: Butterworths, 2003).

(v)   *Consumer*

Weatherill, S., *EU Consumer Law and Policy*, 2nd edition (Cheltenham: Edward Elgar, 2005)

(vi)   *Environment*

Krämer, L., *Focus on European Environment Law*, 2nd ed. (London: Sweet & Maxwell, 1997).

Krämer, L., *EC Treaty and Environmental Law*, 5th ed. (London: Sweet & Maxwell, 2003).

(vii)   *Free movement of goods and services*

Andenas, M., and Roth, W-H., (eds) *Services and Free Movement in EC Law* (Oxford: Oxford University Press, 2002)

Barnard, C., and Scott, J., (eds) *The Law of the Single European Market* (Oxford: Hart Publishing, 2002).

Oliver, P., *Free Movement of Goods in the EC*, 3rd ed. (London: European Law Centre, 1995).

Woods, L., *Free Movement of of Goods and services within the EC* (Aldershot: Ashgate, 2004).

(viii)   *Health*

Hervey, T., *Health Law and the European Union* (Cambridge: Cambridge University Press, 2004)

(ix)   *Remedies*

Brealey, M., and Hoskins, M., *Remedies in EC Law* (London: Longman, 1994).

Heukels, T., and McDonnell, A., *The Action for Damages in Community Law* (The Hague: Kluwer Law International, 1997).

(x)   *Tax*

Farmer, P., and Lyal, R., *EC Tax Law* 2nd edition (Oxford: Clarendon, 2003).

Meussan, G.T.K., *The Principle of Equality in European Taxation* (The Hague: Kluwer, 1999).

(xi)   *The social dimension*

Dashwood, A., and O'Leary, S., *The Principle of Equal Treatment in EC Law* (London: Sweet & Maxwell, 1997).

Ellis, E., *European Community Sex Equality Law* 2nd edition (Oxford: Oxford University Press, 1998).

Giubboni, S., *Social Rights and Market Freedom in the European Constitution* (Cambridge: Cambridge University Press, 2005)

Handoll, J., *Free Movement of Persons in the European Union* (J. Wiley & Son, 1995).

Hervey, T., and O'Keeffe, D., (eds), *Sex Equality Law in the European Union* (Wiley, 1996).

Hervey, T., *European Social Law and Policy* (London: Longmans, 1998).

Kenner, J., *EU Employment Law: From Rome to Amsterdam* (Oxford: Hart Publishing, 2002).

Nielsen, R., and Szyszczak, E., *The Social Dimension of the European Community*, 3rd ed. (Handelshøjskolens Forlag, 1997).

Prechal, S., and Burrows, N., *Gender Discrimination Law of the European Society* (Dartmouth: Gower, 1990).

van der Mei, P., *Free Movement of Persons within the European Community: Cross-Border Access to Public Benefits* (Oxford: Hart Publishing, 2002).

White, R., *Workers, Establishment and Services in the European Union* (Oxford: Oxford University Press, 2004)

(xii)   *Transport*

Balfour, J., *European Community Air Law* (London: Butterworths, 1995).

Greaves, R., *Transport Law of the European Community* (London: Athlone Press, 1991).

Articles, casenotes and reviews

American Journal of International Law.

Cahiers de Droit Européen.

Common Market Law Review.

European Business Law Review.

European Competition Law Review.

European Intellectual Property Review.

European Law Review.

European Public Law.

International and Comparative Law Quarterly.

Journal of Common Market Studies.

Journal of World Trade Law.

Legal Issues of European Integration.

Maastricht Journal.

Yearbook of European Law.

INFORMATION

Information Office of the European Commission, Jean Monnet House, 8 Storey's Gate, London SW1P 3AT. Tel: 0207 973 1992.

European Business Information (Small Firms' Service), 11 Belgrave Road, London SW1V 1RB. Tel: 0171-828 6201.

European Documentation Centres (in most major cities).

European Information Centres (in most major regional centres).

INDEX